Avedon's France: Old World, New Look

Avedon's France

Old World, New Look

Robert M. Rubin
Marianne Le Galliard

Abrams, New York
Bibliothèque nationale de France

Preface

Laurence Engel

In 1961, the Bibliothèque nationale de France was the first institution in France to see Richard Avedon as more than a famous fashion photographer. When it presented three of his portraits in a group exhibition, it recognized him as an artist. Now, fifty-five years later, the establishment is opening its season with a dedication to him. *Avedon's France* reveals another side to the New Yorker. What sort of American was this eternally youthful photographer? He was certainly multifaceted, capable of capturing everything on film: an Indian prince of fashion photography, throwing Dovima, one of his models, among elephants; a philosopher portraitist questioning the truth of faces; a wandering aristocrat lost in the midst of war in Vietnam; and an experimental photographer setting up a studio outdoors to seize a stream of American faces. Seeing through the dark hole of his lens, this incredible Cyclops devoured the world during the second half of the twentieth century.

But this exhibition reveals something else: a certain love story between this American and France. Of course, he wasn't the only one to fantasize about Europe, arriving in the wake of the Marshall Plan. Avedon, the new incarnation of an American in Paris, was enchanted with the country. From the time he set foot in France in 1947 to shoot Christian Dior's New Look, and until the end of his life, rare was the year when he was not found in Paris. In November 1966, when he met Jacques Henri Lartigue, his elder, his passion deepened. Through the vision of the "old" came a "young" one that understood that France stretched back in time, that it was a kind of yesterday's world, one that could already be felt in his work.

What is original about this exhibition is that, far from the image of fashion star, there is revealed a Proustian Avedon, clinging to the surface of time, his gaze studded by society's comedy, the Volpi Ball, for one. For, in his frenzy to be in the here and now, Avedon was searching for something other than what was current. Witnesses and symbols, the masterpieces that the exhibition spotlights: the stills, incorporated into Stanley Donen's movie *Funny Face*, in which one, for example, discovers Audrey Hepburn and her many colored balloons, which her elegant fingers release in front of the Arc des Tuileries. Those shots, so important for Avedon, are like golden sparks hidden within the world's crust. Only the artist can reveal them, as the Kabbalah says. Avedon, like Proust, sought to seize the gold of time, perhaps captured in the suspended moment of photographs, arrested at the intersection of old and new, to echo the exhibition's fine subtitle: "Old World, New Look."

It is only natural that it was Robert M. Rubin, another great New Yorker and lover of France, who proposed and conceived of this exhibition, with help from Marianne Le Galliard, a specialist in Lartigue. Telling the love story between America and France would not have been possible without the curator's personal, almost filial, understanding of Avedon; nor would it have been possible without the amicable collaboration of the Richard Avedon Foundation, Paramount Pictures, and Nicole Wisniak, head of the legendary magazine *Egoïste*. May they be thanked here. We express our gratitude to the Terra Foundation for American Art, to the Fondation Louis Roederer and to Mr. Arnaud Brillois for their support.

France is now probably the most fortunate survivor of an Old World that is being destroyed into something new.

JANET FLANNER, "LETTER FROM PARIS,"
THE NEW YORKER (DECEMBER 23, 1944): 42.

Old World, New Look

Robert M. Rubin

In the spring of 1993, Richard Avedon had just turned seventy. A major retrospective was set to open soon at the Whitney Museum of American Art in New York (*Evidence 1944–1994*) and then travel to Europe. Invited to Arles for Europe's preeminent photography festival that summer, he granted a rare interview to *Le Monde*. The session started smoothly and flowed easily. Michel Guerrin, the paper's critic, knew and admired Avedon's work, and Avedon was eloquent. At first, the photographer talked movingly of his youth and family, especially his sister Louise's mental illness, institutional confinement, and early passing.

When the subject turned to fashion, Avedon shifted gears. He spoke ominously about his "subversive" thoughts about fashion as a "carapace," describing ". . . those women lunching at cafes, full of anxiety in the afternoon, armored in their perfect surfaces at night . . ."[1] — hardly comporting with the exuberant pages of *Harper's Bazaar* magazine in the 1950s, where an Avedon-lensed Parisian imaginary arose from the ashes of World War II. Why was he distancing himself from the work that made him famous? This was a new Avedon. Indeed, *Evidence* would contain only a handful of fashion images, as if that body of work were just an early sideline.

Guerrin led him back to a more spontaneous outburst on the "delirium" of postwar Paris: "I photographed a prewar Paris, a Lubitsch Paris, a Paris that didn't exist . . . it was the moment in my life when it was all beginning . . . the age you first read Proust, Sartre, eat your first truffle. I was presented to Colette by Cocteau!"[2]

I Am Not an Artifact

Avedon, however, was bent on moving the discussion toward other aspects of his work. A few hours later, he lost his cool. He ripped off his microphone, threw it on the table, and announced that the interview was over:

> "I'm getting so fed up . . . it's terrible what you do to me. I'm a photographer and you're interested in goddamn Paris fashion . . . it's demeaning . . . you want to take me as a Horst, as an artifact of the past. . . . I'm a functioning photographer."[3]

After this bit of theatre, Avedon regrouped by cooking pasta for everyone, and then allowed "one last" fashion question. It was a good one. Guerrin asked about Avedon's role in the making of *Funny Face* (1957). Avedon himself had brought up the film earlier, in what would become a standard sound bite in his personal narrative: "[Fred] Astaire ended up playing me in the movie . . . It's all very strange. I'd learned how to be me by pretending to be him and then I had to teach him how to pretend to be me."[4]

The question was: Who pushed the button on the film's famous freeze-frame sequences — Avedon, director Stanley Donen or cinematographer Ray June? Said Guerrin:

> "I remember in the film when she [Audrey Hepburn] just lets go of the balloon[s], the position of the balloons could not be more perfect. I don't know if one-tenth of a second earlier, one-tenth of a second later, it would have been not quite as good. The same with walking down the steps by the Victoire de Samothrace

> [in the Louvre] and [she] goes, "Take the picture, take the picture," with the scarf billowing, "Whoosh!" Again, half a second earlier, half a second later, it would not have been so good."[5]

It was, of course, Avedon who pushed the button. He was not just the source of the film's fashion world ambience. He was also the basis of the Fred Astaire character. His first marriage was the source of the film's story line. His life had become a Hollywood movie, shot on location in Paris.

Avedon's France: a Psychogeography

Avedon's France — rather than *Avedon and France* — was chosen for the title of this exhibition because Avedon's France is a country with its own special geography. It was not exactly invented, but rather reinvented, out of the postwar ruins of its interwar avant gardes, packaged for middlebrow America by magazines like *Harper's Bazaar, Vogue* and *The New Yorker*. The Christian Dior show of 1947 —immediately dubbed "the New Look" — was Ground Zero. Marcel Proust and the Belle Epoque would be thrown into the mix, and remixed. Hence, "Old World, New Look."

French culture underpins virtually all of Avedon's art. Even before he actually set foot on French soil, his formative years were spent learning from, and then working for, Alexey Brodovitch, the art director of *Harper's Bazaar* who had lived and worked in Paris between the wars. Twice a year, beginning in 1947, Avedon would accompany Carmel Snow, the magazine's editor-in-chief, to Paris. Paris editor Marie-Louise Bousquet took Avedon under her wing and into her Thursday salon.

France is where he returned in the late sixties to rebuild his vision, through a collaboration with Jacques Henri Lartigue, after the critical failure of *Nothing Personal* (1964), his second photobook. And France is where he returned to collaborate with Nicole Wisniak for her magazine *Egoïste* in the eighties, after his lucrative but artistically suffocating stint at *Vogue*.

The Avedon conversation has always been as much about the man as the artist. A skilled self-promoter, Avedon was complicit in this. He liked to be referred to as "the world's most famous photographer." He certainly had "elbow," as Brodovitch once described his unfettered ambition. Yet it didn't seem to bother anybody until he actively sought the recognition of the New York intelligentsia — not the middlebrow readers of *Harper's Bazaar,* but rather those who ruled on what was and wasn't Art. In a 1958 *New Yorker* profile of Avedon, he was still unselfconscious enough to say that he made almost as much money as Picasso.[6] Those who didn't would never forgive him for it. In today's art world, where paintings have become negotiable securities and some artists become billionaires, Avedon's machinations are common. It was Avedon's misfortune to be ahead of his time.

Hewing to his long-term plans for posterity, Avedon stepped out of the preserve of fashion magazine work in 1959 and published his first book, *Observations*, with text by Truman Capote. He

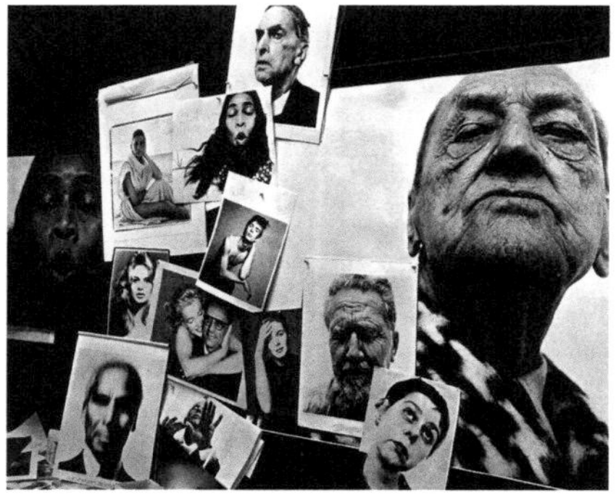

Announcement card, *Richard Avedon Retrospective*, Smithsonian Institution, Washington, D.C., 1962

mounted a revolutionary, though unnoticed, exhibition at the Smithsonian Institution's Photography Gallery in Washington D.C. in 1962.[7] His self-penned capsule biography, published on the occasion as a handout, is an excellent snapshot of his idea of himself at the time:

> This 100-foot collage, which Richard Avedon personally prepared here in the Photography Gallery, represents a cross-section of his creative portrait and fashion photographs. Born in New York in 1923, Avedon received his first formal photography training in the Merchant Marine. After World War II he studied experimental photography under Alexey Brodovitch, and in 1945 joined the staff of *Harper's Bazaar*. In 1956, he was visual director of the movie *Funny Face*. *Observations*, a collection of Avedon's work, was published in 1959. He is on the faculty of the Famous Photographer's School, Westport, Conn.

Note in particular the inflation of the title "visual consultant" — his actual title on the crew of *Funny Face* — to "visual director." The juxtaposition of the terms "creative portraits" and "fashion photography" is also interesting, as if the relationship between art and commerce was a given. Most striking is the scenography: a 100-foot collage. The Smithsonian show was a radical photography installation compared to what the New York art museums and galleries (to the extent that they showed photography at all) were up to. One observer described the show as consisting of "Gigantic stats, contact sheets, proofs of magazine ad pages, telegrams, sample layouts, rich full-toned black and white prints, and a wall sized (rear projection) screen that changed pictures every three seconds."[8] Avedon would do a similar show at the McCann Erickson advertising agency offices in New York, filmed by pioneering *cinema verité* director D. A. Pennebaker for an unrealized documentary. The young dynamo captured by Pennebaker is pure Avedon, with all his elbow, at the peak of his early career.

Observations was well received. But his second book, *Nothing Personal*, was destroyed by drama critic Robert Brustein in an ugly, *ad hominem* attack in *The New York Review of Books*.[9] A decidedly "New York is a small town" story, I nonetheless tell it in some detail below because it is the seminal event leading to his project with Lartigue, the photobook *Diary of a Century* (1970). Avedon's naked ambition, wealth, good looks, and fluency in the gray area between high and low art had become threatening to the gatekeepers of the art world. Terms like "fine," "high" and "low" may seem so Last Century to us today, but in the sixties they demarcated hotly contested territories. He was knocked for a loop by Brustein's vitriol. For several years, he retreated into his magazine work, and avoided making the "artistic portraits" that were the hallmark of *Observations*.

I like to refer to the next phase of Avedon's career as "Avedon, Inc." It began with his move to *Vogue* in 1965, and was marked by an increasing tendency to self-curate rather than just put his work on view. He was aiming for posterity, but he often ended up shooting himself in the foot. Stung by accusations of superficiality, he drew self-conscious lines between his commercial and what he referred to as his "serious" work. He would have been far better off embracing the continuum of his practices.

This awkward revisionism reached a crescendo in the Whitney show of 1994: its puzzling suppression of his so called "fashion work"; the resurrection of some of his early "street photography" that he had wisely chosen to buy back from *LIFE* magazine in 1948 rather than see them published at the time; and, finally, his exact recreation, down to the shades of grey on the walls, of the little room in which his sole monographic Museum of Modern Art (MoMA) exhibition had been held a mere two decades earlier.[10] Avedon would have been better served letting his fashion work speak for itself; leaving the *LIFE* photos in the drawer rather than trying to shoehorn them into a tradition of New York "street" photography, of which he was only tangentially a part; and remixing his presentation of the MoMA photos of his father rather than suspending the moment in curatorial formaldehyde. Through these strained reinventions, he seemed to be trying to force-feed the spectator his importance in the history of photography.

The more Avedon pushed, the more the intelligentsia dug in their heels. MoMA photography curator John Szarkowski, an early supporter of his work, would eventually exclude Avedon from the canon.[11] Far from gaining the recognition he craved, Avedon died frustrated and perplexed by his relative marginality at MoMA, *The New York Review of Books*, and their international counterparts. The exhibits he did obtain, while impressive

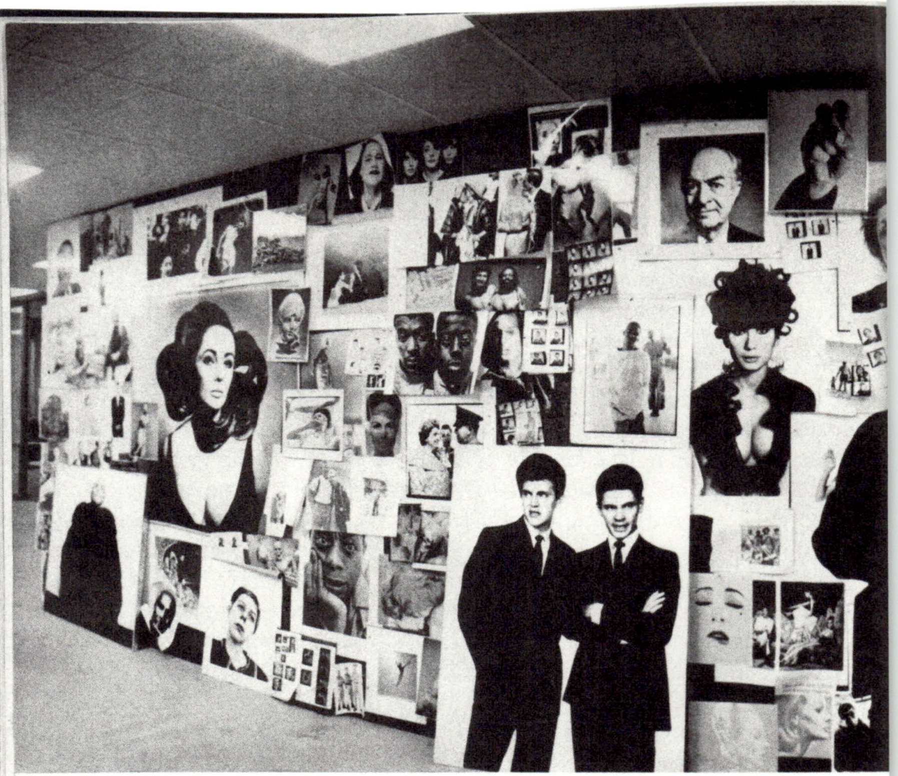

AVEDON SHOW

There has never been a photographic show like this one.

Richard Avedon, photographer, iconoclast, and showman, produced what must be called (for the sake of accuracy) the most spectacular photographic show ever. On leaving the McCann-Erickson ad agency exhibition hall, some—including this writer—were convinced that photo shows will never again be the same. This explosive talent called Avedon will have long-range effects on all men who think seriously about hanging pictures on walls.

The show was part circus, part Happening, part Broadway opening, and all exciting photography. Gigantic stats, contact sheets, proofs of magazine ad pages, telegrams, sample layouts, rich, full-toned black-and-white prints, and a wall-sized (rear-projection) screen that changed pictures every three seconds—these were some of the parts from which the show was made. There was a telegram from former President Eisenhower telling that he couldn't make a sitting, and a note from the Daughters of the American Revolution telling how much they liked Avedon's photograph of them. Plus a door: when it was opened and

52

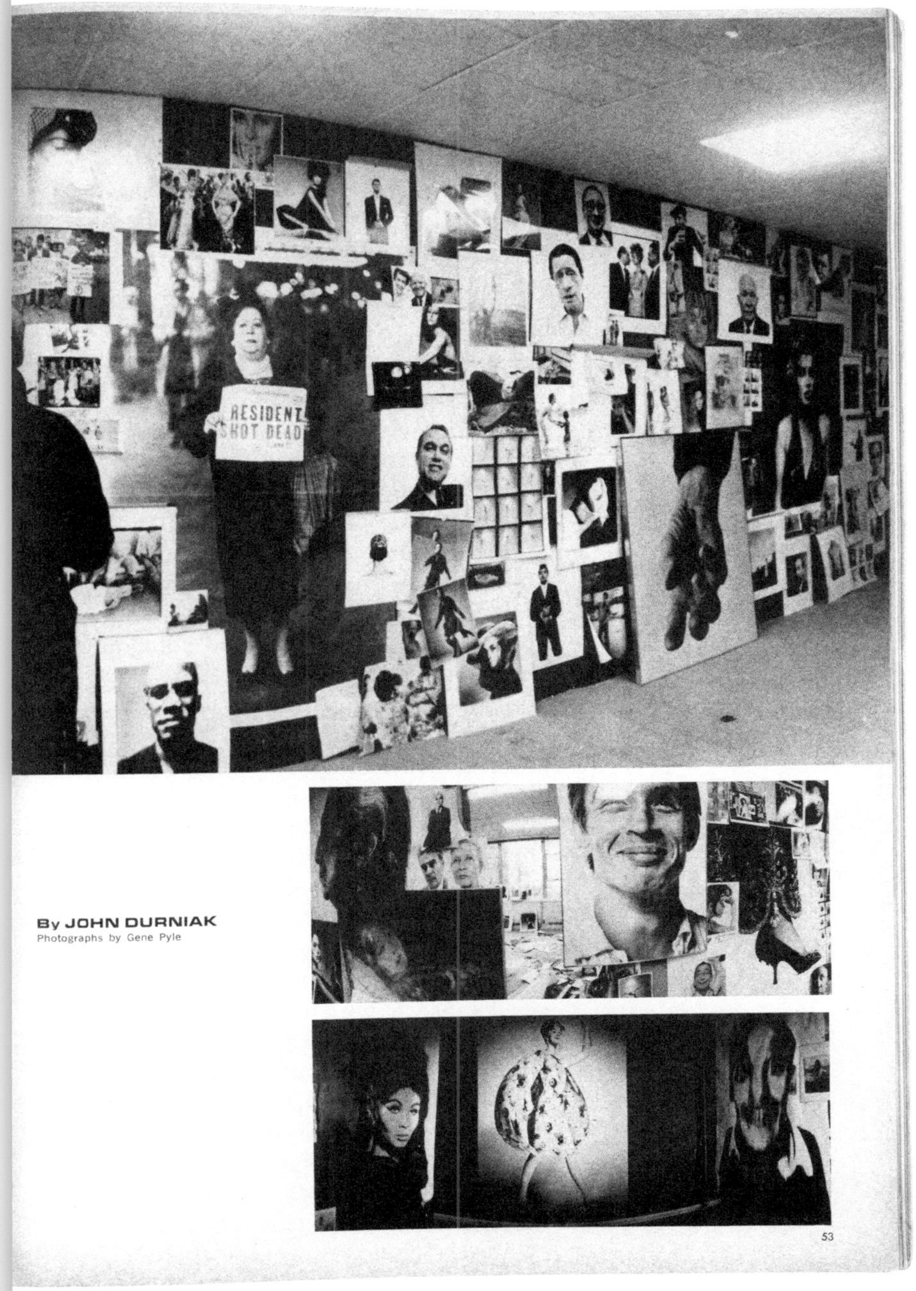

By JOHN DURNIAK
Photographs by Gene Pyle

53

Richard Avedon, McCann Erickson advertising agency installation, 1965, in *Popular Photography*, May 1965, pp. 52–53; text by John Durniak, photography by Gene Pyle

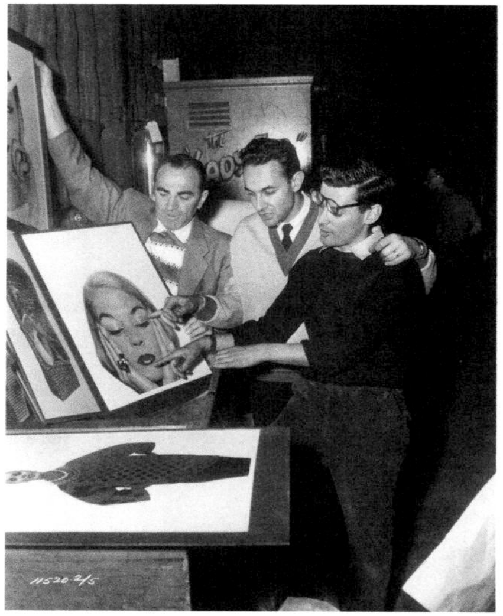

Director Stanley Donen and Avedon select photographs to dress the set of *Quality Magazine* for *Funny Face*, 1957

to us in retrospect, were mere consolation prizes to him. The ones he really wanted never came to pass: a major monographic exhibition at MoMA in the early seventies; a New York venue for his masterpiece, *In the American West*, in the eighties; and, in the nineties, a Paris venue for his Whitney show. In his biographical note in his later photobook, *The Sixties* (1999), no mention is made of *any* museum exhibitions in his lifetime, as if what really mattered was his career as a working photographer. After nearly sixty years, they just didn't add up for him.

Then again, Avedon didn't make it easy. Photography museums were still considered art world ghettos, and he turned down their offers. He wanted to be up there with the great portrait painters in the Louvre, or his brush-wielding contemporaries at the Centre Pompidou or the Musée d'Art Moderne de la Ville de Paris. In time, he is getting there. The big tent of contemporary art has opened to photography-based practices in ways that Avedon significantly prefigured. He rejected the idea of "truth" in photography (we can file that word with "fine," "high" and "low" under Last Century) before the Pictures Generation — Richard Prince, Cindy Sherman and their cohorts — took the final steps of its deconstruction. His work — and not just his commercial work — ushered in the desacralization and hybridization of the photographic image throughout the entire landscape of visual culture, from magazines to museum installations, even as he himself sought affirmation as an artist from the gatekeepers of the White Cube. Succeeding generations will increasingly recognize Avedon not simply as a portrait maker (or, as I prefer to think of him, a history painter) with a keen eye for the Zeitgeist, but also as a harbinger of our image-saturated, digital present. What better way to explore these themes is there than a "photography" exhibition about a movie, a book, and a magazine: *Funny Face, Diary of a Century,* and *Egoïste*?

Funny Face: the New Look of American Lyric Cinema

Trying to characterize Richard Avedon's contribution to *Funny Face* while also giving Donen, the director, his relative due is a complicated matter. The facts are not in dispute: Avedon, as visual consultant, contributed the title credits, and the freeze frame stills in the "Think Pink" musical number and of Hepburn at various Paris landmarks and tourist spots. He advised Donen and June on lighting (both studio and exterior), filters and optical effects generally. He also served as a consultant to the film in terms of "authenticating" its representation of the world of fashion and fashion photography. Avedon's contract was for nine weeks, only one of which was supposed to be on location in Paris. However, rain delays kept him there longer. He was paid a thousand dollars a week (the same as June). Avedon was also paid a flat fee of five hundred dollars for the use of still photographs (several of which can be seen in the film in the offices of *Quality* magazine) and another two hundred and fifty dollars for each still photograph he might make at Paramount's request for additional set dressing.[12] Presumably, this covered the iconic image of Hepburn that Astaire/Avery/Avedon develops and hangs in the darkroom before their first kiss.

Other photographers had consulted on films in ways distinct from being mere "still men," as they were called — set photographers who took pictures for continuity and publicity purposes. Avedon himself cites Eliot Elisofon's work for John Huston on *Moulin Rouge* (1952) and George Hoyningen-Huene's for George Cukor on *A Star is Born* (1954) as precedents for photographers working as visual consultants with movie directors.[13] *On the Waterfront* director Elia Kazan's personal copies of Weegee's photobook *The Naked City* (1945) were bookmarked by Kazan to note interesting visual signifiers that might translate well to his film.[14] Soon afterward, Stanley Kubrick would bring Weegee on in a similar capacity for *Dr. Strangelove* (1964). As Avedon put it, "Fashion photography and photography in general was more inventive at that moment than was Hollywood."[15]

How Avedon came to Donen's attention is emblematic of the way he advanced his commercial and artistic practices together. Other aspiring artists who worked with still cameras, like Robert Frank, took on commercial work quietly, to pay the bills. Still others, like Diane Arbus, embraced editorial work for the likes of *Esquire*, but shot ads and fashion spreads without fanfare. For Avedon, on the other hand, photography existed on a continuum. He came to Donen's attention through his work on the ad campaign for Helena Rubinstein's "Jazz, Red Hot and Cool" lipstick; the lighting piqued the movie director's interest. (There was also

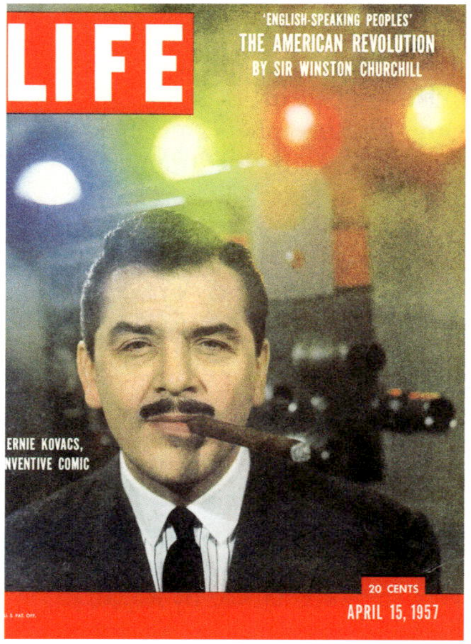

Ernie Kovacs on the cover of *LIFE* April 15, 1957; photograph by Ralph Morse

a tie-in to the ad campaign in which a Dave Brubeck record with an Avedon image as the cover was included with a lipstick purchase.)

Avedon's use of blurry colored lights in the background caused a minor stir in visual arts circles. The *LIFE* photography editor sent a memo around that his staff photographers should take note, resulting in a magazine cover of Ernie Kovacs that "uses the technique of the colored lights in the background to a fare-thee-well." [16] Maidenform then asked Avedon to work that effect into their bra ads. All of this was recounted in an ad industry newspaper column, the source of which was clearly Avedon. It served two purposes: to remind his Madison Avenue clients that, even after *Funny Face*, he was still not too busy to take their commercial work, and to make sure everyone understood that, even though Avedon didn't actually shoot the *LIFE* cover, he was the *auteur* of its visual effects, and should be credited for his impact on current photographic practice. Not coincidentally, that issue also contained a four-page spread on Avedon's work in *Funny Face*.

Avedon's collaboration with Donen was loose but one of mutual confidence (and youth — Donen was thirty, Avedon thirty-three). Donen sought Avedon out —"I wanted certain scenes in the picture to have a soft smoky focus, to look like some of Dick's fashion shoots," he said. [17] The key moment of their collaboration was in the innovative way they froze the shots. At that time, freezing a frame was technically primitive and visually problematic. Taking the 35mm frame and filming it yielded grainy and imperfect results, and Donen was a perfectionist. He made, in effect, an 8 x 10 fashion photograph freeze frame by linking Avedon's 8 x 10 camera to the monstrous VistaVision camera by a set of mirrors, so that whenever Avedon clicked the shutter, he shot the exact picture that was being filmed, perfectly in frame with the running film. Donen may have been inspired by 3-D movies (still something of a gimmick in the fifties), where two cameras with the same angle are used, one looking into a mirror and one looking through, so that the nodal point of the two cameras is exactly the same. Essentially what Donen did was substitute Avedon's still camera for a second movie camera. Now you understand Guerrin's question.

Donen held his ground when Paramount executives balked at the soft focus, particularly the flaring lights in the Paris café scene (shot, by the way, on a Hollywood set). The look both Donen and Avedon wanted ran exactly counter to the studio's obsession with VistaVision-induced clarity. (VistaVision was Paramount's multi-million dollar bet that they could one-up CinemaScope in terms of image sharpness, which studios felt was their best offensive weapon against the incursions of television into their viewing audience.)

In Donen's authorized biography, Avedon recounts that he was barred from setting or adjusting the lights (this being a union job), or even talking to Donen on set, so the two evolved a set of signals based on Avedon fiddling with his necktie:

> They banned me from setting the lights, because I wasn't the lighting director, and I was told I could no longer speak to Stanley . . . [We] worked out a system using my necktie. First I'd swing it over to the direction of the light in question. I'd look at Stanley, Stanley'd look at me. Then, if I opened the knot in my tie, it meant that he should widen the aperture of the light. If I tightened my tie, it meant to narrow the spotlight and move it to the left, so it would flare, but not too much . . . "[18]

Avedon's outlaw status on the set was evident in some of the commentary on the budget sheets: "NOTE: no money allowed this budget [*sic*] for any special Avedon photographs" is typed on the set construction budget under Action Props on the thirty-fourth and last day of shooting. It's repeated on the Special Effects page: "No allowance for freeze frames for fashion montage . . . or tableau portion of THINK PINK Number."[19]

The studio bosses wanted Avedon reined in. In their view, he was ruining the bankable Stanley Donen's movie. In our digital age of manipulated images, it is hard to imagine how provocative, even polemical, the mise-en-scene of this bit of filmic fluff was in postwar Hollywood. But according to cameraman Stanley Cortez, whose credits include *The Magnificent Ambersons* (1942) and *The Night of the Hunter* (1955), this is how it went back then:

> We had to follow the studio's specific styles . . . Louis B. Mayer saw one of Zanuck's pictures in the early days and decided to change all his pictures from soft to hard color as a result . . . the other studios followed suit, so as a result we got "Christmas package"

> colors in Hollywood films of the forties and after. . . . Sometimes people here try to experiment but when the top brass see the first day's work . . . they say, "What the hell happened here?"[20]

Funny Face was considered lightly in the mainstream press when it came out. Bosley Crowther of *The New York Times* weighed in with a cursory review which did not mention Avedon.[21] (Avedon rectified this omission a few weeks later by generating a piece in the *Times* about his involvement.) Magazines such as *Films in Review* went a bit deeper: critic Edward Jablonski noted that the color in Hepburn's dance sequence in the "murky Existentialist boîte" was "masterfully handled." Moreover, he wrote, "the title and credits of *Funny Face* have a visual snap that makes one eager to see the picture itself," and:

> . . . the specific visual elements that adorn and enliven them derive from the typographic and art layouts of the fashion periodicals for which . . . Avedon has worked . . . *Funny Face* is replete with diffusions, distortions, color separations and other photographic hi-jinx before, during and after the developing and printing of the negative.

June, for his part, modestly averred that his job was "the practical realization of suggestions from Donen and Avedon." And Donen "generously" attributed the look of the film to Avedon.[22]

In *Dance* magazine, film critic Arthur Knight explored "the photographic problems of applying slick magazine techniques to a big studio musical," and how the film imparts "a choreographic quality to the fashion sequences" of the film. By far the most detailed period accounting of Avedon's work on the film, Knight's review discusses the freeze frames and the lighting complexities (both exterior and on set), and characterizes Avedon's photographic style as "frozen dance." According to Knight, Donen conceived the idea of shooting the darkroom scene, in which Astaire sings the title song to Hepburn, in a red light (though in reality such lights are yellow), but Avedon "proposed adding the bright beam of the enlarging camera, literally transfixing Miss Hepburn to the wall as Astaire danced around her."[23] Donen later said that "if Avedon had made no other suggestion on the entire show, that single shot idea was worth his entire salary."[24]

Knight singled out the dance scene in the basement café as an example of "a lighting style that knowingly breaks all the rules — at least, the rules by which most films are made today." Those rules meant that "art" films were made in black and white, and commercial films were shot in orthodox color. For Hollywood musicals, orthodox meant what Cortez had termed "the Christmas package." It would be years before Antonioni's first color film *Red Desert* (1964) and other foreign art films would introduce expressionistic color into the mix. Is it a stretch to consider *Funny Face* a necessary precursor to Antonioni's *Blow-Up* (1966)?

Directors and lighting cameramen found the VistaVision/CinemaScope format stultifying. The great cinematographer Leon Shamroy recalled the "terrible days" of CinemaScope, which "wrecked the art of film for a decade," though he also acknowledged that "wide screen saved the picture business."[25] *Funny Face* was seen by some as reaction against the inherent gigantism of widescreen. Although shot in VistaVision, it managed to recover the lost intimacy of Hollywood movies. British critic David Vaughan, writing for *Sight and Sound*, had previously written an obituary for what he termed American Lyric Cinema:

> a pure form of musical comedy that was essentially a cinematic form . . . a freer and easier use of song and dance that had existed before . . . rather than the usual state of affairs in which everything stopped while somebody sang or danced.[26]

Epitomized by *On the Town* (1949), it was already in decline in *Singin' in the Rain* (1952, also directed by Donen). "The true and touching qualities of the [original stage productions] are dissipated in the acres of screen space and aeons of screen time," continued Vaughan.[27] Donen instinctively understood he needed to temper and even reinvent the screen musical to save it from regressing to colorized Depression-era *tableaux vivants*. Avedon was the person to help him do it.

Vaughan perked up when, less than a year later, he reviewed *Funny Face*, writing, "it gives hope that the American Lyric Cinema can survive in spite of CinemaScope."[28] Its "notable visual distinction given by the collaboration of Avedon" is a critical part of the new look to Donen's picture, despite its rather conventional story line and recycled Jazz Age stage music.

Cahiers du Cinéma found the film "extremely seductive," as Jean Domarchi wrote.[29] Though Avedon was not cited, the film was described as being shot in the style of *Vogue* or *Harper's Bazaar*. Hepburn ended up on the cover of the magazine.

The New Wave also weighed in. Alain Resnais, perhaps signaling his future intention to branch out from Holocaust documentaries to musical comedy, included *Funny Face* in his list of top ten films of 1957.[30] *Cahiers's* editor, Eric Rohmer, heralded the film's bold use of color.

Like his British colleagues, Domarchi wrote effusively about Donen's redemption of the musical comedy genre. The film's "deliberate intrusion of photographic technique into the cinema" is a huge success, Domarchi noted, contributing a "fairy tale feeling" to Hepburn's subterranean dance scene. That the "look" of the film was a contentious subject is evident in Domarchi's invocation of Robert Burks and Joseph LaShelle as examples of cinematographers who would be threatened by Donen and Avedon's bold visuals. (Burks shot twelve films for Alfred Hitchcock. LaShelle, one of the great craftsmen of the *film noir* era, was prone to harshly lit close-ups and classical pictorial compositions. It was said he could make even a color film look black and white.[31]) Obviously neither was on Donen's short list for *Funny Face*. Perhaps Donen settled on the veteran June to provide protective coloration for the project — a Hollywood workhorse, a familiar face to studio bosses, versed in the visual orthodoxy of the Hollywood musical. Who could be a better choice to subvert it?

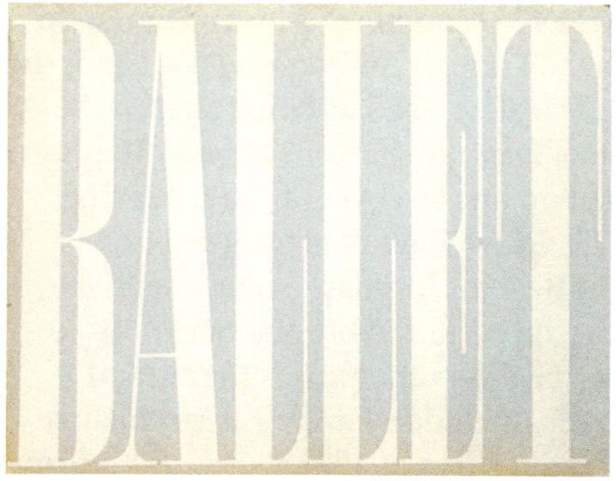

Alexey Brodovitch's *Ballet* (New York: J. J. Augustin, 1945) was a cinematic chronicle in still photographs of the 1930s Ballets Russes.

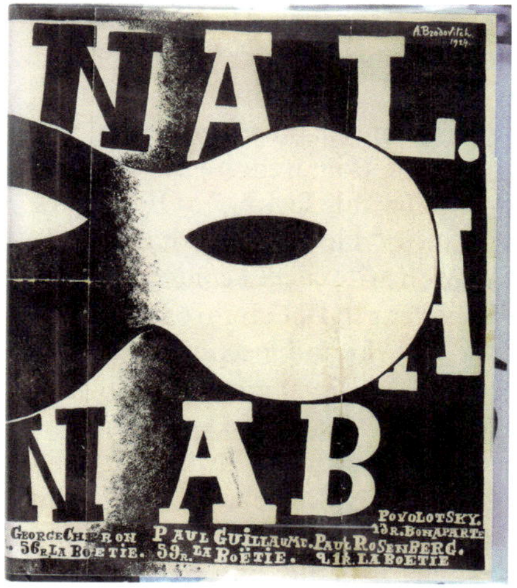

In 2002, Avedon gave his gallerist, Jeffrey Fraenkel, a copy of *Alexey Brodovitch,* the biography by Kerry William Purcell (London: Phaidon, 2002). Avedon used a scan of Brodovitch's 1924 *Bal Banal* poster to make a custom dust jacket (see *pages 244–45*).

The Book that Misses You

Wherever you draw the *auteurist* line between the director's and the visual consultant's respective roles in *Funny Face*, Avedon's contribution was a major factor. But his presence in the film was something else entirely: as already noted, though it bears repeating, he was also the source of the film's story. He had married Dorcas Nowell, a bank teller, whom he transformed into a fashion model despite her alleged resistance to the proposition. Producer Leonard Gershe, who knew Dick and Doe, as they were called, thought it was a great idea for a musical comedy. Later, he would say that he was going for Avedon's "aura," not his life story, in the Fred Astaire character, and Holly-wood- type liberties were indeed taken.[32]

By the time *Funny Face* began filming, Avedon was divorced from Doe and had remarried. Doe had left him for Hollywood and a brief acting career, marrying tough guy movie director Don Siegel along the way. So much for the reluctant Galatea.

Nonetheless, the film's narrative was drawn from Avedon's time in Paris with Doe. And the France of *Funny Face* is Avedon's France, close to the movie in his head, even if it is Gershe's screenplay and Donen's mise en scene. Dorian Leigh's description of her first modeling trip to Paris, five decades after the fact, is actually so close to the script of *Funny Face* that she seems to be confusing the movie with real life (*see pages 73–74*).

Avedon's own memories of his days with Doe in Paris grew more intense with time. In 2001, Avedon's gallerist (and friend) Jeffrey Fraenkel published *Made in France*, a slim, elegant volume of reproductions of early *Harper's Bazaar* engraver's prints. In it, Avedon recalled a visit with Doe to la Boule Blanche, a storied, long-shuttered Parisian nightclub. For more than fifty years after she left him, Avedon dutifully continued to send her inscribed copies of every book he published. In her copy of *Made in France,* he wrote: "This is the book that misses you."[33]

Carmel and Mary Louise: Les Girls

Avedon's France — the France of his imagination, nurtured by magazines — began to take shape in 1934, when Carmel Snow joined *Harper's Bazaar* and rose to become its editor. Once Snow took the magazine in hand, it became the principal conduit to America of French culture as it informed fashion. Snow had a broad view of what went into the mix. Selling clothes for advertisers was a pretext to dive into French culture and revel in its worldly pleasures.

After World War II, Snow enlisted Marie-Louise Bousquet as the magazine's Paris editor. Bousquet presided over one of Paris' most vibrant salons. She and Snow schooled the twentysomething Avedon in the basic elements of *la French touch*. He discovered Proust, who would be a foundational reference for Avedon in his framing of Lartigue's work, and, later, the Volpi Ball, which he photographed for *Egoïste*. Avedon's personal library contains three complete editions of *In Search of Lost Time.* The earliest of these has the old-fashioned Galignani label on the endpapers, indicating that Avedon bought it just after the war, in Paris, on one of his first assignments for *Harper's Bazaar*. One can imagine Bousquet and Snow sweeping into the venerable Rue de Rivoli bookstore, their young innocent abroad in tow, loading him up with the necessary tomes for his "*education sentimentale*." The books in Avedon's library are rarely annotated in his hand, but on the inside front cover of his copy of *Swann's Way*, he wrote the word "asparagus" and the page number corresponding to Proust's oft-quoted description of the vegetable.[34]

After the war Snow went on a mission to resuscitate the French fashion industry. The magazine's wartime coverage had been sober and serious: she had dispatched Henri Cartier-Bresson to London in 1944 to document the ravages of war. With its end, she knew what she had to do. Her efforts earned her a Légion d'honneur, which she wore proudly on her bathrobe. Snow died in 1961, out of power and out of favor, the wear and tear of her alcoholic lifestyle evident in Avedon's portrait of her, taken in 1959. Her reputation as field marshal of the fashion army was quickly eclipsed by the ascendancy of her more mediagenic lieutenant Diana Vreeland.

My Teacher

Even more than Carmel Snow, Alexey Brodovitch was Avedon's professional mentor. He was also something of a surrogate father. It is not hard to see why. Avedon had a troubled relationship with his own father, Jacob Israel Avedon, who would leave Avedon's adored mother when the photographer was not yet thirty.

Jacob's forebears were immigrant Russian Jews. Brodovitch was a White Russian aristocrat. Jacob's father deserted his family after they landed on the Lower East Side of Manhattan. Jacob was sent to a Jewish Child Care Association Orphanage with his two brothers. Before the Revolution, Alexey lived in St. Petersburg and journeyed often with his family to the South of France. He spoke French fluently; Jacob spoke Yiddish. Jacob clawed his way through the New York City Public School system, became a substitute teacher, and eventually started Avedon's Fifth Avenue, a women's specialty shop where young Richard got his first taste of fashion. The business went bankrupt in the Great Depression. After fighting for the Tsar in World War I (lying about his age to enlist against the wishes of his father, who was a General), Alexey served in the White Russian Army and was wounded in battle. He fled to Constantinople and then Paris when Odessa fell to the Bolsheviks. He found himself penniless in Paris and gravitated toward the avant gardes, who were remaking modern culture in the wake of the First World War.[35]

Brodovitch's journey through the first half of the twentieth century must have seemed impossibly glamorous to young Avedon. Here was an aristocratic Francophile who beat out Picasso in the 1924 Bal Banal poster competition. (The Bal Banal was organized by the Union of Russian Artists as a benefit for needy emigré artists. Picasso came in second; both designs were printed and pasted about Paris.) Here was someone who, through the Ballets Russes, collaborated with Picasso, André Derain and Christian Bérard[36] — someone conversant with all the *-isms* in the air: Cubism, Constructivism, Futurism, Purism and Surrealism.

Brodovitch's adoptive paternity allowed Avedon to draw a historical line back in time from postwar New York to 1924 Paris, melting pot of multiple modernisms, and thus to situate himself in the broad historical trajectory of twentieth-century visual culture. As an added bonus, Avedon's chosen métier of photography, the "second child of the arts,"[37] was already in that pot — along with industrial design, graphic design, advertising, posters, billboards and everything else taking Modernism to the less contested terrain of "the street." As Andy Grundberg noted in *Brodovitch* (1989), in addition to the obvious themes behind the Bal Banal poster's mask, its "graphic light-to-dark inversion of its mask shape, type, and background . . . suggests the positive-negative process of photography."[38] Brodovitch's own photographic work, especially his remarkable, largely forgotten photobook *Ballet* (1945), a collection of photographs of the Ballets Russes, was an important influence on Avedon.

In a telling, private gesture, Avedon drew this line from Picasso/Brodovitch to himself quite clearly. When Kerry William Purcell's monograph *Alexey Brodovitch* was published in 2002, Avedon was unimpressed with the dust jacket design (and perhaps miffed that another photographer's work graced the cover). He made a scan of Brodovitch's *Bal Banal* poster and covered the book with it, as if to say: This book is worthy of a more emblematic image of the man than a Lillian Bassman photograph from the pages of *Harper's Bazaar*. After all, this man out-designed Picasso! He sent the re-jacketed book to Fraenkel, and gave another copy to his son John for John's fiftieth birthday. In that copy, next to the designer's name, Avedon simply but eloquently wrote, "My teacher."

Observations and Photobooks

Avedon and Brodovitch's collaboration reached its peak with *Observations* in 1959. Avedon's first book gathered up his "art portraits" with brief texts by Truman Capote, in a stunning Brodovitch design.[39] Removed from the layouts of *Harper's Bazaar*, these pictures — many of which had been used in support of the magazine's cultural reporting — take on an entirely different aspect. For example, Bernard Buffet is made to peer enviously sideways at the bigger, older and more relaxed painter Georges Braque. Connecting unrelated photos by this kind of impish, Eisensteinian montage was one of Brodovitch's signature design moves. Picasso — declared simply "The Winner" by Capote — is followed by a diptych of Coco Chanel and a picture of Marie-Louise Bousquet in bed with her stuffed monkey. Then come *New Yorker* Paris correspondent Janet Flanner (pen name "Genet"), and Marcel Duchamp. Capote dwells for several pages on Jean Cocteau (who, according to the writer, "more than anyone formed French taste in the present century,"), recounting a rather fatuous anecdote about Gide and Cocteau while Marcel Achard, Marcel Jouhandeau, and Jacques-Yves Cousteau pass by. In another chapter, we have Brigitte Bardot, then Martita Hunt and Estelle Winwood in the New York production of *The Madwoman of Chaillot*.[40] (That production, following the play's unprecedented run in Paris, also featured Bérard's sets and costumes.)

If *Harper's Bazaar* was a weather report on Paris fashion and its cultural sources, *Observations* is a more planetary discourse. Avedon's collection of French icons is only one element among several samplings of the great, the good, and the unsung. With respect to France, *Observations* presents a postwar avant garde. The war in question, however, is World War I. All of Avedon's French subjects are a generation or more older than he is: the interwar avant garde, recycled for the postwar reconstruction of the Fashion Capital of the World. Like the Beat poets who made pilgrimages to Paris around the same time, Avedon was looking for a Paris that, to its emerging avant gardes, was already passé.

In an early mockup of the book he had prepared for Truman Capote, Avedon implores the writer not to show it prematurely to fashion photographer Cecil Beaton.[41] His intended audience was not yet "real" critics — art world gatekeepers like, say, Clement Greenberg. Although no longer at the service of a magazine selling dresses and cosmetics, the images of the book still exist in a middlebrow no-man's land somewhere between fine art and fashion reportage. (Many of the images in *Observations* would later be editioned by Avedon, but the concept of limited edition prints had not yet come into practice.[42]) Soon he would seek the approbation of the "serious" art world, but for now he operated comfortably and unselfconsciously in the grey zone where, at the apogee of his fame, in 1958, he was profiled in *The New Yorker*.

Avedon understood how important

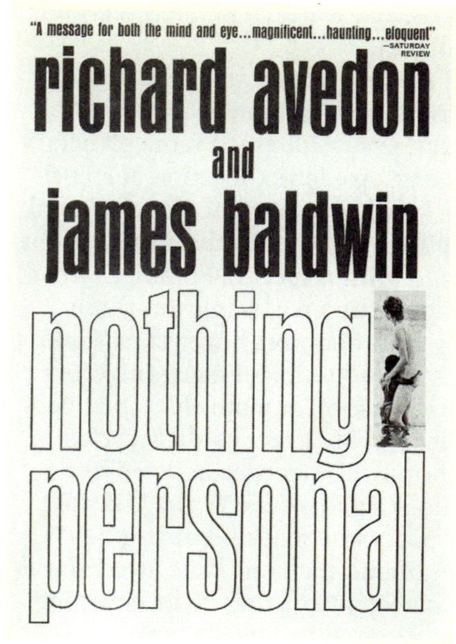

Nothing Personal (New York: Atheneum / Lucerne: C.J. Bucher, 1964) was Avedon's second photobook, a collaboration with his friend from high school, the writer James Baldwin. Pictured: the first paperback edition (New York: Dell, 1965).

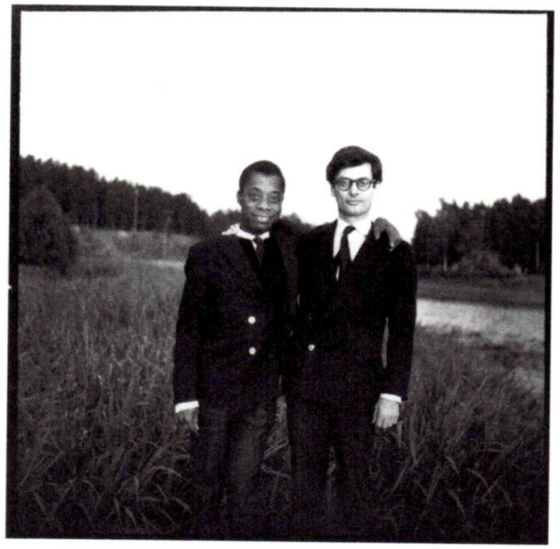

James Baldwin and Richard Avedon, writer and photographer, Finland, June 1, 1964 (contact print)

the photobook would become as the photography market evolved, as important as — and perhaps even more important than — a museum exhibition. The fifties saw an emergent interest in photobooks that mimicked coffee table art books. Audiences could more easily buy a book than travel to the few major cities where photography was exhibited in galleries and museums. As publishing evolved, photobooks would become better printed, easier to produce, and, eventually, collectibles in their own right.[43] Even in its title, *Observations* responds to Henri Cartier-Bresson's earlier *The Decisive Moment* (1952). With its multiple images from the same portrait sitting, laid out on the page with brio by Brodovitch, the book is something of a riposte to Cartier-Bresson's idea that a photograph captures a single, decisive image. Later Avedon would use the phrase, "the constructed moment," to describe his own photographic modus operandi.

One may wonder when Avedon and Brodovitch first became aware of Robert Frank's *The Americans* (1959). No doubt by the middle of the next decade, it (and Frank) loomed large in Avedon's thinking. The parallel histories of the two books speak to the evolution of the photobook. Frank's seminal work first appeared in France in 1958 under the title *Les Americains.* (The *Observations* project was already well under way.) The French edition was published with borrowed texts by Simone de Beauvoir, Erskine Caldwell, William Faulkner, Henry Miller and John Steinbeck, along with a bizarre cover drawing by Saul Steinberg of a New York high-rise apartment building that is difficult to connect with Frank's images. Frank himself was not happy. He recalled the similar disconnect between James Agee's text and Walker Evans' photographs in *Let Us Now Praise Famous Men* (1941), but he was not in a position to win any arguments with French publisher Robert Delpire. Frank wanted no text, and only one photograph per spread. Unlike Brodovitch, whose visual language depended on the juxtaposition and movement of multiple images, Frank was opposed to any montage effects in the layout. Although the individual images in *The Americans* build an overall mood in four discrete chapters, the images are meant to be absorbed one at a time.

A year later, the American edition would jettison all the texts, leaving only the brief, descriptive captions, and add a brief introduction by Jack Kerouac —someone much more in synch with Frank than, say, Simone de Beauvoir. There would be only one photograph per spread. This was exactly how Walker Evans had laid out his photobook, *American Photographs*, to accompany his 1938 exhibition at MoMA — the first monographic exhibition allotted to a photographer in the history of that institution, and a landmark in the history of photography. Frank had financed *The Americans* with a Guggenheim grant. Avedon used to make bitter jokes that his commercial practice was his own Guggenheim. (Diane Arbus also had a Guggenheim grant, and John Szarkowski had two.) Like Kerouac with *On the Road* (finished in 1951 but not published until 1957), Frank had struggled for years to find a publisher.

Kerouac's agreement to write an introduction for the American edition is probably what obtained American publication for the project so quickly after the French edition came out, but the book is hardly a collaboration between Kerouac and Frank in the way that their film *Pull My Daisy* (1959) would be.[44] And even with an assist from Kerouac, it wasn't until a decade later, with the Aperture edition of 1969, that Frank was able to publish exactly the book he envisioned.[45] *Observations*, on the other hand, was an active three-way collaboration between writer, designer and photographer, and Avedon had the means to produce the book he wanted.

Highbrow Smackdown

By 1962, Avedon was well positioned for posterity. On the foundations of his commercial success, he had laid the twin cornerstones of his artistic career: his first photobook and his first monographic museum exhibition at the Smithsonian. He would soon find out that it was easier for a camel to pass through the eye of a needle than for a rich, glamorous fashion photographer to achieve validation as an artist. His fluency in the gray zones of the culture industry — which today seems quite modern — was taken as a treasonous embrace of Mammon. For the gatekeepers of culture, money was, quite simply, a liability.

In 1964, it was Brustein's *New York Review of Books* assessment of his second photobook that derailed the Avedon express. While a competent theatre critic, Brustein had no real credentials in art or photography, and he eviscerated Avedon and Baldwin. Though many would agree

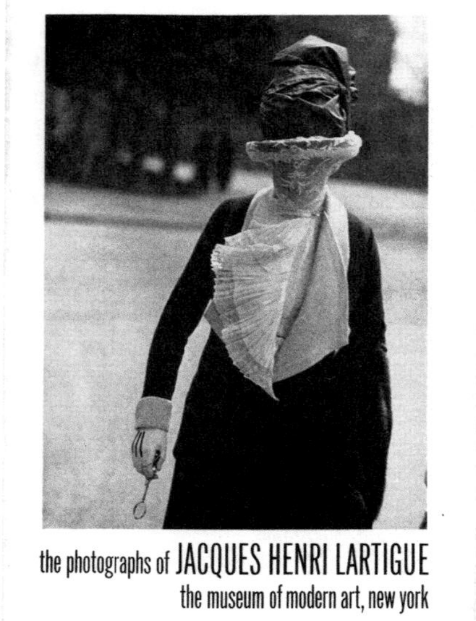

The Photographs of Jacques Henri Lartigue, MoMA Bulletin XXX, no. 1 (New York: Museum of Modern Art, 1963). MoMA's exhibition presented Lartigue as a naïf with a camera.

that *Nothing Personal* is among Avedon's weaker published efforts (and Baldwin's text has not aged as well as Avedon's photographs), Brustein's animus, which oozes from his sentences, is brutal. Avedon, he wrote, is a "show biz moralist" with a "hideously jaundiced eye" caring "less for truth than sensation." He asserted that the book demonstrated "an honorable tradition of revolt gone sour, given over to fame and ambition, discredited by shadowy motives, twisted by questionable ideals, turned into a theatrical game by café society performers."[46] Brustein was even disgusted by the book's high production values.

Truman Capote leapt to Avedon's defense. In a published letter to the editor, he questioned why Brustein would attack the book simply because it is a handsome piece of bookmaking. "Would he rather it was printed on paper-toweling?" Capote archly asked. He pointed out that even if the entire print run sold out, neither Avedon, Baldwin nor the publisher would make "twenty cents."[47] (To be fair, Brustein doesn't really criticize it as a moneymaking operation. He objects to the *expenditure* of money in principle on such a project.) For three years following Brustein's diatribe, Avedon made no art portraits.

Proust, with a Camera, to the Rescue

Fortunately, in 1963, Avedon had been shown the work of a French photographer whose images were, to his eye, the visual equivalent of Proust. By 1968 he was deeply involved in the editing and publishing of his third photobook — one that would, over time, have an impact on photography greater than his first. However, his next project, *Diary of a Century* (1970) contained none of his own photographs, but those of Lartigue.

The extent of Avedon's role in crafting the Lartigue of today has been little understood up until now. Marianne Le Galliard's essay makes clear, finally, the extent to which Avedon is the principal *metteur en scene* of the Lartigue of the twenty-first century, despite Lartigue's reputation being more identified with John Szarkowski. Kevin Moore, who first tackled the subject of Lartigue's successive identities as an artist in *The Invention of Lartigue*, was primarily focused on the ways in which Szarkowksi appropriated Lartigue's chilhood photos to buttress prevailing theories of "fine art" photography. Moore's deconstruction of the seminal 1963 Lartigue exhibition at MoMA is a critical contribution to Lartigue scholarship. Unfortunately, Moore stops there. He refers only generally to the next phase of Lartigue's appropriation by fashion photography. *Diary of a Century* is referred to only a handful of times. Avedon is barely mentioned.

Moore is simply wrong when he lumps *Diary of a Century* together with *Boyhood: Photographs of J. H. Lartigue*, the facsimile family album published in Switzerland in 1966. He writes: "They reinforced and extended Szarkowski's characterization of Lartigue as a photographic naïf."[48] On the contrary, *Diary*'s conception of Lartigue is diametrically opposed to the MoMA notion of Lartigue as naïf. Avedon is quite clear that Lartigue is constructing his photographic moments. How else to explain the endpapers of the book, taken from Lartigue's diaries, which show his meticulous compositions, recalled from memory and committed to paper before he received developed prints back from the lab? Moore's book was published before the Avedon archives were accessible to researchers. He was not aware of the trove of correspondence between the two men about the making of *Diary*. The Lartigue of the twenty-first century is Avedon's, not Szarkowski's.

Diary of a Century was the third and final photobook collaboration of Avedon's career. Never again would he link his artistic fate in any meaningful way to a writer, a designer or an artist. *Diary* would eventually achieve Avedon's major objective: to make Lartigue's body of work a legitimate artistic antecedent to his own. Alongside MoMA's trajectory of the history of photography from Eugène Atget to Walker Evans to Robert Frank and Diane Arbus, Avedon invented a parallel universe: Lartigue, Brodovitch, Avedon.

After the Barricades

Avedon edited *Diary* in Lartigue's Paris apartment while the riots of May 1968 occurred in the streets below. Avedon eventually made it home to New York, via Brussels. Lartigue almost fled to Switzerland, changing his mind only after he had loaded up his car and hit the road. During the next decade, Avedon would be less present in France. Apart from discharging his contractual fashion obligations to *Vogue*, his activity would focus on American politics, especially the war in Vietnam, the death of his father, and, in 1978, a retrospective at the Metropolitan Museum of Art in New York. While in France for *Vogue* the following year, he made memorable photographs of Francis Bacon and Samuel Beckett. In New York, he also produced his fourth photobook (with Doon Arbus), *Alice in Wonderland: The Forming of a Company and the Making of Play* (1973). Designed by Ruth Ansel, Bea Feitler's co-art director at *Harper's Bazaar*, this "book about a play" documents avant-garde theatre director André Gregory's transformation of *Alice and Wonderland* by the Manhattan Project, an "off" theatre company, into a raucous, improvised gathering[49] In terms of subject matter, we are a long way from Lewis Carroll's Wonderland. It marks a 180-degree turn from *Diary of a Century*. Still, Avedon is taking small steps back toward an all-Avedon photobook. Here he features his own photographs, but puts the spotlight on André Gregory and his troupe. The book feels closest in spirit to Brodovitch's *Ballet* from nearly thirty years earlier.

Avedon's next book, titled, simply, *Portraits* (1976), would align much more closely with the Walker Evans/Robert Frank template: one photograph per spread, very simple captions at the bottom of the white space opposite, each image framed rather than bled. *Portraits* was not a collaboration (except to the extent that one considers all portraits to be collaborations between the shooter and the sitter). Capote and Baldwin had been swapped out for a bona fide art critic, Harold Rosenberg, who contributed a deeply art historical introduction in place of Capote's gossipy belles lettres or Baldwin's searing sermonizing intercut with images. The design is minimal, if not invisible. It is as if Avedon had decided: if you can't beat 'em, join 'em.

Besides losing his father and suffering a minor heart ailment shortly thereafter, Avedon experienced a major professional disappointment during this period. For several years, he had been in discussions with Szarkowski for a major show at MoMA, tentatively titled *Hard Times*. The exhibition was intended to instrumentalize Avedon's camera into the realm of politics through a radical exhibition concept. He wanted to time the exhibition with the 1972 Presidential elections. It was to open at MoMA, in order to "validate" it,[50] but then reopen simultaneously in the following days at several high schools around the country. Avedon's studio was using contact printing machines at the time that made serviceable prints from 8 x 10 contact negatives in ten seconds. His idea was to have several such machines at the show, manned by students (performance meets exhibition!), making the prints for "twenty exhibitions in two nights, to quickly get this out to the kids."

This would have been a radical departure from mainstream photography shows, which travel through serial venues and, as Doon Arbus said, "are very precious." Avedon and Arbus envisioned a phone-book-sized catalog of 300–400 images with an image on one side of each spread and a text on the other. That text would be a transcription of an interview with the sitter that was made simultaneously with the sitting. Each would be given fifteen minutes to say whatever was on his or her mind. This was thought to be more authentic than giving the sitter an opportunity to submit something, or even edit what was said spontaneously. The concept of the exhibition and the catalog are more audacious even than the Smithsonian show of 1962 — in any event, too audacious for the cultural establishment of New York. Perhaps if Avedon hadn't insisted on the imprimatur of a major museum, he could have made it happen: he had the connections in the Movement to get it done. But he wanted to have his cake and eat it too. Too bad. Such an exhibition would have been a high water mark in the annals of exhibition design: relational esthetics *avant la lettre*.

Avedon gave us an alternative vision of *Hard Times* with *The Family*, his project with Renata Adler for *Rolling Stone*. In August 1976, Avedon was given the bulk of the magazine for an ambitious photoessay. Although one had to wade through fifty pages of rock & roll news and advertising to get to it, the effort was well worth it: Avedon and Adler were able to connect with the magazine's readership of five hundred thousand.

This time, the subject matter went beyond the counterculture, elaborating an inclusive vision of American power in the year of the American Bicentennial. In a highly original move suggested by Adler, the seventy-three frontal portraits were accompanied by an appropriated reference text — the *Who's Who* listings of the sitters, printed in the same format and typeface as the annual directory.

By comparison, *Portraits* is a generic photobook. It was published to accompany an exhibition at Marlborough Gallery in 1975 that followed Avedon's rupture with Szarkowski. *The Family* was subsequently editioned, and remains among Avedon's most sought-after works. But its notable impact was outside the art marketplace, in its magazine form.

Egoïste

In the late 1970s, Avedon began to take pictures for what would eventually become *In the American West*, a travelling exhibition that originated at the Amon Carter Museum in Fort Worth and was accompanied by an eponymous photobook. Those pictures would first appear in a French magazine, *Egoïste*. Begun in 1977 by Nicole Wisniak, it has published irregularly — seventeen times in thirty-five years—with recent print runs of around twenty-five thousand copies.

For Avedon, after enduring the corporate court of *Vogue* and its parent company, Condé Nast, *Egoïste* was a breath of fresh air. Wisniak gave Avedon artistic freedom but pushed him outside his comfort zone in both subject matter and technique. She was not only his editor and collaborator, but also his sherpa, guiding him through the new landscape of the France of Mitterand at a time when Reagan/Thatcherism ruled the Anglo-Saxon roost. Avedon was back in his element: French intellectuals still went to fashion shows.

When the Soviet Union collapsed and the Berlin Wall fell, Wisniak dispatched him to photograph Berlin on New Year's Eve, 1989. The Wall was open on both sides for the first time since the end of World War II. For the first time as well, Avedon was photographing history in the making. Previously he had made portraits of sitters during political field trips, photographing members of the

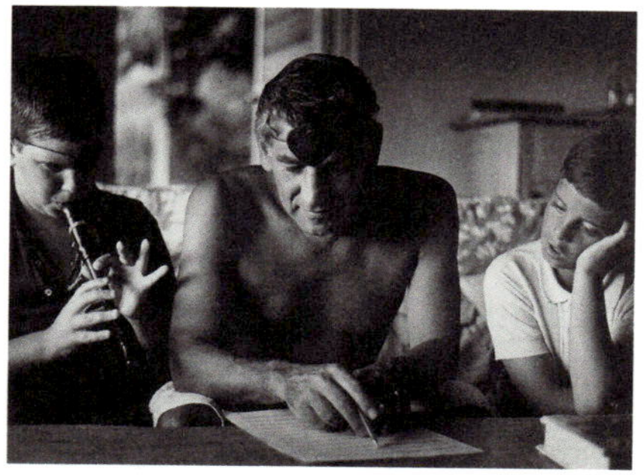

Leonard Bernstein gives a music lesson to John Avedon (right) and Fred Iseman, Round Hill, Jamaica, 1962

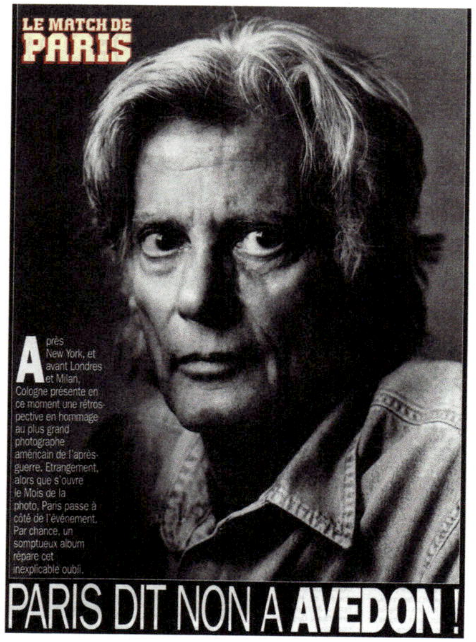

LE MATCH DE PARIS

Après New York, et avant Londres et Milan, Cologne présente en ce moment une rétrospective en hommage au plus grand photographe américain de l'après-guerre. Etrangement, alors que s'ouvre le Mois de la photo, Paris passe à côté de l'événement. Par chance, un somptueux album répare cet inexplicable oubli.

PARIS DIT NON A AVEDON !

Avedon in *Paris-Match*, October 27, 1994; photograph by Irving Penn

civil rights movement in the American South in the sixties, and those involved in the Vietnam war in the seventies.

The publication of those remarkable photos in *Egoïste* led to an invitation to exhibit them in the 1991 Carnegie International at the Carnegie Museum of Art, Pittsburgh. The highly theatrical Carnegie installation was Avedon's bold remix of his *Egoïste* images, a successful transposition from magazine page to museum wall. He reprinted his images in large format and hung them unframed, arranging them along three intersecting planes so that they could be read simultaneously as independent photographs, or as one long historical painting. He enhanced this effect by programming lighting that shifted throughout the day, evoking the Wall's well-known crossing point, Checkpoint Charlie, just as he had used strobe lights on the crowd to take the pictures in the first place.[51]

The Carnegie installation demonstrated how easily Avedon's work — or at least the kind of work he was doing for *Egoïste* — could coexist with the conceptual vanguard of the early nineties. In Pittsburgh his work presented comfortably with neighboring installations by Hiroshi Sugimoto, Louise Lawler, Thomas Struth and Christopher Williams, artists a generation or two younger than him. They are all considered conceptual artists who happen to work in photography, as opposed to, say, Irving Penn, who was and always will be a "fine art photographer." Avedon should have mixed it up more with the contemporary art scene and let his work speak for itself alongside other voices, as he did at the Carnegie.

Unfortunately, Avedon's Whitney show would subsequently present his legacy in an overly controlling monographic vacuum.

Wisniak also accompanied Avedon to the Volpi Ball in Venice. He collaged the photographs he took on that assignment into hyperimages of high society in decline, which he described as "collages that appear to be photojournalism." [52] (The ball was once an elegant fixture of the Venice Film Festival.) Published in *Egoïste*, the Volpi Ball pictures were introduced with a favorite Avedon quote from Proust. And Wisniak made a canny editorial insertion of two unspoiled young women amidst all the melting flesh and gaunt, frightened stares of the ball's older attendees. Avedon's photographs would be a highlight of his exhibition at the Metropolitan Museum in 2002.

Another first for Avedon under Wisniak's aegis: he photographed architecture, including a Moscow cemetery and Franco's tomb in Madrid, and punctuated his photonarratives with images devoid of people. Haunting images of Belle Isle ("Isabelle Adjani") and Drancy ("Kate's Story") provide unusual but effective counterpoint to Avedon's primacy of portraiture.

Avedon signed on as *The New Yorker's* first ever and sole staff photographer in December 1992, the result of an editorial shakeup in the wake of the magazine's acquisition by Condé Nast. The idea of being crowned sole monarch of photography at *The New Yorker* meant a lot to him, but he reverted to a comfort zone which seemed to shrink as he aged. He grew increasingly out of touch. It is strange, for example, that he would have called his 1994 Whitney show *Evidence*, given that the same title had already been used by Larry Sultan and Mike Mandel for their 1977 book of found corporate and government archive photos. Sultan and Mandel's *Evidence* was quickly and firmly established as a basic text of the Pictures Generation — photographers who agreed with Avedon that "All photographs are accurate. None of them are the truth," [53] but worked in a deadpan register that was alien to him.

Wisniak recognized that Avedon's greatness lay in his ambitious, if not always successful, experimentation — his openness, his eagerness to collaborate with people whose eye and judgment he respected. At the beginning of their collaboration, after *Egoïste* published those first images from *In the American West*, Avedon wrote to her:

> You must understand and accept the fact that when it concerns my work, I do nothing out of blind enthusiasm or because I'm a nice fellow . . . [I chose] *Egoïste* for the first viewing of the photographs . . . because I could see what uncompromising care and quality you brought to your work. I was right. The issue is exquisite and the engravings are the equal if not better than my own book." [54]

New Yorker editor Tina Brown, on the other hand, was trading on Avedon's existing star power. Wisniak and Avedon took risks together: from "fashion" shoots of Isabelle Adjani with no clothes other than Avedon's old leather jacket, to naked plus-size girls in exuberantly carnal romps ("Kate's Story"). Not everything worked, but the risks demanded to be taken, and they would collaborate until his death.

Avedon after Avedon

My own interview with Wisniak turned out to be an interesting bookend to her *Egoïste* interview with Avedon in 1984, when they had just met. Held in early 2016, it was an opportunity to consider Avedon's legacy a generation after his passing. In my view, if not hers, Avedon's constructed hagiography elides bitter disappointment at the lack of recognition in his lifetime from those places and institutions that mattered most: the New York art world, especially MoMA, and France. Unprepared to accept the outcomes of cultural politics and the bureaucratic machinations of its flagship cultural institutions as random, he took it all very personally.

Sometimes, it was difficult not to. James Baldwin received his Légion d'honneur in 1986, at the same ceremony as Leonard Bernstein, another close friend of Avedon's (the Bernstein and Avedon families sometimes vacationed together). One can only imagine how Avedon must have felt knowing that his two close friends, Jimmy and Lenny, were both getting the Légion d'honneur, but not him. This would have been right around the time that it became clear to him that *In the American West*, despite his best efforts to museify the project, would muster only a private gallery showing in New York.[55] Despite years of advance planning, as well as the imprimatur of the Amon Carter Museum of Fort Worth, which had commissioned the project, no New York museum could, or would, take it.

At one point in his 1993 interview with Guerrin, Avedon was asked about how he felt about his lack of museum validation in France. His reply: "Maybe it takes a foreigner to discover someone else's national treasure." He went on to invoke Robert Frank's *The Americans,* the "serious genius" of Jerry Lewis, and the fact that "Lartigue had to wait for the Museum of Modern Art . . . and the publication in America of *Diary of a Century.*"[56] The Lartigue and Jerry Lewis points are sound, but Robert Frank? Certainly not. The critical acclaim surrounding Lartigue's MoMA show, and Avedon's subsequent book, helped open French eyes to the art of Lartigue's photography. The New Wave's championing of Lewis as an *auteur* beyond his gift for physical comedy brought him to the attention of New Hollywood filmmakers. On the other hand, the French publication of *The Americans* was a non-event. Frank's difficulties in getting it published had more to do with the embryonic state of photobook publishing at the time than his lack of recognition as an artist. In citing these examples, Avedon may have been seeking a subliminal takeaway: "art" by association.

With the further passage of time, and the fading away of self-inflicted curatorial wounds, Avedon's work will increasingly speak for itself. His impact on the visual culture of the late twentieth century will be acknowledged. The proof is in the pudding. When somebody who sat for Avedon dies, it is generally Avedon's photograph of him or her, above all others, that is selected to accompany the obituary in *The New York Times* or *Le Monde.* Avedon's moments may be constructed, but in these cases they are decisive.

1 Henri Béhar and Michel Guerrin, "Avedon" (an interview with Richard Avedon), *Le Monde* (July 1, 1993). The interview took place during the XXIVe Festival des Rencontres de la Photographie in Arles.
2 Ibid.
3 Original transcript of the interview in English, Michel Guerrin archives.
4 Béhar and Guerrin. Avedon said, "J'avais appris à être moi en prétendant être lui et là je devais lui apprendre à prétendre être moi..." (I had learned to be me by pretending to be him and then I had to teach him to pretend to be me ...)
5 Ibid.
6 Winthrop Sargeant, "A Woman Entering a Taxi in the Rain," *The New Yorker* (November 8, 1958): 49. Avedon was quoted as saying, "Why, you know, I sometimes get almost as much as Picasso for a picture."
7 Apart from a brief mention in *The Rangefinder,* a professional photography magazine, and a gossip column item in *The Washington Star*, I can find no mention of it anywhere.
8 John Durniak, "Avedon Show," *Popular Photography* (May 1965): 52.
9 Robert Brustein, "The Pop Liberalism of Avedon and Baldwin," *The New York Review of Books* (December 17, 1964): 10–12.
10 In 1949 Avedon was commissioned by *LIFE* to shoot street scenes. When he saw the results, he returned his advance, and filed the negatives and contacts away. Although curator Jane Livingston would make an elaborate case in the Whitney Museum exhibition catalog and in her subsequent book,

The New York School: Photographs 1936–1963 (New York: Stewart Tabori & Chang, 1992) for these pictures, arguing that they situated Avedon in the New York tradition of "street photography" that included Diane Arbus and Weegee, Avedon's first instinct was the right one. For the Whitney show, see, for example, Michael Kimmelman, "Farewell Fashion, Hello Art," *The New York Times* (March 25, 1994).

11 Szarkowski granted Avedon a small but important show of photographs of his dying father in 1974. Shortly before that, he wrote a less than flattering appraisal of Avedon's place in photographic history to accompany Avedon's portrait of Isak Dinesen in *Looking at Photographs: 100 Pictures from the Collection of the Museum of Modern Art* (New York: Museum of Modern Art, 1973). In 1978, Szarkowski omitted Avedon entirely from his canonization of the eighty most important photographers of the sixties and seventies in *Mirrors and Windows: American Photography Since 1960* (New York: Museum of Modern Art, 1978).

12 Avedon would also be reimbursed for "model fees and other out-of-pocket expense in connection with such photographs." From the "Contract between Paramount Pictures and Avedon, Richard – Visual Consultant" (February 17, 1956), Paramount Collection, archives of the American Academy of Motion Picture Arts and Sciences (AAMPAS), Los Angeles, California.

13 Stephen M. Silverman, *Dancing on the Ceiling: Stanley Donen and his Movies* (New York: Knopf, 1996), 230–31.

14 Author's collection. The bookmarks in Kazan's copy of *Naked City* are torn strips of paper that appear to be from a discarded draft of the screenplay for *On the Waterfront*.

15 Silverman, 231.

16 Joseph Kaselow, "He Can't Dance," *The New York Herald Tribune* (May 12, 1957).

17 Silverman, 232.

18 Ibid, 233–34.

19 $5500 was in fact allocated elsewhere for the freeze frames of the Audrey Hepburn fashion shoots and the "Think Pink" dance number, 1956, AAMPAD archives.

20 Charles Higham, *Hollywood Cameramen* (Bloomington: Indiana University Press, 1970): 98–9.

21 Bosley Crowther, *The New York Times* (March 29, 1957).

22 Edward Jablonski, *"Funny Face," Films in Review* (April 1957): 170–74.

23 Arthur Knight, the regular film critic of *Saturday Review*, was also assistant curator in the film department of the Museum of Modern Art, and the author of the popular textbook, *The Liveliest Art: A Panoramic History of the Movies* (New York: Scribner, 1957).

24 Knight, *Dance Magazine* (May 1957): 16, 22.

25 Charles Higham, 30–31.

26 David Vaughan, "After the Ball," *Hollywood Cameraman* vol. 26 no. 2 (Autumn 1956).

27 Ibid.

28 David Vaughan, "Funny Face," *Sight and Sound* vol. 27 no. 1 (Summer 1957).

29 Jean Domarchi, "La Métamorphose (*Funny Face*)," *Cahiers du Cinéma* no. 79 (January 1958): 47–49.

30 Alain Resnais, list for "Top Ten Films of 1957," *Cahiers du Cinéma* no. 79: 4.

31 For more on LaShelle, see: http://www.cinematographers.nl/GreatDoPh/lashelle.htm

32 Silverman.

33 Inscribed presentation copy from Richard Avedon to Doe Avedon, author's collection.

34 Collection of John Avedon.

35 For a fuller discussion on Brodovitch, see Kerry William Purcell, *Alexey Brodovitch* (London: Phaidon, 2002).

36 For a biography of Christian Bérard, who owned and embellished the Countess of Castiglione photo album that Avedon would acquire (see pp. 450–53), see: Boris Kochno, *Christian Bérard* (Paris: Herscher, 1987). Kochno was Sergei Diaghilev's personal secretary. Avedon photographed Bérard in 1947.

37 Richard Avedon, "Afterword," *Diary of a Century* (New York: Viking Press, 1970).

38 Andy Grundberg, *Brodovitch (Masters of American Design)* (New York: Harry N. Abrams, 1989). As quoted in Purcell: 26.

39 For a useful discussion of *Observations*, see Jane Livingston's essay in *Evidence 1944–94* (New York: Random House, 1994): 24–34. For a detailed analysis of Brodovitch's work on *Observations* see Purcell.

40 The American production of *La folle de Chaillot* opened in New York in 1948 and ran for more than a year.

41 Capote's mockup is in the author's collection. (See pp. 386–87 for the full text of Avedon's previously unpublished letter.)

42 For example, Avedon wrote Szarkowksi about an idea that David Pittman (who would later produce films such as *Chariots of Fire*, but was then a photographer's agent representing David Bailey, among others) was floating about, of creating limited editions of photo graphs. Avedon letter to Szarkowski (July 5, 1967), Szarkowski archives, Museum of Modern Art.

43 See the multi-volume series by Martin Parr and Gerry Badger, *The Photobook: A History* (London: Phaidon, 2001 and later) on the evolving collectability of photobooks.

44 See Luc Sante, "Robert Frank and Jack Kerouac," in Sara Greenough, ed., *Looking In: Robert Frank's The Americans* (Washington, D.C.: National Gallery of Art/ Göttingen: Steidl, 2009): 202–09.

45 Greenough is a thorough, scholarly account of the making of the various iterations of *The Americans*.

46 Brustein: 10–12.

47 Truman Capote, "Avedon's Reality" (letter to the editor), *The New York Review of Books* (January 28, 1965).

48 Kevin Moore, *Jacques Henri Lartigue: The Invention of an Artist* (Princeton: Princeton University Press, 2004): 199.

49 For further discussion of Avedon's studio photographs of *Alice*, see "André Gregory Sees the Light," Theatre Communications Group: http://www.tcg.org/publications/at/mar05/gregory.cfm/

50 "It needs a museum for a kind of establishment view of it and then to the high schools," Avedon explained to Alan Ginsberg in an interview. For a detailed discussion of the project and additional citations from the interview tapes, see author's essay, "Landsmen Lensmen," in *Avedon: Portraits and Murals* (New York: Gagosian Gallery, 2012): 86–128.

51 See Triennial Co-Curator Lynne Cooke's note on Avedon's installation in Cooke and Mark Francis, eds, *Carnegie International 1991*, (Pittsburgh: Carnegie Museum of Art, 1991): 52.

52 Béhar and Guerrin.

53 Nicole Wisniak, "A Portrait is an Opinion" (interview with Richard Avedon), *Egoïste* N° 9, (January, 1985): 48–53.

54 Richard Avedon letter to Nicole Wisniak, June 11, 1985. Nicole Wisniak archives.

55 *In the American West* travelled to the Corcoran Gallery of Art, Washington D.C.; the San Francisco Museum of Modern Art; The Art Institute of Chicago; the Phoenix Art Museum; the Institute of Contemporary Art, Boston; the High Museum of Art, Atlanta; and the Madison Art Center in Wisconsin. It was exhibited at Pace/MacGill Gallery, and later at the Richard Gray Gallery, both in New York City.

56 Béhar and Guerrin.

Lartigue by Avedon: A Labor of Love

Marianne Le Galliard

January 29, 1967
Ritz Hotel, Saturday

Dear John,
There is no way of disguising the fact that we're having an absolutely terrific time. We've been here for only three days and have been busy every moment, and no work at all, as yet. We've been to both Picasso shows as well as an exhibition of the photographs of Cartier-Bresson and the show of the Bonnards that was once at the Museum of Modern Art. In each case, we've seen the life's work of a single man. It's so overwhelming. All those years of work in one gathering. Picasso's is like the entire history of modern art. Cartier-Bresson's a visual history of humanity for almost forty years. We saw *Natasha* (the second installment of *War and Peace*) better even than the first . . . Natasha is played by the most enchanting girl. All of the shyness and desire and mixture of girl and woman that you tend to forget when you're my age. If you can fall in love with someone in a movie then I predict it will be this girl.

We've dined with Lartigues at their house. Mme Lartigue cooked herself and we stayed till three in the morning looking at photographs he took in 1902 to 1910: all unpublished. His first bicycle was made of wood, he said they all were. He showed us pictures taken last year in the south of France where you stand on the sand with a parachute attached to your back (open) and you are connected by a line to a speed boat. The boat takes off. You start to run and in six steps, with the boat going about thirty miles an hour you TAKE OFF! I'd never heard about this before. It looks like terrific fun. Air skiing! I'm enclosing his invitation to give you an idea of how young in heart someone of seventy-six can be.

Tonight we had dinner with Ginette and Paul-Emile (who send you their love, and Goddard who sends his) and tomorrow we are seeing *The Rise and the Fall of the City of Mahagonny*, an opera of Brecht and Kurt Weill's that is rarely performed. It's the opera in which "Surabaya Johnny" is sung. You used to think it such a sad song when you were a baby. Then back to the Picasso shows for another look. I've bought a catalog and an affiche so that you can get an idea of what it was like. Then dinner with Patrice Habans and his wife. He is the *Paris Match* photographer who photographed the Alps as he skied all the way across them (sleeping in the snow, that really impresses me since I'm addicted to an electric blanket).

It is now Sunday. The air has cleared and the temperature dropped. Mom and I are all wrapped up and ready for a long walk back to the Lartigues for lunch. There isn't time in the day to stop for even a proper letter to you. All our love, always. The current plan is that we arrive in NY Sunday afternoon IF you don't hear otherwise call us Sunday night.

Love, Dad.

By the time Richard Avedon wrote that letter to his son John in 1967, he was no stranger to France. He had been traveling to Paris regularly to photograph the fashion collections since 1947 and knew the capital well, especially the eighth arrondissement between the Champs Élysees and the Seine. He stayed in the small section between the Hôtel San Régis and the fashion house of Dior on avenue Montaigne, first working in the *Harper's Bazaar* studio and then for *Vogue* (which he joined in 1965). But on this trip in 1967, his being in Paris had nothing to do with fashion.

Avedon and his wife, Evelyn, stayed at the legendary Hôtel Ritz (where Marcel Proust lived in the late 1910s, and dined with Jean Cocteau and Colette) and spent their days taking in the cultural high points of the city: Pablo Picasso at the Grand Palais, Henri Cartier-Bresson at the musée des arts décoratifs, Pierre Bonnard at the Orangerie, and *Guerre et Paix* (*War and Peace*)[1] in a Paris movie theatre. They visited the Lartigues, in the sixteenth arrondissement, rue de Longchamp, that Friday, staying late into night and poring over Lartigue's trove of images — from the most recent to the first, "all unpublished," as the letter reads excitedly. The Avedons were invited back for lunch that Sunday.

The meeting would be the third between Richard Avedon and J. H. Lartigue. Sitting at the dining table next to Florette Lartigue (fig. 1), Avedon got better acquainted with Georges Tourdjman, the young photographer who had set up the first meeting of Avedon and Lartigue two months before, in Avedon's New York studio. Despite the warm atmosphere of a friendly Sunday lunch, this was not a merely social occasion: Avedon was back at the Lartigue's to take "another look" at the images he had just seen on Friday, much in the same way he went back for a second look at the Picasso exhibit.

Avedon's letter to his son describes his wonderment at Paris' cultural bounty, and then his immediate, unbridled enthusiasm for Lartigue's persona and work, such as his discovery of a photograph of "Air skiing" (fig. 2), that filled him with childlike excitement. It was apparent to him that he, forty-four, and Lartigue, thirty years his senior, were similarly "young in heart." Avedon would later say that in Lartigue he found the "joyous part" of himself, the "same burst of humor and life" and, most of all, a "father in photography."[2]

Avedon had first learned of Lartigue in 1963, shortly before Lartigue's solo exhibition at the Museum of Modern Art, and had obtained several of Lartigue's images.[3] He put them up on the walls of his apartment, next to his own work, whatever was inspiring him at the moment, and other images from his personal pantheon — such as Cartier-Bresson's *Lock at Bougival*, France (1955), visible in this photo of Avedon at home taken in 1965 (fig. 3). Propped on the back of the couch is a photograph Lartigue took at Combegrasse in 1922 (one of the images exhibited at MoMA, later published in *Diary of a Century* as a double-page spread (*see pages 506–07*). Above that: Lartigue's 1911 photograph of an "elegant lady" in the Bois de Boulogne.[4] On the lower right, laid flat, is an issue of *Cahiers d'Art* on Picasso. These

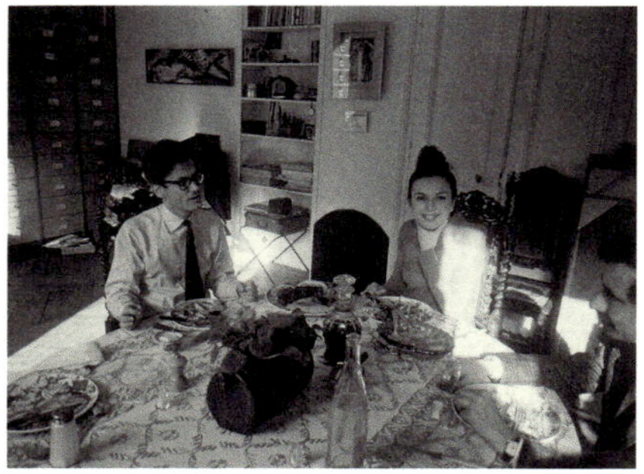

1. Richard Avedon, Florette, and Georges Tourdjman, Paris, January 1967; photograph by J. H. Lartigue

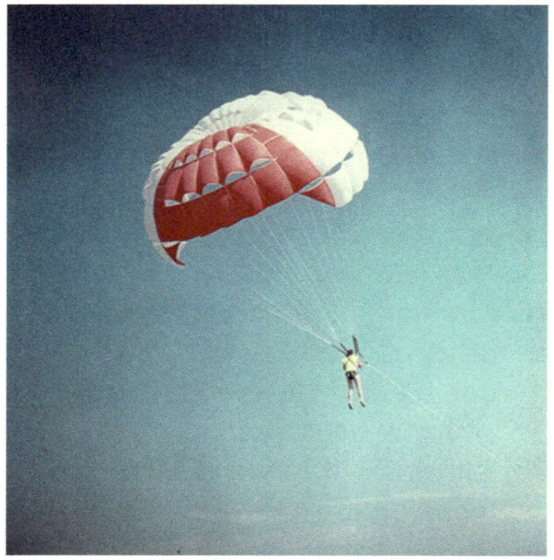

2. Paraskiing, Jean Creff, Antibes, July 1964; photograph by J. H. Lartigue

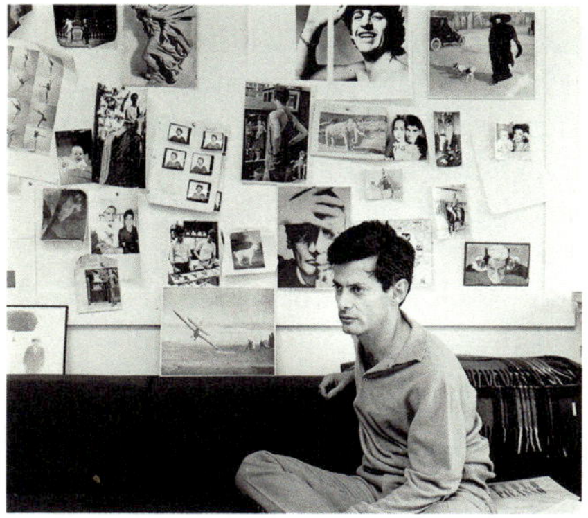

3. Richard Avedon at home, East 58th Street, New York, 1965

references come together like pieces of a puzzle, with Picasso, Cartier-Bresson and Lartigue forming a common cultural foundation for the American artist.

In January 1967, Avedon made a new discovery: Lartigue's most recent work, which looked as fresh to him as the images Lartigue had taken half a century before. It was clear to Avedon that Lartigue had a singular ability to pull together the two poles of the century: the sixties — with its atmosphere of late-century modernity, and the Belle Epoque — the world before the First World War.

Thus inspired, Avedon would produce and edit *Diary of a Century*,[5] the first monograph to deal with Lartigue's work over the course of the century. Its publication in 1970 signified a third phase in the world's recognition of Lartigue. The first phase was his "discovery" by MoMA in 1963, and institutional legitimization as a chronicler of the Belle Epoque (since the museum chose to display only his early work). The second was the publication of his professional fashion photography in *Harper's Bazaar* in 1967[6] — promoted by both Avedon and his former assistant Hiro.[7] And the third was as an artist of the twentieth century, thanks to the success of *Diary*.

Today it is common to speak of Lartigue as being "invented" by John Szarkowski, MoMA's director of photography from 1962 to 1991.[8] To establish a plausible precursor to his own modernist theories, the young Szarkowski presented Lartigue as "an authentic primitive" from the turn of the century, an amateur genius who never intended to make *art* — and thus a forerunner of the modernist tradition exemplified by

Gary Winogrand and Lee Friedlander. Here was a precocious and spontaneous genius of the Belle Epoque, with an amateur's purity of style — and the first monograph of his photographs, *Boyhood: Photos of J. H. Lartigue, the Family Album of a Gilded Age*, published in July 1966, largely followed this line of thought.[9] The photographs are presented as if still in an old family album, seemingly touched by a "slight poetry of nostalgia"[10] as Szarkowski himself described it. MoMA's conception of Lartigue and his work would dominate critical discourse until 1970, when, with *Diary*, Avedon articulated a different vision.

Remarkably, even when *Boyhood* was published, Lartigue was still unknown in France. Public presentations of his work were limited to images of flowers and pretty women for calendars and articles on aviation and automobiles.[11] He made his first trip to America in 1962 on assignment to photograph American life, not exhibit his work. Despite his growing recognition in New York,[12] the French press did not go beyond asking him to re-stage photographs he had shot in the Bois de Boulogne fifty years before.[13]

Around the same time as *Boyhood* was published, *Harper's Bazaar* initiated a different approach, commissioning Lartigue to shoot fashion. For the first time, his talent was freed from the imagery of the Belle Epoque. And three photographers who worked for *Bazaar* and had studied with its former art director, Alexey Brodovitch — Tourdjman, Hiro and Avedon — would become deeply interested in Lartigue's work.

Tourdjman, who had seen Lartigue's 1963 work in *LIFE* magazine, met Lartigue in 1965. In 1966, while assisting Hiro for the Paris fashion collections, he offered to introduce his boss to Lartigue. Their meeting, on July 25, 1966, was memorialized with images of Hiro looking at prints and posing with *Boyhood* in Lartigue's Parisian apartment. In one, Tourdjman captured Hiro taking a photograph of Lartigue in the Bois de Boulogne (fig. 4). A relaxed Lartigue walks toward Hiro as he bends over his camera: an author without artistic intention and a professional working by commission, two types heretofore considered antithetical. The photograph symbolizes a connection in both time and space, from the beginning of the century to the 1960s, from Paris to New York, from Old World to New. The short distance between the two men symbolically spans the entire century, much in the same way *Diary of a Century* will reveal.

It is not surprising that Avedon will place this very photograph at the end of *Diary of a Century*. It illustrates his own connection to the photographer via Tourdjman and Hiro, and acknowledges their contributions to the book. It discreetly mocks the current general discourse of photography — artistic versus commercial practice, and more broadly, the museum-centric approach of MoMA versus Avedon's approach. Above all, as the last image in *Diary*, it came to embody the link between two generations and two different artistic practices: amateurism and commercial work.

On November 9, 1966, orchestrated by Hiro, Avedon met Lartigue for the first official time, in New York. The links between Avedon's and Lartigue's

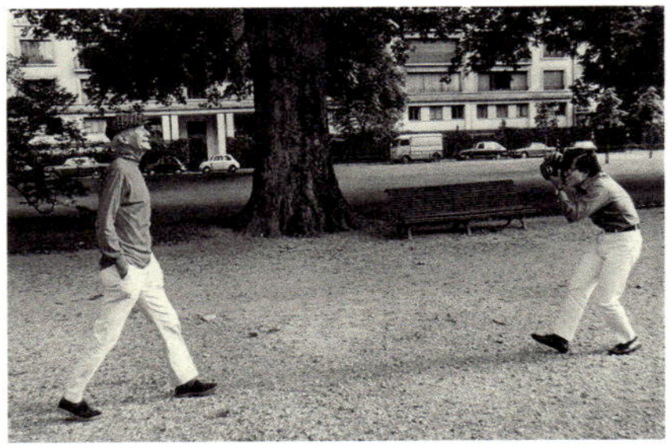

4. Hiro photographing Lartigue, Paris, July 25, 1966; photograph by Georges Tourdjman

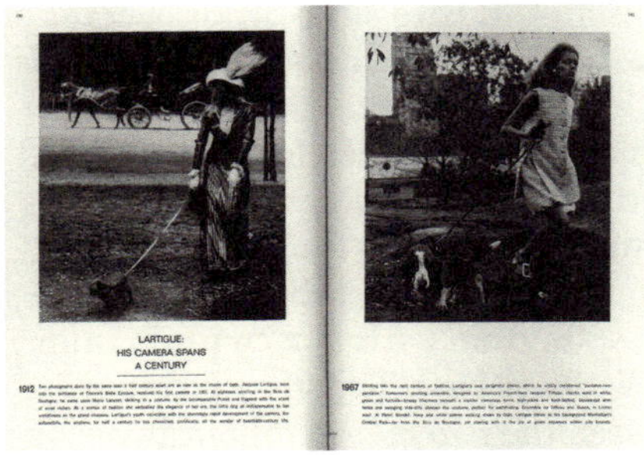

5. "Lartigue: His Camera Spans a Century," *Harper's Bazaar*, March 1967, pp. 190–91

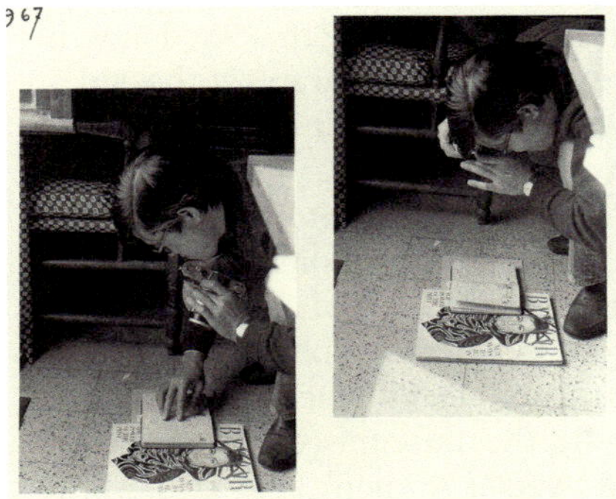

6. Hiro photographing Lartigue's notebook, Opio, March 7, 1967 (album page 0043R67); photograph by J. H. Lartigue

respective bodies of photography would be clear from that meeting on, despite differences in age, social backgrounds, and artistic practices.[14] Lartigue photographed Avedon in an Avedonian pose — mid-flight (*see pages 456–57*). The image hearkens back to Lartigue's early-century snapshots, such as the one of his cousin Bichonnade in 1905 (*see pages 458–59*). This time, however, the model was one of the world's top ten photographers, (according to a poll by *Popular Photography*)[15] who would also become, in essence, the producer of Lartigue's photographic work.

In 1963, when Avedon saw the Lartigue exhibition in MoMA, he had written Lartigue to express how much the work resonated:

> It was one of the most moving and powerful experiences of my life. They are photographs that echo — I will never forget them. Seeing them was for me like reading Proust for the first time.[16]

Avedon again wrote to Lartigue in 1966 about feeling that same resonance upon seeing *Boyhood*:

> Your book is ravishing. A lift to the heart. I have bought ten copies and sent them to my friends. Hiro could not stop talking about your generosity. I felt so badly about not meeting you, when I was in Paris, but I will return at the end of January and I call you then [...] Your book is a serious masterpiece and an inspiration.[17]

Indeed, *Boyhood* brought forth a dramatic turn in Lartigue's career and a considerable expansion of his social world. His work was shown at *Photokina* (with Cecil Beaton)[18] and published in *Camera*.[19] He met Man Ray and Arthur Rothstein, Edward Steichen[20] and then Cartier-Bresson[21] — who invited Lartigue to the opening of his show at musée des arts décoratifs. He was quickly becoming a part of the French photography scene. In rapid succession, he met Albert Plécy and Janine Nièpce, Robert Delpire and William Klein, whose new movie, *Qui êtes-vous, Polly Maggoo?*[22] featuring Avedon was showing in Paris.

Feeling welcome, if not warmly embraced by the world of artistic photography, by 1967 Lartigue himself was comfortable enough to show his more recent work. If MoMA had pigeonholed his photography as Old World, a younger generation of American fashion photographers now took the opposite tack: Lartigue had to be made modern. The inevitable change was catalyzed when *Harper's Bazaar* published his "first official fashion photograph" as Lartigue called it, in March 1967 in "Lartigue: His Camera Spans a Century." A centerfold (fig. 5) features two photographs of elegant women — the first, a lady of leisure walking in the Bois de Boulogne in 1912; the second, a model in Central Park in New York in 1967. As did Hiro's portrait of Lartigue, the image symbolically spans fashion's transformation within the century: 1912 to 1967, Paris to New York, from private photo album to popular fashion magazine. To sum it up, from Lartigue to Avedon.

In Avedon's emotional 1967 letter to his son John, it is remarkable — if not coincidental — that Avedon places his discovery of Lartigue's life and work right next to comments celebrating "the entire history of modern art" embodied in Picasso's work and "a visual history of humanity" in Cartier-Bresson's. Fascinated by the possibility of covering the entire century through the lens of one man, Avedon would throw himself into the effort six months later. *Diary of a Century*, an enormously ambitious project, would consume three years of Avedon's life.

The Odyssey: Creating *Diary of a Century*, June 1967 – December 1970

Even before *Harper's Bazaar* proclaimed a "New Look" and a "new school of photography"[23] headed by Avedon in its April issue, Avedon's own sensibility was being changed by his discovery of Lartigue's diaries (*see pages 50–51*), which were photographed in Paris in March by Hiro. (fig. 6)

Lartigue used the diaries to document his daily activities, adding little sketches to the text to help memorize the compositions of photos taken that day. Dated 1911 to 1914, they triggered in Avedon new insight into how to better present Lartigue's work. *Boyhood* had been criticized by the jury of the Prix Nadar for not showing Lartigue's photographs "in a modern context and in greater numbers, so as to represent adequately sixty years of daily life."[24] Hiro thought "the Museum [MoMA] didn't do justice" to Lartigue's work either. It's time, he said to Lartigue, to "have a spectacular exhibit of all your complete work to date."[25] Avedon began to develop the idea of organizing Lartigue's work as another form of diary.

In June 1967, Richard Avedon became Lartigue's de facto agent, securing him magazine and advertising assignments, and Lartigue visited New York in June

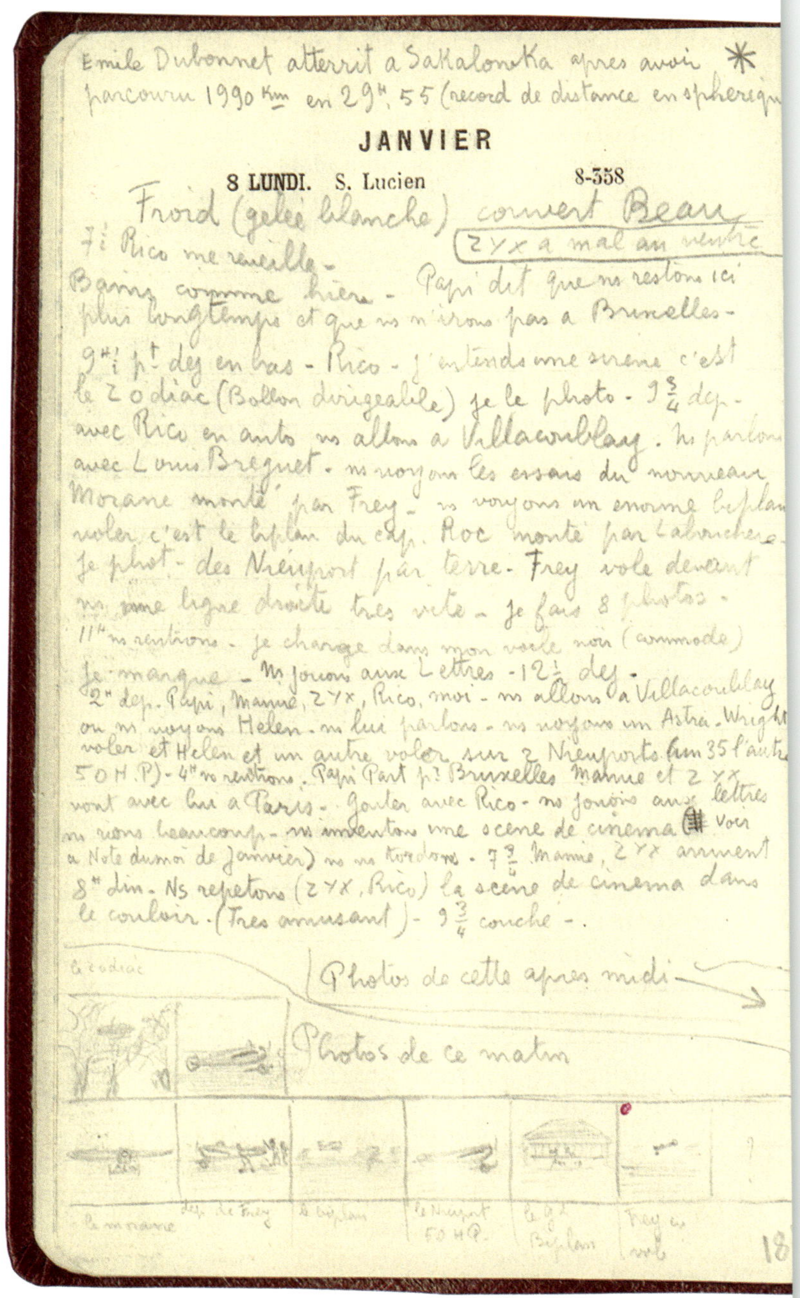

Emile Dubonnet atterrit a Sakalonka apres avoir parcouru 1990 Km en 29H, 55 (record de distance en spherique)

JANVIER

8 LUNDI. S. Lucien 8-358

Froid (gelée blanche) couvert Beau

7 i Rico me reveille - ZYX a mal au ventre

Bains comme hier - Papi dit que ns restons ici plus longtemps et que ns n'irons pas a Bruxelles - 9H i pt dej en bas - Rico - j'entends une sirene c'est le Zodiac (Ballon dirigeable) je le photo - 9 3/4 dep. avec Rico en auto ns allons a Villacoublay. Ns parlons avec Louis Breguet. ns voyons les essais du nouveau Morane monté par Frey - ns voyons un enorme biplan voler c'est le biplan du cap. Roc monté par Labouchere. Je phot. des Nieuport par terre - Frey vole devant ns une ligne droite tres vite - Je fais 8 photos - 11H ns rentrons - je change dans mon voile noir (commode) Je manque - Ns jouons aux Lettres - 12 1/2 dej - 2H dep. Papi, Maman, ZYX, Rico, moi - ns allons a Villacoublay ou ns voyons Helen - ns lui parlons - ns voyons un Astra-Wright voler et Helen et un autre voler sur 2 Nieuports (un 35 l'autre 50 H.P.) - 4H ns rentrons. Papi part pr Bruxelles Maman et ZYX vont avec lui a Paris - Gouter avec Rico - ns jouons aux lettres ns rions beaucoup - ns inventons une scene de cinema (Voir a Note du mois de Janvier) ns ns tordons - 7 3/4 Maman, ZYX arrivent 8H din. Ns repetons (ZYX, Rico) la scene de cinema dans le couloir. (Tres amusant) - 9 3/4 couche -.

Zodiac

Photos de cette apres midi

Photos de ce matin

Le morane | dep. de Frey | le biplan | le Nieuport 50 HP. | le g.d biplan | Frey en vol

18

7. Lartigue's notebook: pages for January 8–9, 1912

JANVIER

9 MARDI. S. Julien 9-357

as. Beau couvert – Pluie le soir à Paris

½ Rico me reveil.
Bains comme hier.
9h Pt dej – en bas –
9½ dep. av. Rico ns allons en auto a Buc (l'auto derappe beaucoup
ns marchons 3km a pied – ns voyons un M. Farman et un Rep
voler – 11h ns rentrons – je change le cinema et je ne pense
pas le faire marcher – 12h l'auto ns conduit (2YX, Rico, moi)
au Pt Trianon (Rico – moi sans pardessus) ns voyons un martin
pecheur – ns revenons a pieds – 1h dej – Mamie, 2YX, Rico, moi
2½ dep. ns allons a Buc – on ns voyons Mmes Folletête –
Je vais avec 2YX et Rico chez Rep. Plusieurs M. Farman
(dont un venant de St Cyr à 400m) et 2 Reps volent –
4h ns rentrons – ns faisons nos sacs. 4½ ns rentrons à Paris –
2YX et moi ns allons reconduire Rico chez lui. ns rentrons
5h Papa arrive de Bruxelles (il devait revenir seulement
à minuit) je décharge et j'arrange le cinema –
7½ din. – Plit vient. J'ecris a Gaumont – je marque –
9½ couché

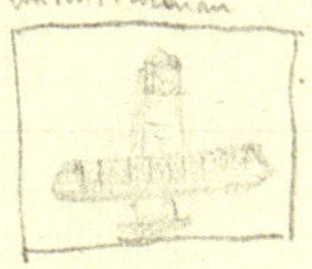

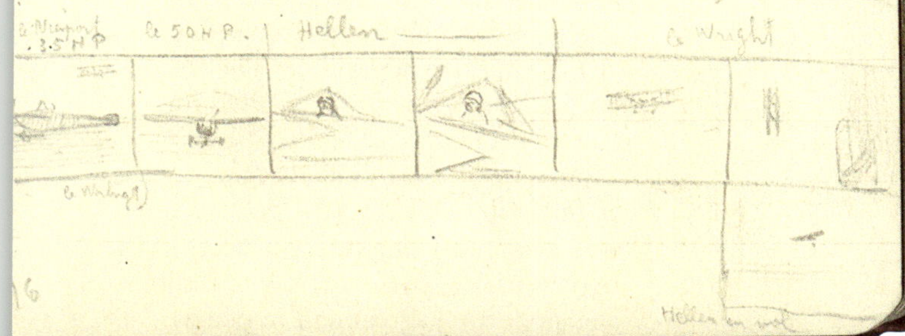

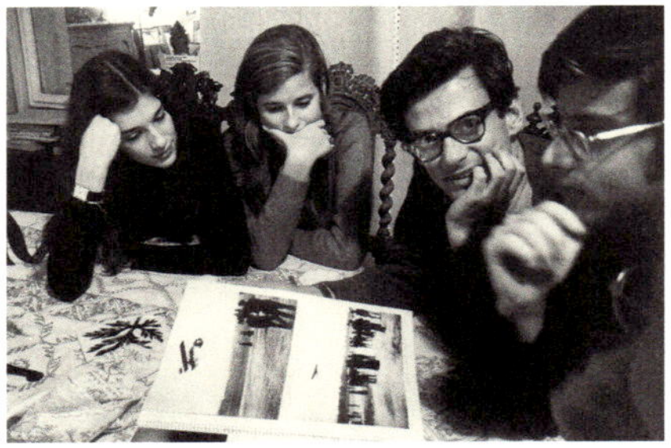

8. Richard and John Avedon and Martine and Sylvia Schildge leaf through a photo album by Lartigue, Paris, January 1968; photograph by J. H. Lartigue

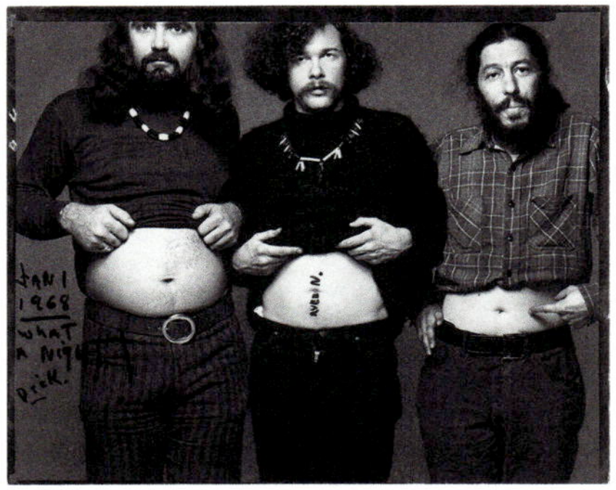

9. In January 1968 Avedon gave a print of his portrait of the Fugs to Lartigue, on which he inscribed, "What a night!" The Fugs: Ken Weaver, Ed Sanders and Tuli Kupferberg, musicians, New York, October, 26, 1967; photograph by Richard Avedon

and October. In following January, Avedon and his son John went to Paris and spent time looking through Lartigue's albums (fig. 8). They took a few back to New York as well.[26] In a gesture of friendship, Avedon presented Lartigue with a print of the Fugs, inscribing it, "Jan 11, 1968. What a night! Dick."(fig. 9)

The book project was launched in March. Avedon was convinced it would be "the single greatest book of photography of the 20th century," "a masterpiece," "the best book of photography and memoirs ever done," and "the biggest book in the world."[27] Naturally Lartigue was caught up in the enthusiasm, his confidence in Avedon absolute. On the advice of the man who was, in effect, his producer, he shot new portraits and started to make contact sheets of some of his unprinted negatives.[28]

By May, design and layout were in the hands of Avedon collaborator Bea Feitler, the co-art director (with Ruth Ansel) at *Bazaar*.[29] Publication was slated for the 1968 Christmas season, in conjunction with a planned traveling exhibition. It was intended that together, the book and exhibition would encompass Lartigue's entire body of work, including portions of his journals. Even before having seen it all, Avedon was determined to make the book an essential reference of twentieth-century photography.[30] The chosen title, *Diary of a Century*, recalled the successful historical book, Alfred Eisenstaedt's *Witness to our Time*, also published by Viking. (By now, Avedon was discussing marketing aspects of the book with the publisher, though there was no formal agreement in place.)

While the streets of Paris were

engulfed in the riots of May 1968 (*see pages 467–77*), Feitler and Avedon worked in Lartigue's apartment, pulling thousands of images from Lartigue's albums.[31] It was the first time someone outside of the family had seen the album pages, many of them unbound. Lartigue's living room was transformed into an editorial office (*see page 474*). Time was of the essence. As Lartigue noted:

> "Dick, with the intensity of a jaguar in pursuit of his prey, wanted to see everything: all my albums, all my unmounted photographs, all the unprinted negatives. More than 100,000 photos to choose perhaps 200."[32]

On the day he was leaving Paris, since Avedon needed a head shot for his travel documents, the group, including Henry Pessar (who was driving Avedon for a flight from Brussels, as Avedon had been unable to get a flight from Paris), converged on a photobooth (*see page 478*). Then, for the rest of the summer, Lartigue continued his "excavations"[33] at home, until he and Avedon met again in Paris in August. After that, Avedon and Feitler worked on the book in Avedon's studio, in New York.

Despite everyone's best efforts, *Diary of a Century* wouldn't be published until 1970. While still fulfilling his contractual obligations to *Vogue*, Avedon continued to work on the book, making layout and editorial choices, overseeing the mockup, conceiving the cover (with Feitler), controlling the quality of printed images, and handling all aspects of negotiations with Viking, including Lartigue's compensation. It took all of 1968 to arrive at an overall organizing principle for such an immense collection of images: the book would unfold decade by decade, with thematic sections (such as family, garden, swimming, travel, airplanes), supported by long excerpts from Lartigue's journals.

The first part of the book, spanning 1900 to 1920, was completed by July. Avedon had initially thought all parts would be finished by August, but he decided the material from the sixties was too weak and asked Lartigue to take new pictures. He encouraged Lartigue to re-photograph certain family members, such as his cousin Simone (*see page 524–25*) and brother Zissou. Though the schedule was important, "YOUR ART COMES FIRST," he wrote to Lartigue, declaring he had never been so excited in his entire life.[34]

By August, the material for 1920 to 1960 was in final form, but the correspondence between the two shows they still considered the sixties problematic. Finally, in September, things were in place enough for Avedon to show the mockup to Thomas Hoving, the director of the Metropolitan Museum. Avedon's goal was to organize a Lartigue retrospective at the Met and Louvre to coincide with the book's release. Avedon was perpetually on edge over the project, and even scolded Lartigue for publishing images in *Photo* magazine over the summer without consulting him.

On a quest for the best possible result — international critical recognition of Lartigue's body of work — Avedon invested tremendous effort into the book up until the last minute. In October, the layout was substantially modified again: pages following the chronological section, which ends with the image of Lartigue's parents in 1949 (*see pages 518–19*), were

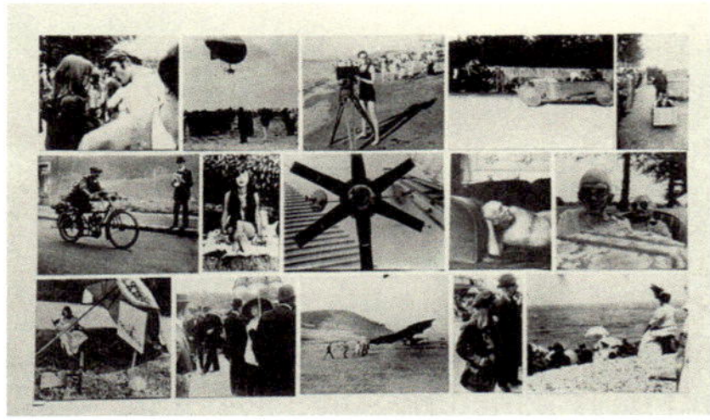

10. Layout, *Diary of a Century*, October 1968

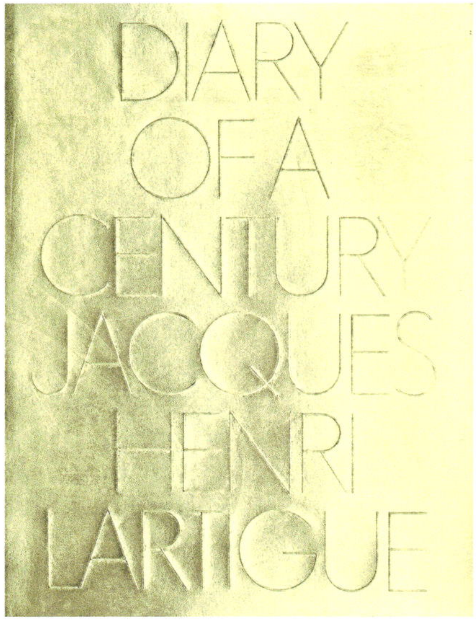

11. Jacques Henri Lartigue, *Diary of a Century*; edited by Richard Avedon and designed by Bea Feitler (New York: Viking Press, 1970)

redesigned in *LIFE* magazine style, with what Lartigue called a "patchwork of snapshots"[35] (fig. 10). Collaged together were portraits of celebrities, automobiles, society women, and family members, all in line with Avedon's vision of an eventual exhibition. The arrangements functioned as virtual map of how the images might be hung on a museum's walls.

Lartigue himself found the new layout "lively, entertaining, fantastic," as he wrote to Avedon.[36] Even Szarkowski was pleased, writing to Lartigue:

> I found it very deeply moving. Nothing like this has been done in photography—it is an astonishing testament to your life and your talent and to photography itself.[37]

Avedon spent the next six months ceaselessly promoting the project to advertising agencies, museum curators, and American television producers, talking it up to friends and colleagues, his enthusiasm inexhaustible. In a letter to Hoving dated November 19, he underscored Lartigue's importance:

> There is no question in my mind that he ranks as one of the finest photographers in the history of the art. Certainly he is unique in that he found his subject matter in his own life rather than searching out "important" themes and subjects.[38]

But in early 1969, the Metropolitan Museum abandoned the idea of a Lartigue exhibit, a casualty of a public relations issues it was having with another photography show.[39] Possible television outlets also lost interest. Nonetheless, Avedon continued his efforts with movie and theatrical producers. In each case, he kept Lartigue informed, and advised him on his negotiations with Viking Press, trying to ensure his work would be commercially protected: "Give nothing away, Jacques!"[40]

In July 1969, the contract with Viking Press was finally signed and the process of editing and translating began.[41] Avedon, at first reluctant to write a preface, overcame a sense of modesty to do so. It would become the Afterword.[42] He also felt the book needed to end differently, so the idea of what he called a "potpourri of many pictures" was abandoned for a more conventional approach, more in keeping with the rest of the book. Always in pursuit of perfection, Avedon paid for all the photographic printing related to the book, so it could be done at his preferred lab.

In January 1970, Avedon and Doon Arbus paid a short visit to Lartigue in Paris, and then Avedon continued to work intensively through March, often seeking clarifications, new texts or more negatives from Lartigue. In New York, he involved himself in the quality of the translations as deeply as he did in the reproduction of images. Meanwhile Lartigue, then dividing his time between Paris and Opio, was undoubtedly excited by the approaching publication and was already envisioning the possibility of publishing his memoirs. But February was more difficult: Avedon was not only dissatisfied with the translations, his Afterword was unilaterally transformed by Viking editors into more of a traditional essay. As usual, however, he had the last word. Lartigue knew nothing about it: he was out of the loop.

Finally, on March 30, the book was complete. Avedon wrote to Lartigue: "Can you believe that we are almost at the end of this odyssey?"[43] Almost: Avedon tinkered with the book until the last possible minute before it was sent to the printer in April. Finally, it was published. "I feel SATISFIED, a rare feeling for me [...] it's over now, and we must all go forward to the next adventure," he wrote.[44] In the same letter, he wished Lartigue good luck for his next book, but the story was not over yet.

The Story of a Man's Life

A direct descendant of Brodovitch's first monograph on Avedon, *Observations*, Avedon's *Diary of a Century* celebrates Lartigue's "entire photographic practice over a century."[45] It came out just before Christmas, in an edition of twelve thousand.[46] The book was imposing and luxurious, with a gold foil dust jacket and majestic capital lettering in relief — DIARY OF A CENTURY JACQUES HENRI LARTIGUE (fig. 11). The endpapers were facsimiles of the diaries.

Lartigue dedicated the book to Florette and thanked Avedon:

> My thanks to Richard Avedon; without his incomparable friendship I would never have been able to realize this book.[47]

Opposite the dedication page was the credit: "Edited by Richard Avedon / Designed by Bea Feitler." Avedon resurfaces at the very end, after two hundred and fifty photographs by Lartigue, with his brief and powerful Afterword (*see pages 528–31*). While the contract with Viking Press was signed only by Lartigue (represented by agent Robert Lantz), the "Author" of the book and sole

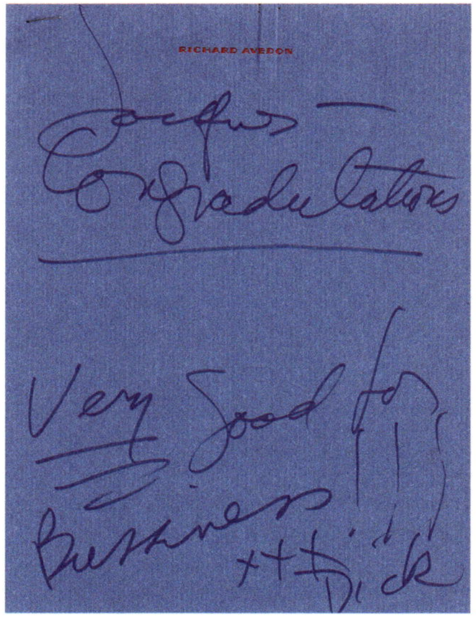

12. Avedon's note to Lartigue, pinned to Anaïs Nin's review of *Diary of a Century* in *The New York Times Book Review*, February 21, 1971

recipient of its royalties, the final word remained with Avedon. A clause stipulated that "the Author agrees to abide by and consent to any artistic decisions and approvals given by Richard Avedon in connection with this agreement."[48]

The book was launched at a party on December 8, 1970 in New York, accompanied by a premiere of Robert Hughes' film, *Portrait of Lartigue*.[49] Present were Feitler, Hiro, Helen Wright (the U.S. agent of Cartier-Bresson), Art Kane, Alfred Eisenstaedt and Grace Mayer from MoMA,[50] but not Lartigue or Avedon. It remains unclear why. Nevertheless, the book launch was a great success. According to Hiro, who wrote to Lartigue the next day, it was "a total SUCCES FOU!!!!!!"[51]

By April, the first edition of *Diary* had nearly sold out. The American and French press were unanimous, calling the book a marvelous homage to twentieth-century life, its wondrous inventions and wrenching changes captured by Lartigue with all his *joie de vivre*.[52] Critics noted the intimacy of its images, the fluidity and elegance of its subjects, the curiosity and humor of the photographer, the quality of its writing, the sensuality of its women as well as its celebrities: Colette, Maurice Chevalier, Picasso, Jean Cocteau. Avedon's narrative on Lartigue enchanted the English-speaking world (the book was reviewed in *The New York Times*, *London Arts Review*, *Evening Standard*, the *Sunday Telegraph*, the *Times*, the *Guardian*…). For Anaïs Nin, among others, Lartigue was not only an important photographer but also a talented diarist. The ever-enthusiastic Avedon sent Lartigue a copy of her review with a note: "Very good for business!!!" (fig. 12).

Indeed, *Diary of a Century* presents a simultaneously intimate and historic narrative of the entire century. On one side, the two world wars function as chronological dividers, with the presence of figures like Emile Loubet, President of France, marking the historical moments from the beginning of the century, and Senator John F. Kennedy (taken in 1953) marking those in the later part. On the other side, the description of Lartigue's life is structured around very personal events and themes — childhood games, his marriage and honeymoon, births, family happenings, death and old age.[53] The fact that Lartigue himself, the witness to so much life and history, was still alive adds poignancy to the story.

Evoking his own photographic practice, Avedon added a narrative thread that focused on fashion, from the *elegante* at the beginning of the century to the tomboy style of the twenties, through the vamp of the thirties (as embodied in Renée Perle, who was involved with Lartigue from 1930 to 1932, and is seen here publicly for the first time (*see pages 510–11*). Then it's on to the idiosyncratic femininity of the sixties, in the form of Penelope Tree, Avedon's favorite model of the period. It is worth mentioning that Avedon's contribution to the book was barely noted in the press, even if Viking's publicity credited him as the book's editor. But from the beginning, Avedon had requested that his presence in the project remain, as he put it, "modest" compared to that of Lartigue.[54]

The book's enduring success, aside from the fact that two years of hard work went into it, is largely due to its ability to simultaneous operate at two levels. While the book offers a faithful presentation of events in Lartigue's life, the story is told through a subtle and artful series of "constructions" to give it greater universality and force. This is Avedon's mark on the project as its *auteur*. He created ruptures, dynamic movements, cinematic transitions, emphases and contrasts — transformations to which Lartigue acquiesced himself. For instance, it is known that Lartigue took very few pictures of soldiers during the First World War. The one found by Avedon is included in the narrative, making a sudden dramatic break in an otherwise undisturbed flow of elegant images. At the same time, the general picture of the twentieth century is slightly distorted, giving the Belle Epoque considerably more weight. With this, Avedon was able to realize his Proustian dream: the prewar Parisian imaginary, with its *elegantes*, salons, sophistication, and high society; mixing writers, dancers and actors.

In a similar transformation, after the Second World War, the book shifts progressively toward America — again a deliberate choice by Avedon. In an even more daring gesture, he virtually eliminates the presence of Lartigue's second wife, Marcelle Paolucci (from 1934 to 1940), from the story of his life in favor of the more photogenic Renée Perle, with whom the photographer was only briefly involved. Avedon's art direction even magically constructs close personal friendships for Lartigue out of the celebrity acquaintances he photographed: Picasso, Cocteau, Marcel Achard, Elsa Maxwell[55] (*see page 523, top*). Good examples of this include the portrait of

Picasso, which was merely an assignment for *Point de vue*, a society magazine; and that of Colette — one of only a few Lartigue ever made. Similarly, despite the tremendous fame of his portrait of Kennedy (*see page 521, bottom*), Lartigue met him only once, at a large society luncheon at the Dubonnets. Generally, Avedon's detailed instructions to Lartigue (*see pages 492–93*) tended to privilege the overall flow and equilibrium of his work over the literal details of his life story. If an image was weak, text was deployed. If a section lacked rhythm, images could be cropped (like Penelope Tree's portrait, *see page 467*), retouched[56] (*see pages 518–19*), or even backdated.

The resulting book reads like a novella, its images underpinning the emotions of the story, "composing and emphasizing the moments," as Ruth Ansel noted.[57] The photographs, in other words, are part of a greater whole. In this respect, the two men show a similar approach to the photo book. Avedon immediately grasped the flowing graphic quality of Lartigue's photo albums as well as their narrative power, which he also found in Lartigue's journal sketches. This power was amplified by the influence of Brodovitch's graphic language, which is evident in the alteration of large and small images, pauses and shifts in pacing with blocks of text, and elements of surprise in the visual flow. Similar to the method they employed at *Harper's Bazaar*, Avedon and Feitler laid out the book pages on Lartigue's table, or pinned them on the wall of Avedon's studio (*see pages 482–83*), recalling the Smithsonian and McCann shows, to be able to "change and adjust them during the day."[58] In many ways building on *Observations*, *Diary of a Century* is also a very cinematic book, evoking what to Avedon was a double paternity: Lartigue as the father progenitor in photography, and Brodovitch as that in design.

Diary presented Avedon's own discourse on photography, openly questioning the modernist narrative advanced by Lartigue's first discoverer, John Szarkowski. To Avedon, Lartigue was an artist in all senses of the word: he not only took pictures, but also edited and designed the album pages, writing out each day on paper, his diaries bearing witness to this. Despite its seeming airiness, Lartigue's work was profoundly rigorous: "Warning. Do not be deceived by his charm. He is not to be taken lightly. He is a very serious man. His next book will prove this."[59] Avedon's Afterword buttresses this rigor, evident throughout the book: Lartigue has no intention of "making art" that contemplates great themes such as "Hunger, War, or The Human Condition," as Avedon wrote. Instead, his photography is an essential part of every day of his seventy years of life. A daily labor, the labor of love. Devoid of any explicit ambition as a photographer — artistic, commercial, or careerist —Lartigue managed to produce, without exactly knowing it, "a single body of work so consistently brilliant."[60] For Avedon, it's the totality of it that makes the work.

Besides a multimedia approach to photography, the two shared a refusal to accept the primacy of technique; a love for movement; and a common interest in the "construction" of images. Simplicity in Lartigue's images was merely an illusion.[61] The still image that appeared to be accidental or spontaneous was, in fact, the final part of a carefully staged performance. Lartigue may not have "borrowed dogs," as Avedon put it, to dress his family, but he was capable of insisting that scenes be played out over and over until they properly expressed his intention. As Avedon wrote in his Afterword:

> the events he photographs ... so many of them are the result of his own invention. He creates them [...] Bichonnade didn't just jump down the stairs like that on her way to ... the Métro. It was Lartigue who *made* her do that [...] He *made* those pictures happen.[62]

For Avedon, all portraits were performances[63] and these artifices had their own quality. While the fictional image was a representation that had been constructed, it nonetheless revealed the essence of the subject. Thus, it was true in its way.[64]

Consecration

If Lartigue's work achieved the status of art after *Diary of a Century*, it was mainly due to its Proustian qualities, enhanced by Avedon.[65] Their power and appeal, immediately perceived by Avedon back in 1963 and then further emphasized by Lartigue himself, helped propel the latter to international fame after *Diary* was published. Lartigue, who in 1962 claimed he had never dared to read Proust, finally "discovered" Proust in 1970 and began to make systematic references beginning in 1974.[66]The press was a great help, seeing *Diary* as "a kind of graphic *Remembrance of Things Past*."[67] The book was described as "a clear vision into the world of Proust" by Anaïs Nin, an author who was herself immersed in the genre of memoir heavy on interiority.[68] The milieu to which Lartigue had been born was, in fact, the Proustian *haute bourgeoisie*, a leisure class dedicated to self-representation, the pleasures of the present, and idleness. And his diaries — with their lightness and touches of imagination, their attachment to time, were fueled by emotional memories of childhood ("enchanted," according to Avedon) and of love.

Avedon, also, exaggerated the changes that took place over the course of the century, which according to his vision started with the "romantic and empty oceans and sands," and ended in the contemporary "overcrowded world."[69] During the editing process, he kept requesting photographs that reflected the vulgarity of the fifties (*see pages 512–13*). Above all, he was looking to create a smooth, resolved arc of time:

> It would be remarkable, incredible, important, if you could photograph Zizou [*sic.*] and Yvonne Printemps for the last decade, because like Proust, it would show the change in their lives and faces and would bring the beginning of the book right to the end — to a powerful and emotional end, in the way you have cars from the beginning [...] planes from the beginning of aviation until today [...] women from the bois until today.[70]

With *Diary of a Century*, the lost time was regained.

Jean Renoir wrote to congratulate Avedon in 1972: "Each page is a reflection of history. I feel that I am being confronted with the monumental account of the tragedy of today's world."[71]

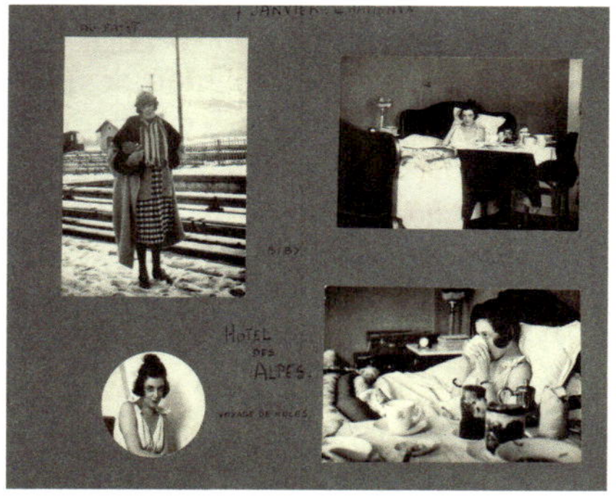

13. Page 0002R20 from the 1920 album by Lartigue, Bibi, Voyage de noces à l'Hôtel des Alpes, Chamonix, January 7, 1920

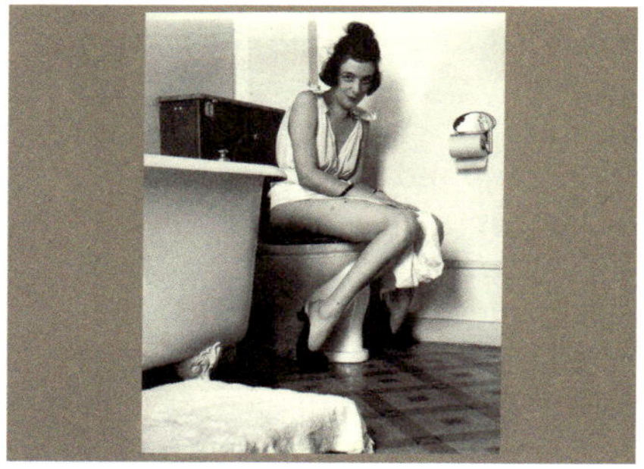

14. Page 0001V20 from the 1920 album by Lartigue

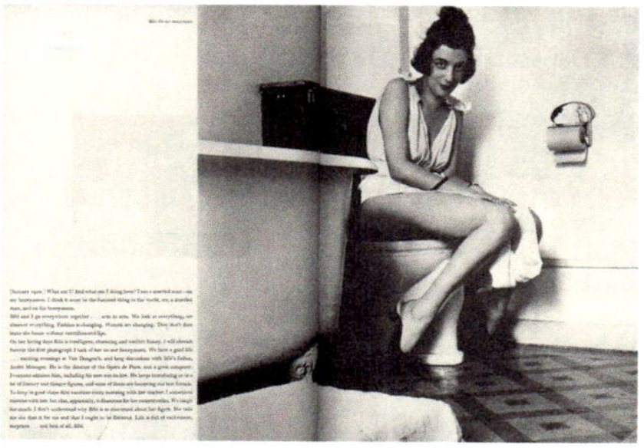

15. Double-page spread, *Diary of a Century*

Photography makes things immortal, preserving them in time, so it is only natural that Avedon preferred books to exhibitions. Hiro recalled Avedon once saying that "the problem with exhibitions is that they come and go. It is good for ego and for museums. The book is about lasting images."[72] In this case, Avedon's big bet paid off: this diary jacketed in gold foil succeeded immediately in immortalizing Lartigue's output as a total, monumental body of work.

The critical reception mainly focused on the single images that had been sanctified by Avedon, often presented as a double-page spread. Paradoxically, the diaries, and most of all, Lartigue's photo albums, remained largely neglected and even isolated from these images thereafter.[73] This graphic dilemma at the heart of the project — between large, self-sufficient single images, and composed, magazine-like pages with groups of small pictures — was a principal preoccupation of Avedon. Since 1964 he had been hobbled by the violently negative critiques of *Nothing Personal*, his second photobook. But by the summer of 1970, under pressure as he prepared for his retrospective at the Minneapolis Institute of Arts, for which he had been making new portraits (notably of his father), Avedon regained his strength and reformulated his vision, as if renewing his own sense of self, thanks to his project with Lartigue. Starting in 1969 his practice had begun to evolve from mixing high and low culture to one primarily focused on artistic legitimacy. In the years to follow, in his artistic work, Avedon would mostly concentrate on producing grand, iconic images.

In 1972, Avedon, his assistant Nicholas

Vreeland (grandson of Diana Vreeland), and his agent Robert Lantz visited Lartigue in Paris. During the visit, Lartigue photographed Nicholas. Avedon would send two of the photos to Nicholas' grandmother, who had recently left *Vogue* as editor-in-chief, and include, as well, a letter filled with admiration for Lartigue (*see page 537*). During the Paris visit the two photographers signed and exchanged copies of *Diary*. "For DICK AVEDON, I kiss him. I thank him. I am his friend. J. H. LARTIGUE," wrote Lartigue above the main title. "For Jacques, with deepest, best regards, Dick," wrote Avedon, in the margin (*see pages 538–39*).

Avedon continued to push for a French edition. By May 1972, there were indeed German and English versions of the book, yet still nothing in France, and many found this lack of recognition irritating. Jean Adhémar, head of the Prints Department at the Bibliothèque nationale de France (BnF), had seen *Diary* and wanted to organize an exhibition of Lartigue's photographs "at any cost" in the library's main exhibition galleries, which had previously hosted a Proust exhibition. In 1973, Jean-Claude Lemagny, BnF's chief curator of prints and photographs, assured Lartigue that efforts to generate his show in France were ongoing. The final publication of the French version of *Diary of a Century* in 1973, albeit with a new title, *Instants de ma vie* (Instants of my life), in a different format, and with a new cover, helped the process.

But there was another, more troubling difference in the French edition: the complete absence of Avedon's and Feitler's names in the credits. Avedon's name, it seemed, wasn't "good for business" in France. There would of course be an *erratum* printed.[74] But the omission certainly marred Avedon's friendship with Lartigue, and the damage would never be repaired. As subsequent editions of the French version[75] contained more alterations and moved farther away from the original, Avedon would lose interest in the project. And his relationship with Lartigue was over, with the exception of an odd visit or letter, between 1973 and 1985.

As Lartigue's career took off post-*Diary*, requests for books, films and exhibitions rolled in. The first show took place in London at the brand new Photographer's Gallery in May 1971, followed by shows at the Neikrug and Witkin Galleries in New York (also newcomers to the scene) in October 1972. The photography market was heating up, and thanks to Lee Witkin[76] and Marjorie Neikrug, Lartigue's prints — worthless before — became sought by collectors.[77] In 1972, Witkin-Berley published a portfolio of ten prints, in an edition of 50, with an introduction by Anaïs Nin. Works by Lartigue were included in various exhibitions, including *Photokina* in Milan in 1970, *Expo'70* in Osaka, *Photographs of Women* at MoMA in 1971, and *Fotografie e pittori* at the Galleria Civica d'Arte Moderna in Turin, in 1973. Within two years of the publication of *Diary of a Century*, the Anglo-Saxon world unanimously recognized Lartigue as a fine art photographer, and he found himself suddenly a star of the international photography scene.

Lartigue would be visited by the likes of Cecil Beaton, David Hockney, Robert Bresson, David Hamilton, Alain Delon,

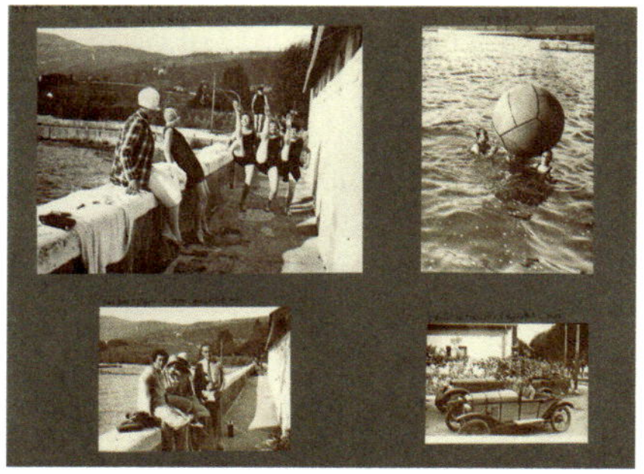

16. Page 0068R25 from the 1925 album by Lartigue, Bains au grand port, Bibi, Les Sunshine Girls, Dédé, September 1925

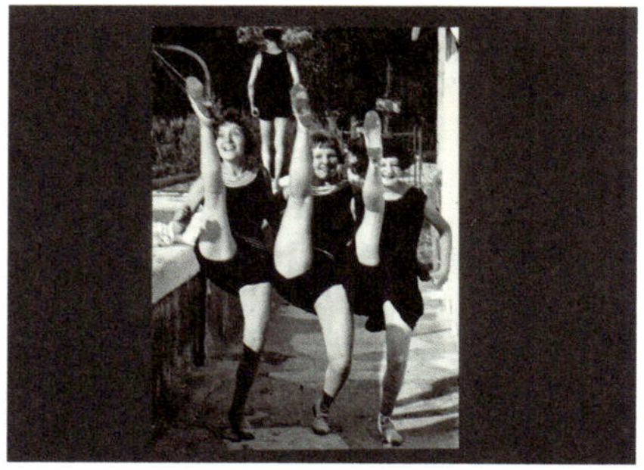

17. 0069V25 from the 1925 album by Lartigue, Les Sunshine Girls, September 1925

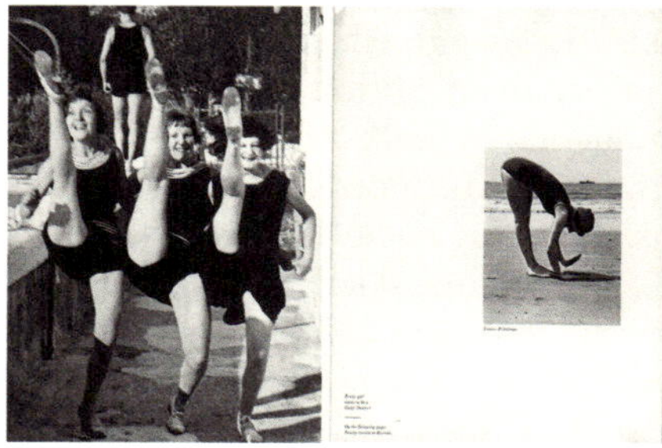

18. Double-page spread, *Diary of a Century*

David Bailey, François Truffaut, Bill Brandt, César, and Gisèle Freund. He counted among his friends celebrities like Michel Tournier, Cartier-Bresson, Sarah Moon, Robert Delpire, Jean-Loup Sieff and Helmut Newton. Four years after *Diary* came out, he was selected to take the official photograph of French President Valéry Giscard d'Estaing, and participated in the third Festival of Arles, along with with Sieff and Hiro. 1975 saw his first major retrospective, *Lartigue 8 x 80* at the musée des arts décoratifs of Paris.[78] Perhaps it was his success in America that made France cautious of embracing his talent, but finally even France lauded him as one of their own.

After the "wake up call" of 1963, as Lartigue would call it in his personal diary,[79] when Lartigue's "hobby" first entered a museum, *Diary of a Century* played the ultimate role in the construction of Lartigue's legacy, becoming in itself the art object that gave his practice a universal scope. Its publication turned him into a key figure in the history of photography, his images recognized as classics. The project undertaken by Avedon also provided Lartigue with new insights into his own work, which resulted in his decision in the 1970s to redo his photo albums.

As vintage prints of his work were becoming rarer and more valuable, Lartigue added more recent prints to his albums, matching those Avedon had chosen to use in *Diary of a Century*. Lartigue had unbound several of his albums for the purposes of making the book, particularly albums from 1920 to 1928, taking out prints he had no negatives for.[80] Using one of Avedon's signature moves — give a new look to the old world — Lartigue undertook a complex and imaginative reorganization of his personal albums, numbering every page, whether still bound or now loose, into a new sequence.

Looking at this now, it is clear that the artist was trying to maintain two parallel visions of his work: that of his own, in keeping with the albums as originally conceived and constructed; and a revised, updated one — Avedon's "new eye"— as he used to call it.

Consider two examples from among many.[81] Today's version of the 1920 album opens with two variations of the same image, the famous shot of Bibi sitting on the toilet in the hotel bathroom. But the original 1920 layout did not include that as its first page. Its first page opened with a vintage print, cropped into a circle, of Bibi's head from that photograph. And in today's version of the album, that page is now page 2 (2 recto, fig. 13), and page 1 is the full shot of Bibi sitting on the toilet (1 verso, fig. 14).

What's notable as well is that the full image of Bibi is the same image that Avedon used to open the 1920s section of *Diary of a Century*. Lartigue didn't make the print until 1970s, and then added it to the album. Moreover, the way the image opens the album directly echoes Avedon's use of it, including how it was cropped and presented on the page (fig. 15).

The second example is from the 1925 album. On page 68 (recto, fig. 16), Lartigue had placed an image of Bibi in front of the Sunshine Girls (upper left). Then, on page 69 (verso, fig. 17) we see this image reoccurs — only this time it's printed full-page, and cropped exactly as it appears in *Diary of a Century* (fig. 18). Notably, Bibi has been completely cropped out of from the picture, and thus the Sunshine Girls replace her as the subject.

These two examples illustrate Lartigue's newly found interest in juxtaposing his pre-*Diary* style of a multiple-image layout and an iconic post-*Diary* full-page display; of intimate and large-scale. In the following years, Lartigue would kept his albums in a constant state of renewal, essentially works in process, right up until he donated his photographic collections to France in 1979.

Diary of a Century opened many doors to the "new world" for Lartigue, in both his life and in his work. A month after Lartigue died, in 1986, Avedon donated the works Lartigue had given him over the years to the Smithsonian Institution — the site of Avedon's first major exhibition, in 1962. Coming sixteen years after *Diary of a Century* was published, and nearly a quarter century after each's respective museum exhibitions — Avedon's at the Smithsonian and Lartigue's at MoMA — this was the last gesture in the two men's relationship. It was a relationship that proved to be both profound and fruitful. With the production of *Diary*, Avedon found his new inspiration, and achieved a personal goal in creating a monumental document on photography. But above all, his efforts gave new life to the work of another — the fruit of a true "labor of love."[82]

With gratitude to Georges Tourdjman, Hiro and Ruth Ansel for their kind, invaluable help with my research.

1 Respectively: *Hommage à Pablo Picasso*, Grand Palais, November 1966–February 1967; *Henri Cartier-Bresson, Photographies 1930–1955*; musée des arts décoratifs; Palais du Louvre; Pavillon de Marsan, November 1966 – January 1967; *Bonnard, Centenaire de sa naissance*, Orangerie des Tuileries, January–April 1967. The movie, *Guerre et Paix*, by Sergueï Bondartchouk, starred Lioudmila Savelieva playing Natasha. Avedon compared it to the King Vidor version of the movie (*War and Peace*) shot in 1956, starring Audrey Hepburn, Mel Ferrer and Henry Fonda. "Ginette" is Ginette Spanier, who had been the director of Balmain since 1947.

2 Avedon, unpublished interview (1994) for the PBS series *American Masters*: Richard Avedon, *Darkness and Light*, 1995.

3 The exhibition at the Museum of Modern Art, *The Photographs of Jacques Henri Lartigue* (July 1–November 3, 1963), included 40 images, primarily from the Belle Epoque.

4 The image was used for the cover of the French edition of *Diary of a Century*, retitled *Instants de ma vie*, in 1973.

5 Jacques Henri Lartigue, *Diary of a Century* (New York: Viking Press, 1970). Viking Press was also the publisher of Richard Avedon's first monograph, *Observations* (1958).

6 "Lartigue: His Camera Spans a Century," *Harper's Bazaar* (March 1967): 190–91.

7 Cf. by the author: "Jacques Henri Lartigue, in the Spirit of the Age," *Études Photographiques*, No. 32 (Spring 2015): 65–83.

8 The word "invent" refers to the discussion of the role Szarkowski played in Lartigue's career in Kevin Moore's *Jacques Henri Lartigue, The Invention of an Artist* (Princeton, Princeton University Press, 2004).

9 J. H. Lartigue, *Boyhood: Photos of J. H. Lartigue, the Family Album of a Gilded Age* (New York: Guichard-Time Life Books, 1966).

10 Szarkowski's full sentence was: "Time works in favor of the honest photograph, and will in fifty years often turn a banal record into a moving souvenir, sweet with the slight poetry of nostalgia." In John Szarkowski, *The Photographs of Jacques Henri Lartigue*, Museum of Modern Art Bulletin, vol. XXX, no. 1 (New York: the Museum of Modern Art, 1963).

11 "Toute l'aviation dans une vie d'homme," *Point de vue, Images du monde* (July 15, 1954): 7–9; *Point de vue, Images du monde* (February 10, 1955): 15–17. In both articles, Lartigue's snapshots are viewed as "photographic archives."

12 *LIFE* published a portfolio on Lartigue in November 29, 1963. The cover was an official portrait President John F. Kennedy, assassinated on November 22.

13 "Paris au féminin, cinquante ans après, le photographe est revenu au Bois," *Marie-Claire*, March 1966: 11–12.

14 It is important to mention that Lartigue never considered himself a photographer but a painter through his entire life.

15 He was voted as such in *Popular Photography Magazine* in 1958.

16 Avedon letter to Lartigue, March 15, 1963. Of Avedon and Szarkowski's meeting, Szarkowski wrote to Avedon on March 13, 1963: "Watching you look at the Lartigue pictures was my pleasure. I am quite serious. Showing great pictures to people who really know what they are looking at is one of the delights of this job."

17 Avedon letter to Lartigue, October 10, 1966.

18 The first European exhibition of Lartigue photography was at *Photokina*, in Cologne, September 29–October 9, 1966.

19 Allan Porter, "Paris 1900," *Camera*, December 1966, no. 12: 7-27.

20 Lartigue visited Edward Steichen in West Redding, accompanied by Hiro, on November 5, 1966. The meeting was organized by Szarkowski.

21 Georges Tourdjman memorialized the encounter between Lartigue and Cartier-Bresson again in November 1966.

22 Since 1954, Lartigue was a member of Gens d'images, an association created by Raymond Grosset (the director of Rapho in Paris) and Albert Plécy (editor-in-chief of *Point de vue, Images du monde*). Robert Delpire, the producer of *Who Are You, Polly Maggoo?* (1966) would curate Lartigue's first exhibition in Paris, which took place in 1975.

23 "Bazaar started the new school of photography with Avedon," declared *Harper's Bazaar* (April 1967): 188–202. And in the same issue: "It is the Paris haute couture houses who [...] send to the world the new look, the new cut, the new material, and

finally the new woman," 154–55.

24 A. Plécy to Ami Guichard, March 28, 1967.

25 Hiro letter to Lartigue, September 14, 1967.

26 Lartigue letter to Avedon, February 20, 1968, in which he wrote that he felt reassured to know that "his book and albums are safe in New York."

27 Avedon letters to Lartigue, respectively, March 19, 23; June 27; July 10, 1968.

28 Lartigue letter to Avedon, February 20, 1968, in which he announced he was going to photograph the designer Paco Rabanne, per Avedon's request.

29 Bea Feitler was thirty years old at the time, had been co-art director of *Bazaar* with Ruth Ansel since 1963.

30 For Avedon, *Boyhood* had many downsides, as he expressed in a letter to Lartigue on March 19, 1968: "Many pages are wasted with unnecessary and weak pictures and many great pictures are lost and the book lacks cohesiveness and strength in its construction."

31 The Lartigues lived near the Lycée Janson de Sailly, a site of student unrest during May 1968 riots.

32 Lartigue, handwritten diary, April 1968.

33 Lartigue letter to Ami Guichard, August 16, 1968.

34 Avedon letter to Lartigue, July 17, 1968.

35 "Méli-mélo d'instantanés" (a patchwork of snapshots) was the expression Lartigue used.

36 Lartigue letter to Avedon, February 18, 1969. Lartigue was delighted that, thanks to Avedon, Szarkowski "has (at last!) changed his mind about my non-old pictures."

37 Szarkowski letter to Lartigue, February 14, 1969.

38 Avedon letter to Thomas Hoving, November 19, 1968.

39 The Met's exhibition *Harlem on my Mind: Cultural Capital of Black America, 1900–1968* (January–April 1969), was deeply criticized for showing no painting or sculpture and relying on photography, among other issues. The catalog was pulled that January for having anti-Semitic language.

40 Avedon letter to Lartigue, March 6, 1969.

41 Avedon letter to Lantz, In May 5, 1969: "All these points should be considered on behalf of the Frenchman." And Avedon letter to Lartigue: " I do want you to know how thoroughly I'm going over everything. So, when the final contract is sent to you it will really be the best we can do."

42 Avedon letter to Lantz, May 9, 1969: "I don't think we need refer to a preface by me or anyone else. If it seems correct for the book, I'll write it with pleasure."

43 Avedon letter to Lartigue, March 30, 1970.

44 Avedon letter to Lartigue, December 15, 1970.

45 Kerry William Purcell, *Alexey Brodovitch* (London: Phaidon, 2002): 170.

46 The book was specially priced at $22.50 until December 31 of that year.

47 Avedon wanted to have the inscription at the end of *Diary*, after the reader had come to know Lartigue.

48 The contract was signed on July 7, 1969. It stipulated: "The Author agrees to abide by and consent to any artistic decisions and approvals given by Richard Avedon in connection with this agreement."

49 By 1968, film companies interested in Lartigue's life story were contacting Avedon. Avedon was the one who connected the filmmaker Robert Hughes with Lartigue.

50 A special edition of *Diary* was made in 1970 for the Museum of Modern Art of New York.

51 Hiro letter to Lartigue, December 9, 1970: "I think the book is absolutely superb, especially the photographs. I can't begin to tell you how much the photographs and your life through them give me a lift [...] Again, we both enjoyed so much seeing you in the film and the book is a total SUCCES FOU!!!!!!"

52 Many reviews quoted the following language used in Viking's marketing materials for *Diary*: "The eye of his camera has seen seventy years of the joys of life. The man who clicked the shutter has captured the twentieth century. Its spirit of fun. Its boundless enthusiasm. Its changing styles. And its marvelous inventions."

53 Old age is a subject dear to Avedon.

54 Avedon letter to Lantz, April 29, 1970: "My name as editor of the Lartigue book should be used in all advertising, but, under no condition, should the billing be too large — always modest in relation to his name." For his own retrospective at the Minneapolis Institute of Arts in 1970, Avedon chose a silver foil coating for the catalog.

55 Picasso, Cocteau, Marcel Achard, and Elsa Maxwell also appear in *Observations*.

56 As examples of how Avedon manipulated the prints, he enhanced the softness of the

images of the society-women in Bois de Boulogne, and darkened the images from World War I. The marks on the images, taken during the Liberation, were left apparent.

57 Ruth Ansel, interviewed by the author in New York, September 15, 2012, said, "The book [*Diary*] is about composing and emphasizing the moments."

58 Avedon letter to Lartigue, July 10, 1968: "We have the layouts up on a big wall in the studio and we keep changing and adjusting them during the day and in the evening. "

59 Avedon in "1901–1968: Notre Siècle," *Magazine Photo*, July–August 1968: 25. The quote is from Avedon who submitted an English text to Lartigue.

60 Avedon, "Afterword," *Diary of a Century*.

61 Ibid., "Lartigue is the most deceptively simple and penetrating photographer."

62 Ibid.

63 As Avedon wrote, "Portraiture is performance." From his essay, "Borrowed Dogs," *Grand Street*, No. 1 (Autumn, 1987): 55.

64 See also author's "La Photographie de Jacques Henri Lartigue comme loisir ostentatoire," in Éléonore Challine, Laureline Meizel, Michel Poivert *(eds.), Histo.Art-6, L'Expérience photographique* (Paris: Publications de la Sorbonne, 2014): 79–94.

65 Lartigue changed his captions to fit the Proustian tone of the book; the little girl on a horse in Pavillon Dauphine became "Marcel Proust's Gilberte."

66 In Lartigue's interview in 1984 by Hervé Guibert in *Le Monde*, he confessed to having enormous admiration for Proust.

67 "Lartigue," *National Observer* (May 1971).

68 Anaïs Nin review of "Diary of a Century," *The New York Times Book Review* (February 21, 1971): 4.

69 Avedon letter to Lartigue, July 3, 1968: "Make the contrast from the beginning of the book when the oceans and sands were romantic and empty to this terrible overcrowded world we live in."

70 Jean Renoir letter to Avedon, March 17, 1972.

71 Avedon letter to J. H. Lartigue, July 10, 1968.

72 Hiro, interviewed by the author in New York, September 12, 2012, said, "The problem with exhibitions is that they come and go. It is good for ego and for museums. The book is about lasting images."

73 Lartigue's memoirs of the beginning of the century, published in 1975 — J. H. Lartigue, *Mémoires sans mémoire* (Paris, Éditions Robert Laffont, 1975); and those from 1932 to 1985, published in 1986 — J. H. Lartigue, *L'Œil de la mémoire* 1932–1985 (Paris: Carrère, 1986) include no photographs. Lartigue's photo albums were shown for the first time in the 2003 Lartigue retrospective, *Lartigue, Album of a Century*, in Centre Pompidou, Musée National d'Art Moderne, Paris.

74 The text of the errata for the French edition of *Diary*: "Following an unfortunate mistake, the page of the book that follows the title page does not include the following credits: edited by Richard Avedon, designed by Bea Feitler. We are all the more sorry for this omission since the outstanding work of selection and presentation of photographs have earned all the recognition of J. H. Lartigue." Lartigue comforted Avedon by reminding him that the dedication was fortunately not omitted.

75 Avedon felt that the revised editions sacrified too much quality, and created tension between the American and French publishers.

76 Lee Witkin was a pioneer; one of the first art dealers to have shown an interest in photography. His gallery (Witkin Gallery), which specialized in photography from its opening in 1969; was on the vanguard in that regard.

77 For example, London's Victoria and Albert Museum sought to purchase photographs by Lartigue as early as May 1971.

78 Lartigue's recognition preceded Avedon's. The latter had to wait until 1978 for his first major museum retrospective at the Metropolitan Museum of Art.

79 Lartigue described the events of 1963 in his personal diary.

80 Lartigue letter to Avedon, May 26, 1968: "I am very happy to have been able to find a way to send to you a first package of photographs that you will soon receive from Brussels: all the negatives . . . and all the prints, without negatives, that I detached from my albums."

81 This topic was the subject of a PhD in 2013 by the author, "Jacques Henri Lartigue in the Eyes of Richard Avedon," overseen by Michel Poivert, University Paris-Panthéon Sorbonne. The analysis of the detailed and complex reorganization of the albums

requires a specific publication.

82 Avedon letter to Robert Bishop, April 21, 1970: "On my part, the book was really a labor of love."

Manipulation is what I do. You can control a chaotic world for a moment in your work, on the paper, on the page.

—

Richard Avedon

Coup de foudre

1946-1965

Before Avedon ever set foot in Paris, the City of Light had been — to paraphrase the model Dorian Leigh — a beautiful picture in his head. For twenty years, Avedon's photographs in *Harper's Bazaar* would be instrumental in refashioning a new, imagined Paris out of the remains of the old city. Stanley Donen's *Funny Face* was a *tour d'horizon* of Avedon's technical innovations in pursuit of this "new look." The film, based loosely on Avedon's career, also added to his burgeoning reputation as "the most famous photographer in the world."

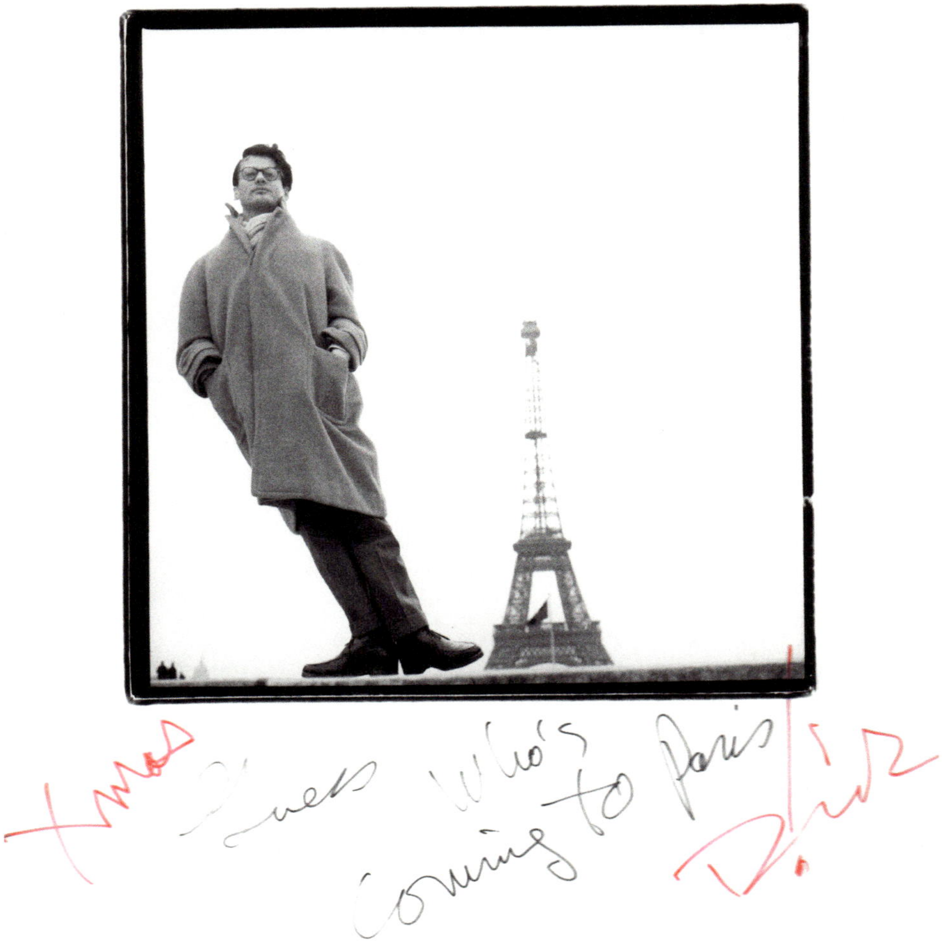

Richard Avedon, Eiffel Tower, Paris, January 27, 1959; print inscribed by Richard Avedon to Nicole Wisniak

Bonjour Paris

Unpublished interview with Dorian Leigh

When we got to Paris, Avedon was standing at the door at Orly's gates, with his arms full of flowers. He had brought along the old taxi, one of the kind that, during the First World War, was rescuing soldiers. There was an old-fashioned chauffeur standing beside him. The car had an open roof. All the way to Paris, he [Avedon] was pouring champagne into the glass. [. . .] It was so exciting. I stood up through the hole in the roof and saw the Arc de Triomphe. The most exciting moment of my life. [. . .] At the hotel, we all got a suite with a little downstairs parlor and a bedroom up the stairway with a door opening right off the lobby [. . .]

Then he said: "Girls, you don't have time to do anything, we're going to have lunch." And we went to St. Cloud and had lunch on a boat. As if Paris already wasn't exciting enough. [. . .] It was the most marvelous thing. It was as though he was setting a scene for a movie. And we were just fitted into this beautiful picture that he had already arranged in his head. And that's what was wonderful about it.

Every scene we did in Paris was, in his mind, a typical little Parisian scene. We posed in front of flower boxes, we went to a little circus, we went to a convent and posed with the children. And he photographed us with baby carriages. Everything was a scene in his head from his movie called "Paris." A wonderful thing about his photographing — of course I didn't realize in those days the difference between his method, because it was so completely new, and other photographers that I'd worked with a great deal, like Irving Penn. They both wanted control. Complete control. But the difference was that Dick participated. He almost was the model. In his head he was doing all of the things. And we were fortunate because we understood each other so well that I'm sure I did every scene just the way he had pictured it. Without his ever saying a word, except "wonderful, wonderful, wonderful."

—

AVEDON STUDIO, UNPUBLISHED INTERVIEW WITH DORIAN LEIGH FOR PBS SERIES *AMERICAN MASTERS*, 1994

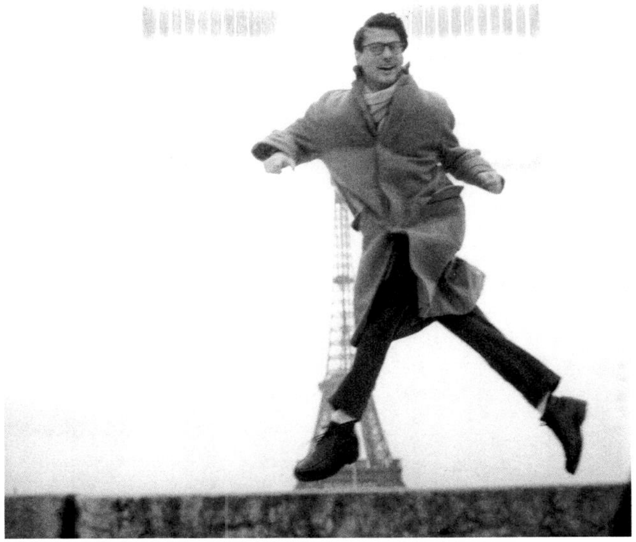

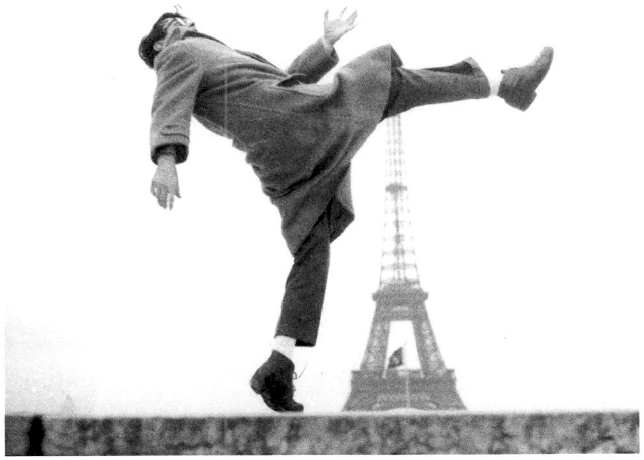

Richard Avedon, Eiffel Tower, Paris, January 27, 1959

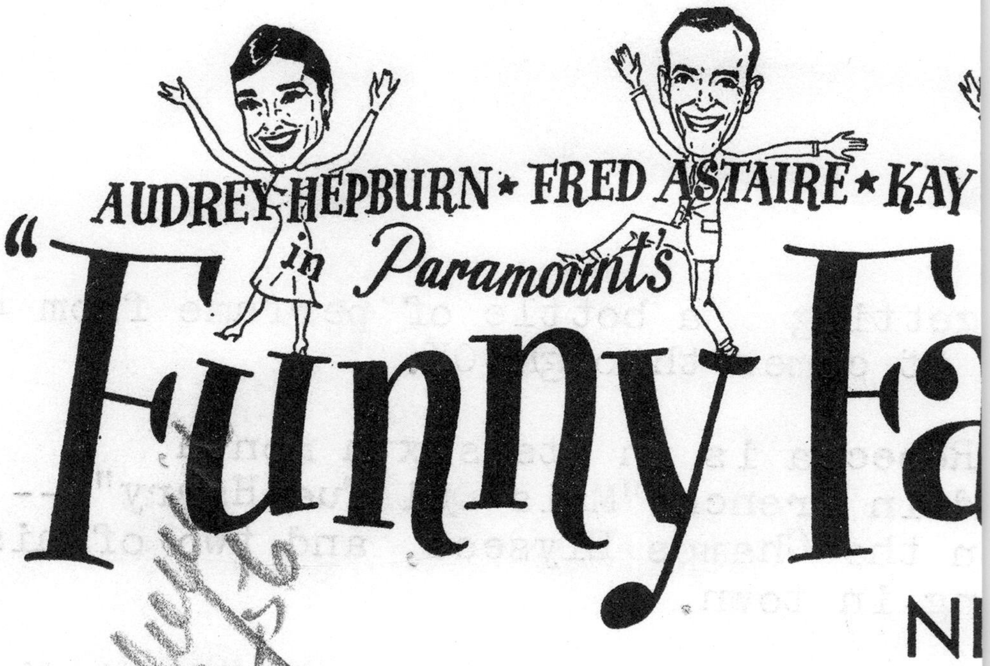

Sunday June 17

Dear Hedda --

From amid the rain and mu
Of the almost three weeks
every day but four. They'

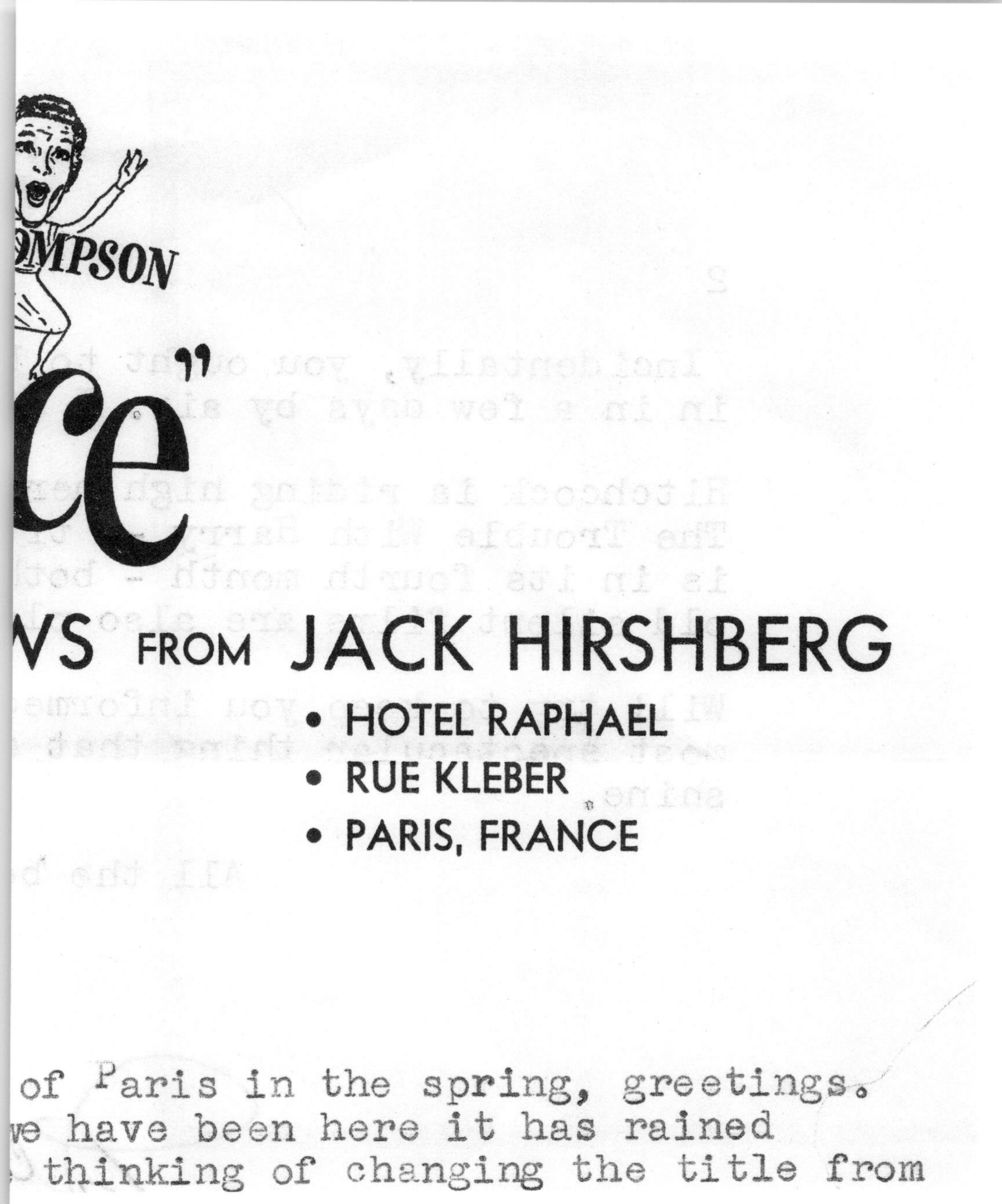

OMPSON

ce"

WS FROM JACK HIRSHBERG

- HOTEL RAPHAEL
- RUE KLEBER
- PARIS, FRANCE

of Paris in the spring, greetings.
we have been here it has rained
thinking of changing the title from

Letter from Paramount Pictures publicist Jack Hirschberg to Hedda Hopper on production letterhead for *Funny Face* (1957), Paramount Pictures (detail)

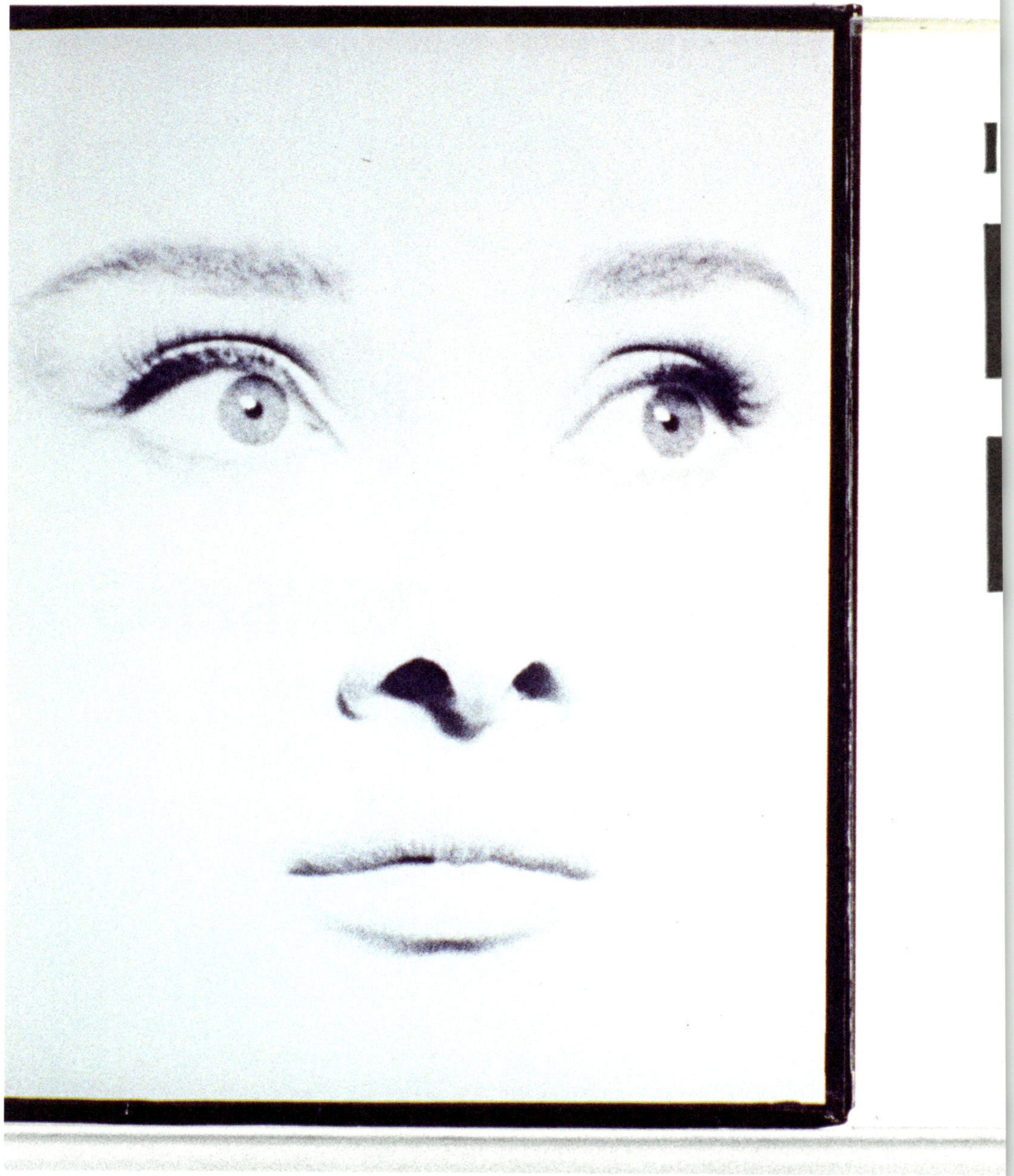

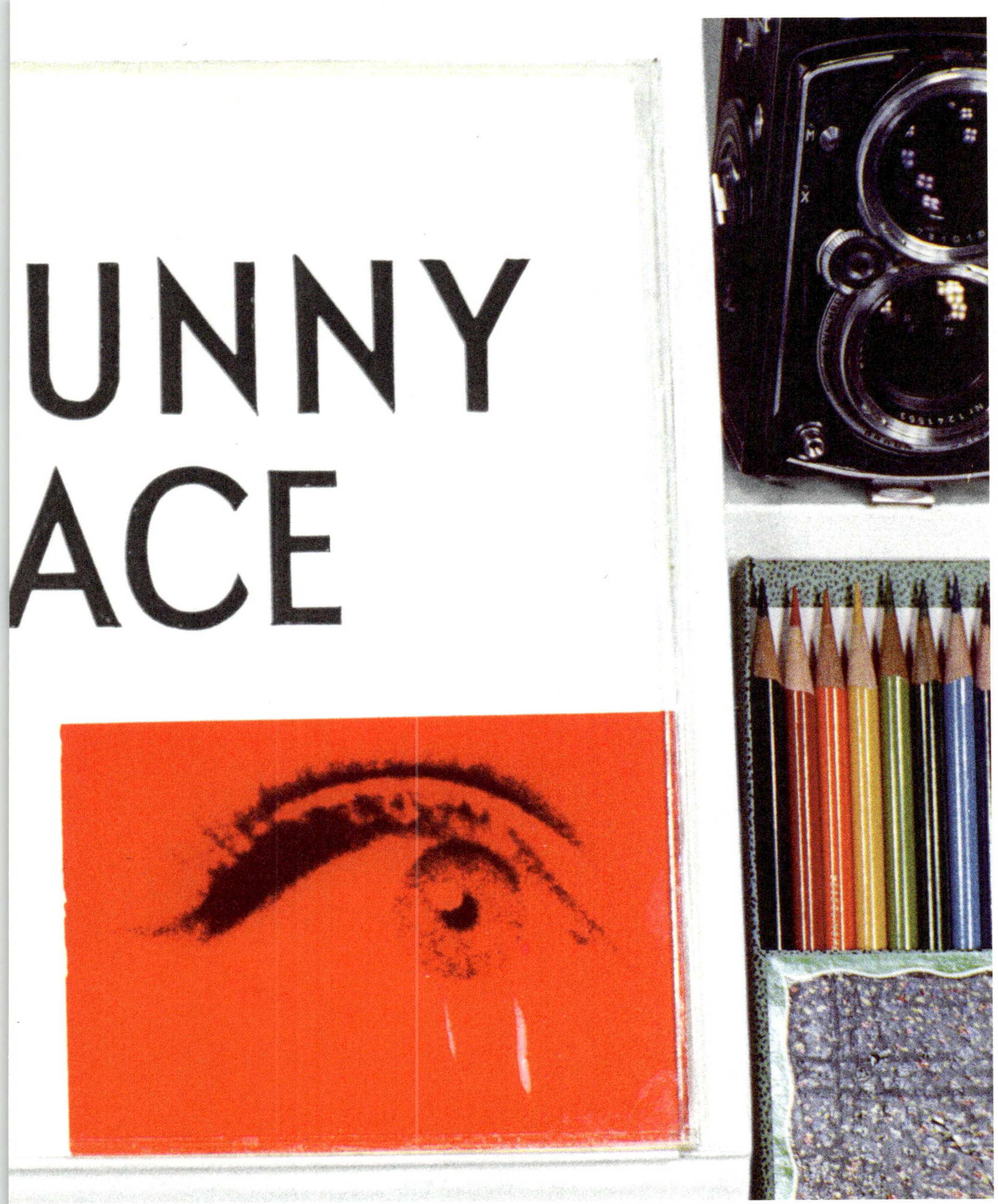

Opening credits for *Funny Face*, designed by Avedon

DOVIMA
SUZY PARKER
SUNNY HARTNETT
JEAN DEL VAL
VIRGINIA GIBSON

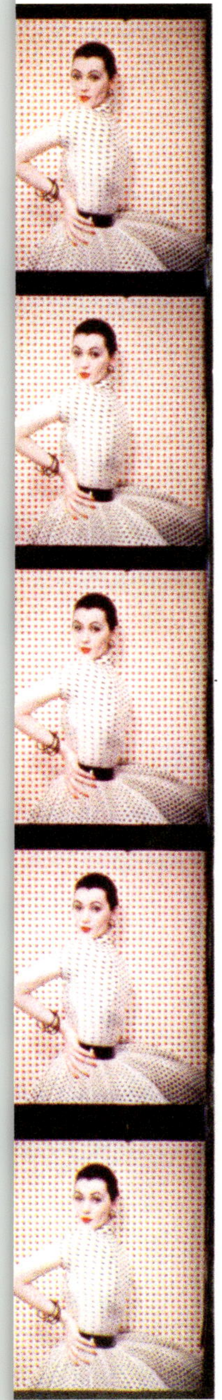

SUE ENGLAND

RUTA LEE

ALEX GERRY

IPHIGENIE
CASTIGLIONI

Opening credits for *Funny Face*, designed by Avedon

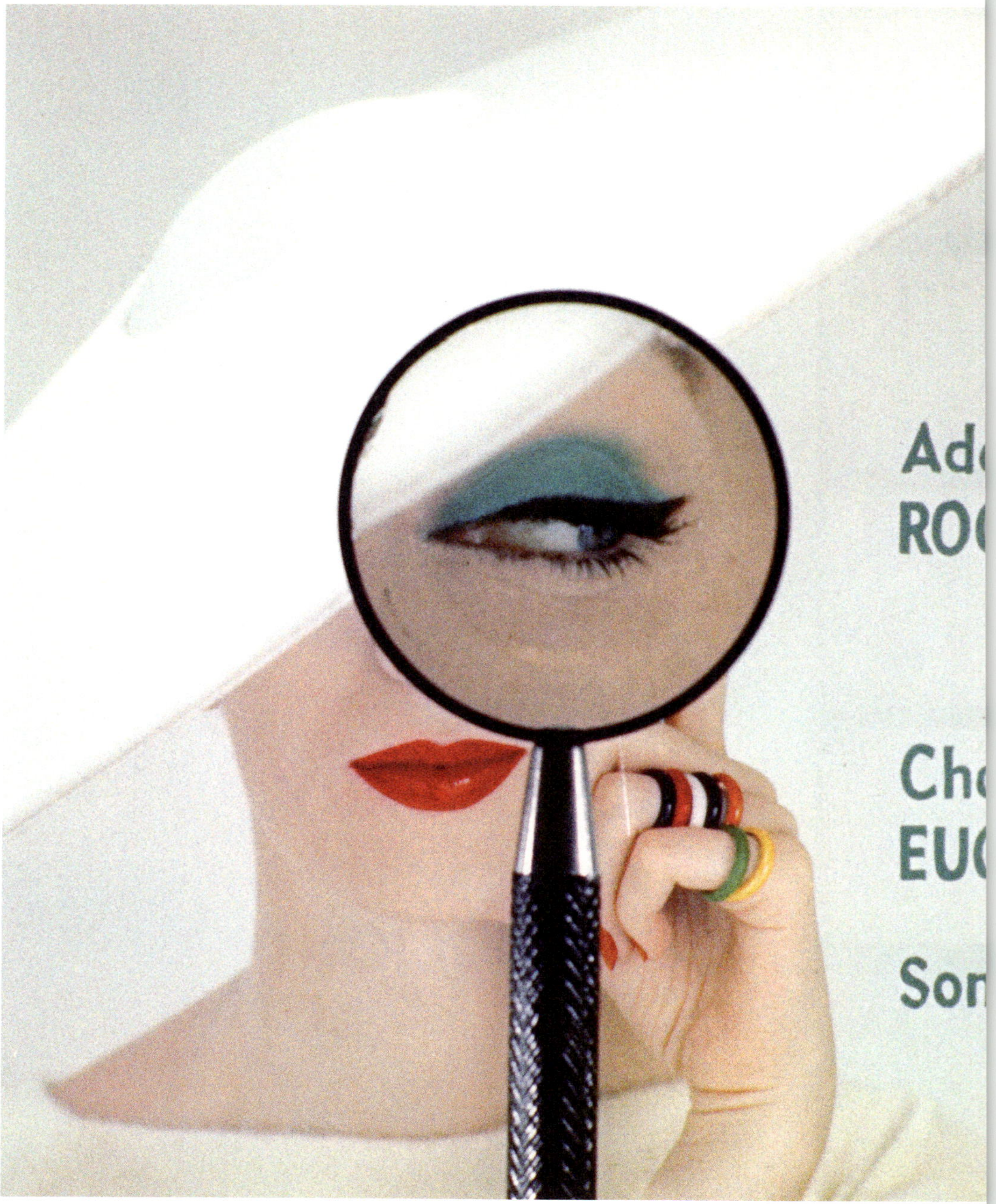

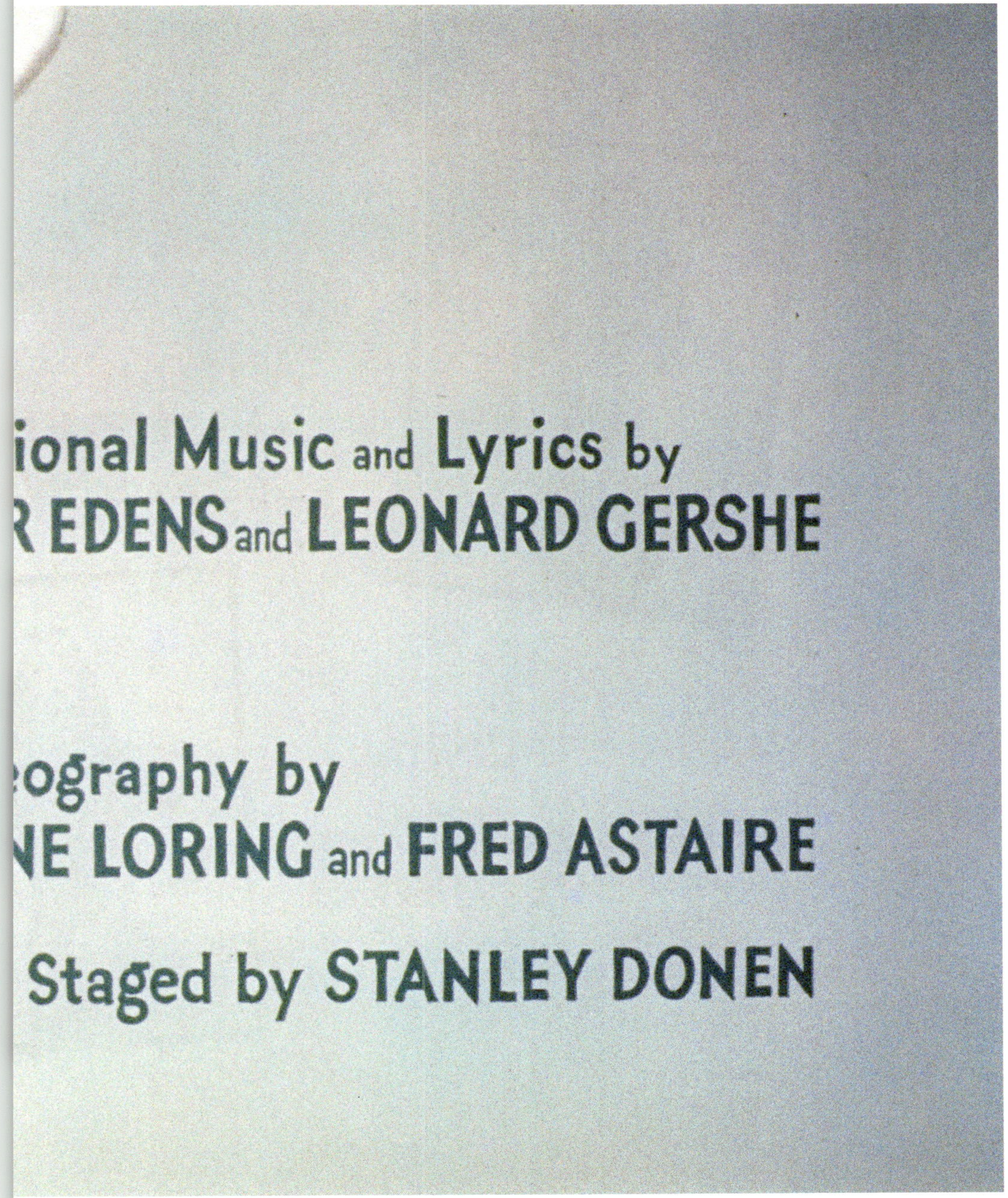

Opening credits for *Funny Face*, designed by Avedon

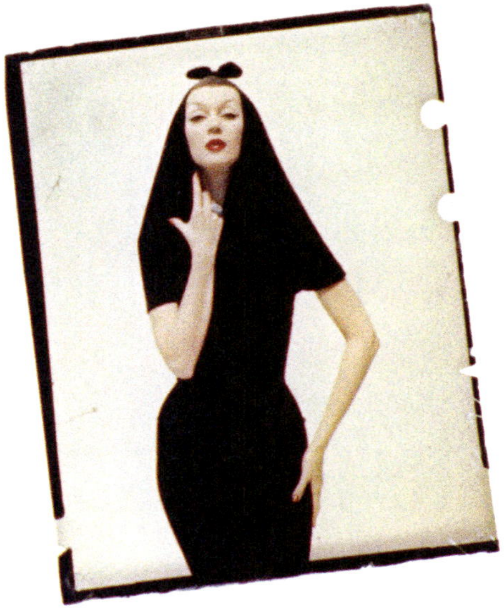

Art Directi
HAL PEREI
GEORGE W.

Edited by . . .
FRANK BRACHT, A.C.E.

Special Photographic Effects
JOHN P. FULTON, A.S.C.

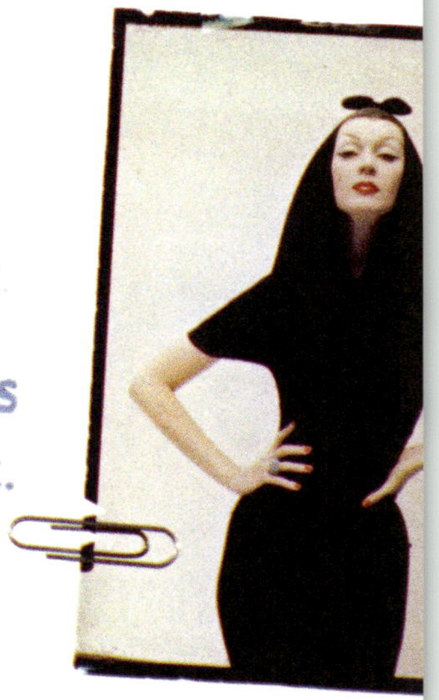

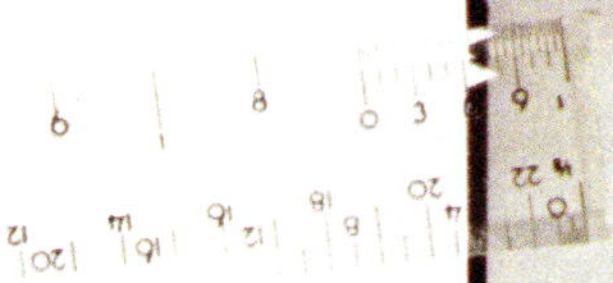

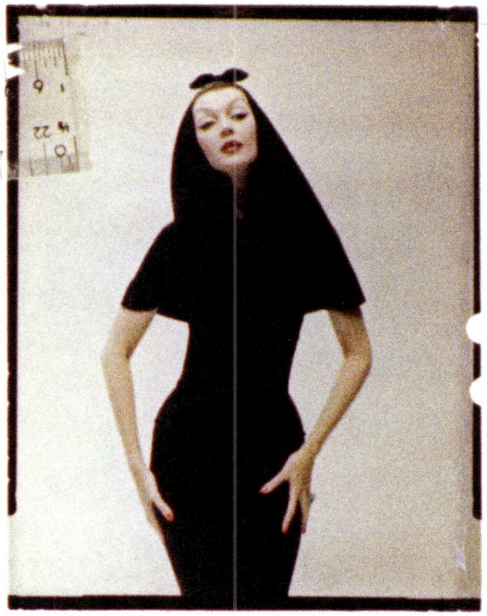

. . .
and
AVIS

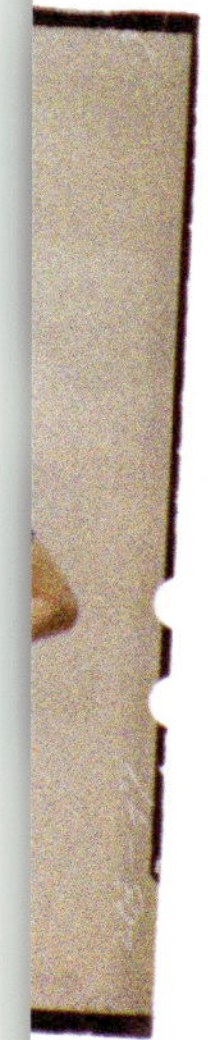

Process Photography . . .
FARCIOT EDOUART, A.S.C.

Set Decoration . . .
SAM COMER and RAY MOYER

Opening credits for *Funny Face*, designed by Avedon

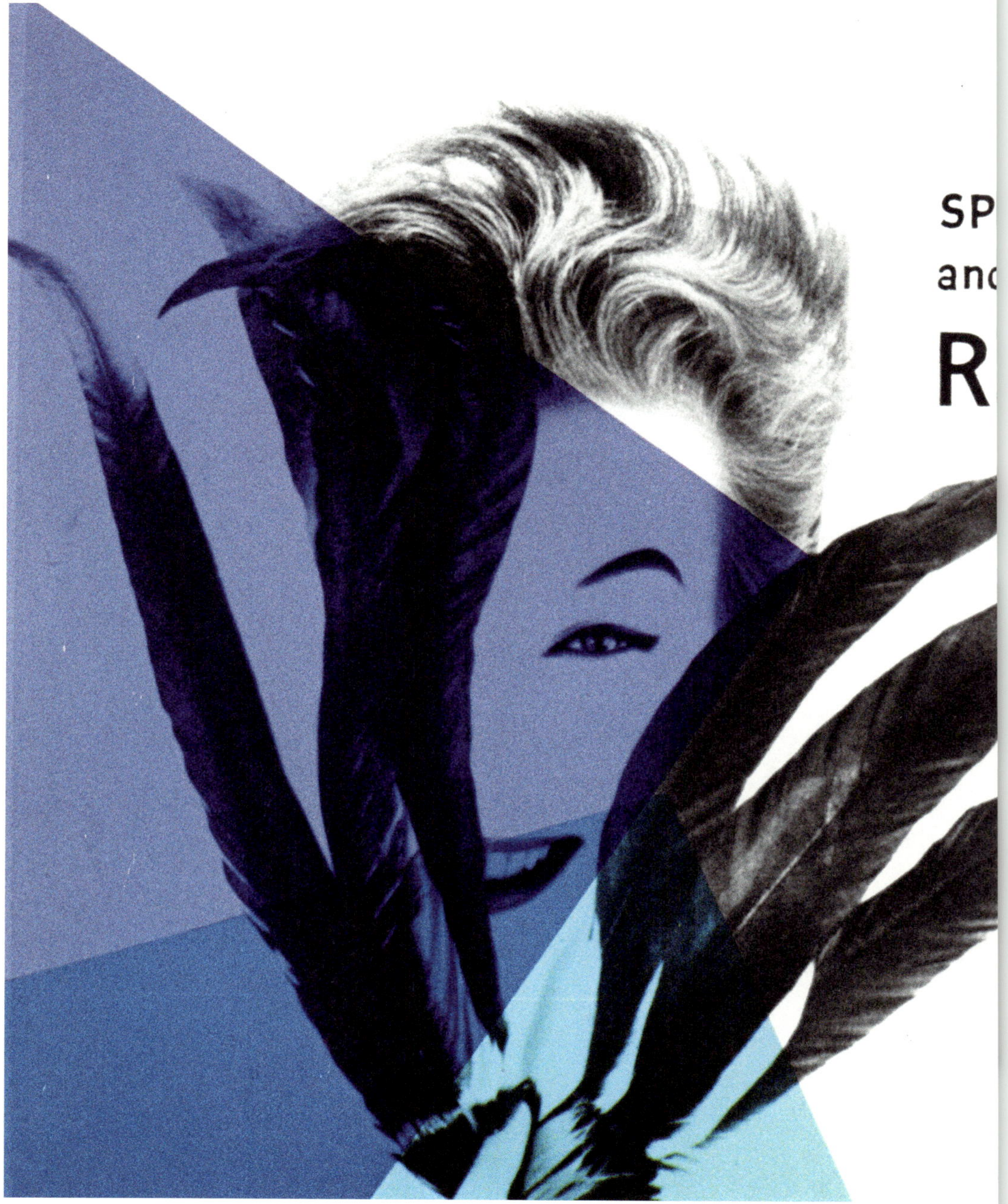

SP

anc

R

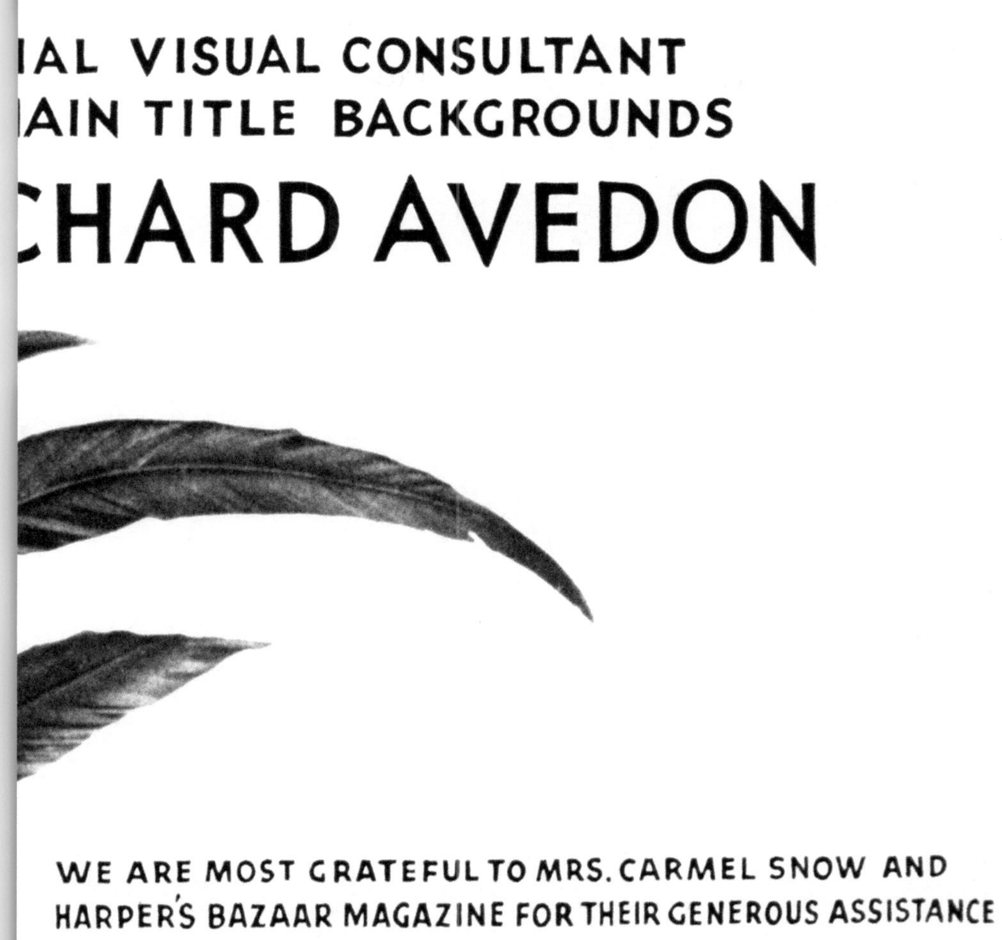

Opening credits for *Funny Face*, designed by Avedon

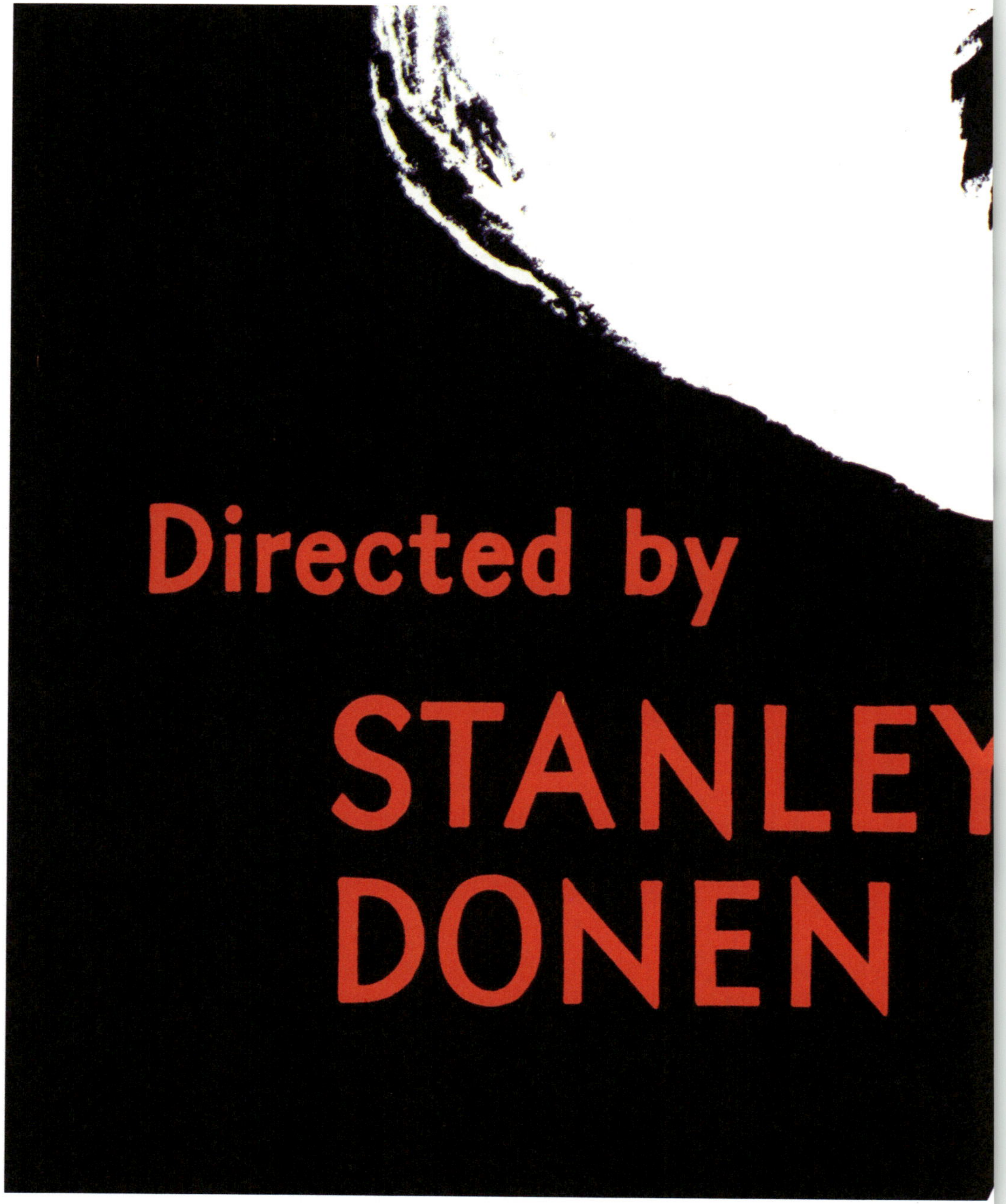
Directed by
STANLEY
DONEN

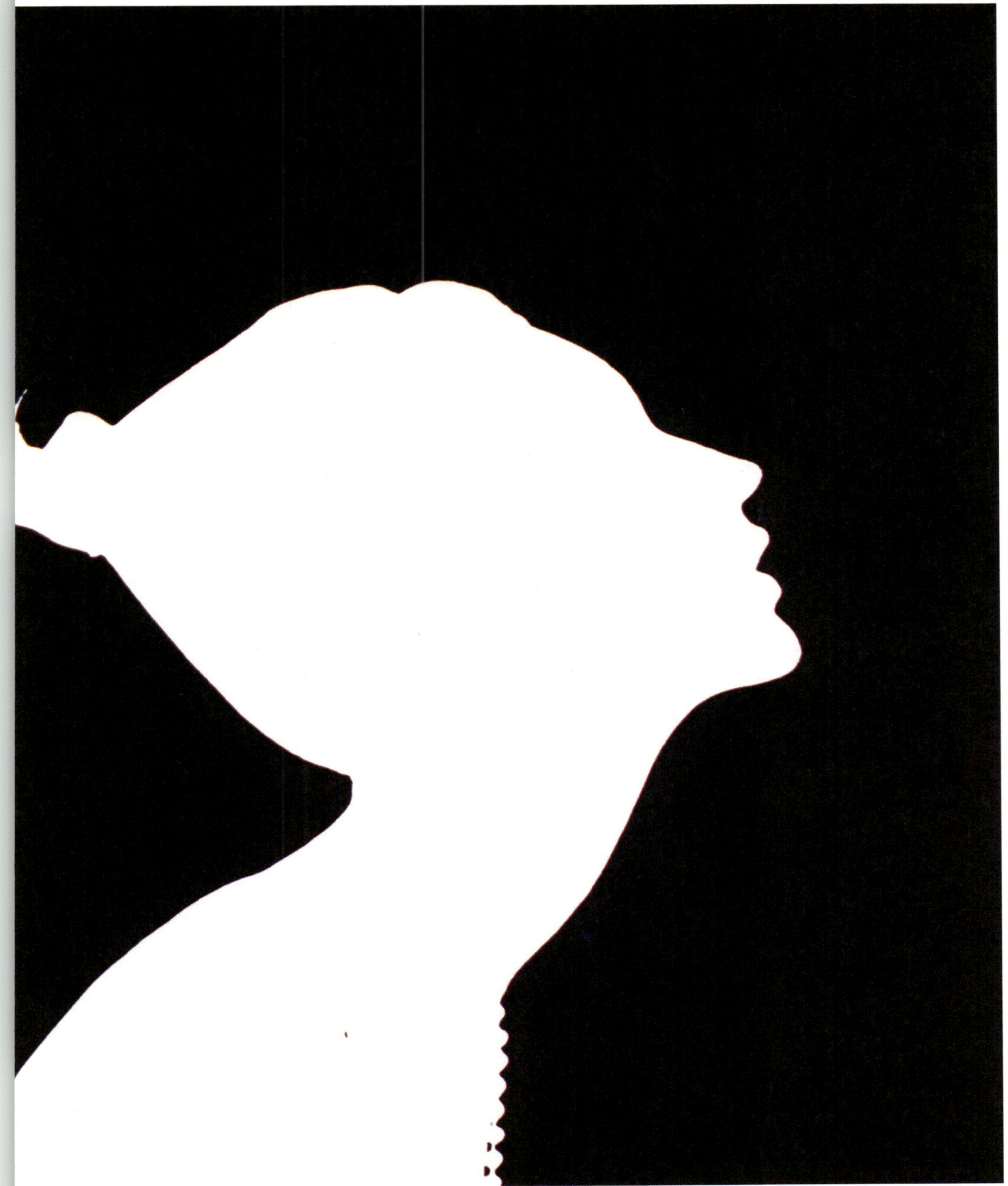

Opening credits for *Funny Face*, designed by Avedon

Seen on TV: *Funny Face*

Funny Face is a late postwar-era representation of American optimism. Its main flaw is excess sentimentality. Its main quality is that it's a defense and illustration of the benefits of technique — in this case, the technique of fashion photographers.

—

JEAN-PATRICK MANCHETTE, "JANUARY 30, 1972," *JOURNAL 1966–1974,* (PARIS: GALLIMARD, 2008): 433.

J. Coffey

July 31, 1956

11520 - FUNNY FACE

S.P.D. WORK REQUIRED

W/A NO.	SLATE	DESCRIPTION
#4	14-4	ADD FLARE TO LIGHTS
#7	109-12) 115-11) 116-4) 119-6) 121-7) 122-12) 128-7) 129-3)	DUPE THESE SCENES TO CHANGE COLOR OF LIGHTS FROM WHITE TO RED
#9	464-2	SPEED UP TO SIX FRAMES PER SECOND FROM BEGINNING TO 5D595R - 14 then 72 FRAMES PER SECOND TO END
#10	28X-9	MAKE 2 THREE WAY SPLIT SCREENS FOR "BON JOUR PARIS" NUMBER
#5 & #11	*	COMPLETE ALL SPECIAL EFFECTS ON ANIMATED, FREEZE FRAMES, AND "THINK PINK" NUMBER:
	353-5	1. AUDREY HEPBURN FISHING FROM BARGE - Freeze and move in
	348-4	2. AUDREY AND LOCOMOTIVE - Freeze and move up
	306R-8	3. AUDREY WITH BALLOONS - Freeze - Change to B&W negative - B&W positive then pop color back into balloons
	394-4	4. AUDREY WITH PIGEON AT VERSAILLES - Freeze and move up
	327-10	5. AUDREY AT FLOWER MARKET - Freeze and move up - Make as many color changes as possible.
	360-6	6. AUDREY AT OPERA HOUSE - Freeze - Matte in - Switch from negative to positive - Many color changes
	366-9	7. LOUVRE - AUDREY IN RED GOWN - Freeze and move up - Make many varied color changes

JUL 31 1956

Requisition sheet for photography special effects, July 31, 1956, Paramount Pictures

Coup de foudre

Freeze Frames

Funny Face

The following seven scenes of Audrey Hepburn by Richard Avedon represent a key moment in cinema and photography. Director Stanley Donen filmed Avedon's photographs, creating a sequence of successive freeze frames that toyed with color palette and exposure and included all the tricks of fashion photography. The result was unlike anything Hollywood had ever seen. The narrative of the movie may be standard fare, but the visuals are avant garde.

Funny Face (01.00:50)

353–5 1. AUDREY HEPBURN FISHING FROM BARGE – Freeze and move in

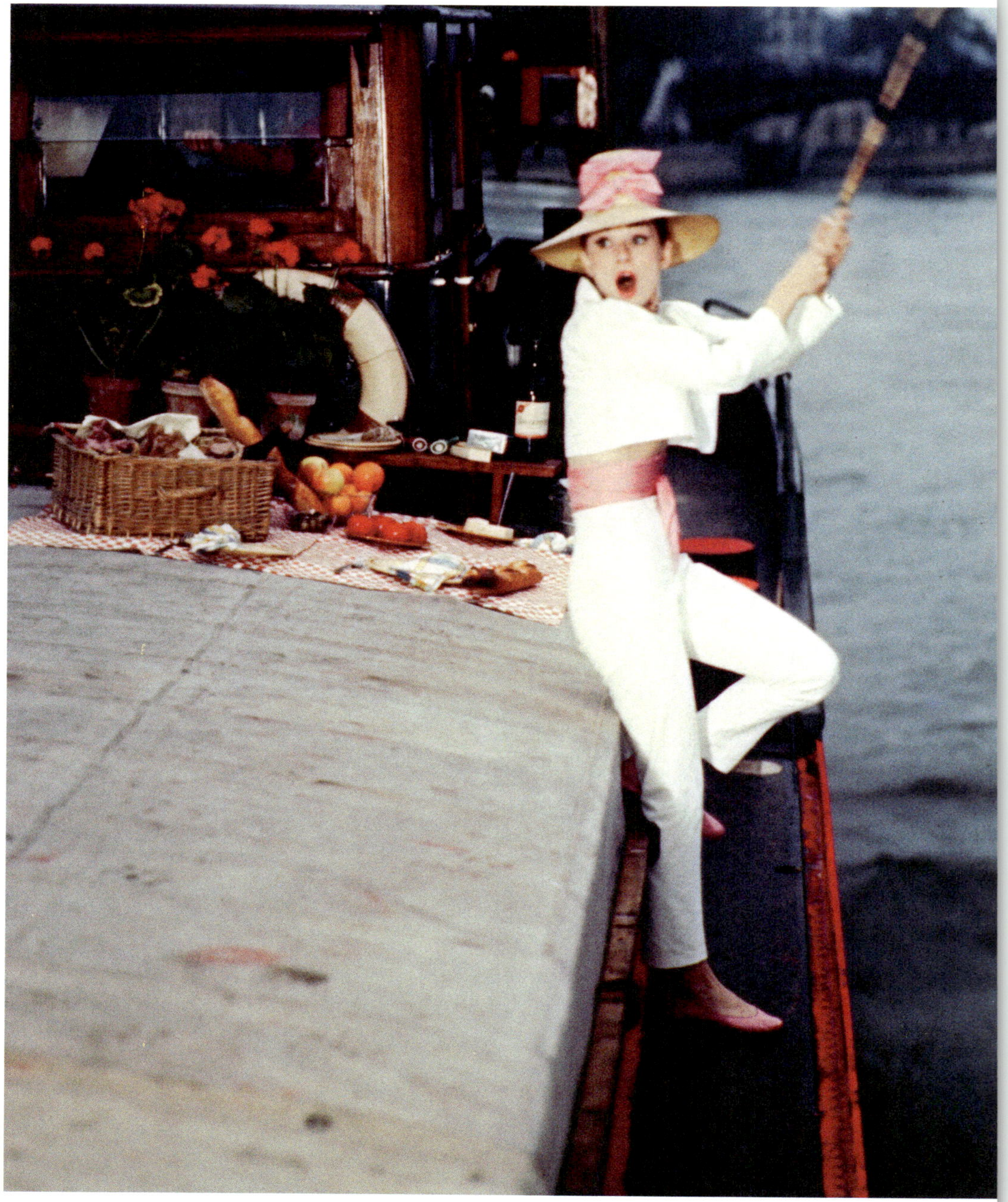

Funny Face (00.59:07)

348–4 2. AUDREY AND LOCOMOTIVE –
Freeze and move up

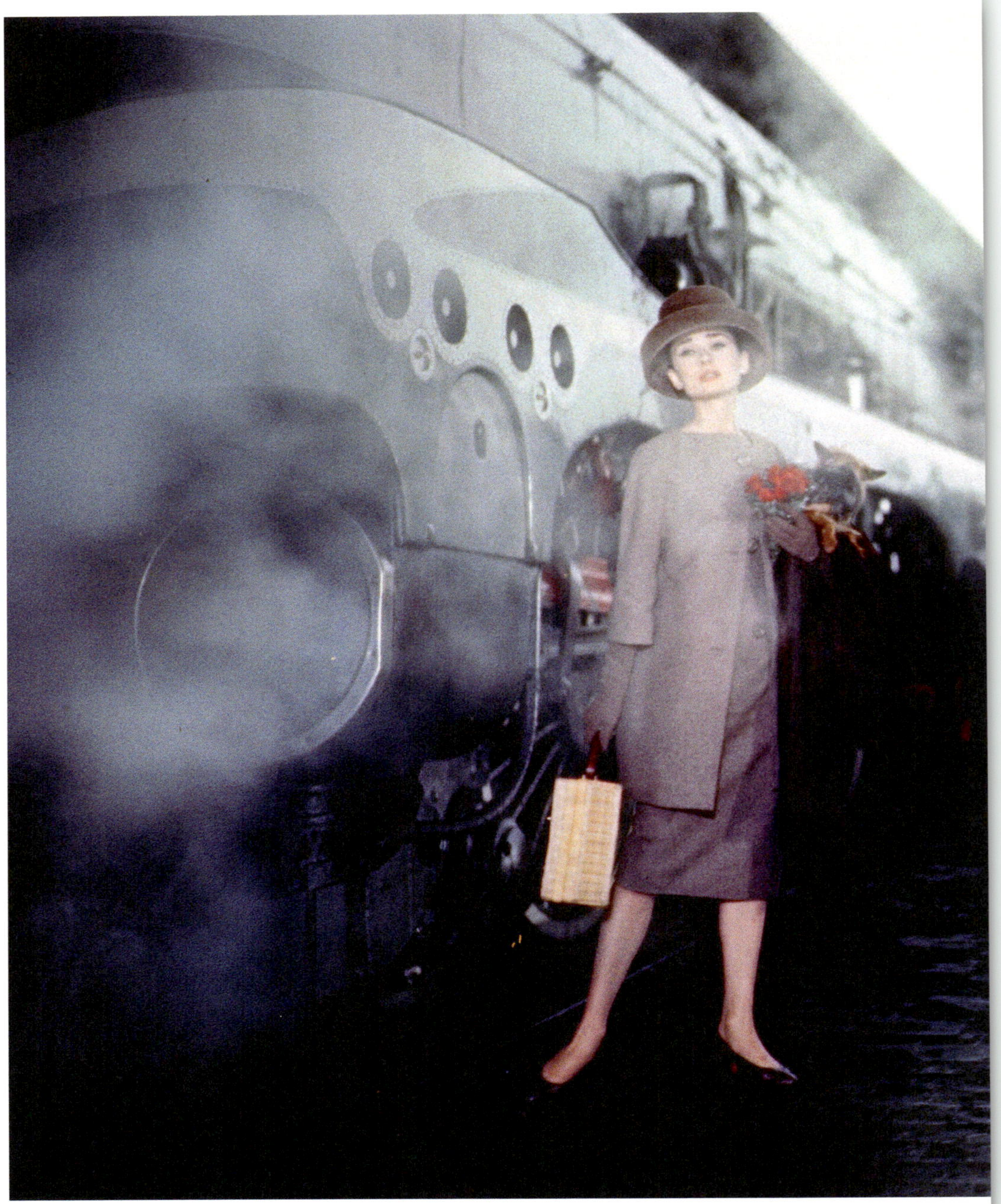

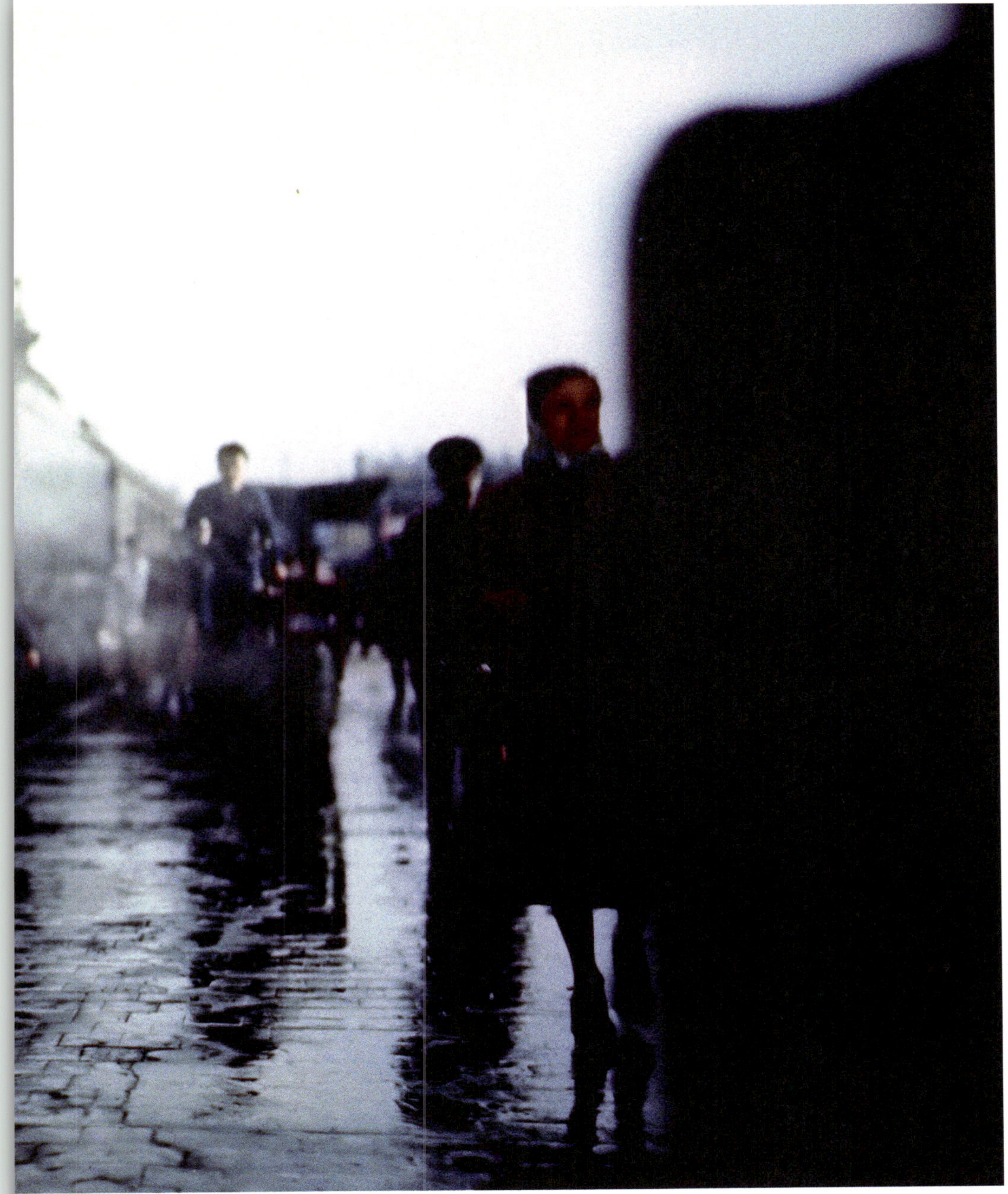

Funny Face (00.58:00)

306R–8 3. AUDREY WITH BALLOONS –
Freeze – Change to b&w negative –
b&w positive then pop color back
into balloons

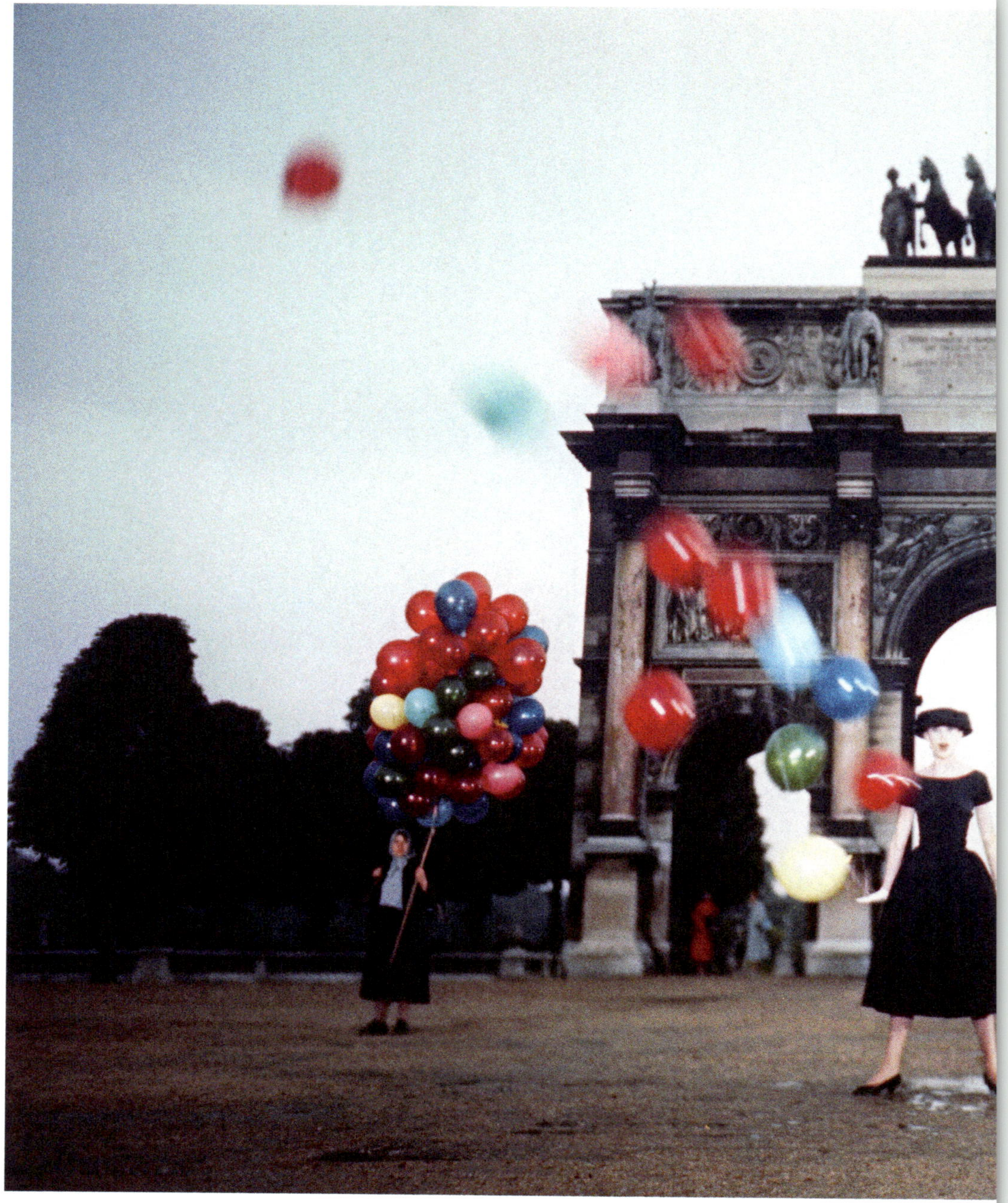

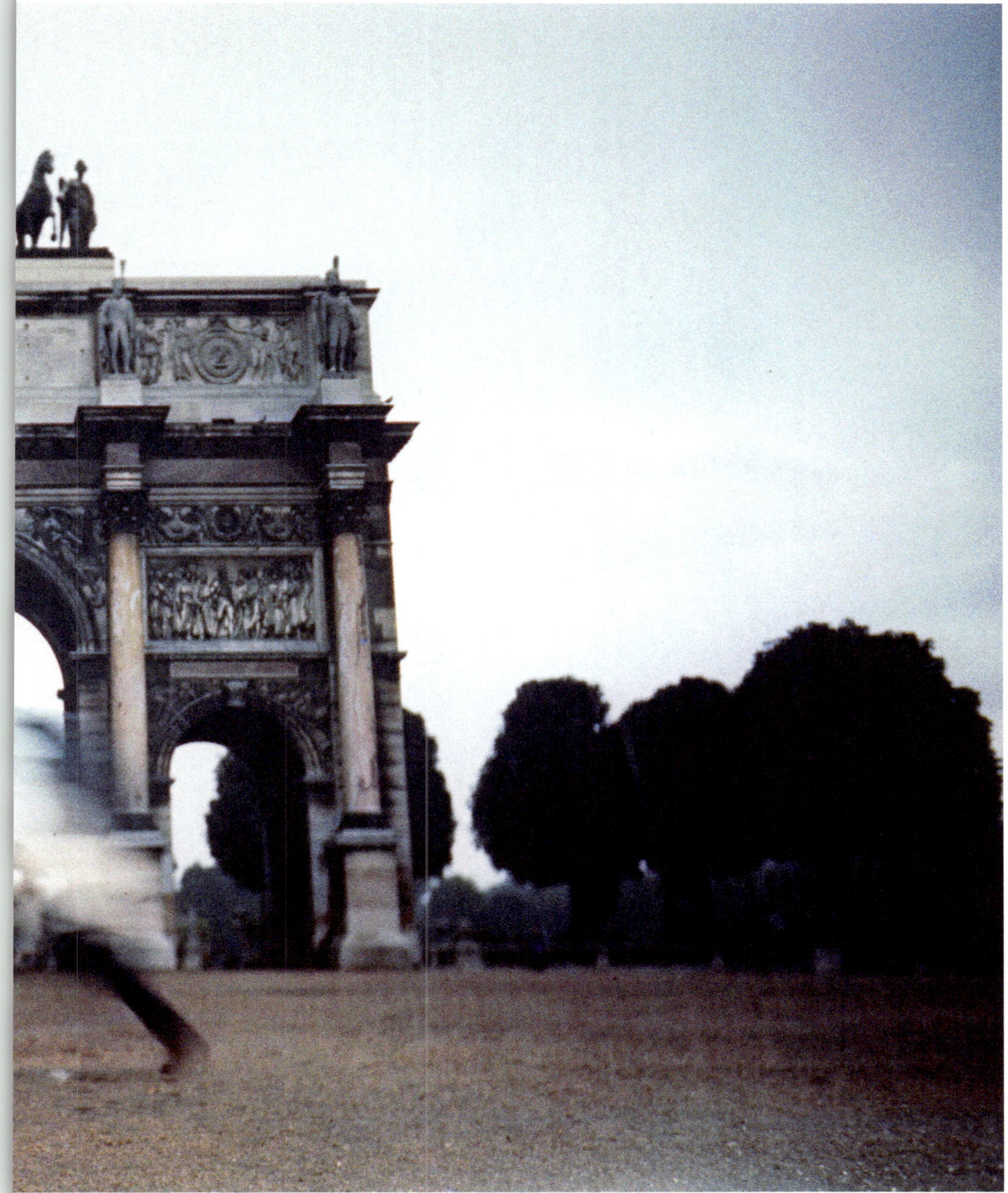

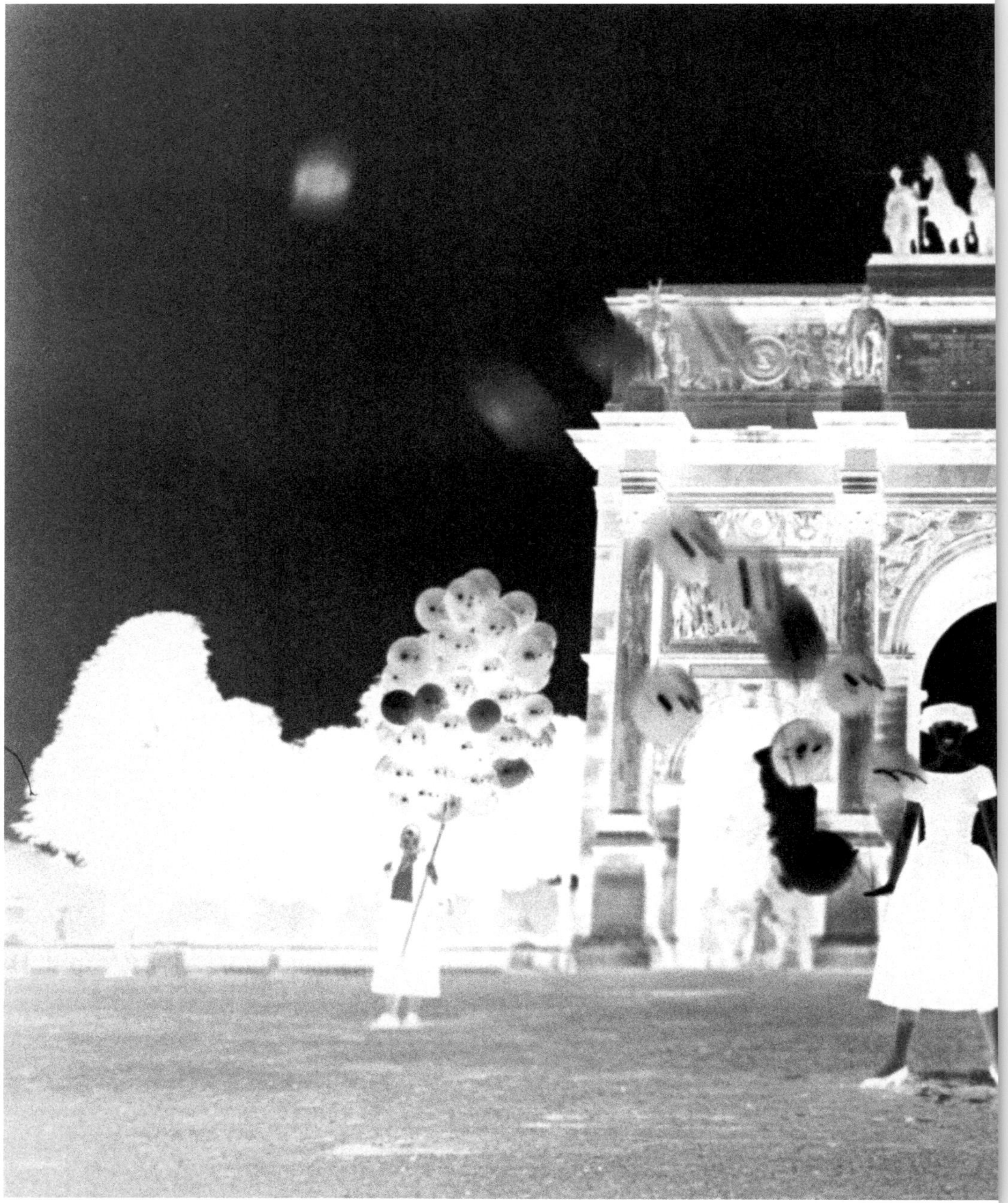

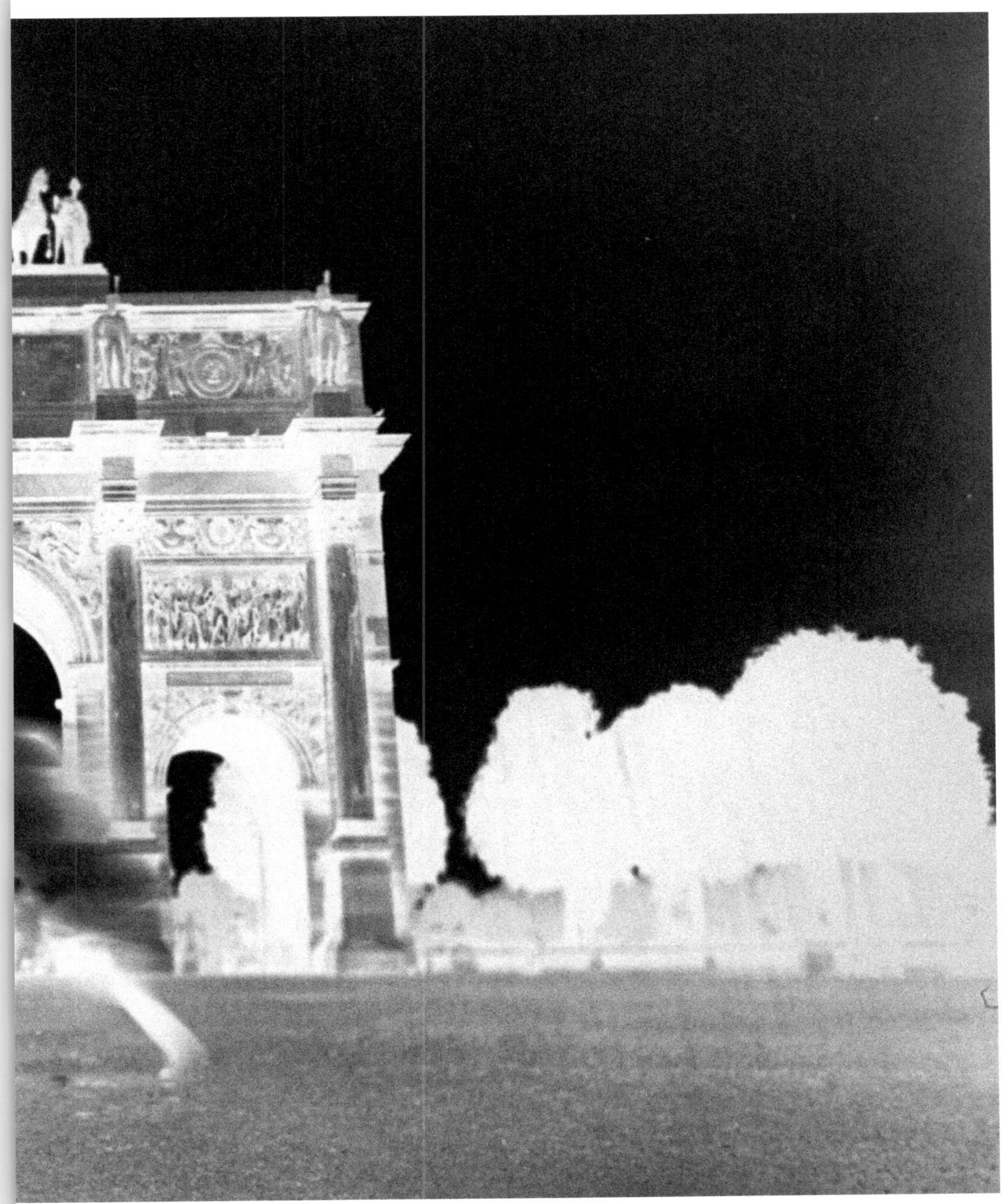

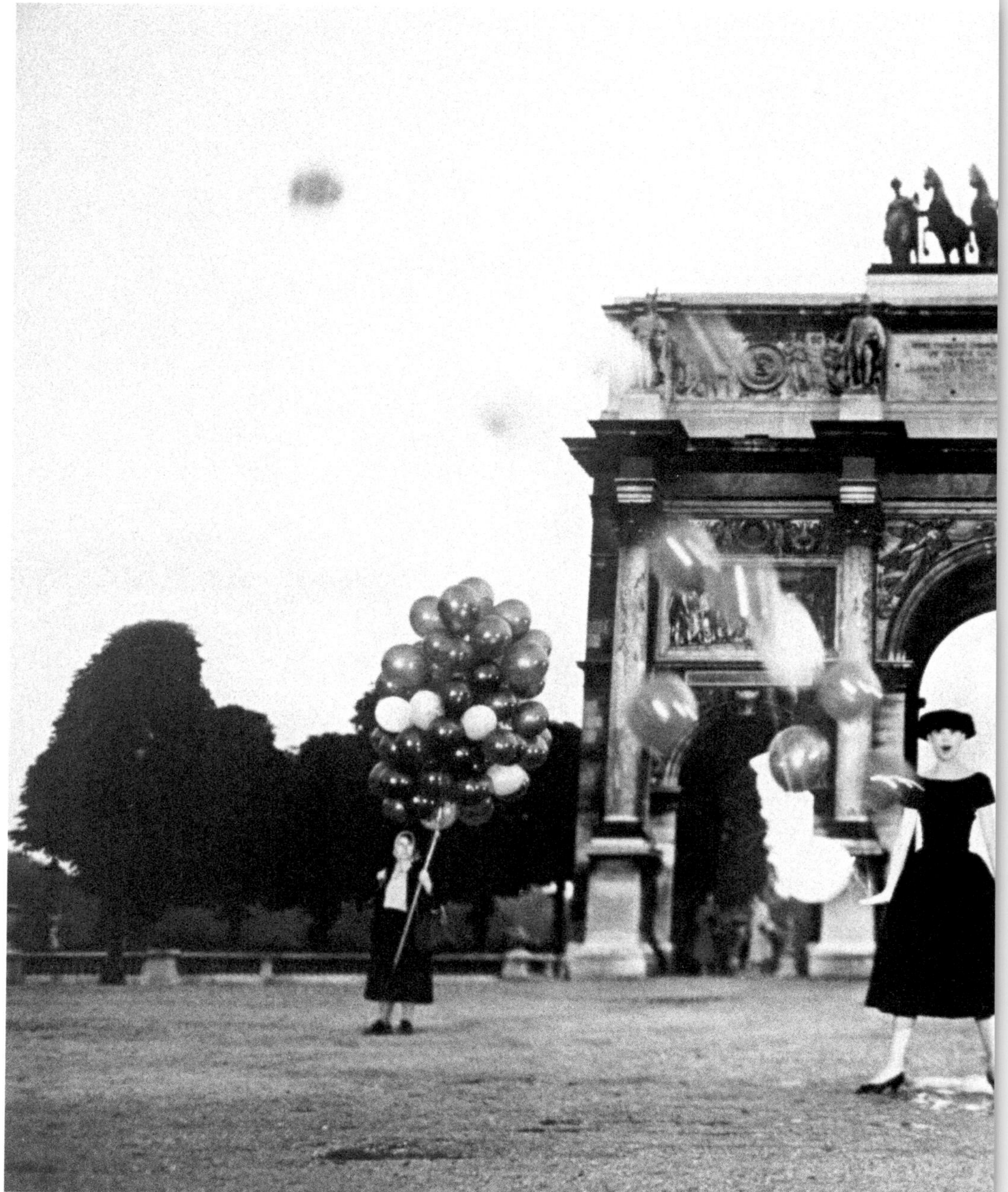

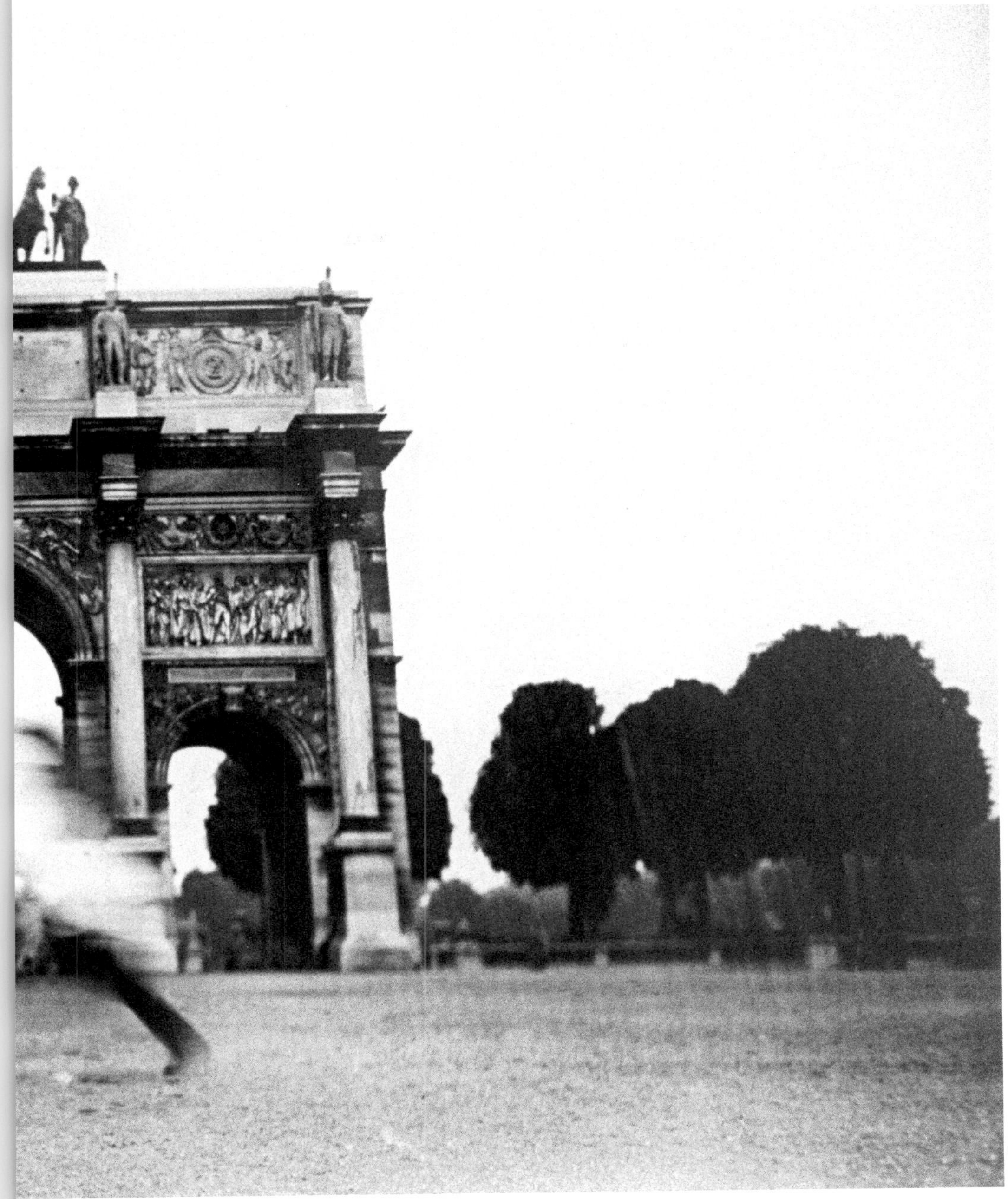

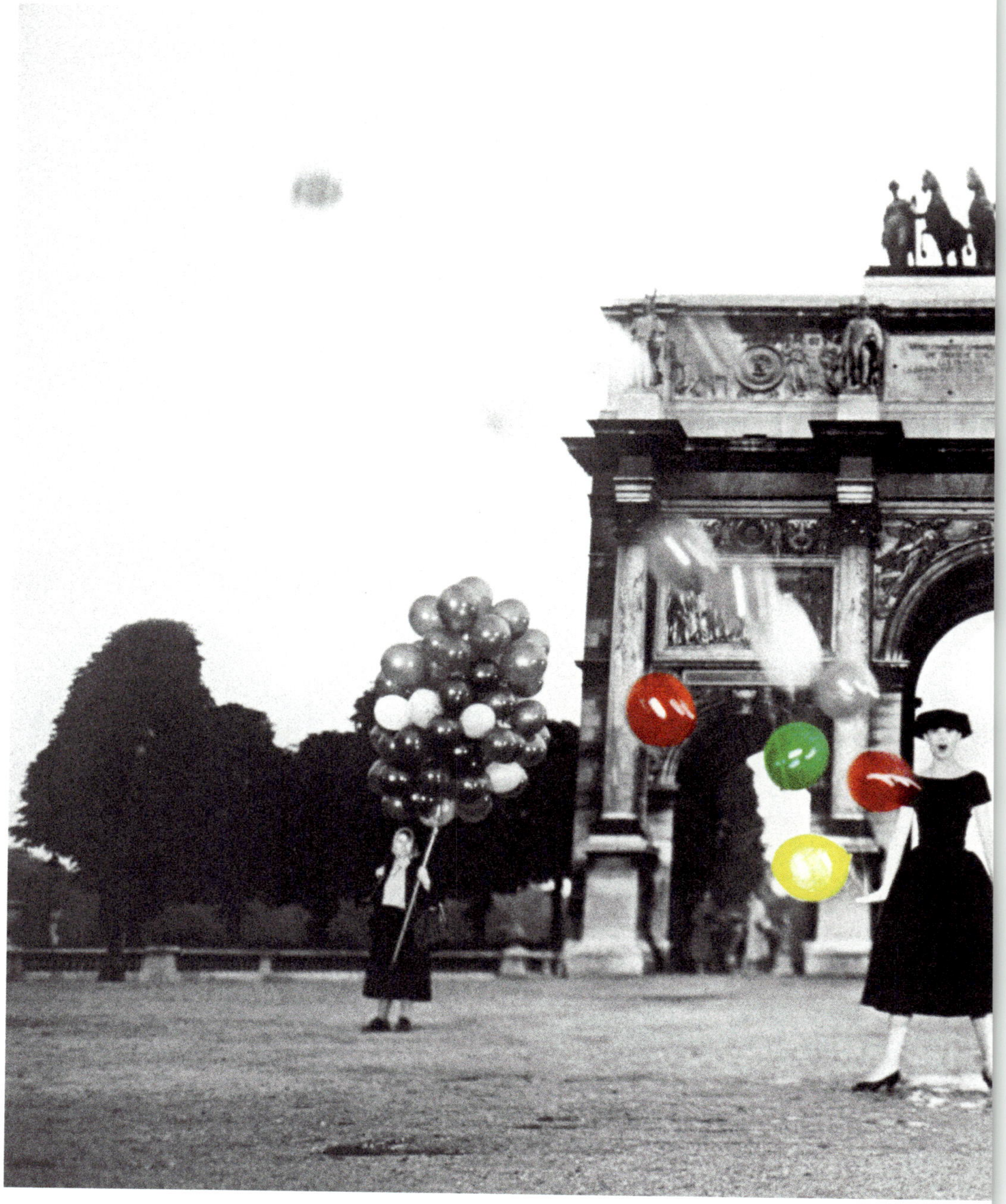

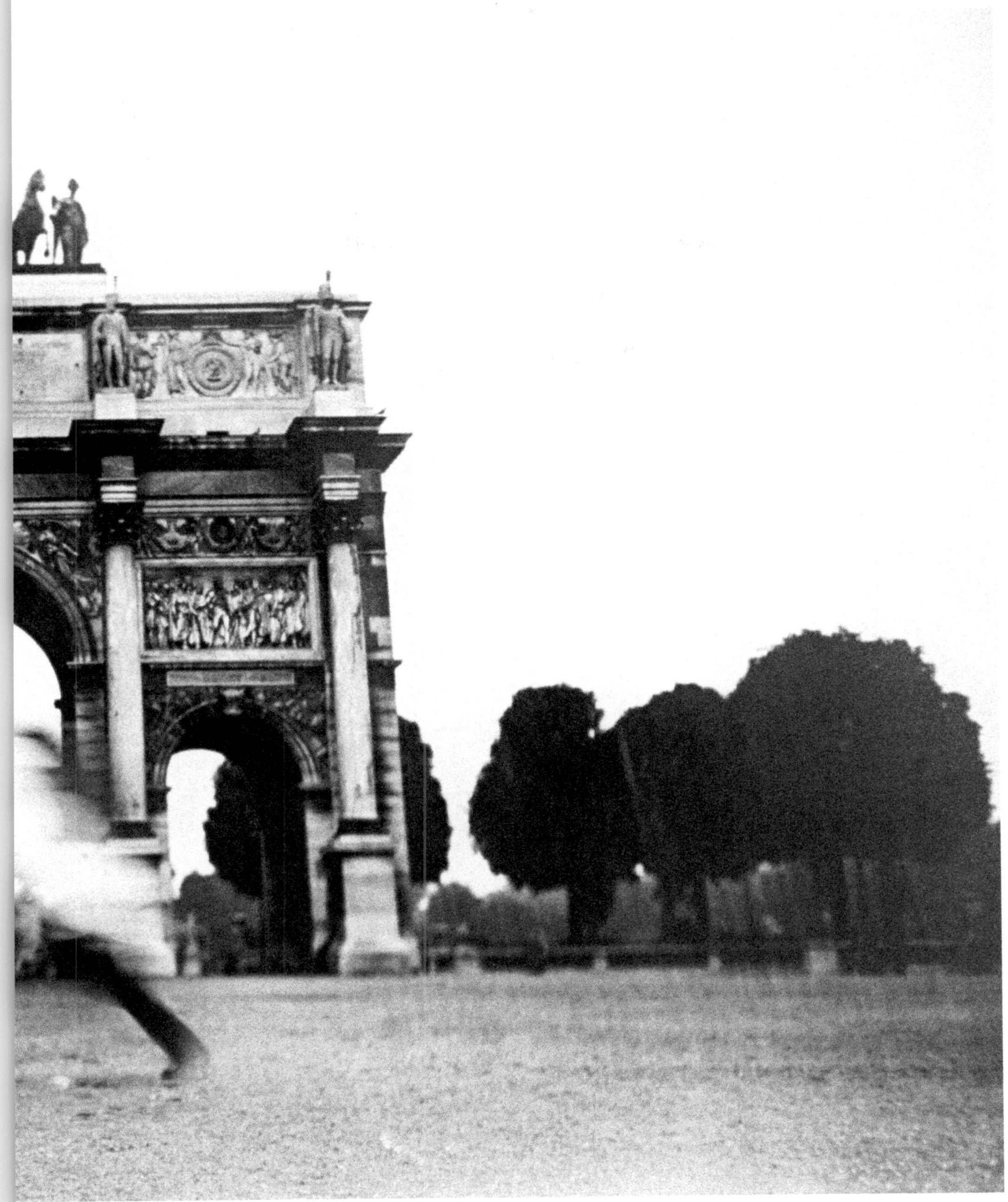

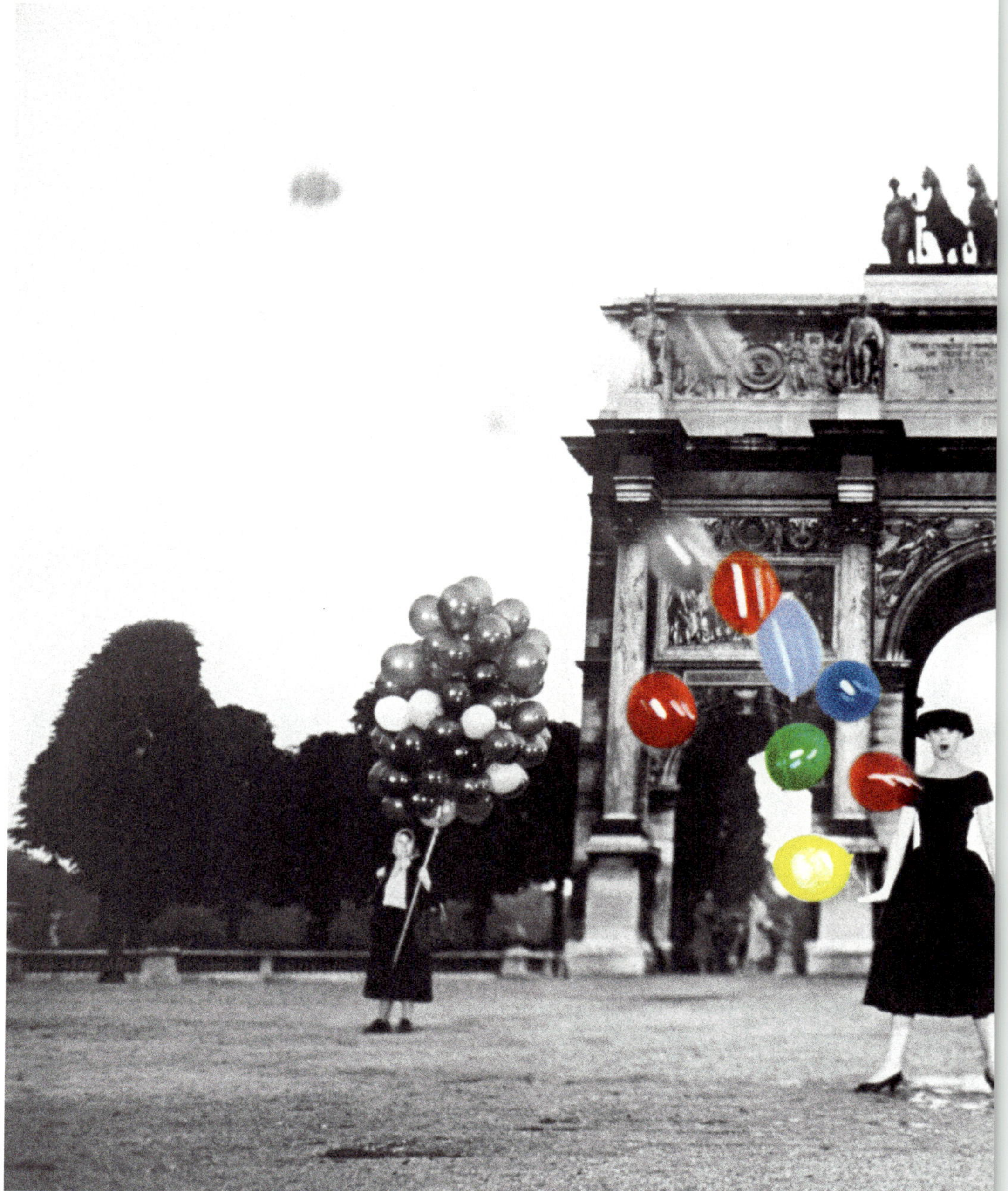

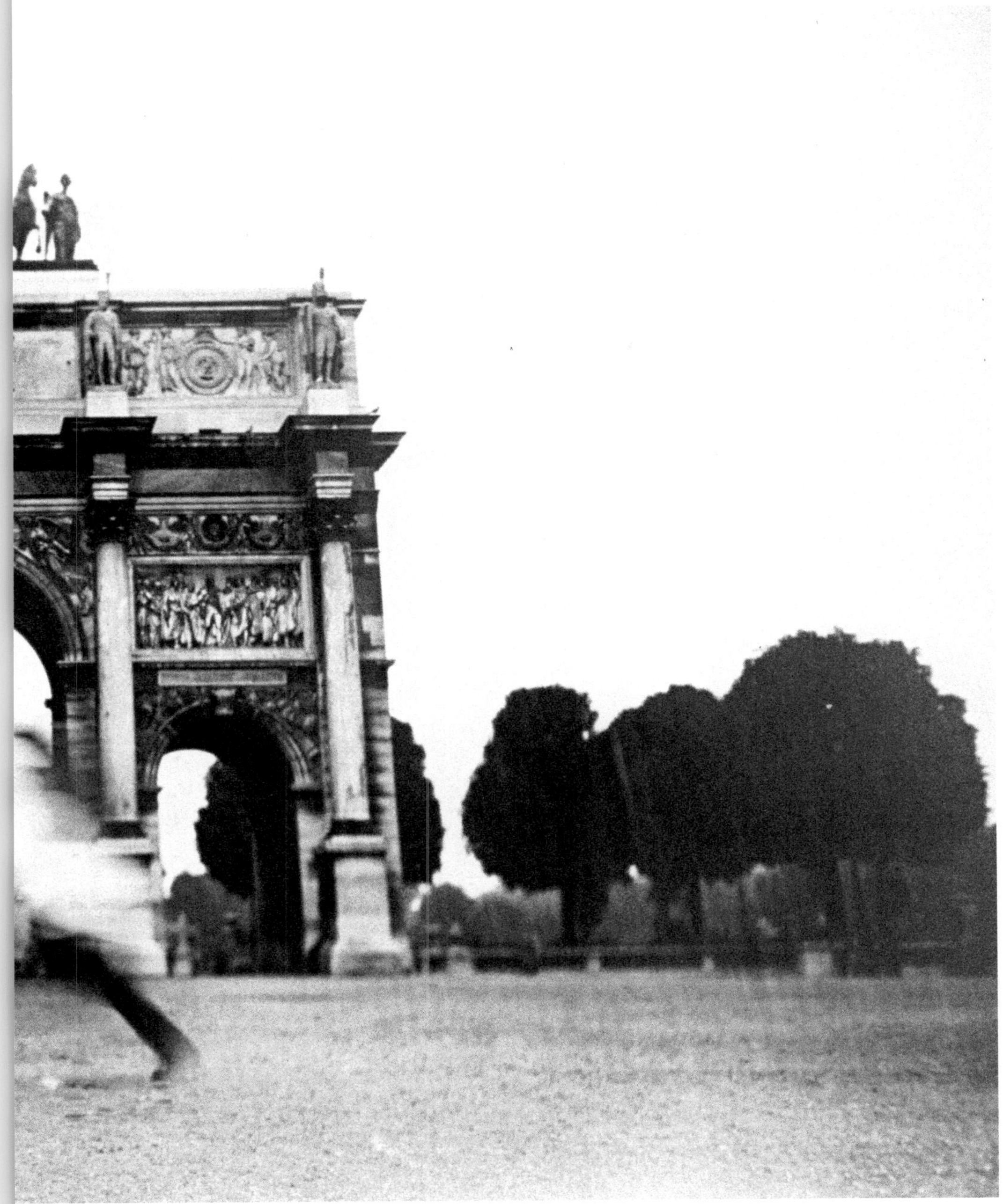

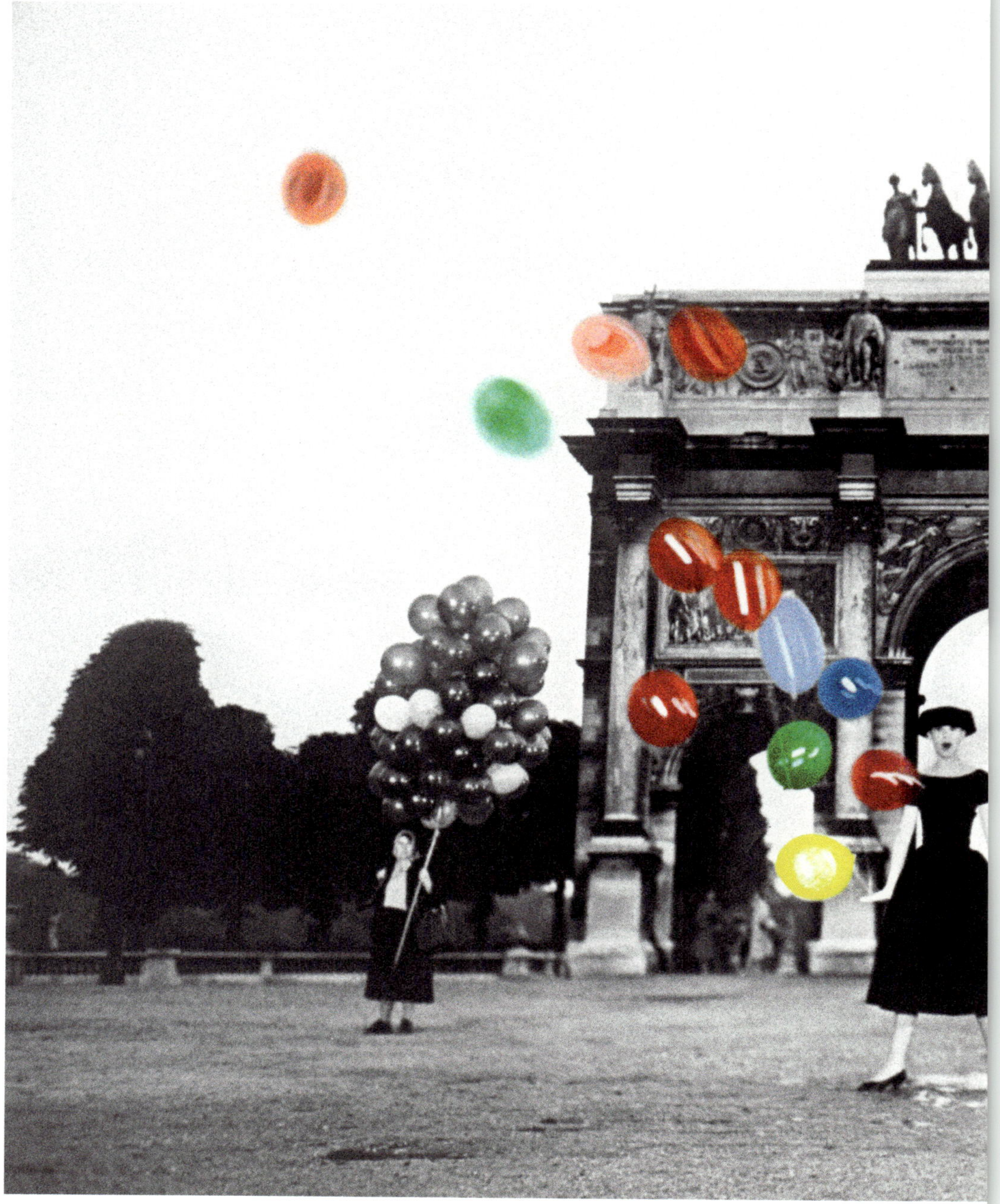

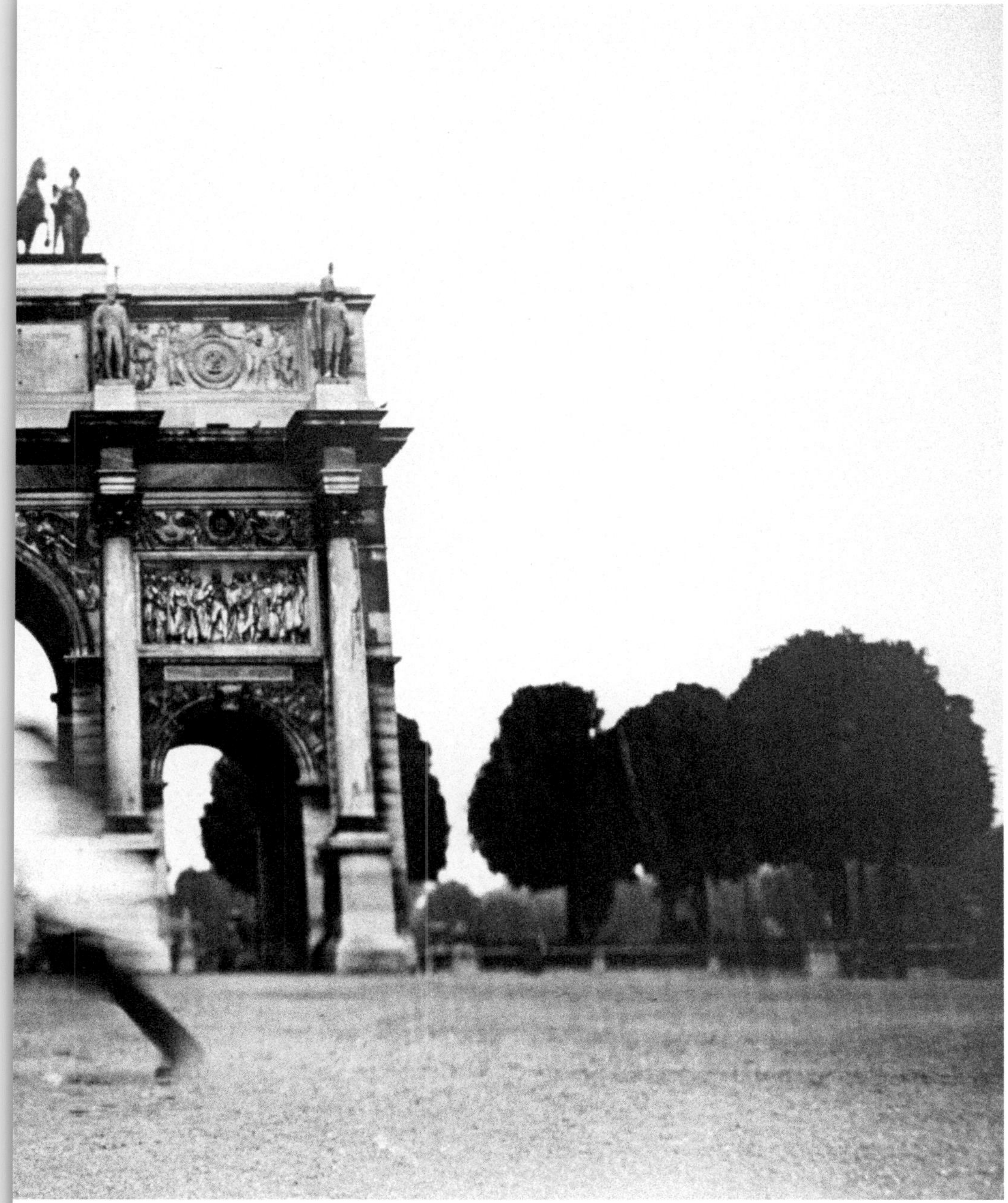

Funny Face (01.01:21)

394–4 4. AUDREY WITH PIGEON AT VERSAILLES – Freeze and move up – Make many varied color changes

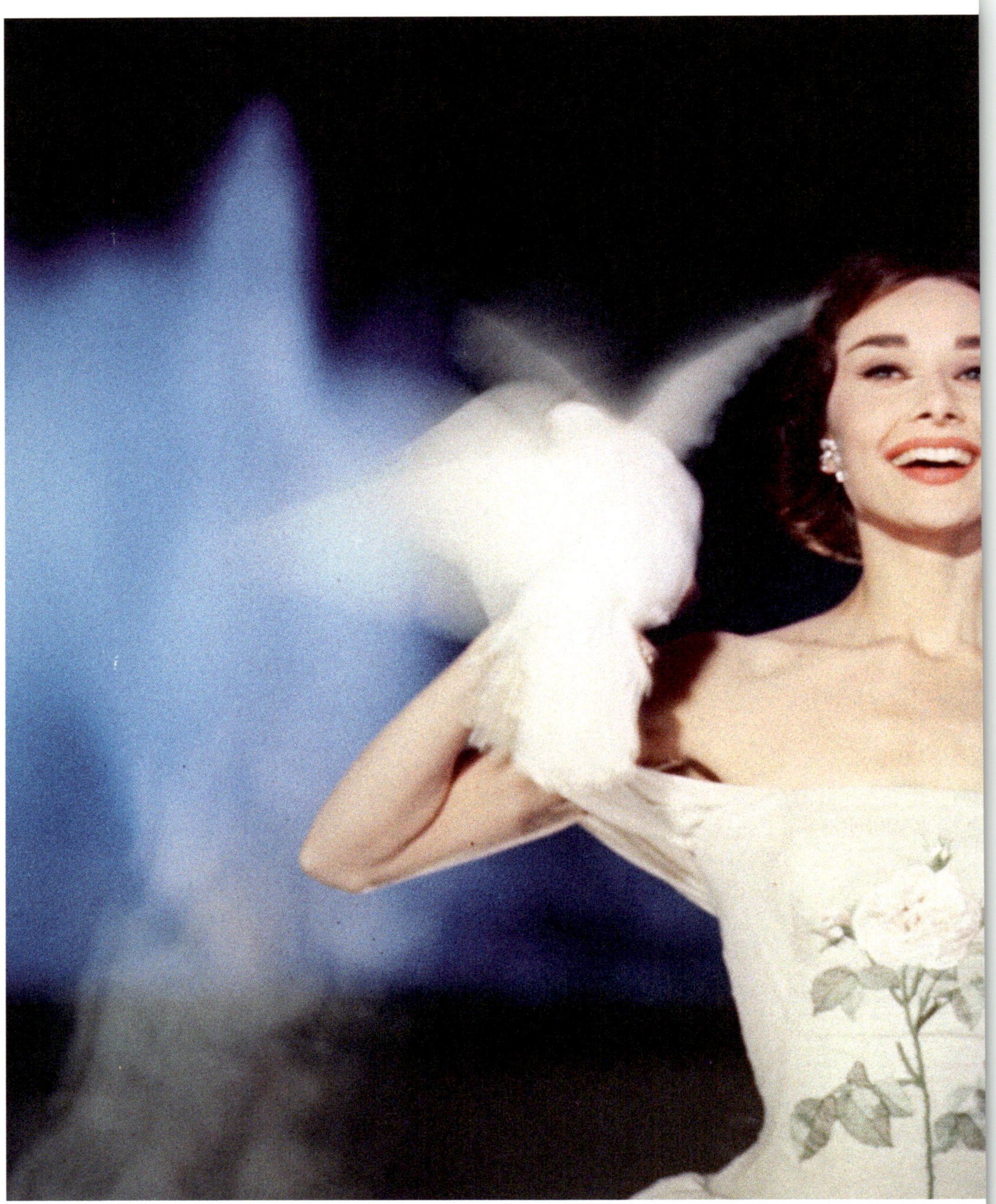

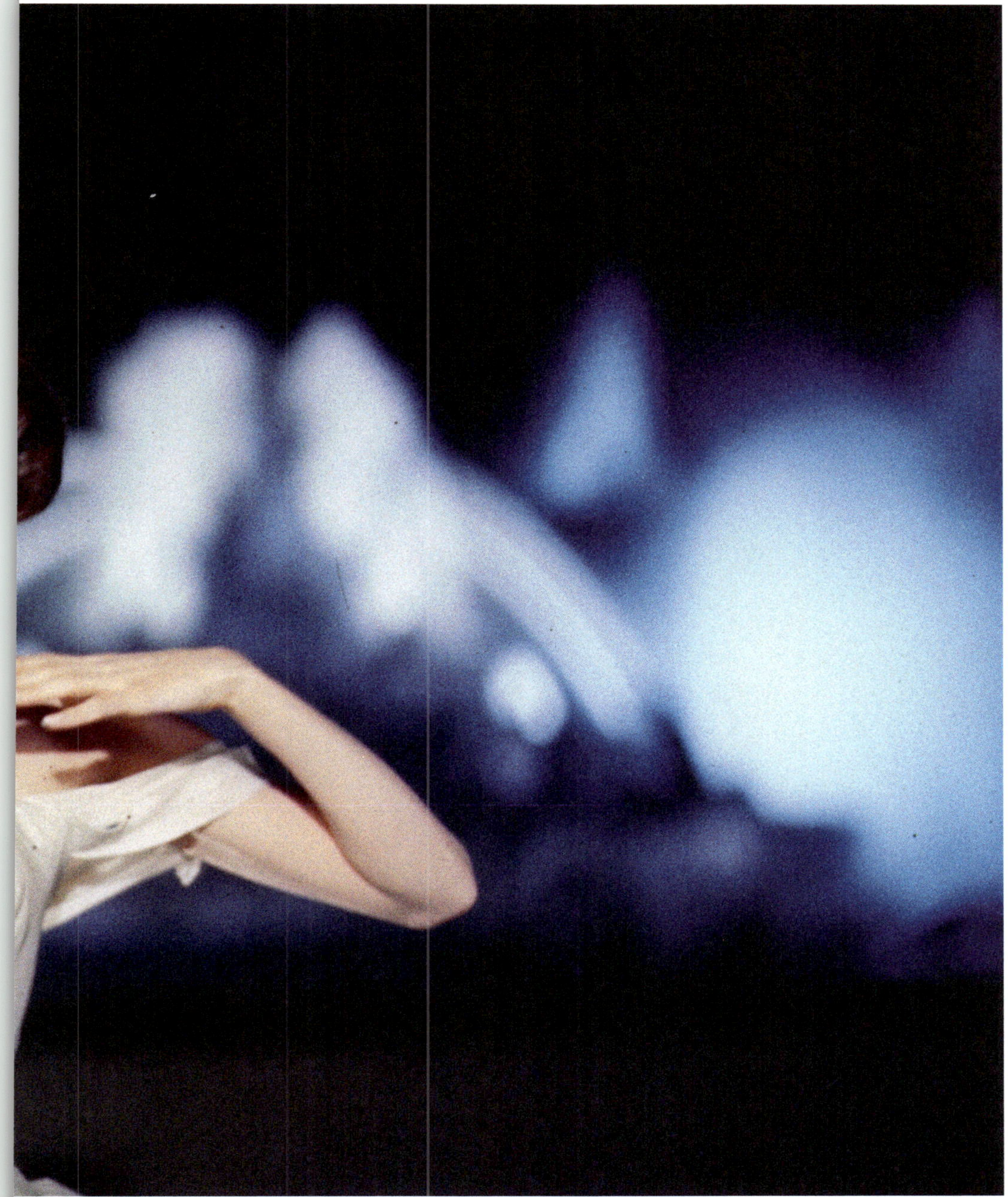

Funny Face (00.59:21)

327–10 5. AUDREY AT FLOWER MARKET – Freeze and move up – Make as many color changes as possible

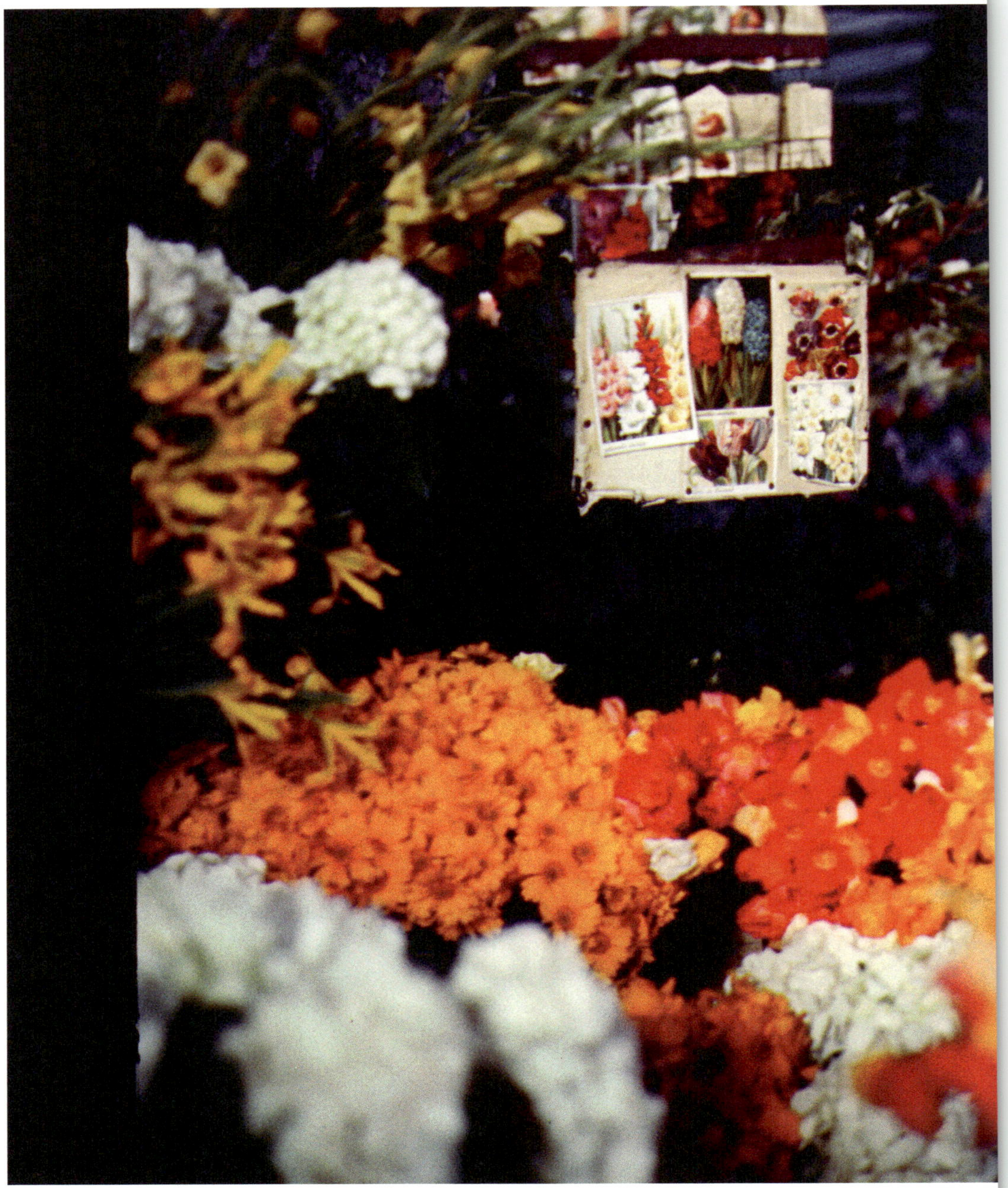

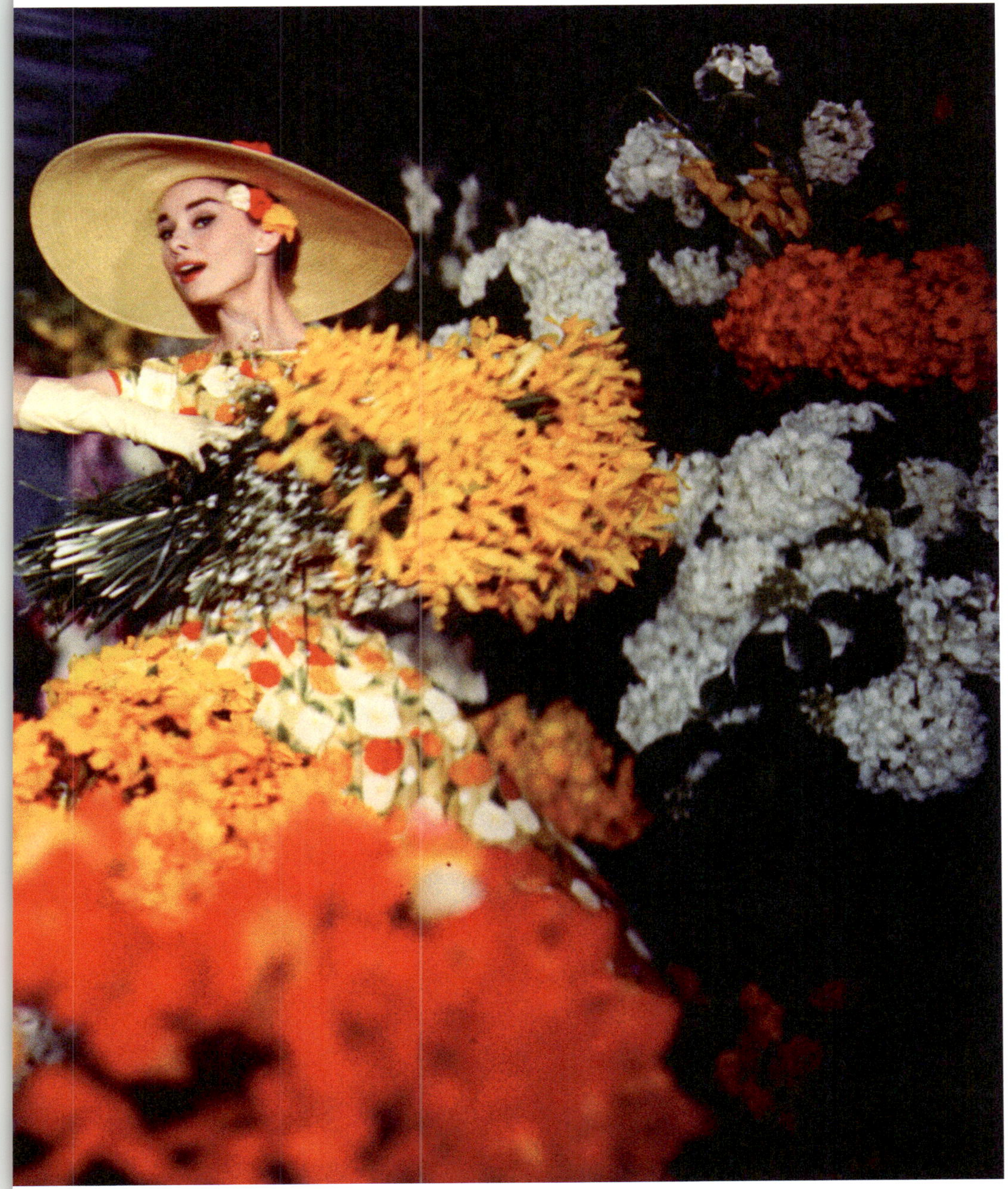

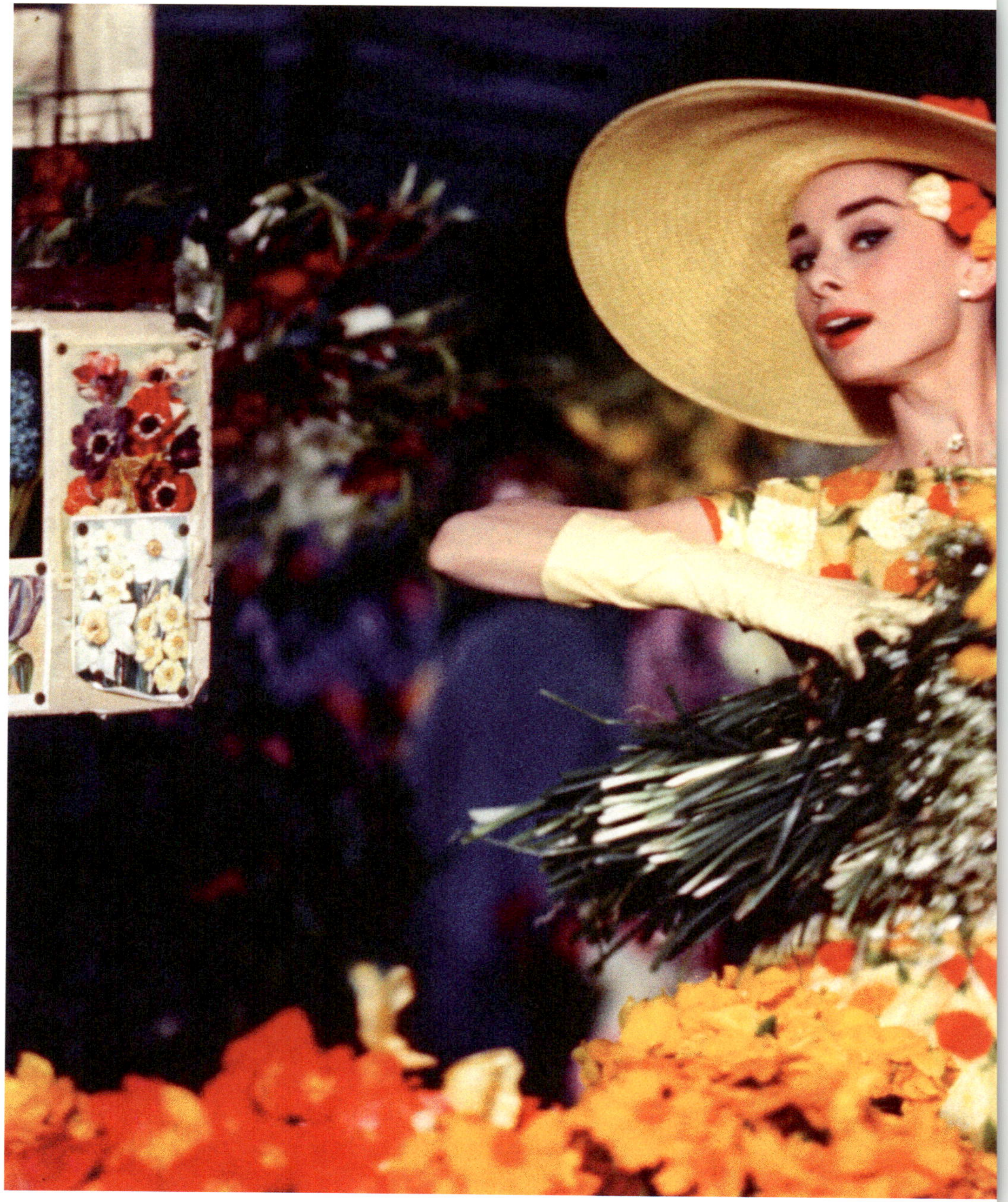

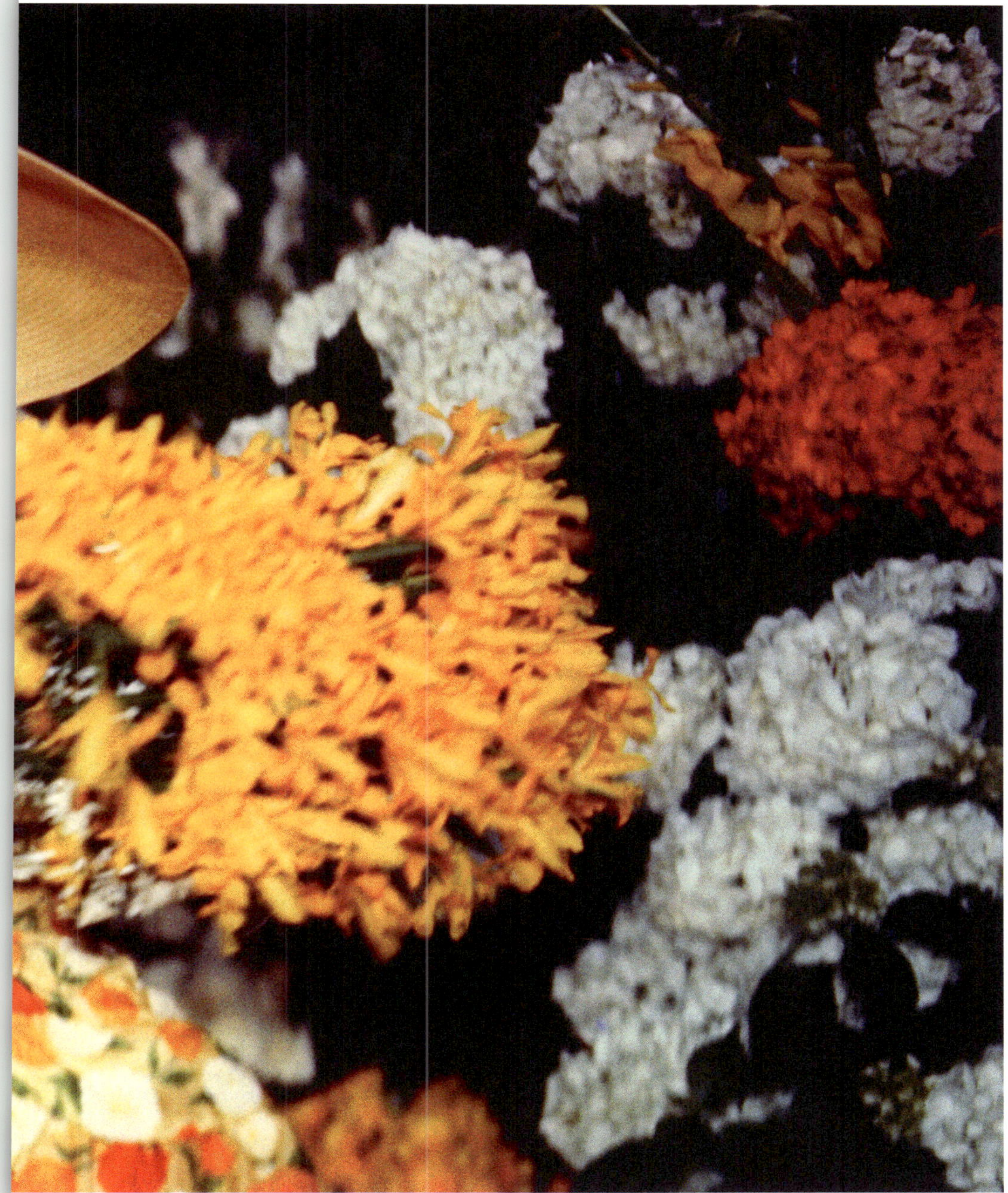

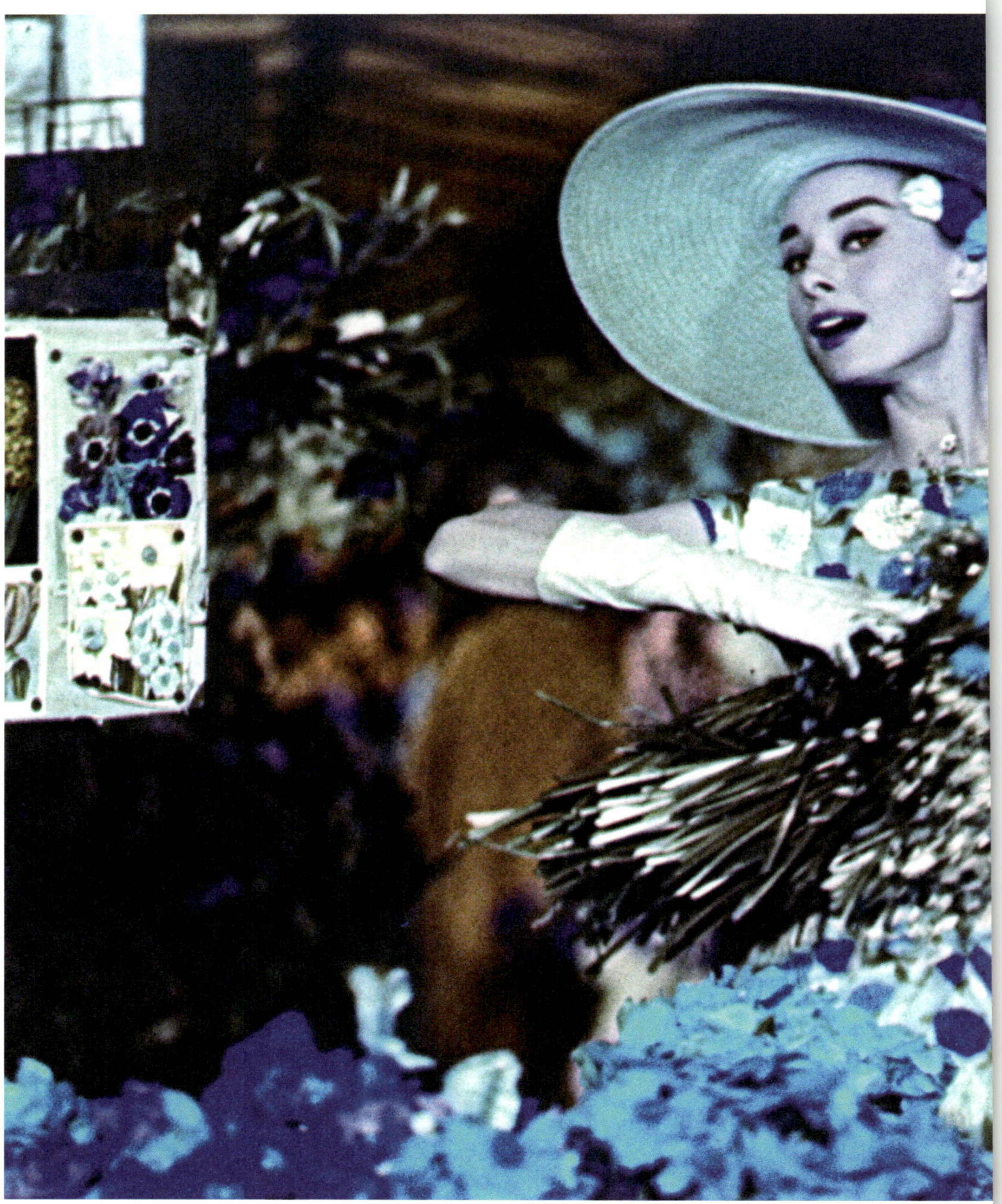

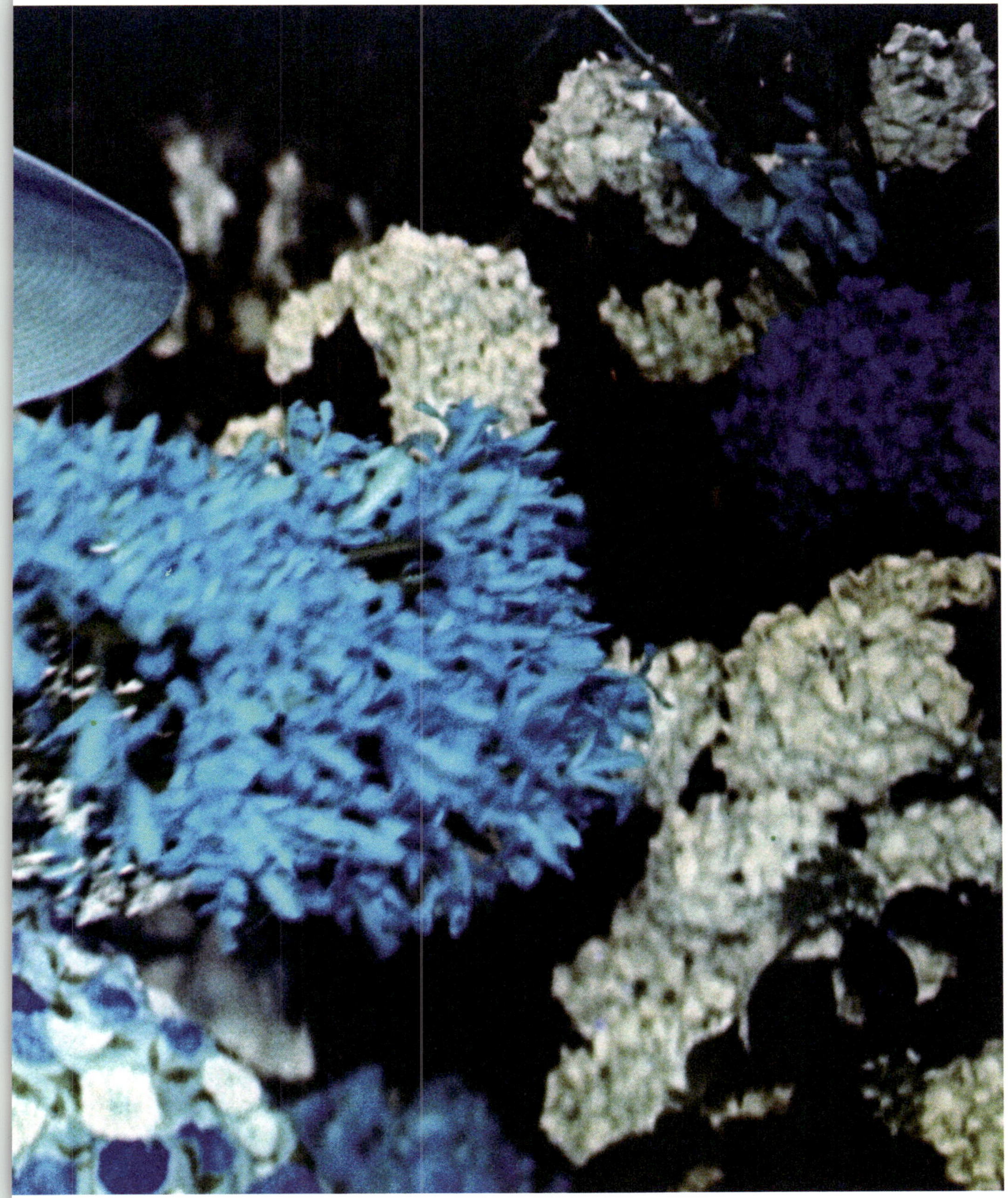

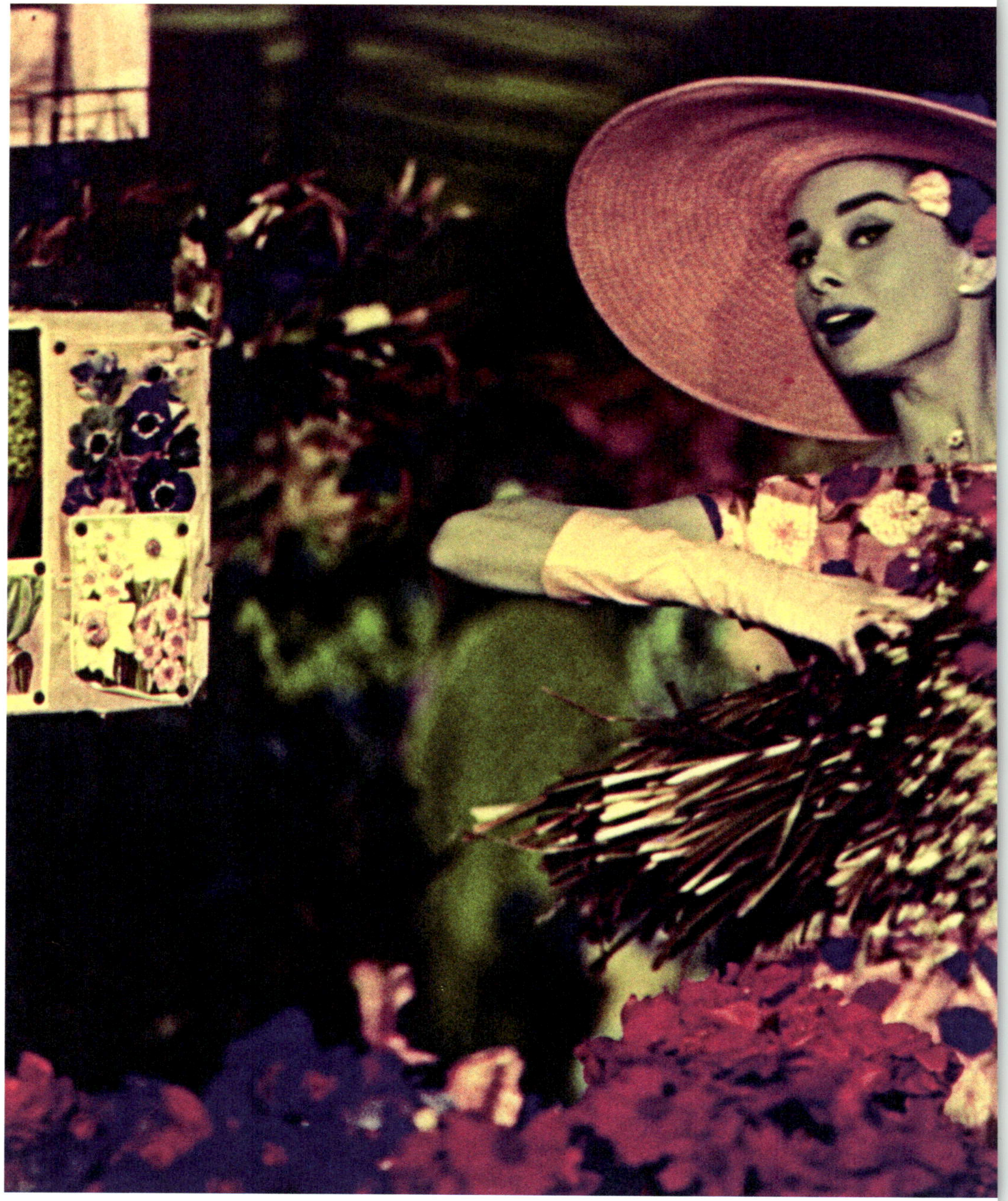

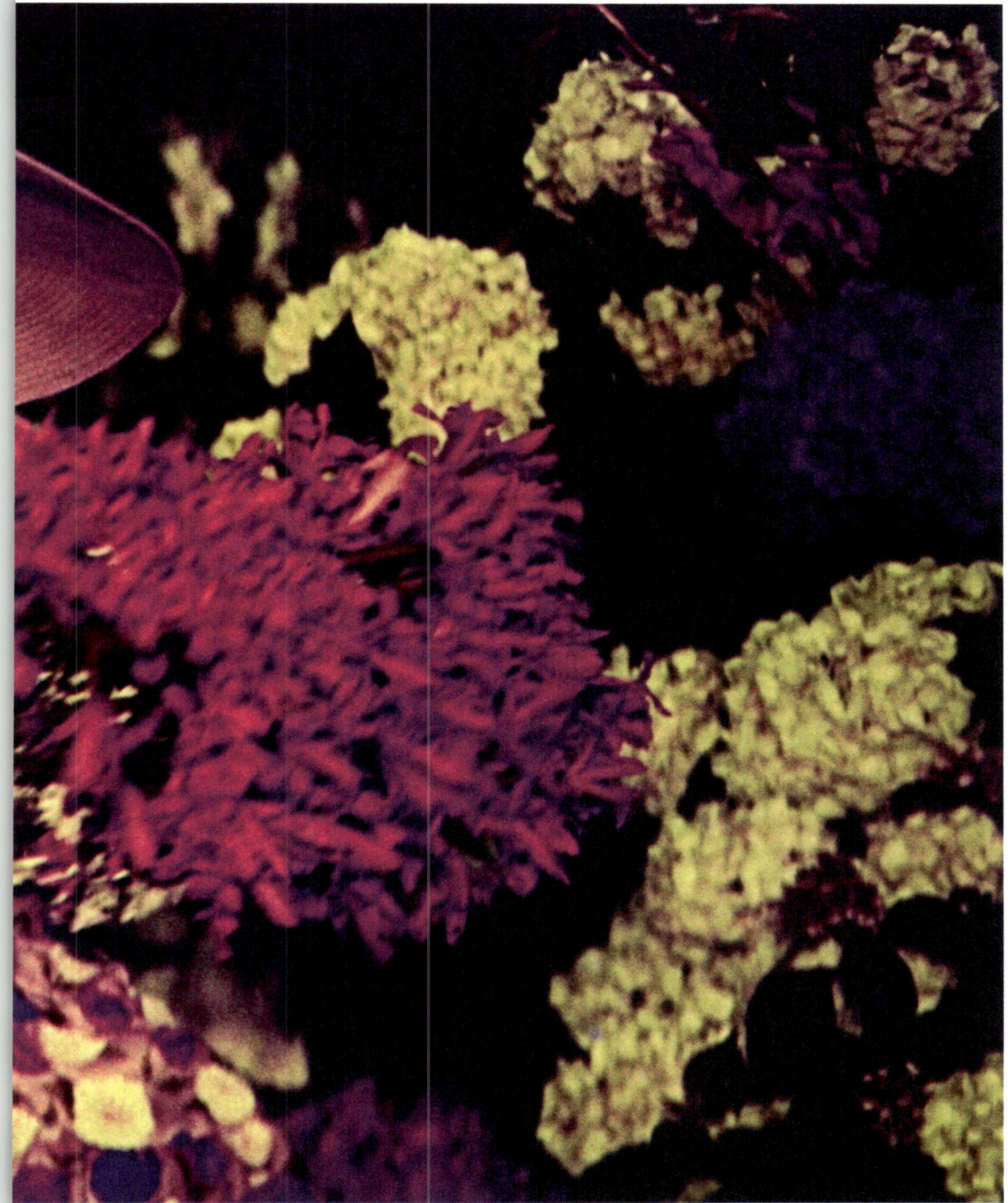

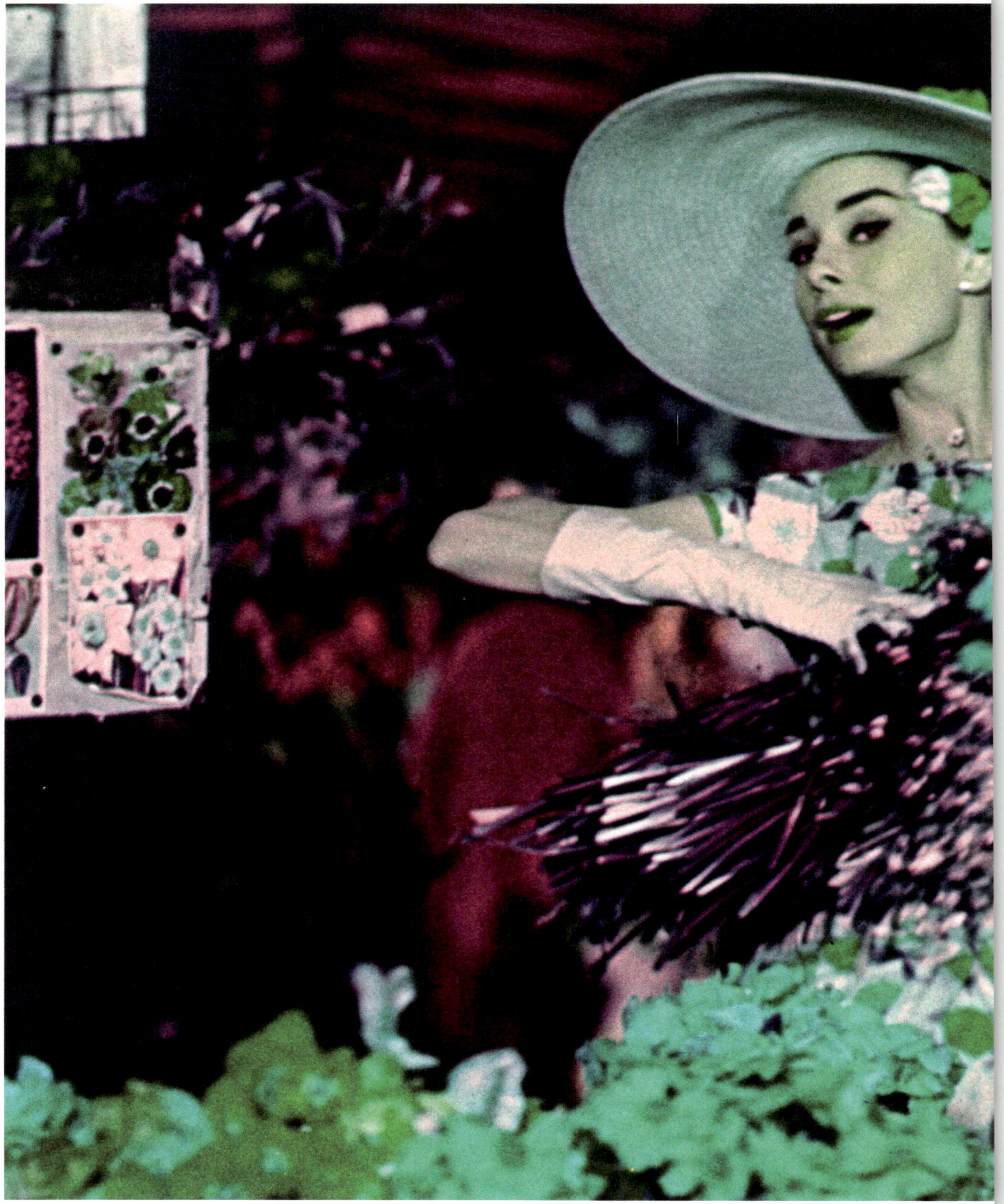

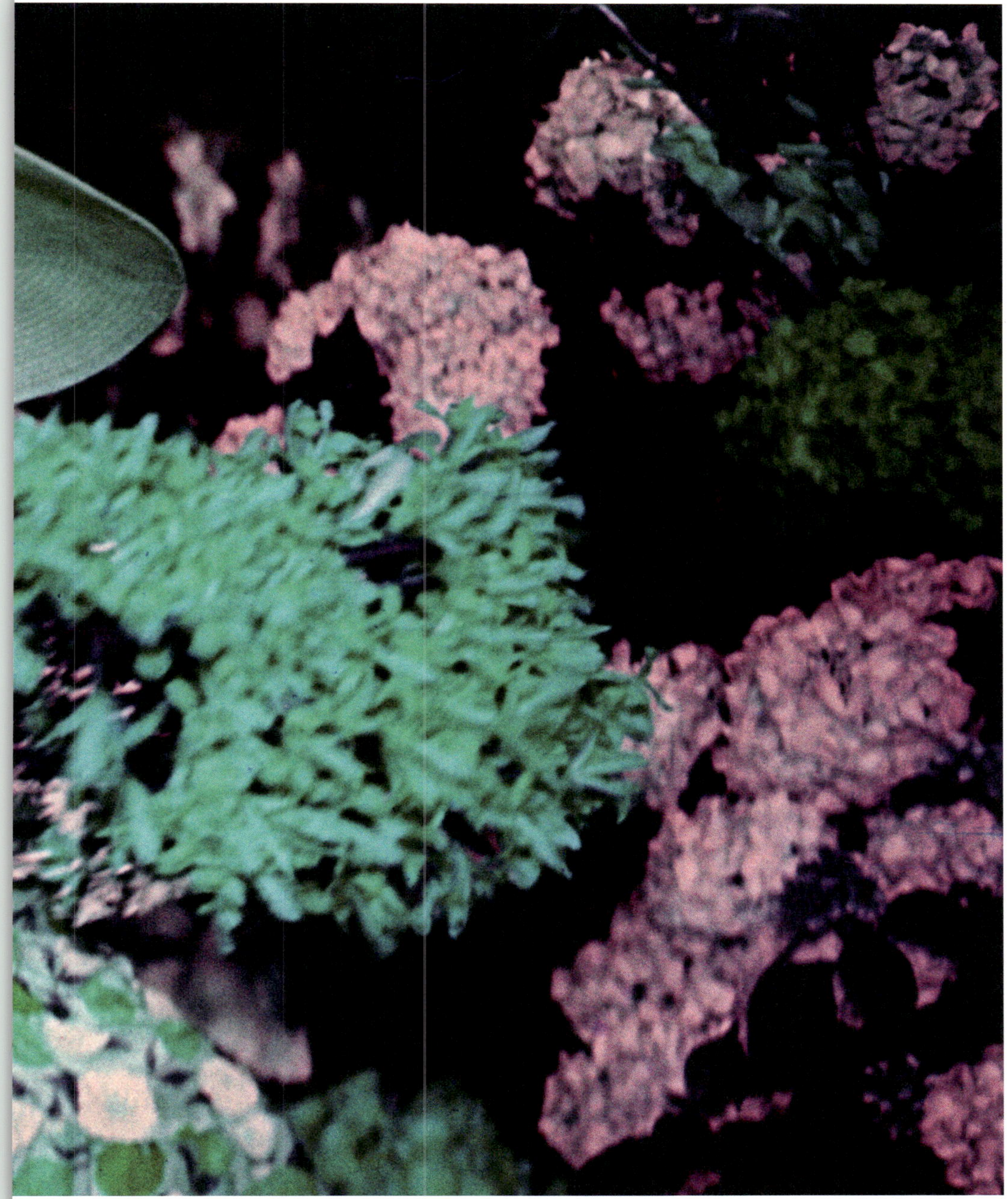

Funny Face (01.00:04)

360–6 6. AUDREY AT OPERA HOUSE – Freeze – matte in – switch from négative to positive – many color changes

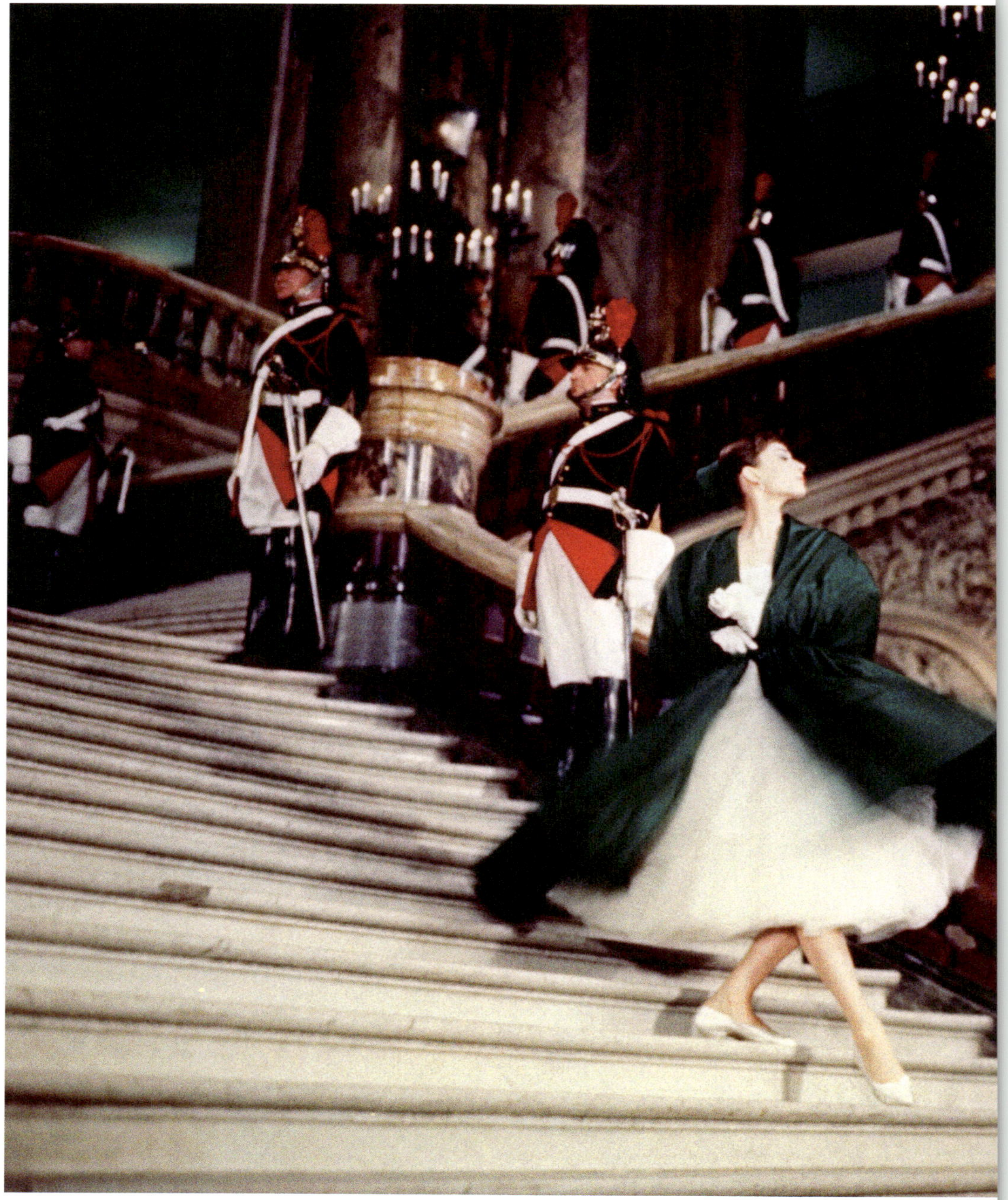

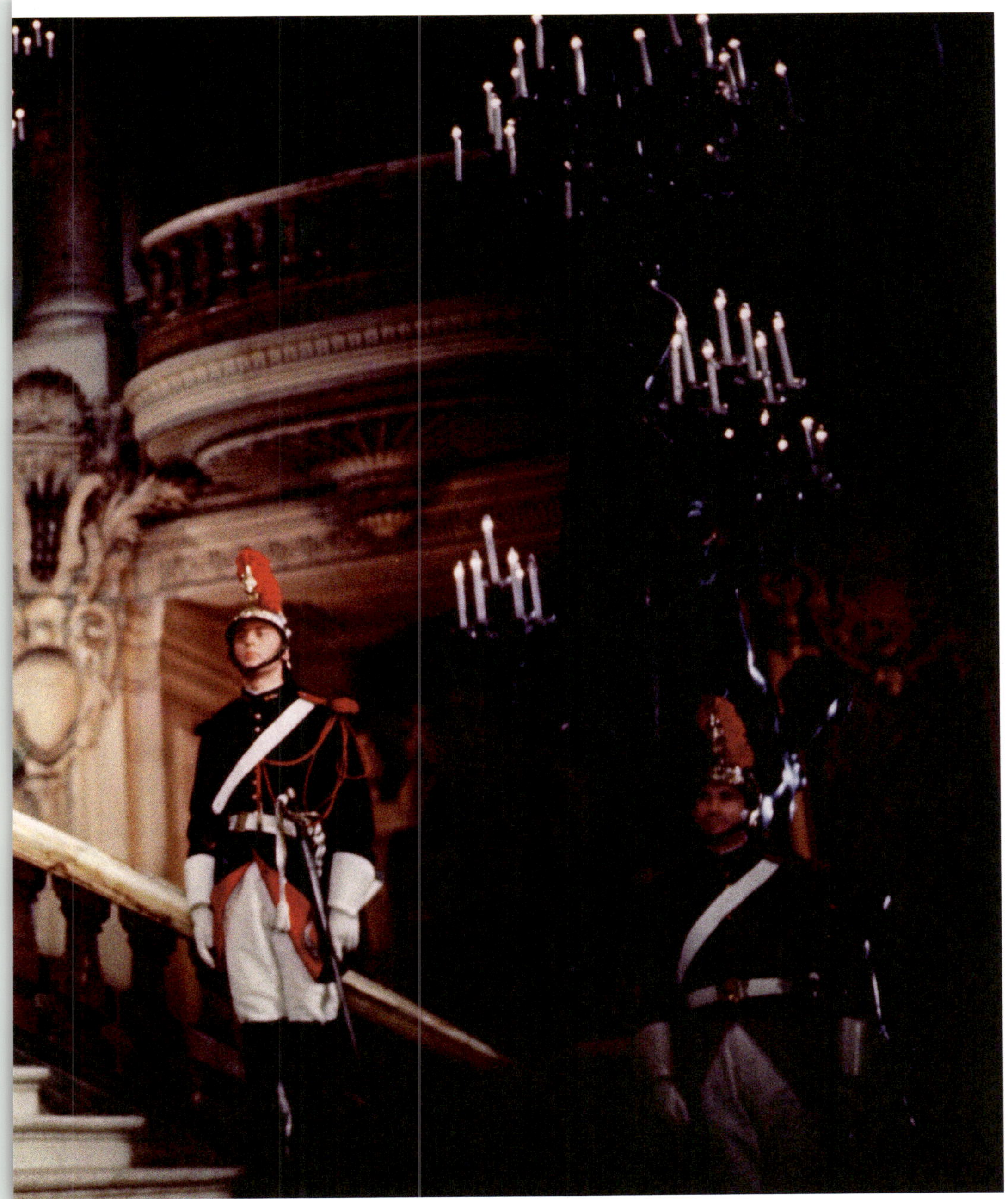

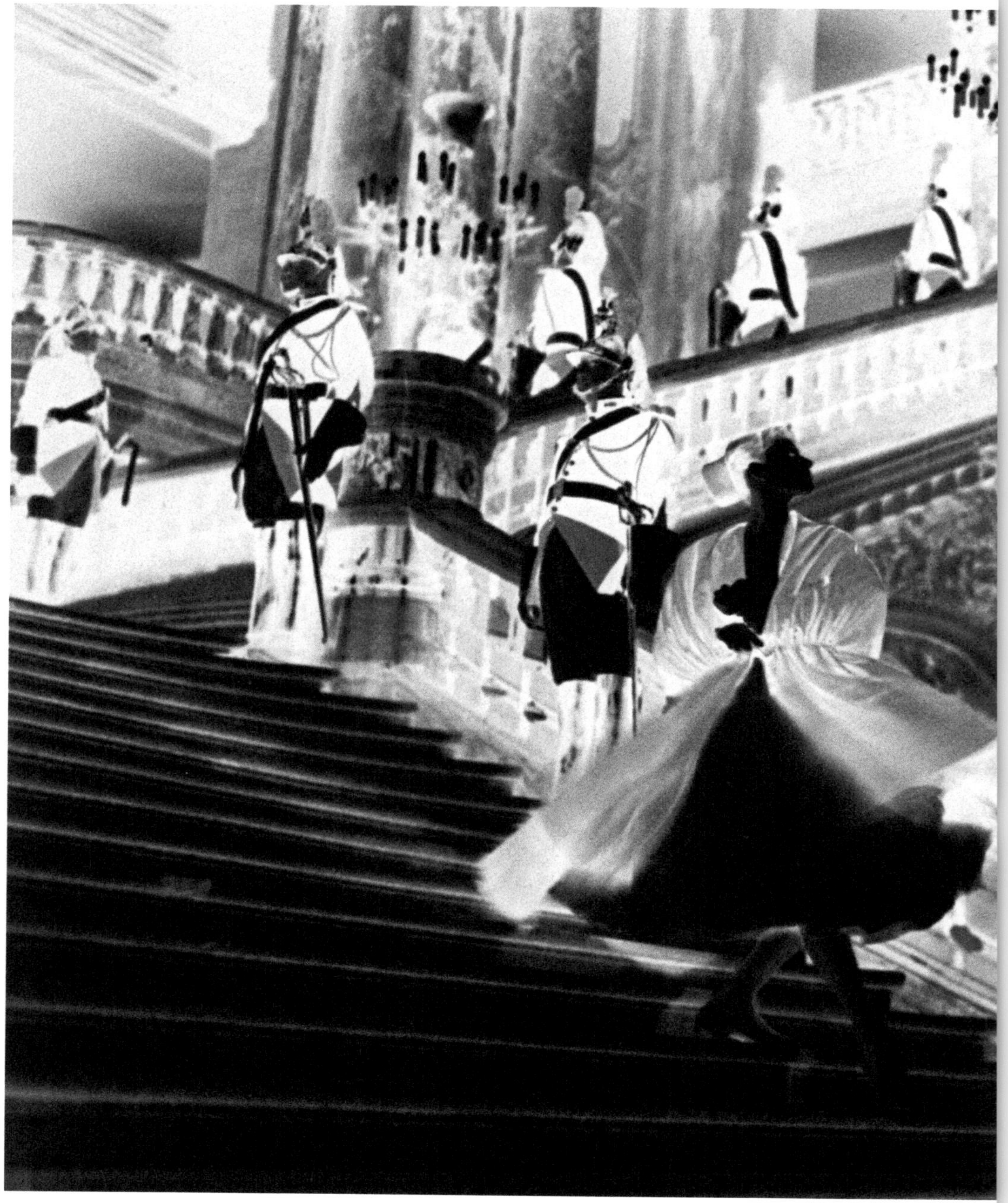

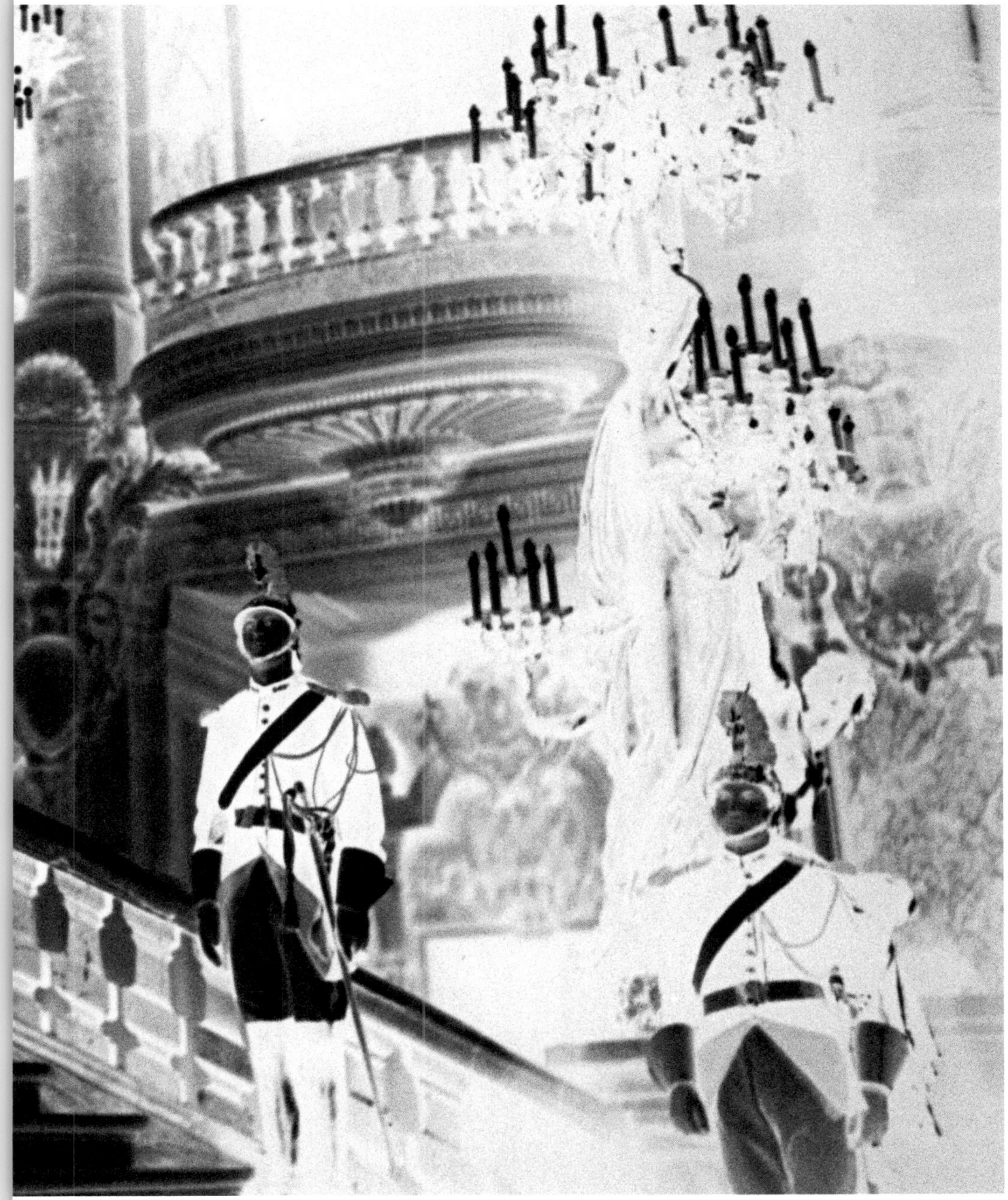

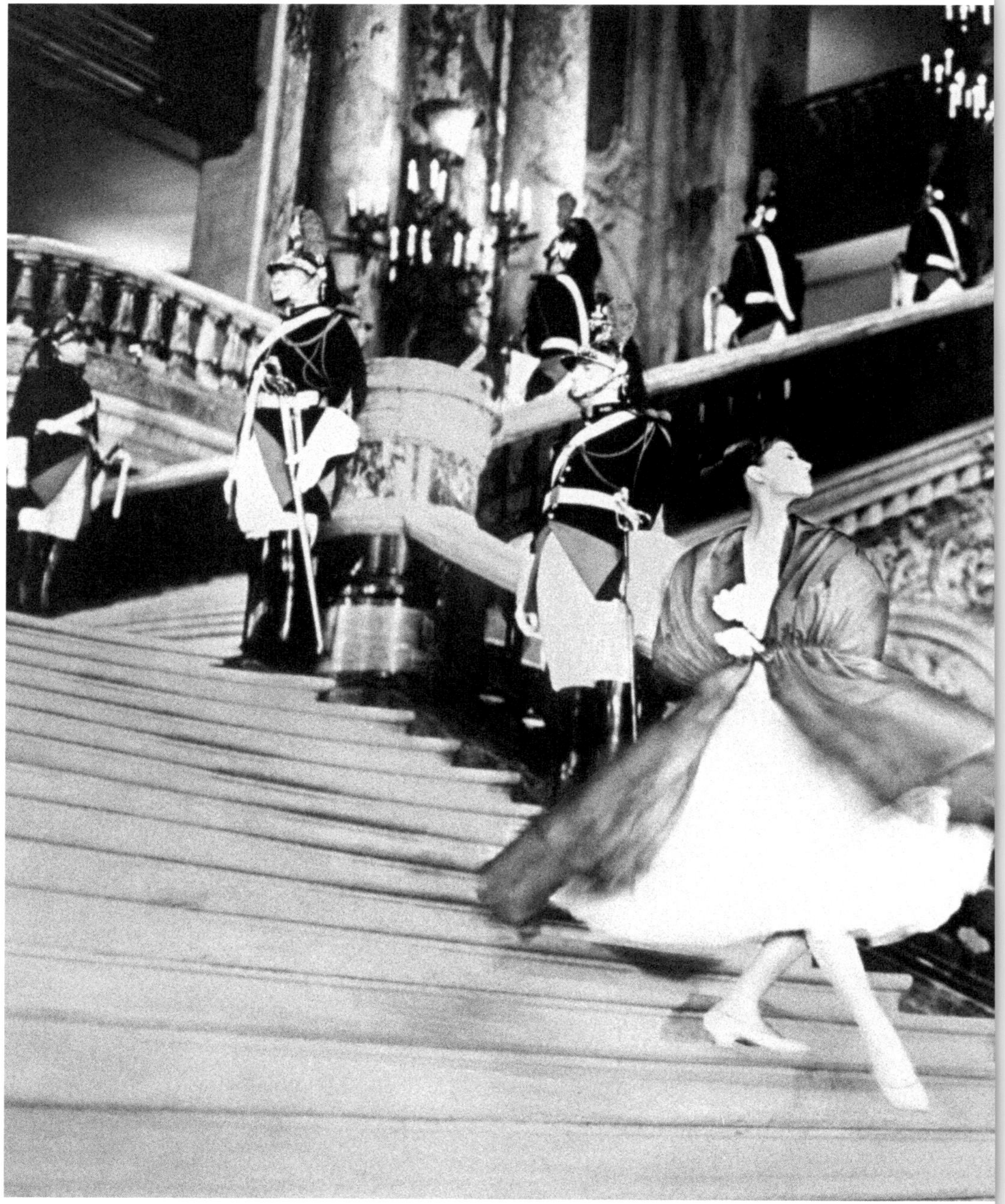

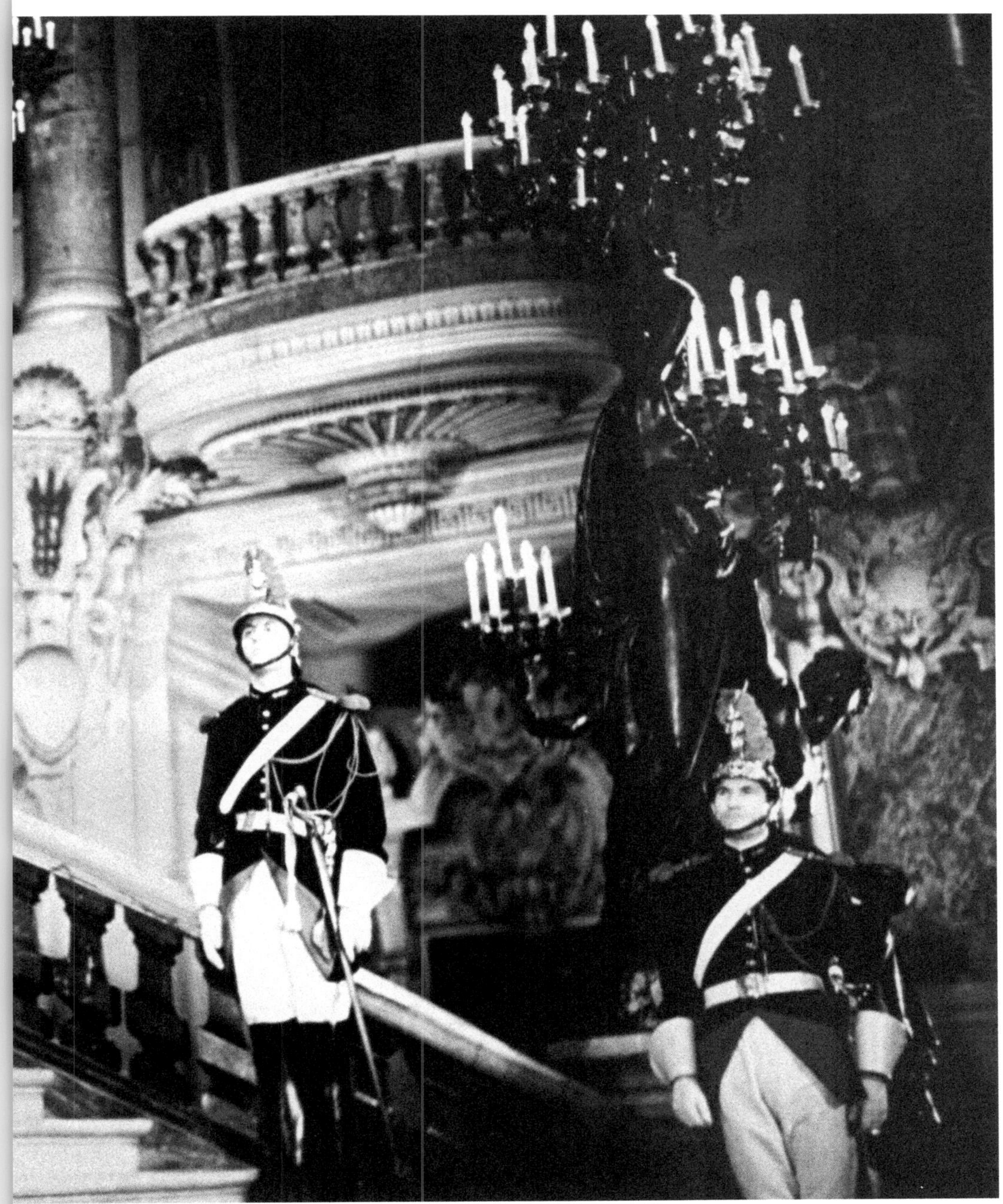

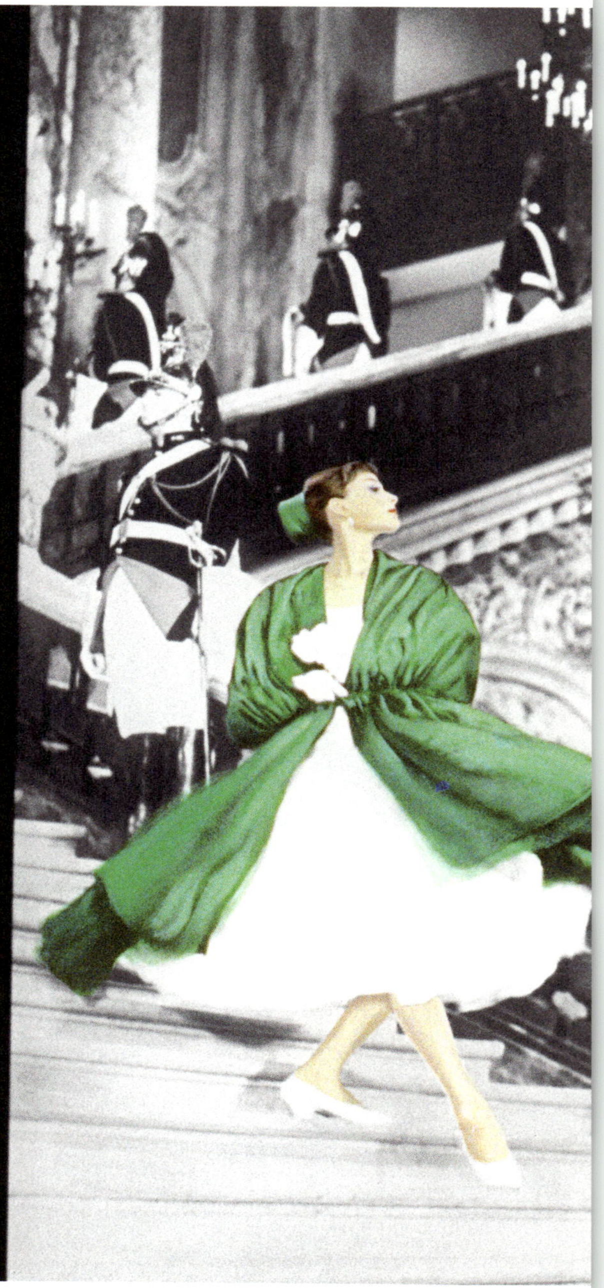

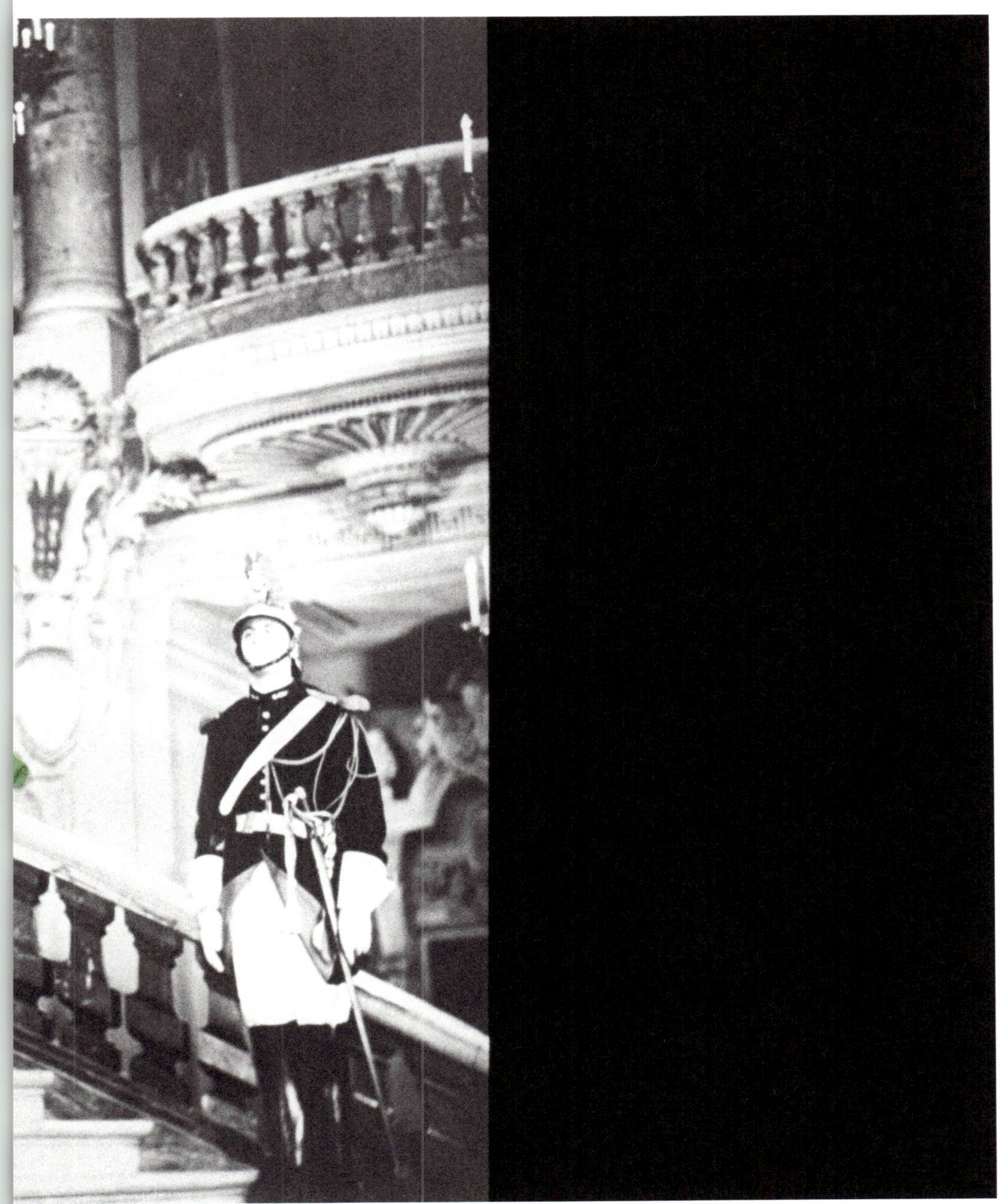

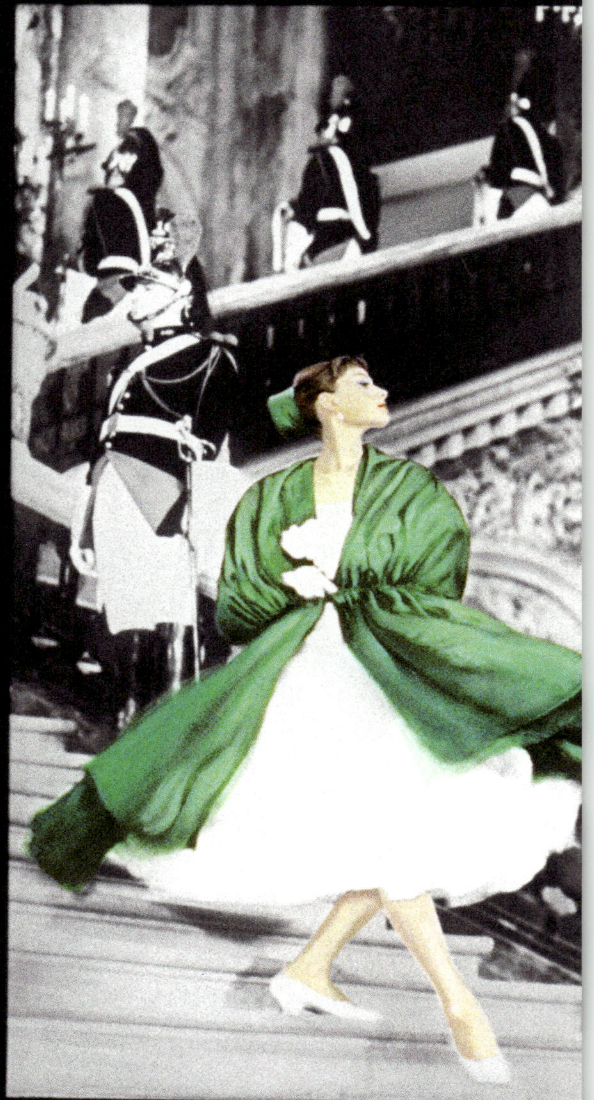

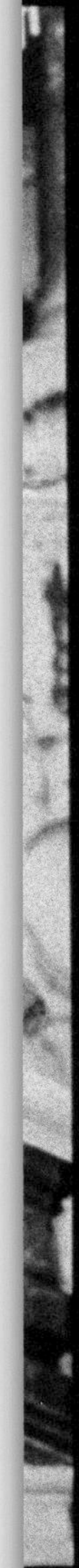

Funny Face (01.02:05)

366–9 7. LOUVRE – AUDREY IN RED GOWN – Freeze and move up – make many varied color changes

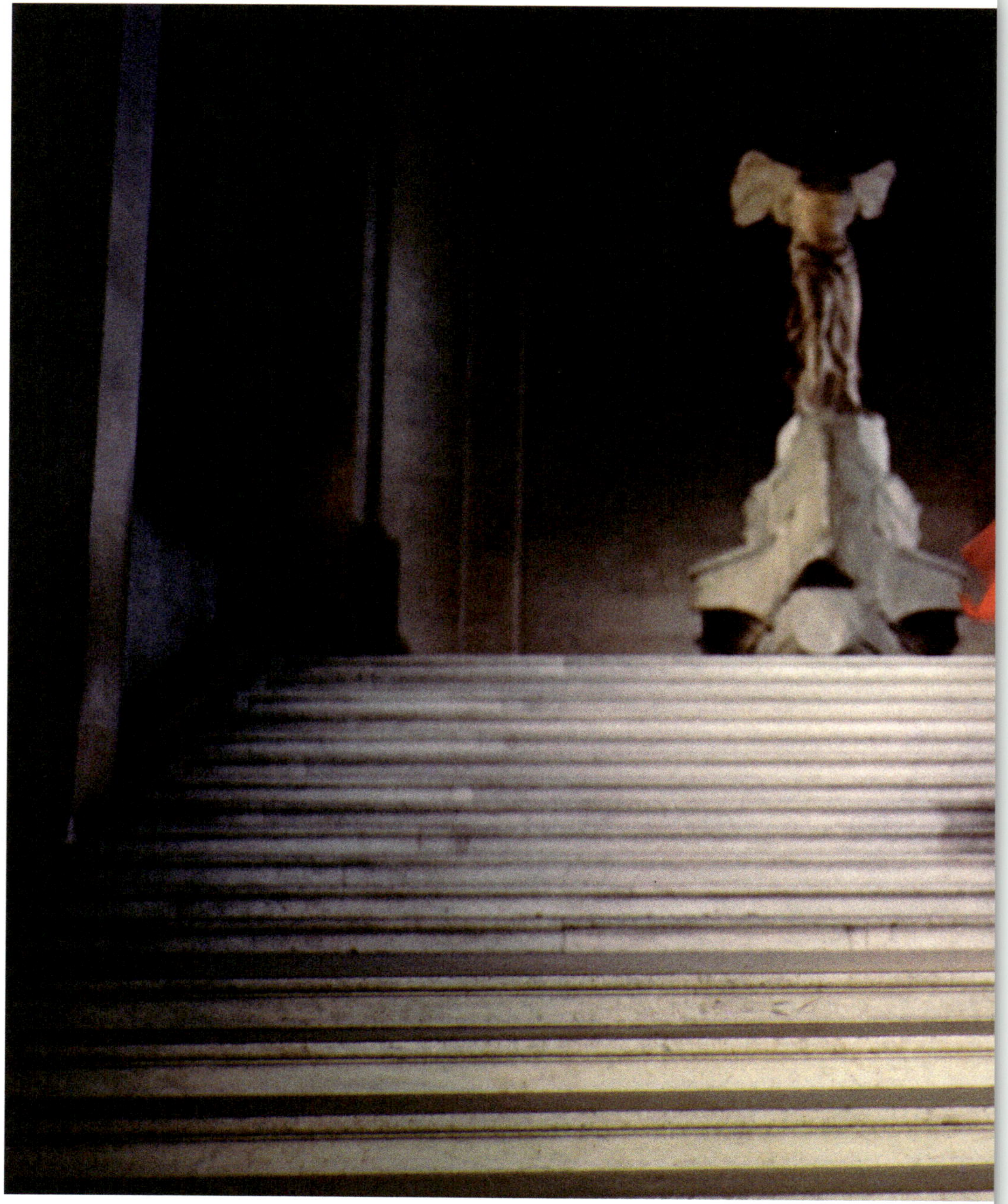

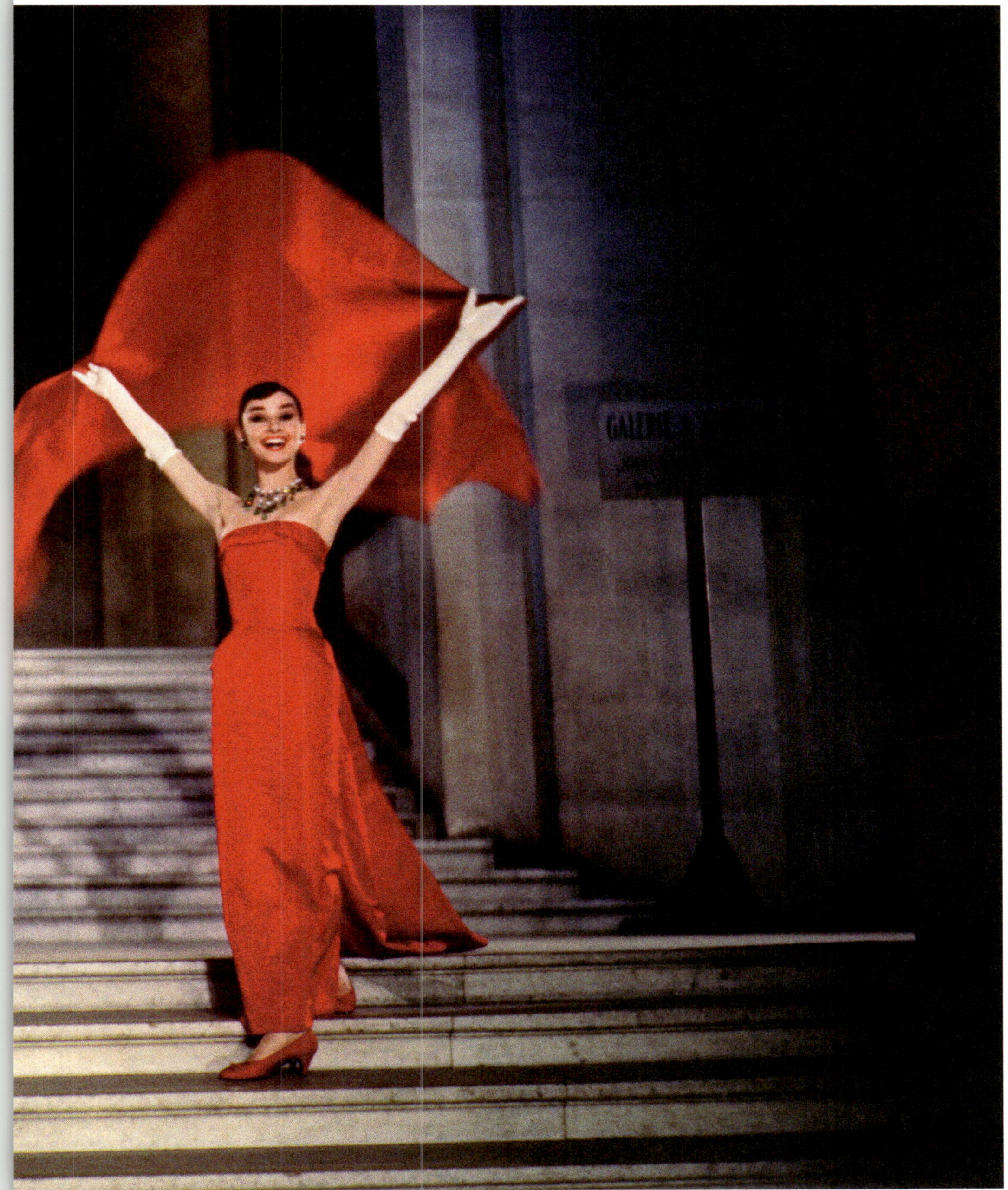

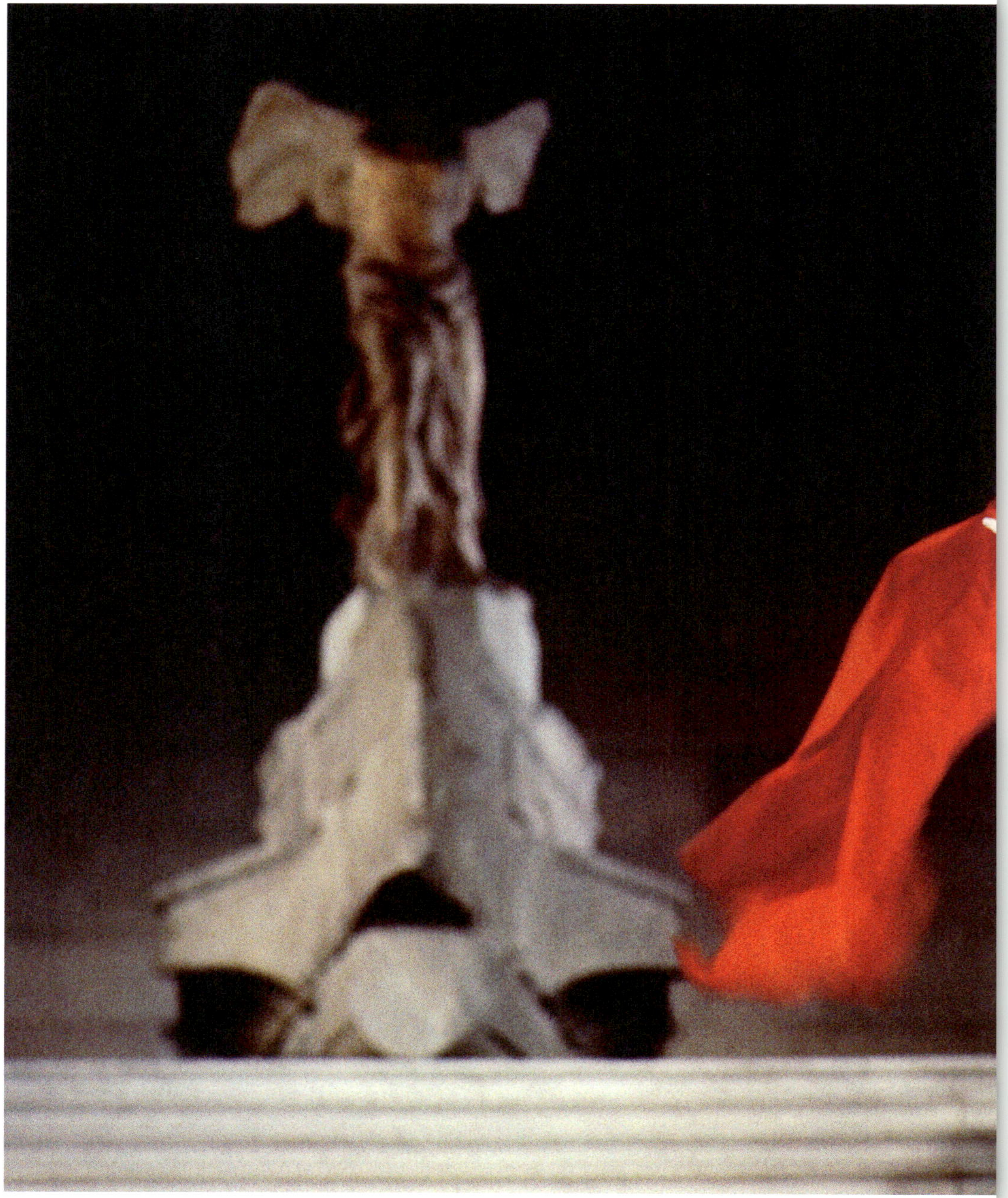

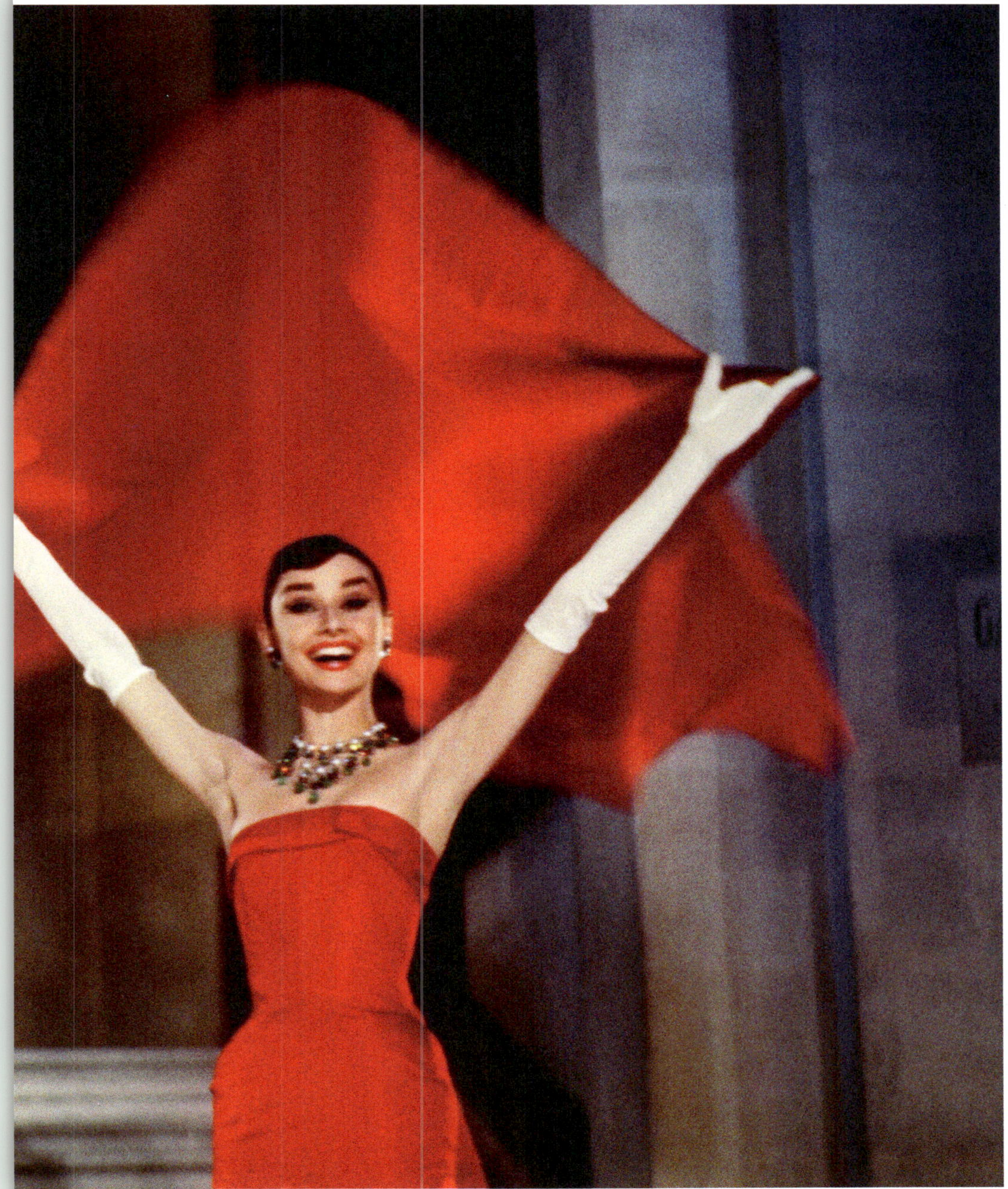

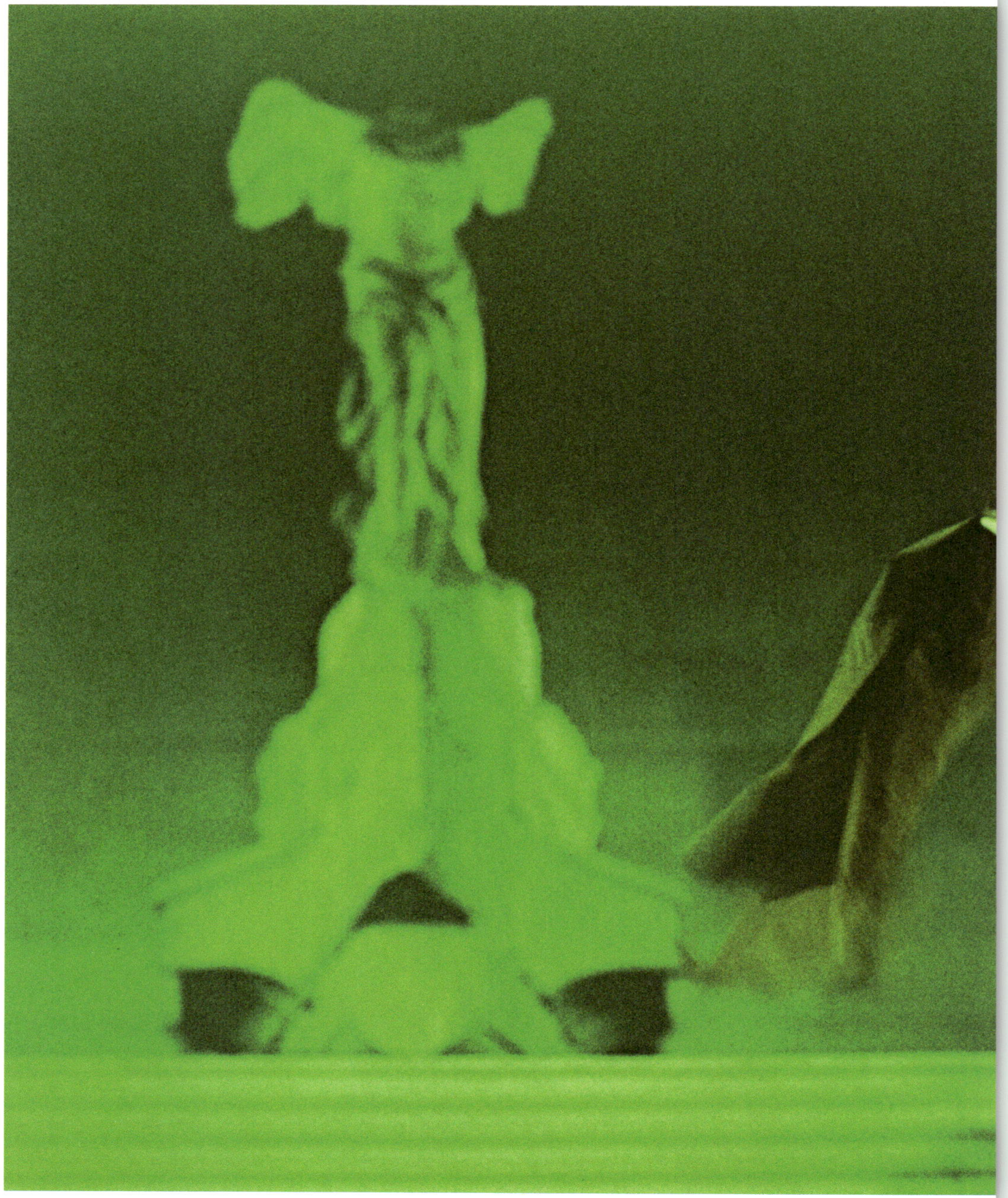

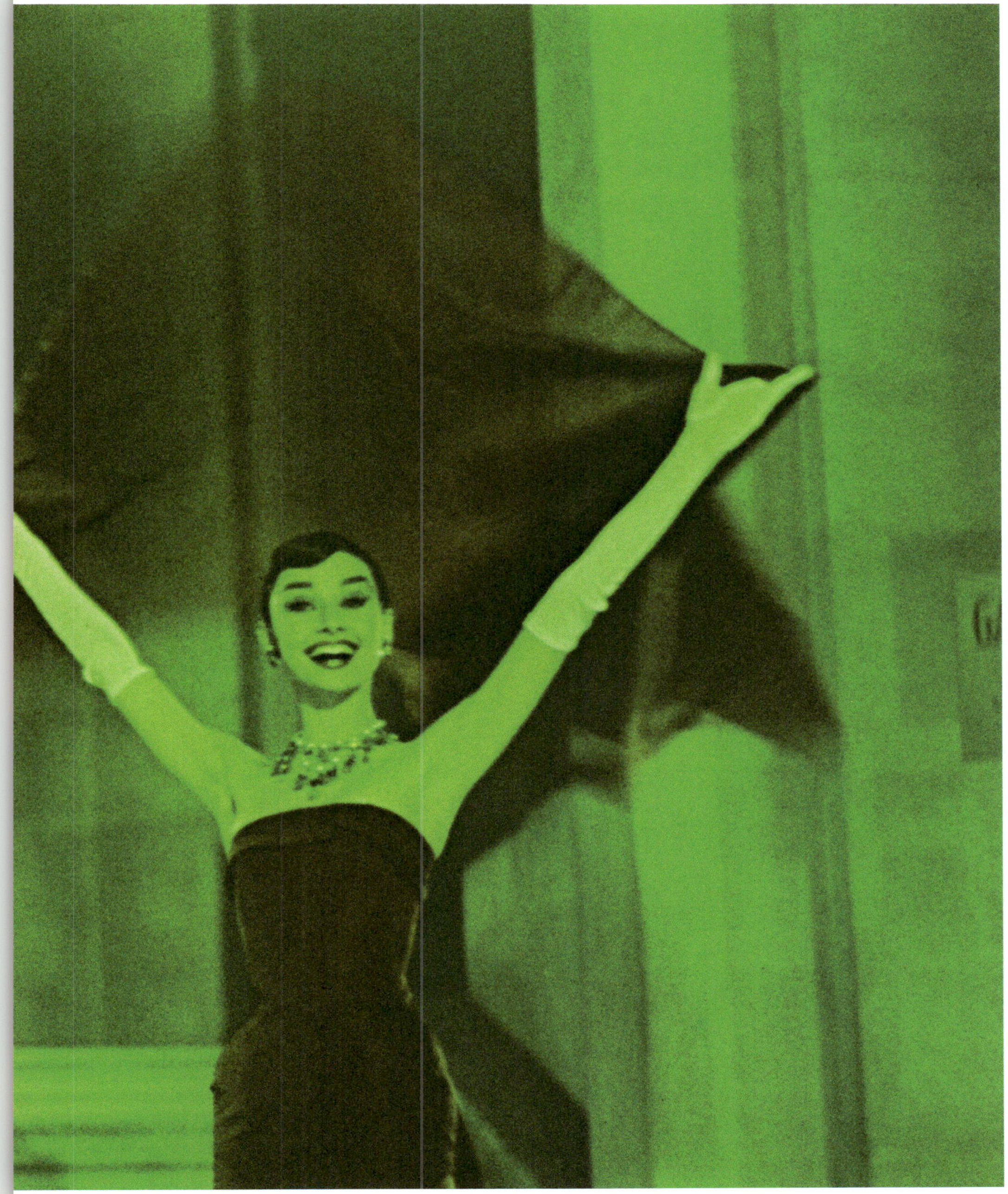

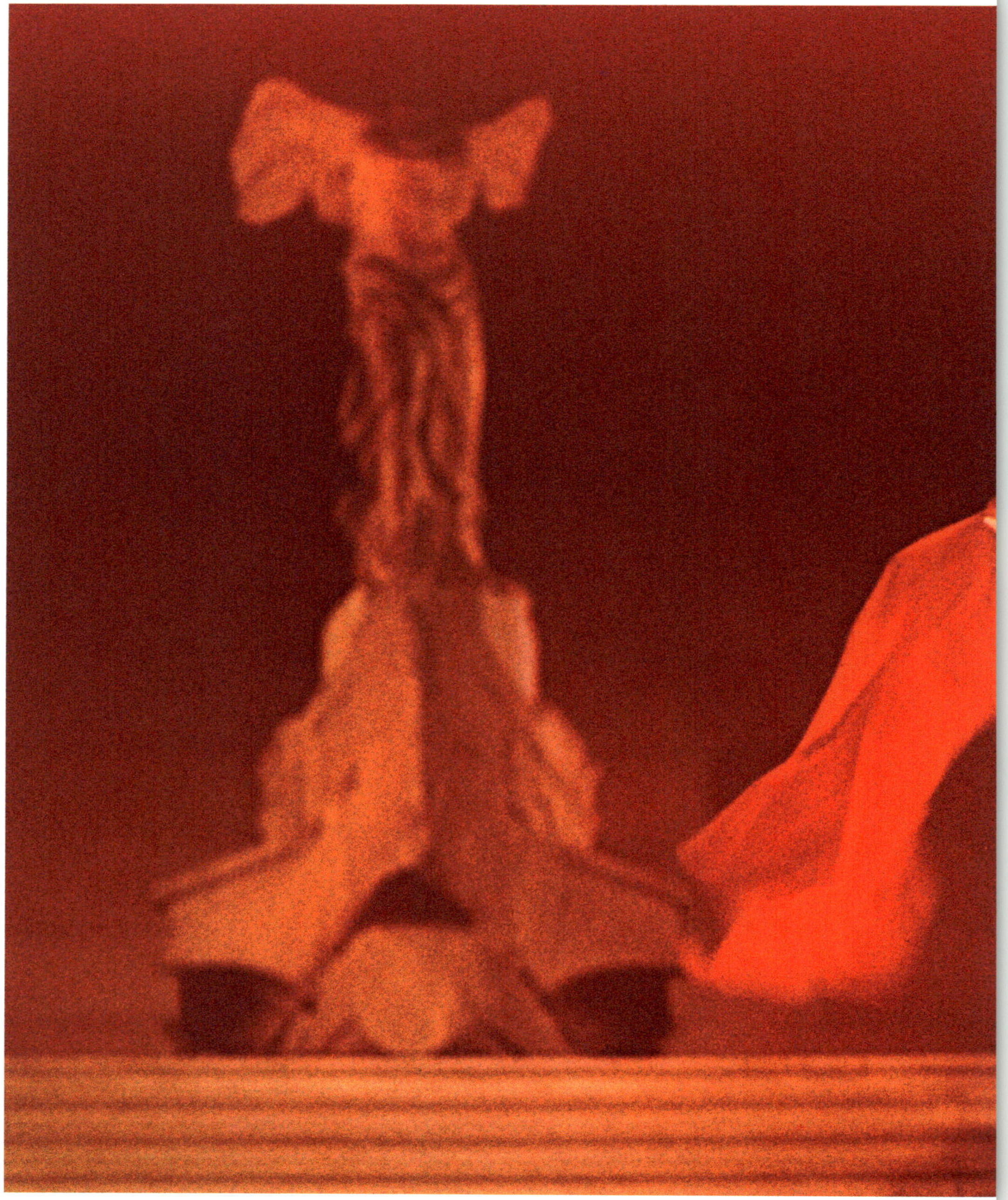

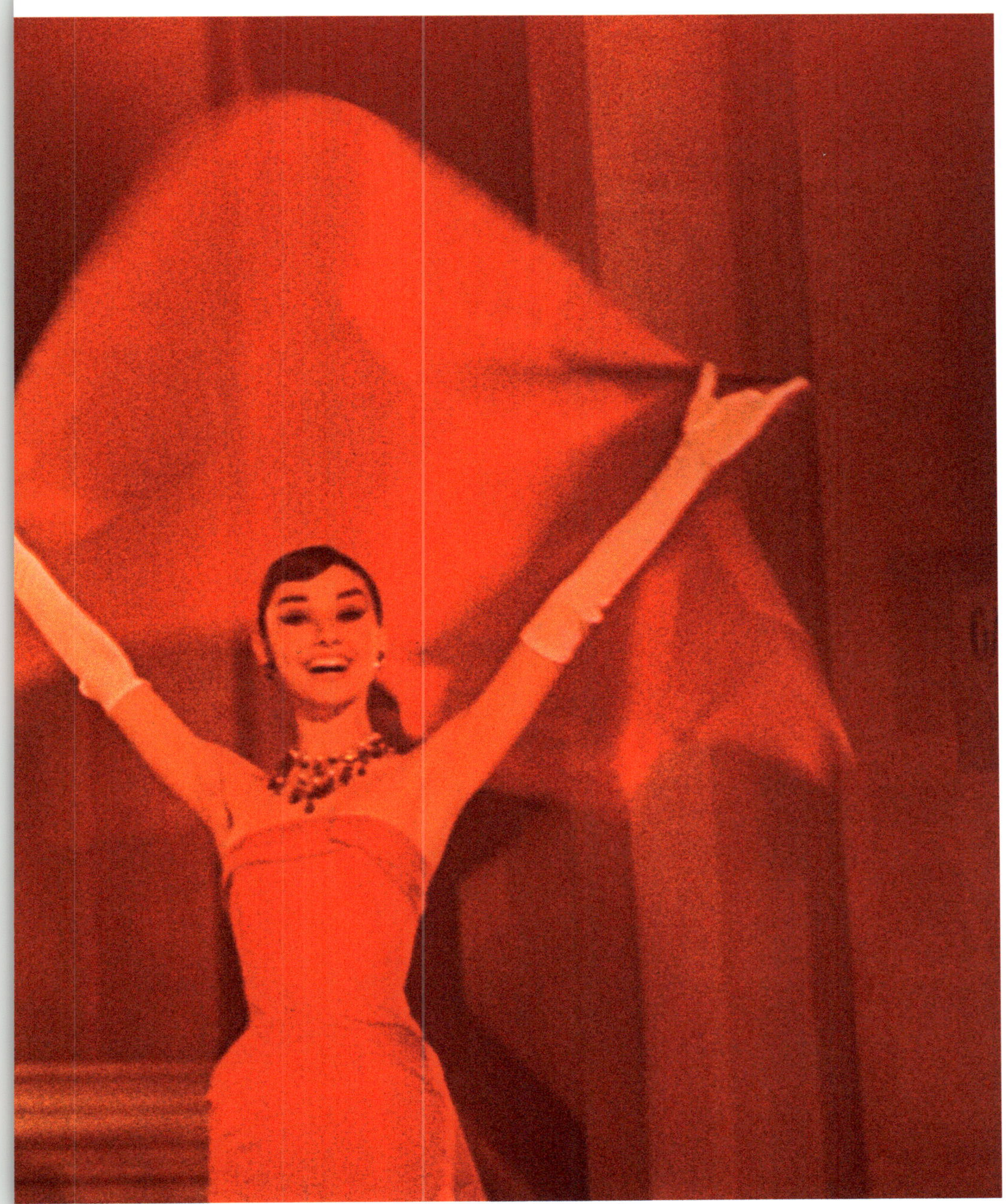

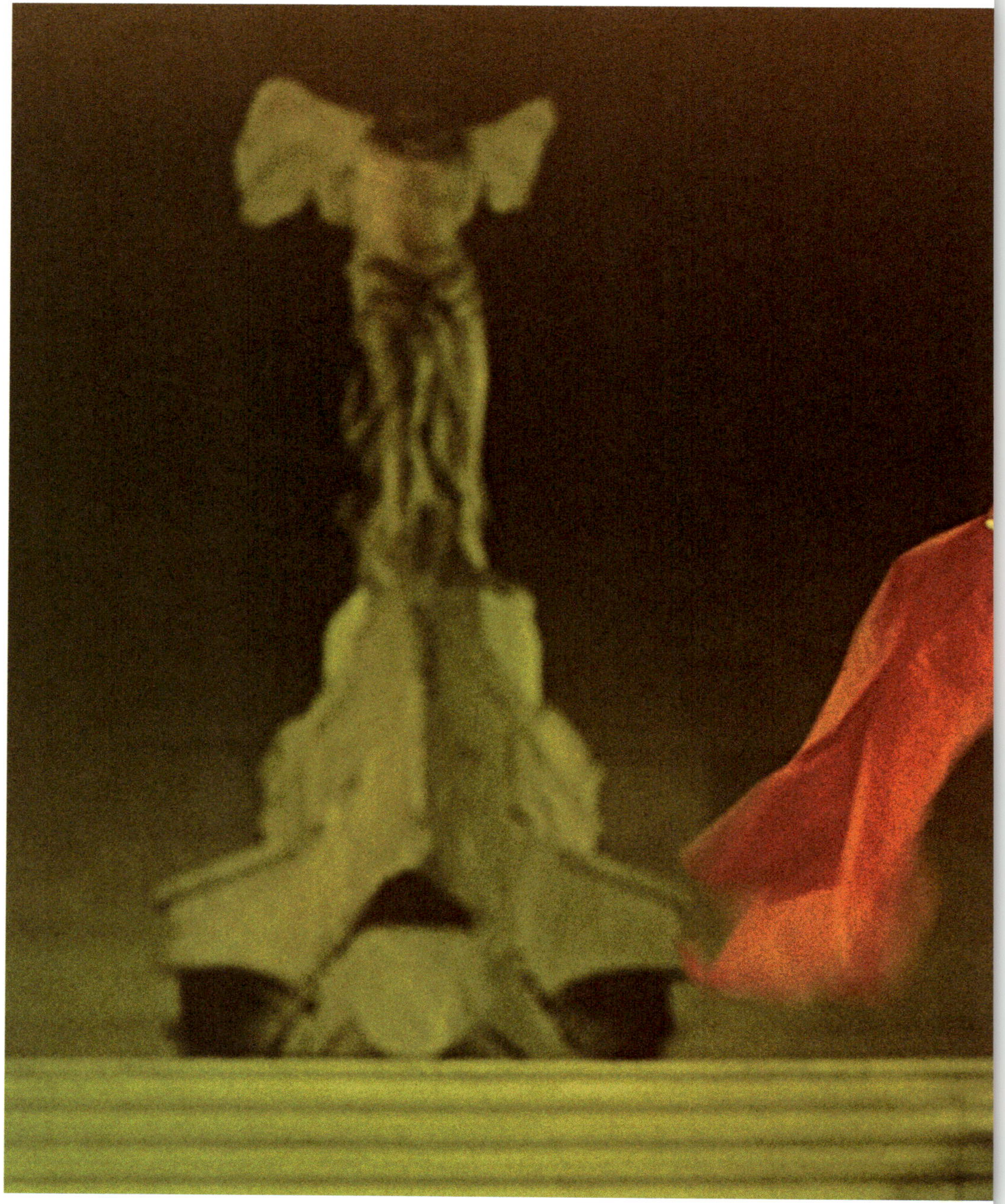

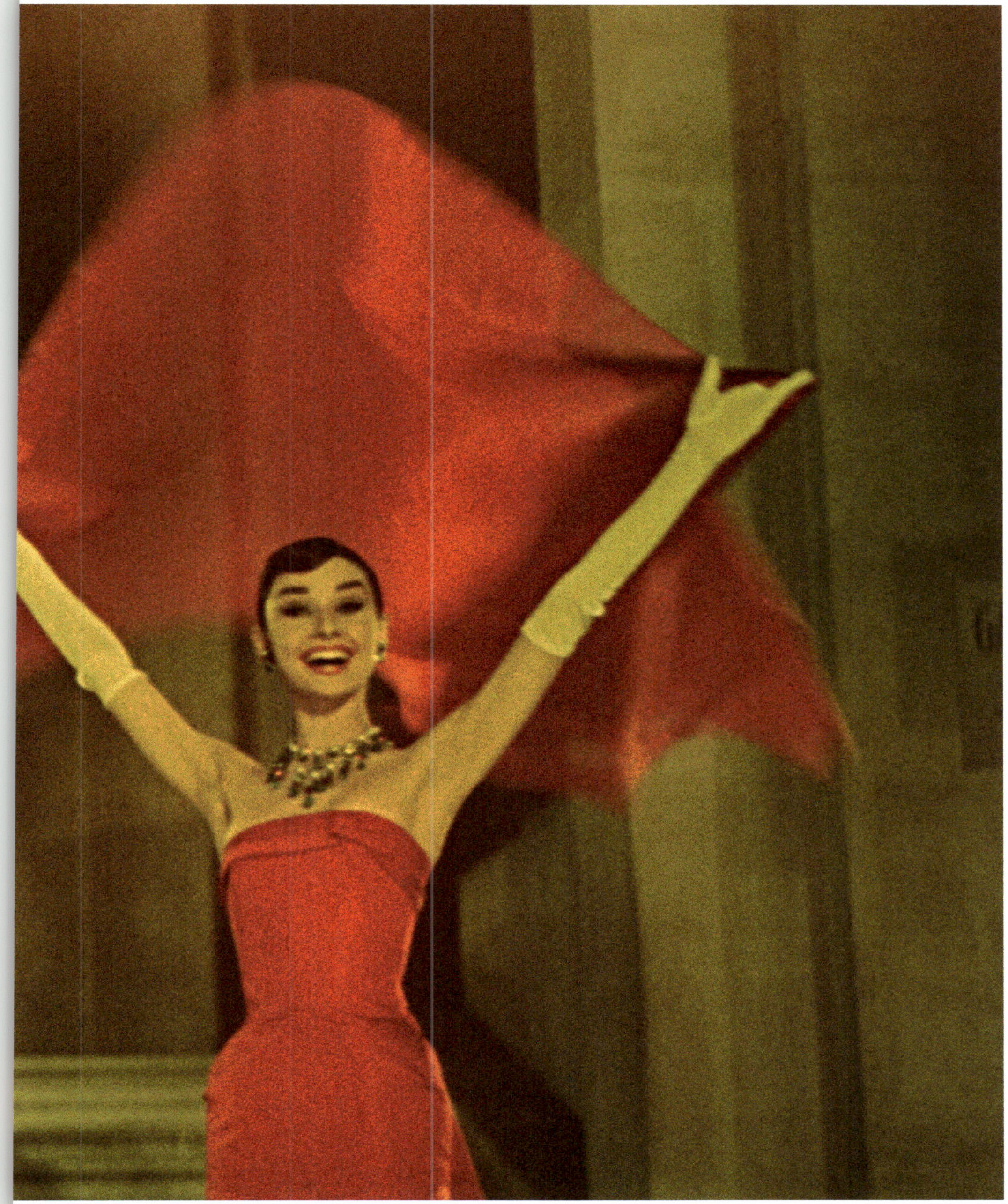

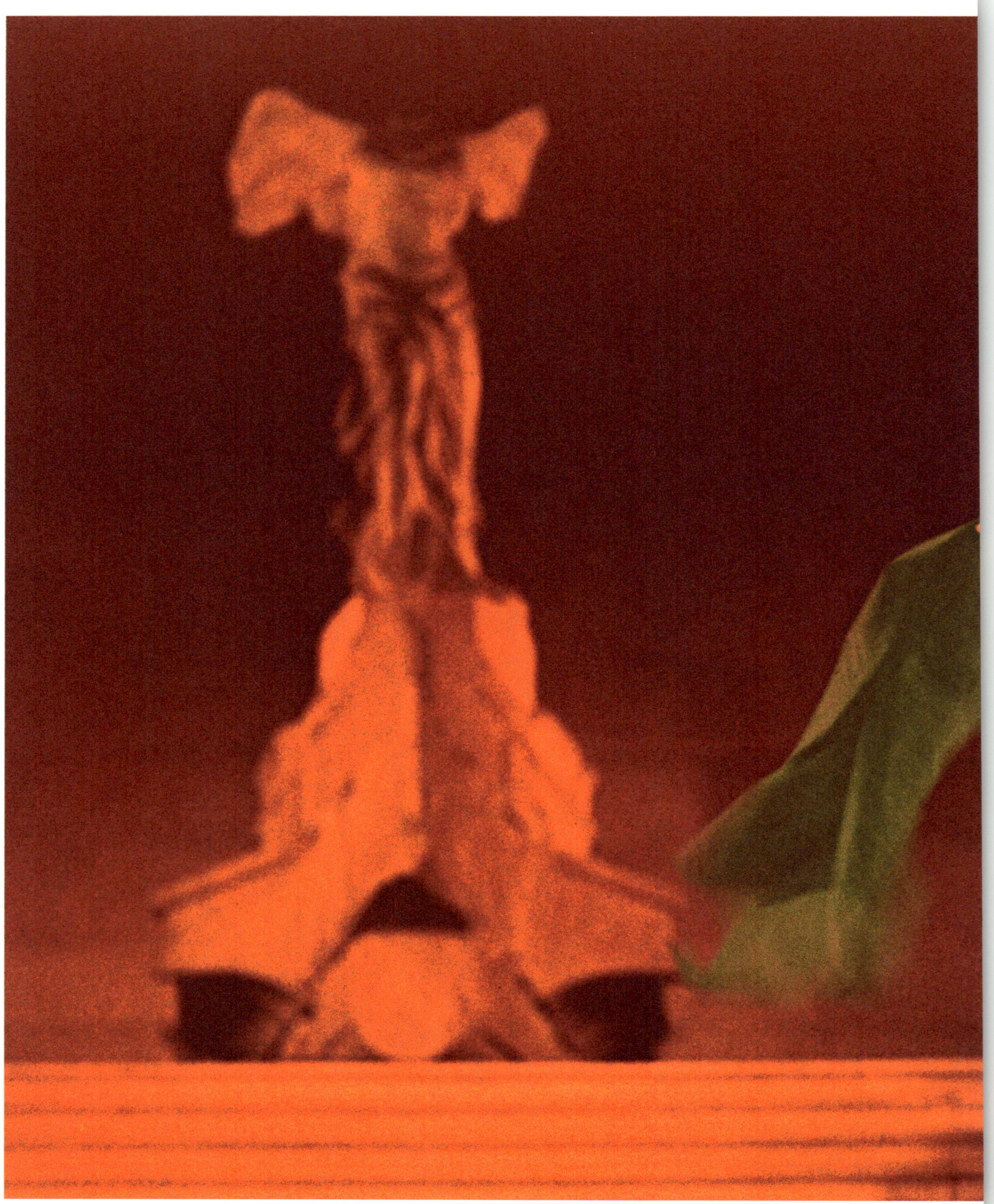

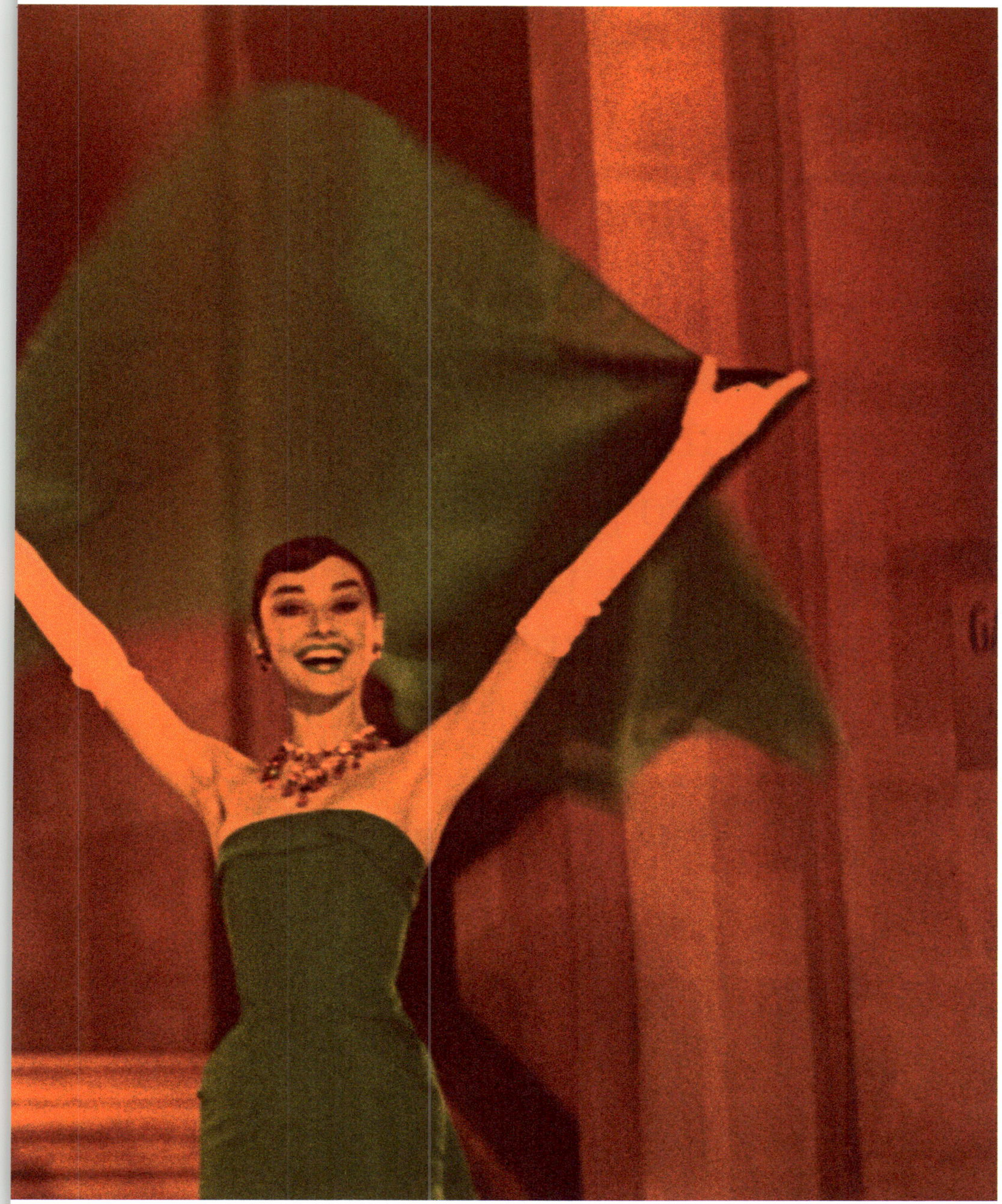

Photographic Feats

Éric Rohmer

There is at least one sequence in this film that's delightful, even if the rest isn't really satisfying. It's the one where Fred Astaire asks Audrey-the-model to pose, or more exactly, to move before the Rolleiflex. A click, and the screen freezes, and the realism of the film gives way, impromptu, to the sophistication inherent in photography. A picture made iridescent, as it were, by a few cleverly arranged blurs, which kill nature with an excess of nature. Aside from this high point, the only other original gags of the film are based on the unique powers of photography, exploited with a willingness — not seen since the advent of color — to treat the question from all sides. I have sometimes argued vehemently against the plastic tendencies of certain filmmakers who, imagining that they are copying the old or the modern masters, are barely creating images worthy of calendars. Here, on the contrary, the effects relate to a technique that feels like pure photography, without any pictorial reference. Indisputable proof that color, far from subduing the art of the image, opens up new enthralling horizons.

—

ÉRIC ROHMER, "PROUESSES PHOTOGRAPHIQUES" (PHOTOGRAPHIC FEATS), *ARTS ET SPECTACLES* [NO. 645] (NOVEMBER 26, 1957).

pp. 162–63, Fred Astaire and Audrey Hepburn on the set of *Funny Face*, Paris, August 1956
pp. 164–65, Audrey Hepburn on the set of *Funny Face*, Paris, August 1956
pp. 166–69, Fred Astaire and Audrey Hepburn on the set of *Funny Face*, Fontaine de Latone, Versailles, France, August 1956
pp. 170–75, Audrey Hepburn on the set of *Funny Face*, Fontaine de Latone, Versailles, France, August 1956
pp. 176–83, Audrey Hepburn on the set of *Funny Face*, Opéra Garnier, Place de l'Opéra, Paris, August 1956
pp. 184–85, Fred Astaire and Audrey Hepburn on the set of *Funny Face*, Opéra Garnier, Place de l'Opéra, Paris, August 1956
pp. 187–203, Audrey Hepburn on the set of *Funny Face*, Paris, August 1956

Funny Face

On the Set

Richard Avedon

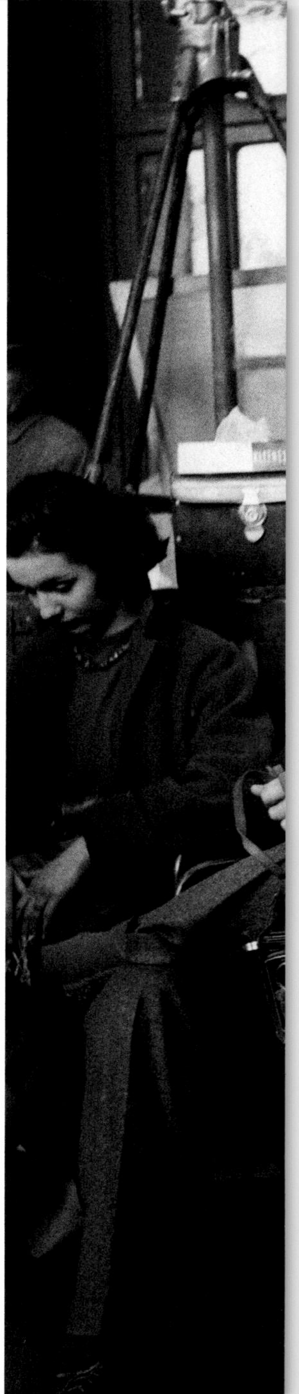

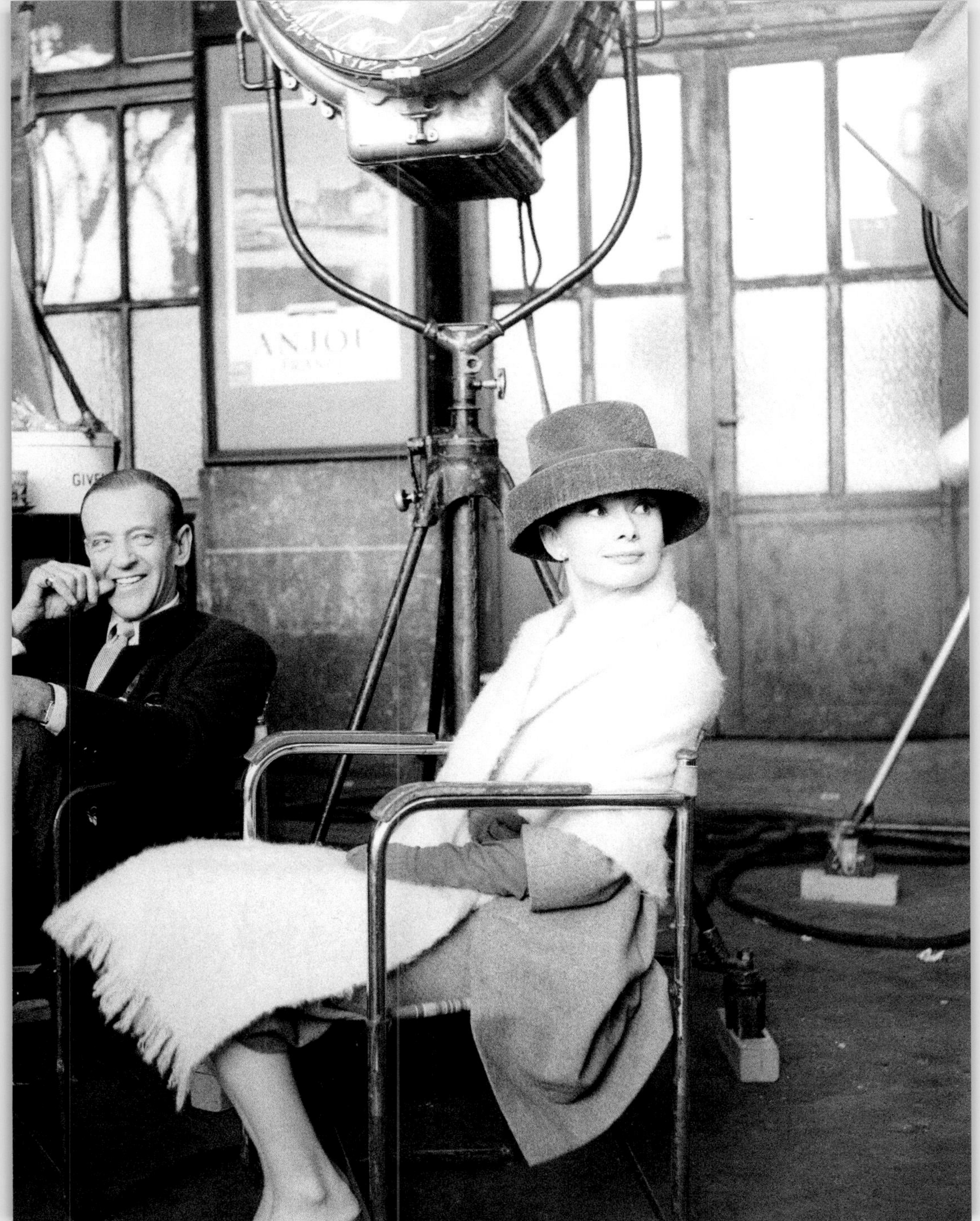

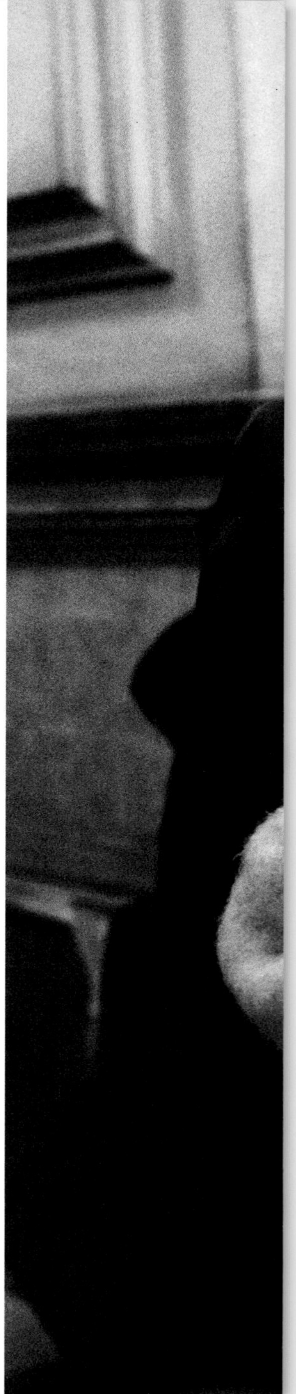

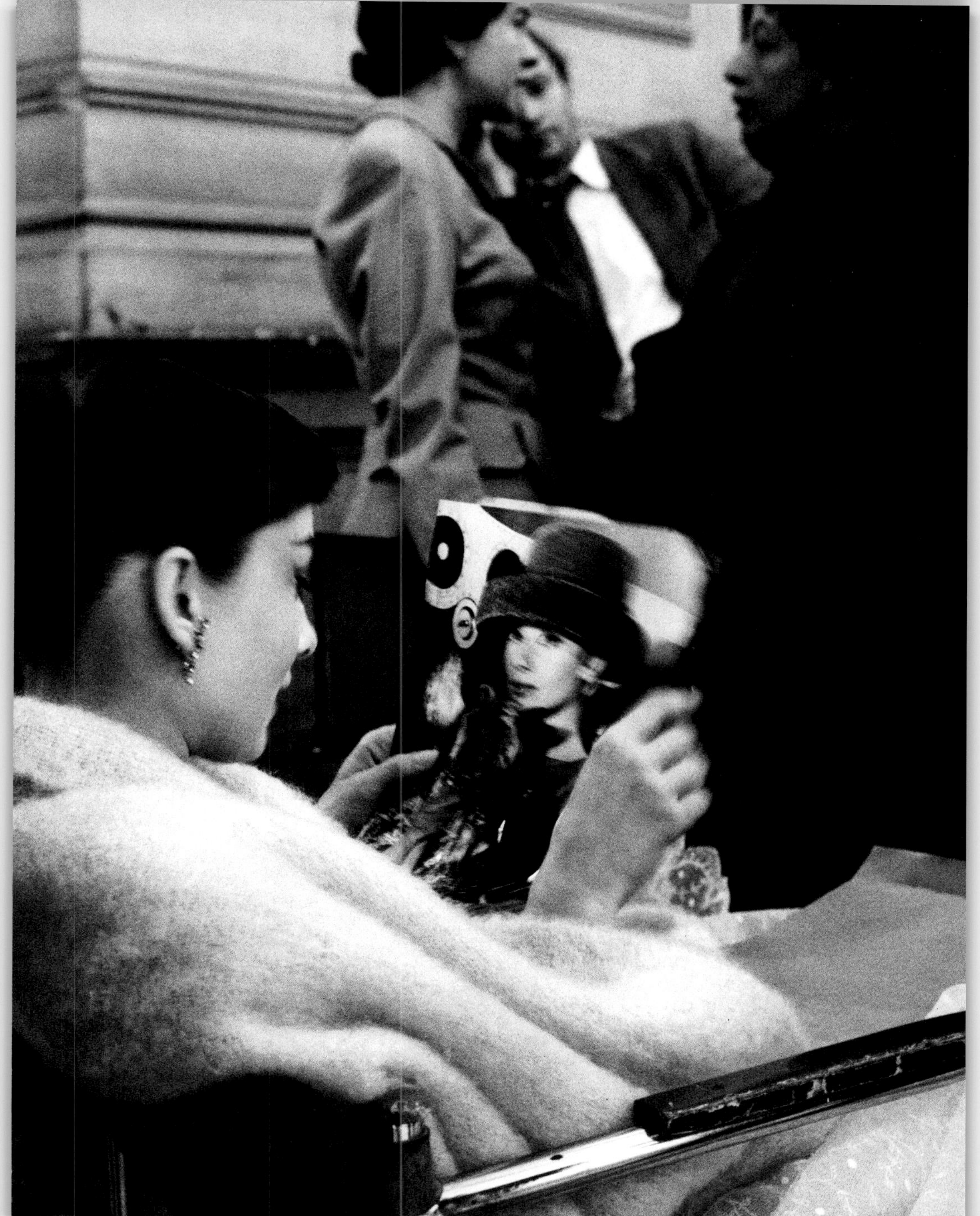

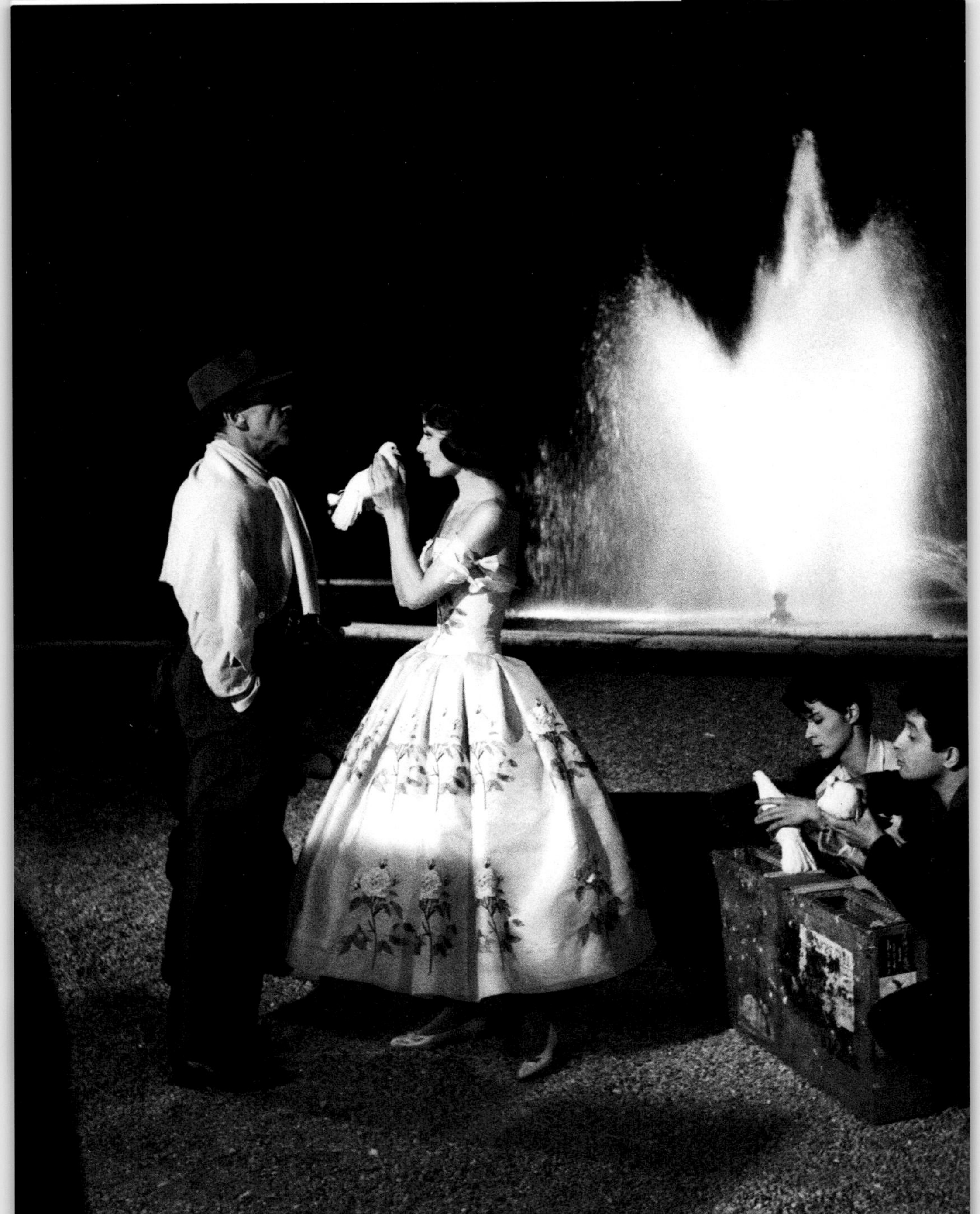

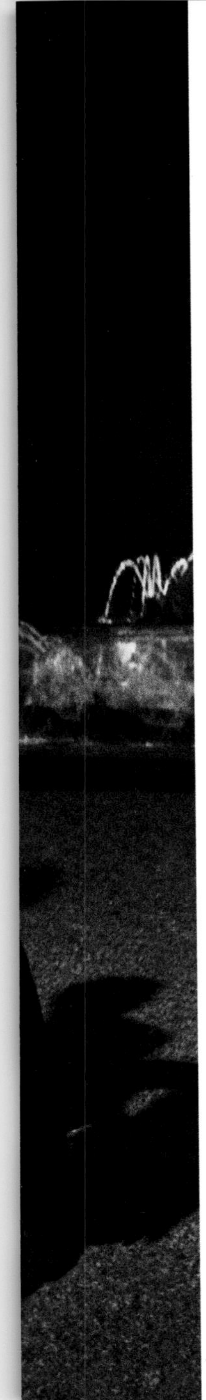

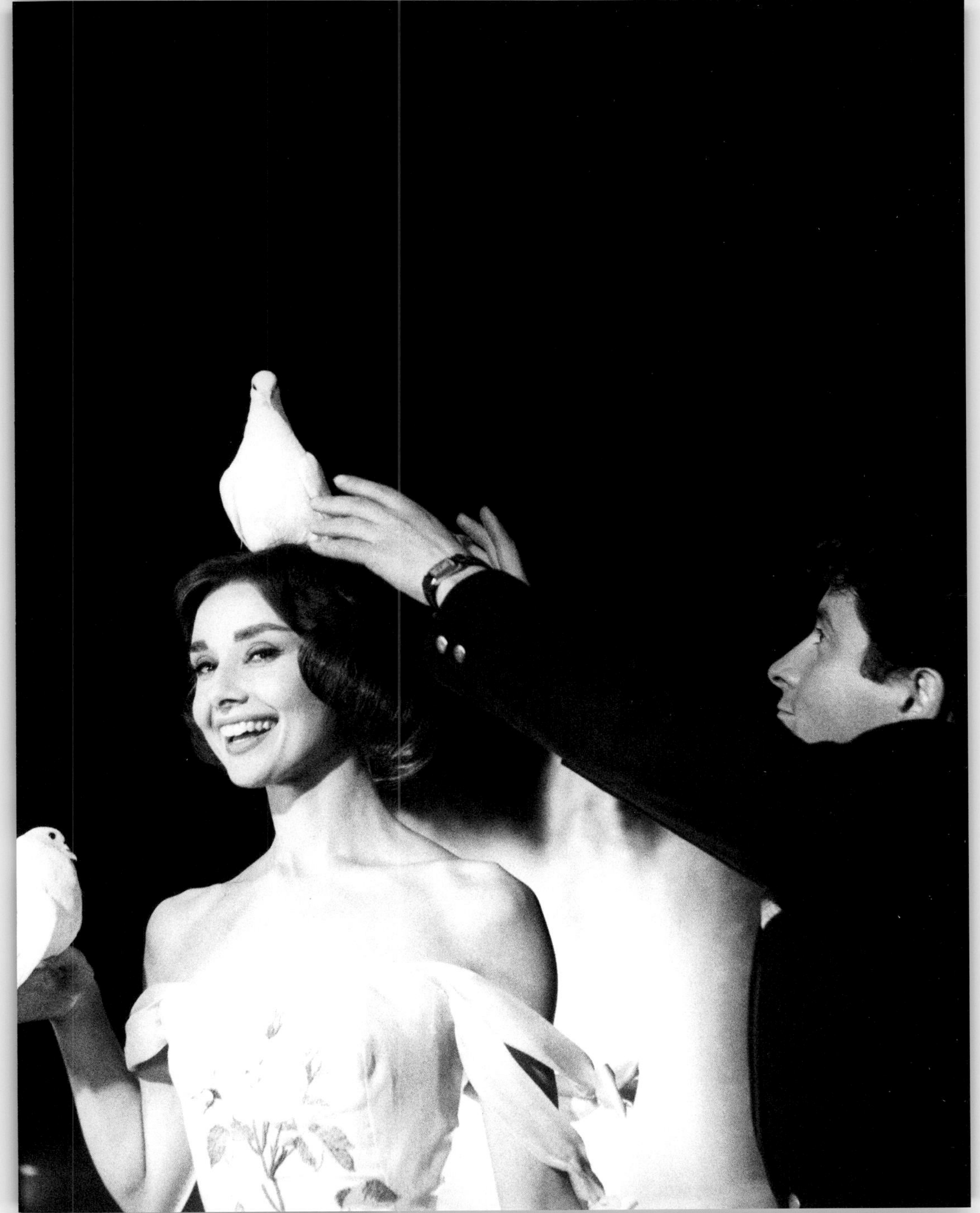

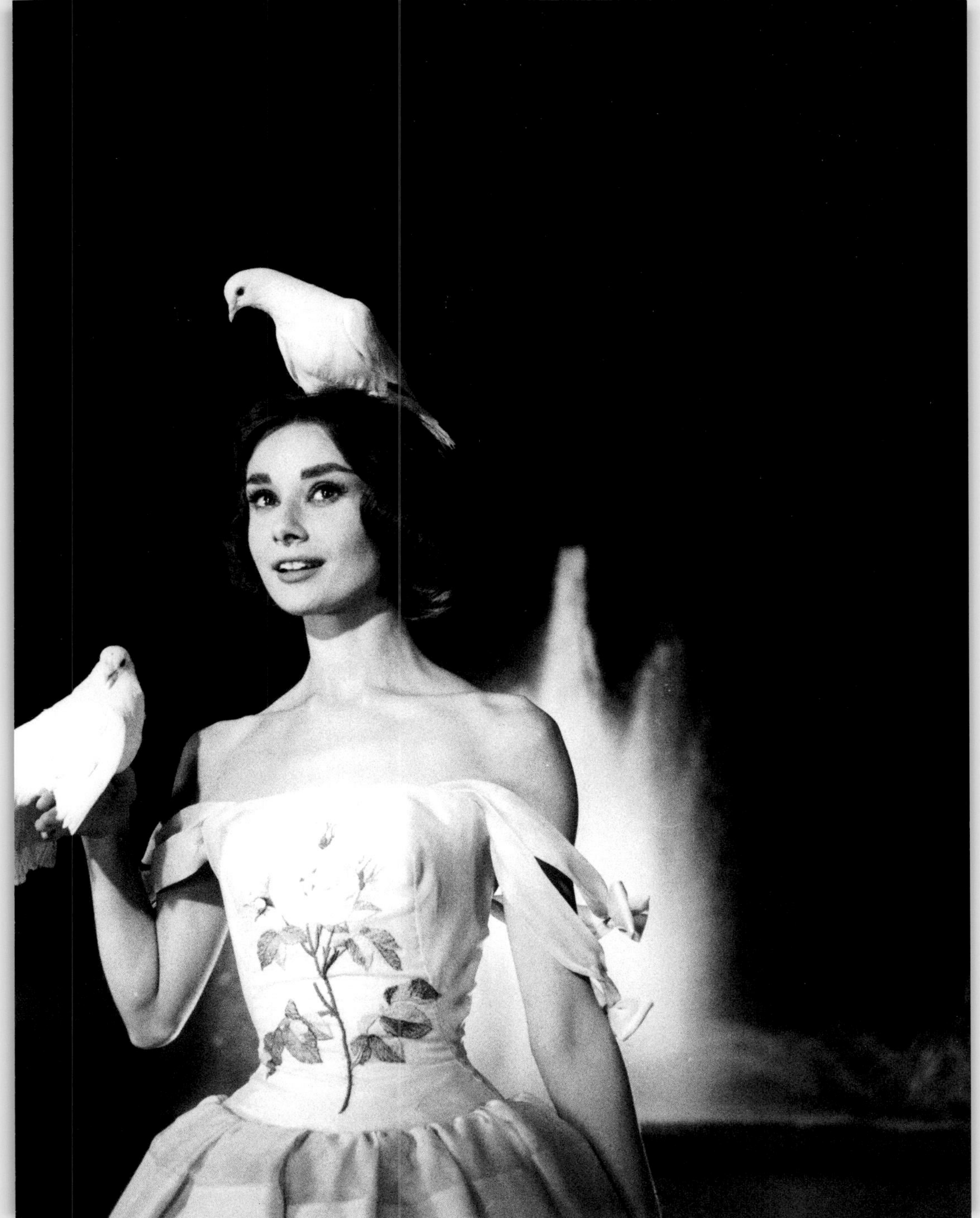

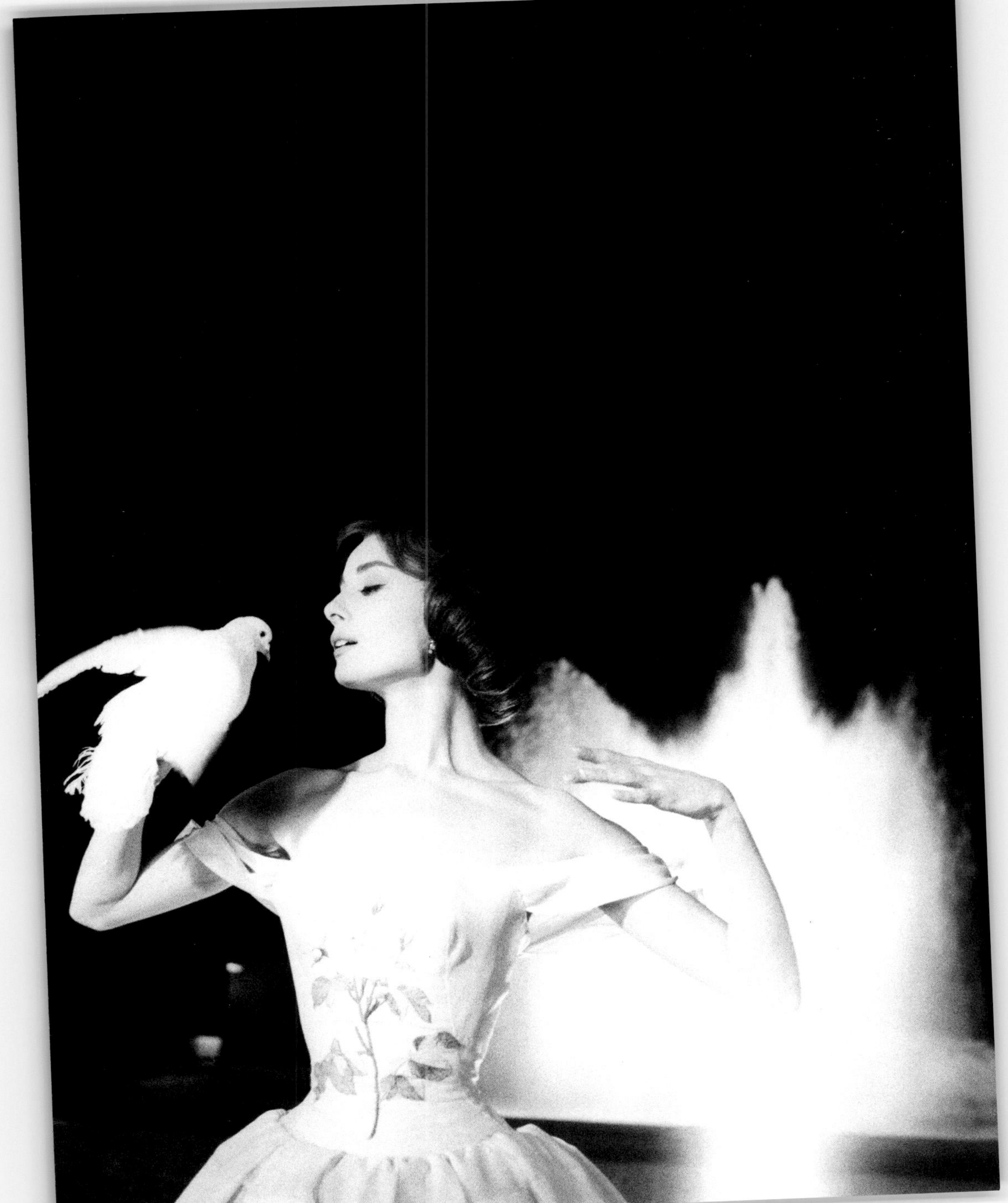

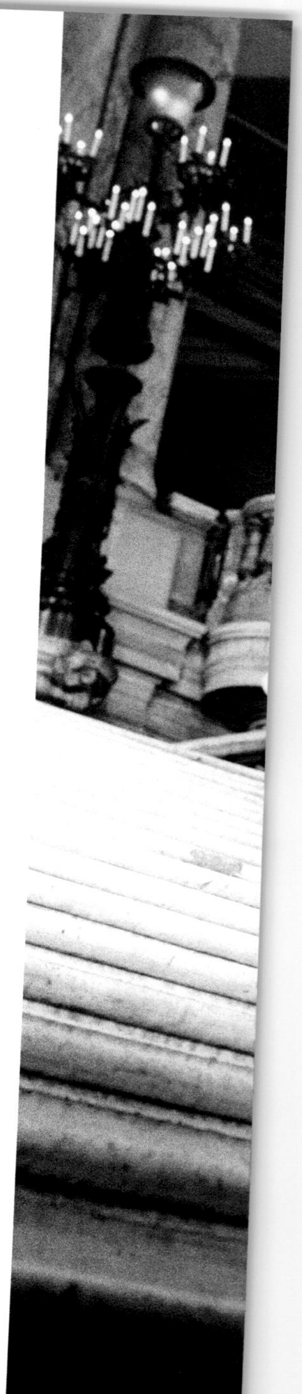

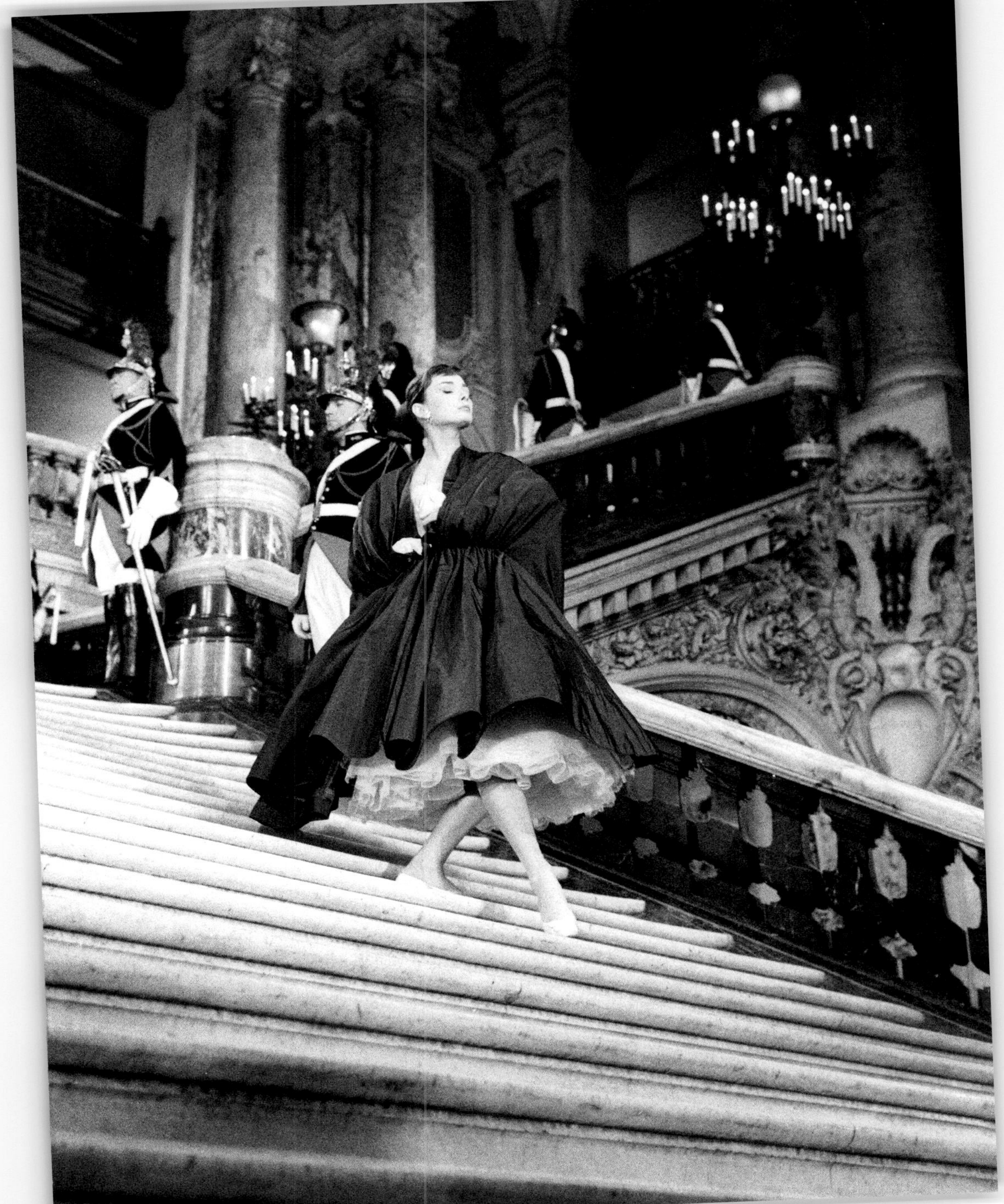

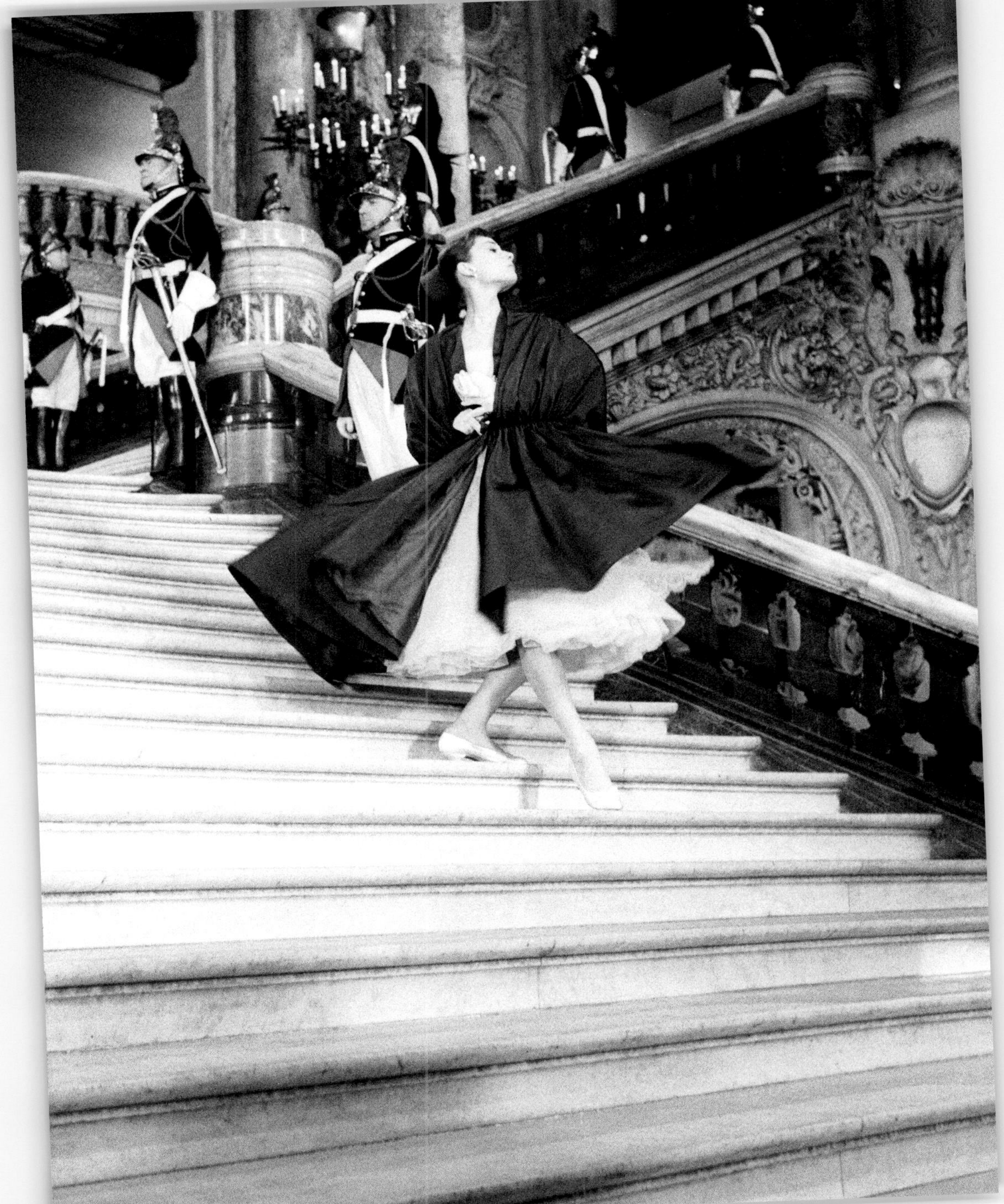

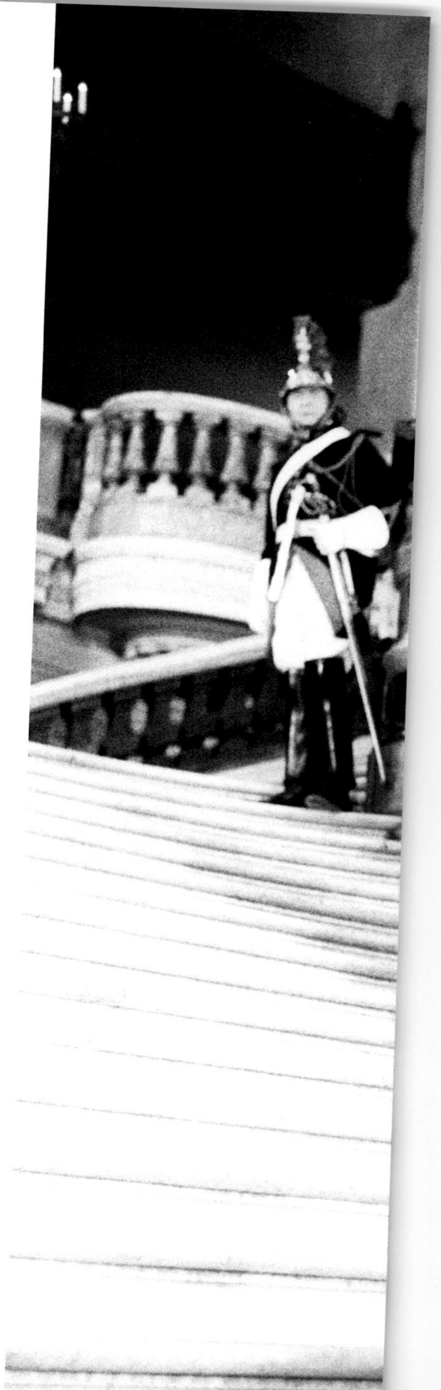

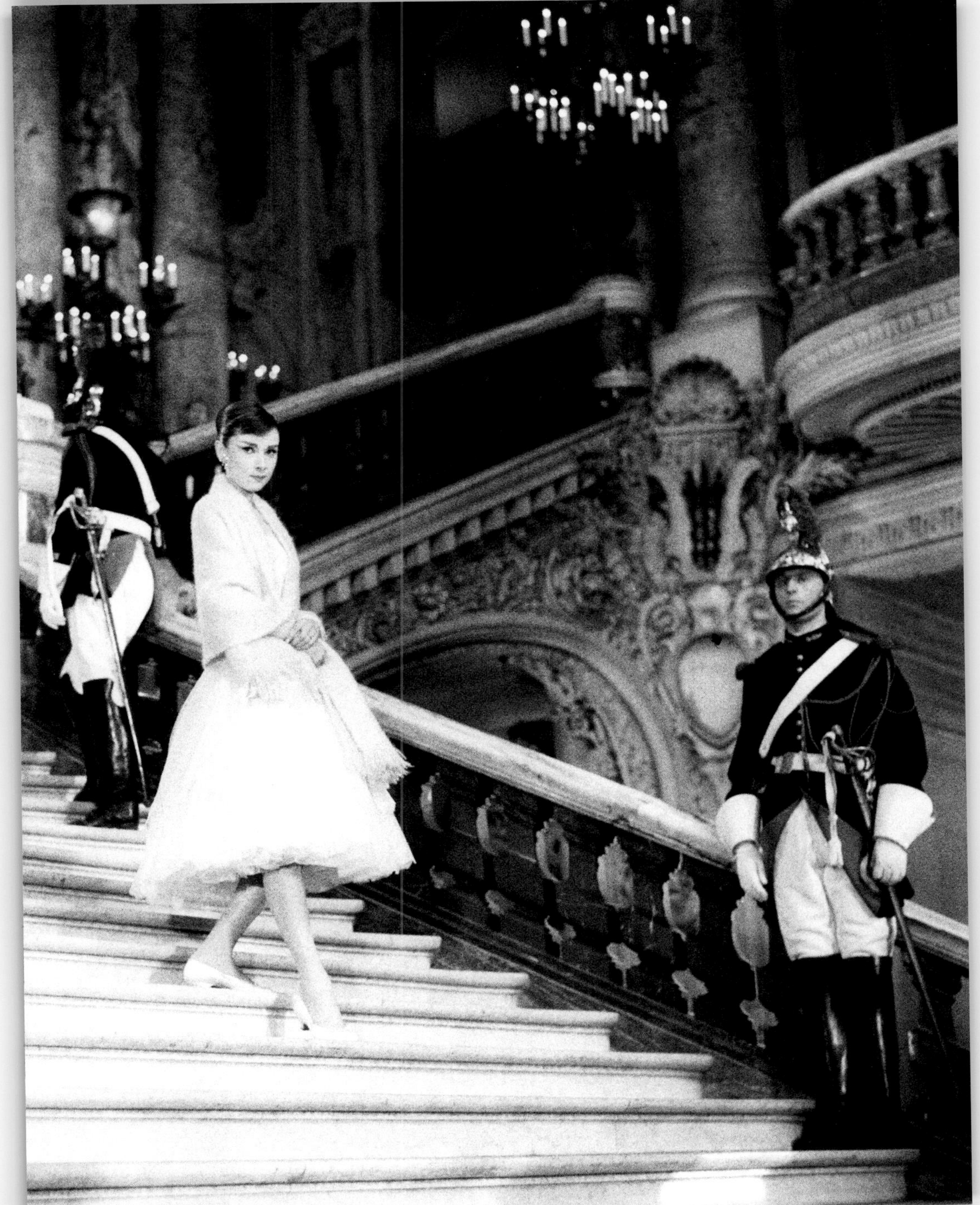

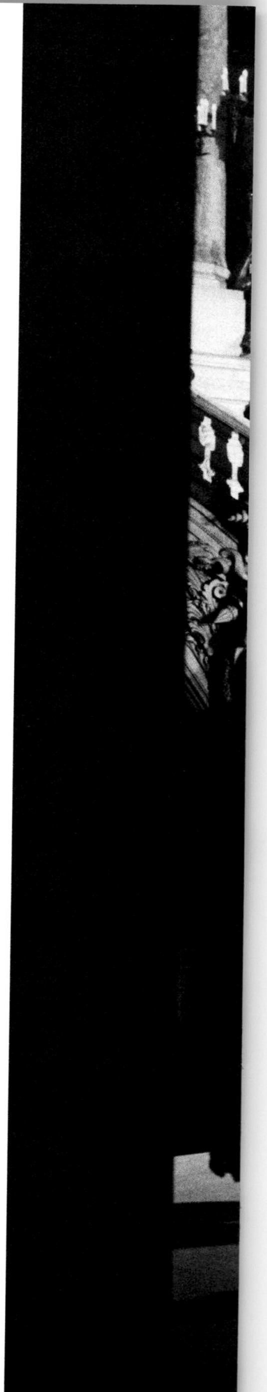

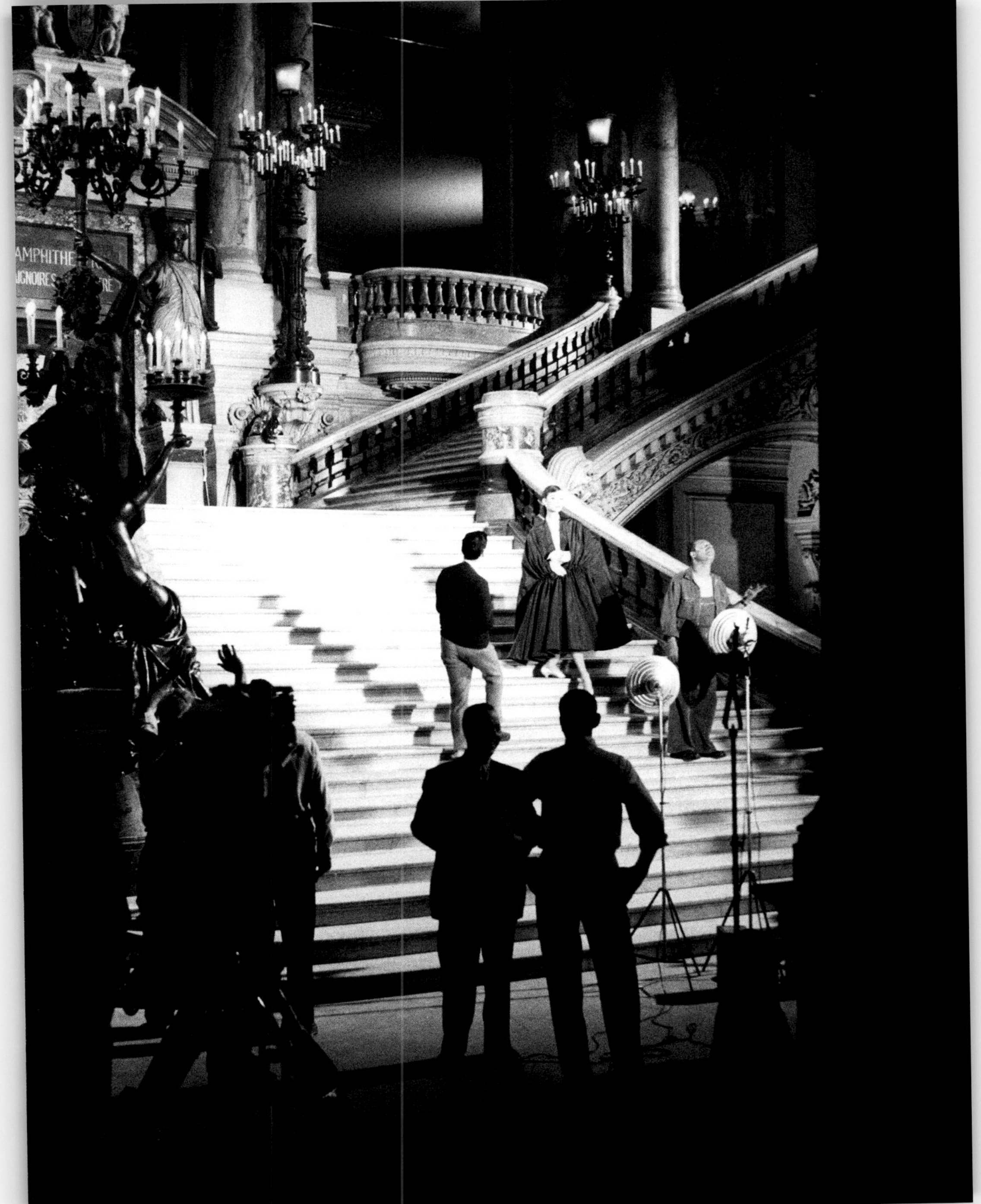

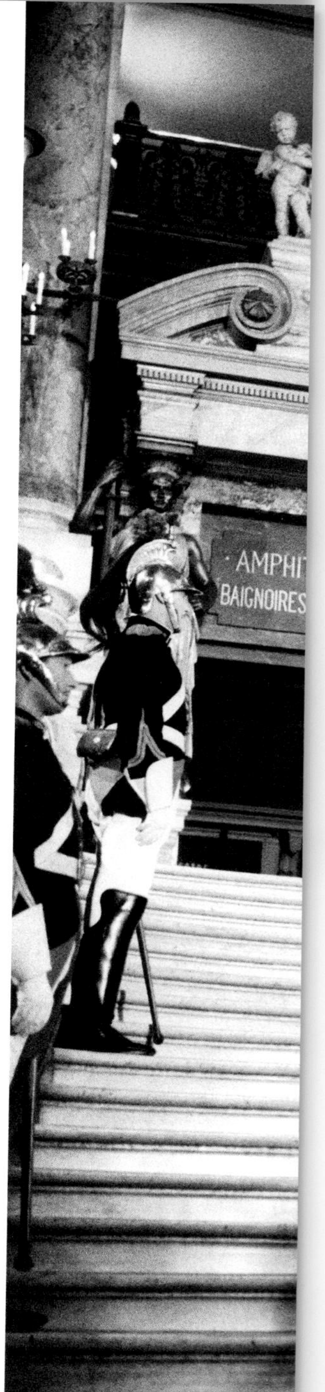
AMPHI
BAIGNOIRES

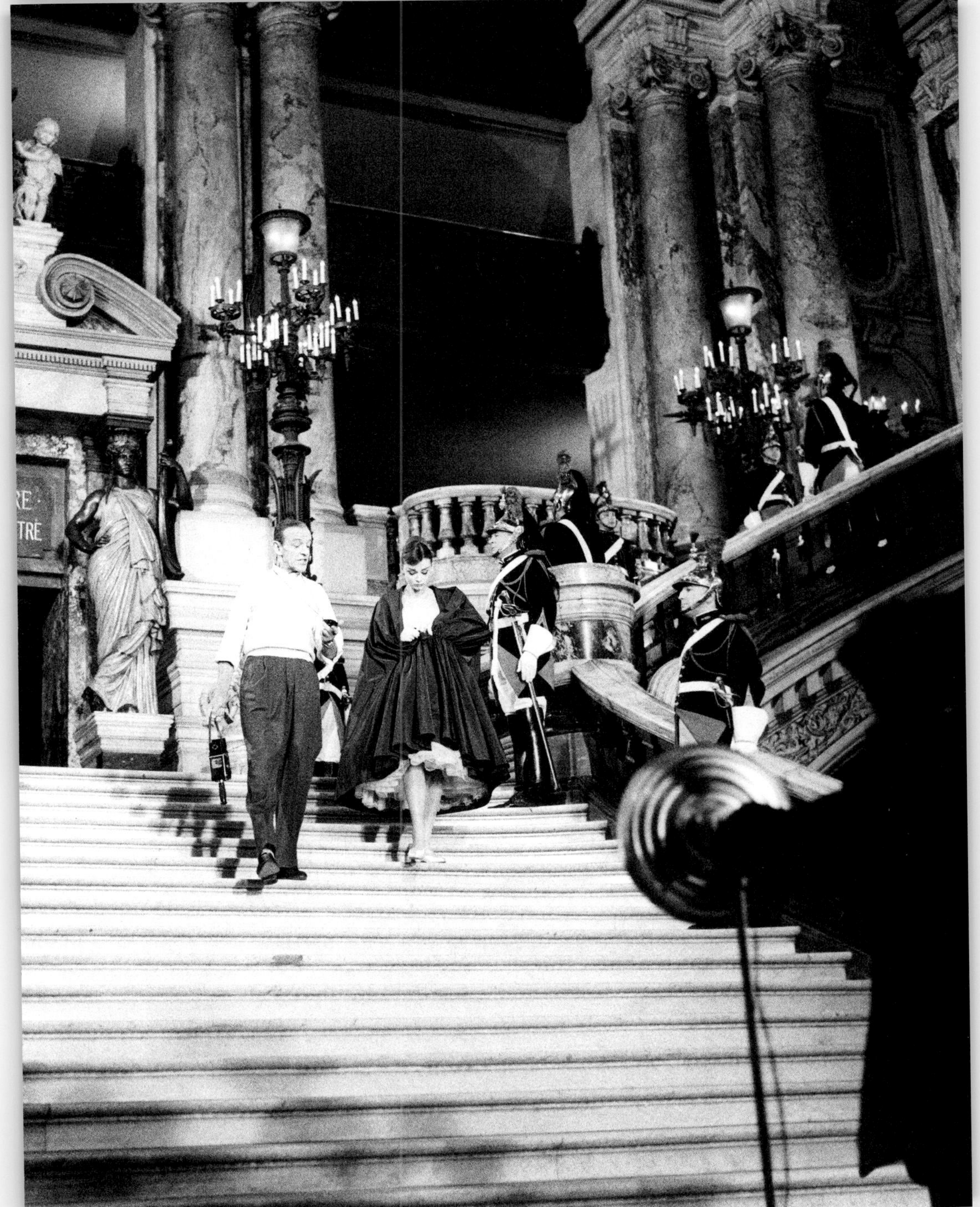

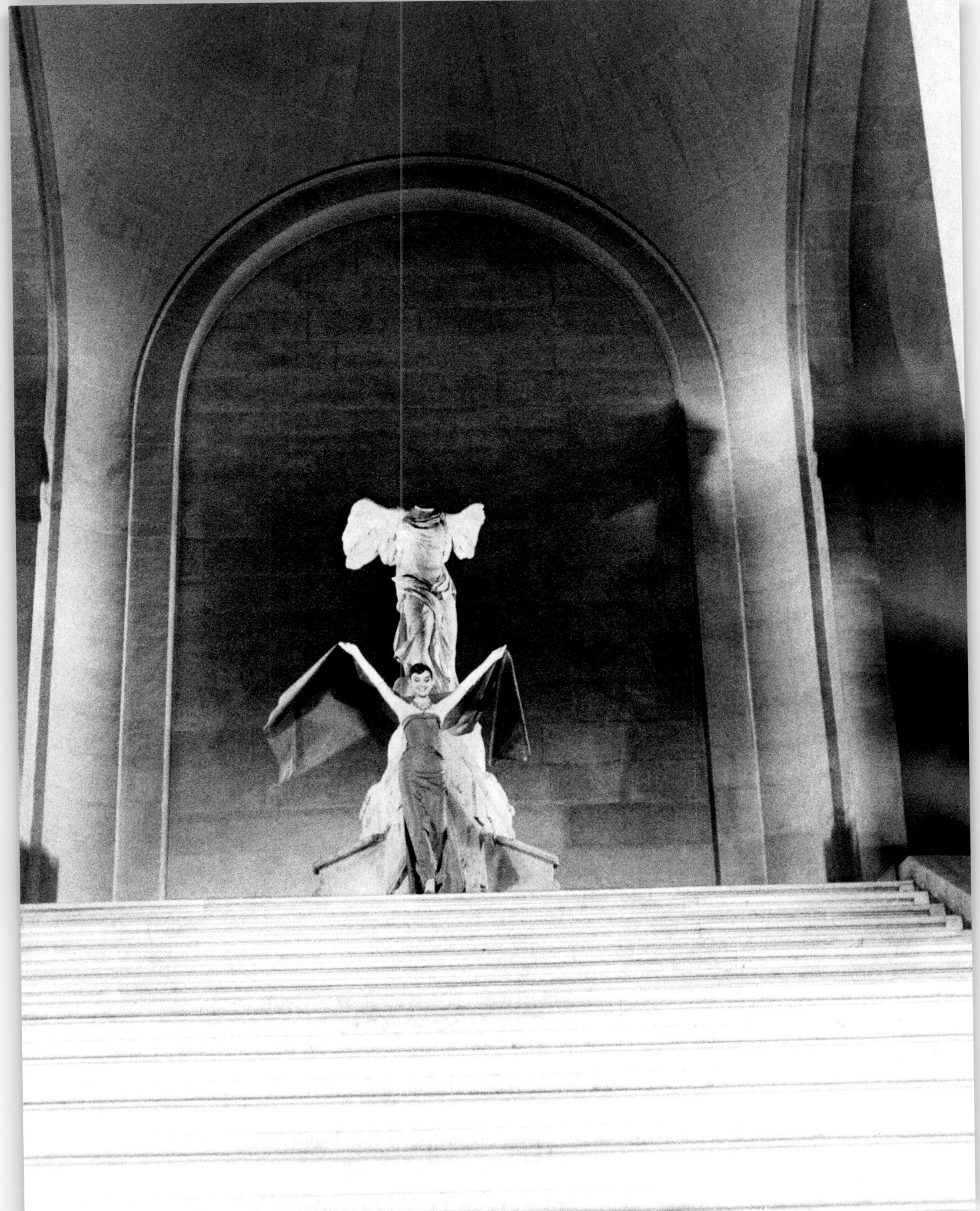

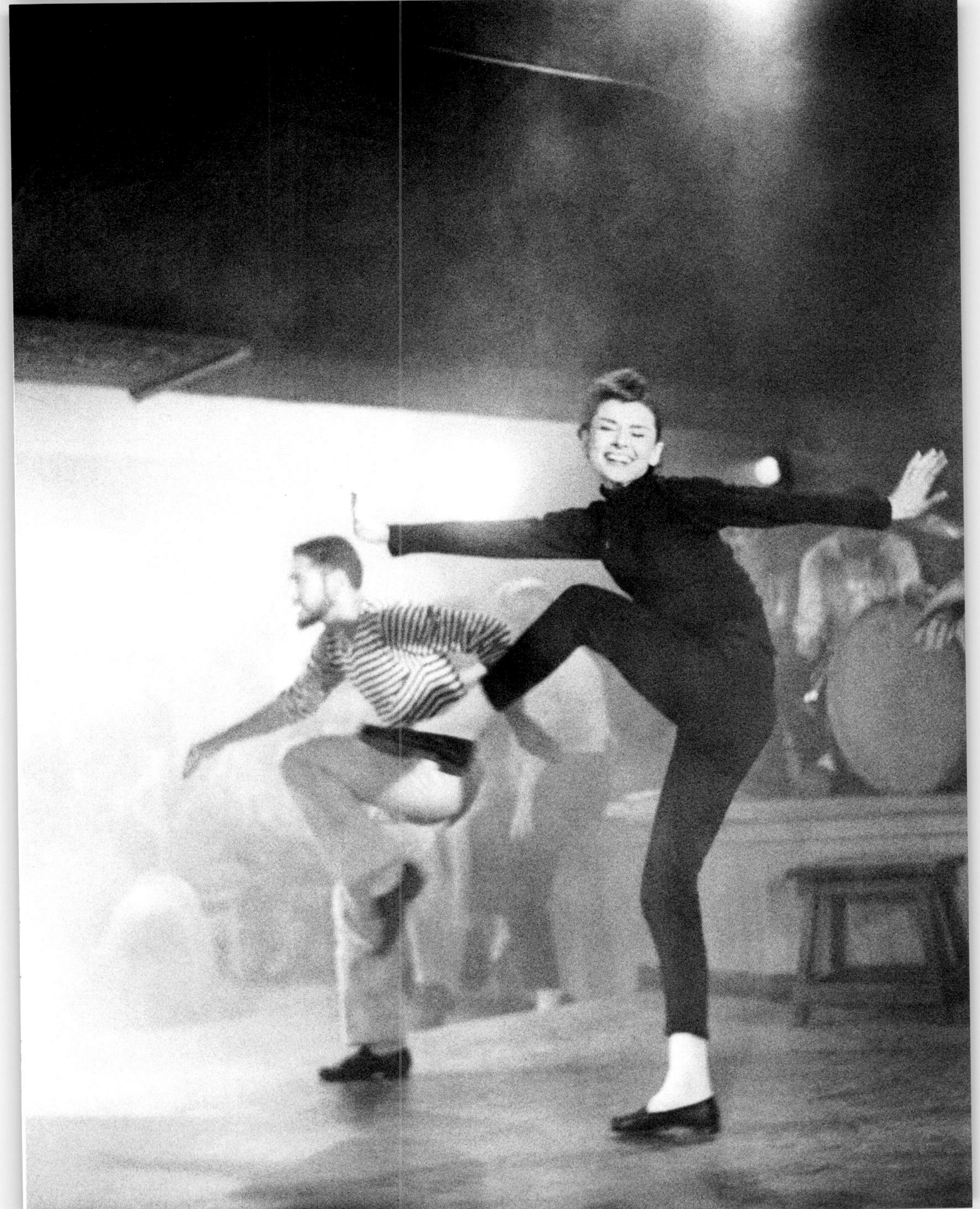

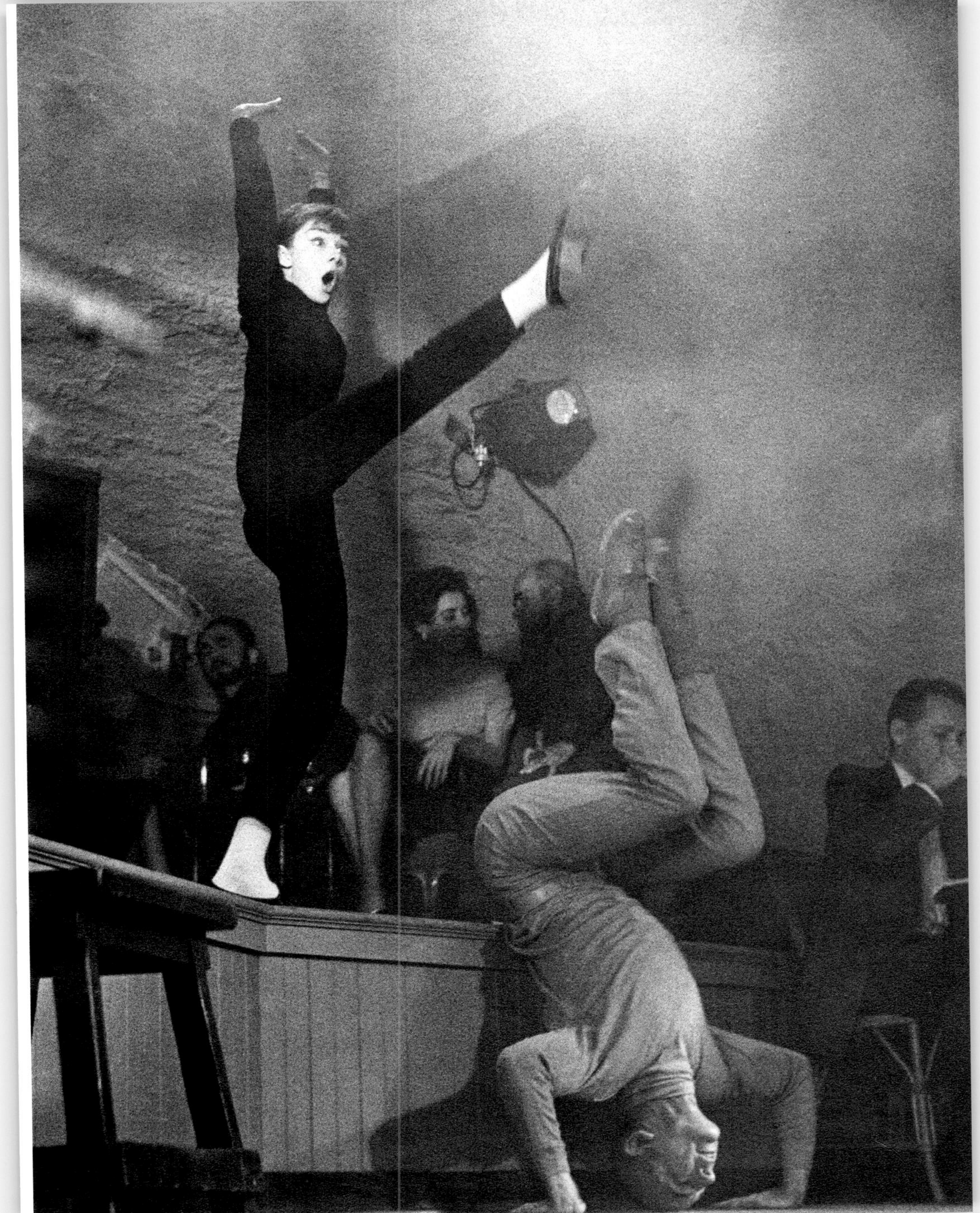

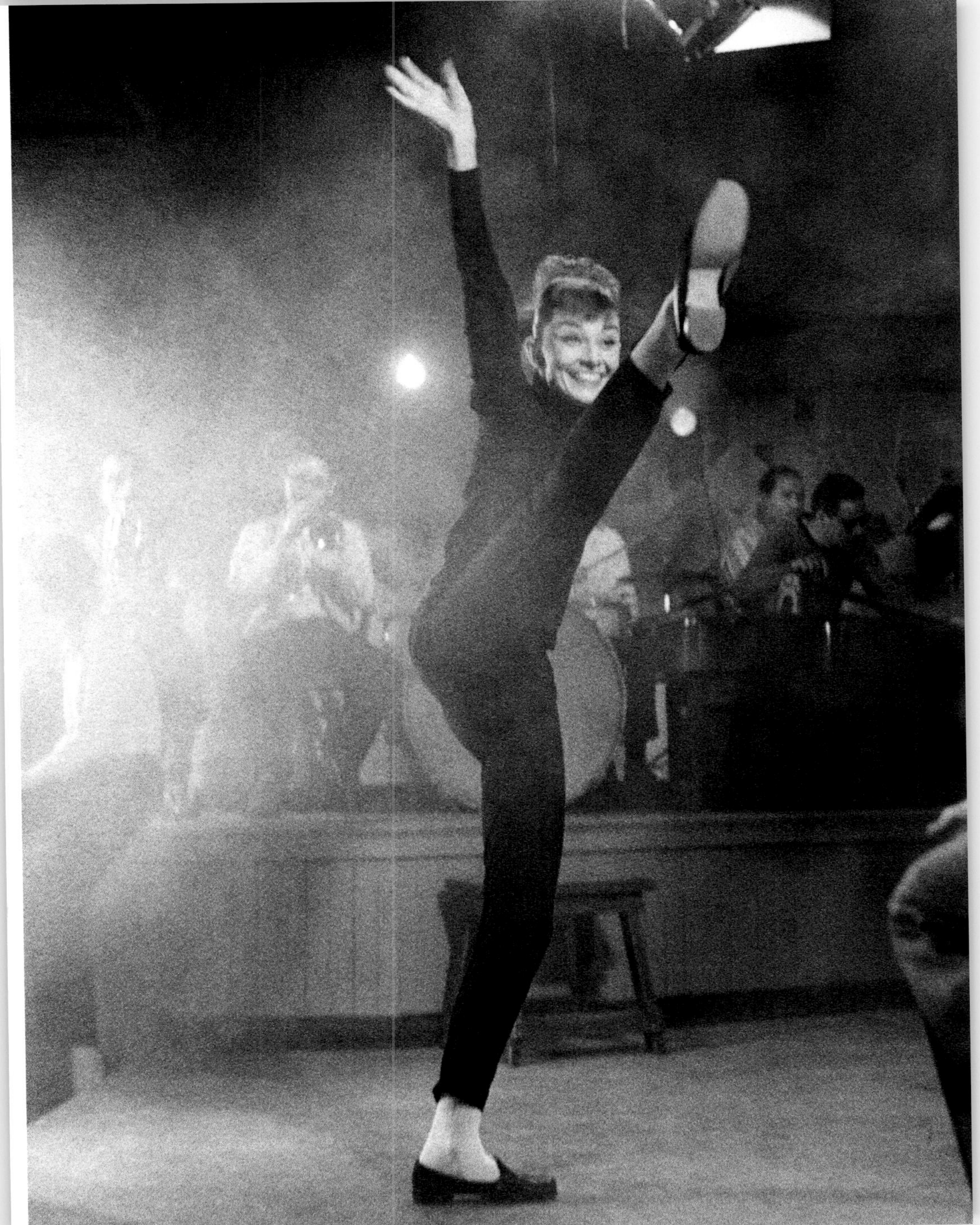

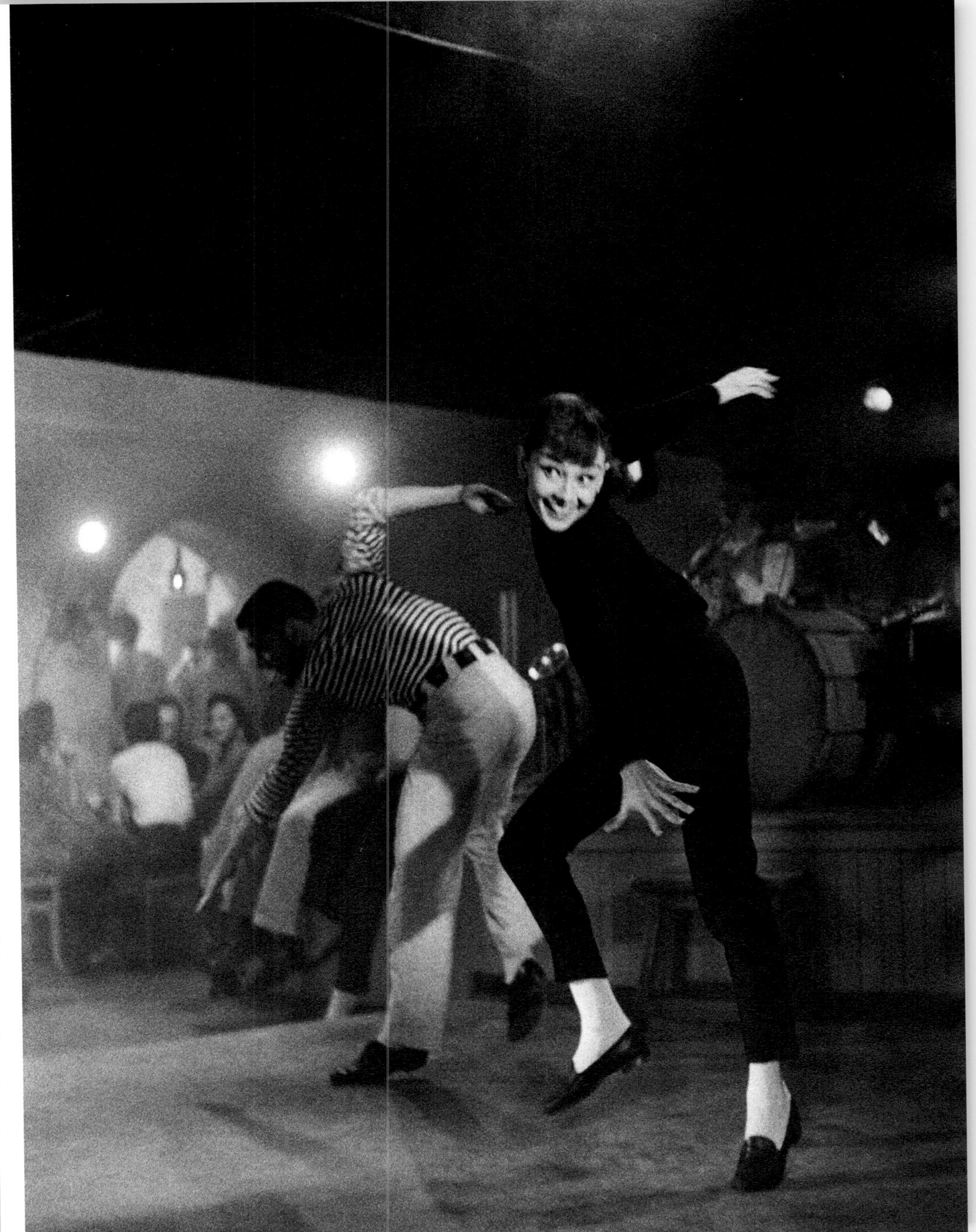

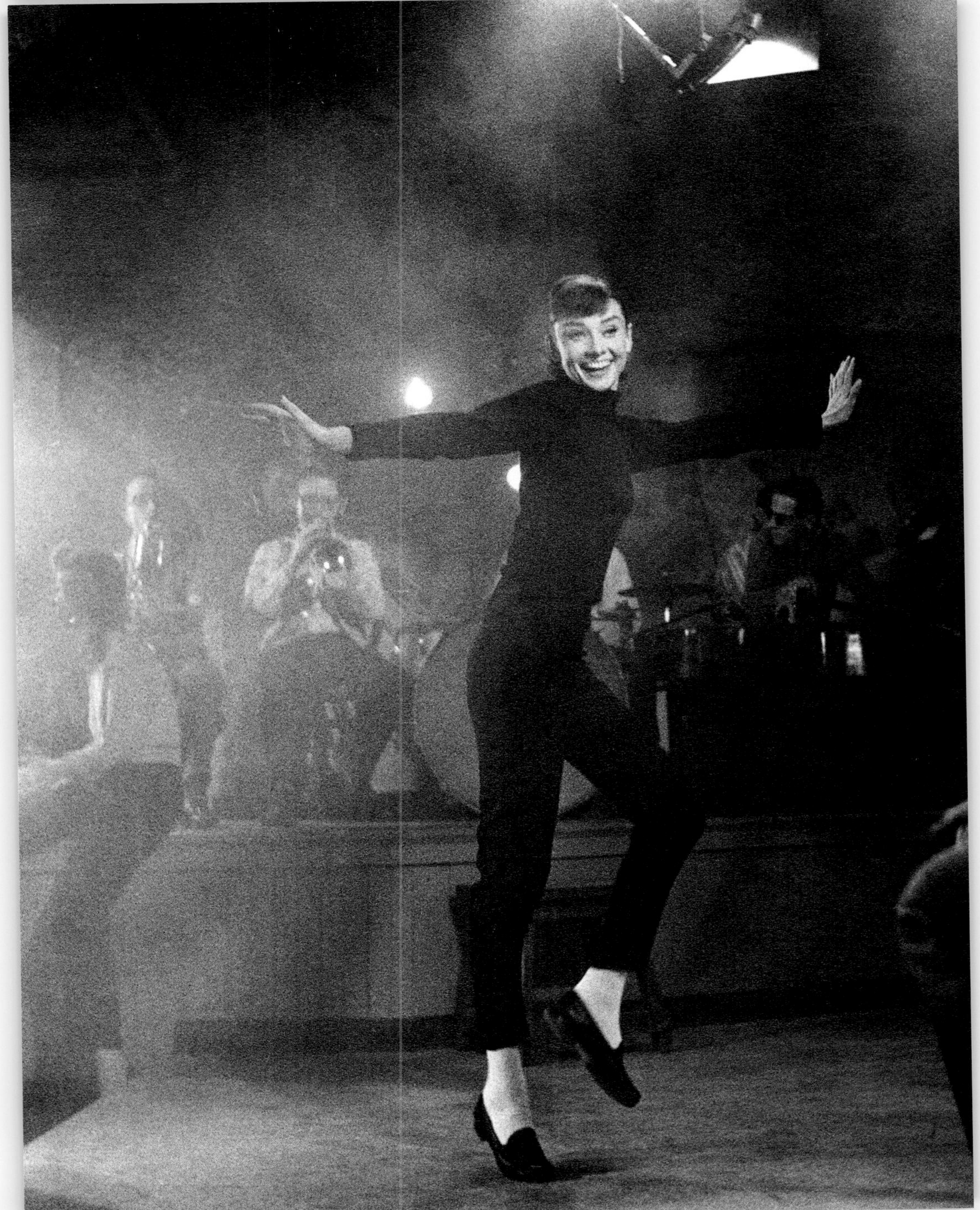

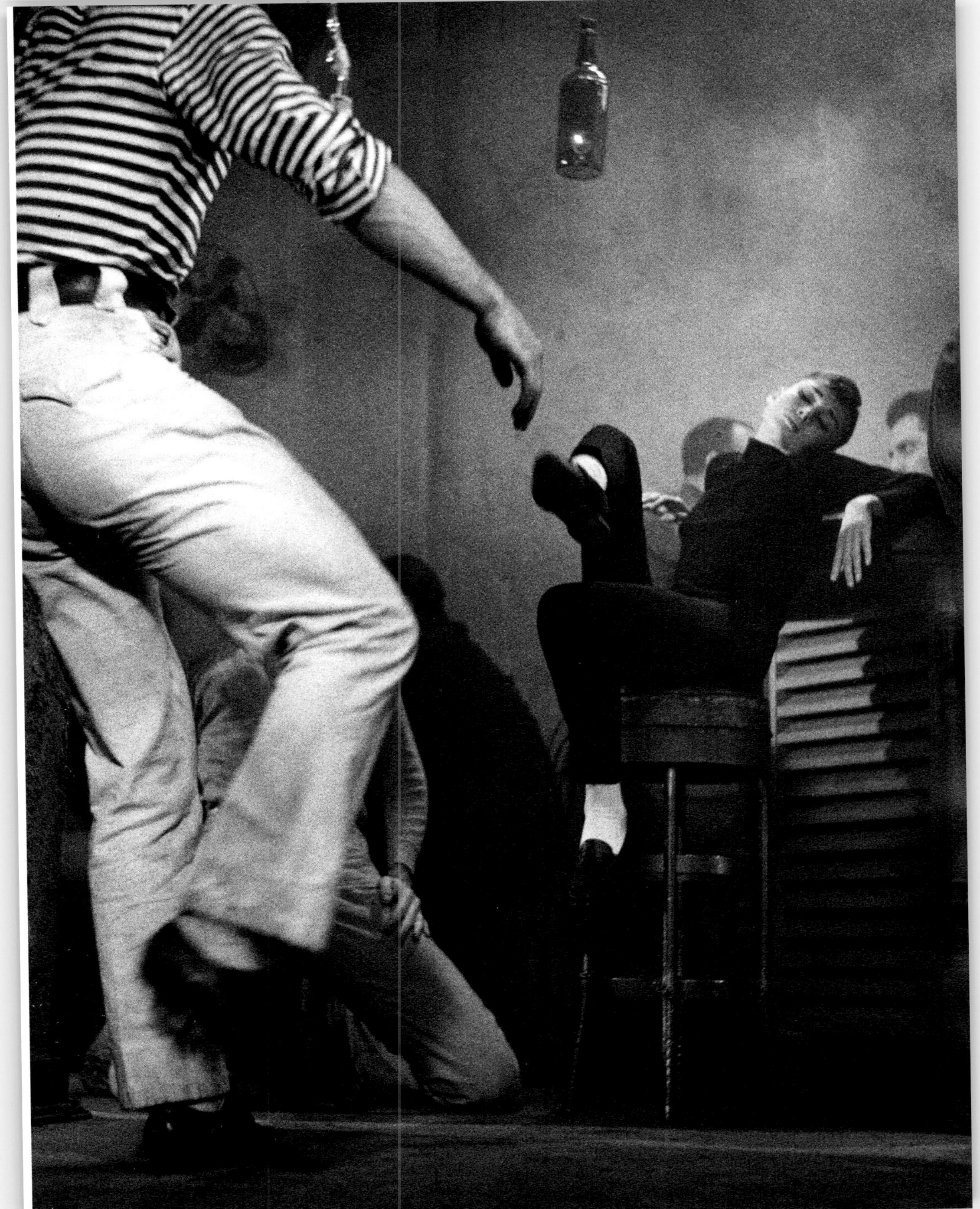

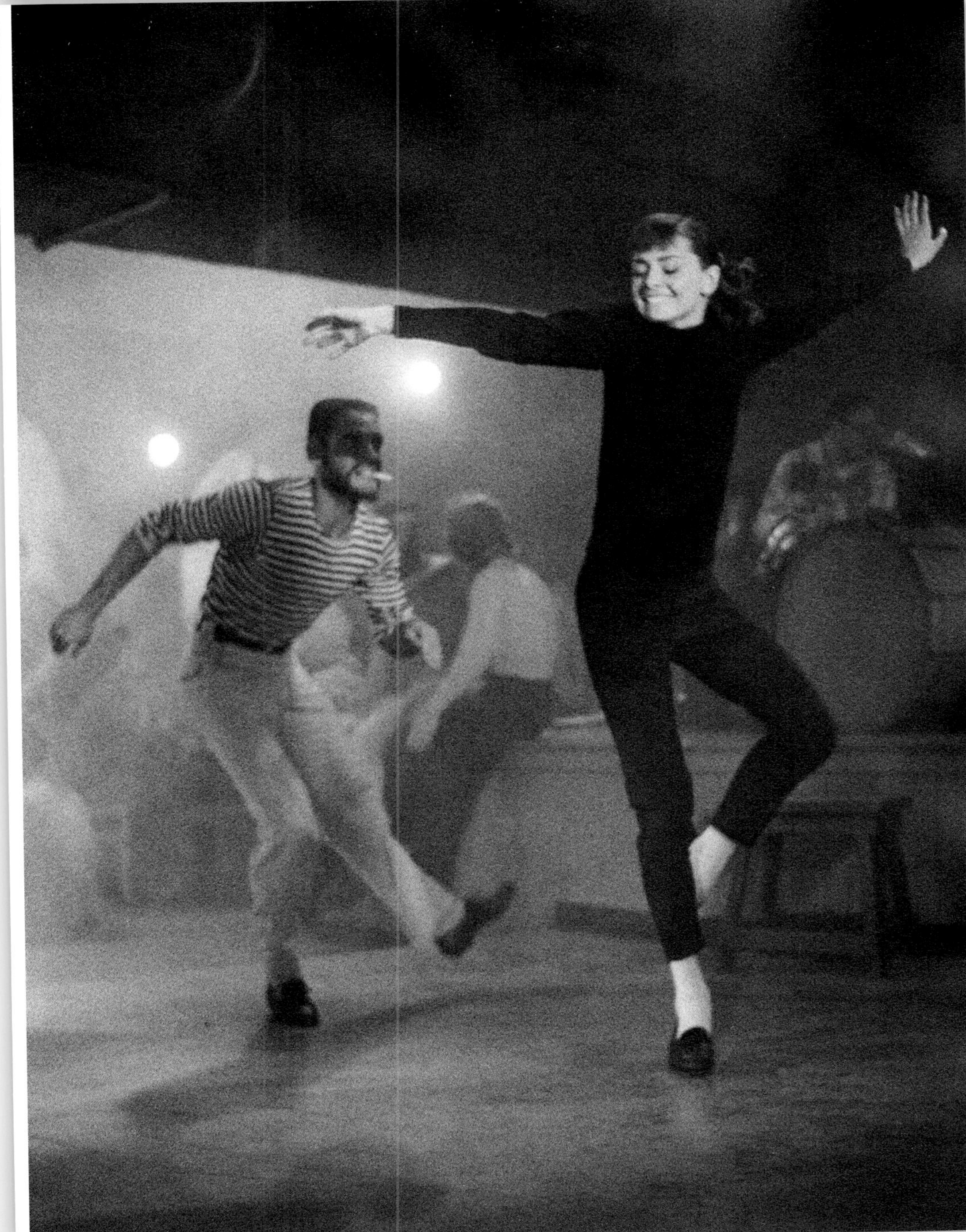

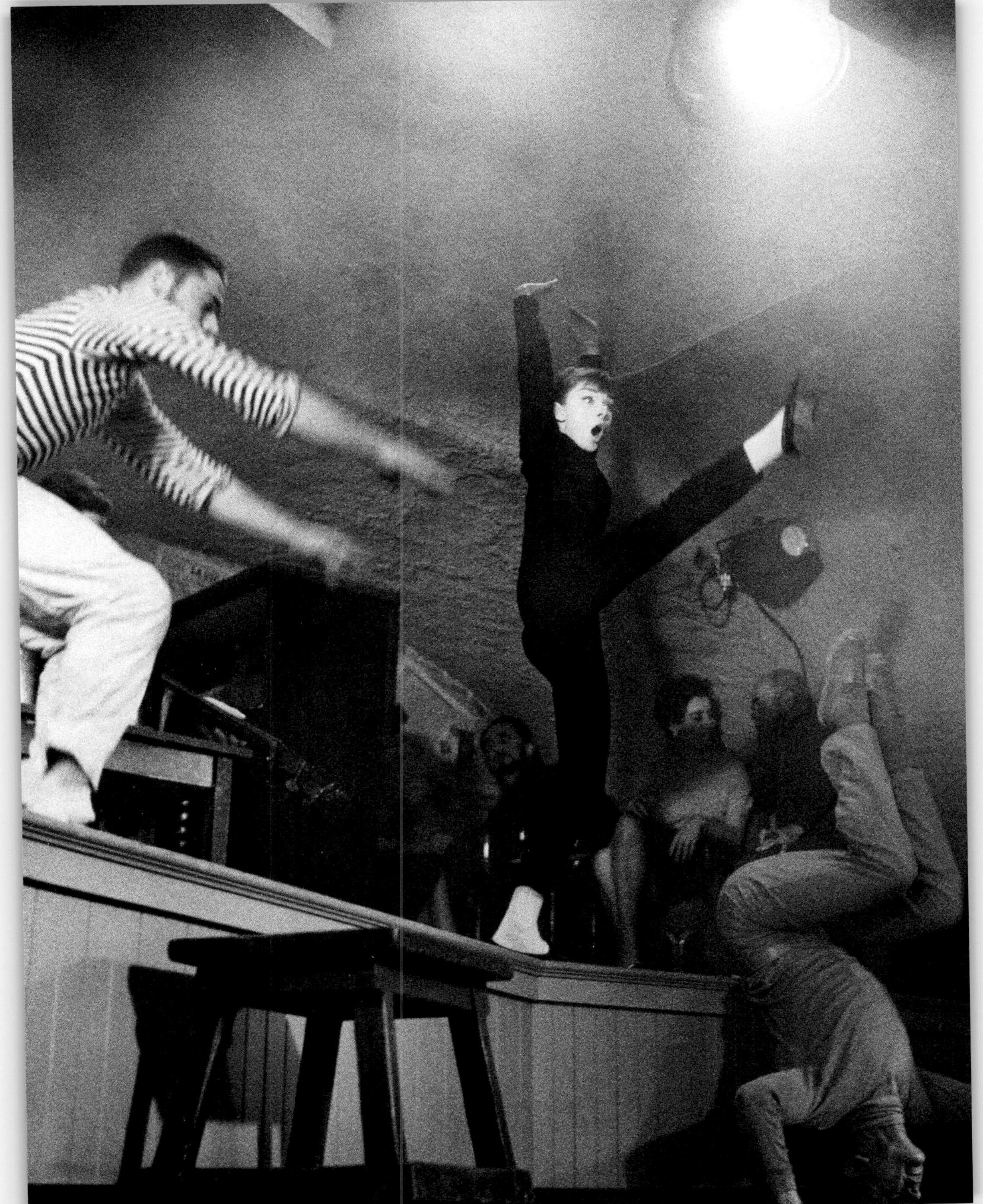

Visitors who want jazz-night-club life will certainly find it on the Left Bank, in the St-Germain-des-Prés quarter, which has become what Montparnasse used to be. Claustrophilia is the St. Germain fashion, which the *boîtes* in basements — some of them authentic eighteeth-century cellars that are still unventilated, after all these years. … The Club St. Germain and The Tabou, the first of the troglodyte caverns called Existentialist — meaning merely jive — are still feverishly popular.

—

JANET FLANNER, "LETTER FROM PARIS," *THE NEW YORKER* (MAY 21, 1949): 98–99.

Interview with Stanley Donen

Bertrand Tavernier

TAVERNIER: *Funny Face* takes a slightly different approach to traditional musicals . . .

DONEN: Yes, *j'adore ce film*. Of all the musicals I've directed, it might not be the best one, but it's my favorite. What excited me most was making a film about a photographer, about photography. I dove into it with great delight and became a great friend of Richard Avedon. I barely knew him when Roger Edens purchased a story intended for a play that had never been performed, and that revolved around the life of a fashion photographer. It had been written by someone who knew Dick Avedon very well. When I was offered the story, I said, "Okay, but why not use Avedon himself?"

Avedon played a huge part in the aesthetic creation of the film. Not so much in the ideas: the dance in the darkroom wasn't his idea, for example. But in the dramatic as well as visual atmosphere. He provided us with all sorts of details about fashion photography, because we really wanted to recreate the true feeling of haute couture, and go against the way Hollywood usually pictured it — even if this fashion world can seem "made in Hollywood" to you. Anyway, Dick was really very helpful with this desire for realism. And he also collaborated very closely on everything regarding photography: the use of filters, the work in color.

I have always been fascinated and excited by all these technical issues, and I got on very well with Dick. At first, we were given some impressive equipment and very qualified technicians, so that we could conduct our experiments freely, but it was a disaster. So we decided, Avedon and I, to do our research on our own, with less cumbersome equipment. I think that the photography in *Funny Face* was superb and technically fabulous. The tricks and the use of filters weren't gratuitous. They suited the subject perfectly, which was both light and important, funny and serious. In a way, it was a story about the struggle between simplicity and sophistication.

—

BERTRAND TAVERNIER, INTERVIEW WITH STANLEY DONEN, *CAHIERS DU CINÉMA*, NO. 143 (MAY 1, 1963).

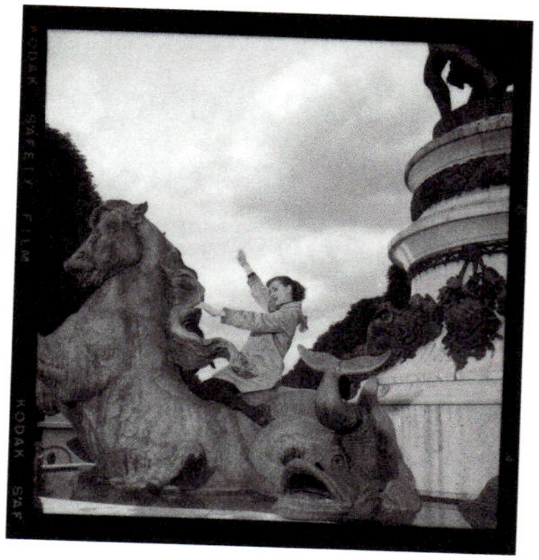

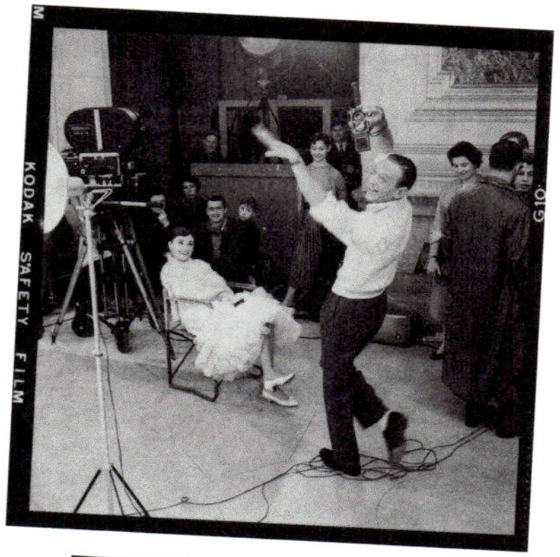

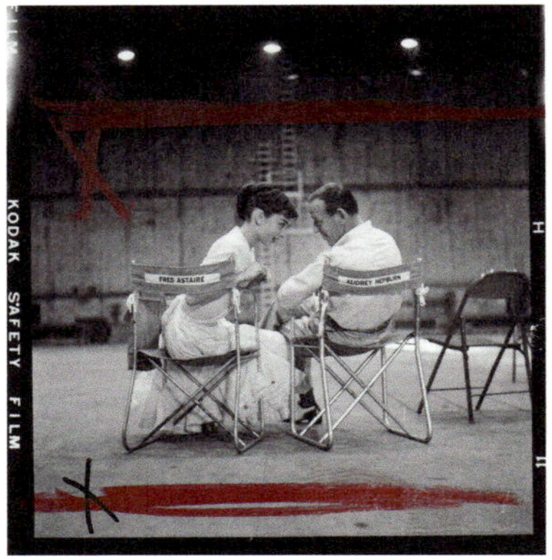

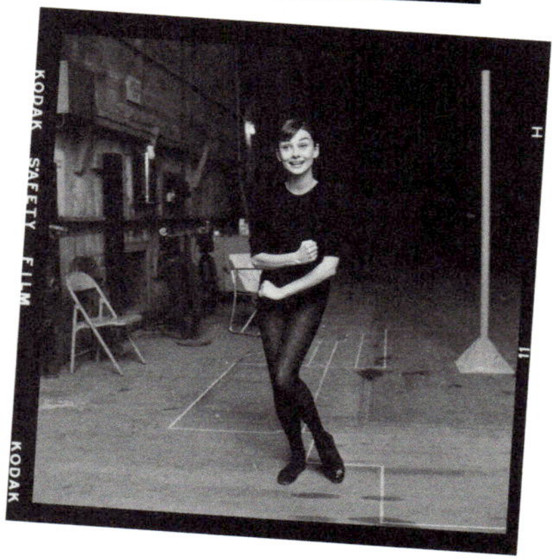

Top left, Audrey Hepburn on the set of *Funny Face*, Fontaine de l'Observatoire, Paris, June 1956
Bottom left, Audrey Hepburn and Fred Astaire on the set of *Funny Face*, Los Angeles, April 1956
Top right, Audrey Hepburn and Fred Astaire on the set of *Funny Face*, Musée du Louvre, Paris, June 1956
Bottom right, Audrey Hepburn on the set of *Funny Face*, Los Angeles, March 1956 (contact prints)

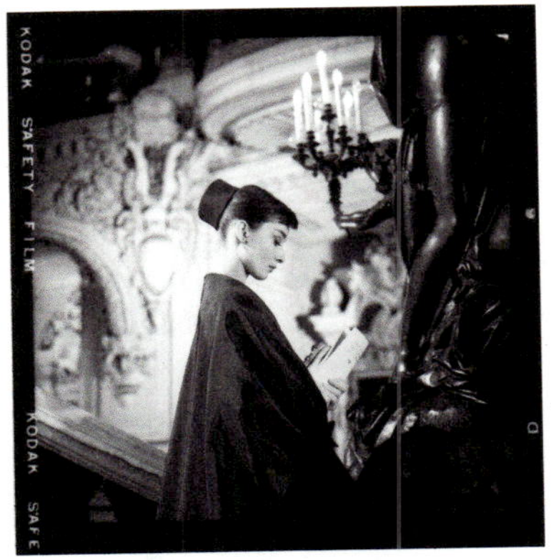

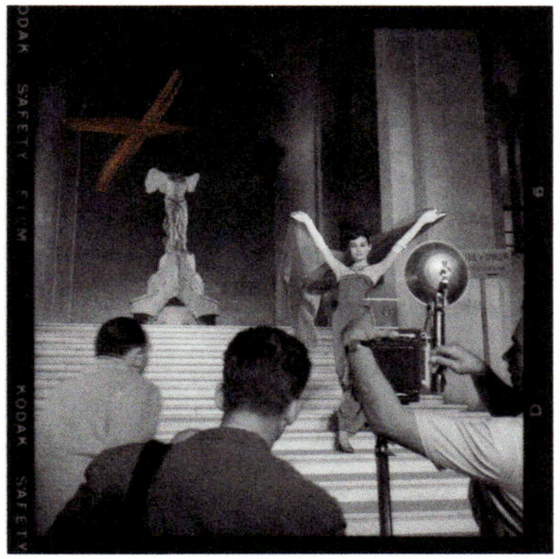

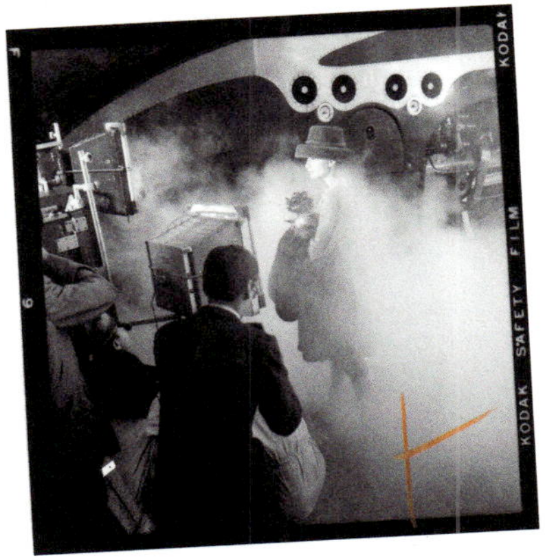

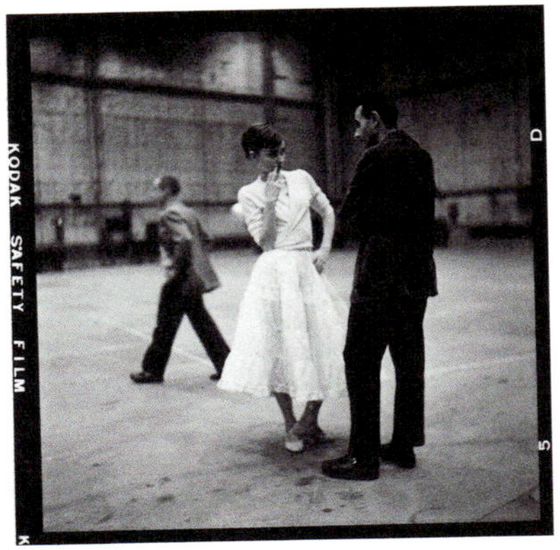

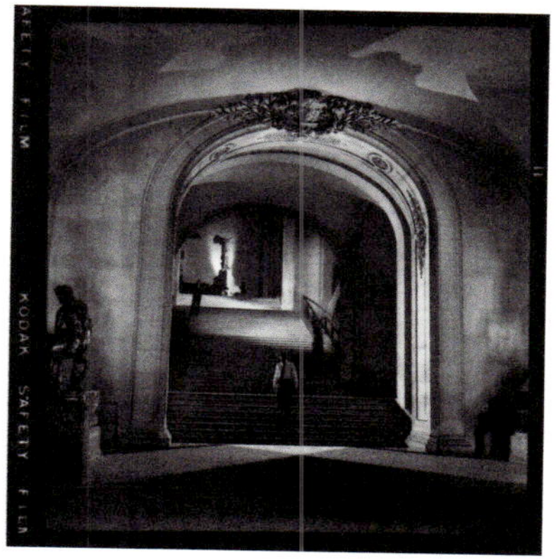

Top, left and right, Audrey Hepburn on the set of *Funny Face*, Musée du Louvre, Paris, June 1956
Middle left, Audrey Hepburn on the set of *Funny Face*, Paris, June 1956
Bottom left, Fred Astaire on the set of *Funny Face*, Musée du Louvre, Paris, June 1956
Bottom right, Audrey Hepburn and Stanley Donen on the set of *Funny Face*, Los Angeles, March 1956 (contact prints)

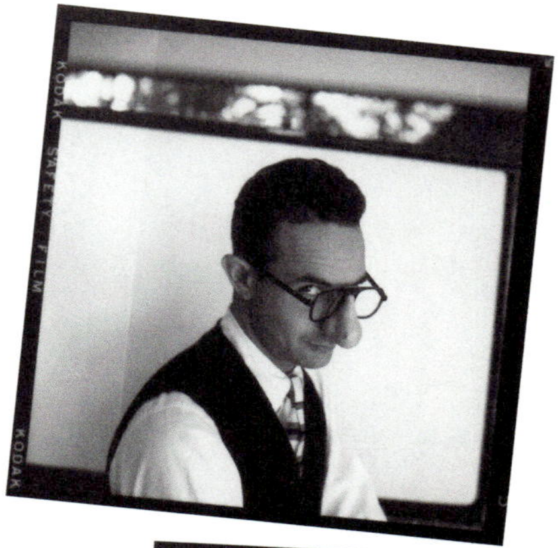

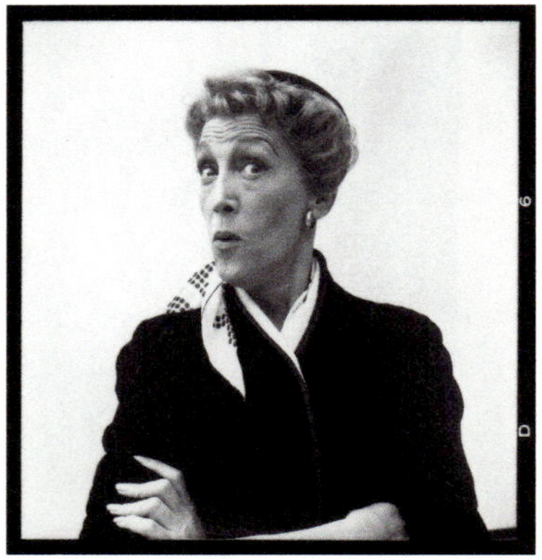

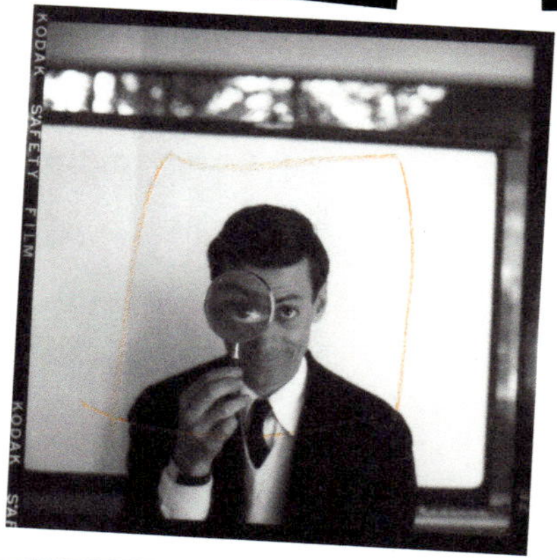

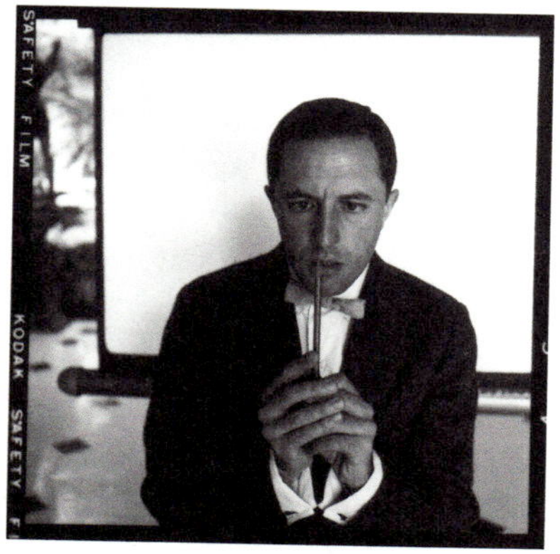

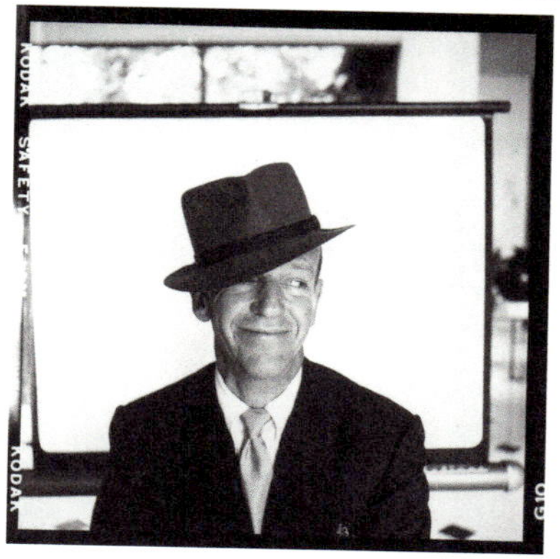

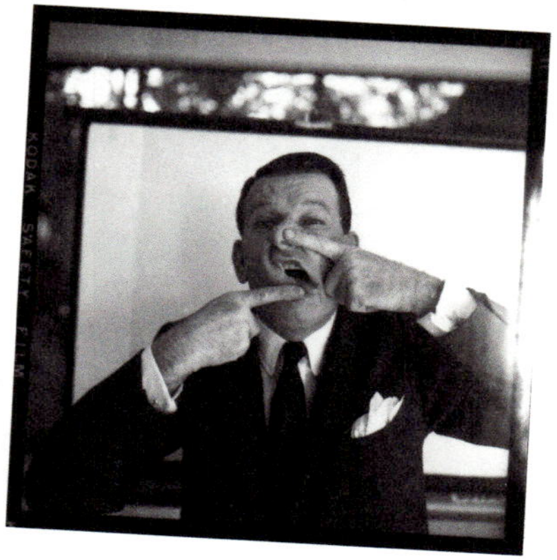

Top left, Stanley Donen, director, *Funny Face*, Los Angeles, June 1956
Middle left, Richard Avedon, consultant and photographer, *Funny Face*, Los Angeles, June 1956
Bottom left, Fred Astaire, actor, *Funny Face*, Los Angeles, June 1956
Top right, Kay Thompson, actress, *Funny Face*, Los Angeles, June 1956
Middle right, Leonard Gershe, writer, *Funny Face*, Los Angeles, June 1956
Bottom right, Roger Edens, producer, *Funny Face*, Los Angeles, June 1956

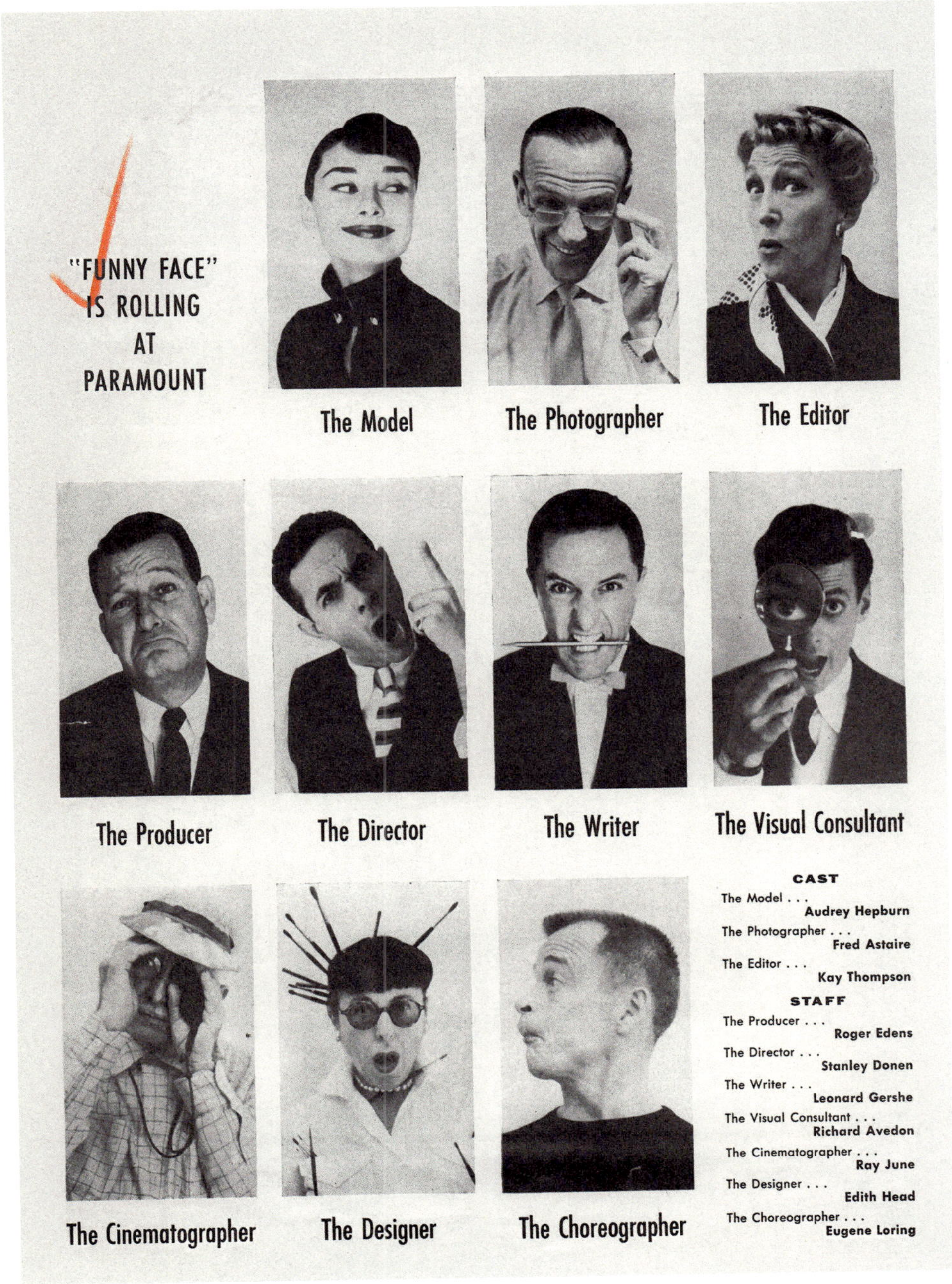

Publicity material for *Funny Face*

I’m drawn to photographs in which the light is raw and the defenses are down. I find passport pictures beautiful.

—

Richard Avedon

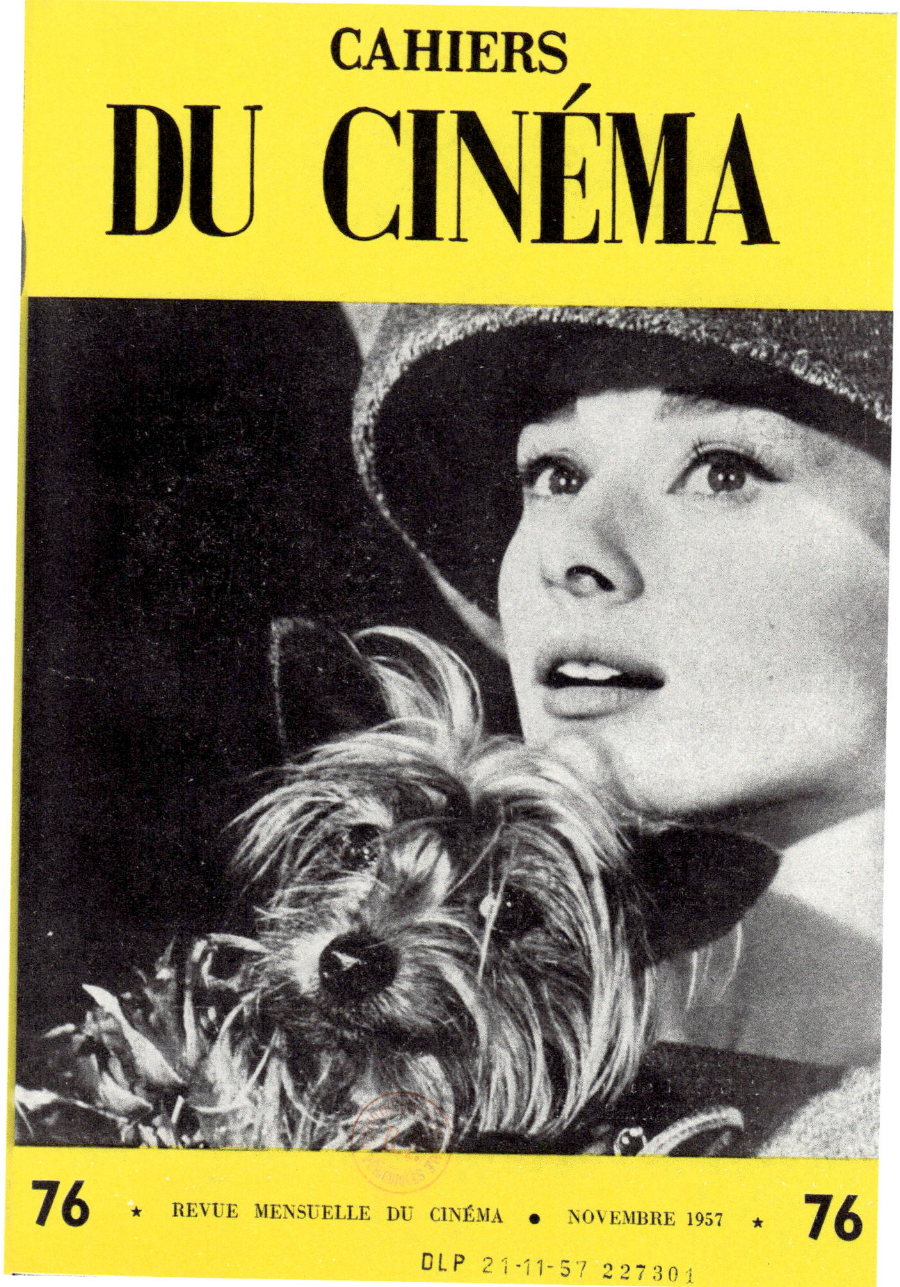

Cahiers du Cinéma, no. 76, November 1957

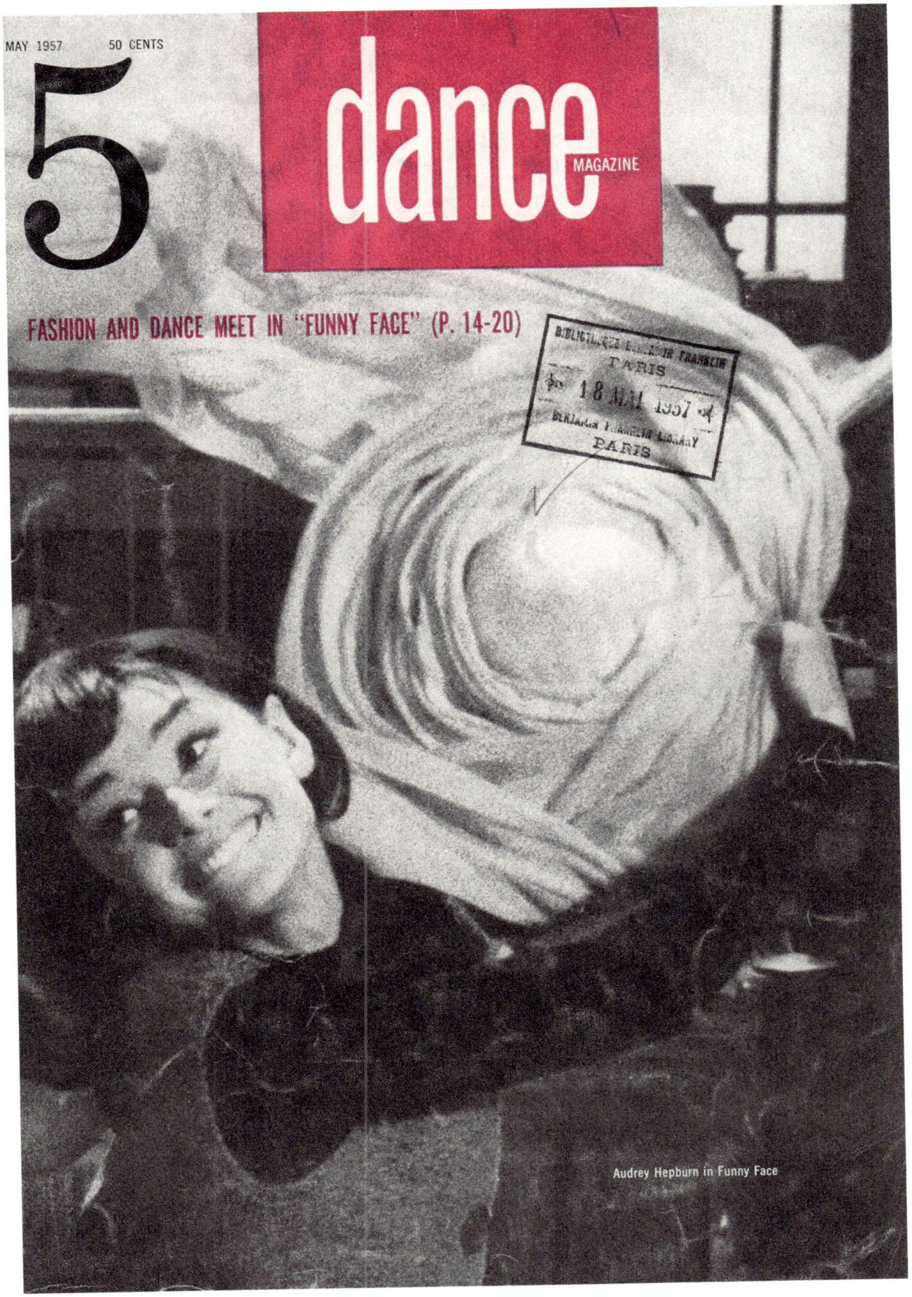

Dance Magazine, May 1957

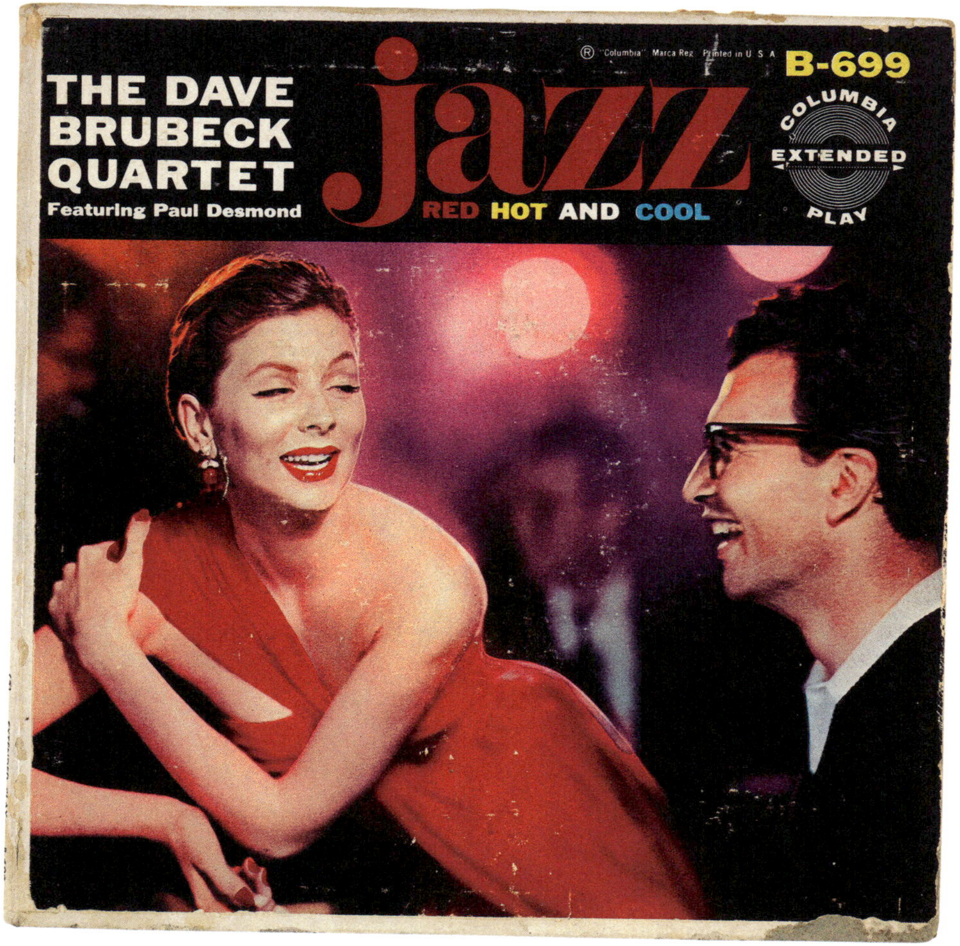

Avedon photographed the cover of the *Jazz, Red Hot and Cool* EP by The Dave Brubeck Quartet featuring Paul Desmond (Columbia, 1955). As a merchandising tie-in, a six-inch EP with excerpts from the LP was included with the purchase of Helena Rubenstein's Jazz lipstick.

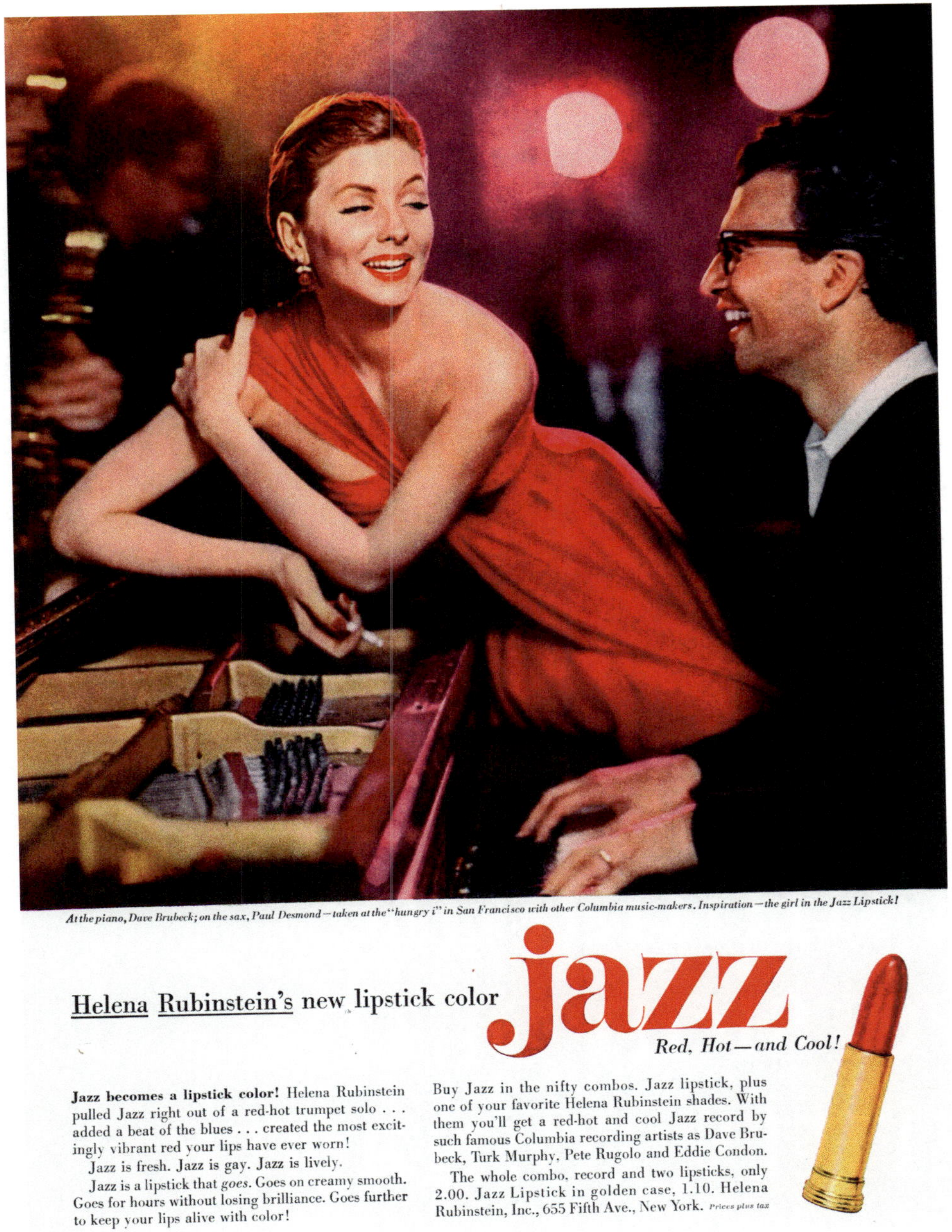

The "Jazz, Red, Hot and Cool" ad for Helena Rubinstein's lipstick, 1955; photograph by Richard Avedon

This is precisely how and where photography begins: in Paris, in this daylight, with an 8 x 10, in such a studio — a miniature version of the gritty romantic places that Nadar had worked in, and Daguerre before him. I wanted to use that frame and history as a reference for pictures that were new…

—

Richard Avedon

pp. 222–25 *(verso, recto)*, Suzy Parker, evening dress by Dior, Paris, August 1956
pp. 226–27 *(verso, recto)*, Barbara Mullen and Gardner McKay, evening dress by Balmain, Shéhérazade, Paris, August 1956
pp. 228–29 *(verso, recto)*, Suzy Parker with Robin Tattersall and Gardner McKay, evening dress by Dior, Maxim's, Paris, August 1956
pp. 230–31 *(verso, recto)*, Suzy Parker, evening dress by Dior, Paris, August 1956

Made in France

Richard Avedon

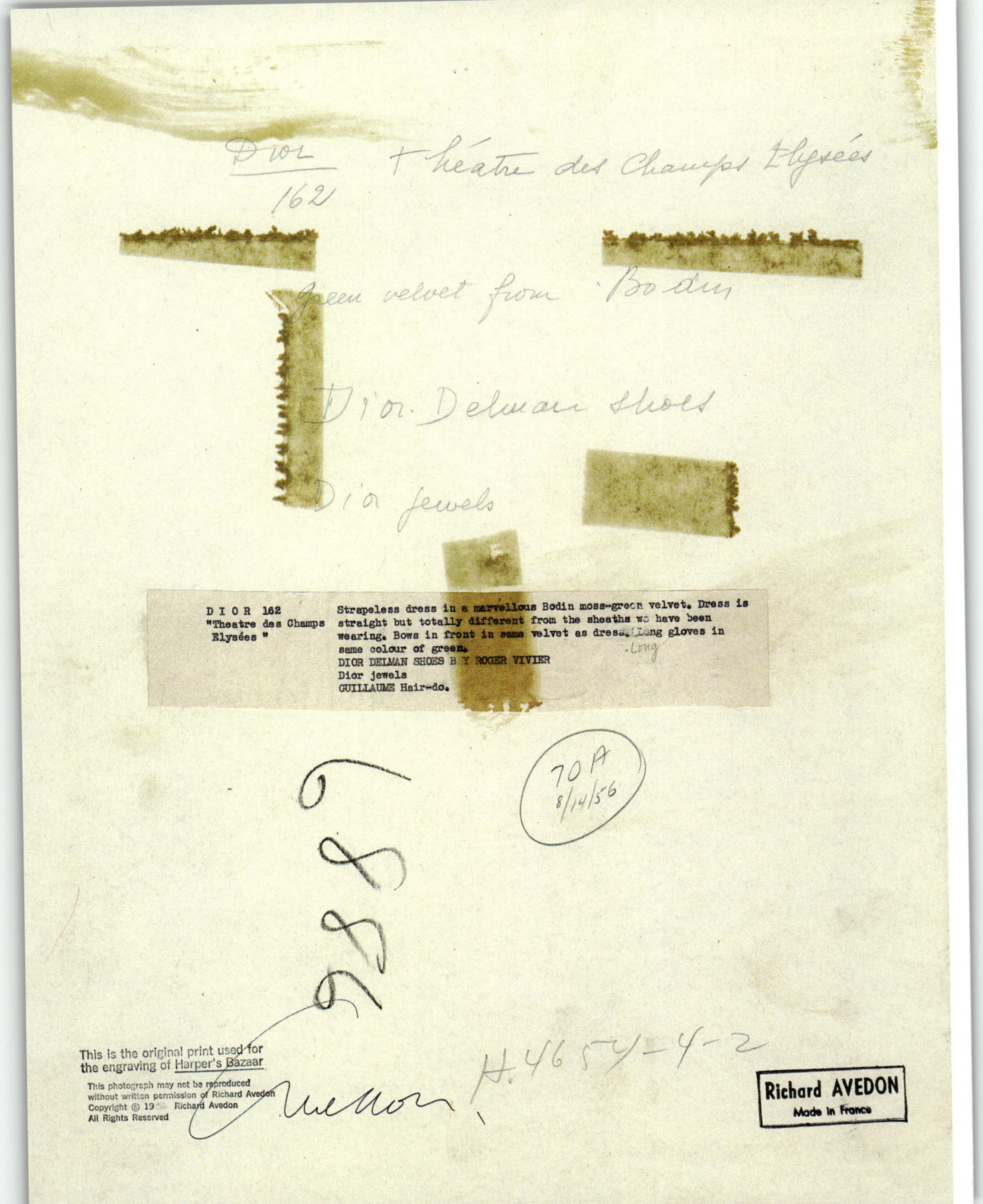

Dior
162
Théatre des Champs Elysées

green velvet from Bodin

Dior Delman shoes

Dior jewels

D I O R 162 "Theatre des Champs Elysées "	Strapeless dress in a marvellous Bodin moss-green velvet. Dress is straight but totally different from the sheaths we have been wearing. Bows in front in same velvet as dress. Long gloves in same colour of green. DIOR DELMAN SHOES B Y ROGER VIVIER Dior jewels GUILLAUME Hair-do.

70A
8/14/56

This is the original print used for the engraving of Harper's Bazaar

H.4654-4-2

Richard AVEDON
Made in France

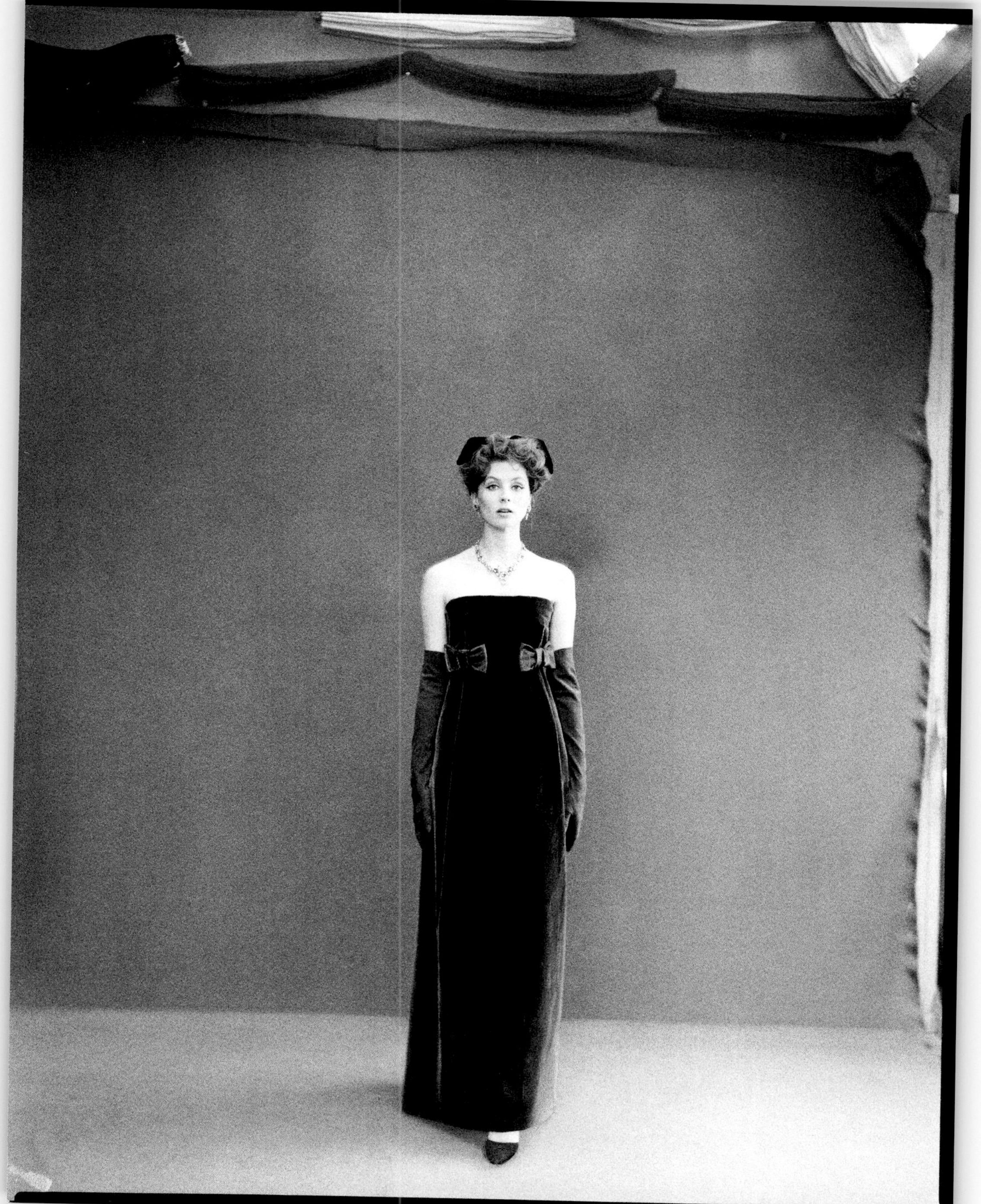

Dior 93 Menuet ; lace from Dognin

Dache necklace (better not mention because of Dior !!)

PARIS OFFICE
HARPER's BAZAAR
August 12th

PHOTOGRAPHS BY RICHARD AVEDON

DIOR 93 "Menuet"

Black chantilly lace dress made over the palest flesh coloured chiffon. This wonderfully feminine dress is strapless. Black lace scarf. Velvet belt tied in bow with two ends falling down front. GUILLAUME Hair-do.

6885

69
8/14/56

Avedon

H 4639-2-1

Richard AVEDON
Made in France

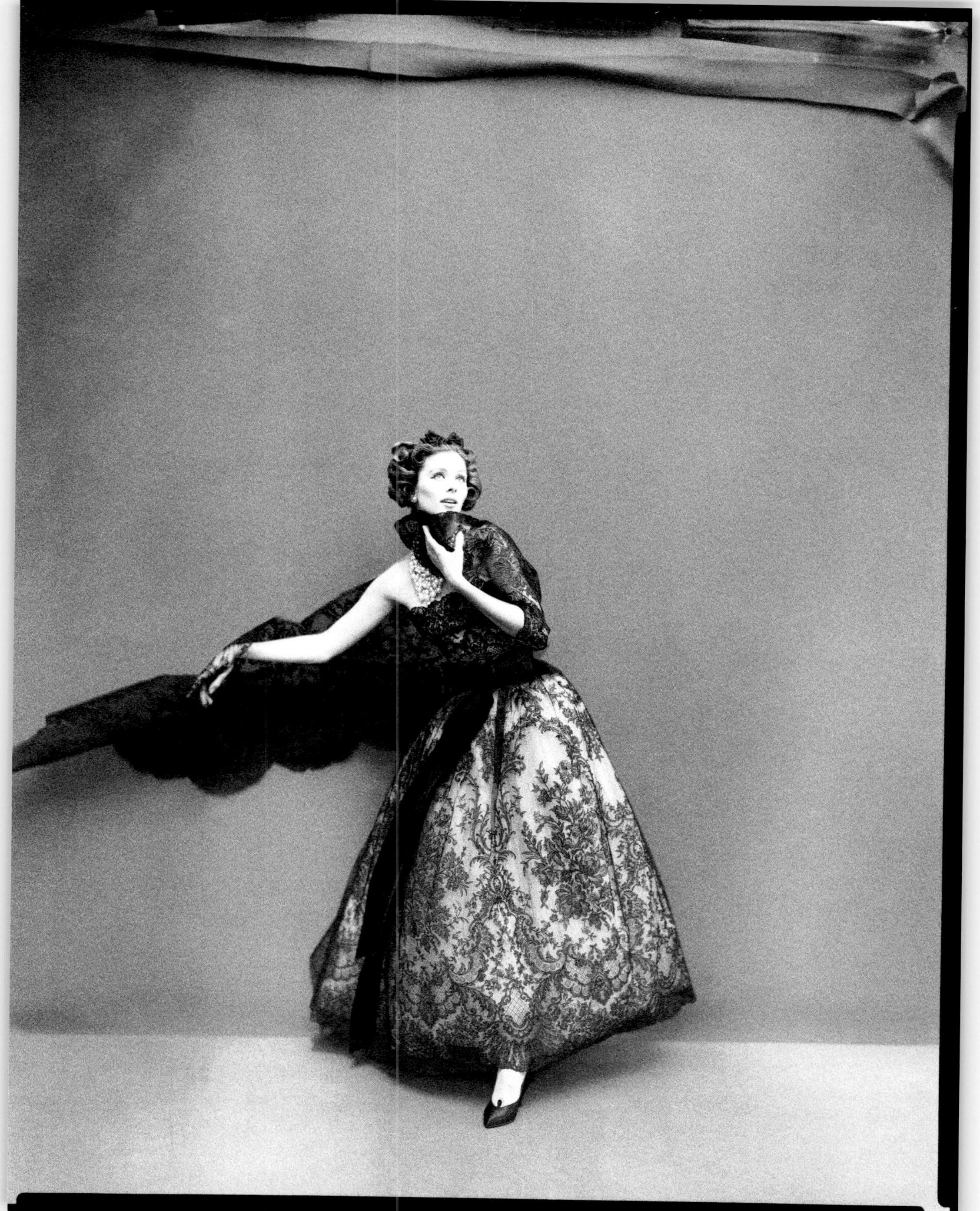

BALMAIN
407

Short dinner dress in white satin from Lesage. Dress is deliciously embroidered in Chinese blue red and cream coloured beads. Chinese blue satin at bosom and hemline. The hem of Chinese satin comes from where embroidery stops. Chinese blue satin scarf.
(Embroidery from Lesage)
GUILLAUME hair-do.
Arpad rhinestone and crystal bracelet.
Photo taken at Shéhérazade night club

HARPER'S BAZAAR
Feature Paris 586
Issue Oct.
Number 10-63
Date 8-16-56

This is the original print used for the engraving of Harper's Bazaar

Richard AVEDON
Made in France

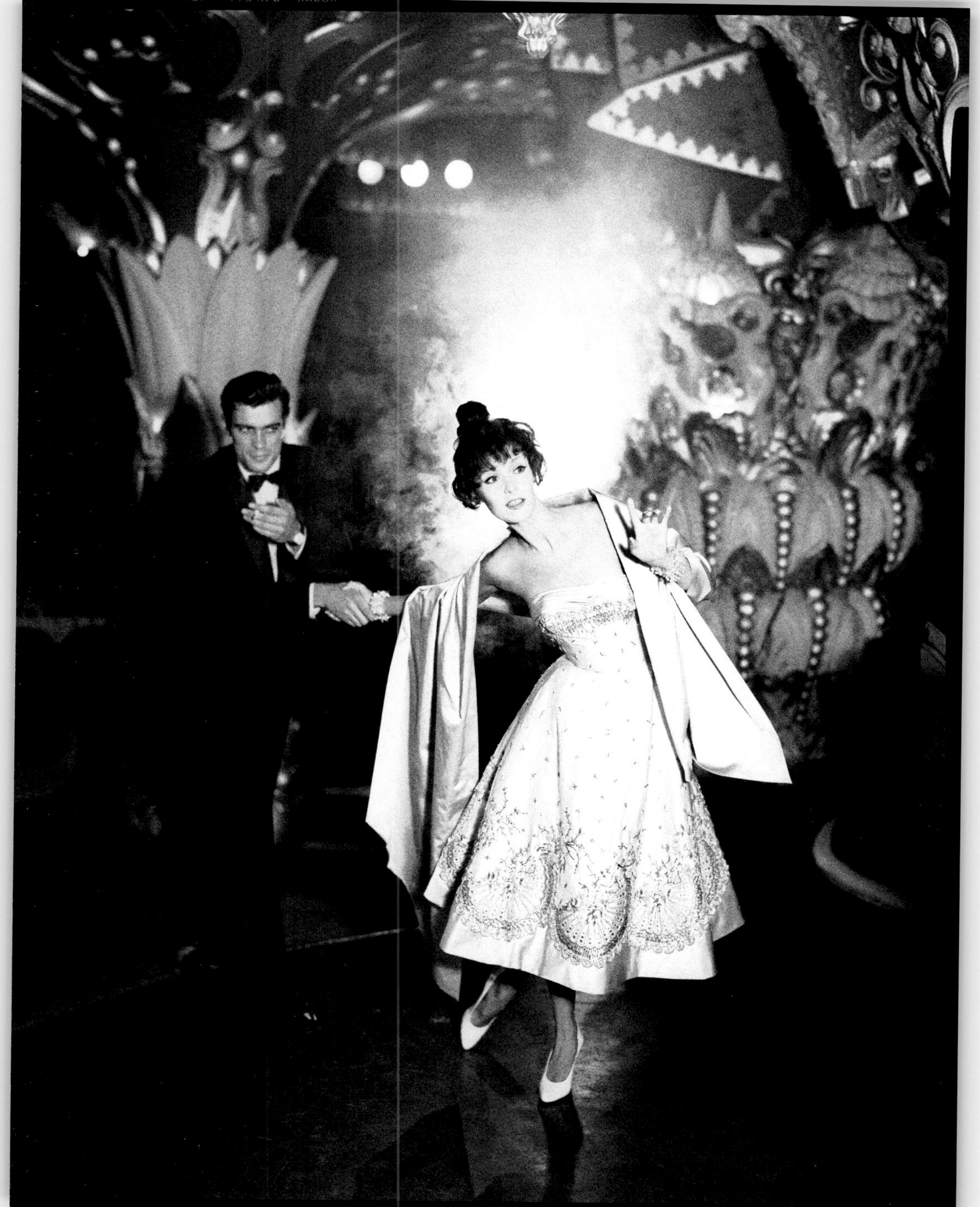

AUGUST 9, 1956

PHOTOGRAPHS BY RICHARD AVEDON

DIOR
107
"Opera de Vienne"

Very beautiful red satin dress, printed with a grey pattern like lace. Although this is a sweeping full evening dress, with off-shoulder décolleté — a dress to be worn at the opera, etc. — it has sleeves coming to the elbow. This elbow-length sleeve is repeated in many of Dior's full evening dresses

Photo taken at Maxim's bar.
Dior Delman shoes by Roger Vivier –
Dior 107 "Opera de Vienne"
to face
Patou "Aladin"

Hair do by Guillaume

6792

65 f
8/6/56

(A)
P. 4

This is the original print used for the engraving of Harper's Bazaar

Avedon

Avedon

H 4577-2-2

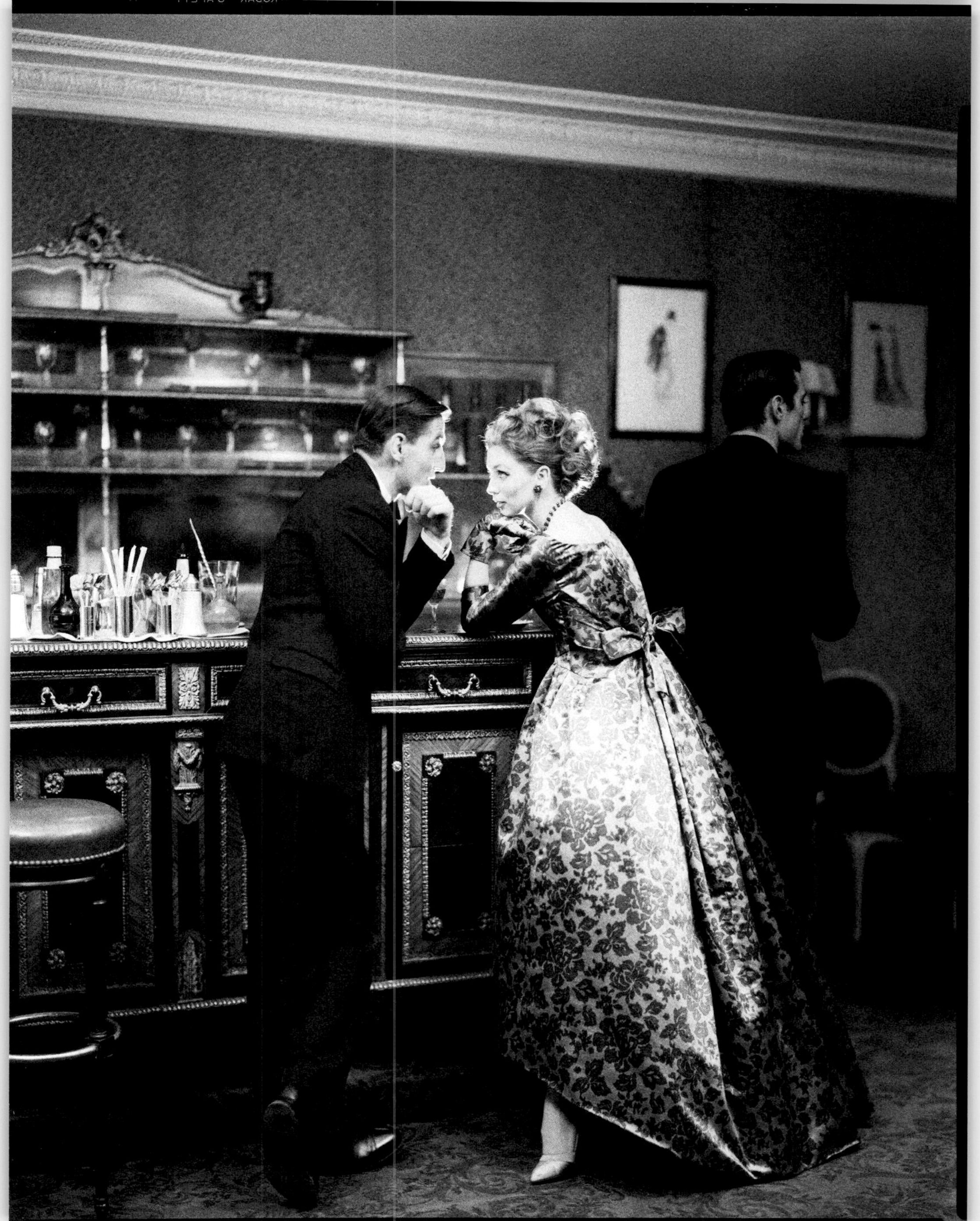

PARIS OFFICE
HARPER'S BAZAAR
August 12th, 1956

PHOTOGRAPHS BY RICHARD AVEDON

DIOR 100
"Musique de Nuit"

Long dinner dress in smoke or elephant grey faille from Lajoinie. Note thet the Vee décolleté shows rounded bosom. Note also that although this is a full décolleté dress, sleeves reach to below elbow. Wide faille stole fringed at edges. This elbow sleeve is in many full Dior evening dresses.
GUILLAUME Hair-do. Suzy Parker

6886

69D
8/14/56

This is the original print used for the engraving of Harper's Bazaar

Avedon p. 144

Richard AVEDON
Made in France

HARPER'S BAZAAR
Feature Avedon - Paris 1412
Issue Oct.
Number 10-70
Date 8-17-56

H4644-2-2

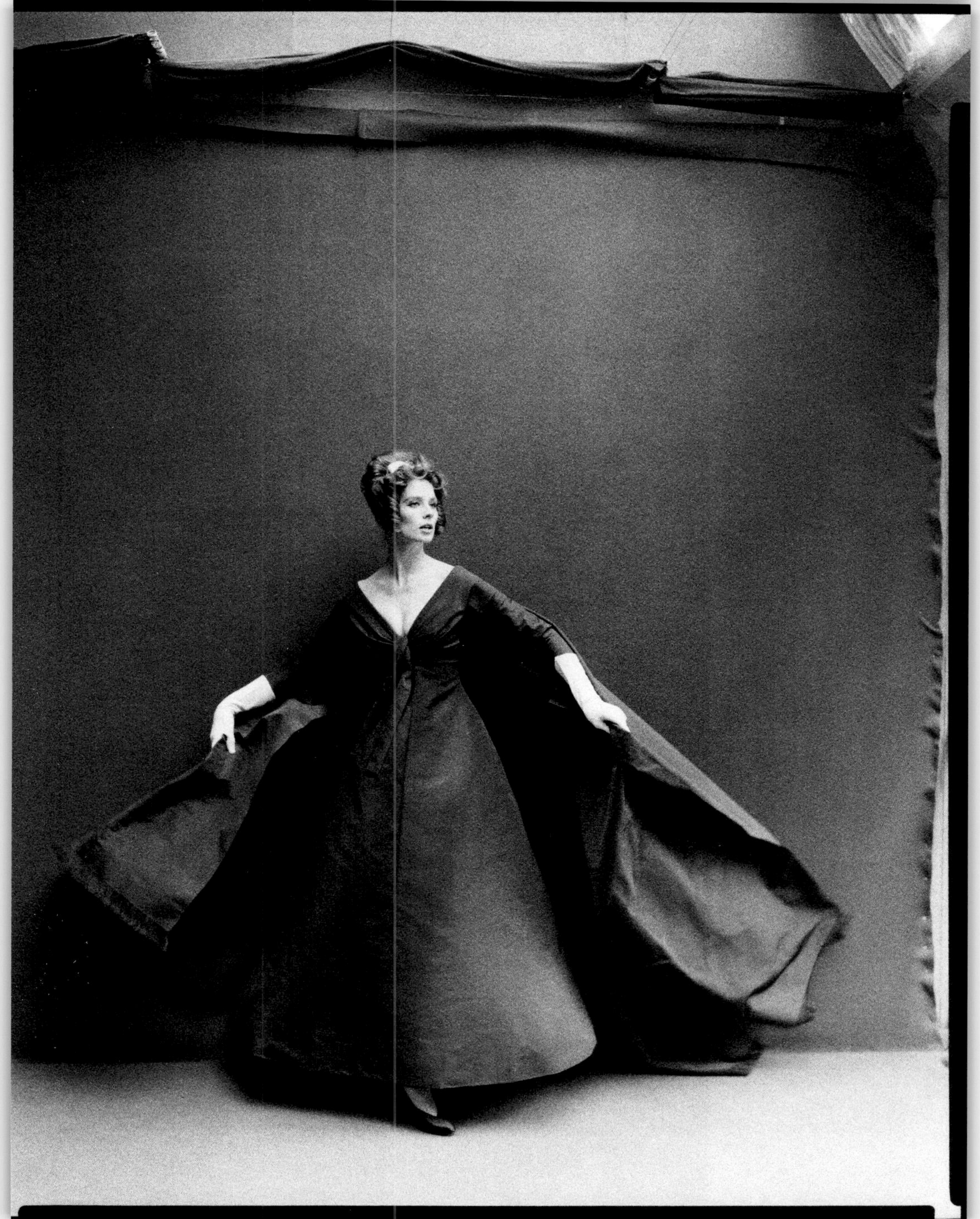

Avedon:
Carmel Snow said: Do you realize what *Harper's Bazaar* and your work mean to the economy of France? We have to recreate the sense of an illusory Paris.

Guerrin:
A sense of . . . Champagne?

Avedon:
Exactly. I photographed a prewar Paris, a Lubitsch Paris, a Paris that did not exist. And it worked ! The buyers came, the world came back to Paris hungrily.

—

HENRY BÉHAR AND MICHEL GUERRIN, "AVEDON" (INTERVIEW WITH RICHARD AVEDON), *LE MONDE* (JULY 1, 1993).

The 8 x 10 is what Nadar, Brady and Atget used — a direct descendant of the camera obscura — and the only things that have changed since its invention are the speed of the film and the sharpness of the lens. It has a very shallow depth of field, which means you can throw the background out of focus, reducing the sum of detail and creating an ambiguous narrative relation between the knowable (what's sharp) and the unknowable (what's blurred), which is what René Clair does, with gauze, in a film like *Le Million*.

—

Richard Avedon

Made in France

Richard Avedon

There's a picture I wish I could have taken, but I didn't have a camera with me. It was my first or second time in Paris, an August after the war. I was with my first wife, Doe. We wanted to see a sex show. One evening, drifting around Montmartre, we went into a cabaret called the Boule Bleue. It was like every *apache boîte* in every Signoret movie, though at that time of year the house was empty. The waiter immediately brought us a bottle of champagne — it was included in the cover. Then suddenly a crowd arrived — a party of deaf-mutes. I have no idea where they came from, because they weren't communicating in a spoken language; they were signing. They took their seats and the show began. It was everything you could dream of: an emcee in a white tux with a top hat and cane, musclemen in gold jock straps, bare-breasted girls in spangles and plumage.

At the climax of the striptease, the dancers left the stage and fanned out into the house, taking partners from the audience. The deaf-mutes couldn't hear the music, but they could feel it through their bodies and through the half-naked bodies pressed against theirs. They were ecstatic. After a while, a drumroll signalled the finale, the music stopped, the performers and the band abruptly vanished, stranding the deaf-mutes on the dance floor, and for a minute they seemed baffled. Then someone ushered them out to their tour bus. All but one. He stayed behind, looking lost, even trapped, and wandered over to the deserted orchestra pit, picked up a horn, and blew a sound on it — a strange, raucous, terrible sound that resembled his expression. For some reason, this scene reminds me of who I really was in Paris, with Carmel Snow, taking these pictures of clothes.

—

RICHARD AVEDON, *MADE IN FRANCE*
(SAN FRANCISCO: FRAENKEL GALLERY, 2001).

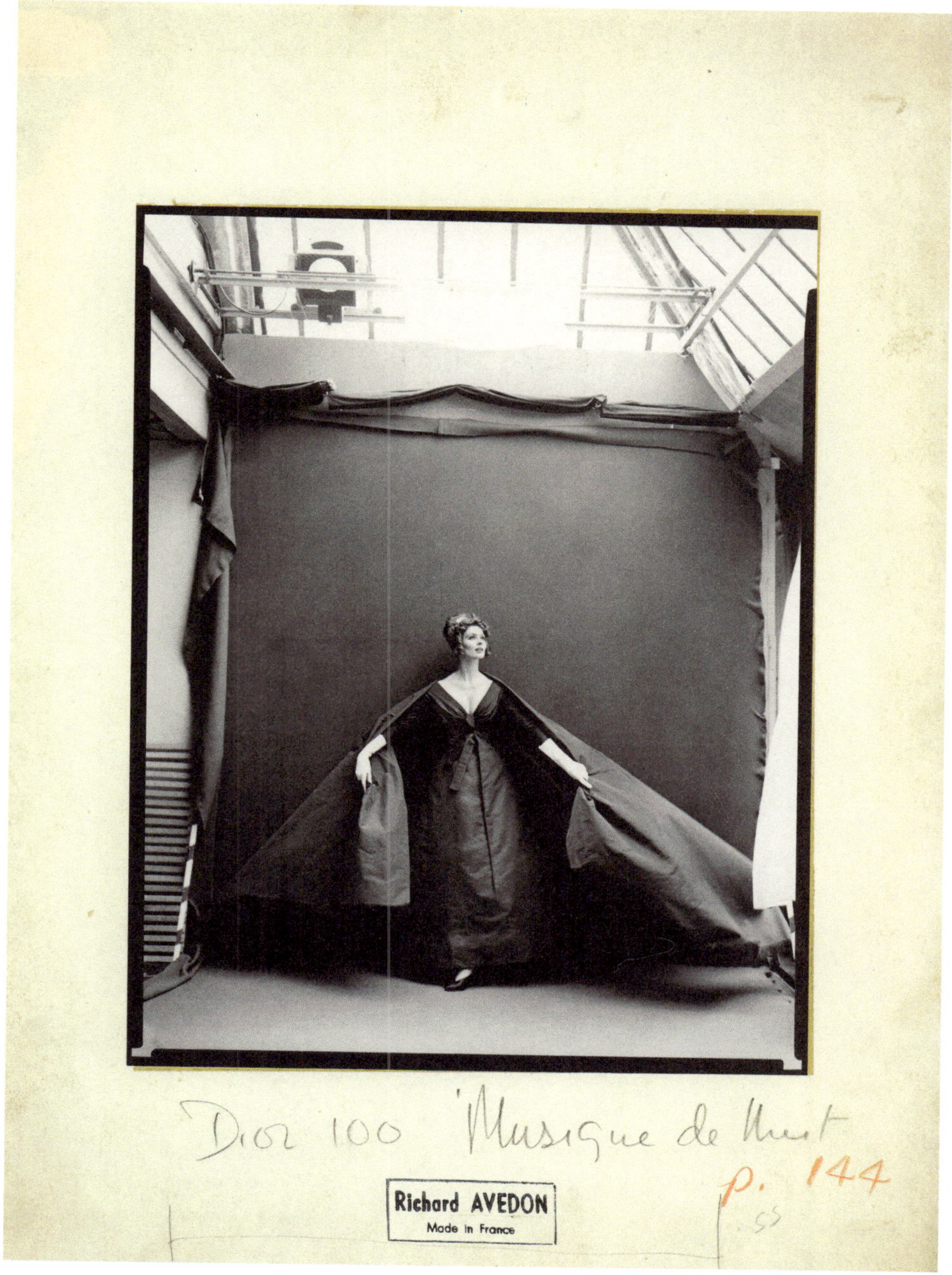

Richard Avedon: Made in France, text by Judith Thurman (San Francisco: Fraenkel Gallery, 2001). Printed in a limited edition of 100, signed and numbered, including a signed original Avedon print. Slipcased in a custom wooden box

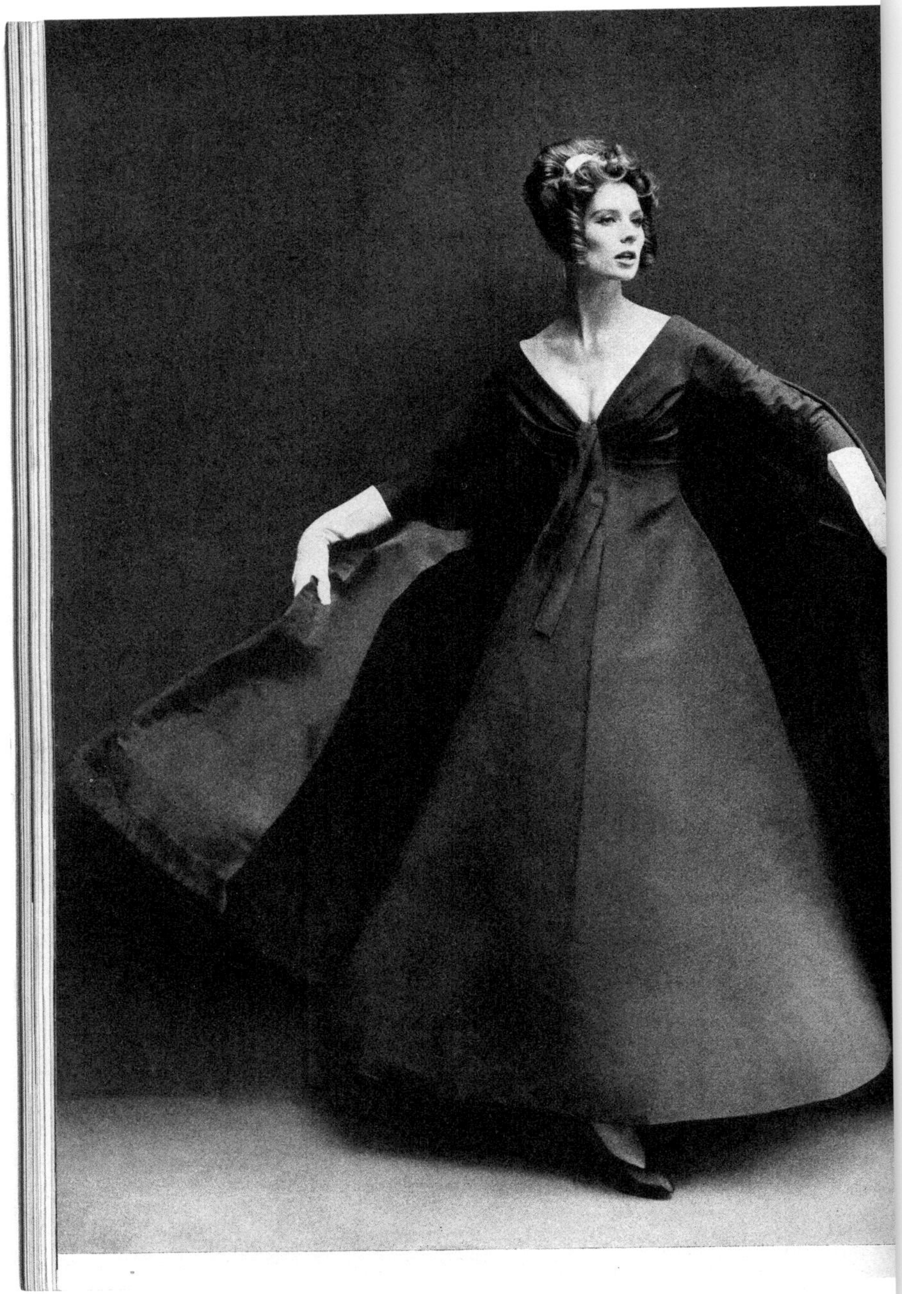

RICHARD AVEDON

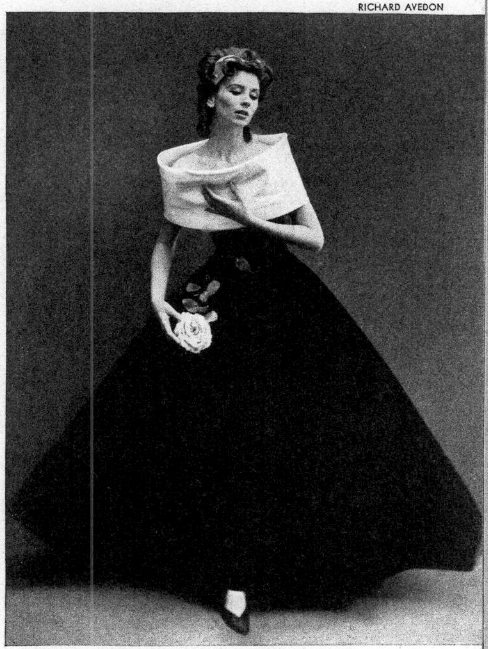

Dior's Sleeved Décolleté (opposite): His prettiest evening news, in the smoke gray faille he and all Paris loves—a bell-skirted evening dress, beautifully V'd to bare the shoulders, then sleeved past the elbow. And it floats, here, in a scarf as big as a cape. Lajoinie faille. At Bergdorf Goodman; I. Magnin.

Griffe's Fichu Top (above): A deep, shining circle of white satin, settled on the shoulders of his romantic ball-dress, its skirt a sweep of black velvet, pinned with a single blush pink rose. Ducharne satin; Bianchini velvet. At Bergdorf Goodman.

Coup de foudre

Teachers

Alexey Brodovitch
Les Girls

Avedon had three mentors in the formative years of his career. Russian émigré Alexey Brodovitch, art director of *Harper's Bazaar* from 1934–1958, recognized talent in the I.D. photographs and portraits Avedon took while in the Merchant Marine. Brodovitch was instrumental in bringing the visual culture of the European avant-garde to the U.S. Avedon, his eager pupil, soaked it up. Carmel Snow not only introduced the twenty-something Avedon to the work of Marcel Proust, she also introduced him to the *Bazaar's* Paris editor, Marie-Louise Bousquet. And it was Bousquet who guided the young photographer to capture a Paris "that didn't exist," as Avedon later recalled.

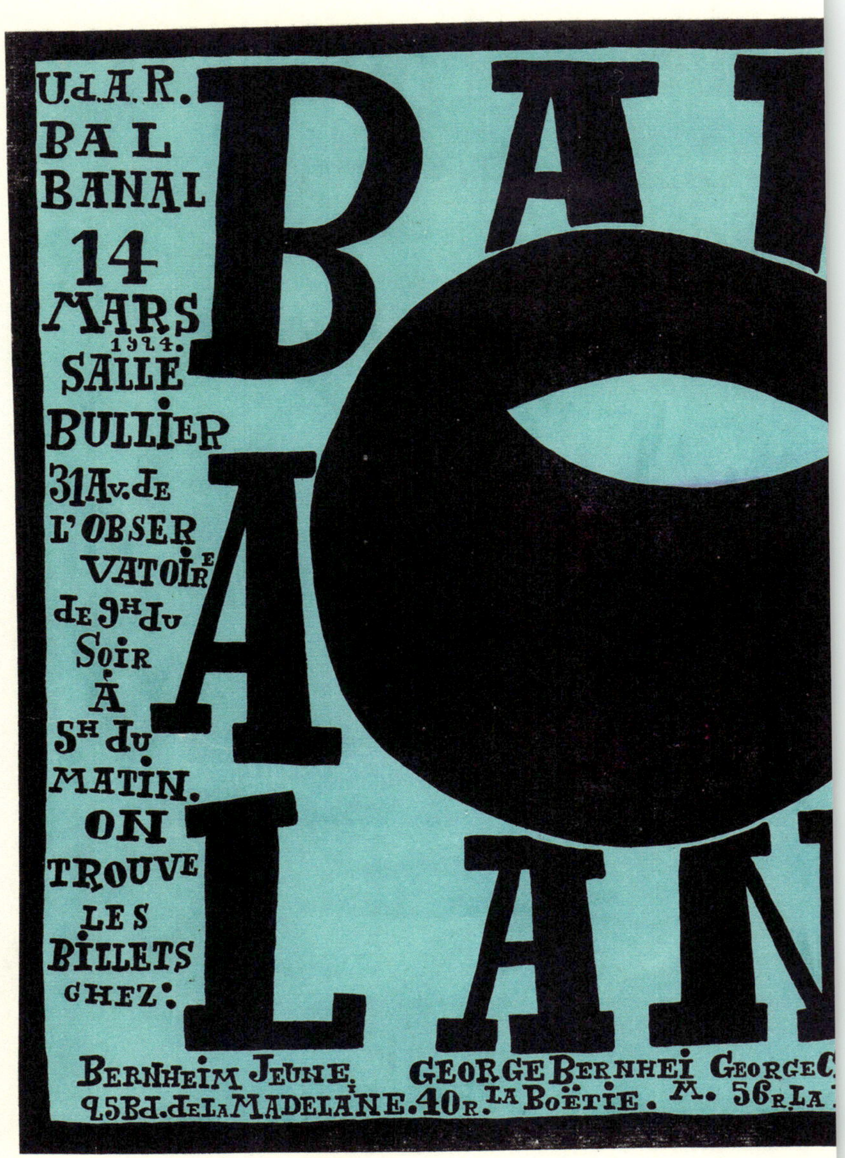
U.d.A.R.
BAL
BANAL
14
MARS
1924.
SALLE
BULLIER
31 Av. de
L'OBSER
VATOIRE
de 9h du
Soir
À
5h du
MATIN.
ON
TROUVE
LES
BILLETS
CHEZ:
BAL
A
LAN
BERNHEIM JEUNE, GEORGE BERNHEIM. GEORGE C
95 Bd. de la MADELAINE. 40 R. LA BOËTIE. 56 R. LA

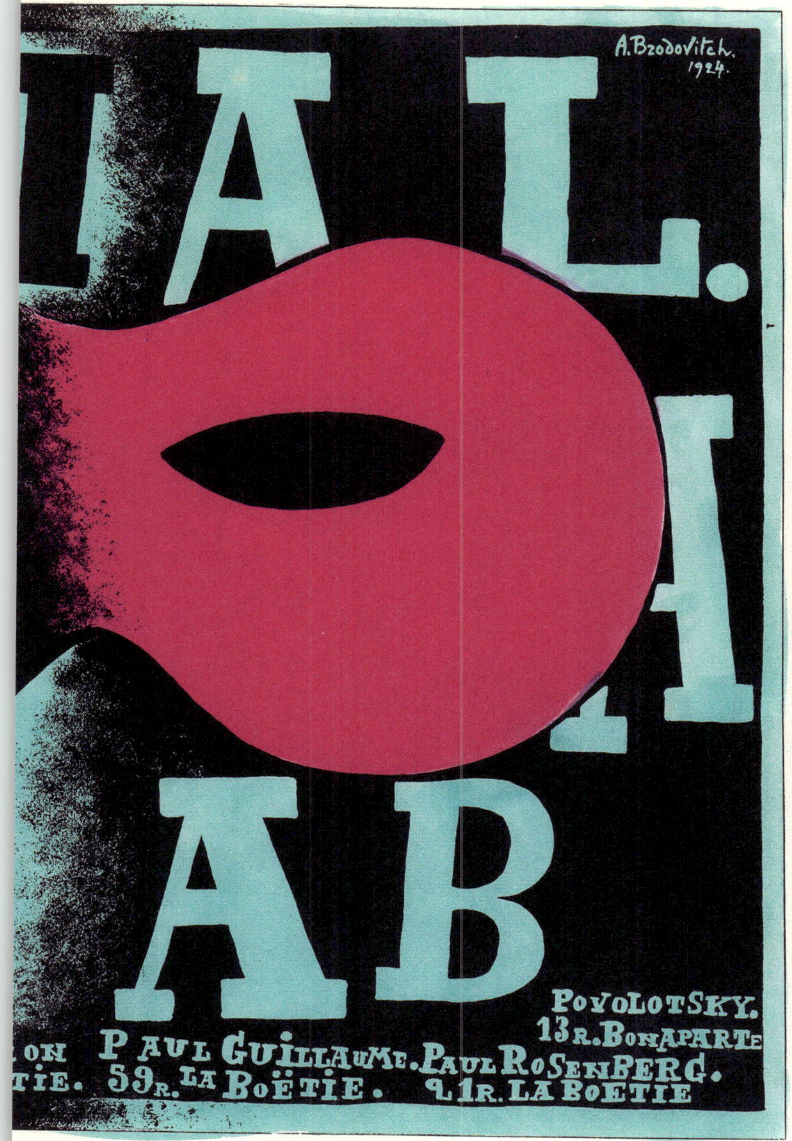

Alexey Brodovitch's winning entry in the poster competition for the *Bal Banal* artists' soiree, 1924

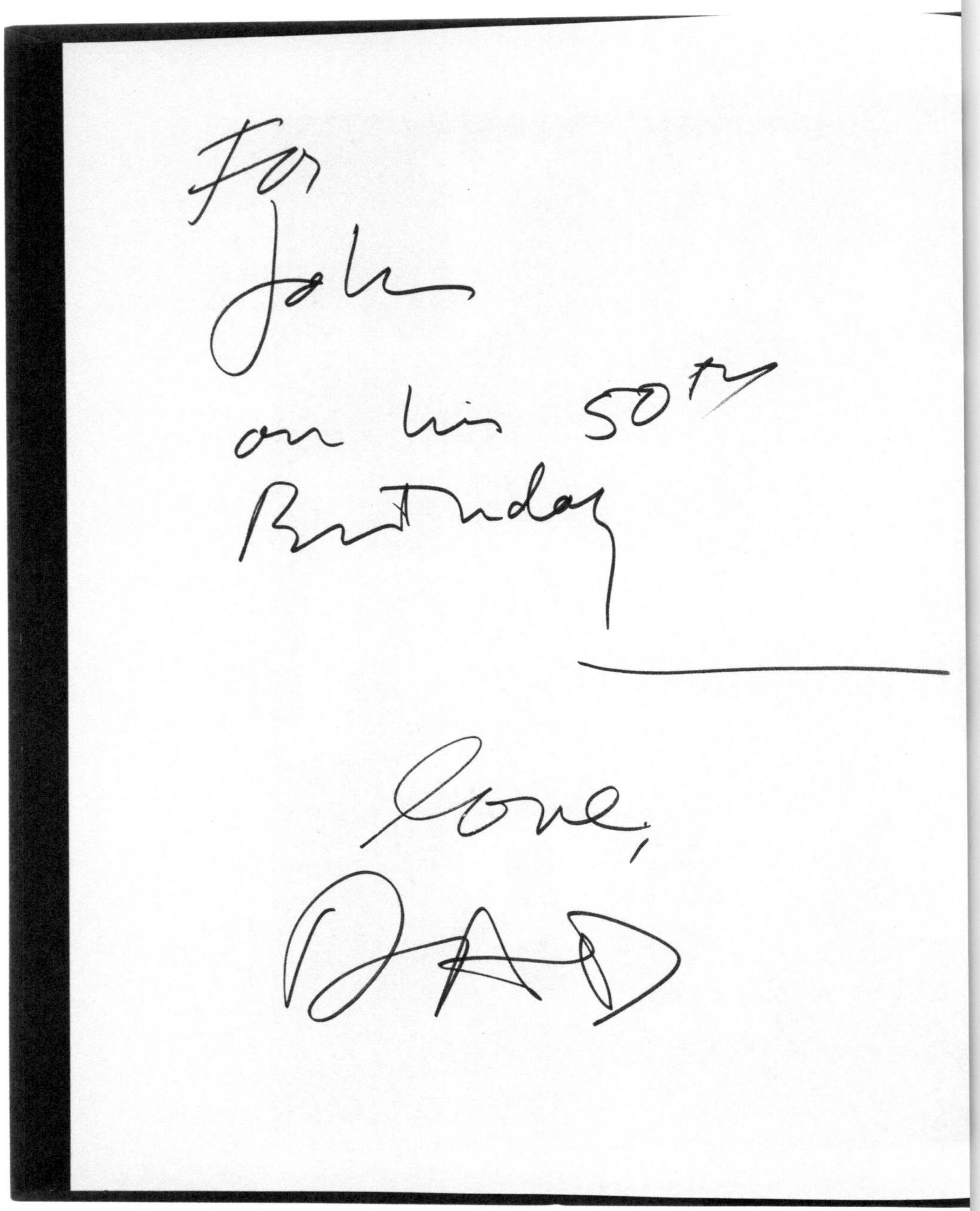
For John on his 50th Birthday

Love, DAD

Alexey Brodovitch

my Teacher

Avedon gave his son John a copy of Kerry William Purcell's biography, *Alexey Brodovitch*, as a fiftieth birthday present.

February 1940

Paris openings

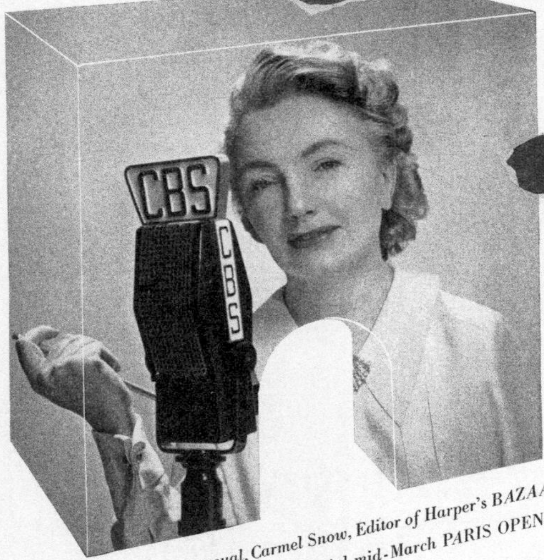

1940

This year, as usual, Carmel Snow, Editor of Harper's BAZAAR, is in Paris, editing the special mid-March PARIS OPENINGS issue of Harper's BAZAAR.

And, again as usual, Mrs. Snow will broadcast the latest fashion news from the very midst of the collections. She will speak over the Columbia Broadcasting System at 2:15 to 2:30 P. M., E. S. T. on February 5th. This is a truly great date in fashion history—and one which, for pure drama as well as for important fashion facts, you must not miss.

Fashion news, like all other news, is slow coming through these days—but this quarter-hour will be packed with information straight off the griddle.

Harper's BAZAAR

For the complete picture of Fashions for Spring, read

MARCH 1st . . *American Spring Fashions*

MARCH 15th . . *The Complete Story of the Paris Openings*

APRIL 1st . . *Beauty and the Bride*

"Paris Openings, 1940," with Carmel Snow, *Harper's Bazaar*, February 1940, p. 117

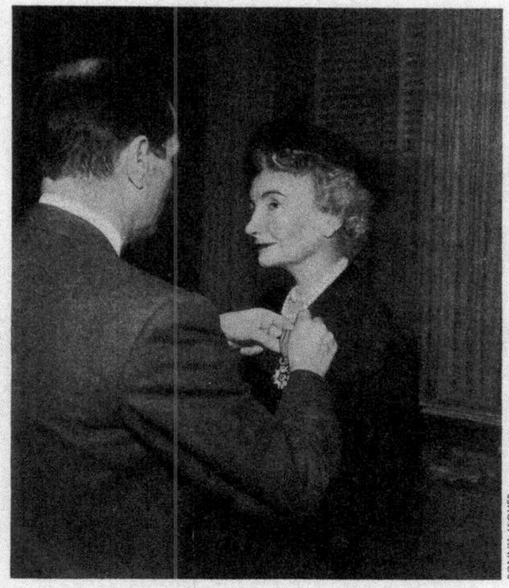

Harper's Bazaar's Editor Receives the LEGION OF HONOR

• It is with great pride that we report that our editor, Carmel Snow, has been made Chevalier of the Legion of Honor. On April 13, in a simple ceremony, M. Ludovic Chancel, Consul General of France, presented the decoration in the name of the President of the Republic, citing Mrs. Snow's long friendship for France, her influence since the end of the war in re-establishing the prestige of French art, French crafts and French design in the United States. Carmel Snow estimates that she has covered the Paris collections at least sixty times. She visited France twice during the war, once in the winter of 1940, and again in the dark winter of 1944–45, when she flew to Paris to carry to her old friends and through them to thousands of workers in the fashion trades a message of confidence and friendship. The little red ribbon which Mrs. Snow wears in her buttonhole is a recognition that international understanding is promoted not only over the conference tables, but in daily business, and particularly by a respect for and generous understanding of talent and skill.

'S BAZAAR, JUNE 1949

"Harper's Bazaar's editor receives the Legion of Honor," *Harper's Bazaar*, June 1949, p. 53. Snow's medal is being pinned by the Consul General of France, Ludovic Chancel.

Les Salons de Paris

Denise Bourdet

Today Marie-Louise Bousquet, director of *Harper's Bazaar* in France, holds her court at the Place du Palais-Bourbon, in two small airy rooms, furnished in Louis-Philippe, that have become the meeting place of all Americans who pass through Paris. The hostess is known for her welcoming attitude and agrees that the friends of her friends bring their own friends, but to avoid getting mixed up with all these new names, she makes everyone sign a register when they come in. This way, the first time she meets them, she doesn't risk confusing Munroe Willer [*sic.*], the director of the Museum of Modern Art in New York, with the cartoonist [Saul] Steinberg, or Thornton

Wilder and [John] Steinbeck, Ray Milland and Humphrey Bogart, or mistaking Truman Capote for a little shy boy. Since English is the most commonly spoken language there, the English visit in force: many female novelists, Elizabeth Bowen, Rebecca West, Nancy Mitford, Violet Trefusis, but also Duff Cooper, Evelyn Waugh, Christopher Fry, Cyril Connolly, Raymond Mortimer, who follow George Moore and Maurice Baring. The newcomer at the Place du Palais-Bourbon might perhaps be surprised that the French are now in the minority, but will soon realize that Parisian society is not only made of Parisians and that to be stylish one must be cosmopolitan.

—

DENISE BOURDET, "LES SALONS DE PARIS," *PRIS SUR LE VIF* (PARIS: PLON, 1957): 2–3.

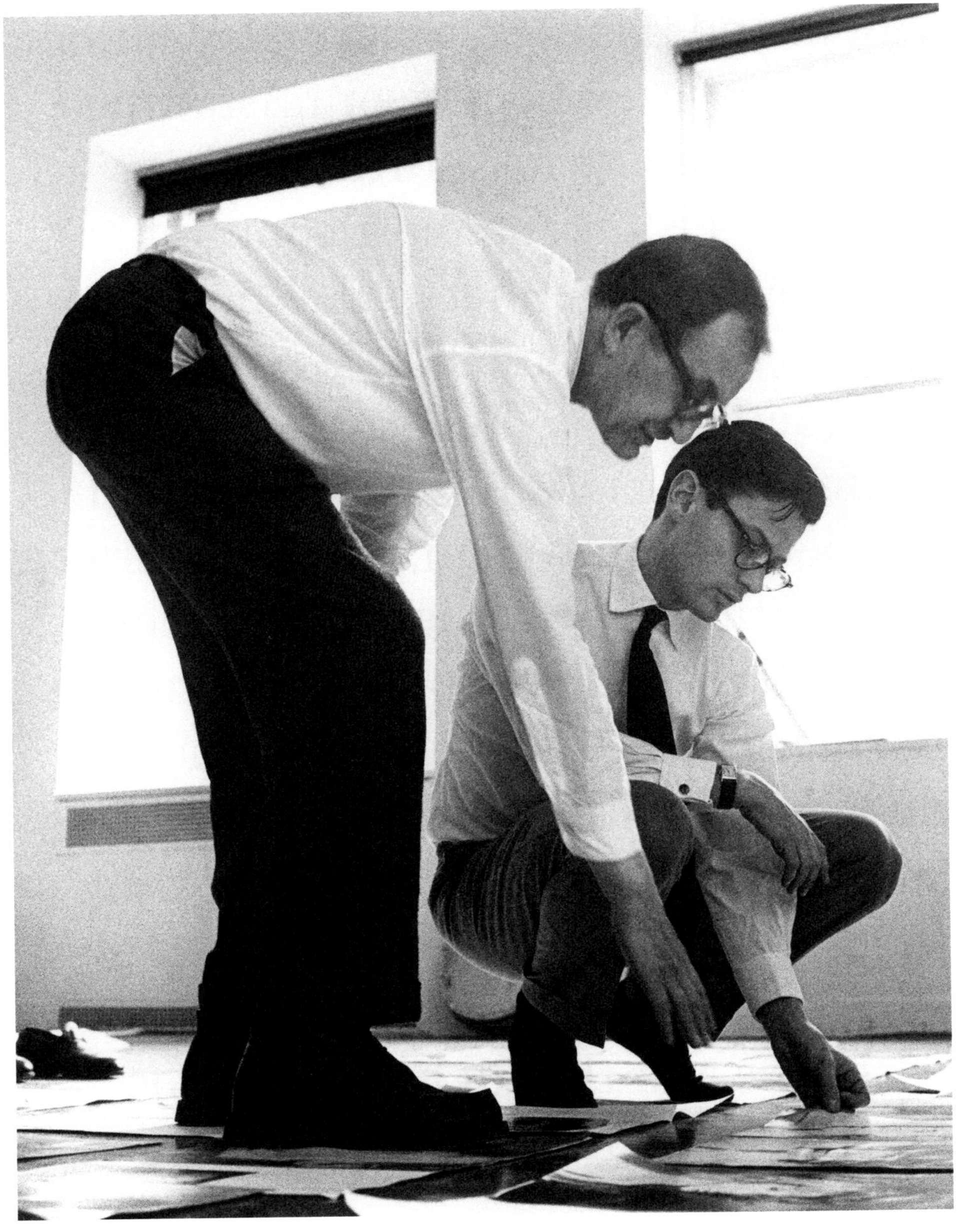

Brodovitch and Avedon at work on *Observations*, 1958; photograph by Hiro

The World of Carmel Snow
Calvin Tomkins

Brodovitch and Snow were turning the editorial pages of the magazine into a unified sequence, with photographs, illustrations, and text working together throughout. Their goal was to give these pages a cinematic continuity — dramatic layouts followed by relatively serene ones, medium-distance photographs played off against extreme closeups, fashion news interspersed with information about books and plays and socialites and movie stars — that would constitute a monthly run-through of popular and high culture with its own ebb and flow, cadence and rhythm. It was the first appearance of a concept that came to be widely imitated but never surpassed: the magazine editor as auteur.

[. . .] At the postwar collections, Carmel always occupied the seat of honor, perched on

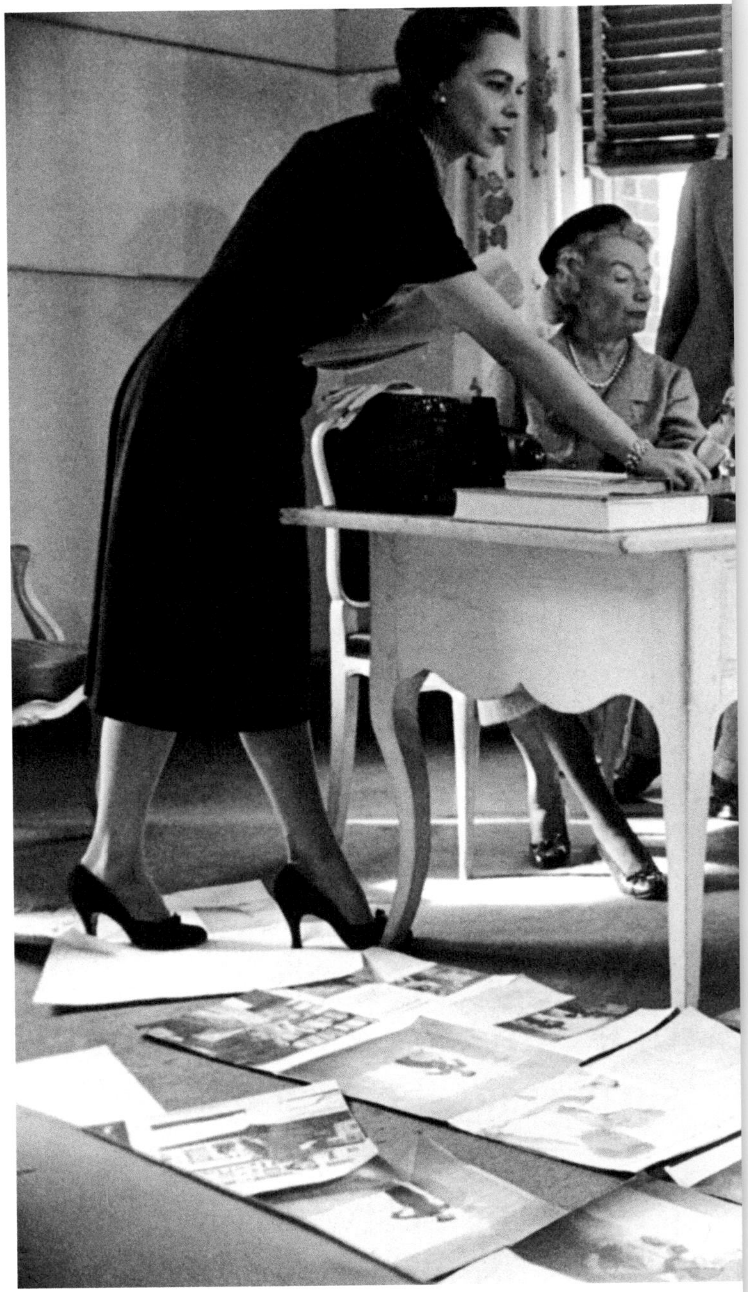

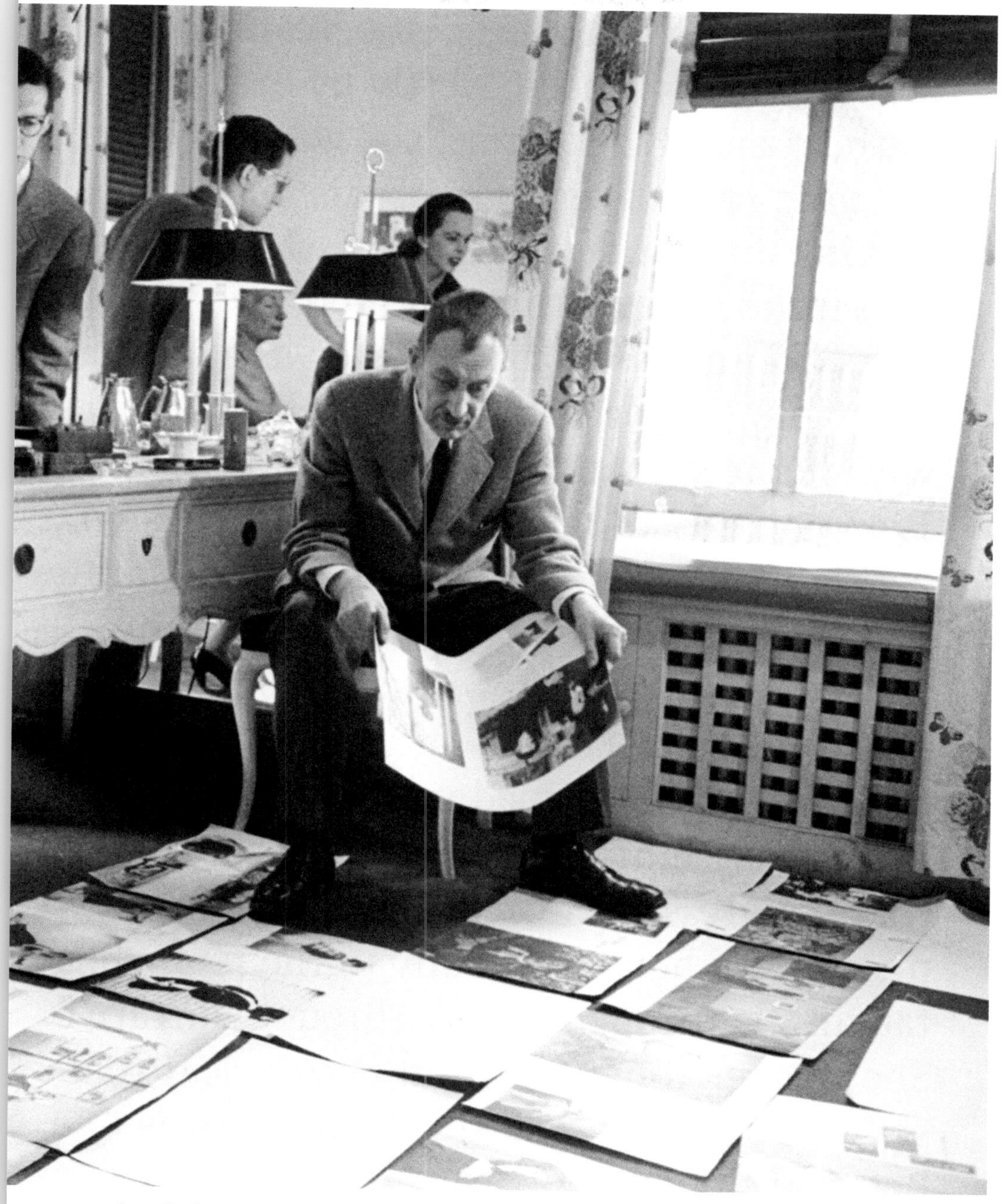

Snow, Brodovitch, and staff lay out an issue of *Harper's Bazaar* in New York, December 1952. Snow's desk was reproduced in almost an exact replica for the set of *Quality Magazine* in *Funny Face*; photograph by Walter Sanders a sofa with her entourage, impeccably dressed and coiffed, watched covertly by every buyer in the room. By this time, she was famous for nodding off to sleep at intervals but always waking up for the best dress or the significant innovation. Richard Avedon, twenty-four years old and just getting started as a fashion photographer for *Bazaar*, remembers going with her to his first fashion show at Dior, in 1947 — the year of the New Look. "I was on her right on the gray velvet settee, and Marie-Louise Bousquet" — *Bazaar*'s Paris editor, a red-wigged dynamo whose famous salons attracted *le tout-Paris* — "was on her left, and Bébé Bérard was curled up on the floor at her feet, with his dirty dog. And the whole time, as dress after dress came out, she told me stories about everybody in the room. She taught me through gossip, through narrative. She was terribly funny. But it was clear that she was adored, a real star, and this was before fashion people were stars.

[. . .] "She took me into a world I couldn't have understood without her, and somehow got across to me what I was then able to get into my pictures. [. . .] She always went for the human quality. She was accessible day or night, she seemed to have all the time in the world, and you'd do anything you could to please her. Vreeland was a genius in her own way, but very different — cold, removed, flamboyant, where Carmel was humane and warm and funny. Vreeland had contempt for photography, interestingly enough. She was a snob, and very condescending. She'd say hello to the woman scrubbing the floor, and know her first name, but for years she called me Aberdeen. I never felt that sort of condescension from Carmel or from Brodovitch. They always lifted me up."

—

CALVIN TOMKINS, "THE WORLD OF CARMEL SNOW," *THE NEW YORKER* (NOVEMBER 7, 1994): 156.

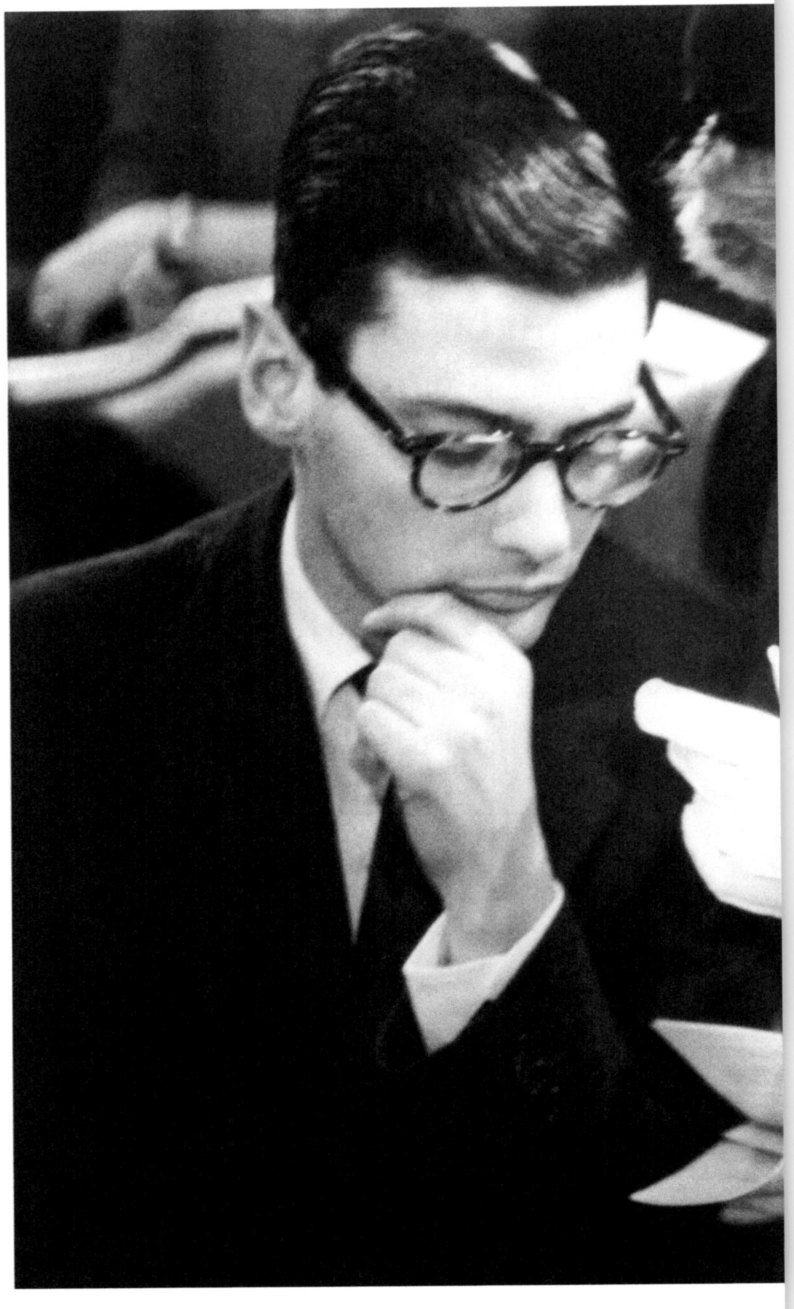

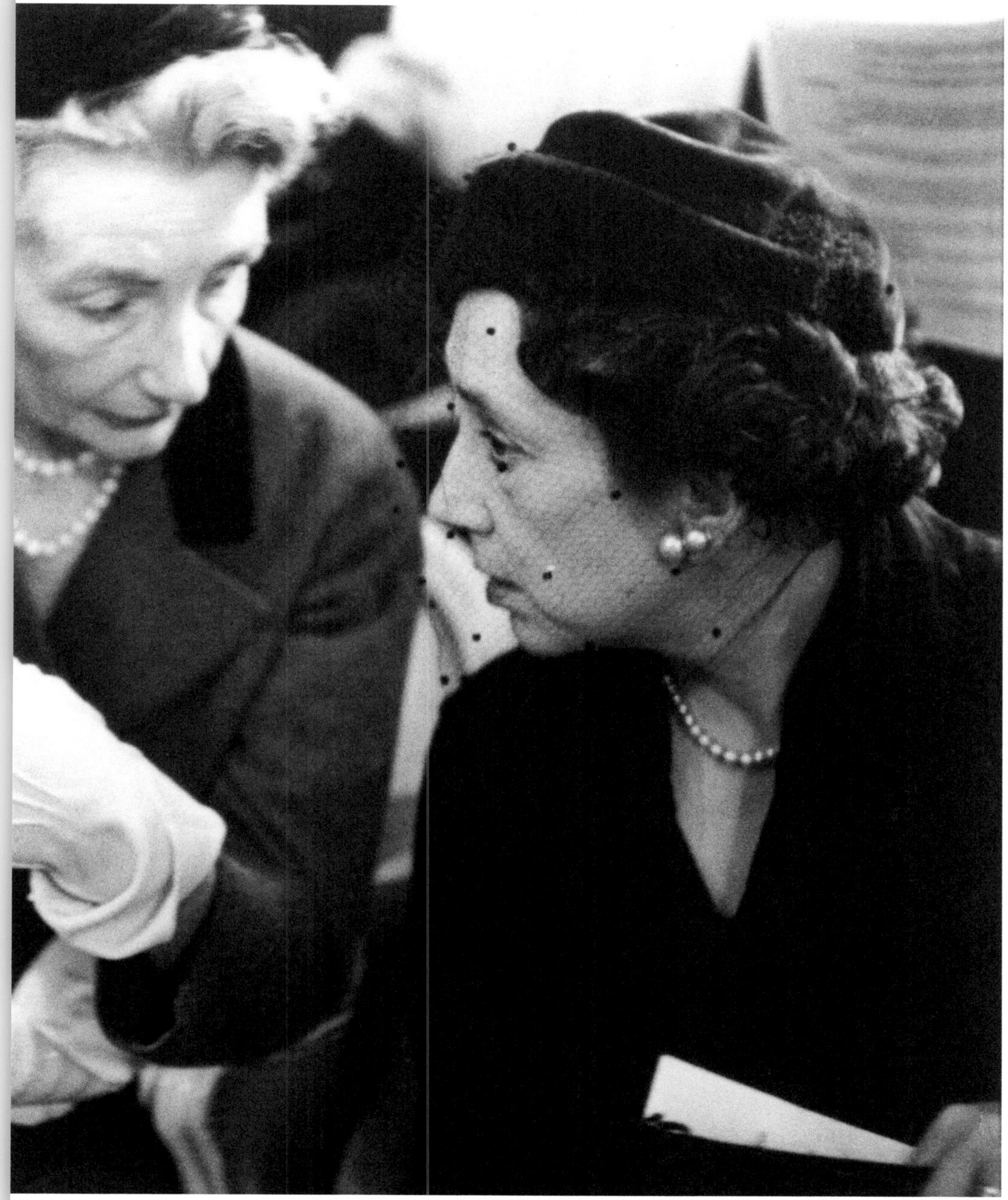

Richard Avedon, Carmel Snow, and Marie-Louise Bousquet, House of Dior, Paris, August 12, 1948;
photograph by Henri Cartier-Bresson

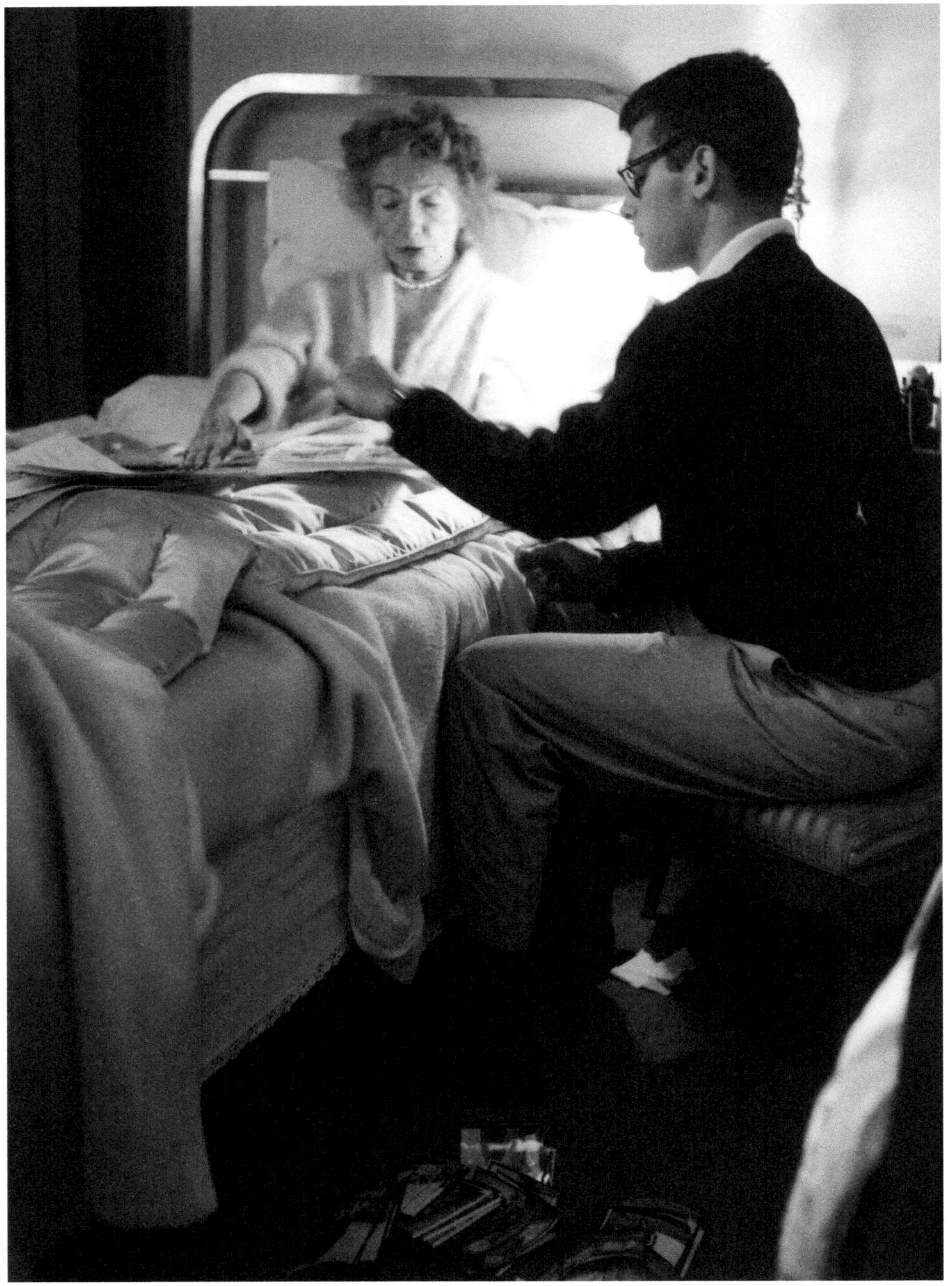

Richard Avedon and Carmel Snow, Hôtel San Régis, Paris, January 1, 1953; photograph by Robert Doisneau

"Carmel Snow, our editor from 1932 to 1958, has been a legend in her time. Her unpredictable and beguiling Irish wit, the dignity and chic of her presence came to epitomize the world of fashion in all its capitals. Her authority was spirited, prophetic and absolute. Her many awards, including the Légion d'honneur and the *Ordine della Stella della Solidarietà Italiana*, could not measure her contribution. Beyond all was her almost mystical intuition with people; her ability to bypass barriers in her search for the gifted – writers, photographers, editors, artists, designers – and to kindle them toward excellence. This, and much more, is her legacy to us."

EDITORS,
HARPER'S BAZAAR, (JUNE 1961): 49.

It's not by chance that the *Bazaar* publishes fiction and articles on travel and the theatre and movies and music in its pages. All these go to make up the climate of fashion, and to be in fashion one must be very aware of the weather.

—

CARMEL SNOW WITH MARY LOUISE ASWELL,
THE WORLD OF CARMEL SNOW
(NEW YORK: MCGRAW-HILL, 1962): 196.

Coup de foudre

The Climate of Fashion

Harper's Bazaar

Carmel Snow took an expansive view of "fashion" In *Harper's Bazaar*. France, of course, was its Mecca and medina. The magazine covered everything from the Cirque Medrano to Eugene Ionesco, from Jean Cocteau to Jacques Cousteau, from Zizi Jeanmaire to Louise de Vilmorin — and all the artists, writers, movie stars, and couturiers in between. *Observations*, Avedon's first book, is the culmination of this phase of Avedon's career. The strong French presence throughout its pages indicates the central importance of his semiannual Paris pilgrimages to his work.

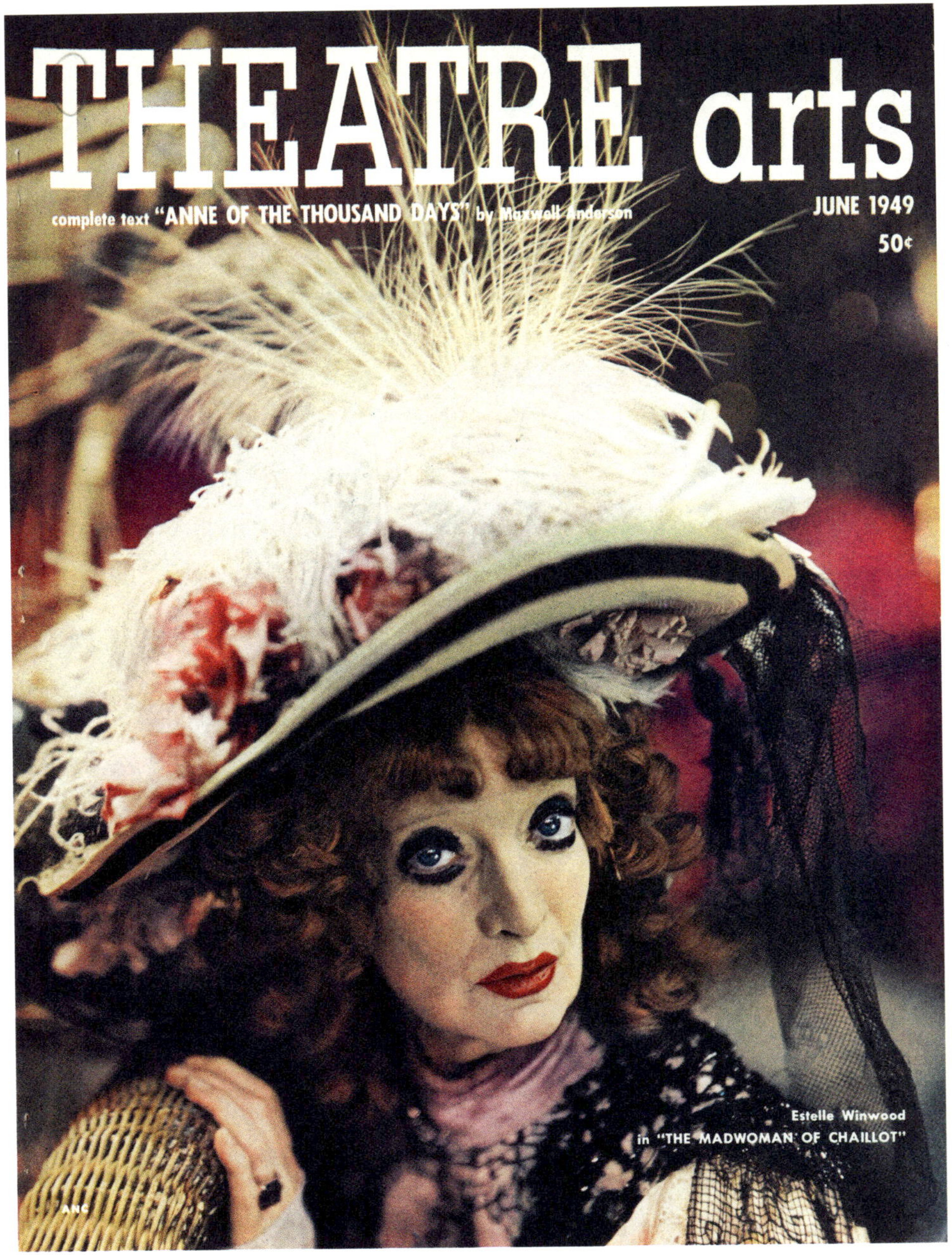

Estelle Winwood in *The Madwoman of Chaillot* on the cover of *Theatre Arts*, June 1949; photograph by Richard Avedon

As the old lunatic, Moreno wears a startling makeup — the white face of a clown, with the wise, black, saucer eyes of an owl. Her foolish finery — such as her great hat, with its mad white bird, her sumptuous, silly dress of red-and-green silk, with torn black lace drooping at half-mast — and the astonishingly beautiful basement room are the careful, *démodé* romantic creations of the painter Christian Bérard. His old-fashioned, elegant white dress for the dog-loving lunatic is like a page of embroidery from Marcel Proust.

—

JANET FLANNER, "LETTER FROM PARIS,"
THE NEW YORKER (FEBRUARY 9, 1946): 46.

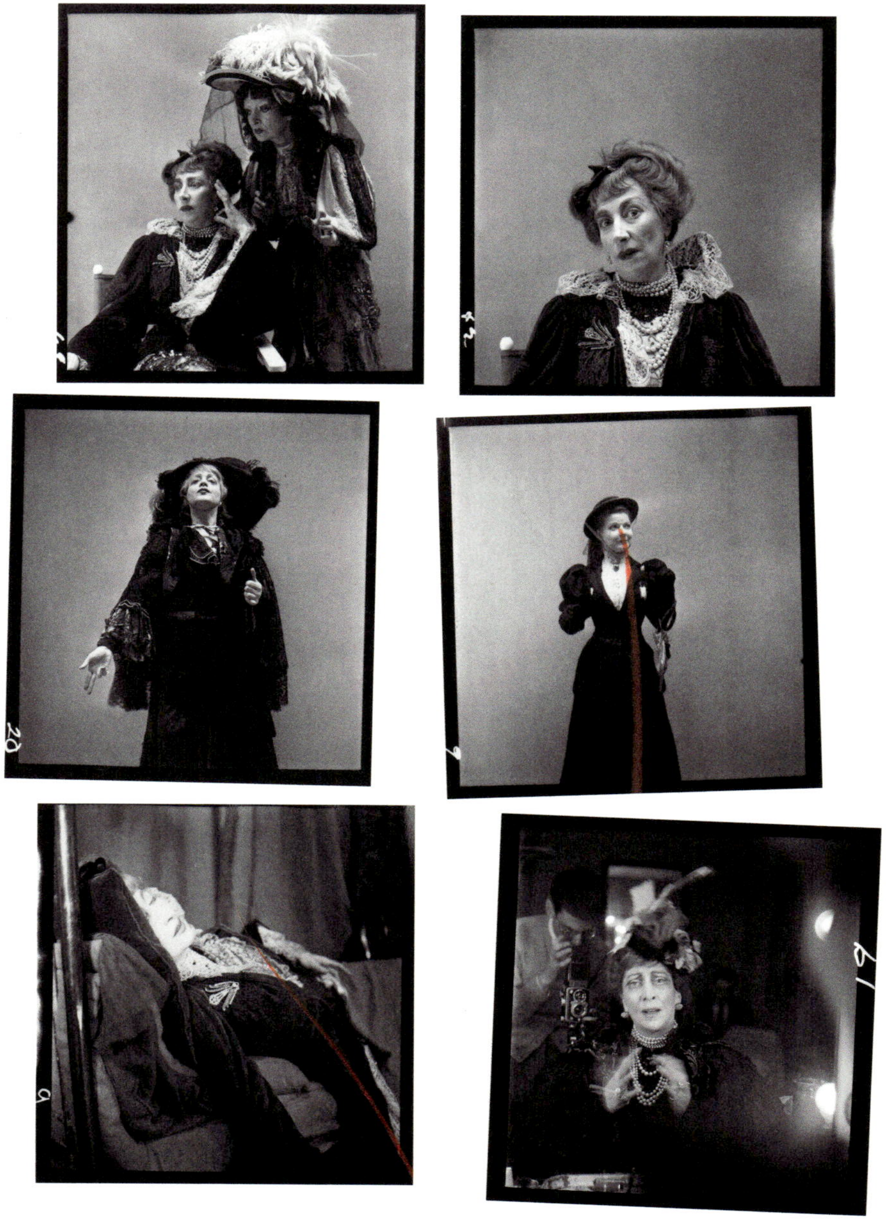

Estelle Winwood, Martita Hunt, Nydia Westman, and Doris Rich in Giraudoux's *The Madwoman of Chaillot*, New York, February 18, 1949 (contact prints)

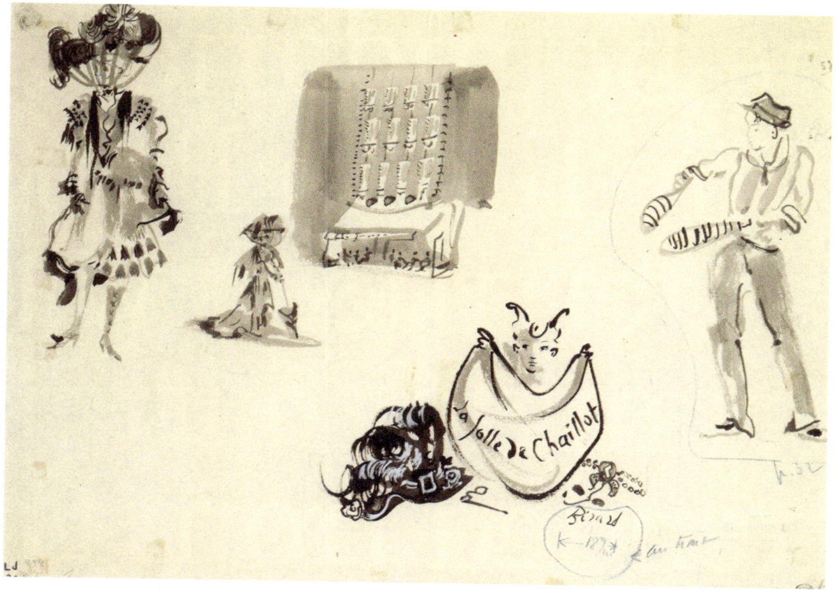

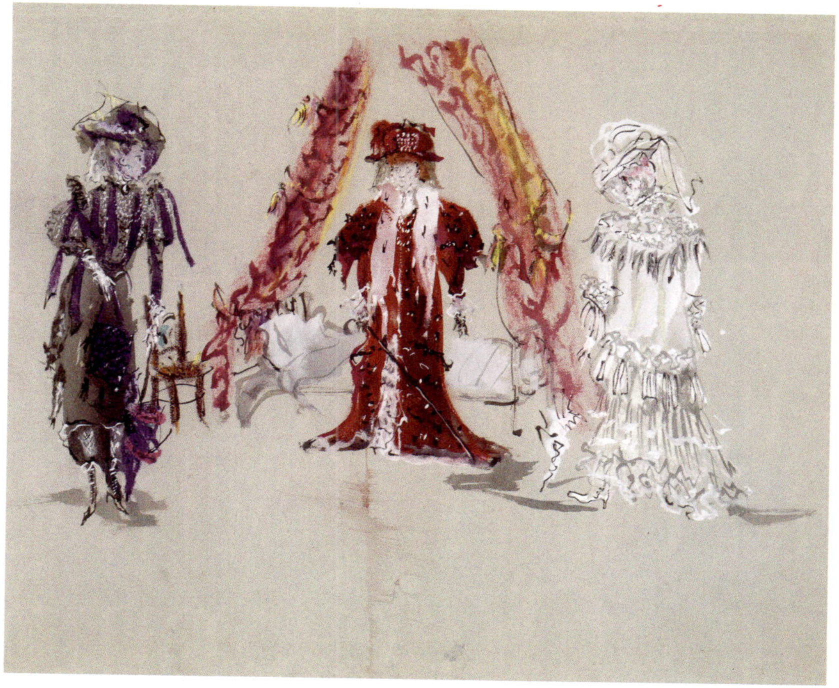

Costume and set sketch boards by Christian Bérard for *Madwoman of Chaillot*, 1945

The boundaries of my life in Paris was terrific. It was a triangle that extended from the Hôtel San Régis to the studio, which was across the Place François 1er and on the other side of Rue Goujon to Dior's, which was behind the studio. Whenever I had a break, I could stand on the balcony and lean over and look down at the midinettes sewing.

—

Richard Avedon

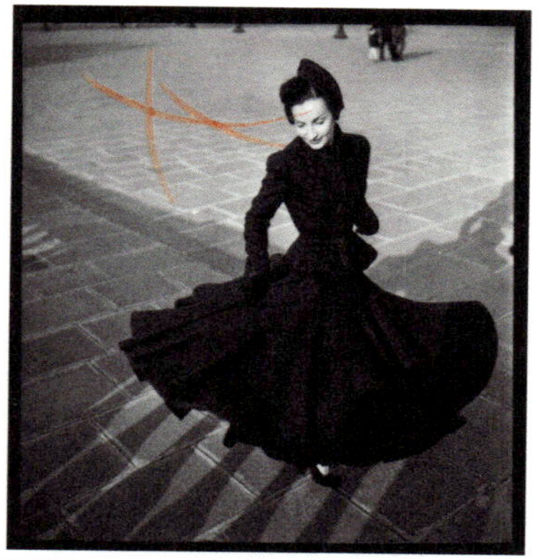

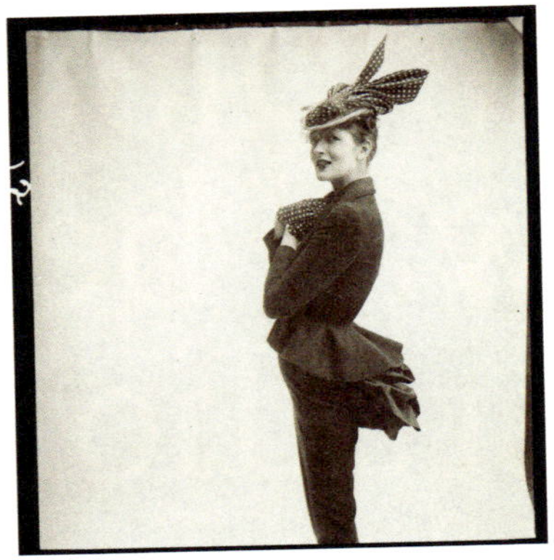

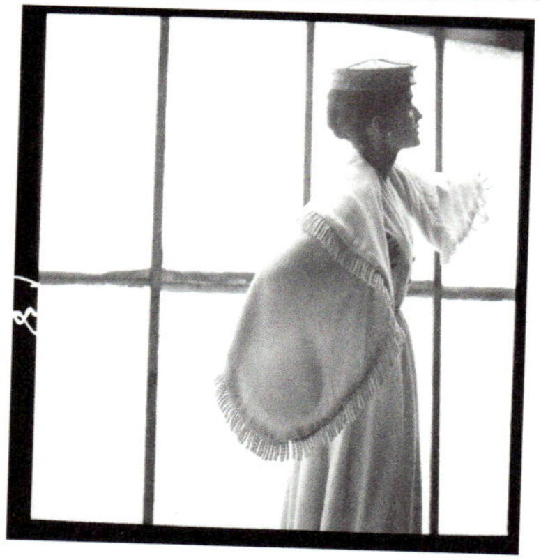

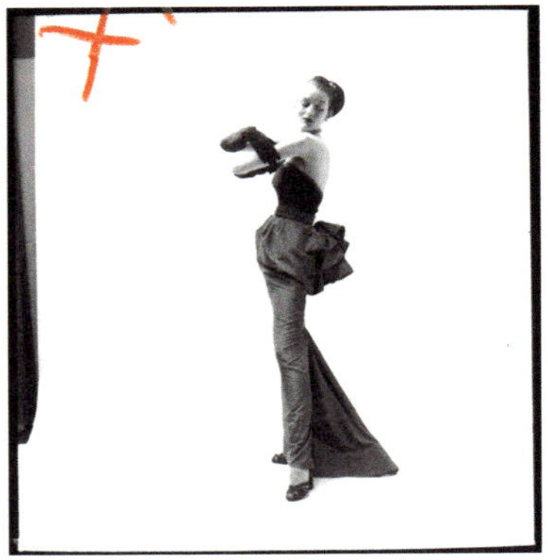

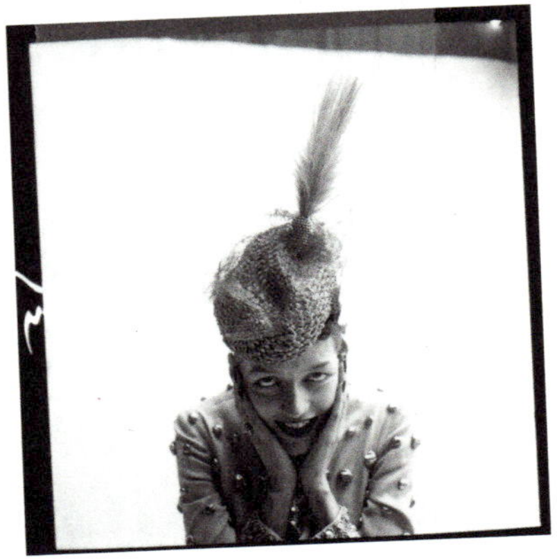

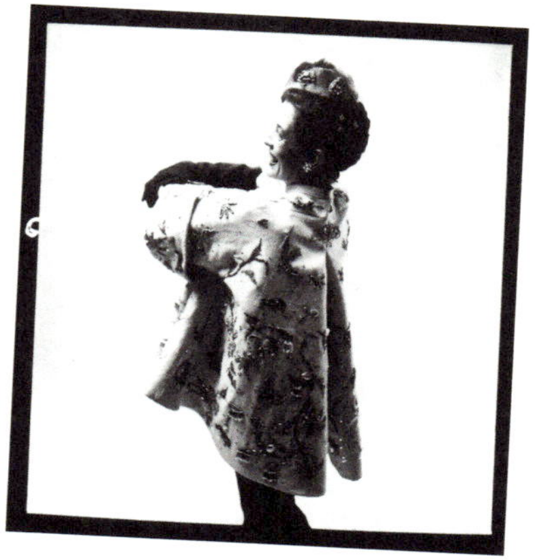

Top left, Renée, "The New Look of Dior," Place de la Concorde, Paris, August 1947
Middle left, Maxime, Comtesse de La Falaise, suit and hat by Fath, Paris, January 1948
Bottom left, Maxime, Comtesse de la Falaise, Paris, 1948
Top right, Maxime, Comtesse de la Falaise, suit and hat by Fath, Paris, January 1948
Middle right, Maxime, Comtesse de la Falaise, taffeta evening gown by Dior, Paris, February 1948
Bottom right, Maxime, Comtesse de la Falaise, embroidered linen evening coat by Dior, Paris, February 1948 (contact prints)

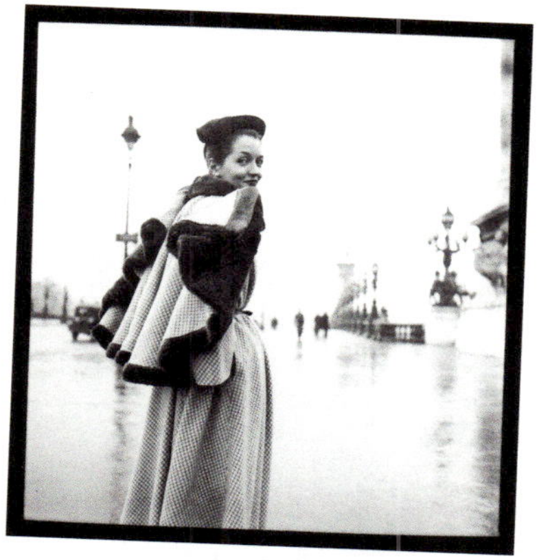

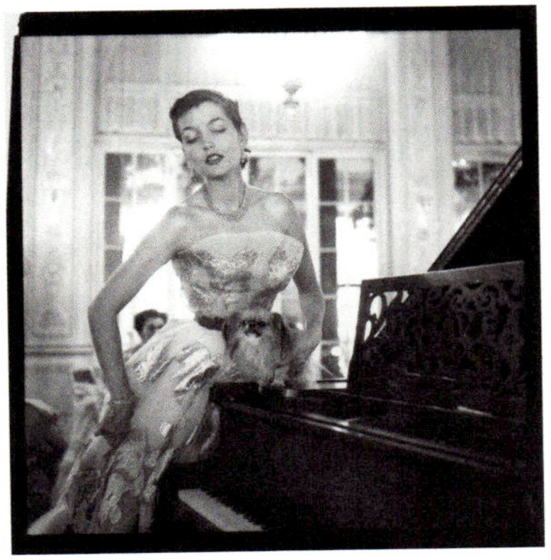

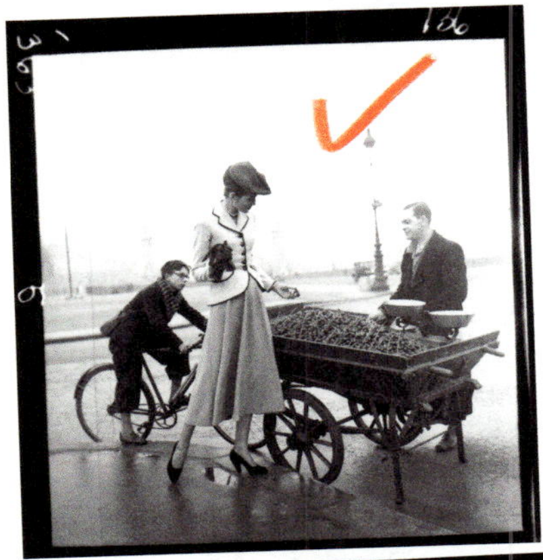

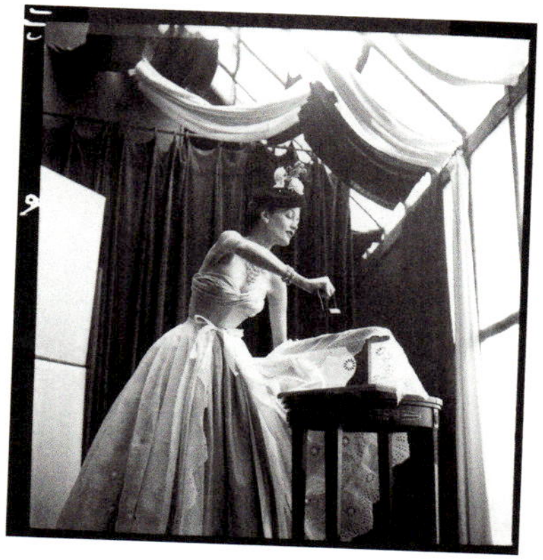

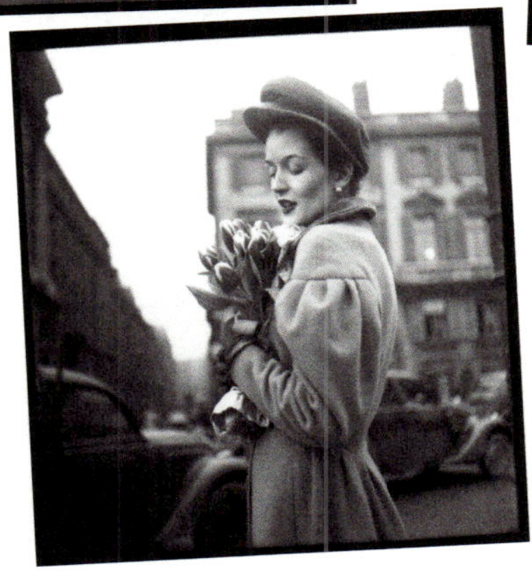

Top left, Maxime, Comtesse de la Falaise, checked dress and cape by Fath, Paris, February 1948
Middle left, Maxime, Comtesse de la Falaise, linen jacket by Fath, Paris, February 1948
Bottom left, Maxime, Comtesse de la Falaise, drop-sleeve coat by Schiaparelli, Paris, February 1948
Top right, Maxime, Comtesse de la Falaise, Biarritz, France, 1948
Bottom right, Maxime, Comtesse de la Falaise, Paris, April 1948 (contact prints)

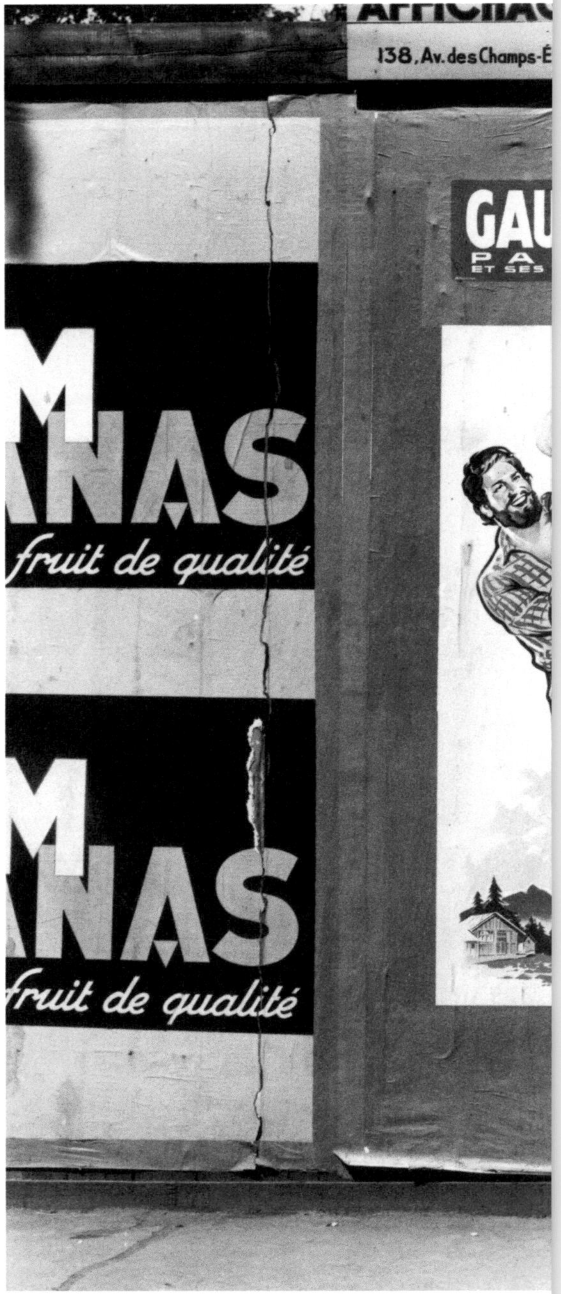
138, Av. des Champs-É
GAU
PA
ET SES
M
NAS
fruit de qualité
M
NAS
fruit de qualité

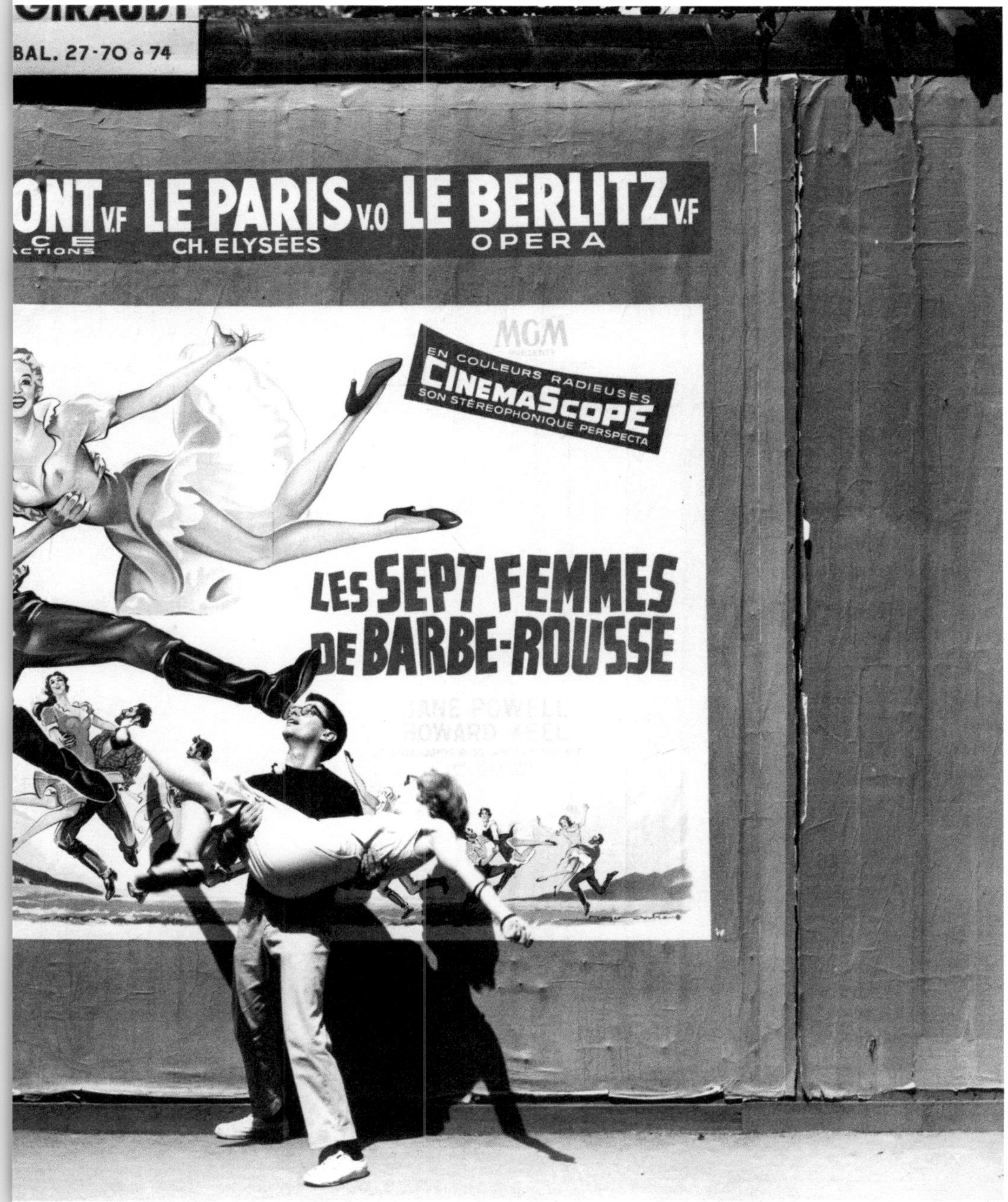

Richard and Evelyn Avedon, Paris, c. 1950s

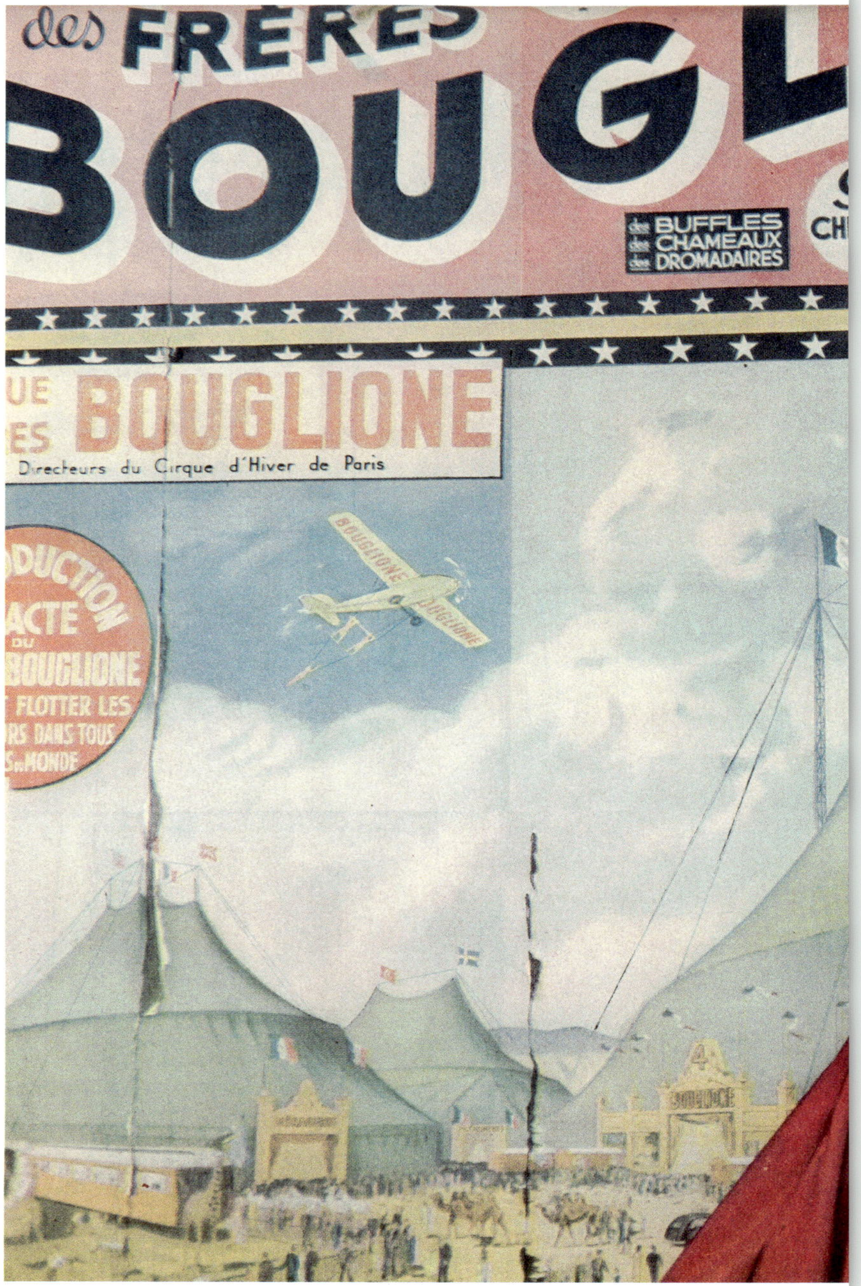
des FRÈRES
des BUFFLES
des CHAMEAUX
des DROMADAIRES
BOUGLIONE
Directeurs du Cirque d'Hiver de Paris
BOUGLIONE
FLOTTER LES

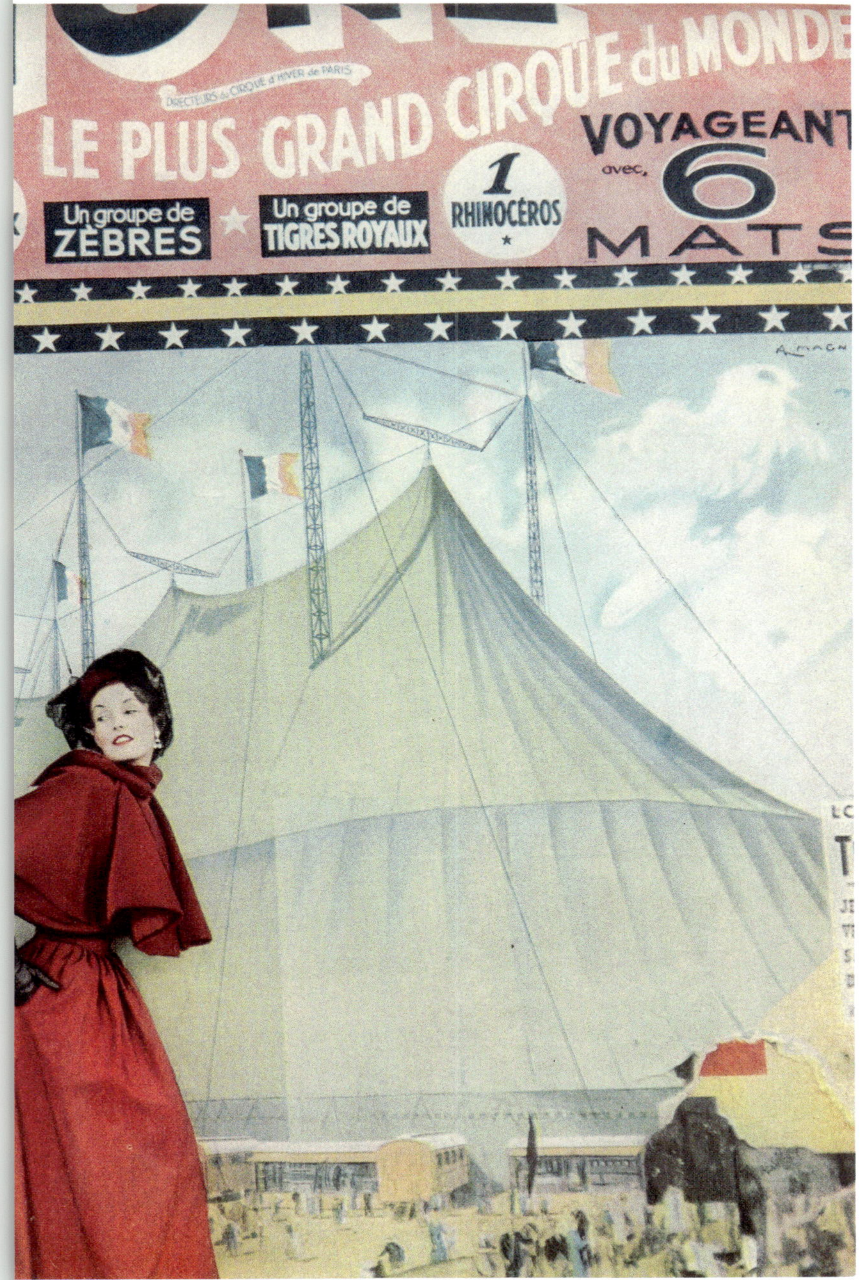

Harper's Bazaar, November 1948, p. 138

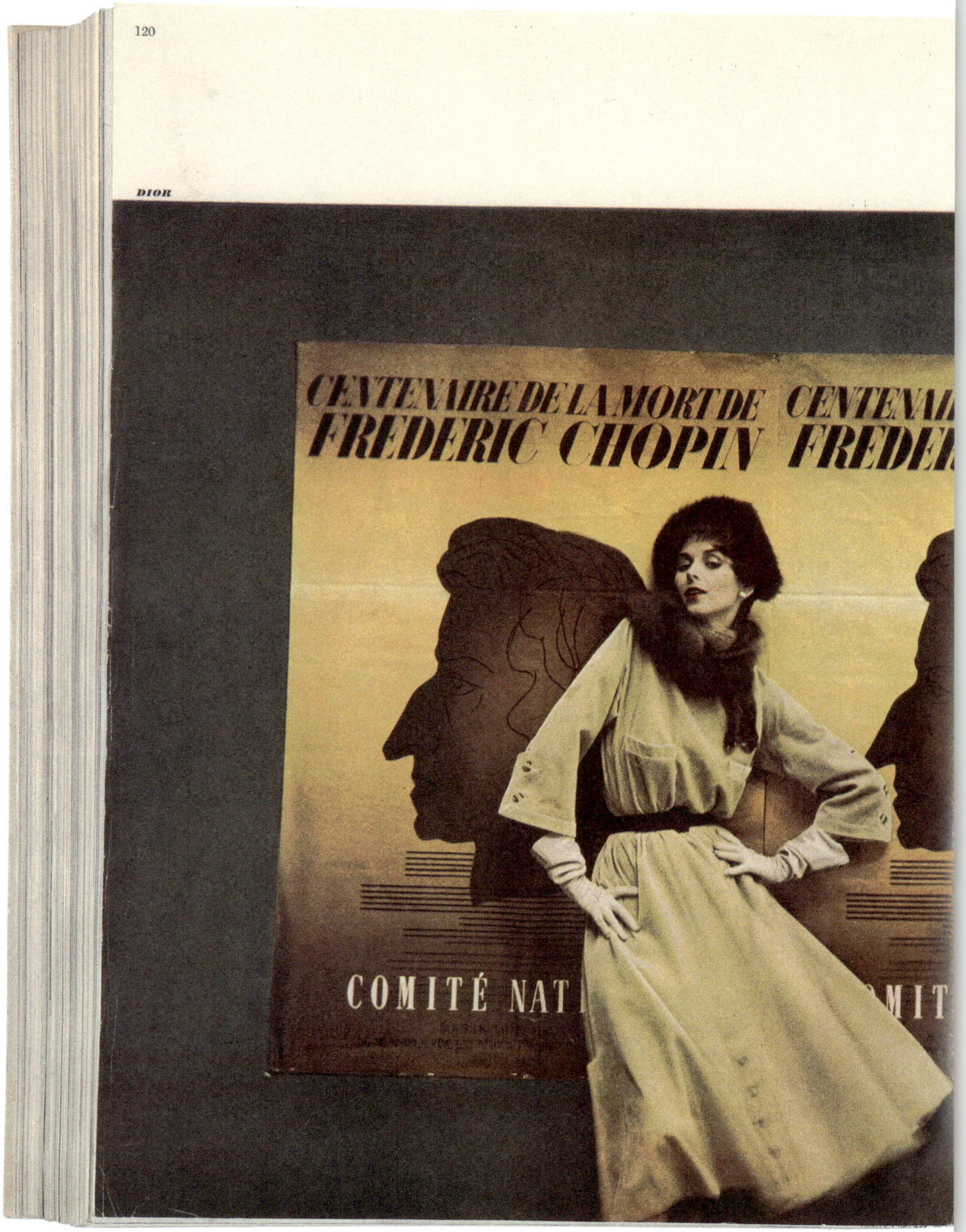
120
DIOR
CENTENAIRE DE LA MORT DE
FREDERIC CHOPIN

UNDER YOUR FUR COAT

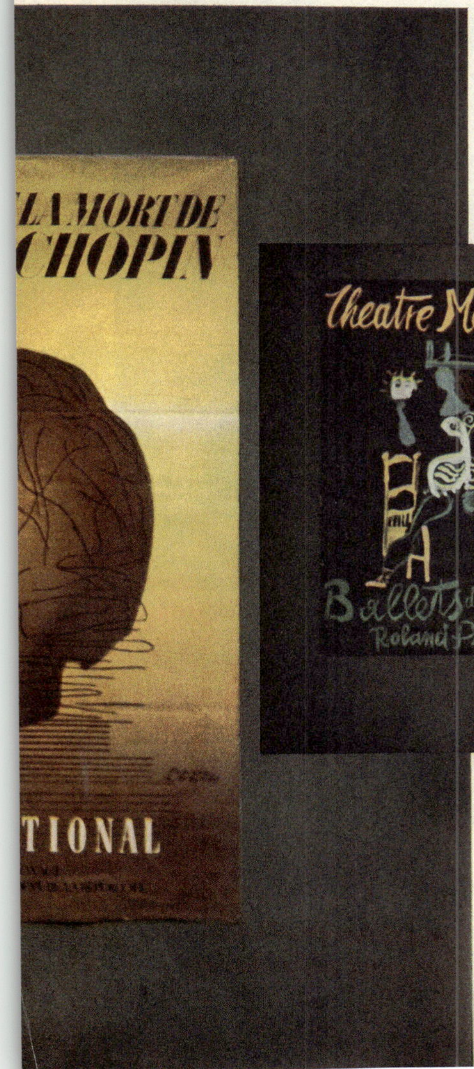

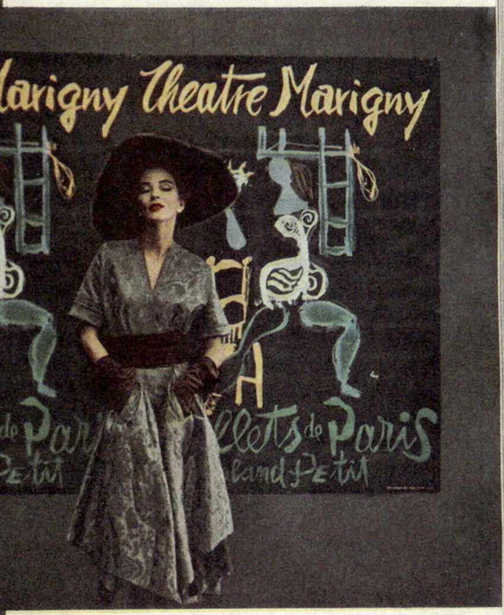

DIOR

• Left: Dior's fawn velveteen dress trimmed only with buttons and with his new low pockets. Russeks. The hat and scarf are in sable.
• And above: Dior's gray brocade dress—very smart under fur—very smart with its brown belt and Chinese hat in brown beaver. The dress, I. Magnin. Charles of the Ritz "Hibiscus" lipstick.

KODACHROMES BY RICHARD AVEDON

Harper's Bazaar, November 1949, pp. 120–21

184

SCHIAPARELLI

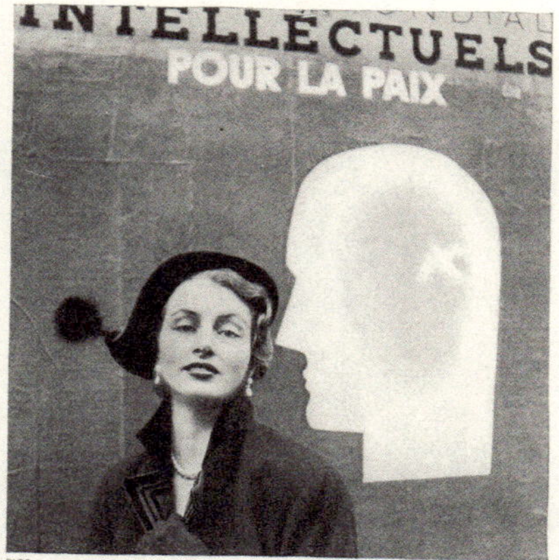

DIOR

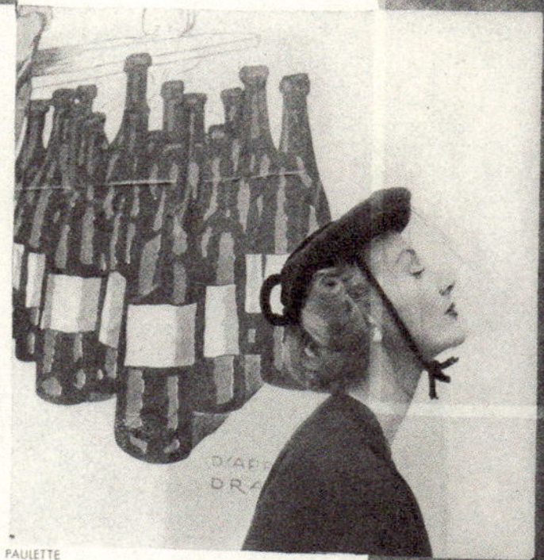
PAULETTE

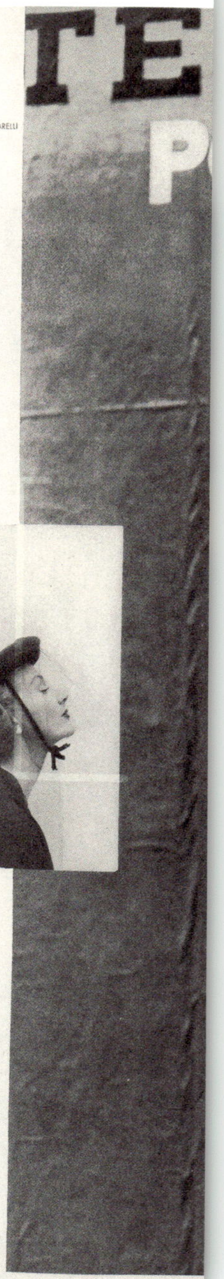

THE CHIC LITTLE SHAPE

• At the top, Dior's sidewise swoop of black velvet, ending in a fat brush. This is one of the hats the Americans fell upon; it's ideal for our short coiffures. Carson Pirie Scott.
• Center, the flattop by Paulette—a round of black felt, set straight on, with a center of black velvet and grosgrain, a tulle veil and a felt chin strap which you can take or leave.
• Directly opposite, Schiaparelli's black patent leather hat with a pie-section crown,→ thick brim, the look of a galvanized tin helmet. All three hats are at Bergdorf Goodman.

PHOTOGRAPHS BY RICHARD AVEDON

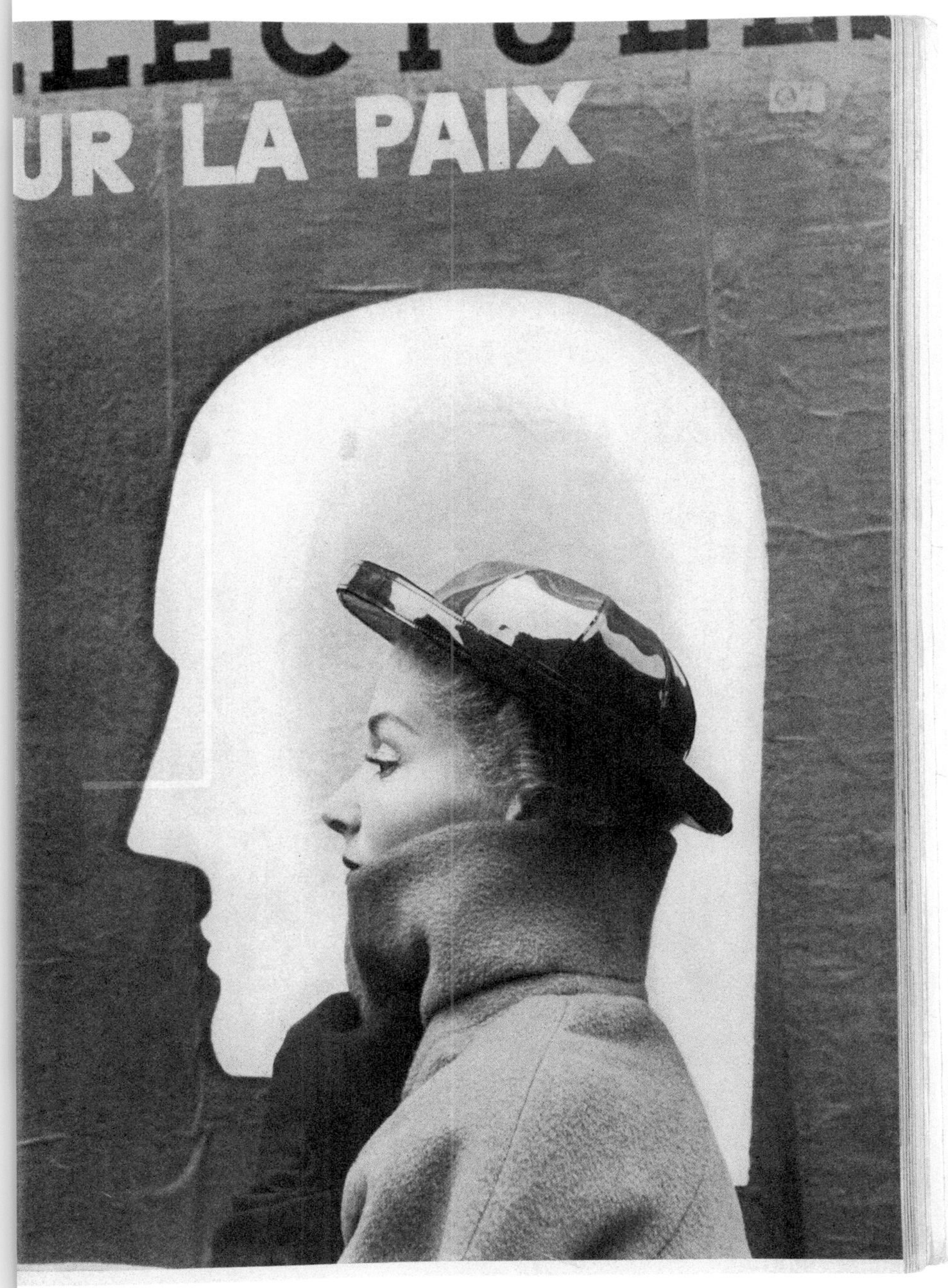

Harper's Bazaar, October 1948, pp. 184–85

182

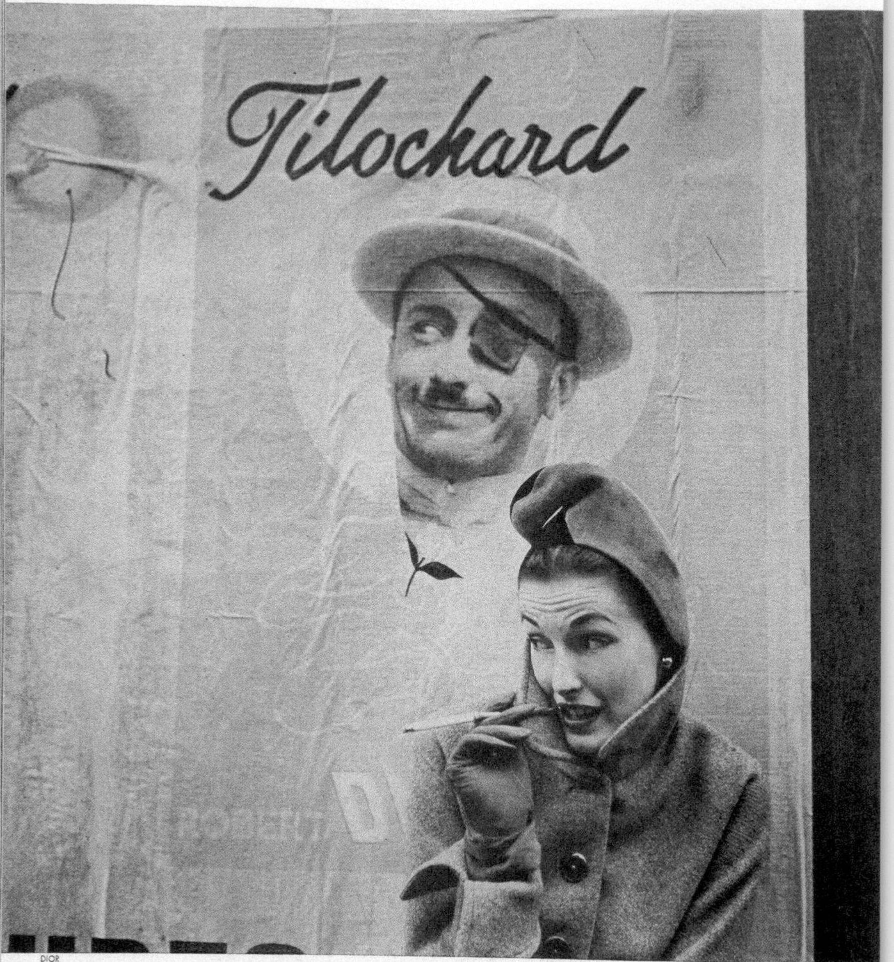

DIOR

RICHARD AVEDON

THE GAY LITTLE HAT The old hatty hats that were the pride of the Parisian milliner are challenged by hats like these—young, cute, impudent and getting more American by the second. • Above, Dior's very young version of the turban, a turban-skullcap in black and beige felt.

HARPER'S BAZAAR, OCTOBER

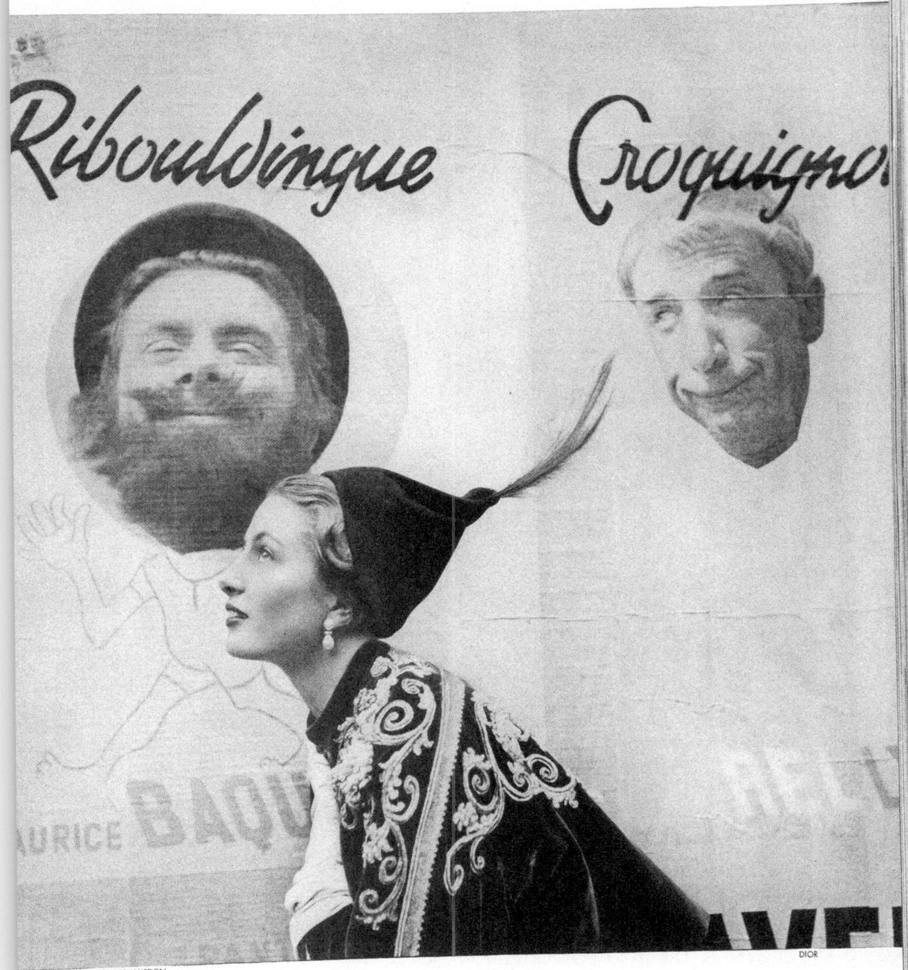

RICHARD AVEDON

DIOR

• Dior's flyaway dunce cap, in green velvet, with a wisp of paradise to tantalize your vis-à-vis and torture the man you left behind you. It is worn with a green velvet jacket embroidered in Dior's new bold gold scrolls —all embroidery in his collection is bold. Both hats (the feather neo-paradise), Bergdorf Goodman.

Harper's Bazaar, October 1948, pp. 182–83

p. 287, Alexey Brodovitch, graphic designer, Le Thor, France, February 9, 1970
pp. 288–89, Carmel Snow, fashion editor, New York, October 16, 1959
pp. 290–91, Marie-Louise Bousquet, fashion editor, Paris, 1950
pp. 292–93, Christian Bérard and Renée, suit by Dior, Le Marais, Paris, August 1947
pp. 294–95, Estelle Winwood, Martita Hunt, Nydia Westman, and Doris Rich in Giraudoux's *The Madwoman of Chaillot*, New York, February 18, 1949
p. 296, Marcel Jouhandeau, writer, Paris, August 20, 1950
pp. 298–99, Janet Flanner, writer, New York, March 19, 1954
pp. 300–01, Georges Braque, artist, and his wife Augustine, Paris, January 27, 1959
pp. 302–303, Pablo Picasso, artist, April 16, 1958
pp. 304–305, Bernard Buffet, painter, and his wife Annabel, Paris, January 27, 1959
p. 306, Igor Stravinsky, composer, New York, January 8, 1959
p. 308–09, Marcel Duchamp, artist, New York, January 31, 1958
pp. 310–11, Eugène Ionesco, playwright, Paris, January 27, 1959
pp. 312–13, Alberto Giacometti, sculptor, Paris, March 6, 1958
pp. 314–15, Jeanne Moreau, actress, Paris, July 30, 1962
pp. 316–17, Jacques Tati, actor, Paris, January 27, 1959
pp. 318–19, Jean Anouilh, playwright, Paris, January 27, 1959
pp. 320–21, Maurice Chevalier, actor, Paris, January 27, 1959
pp. 322–23, Marc Chagall, painter, Paris, January 27, 1959
pp. 324–25, François Truffaut, director, New York, January 26, 1960
pp. 326–27, Captain Jacques-Yves Cousteau, New York, October 23, 1956
pp. 328–29, Henry Miller, writer, Pacific Palisades, California, September 24, 1968
p. 331, Gabrielle Chanel, couturier, Paris, March 6, 1958
pp. 332–33, René Clair, director, New York, July 6, 1958
pp. 334–35, François Villon, poet, Paris, April 16, 1958
pp. 336–37, Emilien Bouglione, animal trainer, Cirque d'Hiver, Paris, July 30, 1955
p. 339, Jean Cocteau, artist, Beaulieu, France, April 1, 1958

French Portraits I

Richard Avedon

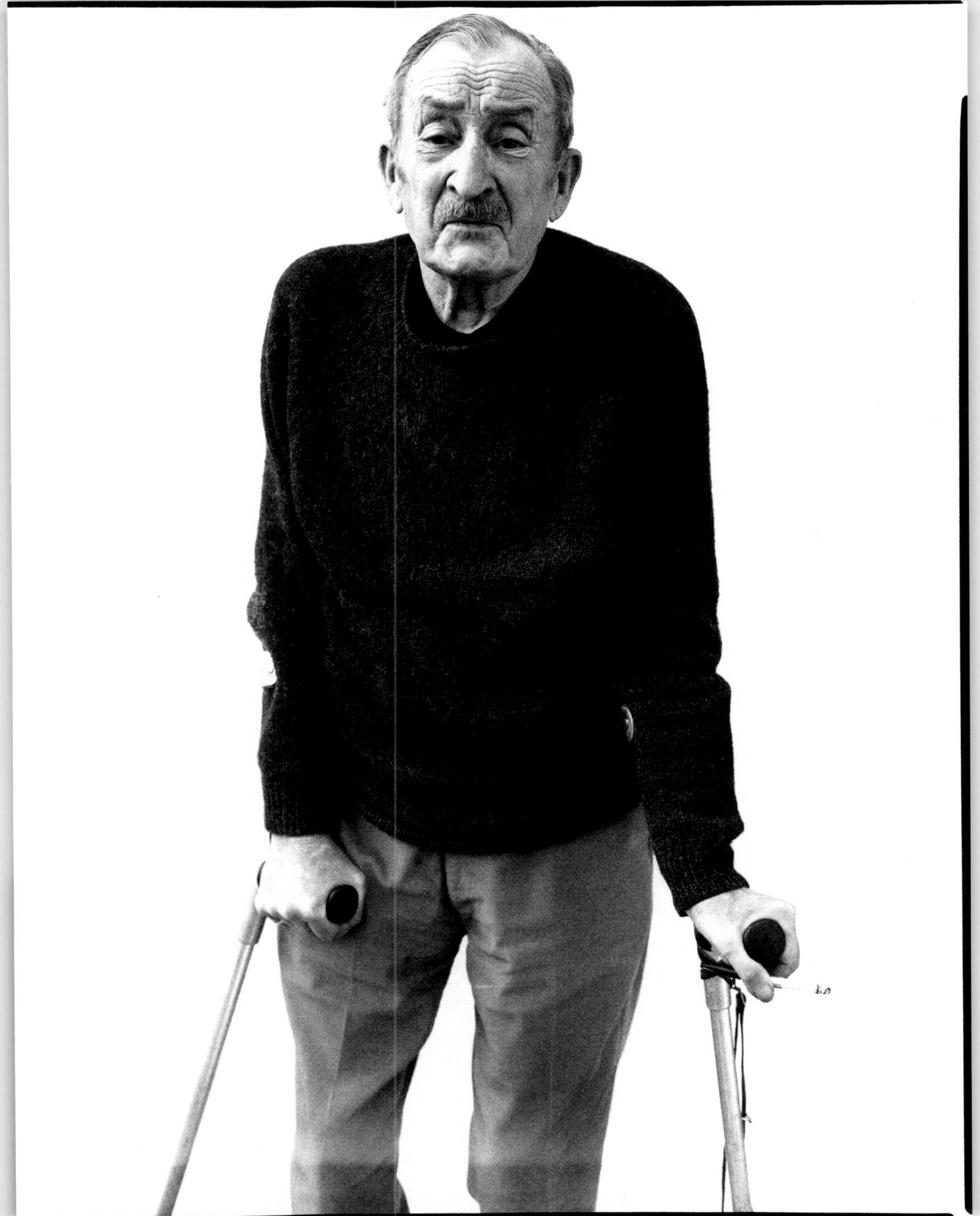

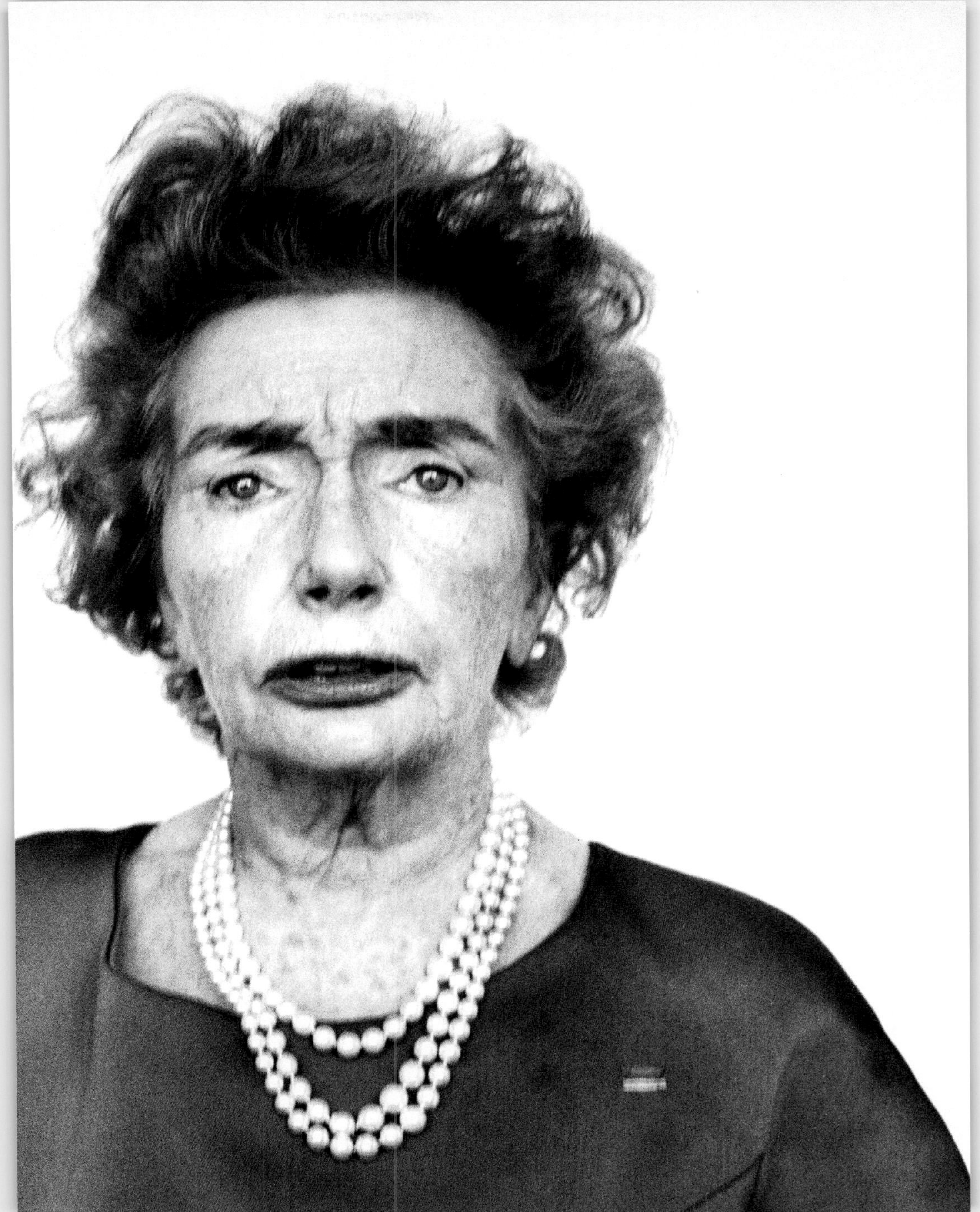

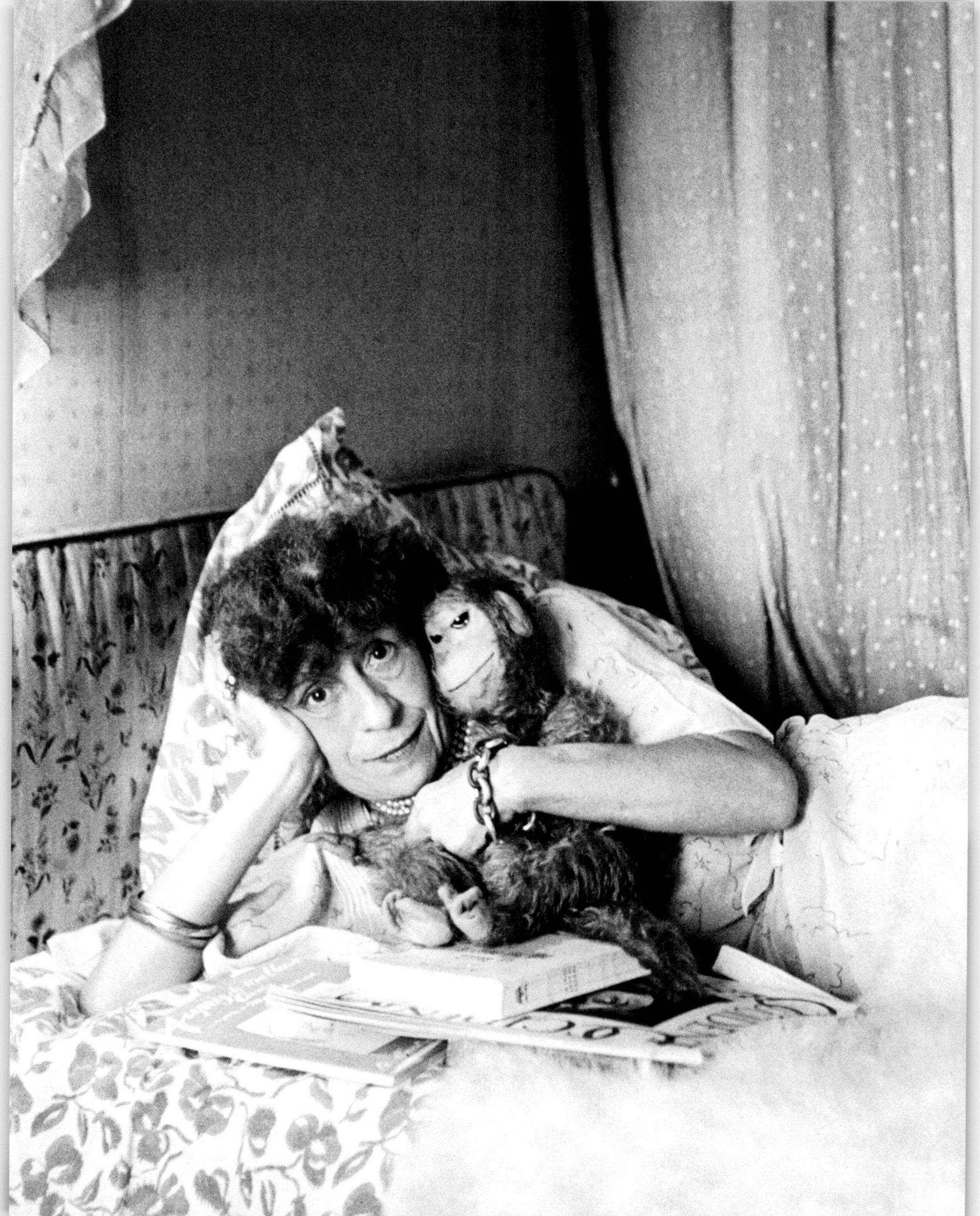

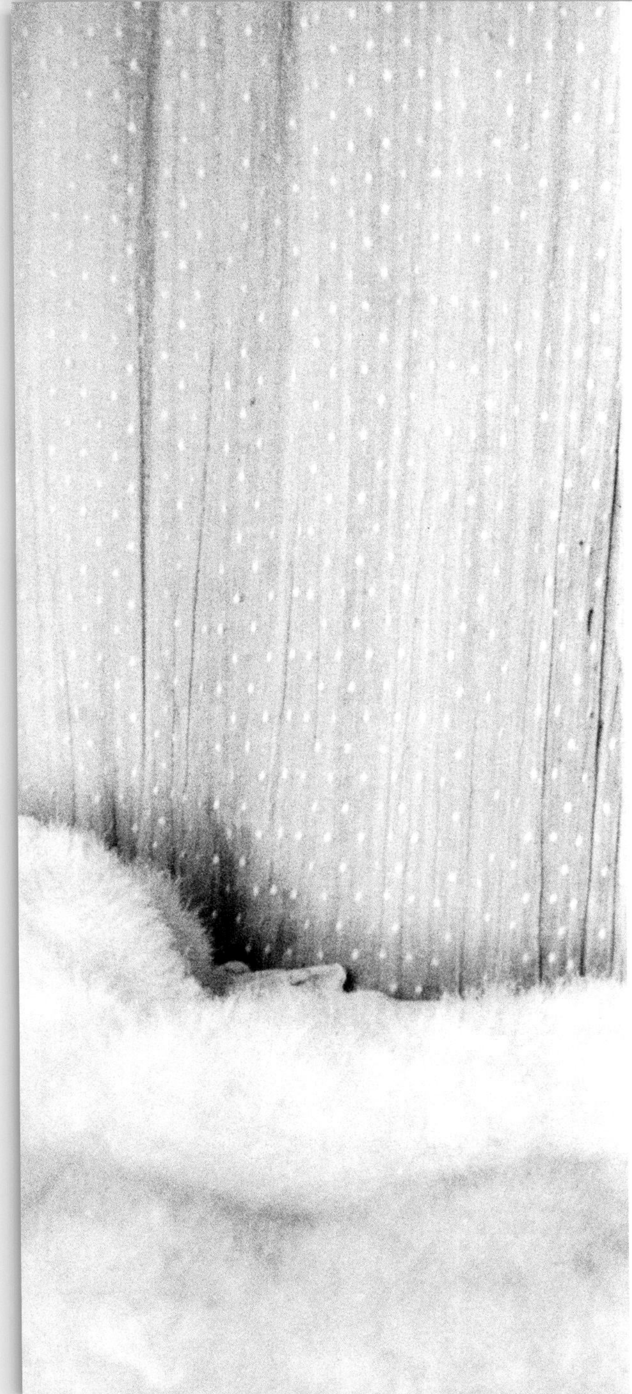

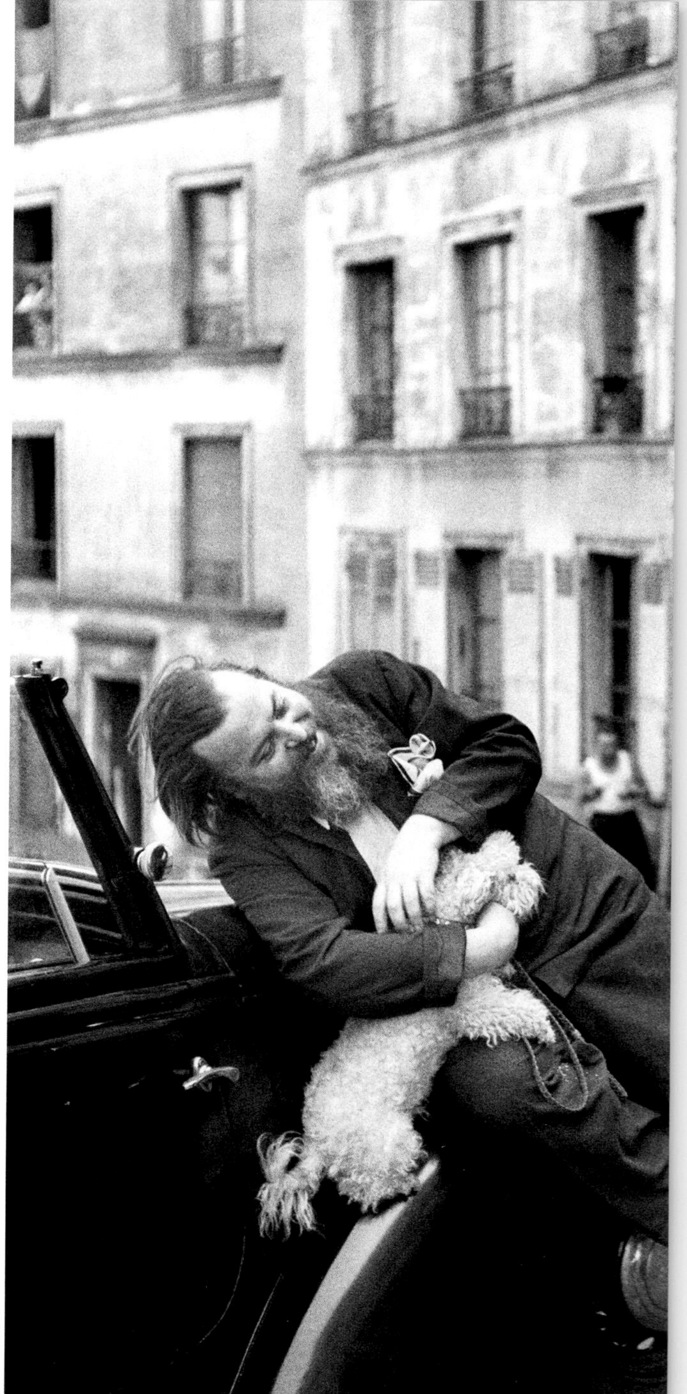

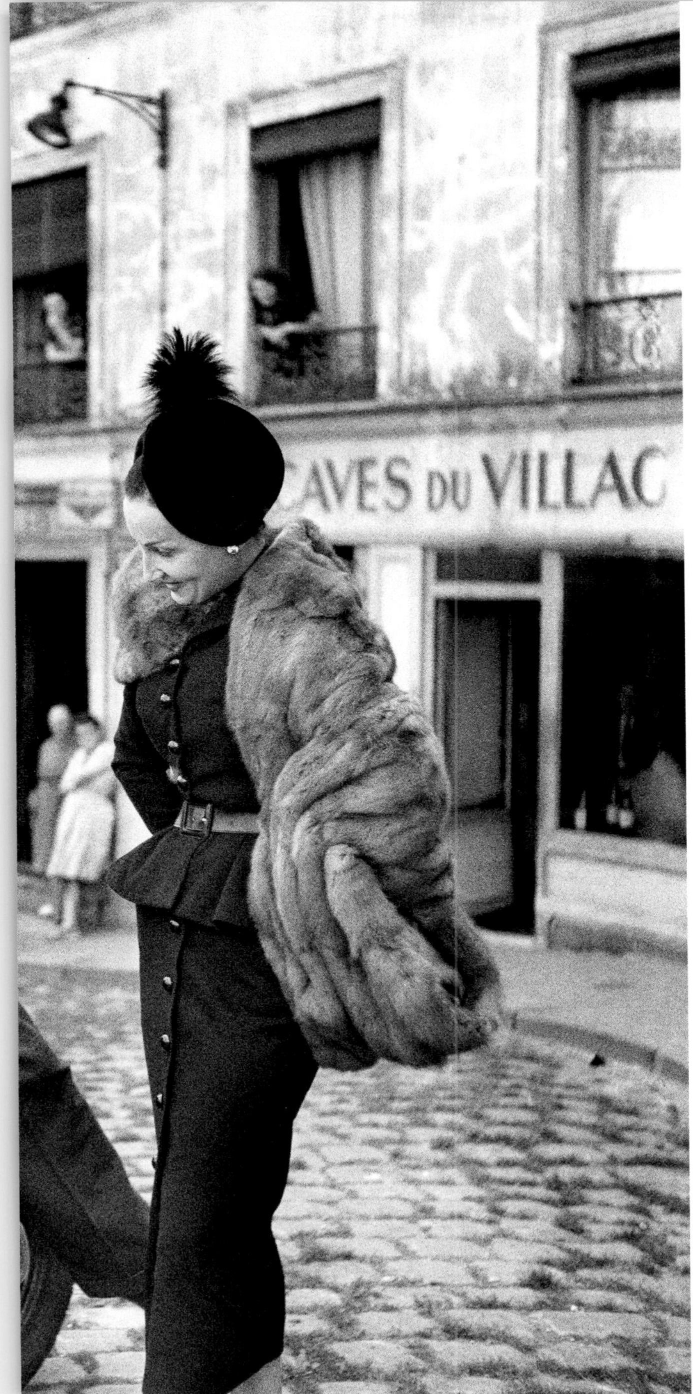
CAVES DU VILLAG

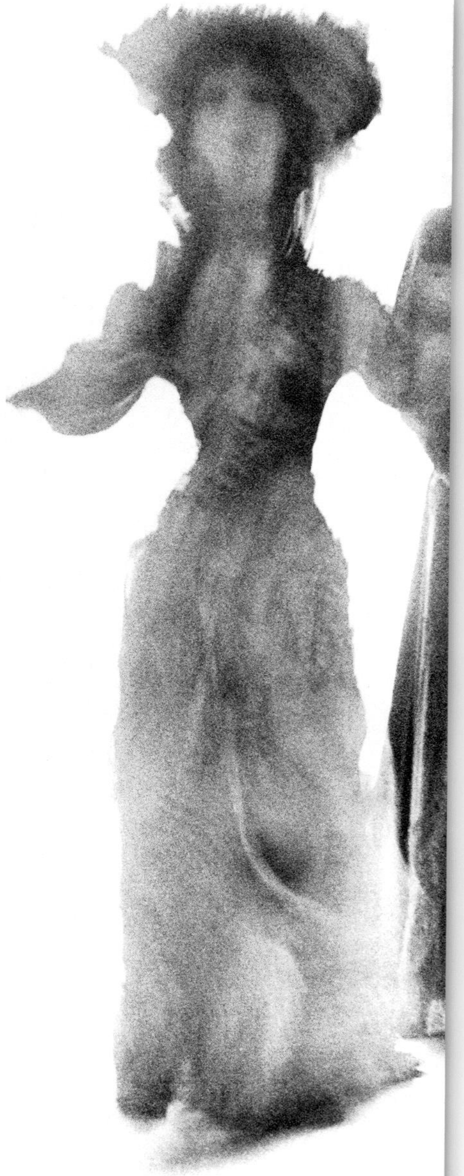

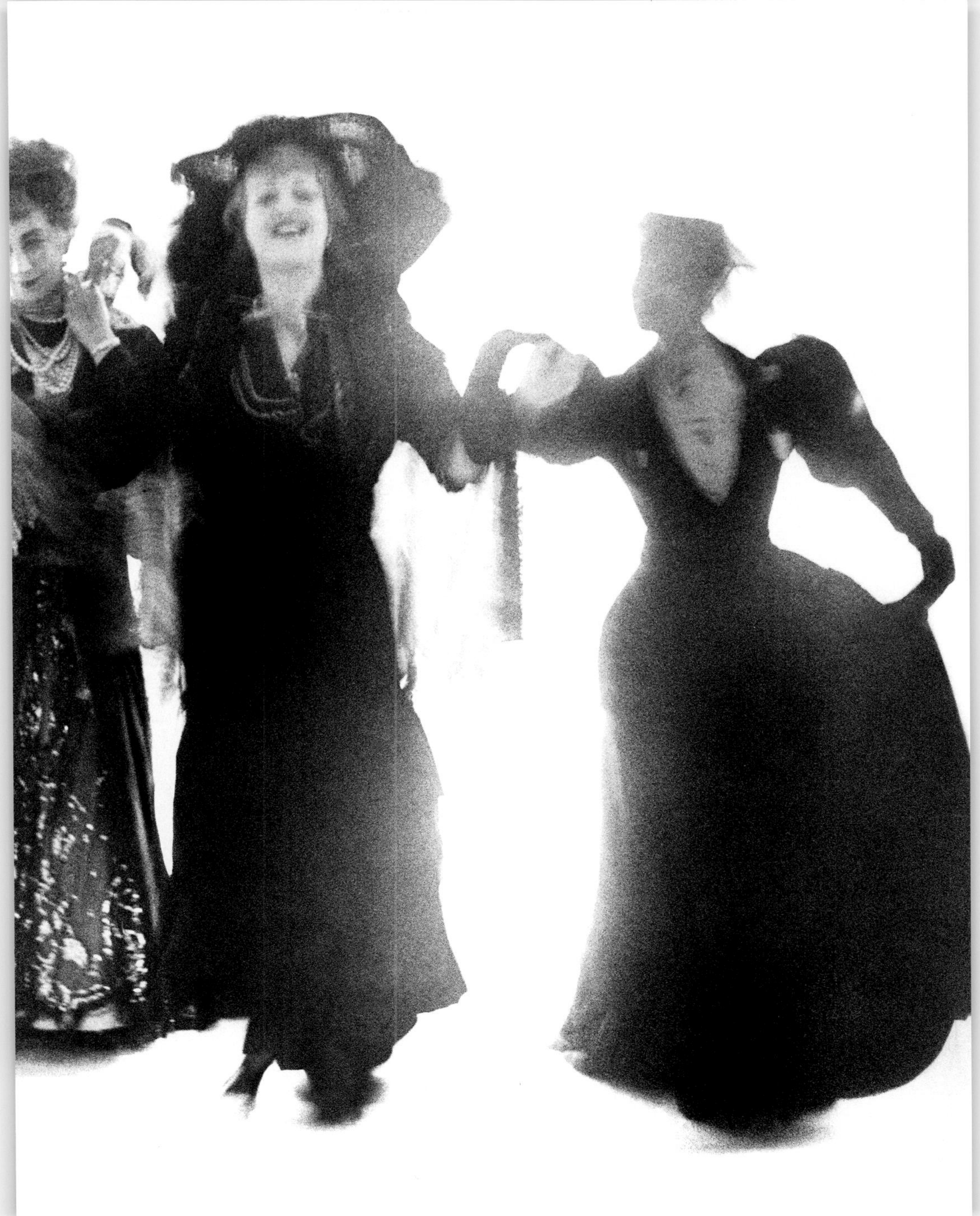

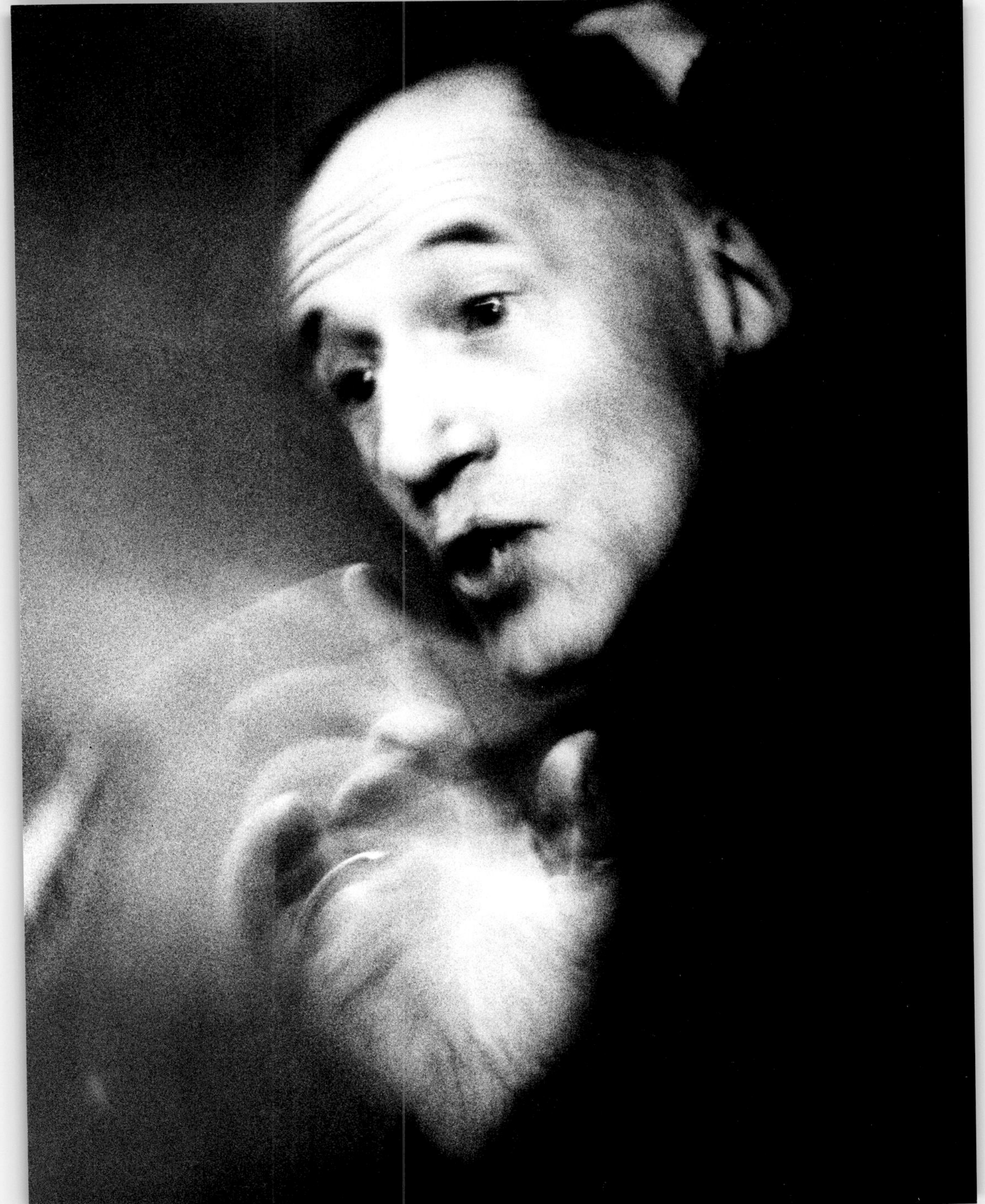

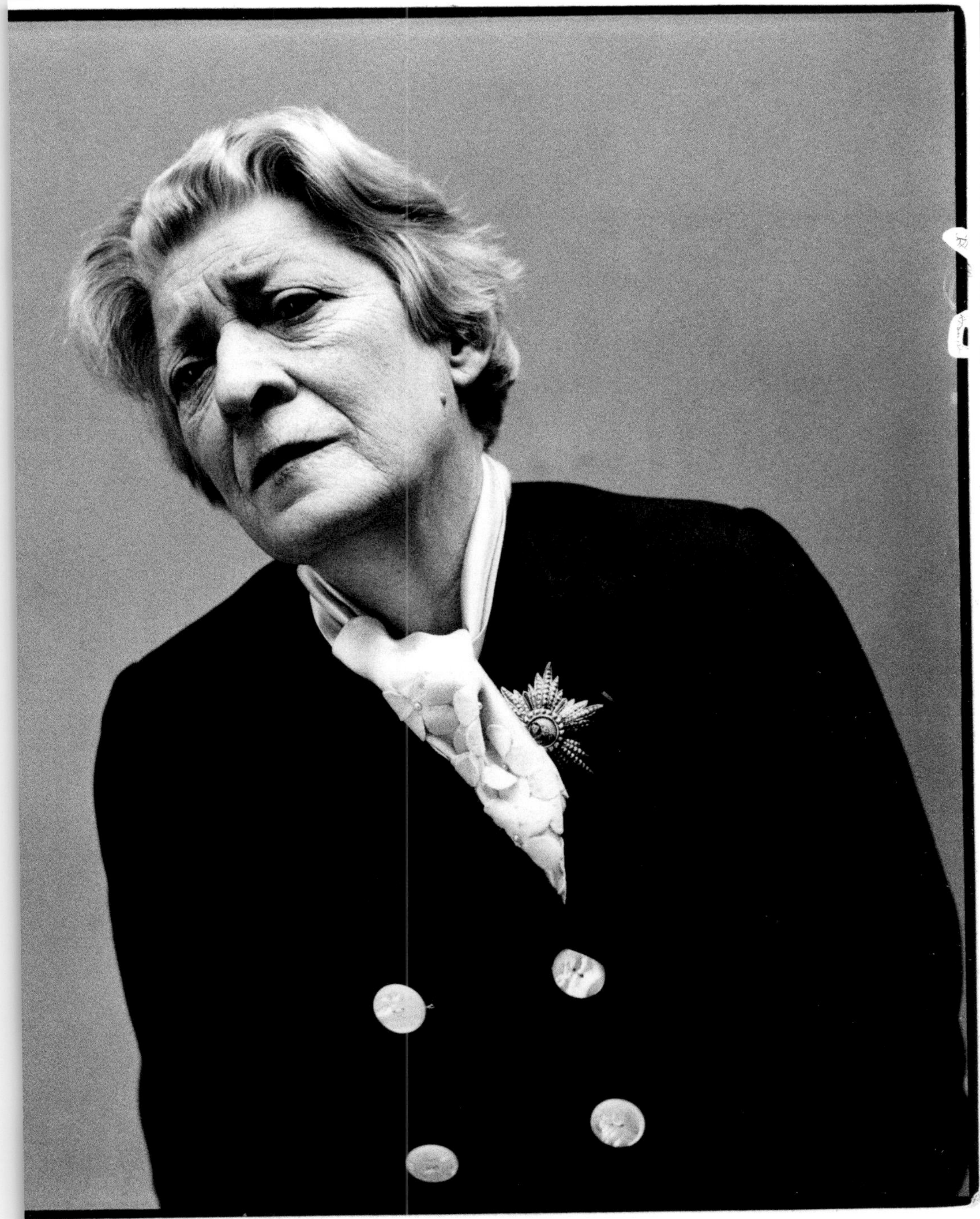

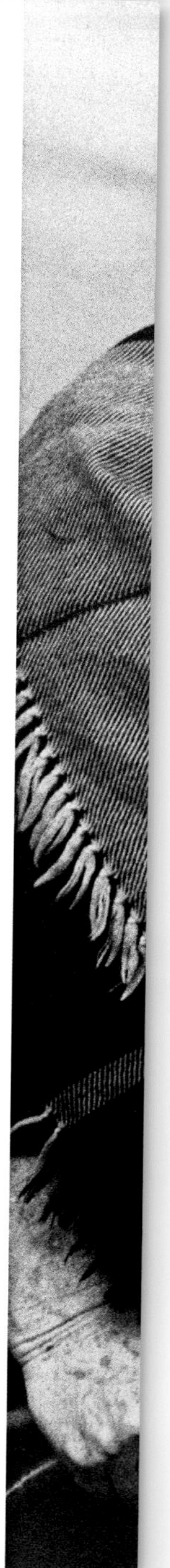

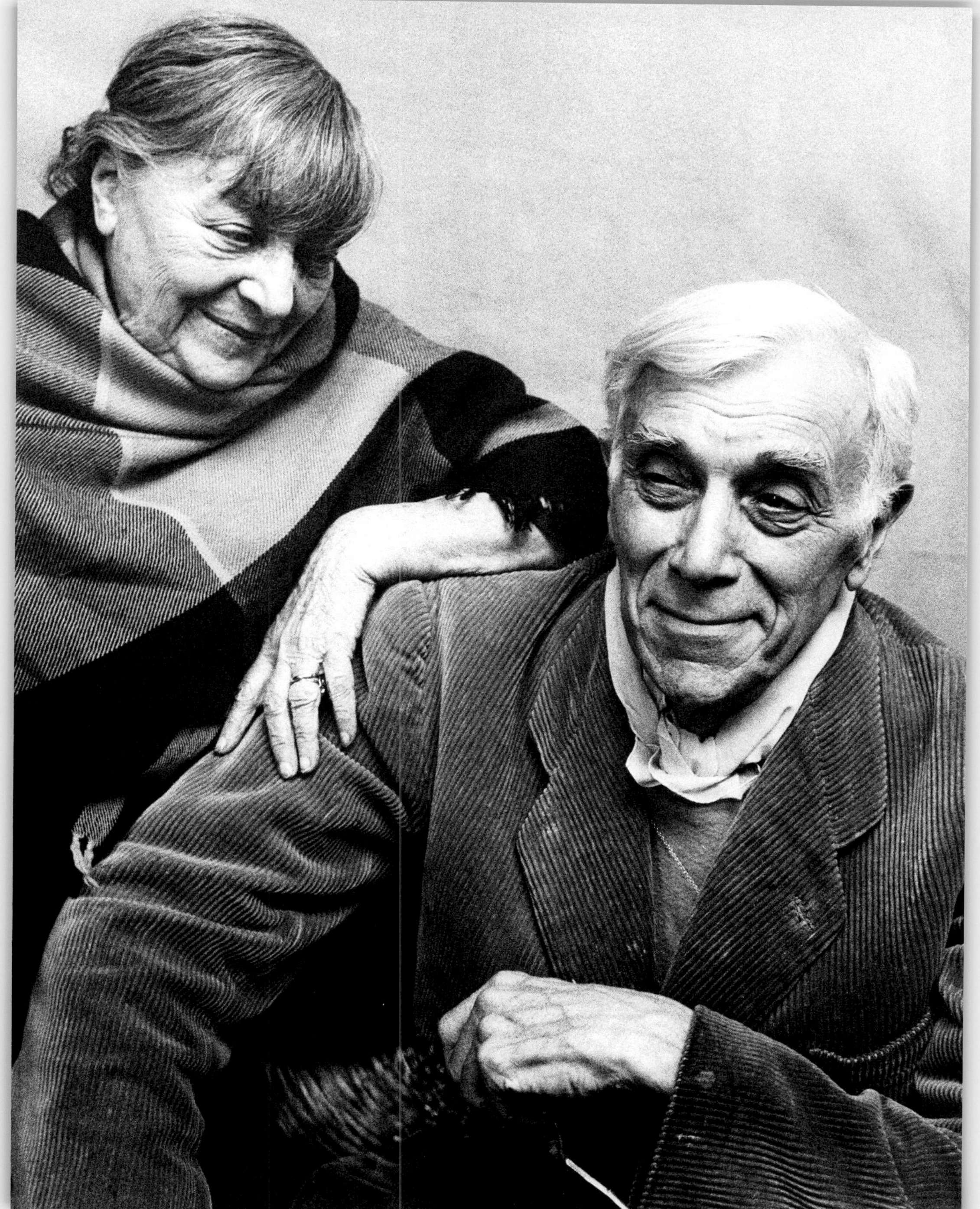

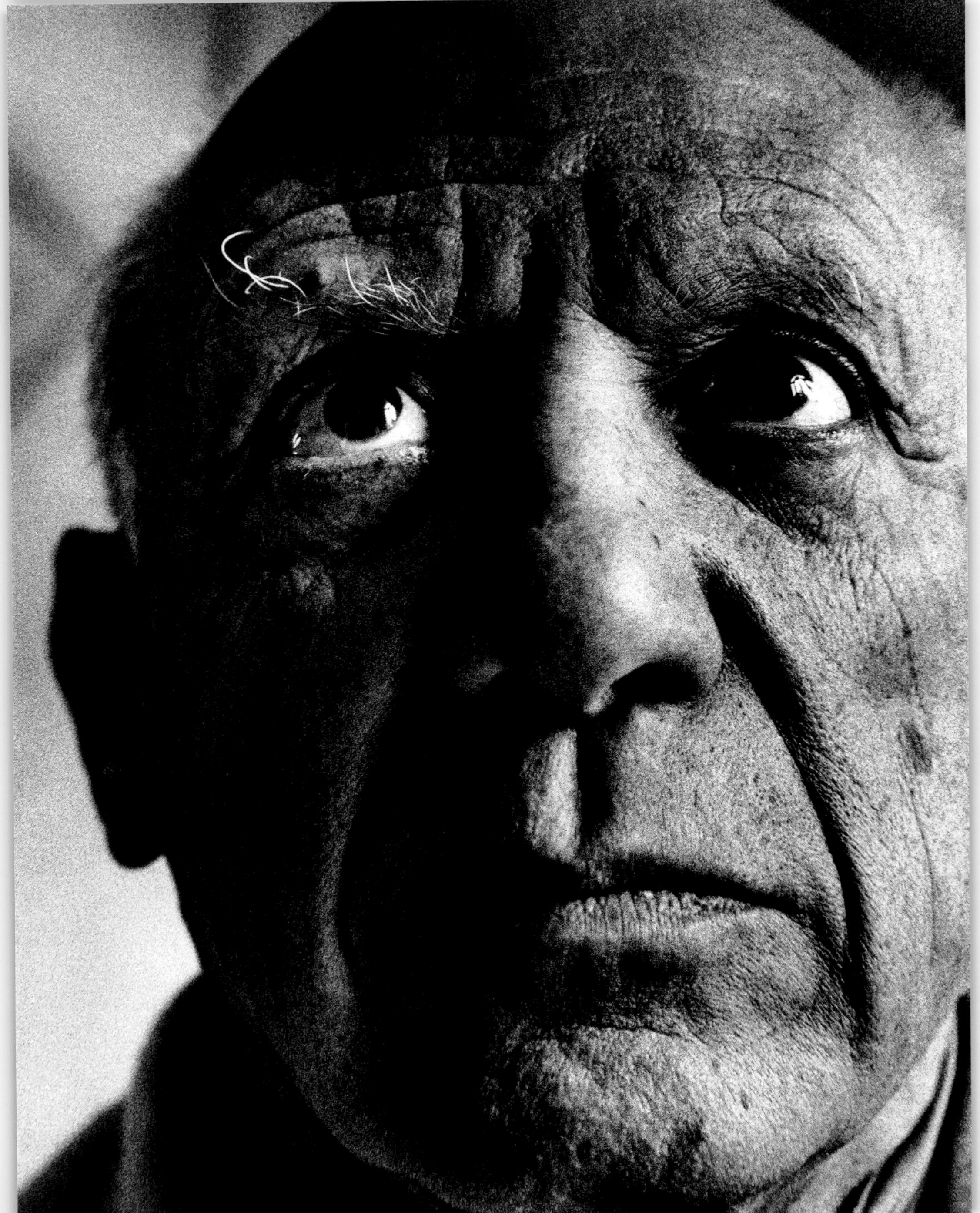

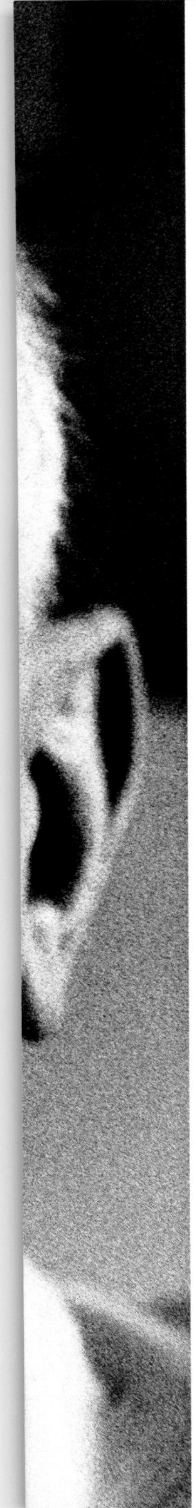

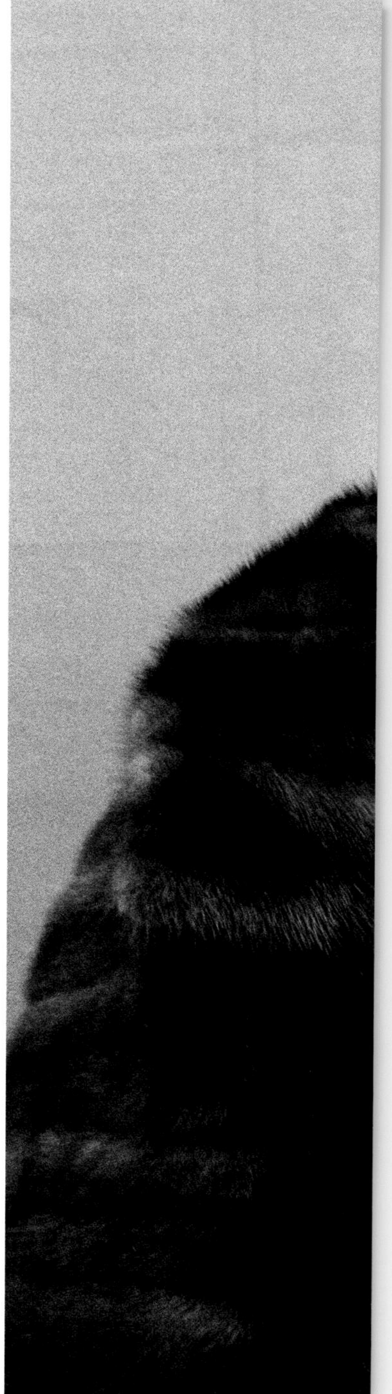

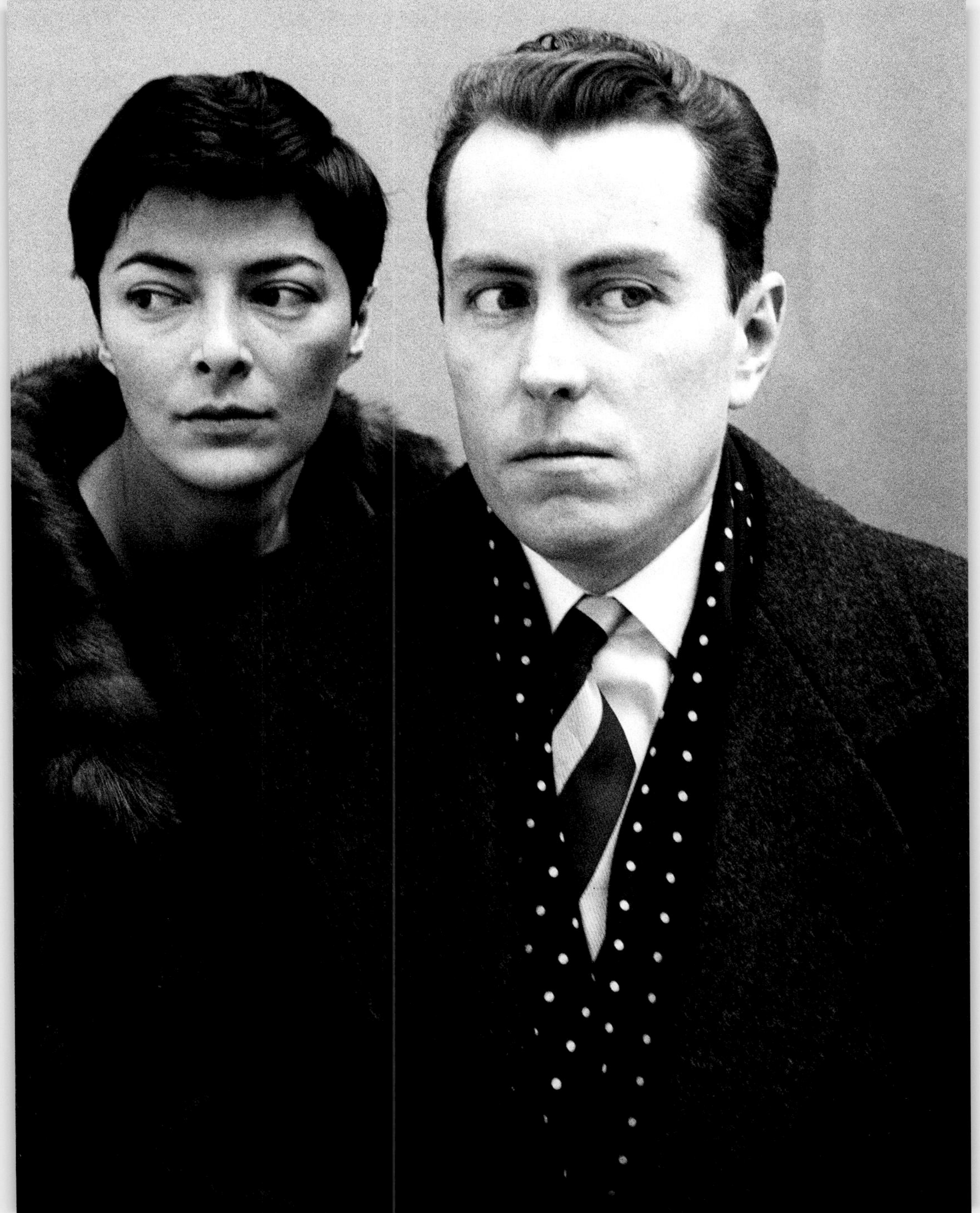

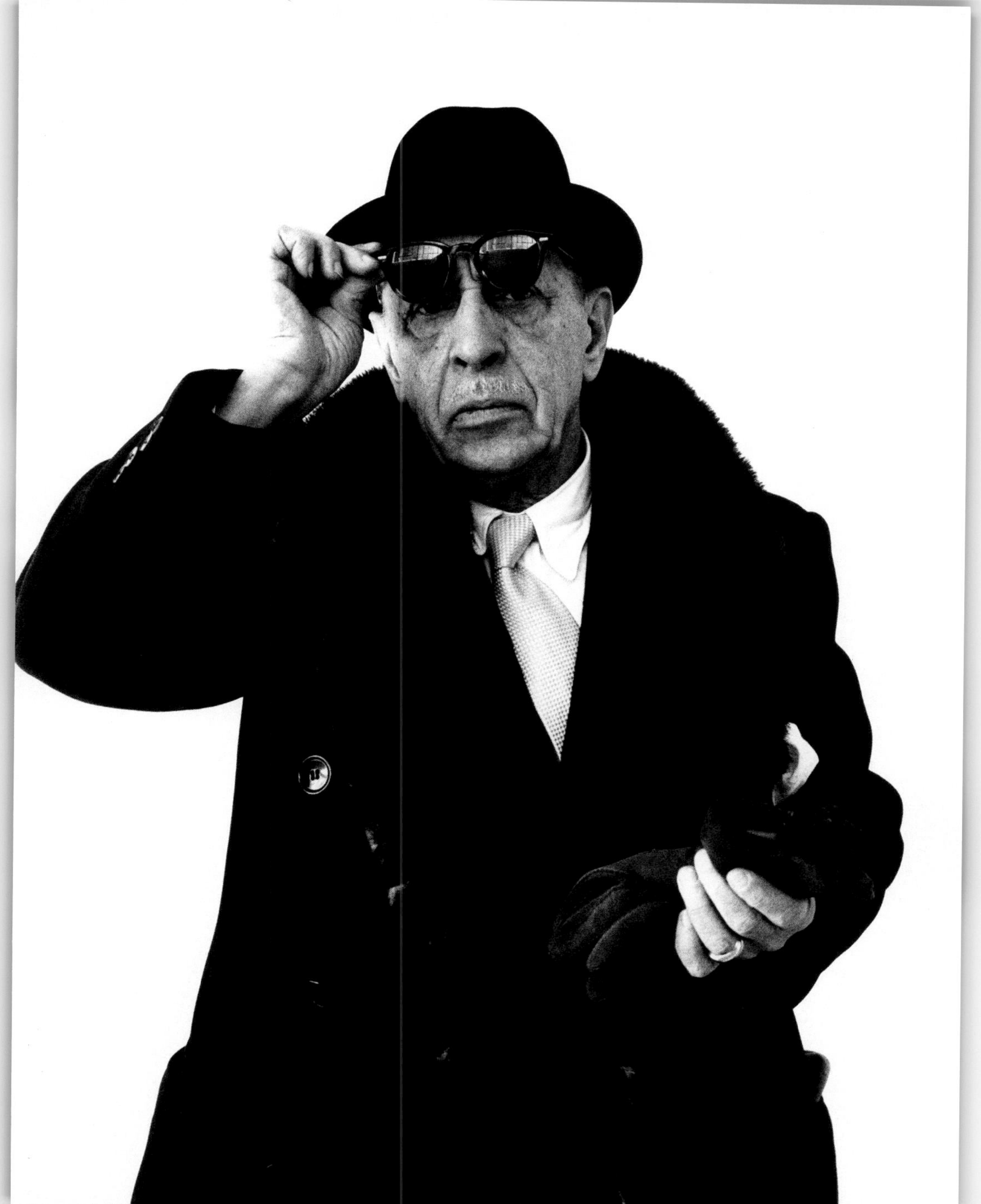

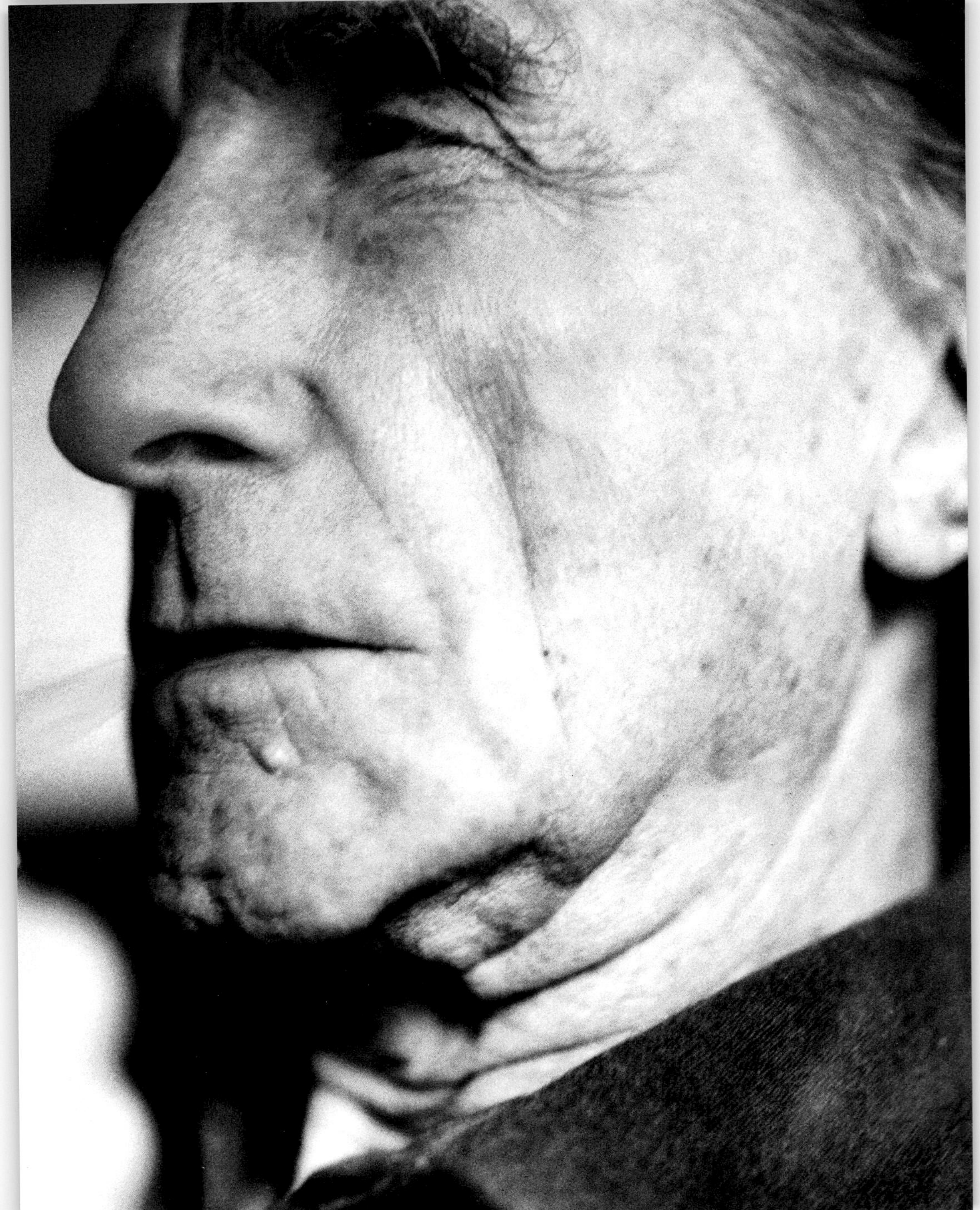

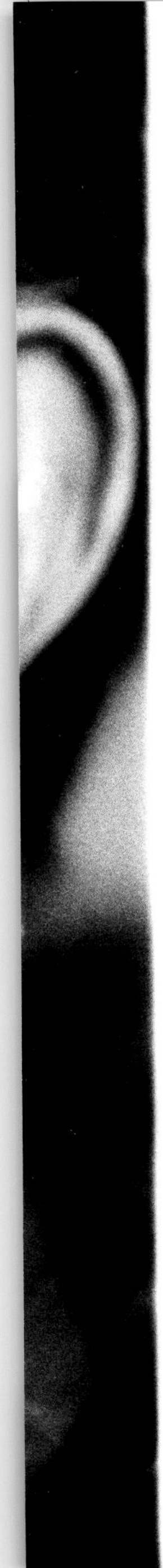

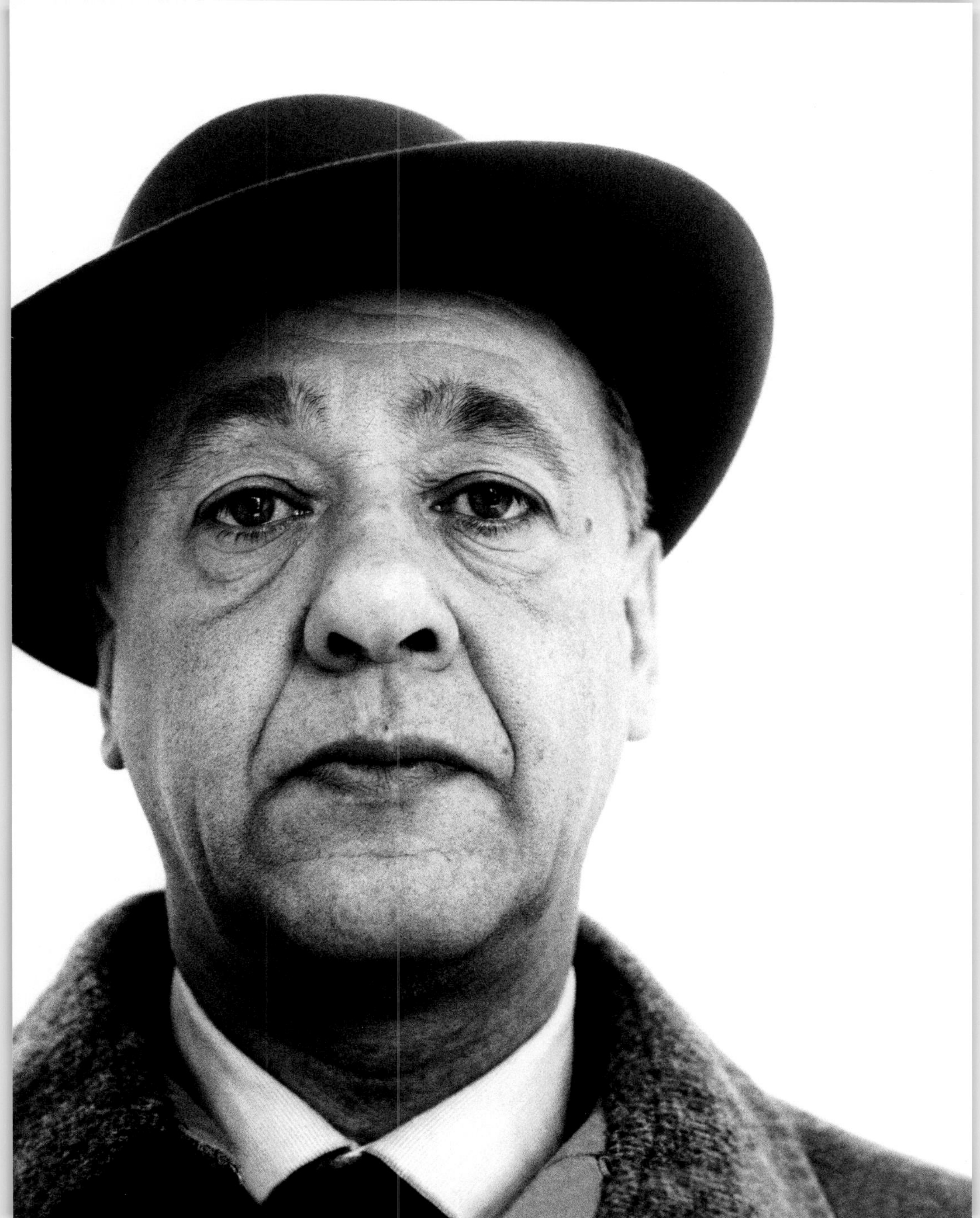

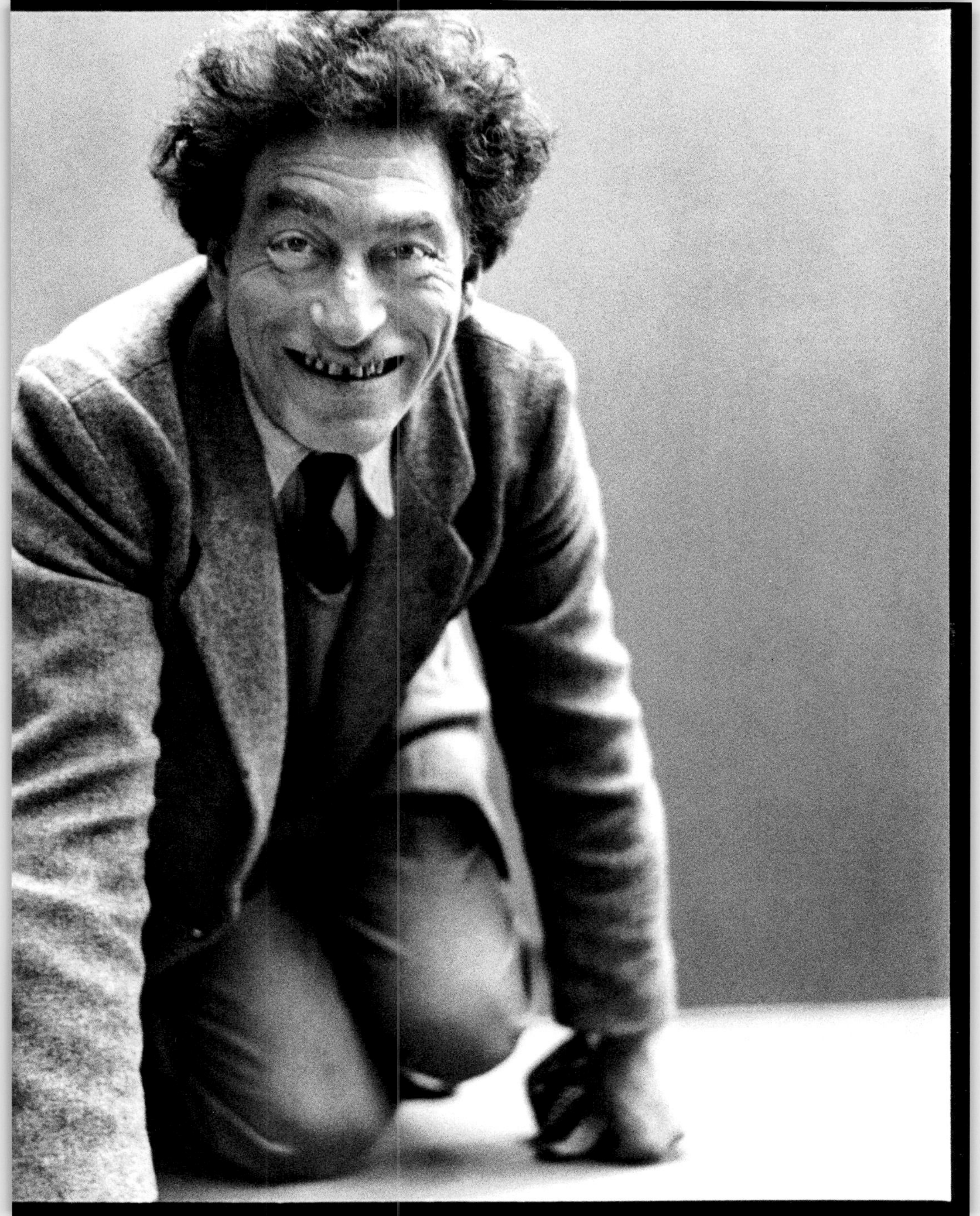

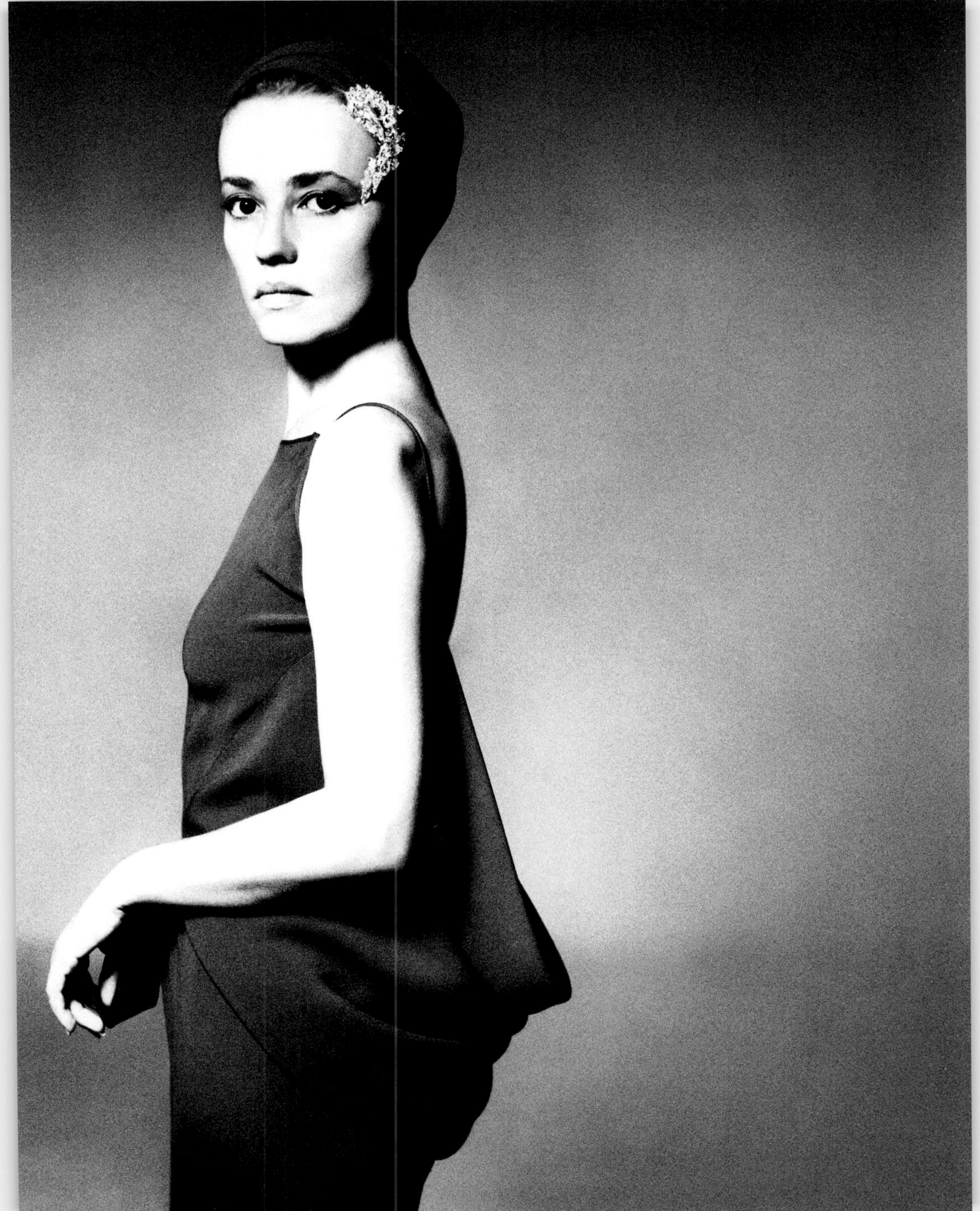

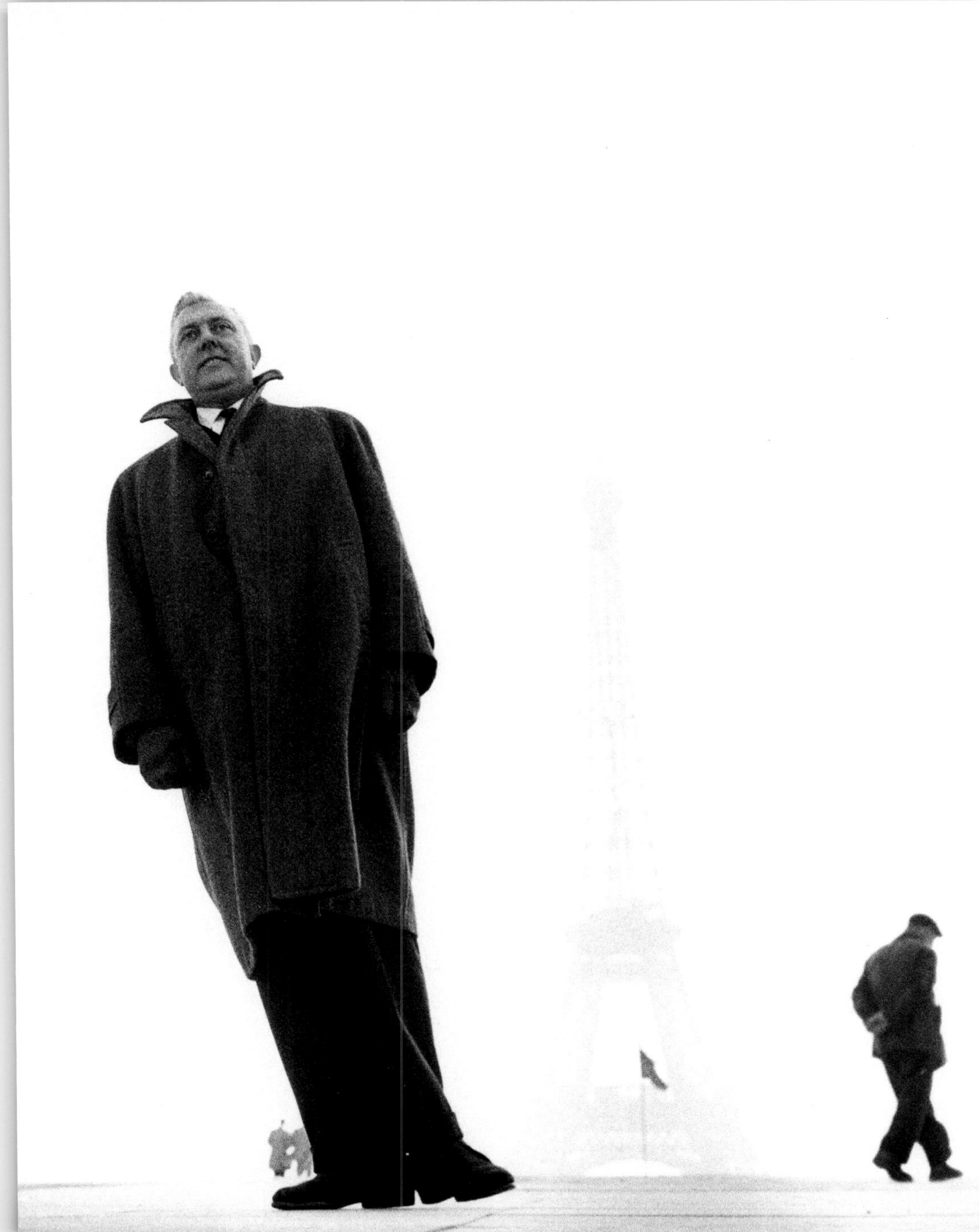

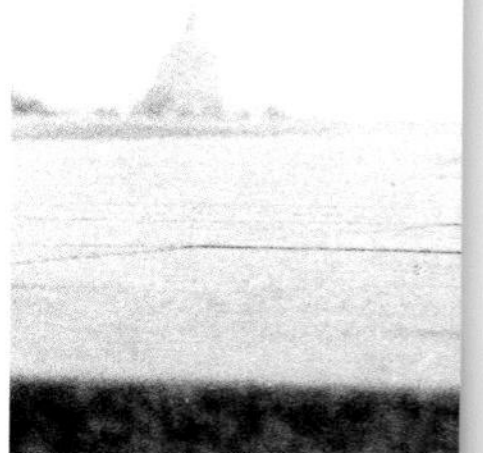

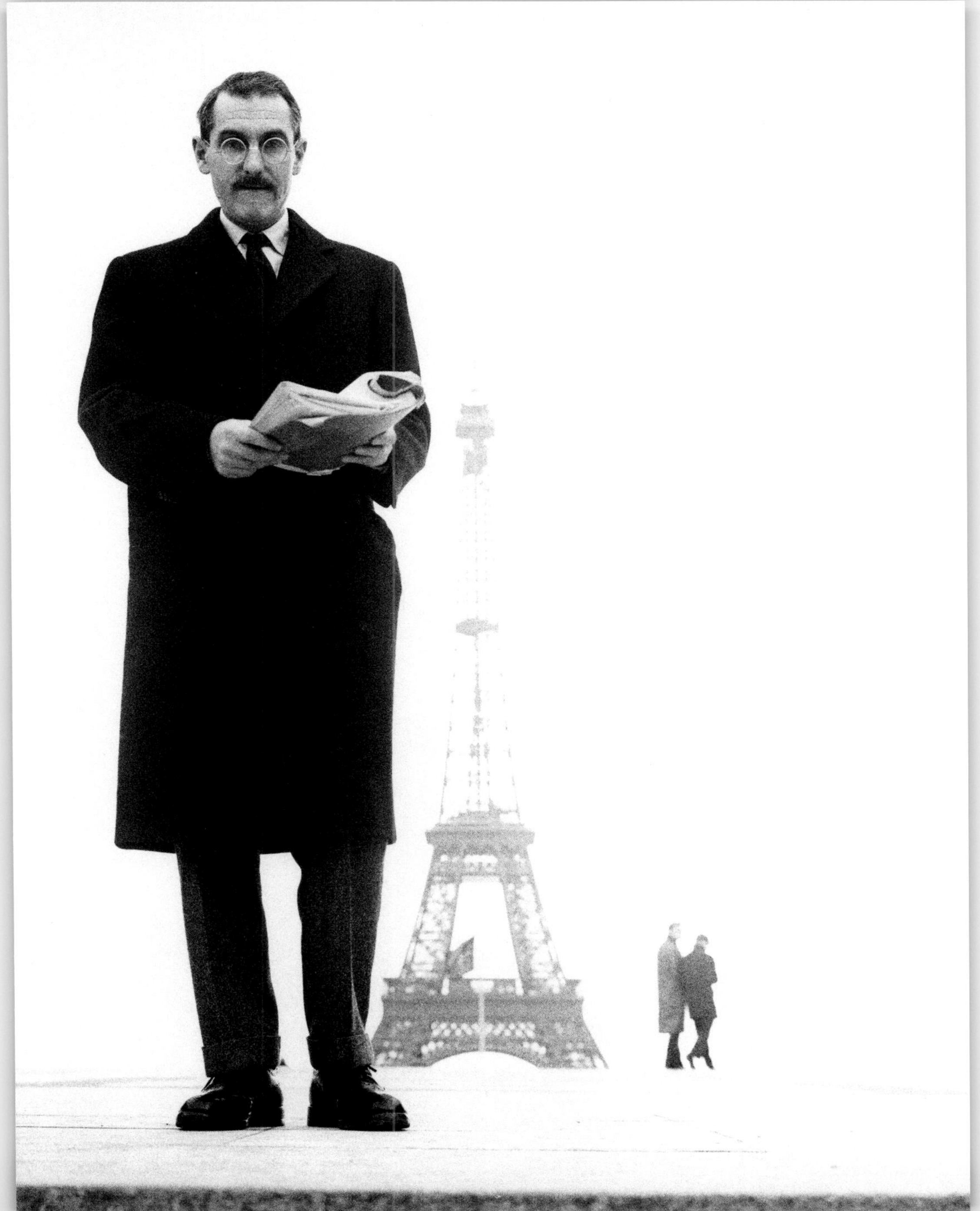

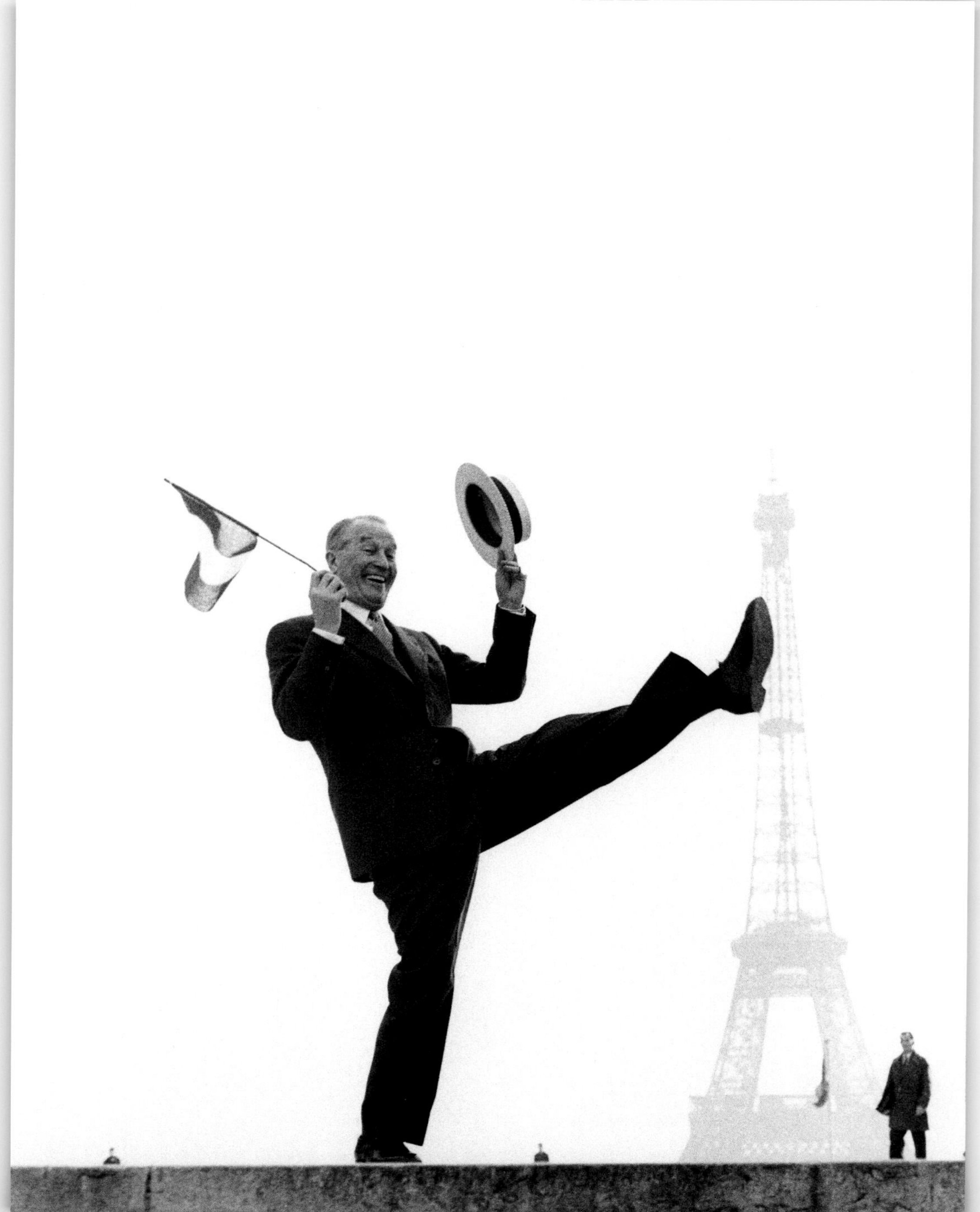

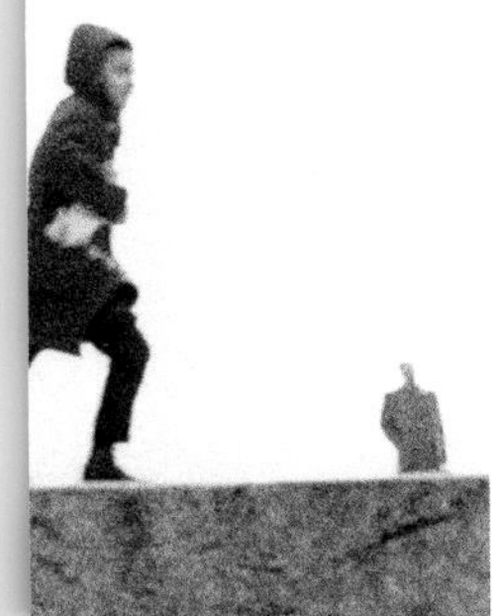

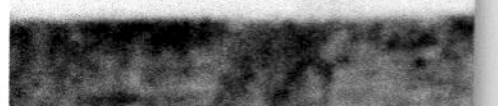

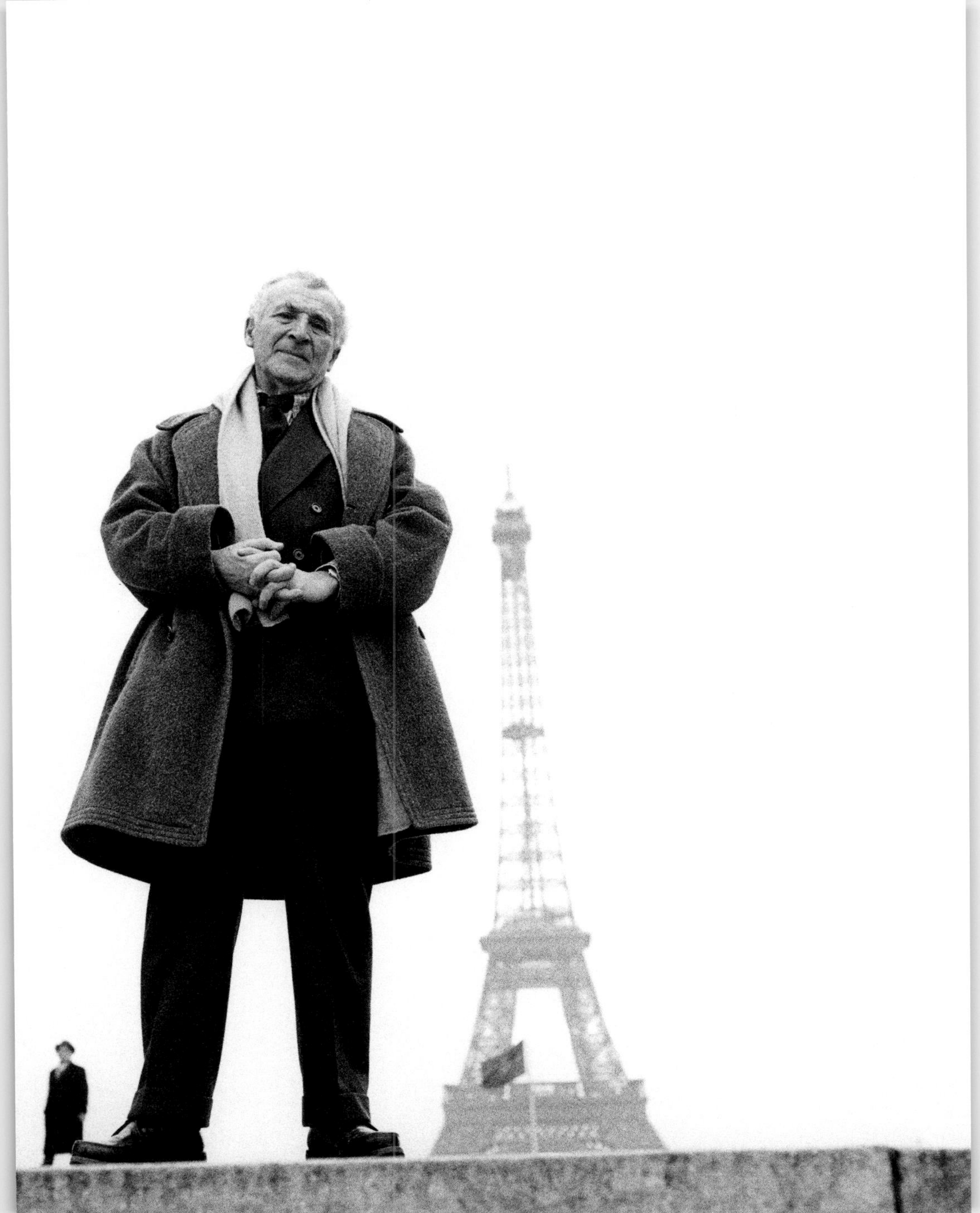

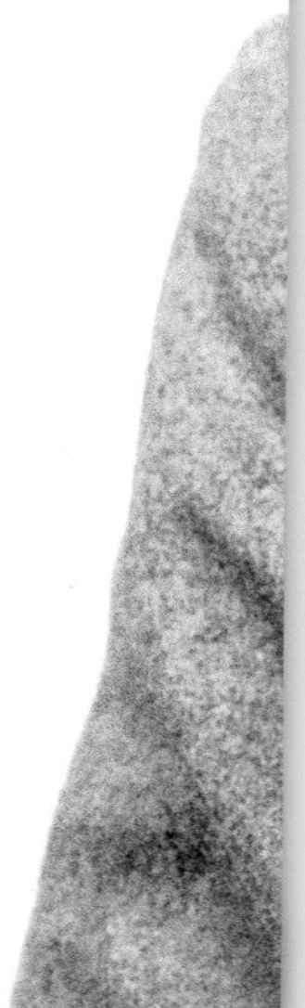

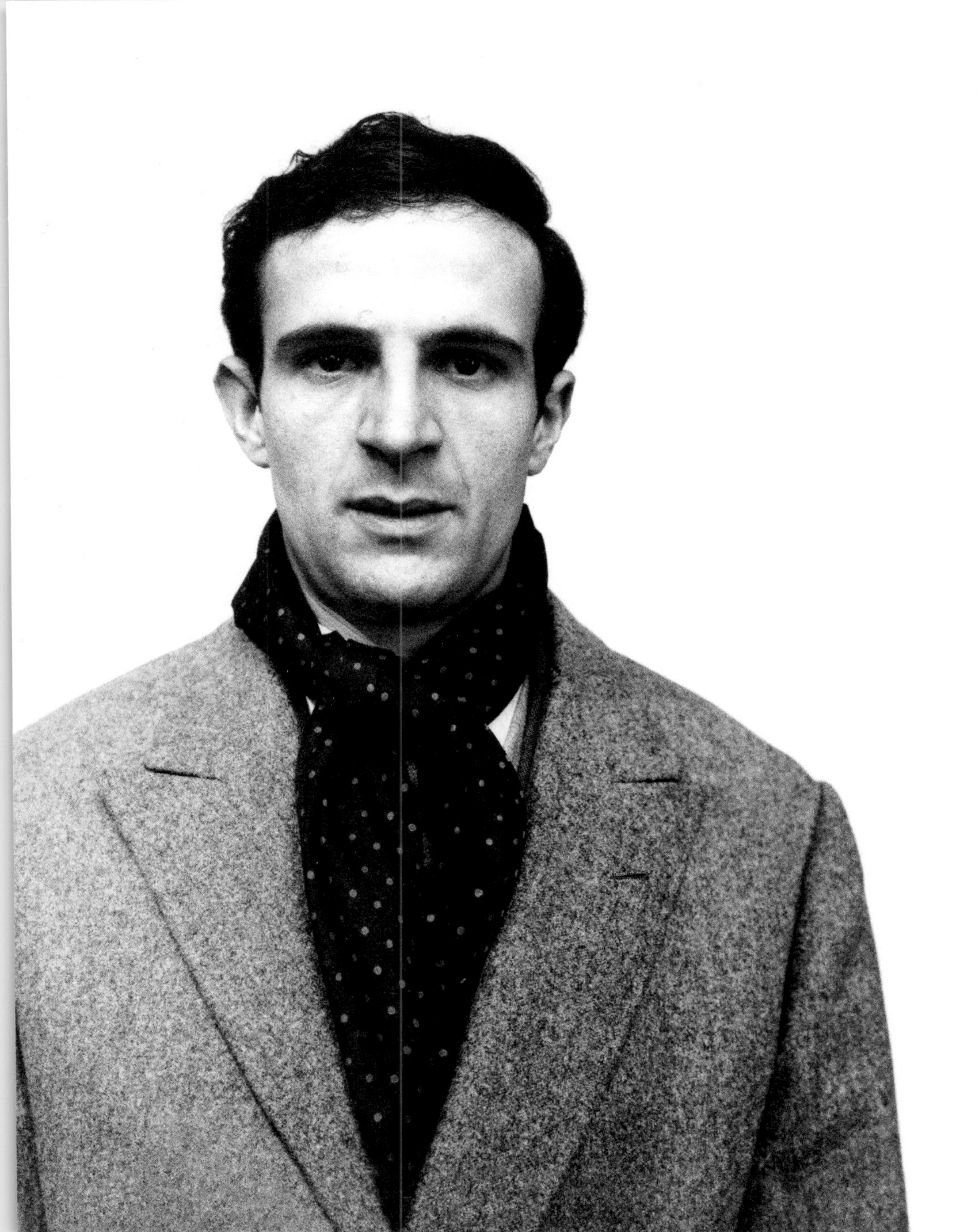

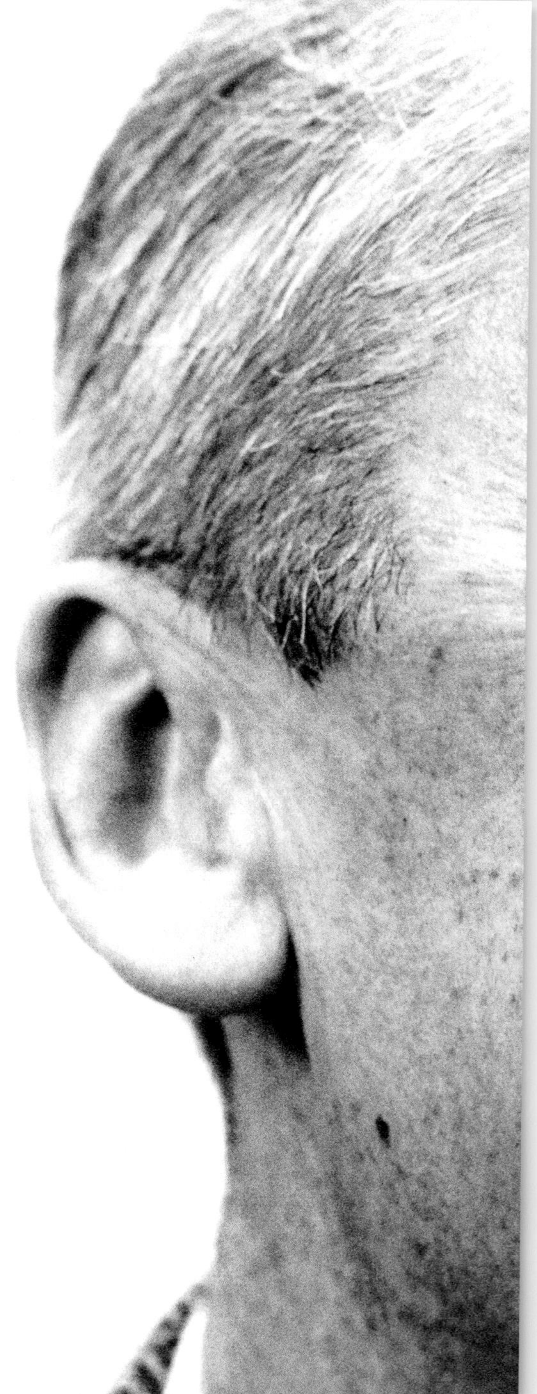

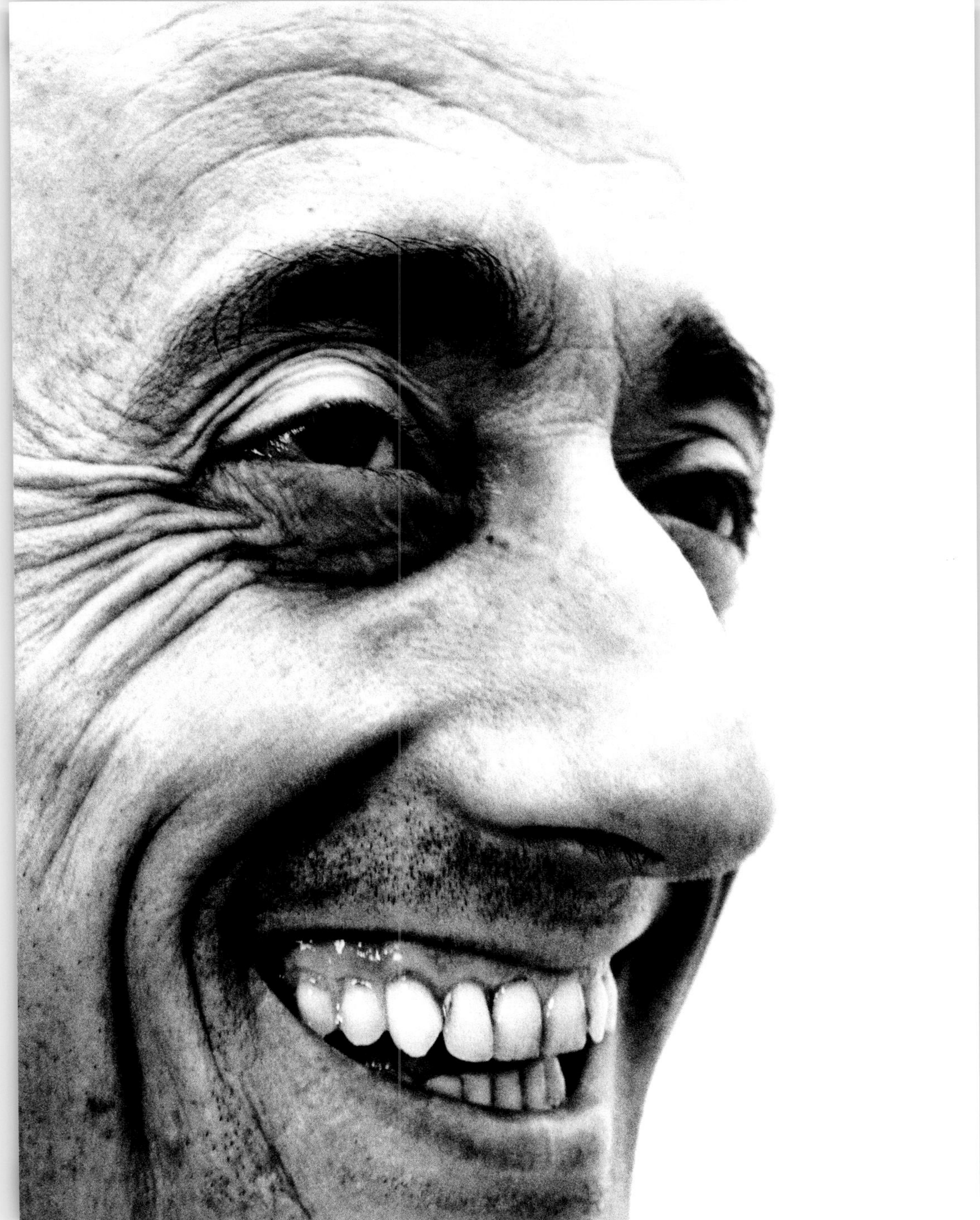

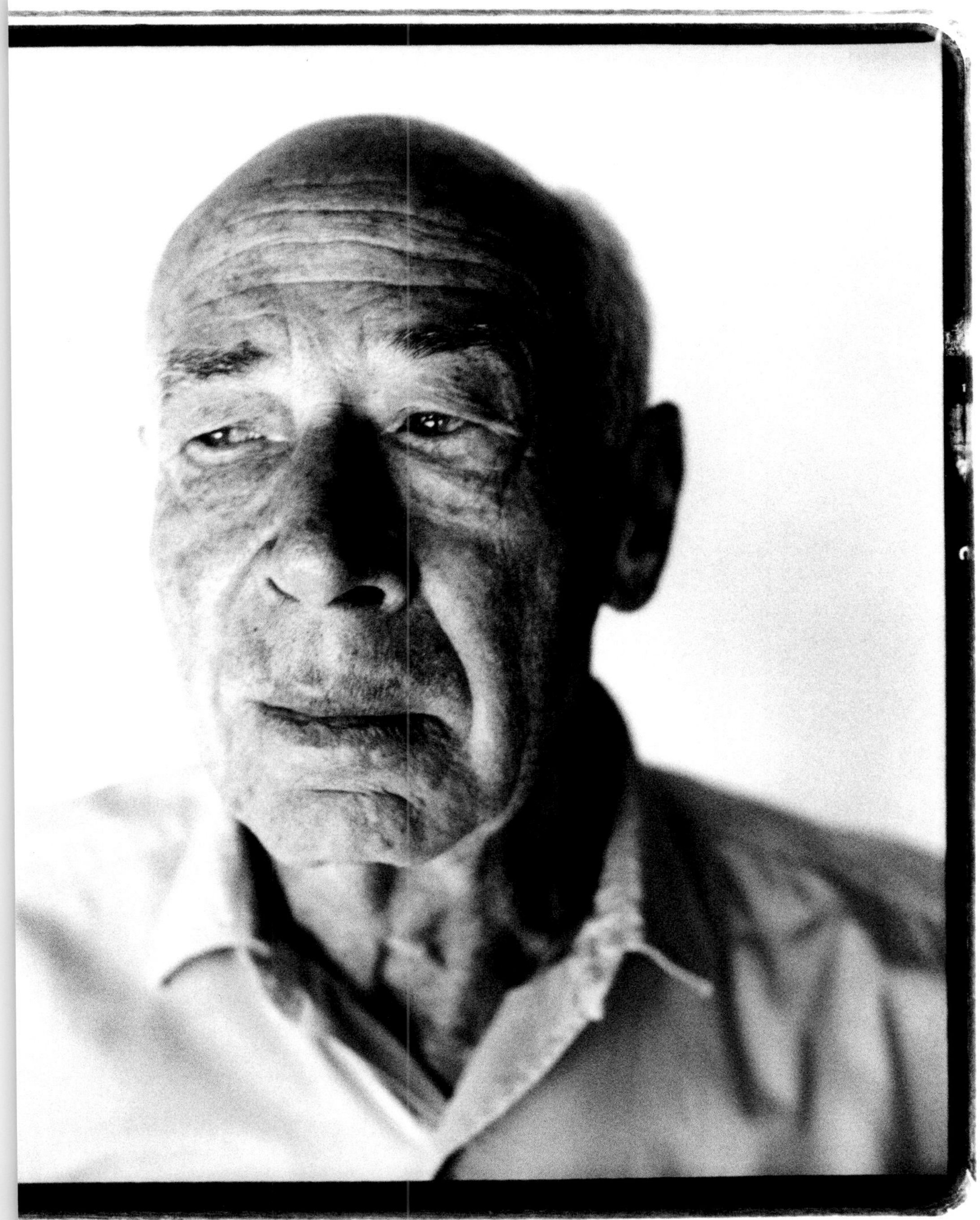

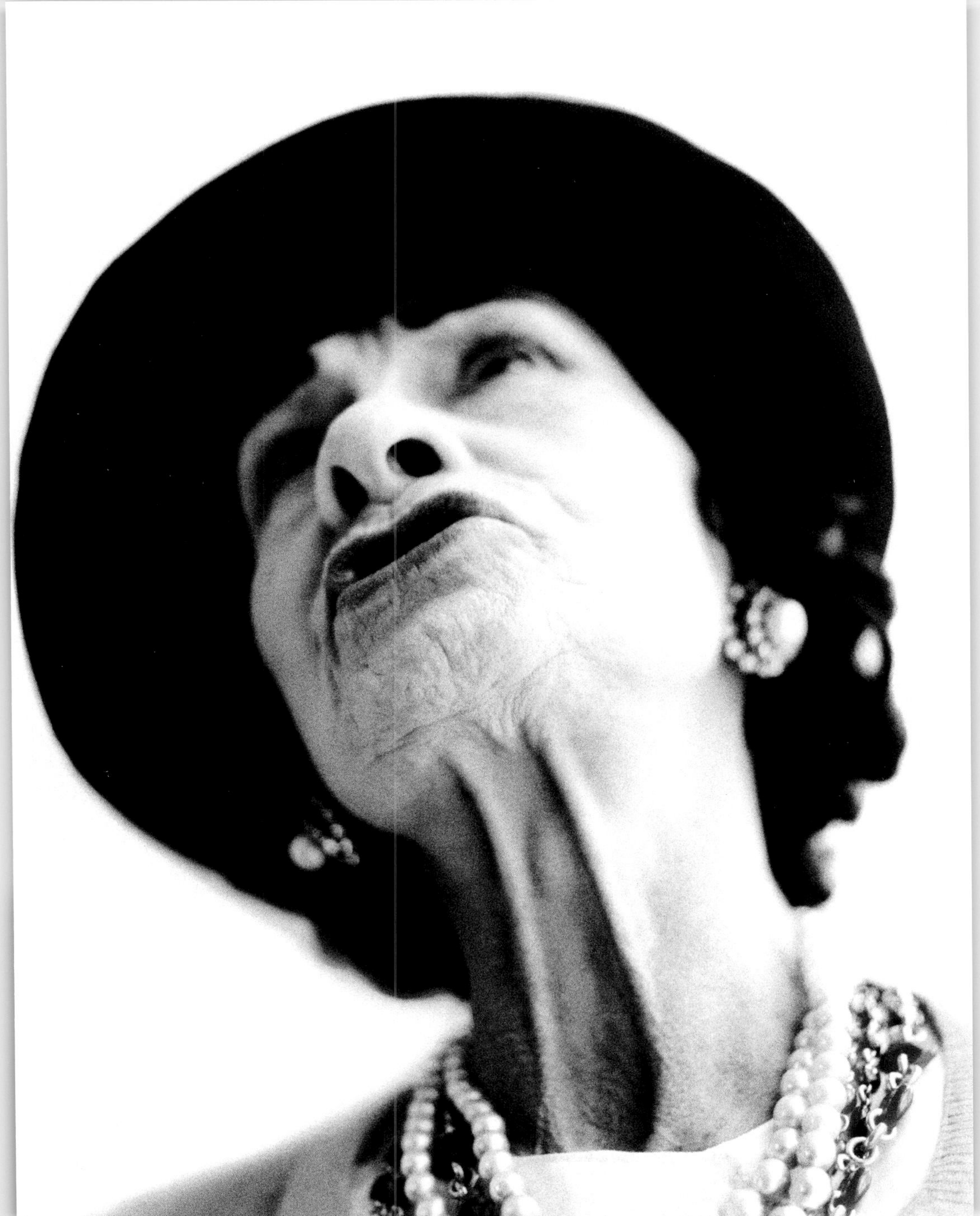

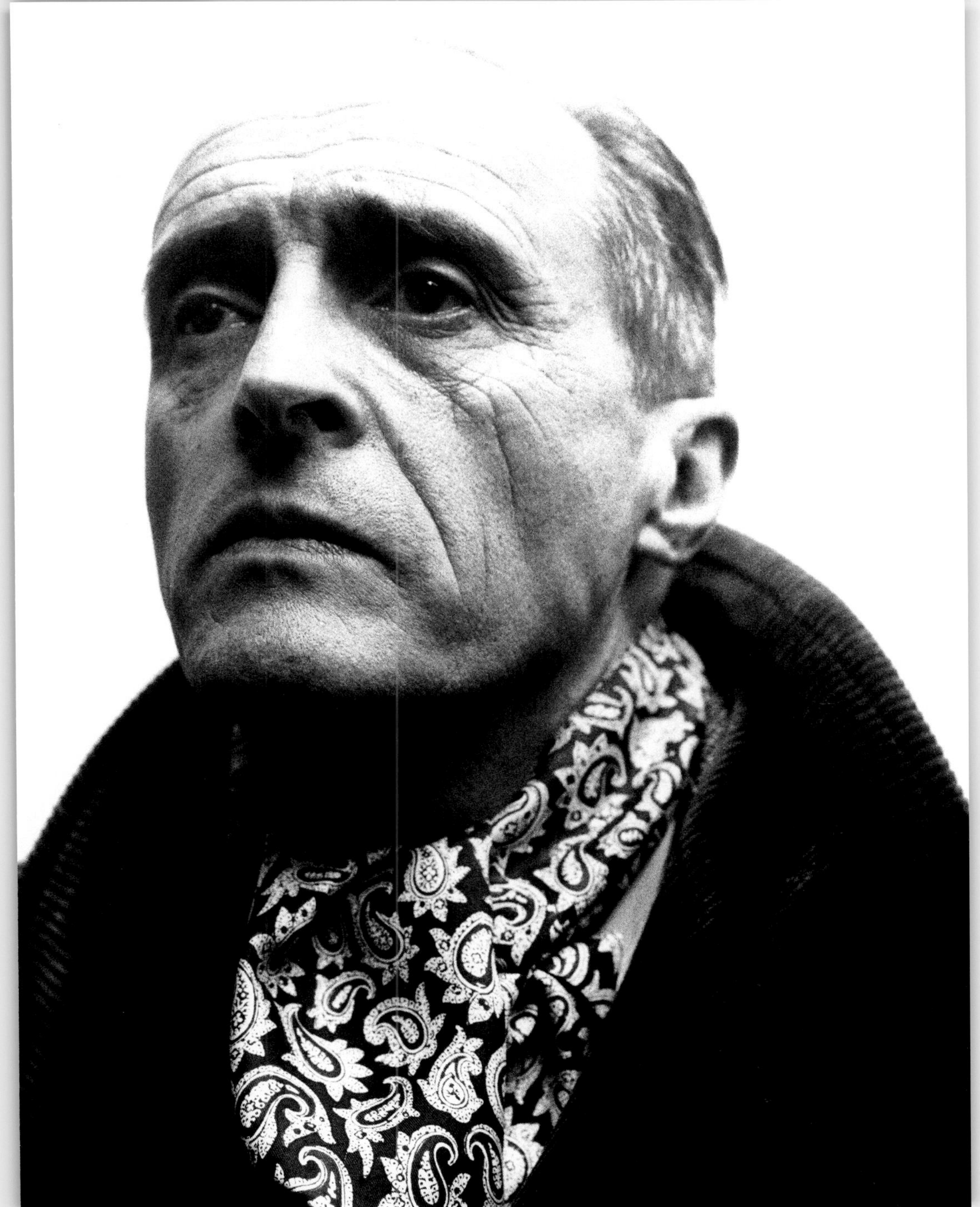

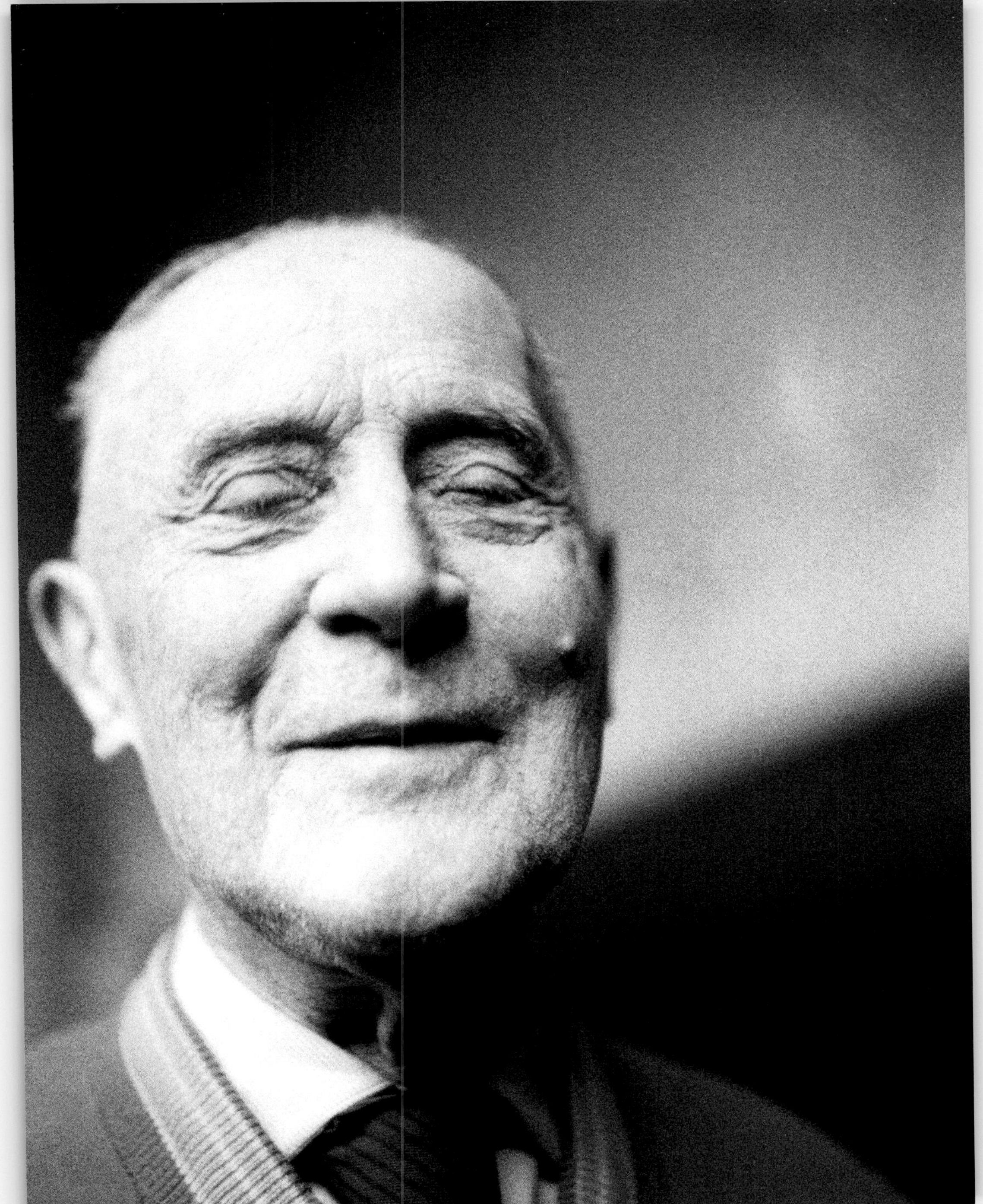

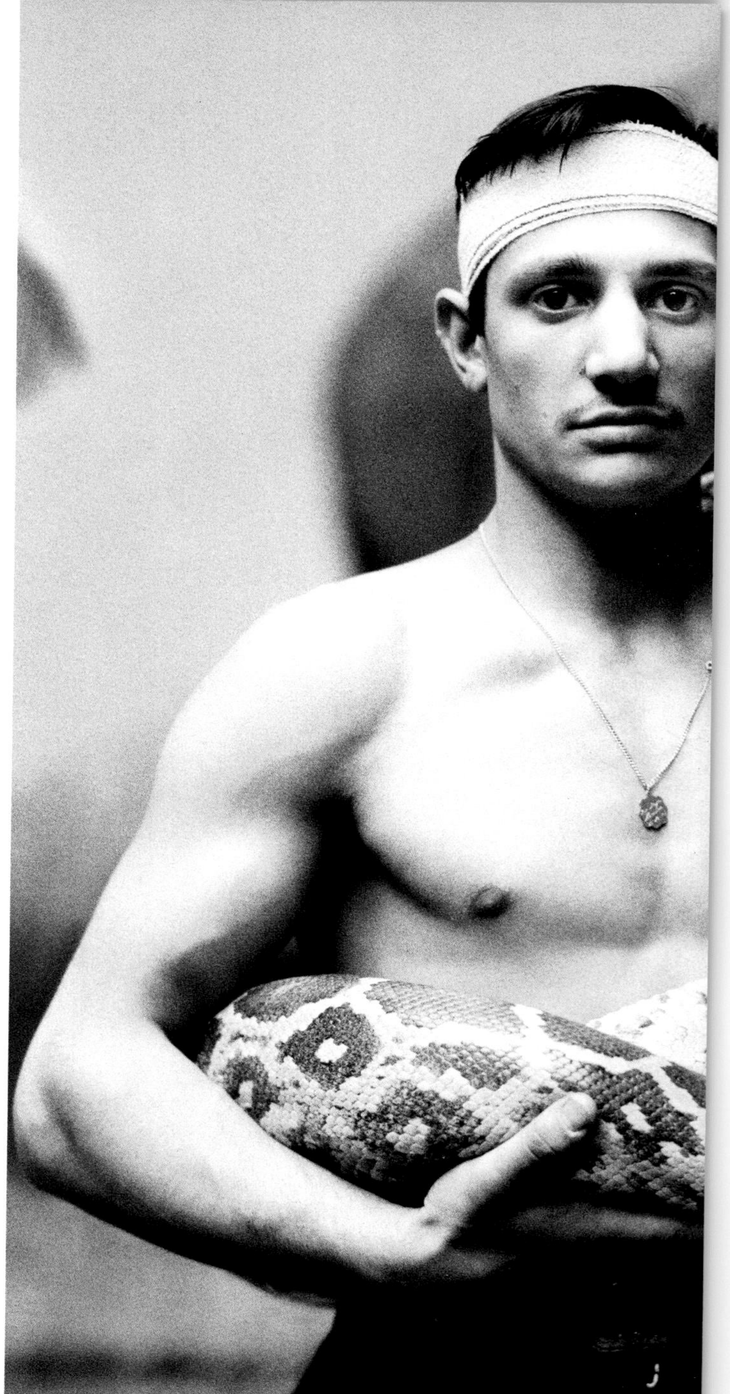

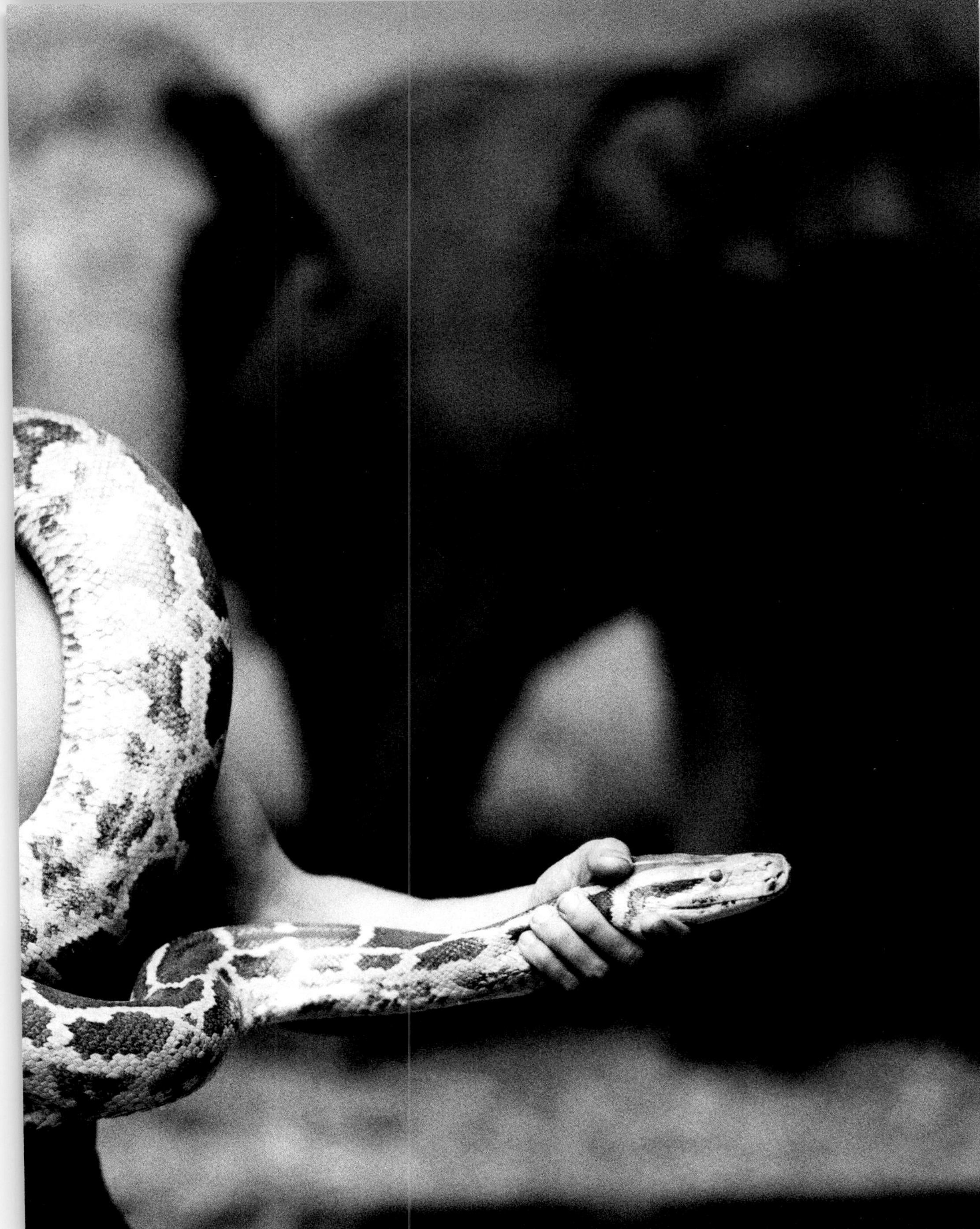

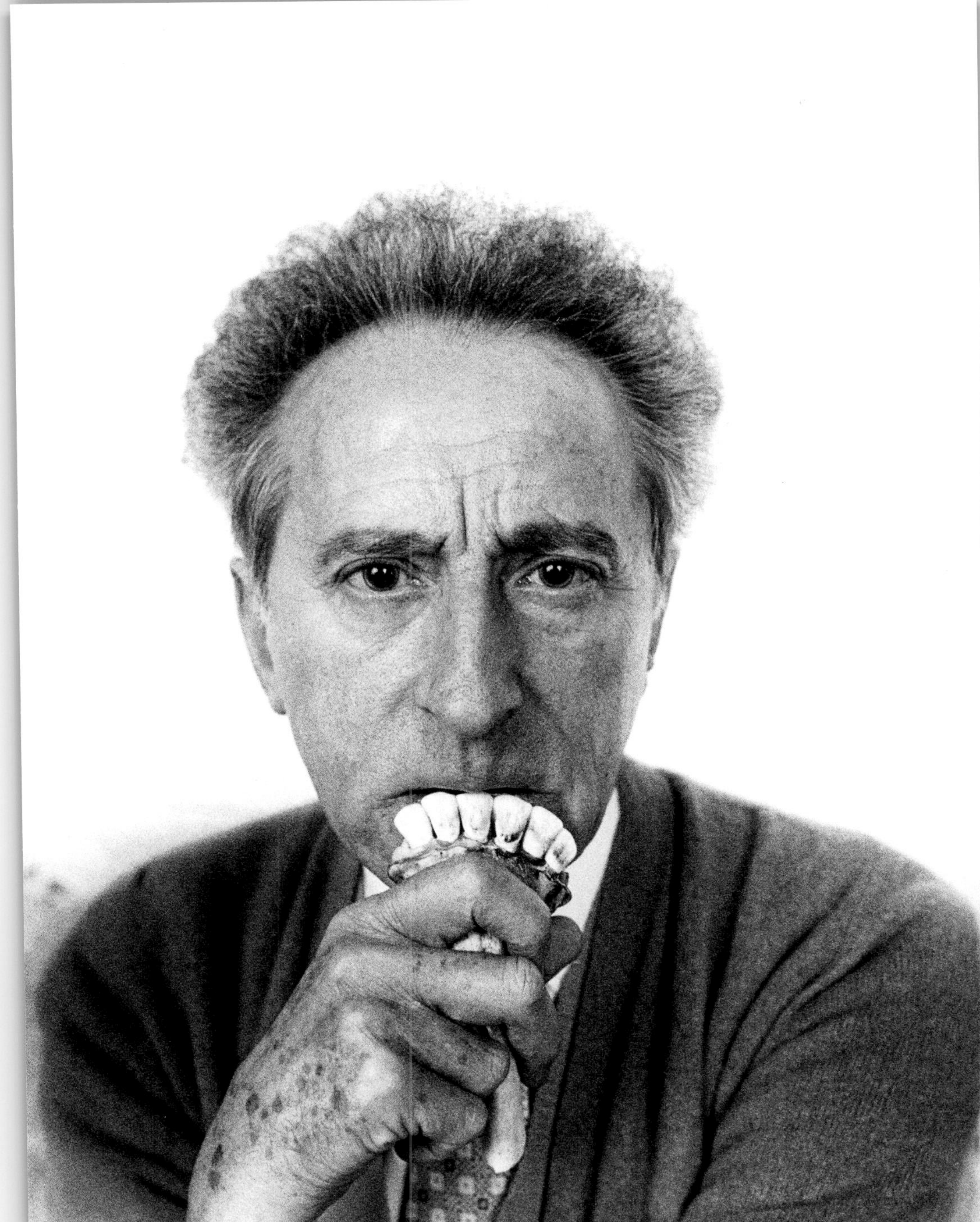

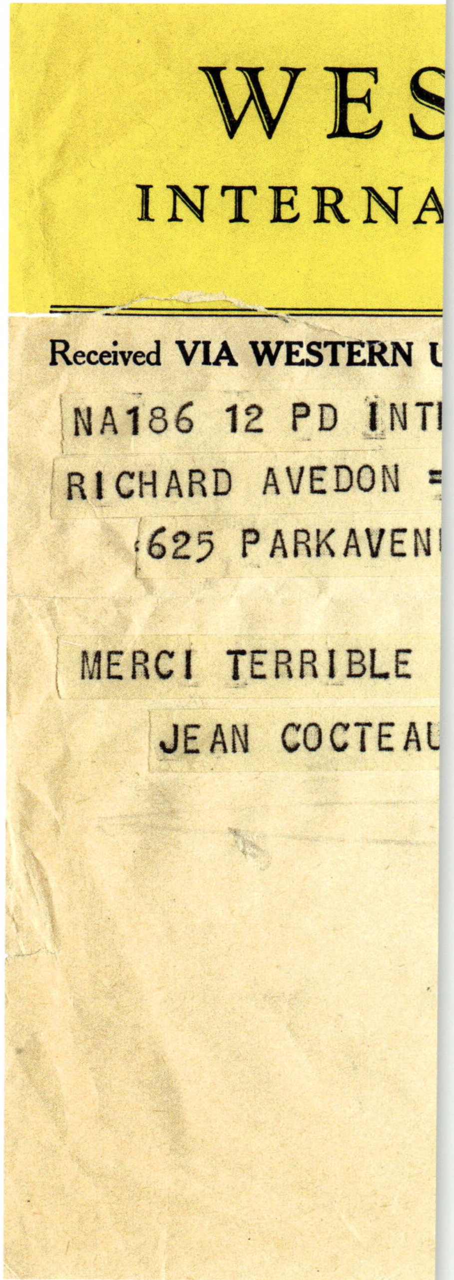

WES

INTERNA

Received VIA WESTERN U

NA186 12 PD INT

RICHARD AVEDON =

625 PARKAVEN

MERCI TERRIBLE

JEAN COCTEAU

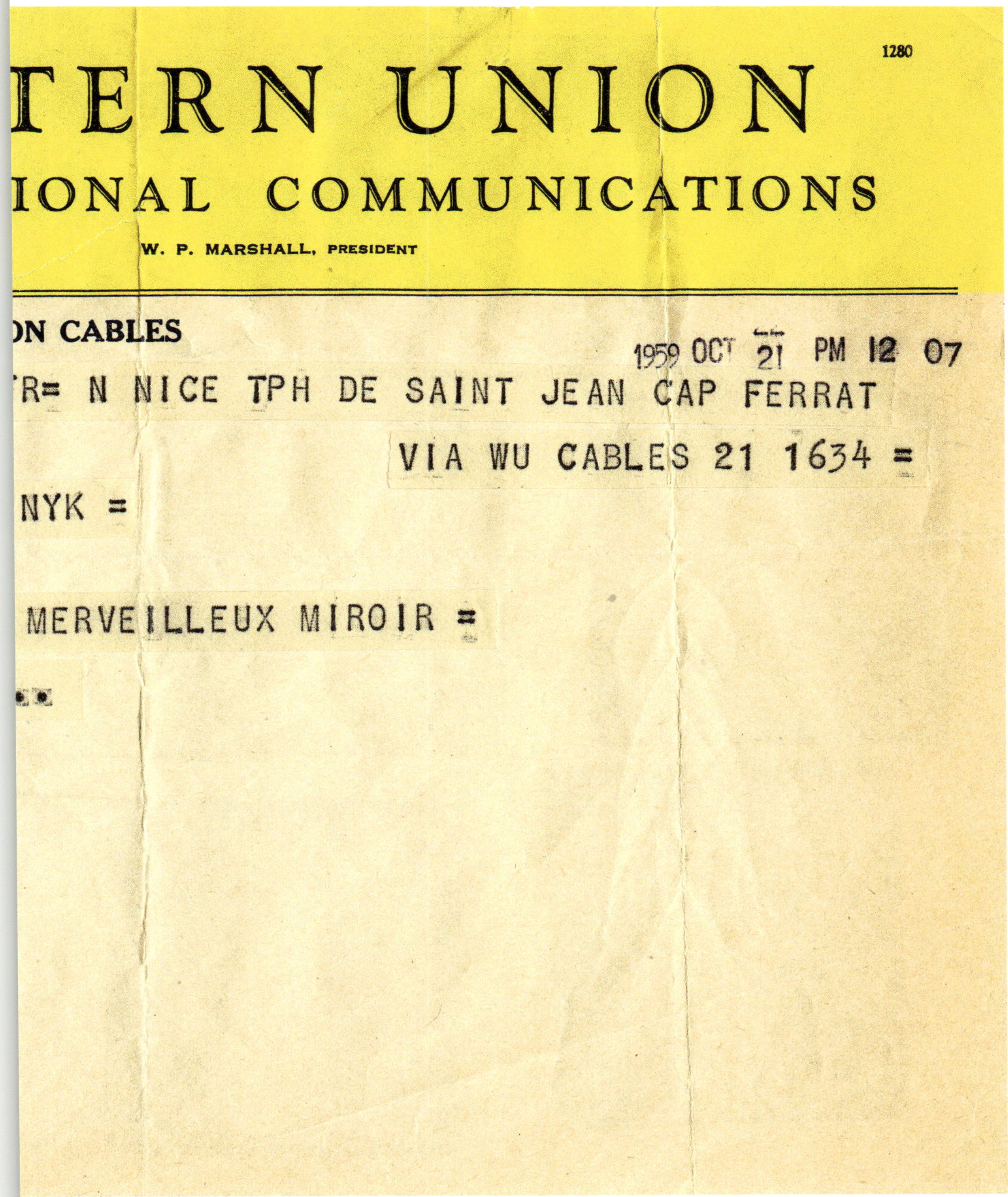

1280

TERN UNION

IONAL COMMUNICATIONS

W. P. MARSHALL, PRESIDENT

ON CABLES

1959 OCT 21 PM 12 07

TR= N NICE TPH DE SAINT JEAN CAP FERRAT

VIA WU CABLES 21 1634 =

NYK =

MERVEILLEUX MIROIR =

Jean Cocteau's telegram to Richard Avedon after seeing his portrait by Avedon for the first time, October 21, 1959

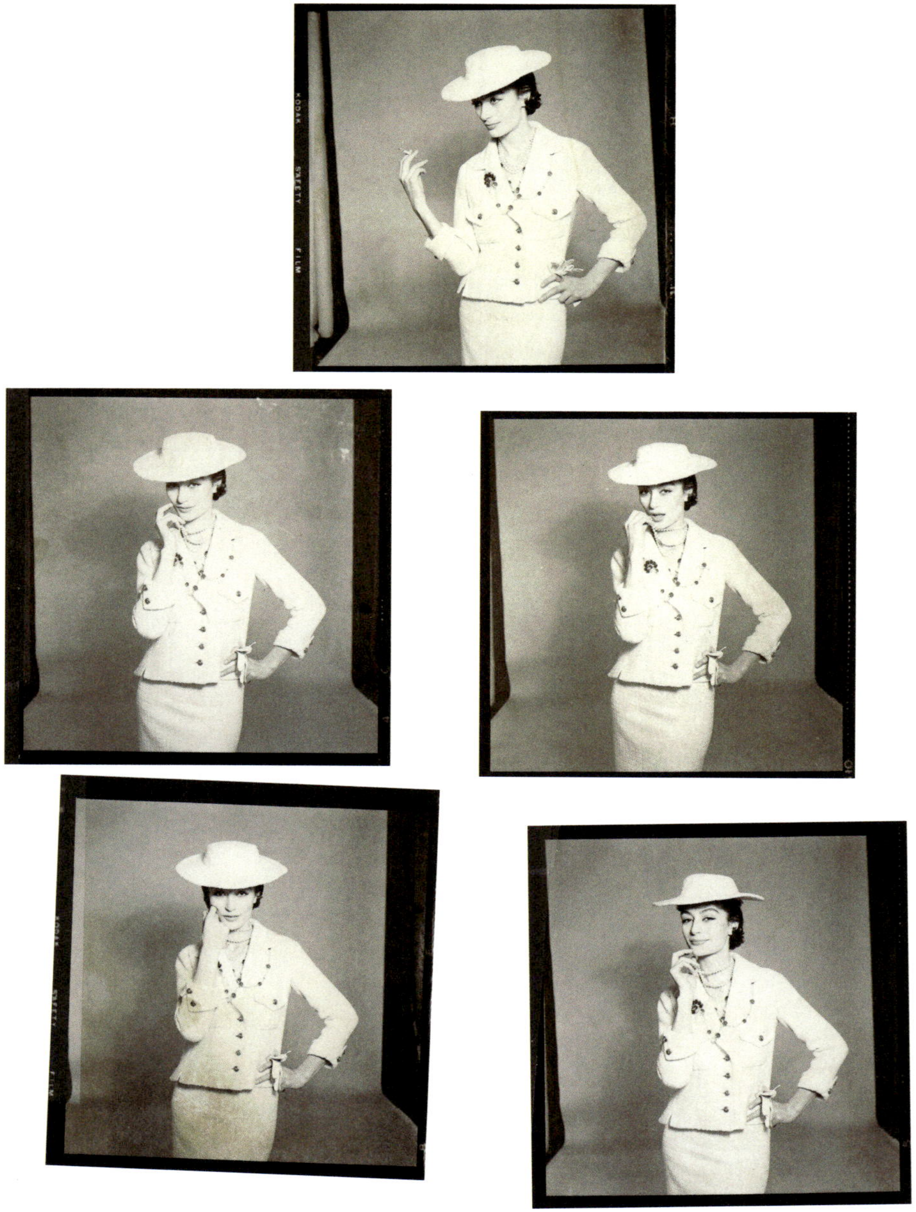

Anouk Aimée, actress, Paris, January 27, 1959 (contact prints)

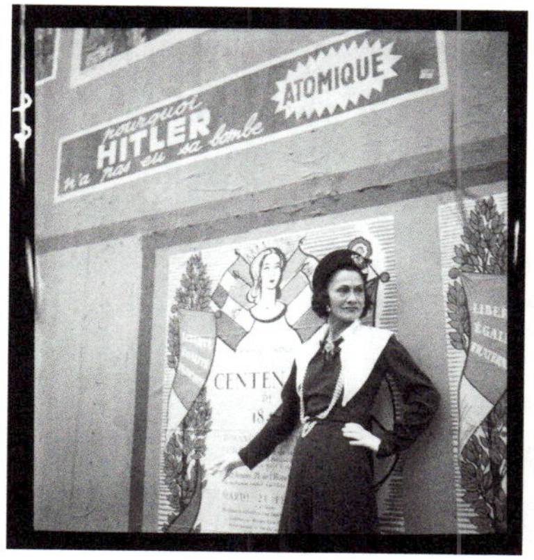

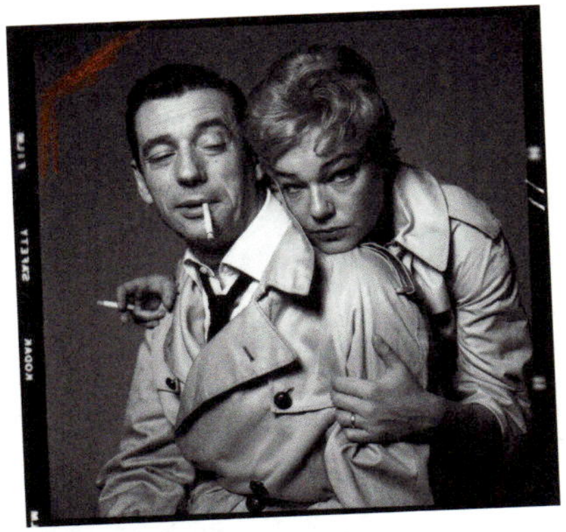

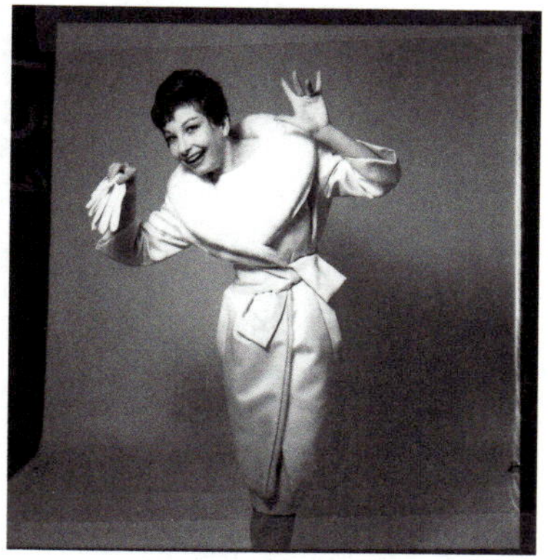

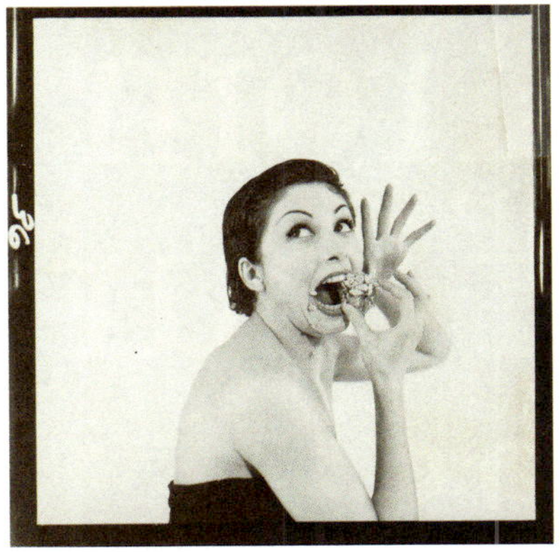

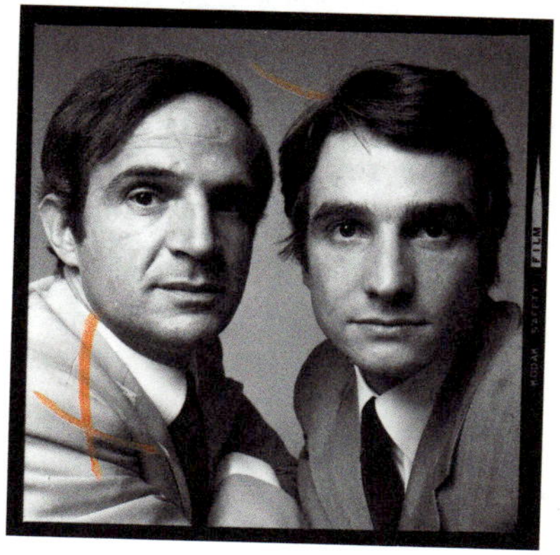

Top left, Gabrielle Chanel, couturier, Paris, June 1948
Bottom left, Renée "Zizi" Jeanmaire, dancer, in *La Croqueuse De Diamants*, Paris, November 28, 1950
Top right, Yves Montand and Simone Signoret, actors, October 23, 1959
Middle right, Renée "Zizi" Jeanmaire, dancer, Paris, January 1959
Bottom right, François Truffaut and Jean-Pierre Léaud, director and actor, Paris, June 20, 1971 (contact prints)

I grew up with a first cousin, two years older than I. I was deeply in love with her from the age of four until I was eighteen. . . .

When the Cocteau movie, *Les Enfants Terribles*, came out, we knew we were those children. We saw it over and over.

—

Richard Avedon

(*Continued*) identically printed, they even have the elusive shimmer of water itself. . . . At the very opposite pole is the marvelous *Gazar*—a coarse, starchy gauze, with a texture like glamorized tarlatan, but woven of the finest silk. Whether in clear color or in print, *Gazar* imparts to the dress a look at once sculptured and airy, and of the most sophisticated freshness. It personifies the venturesome spirit of French dressmaking. Woolens, too, reflect the feeling for transparency, for loose, coarse weaves—the cobweb mohairs, the wools with the wide weave of tapestry crash, sometimes so open they have to be mounted on foundations of organdie or Shantung. Yet everywhere, in every collection, there is an unmistakable pull in another direction: toward tight, dry worsteds that look like traditional men's suitings placed under a magnifying glass, and so raised to the feminine level. In shepherd's checks, Prince of Wales plaid and herringbones, they sound a sustained new note—an overtone to the deliberately casual lines of Paris now.

Suits and Coats: Cardin's fresh-air necklines, on both suits and coats, cut almost as wide as the shoulders themselves above full-blown, tubular sleeves, are a confirmation of his talent and individuality. Most of his suit jackets stop smack at the waist. In contrast, Lanvin-Castillo's Eton jackets now graze the hipbones, and the braided blazer suits at Nina Ricci have jackets longer still. . . . The newest coat in Paris, immensely chic, is the slim, firmly sashed, big-collared overcoat, sometimes shorter than the dress it covers. In white satin gabardine collared in mink; in black silk with a black-and-white scarf at the neck; in clay-colored wool—it is a triumph of St. Laurent of Dior.

Dresses: The pleated dress is omnipresent, sometimes with the pleats so densely concentrated, so thickly folded in upon themselves in deep box pleats, that in motion they appear to fight their way out. At Cardin, pleats are turned (*Continued on page 96*)

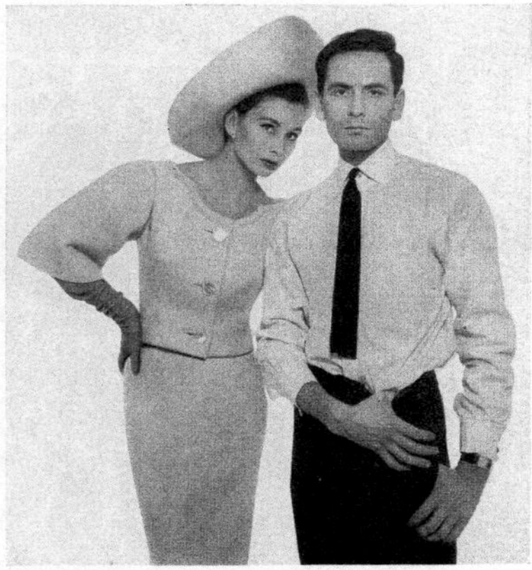

pierre cardin (above) first showed an entire collection of his own two years ago, and instant recognition was followed by more resounding success each season. For spring 1959 he airily widens the top of the silhouette with great bursts of sleeve extended from an open neckline, as in this short jacket suit of coarse, creamy Lesur wool with ocean pearl buttons. A big, back-blown Breton in pale rice straw. Suit and hat at Saks Fifth Avenue; Filene's.

yves st. laurent (opposite), Dior's 23-year-old heir, looks wide-eyed at the world from behind large dark-rimmed spectacles, but designs with the singular beauty and sophistication of his master. A jacket, deliberately cut so narrow it can never be buttoned, is tossed on the shoulders of a sleeveless dress, in Rodier gray and white shepherd's check wool. At Lord and Taylor; Nan Duskin; Filene's; Marshall Field; Neiman-Marcus; I. Magnin.

RICHARD AVEDON

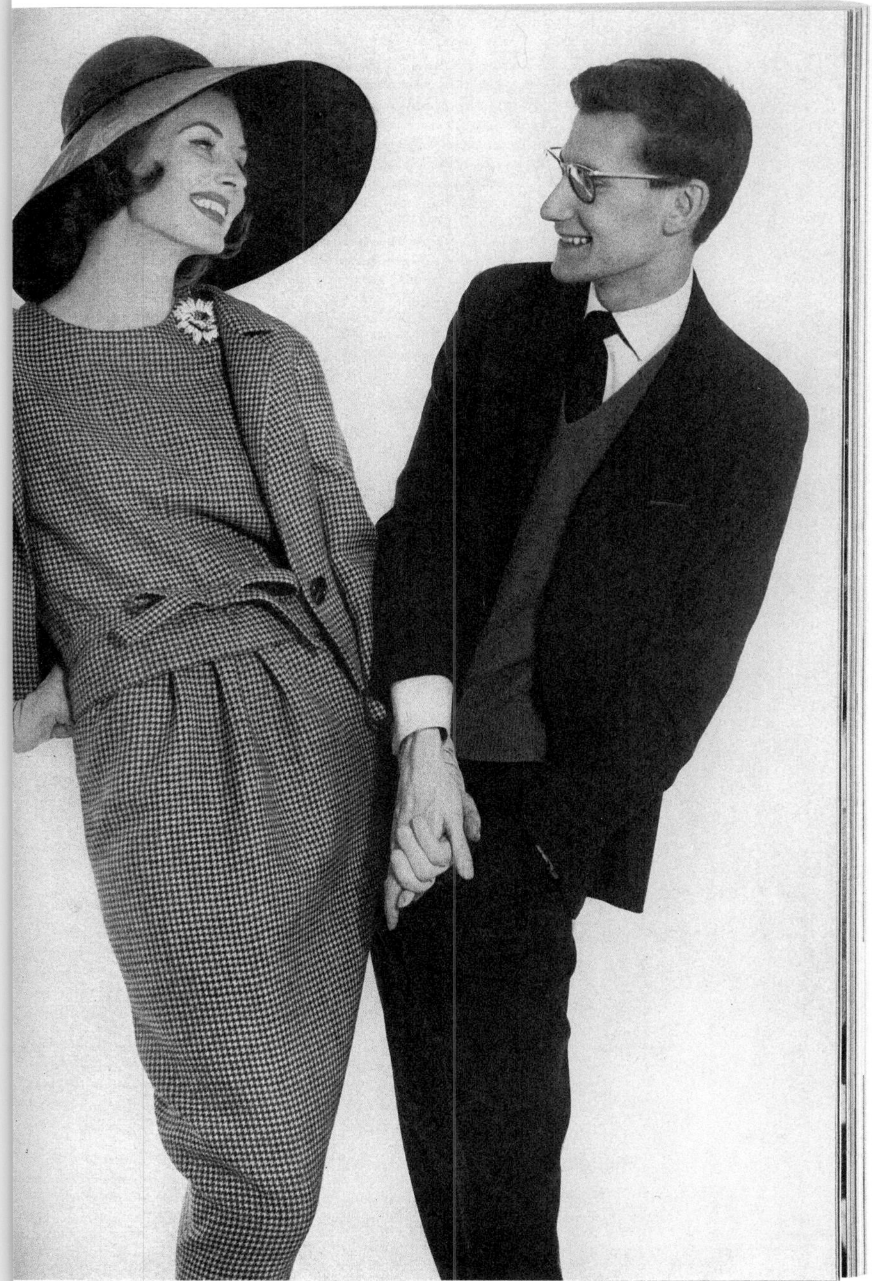

Harper's Bazaar, March 1959, pp. 94–95: Pierre Cardin, Yves Saint Laurent and Suzy Parker

(*Continued*) under at the hem. Chanel distributes them in tiers. The freshest version appears at Dior: fluid box pleats caught at the waist, with a wide, pleated bertha collar circling the shoulders—in clear-colored Shantung, the most fetching dress in the world for a Sunday in the country. . . . Evening dresses have lost weight with becoming results. Chiffon, organza, organdie and the exciting new *Gazar*, in short dresses with blown skirts as light as thistledown, are delicious for dancing. Scattered among them are full-length balldresses—and the brand-new evening length that uncovers the ankle but shows not a glimpse of the calf. . . . Coral, the stone itself as well as the color, is a new evening highlight. . . . Fresh as fury: a flock of white dresses in organdie, lawn and linen, frilled, lacy and beribboned, deliberately ingenuous but not in the least childlike. The favorite at Dior, of white eyelet embroidery and christened *Visite à Grand'mère*, is precisely the kind of dress that women will buy for their daughters—and then wear themselves.

Headlight: New in Paris, and contributed in great measure by Alexandre, is the coiffure as a vital fashion ingredient. Hair is manipulated as though it were cloth—draped in smooth bands over the ears or drawn taut into an offside bun above the temples. Always there is a narrowness at the temples, with the face as distinct as the face of a flower.

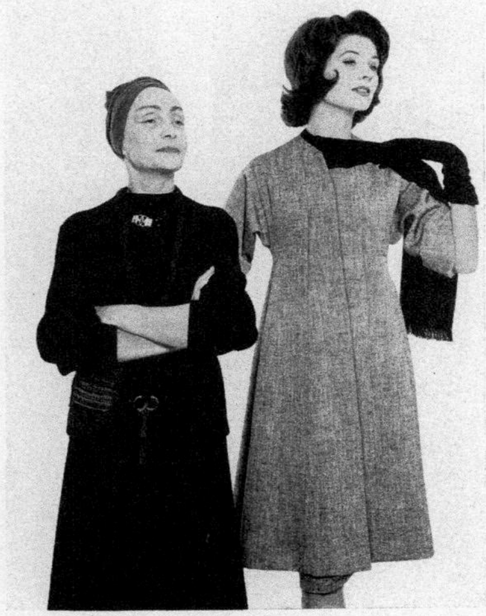

alix grès (above) is a designer's designer. Shy and unaffected, she has gone her own way sculpting clothes of classic beauty for almost three decades. A recent trip to India for the Ford Foundation inspired this coat reminiscent of Nehru's—a width of sleeve and an intricate, flaring tunic line that falls within a hem's length of the slim skirt. In navy blue and white Lahondes worsted, with a navy blue Shantung blouse. At Lord and Taylor.

gabrielle chanel (opposite), whose unerring taste and prophetic realism brought about a new century of fashion, poses with a favorite suit from her present collection: navy blue and white Prince of Wales wool plaid from Dumas Maury lined and outlined in the black and white checks of the silk surah blouse. At Lord and Taylor; Marshall Field; I. Magnin. Other Chanel favorites: her massed pearls, gold chain belt, "No. 5" perfume.

suzy parker (opposite), the slim auburn-haired actress whose beauty takes on the many moods of Paris Present, brings an intangible and compelling allure of her own to each of the designs of the French couturiers with whom she is photographed on these four pages.

RICHARD A

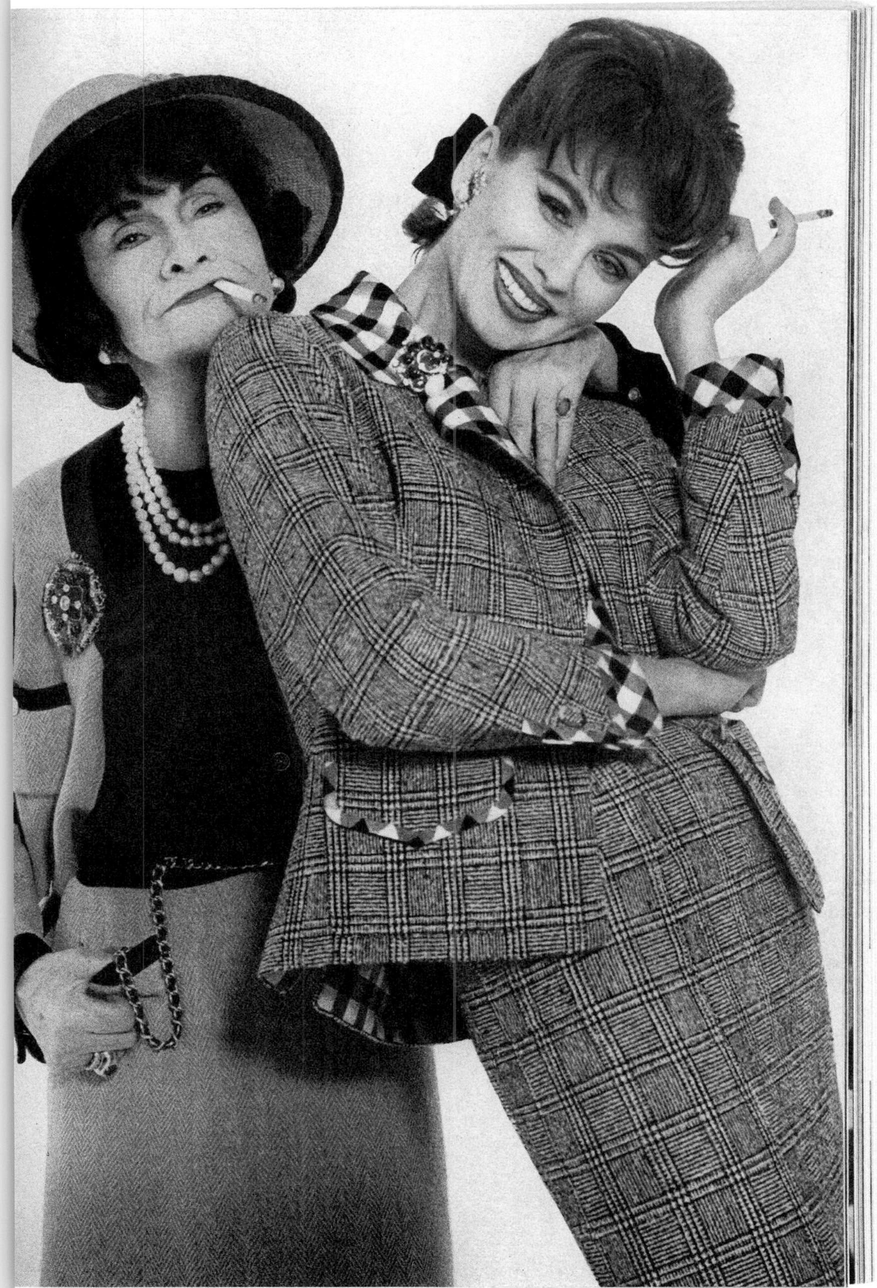

Harper's Bazaar, March 1959, pp. 96–97: *(left)* Alix Grès and Suzy Parker, *(this page)* Chanel and Suzy Parker

FANNY

Joshua Logan, director of the new, nonmusical, color film version of *Fanny*, photographed on location in the old port of Marseilles, is upstaged (opposite) by the principals of his waterfront cast: Horst Buchholz as the sea-struck Marius; Leslie Caron in the title role of the fishmonger's spirited daughter; Charles Boyer as the irascible barkeeper, César; and Maurice Chevalier, especially padded around the midriff for the part of Panisse, the sentimental sailmaker who gives Fanny's illegitimate son a name and a foster father. Written thirty years ago as a trilogy by French academy playwright Marcel Pagnol, *Fanny* was immediately produced as both a play and a film to remain a Gallic favorite ever since. In 1953, Mr. Logan had it adapted for the Broadway musical and hoped even then to present it one day in dramatic form, an ambition to be realized when the Warner Brothers feature opens in New York at the end of the month and nationally soon after.

RICHARD AVEDON

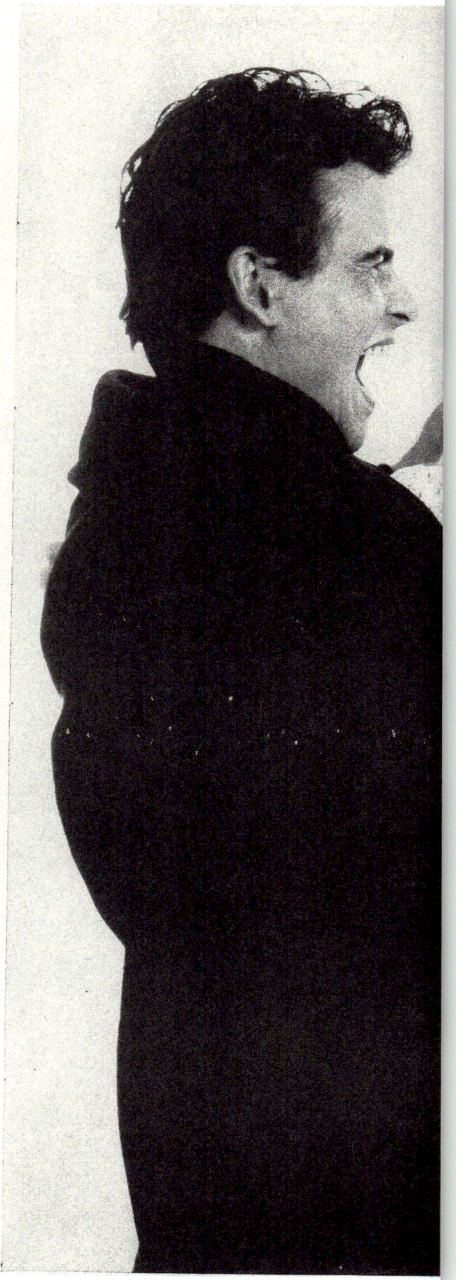

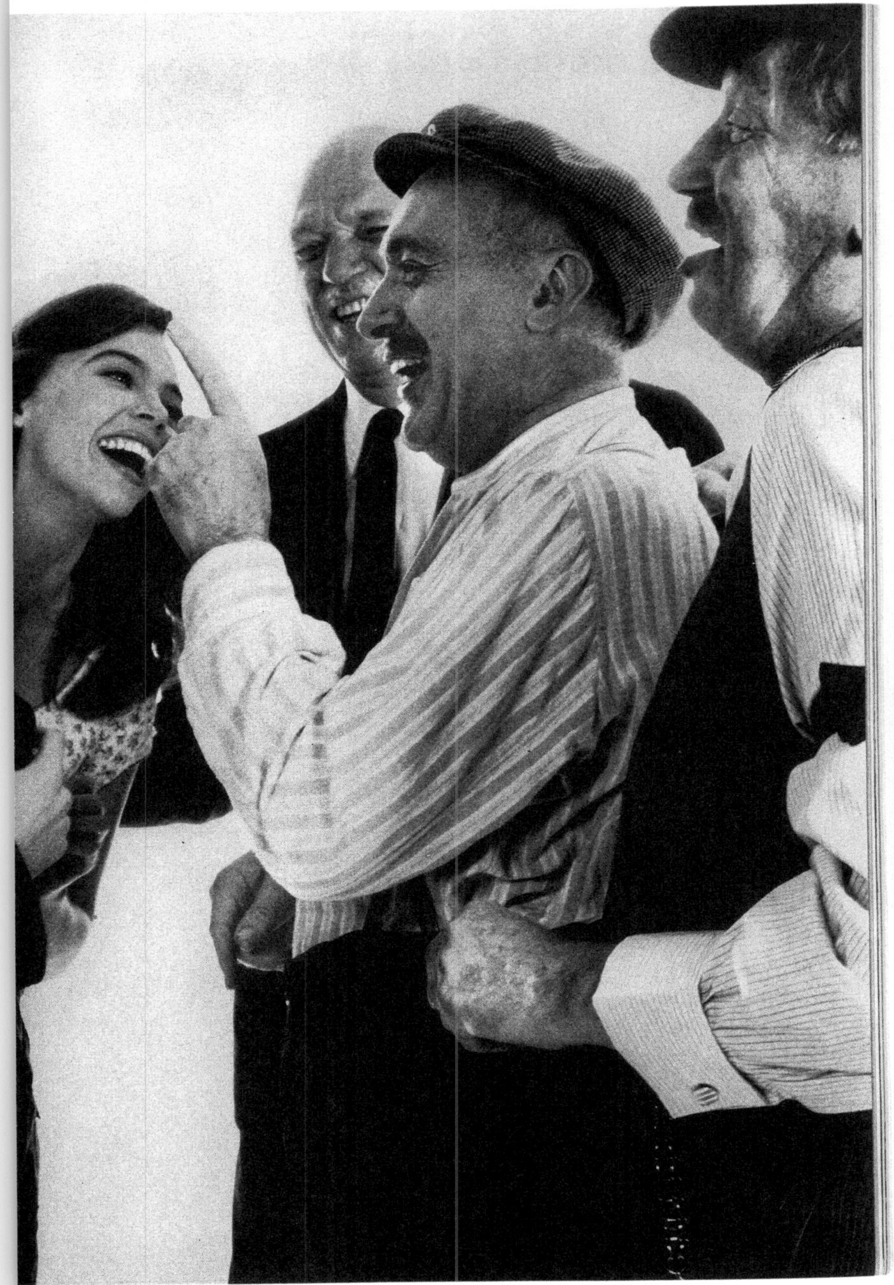

Harper's Bazaar, June 1961, pp. 70–71: The cast of *Fanny*

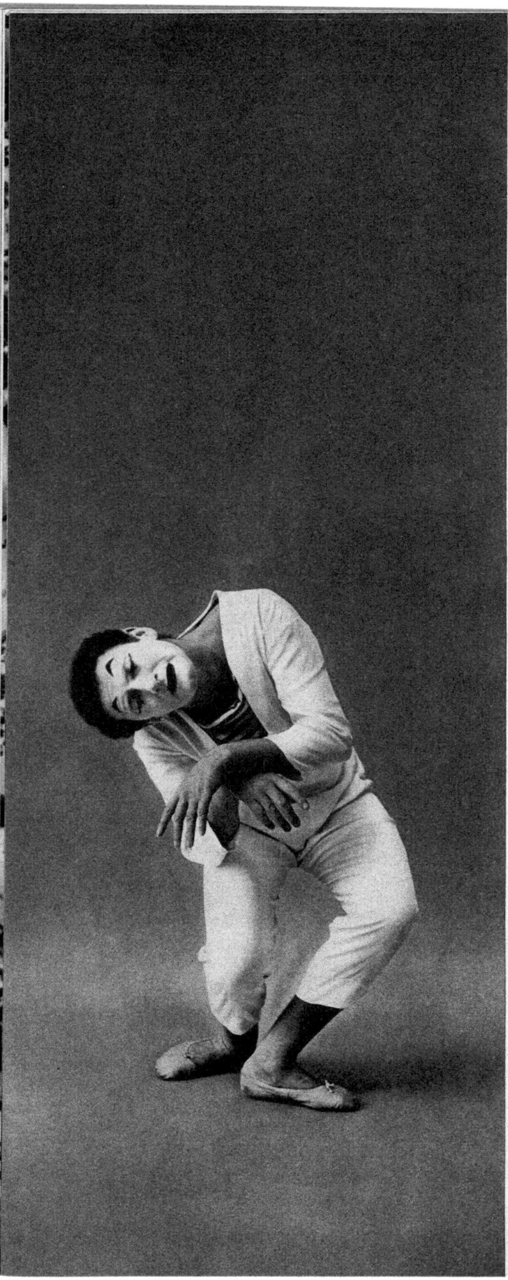

The Clown

• Marcel Marceau revives with infinite freshness and exuberance the all-but-lost art of pantomime—of that droll, wise, often pathetic silent miming in the great tradition of Chaplin and Keaton. M. Marceau, who was a member of the French resistance during the war, is on tour in the United States and Japan. On December 4th, he will perform over the NBC television network.

The Dancer

• Antonio, once a member of the Spanish dance team of Antonio and Rosario, had been absent from the New York stage for seven years when he returned here in October. Then, in a series of electrifying performances, his display of intensity, precision and style took the critics by storm: the precocious and mannered young dancer of 1948 had grown into an artist of the first rank.

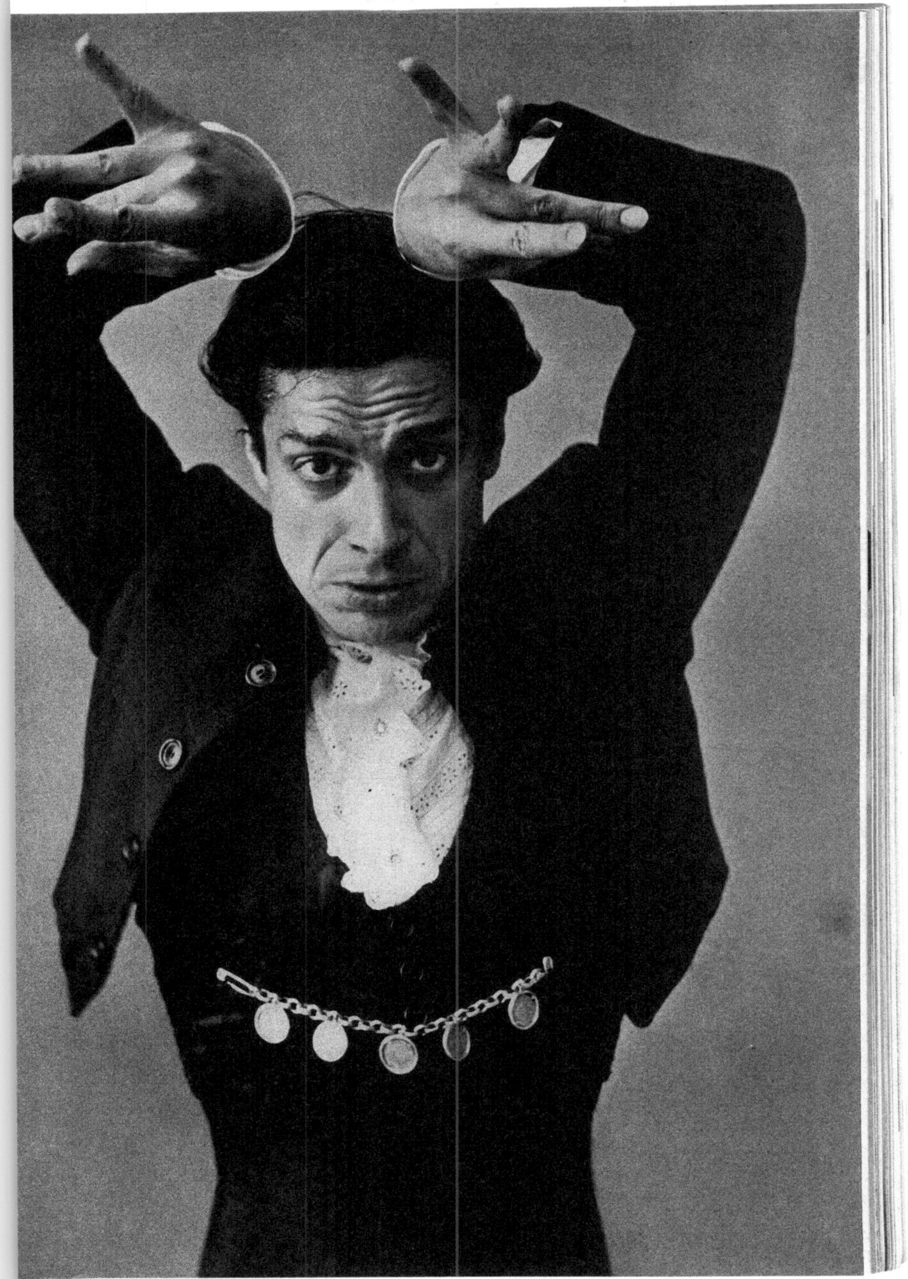

Harper's Bazaar, December 1955, pp. 86–87: *(left)* Marcel Marceau; *(this page)*, Antonio, dancer

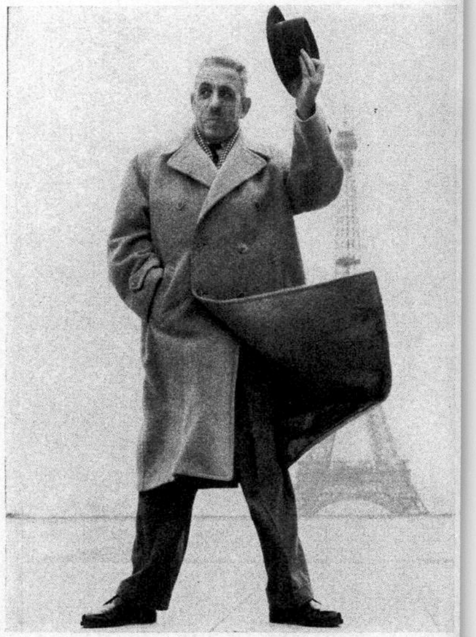

chagall, poulenc, mauriac

Marc Chagall (opposite page), Francis Poulenc (above) and François Mauriac (right) recently joined the roster of distinguished foreigners elected to honorary membership of the American Academy and National Institute of Arts and Letters. • An exhibition of Chagall's paintings, gathered from all over the world, is being sponsored by UNESCO in Hamburg. The show will move to Munich in April, Paris in June. • Poulenc, a charter member of "Les Six," has written the score for *La Voix Humaine,* an opera with settings by Cocteau and Denise Duval in the leading role. After its Paris run, it will be given at the Little Scala, Milan. • François Mauriac, a winner of the Nobel Prize, has just published a book of religious meditations. Soon to come: another installment of his journal and a new novel.

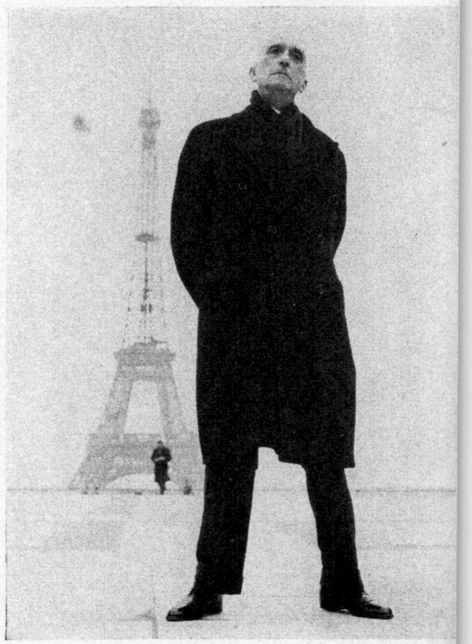

RICH

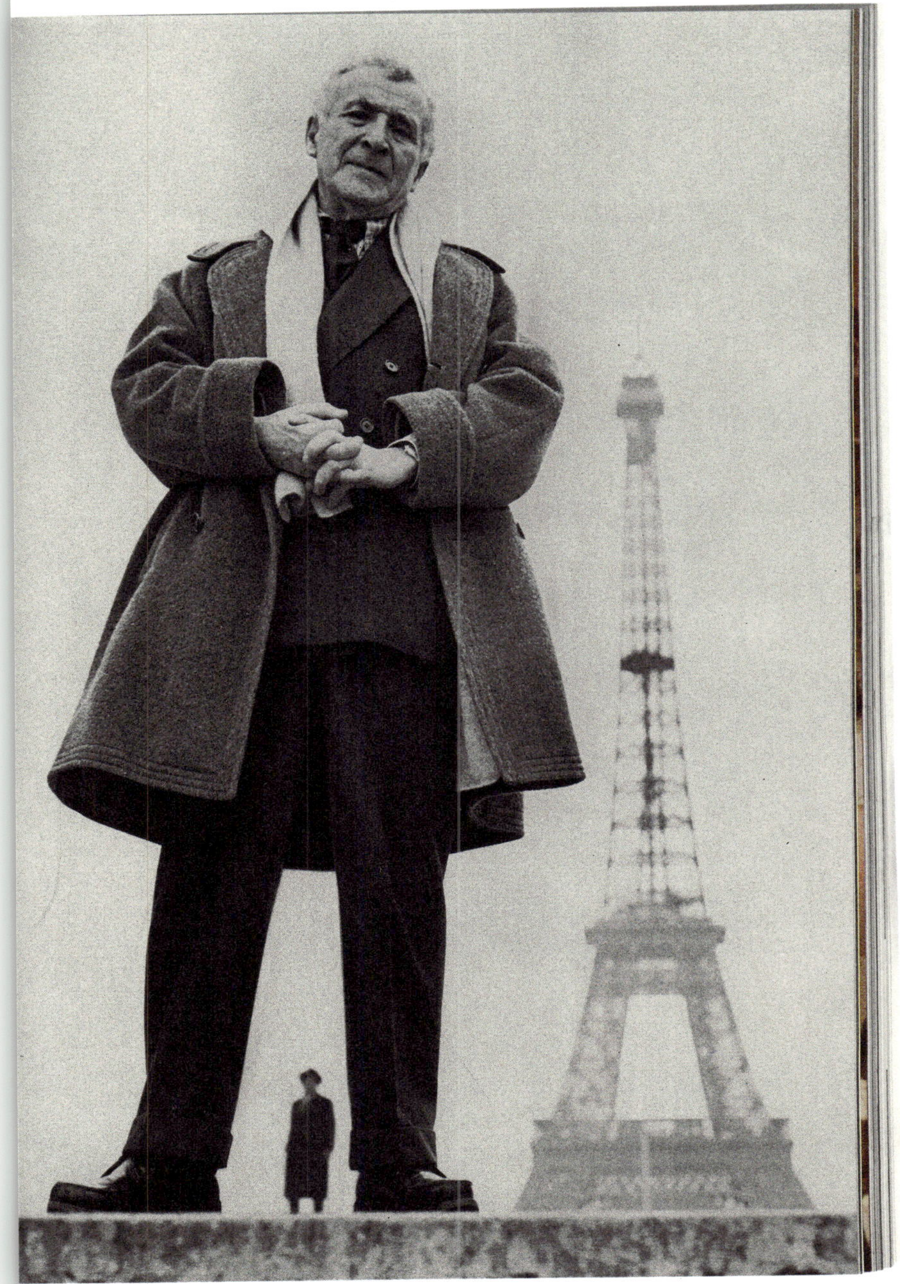

Harper's Bazaar, March 1959, pp 98–99: *(top left)* Marc Chagall *(bottom left)* Francis Poulenc, *(this page)* François Mauriac

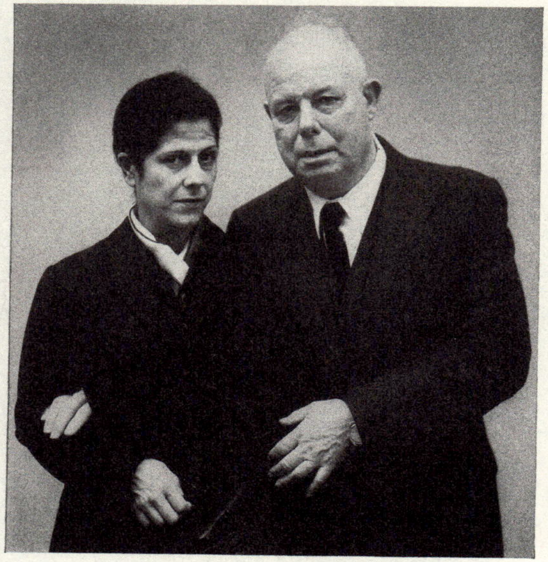

Jean Renoir (left, with his closest associate, Mme. Dido Renoir) is a son of the painter, and for thirty-four years has been one of the great artists of the cinema. His works comprise large reaches of experience—from the poignant melancholy of *La Partie de Campagne* to the spacious humanity of *La Grande Illusion*. M. Renoir, who divides his time between France and Hollywood, has a play (adapted from Odets) and a ballet running in Paris and is starting two films: *Déjeuner sur l'Herbe* and Simenon's *Three Rooms in Manhattan*. • Georges and Rosamond Bernier (he a Parisian, she a Philadelphian) are the founders and editors of what may well be the world's liveliest and best-looking art magazine, *L'Oeil*. Four years ago, it appeared unannounced on every newsstand in Paris—for the price of a *sandwich au jambon*—and made an instant hit. Now it numbers among its champions and subscribers Picasso, Braque, Miró, Léger and the libraries of Leningrad and Moscow. M. Bernier is also a director of Knoedler's; his wife's diverse past has included the harp, archaeology and animal taming in Mexico.

RICHARD AVE

HARPER'S BAZAAR, MARCH

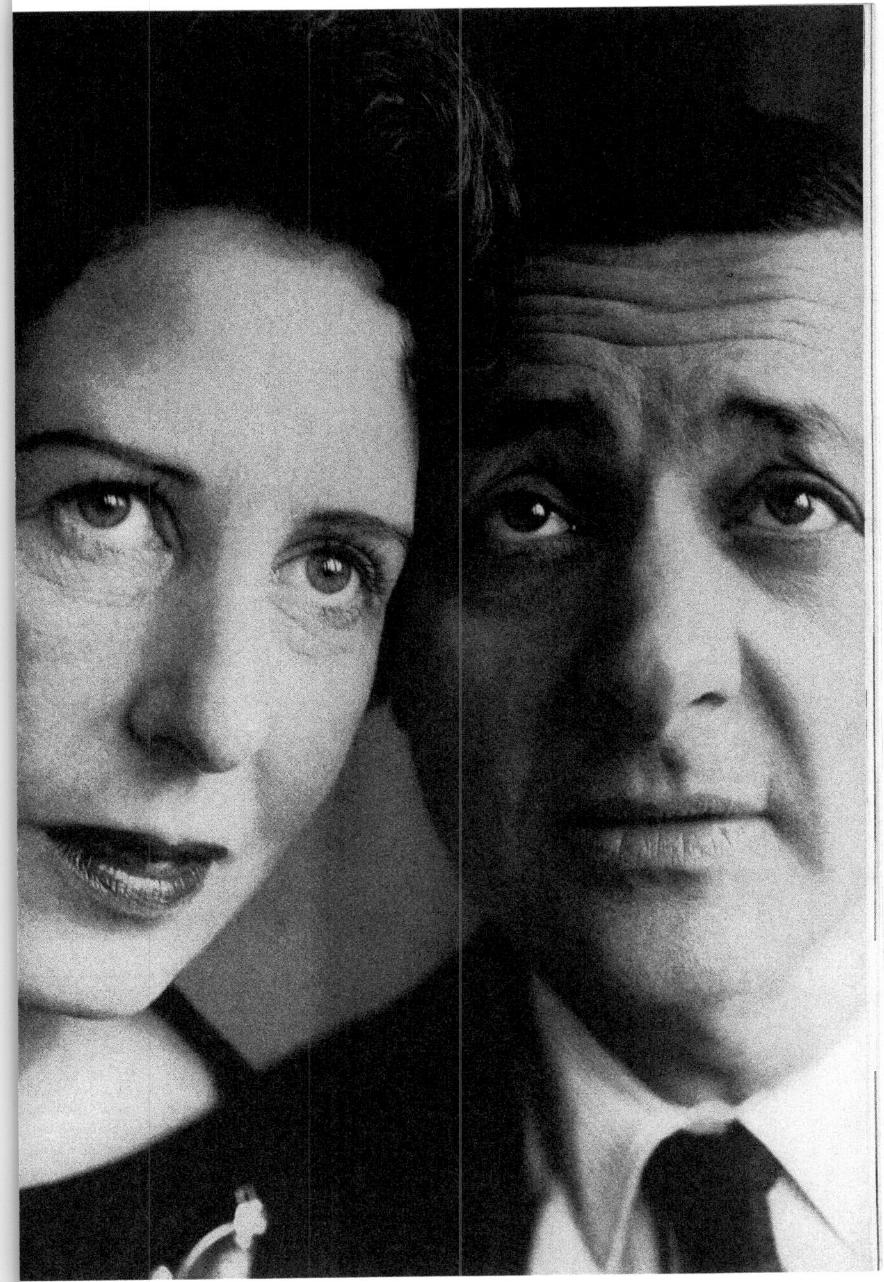

Harper's Bazaar, March 1959, pp. 158–59: *(left)* Jean and Dido Renoir, *(this page)* Georges and Rosamond Bernier

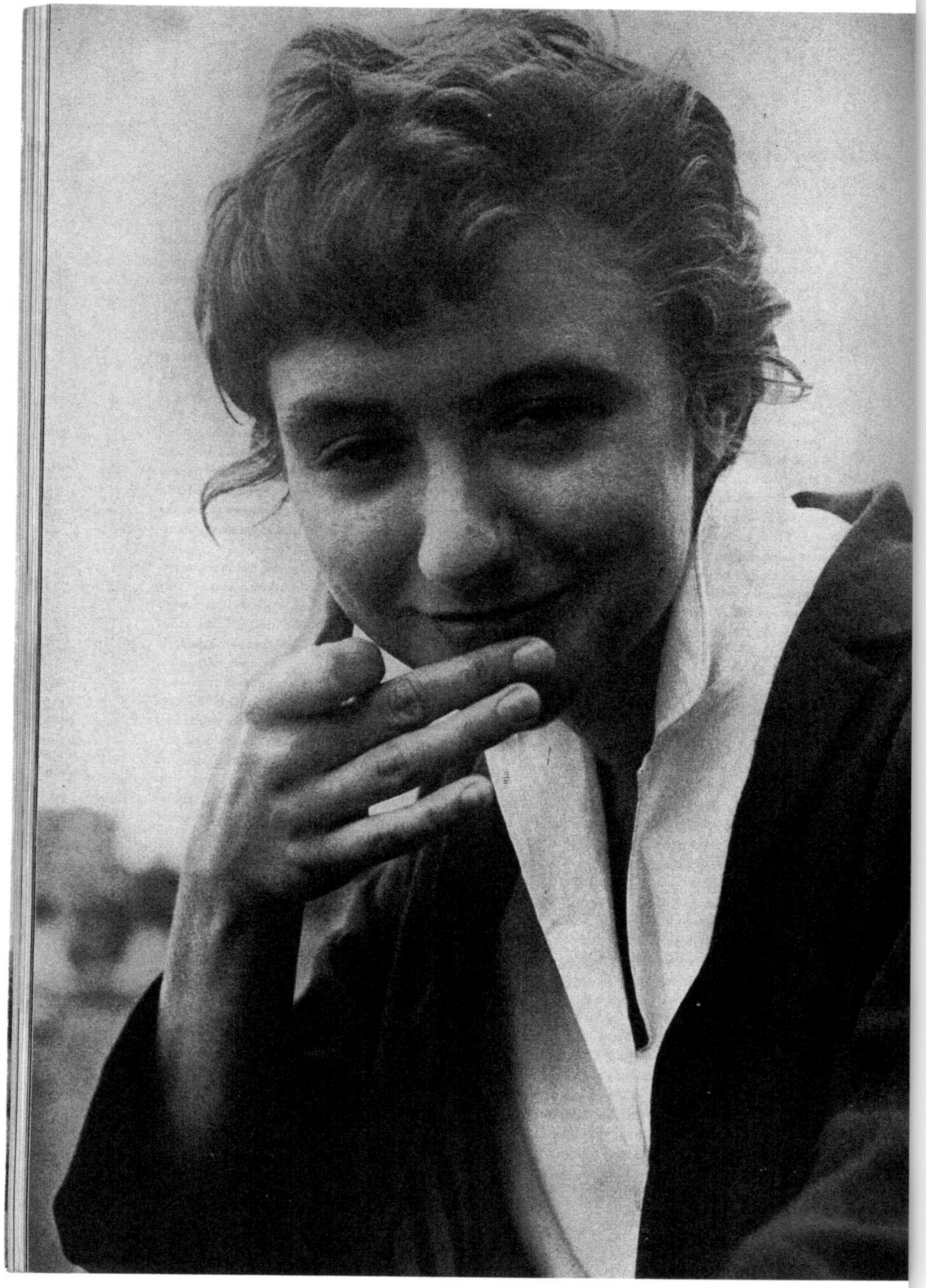

Françoise Sagan, smiling her secret smile (opposite), has set literary France on its ear with *Bonjour Tristesse*, a novel she wrote after flunking out at the end of her freshman year at the Sorbonne. This spring it won her the Grand Prix des Critiques, and by the end of the summer it had become a best-seller that was being talked about and enjoyed everywhere. Sagan is a pen name; she was born Françoise Quoirez (the best French tongues could do with her family's Spanish name of Juárez). Her novel isn't autobiography; it's a surprisingly mature picture of the relations between the old and the young, and a wonderful piece of story-telling.

Louise de Vilmorin (below) has long been known in France for managing to be at once a beauty, a fashionable figure and *une femme de lettres*. Two of her astringently witty and swiftly told short novels, *Madame de* and *Julietta*, translated into English, are winning her an international reputation. This year she has shut herself up on her family's property, famous for its gardens, at Verrière le Buisson, to work on two new novels and a film scenario.

RICHARD AVEDON

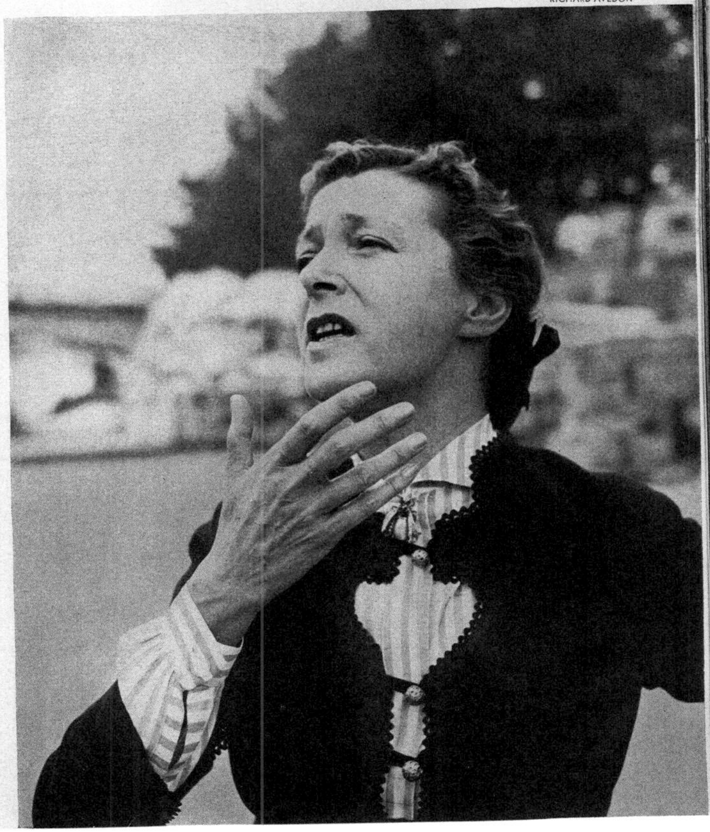

Harper's Bazaar, November 1954, pp. 144–45: *(left)* Françoise Sagan, *(this page)* Louise de Vilmorin

THE GIFT OF PARIS

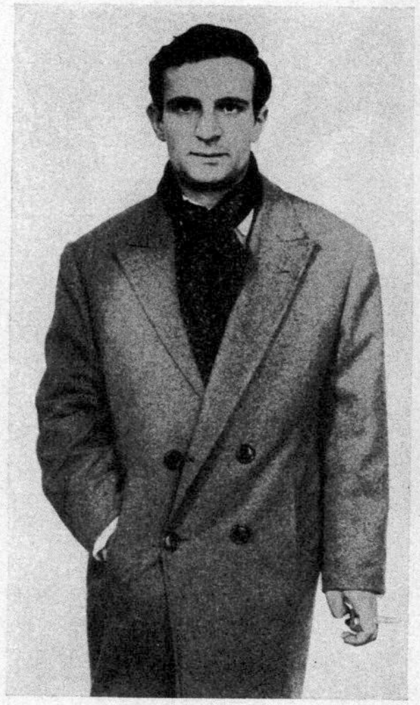

A city of head and heart, Paris is the essence of France. Again and again, its many gifts spark a fire that lights the world: New Wave director François Truffaut (above) won international fame at twenty-seven with The 400 Blows. Coming: Tirez sur le Pianiste. Author Alain Robbe-Grillet (opposite left), of the New Realists movement, rejects "mannered writing in favor of writing as a quest." His novels, including Les Gommes, winner of the 1954 Prix Fénéon, and Le Voyeur, winner of the 1955 Prix des Critiques, negate the psychological approach. In the Labyrinth arrives soon via Grove Press. Director Alain Resnais has been showered with cinematic honors since his 1948 Van Gogh documentary. His current, controversial Hiroshima, Mon Amour will be followed by L'Année Dernière. Director Claude Chabrol, whose prize winners, Le Beau Serge and Les Cousins, pioneered the New Wave, didn't even know how to focus a camera three years ago. His latest: Les Bonnes Femmes.

RICHARD AVEDON

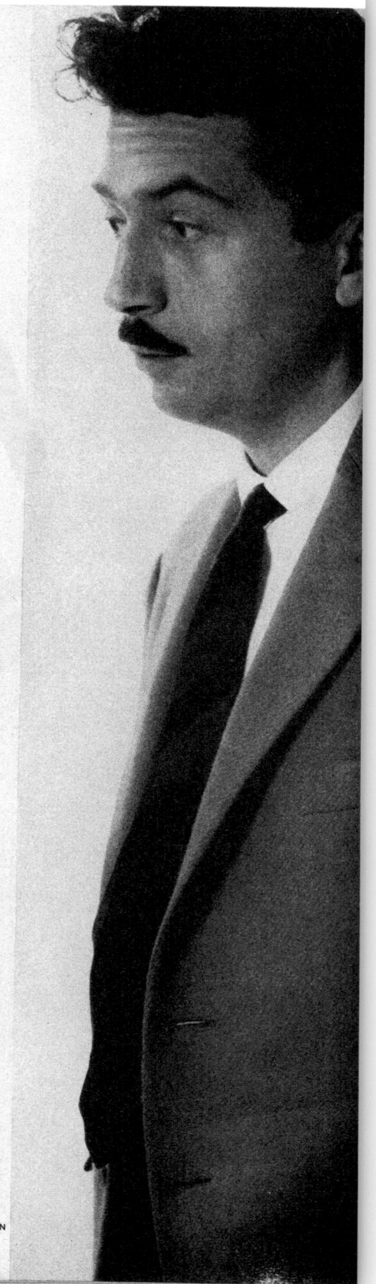

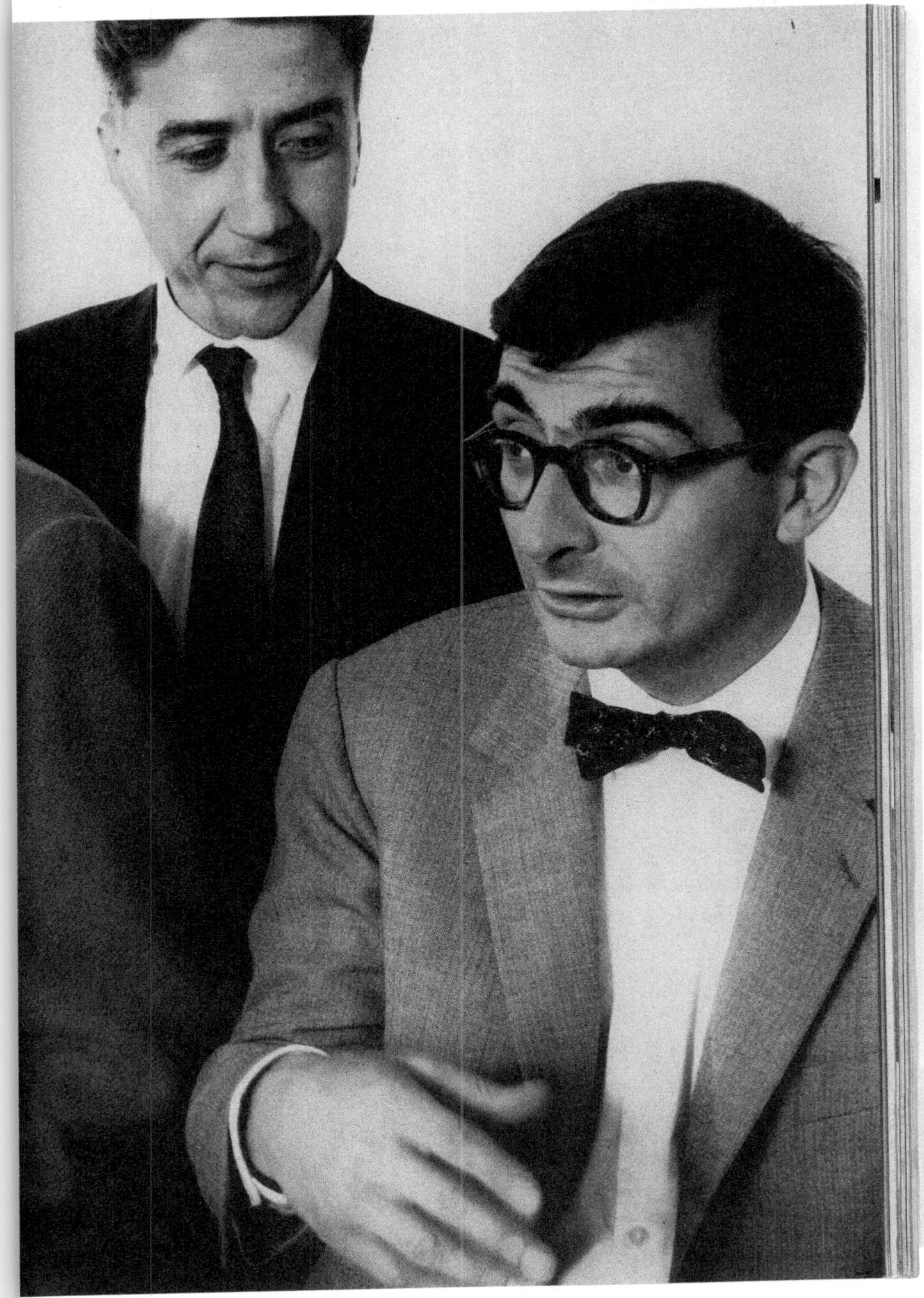

Harper's Bazaar, September 1960,
pp. 194–95: *(left)* François Truffaut, *(this page)* the trio Alain Robbe-Grillet, Alain Resnais and Claude Chabrol

HERE AND NOW French cinema stars Yves Montand and his wife, Simone Signoret (right), are the newest lights in the Hollywood galaxy. Montand, specialist in the gutsy roles he spikes with a slight flavor of garlic and Gable (*Wages of Fear, Heroes and Sinners*), is currently on set with Marilyn Monroe for the Twentieth Century-Fox production of *Let's Make Love*. Signoret, whose blonde lushness gives her the look of a trench-coated eighteenth-century Boucher, has been adroitly juggling contract offers. Her perceptive portrait of the misunderstood mistress in *Room at the Top* is already a modern film classic.

RICHARD AVEDON

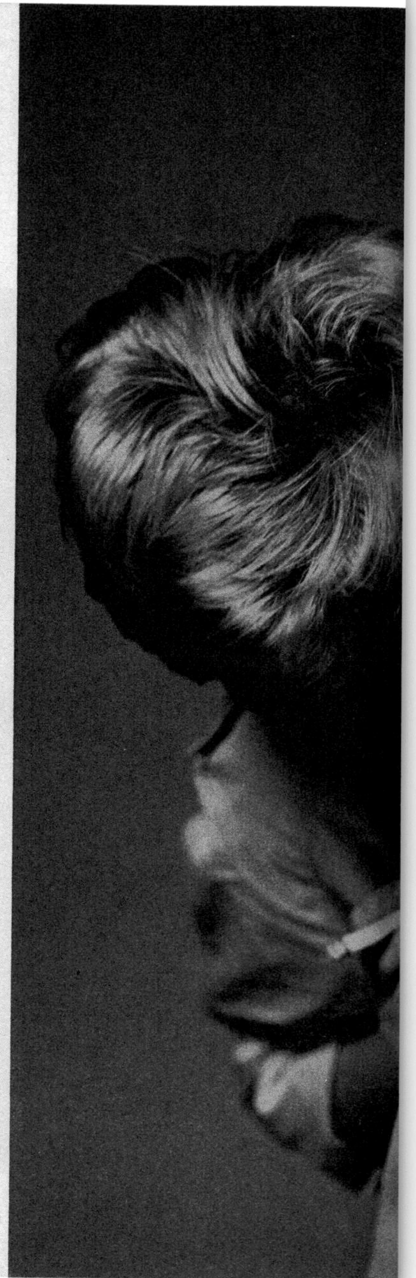

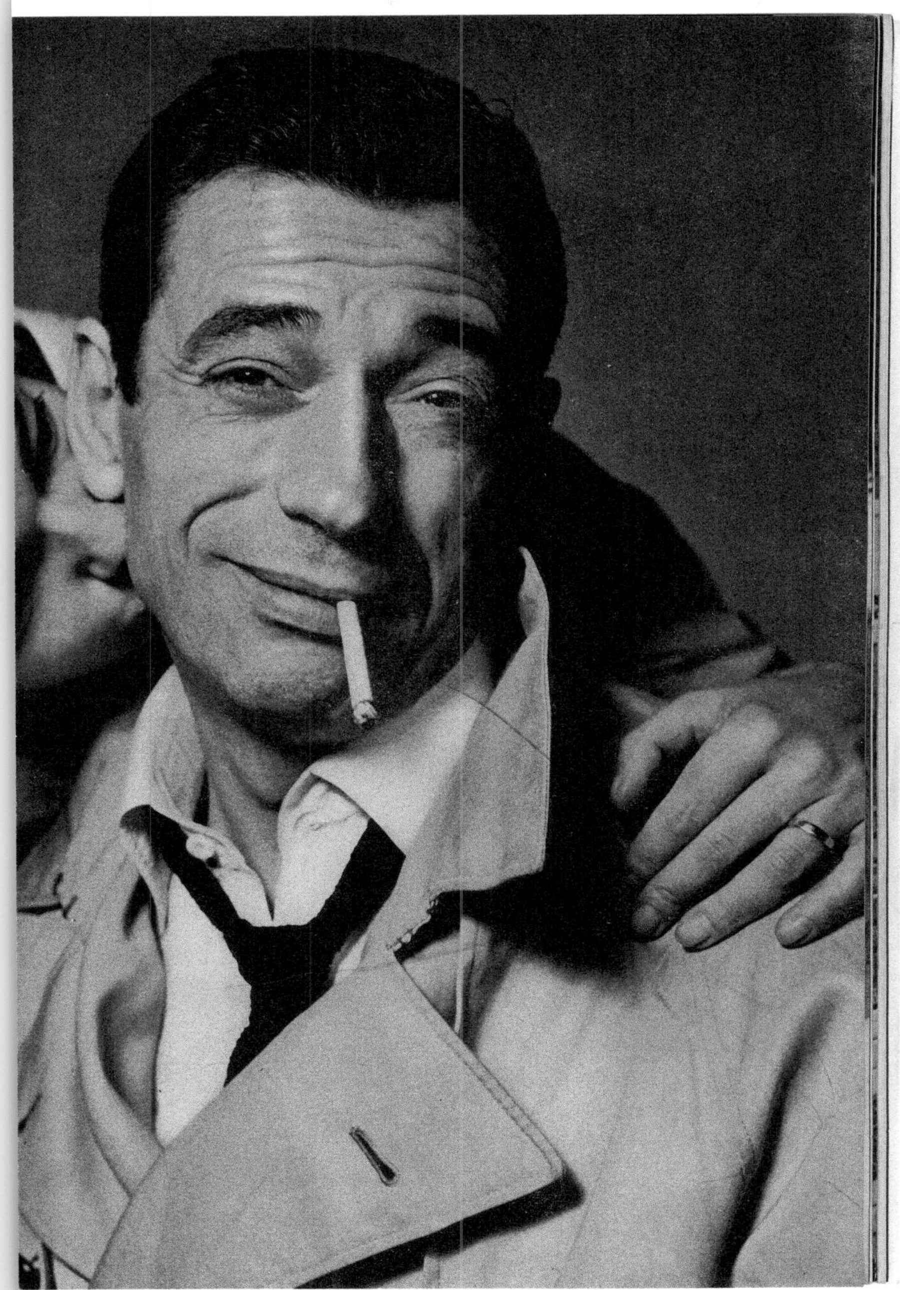

Harper's Bazaar, March 1960, pp. 176–77: Simone Signoret and Yves Montand

TO RUFFLE IS 6 . . . *to beat a drum* . . . TO ROUSE UP A RIFF OF LAUGHTER. CHARLES AZNAVOUR, THE PIED PIPER OF PARIS, SHOT THE WORKS WITH HIS PERFORMANCE IN SHOOT THE PIANO PLAYER. RIGHT NOW, HE'S RUFFLING AMERICA TWO WAYS MORE: WITH HIS MERCURY RECORD, THE TIME IS NOW, A GROUP OF CHANSONS AND BALLADS WHICH HE DELIVERS IN ENGLISH; AND WITH A SERIES OF MERCURIAL ONE-NIGHT PERFORMANCES HERE AND AROUND THE WORLD.

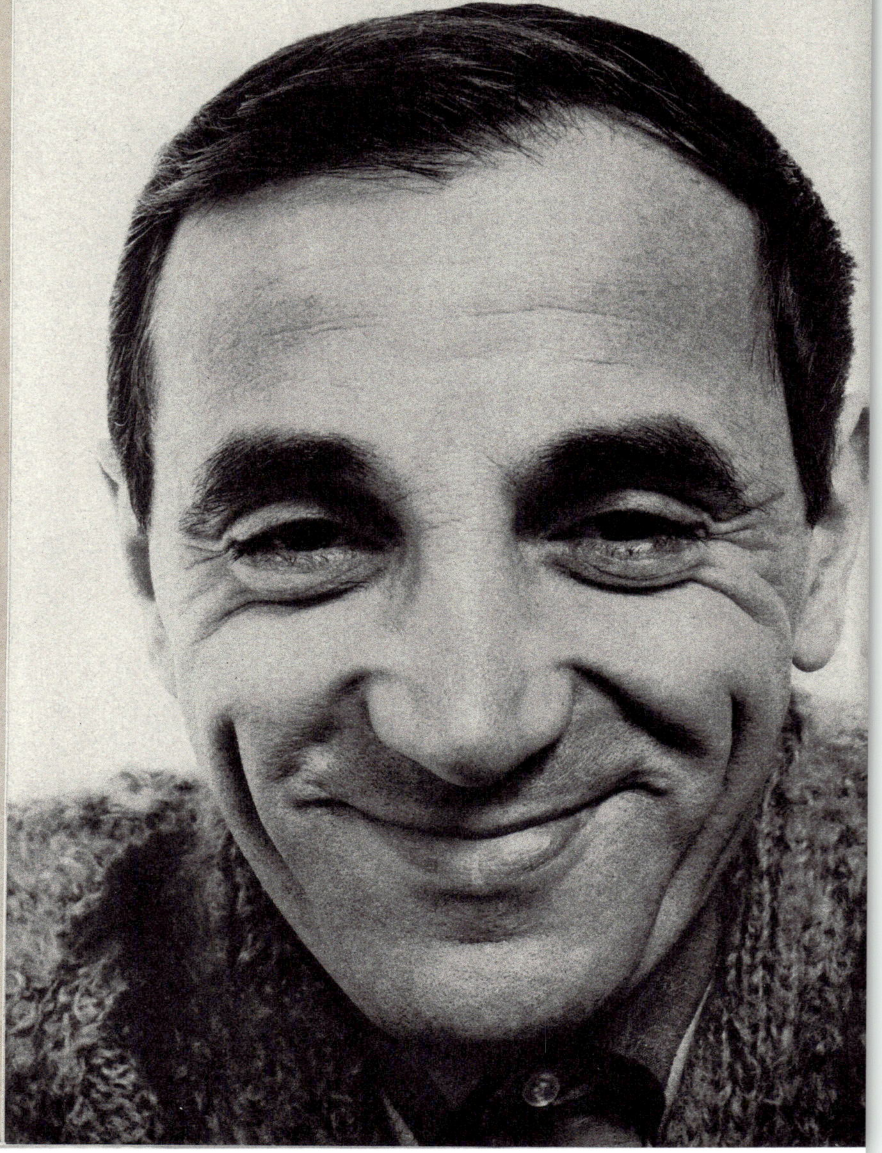

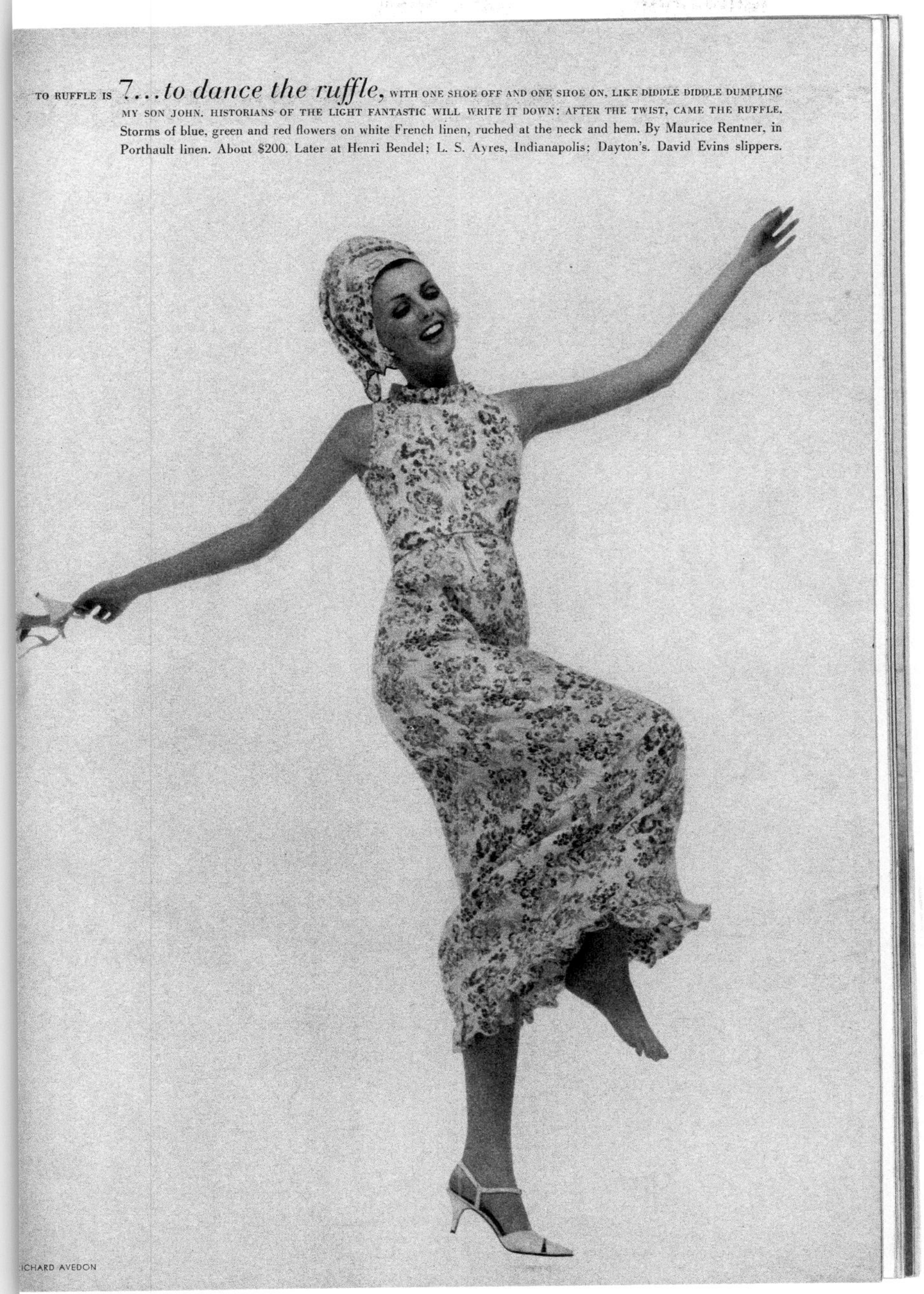

TO RUFFLE IS *7...to dance the ruffle,* WITH ONE SHOE OFF AND ONE SHOE ON, LIKE DIDDLE DIDDLE DUMPLING MY SON JOHN. HISTORIANS OF THE LIGHT FANTASTIC WILL WRITE IT DOWN: AFTER THE TWIST, CAME THE RUFFLE. Storms of blue, green and red flowers on white French linen, ruched at the neck and hem. By Maurice Rentner, in Porthault linen. About $200. Later at Henri Bendel; L. S. Ayres, Indianapolis; Dayton's. David Evins slippers.

ICHARD AVEDON

Harper's Bazaar, April 1963, p. 126–27: *(left)* Charles Aznavour, *(this page)* Dorothy McGowan

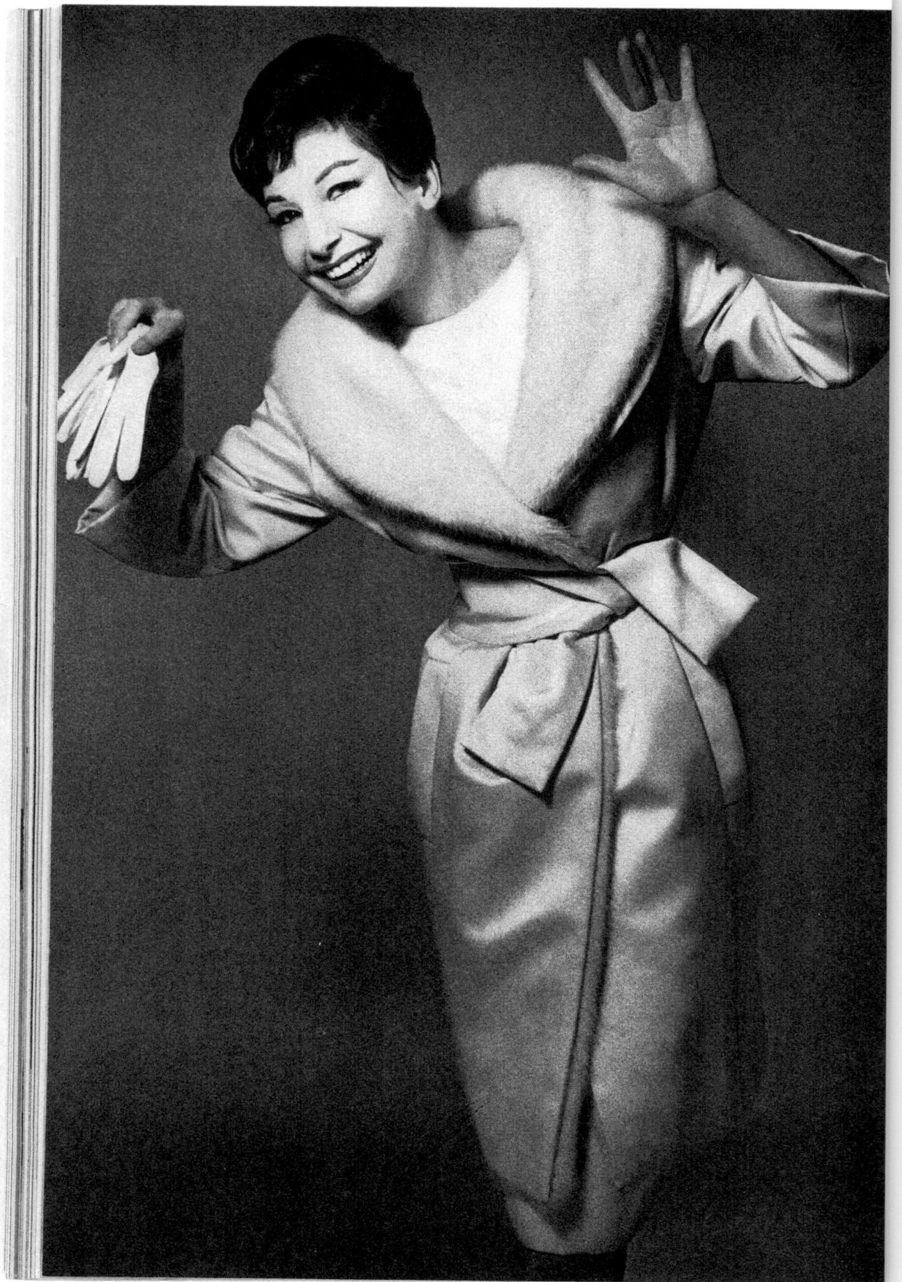

the storm of white

zizi jeanmaire (opposite), who made a wholly contemporary vixen of Carmen in a single ballet, opens another new era from Dior—the belted overcoat. It is cinched tight and cut off a good three inches short of the dress hem. This coat, which will clearly be repeated for every time of day, is marvelous and arresting in white for night—shining Abraham silk gabardine with a magnificent collar and under-binding of mink. At Bergdorf Goodman; I. Magnin.

anouk aimée (below), the eternal feminine . . . compassionate Circe of the forthcoming film, *Les Dragueurs,* shows the delicious white suit with which Chanel opened her collection. The curve of the jacket into the body is new. The rest is a reiteration of the Chanel articles of faith—ease, a play of jewels, bright buttons. The wool is a Hurel basketweave which is repeated in the flat sailor. Suit and hat at Saks Fifth Avenue; Neiman-Marcus.

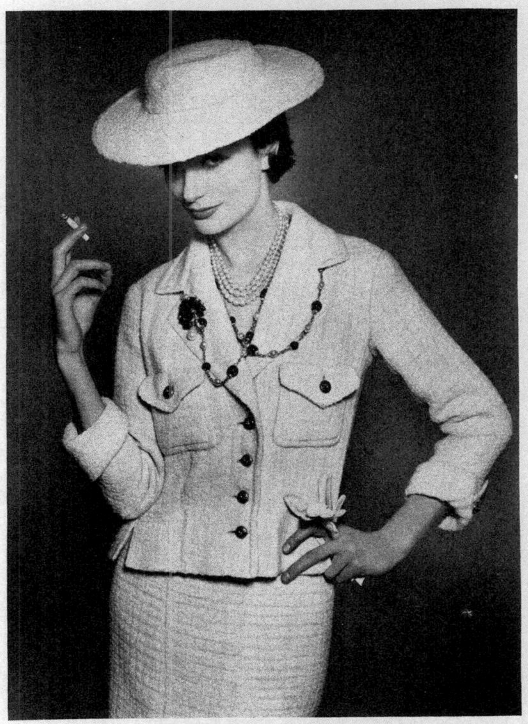

) AVEDON

S BAZAAR, MARCH 1959

Harper's Bazaar, March 1959, pp. 106–07: *(left)* Zizi Jeanmaire, *(this page)* Anouk Aimée

There was a connection between artists, beauty, theatre, rich people. They all worked together. For instance, Diaghilev hired Picasso, Chagall. There was Misia Sert, this great beauty and rich woman who raised money and got artists together. Bérard was very closely involved with Dior [. . .]

Françoise Sagan, the new young writer in Paris was sitting at Dior's looking at clothes at the opening. There was no question that people like, not just Cocteau, but Marcel Achard, and French intellectuals would go to Dior and Balenciaga to see what was happening.

—

Richard Avedon

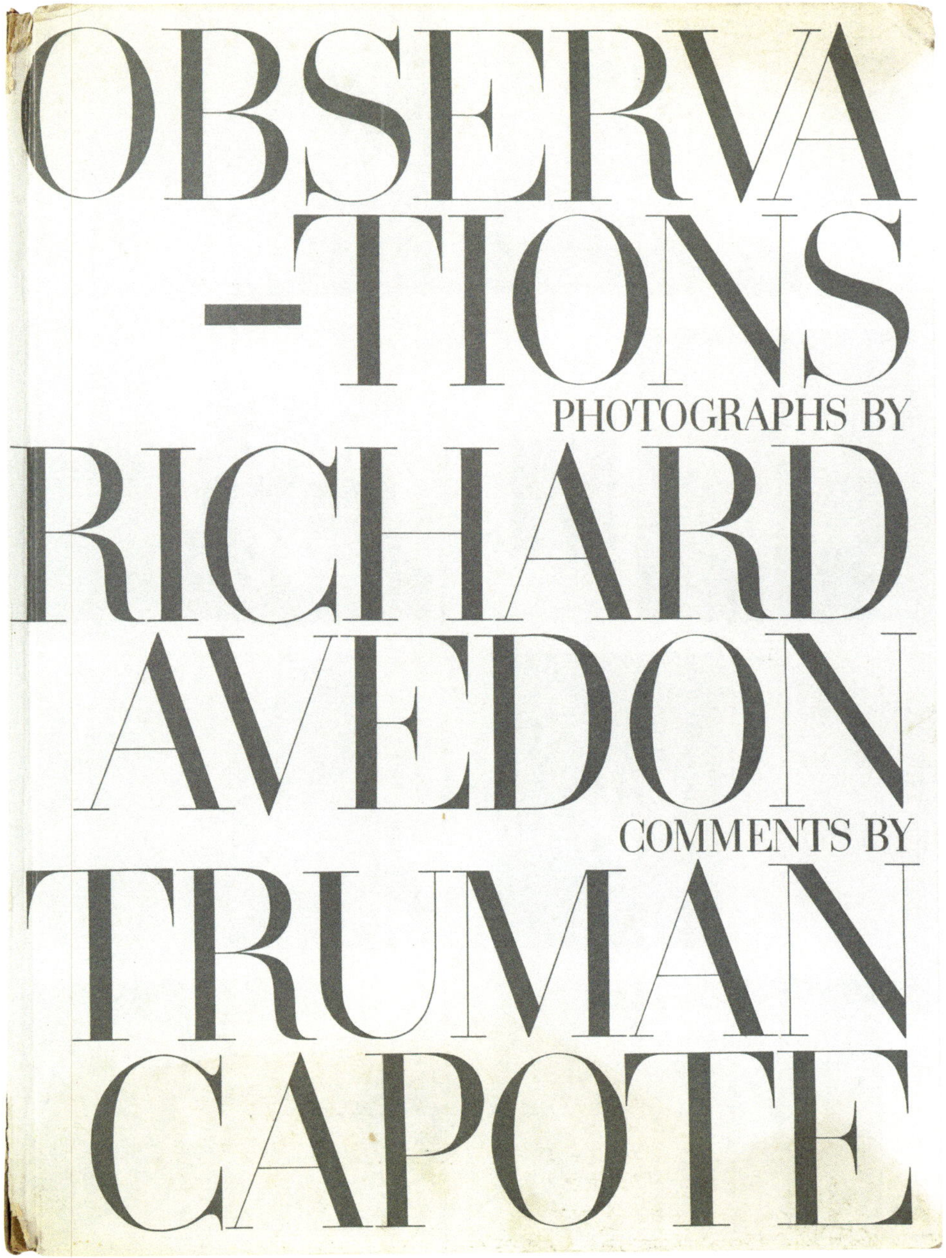

Observations (New York: Simon and Schuster, 1959) was Richard Avedon's first book of portraits; text by Truman Capote, design by Alexey Brodovitch.

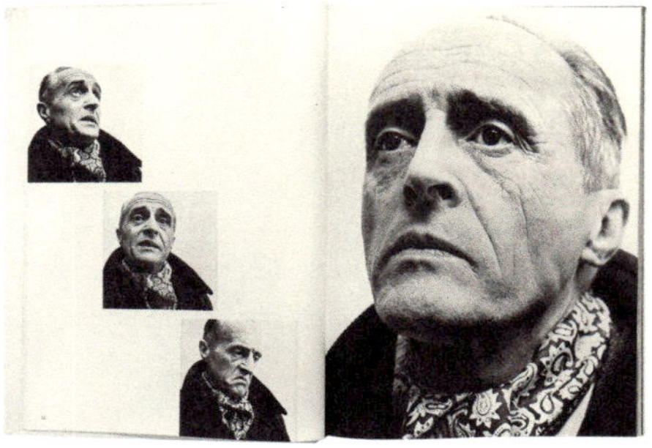
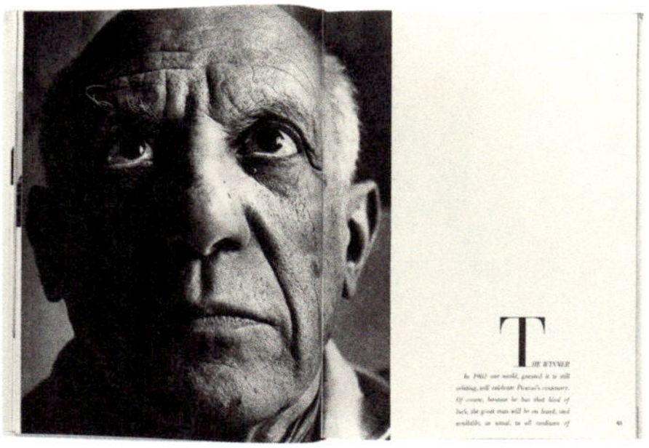
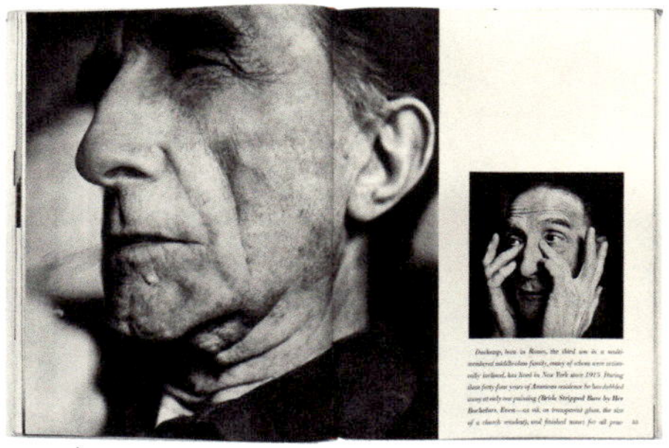
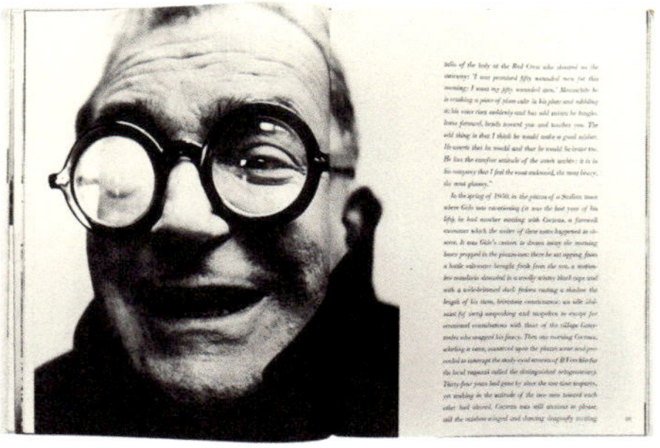
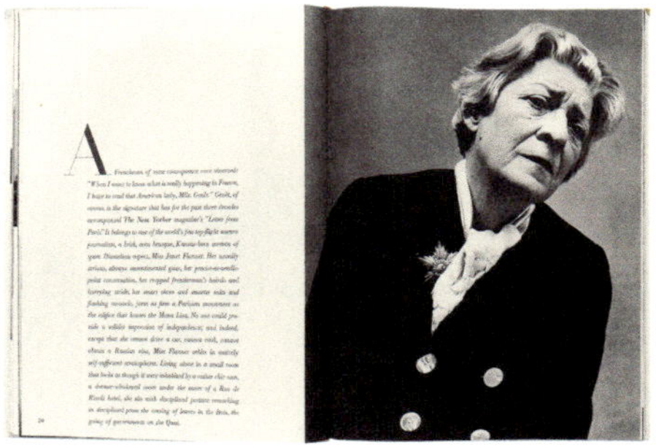
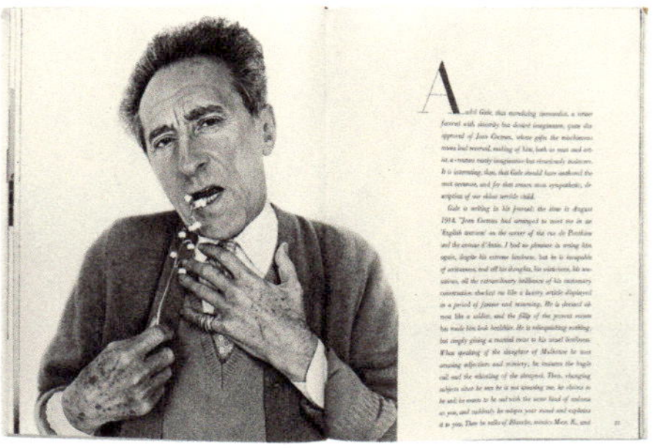
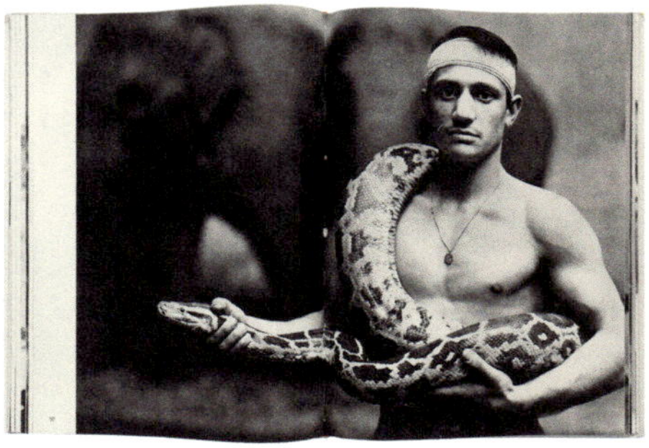
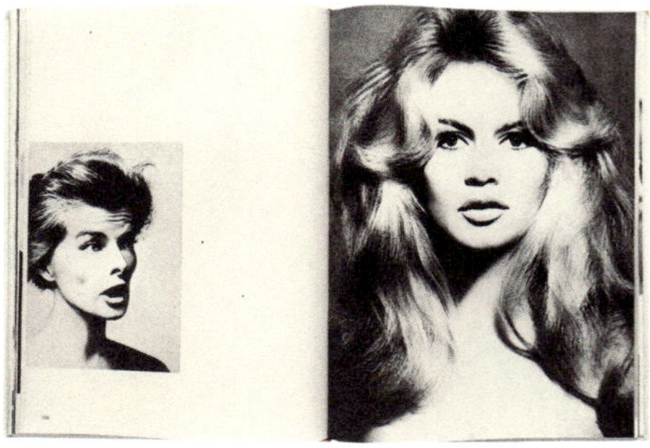

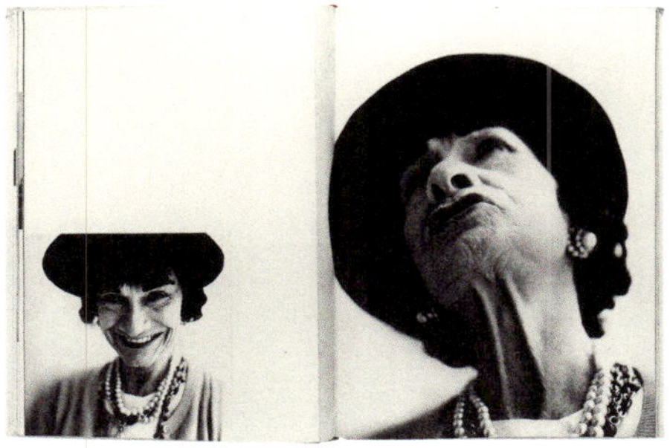
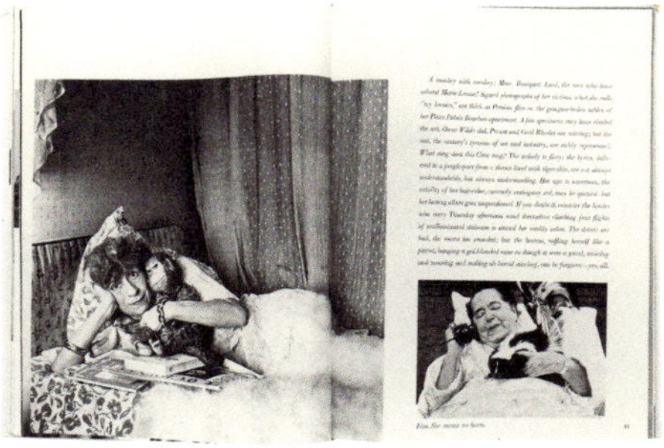
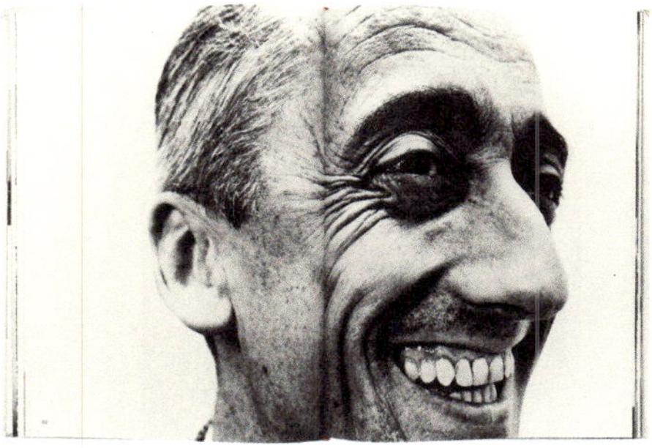
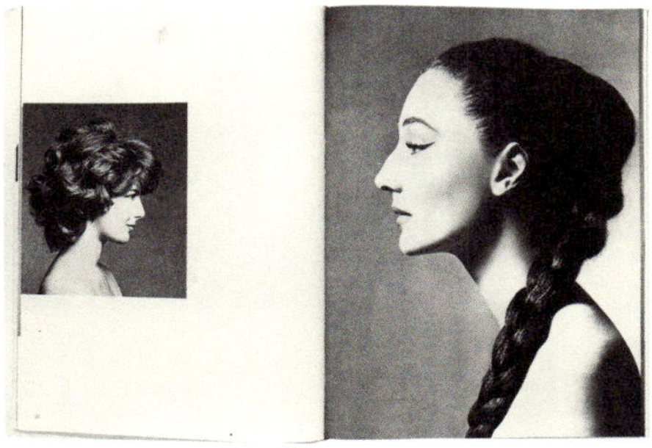
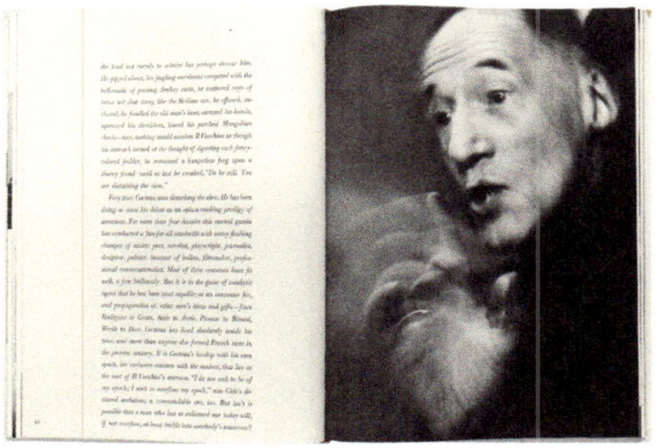
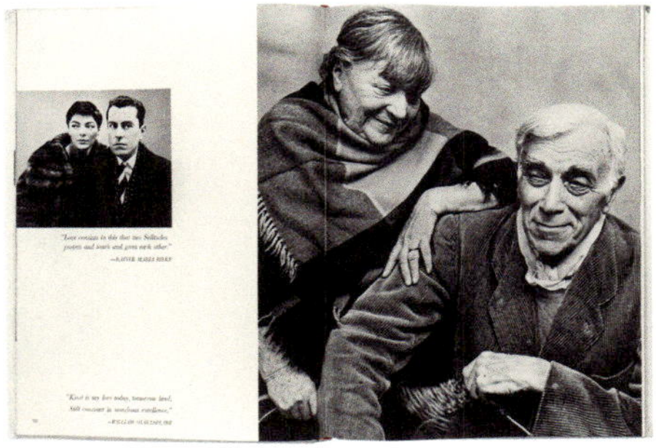
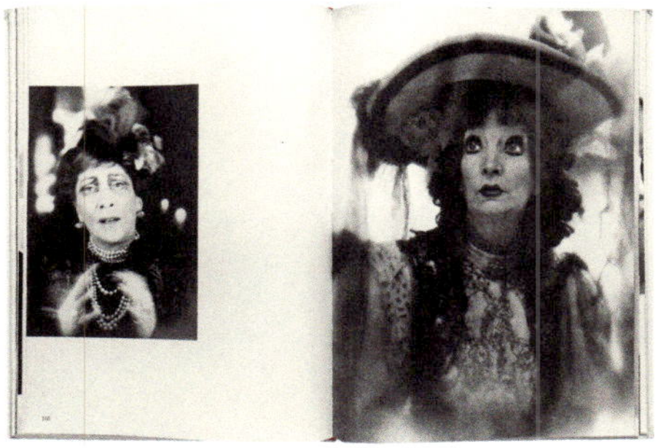
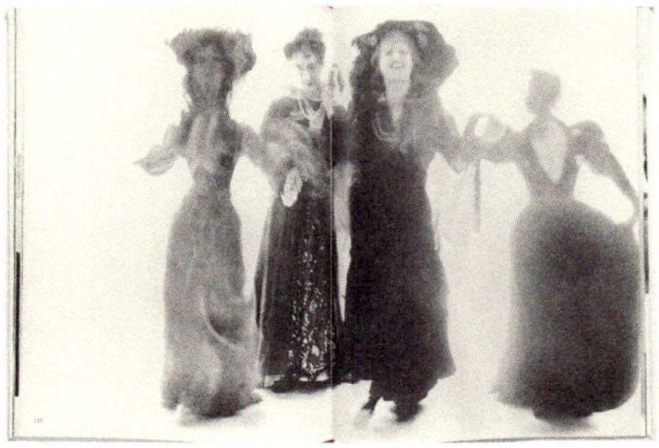

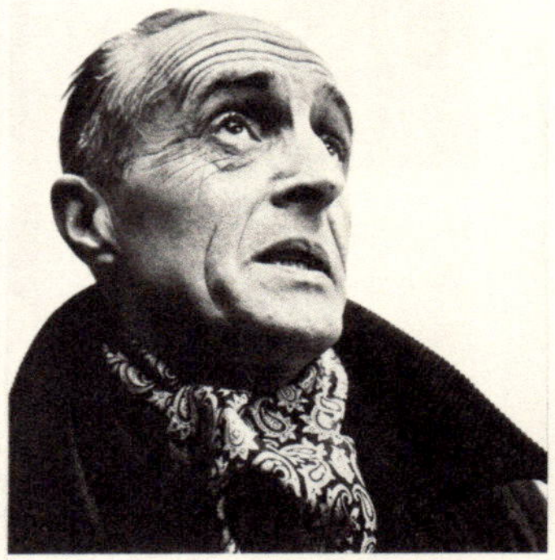

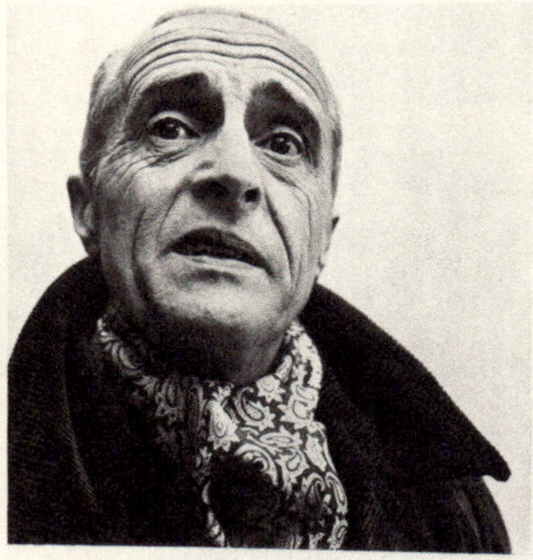

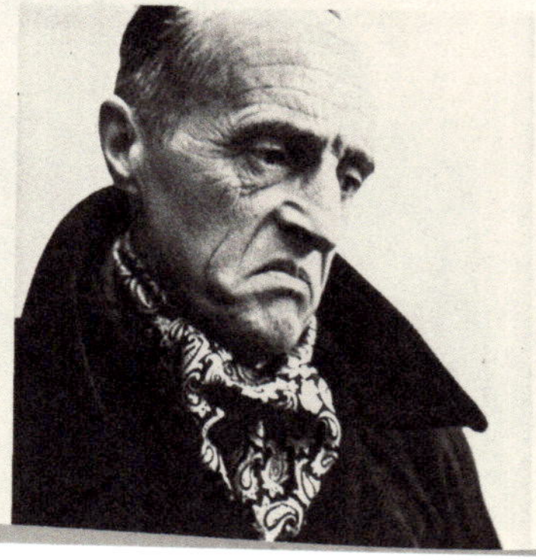

12

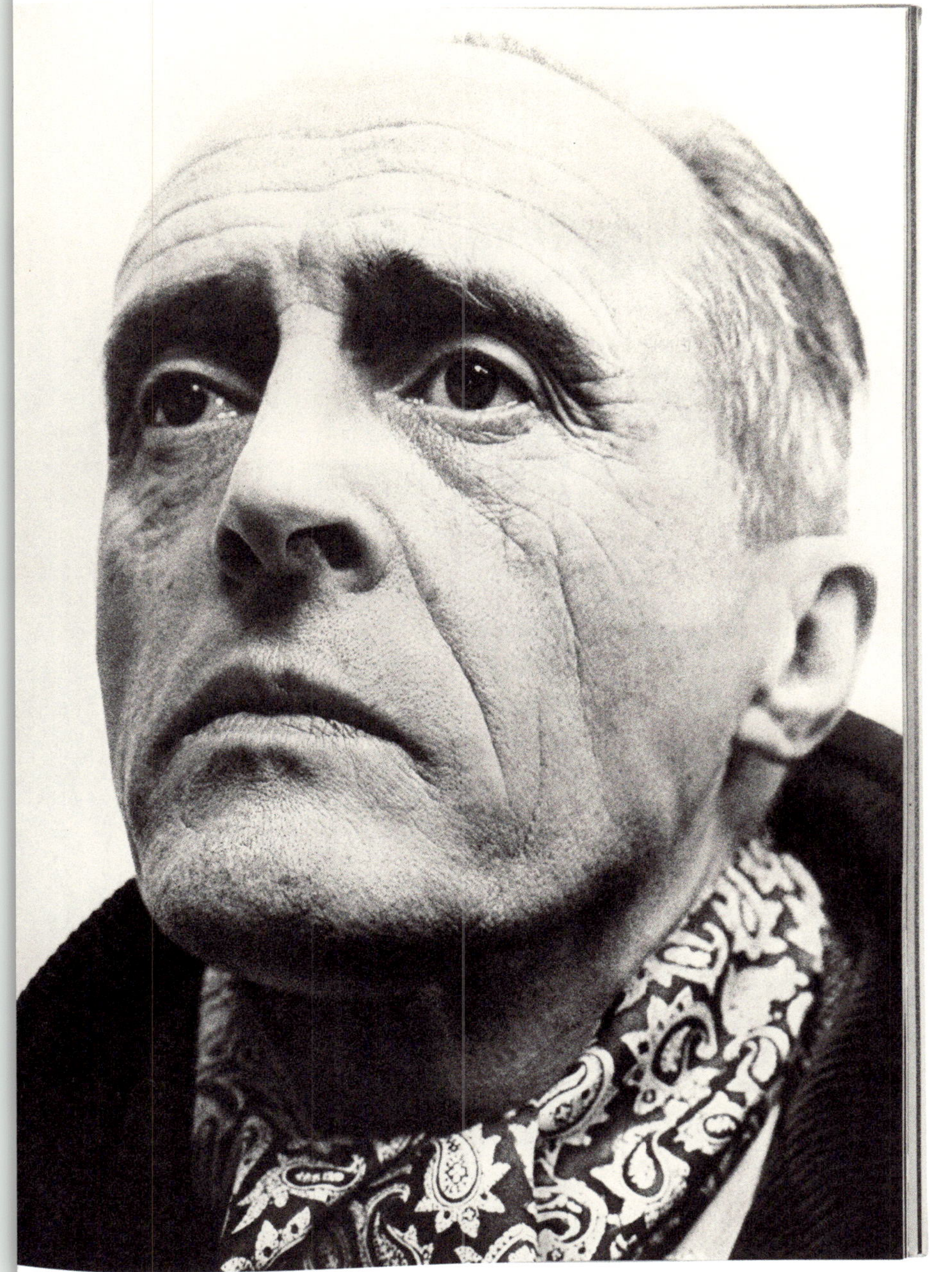

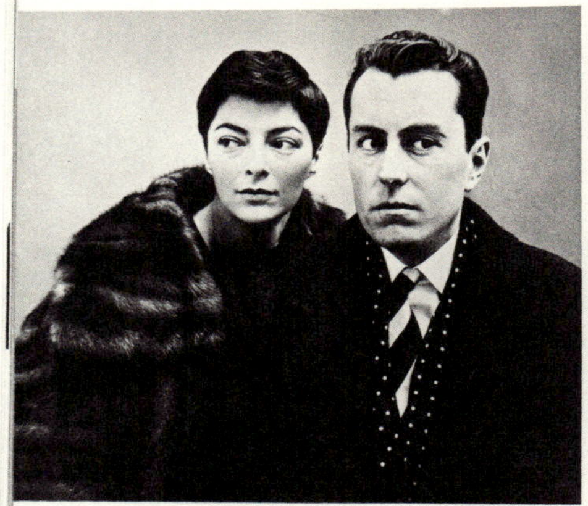

"Love consists in this that two Solitudes protect and touch and greet each other."

—RAINER MARIA RILKE

"Kind is my love today, tomorrow kind,
Still constant in wondrous excellence."

—WILLIAM SHAKESPEARE

38

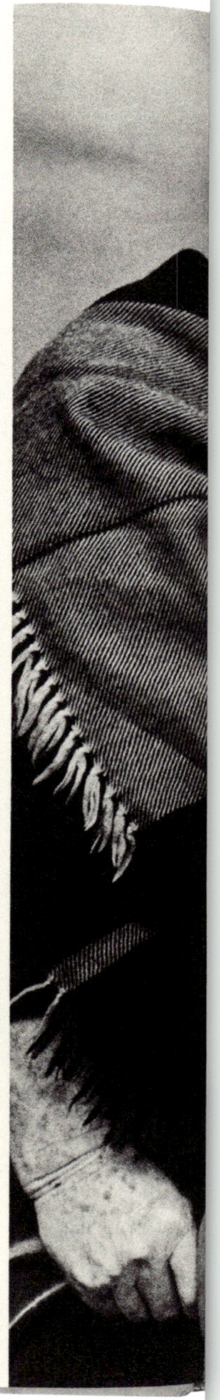

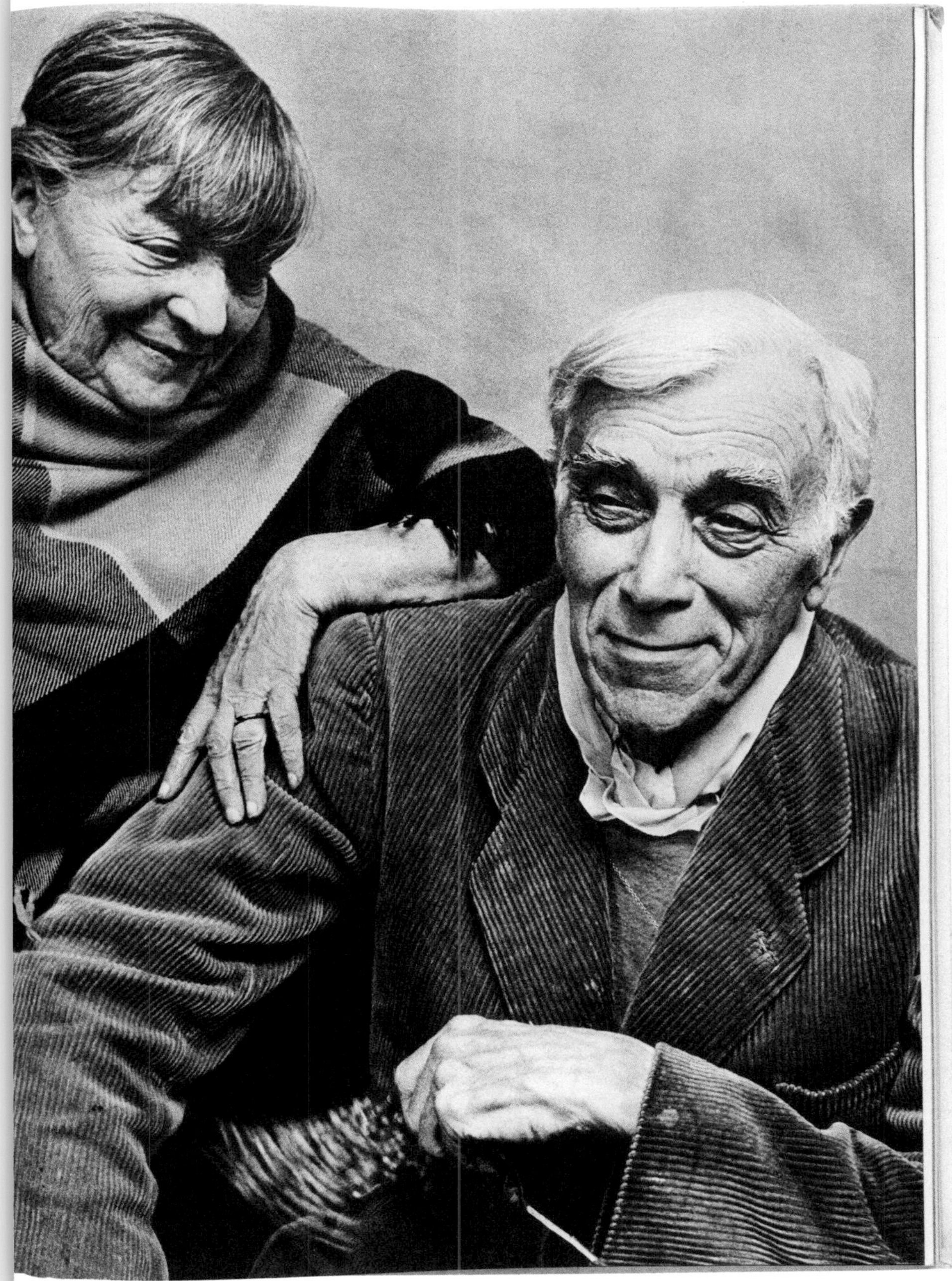

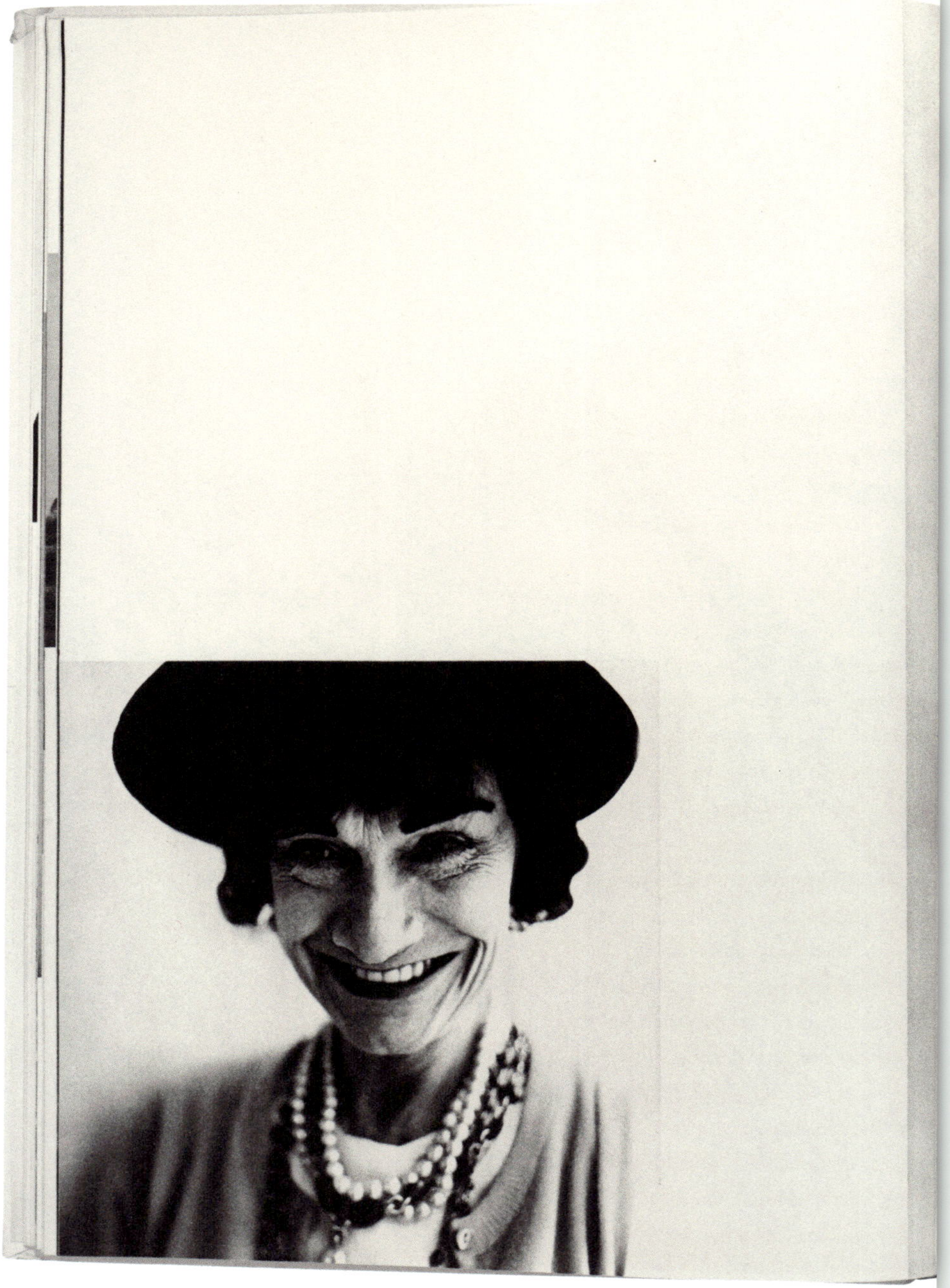

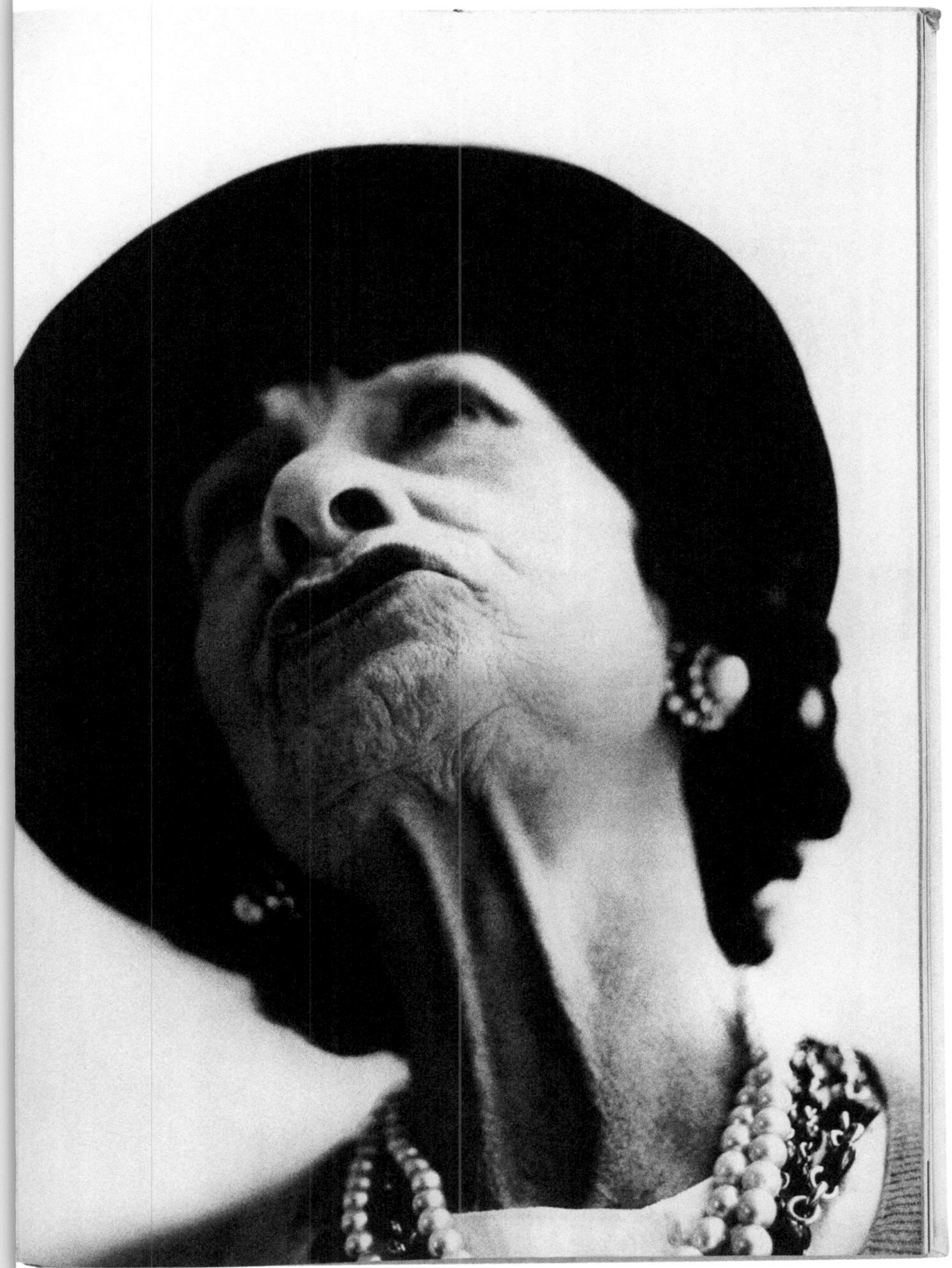

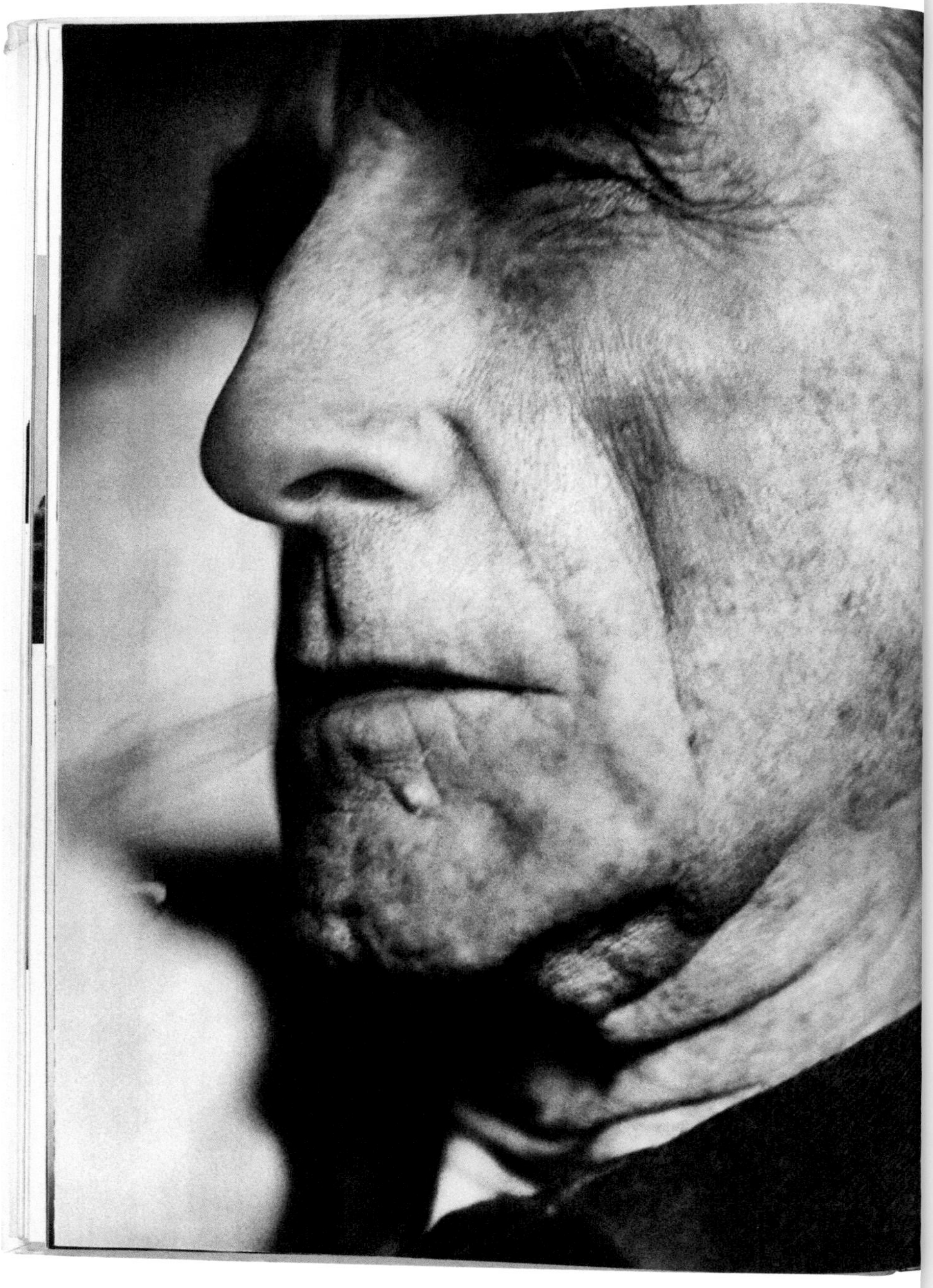

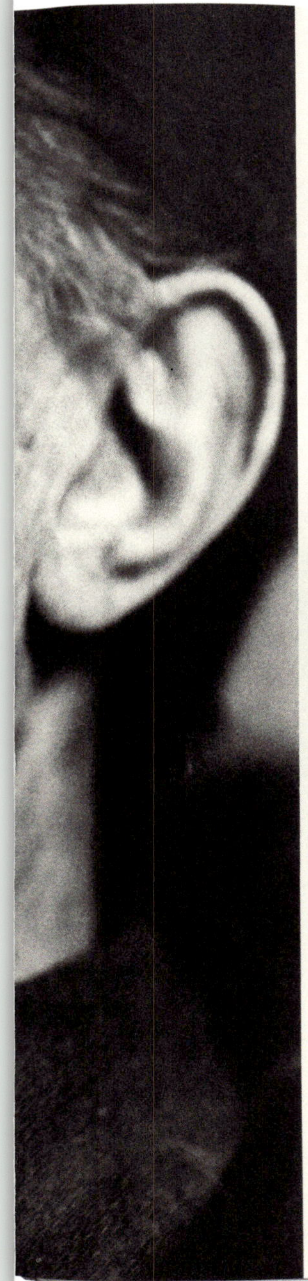

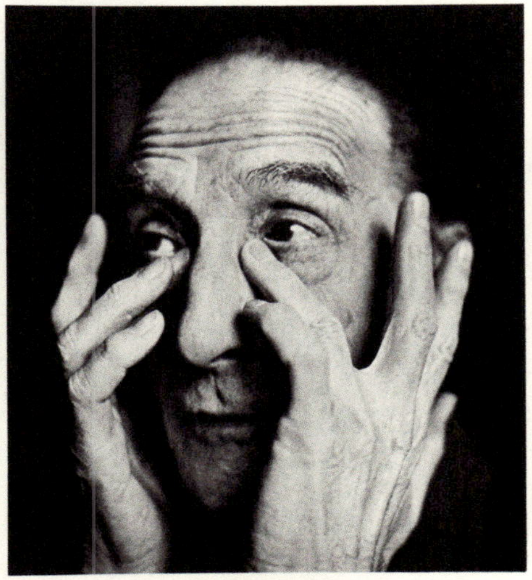

Duchamp, born in Rouen, the third son in a multi-membered middle-class family, many of whom were artistically inclined, has lived in New York since 1915. During these forty-four years of American residence he has dabbled away at only one painting (**Bride Stripped Bare by Her Bachelors, Even**—*an oil, on transparent glass, the size of a church window), and finished none; for all prac-* 53

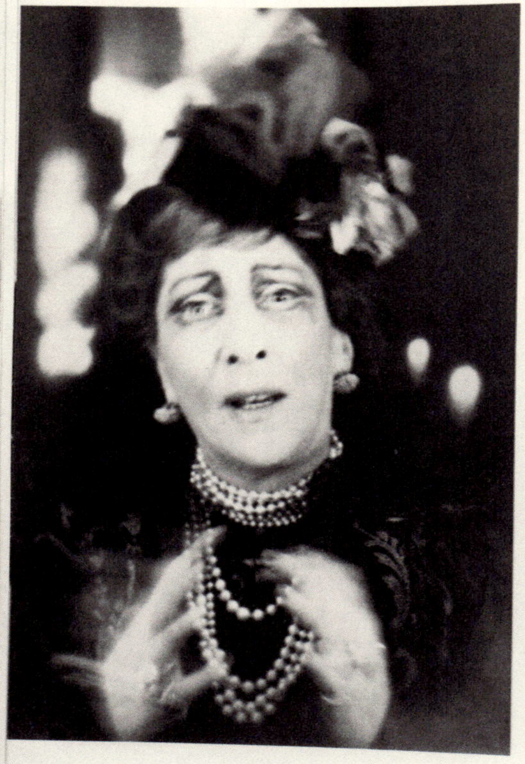

108

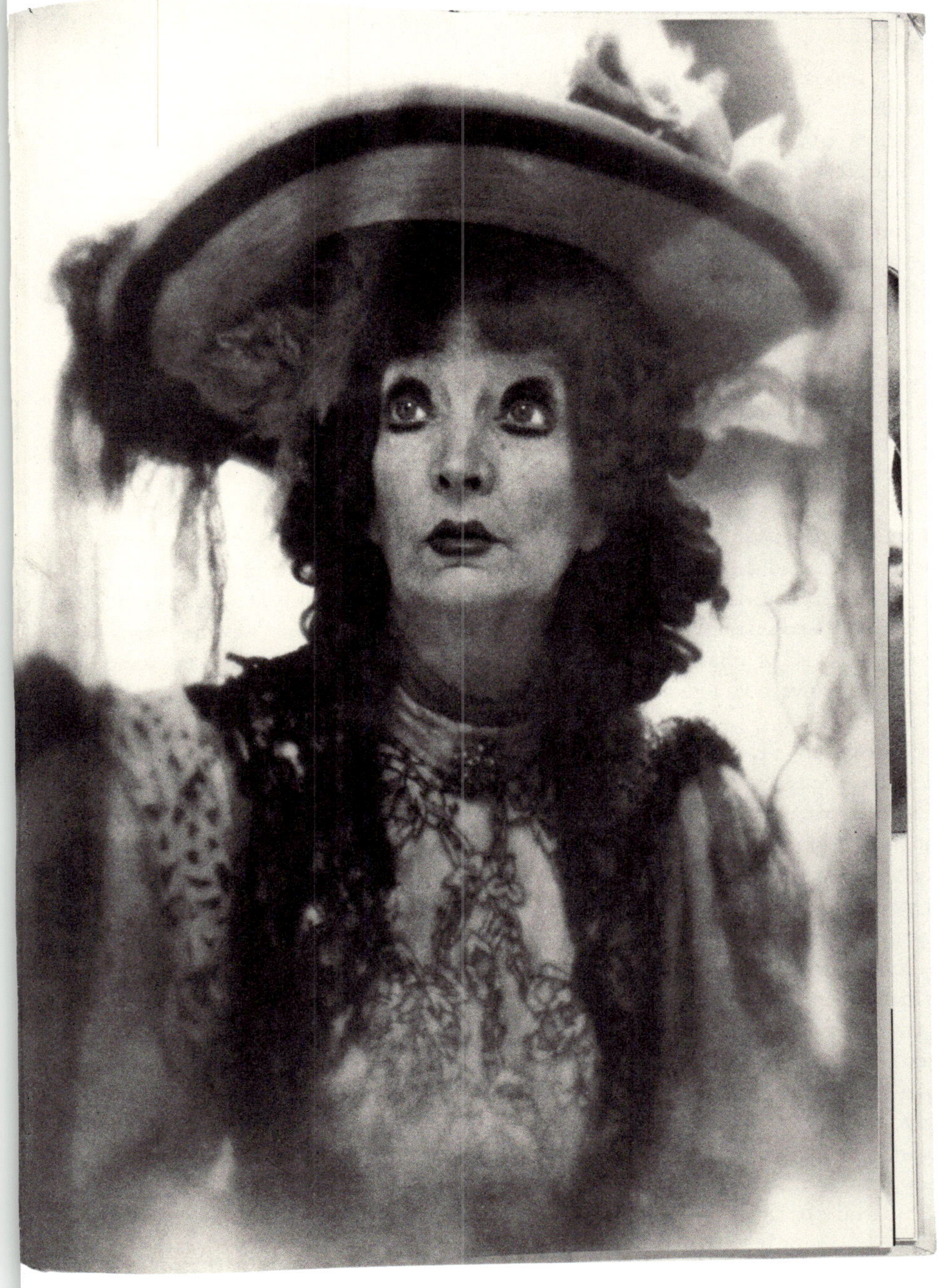

Dear Truman,

This is so impossible for me to do that. I'm just going to turn Ella on loud and do it and not read it and just mail it. I mean I am thirty-five years old born in and never left New York for longer than three months. Public schools. My grandparents lived in the same building as Rachmaninoff. When I was about ten I'd sit on the backstairs with his garbage and listen to him practice for hours and hours. One day I asked for his autograph and if I could take his picture with my box camera in front of the house. That was probably the beginning of the book.

I collected Vanity Fair and Vogue and the Bazaar and when I should have been trying to finish school I kept pasting Steichen and Muncaczi's [*sic.*] pictures all over the walls of my room and running away. Terrible student but liked to write. Editor of high school magazine and poet laureate of New York high schools in my senior year with something called "Spring in Coventry" but couldn't get enough credits together to graduate. My father predicted that I would join the Army of Illiterates. Became errand boy. Merchant Marine. Very lonely. Got photographic training in Merchant Marine. After discharge went directly to Harper's Bazaar. Showed experiments to Brodovitch. Took his courses at the New School. He gave me a chance in 1945. It had never occured to me to want to work for anyone but Brodovitch. Theatre Arts. Funny Face. Etc.

I'm very lucky to have found photography as I am inarticulate in every way but with a camera. With a Rolleiflex I can say everything I feel. There isn't a picture in the book that isn't an expression of a feeling or an opinion. Most of the photographs are expressions of admiration. The only warm thing I feel for the Windsors is for their loneliness. This is probably the only sentimental view in the book as they are probably not lonely at all. For that reason it is probably the most "flattering" picture in the book. Think about the life and the force and the drive and the desire in Chanel's throat. I cannot say this except in the most banal terms. To me there is nothing that can happen to a face that isn't extraordinary and beautiful because it is part of the whole human thing. Dinenson [*sic.*] and Maugham are beautiful on a level way way above Audrey. The smile from the corner of Maugham's mouth down puts anything on Jackie Kennedy's face out of business. You must know there is no hostility in the Bogart or Zavatini [*sic.*] sittings. It is important to understand where the hostility lies. In this collection it is only with Maxwell and Frank Lloyd Wright.

I feel most successful when I am able, doing a portrait sitting, to get a little of the inside of the sitter outside. The selection of a picture say of Ezra Pound or Marianne Moore is the most difficult and dangerous thing to do, and certainly more decisive than the taking of the sitting. When I am photographing someone, I know the moment I have the image that says what I want to say. The strength comes in not printing one that is possibly more of a "photograph" and less of a statement.

Anyone five years old can take a technically good photograph. We are drowning in photographs of all kinds. The daily and weekly publications eat up photographs like those great electric garbage trucks. There was a time in photography when it was enough to record what happened. In this period, a photographer's statement has to be so personal, such a personally definitive view, that once seen, it cannot ever be torn out of memory. I feel I've achieved that about five times in the thousands of pictures I've taken. That is what I hope to be able to do more and more often. That is, get in a picture the whole picture. The past present future. The longing, the finding, mostly the longing, somehow trying to get the entire man caught and held in one moment.

I hate photographing the young. Nothing shows on their faces. Nothing has happened.

Truman, on rereading this, it is all so icky. I'm only doing it because it'll suggest something to you. Meanwhile Phylise Jackson [*sic.*] at MCA has spoken about the little type at the bottom to Simon and Schuster and the contract is being drawn up. The moment it is signed I'll send you my body and anything else happy! Our deadline is January first. That gives Jackson a chance to sell sections around etc. and also meets the publisher's deadline.

We love your cards. So many of them. They're all around the mirror, reminding me that you're working and that I better be working to. I just keep photographing EVERYBODY!

I'm enclosing the only other statement I've made on "the art of it.". Please write but soon. July 23rd to Aug. 5th I'll be in Paris, then who knows, we may be free to visit you.

Letter from Richard Avedon to Truman Capote, 1958. Found in the back of the mockup for *Observations*.

I lit each restaurant, each street as if I were lighting a movie.

—

Richard Avedon

Directed by Avedon: (Paris Pursuit)

While Avedon did not venture further into Hollywood after *Funny Face*, cinematic themes continued to pervade his work. The cover of *Harper's Bazaar* in September 1959 credits Avedon as the director of "Paris Pursuit: a Love Farce." What follows is a light photoplay — a *ciné-roman* — in a screenplay format used to camouflage the necessary evil of fashion credits.

The series features Buster Keaton (photographed by Avedon often), and Art Buchwald makes a cameo appearance.

HARPER'S

BAZAAR

PRESENTS

AUDREY HEPBURN

MEL FERRER

PARIS PURSUIT

A LOVE FARCE

FEATURING THE PARIS COLLECTIONS

WITH BUSTER KEATON DIRECTED BY RICHARD AVEDON

PLUS THE AMERICAN FASHION OPENINGS

SEPTEMBER 1959
60 CENTS

HARPER'S BAZAAR PRESENTS:

PARIS PURSUIT

The Cast:

Jemima Jones, a traveling actress	Audrey Hepburn
Simone, Jemima's cat	Herself
Dallas O'Hara, Esq., a traveling millionaire	Mel Ferrer
Big Thunderbrow, O'Hara's brave valet	Buster Keaton
A Cocotte	Zsa Zsa Gabor
A Seine-side Beatnique	Annette Stroyberg
The Man in the Hat at Maxim's	Art Buchwald
The Tunic	Dior, Cardin, Chanel, everywhere
The Emphatic Sleeve	Grès, Laroche, Patou, Ricci
The Sheltering Collar	Balmain, Grès, Griffe, everywhere
The Bloused Coat	Cardin
The Flirty Skirt	Dior
The Wide Belt	Dior, Ricci
The Lowering Waist	Cardin, Dessès, Goma, Heim, Lanvin
The Lengthening Jacket	Cardin, Heim, Lanvin
The Braided Tweeds	Chanel, Dior
The Hooded Costume	Dior, Goma, Grès
The Ribbon Plaids	Balmain, Dior, Lanvin, Laroche
The Froth of Black After Dark	Chanel, Dessès, Dior, Griffe
The White for Night	Balmain, Dior, Patou, everywhere
Coiffures	Enrico Caruso

Directed by Richard Avedon

Harper's Bazaar, September 1959 cover, and "Paris Pursuit" opener, p. 145

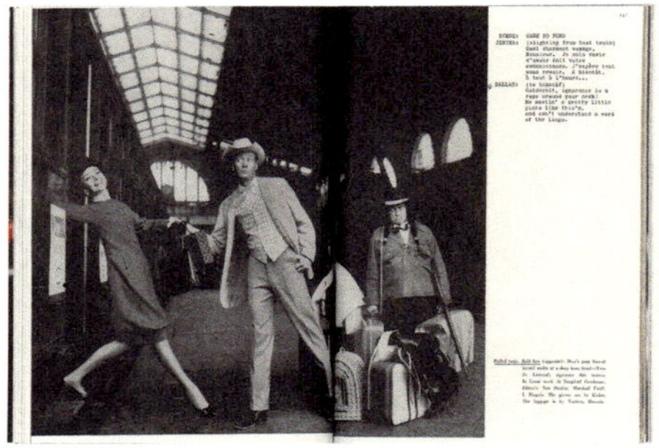

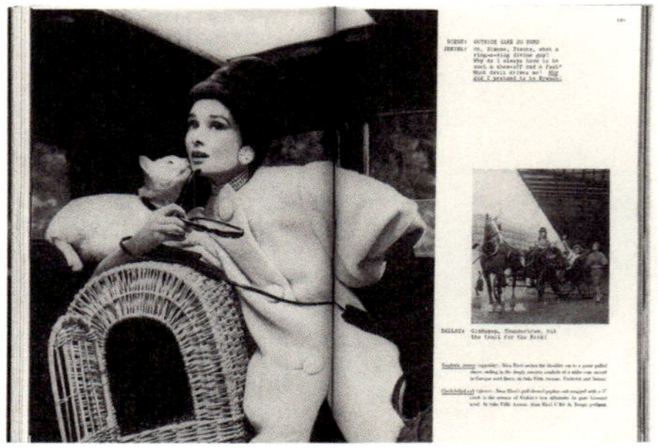

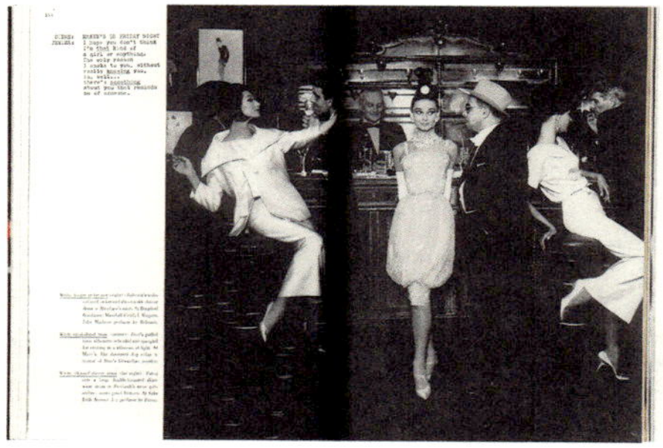

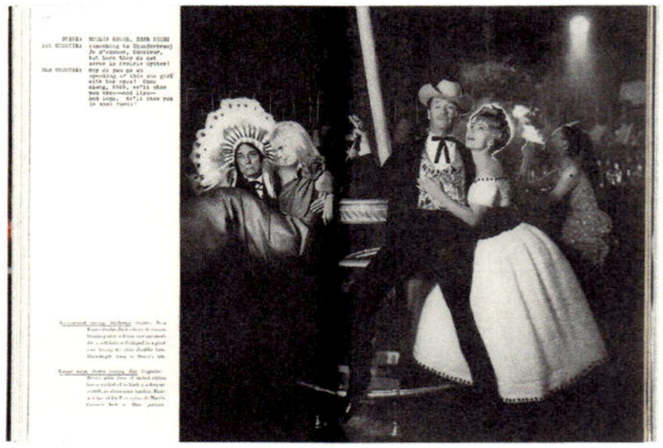

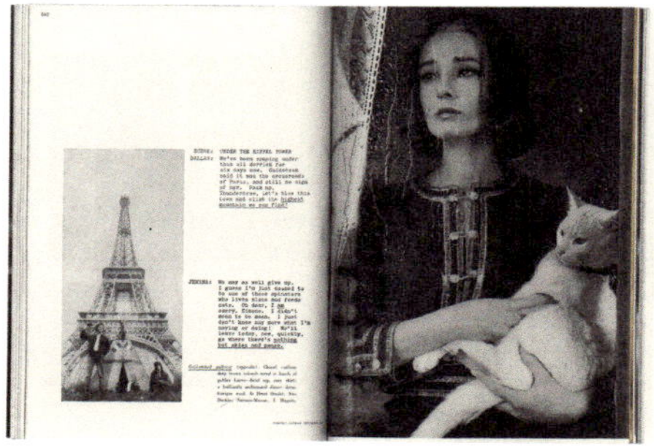

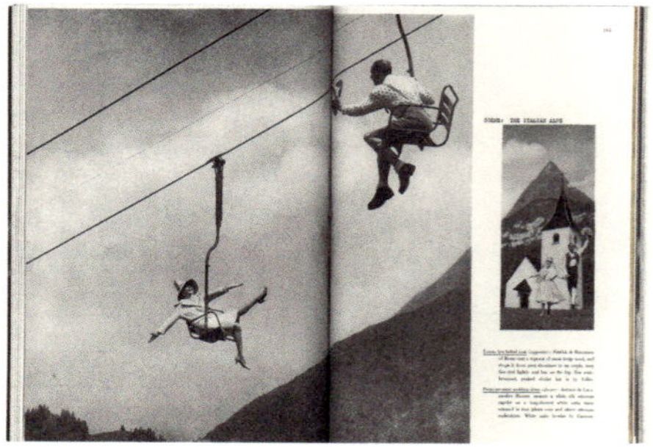

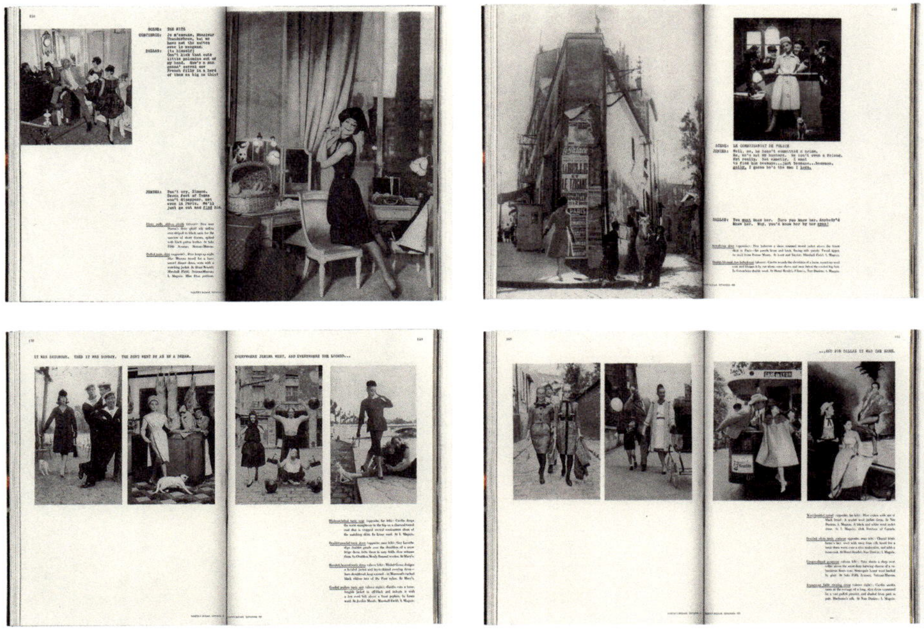

“Paris Pursuit” spreads in *Harper’s Bazaar*, September 1959, pp. 146–65

SCENE: MAXIM'S ON FRIDAY NIGHT

JEMIMA: I hope you don't think
I'm that kind of
a girl or anything.
The only reason
I spoke to you, without
really knowing you,
is, well...
there's something
about you that reminds
me of someone.

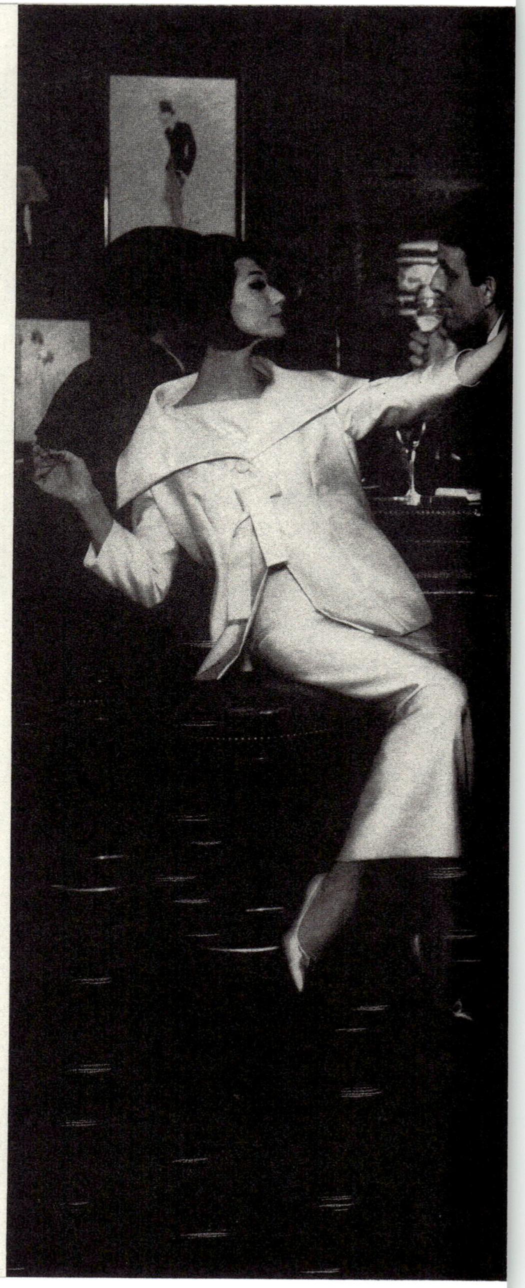

White, longer jacket suit (right): Balmain's wide-collared jacket and above-ankle dinner dress in Abraham's satin. At Bergdorf Goodman; Marshall Field; I. Magnin. Jolie Madame perfume by Balmain.

White crystallized tunic (center): Dior's puffed tunic silhouette is beaded and spangled for evening in a shimmer of light. At Macy's. The *diamanté* dog collar is typical of Dior's Edwardian jewelry.

White, bloused dinner dress (far right): Patou cuts a long, double-breasted shirtwaist dress in Pétillault's satin gabardine; ocean pearl buttons. At Saks Fifth Avenue. Joy perfume by Patou.

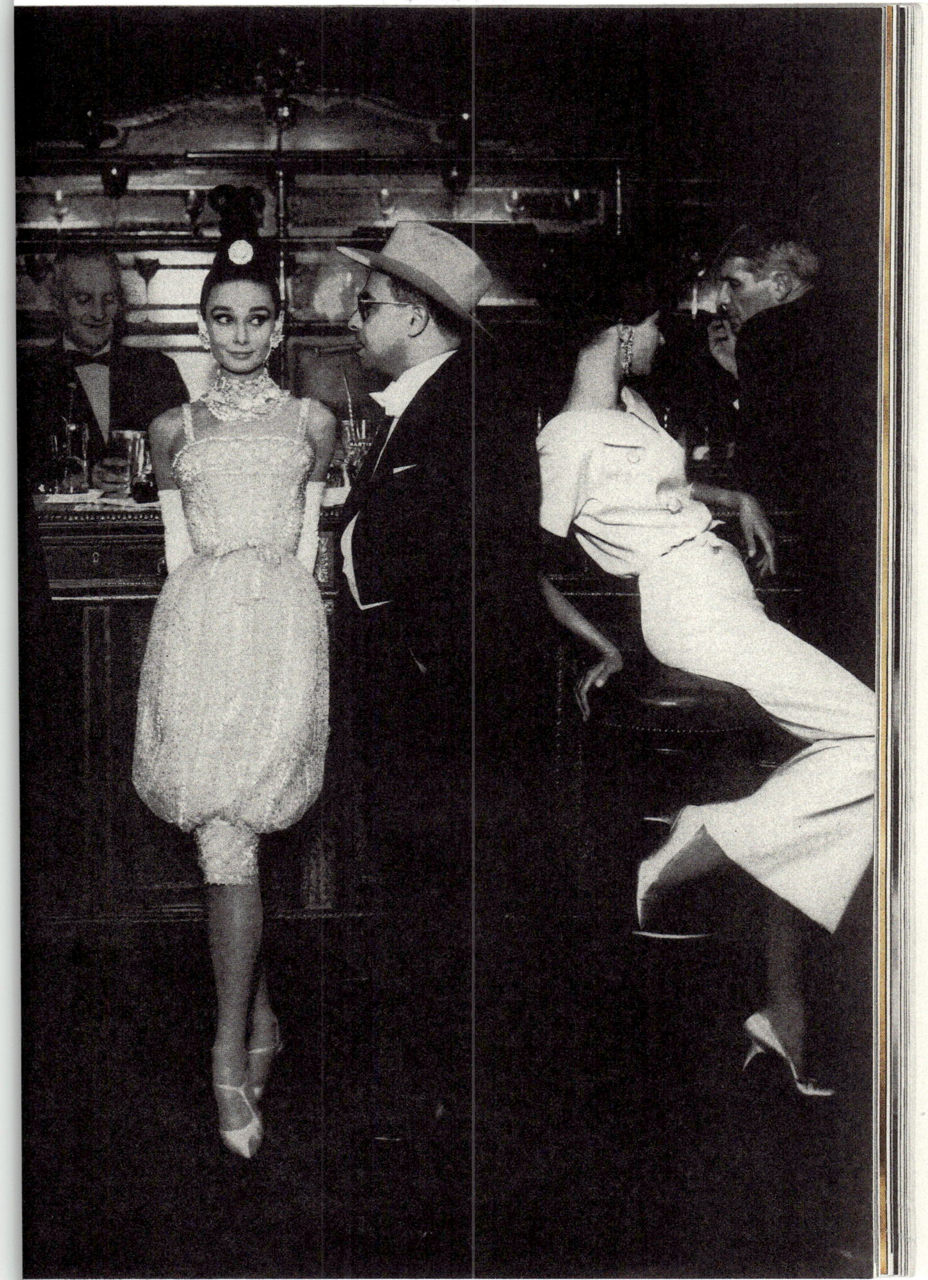

"Paris Pursuit," *Harper's Bazaar*, September 1959, pp. 154–55

SCENE: MOULIN ROUGE, SAME NIGHT

1st COCOTTE: (speaking to Thunderbrow) Je m'excuse, Monsieur, but here they do not serve la Prairie Oyster!

2nd COCOTTE: Why do you go on speaking of this one girl with her eyes! Come along, bébé, we'll show you eyes—and lips— and legs. We'll show you le vrai Paris!

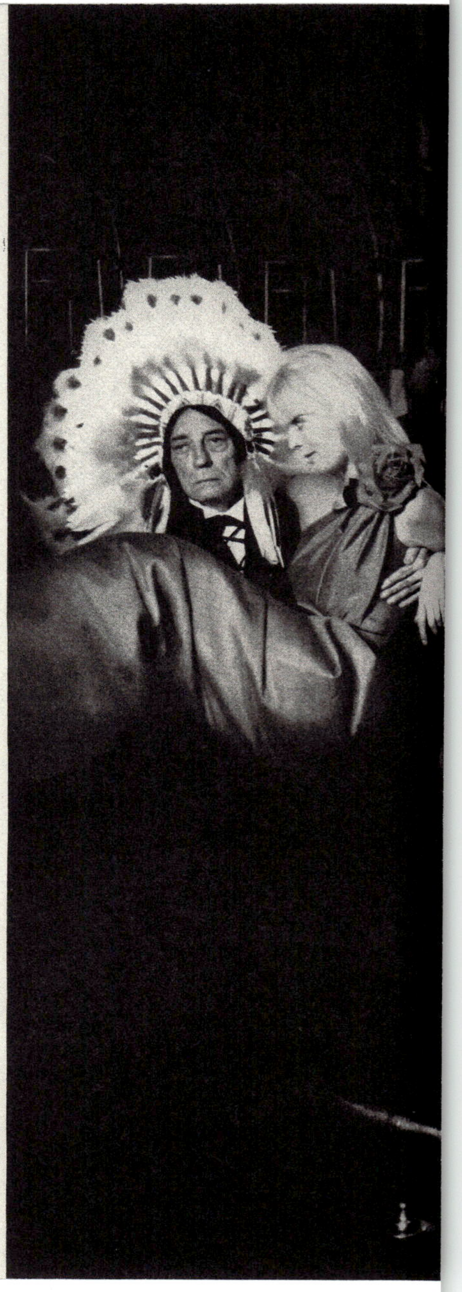

Asymmetrical evening décolletage (right): Nina Ricci's slender, fluid column of crimson Shantung satin is drawn over one shoulder in soft folds and clasped by a giant rose, leaving the other shoulder bare. Floor-length dress, in Staron's silk.

Longer waist, shorter evening skirt (opposite): Heim's white dress of ruched ribbon lace is marked off in black at a deep-set midriff, an above-ankle hemline. Marescot lace of Du Pont nylon. At Macy's. Carven's Vert et Blanc perfume.

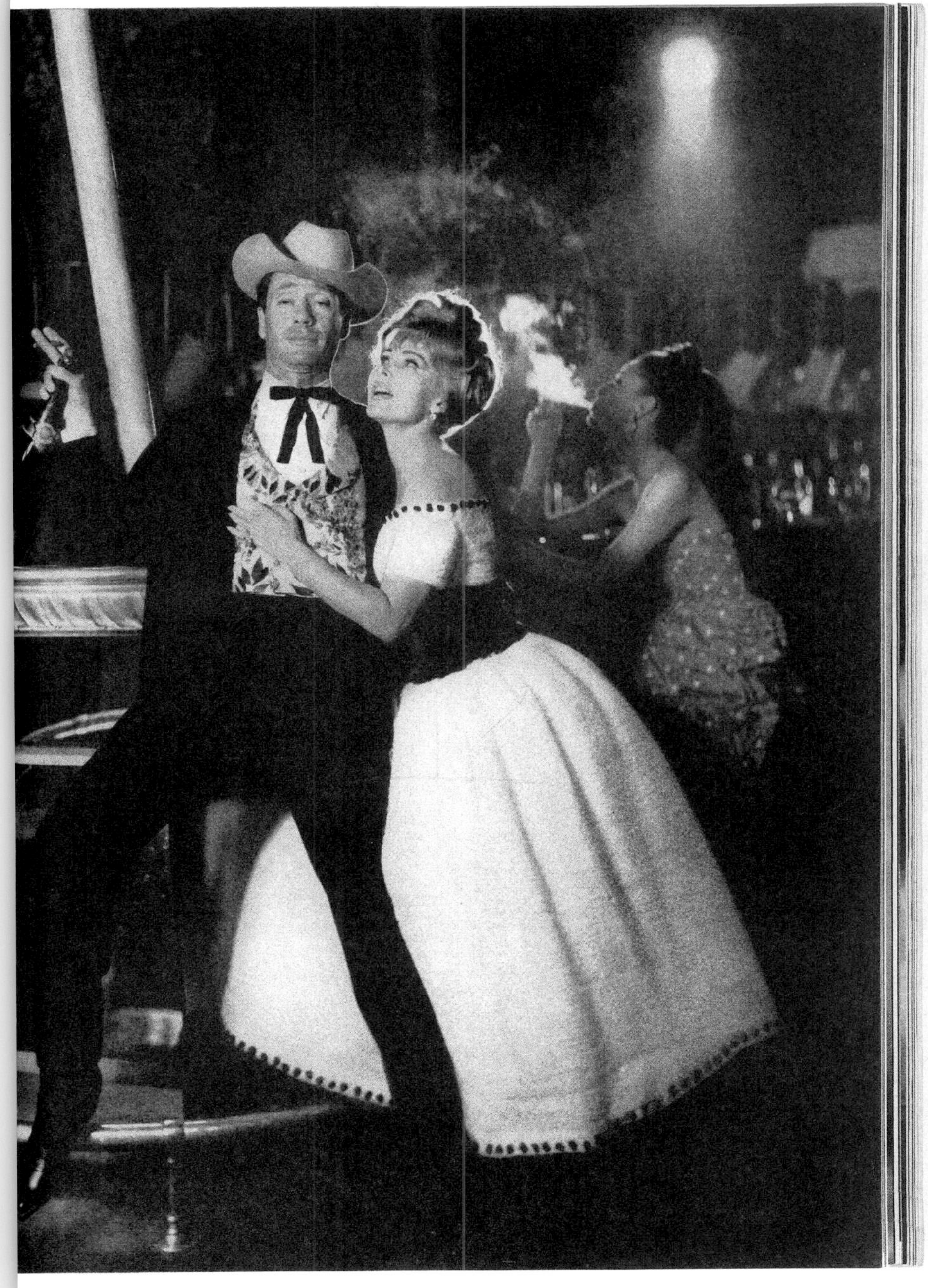

"Paris Pursuit," *Harper's Bazaar*, September 1959, pp. 156–57

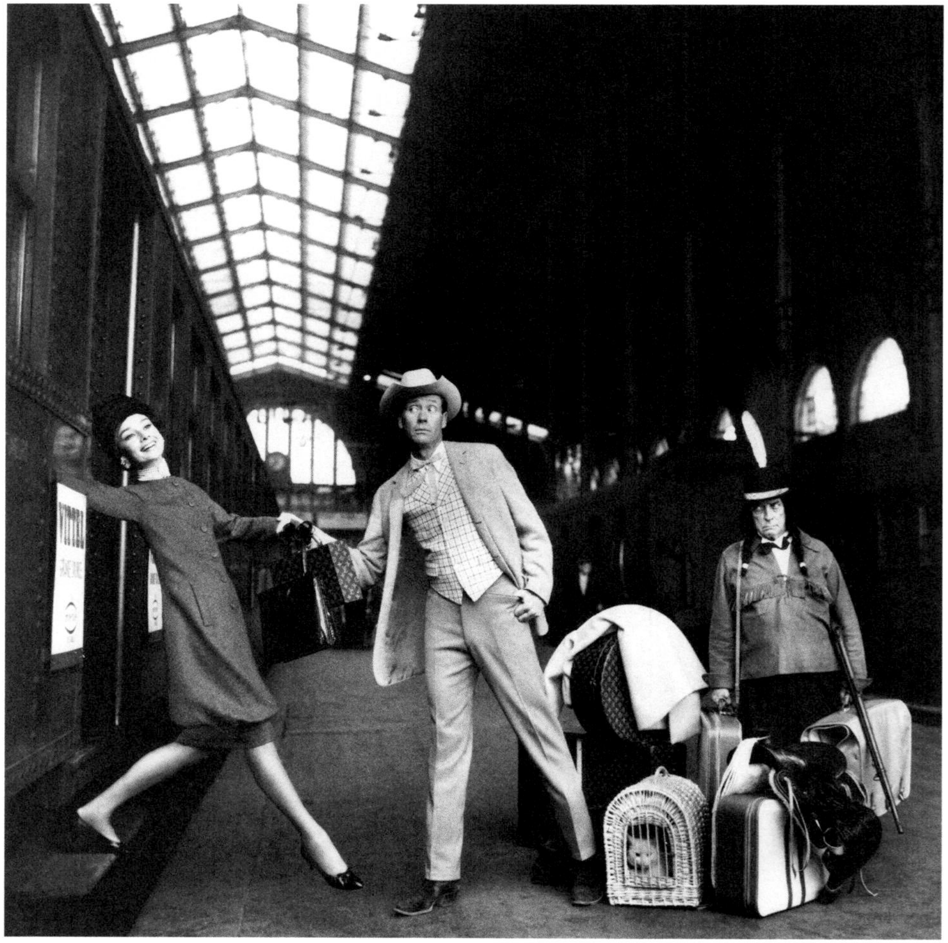

Audrey Hepburn, Mel Ferrer and Buster Keaton in "Paris Pursuit" for *Harper's Bazaar*, Paris, August 9, 1959

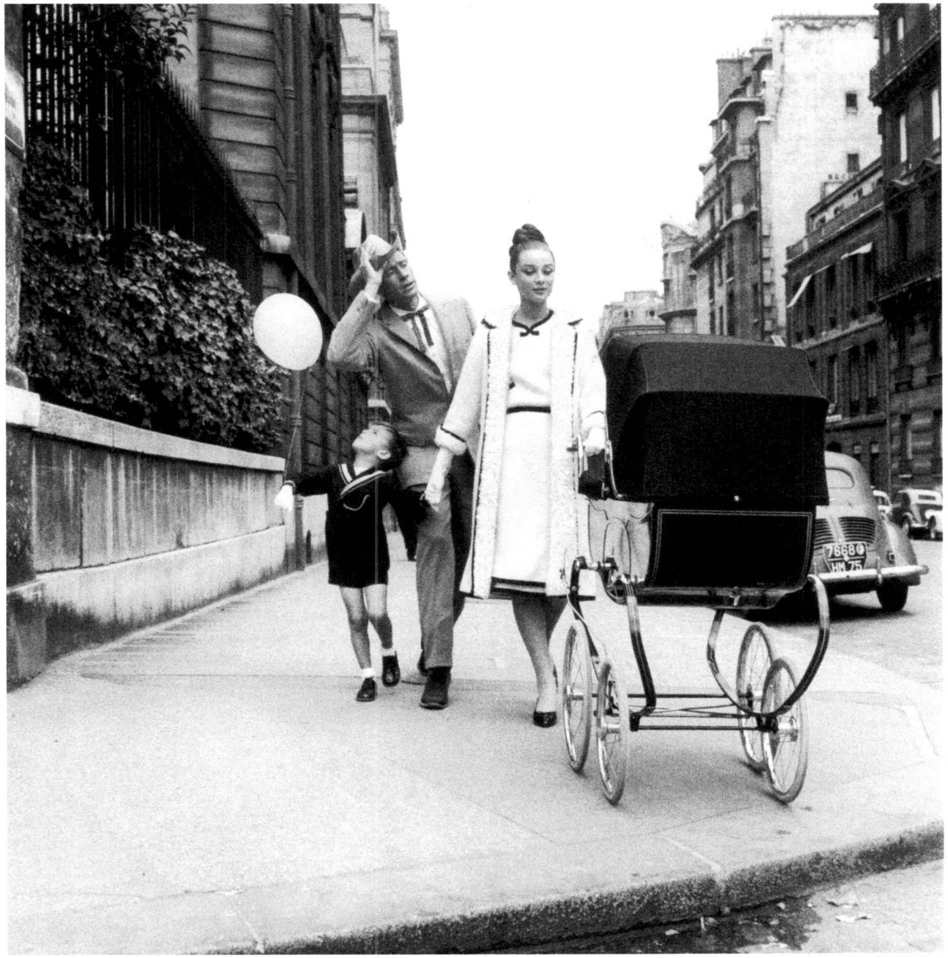

Audrey Hepburn and Mel Ferrer in "Paris Pursuit" for *Harper's Bazaar*, Paris, August 9, 1959

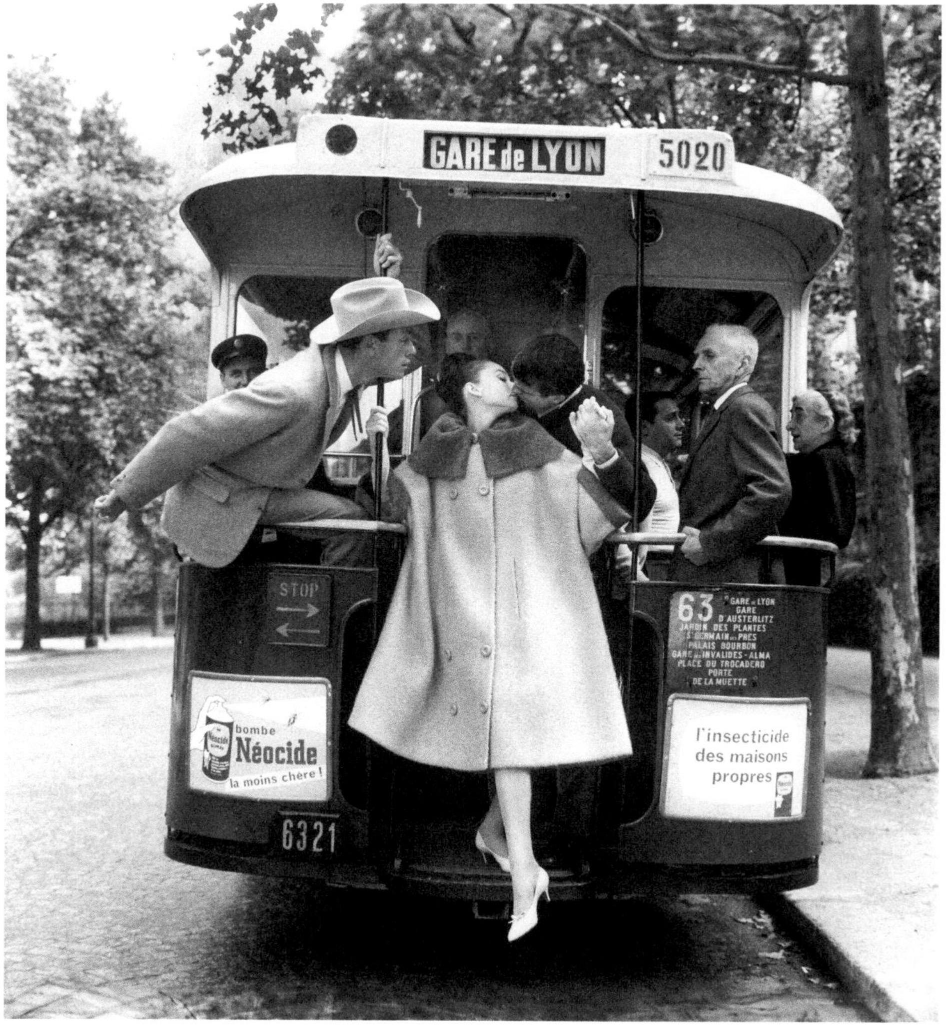

Audrey Hepburn, Mel Ferrer and Buster Keaton in "Paris Pursuit" for *Harper's Bazaar*, Paris, August 9, 1959

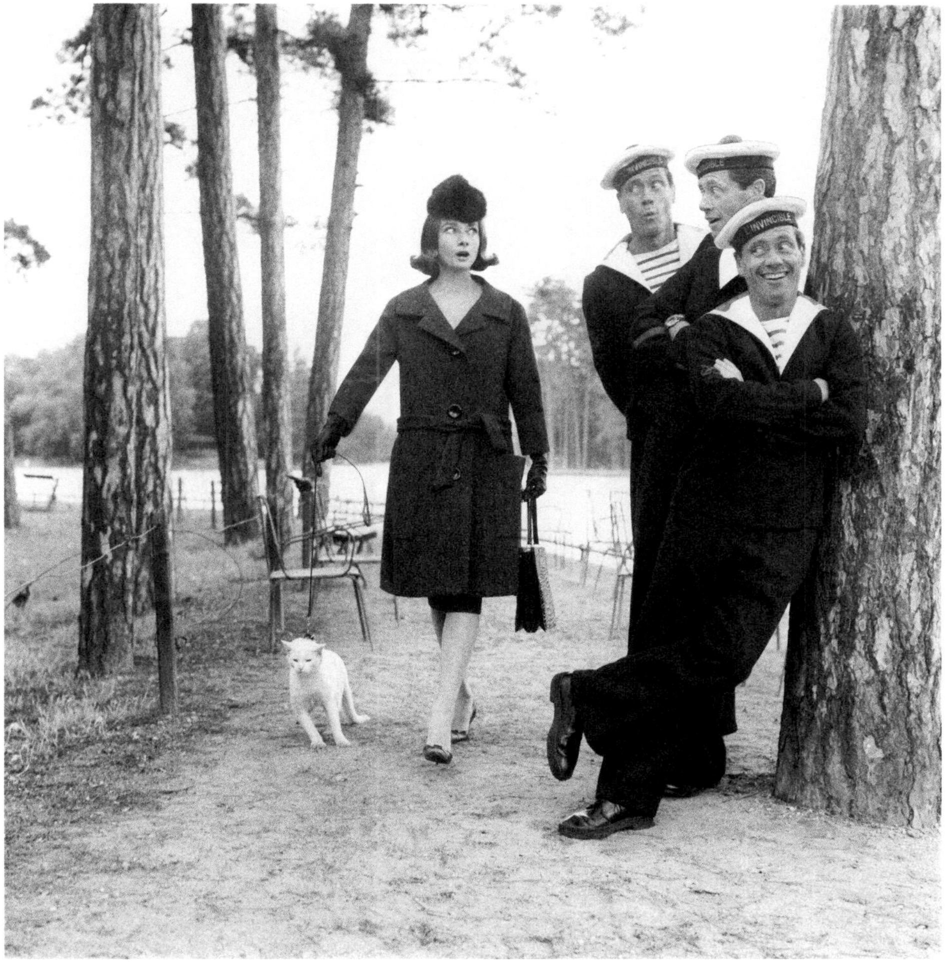

Audrey Hepburn, Mel Ferrer and Buster Keaton in "Paris Pursuit" for *Harper's Bazaar*, Paris, August 9, 1959

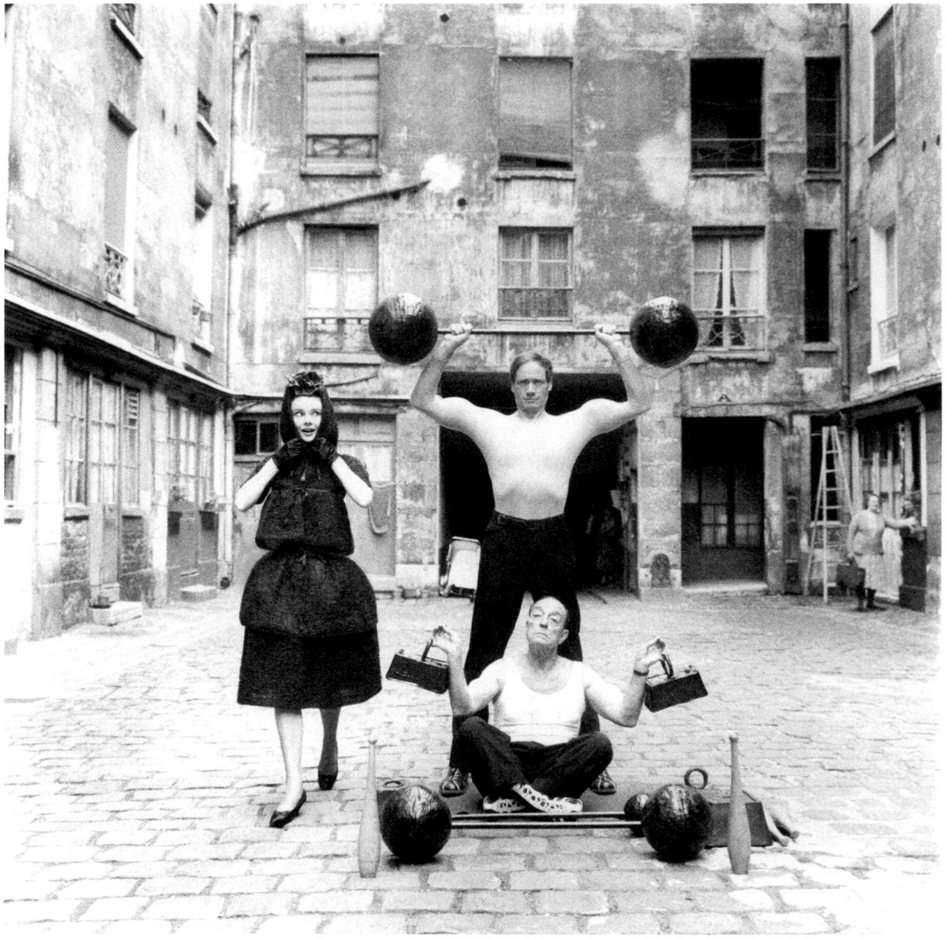

Audrey Hepburn, Mel Ferrer and Buster Keaton in "Paris Pursuit" for *Harper's Bazaar*, Paris, August 9, 1959

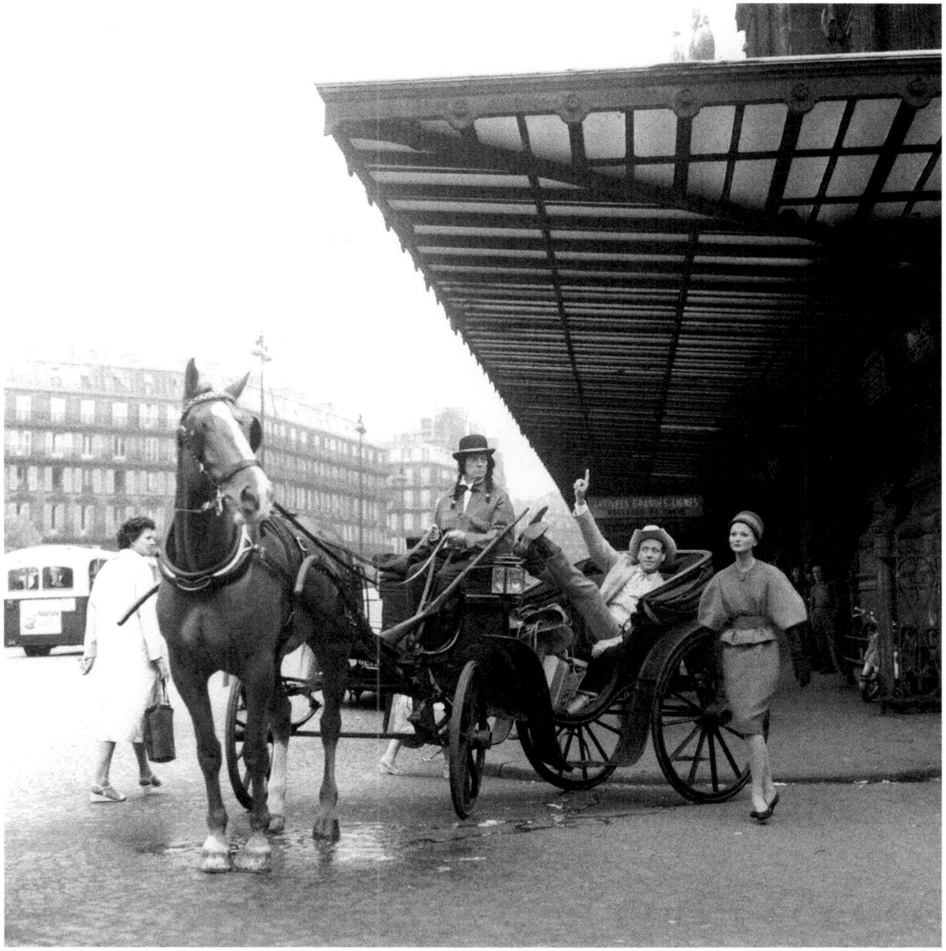

Audrey Hepburn, Mel Ferrer and Buster Keaton in "Paris Pursuit" for *Harper's Bazaar*, Paris, August 9, 1959

Coup de foudre

In the Photobooth

There are nearly as many photo strips of Avedon and his circle floating around as there are self-portraits. His work often blurs the lines between the artistic and the vernacular. The first assignment Avedon gave his students was to take pictures in a photobooth, underlining the importance of the eye over the apparatus. Yet when Avedon was asked by *Esquire* magazine to make portraits in his studio using a Mutoscope Photomatic photo booth, he characteristically retouched them. For Avedon, all photographic moments — however spontaneous they seemed — were carefully constructed.

25c A CELEBRITY

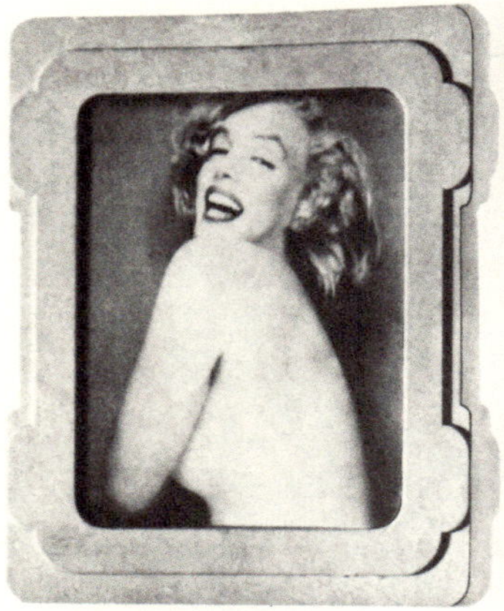

Marilyn Monroe and very little else

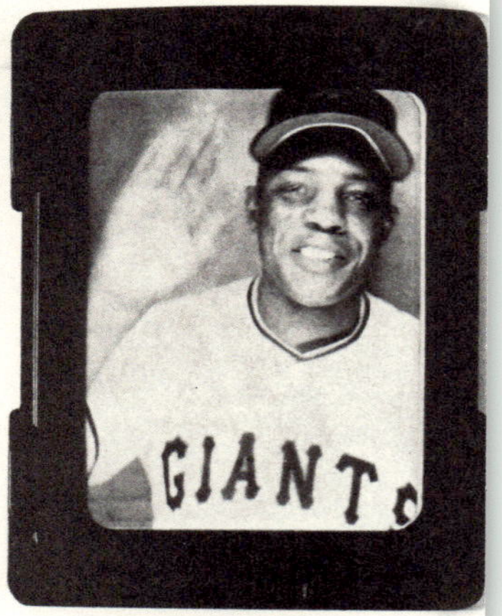

Willie Mays and uniform

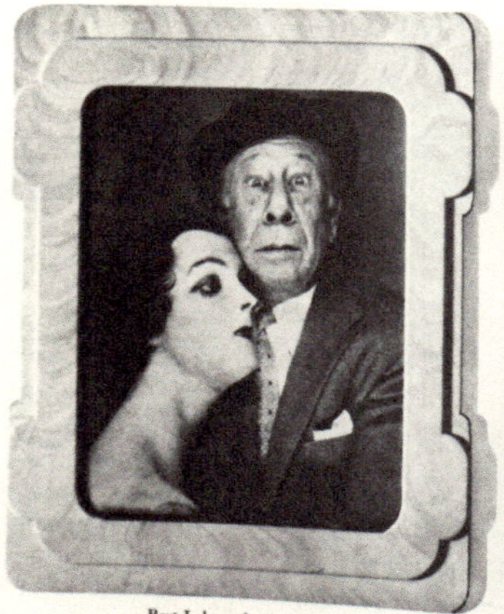

Bert Lahr and quiet friend

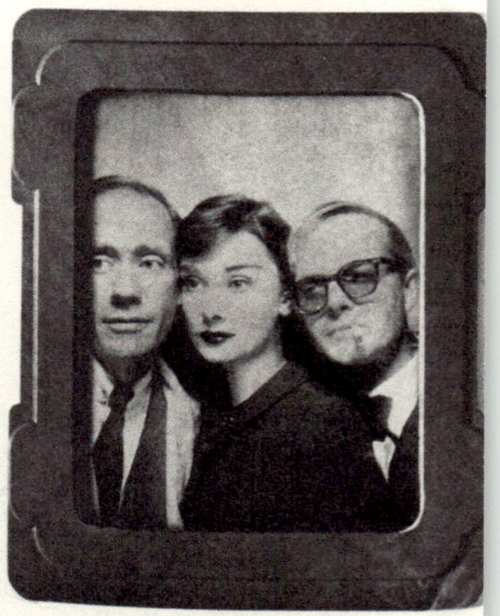

Mel Ferrer, Audrey Hepburn, Truman Capote

58

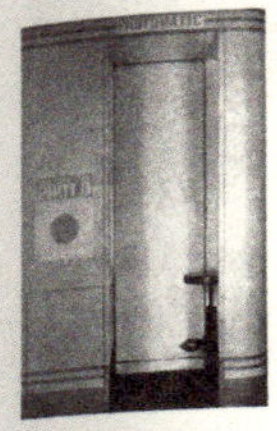

RICHARD AVEDON, probably the world's best-known fashion photographer and the man whose career inspired the film *Funny Face*, has long asserted that true photographic talent cannot be restrained by a camera's technical limitations. With Brownie, box or crude pinhole camera, great photos can be taken, says he. To put Avedon's theory to the test, Esquire installed a 25c Photomatic machine at his studio, asked him to photograph the celebrities seen here

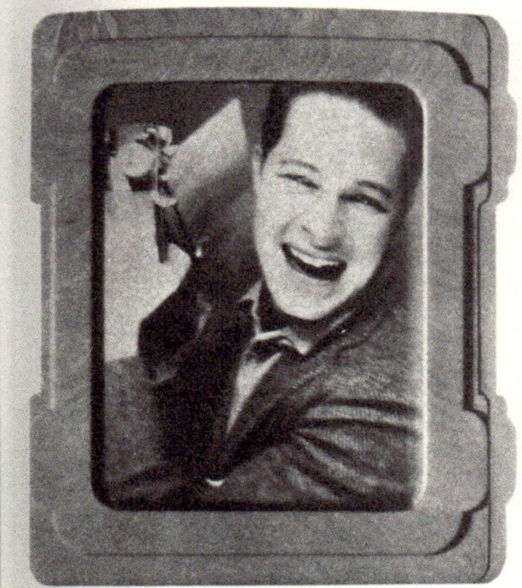

George Axelrod and enervating typewriter

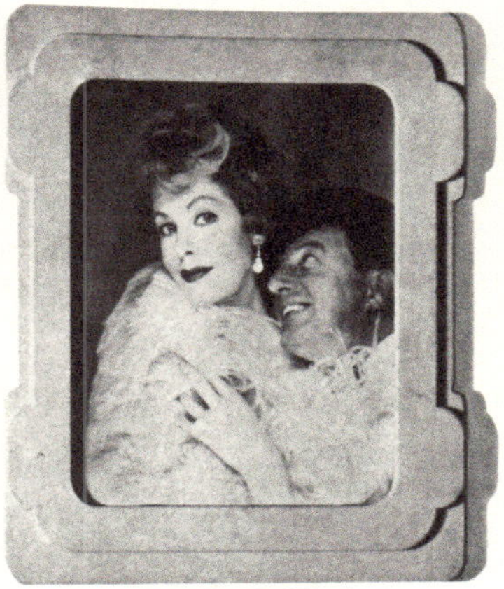

Arlene Dahl and Ray Bolger

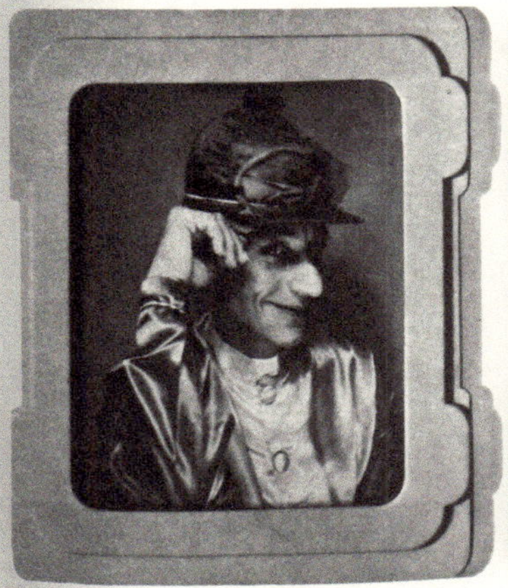

Eddie Arcaro and silks

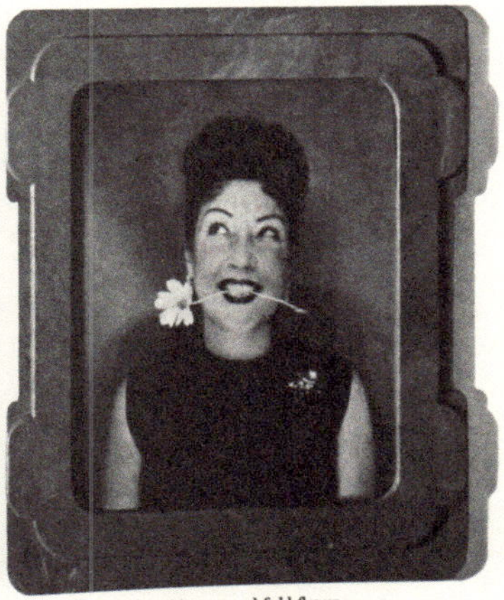

Ethel Merman and field flower

59

Avedon Photomatic photography spread, *Esquire*, November 1957, pp. 58–59

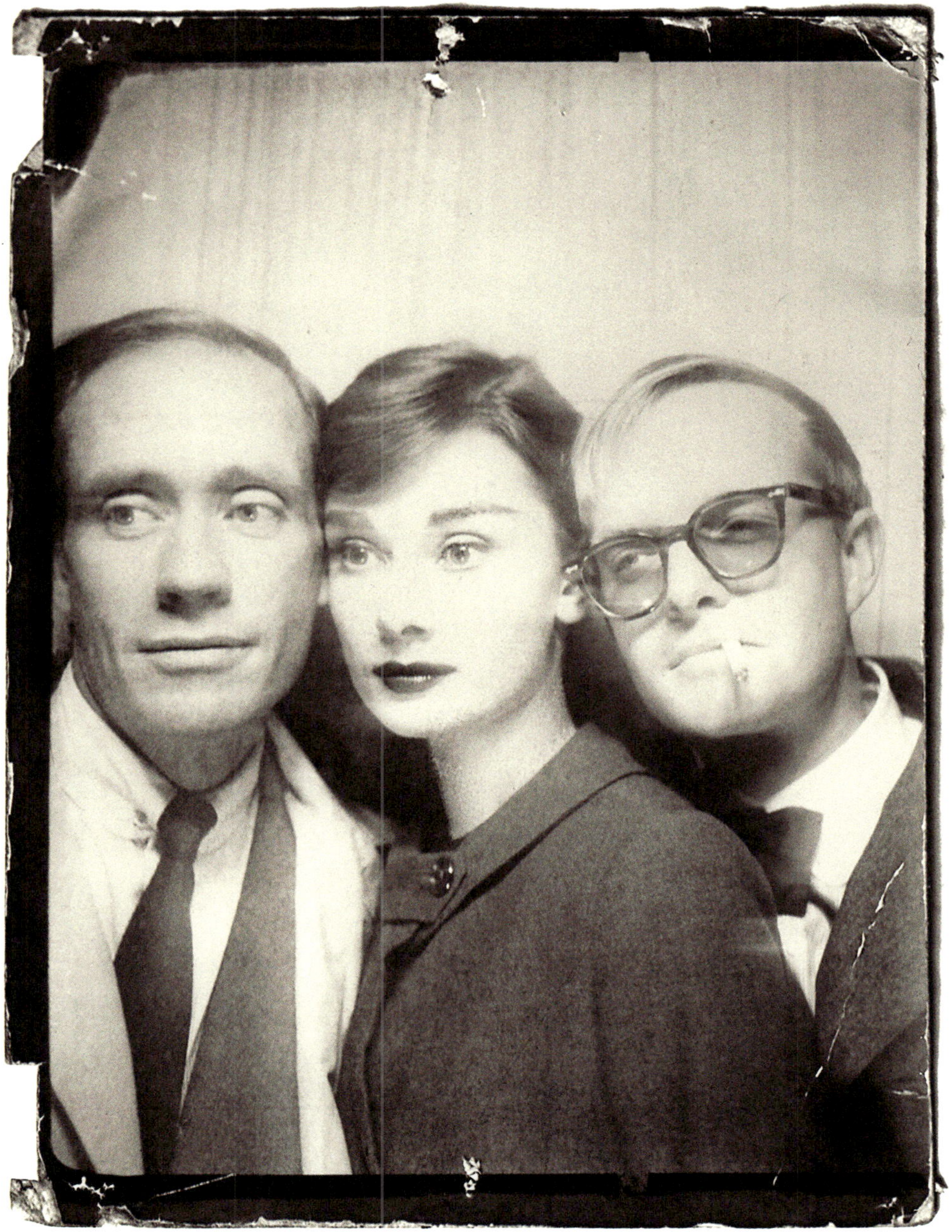

Avedon Photomatic photograph of Mel Ferrer, Audrey Hepburn, and Truman Capote, 1957

p. 415, Evelyn Avedon, wife of Richard Avedon, Apartment 60, Hôtel San Régis, Paris, August 1955
p. 417, Photo booth self-portrait with James Baldwin, New York, September 1964
pp. 418–19, James Baldwin, writer, Harlem, New York, 1945

French Portraits II

Richard Avedon

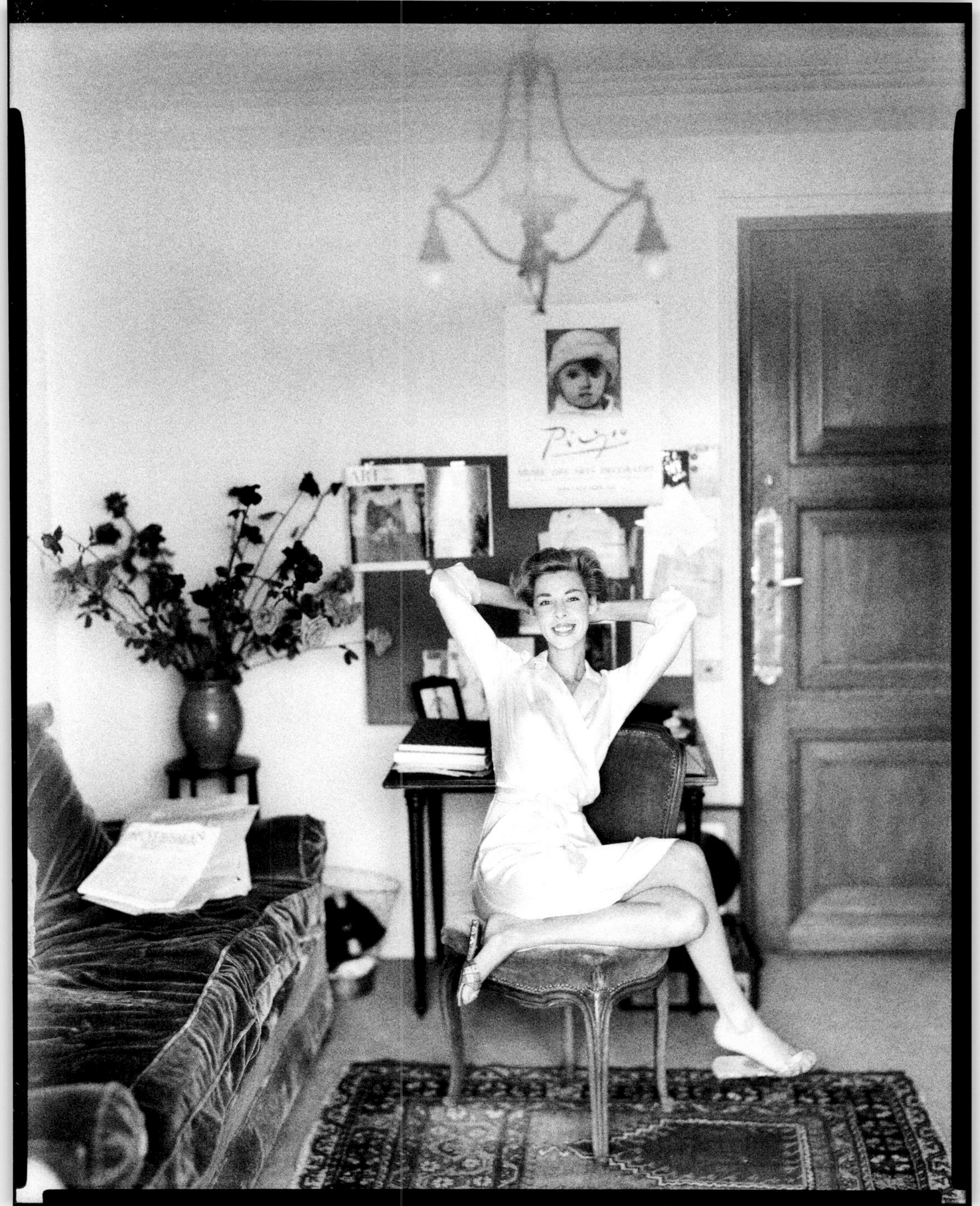

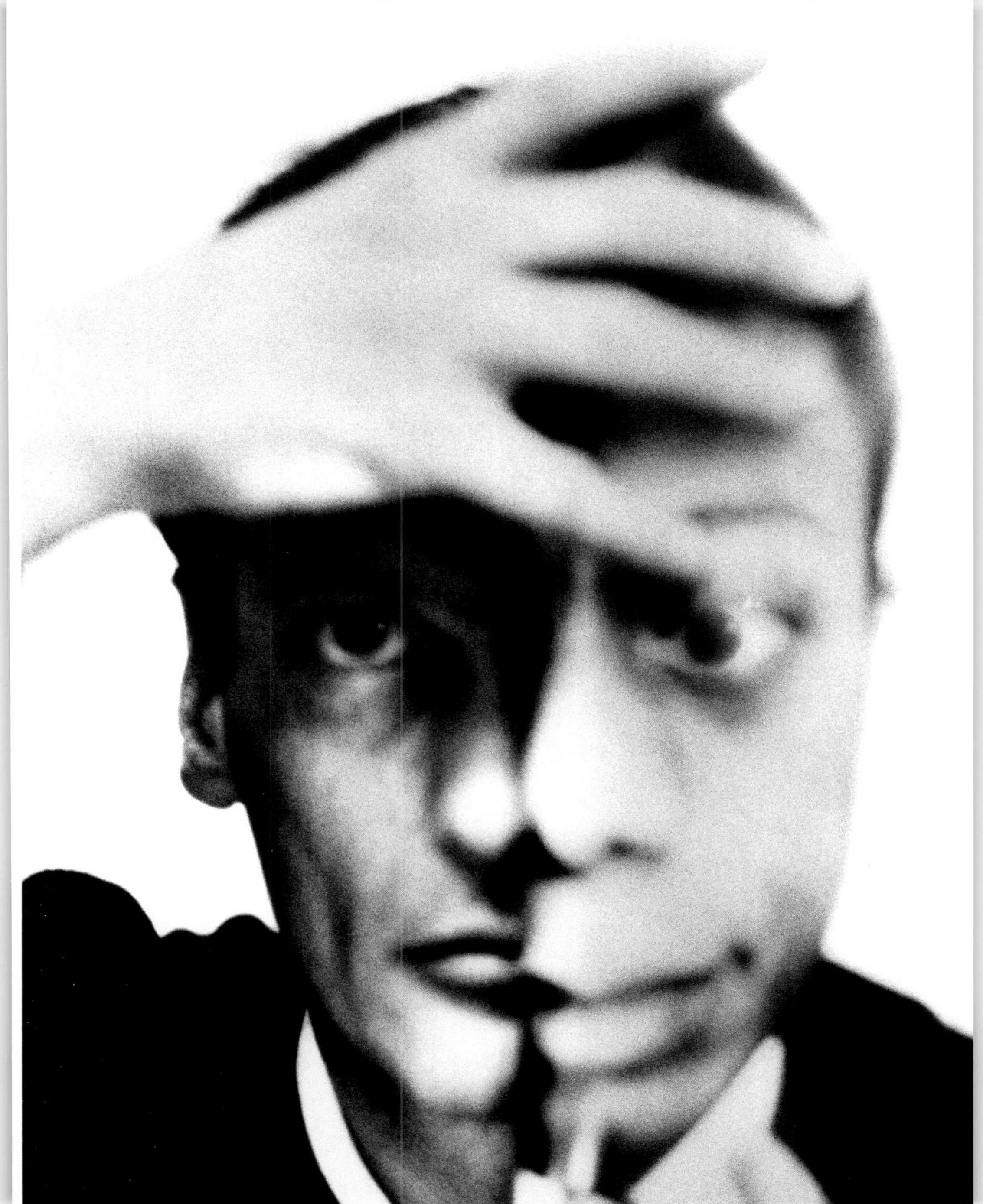

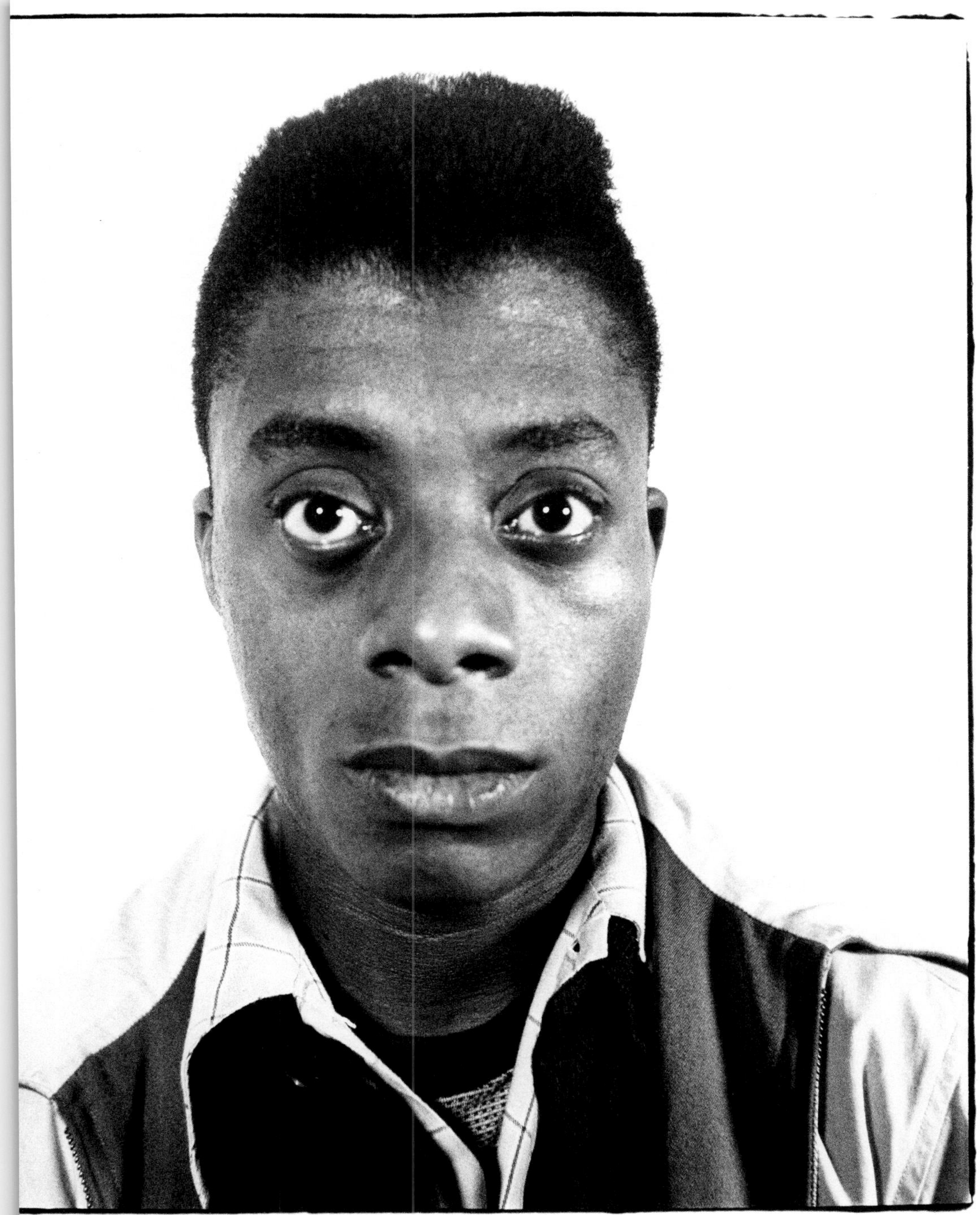

I have never understood why photography should be ghettoized in a photography museum, isolated from any other art forms like lithographies, sculpture, painting. Keeping photography down. In the fifties, my wife didn't want to hang my photographs in our house.

—

Richard Avedon

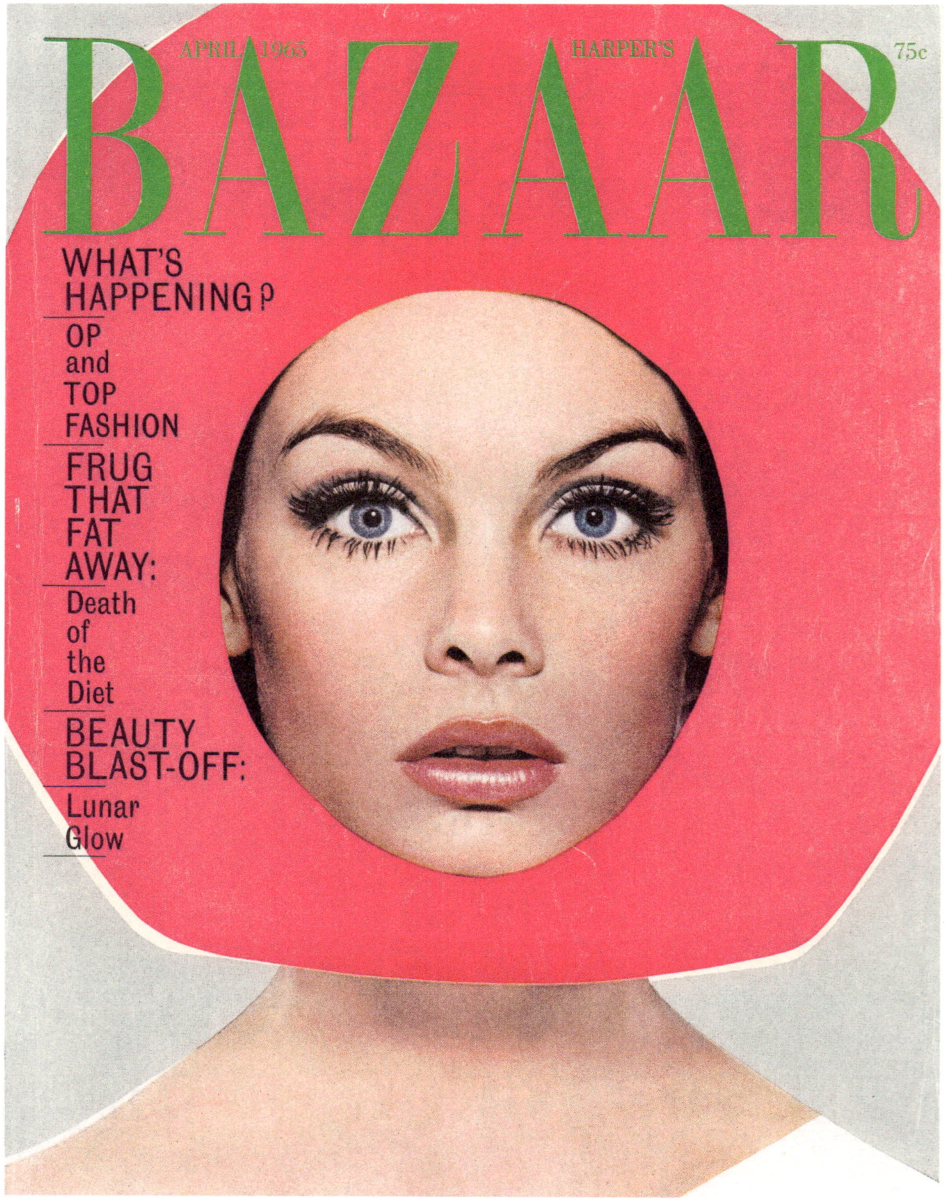
APRIL 1965
HARPER'S
75c
BAZAAR
WHAT'S HAPPENING?
OP and TOP FASHION
FRUG THAT FAT AWAY: Death of the Diet
BEAUTY BLAST-OFF: Lunar Glow

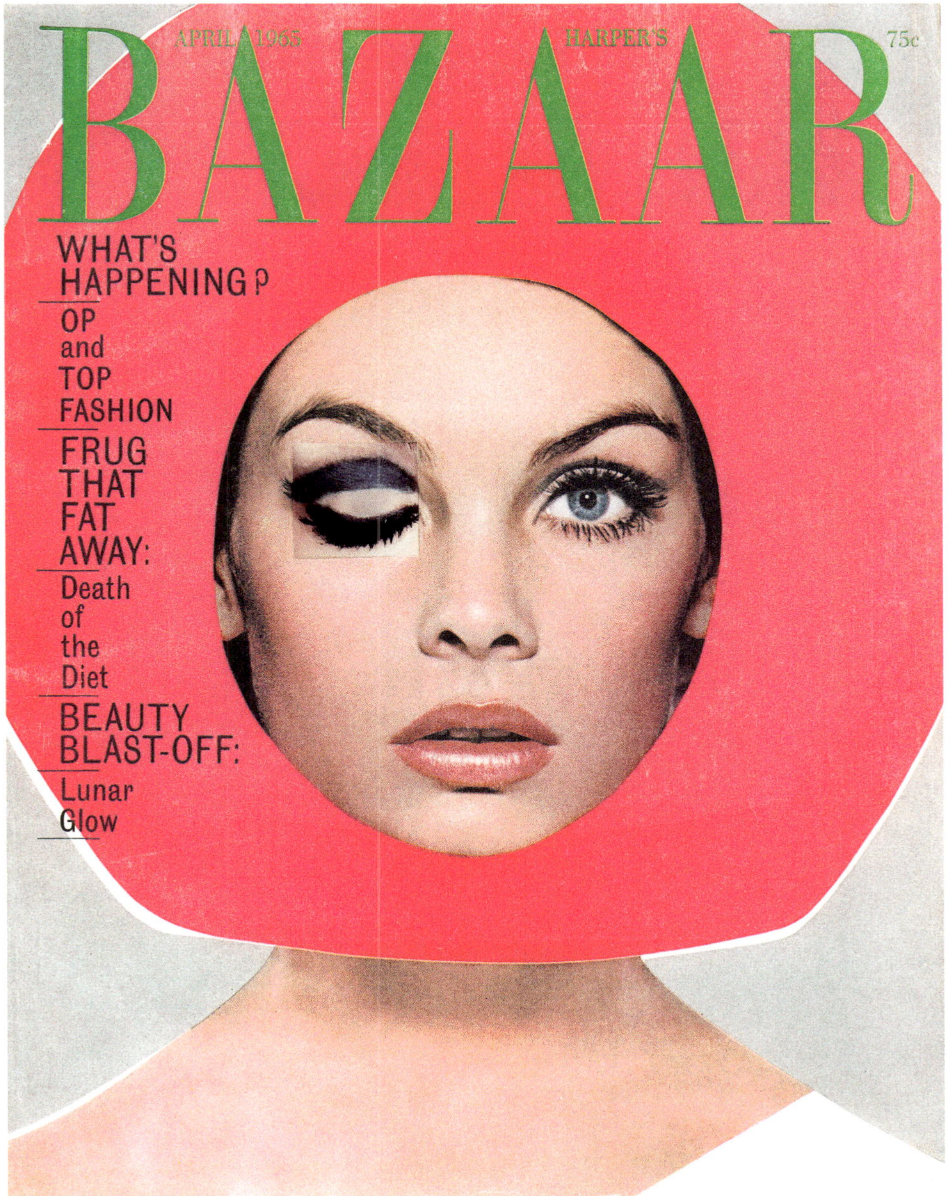

Harper's Bazaar, April 1965, guest edited and with cover photograph by Avedon. The issue featured a pasted-on "winkie" on the cover model's right eye.

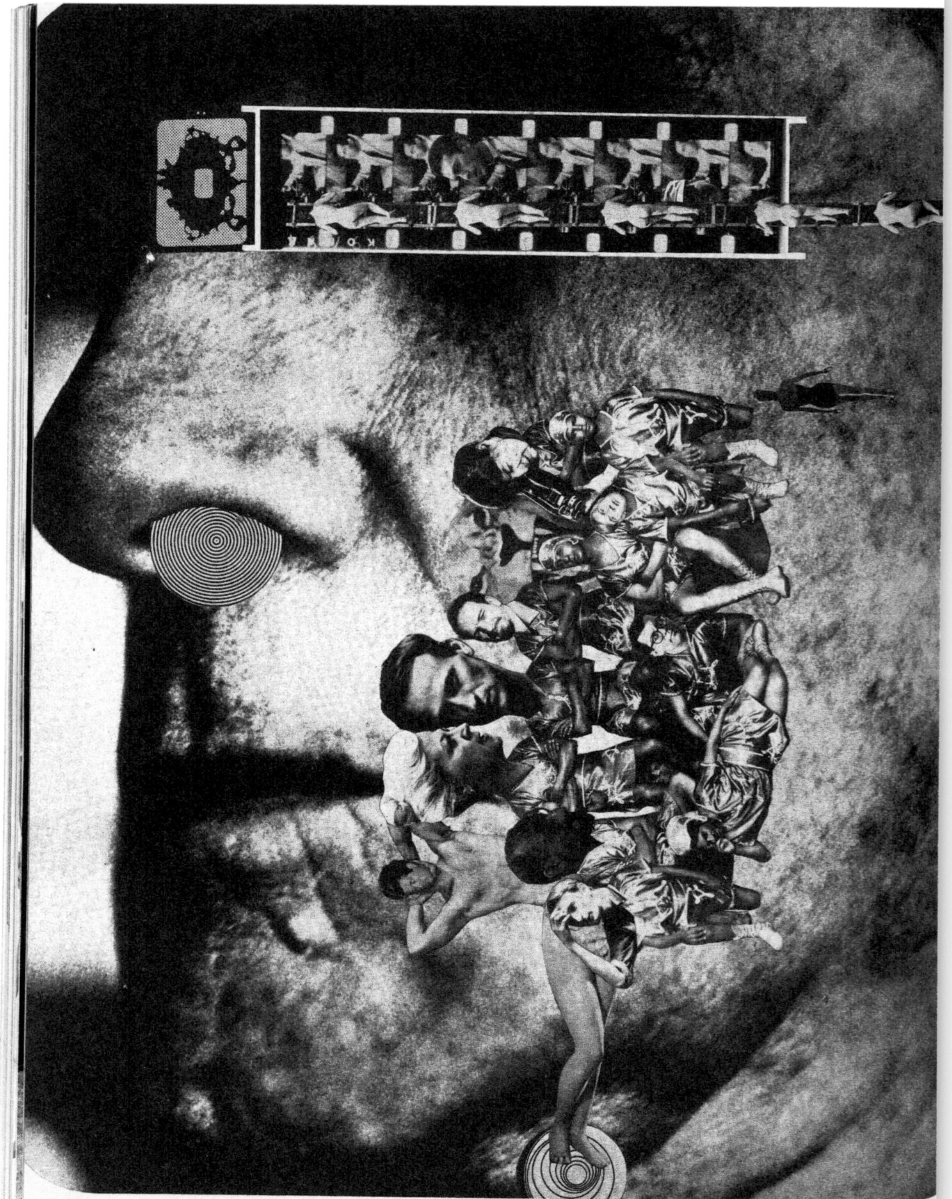

UNDERGROUND FILM MAKERS. Expressly for *Harper's Bazaar*, Stan Vanderbeek made this original montage using photographs of foremost film makers

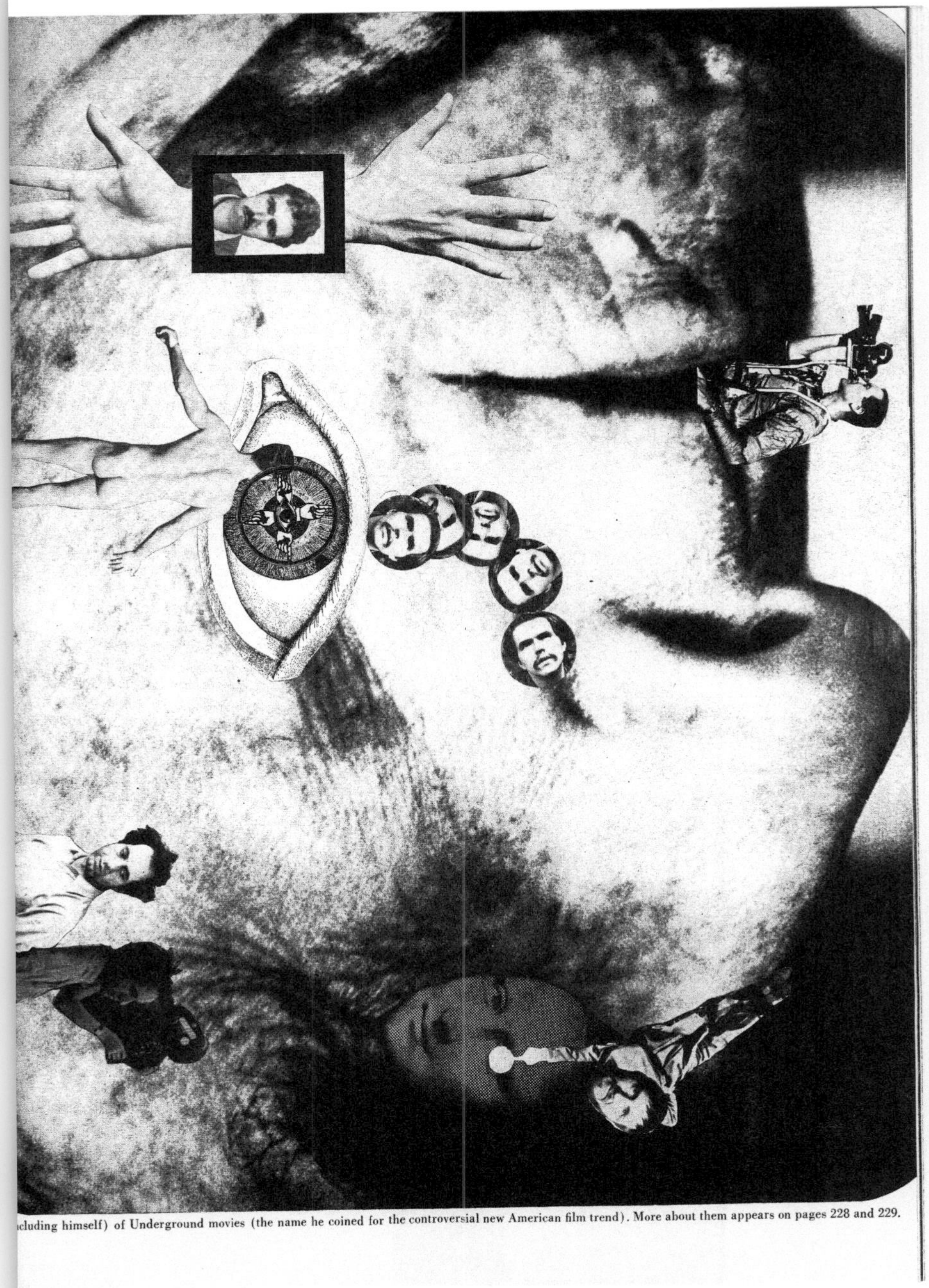

ıcluding himself) of Underground movies (the name he coined for the controversial new American film trend). More about them appears on pages 228 and 229.

Harper's Bazaar, April 1965: collage by Stan Vanderbeek on an Avedon photograph

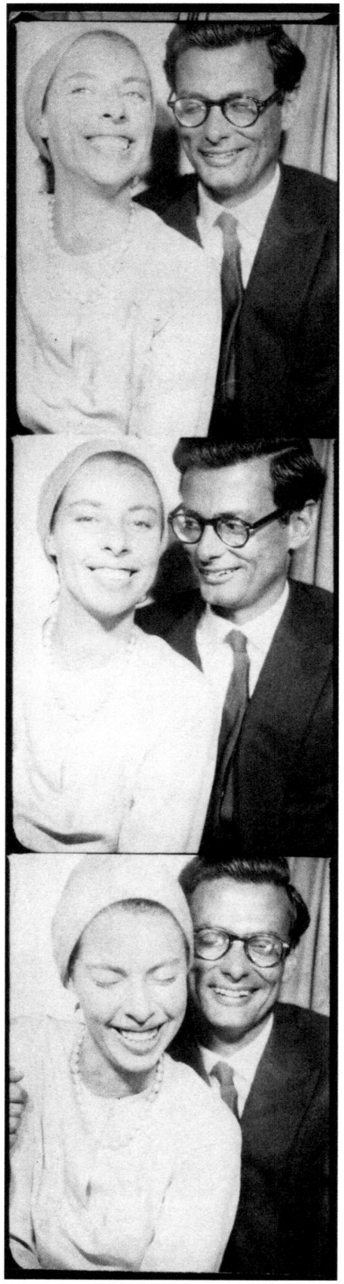

Evelyn and Richard Avedon, New York, September 1951

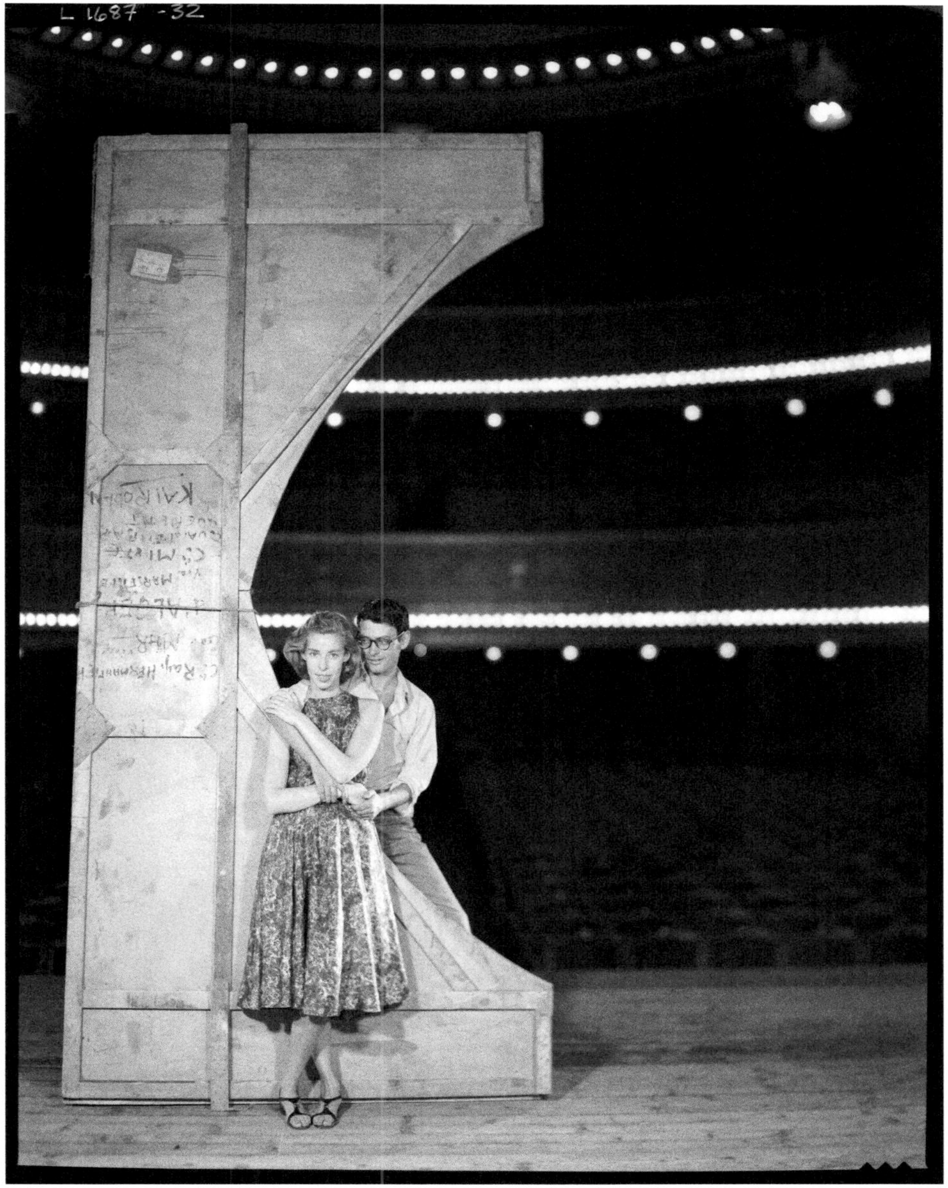

Evelyn and Richard Avedon, Paris, 1955

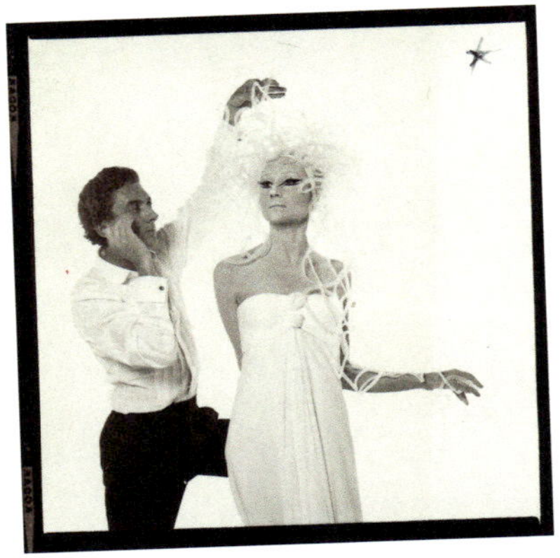

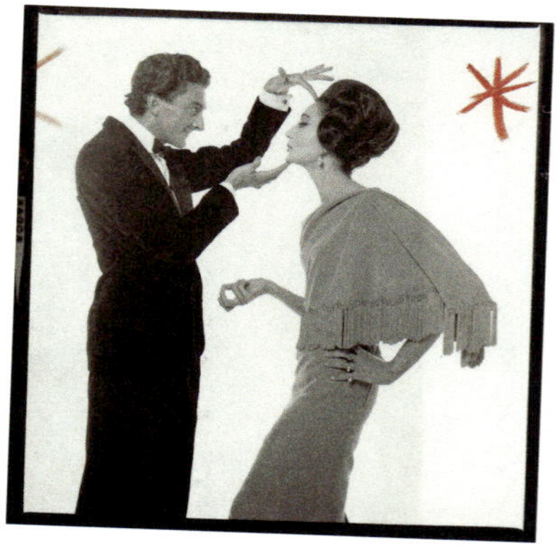

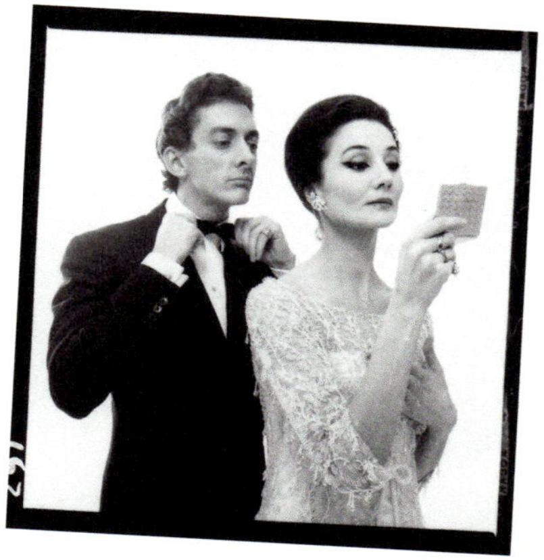

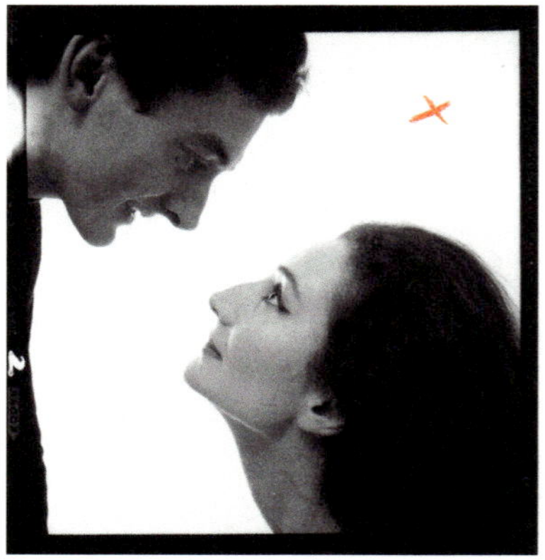

Countess Jacqueline de Ribes and Raymundo de Larrain, New York, May 16, 1961 (contact prints)

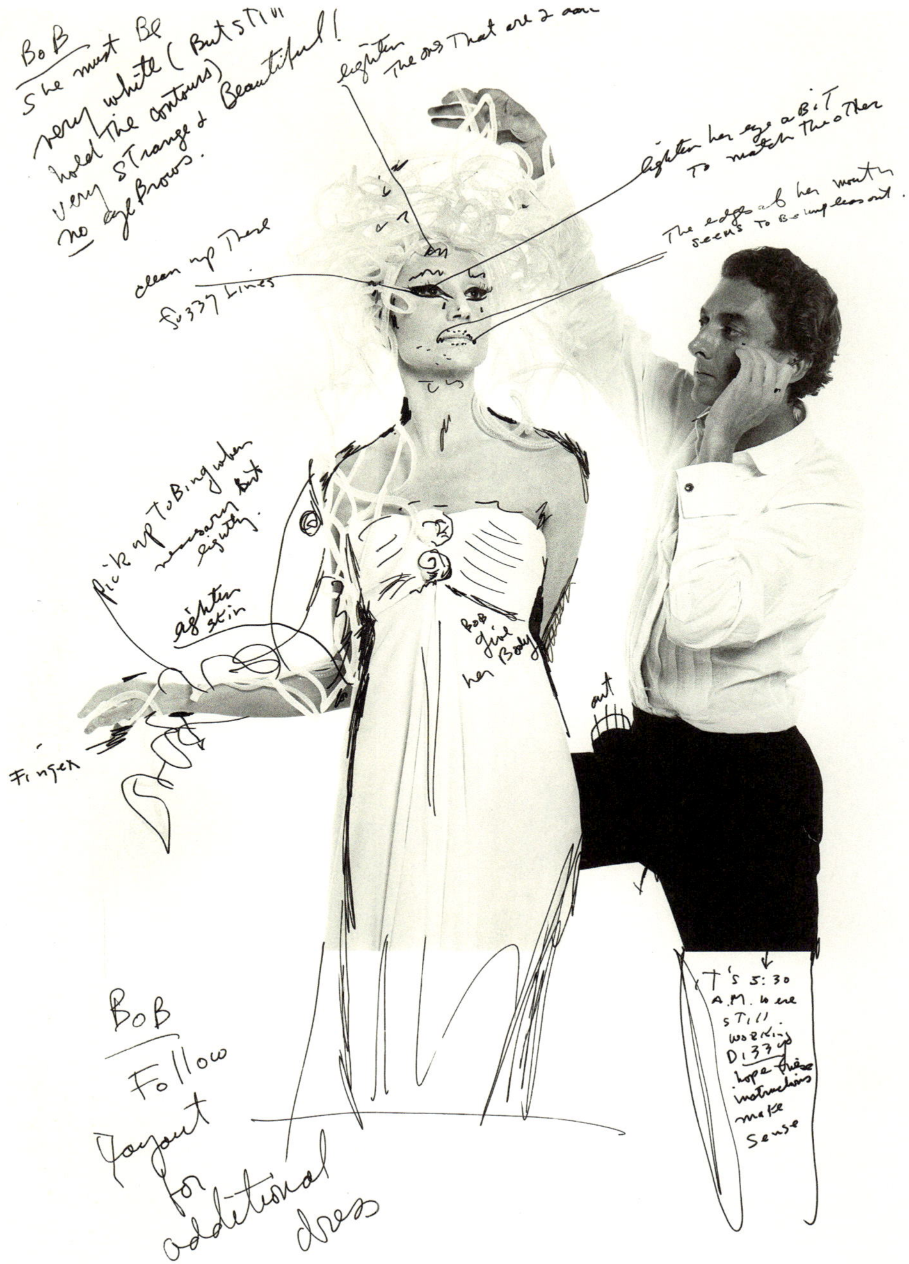

Countess Jacqueline de Ribes and Raymundo de Larrain, New York, May 16, 1961
(work print annotated by Richard Avedon to the retoucher)

pp. 434–37, Countess Jacqueline de Ribes and Raymundo de Larrain, New York, May 16, 1961
p. 439, Rudolf Nureyev, dancer, Paris, July 25, 1961
pp. 440–41, Rudolf Nureyev, dancer, Paris, July 25, 1961
pp. 442–43, Margot McKendry and China Machado with members of the French Press, dresses by Lanvin-Castillo and Heim, Paris studio, August 24, 1961
pp. 444–45, Claude and Paloma Picasso, children of Pablo Picasso, Paris, January 25, 1966
pp. 446–47, Penelope Tree, mask by Ungaro, Paris, January 24, 1968

French Portraits III

Richard Avedon

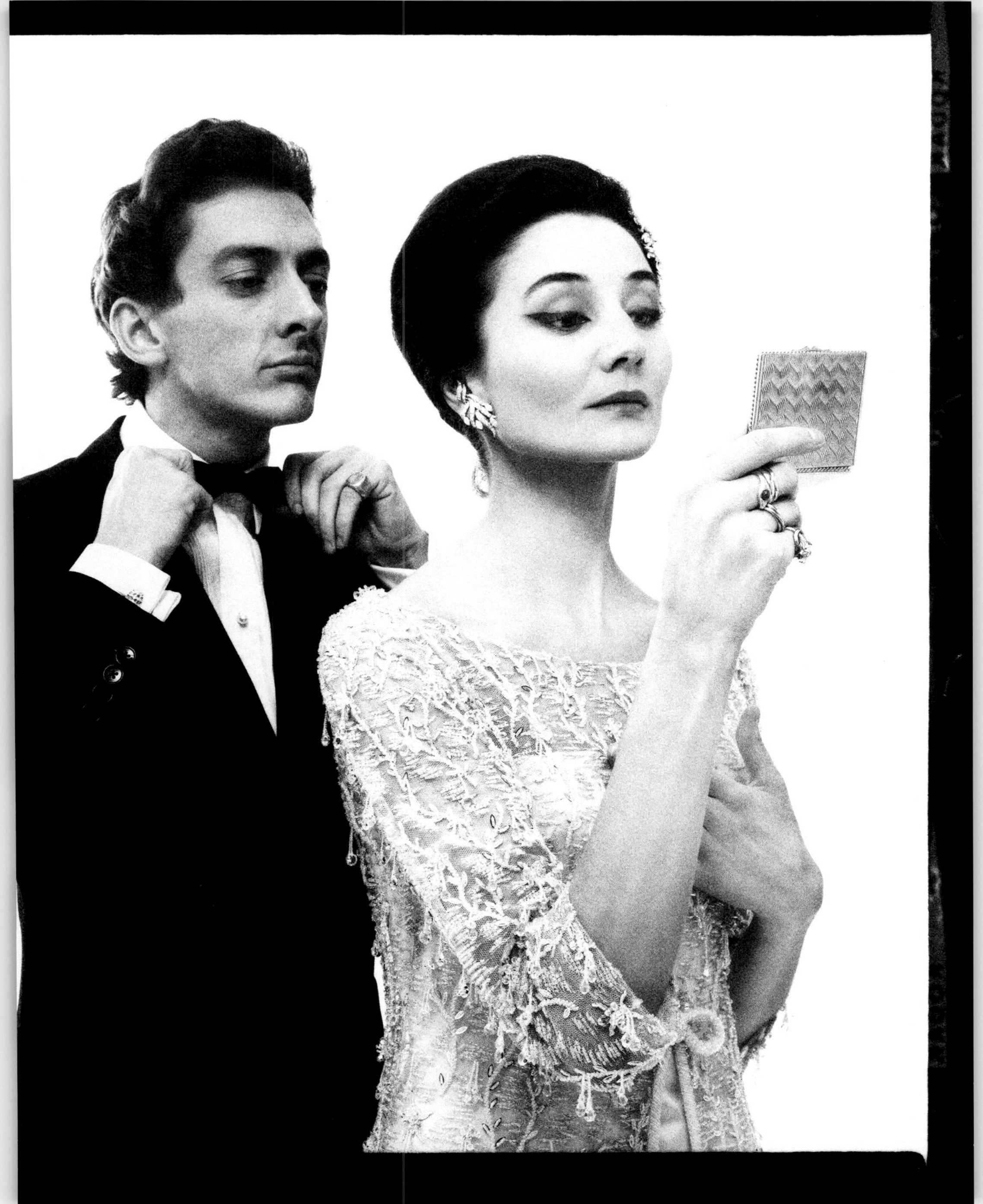

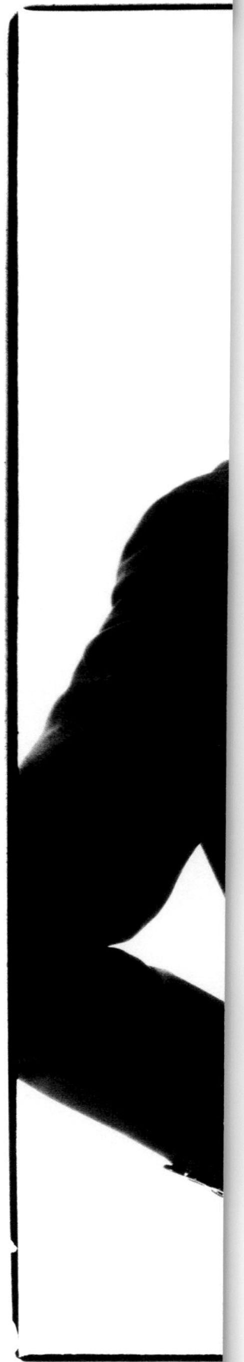

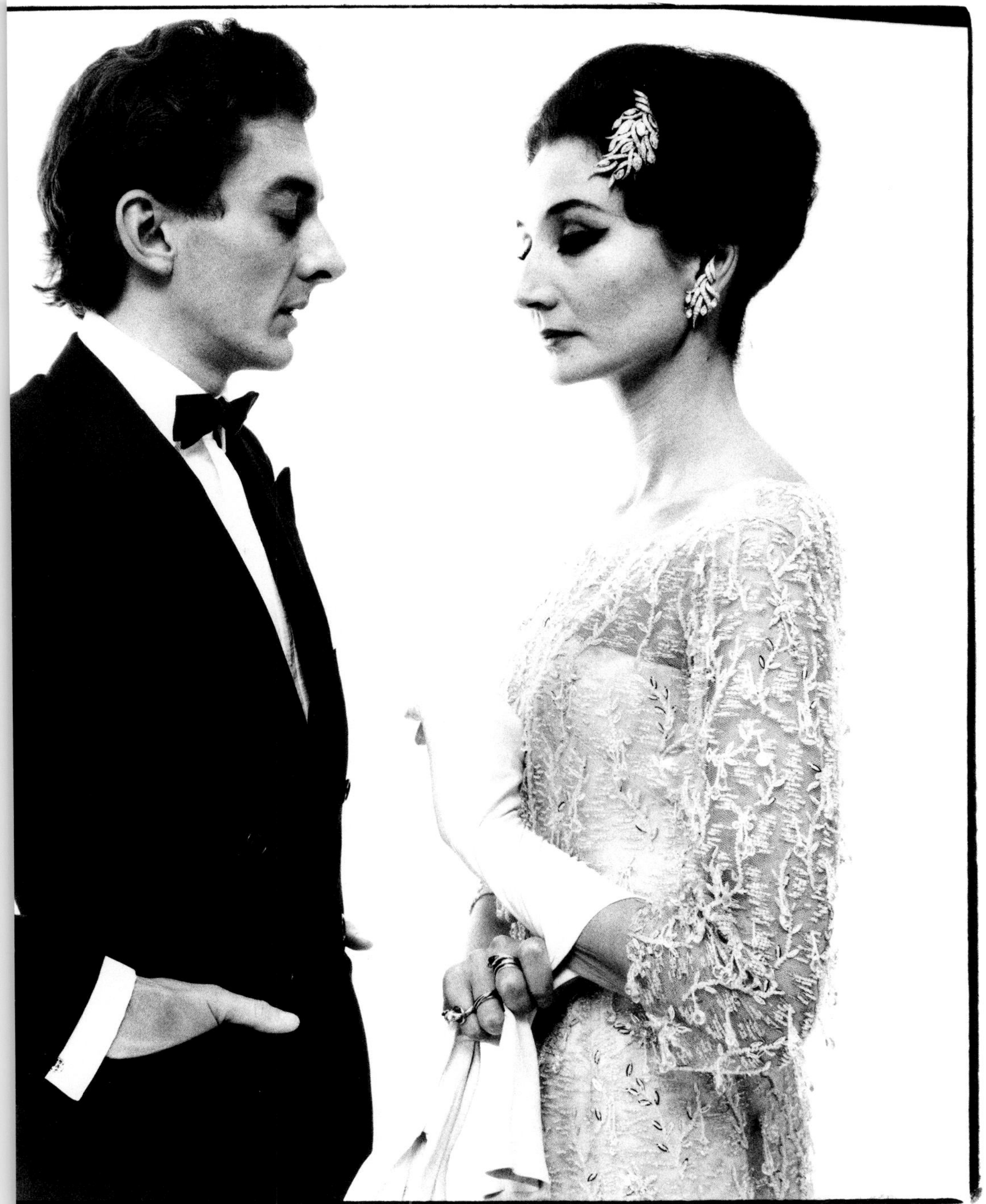

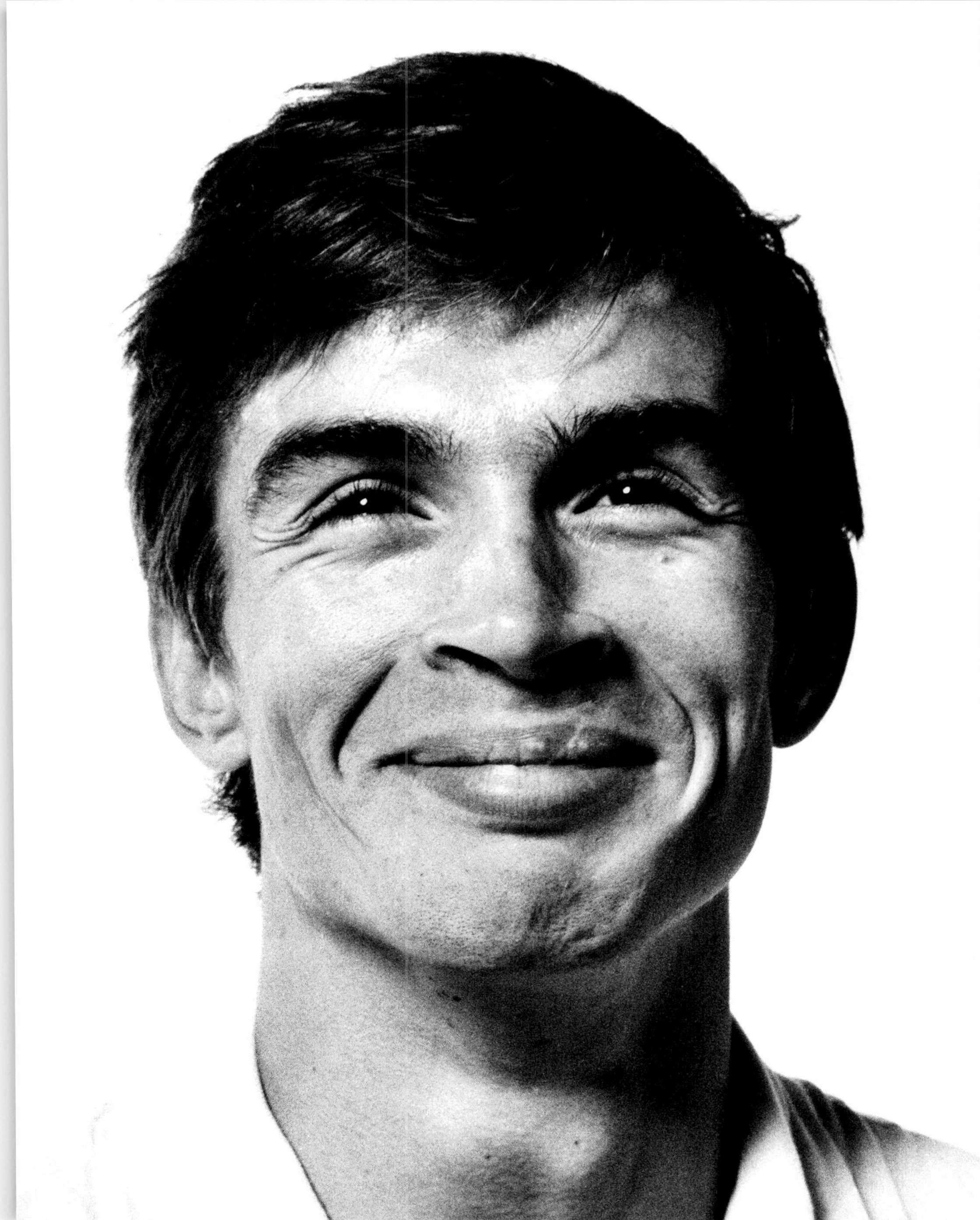

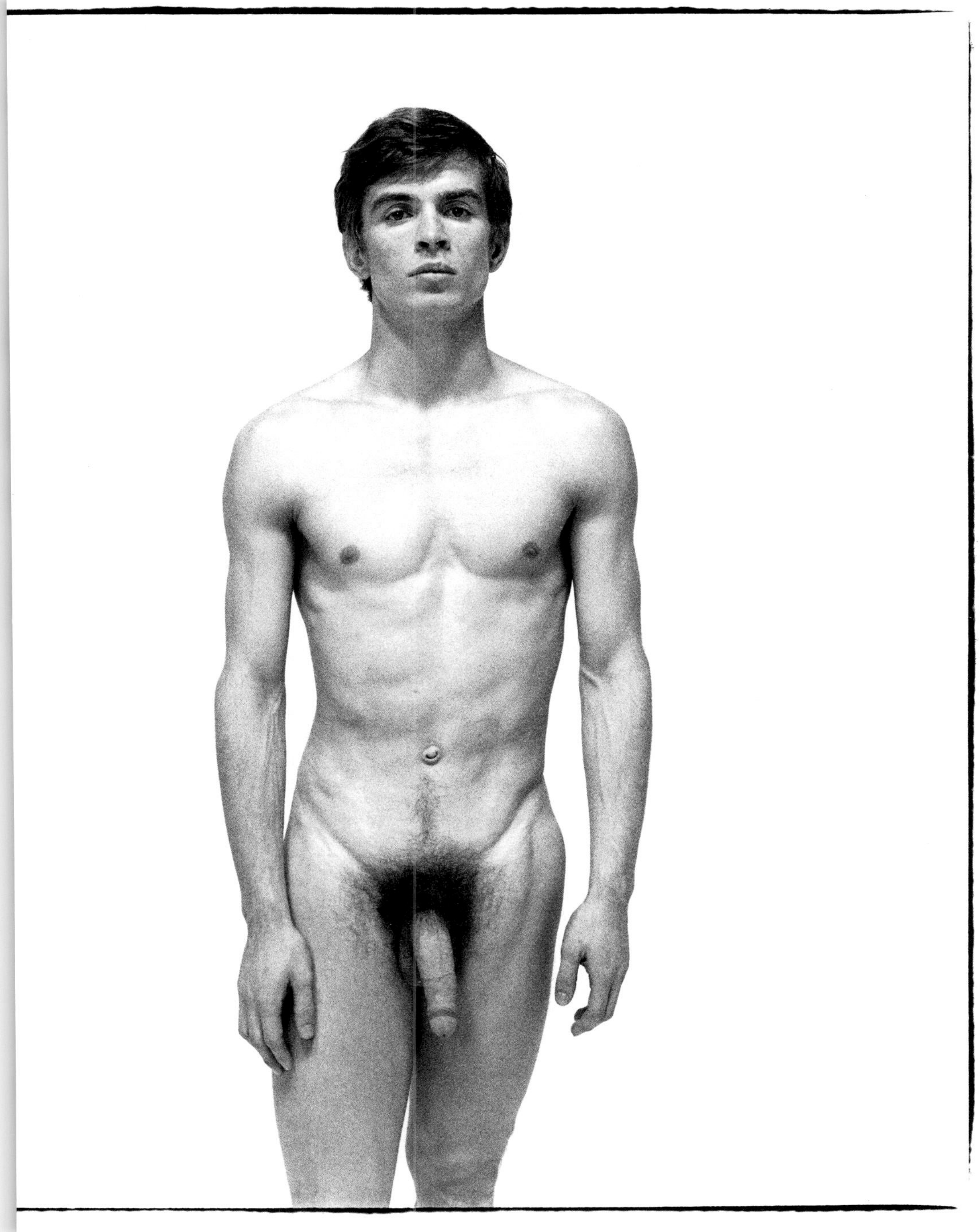

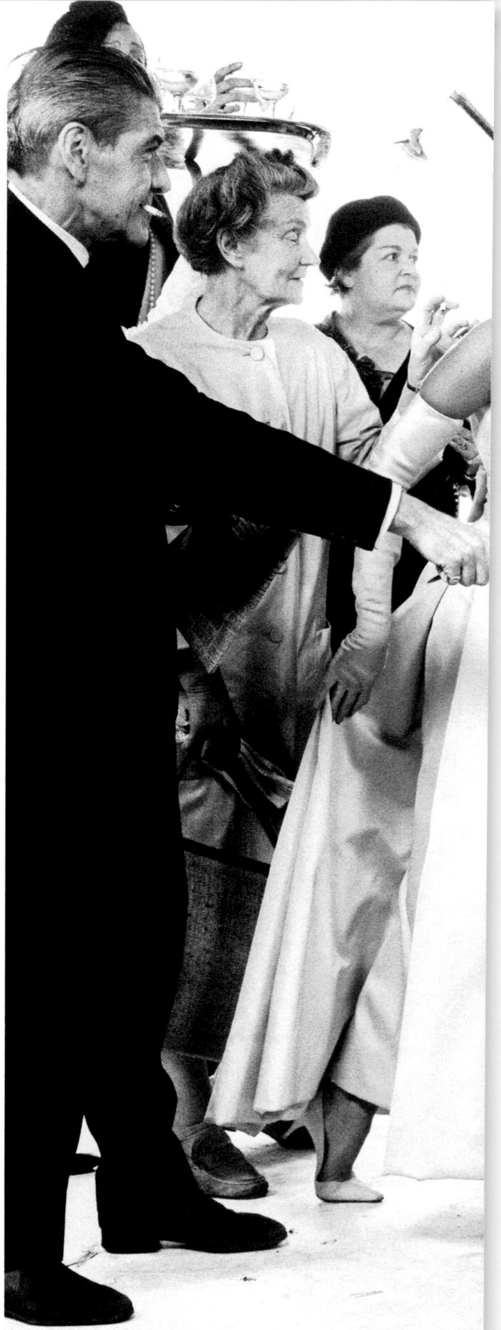

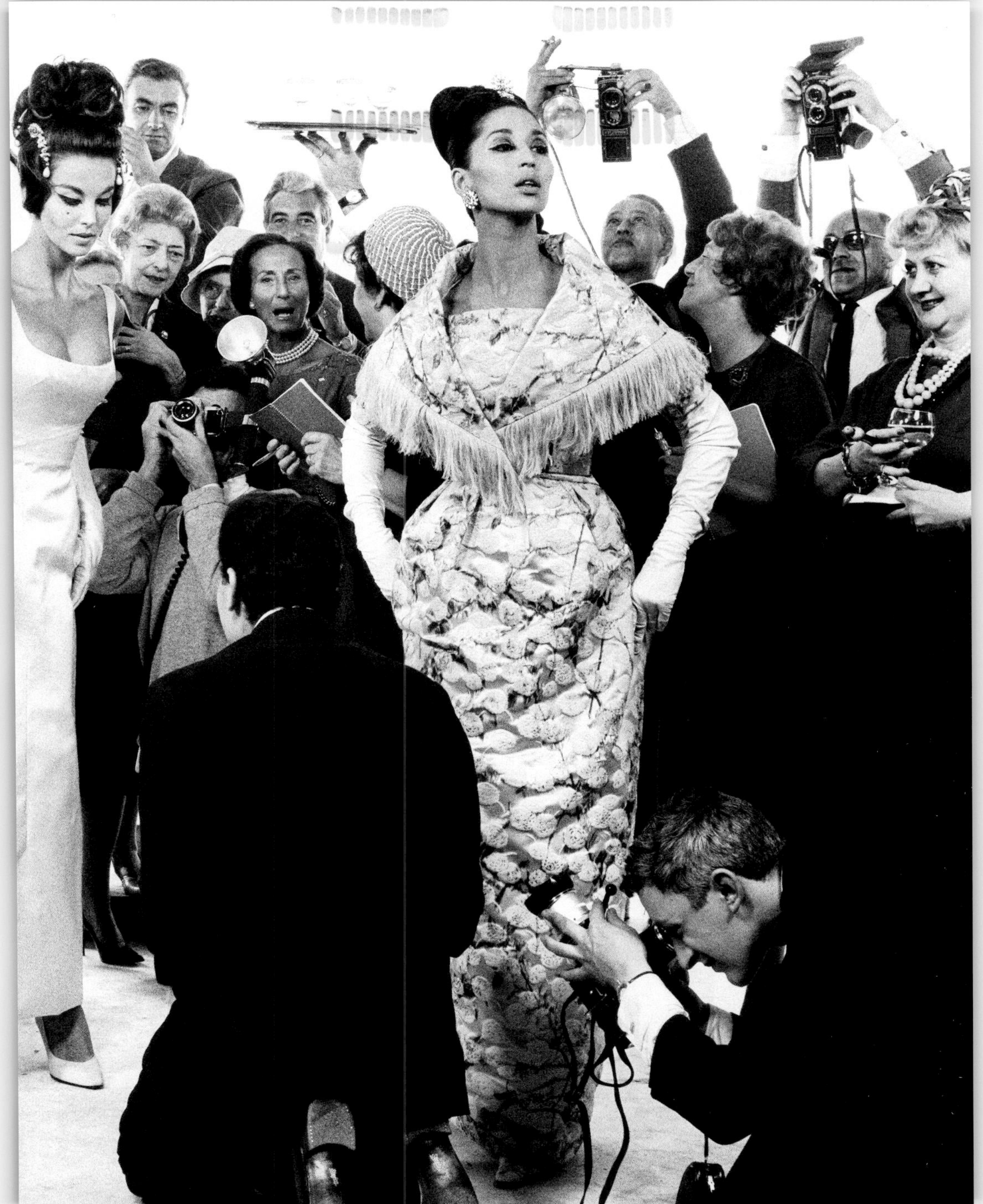

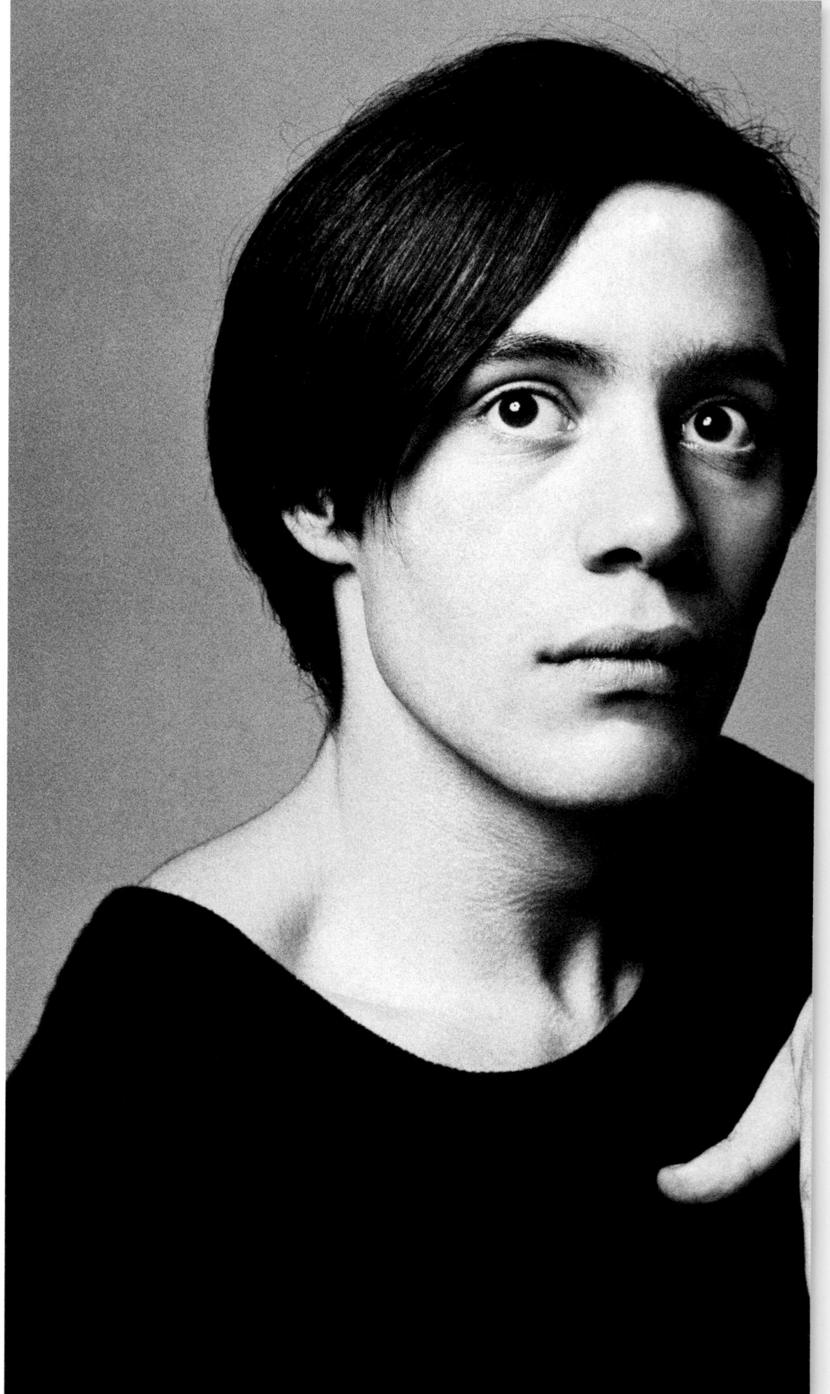

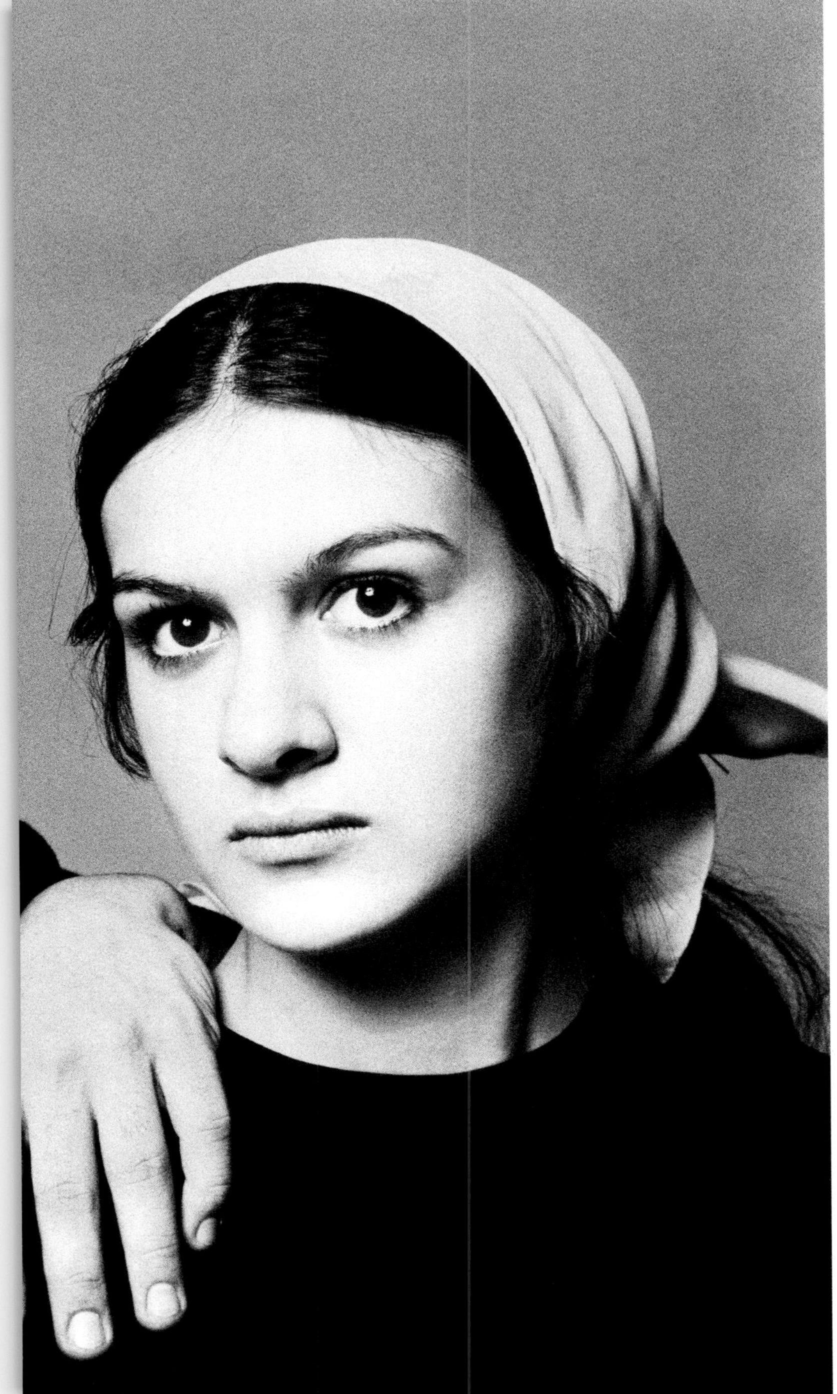

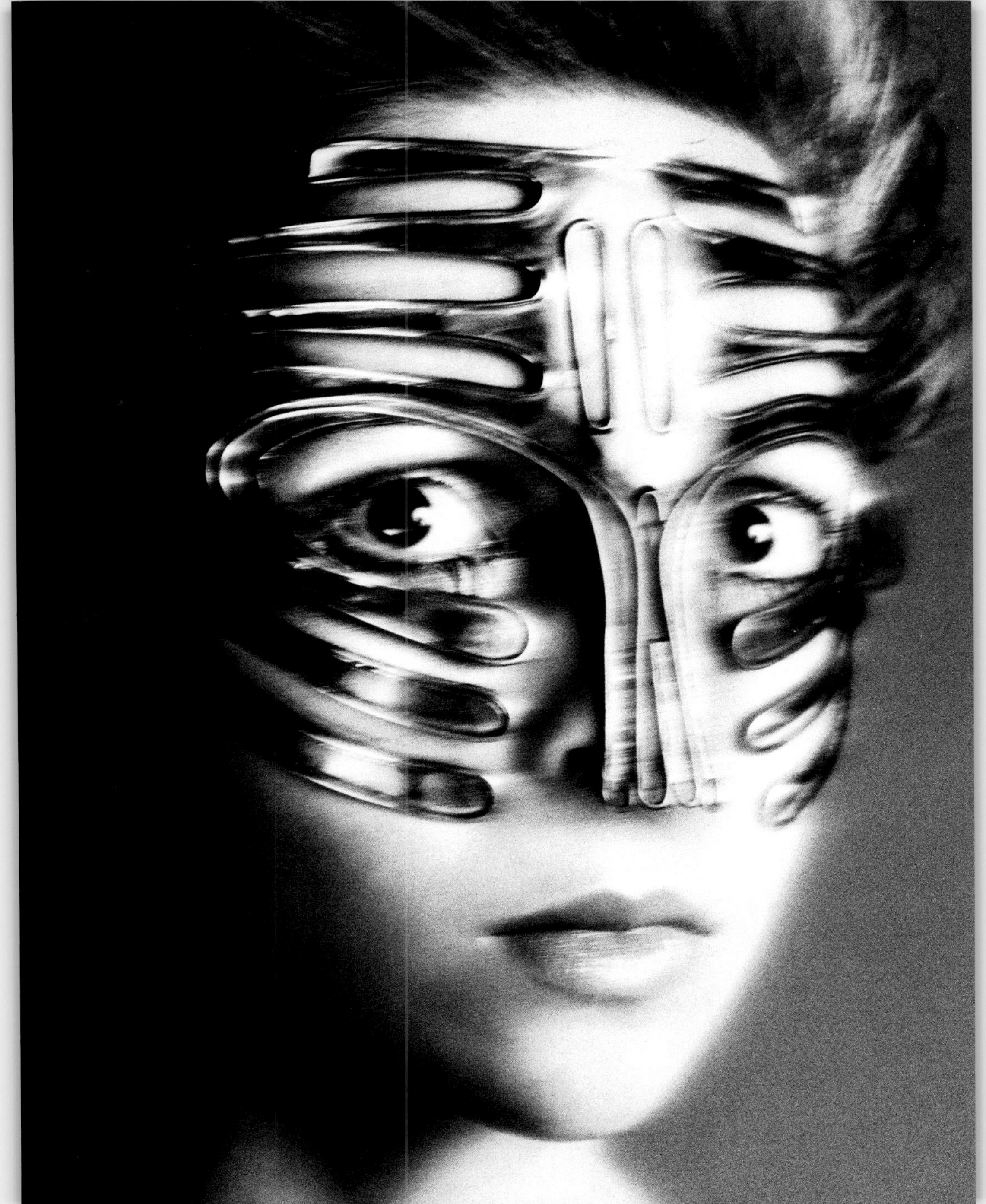

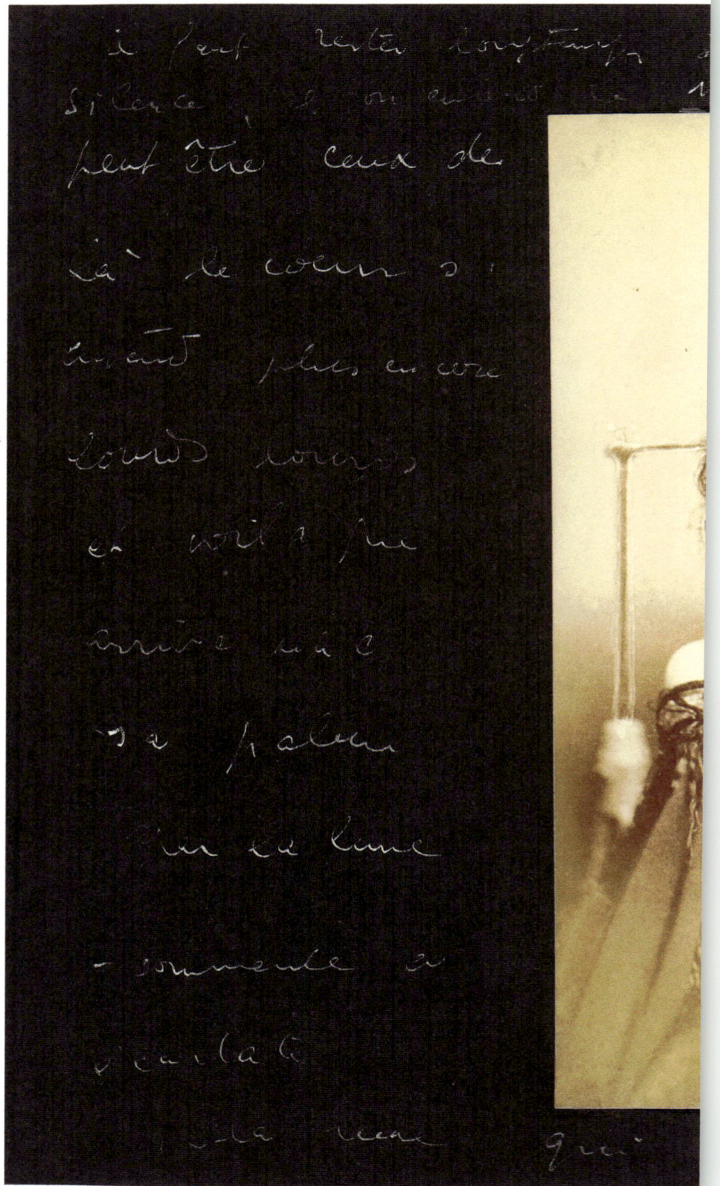
peut être ceux de
là le coeur s
battant plus encore
lourds lourds
et voilà que
arrive une
sur la lune
commence à
écarlate

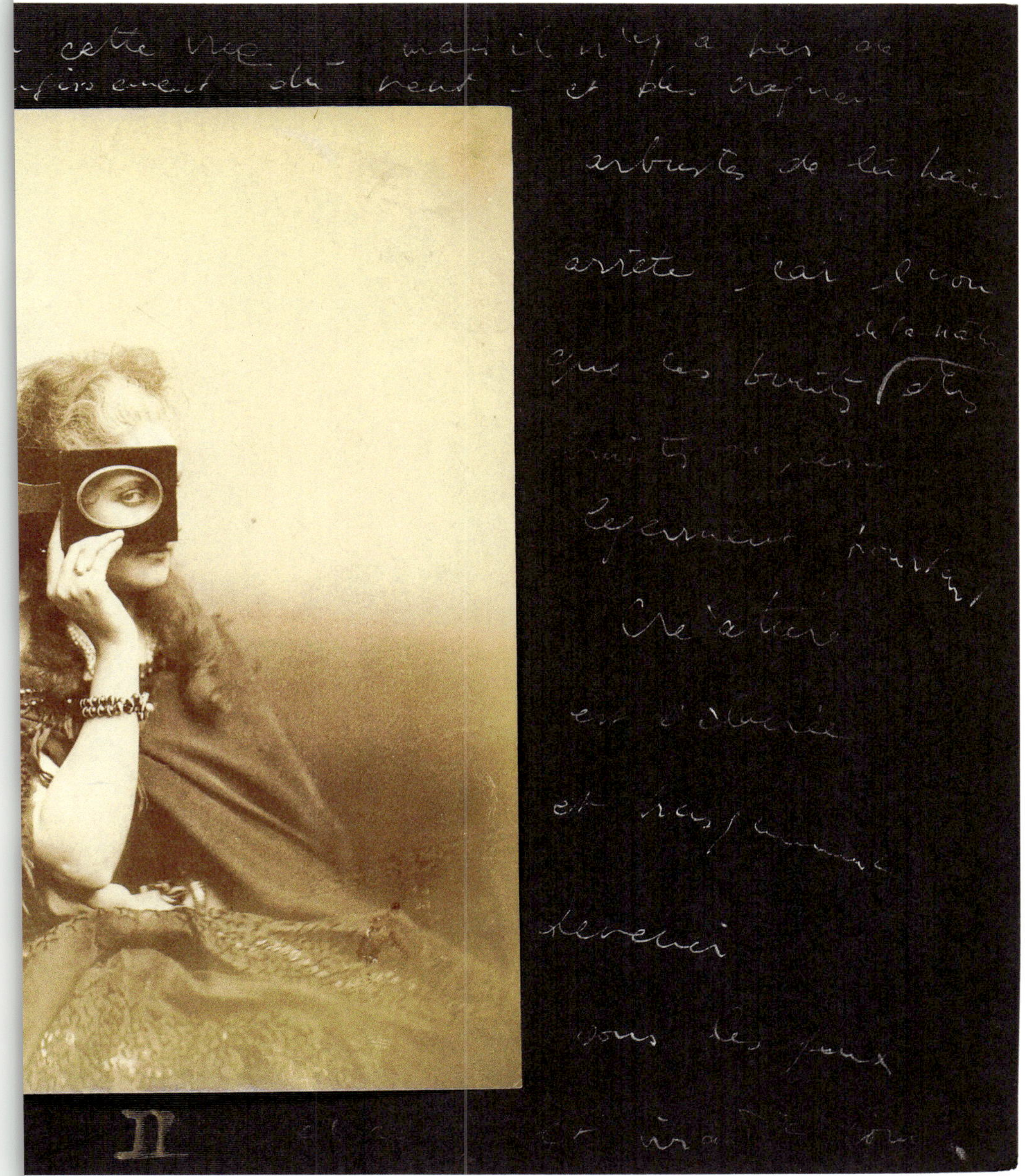

Scherzo di Follia (Games of madness), was an album of photographs by Pierre-Louis Pierson of the Countess di Castiglione (mistress to Napoleon III) from 1863–1866. In the 1930s, Christian Bérard acquired some of the photos, mounted and embellished them. Avedon purchased them for his own collection decades later. Shown here: page 2.

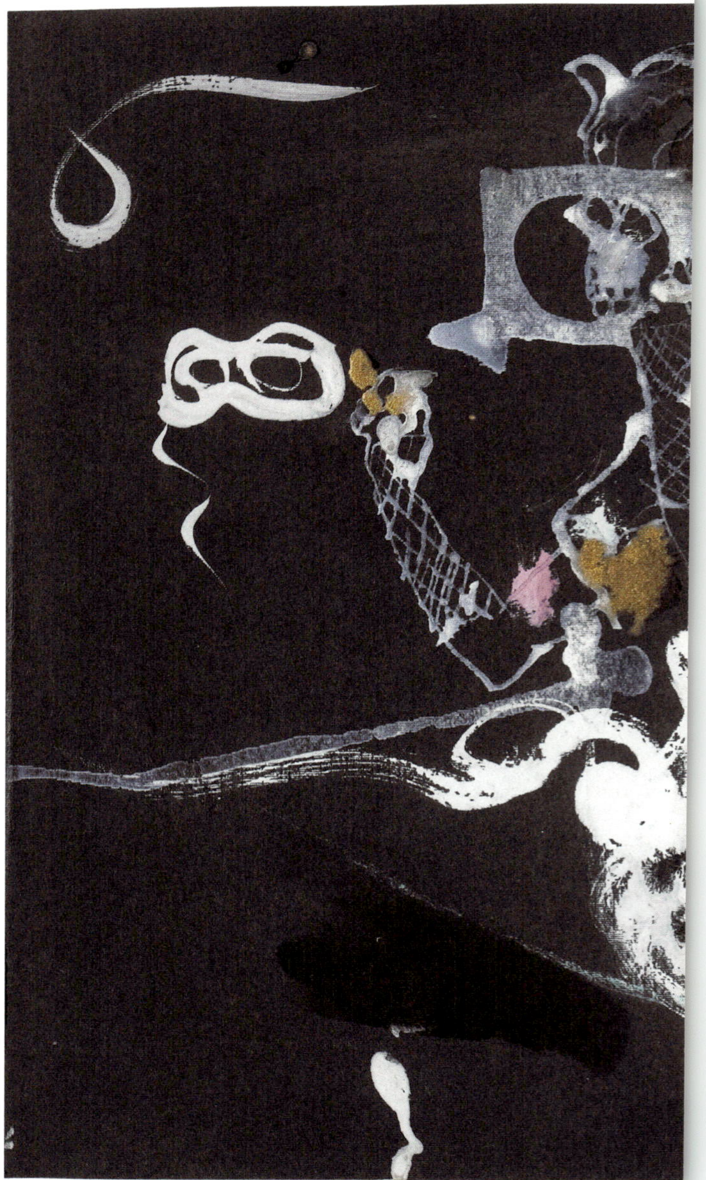

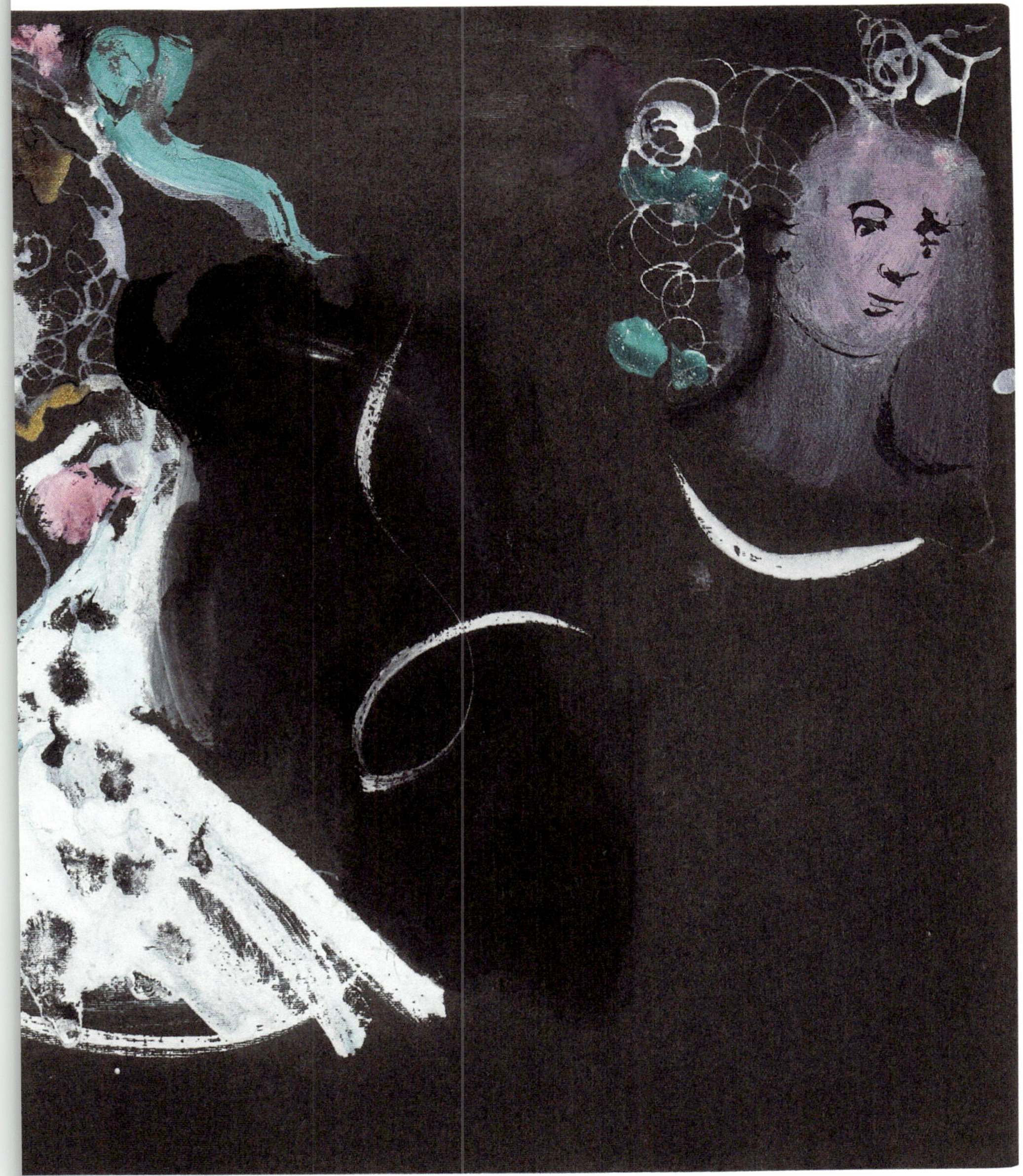

Title page, *Scherzo di Follia*, illustrated by Christian Bérard in 1930

Lartigue: Made in USA

1966–1970

Richard Avedon and Jacques Henri Lartigue met for the first time in November 1966, in Avedon's studio in New York. Immediately, Avedon found himself under the lights for Lartigue, and leaped into a pose that was just like the poses Lartigue's first subjects took at the beginning of the century. In January 1968, Lartigue was invited to go behind the scenes and photograph the model Penelope Tree as she was readied for a Paris fashion shoot with Avedon. One of these images would appear, cropped, in Lartigue's *Diary of a Century.*

In May of that year, during the process of creating *Diary*, Avedon and Bea Feitler worked in Lartigue's Paris apartment while riots erupted in the streets below. The historical irony should not be lost on us.

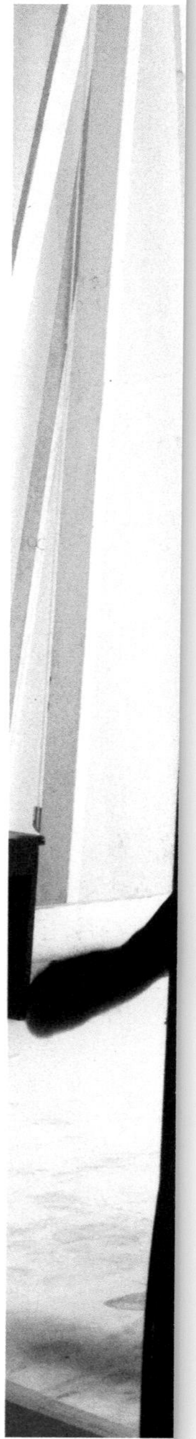

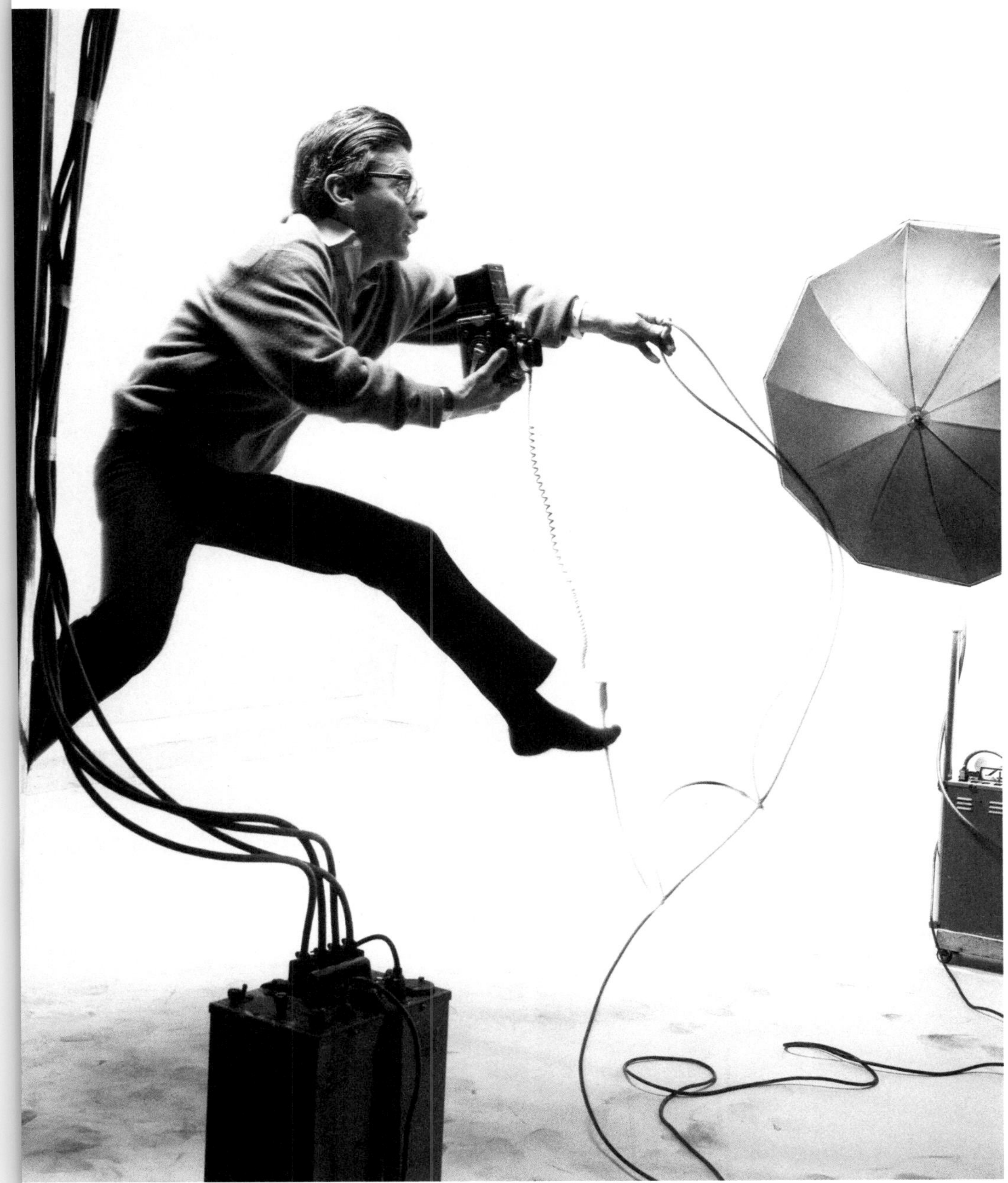

Richard Avedon, New York, November 1966; photograph by J. H. Lartigue

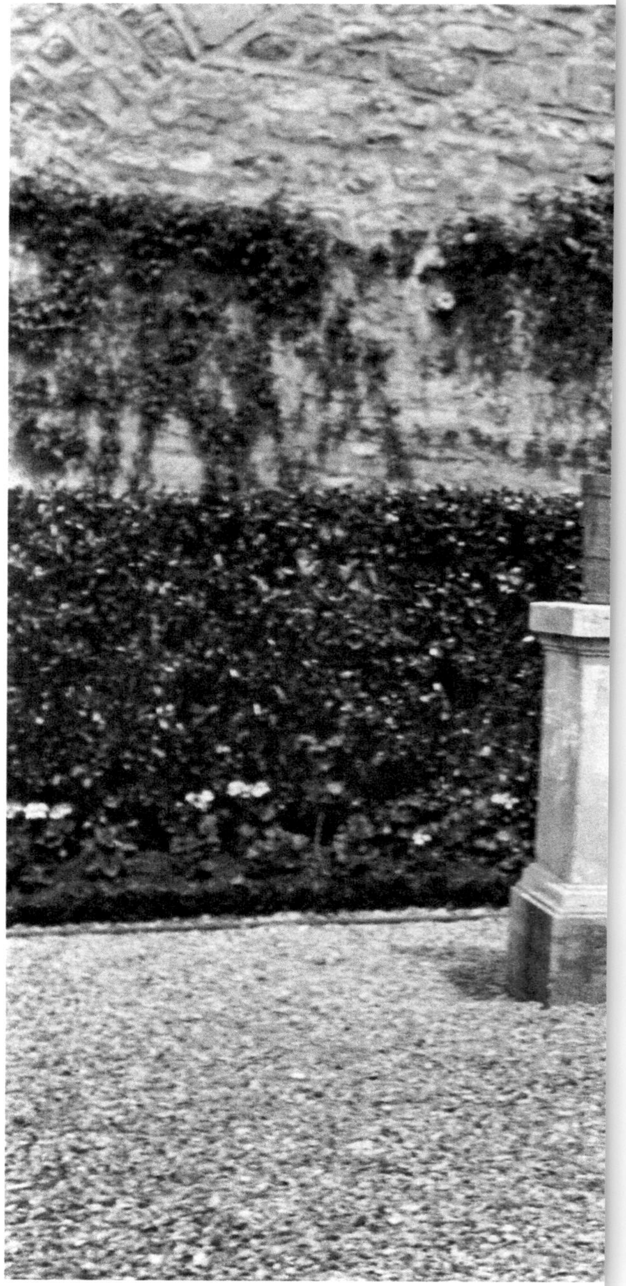

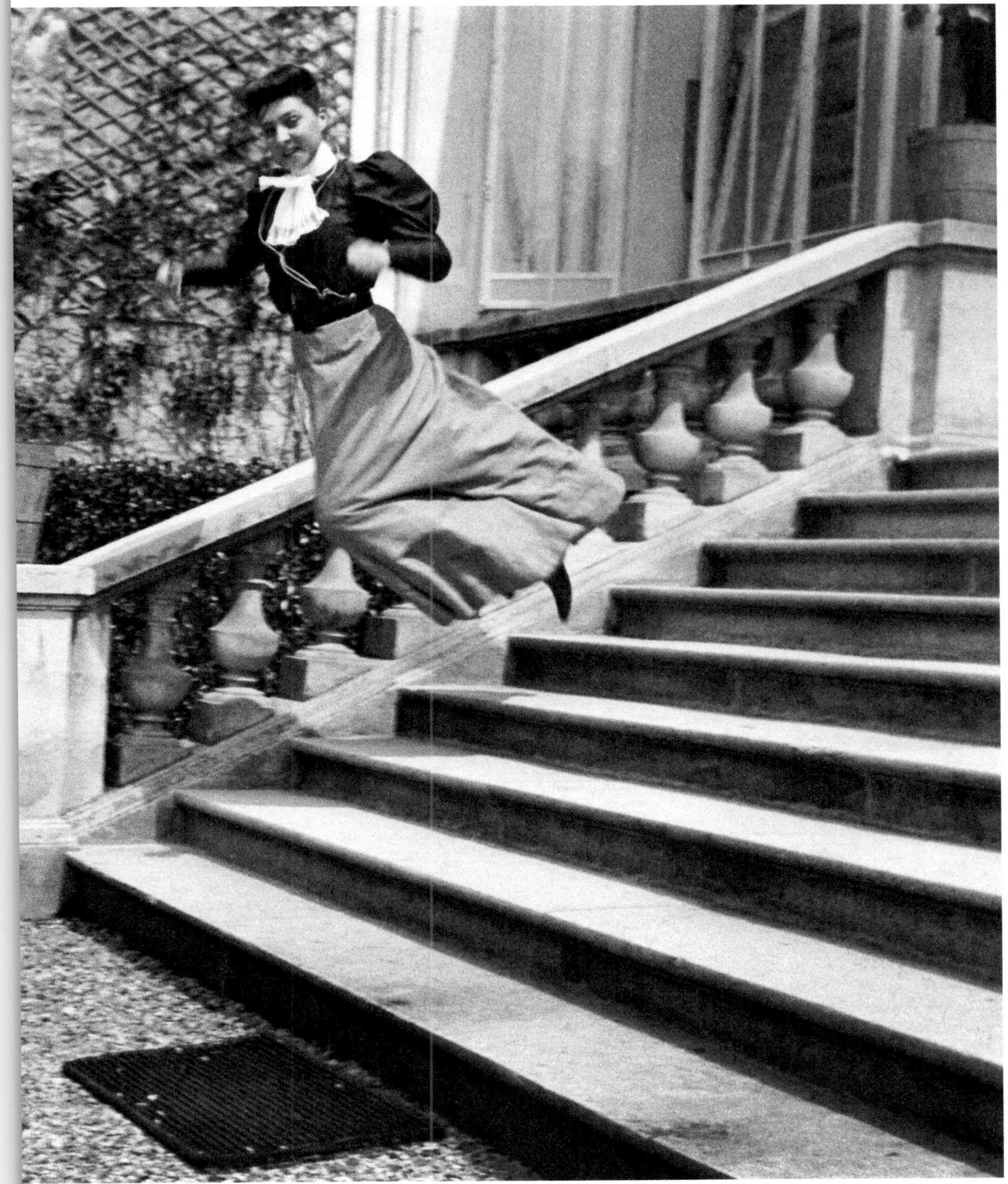

Bichonnade, Paris, 1905; photograph by J. H. Lartigue

Lartigue had to wait until his first exhibition, and the publication in America of *Diary of a Century*, a book I edited, for him to achieve real recognition in France. Maybe it takes a foreigner to discover someone else's national treasure.

—

Richard Avedon

1966 NOVEMBRE : NEW. YORK

120

← STUDIO AVEDON

AVEDON KECIA

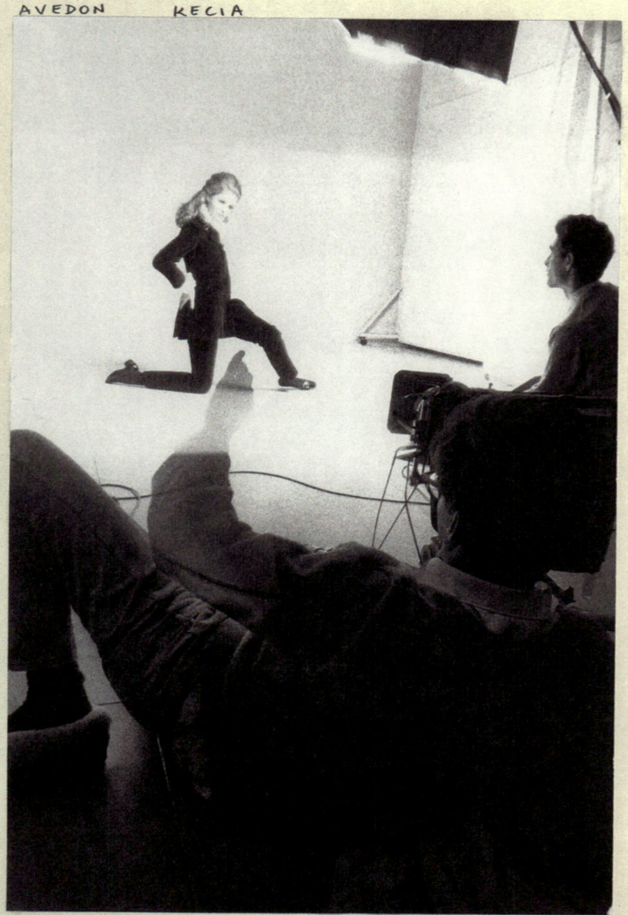

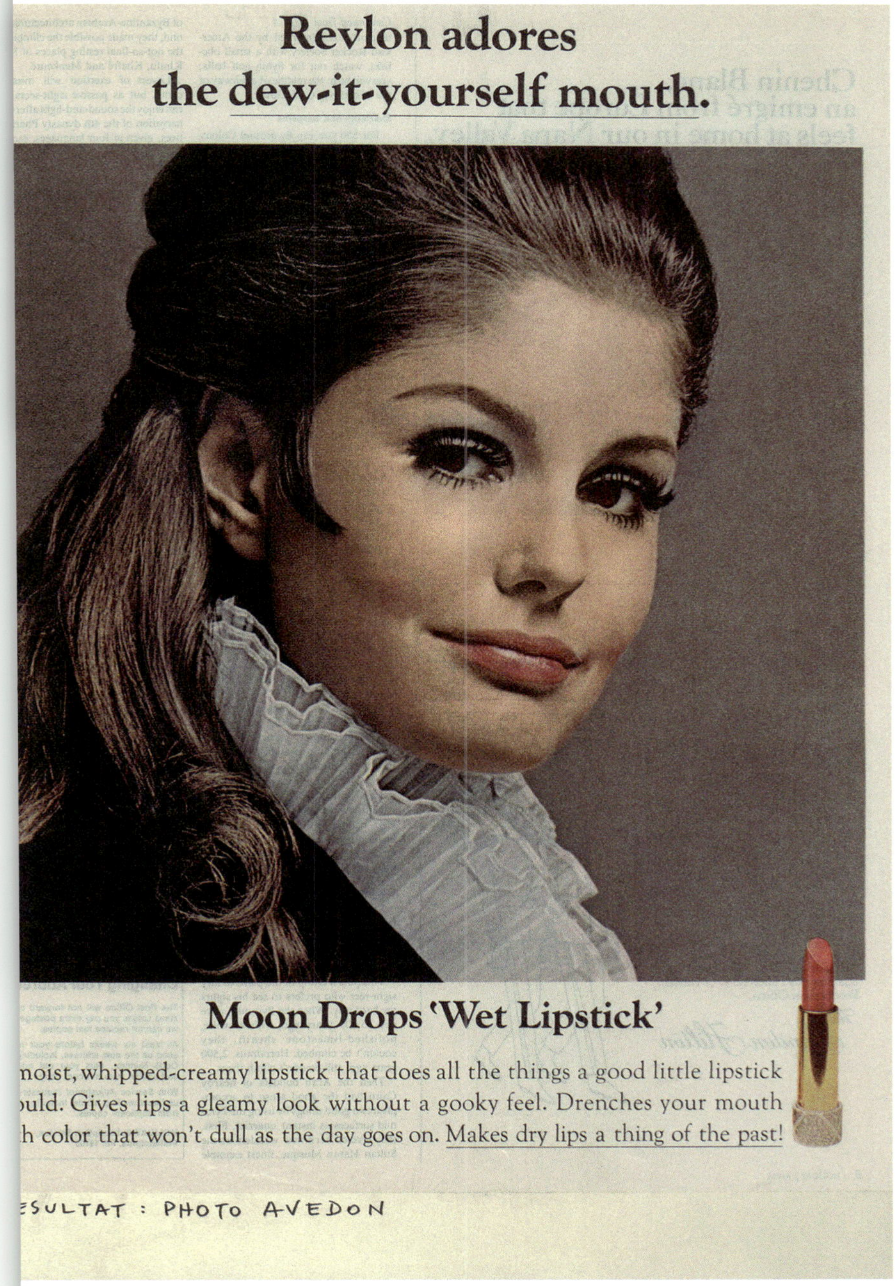

(Left) The Avedon studio, New York, November 1966; photograph by J. H. Lartigue,
(right) photograph by Richard Avedon (album page 0120R66)

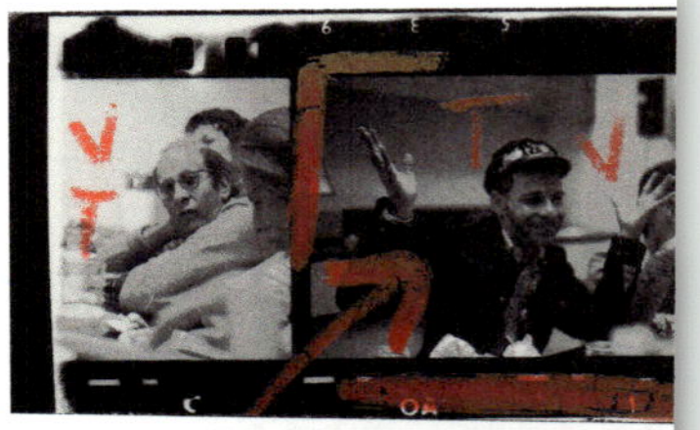

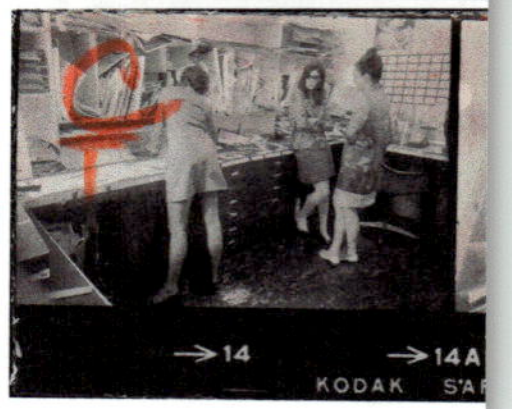
→14
→14A
KODAK

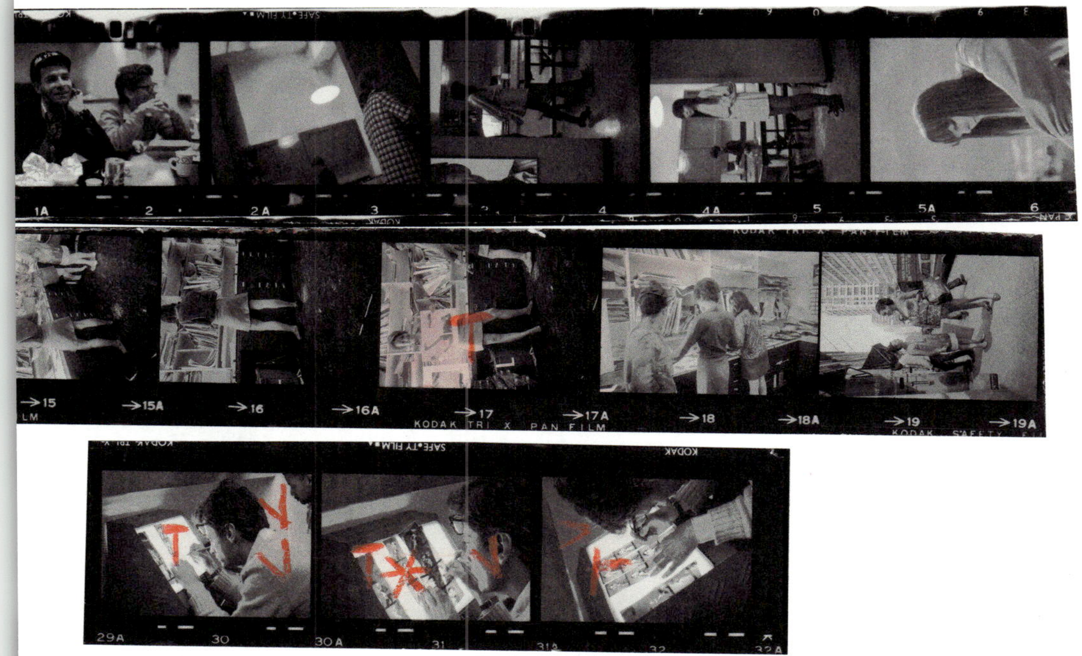

J. H. Lartigue's composite contact sheets of the Avedon Studio, New York, November 1966

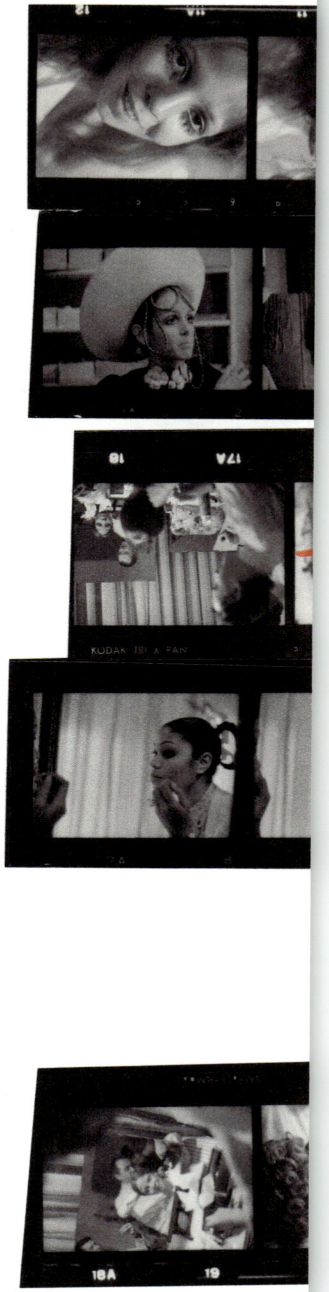
18A
19

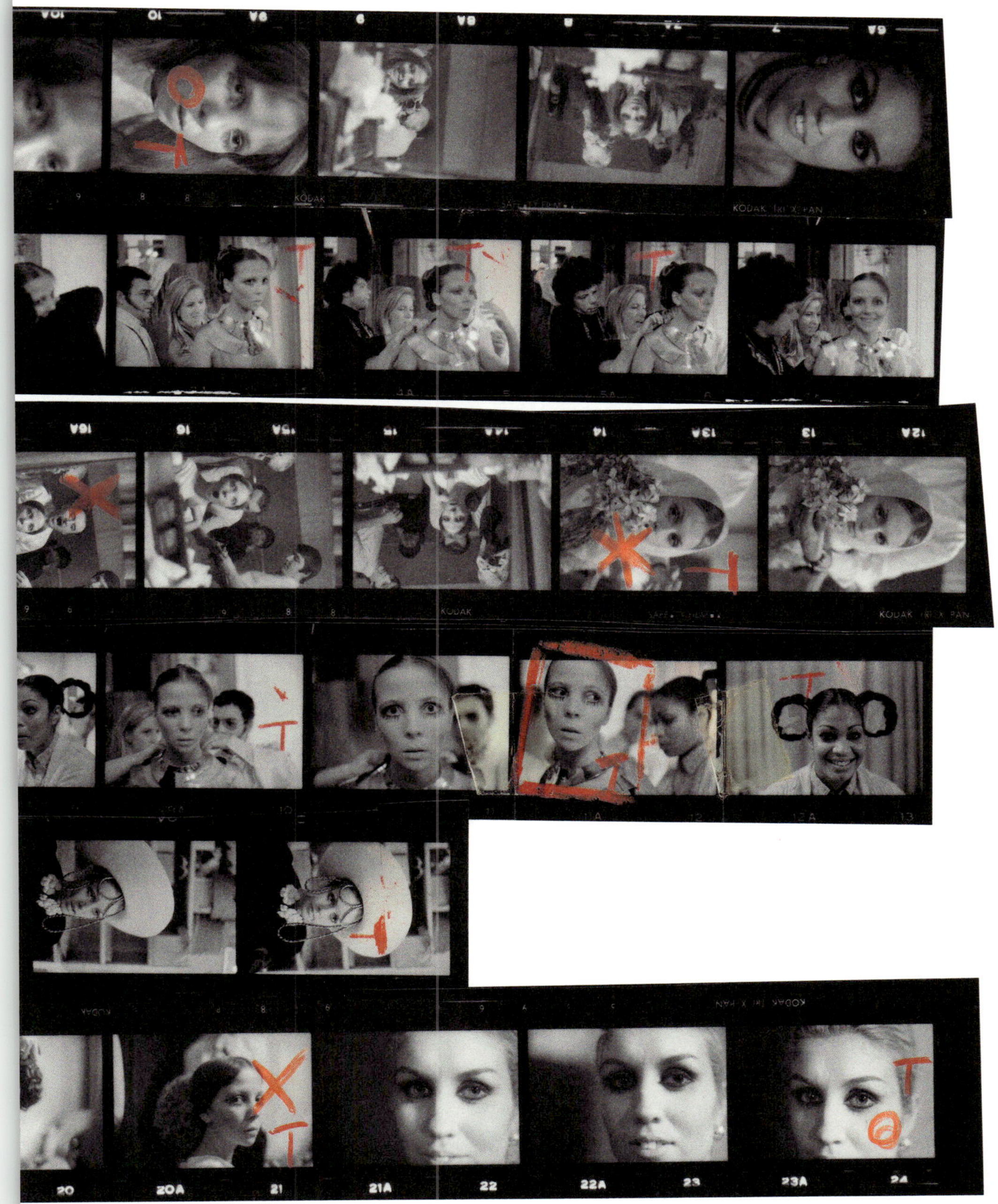

J. H. Lartigue's composite contact sheets of the models Twiggy and Penelope Tree getting ready for a photo session with Avedon at the *Vogue* Studio, Paris, January 1968

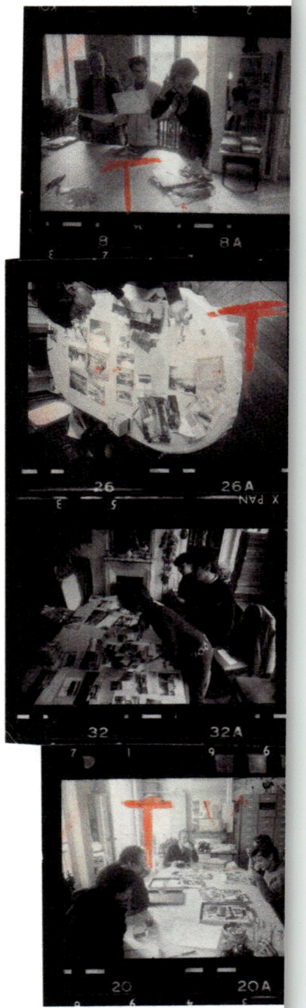
8
8A
26
26A
X PAN
32
32A
20
20A

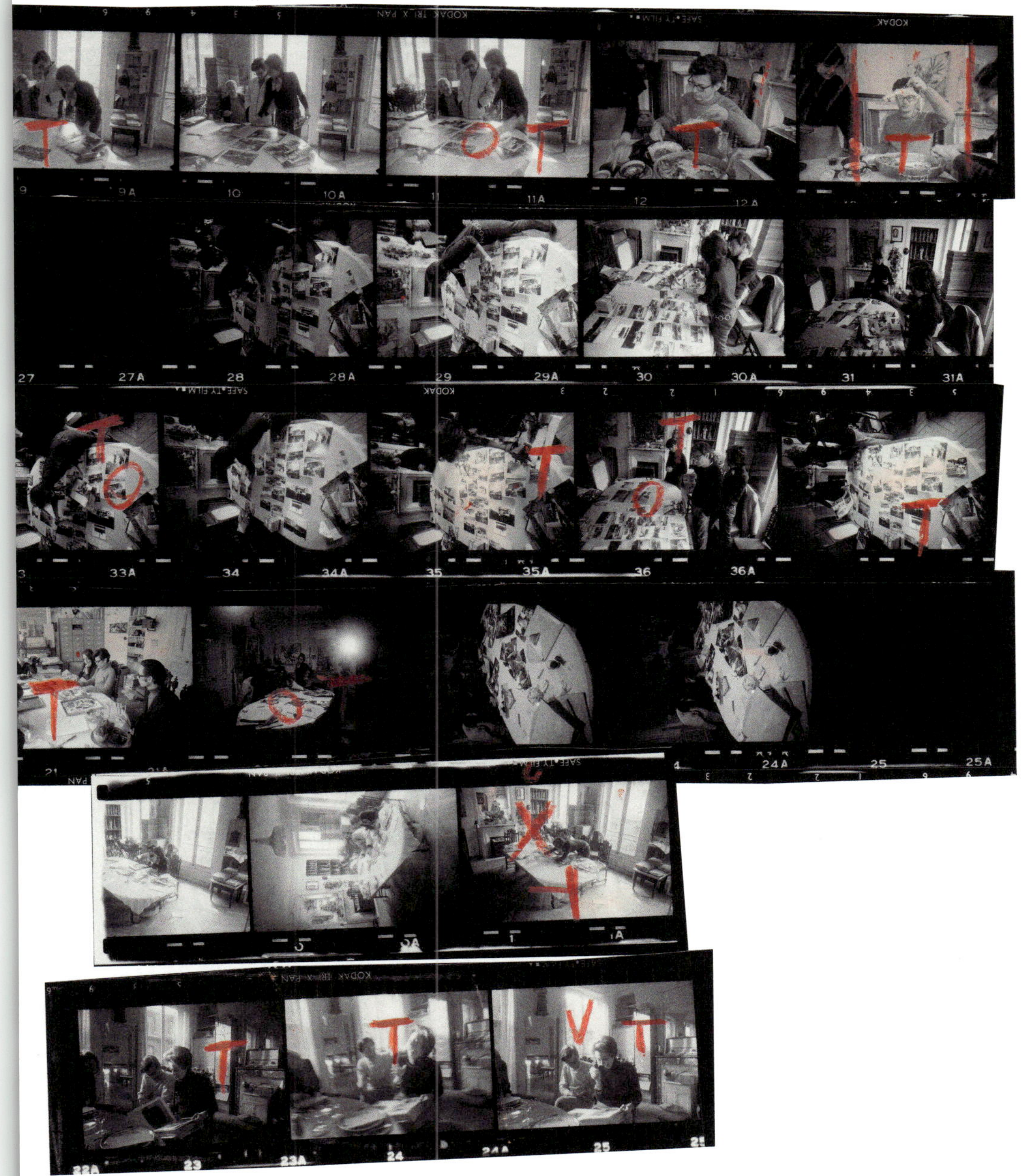

J. H. Lartigue's composite contact sheets of Jacques Henri Lartigue, Richard Avedon and Bea Feitler at work on *Diary of a Century*, Paris, May 1968

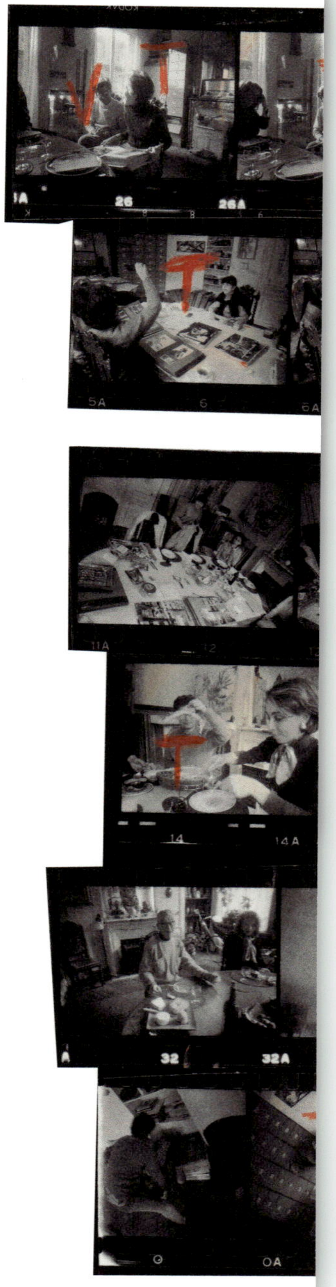

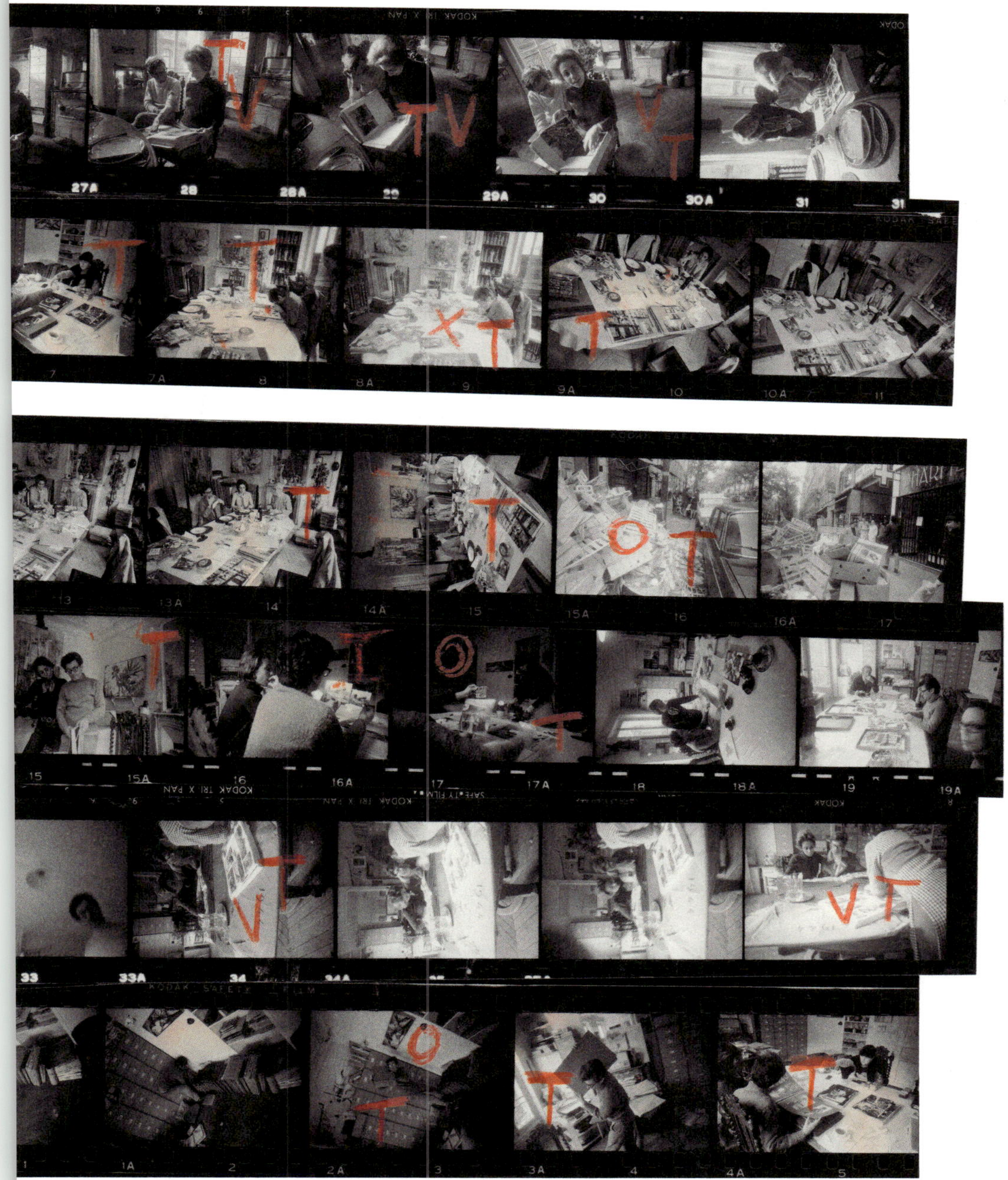

J. H. Lartigue's composite contact sheets of Jacques Henri Lartigue, Richard Avedon and Bea Feitler at work on *Diary of a Century*, Paris, May 1968

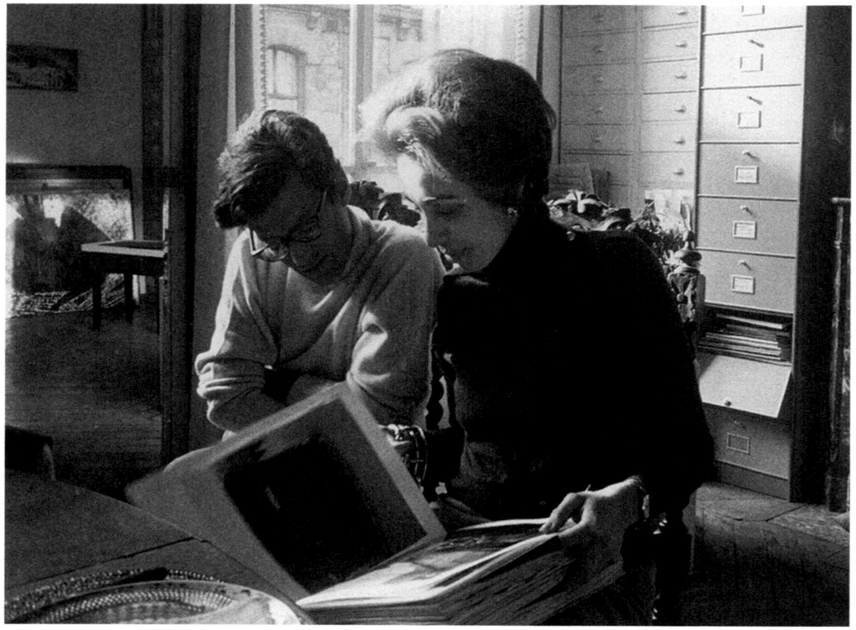

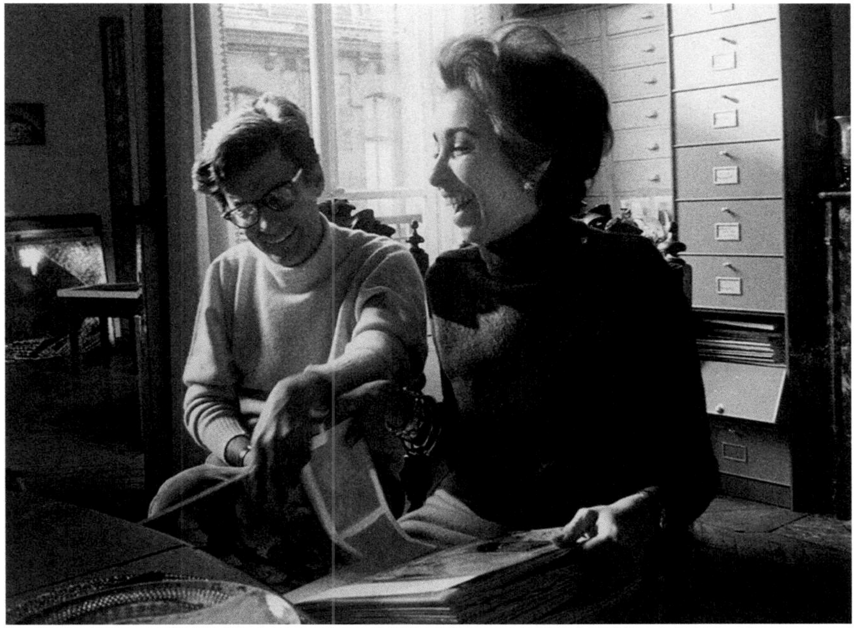

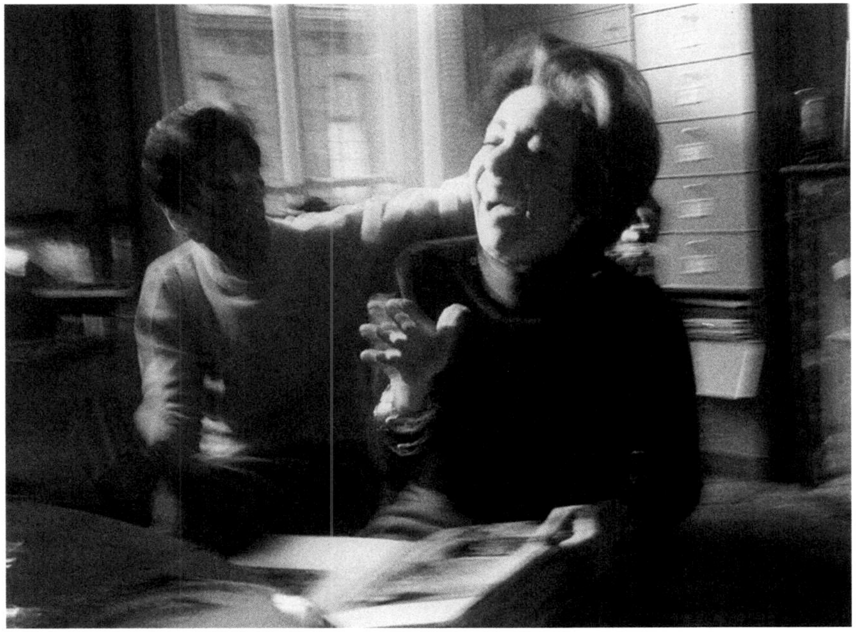

Richard Avedon and Bea Feitler, Paris, May 1968; photographs by J. H. Lartigue

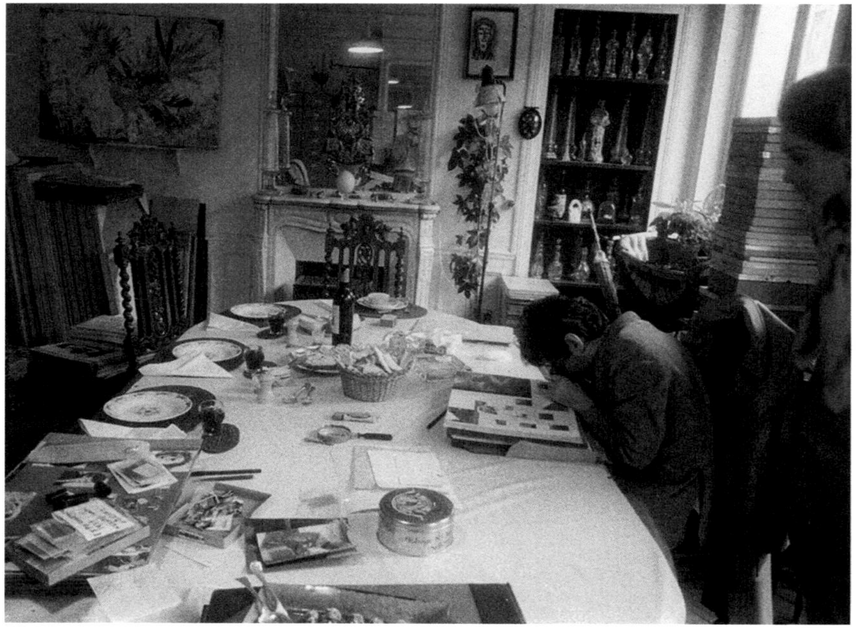

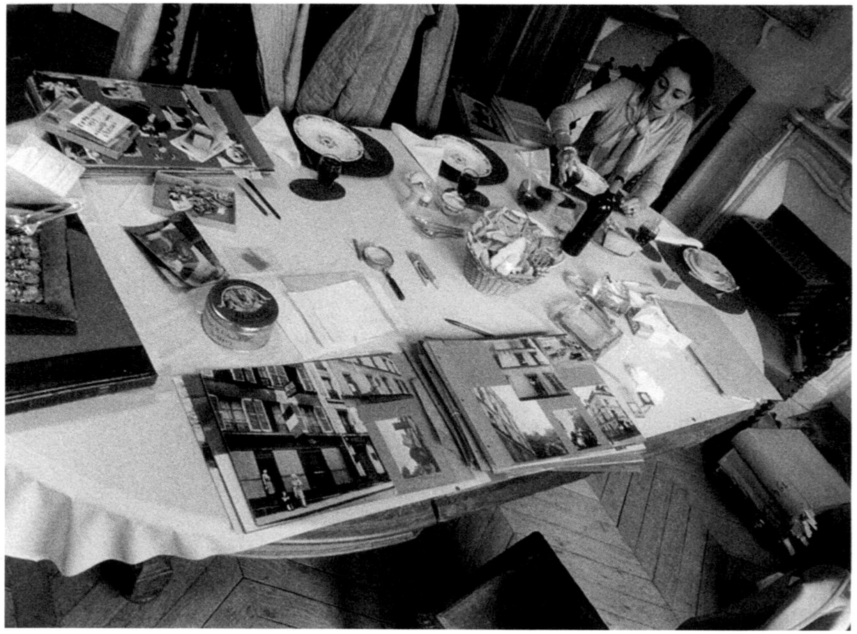

Richard Avedon and Bea Feitler, Paris, May 1968; photograph by J. H. Lartigue

Richard Avedon!
The one I have admired for
so many years as the greatest
photographer in the world.
Bea Feitler, the editor-in-chief
of *Bazaar*, which for three or
four dozens of years has been
stroking my enthusiasm.
Both come to Paris for me!
To choose my photographs.
To see them all with them,
with their new eyes, their
eyes which see so well.

—

JOURNAL OF JACQUES HENRI LARTIGUE,
HANDWRITTEN ENTRY DATED MAY 1968.

RICHARD AVEDON   BEA FEITLER

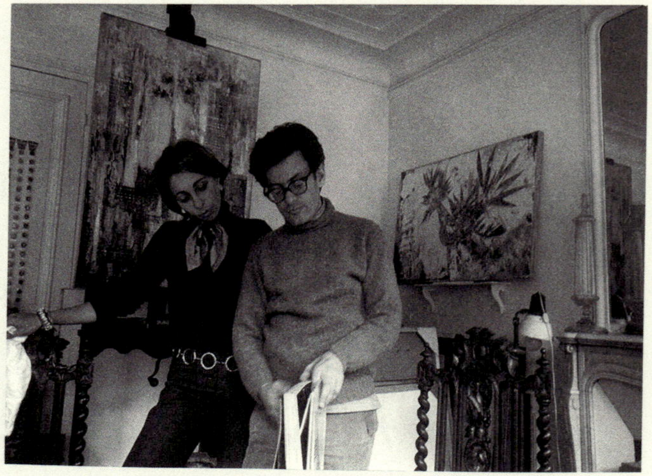

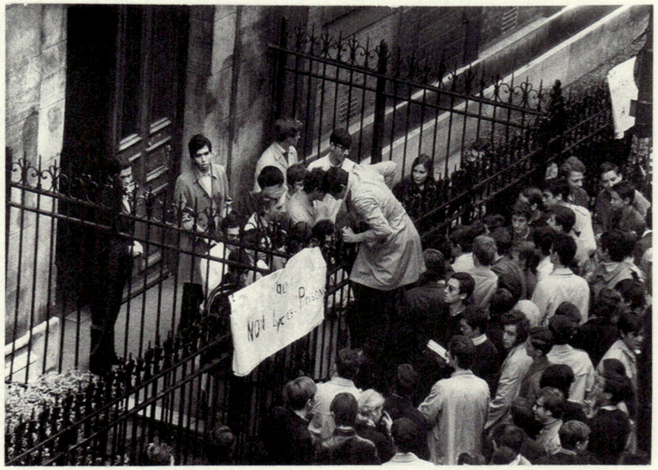

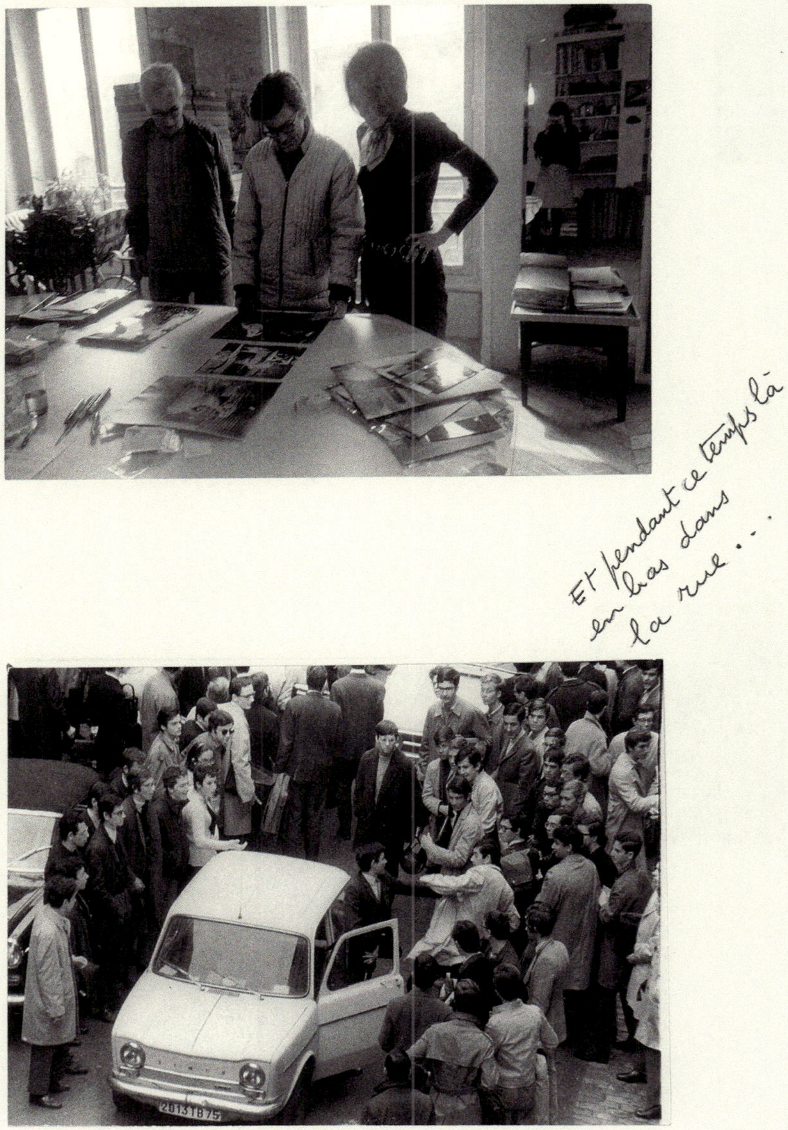

Richard Avedon and Bea Feitler work on *Diary of a Century* while "meanwhile, down in the streets . . ."
Paris, May 1968 (album page 0028V68); photographs by J. H. Lartigue

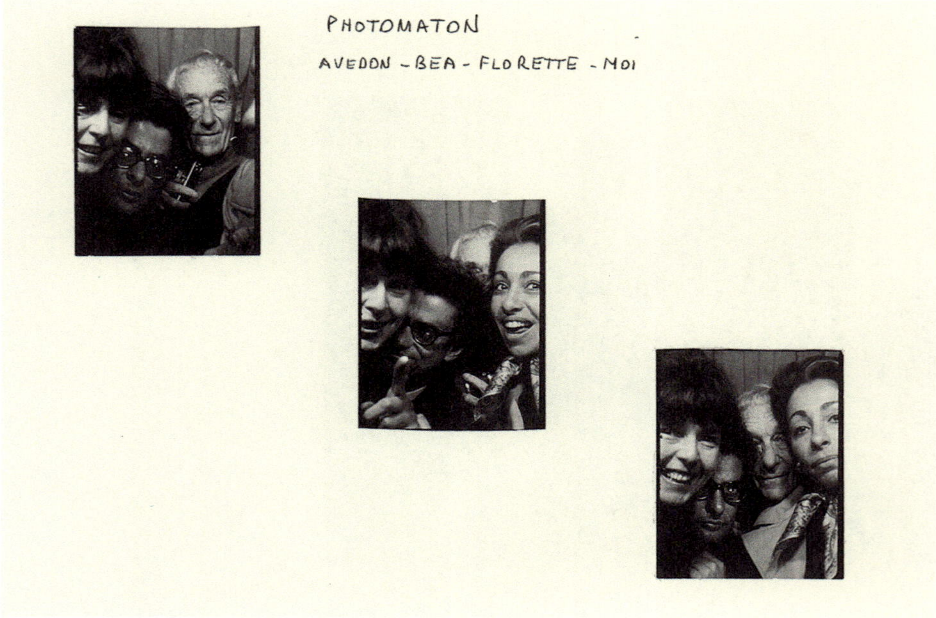

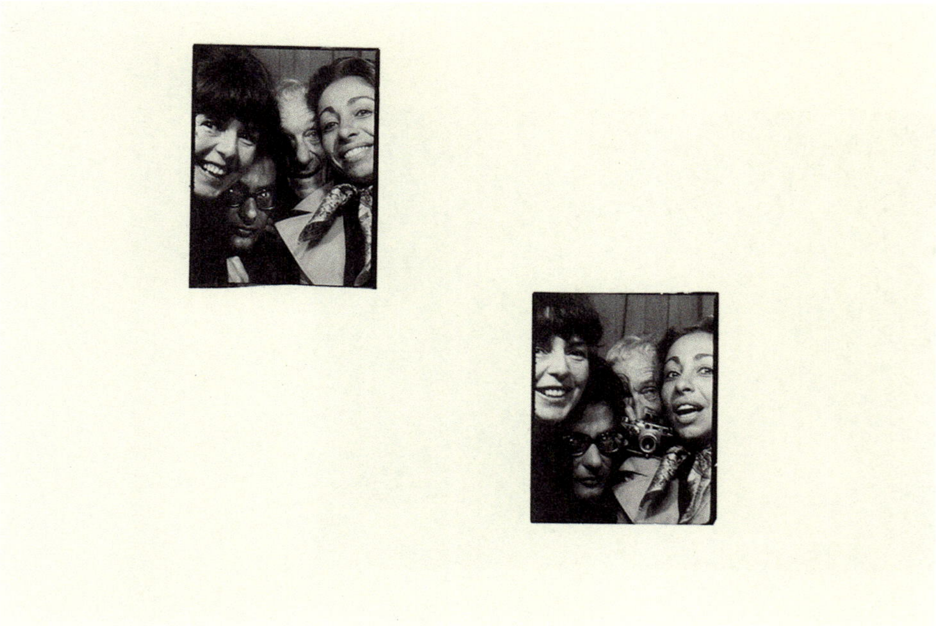

Photomatic pictures of Avedon, Bea Feitler, Florette and J. H. Lartigue, Paris, May 1968

Departure day for Dick Avedon, Bea and their heavy suitcases filled with some of the albums of mine that they are bringing to America. Half of my photographs from so many years of my life are going to be rescued! Yes, it is loosening my heart. Dick needs a picture, we all walk to a small Photomaton, on place Victor Hugo, down an avenue disfigured by the garbage collectors' strike, through mountains of garbage, empty crates, trash rotting on the sidewalk.

—

JACQUES HENRI LARTIGUE, *L'ŒIL DE LA MÉMOIRE*, 1932–1985 (PARIS: CARRÉRE, 1986), 401.

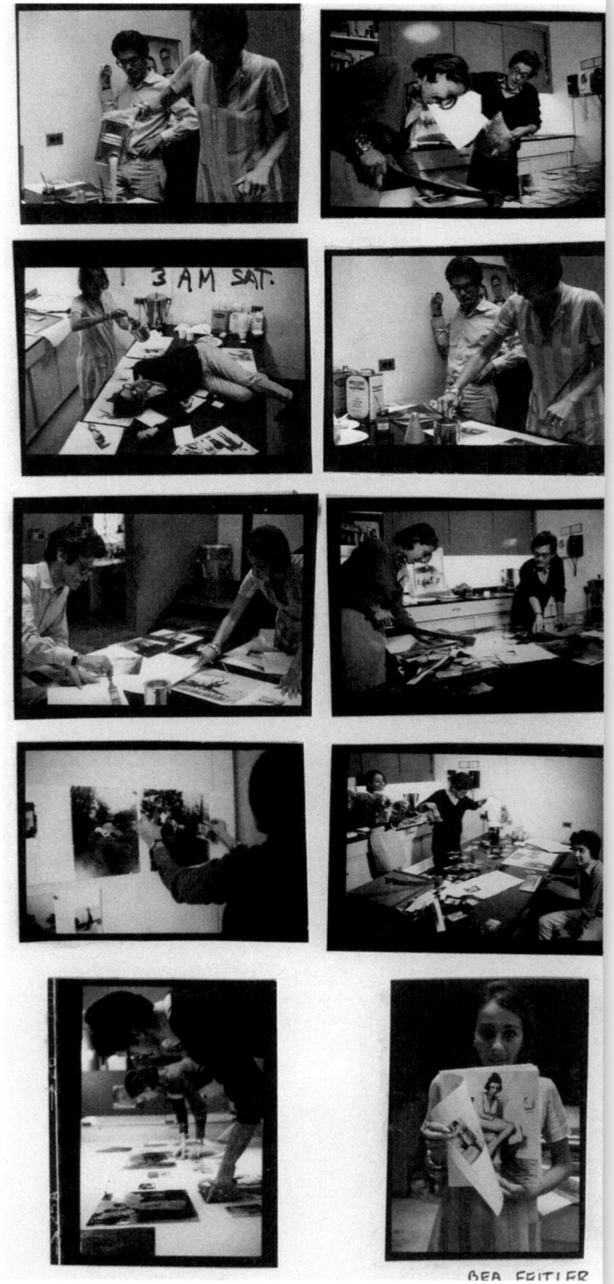
3 AM SAT.
BEA FEITLER

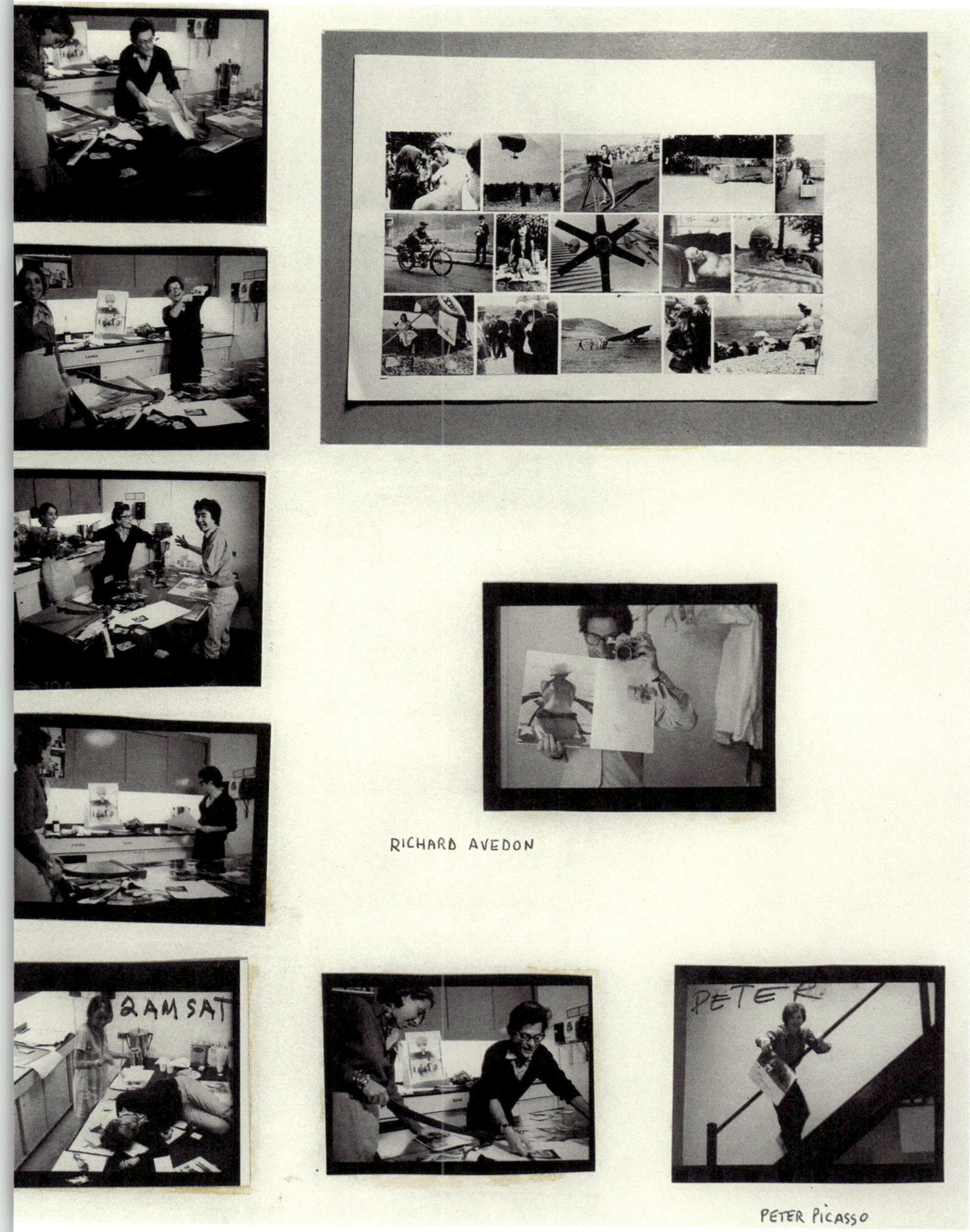

Avedon and Bea Feitler at work on the layout for *Diary of a Century*, New York, November 1968 (album page 0058R68)

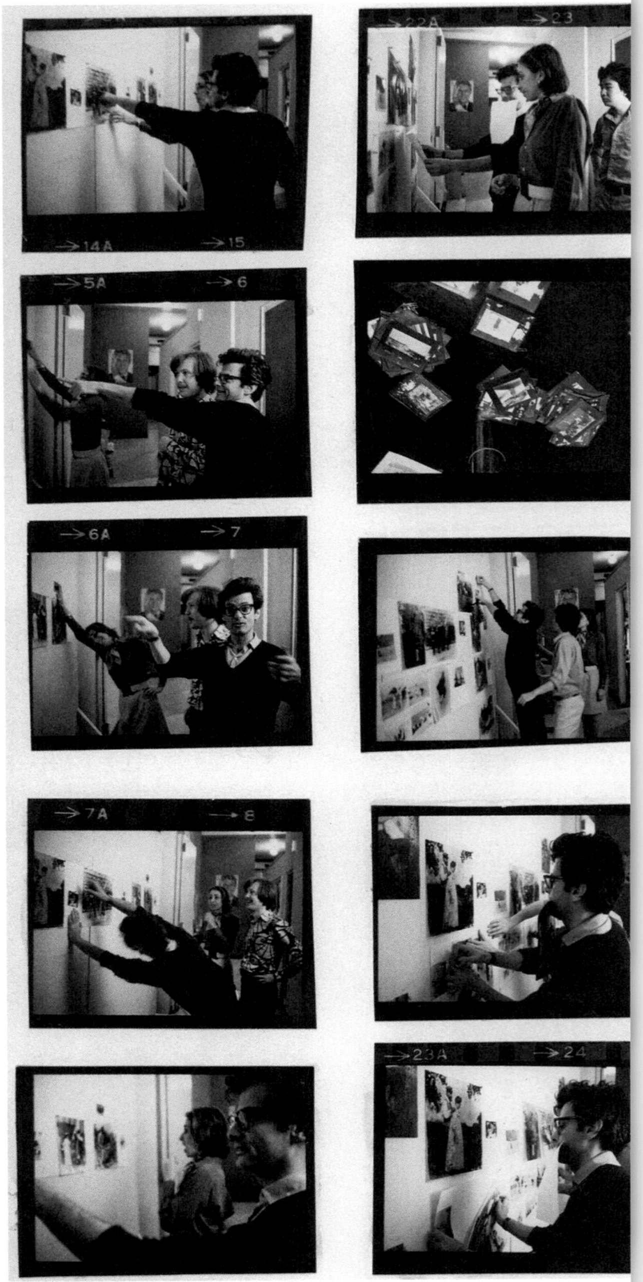
→14A →15
→22A →23
→5A →6
→6A →7
→7A →8
→23A →24

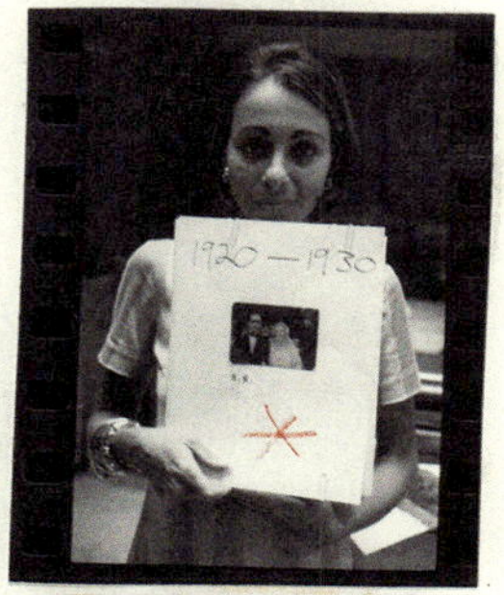

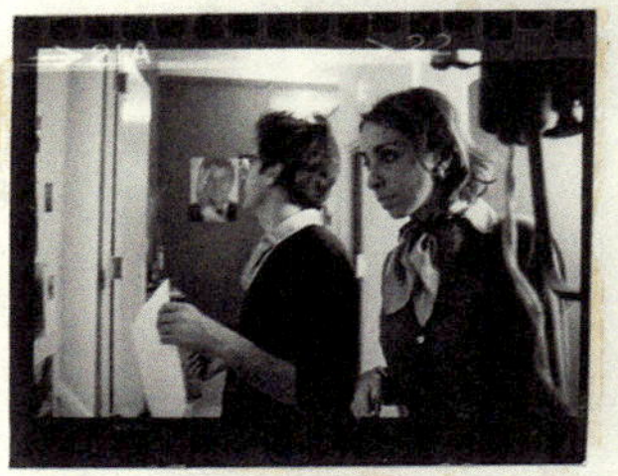

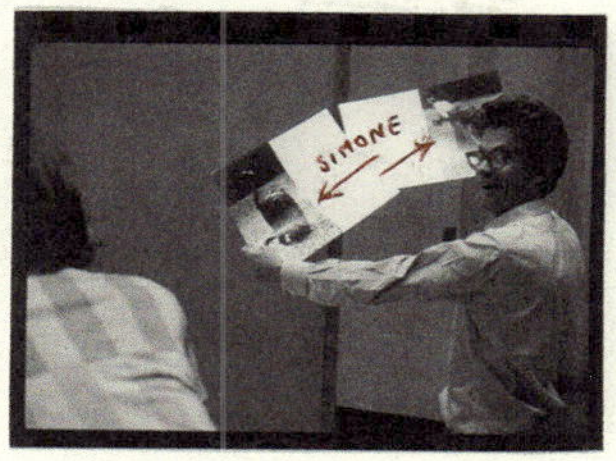

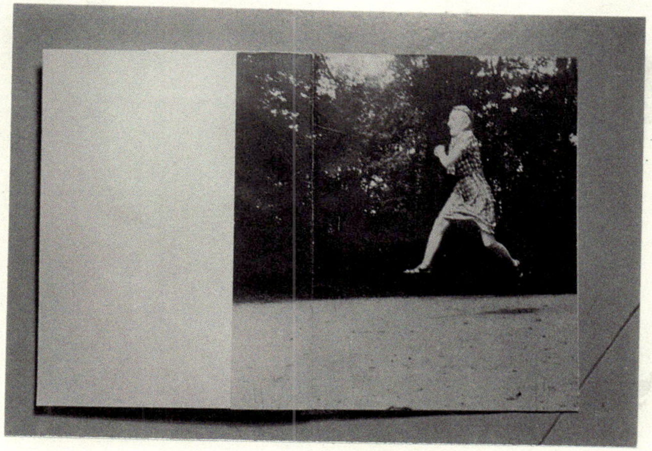

Avedon and Bea Feitler at work on the layout for *Diary of a Century*, New York, November 1968 (album page 0058V68)

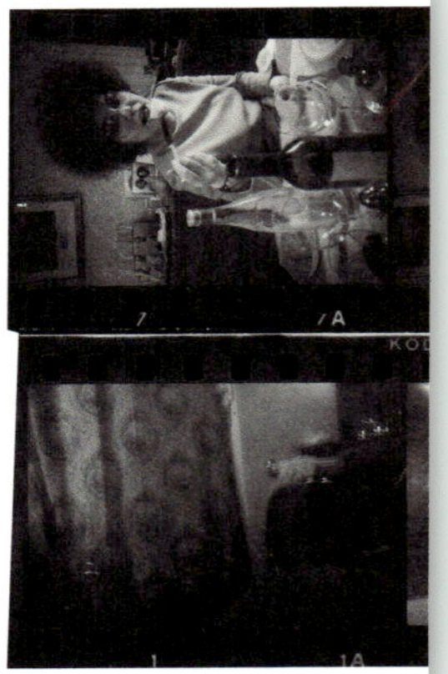

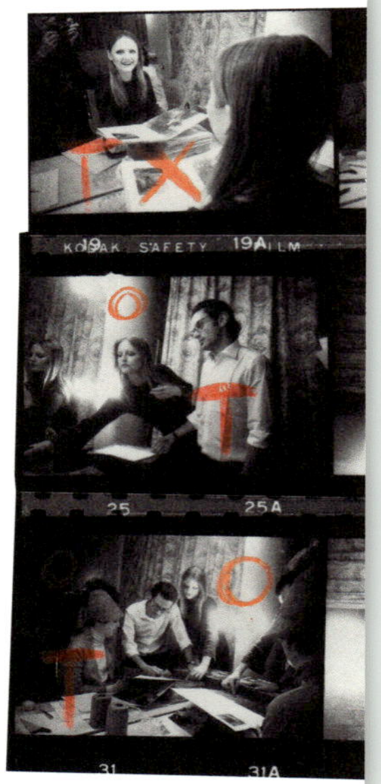
KODAK SAFETY FILM
19
19A
25
25A
31
31A

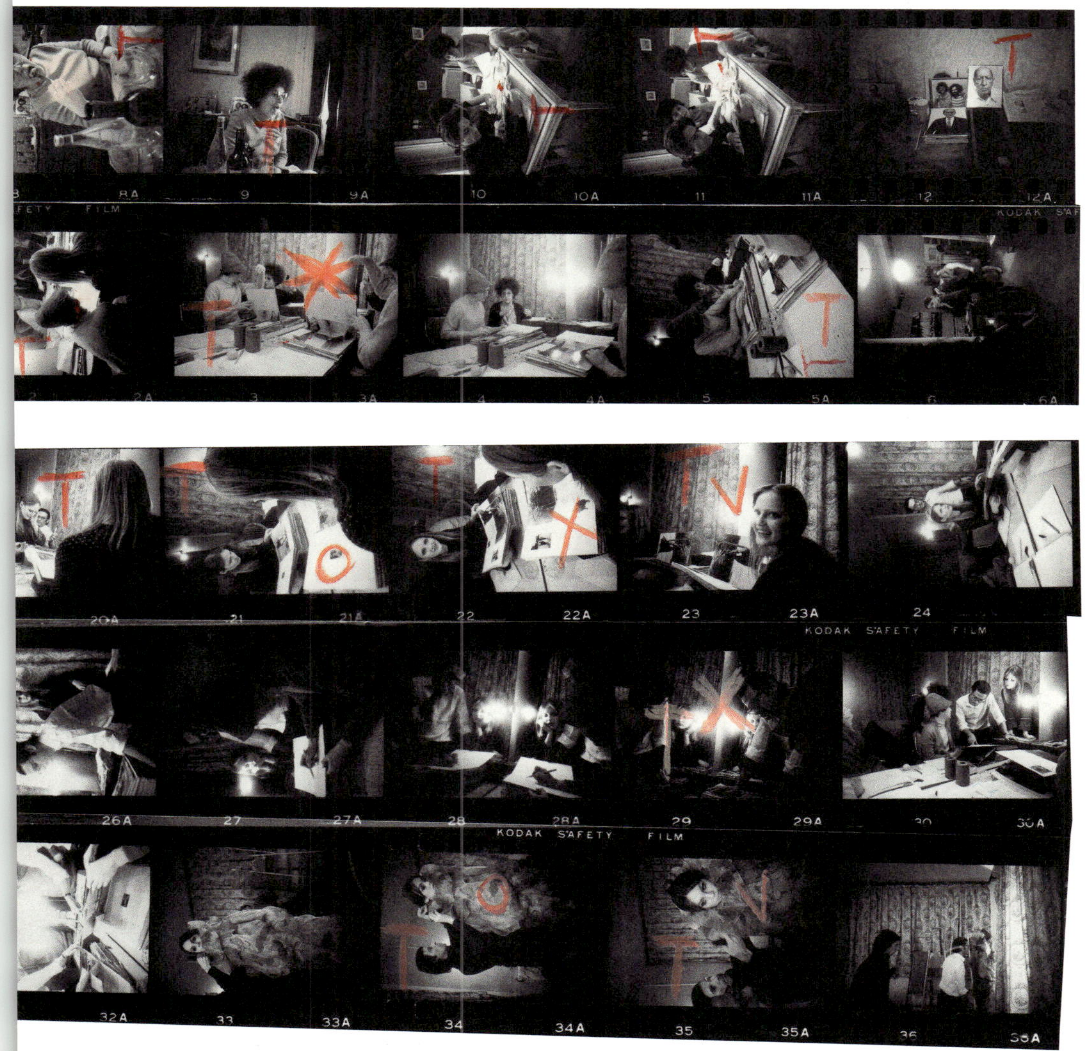

J. H. Lartigue's composite contact sheets of Avedon and Doon Arbus fine-tuning the layout for *Diary of a Century*, Paris, January 1970

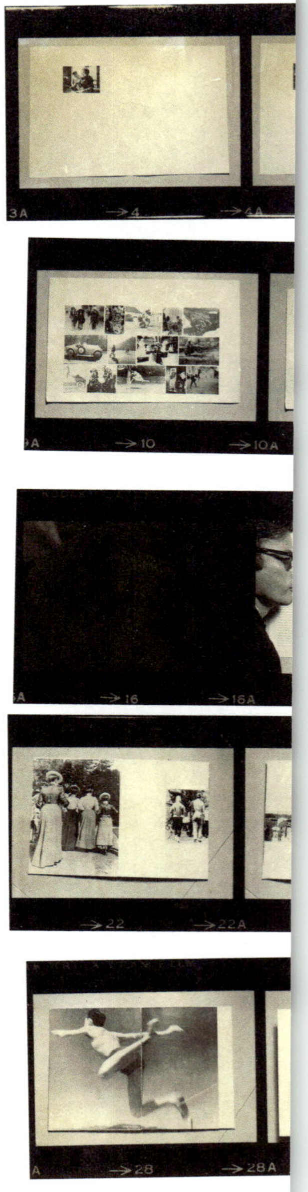
3A →4 →4A
→10 →10A
→16 →16A
→22 →22A
→28 →28A

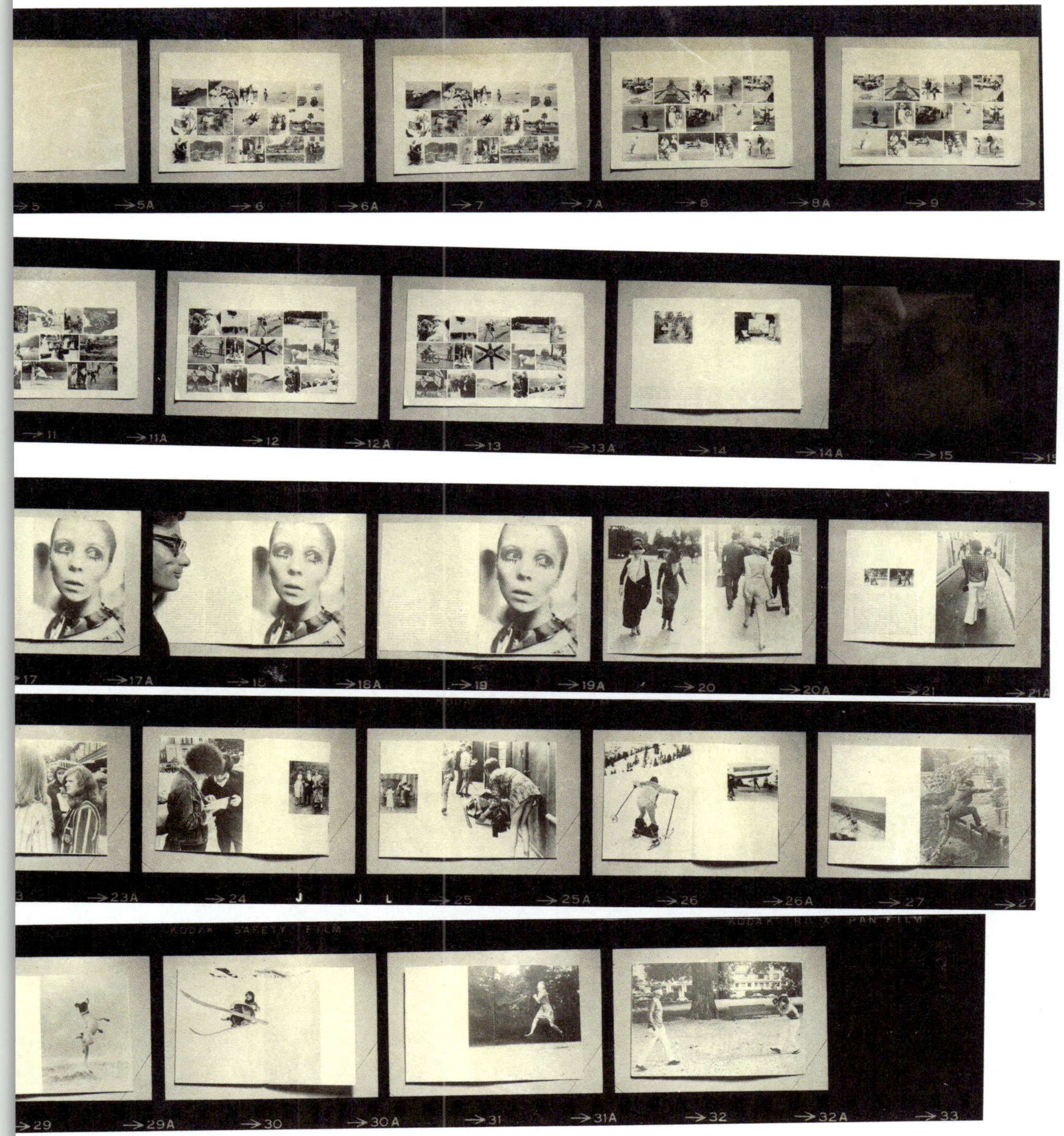

Contact sheets of Avedon and Feitler's mockups for *Diary of a Century*, New York, October 1968

Method is not important, result is.

—

Richard Avedon

Lartigue: Made in USA

Diary of a Century

J. H. Lartigue's, *Diary of a Century*, was edited by Richard Avedon, designed by Bea Feitler, (New York: Viking Press, 1970). The book's cinematic structure was intended by Avedon to resemble a film script, in the manner of Brodovitch's *Observations*.

Notes for *Diary of a Century*
Richard Avedon

Text for pages 4, 7, 8, 12, 13:
The beginning, the first camera, the family, mother and father, the secret garden, the childhood life of the château. One continuous text piece.

Page 28:
Short text on efforts to move in space–flying, riding, bicycles, etc.

Pages 30, 33, 35:
Text on Zissou

Pages 36–37:
Beginning of cars; excitement of racing; excitement of cars, etc.

Page 42:
Text on beginning to fly – kites, family building, planes in back yard, etc.

Page 50:
Short text on plane and balloons – dirigibles, etc.

Pages 52, 53, 54, 56, 62:
One long text piece on women and the Bois.

Pages 66, 68, 70, 71:
Back to château, sports, games: write about Simone.

Pages 72, 75:
Short text about tennis and about Suzanne Lenglen – not too long.

Page 76:
Just a long caption maybe about Monsieur Folletette or the flying dogs or high speed photography – some kind of anecdote.

Page 84:
Family outings and cars and speed and races and your father.

Pages 94, 97:
Long caption about Longchamps, horse racing and the "BIG" women who went, etc.

Page 100:
Long caption explaining "bicycles with wings."

Page 108:
St. Moritz, snow and the beginning of change in the life; the atmosphere just before the war – but don't mention the war directly, let the picture on page 114 be a surprise when it comes.

Page 121:
The war years, the armistice.

Page 128, 130, 132, 135:
This text is very important on the change after the war. The 20s, marriage to Bibi. Explain who Messager was. The atmosphere in Paris, etc.

Page 136:
Long caption about the 20s and the entertainment world.

Page 139, 140, 145, 150:
Make very clear who everyone is as one of this generation knows who Guitry, Printemps, Gaby de Lys, Chevalier, Van Dongen, or Colette are. These could be separate captions for each spread or a text piece that explains everyone. But I think the captions with a little introduction on page 136 would be best.
I KNOW THAT GABY DE LYS IS OUT OF ORDER, CHRONOLOGICALLY, BUT SHE MUST BE THERE FOR THE SAKE OF THE BEAUTY OF THE BOOK. We will just not put a date near her picture. Please, Jacques, let us leave her there. I know it really helps the strength of the book.

Pages 152, 156, 157, 158, 160:
Write about Dany – the birth of a son, becoming a father, new family

life, your life with Bibi and Dany and your painting.

Pages 166–167:
Where is Bibi in this picture? Short caption.

Pages 170–171:
Give us the correct names of everyone in the bed. Actually, I know everyone except Zissou's wife.

Pages 172, 173, 174:
Are absolutely beautiful as they are a remarkable piece of text. If only the rest of the book could be as good.

Page 176:
Short text telling of the new child's birth and death. So that after Messager's death and then the baby's death, we are ending the decade that started in such a happy way with Bibi on the toilet on a very sad, poignant note.

Page 180, 182:
Tell about parting with Bibi and going South to paint and meeting Renée, your life with Renée, how you taught her to be a painter and how the affair ended.

Pages 192, 202:
The short text on life and women and movie making in the South of France. Remember that this text comes just before the World War II pictures and should prepare us for the mood that was in the air before the Second War.

Pages 204, 207, 208, 210, 212:
Since you have few pictures of the war, you might write a big text about what it was like for you during the occupation of Paris and the liberation. Maybe less about the actual war and more about the occupation and the liberation since that's what the photographs are about.

Pages 215, 216, 219, 220, 223:
FLORETTE and then the first grandchild and the aging of everyone, the end of your childhood, the end of old life with a beautiful finale opposite the last picture of your parents.

Pages 224, 226, 227, 228, 230, 234:
This section could start with a long text piece on Warner & Co., vulgarity, South of France, Big America, Movie People invasion, parties, Elsa Maxwell, the Windsors, Picasso, Cocteau, Kennedy, etc., Fashion changed, changes in the life style. Don't make a big point of Kennedy as I think it would be a wrong note.

Page 236:
About change in women in the 60s: miniskirts; everyone has a camera; everyone has a car ; quick jet trips to America ; meeting Hiro – anything you want about now.

Page 246:
This is the most important piece as it ends the book and I hope you will end it with a beautiful tribute to the human spirit – the life force which lasts through all change which is implicit in the pictures of the dog, Simone, and you. All strong and straight and still in your "youth." If you agree with me I think it would be very good to write with sympathy of the student revolutionaries, the landing on the moon – this NEW, NEW world.

Page 252:
Will have your beautiful dedication to Florette and to me. I think it will mean so much more at the end of the book, once the reader has learned to know you, than at the beginning when you are a stranger to them.

Avedon's list of instructions sent to Lartigue regarding the texts, captions, and image placement, 1969.

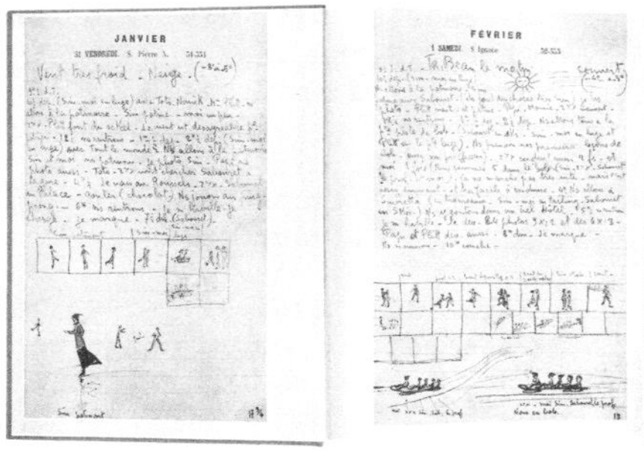
JANVIER
FEVRIER

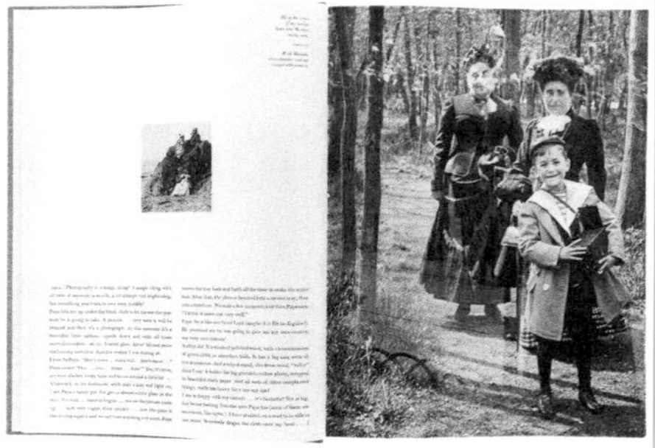

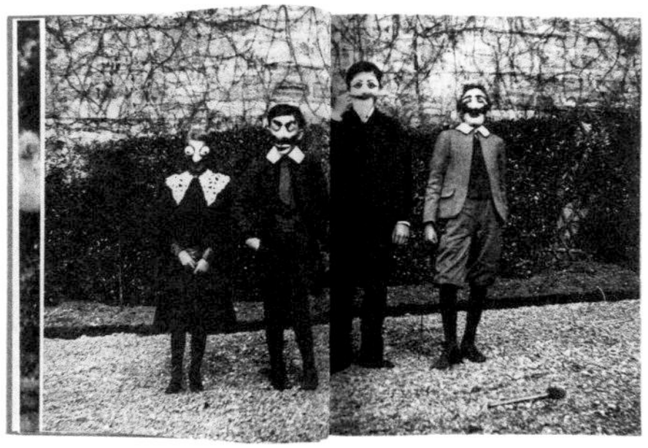

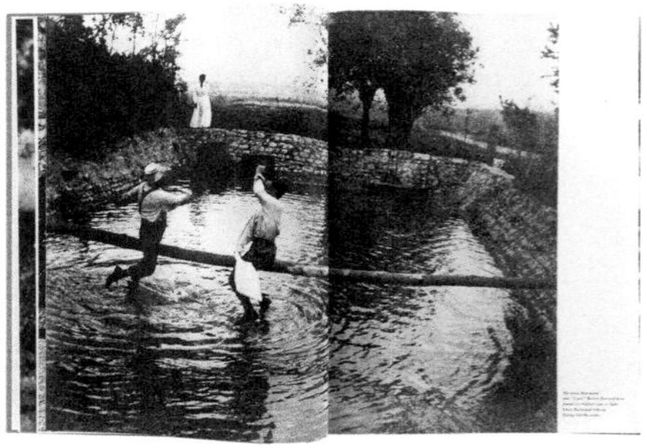

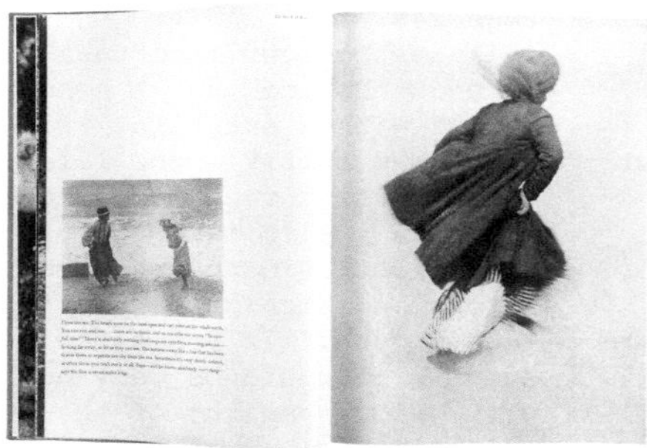

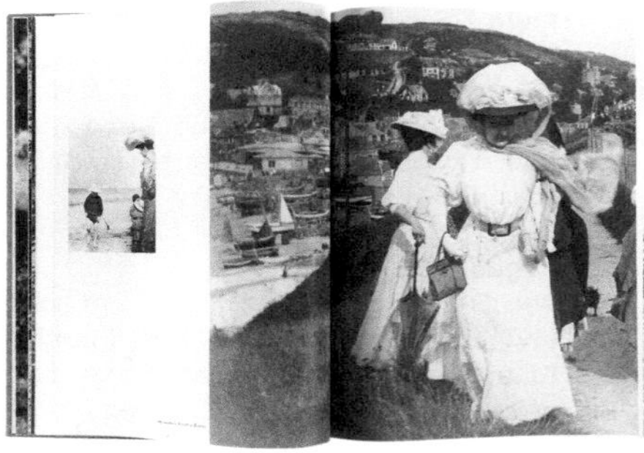

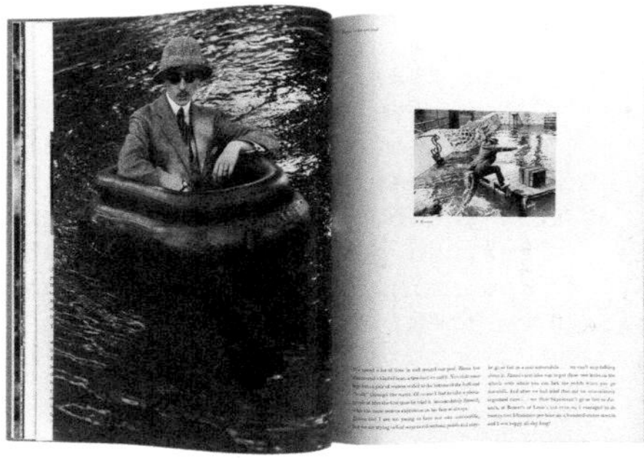

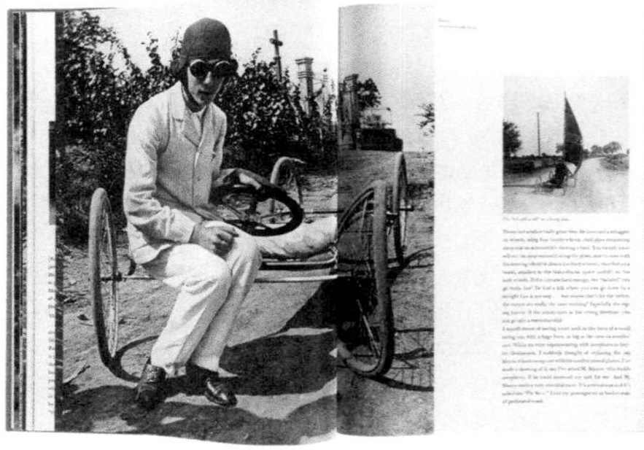

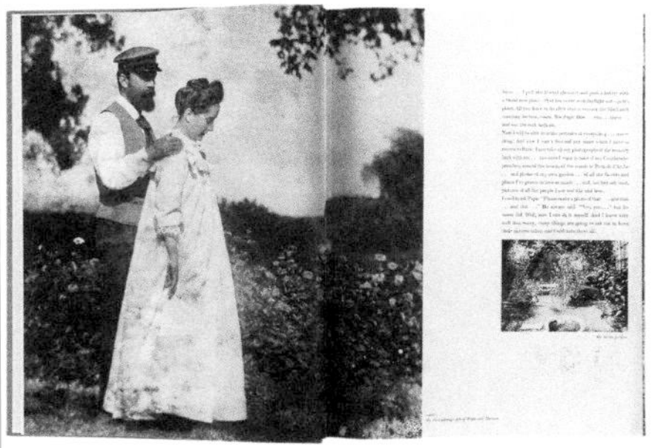

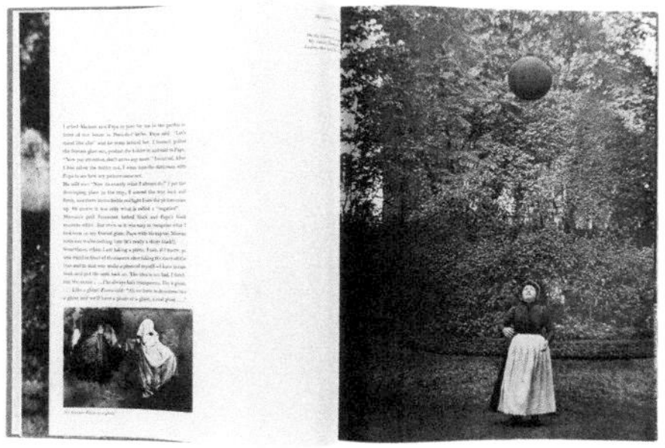

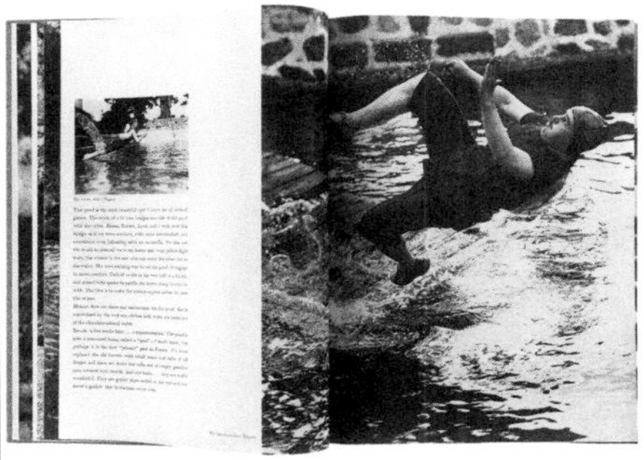

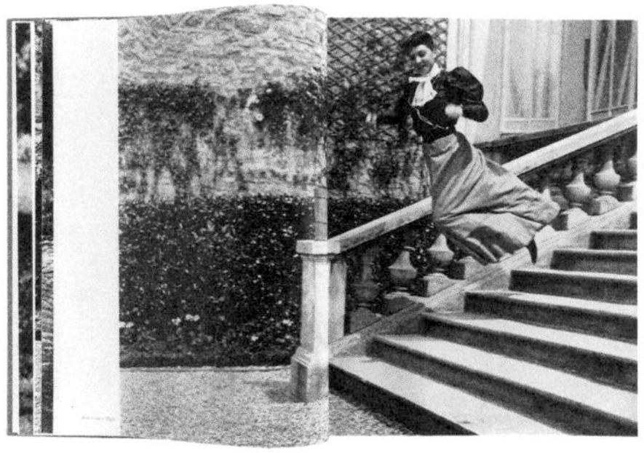

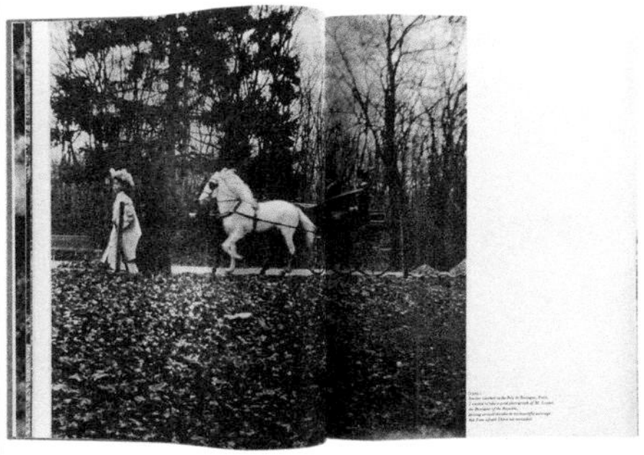

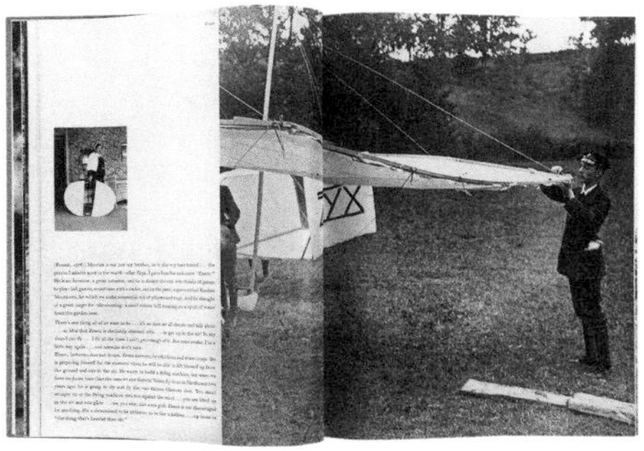

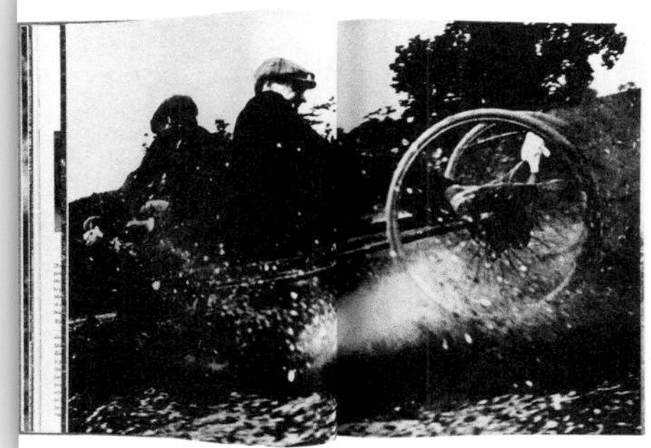

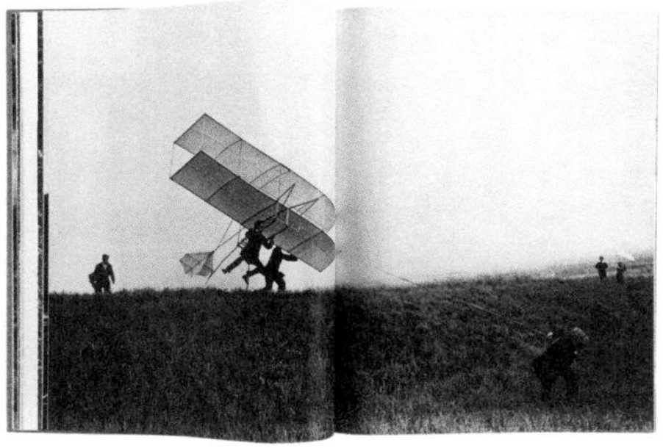

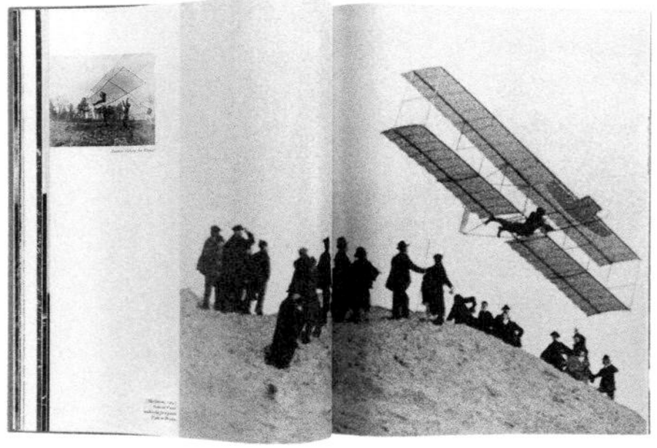
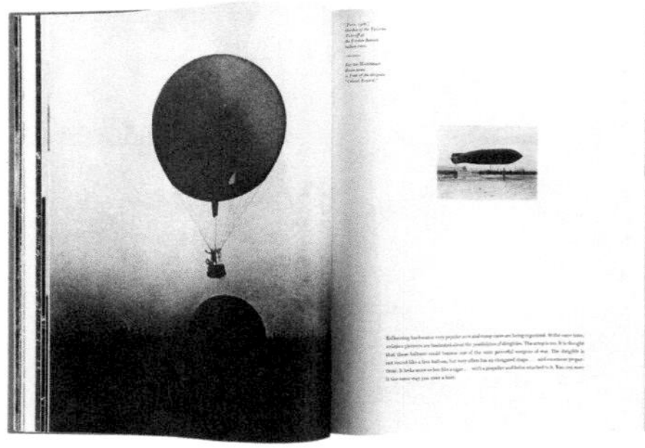
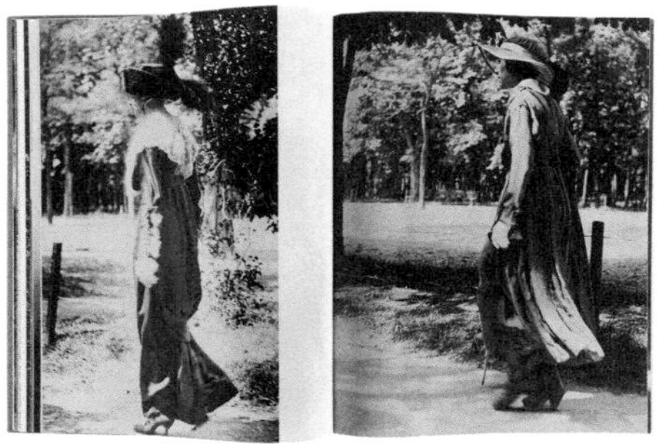
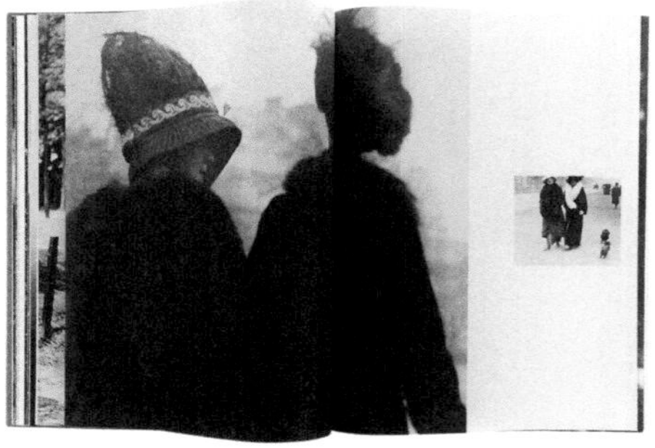
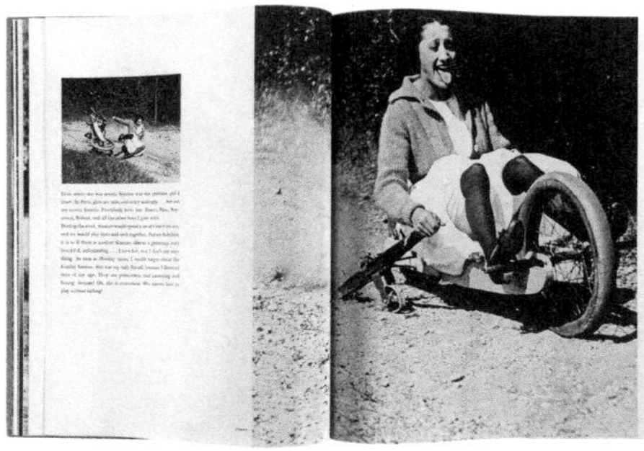
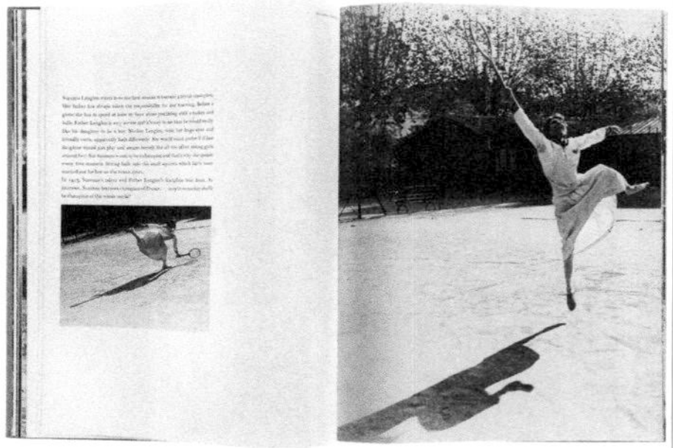
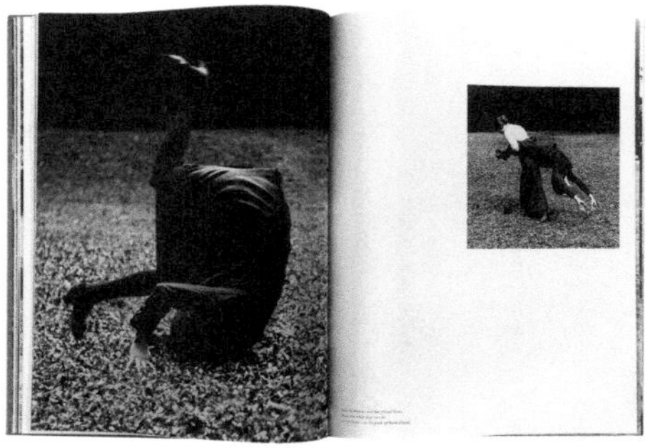
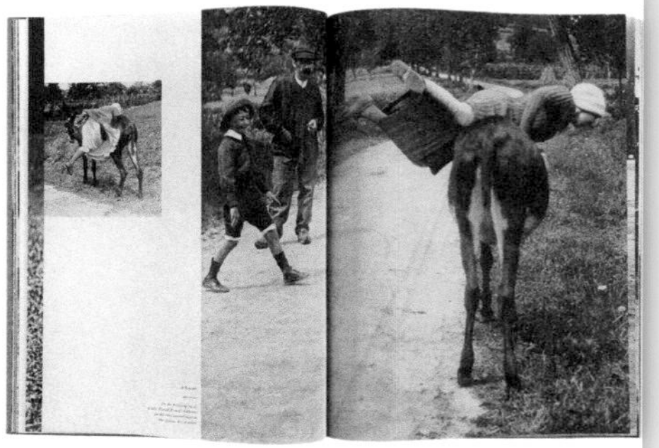

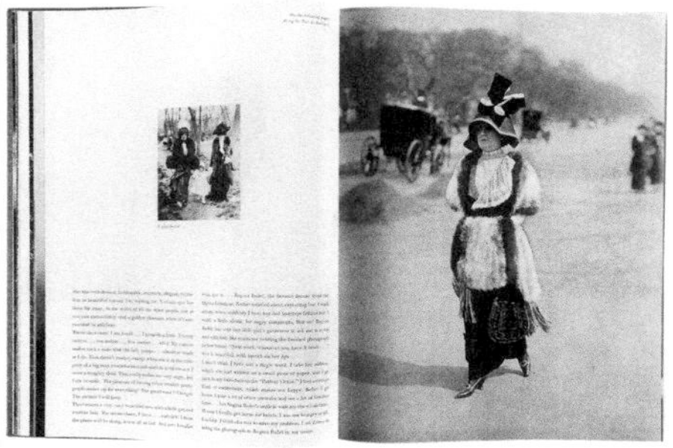

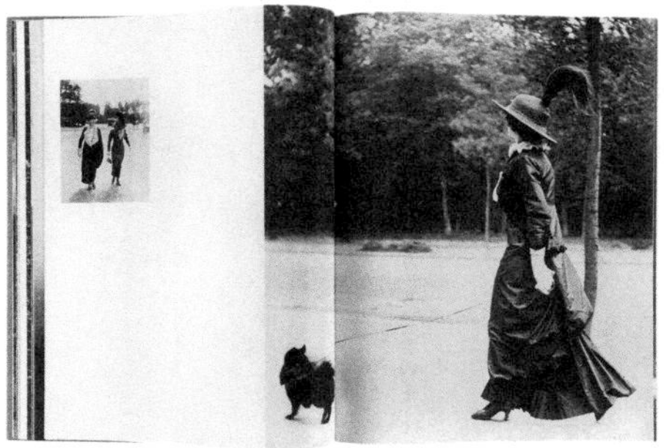

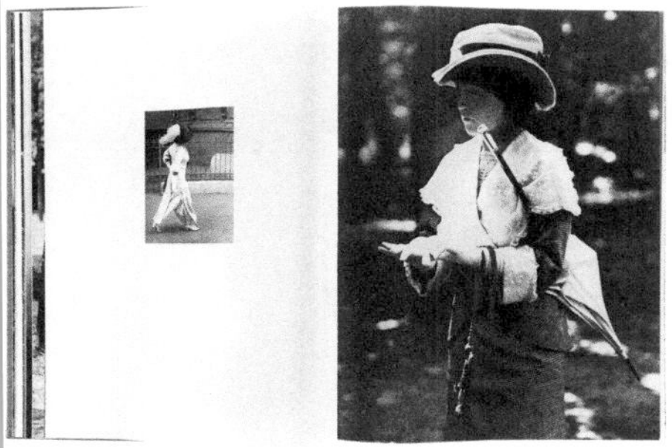

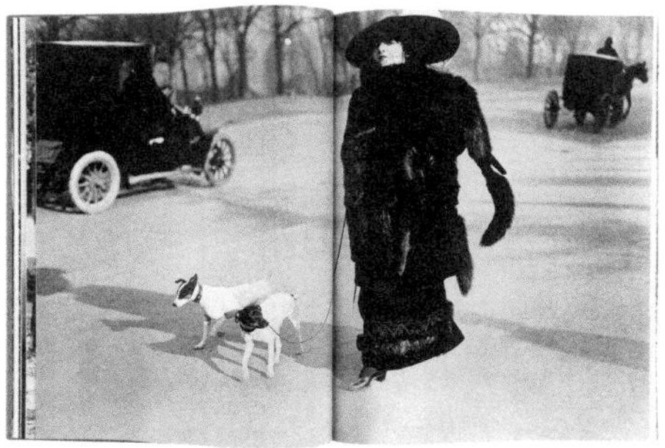

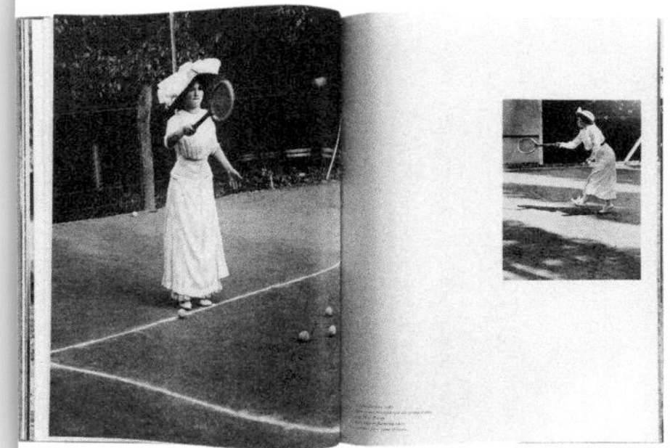

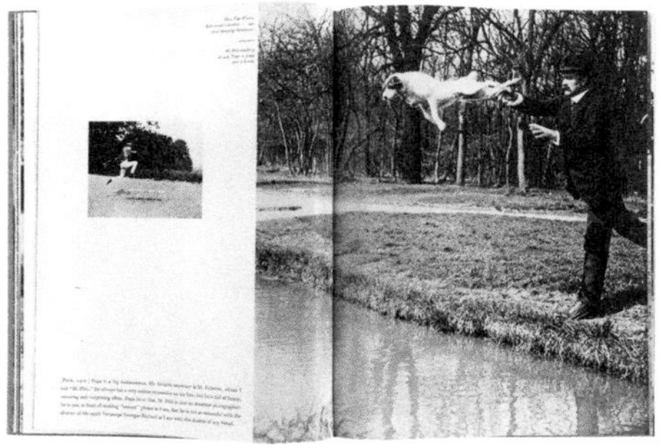

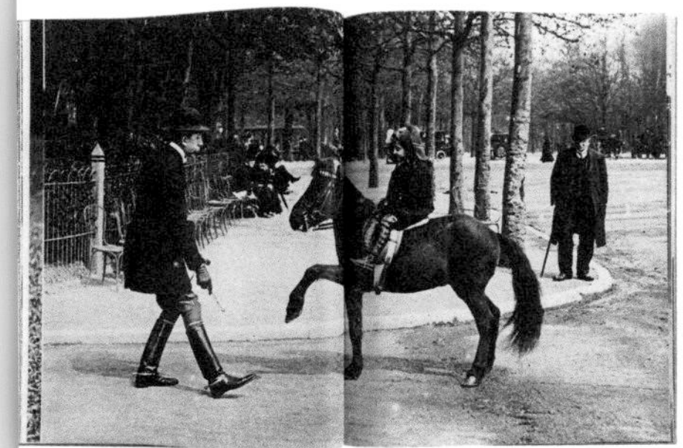

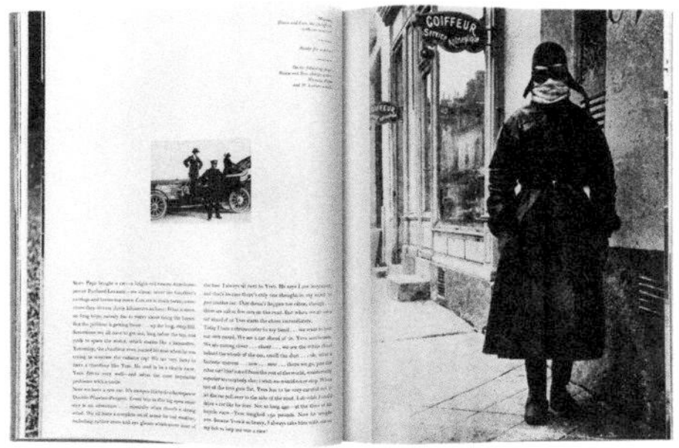

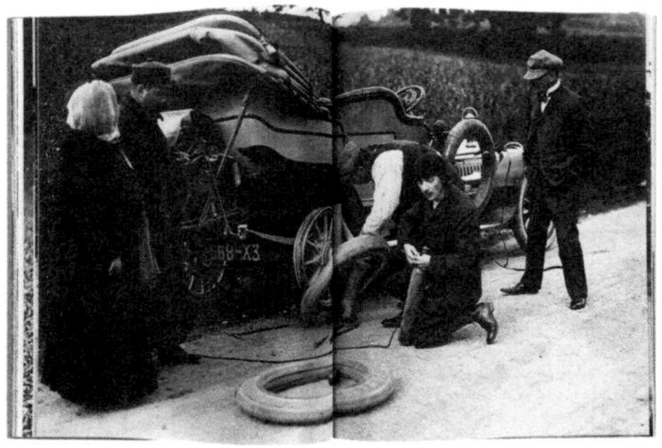

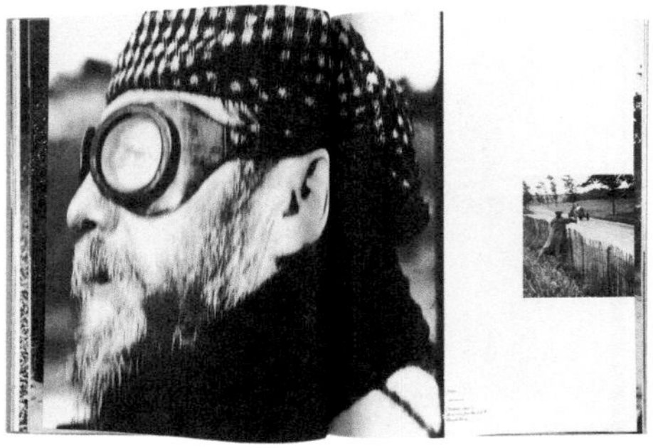

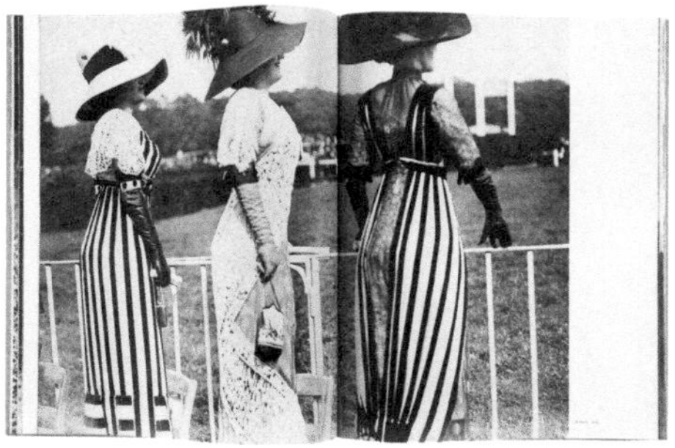

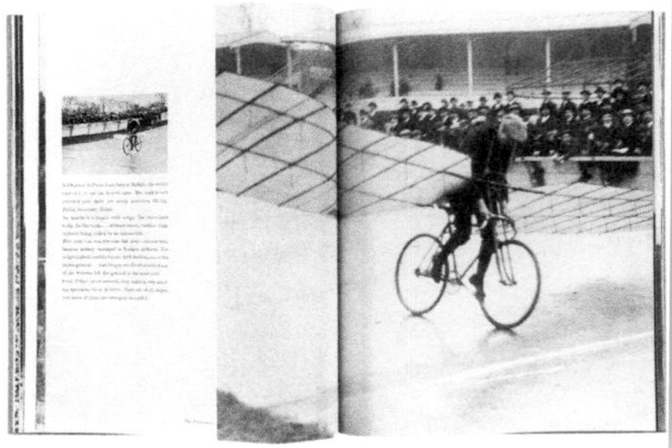

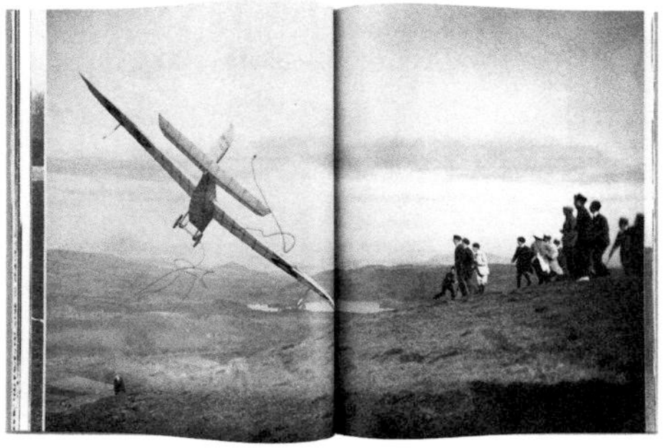

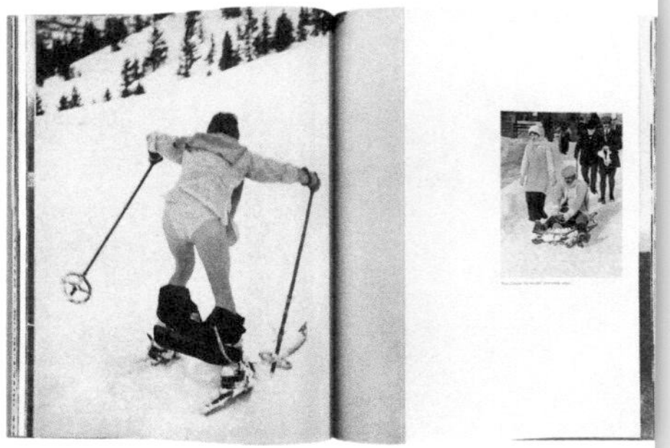

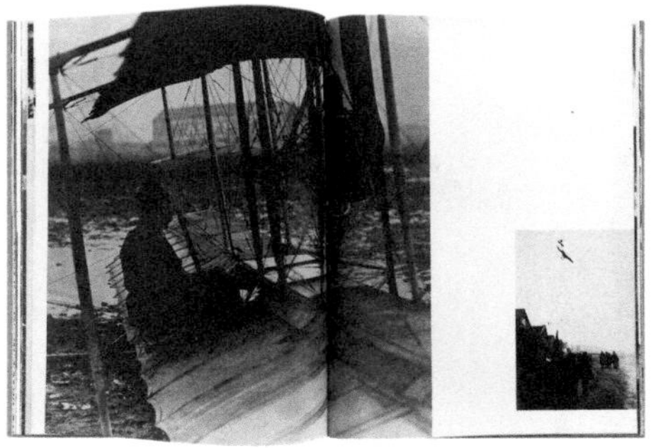

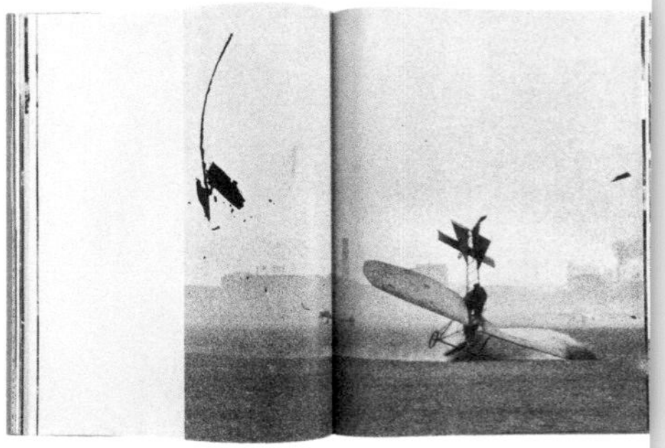

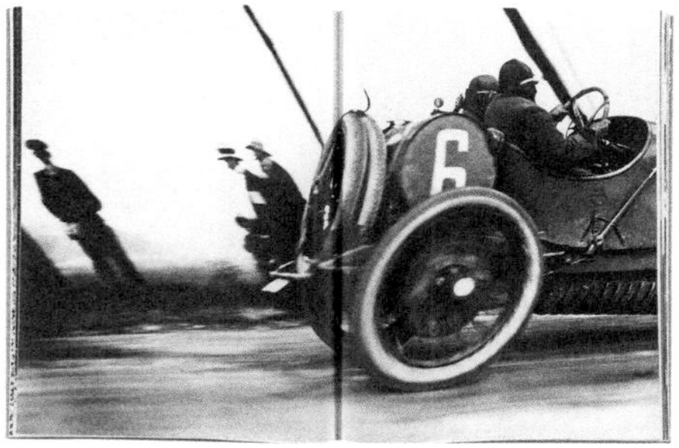
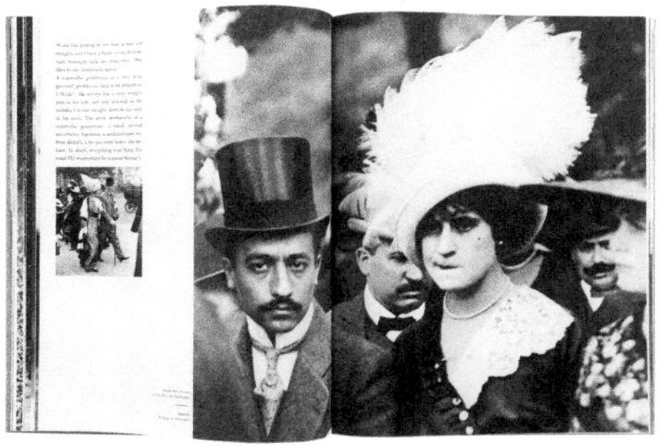
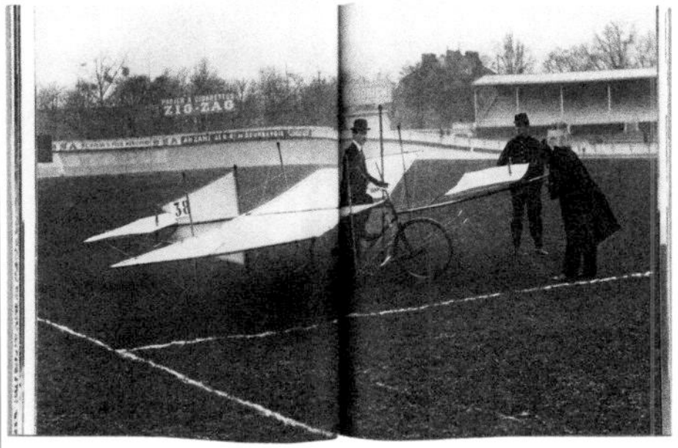
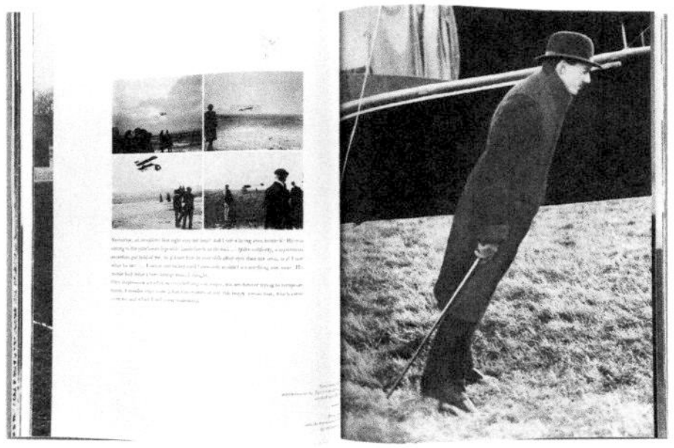
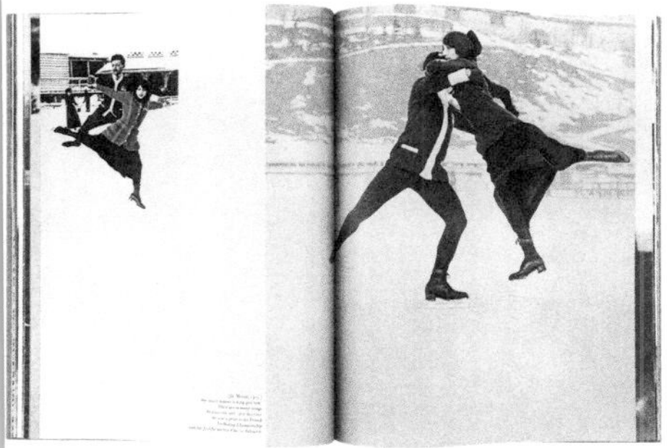
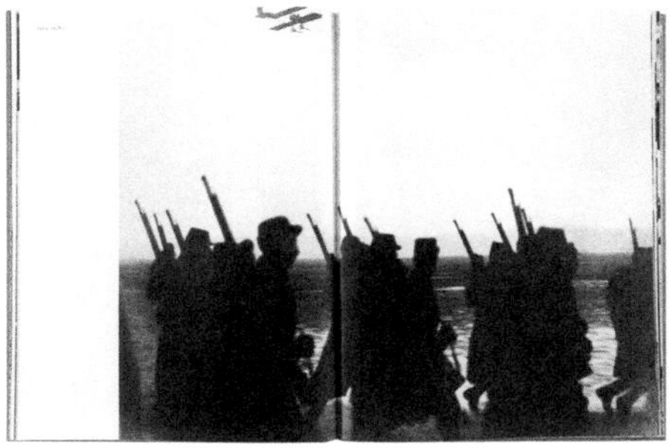
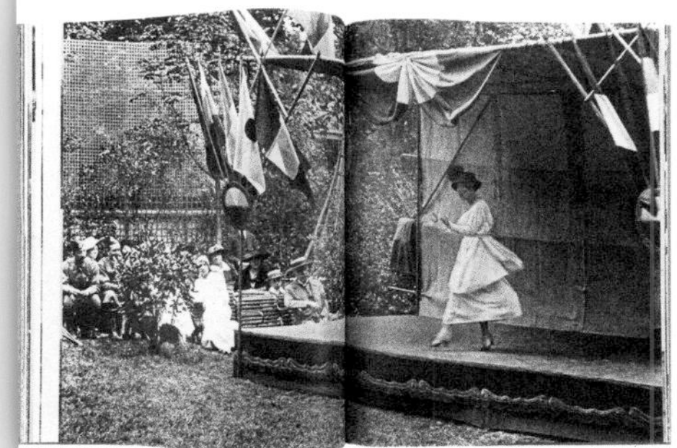
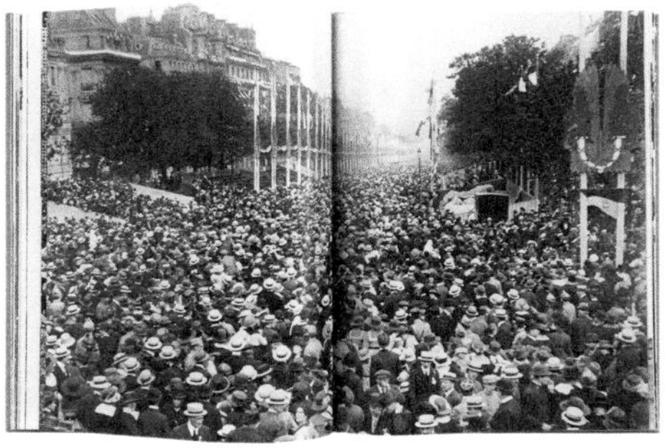

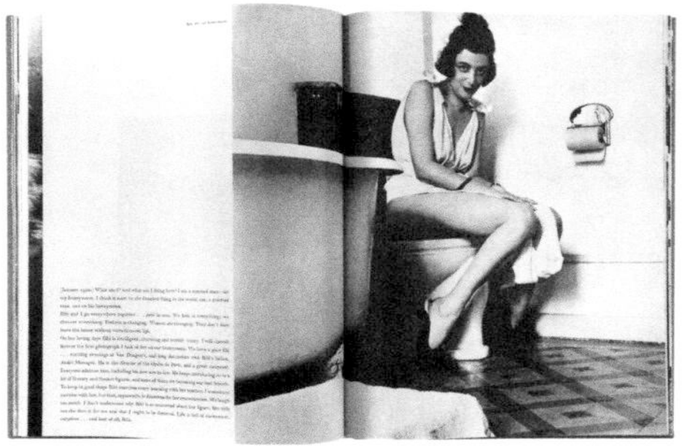

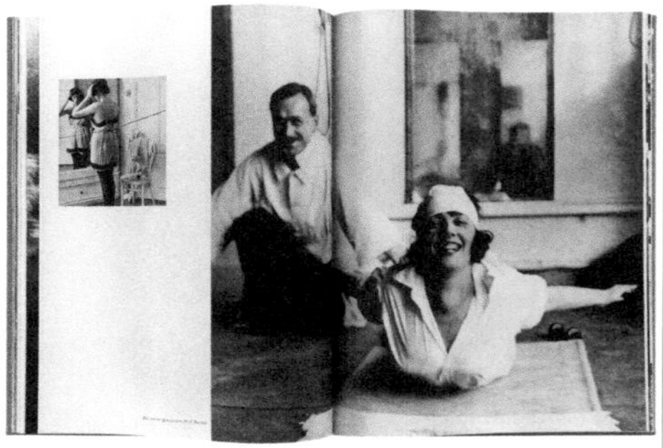

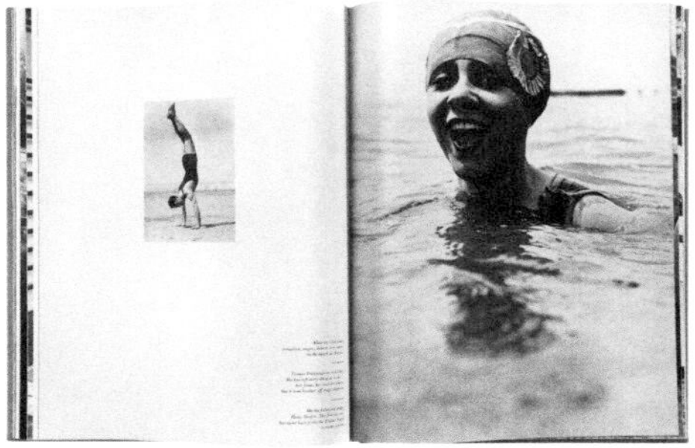

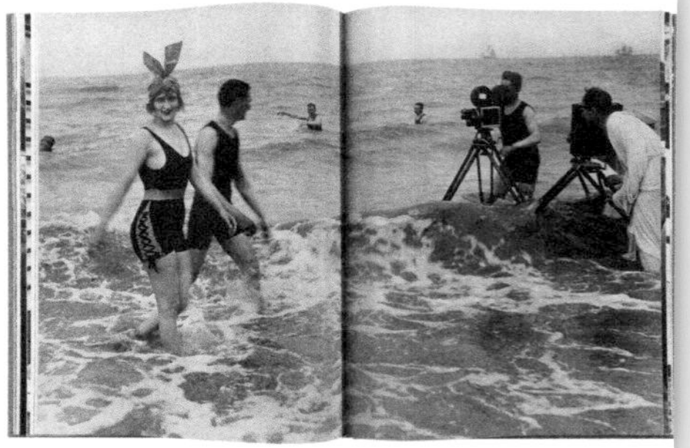

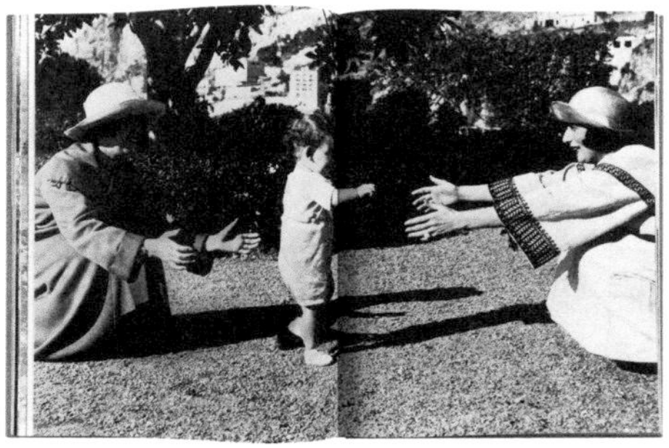

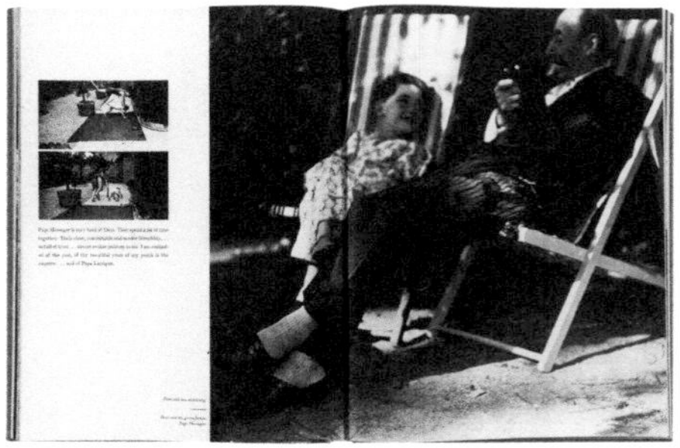

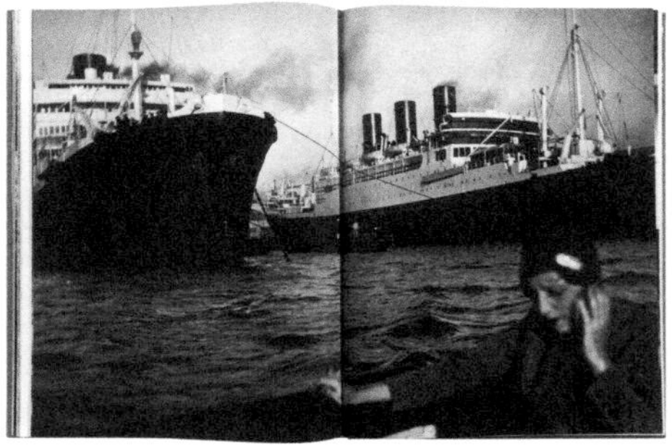

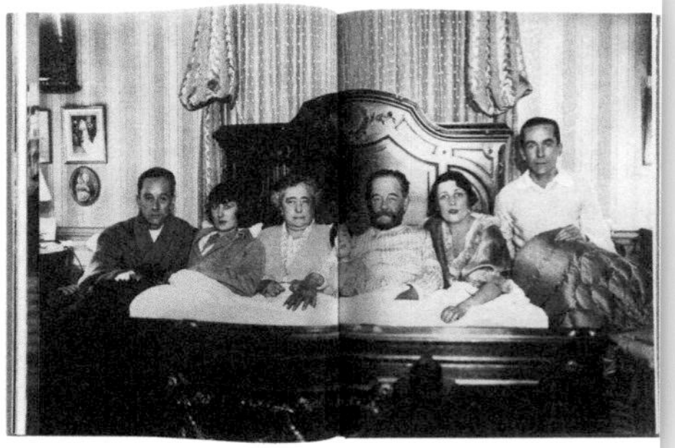

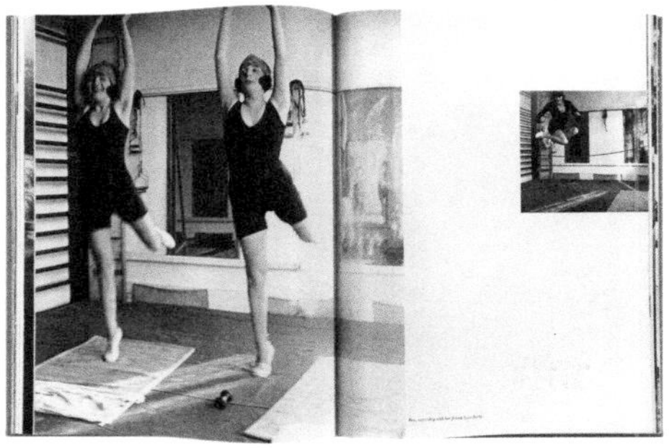

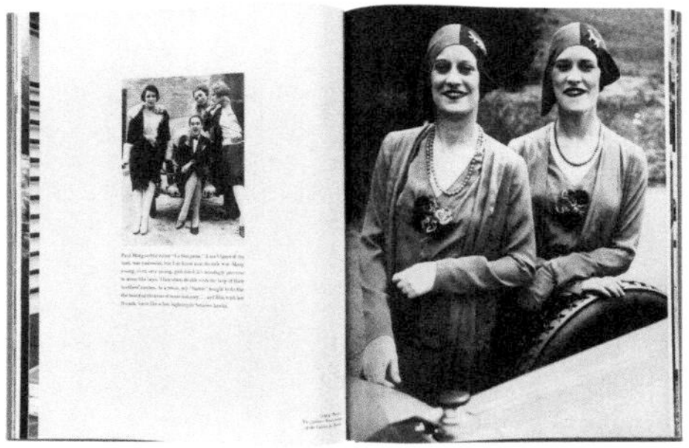

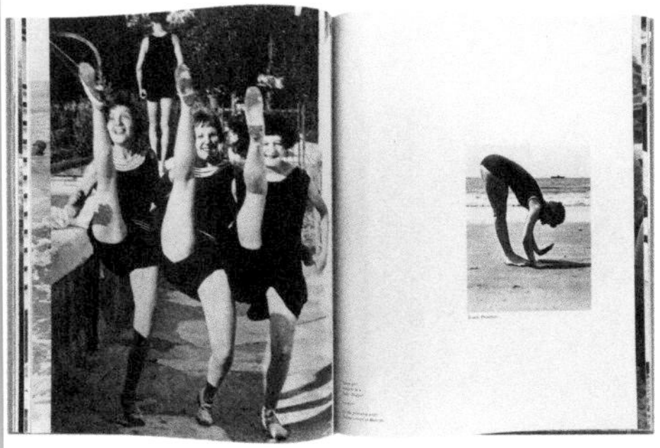

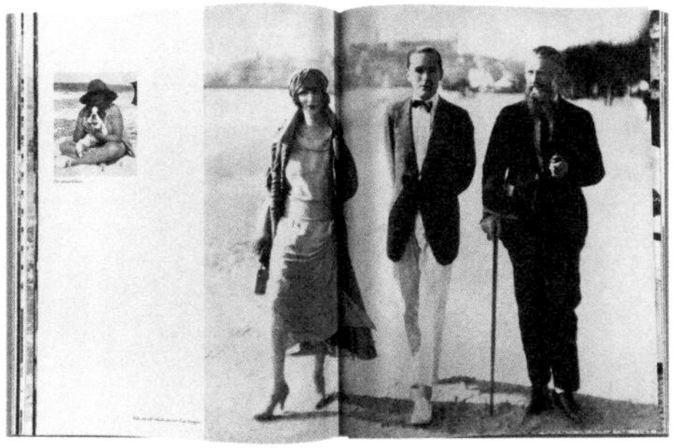

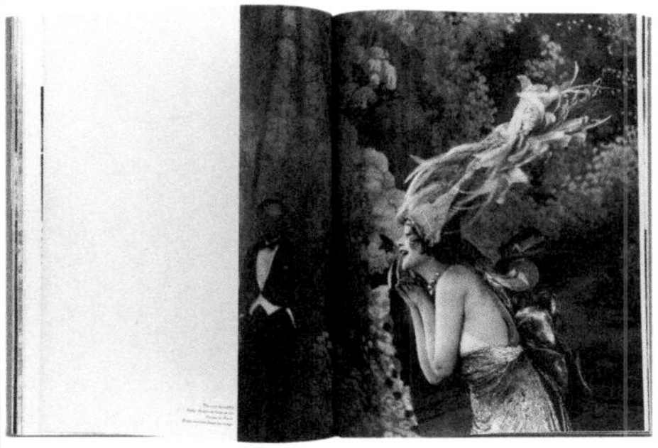

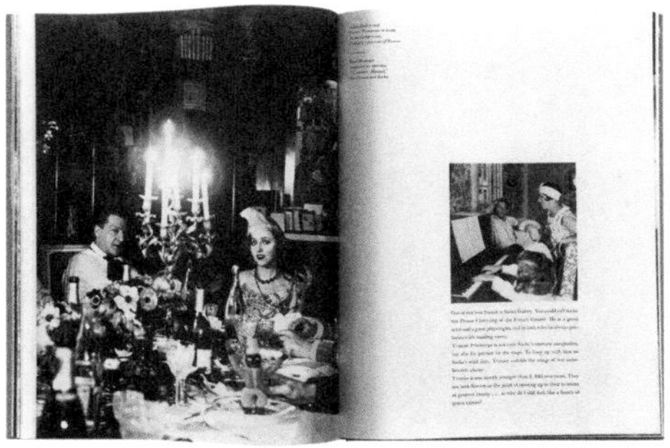

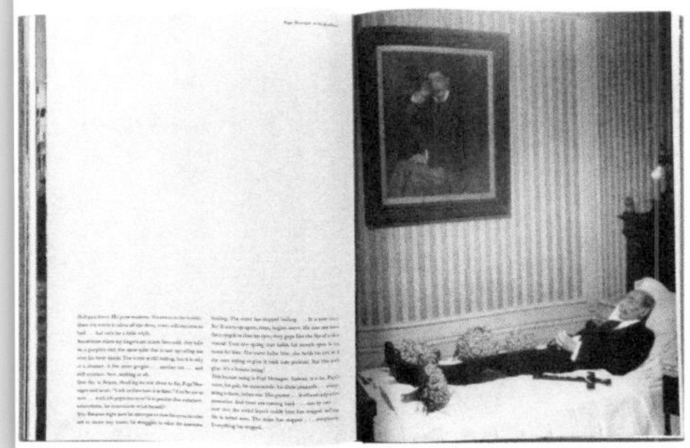

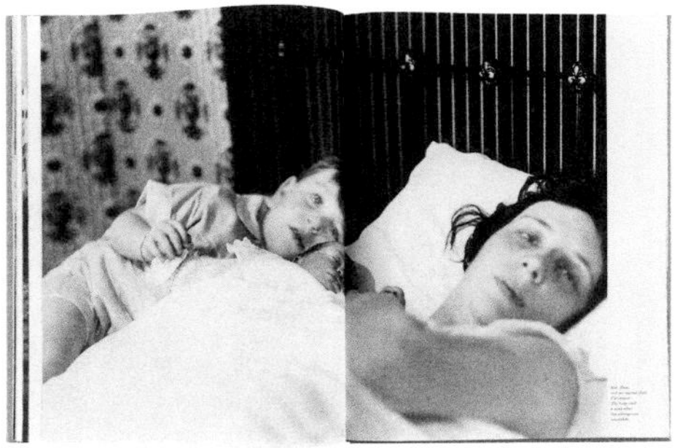

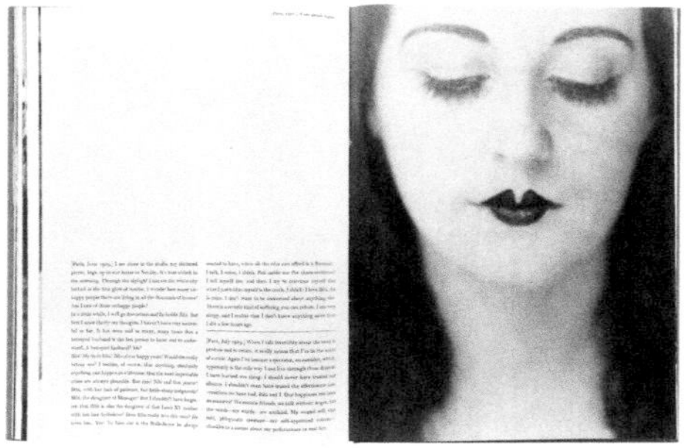

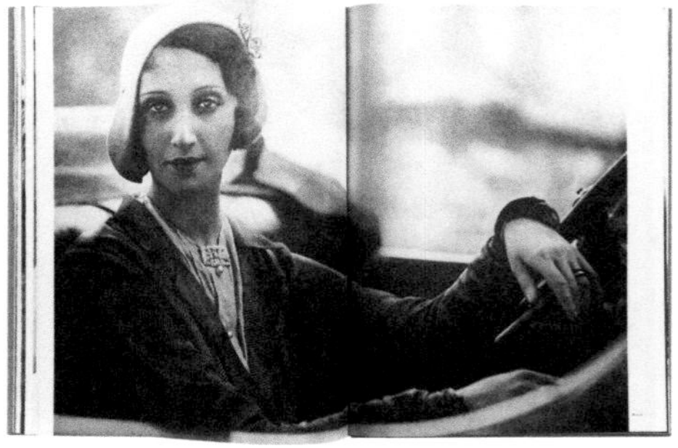

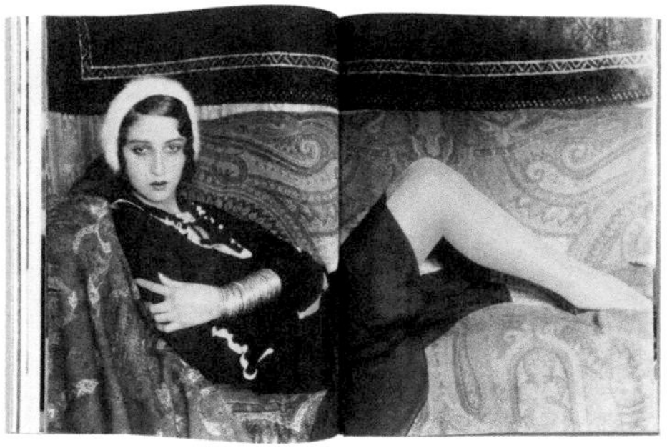

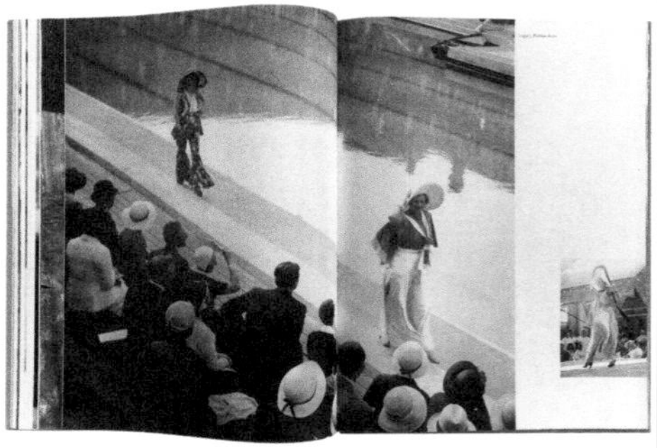

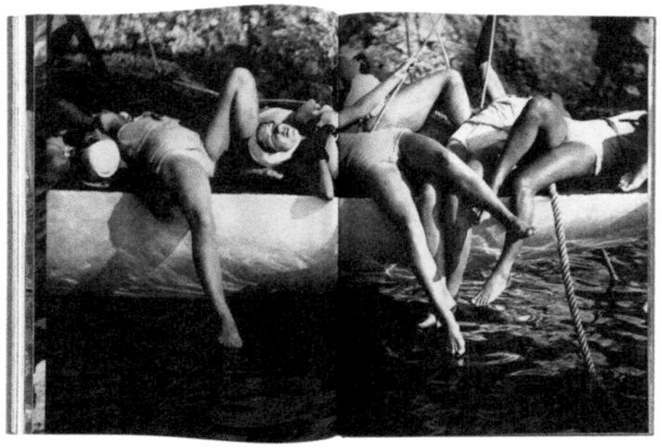

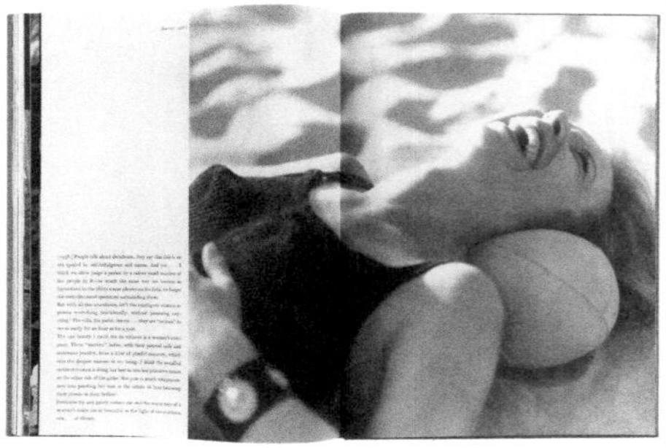

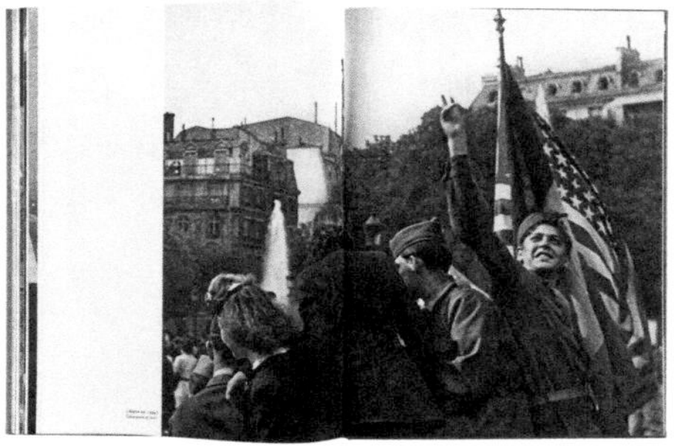

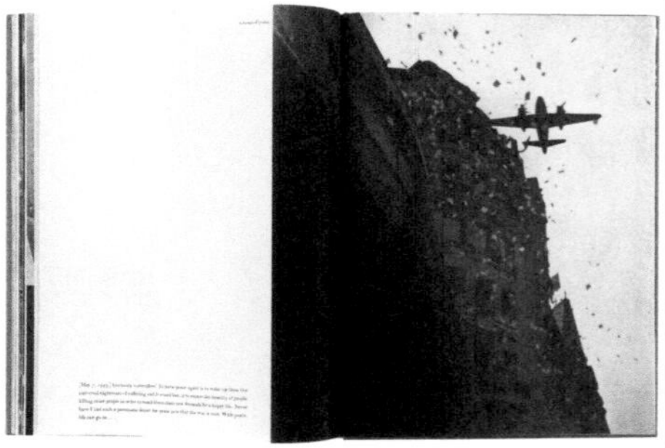

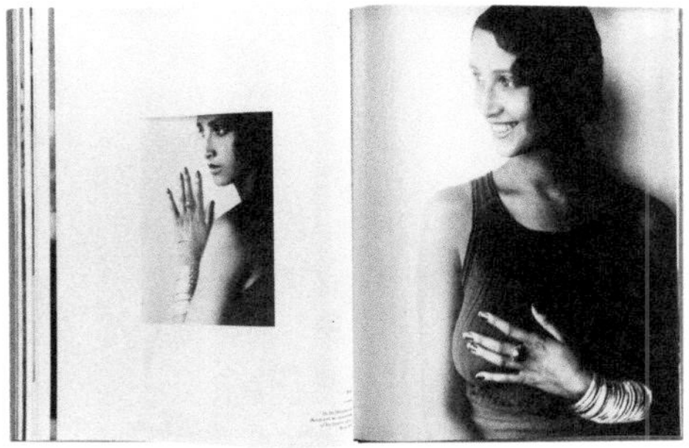

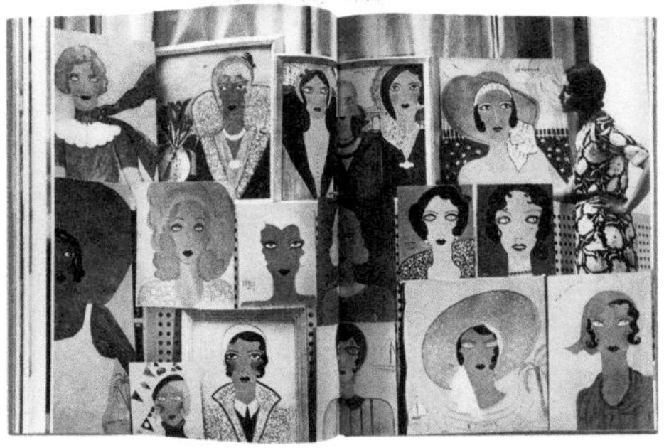

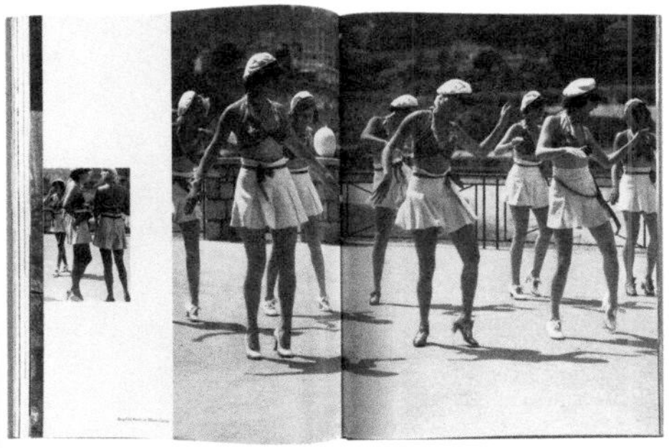

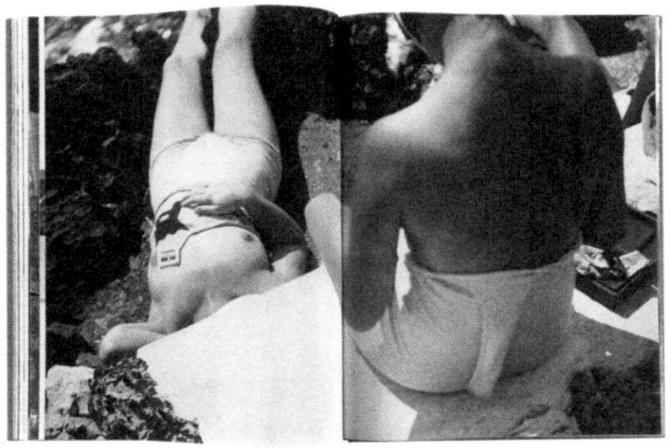

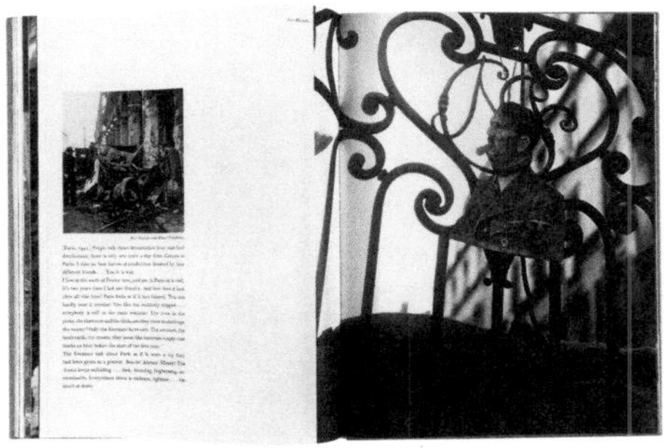

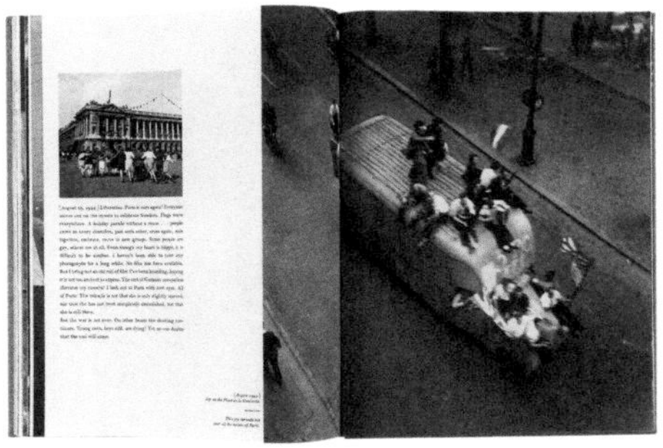

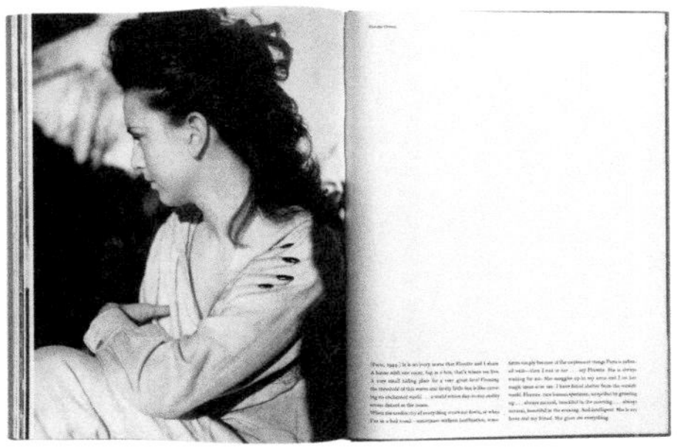

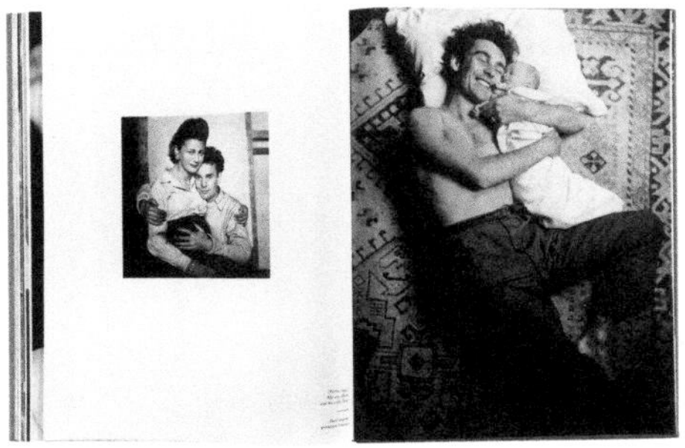

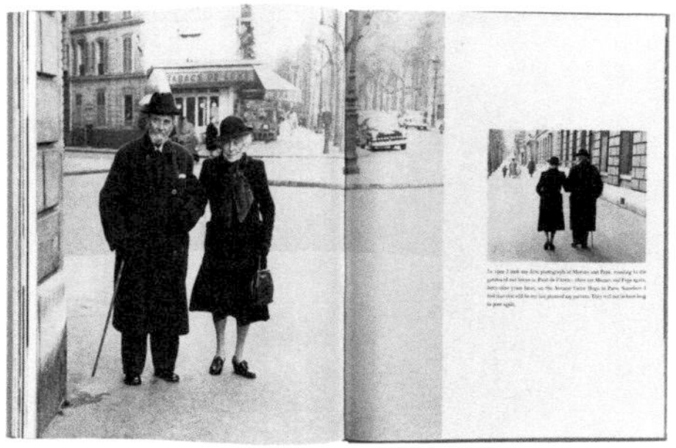

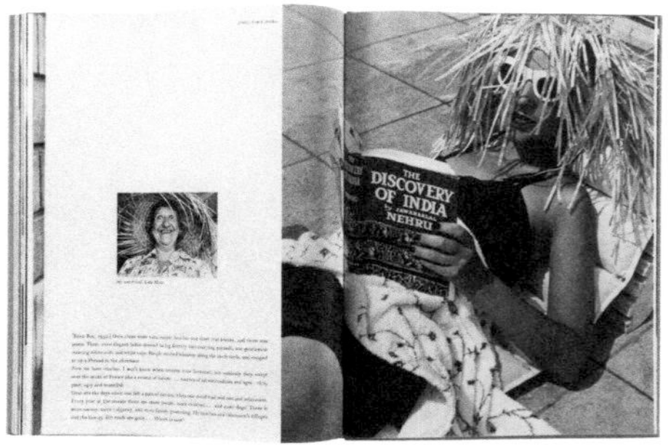
THE DISCOVERY OF INDIA
NEHRU

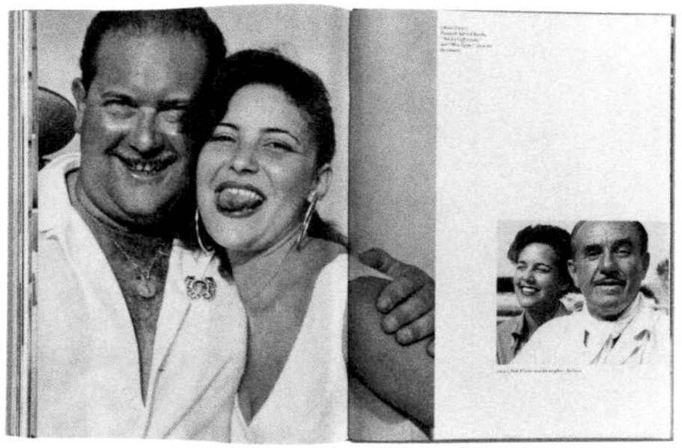

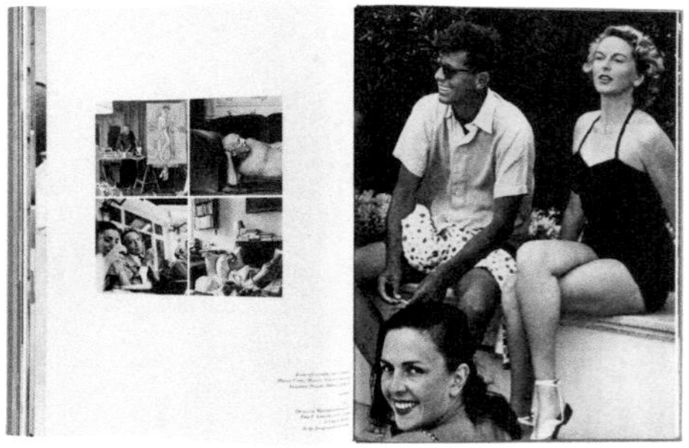

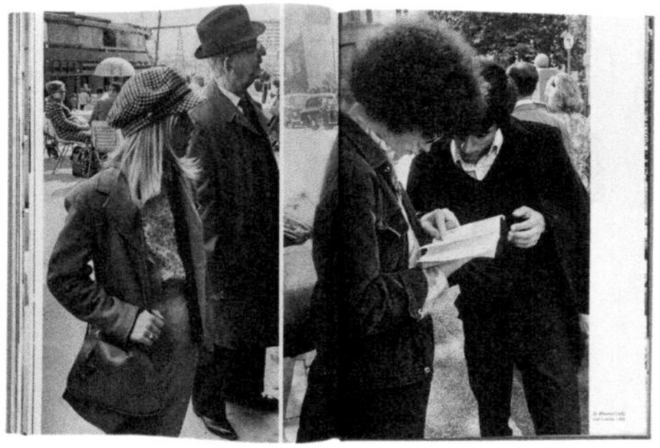

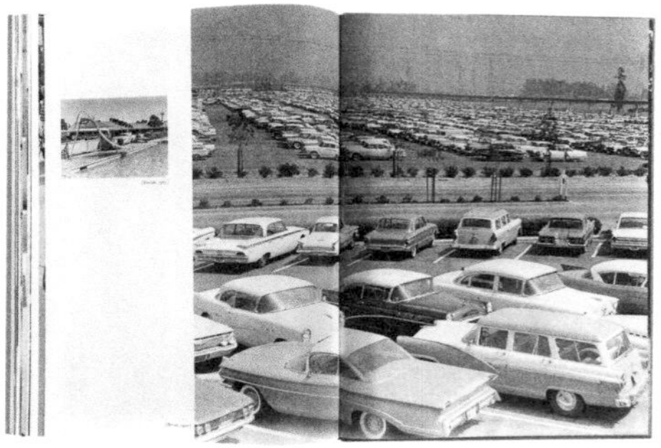

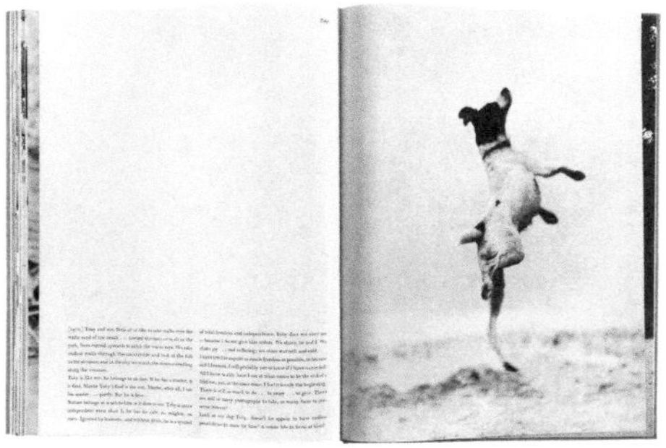

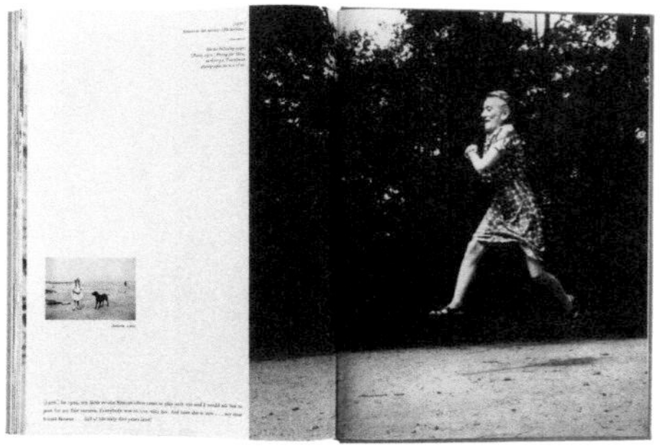

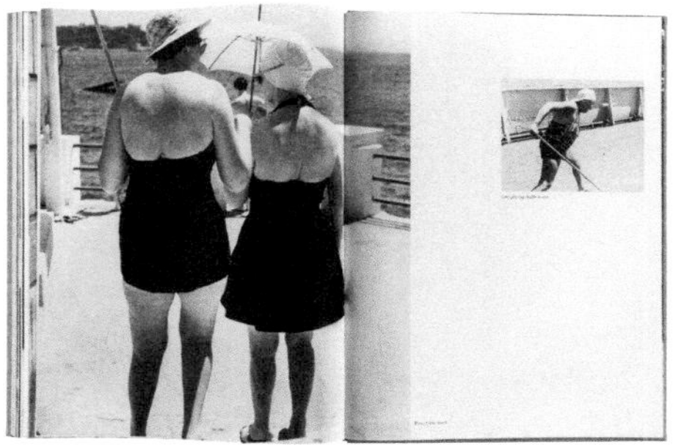

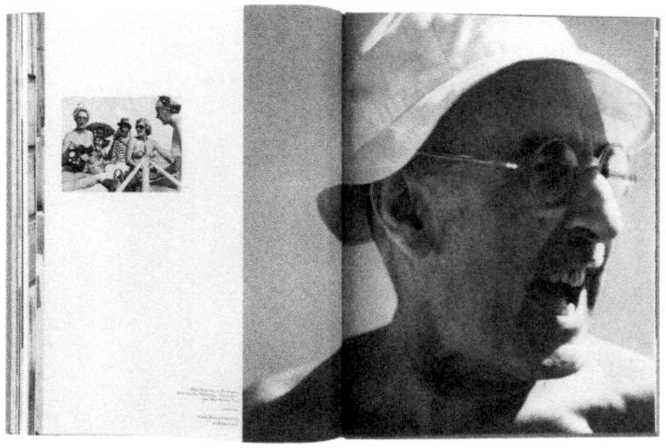

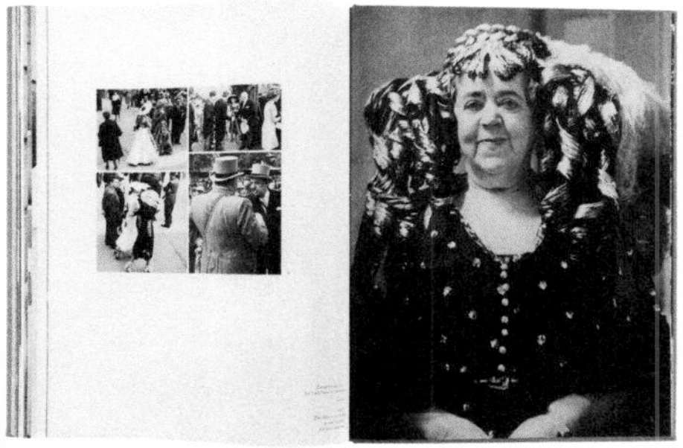

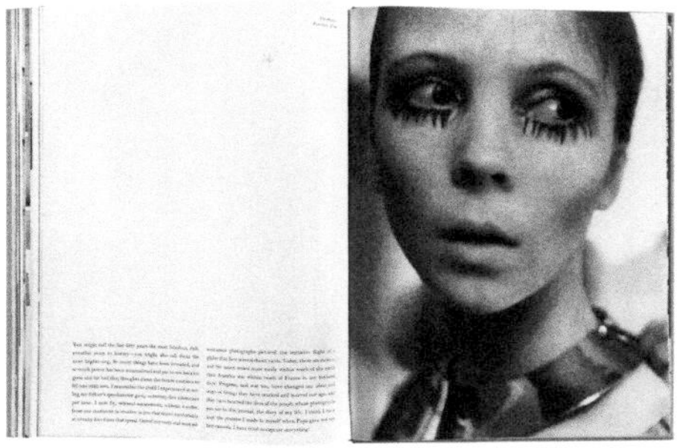

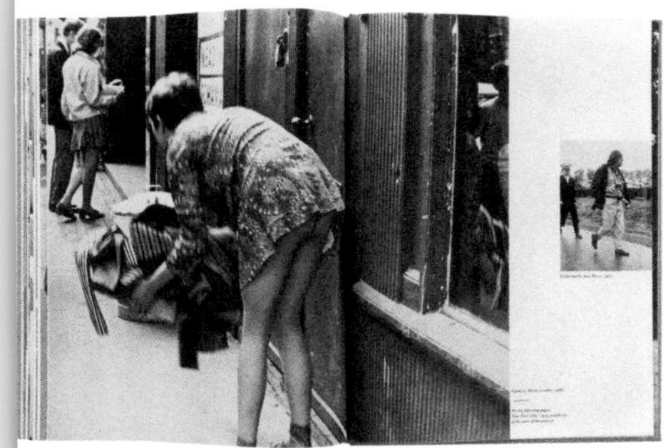

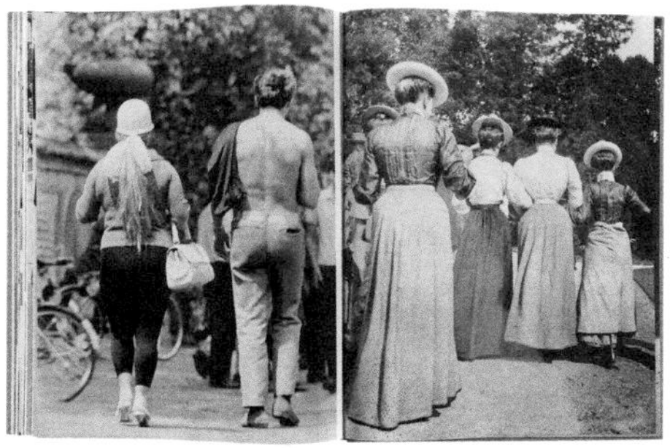

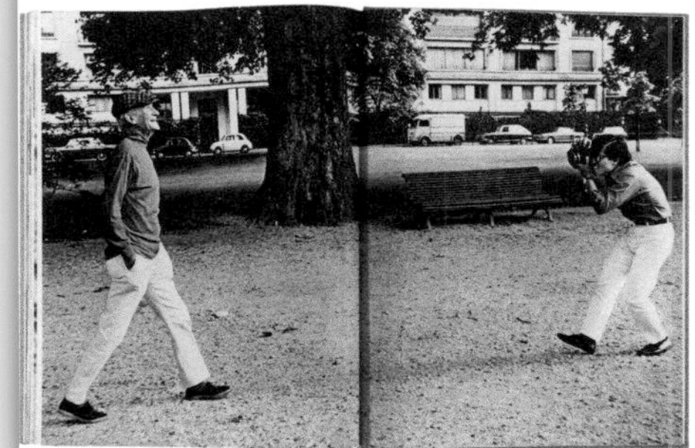

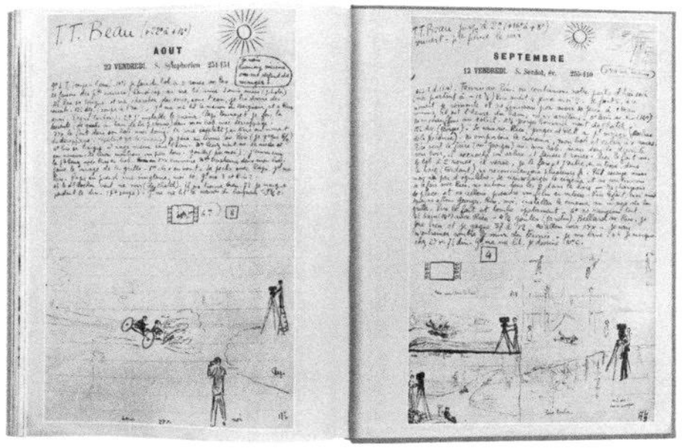
AOUT
SEPTEMBRE

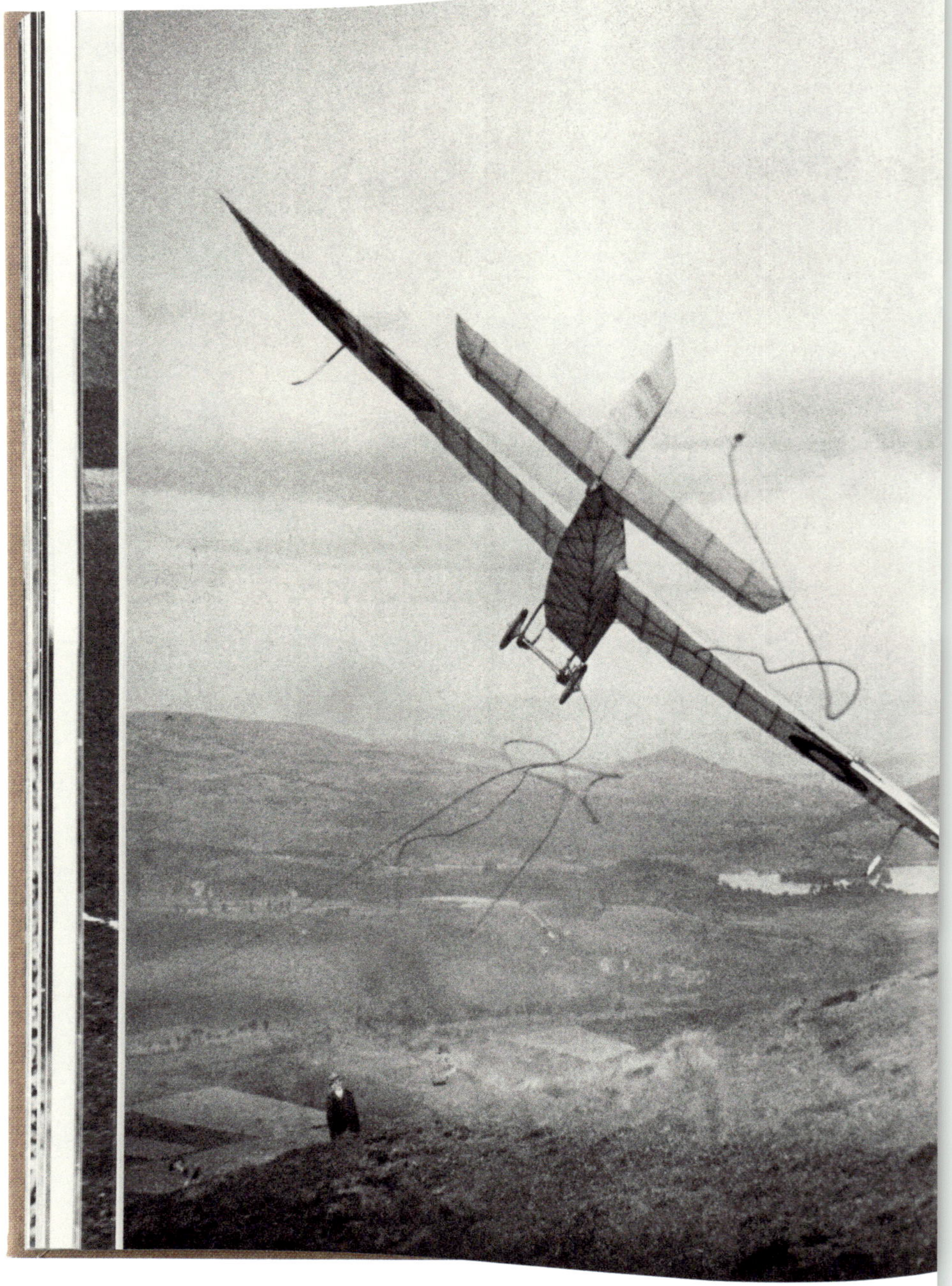

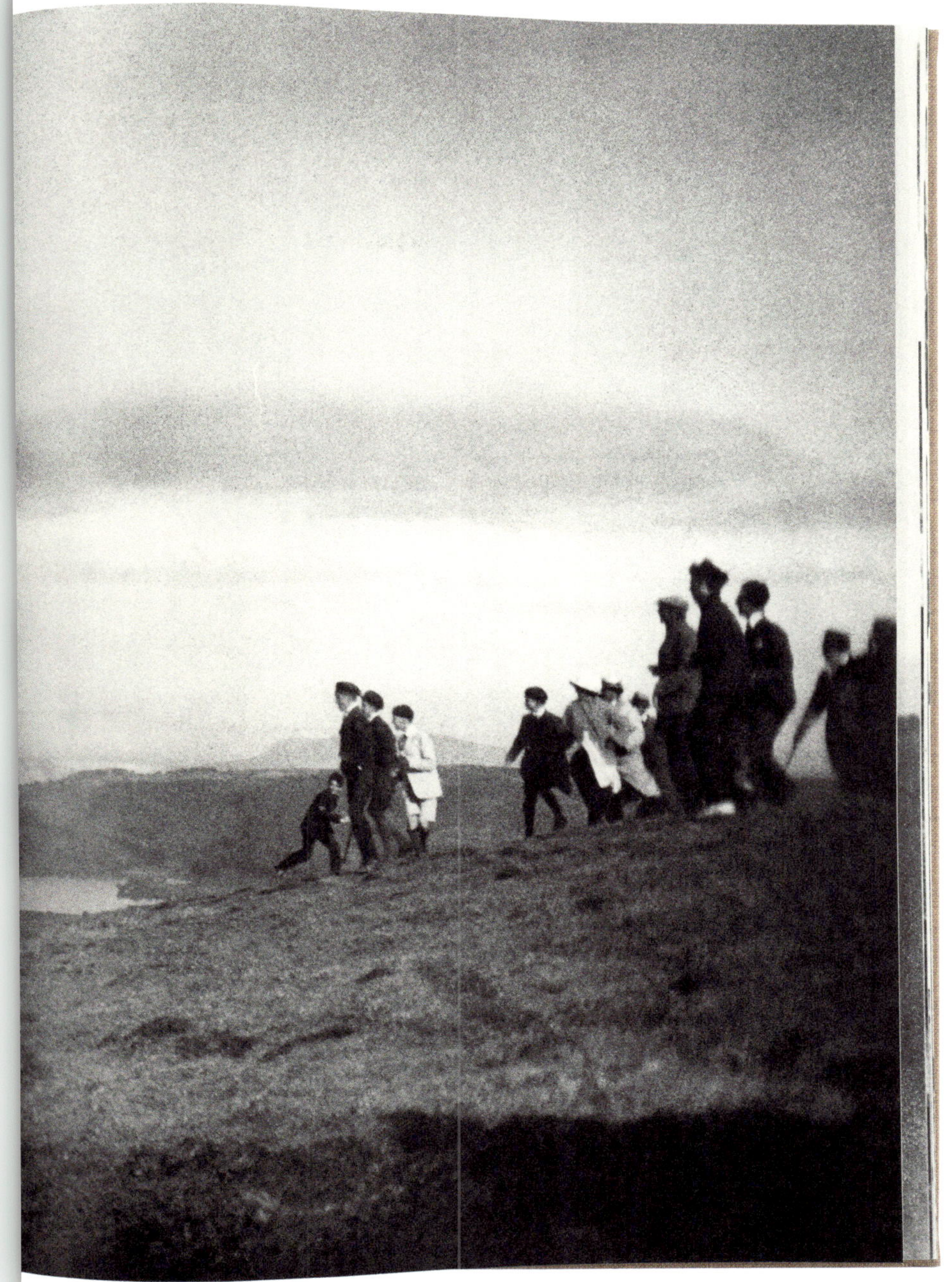

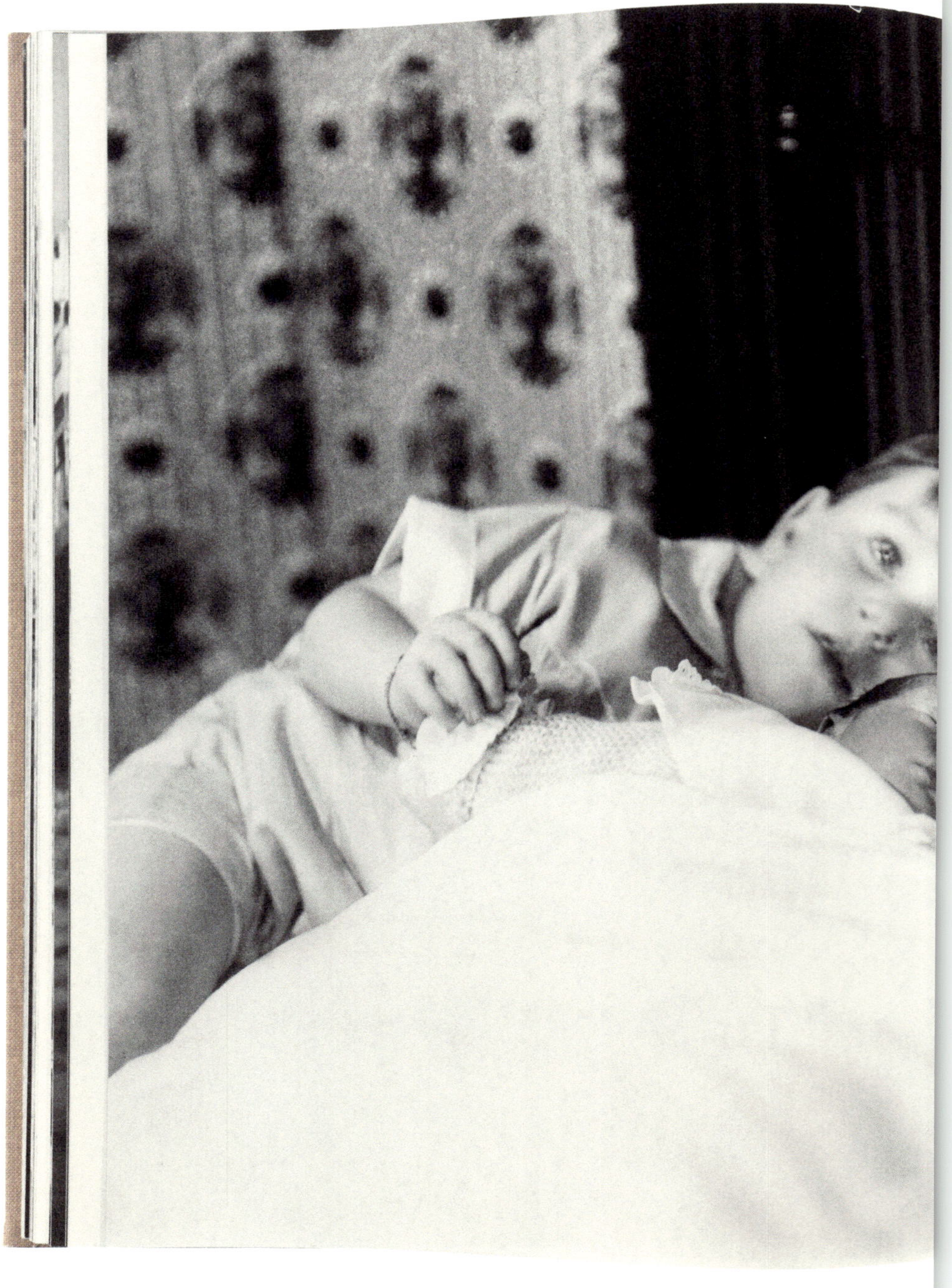

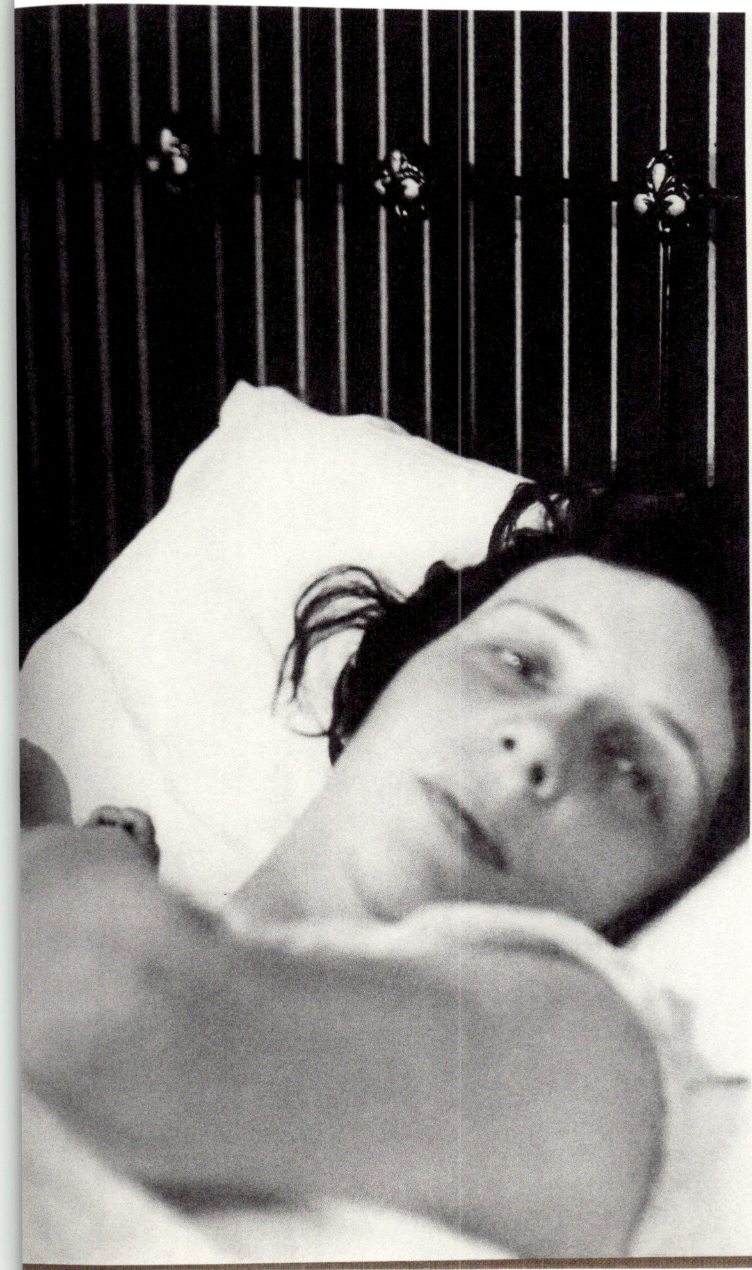

Bibi, Dani
and our second child,
Véronique.
The baby died
a week after
this photograph
was taken.

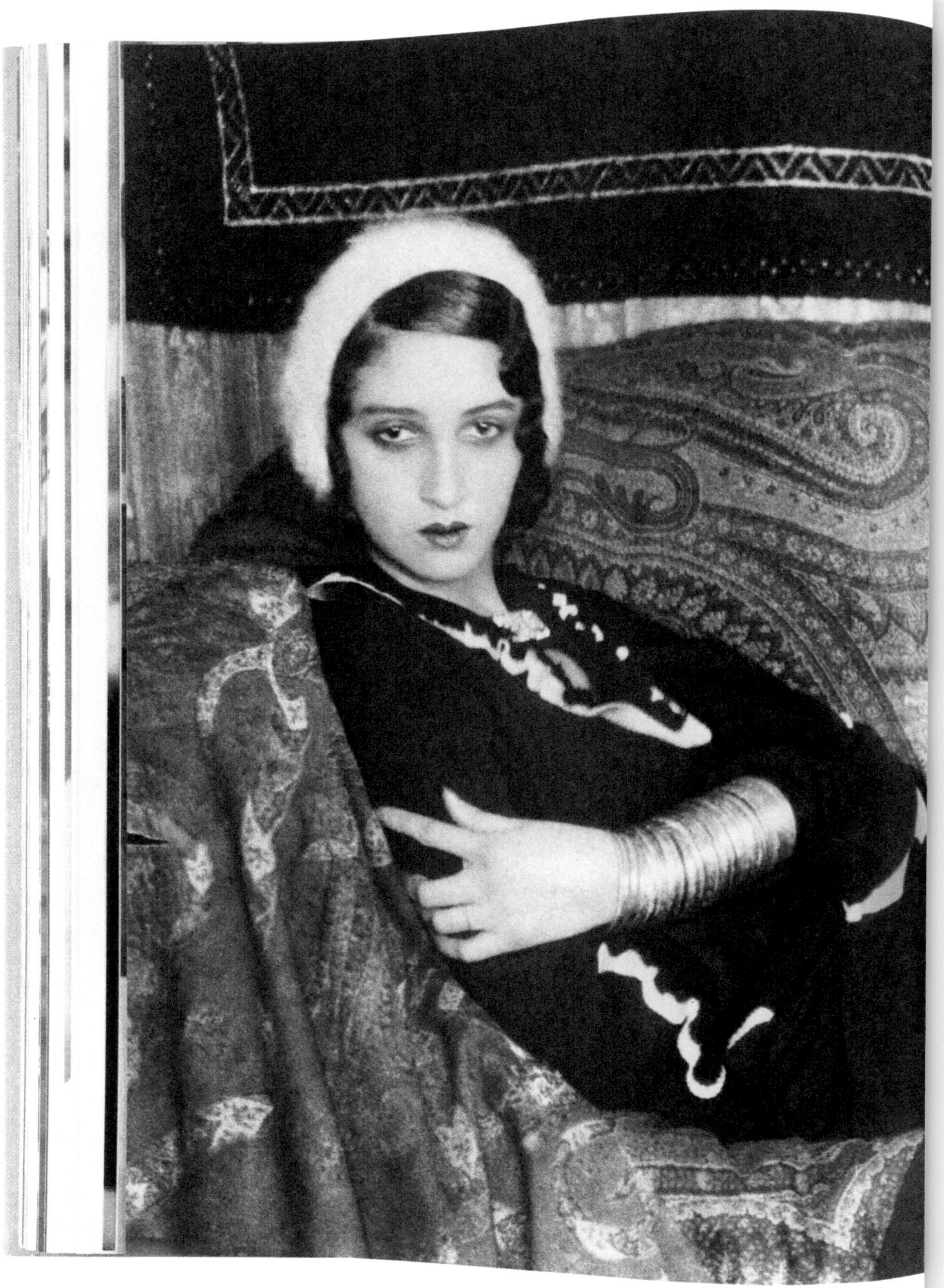

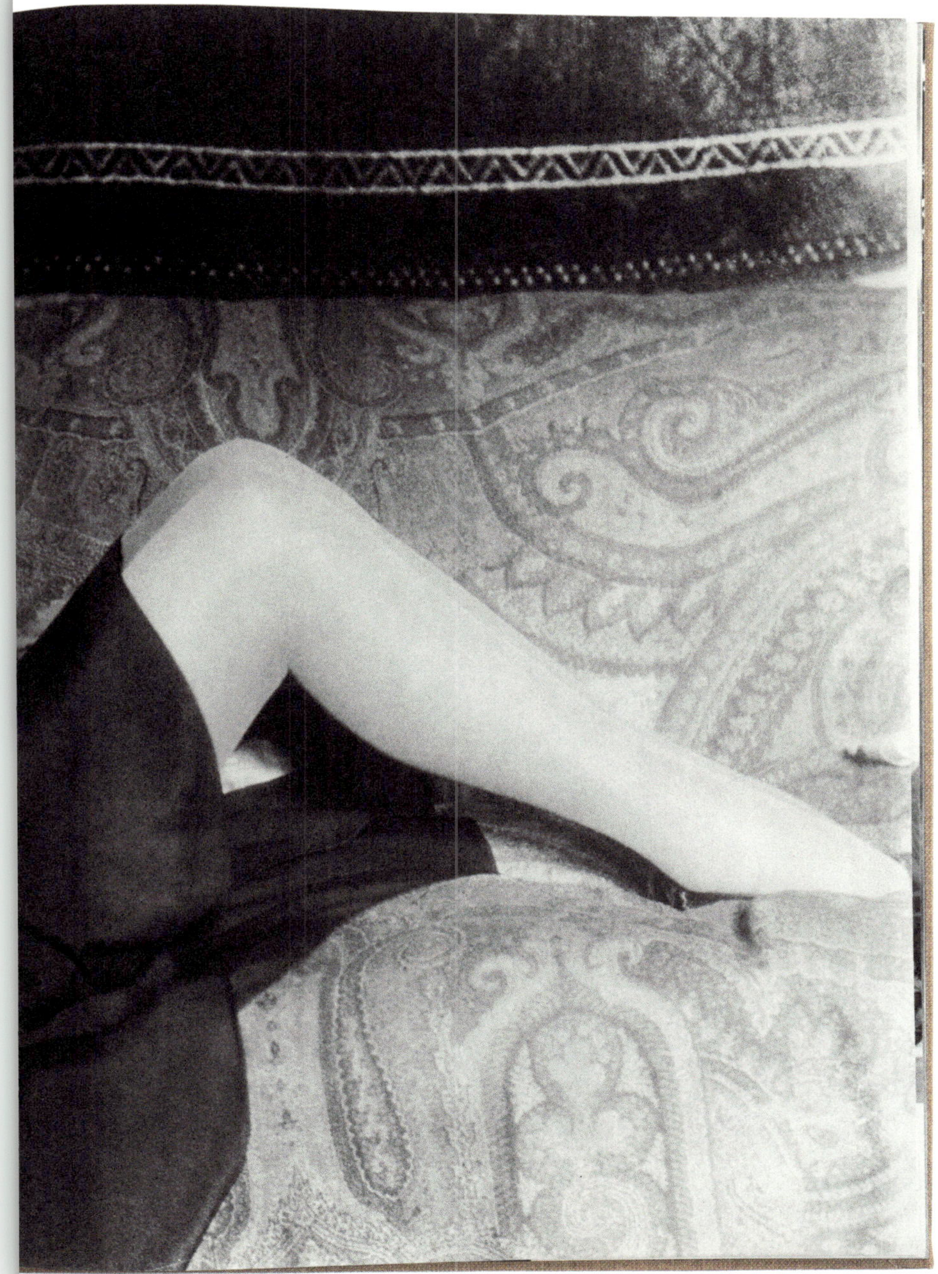

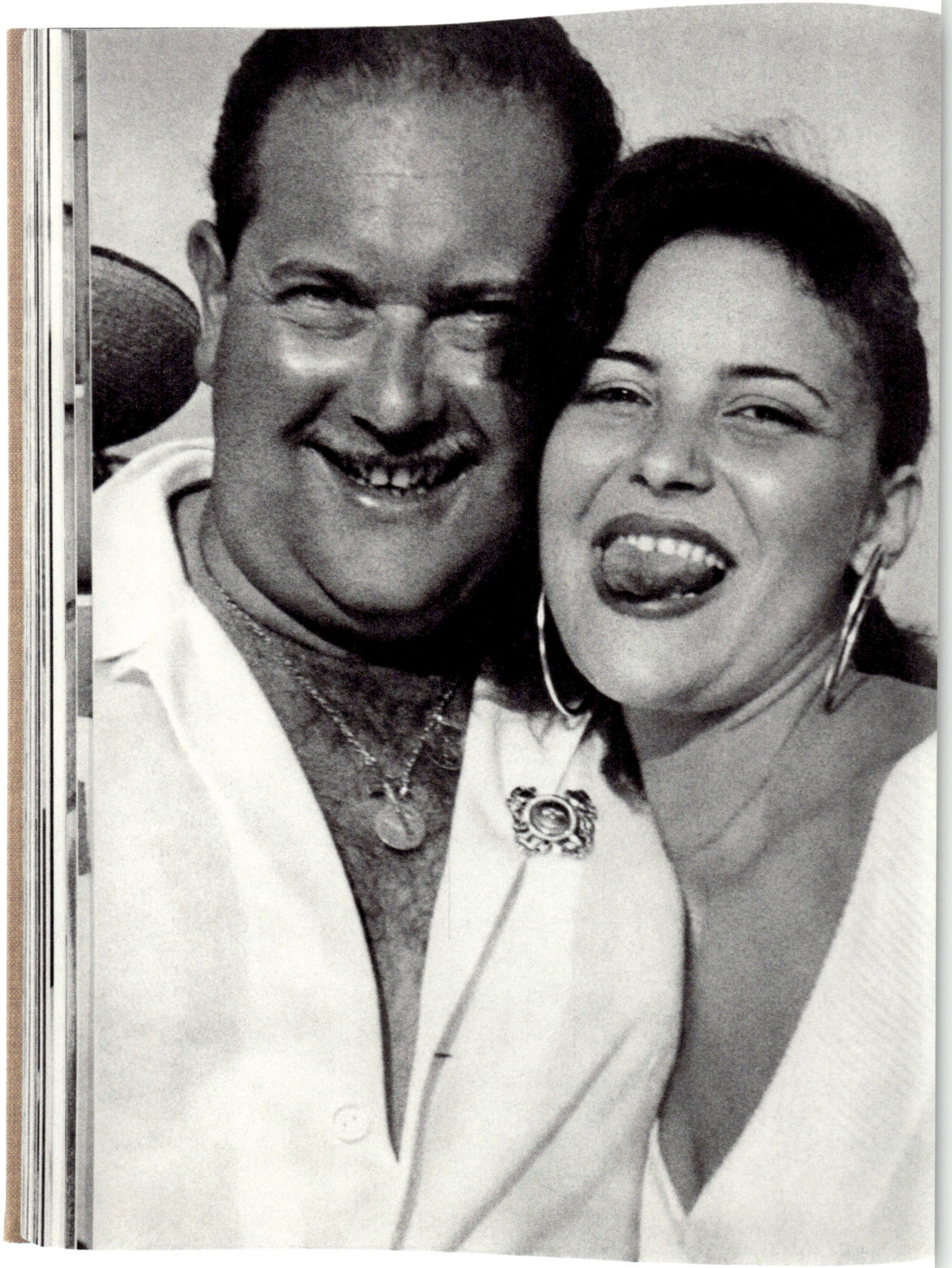

[Monte Carlo.]
Financier Gérard Bauche, "Roi des Coffre-forts," and "Miss Egypt," clown for the camera.

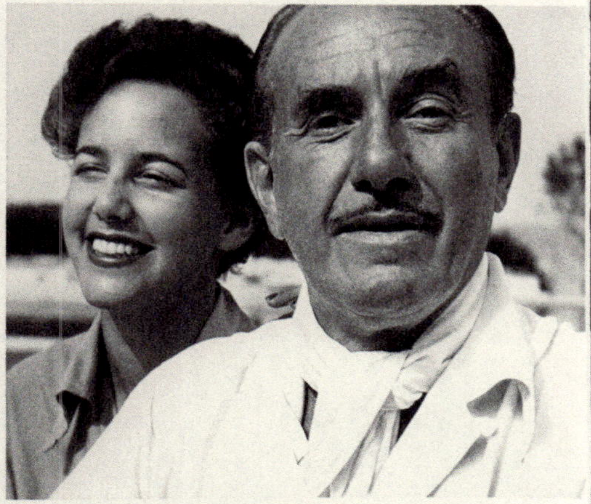

[1953.] *Jack Warner and his daughter, Barbara.*

The photographs that move me the most are stylized but what's happening is not graspable, and certainly, the how it was done is not said. … the craft is invisible.

—

Richard Avedon

The Hand of Avedon

Much as they did when creating an issue of *Harper's Bazaar*, Avedon and Feitler edited *Diary* by spreading prints on the table and pinning layouts to the studio wall. The small-size mockups of the book, with handwritten notes by Avedon, traveled between Paris and New York.

Lartigue's familial circle would be merged with the wider world of celebrities he had encountered. Parents, wives, and cousins mixed freely (if only on paper) with John Kennedy, Elsa Maxwell, Marcel Vertes, Pablo Picasso, Jean Cocteau, Marcel Achard, and Penelope Tree.

TRAVAIL DE DICK AVEDON

POUR MON LIVRE "DAIRY of a CENTURY"

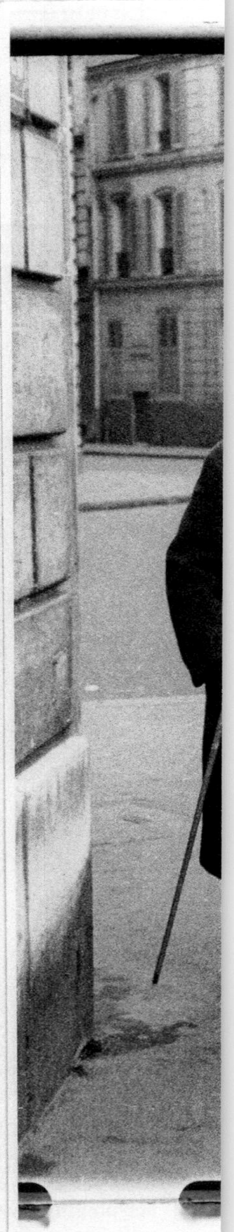

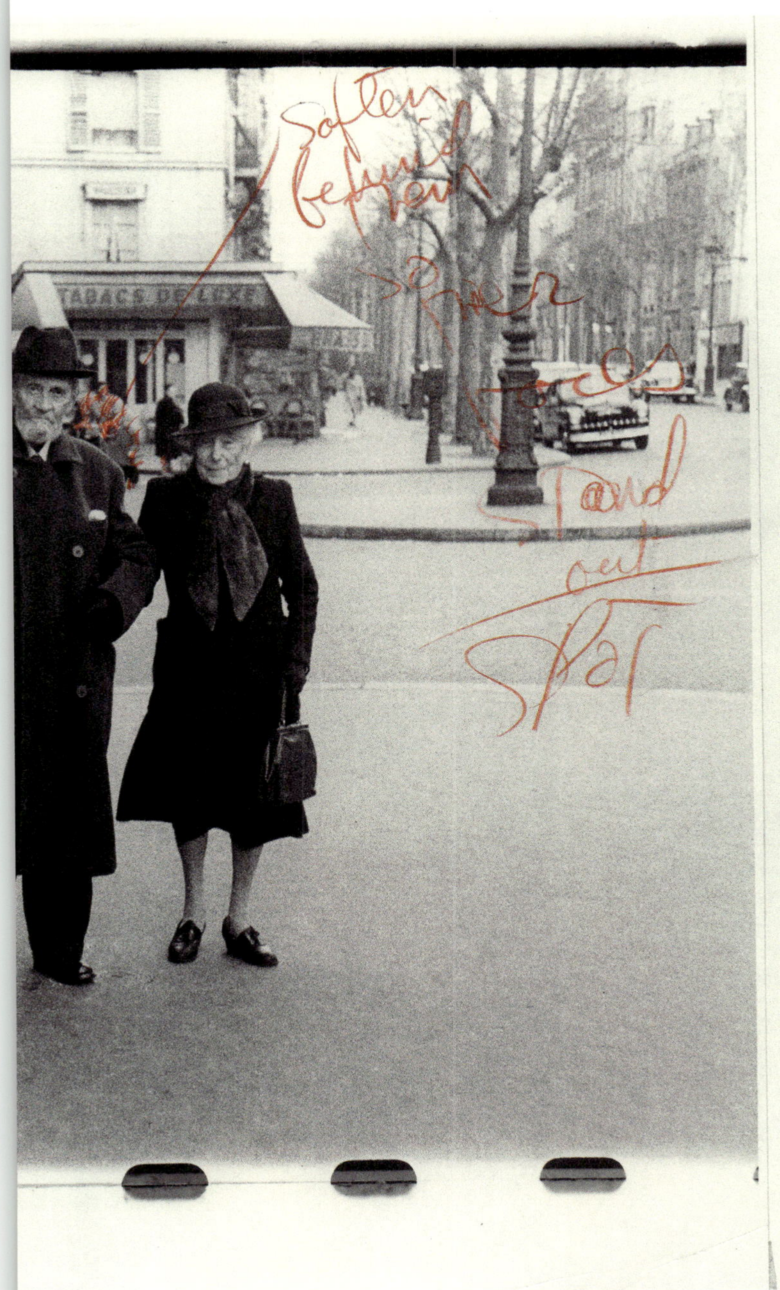

Lartigue wrote, "Dick Avedon's work on my book Diary of a Century" next to the photo Avedon had marked for the retoucher (album from 1949, page 0046R49). The page was added to the end of the 1949 album; photograph by J. H. Lartigue

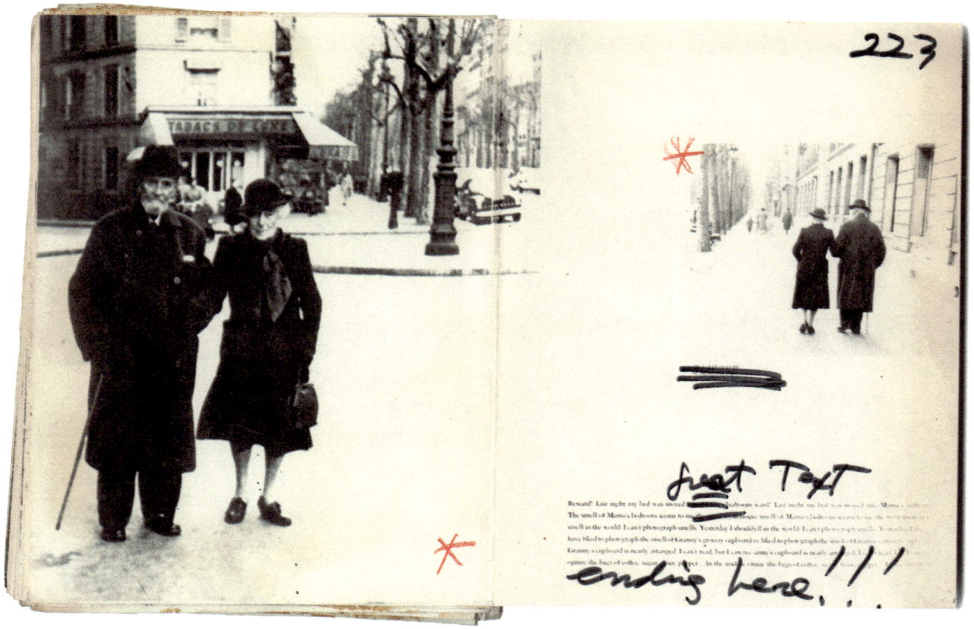

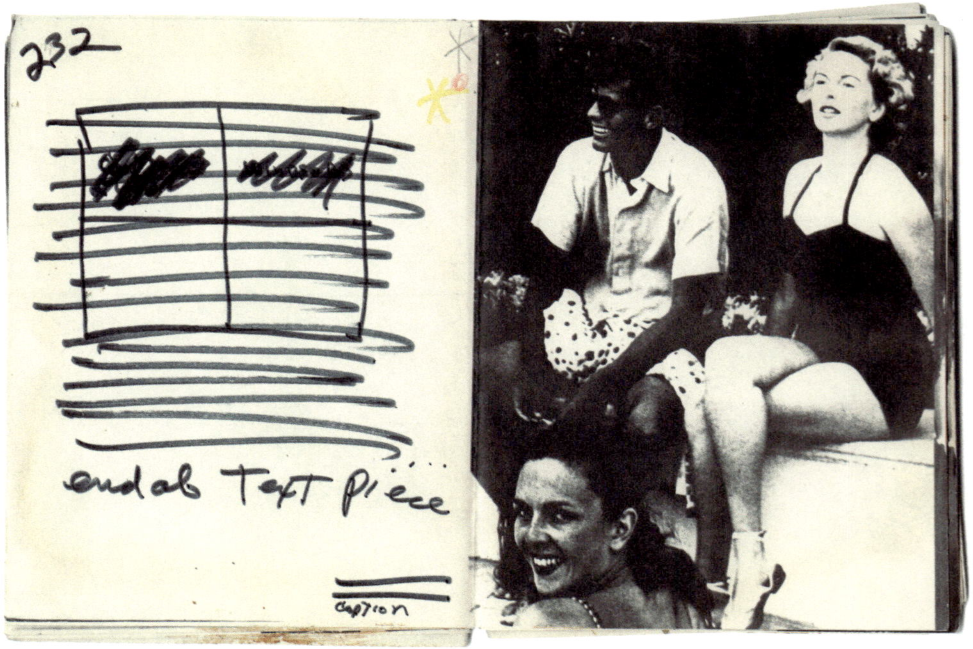

Avedon's mockups from 1969 for *Diary of a Century*

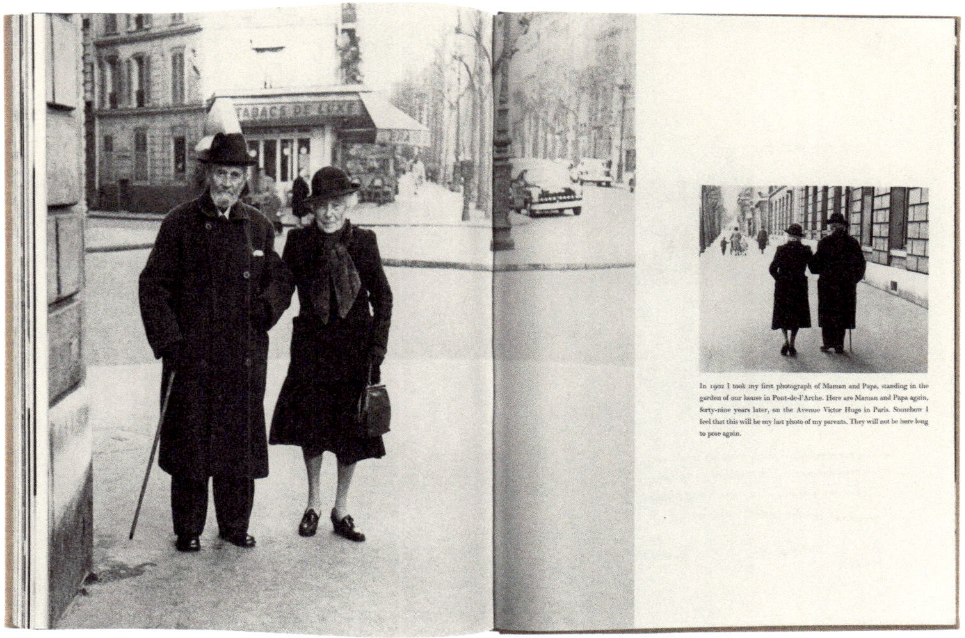

In 1902 I took my first photograph of Maman and Papa, standing in the garden of our house in Pont-de-l'Arche. Here are Maman and Papa again, forty-nine years later, on the Avenue Victor Hugo in Paris. Somehow I feel that this will be my last photo of my parents. They will not be here long to pose again.

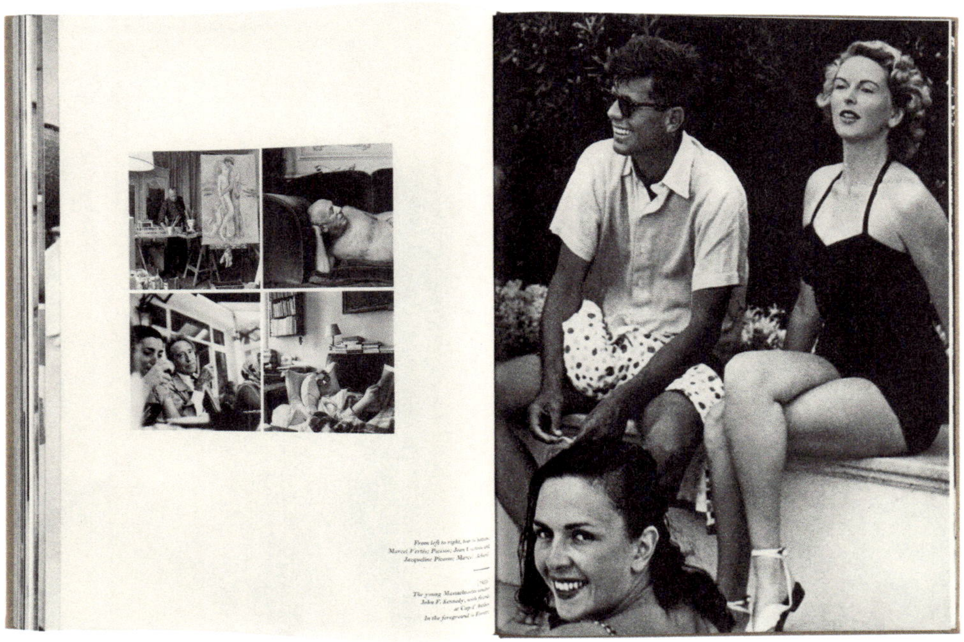
From left to right,
Marcel Vertès; Picasso; Jean
Jacqueline Picasso; Marc

The young
John F. Kennedy,
at Cap
In the foreground

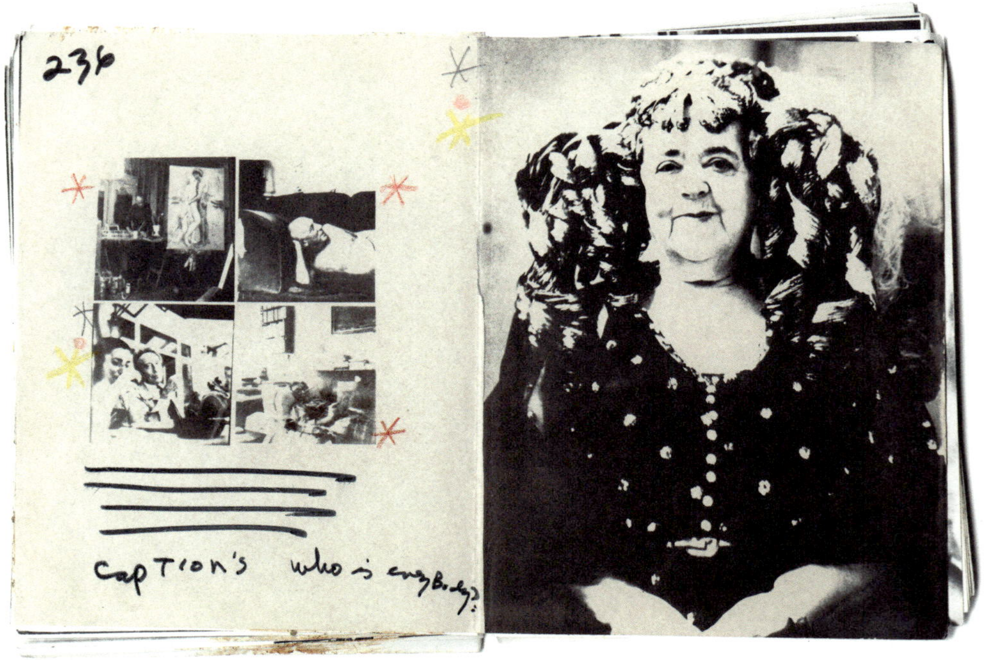

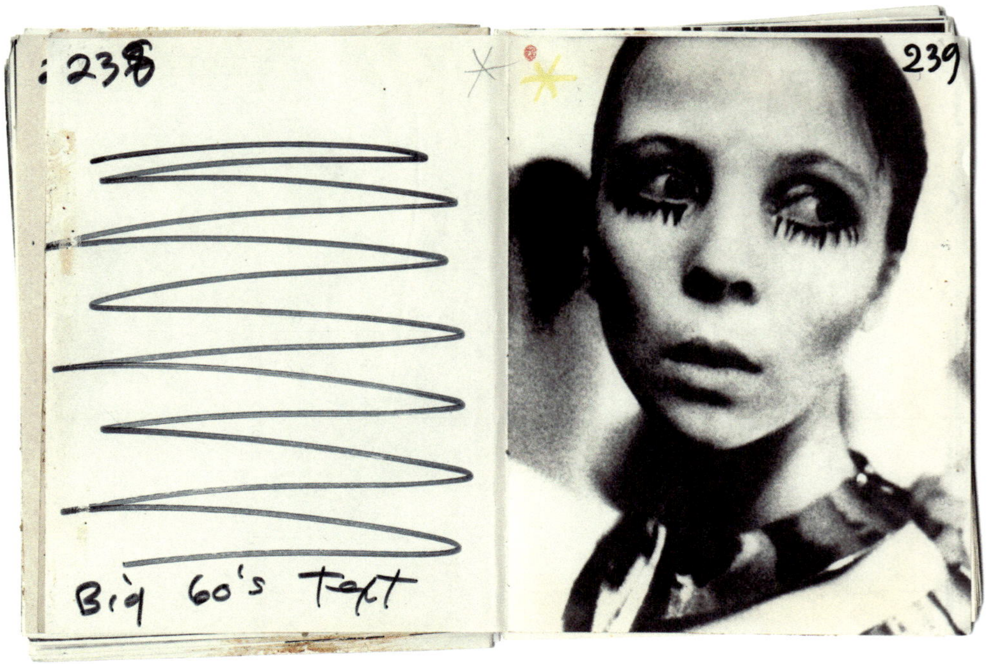

Avedon's mockups from 1969 for *Diary of a Century*

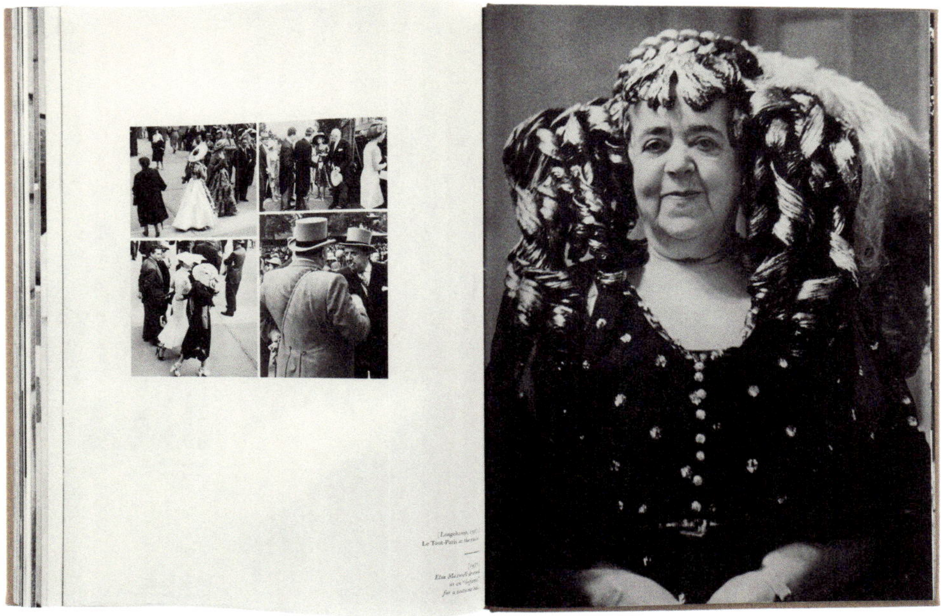

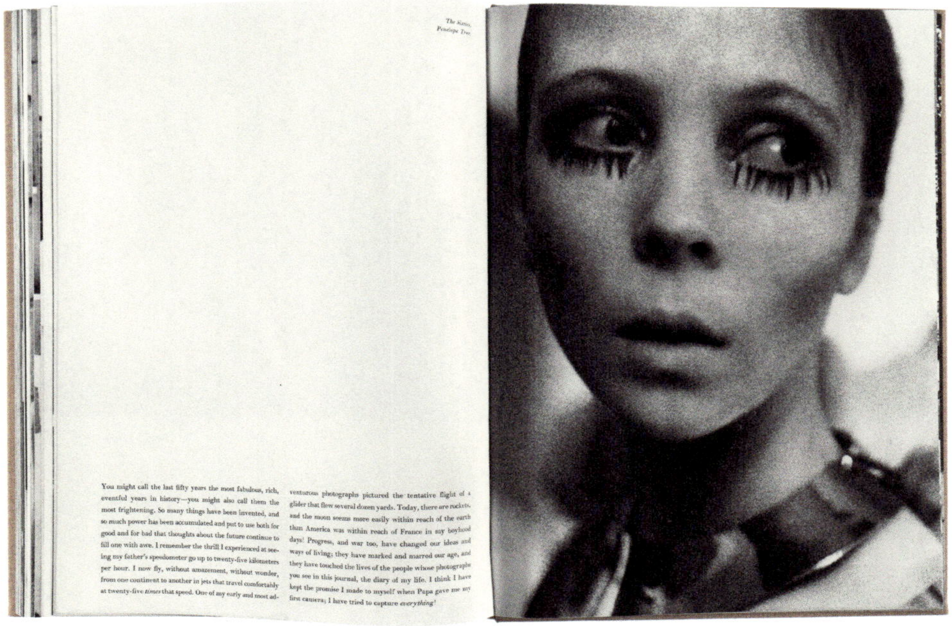

You might call the last fifty years the most fabulous, rich, eventful years in history—you might also call them the most frightening. So many things have been invented, and so much power has been accumulated and put to use both for good and for bad that thoughts about the future continue to fill one with awe. I remember the thrill I experienced at seeing my father's speedometer go up to twenty-five kilometers per hour. I now fly, without amazement, without wonder, from one continent to another in jets that travel comfortably at twenty-five *times* that speed. One of my early and most adventurous photographs pictured the tentative flight of a glider that flew several dozen yards. Today, there are rockets, and the moon seems more easily within reach of the earth than America was within reach of France in my boyhood days! Progress, and war too, have changed our ideas and ways of living; they have marked and marred our age, and they have touched the lives of the people whose photographs you see in this journal, the diary of my life. I think I have kept the promise I made to myself when Papa gave me my first camera; I have tried to capture *everything*!

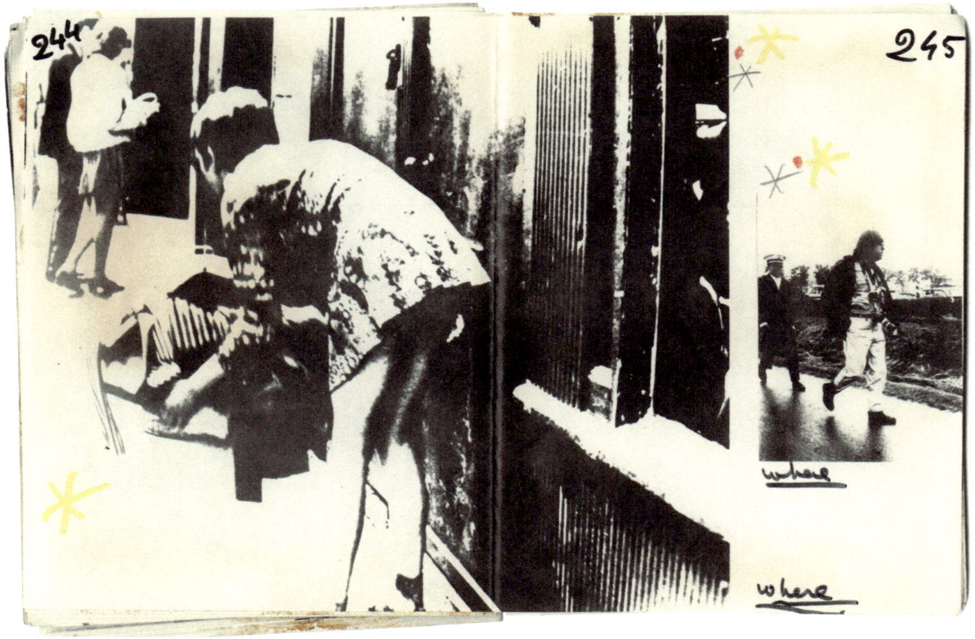

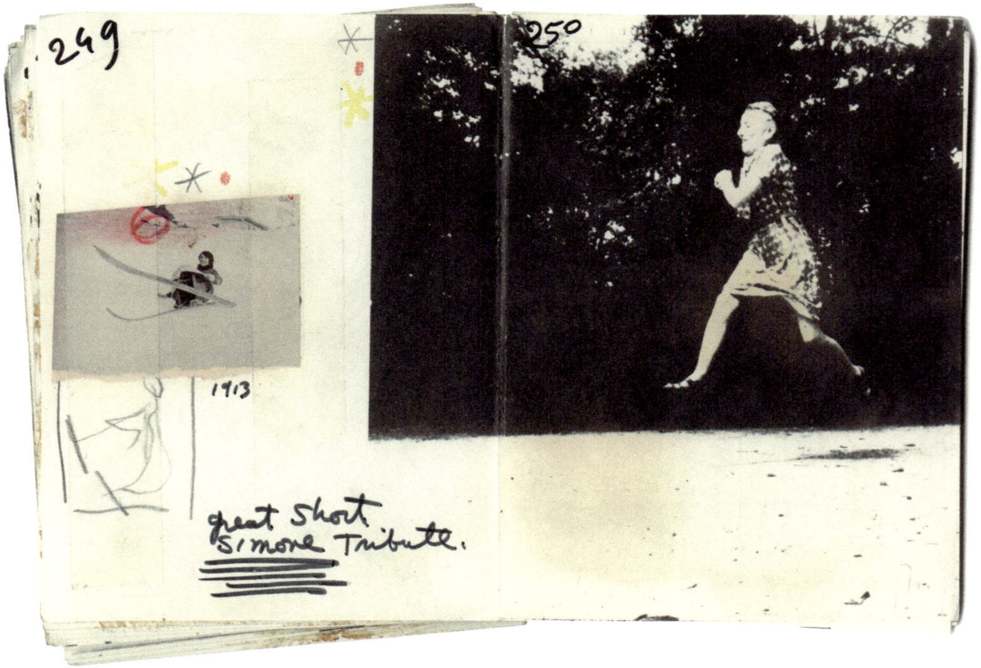

Avedon's mockups from 1969 for *Diary of a Century*

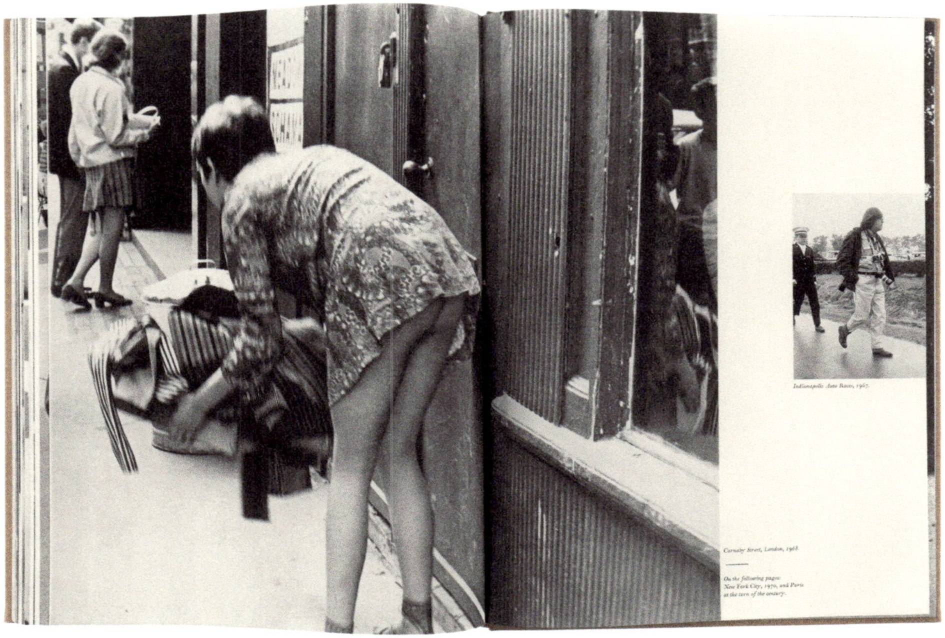

Indianapolis Auto Races, 1967.
Carnaby Street, London, 1968.
On the following pages: New York City, 1970, and Paris at the turn of the century.

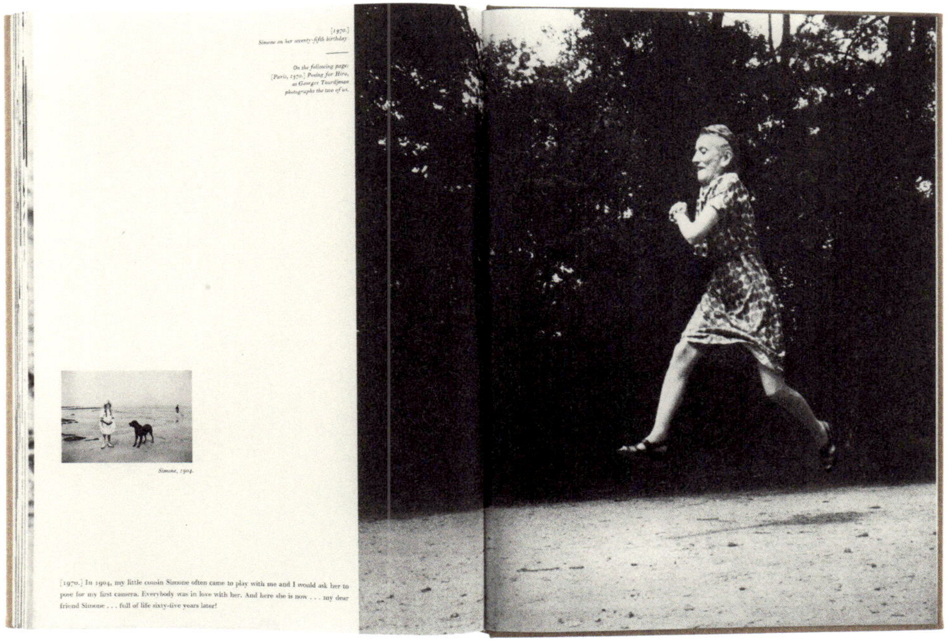

[1970.] Simone on her seventy-fifth birthday
On the following page: [Paris, 1970.] Posing for Hiro, as Georges Tourdjman photographs the two of us.
Simone, 1904.
[1970.] In 1904, my little cousin Simone often came to play with me and I would ask her to pose for my first camera. Everybody was in love with her. And here she is now . . . my dear friend Simone . . . full of life sixty-five years later!

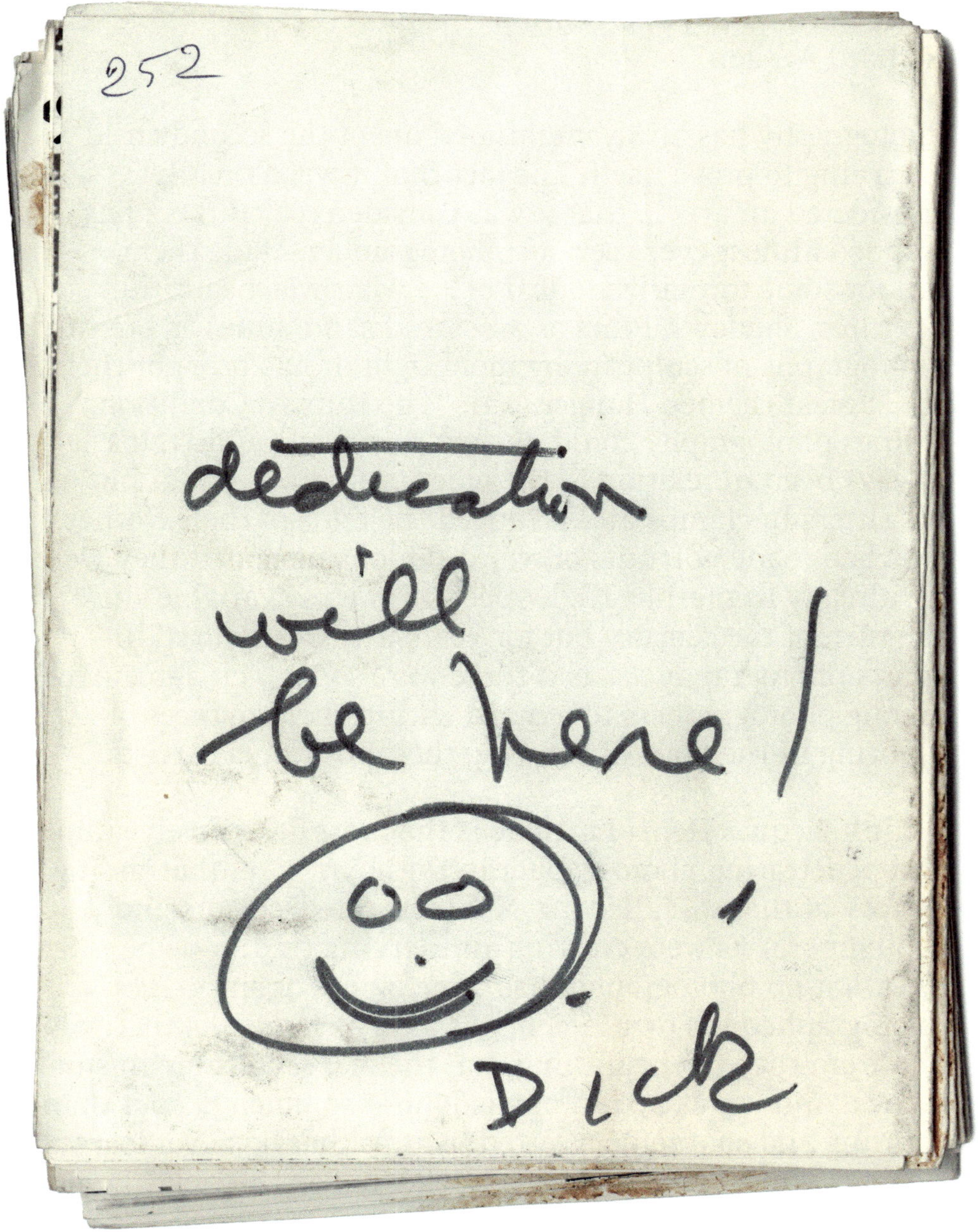

In this 1969 mockup for *Diary of a Century*, Avedon indicated his wish to put the dedication by Lartigue on the last page.
In the final version of the book, it appears at the beginning.

Afterword, ***Diary of a Century***

Richard Avedon

Photography has always reminded me of the second child . . . trying to prove itself. The fact that it wasn't really considered an art . . . that it was considered a craft . . . has trapped almost every serious photographer. Made them fall for some formalized ideal of . . . what was beautiful. Textures. Shadows. Pears as asses and sand dunes as breasts. Photographs of sculpture by moonlight. It has brought them to . . . great themes. Hunger. War. "The Human Condition." Things photography could do that painting couldn't. It's always been in relation to the older brother . . . Nadar put his sitters in clamps and arranged the folds of their clothes. Steichen made portraits of world-famous men as if they were . . . already in marble. High-speed film was available since the turn of the century but for years it was only used in sports photography . . . as if there were some tacit agreement among photographers to remain within the provinces of painting in the hope of assuring their position as artists.

I think Jacques Henri Lartigue is the most deceptively simple and penetrating photographer in the short . . . embarrassing history of that so-called art. While his predecessors and contemporaries were creating and serving traditions he did what no photographer has done before or since. He photographed his own life. It was as if he knew instinctively and from the very beginning that the real secrets lay in small things. And it was a kind of wisdom — so much deeper than training and so often perverted by it — that he never lost. There is almost no one in this book who isn't a friend . . . no moment that wasn't a private one.

Lartigue never exhibited his pictures until 1962. He never thought of himself as a photographer. It was just something he did every day . . . every day for seventy years. Out of the love of it. And every day his eye refined and his skill with a camera grew. He was an amateur . . . never burdened by ambition or the need to be a serious person.

But it would be a great mistake to credit his artistry merely to the fact that he was not corrupted by professionalism. Or to say that his work is the product of accident . . . that his photographs are extraordinary because the people around him were. Or the time in which he lived. Hundreds of children with similar backgrounds were given cameras in those days — but they never became Lartigues. And accidents are capricious. They just don't happen that often. They can't produce a single body of work so consistently brilliant. Lartigue is not a reporter and his best photographs are not those gained by chance.

From the earliest possible age Lartigue kept a little diary. At the top of each page there was always a drawing of the sun or a cloud . . . and some initials: *T. B., B., T. T. B.* They stood for *Très beau. Beau. Très très beau* . . . That was the weather. It was always a good day. It almost never rained. Ever . . . And then there would be a quick description of what he did that day. Who visited the house. Where they went . . . And half the page devoted to drawings of what he'd photographed, because the developing was a very risky process and often the pictures didn't come out. So, afraid that he might never see the pictures that he'd taken, he would draw from memory what he'd photographed. And in the diaries, which went on for many years, you can see the photographs that have since become masterpieces . . . drawn. And the miracle of these little drawings is that he had captured exactly the way a scarf had been caught by the wind the moment he clicked the shutter. And they're accurate. Absolutely accurate. Which means a perfect memory . . . And a complete sense of what he'd wanted. And this obsessiveness went on every year of his life. The files. The scrapbooks. They're all over the apartment. The perfection of those files. In a second, he can find any glass negative from . . . 1911 — neatly kept in perfect condition.

And the events he photographs . . . so many of them are the result of his own invention. He creates them. For example, I had invited him to lunch at my studio one day . . . he and his wife, Florette. It was a bit of an occasion . . . so we had special food. A little French . . . And he was in full form. Laughing. Telling stories. And suddenly, at the peak of his spirits, he reached over for a carrot and toasted us all with it. I took another carrot and toasted him back. And as I raised my hand, his camera came out and . . . click. A picture of me toasting everyone with a carrot!

And that's the secret. Bichonnade didn't just jump down the stairs like that on her way to . . . the Métro. It was Lartigue who *made* her do that. And he was ten years old at the time . . . And his suggestions are rarely direct. They're oblique. They come from impulses, not ideas. I'm sure he didn't say, "Bichonnade, jump down the steps." I'm sure he leaped down the steps himself and she followed him but by the time she did, he was there with his camera . . . Obviously Simone didn't go into the Bois on her seventy-fifth birthday and leap around. Nor did the entire family just happen to climb into bed together. He *made* those pictures happen.

His photographs are so . . . palpable. They imply things that happened before and after the photographs were taken. They remind us of what we were never there to know . . . The uncles fighting — probably my favorite photograph in the entire book. There are two uncles. They're sitting on a pole that's extended over the pool . . . and they're having a pillow fight. In the distance is a woman. We don't know who she is. And somehow . . . from the angle of the photograph . . . it seems to have been taken by a little boy who's been told to take his nap . . . and he's looked out of the window because he's heard laughter . . . that grownup laughter. I mean I think uncles are the most important thing you can have . . . as a child. And the quality the print has taken on over the years . . . with the edges sort of burnt away. If there was be a sort of physical quality of memory . . . a physicalization of memory. It's like a photograph in a dream . . . And what did that fight mean? Was it really all in fun? And which uncle did the woman love?

I feel that's how it was all supposed to be . . . Fathers who gave their sons secret gardens. Brothers who flew airplanes . . . built them and flew them . . . and jumped off walls with umbrellas . . . and wives who posed for their wedding portraits on the toilet. It's just staggering how lost that all is . . . to the whole world. Lartigue has shown us a laughter that is past and the laughter we have traded it for. He has shown us leisure as an adventure and as an indulgence and made us know the full impact of what is lost.

—

RICHARD AVEDON, "AFTERWORD," JACQUES HENRI LARTIGUE, *DIARY OF A CENTURY* (NEW YORK: VIKING, 1970).

2/ Ces photos sont des merveilles
et des chef-d'œuvres-
Toi et Bea êtes ressemblants et
ravissants - SAKATA et...??...
Très bien aussi -
En vous regardant j'ai *vraiment*
envie d'être avec vous!
Et pourtant je suis presque content
de ne pas y être: parceque je
crois (?) que vous travaillez
mieux sans moi. - Et parceque
lorsque je verrai votre travail
je le jugerai avec *un œil neuf*
J'ai beaucoup de choses à faire
à Paris -
Mais, ici, il fait beau beau beau
Resultat: Je ne sais pas si nous
partons dans 2 jours.... ou si nous
restons jusqu'au 15 Juillet -.
Ecris-moi le plus souvent possible

WE SEND ALL OUR LOVE FLORETTE JAC

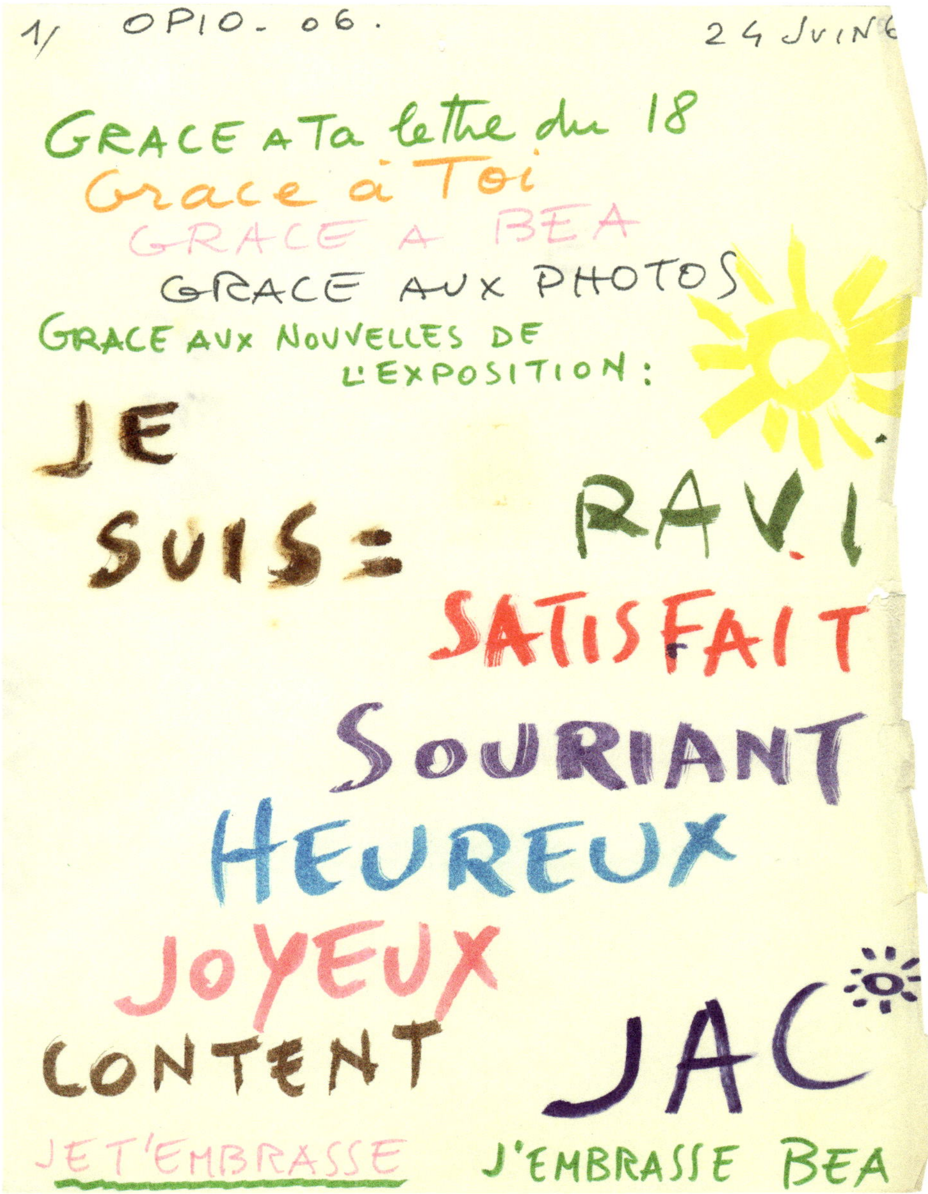
1/ OPIO - 06. 24 JUIN

GRACE A Ta lettre du 18
Grace à Toi
GRACE A BEA
GRACE AUX PHOTOS
GRACE AUX NOUVELLES DE L'EXPOSITION:

JE SUIS: RAVI
SATISFAIT
SOURIANT
HEUREUX
JOYEUX
CONTENT

JAC

JE T'EMBRASSE J'EMBRASSE BEA

Letters from Lartigue to Avedon: February 20, 1968 and June 24, 1968

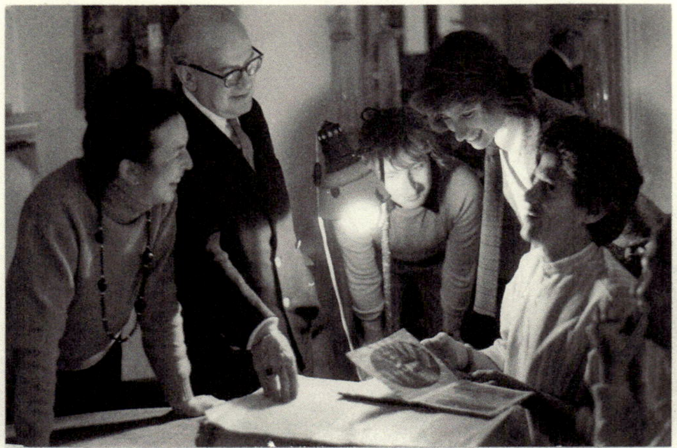

FLORETTE ROBBY LANTZ J.L.SIEFF DICK

DICK SIGNE MON LIVRE "DAIRY OF A CENTURY"

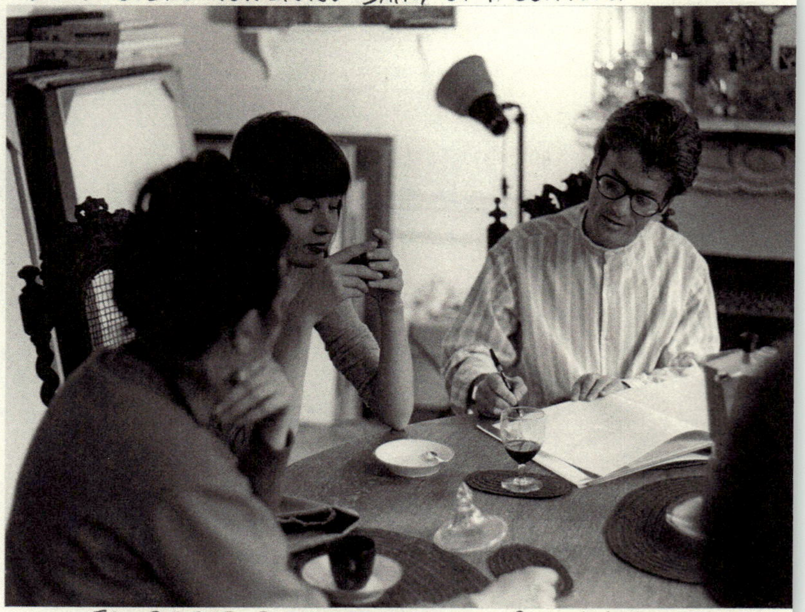

FLORETTE BARBARA DICK AVEDON

On February 13, 1972, Avedon, his agent Robert Lantz, and his assistant, Nicholas Vreeland, visited Lartigue at home in Paris. There, the two photographers inscribed copies of *Diary of a Century* for each other.

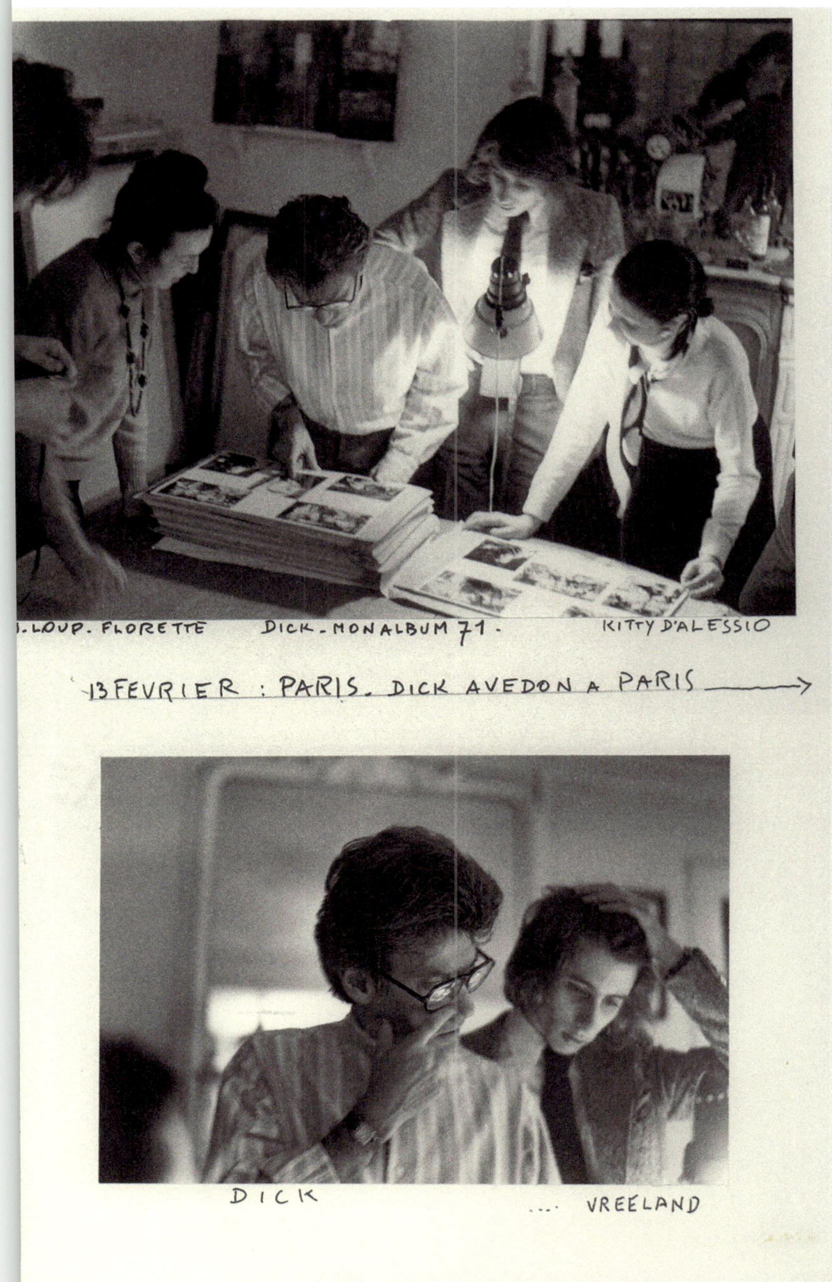

Also present were Florette Lartigue and the photographer Jean-Loup Sieff (album page 0011V72); photographs by J. H. Lartigue

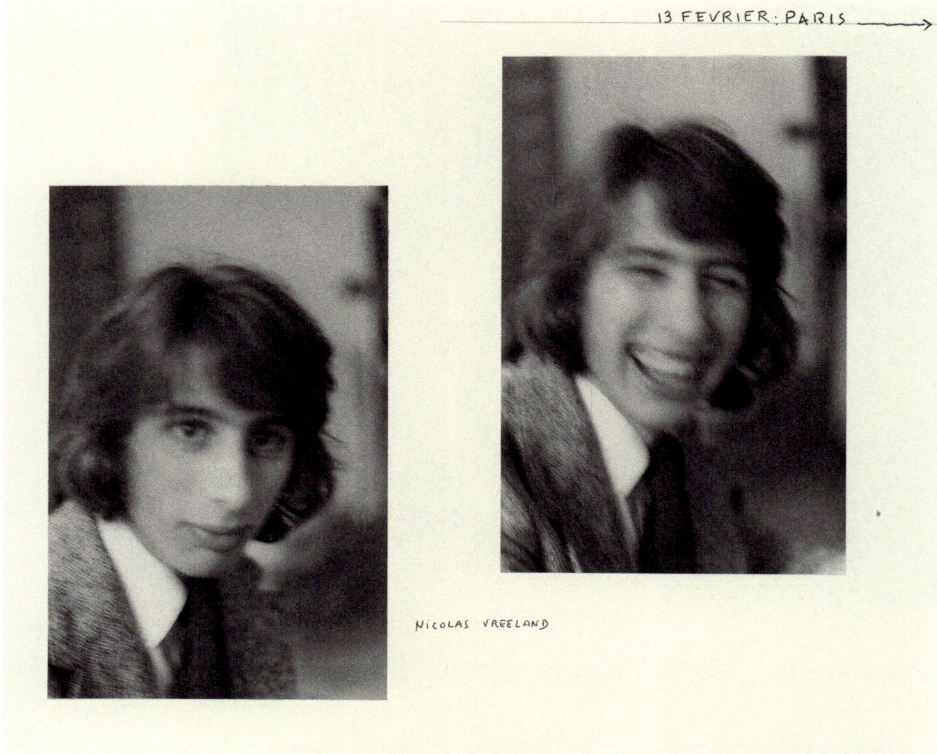

Nicholas Vreeland, Paris, February 13, 1972 (album page 0012V72); photographs by J. H. Lartigue

407 EAST SEVENTY FIFTH STREET
NEW YORK, N.Y. 10021

March 29, 1972

Dearest Diana,

Here are two pictures of Nicky by Lartigue taken one Sunday during lunch, in Paris. I love them side by side because of the sudden change of expression which is so very like Nicky. Also, these are actual Lartigues, and that moves me enormously. He's over 80 now and still going strong.

Love,

Avedon had the prints sent to Nicholas's grandmother, former *Vogue* editor Diana Vreeland, along with a note dated March 29, 1972.

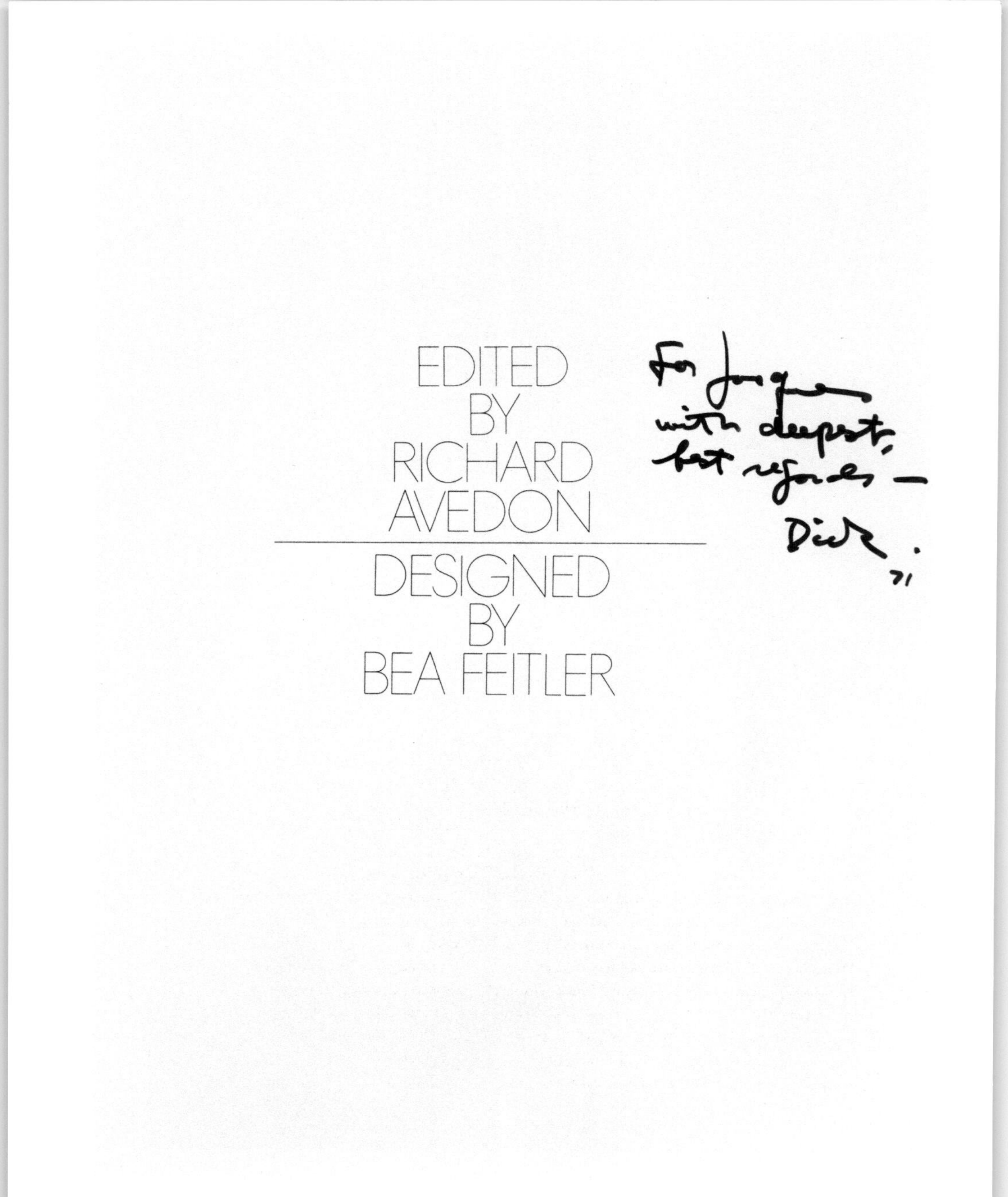

EDITED BY RICHARD AVEDON

DESIGNED BY BEA FEITLER

For Jacques with deepest, best regards — Dick. '71

Avedon's inscription to Lartigue in *Diary of a Century*: "For Jacques, with deepest, best regards — Dick."

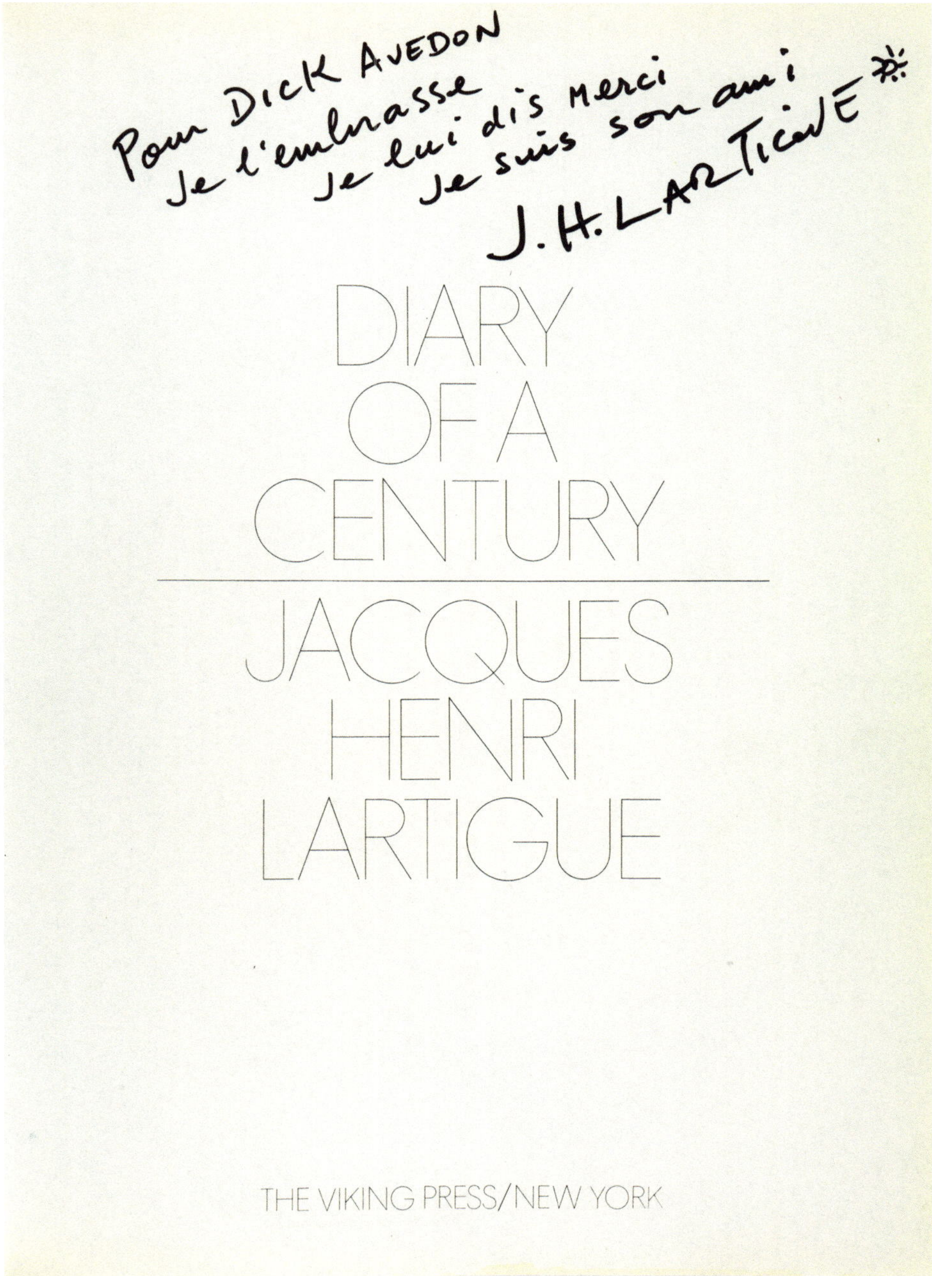
Pour DICK AVEDON
Je l'embrasse
Je lui dis merci
Je suis son ami
J.H. LARTIGUE

DIARY OF A CENTURY

JACQUES HENRI LARTIGUE

THE VIKING PRESS/NEW YORK

Lartigue's inscription to Avedon in *Diary of a Century*:
"For DICK AVEDON. I kiss him. I thank him. I am his friend. J. H. LARTIGUE."

I couldn’t work for two years. I edited a book of photos by Lartigue. I taught. But I couldn’t photograph. Finally I got back in and I’ve never stopped because it’s what I like to do.

—

Richard Avedon

After the Barricades

1970–1985

Between his return to America in May 1968, and when he met Nicole Wisniak, the editor and director of *Egoïste*, in 1984, Avedon's engagement with France was less intense. Nonetheless he produced some striking images in the interim. He also published his seminal text, "Borrowed Dogs," which remains his principal manifesto. It is interesting to compare the essay to the recently discovered letter Avedon wrote to Truman Capote (*see pages 386–87*), in which he characterizes his first attempts at articulating artistic ideas as "icky." By the time he'd written "Borrowed Dogs," Avedon had evolved a sophisticated presentation of his practice, replete with art-historical comparisons that situated his photographic portraiture within the broader context of painting and drawing.

p. 547, Viva and Michel Auder, actress and filmmaker, New York, October 9, 1969
pp. 548–49, Jean Genet, French novelist and playwright, with an unidentified Black Panther, New York, March 11, 1970
pp. 550–51, Jeanne Moreau, actress, New York, December 18, 1993
pp. 552–57, Catherine Deneuve, actress, Los Angeles, September 22, 1968
pp. 558–59, Jean Renoir, director, Beverly Hills, California, May 11, 1972
p. 561, Aurore Clément, actress, New York, September 27, 1974
p. 563, Loulou de la Falaise, fashion consultant, Paris, April 16, 1978
pp. 564–65, Samuel Beckett, writer, Paris, April 13, 1979
pp. 566–67, Francis Bacon, artist, Paris, April 11, 1979

After the Barricades

French Portraits IV

Richard Avedon

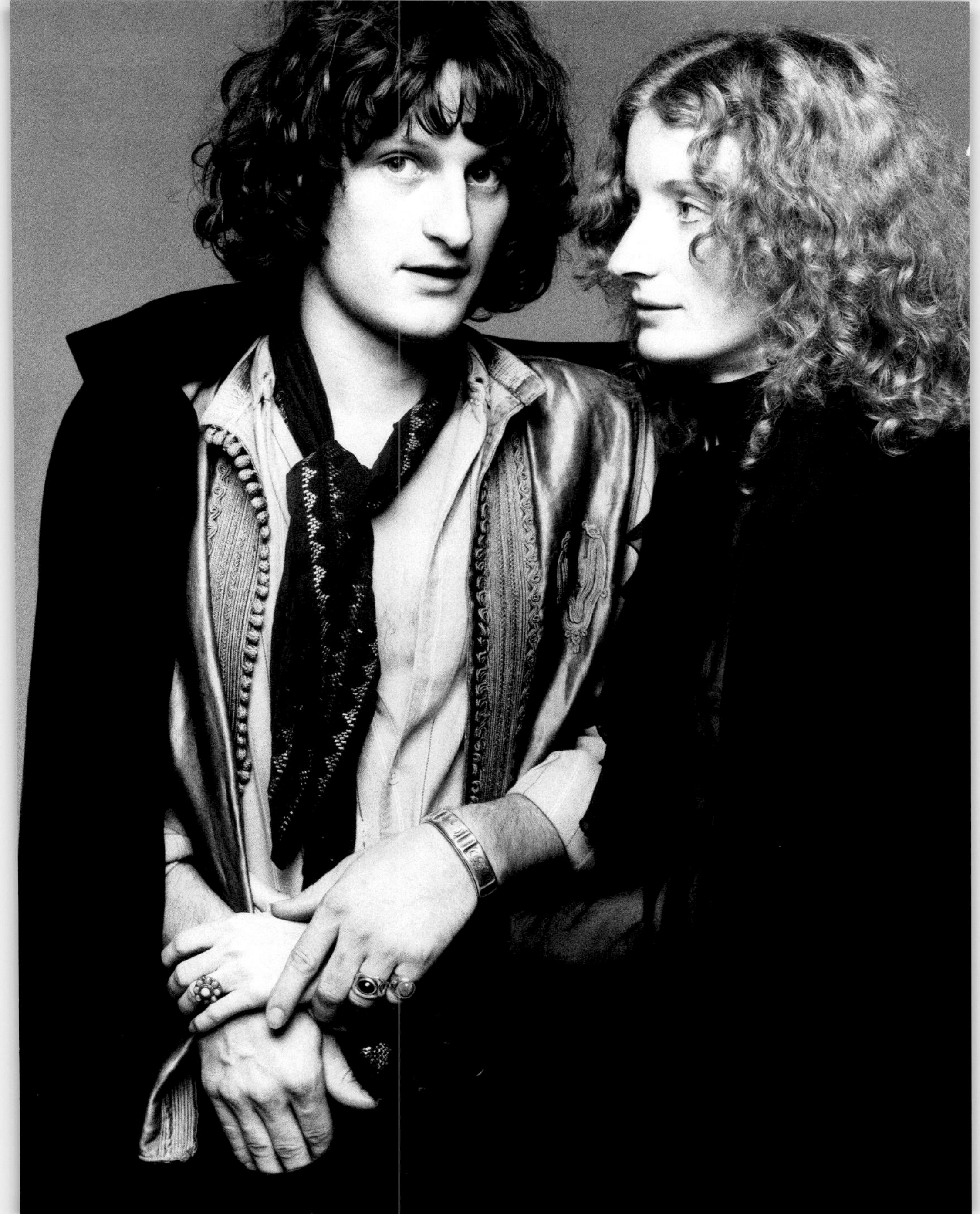

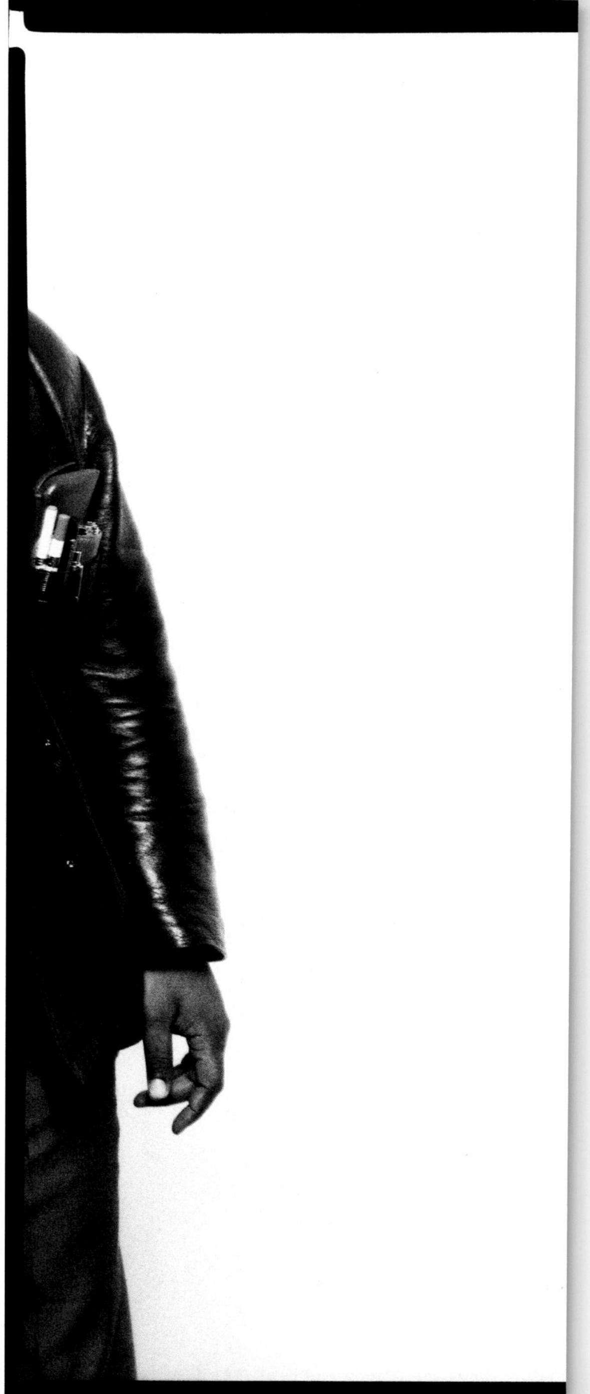

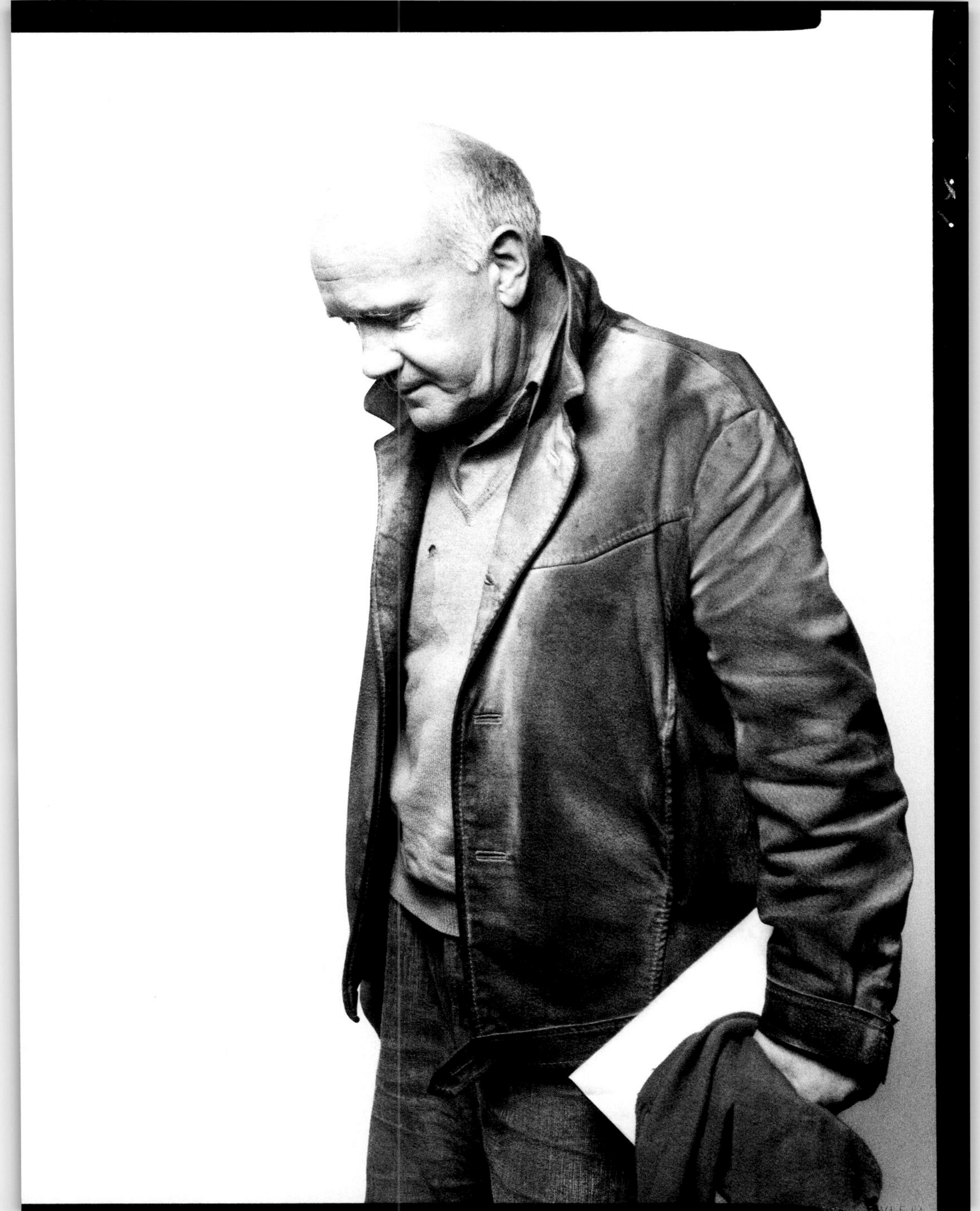

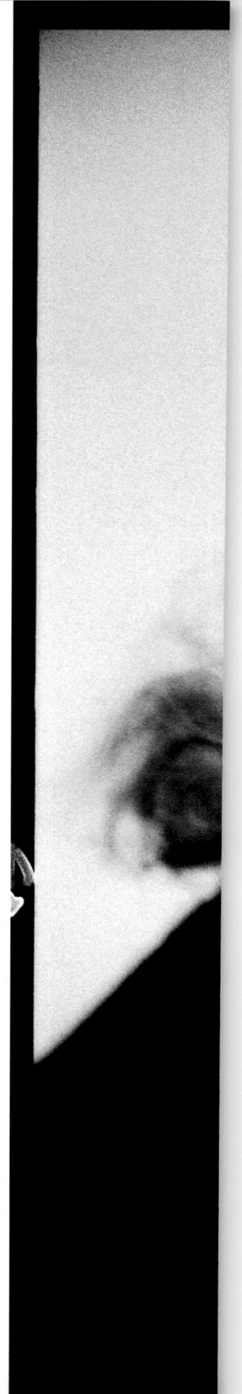

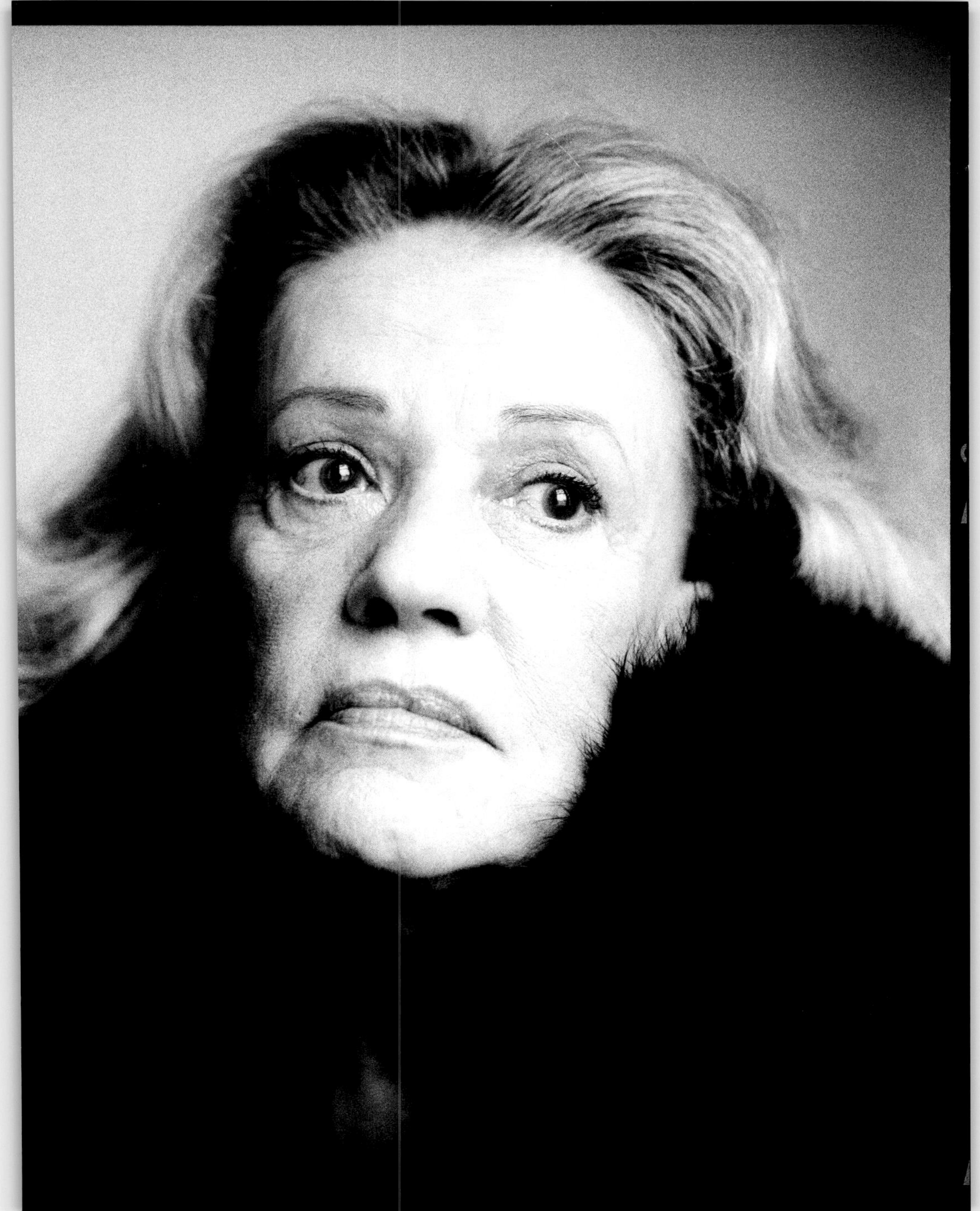

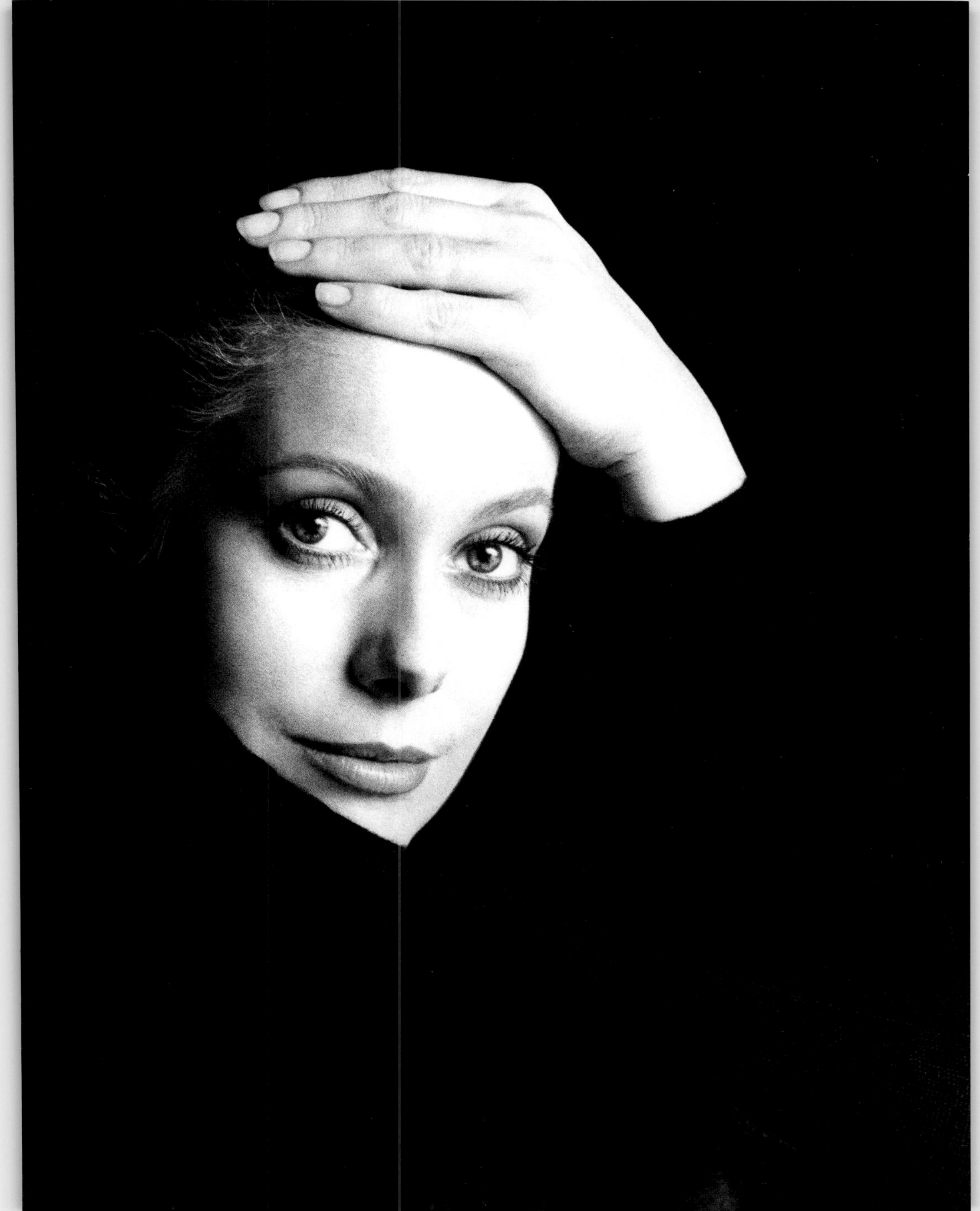

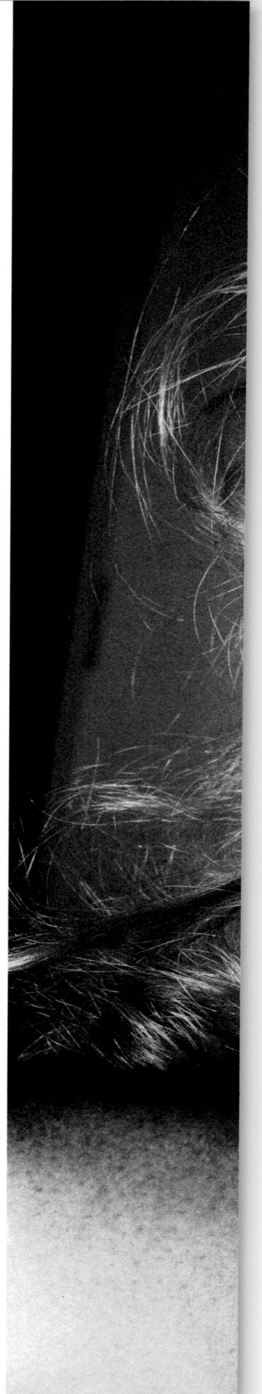

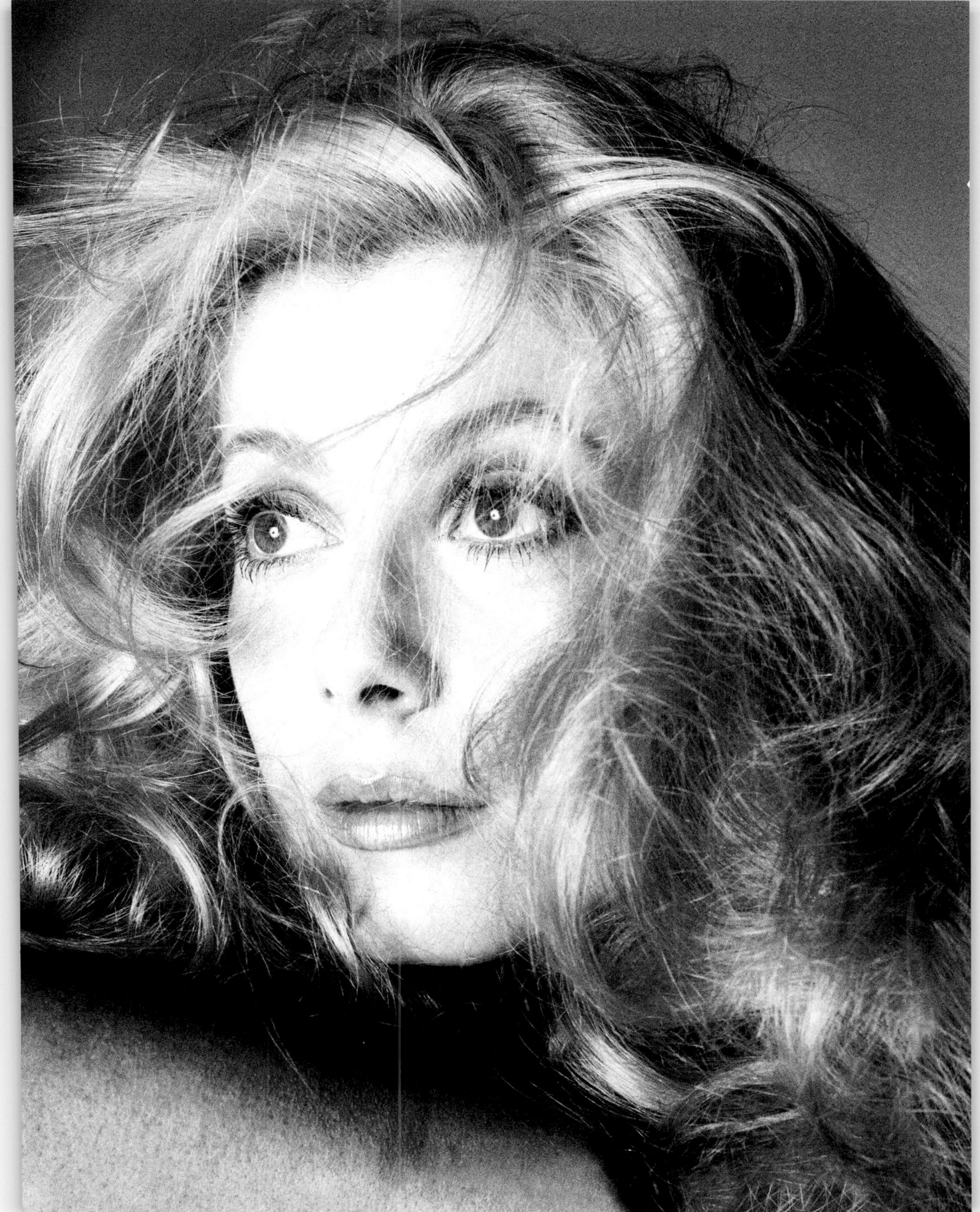

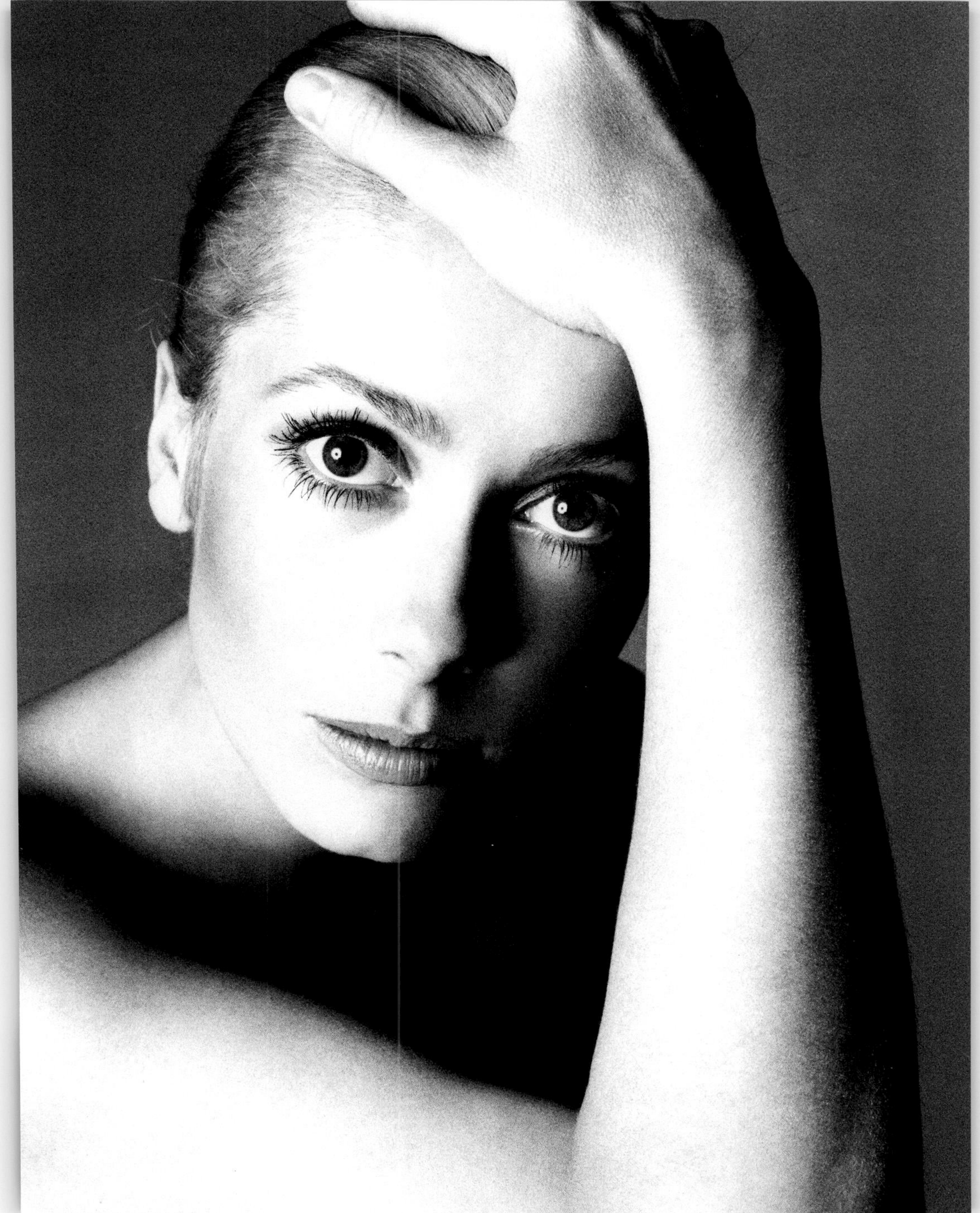

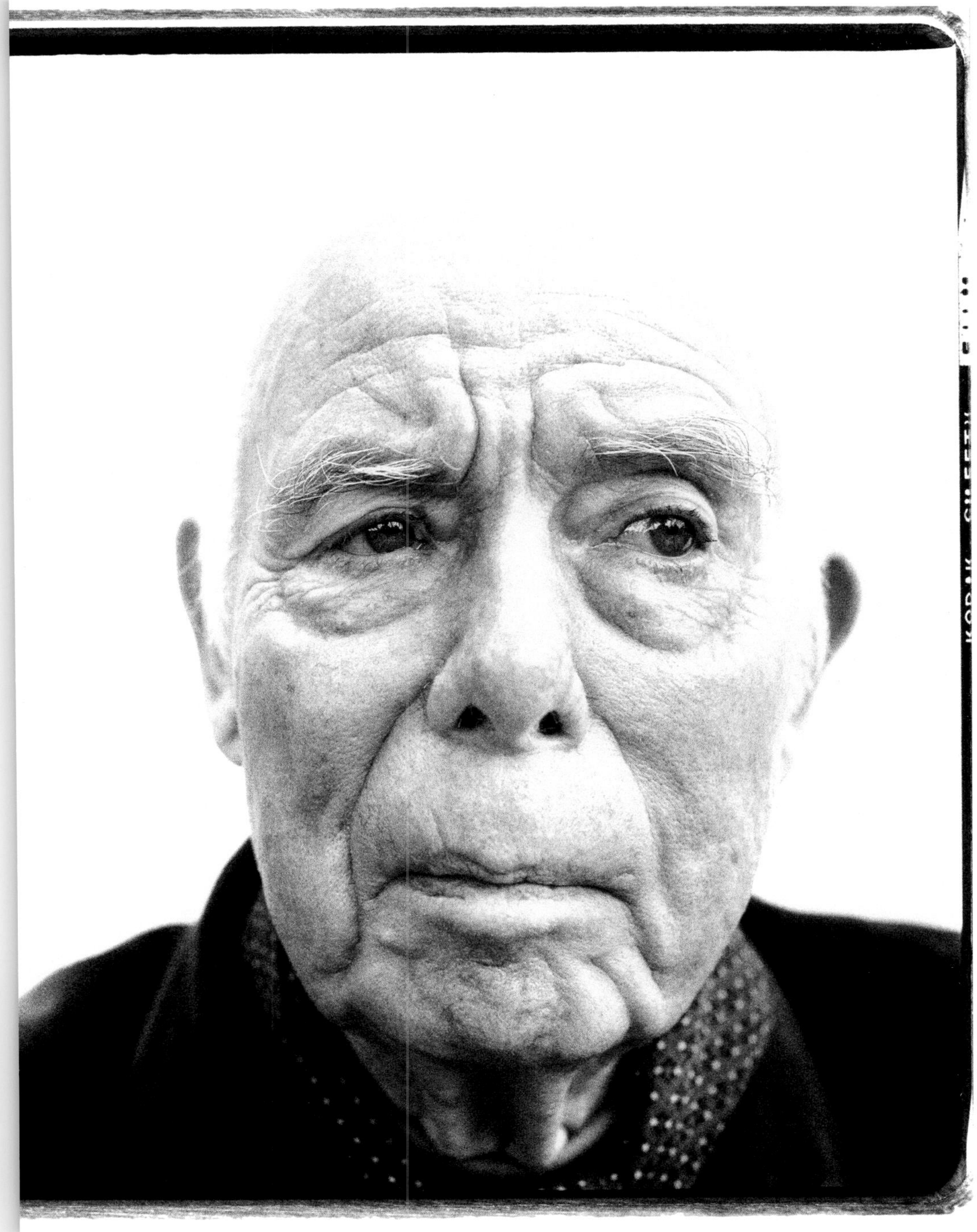

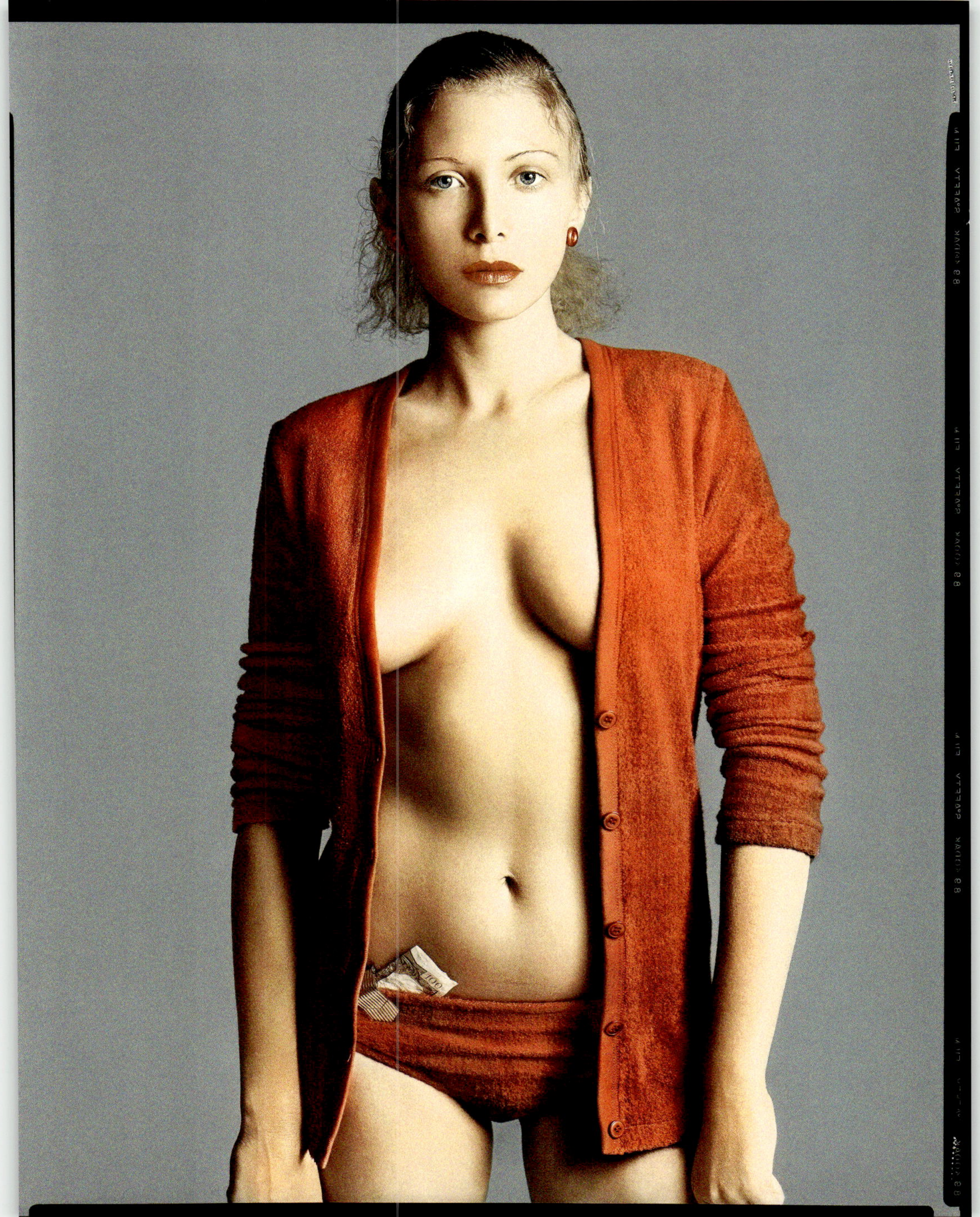

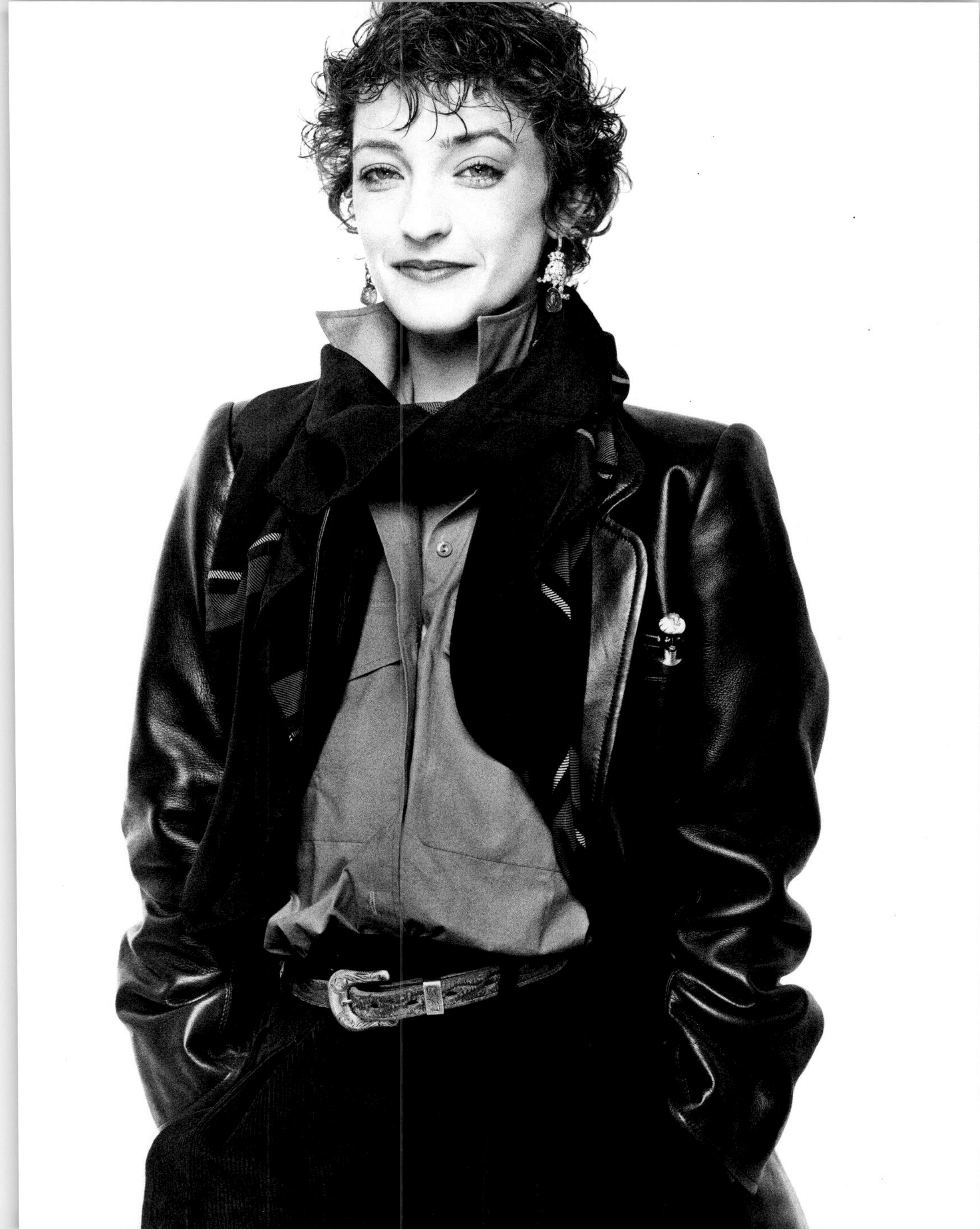

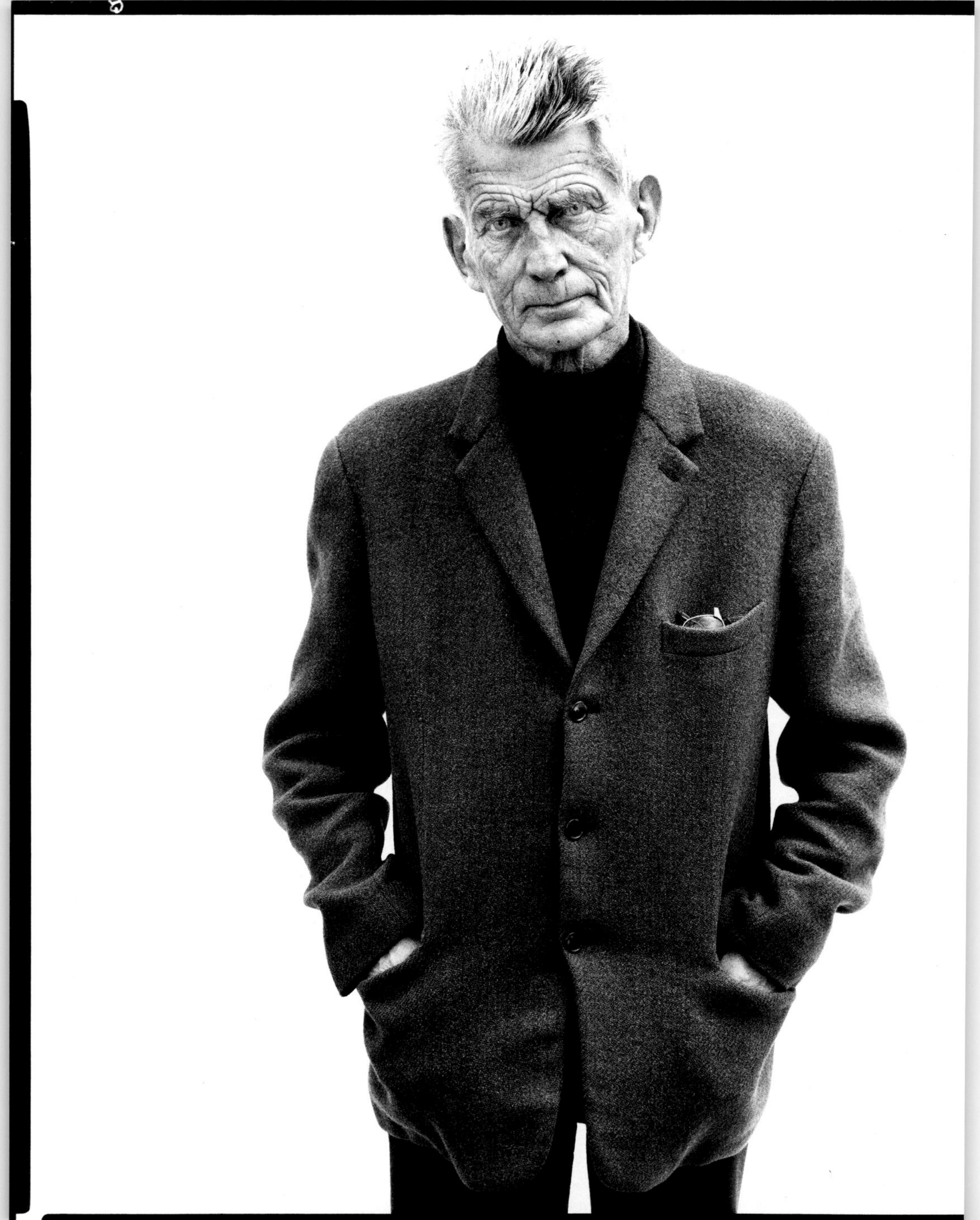

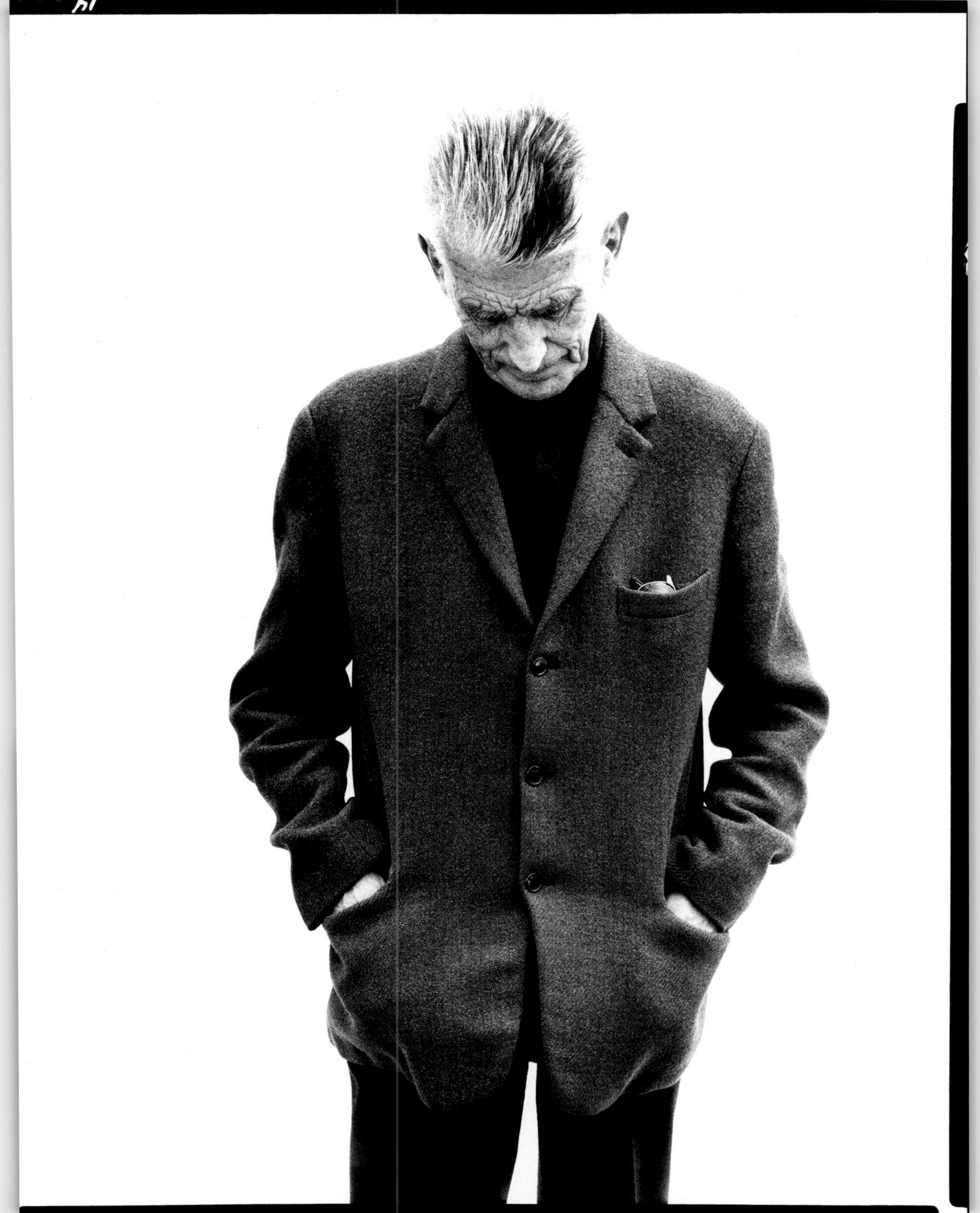

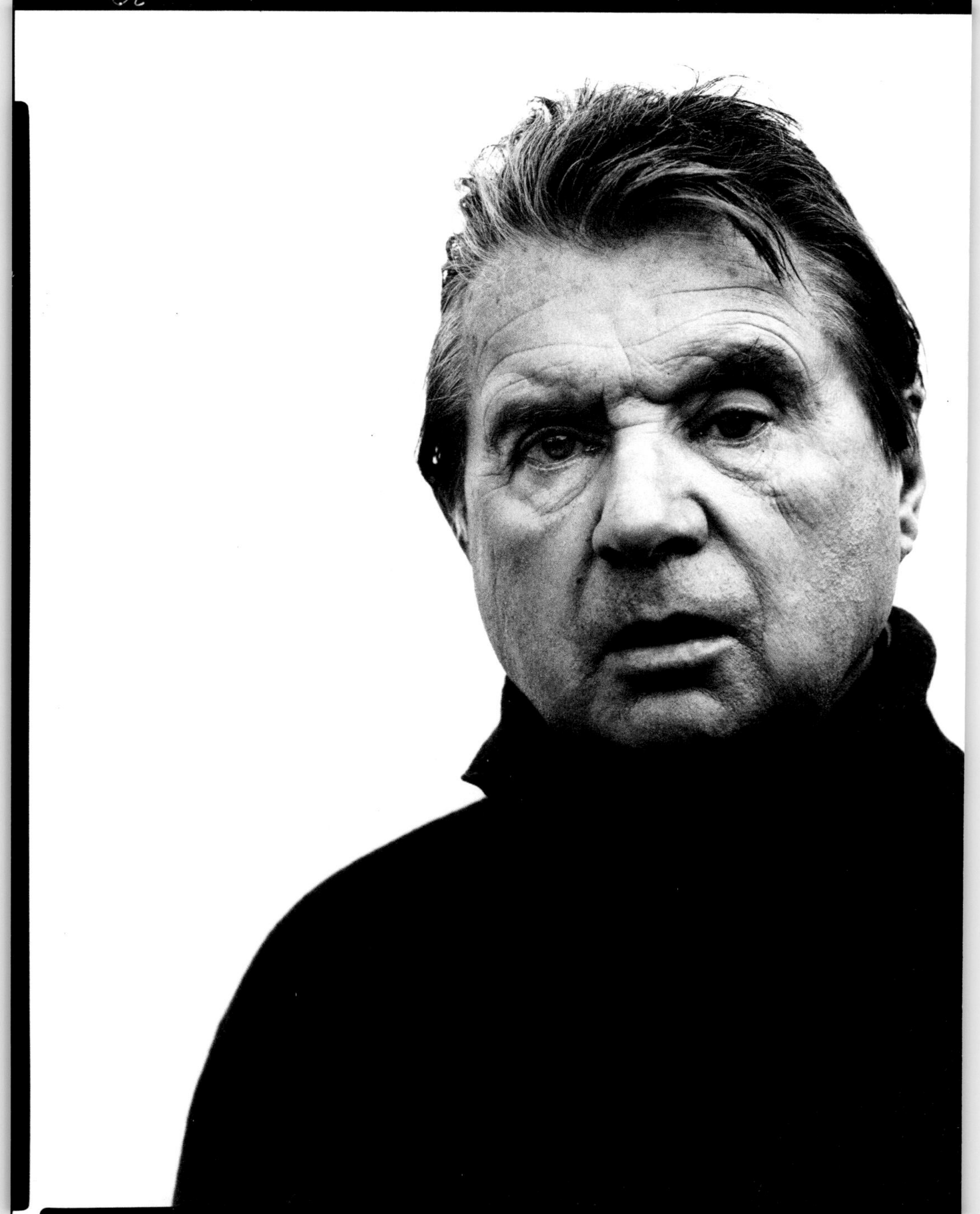

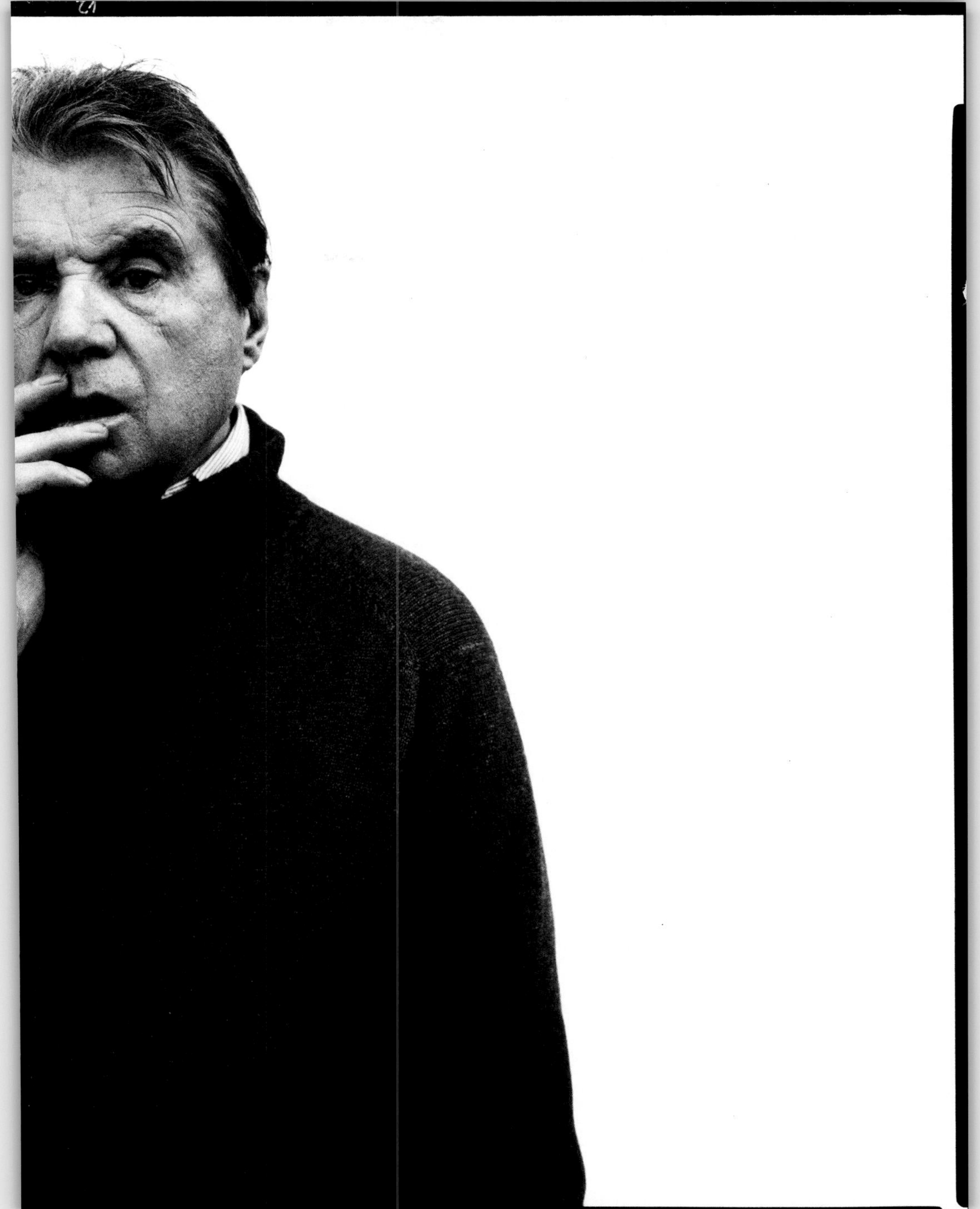

Avedon
Roland Barthes

Look at a photograph by Avedon: you will see the paradox of all great art at work, of all distinguished art: the extreme finitude of the image opens to the extreme infinity of contemplation, of stupefaction. Of how many pictures do we say, rather stupidly, that they are "alive," "lively," etc., all mythical values mobilized by advertising for photographic equipment! But Avedon's art is to create *immobile* photographs, which are therefore *inexhaustible* as objects of fascination: what fascinates is both dead and alive, and that is why it is fascinating. The bodies that Avedon photographs are in a sense corpses, but these corpses have living eyes, that look at you, and think: this realistic art is also a fantastic art.

Hence an engaged production, which immediately opens up a social critique, without, however, falling into the stereotype of engagement: in some of the photos that I have seen, Avedon reveals the opacity, harshness and involuntary sadness of the American *establishment*, everything that makes the successful man a closed body, who has given too much to power and not enough to pleasure; but in another part of his work, and sometimes in the same pictures (and why shouldn't it be so? history is complicated) without abandoning his style, he gives us something else entirely to look at: the thoughtfulness, the sweet severity, intelligence freed from the poses of intelligence, all concentrated in the eyes, that never lie. This is why when looking at a photograph by Avedon, you always communicate with the model: not only does it speak to you, or, even better, because more heartbreaking, it *wants* to speak to you; but you also answer, you want to answer, unable as you are to detach yourself from this image, which holds you without repeating itself (is it therefore an *amorous* relationship that we have with these photos?).

I have spent a whole evening looking at pictures by Avedon; the day before, I had gone to the cinema, where I had been a bit bored, and I was comparing (albeit with some injustice) these two arts. Avedon's art leads to a theory of Photography, unjustly sacrificed today to the flourishing theory of cinema or even comics. As a production, Photography is trapped by two unbearable alibis: sometimes it is sublimated in the guise of "art photography," which precisely denies photography as an art; sometimes it is masculinized, under the guise of news photography, which draws its prestige from the object it has captured. But Photography is neither a painting nor a photograph; it is a Text, that is to say a complex, extremely complex, meditation on meaning.

Here is, for example, everything I *read* in a photograph by Avedon, the seven gifts it gives me: first, the true, the truth, the feeling of truth, the exclamation of truth ("how true!"); then character (thoughtfulness, sadness, severity, satisfaction, joy, etc.); then, type (the politician, the writer, the manager); then, Eros, an engagement, either seductive or repulsive, with affect; then death, the calling to be a corpse; then also, the past, what *has been* captured, can no longer come back, can no longer be touched; finally, the seventh sense, which is precisely the sense that resists all others, the unspeakable supplement, the evidence that in the image, there is always *something else*: the endless, intractable of Photography (desire?).

Avedon's pictures take me on this journey, over and over again; it is never ending; they are simultaneously opulent and bare, they ceaselessly give and ceaselessly hold back; in other words, they are the very figure of dialectic: the greatest intensity of sense and in the end the very lack of sense: something of a restrained *jouissance*. At first, sense thrives, excitement abounds; and then, led by a supremely discreet but nonetheless inflexible hand, that of Avedon, sense exhausts itself: no *reliable* qualifier remains for the body that is represented. If I was photographed by Avedon, I would (at last!) have no desire to judge my own body (like everybody, I have a prickly relationship with its image), nor to find myself too *this* and too little *that*: my body would only insist on being, on persisting: Avedon's photography does not play (and certainly does not play with the photographic image): nobody is ugly, nobody is beautiful (with one exception, that confirms the validity of his whole project, the two naked young men of Andy Warhol's Factory). In short, I would be *such*, and in the *such* of my body, I would maybe feel something of the serenity of the great oriental sages.

—

ROLAND BARTHES, "AVEDON,"
PHOTO (JANUARY, 1977): 58–75.

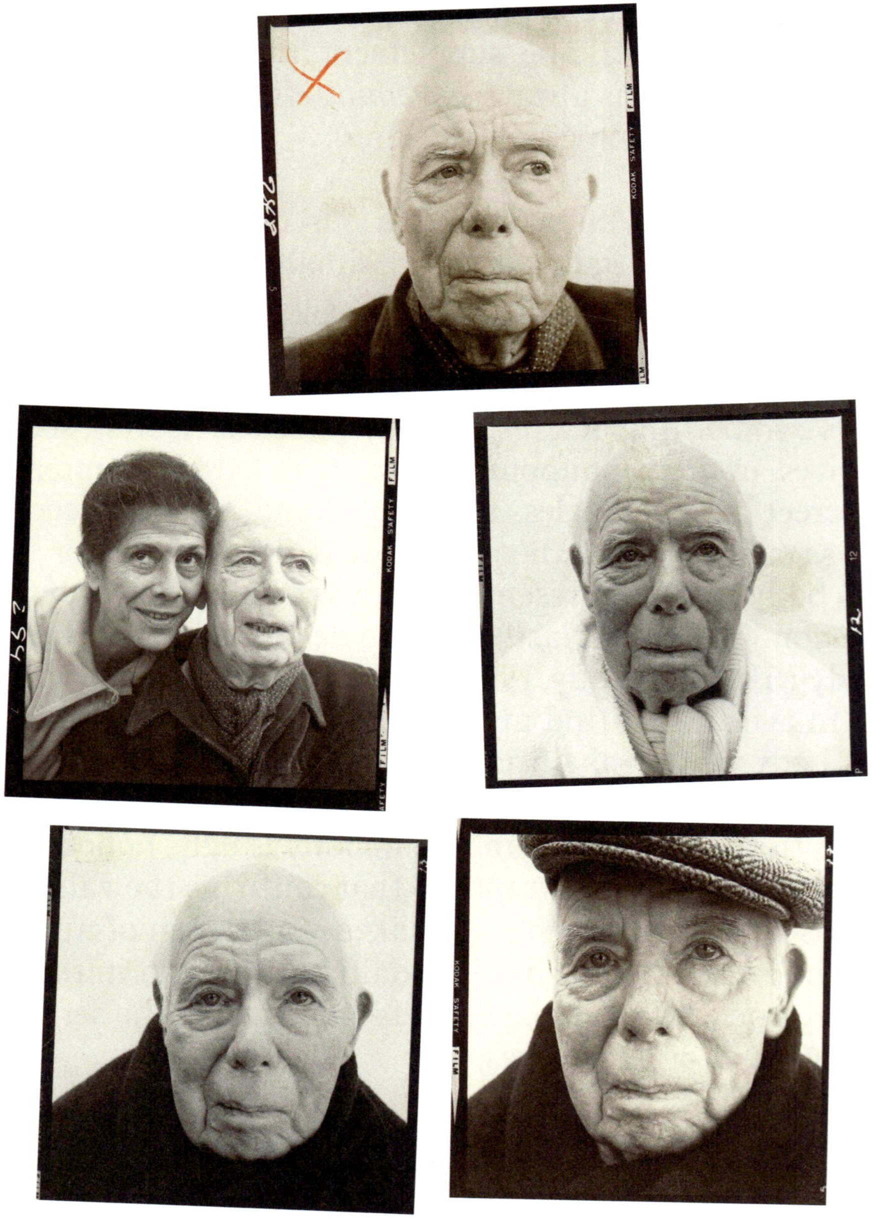

Jean Renoir, director, and his wife, Dido Freire, Beverly Hills, California, March 3, 1974 (contact prints)

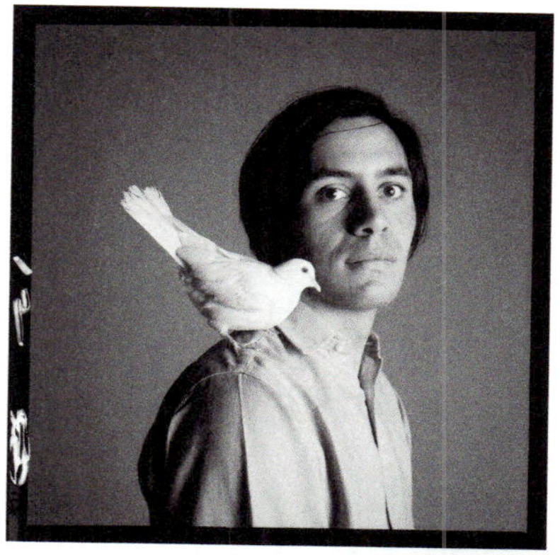

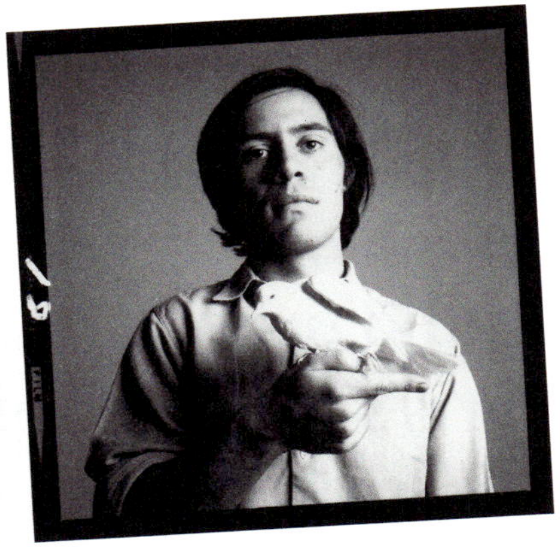

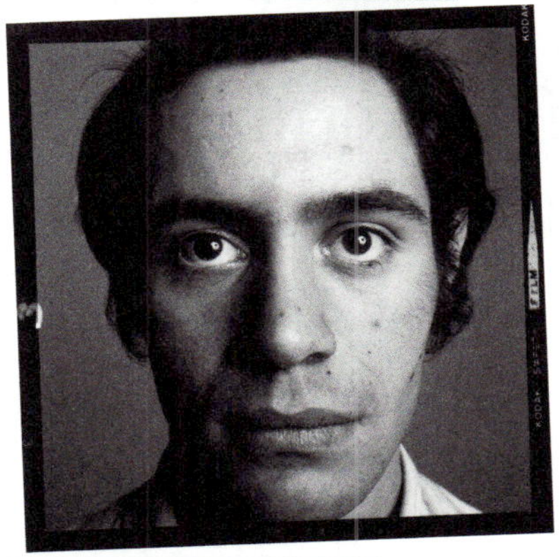

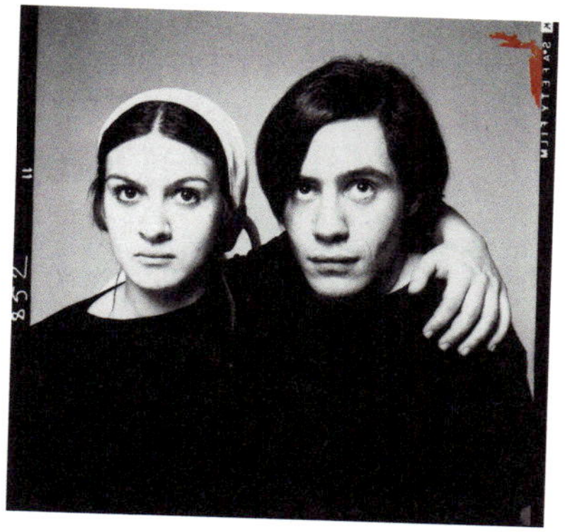

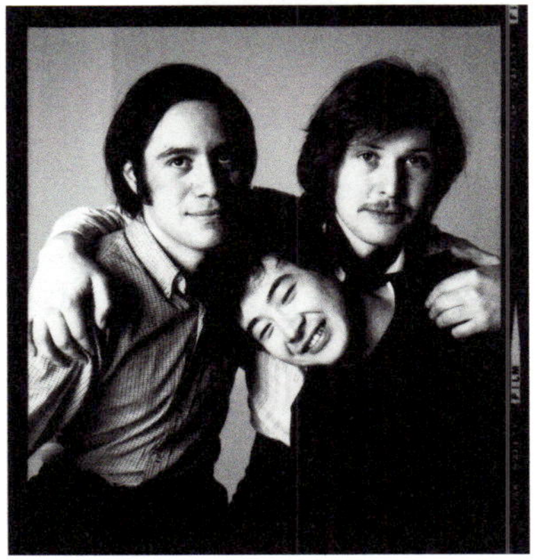

Top left and right, Claude Picasso, son of Pablo Picasso, New York, November 29, 1967
Middle left, Claude Picasso, New York, January 15, 1968
Bottom right, Claude and Paloma Picasso, children of Pablo Picasso, Paris, January 25, 1966
Bottom left, Avedon Studio staff, Claude Picasso, Peter Waldman and Eiichiro Sakata, 1969 (contact prints)

Interview with Richard Avedon

Henry Béhar and Michel Guerrin

In 1979, I went to Paris to photograph Francis Bacon. The sitting was scheduled for a Sunday morning. I had set up my studio outside, on the shady side of Paris's museum of modern art, at the Trocadéro. Bacon arrived in a striped shirt, leather pants and a plaid jacket, dressed from head to toe, dressed to be photographed. We had a charming conversation about the differences between life in London and Paris. The weather was great, the exchange was warm and very civilized. Then I started the portrait. I explained the nature of the diptych that I wanted to make, I had even drawn a small sketch. I asked him to swap his jacket for my dark, solid sweater, then to bring his hand into the portrait. If I had asked a politician to do the same, a banker, or someone else, anyone else, the subject would have given himself a wise and distinguished air, he would have held up his chin with his hand, or brought it up to his forehead. Bacon immediately played the role of secret Bacon, using the purest and sparest gesture, losing none of his authenticity. I didn't have to tell him a thing. He had understood the very heart of my portrait and what it required of him; yet he remained true to himself. No one could play Bacon other than Bacon. On that sunny Sunday, facing the Eiffel tower, his performance was commendable, perfect.

—

HENRY BÉHAR AND MICHEL GUERRIN, "AVEDON" (INTERVIEW WITH RICHARD AVEDON), *LE MONDE* (JULY 1, 1993).

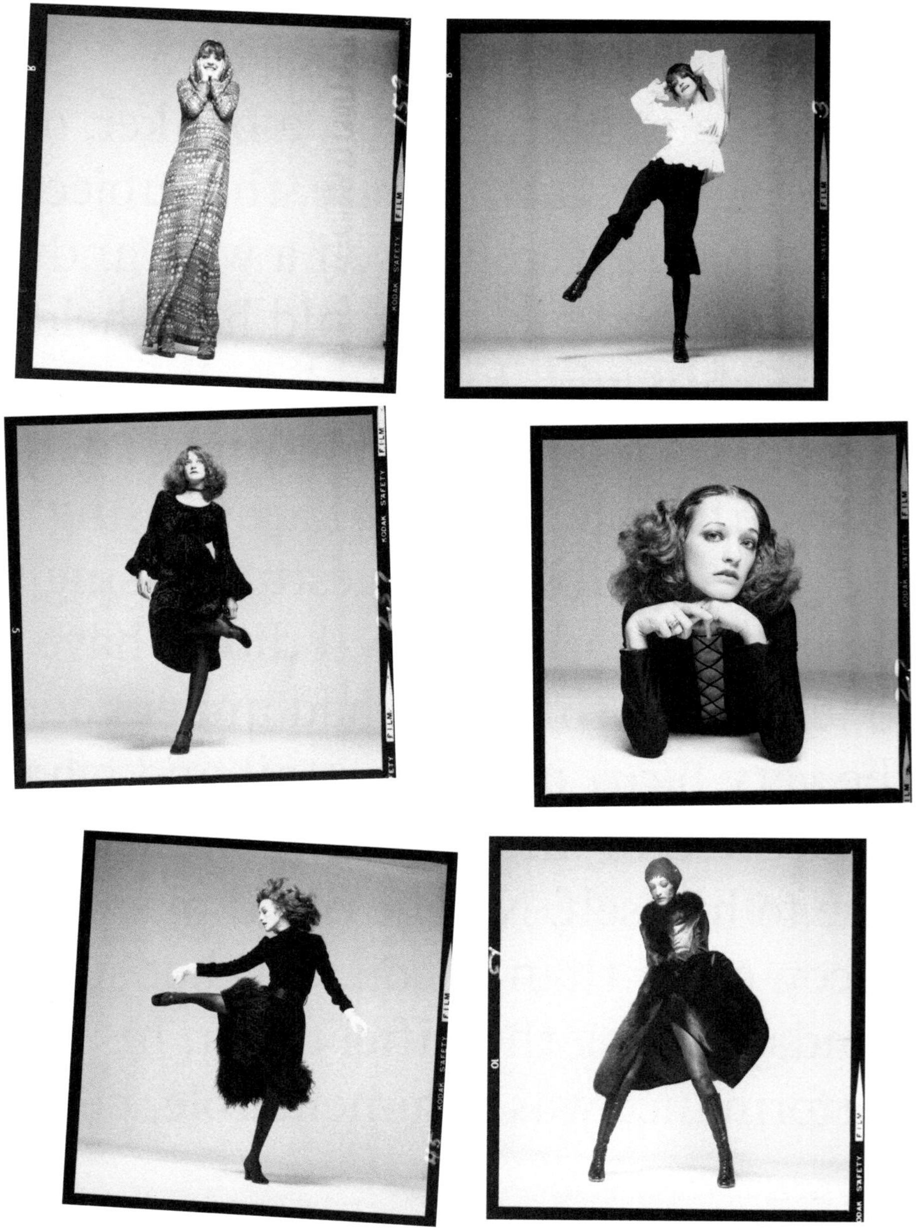

Loulou de la Falaise, fashion consultant, New York, June 23, 1970 (contact prints)

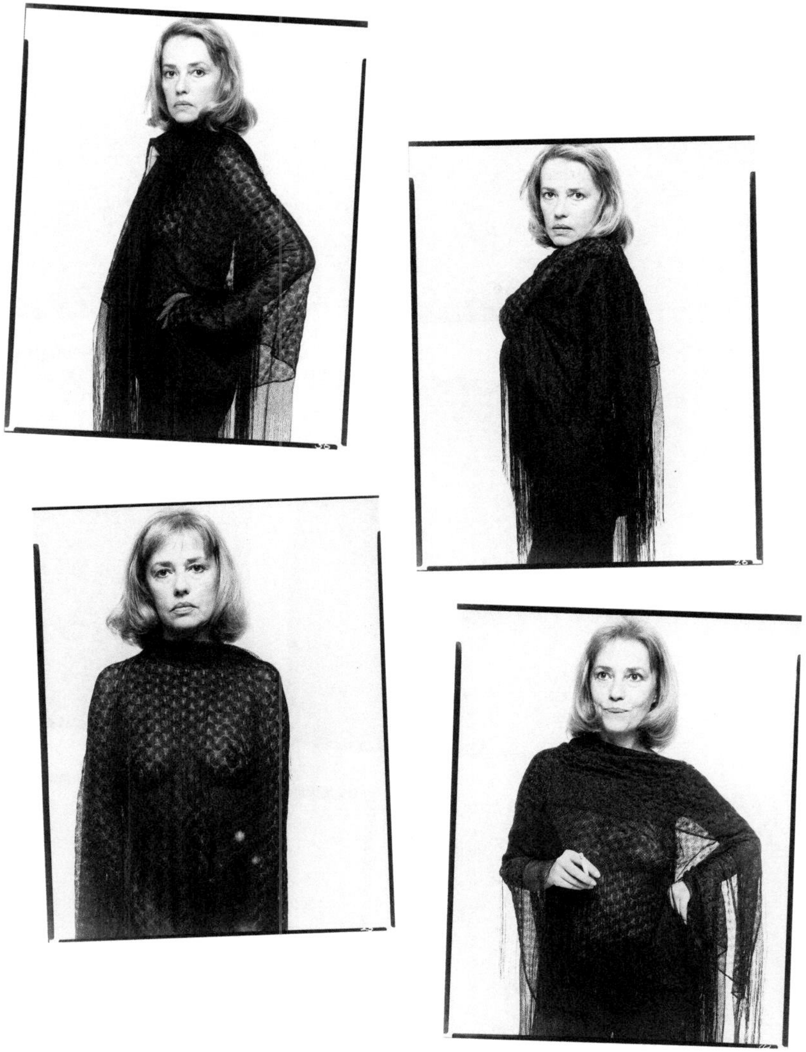

Jeanne Moreau, actress, New York, October 7, 1970 (contact prints)

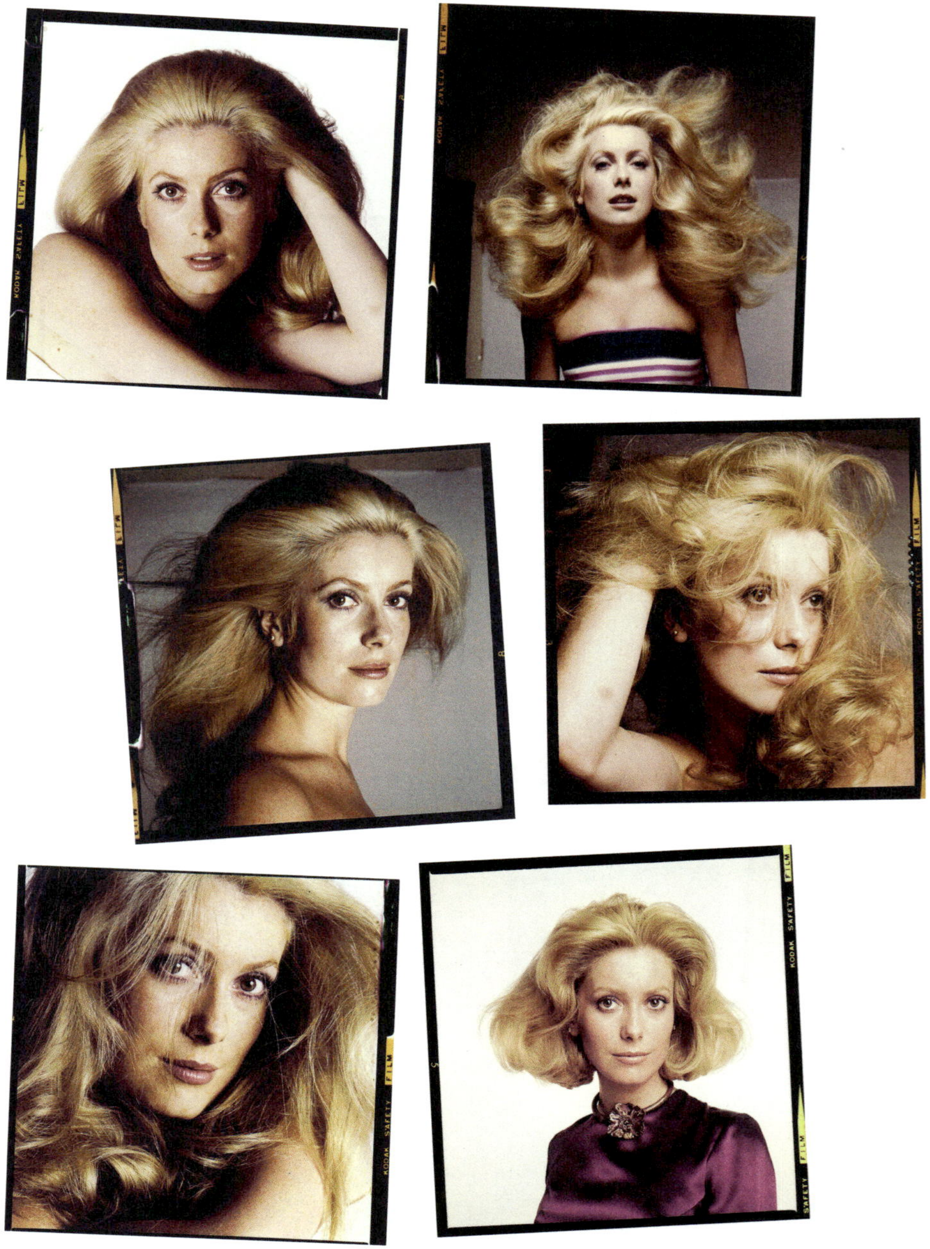

Catherine Deneuve, actress, Los Angeles, September 22, 1968 (contact prints)

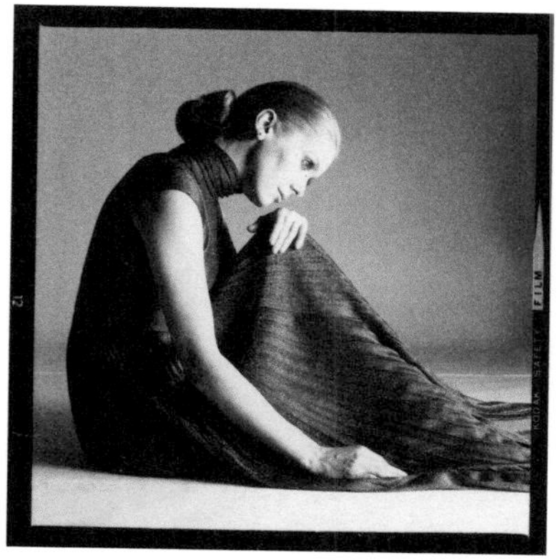
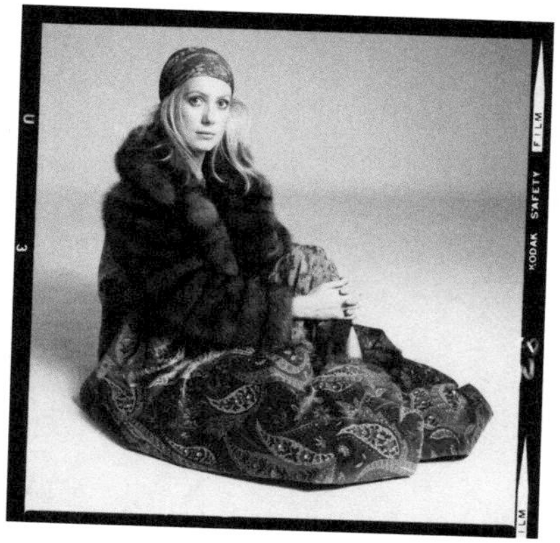
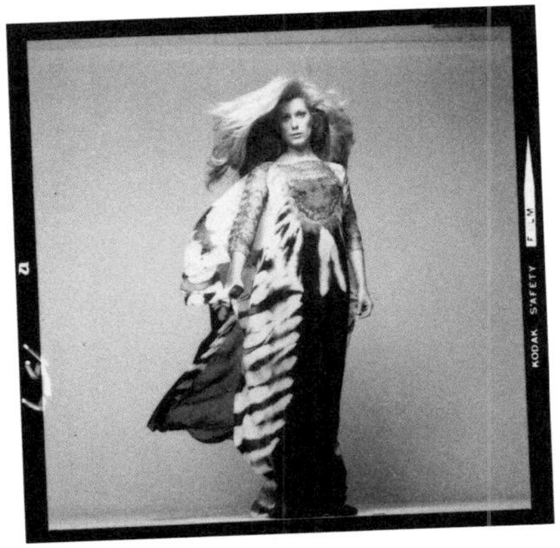
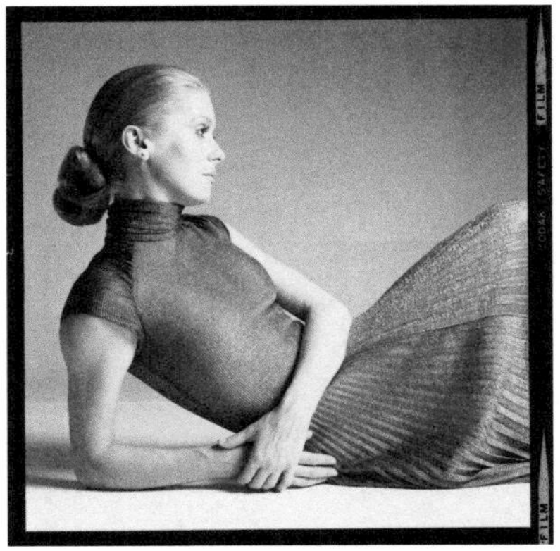
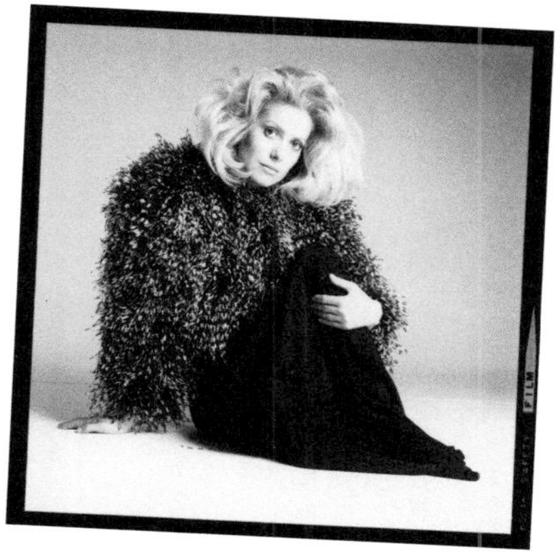
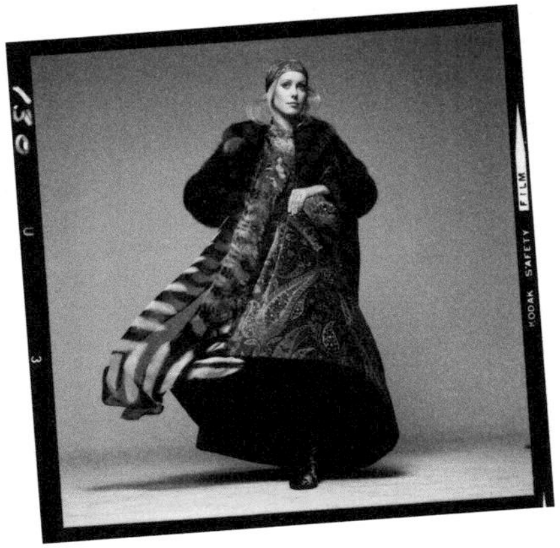

Catherine Deneuve, actress, Los Angeles, September 22, 1968 (contact prints)

It is the faces of others which teach me what mine is like.

—

Richard Avedon

After the Barricades

Borrowed Dogs

Richard Avedon

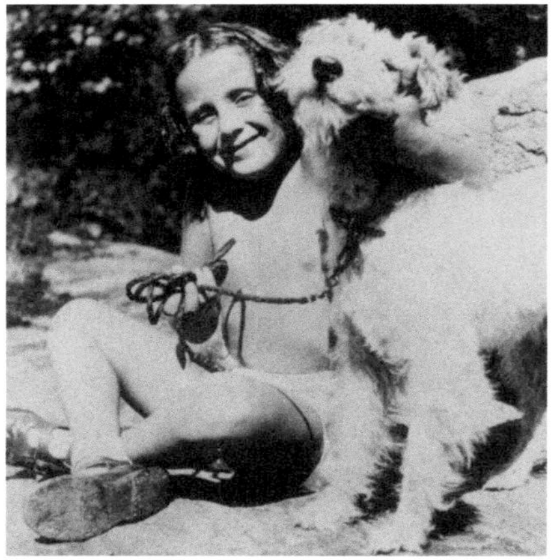

Louise Avedon with a borrowed dog, c. 1933

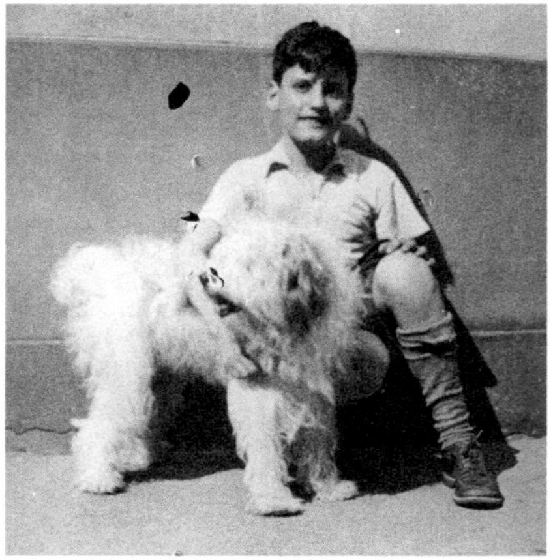

Richard Avedon with a borrowed dog, c. 1935

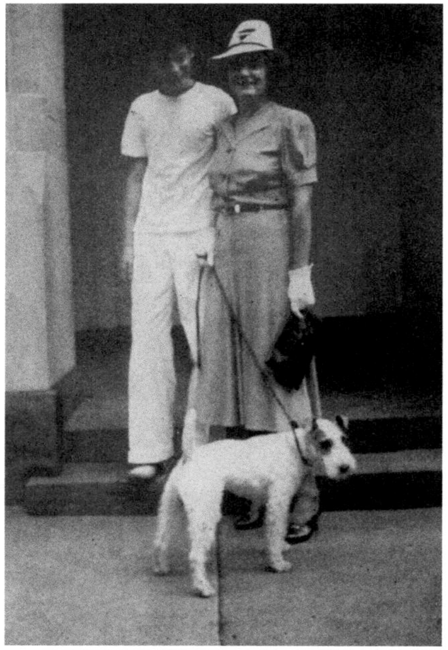

Richard Avedon and his mother, Anna, with a borrowed dog, c. 1937

When I was a boy, my family took great care with our snapshots. We really planned them. We made compositions. We dressed up. We posed in front of expensive cars, homes that weren't ours. We borrowed dogs. Almost every family picture taken of us when I was young had a different borrowed dog in it. The photographs on these pages are of my mother, my sister and myself. It seemed a necessary fiction that the Avedons owned dogs. Looking through our snapshots recently, I found eleven different dogs in one year of our family album. There we were in front of canopies and Packards with borrowed dogs, and always, forever, smiling. All of the photographs in our family album were built on some kind of lie about who we were, and revealed a truth about who we wanted to be.

When I began to look at the portraits of Egon Schiele — I hadn't really known his work until the Museum of Modern Art's *Vienna 1900* show in 1986 — I was excited. It seemed to me one of the highest examples of portraiture without borrowed dogs. So when I began thinking of what I might say about him. I thought I would contrast Schiele's candor and complexity with the entire tradition of flattery and lies in portrait-making.

I've always thought that Rembrandt was the master of empty ennoblement in portraiture, and that he was the most dangerous "Master of the Borrowed Dog" simply because he is the most perfect and seductive of painters. So when I was invited to give this lecture at the museum by Kirk Varnedoe, curator of the show, I was prepared to say hard things about Rembrandt, and it just didn't seem like a swift thing to do. Since I had no other thoughts on the subject, I decided to decline Varnedoe's offer.

Now, what I'm about to tell you is true in every detail.

The morning that I made up my mind not to attempt to speak in public about Schiele, I walked from my study into my bedroom (I'd been having carpenters build bookshelves under my bed), and there by the window was Rembrandt himself, standing in my bedroom in Rembrandt light. There, holding a hammer, dressed as a carpenter, was the genius himself. I reached for Kenneth Clark's book on Rembrandt and showed Rembrandt, the carpenter, the chapter on his self-portraits. The carpenter agreed that they were absolutely on him. He said, "This one, of course, when I was younger." I set up my camera, asked him to imitate the drawings I'd shown him, and did a few snapshots. (All this happened in five minutes.) Rembrandt the carpenter acted Rembrandt the painter exactly. It seemed undeniable to me that Rembrandt must have been acting when he made his own self-portraits. It was so clear. Rembrandt was telling me that he was acting when he drew himself. Not just making faces, but always, throughout his life, working in the full tradition of performance. Elaborate costumes, a turban, a beret, a cloak, the rags of a beggar, the golden cloth of a sultan, and someone's dog — really performing in a very self-conscious way. And then I realized, thanks to Rembrandt the carpenter, that it was precisely this quality of performance that links Rembrandt and Schiele, but which Schiele took to an inspiring and radical extreme. And that performance ought to be the real subject of my talk, just as it is the real subject of all portraits that interest me. So I changed my mind.

Because portraiture is performance, and like any performance, in the balance of its effects it is good or bad, not natural or unnatural. I can understand being troubled by this idea — that all portraits are performances — because it seems to imply some kind of artifice that conceals the truth about the sitter. But that's not it at all.

The point is that you can't get at the thing itself, the real nature of the sitter, by stripping away the surface. The surface is all you've got. You can only get beyond the surface by working with the surface. All that you can do is to manipulate that surface —gesture, costume, expression — radically and correctly. And I think Schiele understood this in a unique, profound, and original way. Rather than attempting to abandon the tradition of the performing portrait (which is probably impossible anyway), it seems to me that Schiele pushed it to

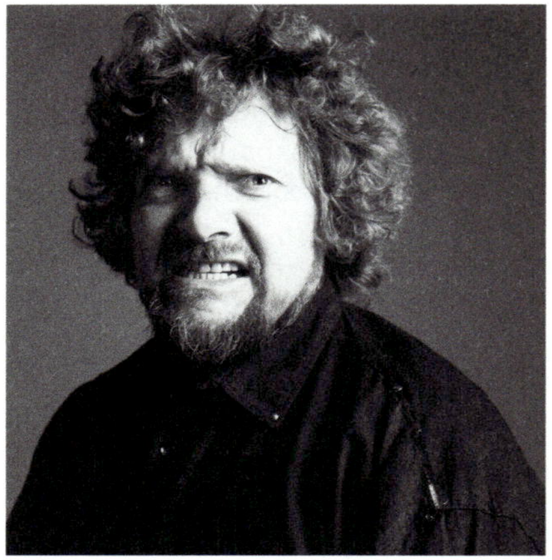

Johann Lukstein, carpenter, New York, September 12, 1986, Richard Avedon

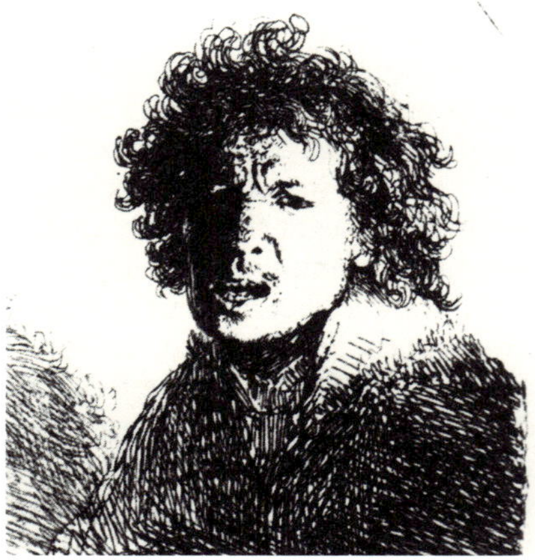

Self-portrait open mouthed, as if Shouting: Bust, 1630, Rembrandt

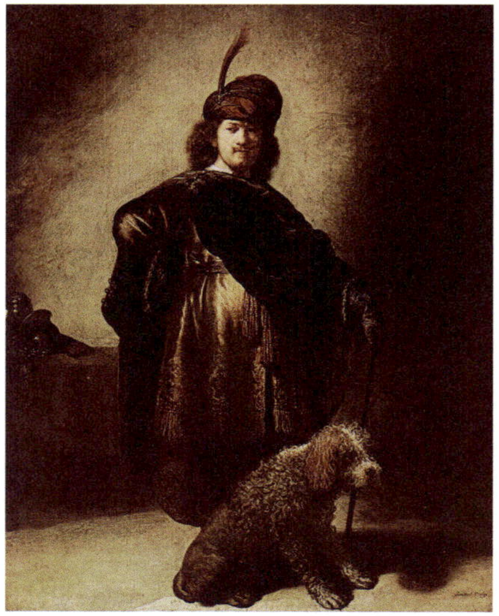

Self-portrait in Oriental Attire with Poodle, 1631–33, Rembrandt

extremes, shattered the form by turning the volume up to a scream. And so what we see in Schiele is a kind of recurring push and pull: first toward pure "performance," gesture and stylized behavior, pursued for its own sake, studied for its own sake. Then these extreme stylizations are preserved in form, but disoriented, taken out of their familiar place, and used to change the nature of what a portrait is.

I think this begins with hands and gesture. All portrait artists have to think about what to do with hands. It's not at all that a portrait is a kind of arrested moment in a stream of gesture. Gesture just doesn't proceed in lock step with thought. On the contrary, gesture in life always follows thought and precedes words. You extend your hand, then say "Hello" — if you reverse the order, something else is going on. In a fixed image, there's no possibility of one act informing the other. Nor is gesture in a portrait just pantomime where you invent the right meaningful gesture. Where the hands go is intimately tied up with the whole expressive quality of design, the graphic rhythm of the image as a whole, as well as its psychological and emotional content.

So the first thing one sees in Schiele is this kind of marionette imagery. This kind of laboratory of splayed fingers that seem oblique and purposefully unrevealing — of the kind of experiment you do when you try to find some random or chance or unpredictable element to break a stereotyped form.

On second look, it becomes clear that this new language of hands really affects things in a fundamental way. First of all, what started out as pantomime has become part of a larger graphic scheme — a jagged, spindled rhythm that you see as clearly in Schiele's flowers as in his figures. And then, eventually he used apparently aberrant or oblique gestures to create a new, meaningful language of gesture that, for me, is much more convincing than the traditional postures. Beginning in pure marionnette theater, ending with an image and gesture to do with intellect — (this pulling down of the eye) — that's much truer and more beautiful than, say — to scrape the bottom of the barrel — Rodin's *Thinker*.

The ultimate expression of this kind of performance — extreme stylized behavior — is, of course, fashion, where everything — the entire body, hair, makeup, fabric — is all used to create a performance. So many portraits in the history of art are fashion portraits, fashion images, as in so many beautiful Klimts. Schiele understood fashion and seems to have been fascinated by it. But he also, more excitingly, chose neither to succumb to it nor reject it. In the same way that the apparently stylized and abstract language of gesture in the marionnette pictures, once controlled, became the means toward a new language of gesture, it seems to me that Schiele never abandoned the theatrical conventions of fashion, but instead intensified those conventions in a way that transformed their meaning. I think the masterpiece of this particular — and particularly daring — aspect of Schiele's work occurs in the picture of himself in a jail cell. Here, in the extreme of humiliation and pain, imprisoned for the daring and power of his work, he draws himself in an explosion of form, equal to the most extravagant ideal of fashion. No man's garment flows so lyrically in the best of times, let alone the worst.

One of the other elements of performance is, of course, the prop. And of course it's significant that Schiele in his portraits, for the most part, deprived himself of props and scenery. He used empty backgrounds. They're so spare.

As one who is addicted to white backgrounds, it seems odd to me that a gray or tonal background is never described as an empty background. But in a sense, that's correct. A dark background fills. A white background empties. A grey background does seem to refer to something — a sky, a wall, some atmosphere of comfort and reassurance — that a white background doesn't permit. With the tonal background, you're allowed the romance of a face coming out of the dark. I don't think you find portraits with white backgrounds before Schiele. Maybe in drawings. Never in paintings, with the possible exception of the white icons of

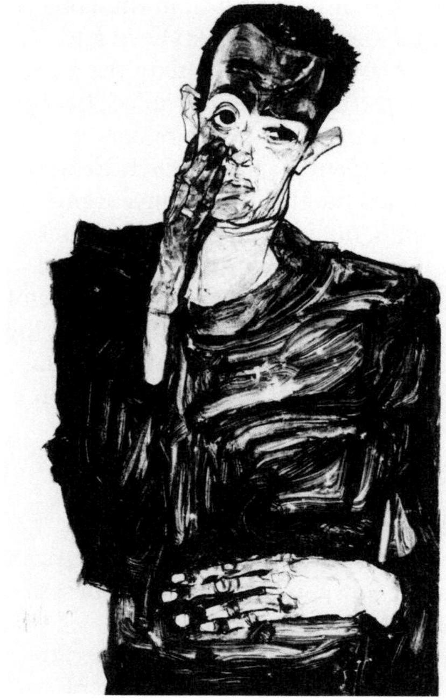

Self-Portrait, 1910; Egon Schiele

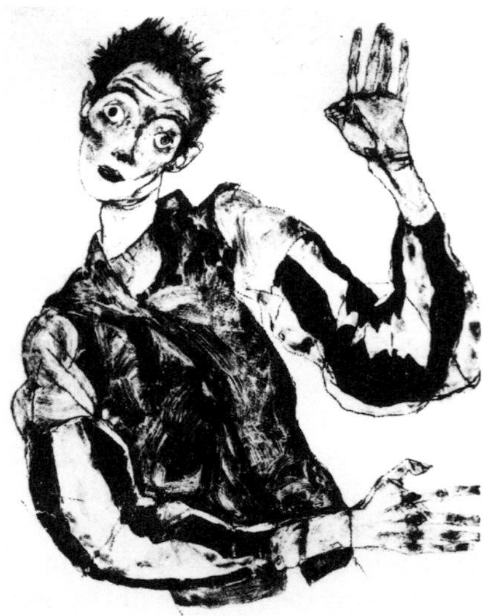

Self-Portrait with Red Hair, 1915; Egon Schiele

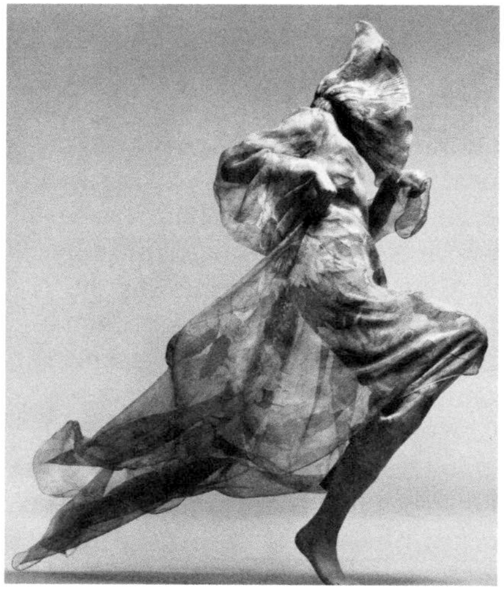

Jean Shrimpton, evening dress by Cardin, Paris, January 26, 1970; Richard Avedon

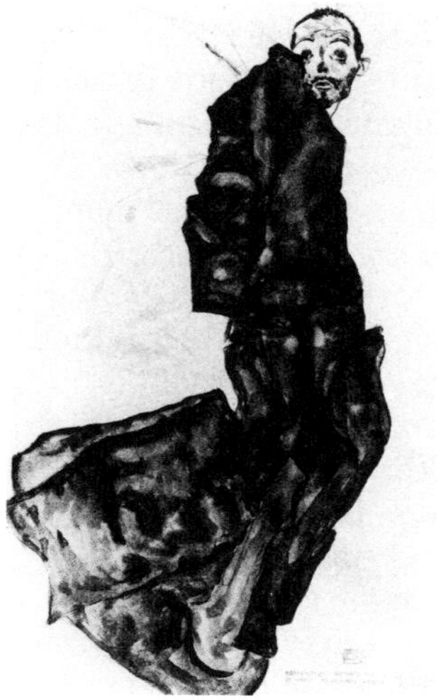

Self-Portrait as a Prisoner, 1912; Egon Schiele

Novgorod. And that, I think, is the point. It's so hard with a white background not to let the graphic element take over. It's so hard to give emotional content to something so completely and potentially caricatural, dominated by that hard, unyielding edge. And that, of course, is the challenge and importance of it. If you can make it work successfully, a white background permits people to become symbolic of themselves.

All of these things—the new language of gesture, the reversal of fashion, the daring white background—are elements that excite and move me in Schiele's work. But what really excites me in his work is what he does with sex. Of all of Schiele's pictures, the one that has come to mean the most to me is the self-portrait masturbating. It seems to me to be a real revolution in the way we imagine sex and erotic life in art. It brings together two different but deeply related things in a very stirring way. First, it's raw and truthful about sex. It reveals something previously hidden about erotic life in art. But in a more subtle way, it's truthful about the implicit eroticism of all portraiture.

I think there's an element of sexuality in all portraiture: the moment you stop to look, you've been picked up. You look in a way you're not allowed to look in life. Is there any situation in life where you can look at the Duchess of Alba for half an hour without ending up dead at the hands of the Duke? A confrontational, erotic quality, I think, should underline all portraiture. But this confrontational quality of portraiture is almost never explored, so far as I know, in explicitely erotic images. They tend to be always voyeuristic rather than confrontational.

Rather than making "sexy" images, it seems to me that Schiele began with the knowledge of the complexity implicit in the sexuality of all portraiture, and then again turned up the volume. It's as though he is saying "You want to see? I'll give you something to look at. And my painting will look at you looking at me." Is there an image in art before this of a man, rather than a woman, masturbating? Schiele engaged in the performance of masturbation presents it as a performance. He seems to have understood the erotic nature of all portraiture and been at once excited and revolted by it. For all the high degree of sexuality in his work, there's an interesting lack of sensuality.

All of this — all this knowledge about being a portrait painter, and about performing this act, about watching himself performing the act, and painting himself performing the act, and then about looking at the painting he made — seems to me, wrapped up in this image. It also seems, to me, a bad performance, though a radical one. This picture fails as a metaphor from the neck up because of Schiele's youthful addiction to sentimentality in the treatment of his own face. It's in the face that we see The Loneliness of the Masturbator — this head expresses a much more banal conception that does the subtlety of this body. It seems to me to limit the picture's power by making masturbation acceptable in art only as a pleasureless act, instead of a frenzied, complicated, pleasurable, destructive wacking-off. Imagine a different Schiele head on this Schiele body.

Forgive me. I know I've gone too far.

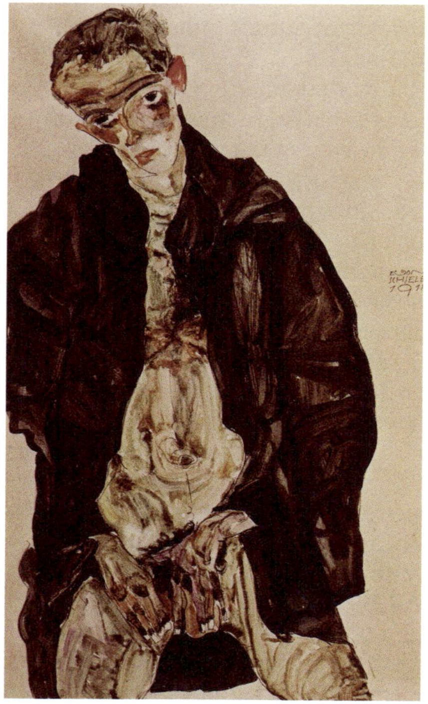

Self-Portrait in Black Cloak Masturbating, 1911; Egon Schiele

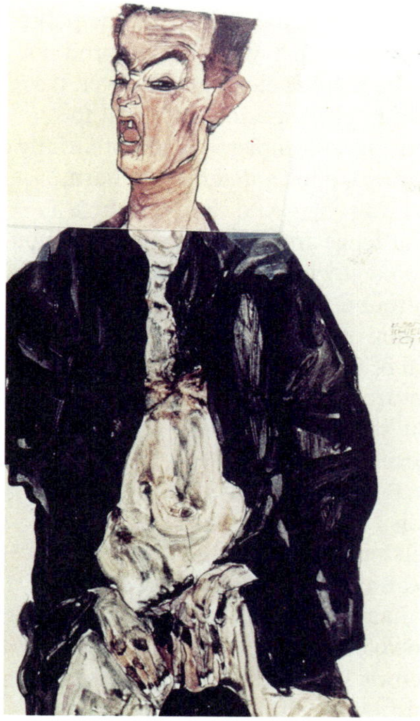

Avedon's collage of artwork by Egon Schiele

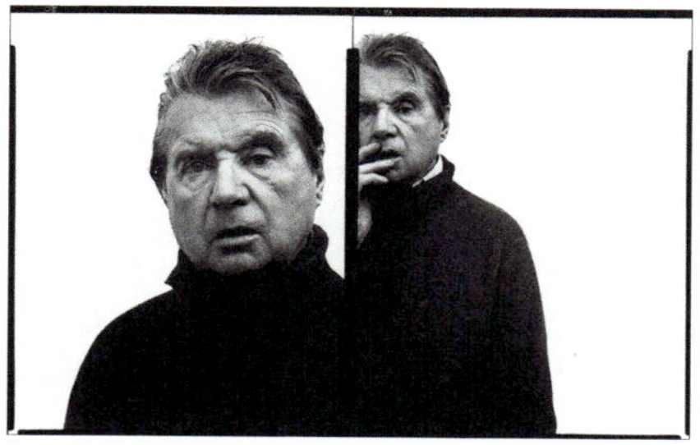

Francis Bacon, artist, Paris, April 11, 1979; Richard Avedon

Presuming to say what Schiele should have done or might have done is out of the question. But let me end with a story that may say something about all of this: performance, gesture, fashion as performance, and the afterlife of Egon Schiele.

In 1975, I had arrived at the point in my own career where I was no longer interested in doing portraits of persons of power and accomplishment. However there were three men whose work I admired enormously and whose portraits I wanted to make: Francis Bacon, Jorge Luis Borges and Samuel Beckett. Their portraits turned out they involve three different kinds of performance: Borges gave an unphotographable performance,

Beckett refused to perform and Bacon offered a perfect performance.

I photograph what I'm most afraid of, and Borges was blind.

On the plane to Buenos Aires, I discovered that Borges's mother, with whom I knew he had lived all of his life, had died that evening. I assumed, of course, that the sitting would be canceled. But he received me as we had planned, the next afternoon at four o'clock. I arrived at his apartment and found myself in the dark. He was sitting in gray light, on a small settee, and signaled with his hand for me to sit beside him. Almost immediately, he told me that he admired Kipling and asked me to read to him. "Go to the bookcase and find the seventh book from the right on the second shelf," he said. I did. He told what poem of Kipling's he wanted to hear — "The Harp Song of the Dane Women" — and I read it to him. He joined in occasionally. Did I know Anglo-Saxon? he asked next. Which would I prefer, legend or elegy? Elegy, I chanced. He explained to me, as he prepared to recite, that his dead mother lay in the adjoining room. Her hands had clenched in pain just before her death, he explained, and then he described how he and their servant had straightened out each of his mother's fingers, one by one, until her hands lay in peace on her breast. Then he recited the Anglo-Saxon elegy, his voice rising and falling in the dark room.

The first time I saw him in light, it was my light. I was overwhelmed with feeling and I started to photograph. But the photographs turned out to be emptier than I had hoped. I thought I had somehow been so overwhelmed that I had brought nothing of myself to the portrait.

Four years later, I read an account by Paul Theroux of his visit to Borges. It was my visit: the dim light, the trip to the bookcase, Kipling, the Anglo-Saxon recital. In some way, it seemed Borges had no visitors. People who came from the outside could exist for him only if they were made part of his familiar inner world, the world of poets and ancients who were already his true companions. The people in that world knew more, argued better, had more to tell him. The performance permitted no interchange. He had taken his own portrait long before, and I could only photograph that.

In 1979 I went to Paris to photograph Samuel Beckett. As we were about to walk around the corner to the camera and white paper, Beckett spoke. "This is very painful for me," he said. I chose to believe him — though the remark might have been meant in another way — and stopped the sitting before it began. I'm still not certain that I did the correct thing.

My sitting with Francis Bacon was planned for a Sunday morning in Paris. I had set up my outdoor studio on the shady side of the Musée d'Art Moderne at the Trocadéro. Bacon came in a striped shirt, leather pants and a checked jacket, dressed to kill, dressed to be photographed. And we had a charming conversation about the differences between living in Paris and London. It was a sunny day, and a really lovely, civilized exchange. Then I began the portrait. I explained the nature of the diptych I wanted to achieve. I'd made a little sketch of what I hoped to do. I asked him to exchange his jacket for my plain, dark sweater. And then I asked him to bring

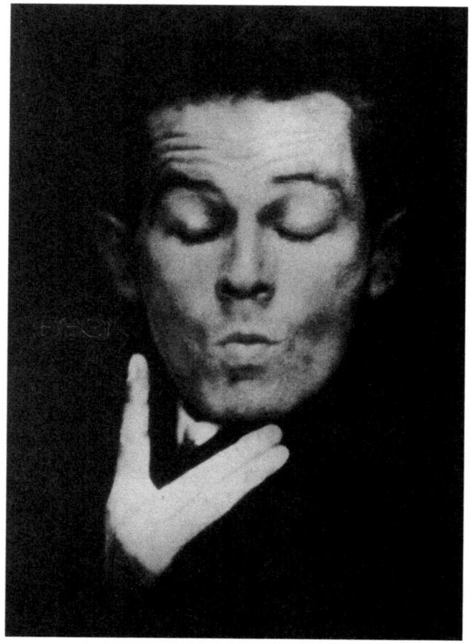

Egon Schiele

his hand up into the portrait. If I'd asked the same of a politician or a banker, or for that matter, any one of us, the tendency would be for the subject to want to look distiniguished, sage, to rest a chin on a hand, or bring a hand to a forehead. Bacon immediately acted the role of the private Bacon with the greatest purity, economy of gesture, and yet filled with authentic feeling. Without my saying a word, he understood what my portrait was about, what it called for from him, and he still remained true to himself. No one could act Bacon but Bacon. On this perfect, clear Sunday, facing the Eiffel Tower, he achieved an honorable and perfect performance. Now that I look at the picture again, I see how much this gesture of internal conflict comes out of the modern tradition Schiele began. I certainly wasn't aware of it at the time, and I very much doubt that Bacon was either. But now I like to think that while we were performing, Schiele was pulling the strings.

Richard Avedon, "Borrowed Dogs," *Grand Street* 7, no. 1, (Autumn, 1987): 52–64.

Nouveau Souffle: *Egoïste* 1985-2004

In 1985, Avedon began working for *Egoïste*, where his work would be fearlessly experimental. He appeared in nine issues of the magazine between 1985 and 2004, portraying some of France's (and Europe's) most provocative figures — François Pinault, "Danny the Red" Cohn-Bendit, and John Galliano — along with such surprising subjects as Abbé Pierre, Soeur Emmanuelle, and the winemaking team at Château Lafite.

Issue 9 featured his self-portrait on the cover and "Un Portrait est une Opinion" (A Portrait is an opinion), his interview with Nicole Wisniak (*see pages 604–09*). *Egoiste* was the first magazine anywhere to publish images from Avedon's *In the American West* (*see pages 622–27*).

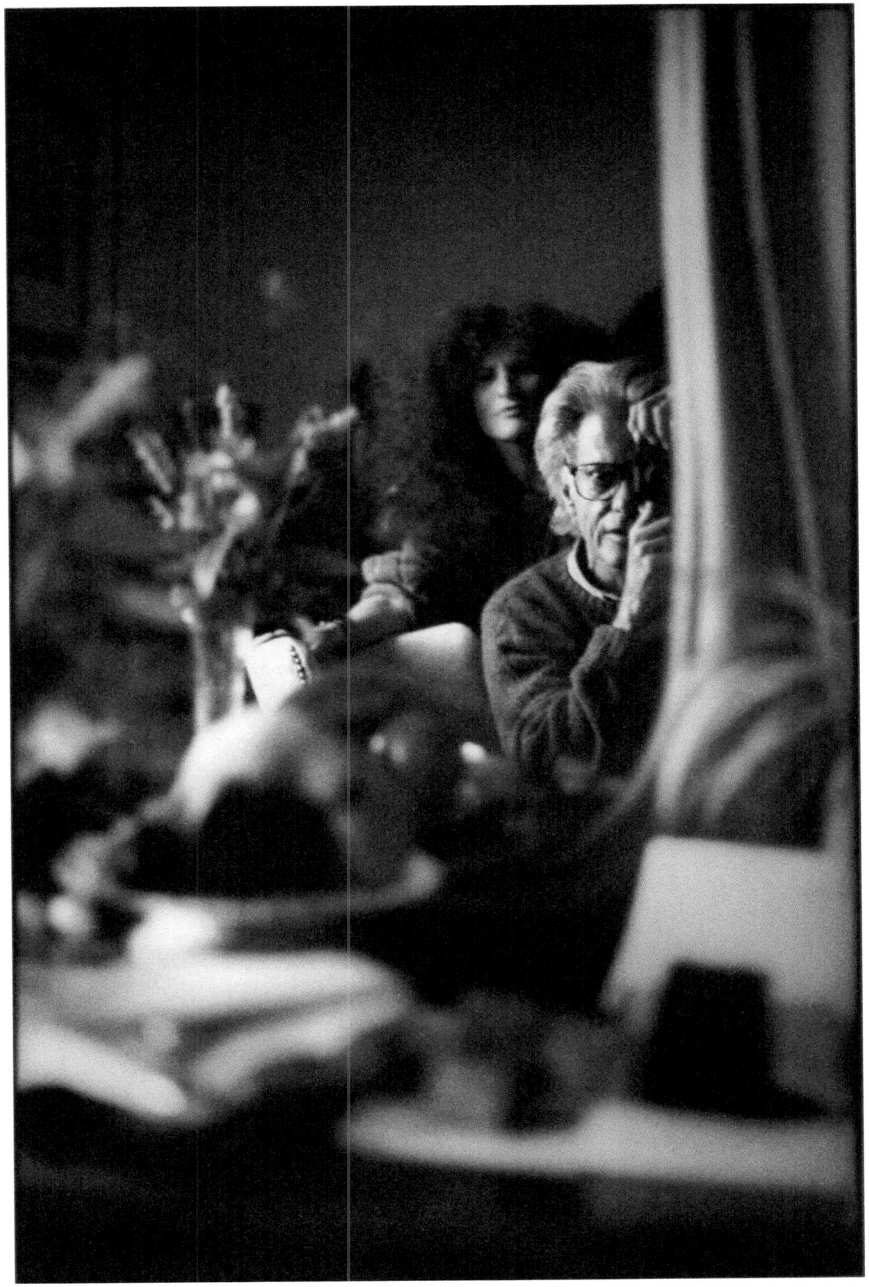

Nicole Wisniak and Avedon, Paris

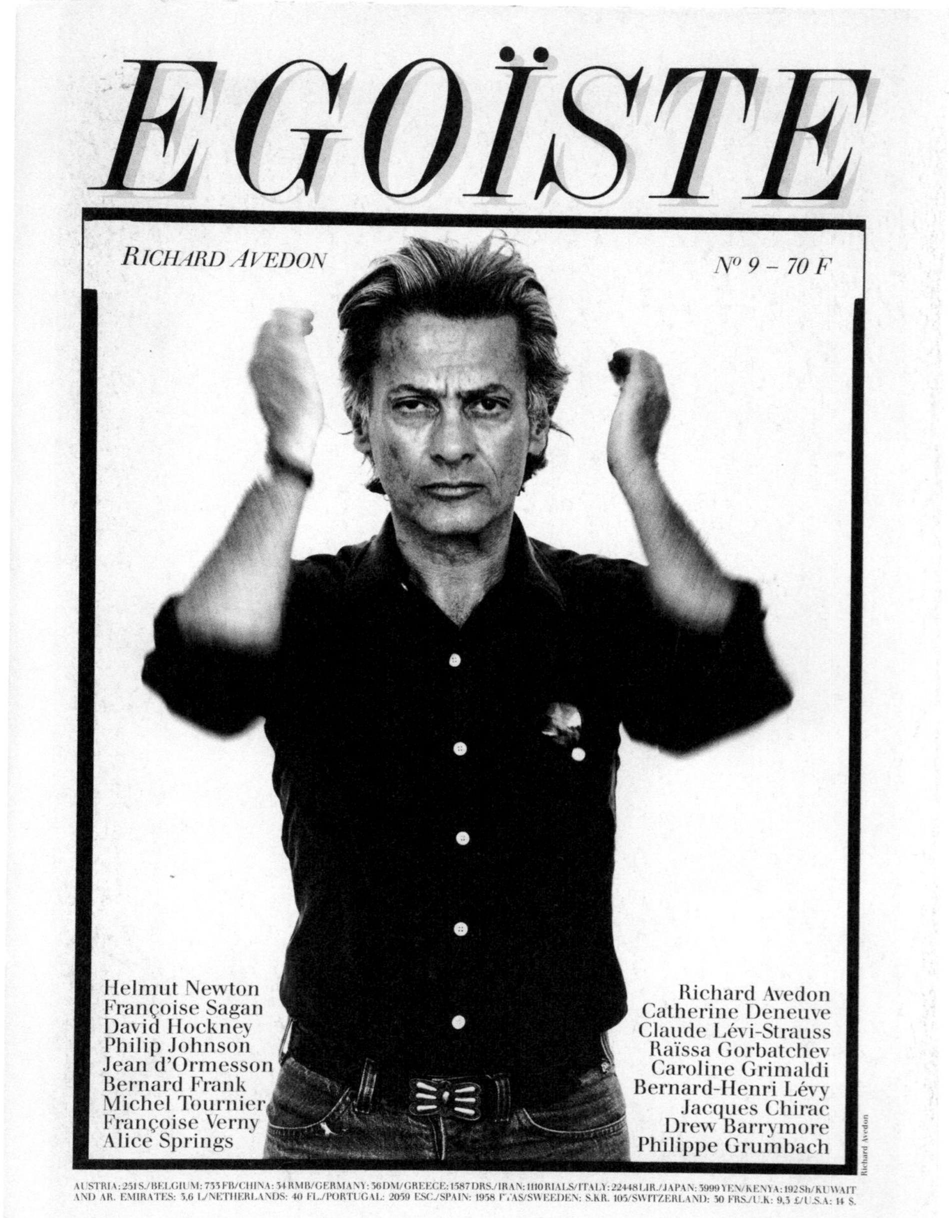

Egoïste, N° 9, 1985. Avedon's work appeared on the cover of *Egoïste* ten times.

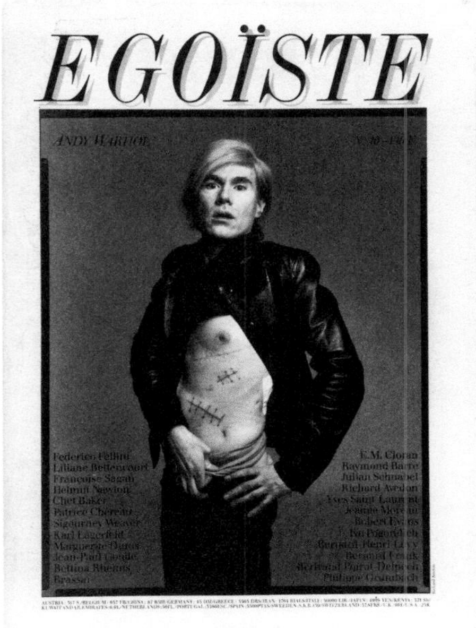

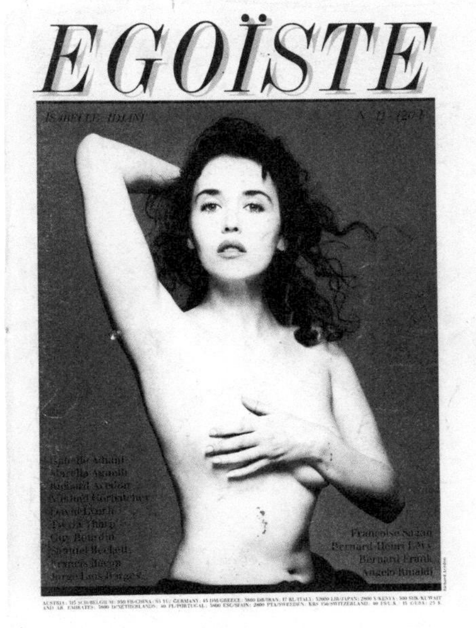

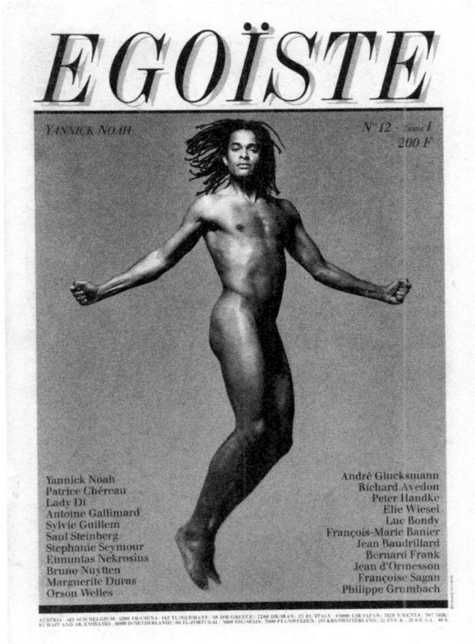

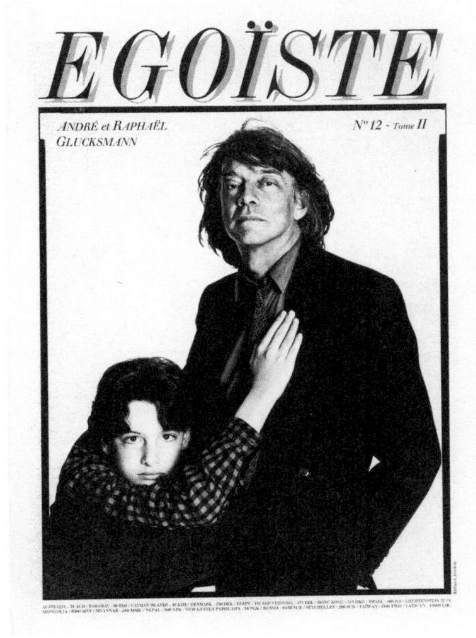

Egoïste covers by Avedon: Andy Warhol, N° 10, 1987; Isabelle Adjani, N° 11, 1989; Yannick Noah, N° 12, Tome I, 1992; and André and Raphaël Glucksmann, N° 12, Tome II, 1992

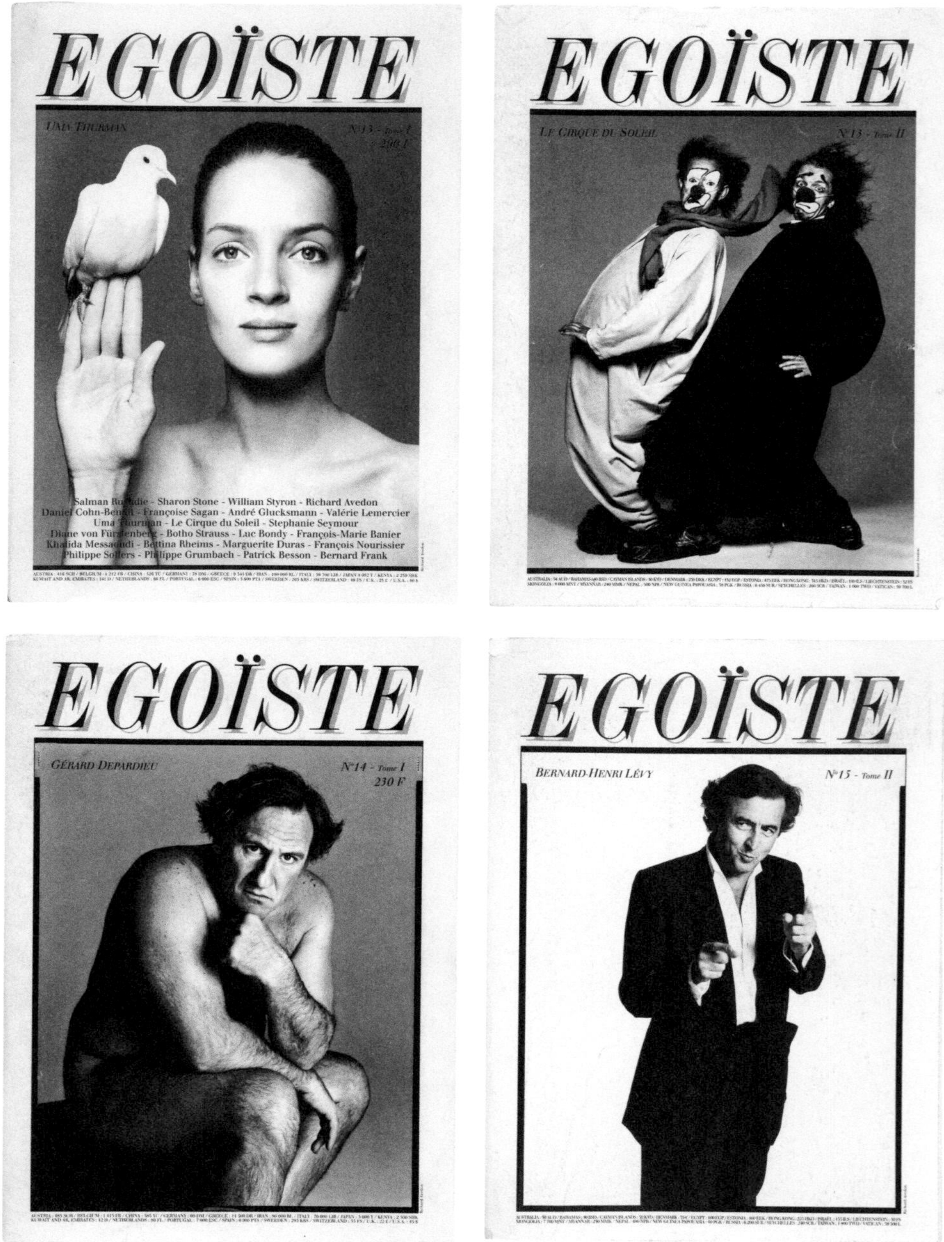

Egoïste covers by Avedon: Uma Thurman, N° 13, Tome I, 1997; Le Cirque du Soleil, N° 13, Tome II, 1997; Gérard Depardieu, N° 14, Tome 1, 2000; and Bernard Henri Lévy, N° 15, Tome II, 2006 (*posthumous*)

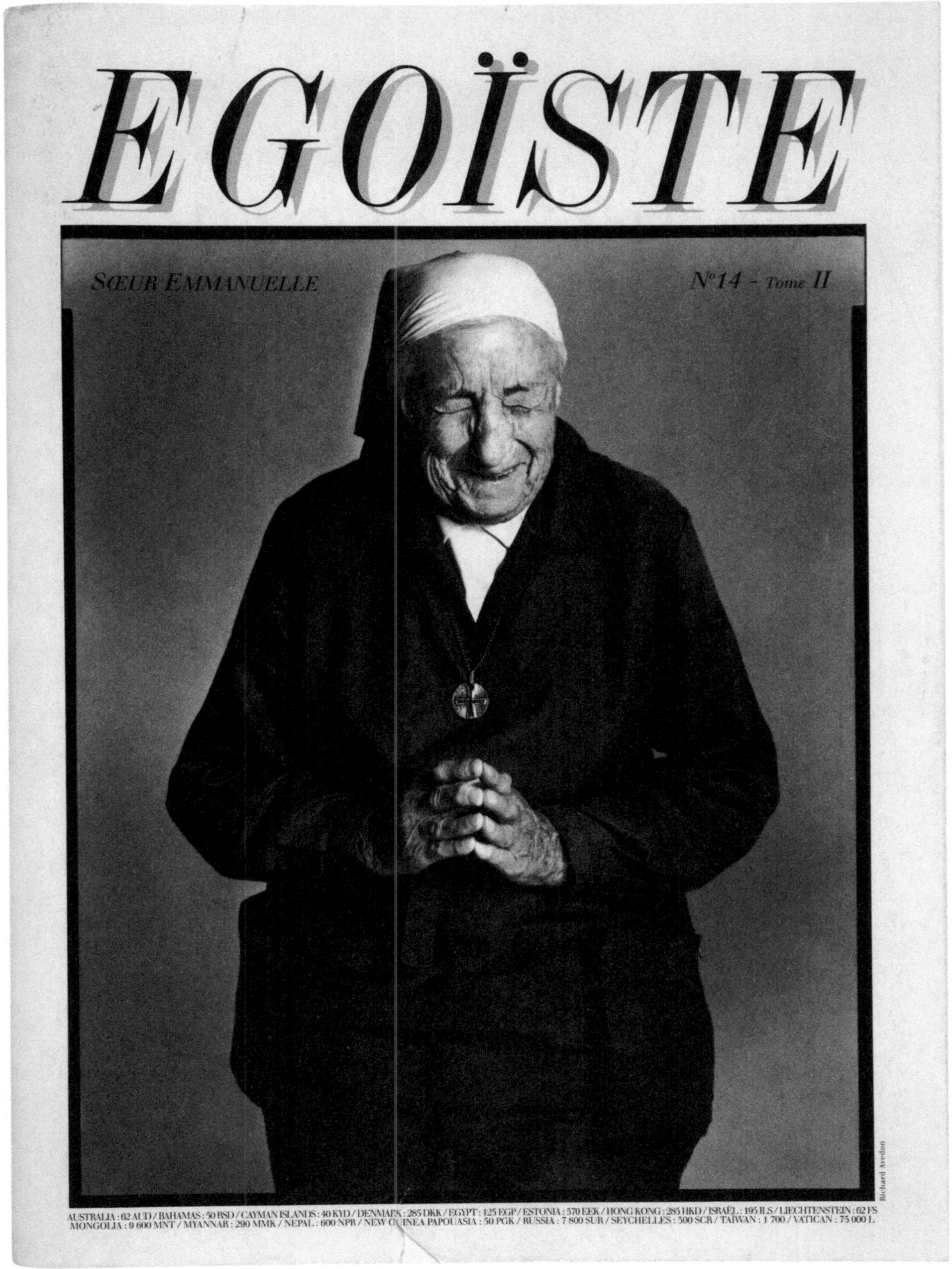

Egoïste, cover by Avedon: Sœur Emmanuelle, N° 14, Tome II, 2000

Egoïste is the only magazine in the world to give me completely free expression.

—

Richard Avedon

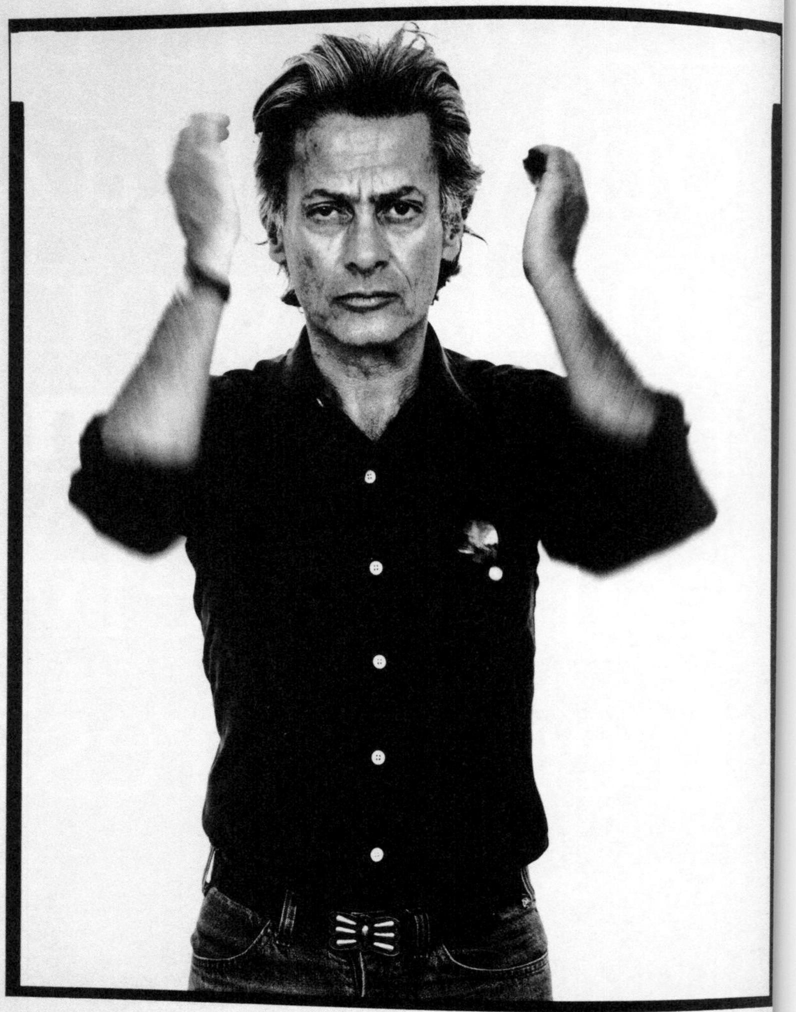

Richard Avedon, Photographe, Autoportrait – Provo, Utah – 20 Août, 1980.

48

MISE AU POINT

Richard Avedon – Nicole Wisniak

Un Portrait est une Opinion

Nicole Wisniak: *Pensez-vous qu'un photographe soit une personne obsédée par l'idée que les choses peuvent disparaître?*

Richard Avedon: On ne peut pas généraliser. Tout ce qui me reste de Humphrey Bogart, c'est la photo que j'ai faite de lui, c'est-à-dire de la pellicule, mais je ne crois pas que c'est pour cela que je fais des photographies. C'est parce que je vois tout le temps et que, très souvent, je n'écoute pas. Je suis en train de parler avec quelqu'un et, tout d'un coup, je ne suis plus là. A partir d'un certain moment, je me contente de faire semblant; mes amis savent exactement quand cela se produit.

Je vois les gens et les choses comme les musiciens entendent, c'est-à-dire d'une manière extrasensorielle et sans porter de jugement. Je ne fais pas de différence entre ce qui est beau et ce qui ne l'est pas. Ma perception n'est que la répétition, la confirmation des choses, des nombreuses choses qui me sont nécessaires. C'est un élan, un geste qui relève de l'obsession, et donc inexplicable! Je suis un photographe instinctif, au premier degré. C'est mon langage. Je m'exprime à travers mes photographies d'une manière plus complète et plus profonde qu'à travers des mots.

N.W.: *Mais cet œil surdoué est parfois sans pitié. Vous faites apparaître, dans vos portraits, des traits de caractère que vos modèles auraient préféré dissimuler. Pensez-vous qu'il soit possible de garder son identité masquée devant votre appareil?*

R.A.: Je ne cherche pas automatiquement à découvrir la face cachée d'une personne. Mais le fait que quelqu'un cherche à me cacher quelque chose rend ce quelque chose intéressant. Suffisamment pour que j'aie envie de faire son portrait, le portrait de quelqu'un qui a un secret et veut le cacher. Il n'y a pas de vérité en photographie. Et il n'y a pas qu'une seule vérité chez quelqu'un. Mes portraits sont davantage un reflet de moi-même que des personnes que je photographie. J'ai longtemps pensé qu'il s'agissait d'une collaboration, et que ce qui en surgissait était l'addition de l'expression souhaitée par le modèle et de celle voulue par le photographe. Je ne le pense plus du tout. Le photographe a un contrôle total, il est confronté à un problème compliqué, d'ordre moral: car tous les sujets qui posent devant son appareil photographique en attendent quelque chose et je contribue à les décevoir dans la mesure où ils peuvent croire que je vais combler ce désir. Si on écrit sur vous, ou si on peint votre portrait, vous pouvez dire: Ce n'est pas moi, c'est Bacon, c'est Soutine! Ce n'est pas moi, c'est Céline!

N.W.: *Picasso a exprimé cela en parlant de Gertrude Stein: "Elle n'était pas ainsi quand je l'ai peinte mais c'est ainsi qu'elle sera, tôt ou tard."*

R.A.: C'est plutôt exagéré de sa part, plutôt prétentieux. Mais maintenant qu'elle est morte il faut reconnaître que c'est, visuellement, exact. C'est une terrible responsabilité pour un photographe. Comme le sujet était là, le sujet ne pourra jamais dire: ce n'est pas moi. C'est encore pire quand il s'agit de photographies pour les journaux, quand il s'agit de photos prises sans l'autorisation du sujet. Moi en tout cas, au moins, je demande: "Puis-je faire votre portrait?"

Je ne suis pas parvenu à résoudre ce problème compliqué parce que je crois à toutes sortes de responsabilités morales. Je suis convaincu que je n'ai pas le droit de dire: "C'est comme ça", et, d'un autre côté, je ne peux pas m'en empêcher. C'est pour moi la seule façon de respirer et de vivre. Je pourrais dire que c'est la nature même de l'art qui m'amène à me conduire ainsi, mais il n'y a jamais eu un art comparable à la photographie. Il est impossible de faire la photographie d'une personne hors de la présence de cette personne, et c'est cette présence même qui suppose la vérité. Mais un portrait n'est pas une ressemblance. A partir du moment où une émotion ou un fait devient une photographie, ce n'est plus un fait mais une opinion. La notion d'inexactitude n'existe pas pour un photographe. Toutes les photographies sont exactes; aucune n'est vraie.

N.W.: *Depuis plusieurs années vous travaillez sur un livre qui concerne les travailleurs. Avez-vous entrepris ce nouveau travail parce que vous étiez lassé de ce qu'on appelle l'élite?*

R.A.: Non, pas du tout. Cela fait longtemps, de nombreuses années, que je travaille, comme portraitiste, à faire des portraits d'Américains. Mais je croyais ne pouvoir photographier que ce que je connaissais et comprenais; je comprenais les artistes, les gens capables de prouesses. Le pouvoir, la beauté, je croyais connaître tout cela. J'ai dit, dans une interview, que j'ignorais totalement ce que c'était que d'être noir ou de travailler en usine et que je ne pouvais donc pas photographier cela. Bien entendu ce n'était pas vrai. Mais cela m'a pris beaucoup de temps pour comprendre, au fond de moi-même, que les gens ont les mêmes préoccupations et que se retrouver, par exemple, face à un pompiste est très peu différent de se retrouver, disons, face à un écrivain. C'est uniquement une question de langage. En fait, les gens que j'ai photographiés pour ce nouveau livre m'ont semblé plus généreux, moins méfiants, souvent plus faciles à voir.

N.W.: *Mais tout le monde n'est pas un bon sujet pour vous. Comment choisissez-vous les gens que vous photographiez?*

R.A.: Rares sont les bons sujets pour moi. Et rares étaient les gens ressemblant à un Modigliani. Et rares étaient les sujets convenant à Matisse. Il s'agit là d'une question difficile parce que ce n'est pas quelque chose que je mets en équation. Ce qui m'intéresse ce sont les points communs entre des êtres humains qui ont une expérience de la vie tout à fait différente mais qui, pour des rai-

49

Richard Avedon interview by Nicole Wisniak, "Un portrait est une opinion" (A portrait is an opinion), *Egoïste*, N° 9, 1985, pp. 48–49 sons inattendues et inexplicables, se ressemblent. Dans mon nouveau livre, vous verrez un homme, un ouvrier du Colorado, qui ressemble à James Galanos. Or Galanos est un styliste de Beverly Hills qui dessine des robes, notamment pour la femme du Président. Et l'homme du Colorado, lui, est un ouvrier qui s'occupe des emballages. Ça, ça me fascine. Si vous regardez les portraits des "Sept de Chicago"*, vous trouverez des ressemblances avec le "Mission Council"**. Le paradoxe, l'ironie, la contradiction, voilà ce qui m'intéresse dans une photographie. Les contradictions par exemple à l'intérieur d'un seul personnage: le contraste possible entre la délicatesse, l'innocence des mains d'un sujet et le manque de franchise, le côté fuyant du visage.

N.W. : *Il y a aussi des contradictions dans votre travail. Vos photos de mode et, ensuite, vos portraits, qui semblent montrer un aspect plus dramatique de la vie.*

R.A. : Je ne crois pas que l'un et l'autre soient contradictoires bien que ce soit une opinion généralement retenue à propos de Diane Arbus et de moi-même: le fait que le côté sérieux, ou, si vous voulez, le côté "tragique" de nos portraits, soit une réaction contre les exigences ou les futilités de la mode. Et je trouve qu'il y a une tendance à classer les photographes comme on n'oserait jamais classer les écrivains. Si un auteur écrit une comédie ou une tragédie, puis un essai ou un ouvrage politique, personne ne le met en cause. Personne ne se demande pourquoi un philosophe écrit un roman ou un poème, ou pourquoi Picasso a fait les costumes d'un ballet! Ce libéralisme ne s'étend pas aux photographes de mode. J'ai toujours eu à me justifier là-dessus, moins maintenant, mais quand même...

La photographie de mode n'est pas un art qui peut se développer indéfiniment. Il évolue toujours à la surface des choses et cela désormais ne m'attire plus. Quand j'étais jeune, mes conceptions sur le plan artistique étaient les mêmes que celles des magazines pour lesquels je travaillais – Harper's Bazaar. Il publiait ce que je voulais exprimer. (Ça a duré vingt ans – c'est quand même un peu gênant, non?)

Puis, il y eut un moment où les aspirations des magazines de mode ne me concernèrent plus, ne m'intéressèrent plus. Cela demeurait cependant pour moi une nécessité économique; la photographie de mode fait partie de ma vie professionnelle. Cela ne présente pas de difficultés. J'en vis et cela finance d'autres travaux que je préfère.

N.W. : *Et cela fait vivre votre studio?*

R.A. : Pendant mon enfance et mon adolescence, dans les années trente et quarante, il était admis qu'un homme devait faire vivre ses parents et sa famille; c'était lui qui devait gagner de quoi nourrir les siens. Et j'ai toujours gardé cette idée ancrée en moi. Je n'ai rien d'un bohème. Je sais que je suis responsable de ma famille. Et je l'ai su très tôt.

N.W. : *Etre photographe, était-ce le moyen le plus évident de gagner sa vie au début des années cinquante?*

R.A. : Mon père voulait que je devienne un homme d'affaires. Il avait terriblement souffert en tant que Juif russe au début du siècle à New York. Enfant, il avait eu une vie épouvantable, avec ses cinq frères et sœurs abandonnés par leur père et envoyés dans un orphelinat; il y avait en lui un sentiment du tragique très développé et un sens exagéré du danger. Il voulait que je sois prêt à affronter ce qu'il appelait "la bataille" avec le maximum d'atouts: l'éducation, la force physique et l'argent.

Je suis une parfaite mosaïque de ma mère et de mon père. Elle a quatre-vingt-cinq ans, elle est devenue sculpteur à soixante-quinze ans en travaillant sur le granite et le marbre. Ma mère aimait les arts (pendant la dépression, elle volait des lilas!), elle avait une activité politique et elle m'a toujours encouragé à devenir un artiste. Elle a été mon plus grand soutien, et elle l'est encore, sans réserve. D'un artiste, elle dit: "Il est authentique" ou "Il n'est pas authentique".

De toute façon, la photographie était la seule chose que je puisse faire. Je suis photographe depuis au moins l'âge de treize ans. Ma famille travaillait dans la mode et mes parents étaient abonnés à Harper's Bazaar, Vogue et Vanity Fair. J'ai vu, quand j'étais enfant, des photos de mode et des portraits d'acteurs de Steichen, du baron de Meyer et de Man Ray dans chaque numéro, et j'ai commencé à les imiter en faisant des photos de ma petite sœur. Elle était très, très belle, de deux ans ma cadette. Sa beauté fut le grand événement de notre famille et sa beauté aussi détruisit sa vie. Elle fut élevée comme s'il n'y avait personne à l'intérieur de sa parfaite enveloppe, comme si elle était seulement un long cou, des yeux d'un brun profond. Je pense qu'elle croyait n'être qu'une peau, des cheveux et un corps magnifique. Il se trouve que je n'avais pas regardé une photographie d'elle depuis trente ans; ce n'est que la semaine dernière que j'ai ouvert un paquet de mes premières photos, faites alors que j'étais adolescent. Chaque famille croit que sa fille ou son fils sont les plus beaux enfants du monde, mais ma sœur Louise (je l'ai photographiée entre quatorze et dix-huit ans) était réellement une beauté de classe internationale et je l'ignorais jusqu'à la semaine dernière. J'ai découvert qu'elle était le prototype de ce que j'estimais être la beauté pendant mes premières années comme photographe de mode. Tous mes premiers mannequins: Dorian Leigh, Elise Daniels, Carmen, Marella Agnelli, Audrey Hepburn, étaient brunes et avaient de jolis nez, de longs cous et des visages ovales. Elles étaient toutes des souvenirs de ma sœur. Ma conception de la beauté s'est formée très tôt à partir d'elle.

> ## Mes premiers mannequins étaient toutes des souvenirs de ma sœur

N.W. : *Où est-elle maintenant?*

R.A. : Elle est morte. Elle est morte dans un asile d'aliénés à l'âge de trente ans. Elle s'était complètement repliée sur elle-même à la fin de son adolescence.

N.W. : *Vous croyez que c'est sa beauté qui l'a tuée?*

R.A. : Dépersonnalisée. Probablement détruite, je pense, sous l'effet de sa beauté. C'est aussi isolant que le génie, ou une malformation. Mais, au contraire du génie, la beauté vous éloigne du monde sans vous offrir de vraies compensations. J'ai toujours été conscient de la parenté entre la folie et la beauté. Cela contribue-t-il à expliquer un peu ce qui paraît contradictoire dans mon travail? Ce n'en est qu'un aspect. Ça n'a rien à voir avec la discipline photographique ou quoi que ce soit, mais vous comprendrez ce que je veux dire en regardant mes portraits: une possibilité d'échec, de danger, de poésie dans la vie , et la frontière fragile qui sépare l'ensemble.

Quand ces éléments ont commencé à se mélanger dans mes photos de mode, je devins inutilisable pour les magazines. Il fallait que je corrige ma manière de travailler ou que j'abandonne.

N.W. : *Mais vous êtes parvenu à éliminer cette obsession de votre travail commercial?*

R.A. : Complètement. Je fais de la publicité ou du rédactionnel avec facilité. Je travaille dur et j'essaie de faire du mieux possible. Mais je n'y investis maintenant qu'une très petite part de moi-même.

N.W. : *Vous pensez que les magazines sont dangereux pour les photographes?*

R.A. : Cyril Connolly, le critique anglais, a écrit un livre intitulé "Enemies of Promise". J'avais pris l'habitude de le recommander à mes étudiants. Ils n'ont jamais exactement compris pourquoi. Il parle, dans ce livre, des éditeurs, des magazines, du marché de l'art comme d'"ennemis des promesses". C'est une très belle image.

Je pense que tout peut être dangereux. Cela dépend uniquement de la manière dont on se comporte. Du jour où j'ai été convaincu que je ne parvenais plus à exprimer les choses comme je les ressentais par la photographie de mode, je me suis mis à faire un autre genre de photographie, pour moi-même. C'est d'ailleurs absurde pour un artiste d'entretenir l'illusion qu'un magazine peut être le lieu où s'épanouira sa vie créative.

N.W. : *Depuis quarante ans vous photographiez des peintres, des hom-*

**Les sept animateurs de la manifestation de Chicago contre la guerre du Vietnam, accusés de conspiration contre le gouvernement fédéral et jugés en 69.*

***Les onze conseillers civils et militaires américains en mission à Saïgon, pendant la guerre du Vietnam, en 71.*

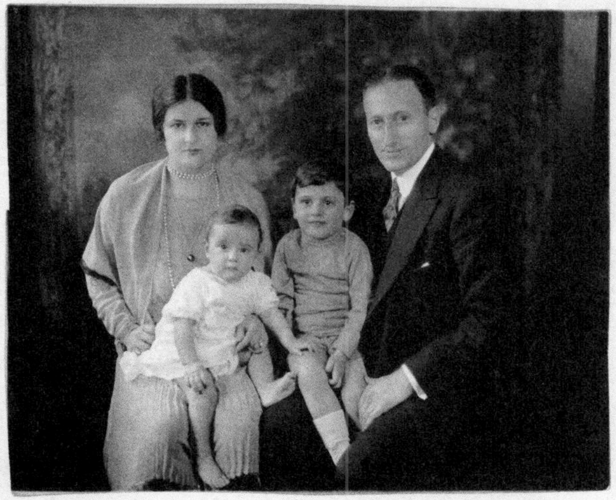

De gauche à droite : Anna, Louise, Richard et Jacob Israël Avedon en 1926.

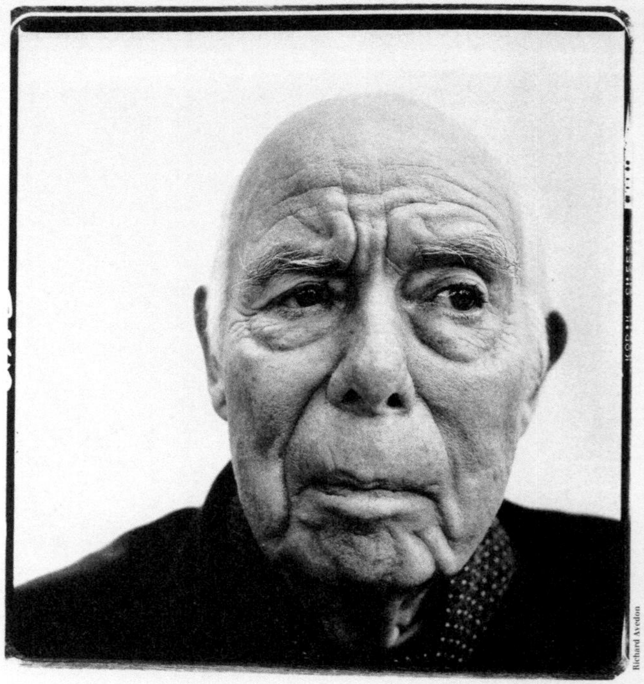
Richard Avedon

Jean Renoir, Beverly Hills, Californie 1972

La tempête se concentre sur mes photos...

mes politiques, des artistes, des travailleurs, des gens célèbres ou inconnus. Qu'est-ce qui nourrit votre curiosité pour les gens ?

R.A. : Je ne pense pas que les explications psychanalytiques suffisent. Mais il y a un peu de vrai dans tout cela, dans Freud, dans Pavlov, dans la génétique, dans l'environnement. J'ai été élevé avec une cousine germaine qui avait deux ans de plus que moi. J'en ai été profondément amoureux de quatre à dix-huit ans. Il n'y avait qu'avec elle que je pouvais respirer librement. Nous étions très précoces. Quand le film de Cocteau "les Enfants terribles" sortit, nous comprîmes que nous étions ces enfants-là. Nous avons vu et revu ce film plusieurs fois. Nos sentiments étaient si intenses, si interdits, si complices, qu'il devint évident pour moi – je ne peux pas parler pour elle – que si je voulais m'épanouir, devenir adulte et prendre place dans le monde, il fallait que nous brisions cette serre parfaite. Pendant toutes ces années où un jeune homme fait l'apprentissage de la vie hors de sa famille, je ne connus qu'une seule personne. Je pense que mon caractère, tout entier, s'est formé dans cet amour envahissant. Et ma vie s'est poursuivie ainsi, une personne à la fois.

N.W. : *Cette relation – une personne à la fois – c'est celle que vous répétez dans votre studio en faisant des portraits ?*

R.A. : Oh, oui ! Avec une grande intensité – mais avec la photographie il s'agit d'une intensité gratuite. C'est ainsi que je ne suis jamais devenu l'ami – ou très rarement – de quelqu'un que j'ai photographié. Pendant des années et des années, je n'ai jamais imaginé, en rentrant dans une pièce où se trouvait quelqu'un que j'avais photographié auparavant, que ce quelqu'un puisse me reconnaître. Il y a des moments d'une intensité gênante, de cette intimité si particulière, dans ce double besoin que nous avons : le besoin pour le sujet de s'offrir à l'appareil de photo et à moi-même, et le besoin pour moi d'accepter ce don afin de pouvoir m'exprimer. C'est quelque chose de compliqué, et je dis d'immérité. Je n'ai jamais présumé qu'il puisse y avoir autre chose que cette photo entre mes modèles et moi. Cela dure moins d'une heure et ensuite c'est terminé, complètement.

N.W. : *Mais vous n'avez jamais été séduit par l'une de ces personnes ?*

R.A. : Quand mon livre "Portraits" fut sur le point d'être achevé, il restait certains artistes dont le travail m'avait touché, que je n'avais pas photographiés ; l'un d'eux était Jean Renoir. Renoir vivait à Beverly Hills et j'ai été le voir. Sa maison ressemblait exactement à ce que j'ai toujours pensé qu'une maison dût être. On se serait cru dans le sud de la France, pas à Beverly Hills : il y avait des fleurs partout et le soleil traversait les fenêtres. Une longue table était placée au milieu de la pièce. (Une longue table au centre d'une maison, cela a toujours eu une grande signification pour moi.) Quand j'arrivai, on me conduisit à sa chambre à coucher. Il était en train de s'habiller sans que ma présence semblât le déranger. Il était très malade à ce moment-là et il marchait avec difficulté, à l'aide d'un déambulateur. Il y avait quelque chose de très émouvant dans son visage, comme dans sa vie, son œuvre et ses convictions. Il était une des dernières personnes qui m'impressionnaient vraiment. Quand la séance de travail fut terminée (à cette époque je travaillais avec une intensité incroyable, mon cœur battait la chamade pendant que je travaillais), Renoir me dit : "Voulez-vous vous joindre à nous ?"

Je m'assis donc devant la table et quelques amis arrivèrent avec de la vodka et un gâteau du dimanche et Renoir s'assit. Derrière lui il y avait un portrait de lui petit, peint par son père, et les poteries qu'il avait faites alors sous sa surveillance.

Un jeune metteur en scène tchécoslovaque qui était là en visite commença à parler cinéma avec Renoir. Il m'arriva alors ce qui m'arrive très souvent : je fus soudain pétrifié, je ne pouvais plus penser ni parler. Je ne me sentais pas à ma place. Je pensais : que pourrais-je dire qui enrichisse en quoi que ce soit ce qui se passe autour de cette table ? D'ailleurs rien de bien particulier ne se passait ! Je trouvais que je réussissais assez bien à camoufler ce que je ressentais et je savais que je n'étais nullement obligé de parler. Je pouvais, en toute tranquillité, rester silencieux. Mais, intérieurement, j'étais paralysé. Je souriais, essayant de faire croire que j'étais parfaitement à mon aise, tout en pensant : quel droit ai-je d'être assis à cette table ? Je suis venu pour faire une photographie, je devrais m'en aller ; je ne suis pas un ami des Renoir et c'est dimanche.

Renoir se leva pour aller aux toilettes et j'en profitai pour prendre congé de tout le monde. Mais, alors que je m'approchais de la porte, il sortit de sa chambre dans son déambulateur, me barrant la route. Je lui tendis la main en disant : "Monsieur Renoir, merci beaucoup de m'avoir permis de vous photographier". Alors il me regarda droit dans les yeux et je n'oublierai jamais ses paroles : "Ce n'est pas ce qu'on dit qui compte ; ce sont les sentiments qui s'échangent au-dessus de la table". Mon visage se figea. Je marchai jusqu'à ma voiture et me mis à pleurer. Imaginez : un homme de plus de quatre-vingts ans, malade comme il l'était, conscient de ce qui m'arrivait à cette table, s'en préoccupant et me le disant.

Oui, c'est le genre de critère selon lequel j'apprécie le comportement humain : être capable de cette acuité à chaque instant. Cette vigilance et cette sensibilité. Je pense qu'il n'y a rien de plus important dans la vie que cette histoire : un homme de cet âge, dans l'environnement des œuvres de son père, qui a créé son œuvre personnelle, vivant dans cette maison baignée par les rayons du soleil qui trouent les fenêtres, avec sa femme auprès de lui, cette carafe de vodka et les rondelles de citron, des amis, son fils devenu professeur et les enfants mêlés aux adultes, un dimanche, et qu'il soit quand même capable d'être aussi attentif à un étranger.

N.W. : *En repensant à l'ensemble de votre carrière, êtes-vous plutôt satisfait, ou avez-vous des regrets ?*

R.A. : Je n'ai jamais ressenti que ce que je faisais était suffisamment bon et, franchement, je continue, en grande partie, à penser cela à propos de tout ce que je fais : ce n'est pas satisfaisant, rien n'est satisfaisant, et de loin. Mais ce n'est pas un regret. Je pense que j'en sais davantage que je ne peux accomplir.

N.W. : *Cela vous fait-il souffrir ?*

R.A. : Non. Cela me fait travailler !

N.W. : *Qu'est-ce qui vous rend anxieux ?*

R.A. : Mes inexplicables changements d'humeur. D'un moment à l'autre, je change : de quelqu'un qui se croit capable de faire face à n'importe quoi à quelqu'un qui ne peut plus penser du tout. Cela n'a rien à voir avec la réalité. J'aime bien imaginer que c'est chimique. J'ai longtemps pensé que c'était freudien *(Il rit.)* Je sais maintenant que je suis au mieux de ma forme pendant ces séances brèves et intenses. Je crois que faire des photographies, c'est plus intense et plus bref qu'écrire. Tout ce que je fais, il me semble, relève de la passion et puis, soudain, c'est fini, je ne suis plus là – ce qui ne veut pas dire, nécessairement, que c'est la dépression. Je peux prendre l'avion ou dormir ou faire des puzzles, mais il faut que je m'arrête. Je ne suis pas capable de vivre au niveau le plus intense pendant longtemps. Je crois qu'il pourrait m'arriver de craquer. C'est probablement pour cela que je continue à faire un peu de photographies de mode, pour me détendre.

N.W. : *Avez-vous jamais pensé que vous pourriez devenir fou ?*

R.A. : Peut-être, quand j'étais jeune, oui. A certains moments, quand la pression était très forte, dans des situations auxquelles il me semblait impossible de faire face, je pensais : je n'y arriverai pas. Mais je suis toujours parvenu à m'évader dans la réalité, dans le travail. Beaucoup de choses m'ont intéressé pendant soixante-deux ans, beaucoup de choses dans tous les domaines de ma vie. Elles ont trouvé leur expression dans mes photographies.

N.W. : *Mais pas sur votre visage. Vous semblez très serein.*

R.A. : Peut-être est-ce parce que la tempête se concentre sur mes photos, pas sur mon visage. C'est une drôle d'idée. *(Il rit.)*

Richard Avedon interview by Nicole Wisniak, "Un portrait est une opinion" (A portrait is an opinion), *Egoïste*, N° 9, 1985, pp. 52–53

A Portrait is an Opinion
Interview with Richard Avedon by Nicole Wisniak

NICOLE WISNIAK: Do you think a photographer is a person obsessed by the fact that things disappear?

RICHARD AVEDON: I can't generalize. All that remains of my father is my photograph, that is to say film, but I don't think that's why I photograph. I see all the time — I very often don't listen. I can be in conversation with someone and at a certain point, stop hearing what is said, start pretending to listen. My good friends know when that happens.

The way I see is comparable to the way musicians hear, something extrasensory. Not judgemental. I don't differentiate between an idea of what is beautiful and what is not. What I see is a reaffirmation of the many things that I need to feel. It has to do with obsessive qualities, not explainable. I am a natural photographer. It is my language. I speak through my photographs more intricately, more deeply than with words.

NW: But this overdeveloped eye is sometimes pitiless. You reveal in your portraits facets of character that people would perhaps have preferred not to show. Do you think it is possible to hide one's self in front of your camera?

RA: I am not necessarily interested in the secret of a person. The fact that there are qualities a subject doesn't want me to observe is an interesting fact. Interesting enough for a portrait. It then becomes a portrait of someone who doesn't want something to show. That is interesting. There is no truth in photography. There is no one truth about anyone's person. My portraits are much more about me than they are about the people I photograph. I used to think that it was a collaboration, that it was something that happened as the result of what the subject wanted to project and what the photographer wanted to photograph. I no longer think it is that at all. The photographer has complete control, the issue is a moral one and it is complicated. Everyone comes to the camera with a certain expectation and the deception on my part is that I might appear to be indeed part of their expectation. If you are painted or written about, you can say: "But that's not me, that's Bacon, that's Soutine; that's not me, that's Celine."

NW: Picasso answered to that when he said of Gertrude Stein: "That's not how she was when I painted her, but that's how she will be sooner or later."

RA: That's pretty grand of him. On the other hand, now that she is dead, virtually that is all she is. It is a terrible responsibility for a photographer. The subject was there — the subject can never say — "that is not me." It is even worse in the case of photojournalism, when the photograph is taken without permission. At least I say, "May I do a portrait of you?"

It is complicated and unresolved in my mind because I believe in moral responsibility of all kinds. I feel I have no right to say, "This is the way it is," and in another way, I can't help myself. It is for me the only way to breathe and to live. I could say it is the nature of art to make such assumptions, but there has never been an art like photography before. You cannot make a photograph of a person without that person's presence, and that very presence implies truth. A portrait is not a likeness. The moment an emotion or fact is transformed into a photograph it is no longer a fact but an opinion. There is no such thing as inaccurary in a photograph. All photographs are accurate. None of them are the truth.

NW: You have now been working for many years on a new book on the working class. Did you begin this new work because you were fed up with the elite?

RA: No, not at all. I have been working for many many years as a portrait photographer, on portraits of Americans. But I used to believe that I could only photograph what I knew and understood. I understood artists, people of high achievement, power, beauty — at least I thought I understood those things. I said once in an interview that I had no idea what it was like to be black, or what is was like to be a factory worker, and so I couldn't photograph them. Of course, it was not true. But it took me a long time to know in my stomach that people share the same concerns, and that confronting an oil worker is very little different than confronting, say, a writer. It's just a question of language. As a matter of fact, the people I have photographed for this book seemed more generous with their selves, less guarded, often easier to see.

NW: But not anybody is a good subject for you. How do you choose your subjects?

RA: Very few people are suitable subjects for me. In the same way that not everyone looks like a Modigliani, or would have been a correct model for Matisse. It's a difficult question because I don't formalize these things. I am interested in connections between people of remote experience, in similarities that are unexpected, unexplained. When you see this new book, you will see a man, a worker in Colorado, who has qualities exactly like James Galanos. Galanos is a dress designer in Beverly Hills who dresses the wife of the President. The man in Colorado is a factory worker who wraps packages. That fascinates me. If you look at the portraits of the Chicago Seven, you will find similarities to the Mission Council. Paradox, irony, contradiction — these interest me in a photograph. Contradictions within one person: the contrast possibly between the gentleness and the delicacy of the hands of a subject and the suspicion and the lack of trust on his face.

NW: There is also a contradiction in your work — between your fashion pictures and then the portraits, which seem to show a more tragic side of life.

RA: I don't think one is at all a reaction to the other, which is a view sometimes held about Arbus and myself: that the serious, or if you want, the "tragic" quality of our portraits is a reaction to the artificial demands of fashion. I think there is a tendency to categorize photographers with assumptions that would never be made of writers. If an author writes a comedy or a tragedy and then an essay or is politically concerned, no one questions it. No one asks why a philosopher writes a novel or a poem, or why Picasso did ballet costumes. That generosity is not extended to fashion photographers. I've always had to deal with that — less now, but still.

Fashion photography is not an art that can grow indefinitely. It is constantly taking and dealing with the surface of things, and that doesn't attract me anymore. When I was young, my needs as an artist were exactly the needs of the magazine I worked for — *Harper's Bazaar*. They published what I wanted to express. (That went on for twenty years — embarrassing!) At a certain point, the necessities of fashion magazines were no longer mine, no longer interesting.

As a commercial photographer, fashion is a necessary part of my commercial existence. I find it easy. It underwrites and supports my life and other work that I prefer to do.

NW: So you do it to support your studio?

RA: When I grew up in the thirties and in the forties, the definition of what it was to be a man was to support your parents and your family, and to go into the world and be what they called the Breadwinner. And I have always had that very deep inside of me. There is nothing bohemian about me at all. I know that I am responsible for my family. That started very early in me.

NW: To be a photographer — was it the most obvious way to earn money in the early fifties?

RA: My father wanted me to be a businessman because he had suffered terribly as a Russian Jew in New York City at the turn of the century. He had a terrible life as a child, one of six children deserted by his father, sent to an orphan asylum. He had a tragic quality, and an exaggerated sense of danger. He wanted me to be prepared for what he called the Battle in the ways that he felt one had to be prepared: through education, physical strength and money.

I am a complete composite of my mother and father. She is 85, she began to be a sculptress at 75, working with granite and marble. My mother loved the arts, was politically active, and always encouraged me to be an artist. She was and is completely supportive. During the Depression, she stole lilacs. She says about artists, “He is the real thing,” or “He’s not the real thing,” and that’s that.

Anyway, photography was the only thing I could do. I have been a photographer since at least the age of thirteen. My family was in the business of fashion and my parents subscribed to *Harper’s Bazaar*, *Vogue*, and *Vanity Fair* when I was a child. I saw fashion photography and theater portraits by Steichen, Munkacsi and Man Ray in each issue and I began to imitate them by photographing my little sister. She was very, very beautiful, two years younger than I. Her beauty was the event of our family and the destruction of her life. She was treated as if there was no one inside her perfect skin, as if she was simply her long throat, her brown, deep eyes. I think she believed she existed only as skin, and hair, and a beautiful body. Interestingly enough, I had not looked at a photograph of her in thirty years, and only last week opened a package of my earliest pictures, taken when I was an adolescent.

Every family thinks their daughter and son are the most beautiful children in the world, but my sister Louise (I photographed her from fourteen to eighteen) was truly a world class beauty, and I never knew it until last week. What I discovered was that she was the prototype of what I considered to be beautiful in my early years as a fashion photographer. All my first models: Dorian Leigh, Elise Daniels, Carmen, Marella Agnelli, Audrey Hepburn, were brunettes and had fine noses, long throats, oval faces. They were all memories of my sister. My sense of what was beautiful was established very early, through the way in which I experienced her.

NW: Where is she now?

RA: She is dead. She died in a mental institution at the age of thirty. She withdrew completely in her late adolescence.

NW: You mean she was killed by her own beauty?

RA: Depersonalized, maybe. Destroyed, possibly; I think really by the power of her beauty. It is as isolating as genius, or deformity. Unlike genius, it [beauty] is one of the qualities that removes you from the world, but offers no real compensation. I have always been aware of a relationship between madness and beauty. Does this help to explain some of what appear to be contradictions in my work? It's only one part. It has nothing to do with the discipline of work, and other things, but if you look to the portraits, you will find that connection. A possibility of failure and danger and poetry in life — and the thin line that separates it all.

When these qualities began to emerge in my fashion pictures, I was no longer usable by the fashion magazines. I either had to adjust the way I worked or stop.

NW: But you disciplined this obsession in your commercial work.

RA: Obsession? Completely. Commercial work and editorial work are easy for me to do. I work hard at it. I try to do it the best way possible. But I now have a very small part of myself invested in it.

NW: Do you think magazines are dangerous for photographers?

RA: There is a book by Cyril Connolly, the English critic, called *Enemies of Promise*. I used to give it to my students. They never knew quite why. He speaks of publishers, magazines, the business of art, as enemies of promise. It's a beautiful phrase.

I think everything is dangerous, or not. It depends entirely on what you do with it. The moment I realized I could no longer express things as I saw them through fashion photography, I moved to another kind of photography for myself. For an artist to have the illusion that a commercial magazine is a possible place to spend his creative life makes no sense.

NW: For forty years you have photographed painters, politicians, artists, workers, famous and unfamous people. What feeds your curiosity for people?

RA: I don't think analytic explanations suffice, but there is a little bit of truth in everything — in Freud, in Pavlov, in genetics, in environment. I grew up with a first cousin, two years older than I. I was deeply in love with her from the age of four until I was eighteen. It was only with her that I could breathe freely. We were precocious from the start. When the Cocteau movie, *Les Enfants Terribles*, came out, we knew we were those children. We saw it over and over. Our feelings for each other were intense, so forbidden, so conspiratorial. I knew for myself — I can't speak for her — that if I was ever to complete myself, grow up and out into the world, we had to shatter our perfect hothouse. In all the years that a young man first experiences life apart from the family, I knew only one person. I think my entire character was formed through that powerful relationship. And my life has gone on, one person at a time.

NW: This relationship with one person at a time is replayed in your studio, when you do a portrait?

RA: Oh yes! Very intensely — but in photography it is an unearned intensity. For example, I have never become a friend — or very rarely — of anyone I have photographed. I would never, for many many years, enter a room after photographing a celebrated person and assume that if he were there, he would acknowledge me. The kind of embarrassing intensity of these peculiar intimacies and needs — the needs of the subject to give something to the camera and to me, and my need to take that in order to express myself — is complicated and unearned. I have never felt that I had the right to presume that there was anything but the picture between us. It's less than an hour, and it's over — completely.

NW: Haven't you ever been seduced by some of these people?

RA: As my book *Portraits* was being completed, there were certain artists whose work had affected me, whom I had not photographed, and one of them was Jean Renoir. Renoir lived in Beverly Hills and I went to him. His home looked like everything I'd always thought a home should be. It looked like south of France. It didn't look like Beverly Hills. There were flowers in and out of the rooms and sunshine coming through the windows. And a long table in the middle of the room. A long table at the center of a house has always had great meaning for me. When I arrived, I was shown to the bedroom. He was naked, being helped to dress, completely unembarrassed by my presence. He was old and quite sick at that time and he walked with difficulty, with a walker. There was something so moving about his face, and about his life and his work and what he stood for. He was one of the last people I felt in awe of. When the sitting was over (in those days I worked with incredible intensity, I mean my heart would pound out of control while I photographed), Renoir said, "Won't you join us?"

So I sat at the table and some friends arrived with vodka and a Sunday cake and Renoir sat down. Behind him was a portrait of him as a child painted by his father and the potteries he had made as a child guided by his father.

A young Czechoslovakian director who was there visiting started to talk with Renoir about film. What happened to me used to happen to me very often — I froze, I couldn't speak or think. I felt inadequate. I thought — what can I say, or contribute, to anything that happens at this table? Well, actually nothing so grand was happening. I considered myself very good at disguising my feelings and I knew there was no necessity for me to speak. I could legitimately be a quiet person. But I was paralyzed inside. Smiling, trying to appear comfortable, thinking — what right do I have to be at this table? I came to do my photograph, I should leave. I am not a friend of the Renoirs, this is Sunday.

Renoir stood to go to the bathroom and I used that occasion to say goodbye to everyone. As I approached the front door, he came out of his bedroom with his walker, blocking my way. And we were stuck there, in the narrow hall. I extended my hand and said, "Monsieur Renoir, thank you very much for allowing me to photograph you." He looked straight into my eyes and I'll never forget his words: "It's not what we say that matters, it's the feelings that cross the table."

My face froze. I walked to the car and wept. Imagine a man in his eighties, sick as he was, knowing what was happening to me at that table, and to care, and to say it. Well, that's my kind of standard for human behavior. To be able to be that present in each moment. The quality of paying attention that he had, and then the compassion. I think that there is not much more to life than that story: to be that age, surrounded by your father's works of art, to have created your own, to live in a house with sunshine falling through the windows, and a wife, and a jar of vodka with spirals of lemon in it, and friends and your own son who has become a teacher and his children sitting with the grown-ups, on Sunday — and to still pay that kind of attention to a stranger.

NW: Do you have any regrets?

RA: I never felt that anything I ever did was good enough and frankly, a large part of me still thinks exactly that way about everything I do — it is not good enough — nothing is ever even near good enough. But that's not regret. I just feel that I know more than I could put into my work.

NW: Does it make you suffer?

RA: No. Not that. It makes me work.

NW: What makes you anxious?

RA: That unexplainable shifts in my feelings. From moment to moment I can shift from someone who thinks he can deal with anything to someone who can't think. It has nothing to do with reality. I like to believe it's chemical. I used to think there was a Freudian answer [*laughs*]. What I do know about myself is that I am best in intense short takes. I mean the way in which making pictures is very intense and short, compared to writing.

Everything I do, it seems to me, has passion about it, and then suddenly the drop and then withdraw, which is not necessarily depression. It can be planes or sleep or doing puzzles, but I have to pull back. I am not capable of living at my most intense level for a long period of time. I think I might crack. That's probably why I still do a bit of fashion photography—to relieve the tension.

NW: Did you ever think you might possibly go insane?

RA: Maybe, when I was young, yes. At certain periods, when there were real-life pressures, situations that seemed impossible to face, I thought: I am not going to make it. But I always had the ability to escape into reality, into work. Many things have called to me in 62 years, many things in all areas of my life, and they have found their proper home in my photographs.

NW: But not on your face. You look very serene.

RA: That's because, perhaps, the storm approaches my pictures instead of my face. That's a funny thought [*laughs*].

—

NICOLE WISNIAK, "A PORTRAIT IS AN OPINION" (INTERVIEW WITH RICHARD AVEDON), *EGOÏSTE* N° 9, JANUARY 1985, 48–53.

America has retained power, both political and cultural, but it is now power as a special effect. In the image of Reagan, the whole of America has become Californian. Ex-actor and ex-governor of California that he is, he has worked up his euphoric, cinematic, extroverted advertising vision of the artificial paradises of the West to all-American dimensions. . . .

The Third World, which no one mourns, has been obliterated. Long live the Fourth World, the world in which you can say, "Right, Utopia has arrived. If you aren't part of it, get lost!"

—

JEAN BAUDRILLARD, *AMERICA*
(LONDON/ NEW YORK: VERSO, 1989): 107–108, 112.

IN THE AMERICAN WEST

PAR

RICHARD AVEDON

Ces cinq photos font partie d'un travail qui a duré cinq ans et qui trouvera son aboutissement dans une exposition qui sera ouverte en Septembre au Musée Amon Carter de Fort Worth, Texas; elles seront, simultanément, reproduites dans un livre édité aux Etats-Unis par Harry N. Abrams Inc. Elles sont publiées ici pour la première fois.

Page 55
– Boyd Fortin, Rattlesnake Skinner. Sweetwater, Texas – March 10, 1979.

Page 56
– Benson James, Drifter. Route 66, Gallup, New Mexico – June 30, 1979.

Page 57
– James Kimberlin, Oil Worker. Hobbs, New Mexico – October 7, 1980.

Page 58
– Juan Patricio Lobato, Carney. Rocky Ford, Colorado – August 23, 1980.

Page 59
– Sandra Bennett, 12 years old. Rocky Ford, Colorado – August 23, 1980.

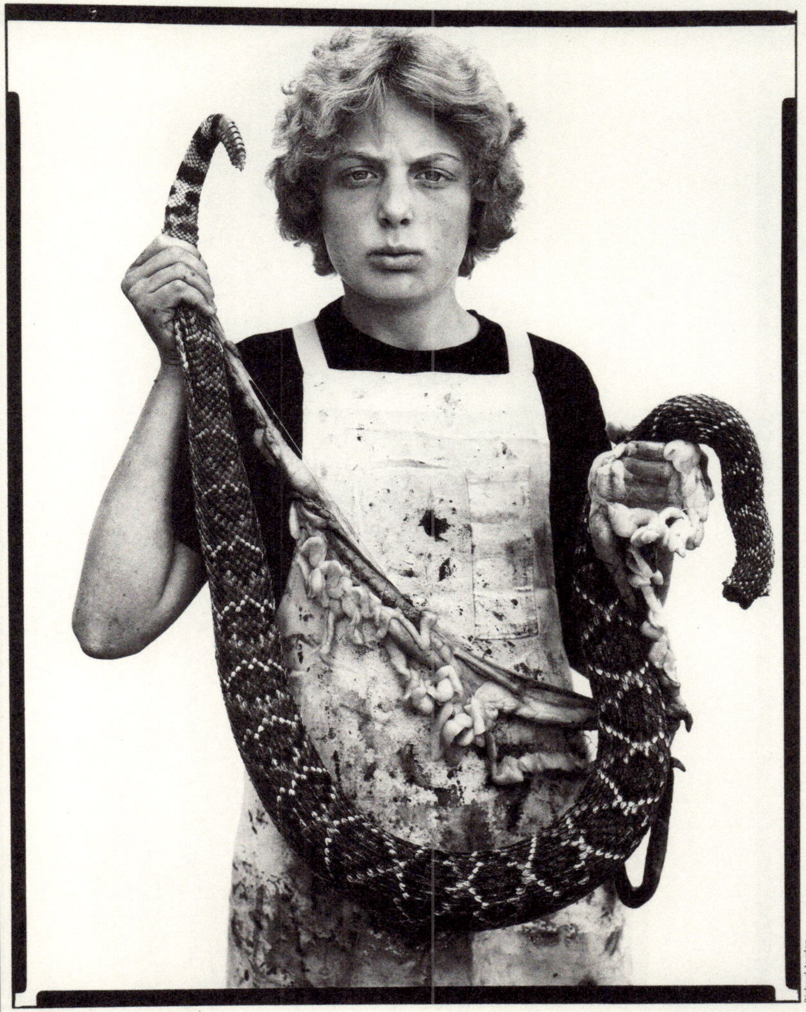

Richard Avedon

55

"In the American West par Richard Avedon," *Egoïste*, N° 9, 1985, pp. 54–55

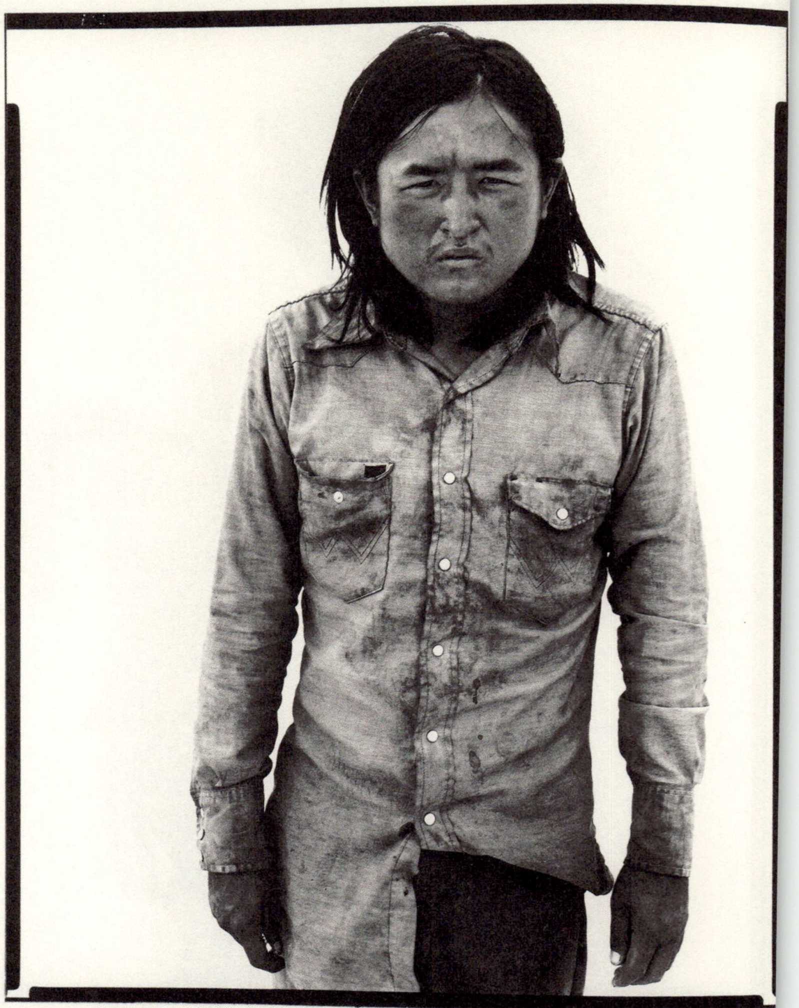

56

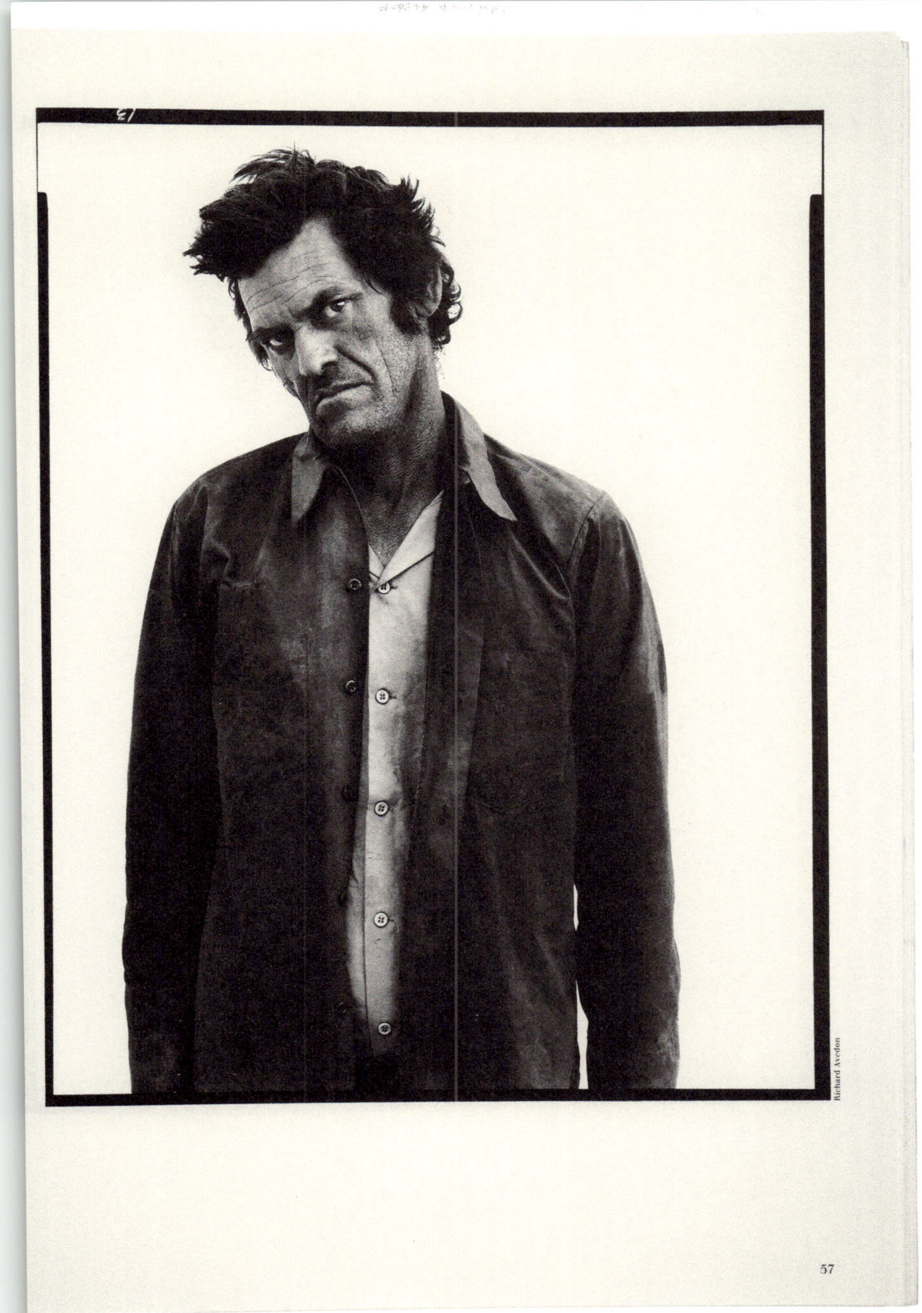

“In the American West par Richard Avedon,” *Egoïste,* N° 9, 1985, pp. 56–57

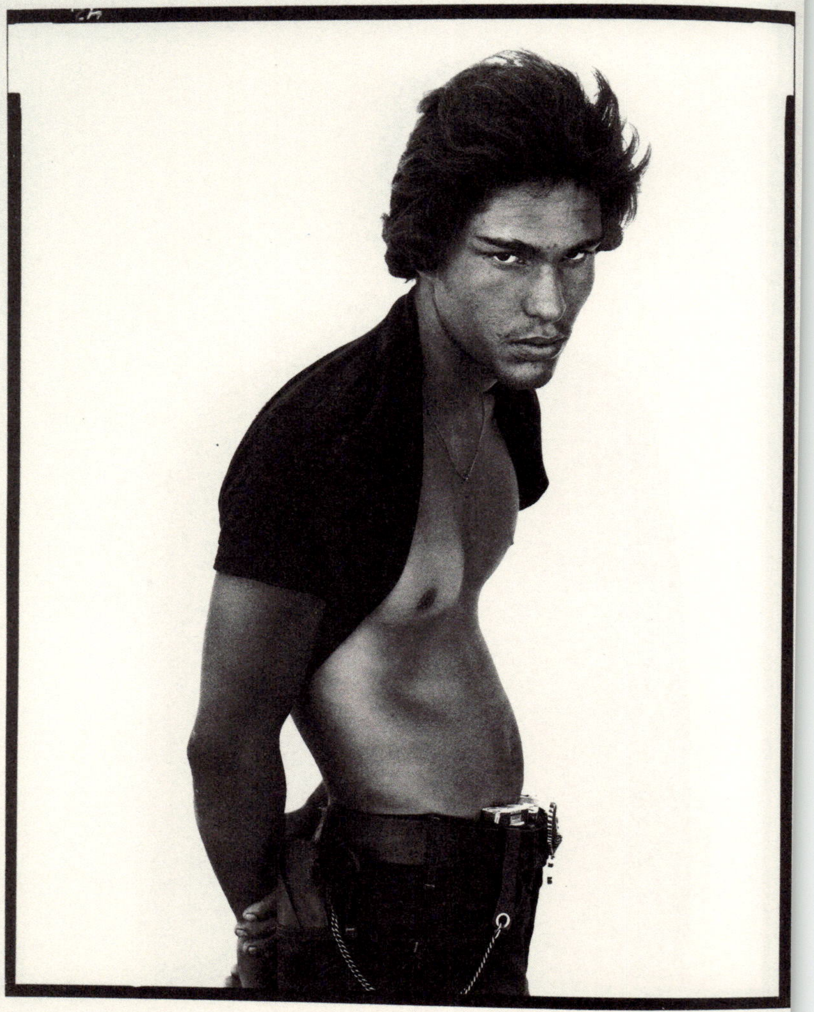

58

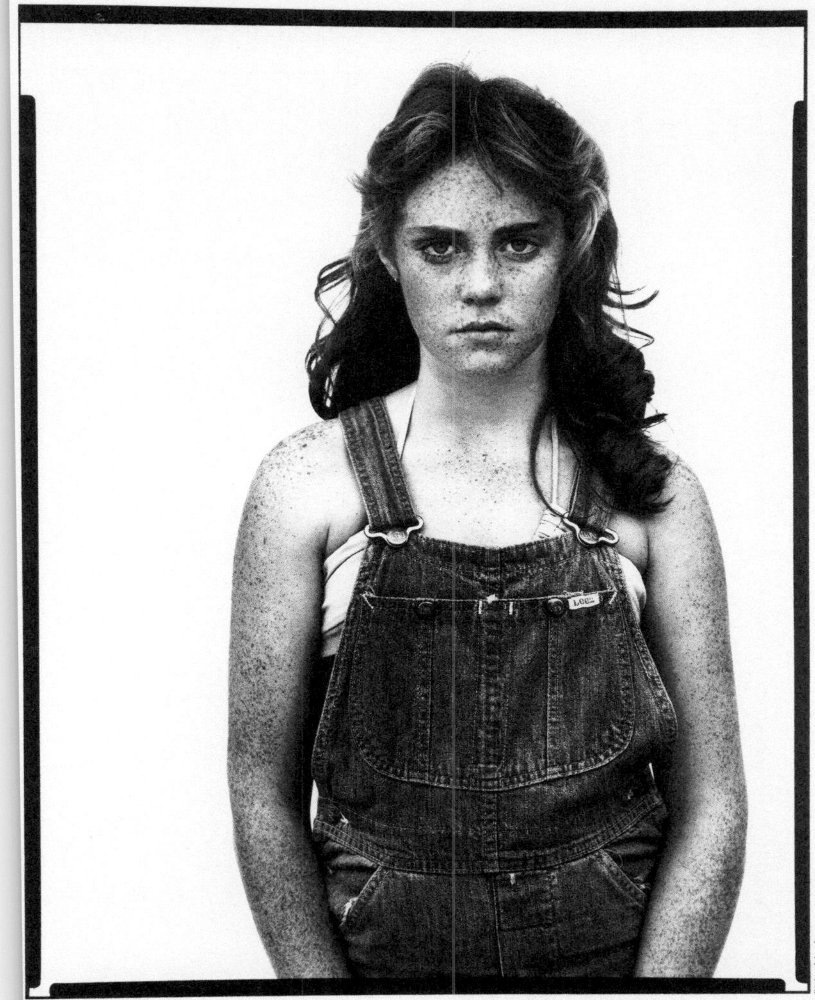

Richard Avedon

59

"In the American West par Richard Avedon," *Egoïste,* N° 9, 1985, pp. 58–59

They tried nevertheless to preserve, fixed upon them in a state of permanency, one of those fugitive expressions which one assumes for a second when posing for a photograph, either in order to show off some good point in one's appearance to the best effect or to overcome a deformity; they seemed to have become, once and for all, unalterable snapshots of themselves.

—

MARCEL PROUST, *LE TEMPS RETROUVÉ* (PARIS: GALLIMARD, 1927): 102–03.

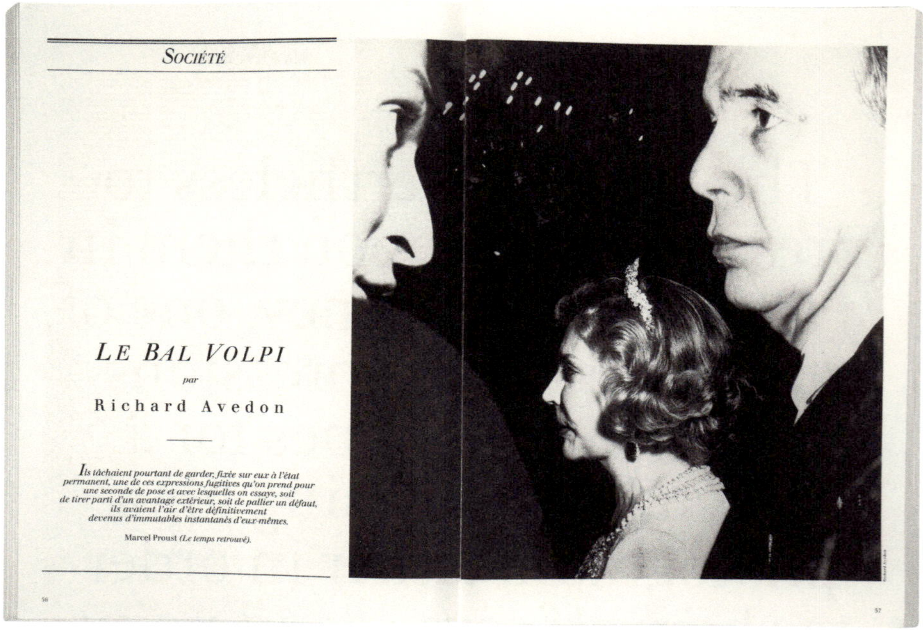

SOCIÉTÉ

LE BAL VOLPI

par

Richard Avedon

Ils tâchaient pourtant de garder, fixée sur eux à l'état permanent, une de ces expressions fugitives qu'on prend pour une seconde de pose et avec lesquelles on essaye, soit de tirer parti d'un avantage extérieur, soit de pallier un défaut, ils avaient l'air d'être définitivement devenus d'immutables instantanés d'eux-mêmes.

Marcel Proust *(Le temps retrouvé).*

56

57

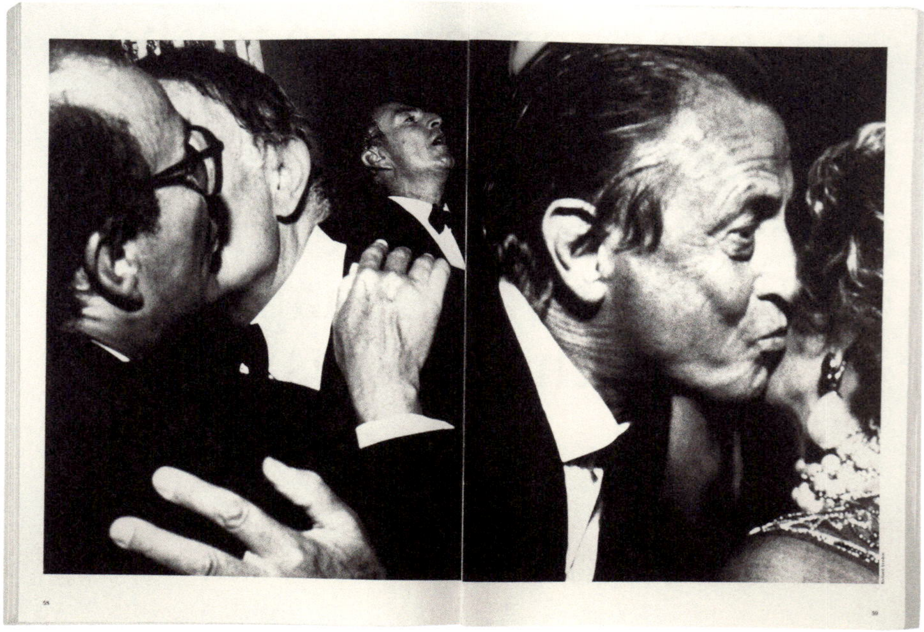

58

59

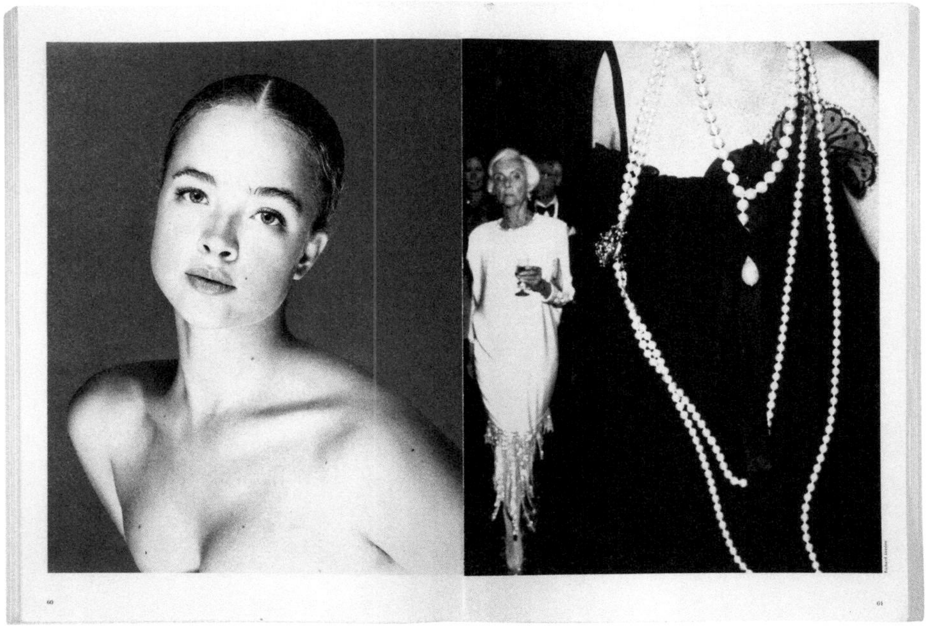

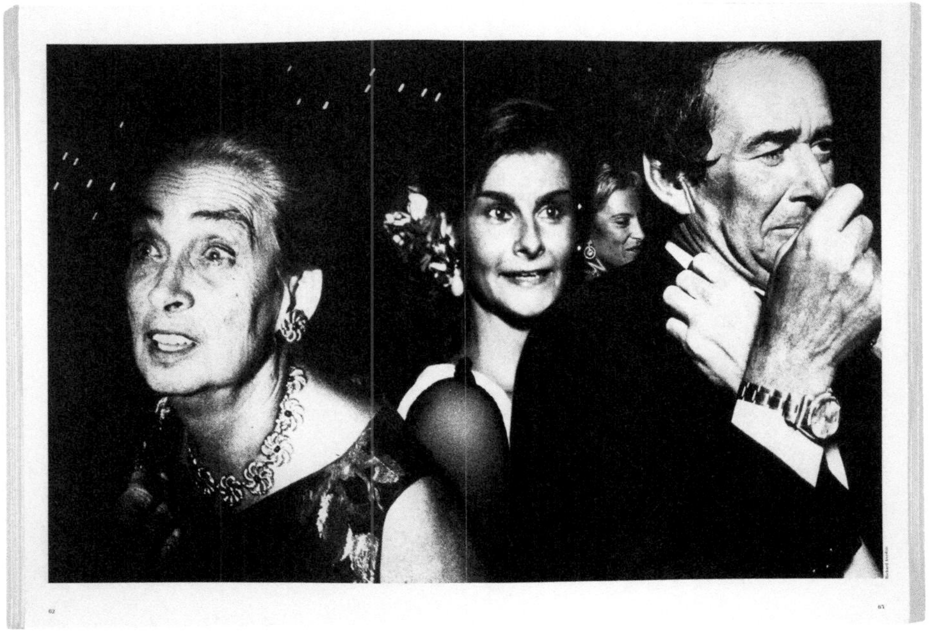

"Le Bal Volpi par Richard Avedon," *Egoïste,* N° 12, Tome I, 1992, pp. 56–63

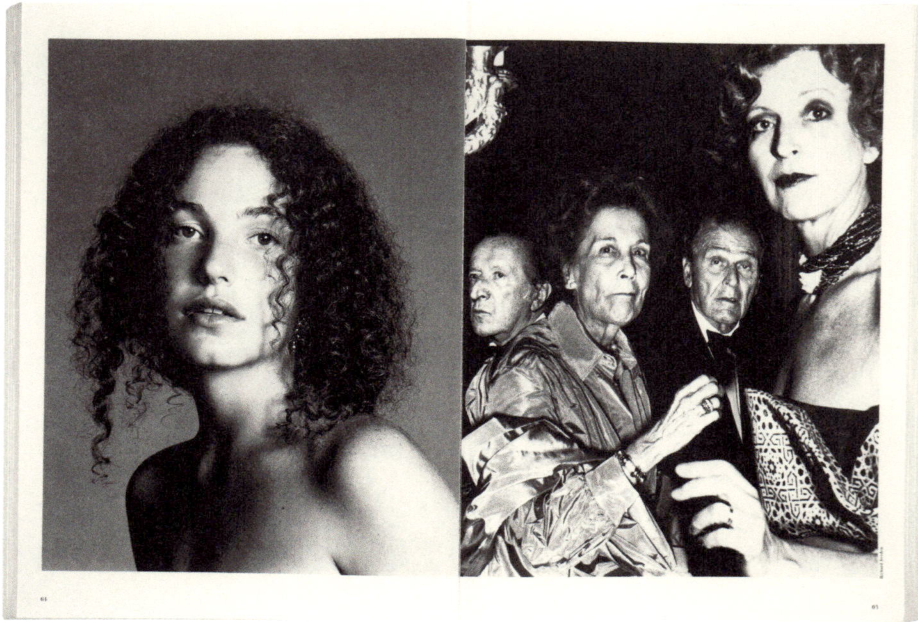

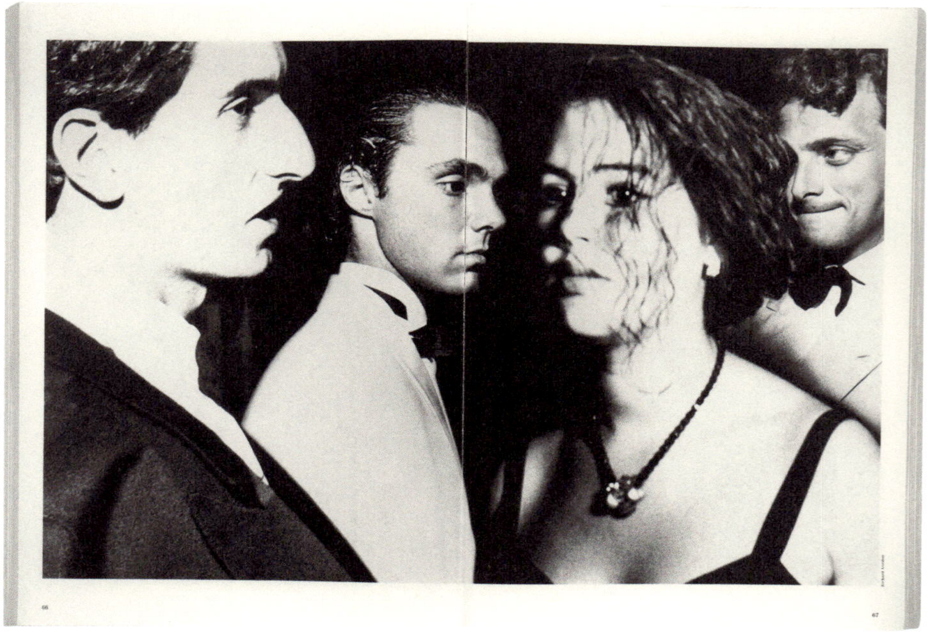

“Le Bal Volpi par Richard Avedon,” *Egoïste,* N° 12, Tome I, 1992, pp. 64–67

Proust
Richard Avedon

Everything has to be measured against Proust . . . when I first read him I wanted to do one photograph that would take my whole life . . . I learned things from Proust long before I experienced them myself, but it was sort of a signpost for what was coming . . . When I did experience it, it was almost a cliché for me . . . as if I had been laying in wait, just lurking around, waiting for this inevitable thing that I had been taught by that last book of Proust (*Le Temps Retrouvé* [Time Regained]) . . . I had photographed the aging process when I was young with more enthusiasm and creative freedom than I do now as I get close to that very thing myself. . . .

Then I was invited to something called the Volpi Ball. The last aristocratic ball in Europe, in Venice. The gondolas blocked the Grand Canal to Palazzo Volpi. Women and men in evening clothes standing for hours in order to get into the palace, which had been painted and decorated, made beautiful. It was the last ball of its kind — not for charity. This was total indulgence. European royalty came from all over: Belgium, France, England, Spain. I photographed all night. Which was difficult because I'm known in that crowd so I wasn't a fly on the wall.

The aging beauties of Proust, the aging aristocracy were no news to me. But I got very interested that night in the young there. There is one photograph of a very beautiful young girl and I deliberately put her a little bit out of focus because the men were looking at each other in such a way that she was lost in that world. If you look closely at that picture you will see two men in the background looking at each other in their white tuxedos. Another man in profile looking past her and she's lost in the middle of this. That was interesting. Interesting about the nature of the world a young girl is thrown into, particularly in that aristocratic environment where narcissism is so rampant. So you can be surprised. I'm always surprised.

RICHARD AVEDON, UNPUBLISHED INTERVIEW
WITH DORIAN LEIGH FOR PBS SERIES *AMERICAN MASTERS*, 1994.

I created the parties in my darkroom. I just put people where I thought they'd be happier. They're paste-ups, a kind of collage, but the collaging disappears and they become photographs of the parties I wanted them to be.

—

Richard Avedon

pp. 638–39, Volpi Ball #4, Venice, Italy, August 31, 1991
pp. 640–41, Volpi Ball #3, Venice, Italy, August 31, 1991
pp. 642–43, Volpi Ball #5, Venice, Italy, August 31, 1991
pp. 644–45, Volpi Ball #1, Venice, Italy, August 31, 1991
pp. 646–47, Volpi Ball #2, Venice, Italy, August 31, 1991
pp. 648–49, Volpi Ball #1, Venice, Italy, August 31, 1991
pp. 650–51, Volpi Ball #6, Venice, Italy, August 31, 1991

Egoïste

Volpi Ball

Richard Avedon

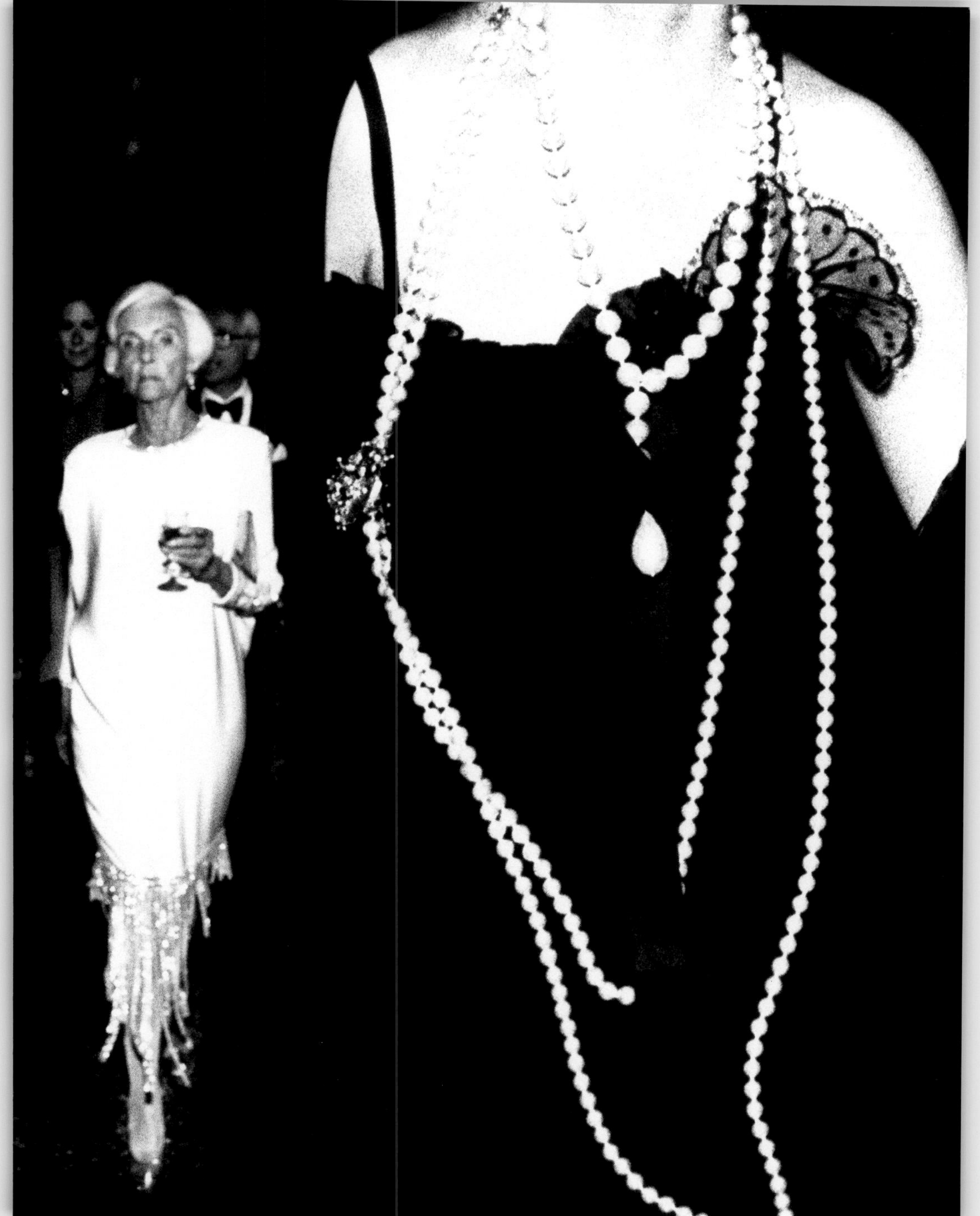

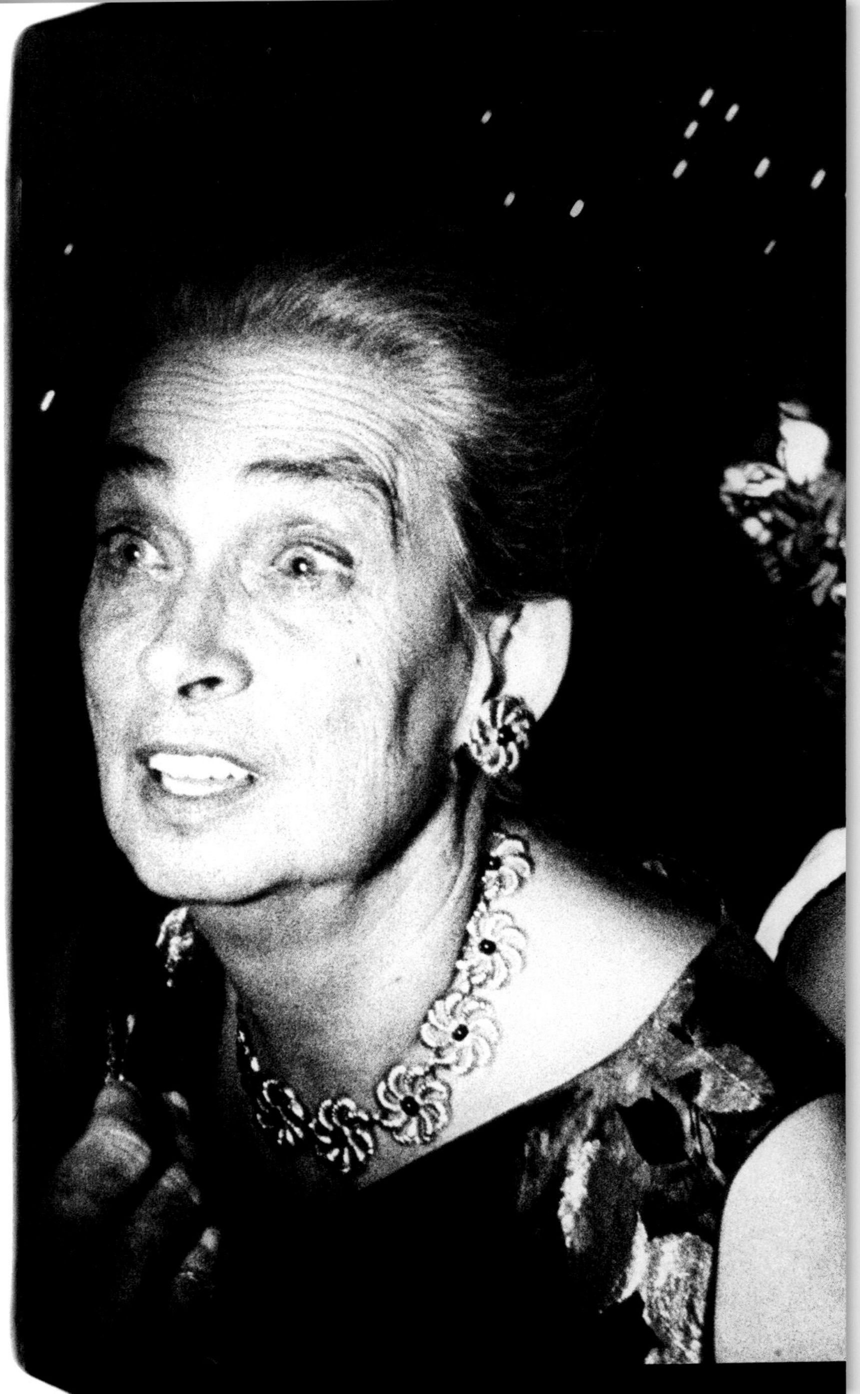

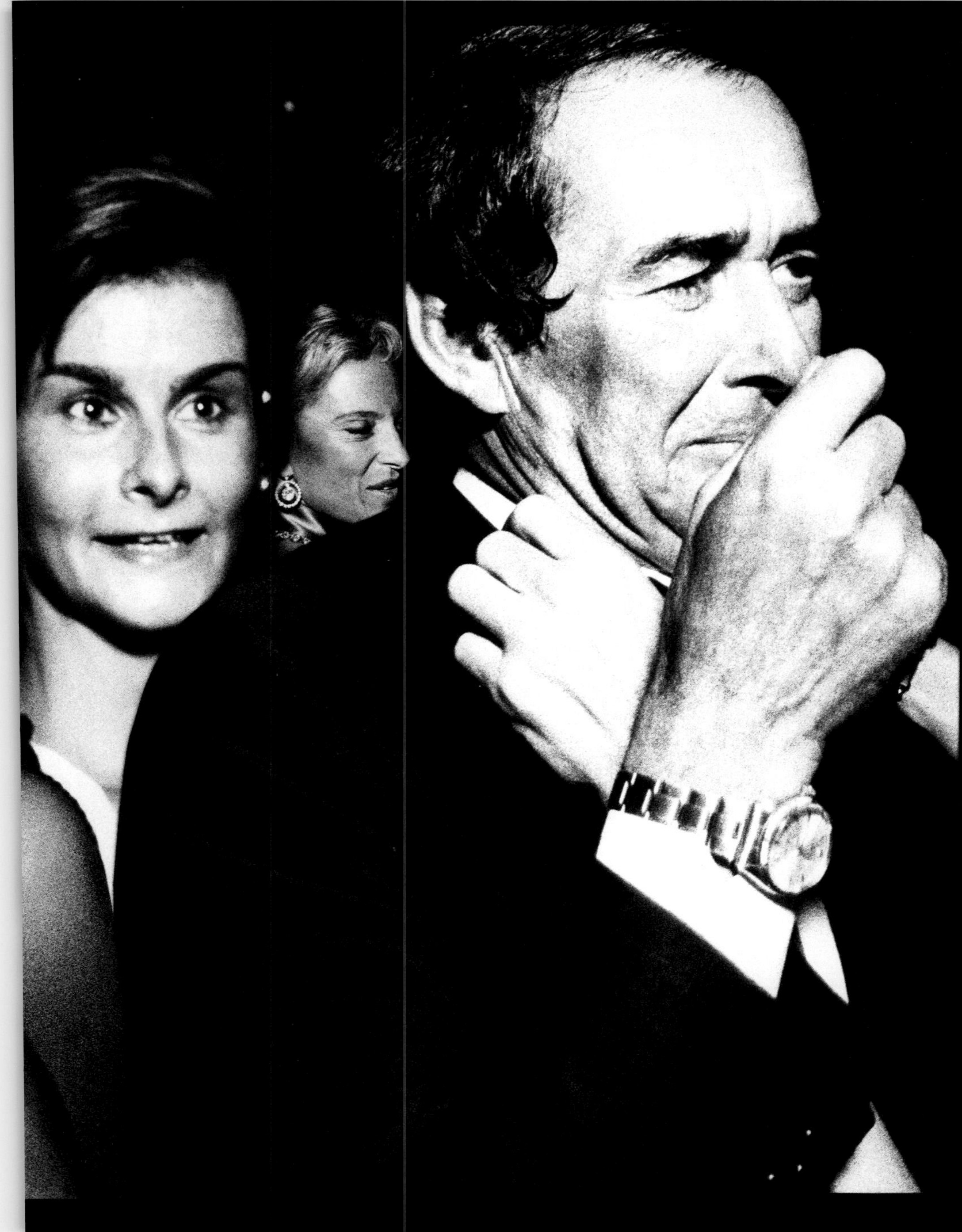

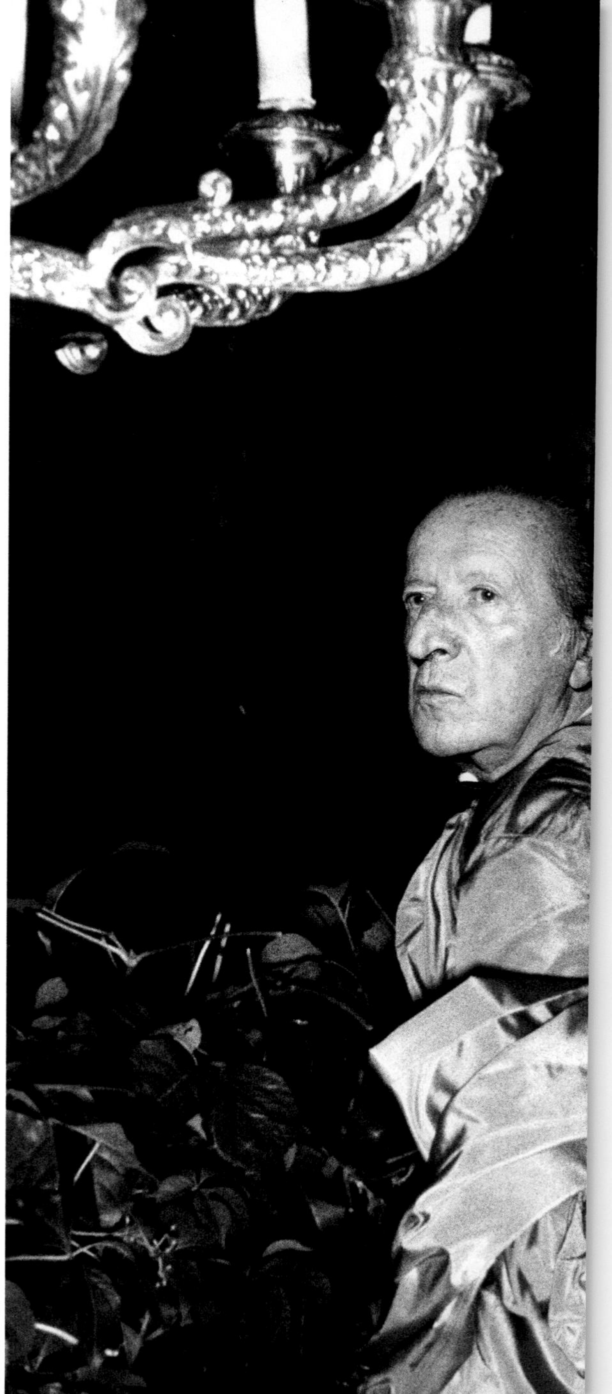

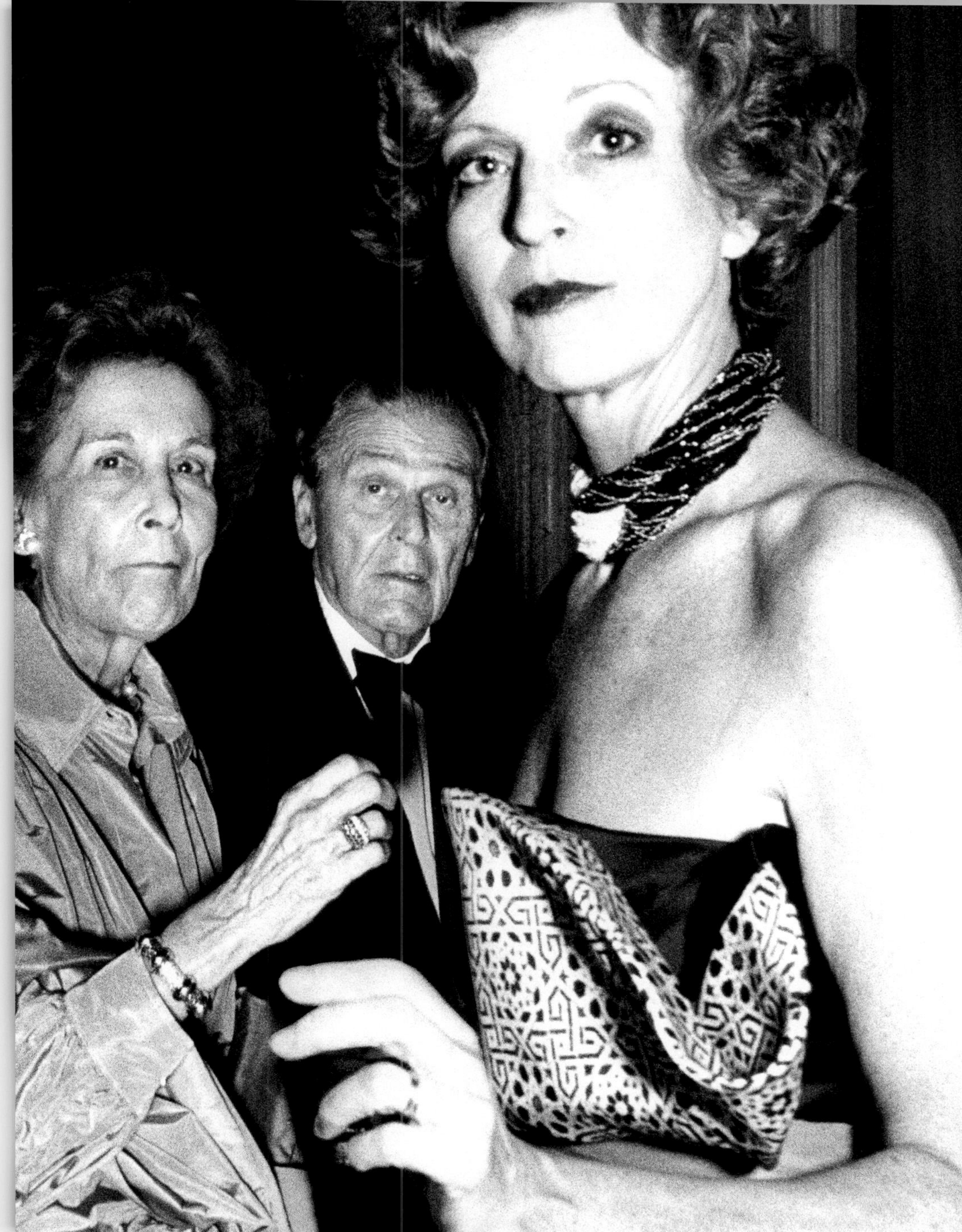

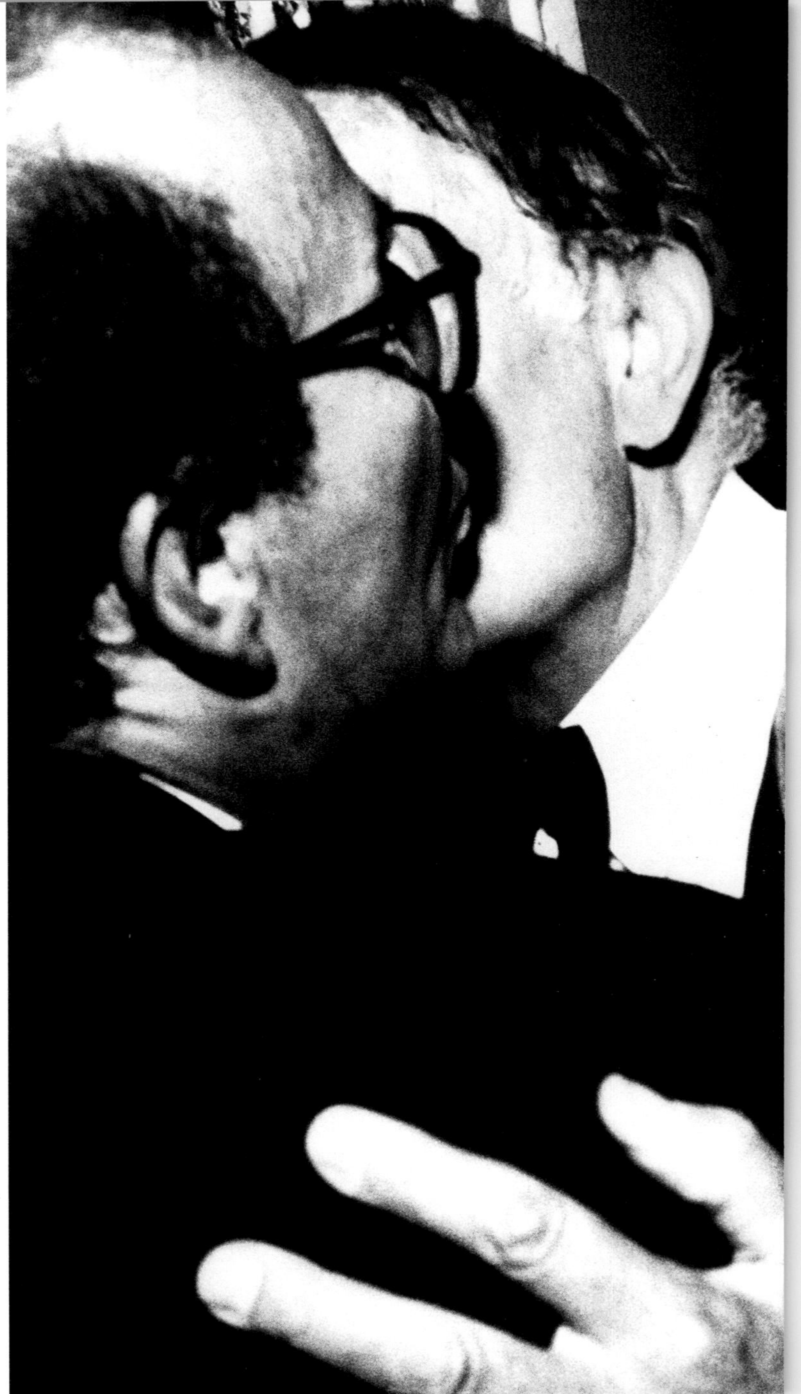

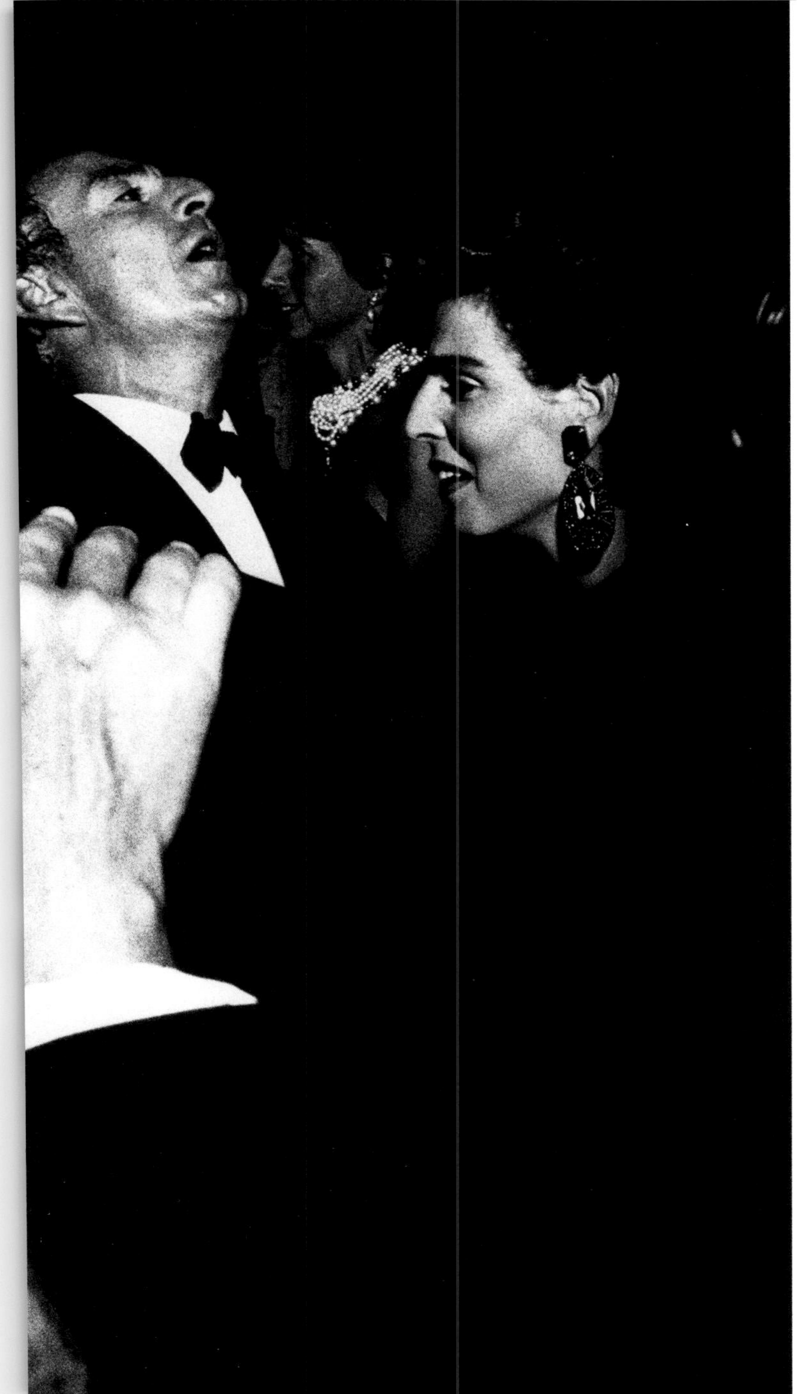

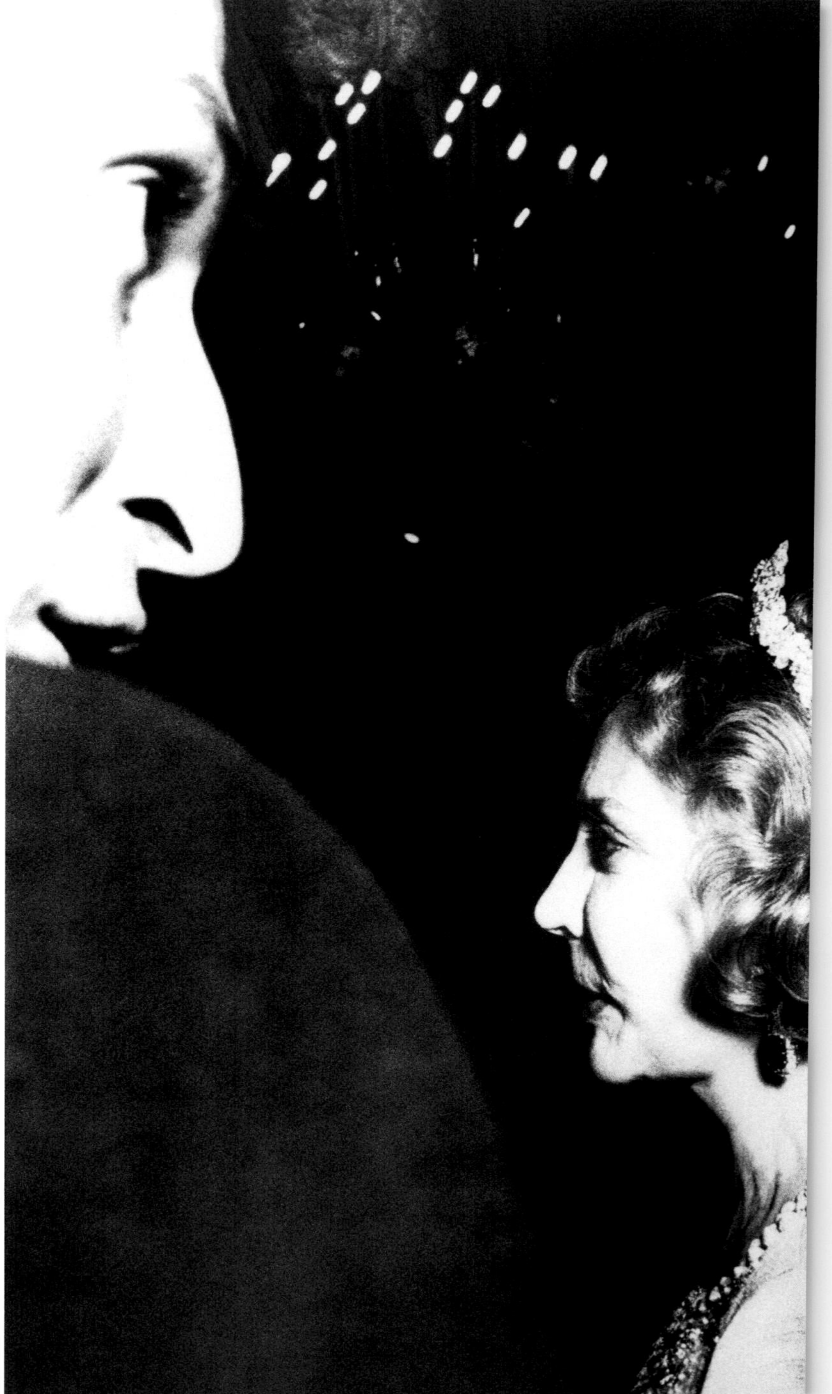

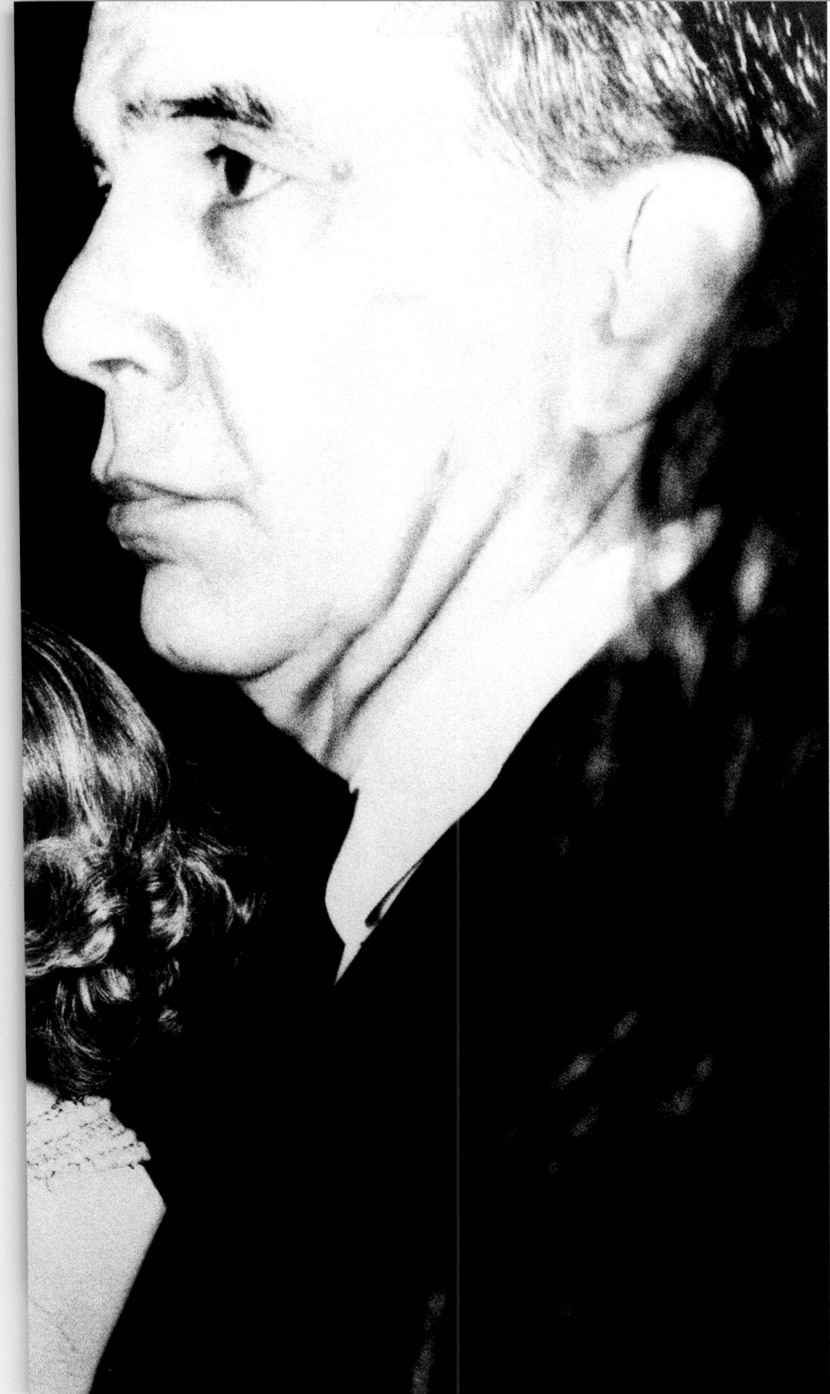

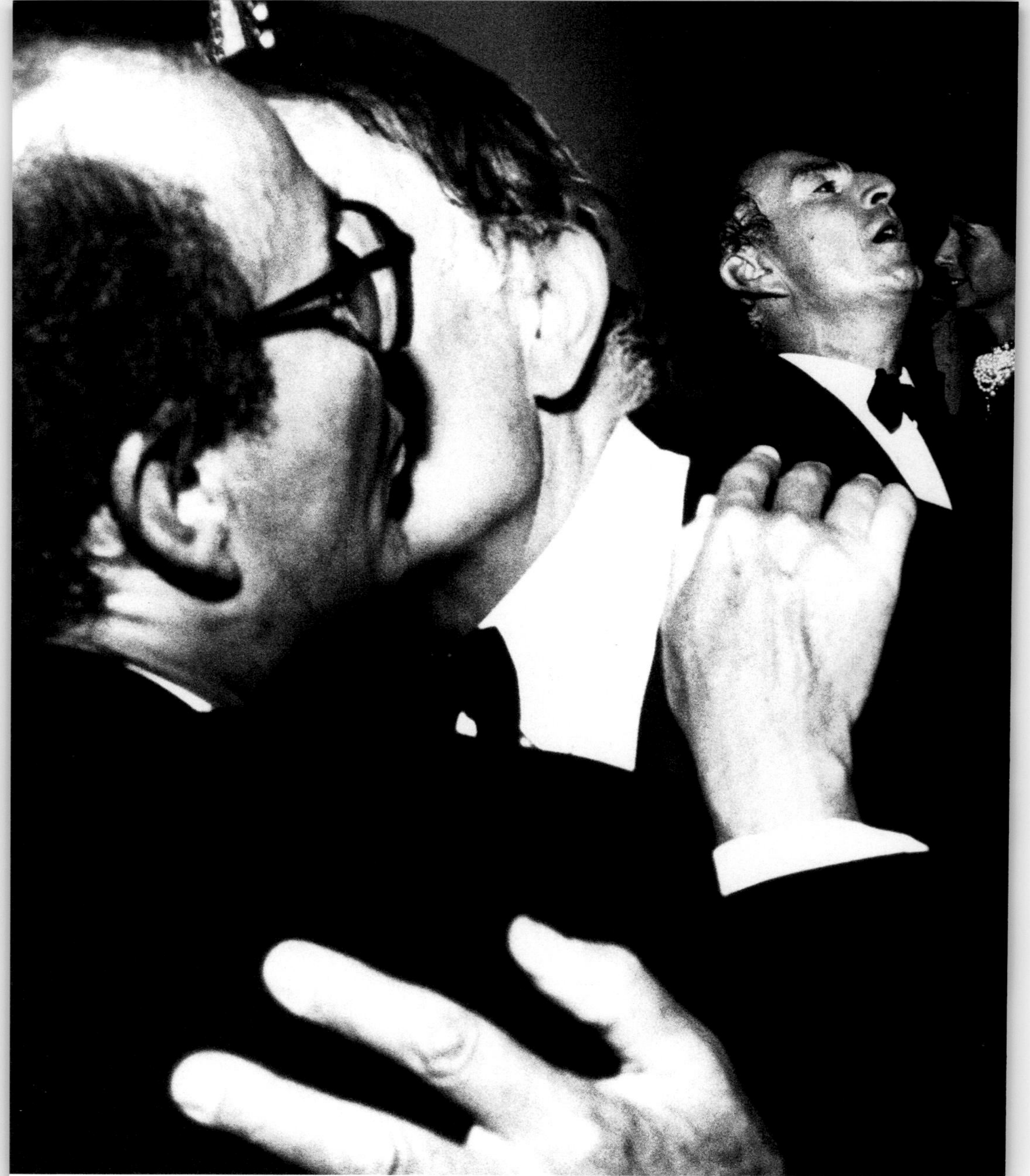

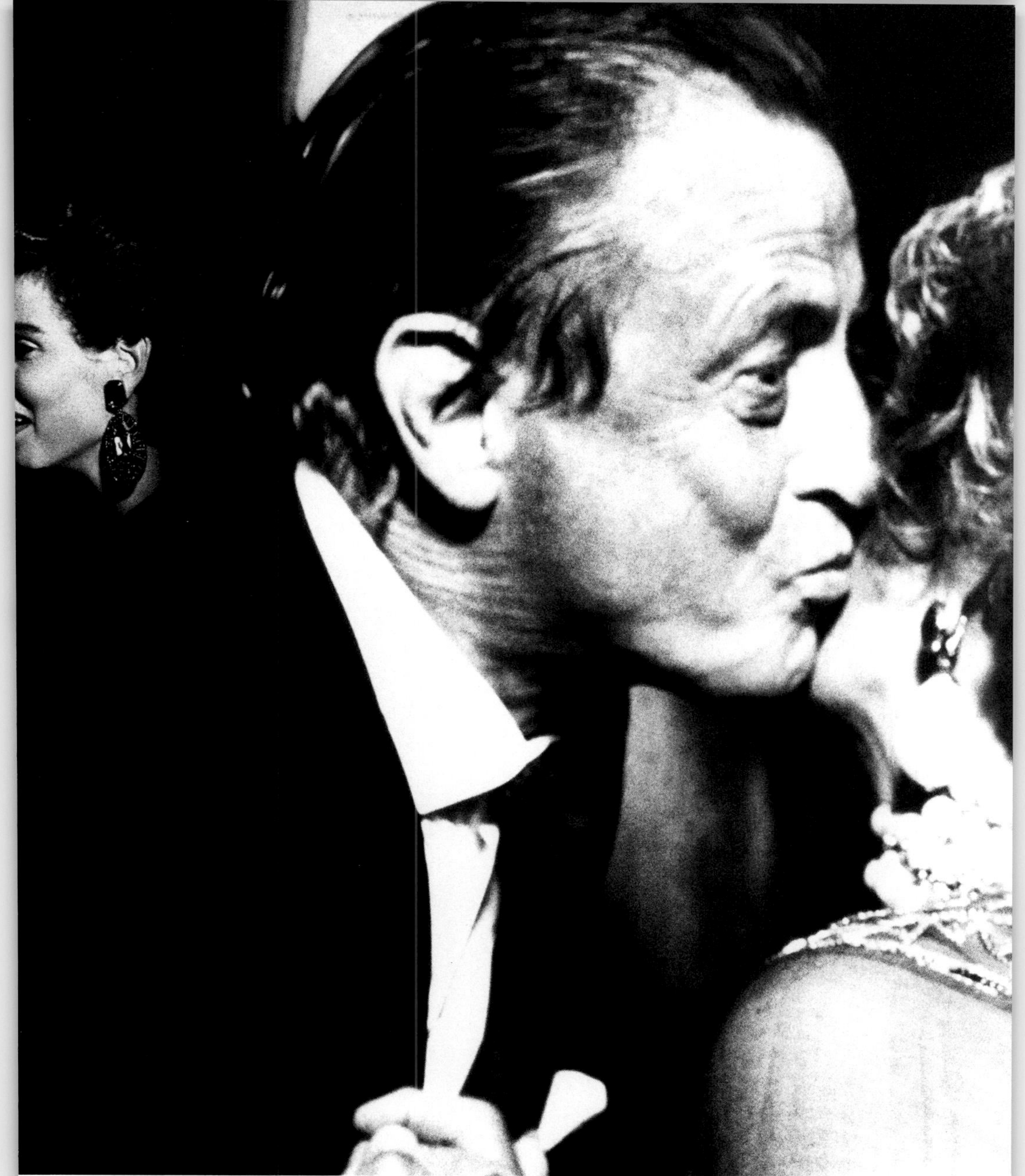

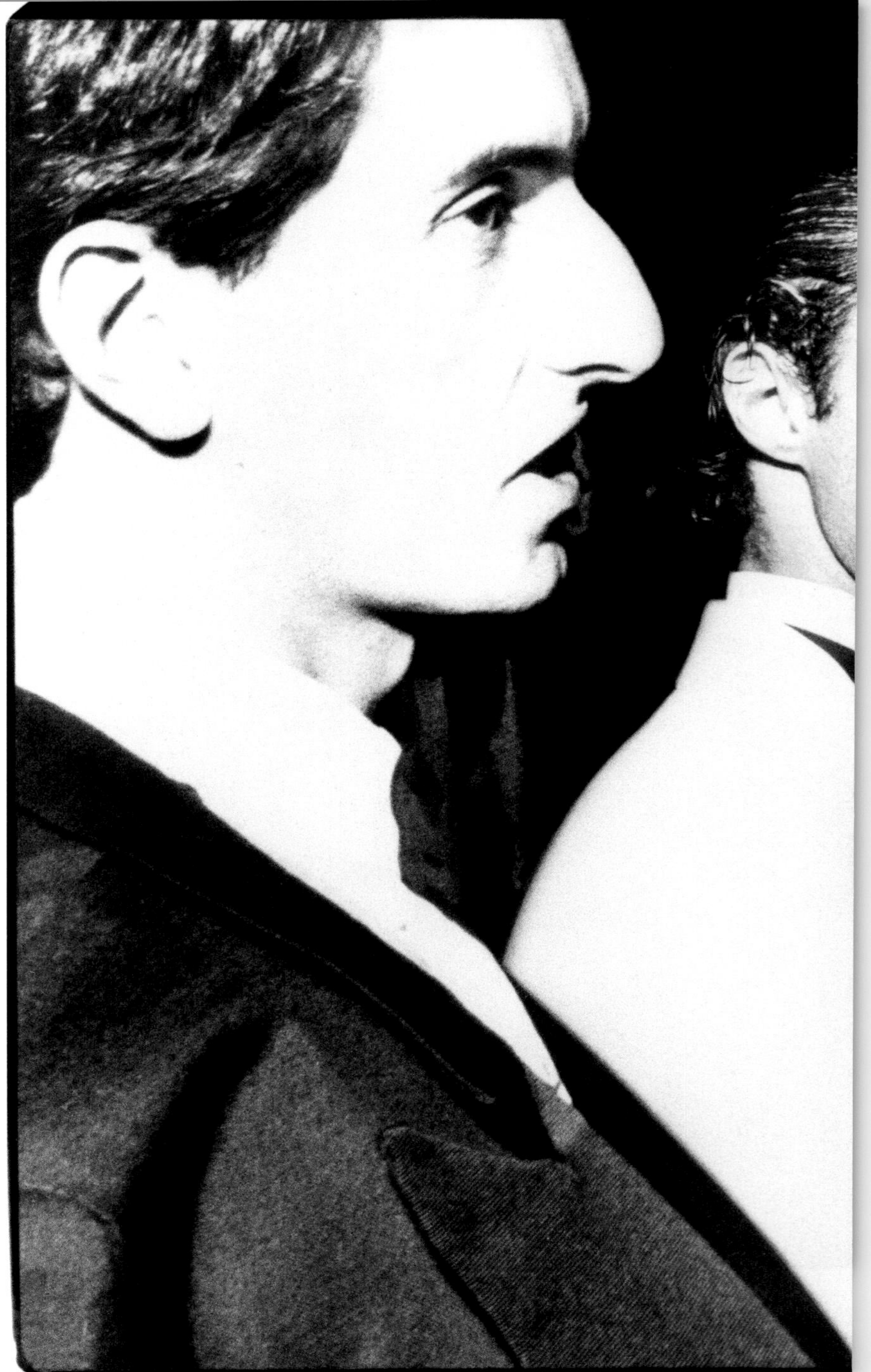

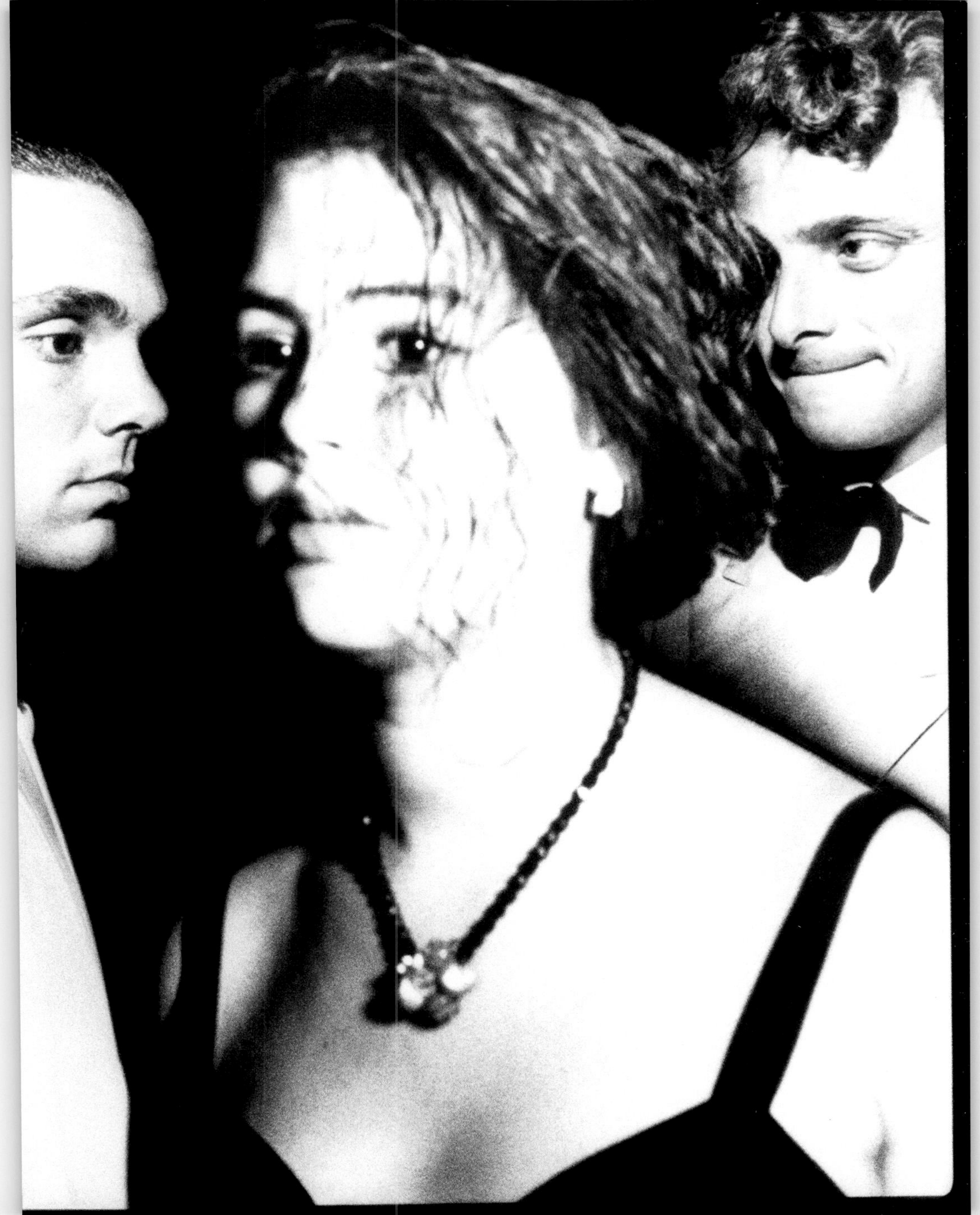

pp. 655–57, Yannick Noah, tennis player, Rome, May 14, 1992
pp. 658–63, Sylvie Guillem, dancer, New York, March 11, 1991

Egoïste

Yannick Noah Sylvie Guillem

Richard Avedon

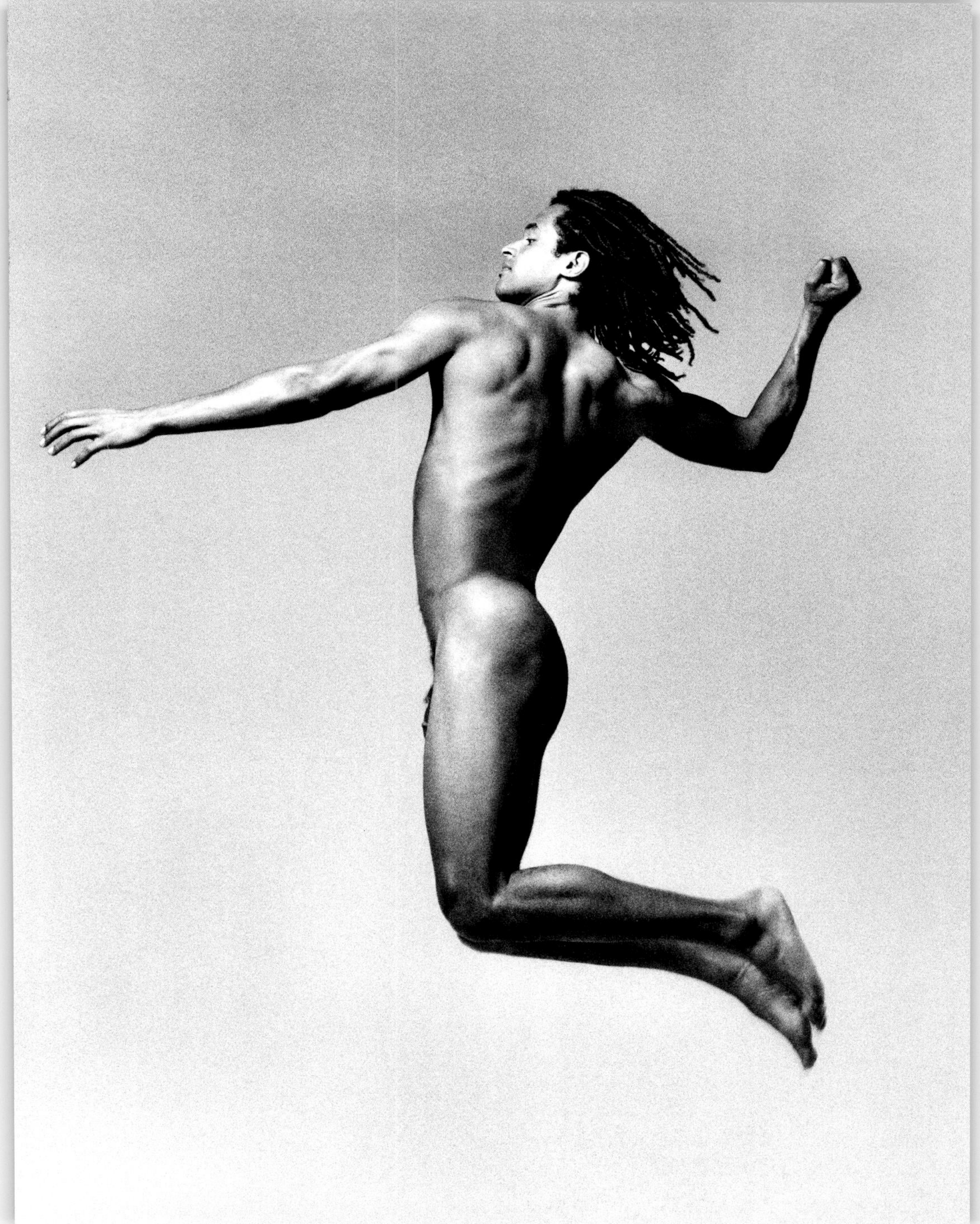

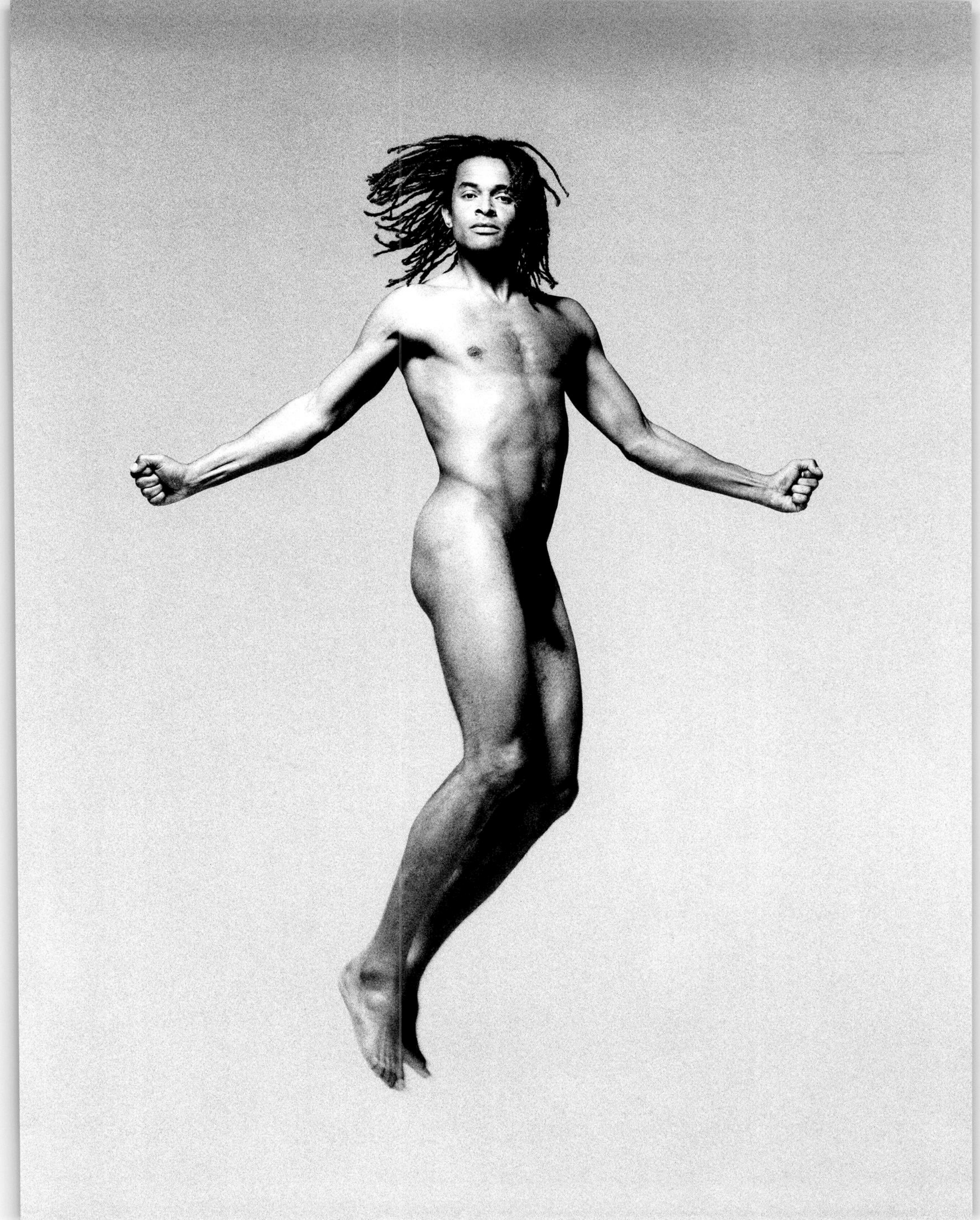

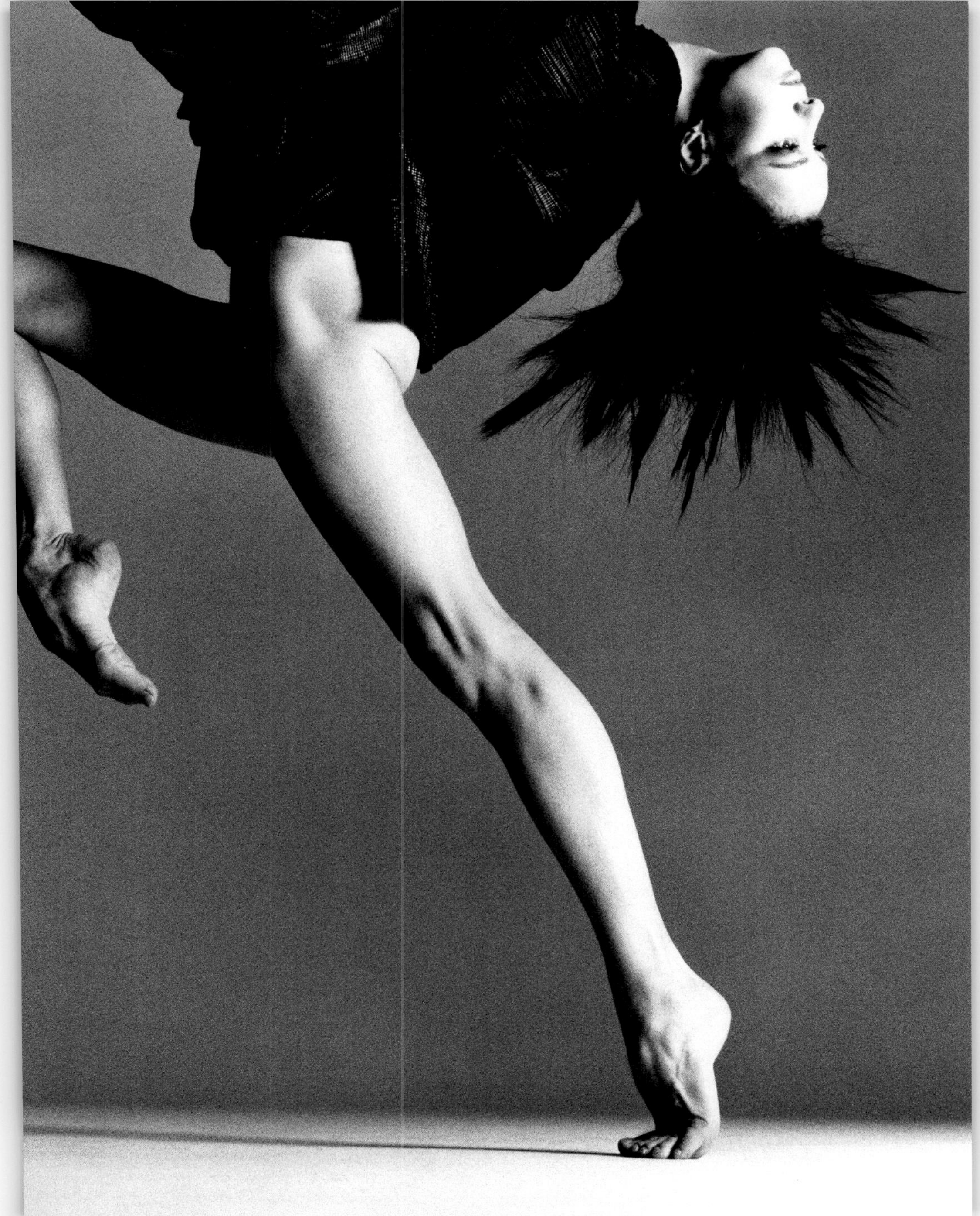

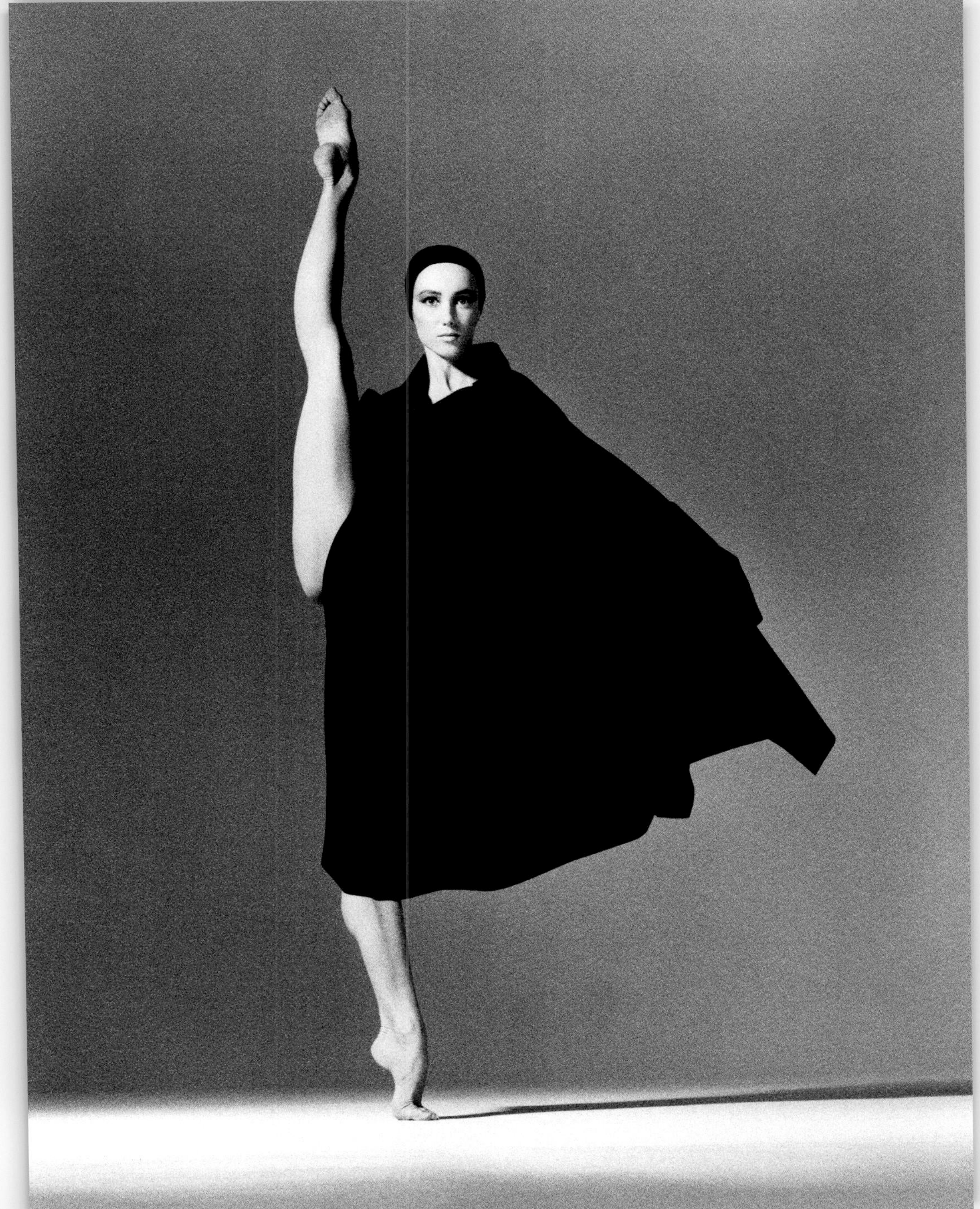

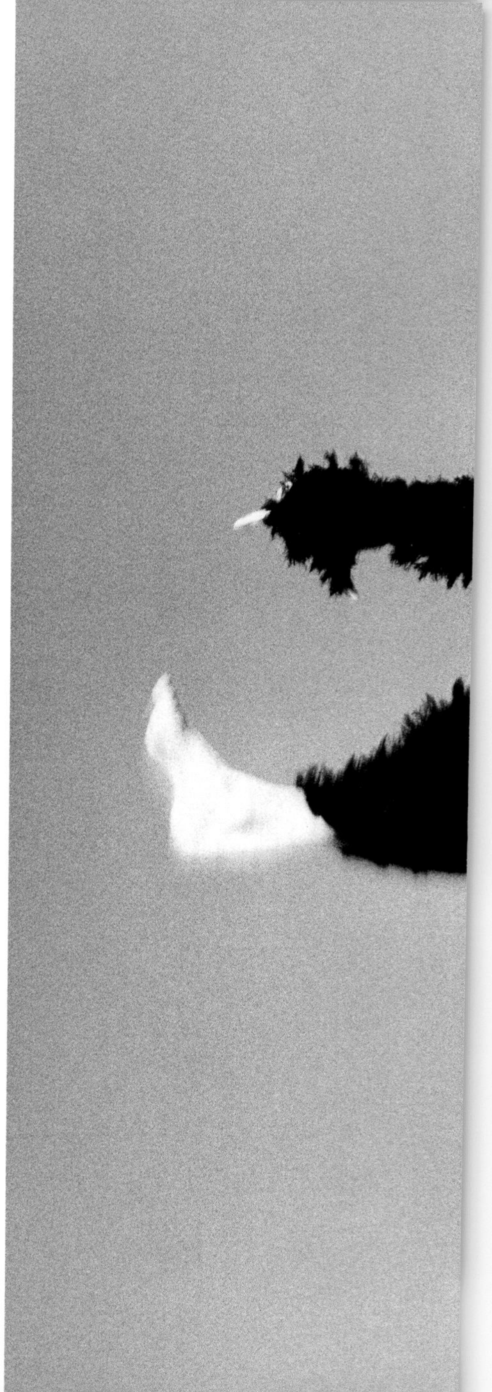

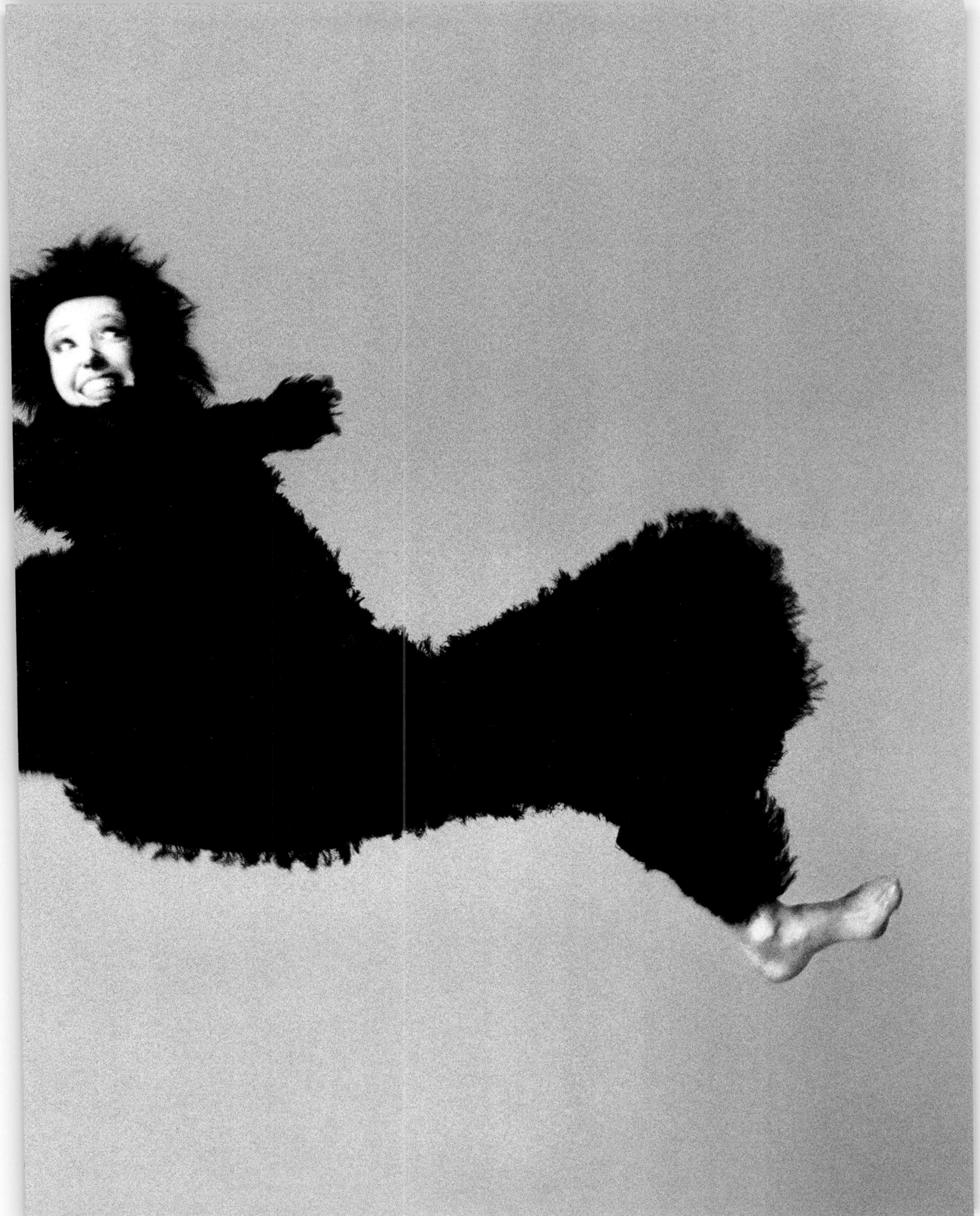

pp. 667–71, Isabelle Adjani, in "Adjani par Avedon," *Egoïste*, Belle-Île, France, November 7, 1988

Egoïste

Isabelle Adjani

Richard Avedon

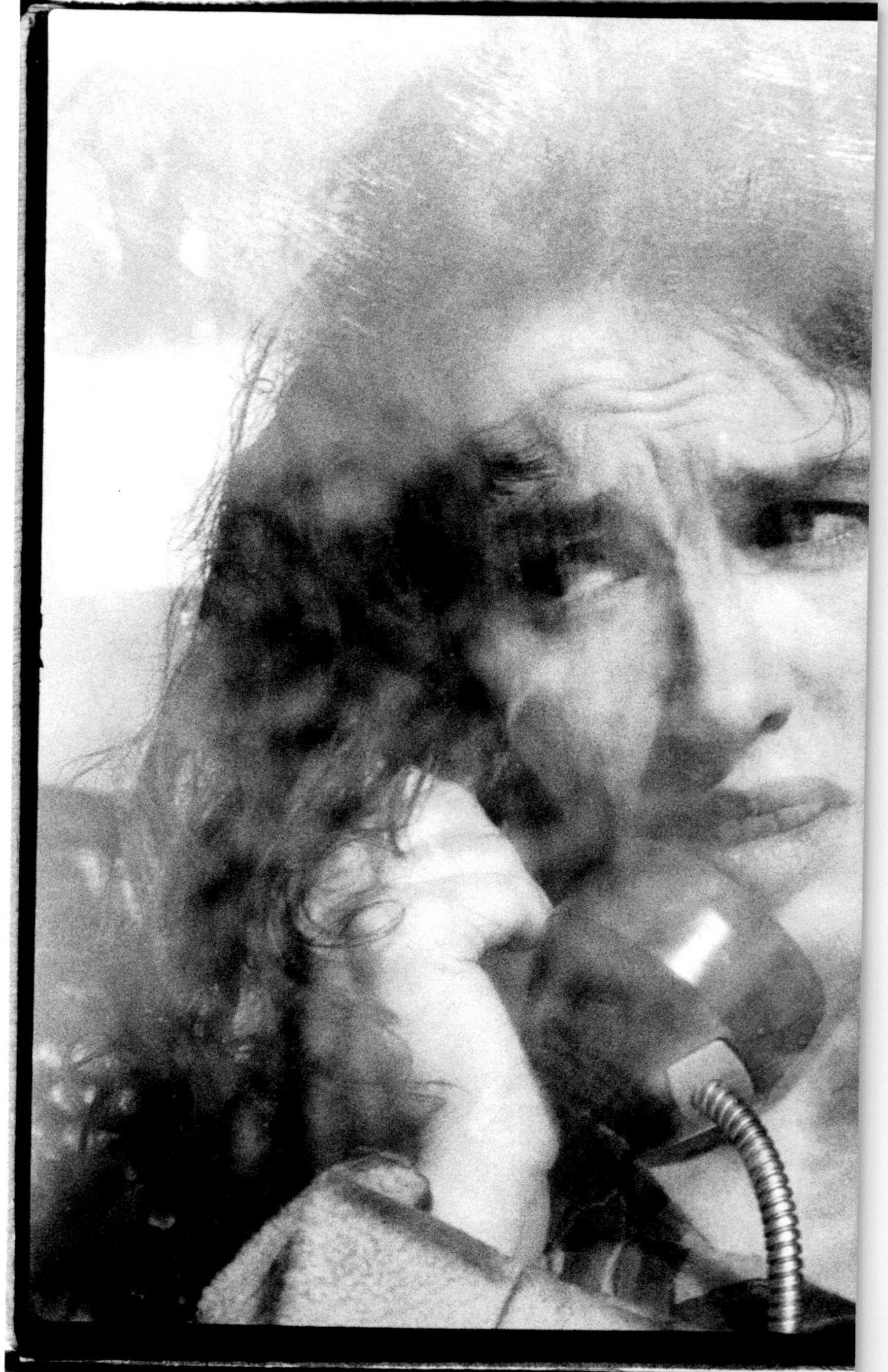

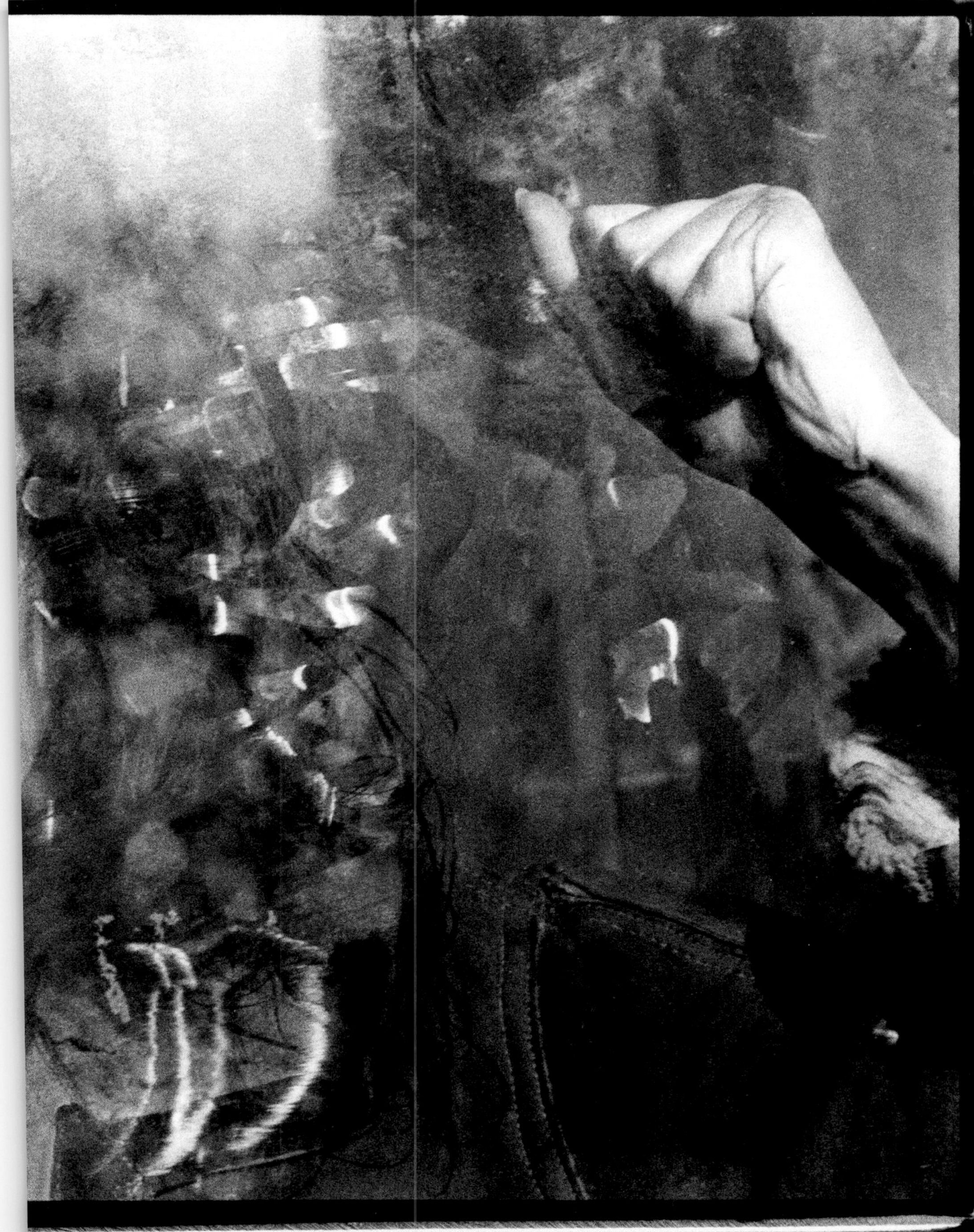

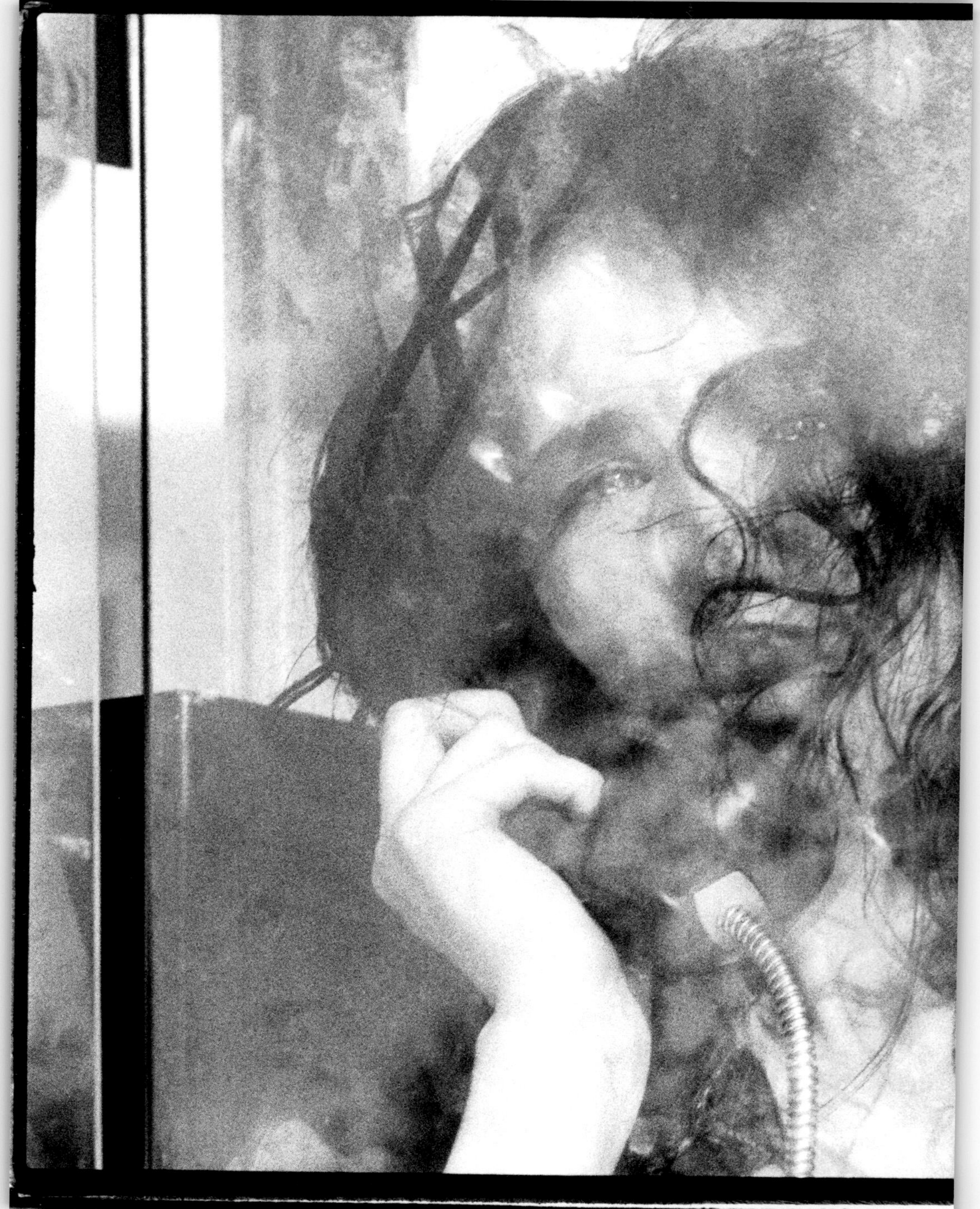

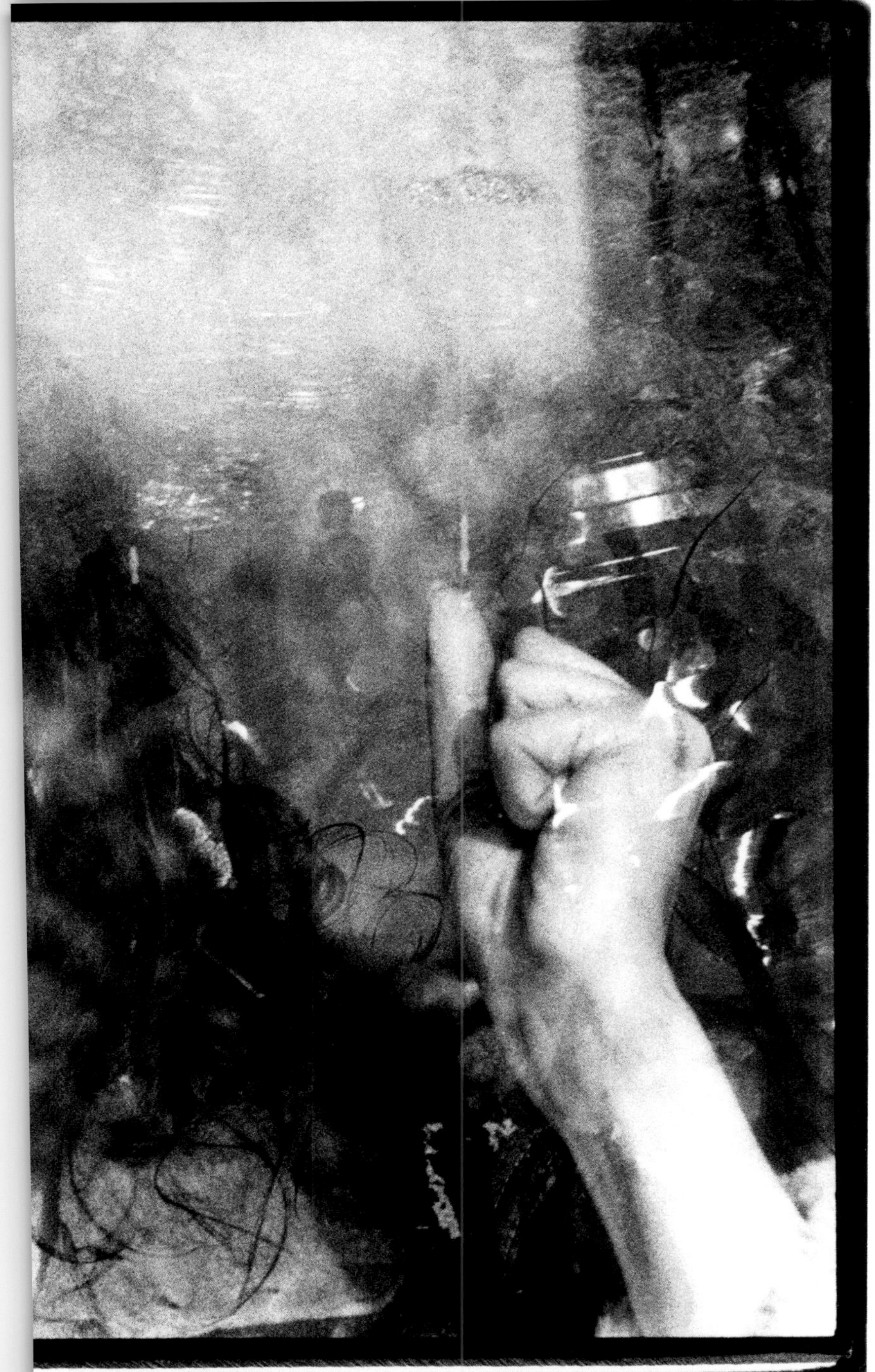

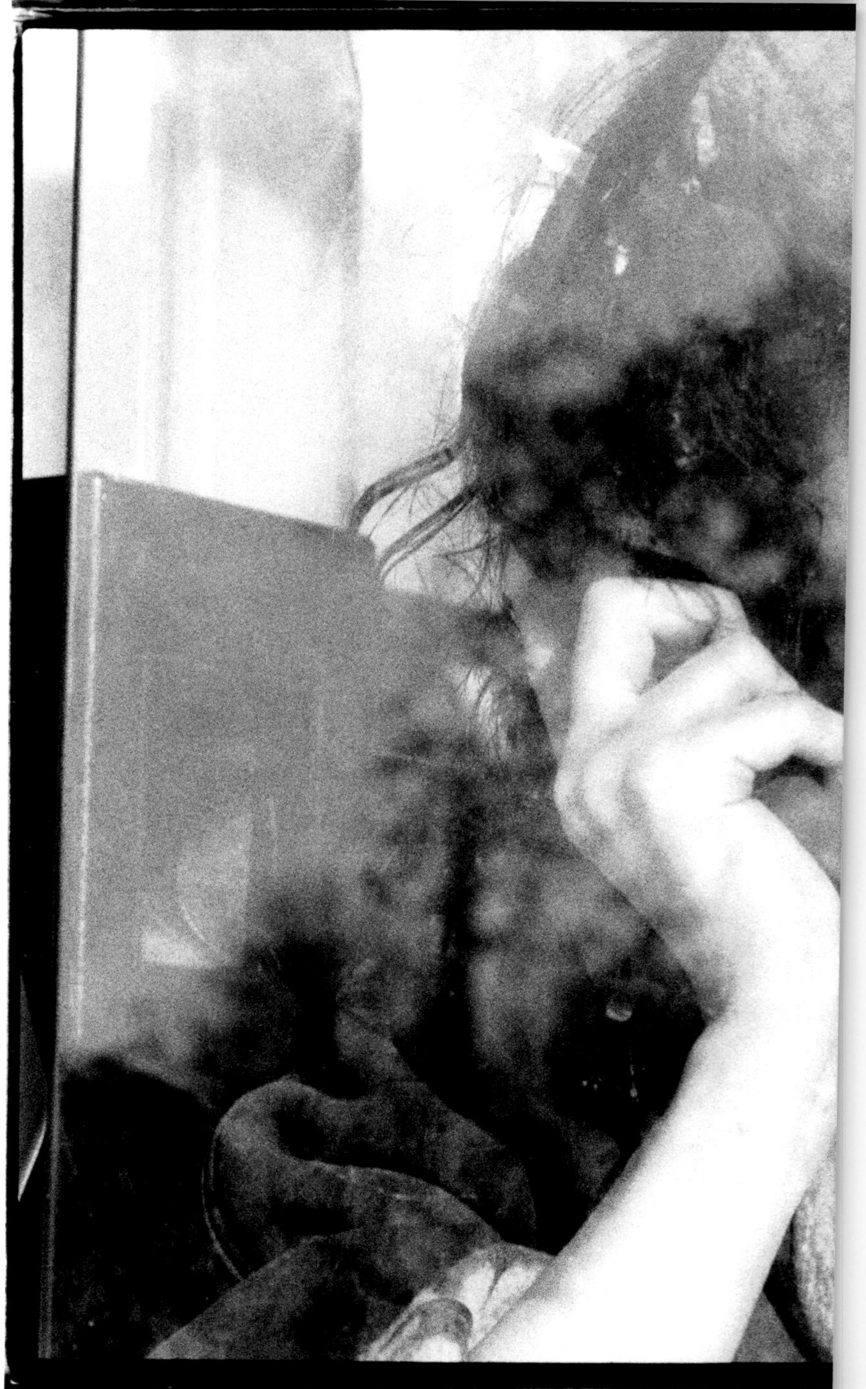

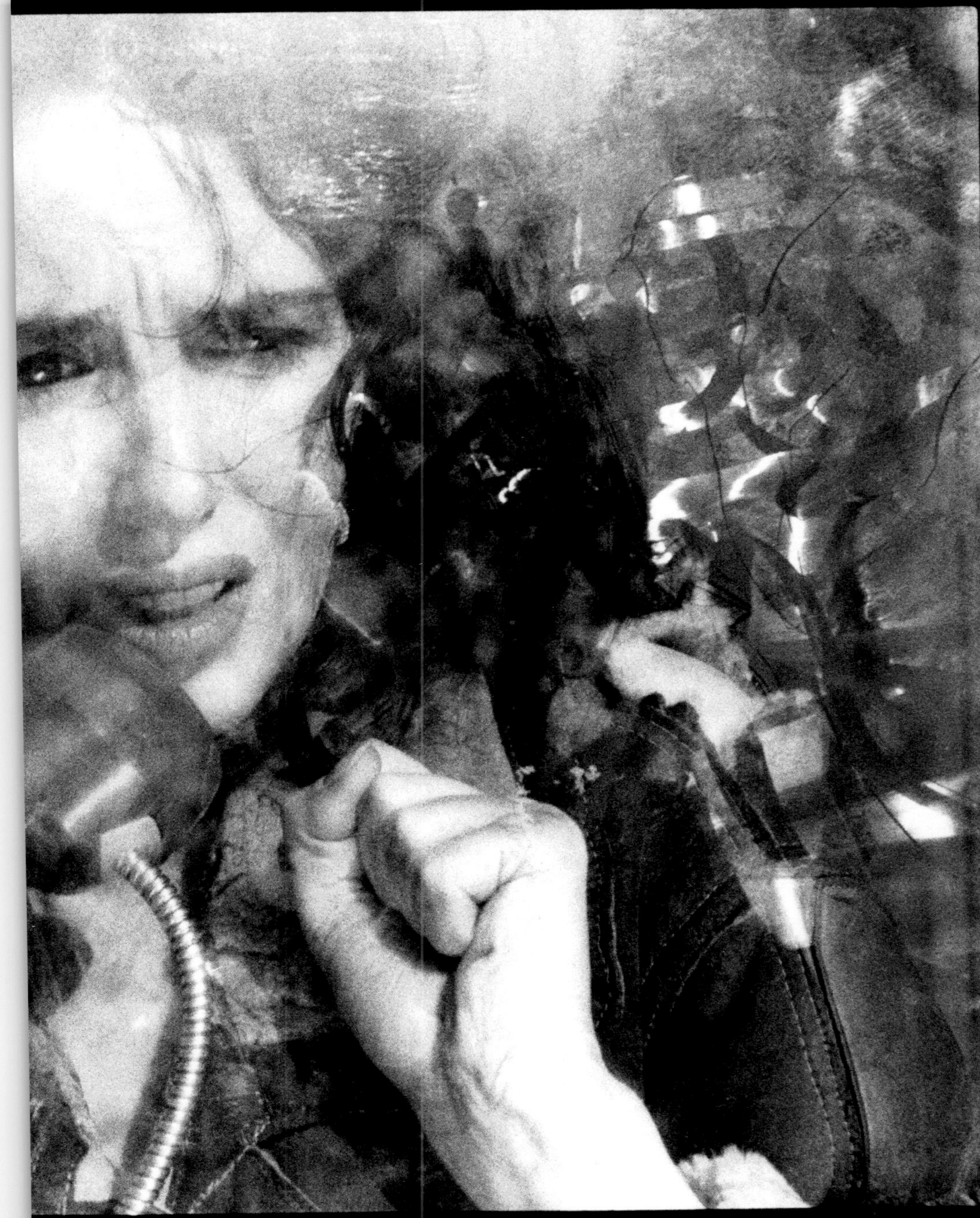

It's a little story in a magazine. Where the photographs need one another to tell the story. It's something I like doing. That could never be in *Vogue*, could never be in *Harper's Bazaar*.

Where else in the world would you have twenty pages that showed nothing but my old leather coat?

—

Richard Avedon

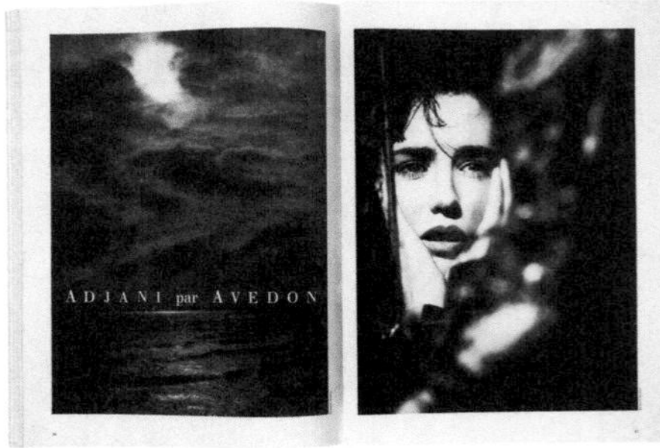
ADJANI par AVEDON

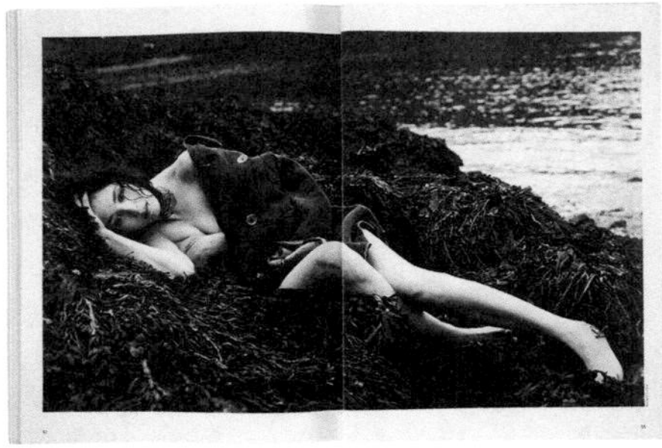

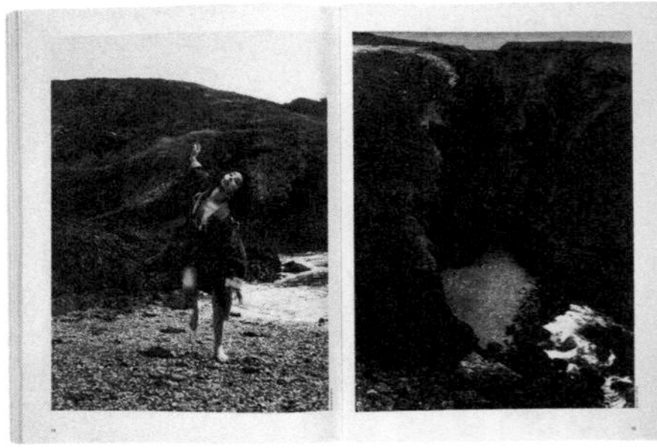

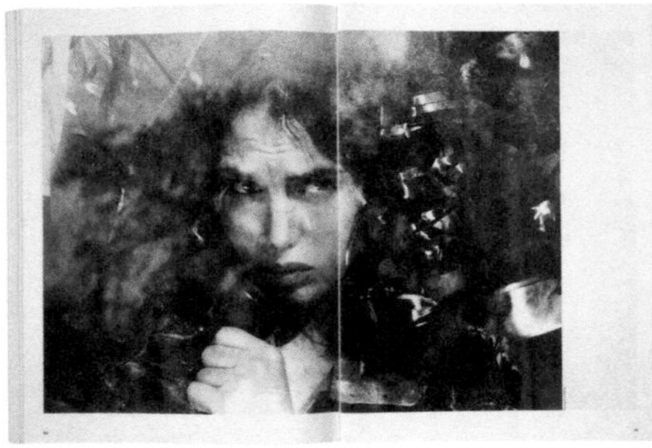

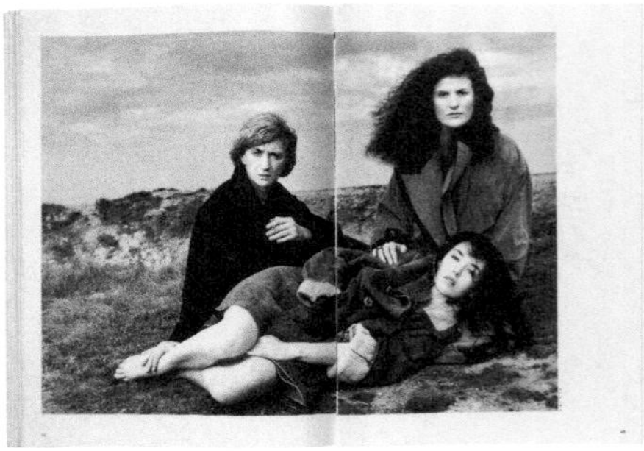

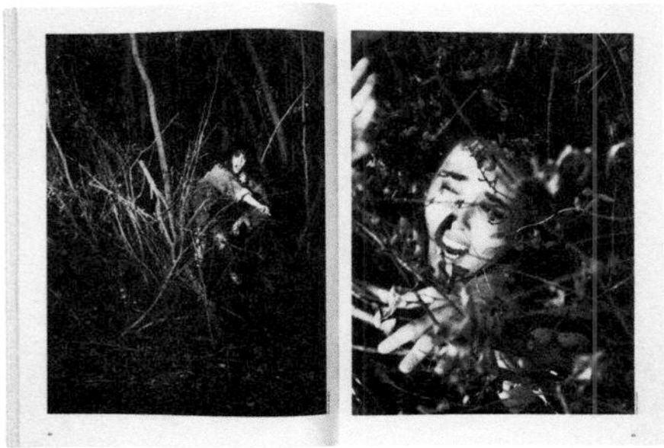

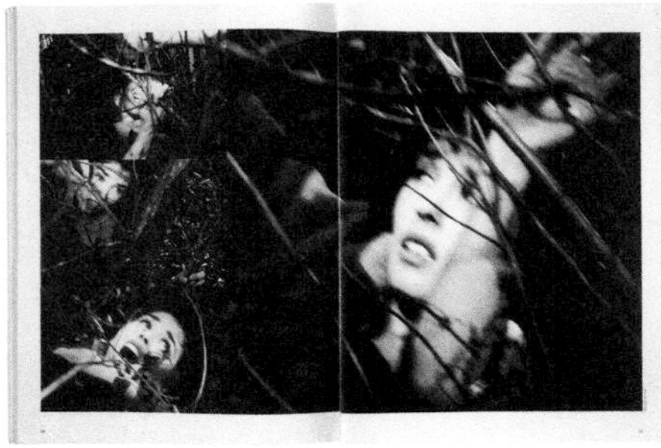

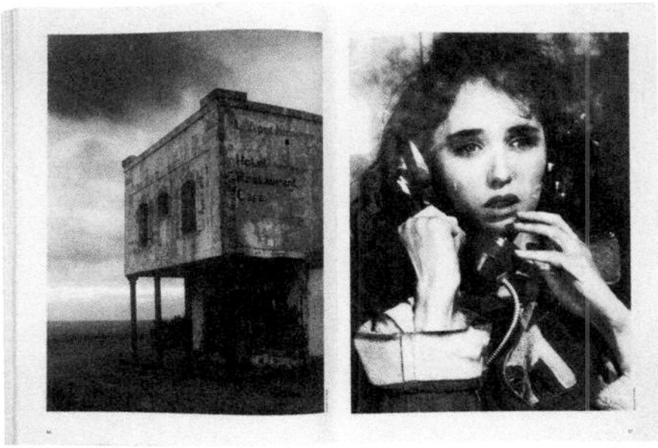

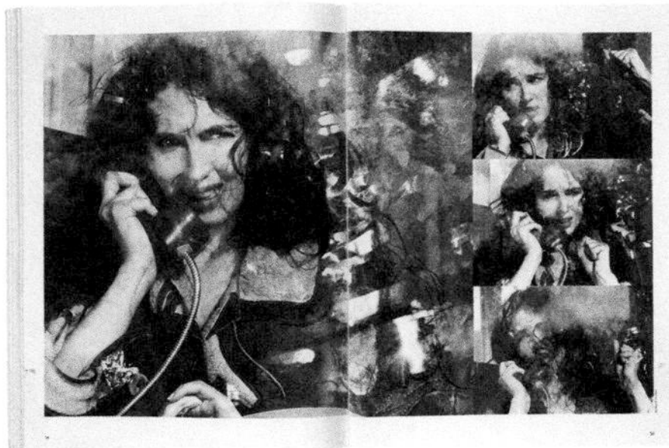

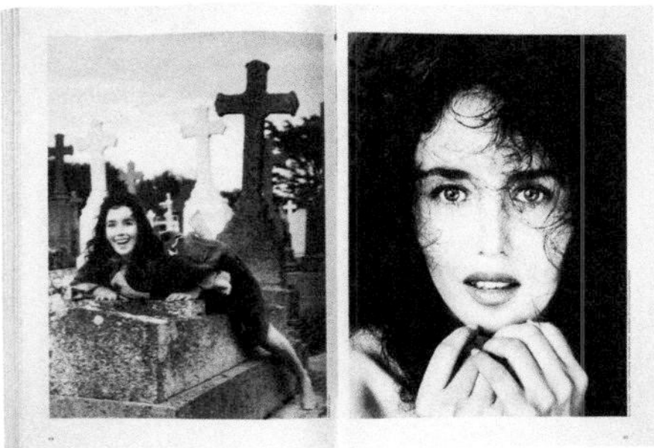

"Adjani par Avedon," *Egoïste,* N° 11, 1989, pp. 46–65

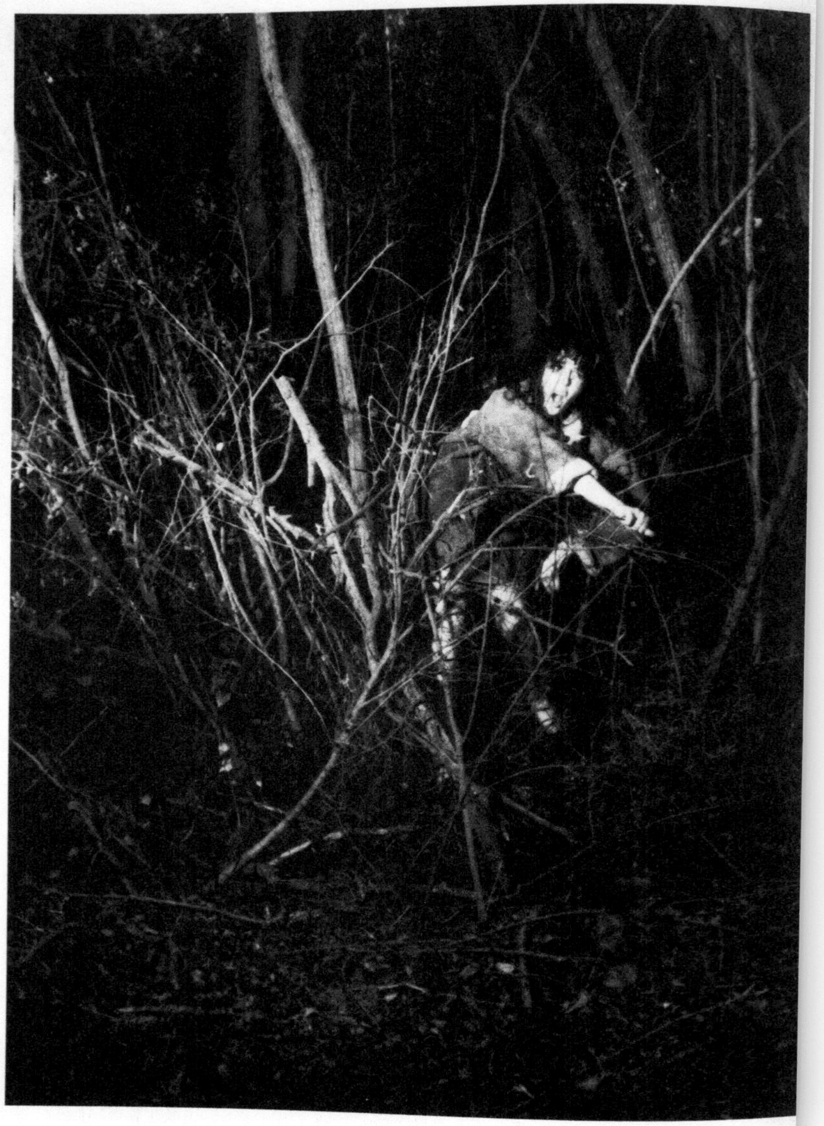

48

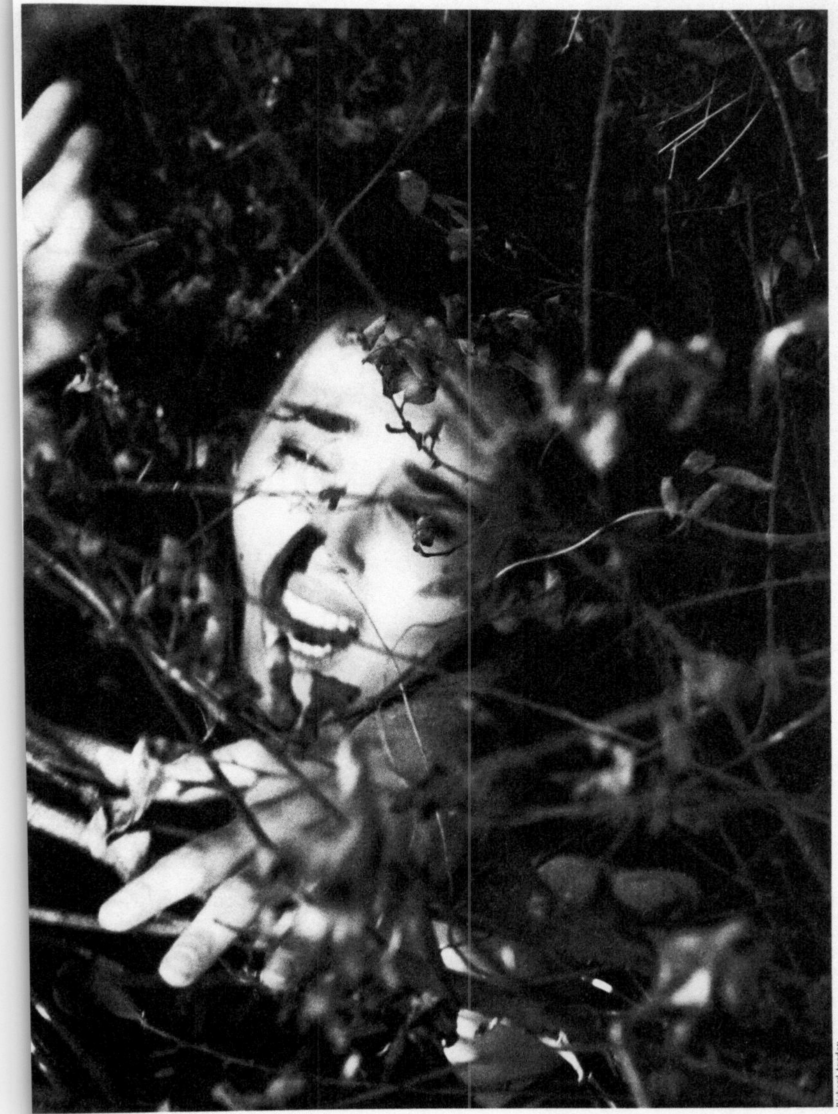

Richard Avedon

"Adjani par Avedon," *Egoïste*, N° 11, 1989, pp. 48–49

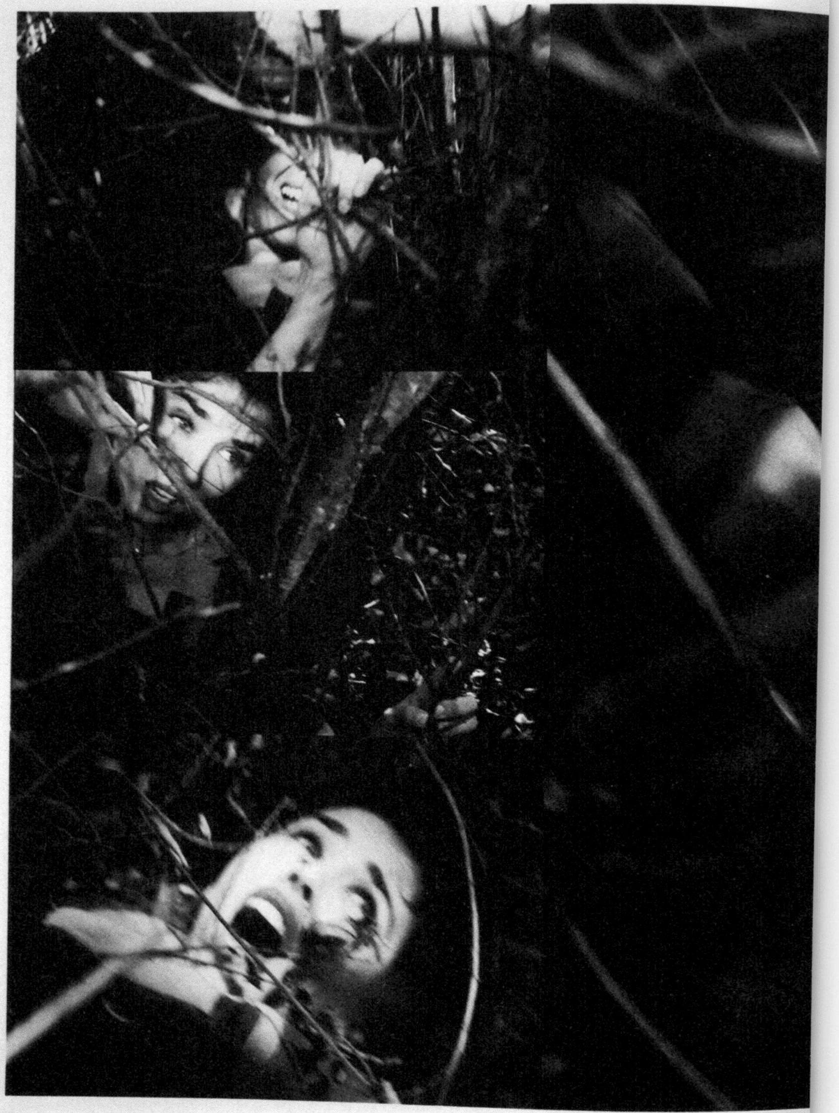

50

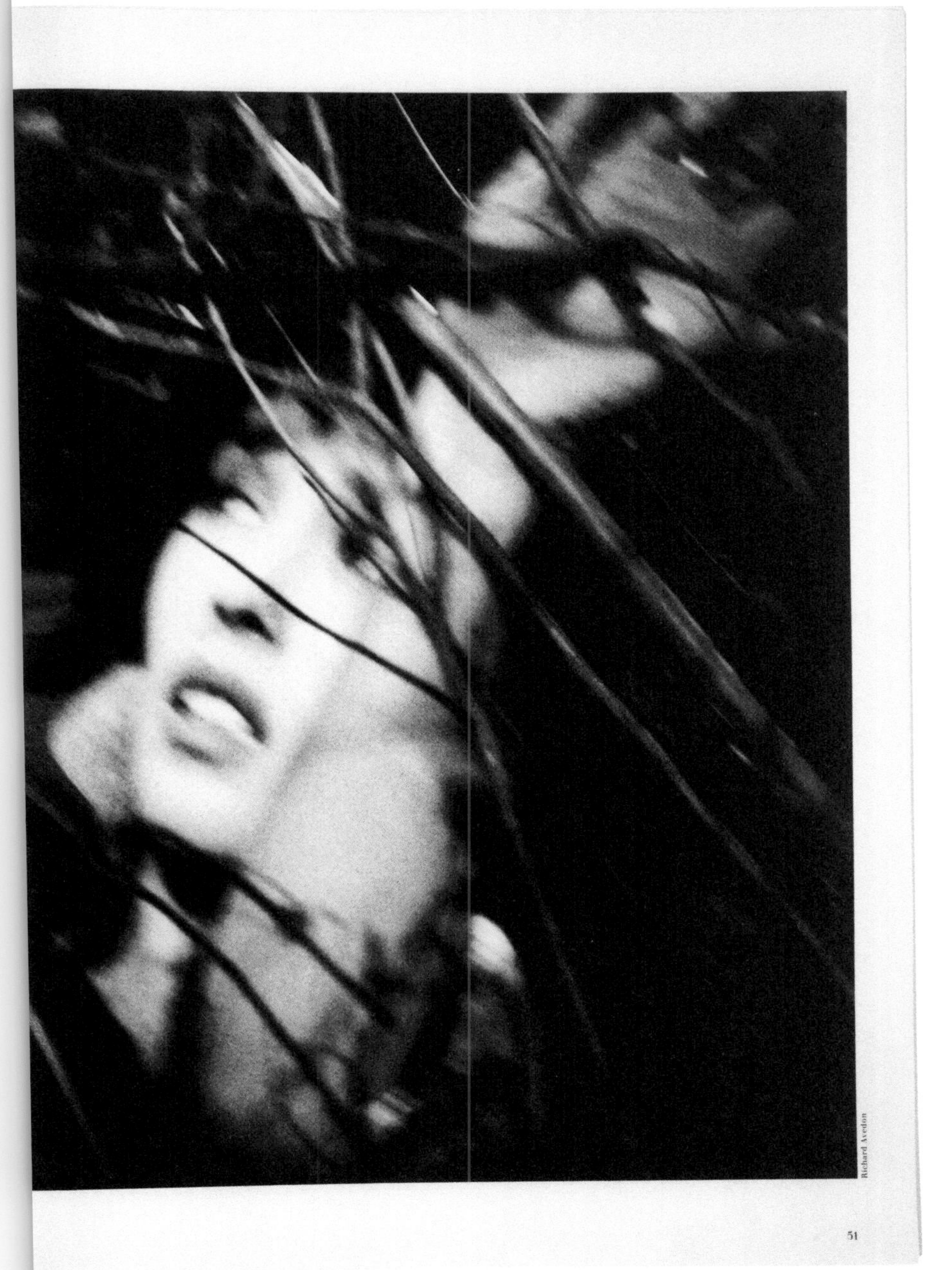

"Adjani par Avedon," *Egoïste*, N° 11, 1989, pp. 50–51

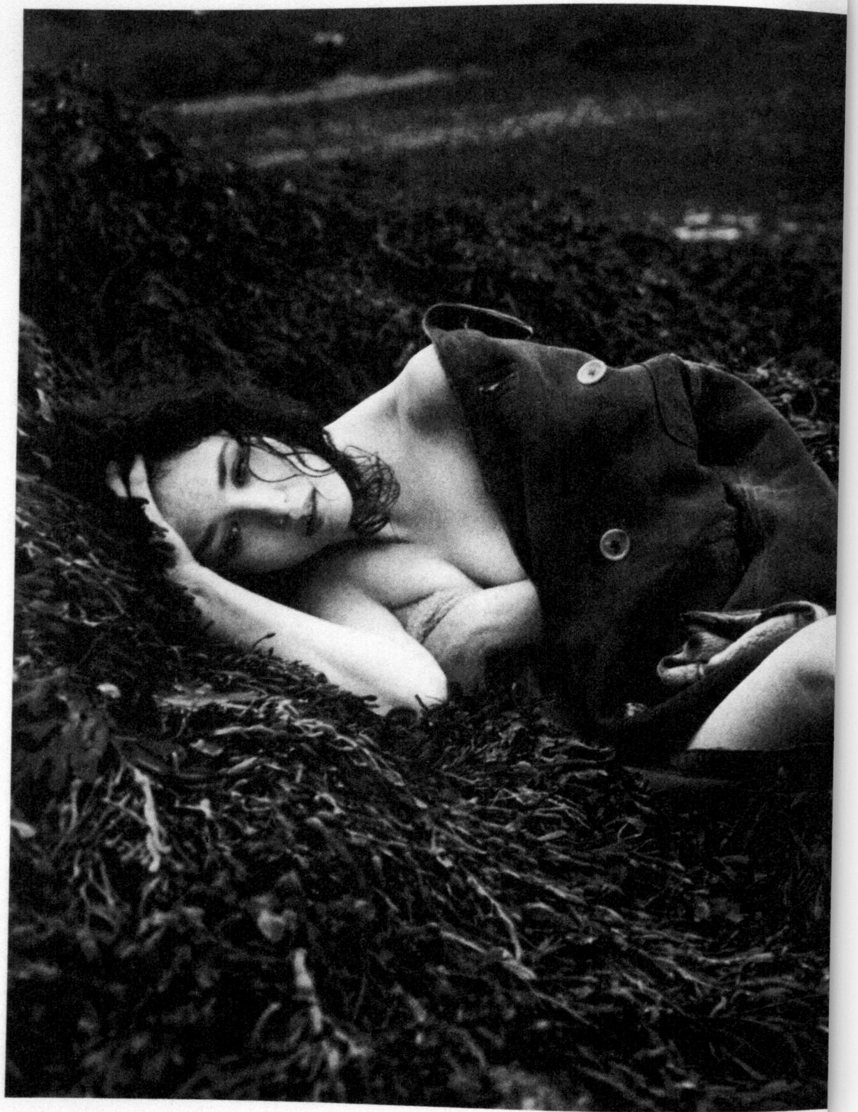

52

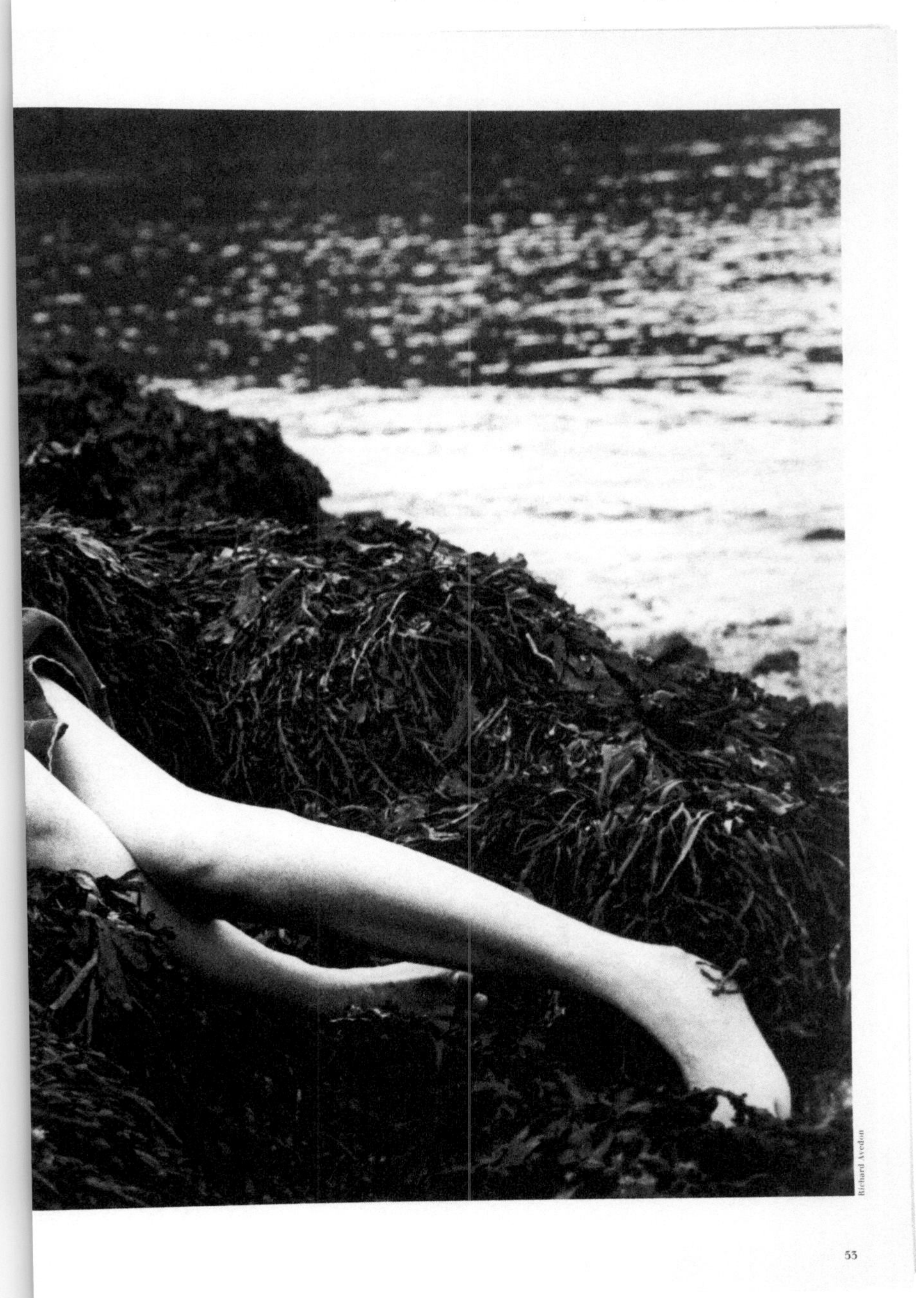

"Adjani par Avedon," *Egoïste,* N° 11, 1989, pp. 52–53

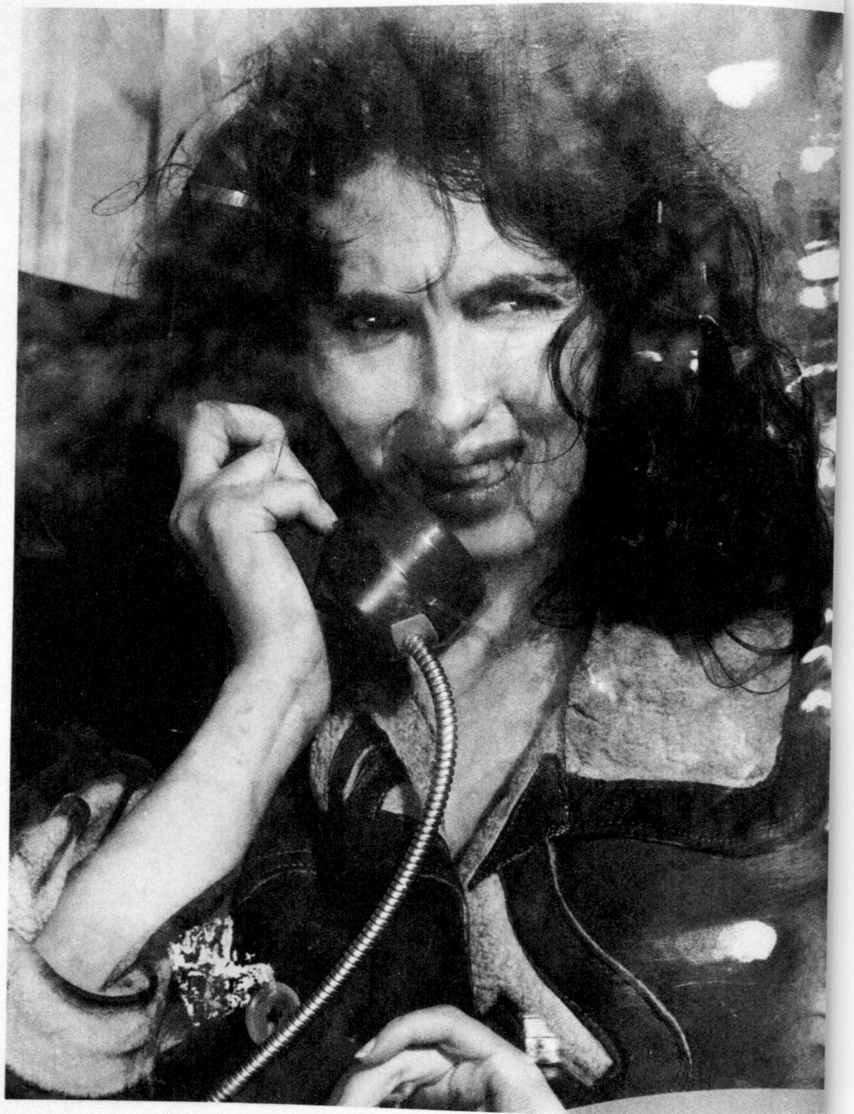

58

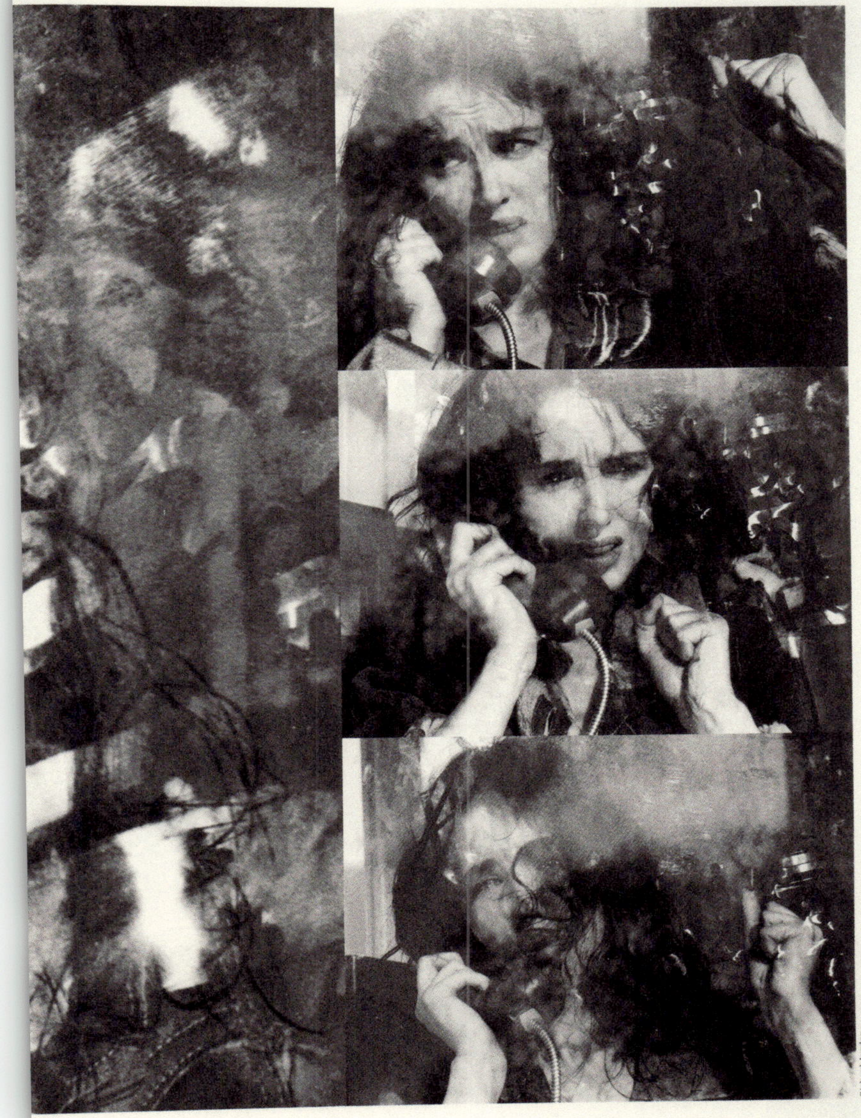

Richard Avedon

59

"Adjani par Avedon," *Egoïste,* N° 11, 1989, pp. 58–59

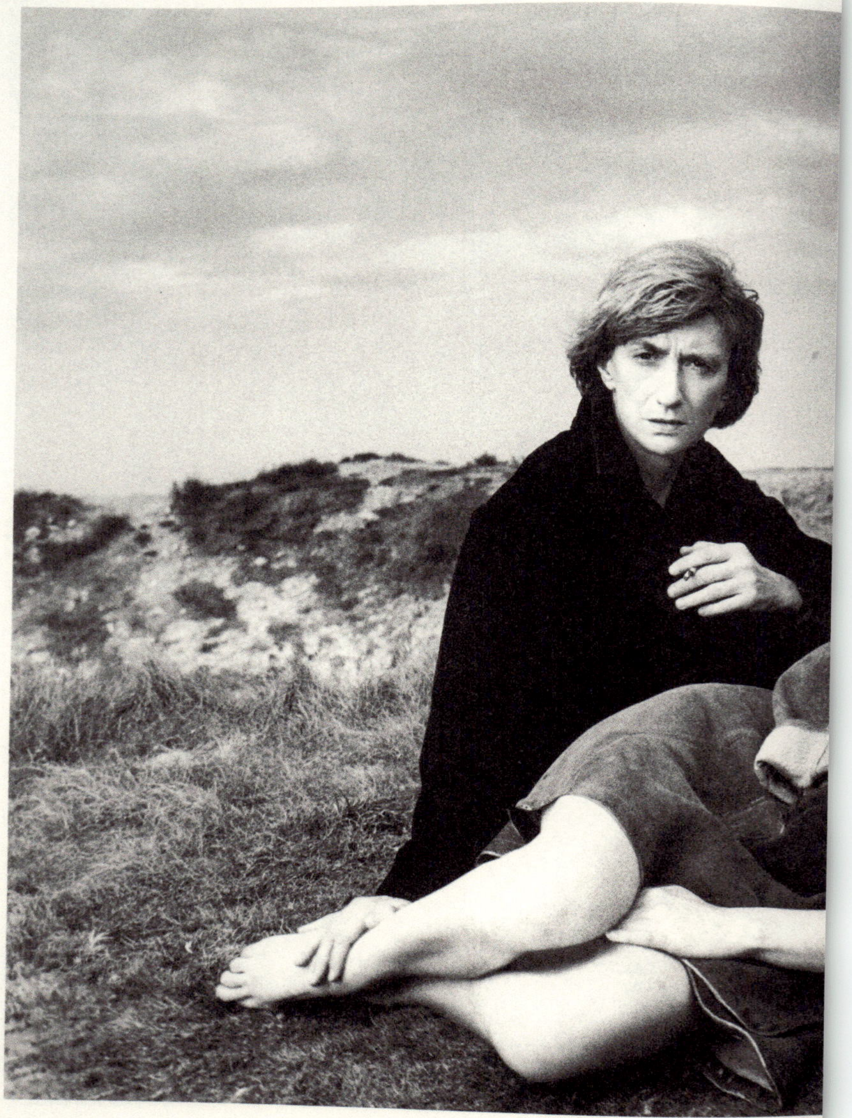

62

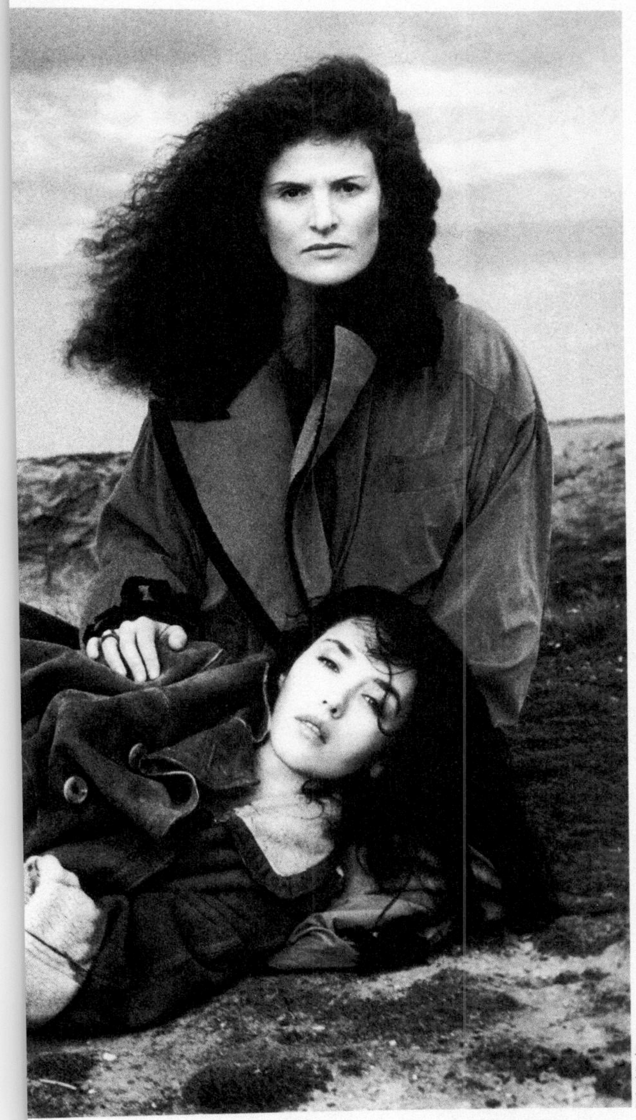

Richard Avedon

63

"Adjani par Avedon," *Egoïste*, N° 11, 1989, pp. 62–63

p. 691, Marguerite Duras, writer, Paris, May 21, 1993
p. 693, Vintner, Château Lafite Rothschild, Pauillac, France, October 16, 2000
p. 695, Sister Emmanuelle, nun, Paris, June 18, 1998
p. 697, Alexis von Rosenberg, Baron de Redé, banker and aristocrat, Paris, June 6, 1998
p. 699, André Glucksmann, activist and writer, New York, April 19, 1992
p. 701, Philippe Sollers, novelist, Paris, May 28, 1998
p. 703, Gérard Depardieu and Françoise Sagan, actor and writer, Paris, November 7, 1998
p. 705, François Pinault, French banking tycoon, Paris, May 28 1998
p. 707, Bernard Frank, writer, Paris, December 6, 1995
p. 709, Daniel Cohn-Bendit, Member of the European Parliament, Brussels, Belgium, December 7, 1995
p. 711, Abbé Pierre, priest, Paris, June 17, 1998

Egoïste

French Portraits V

Richard Avedon

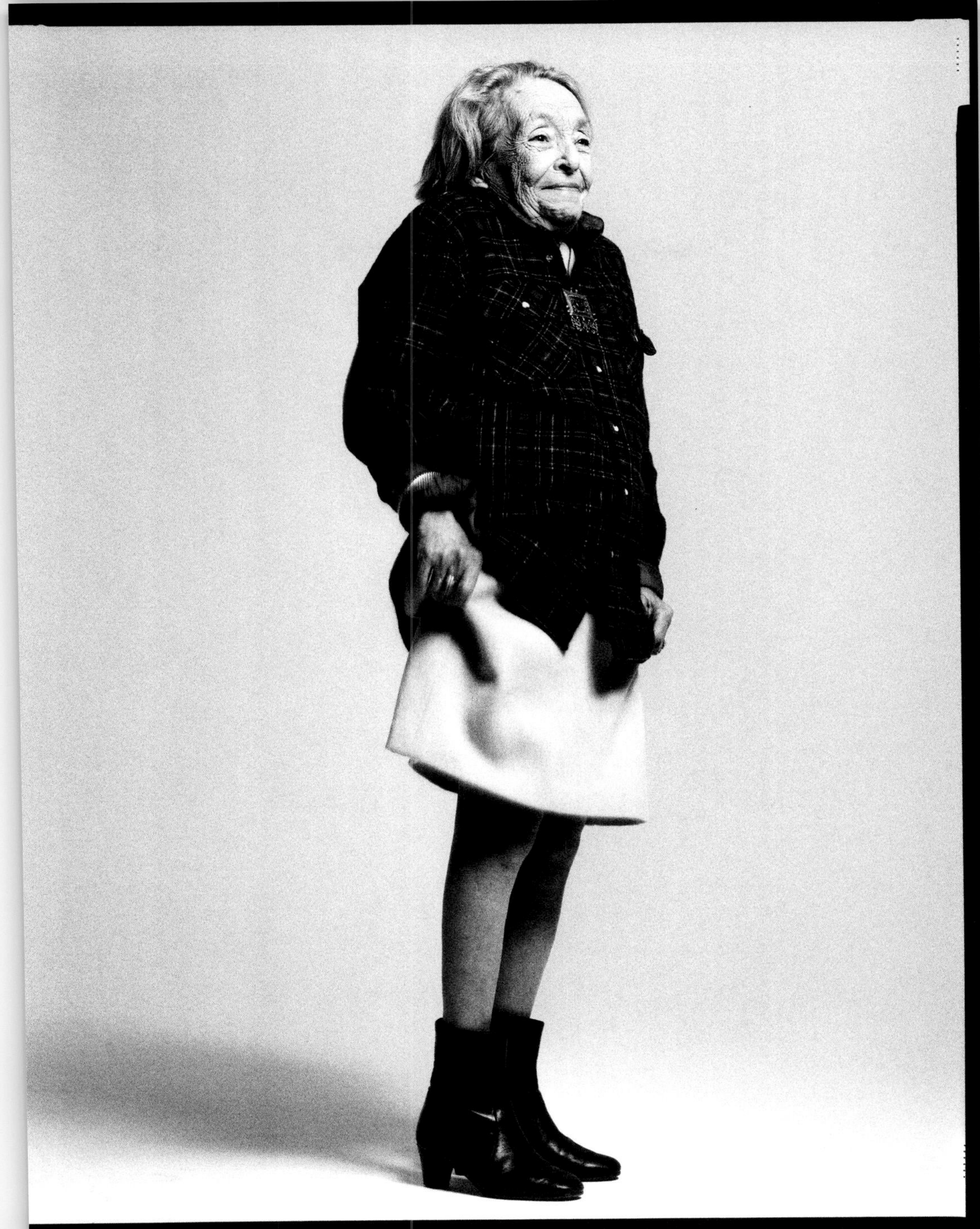

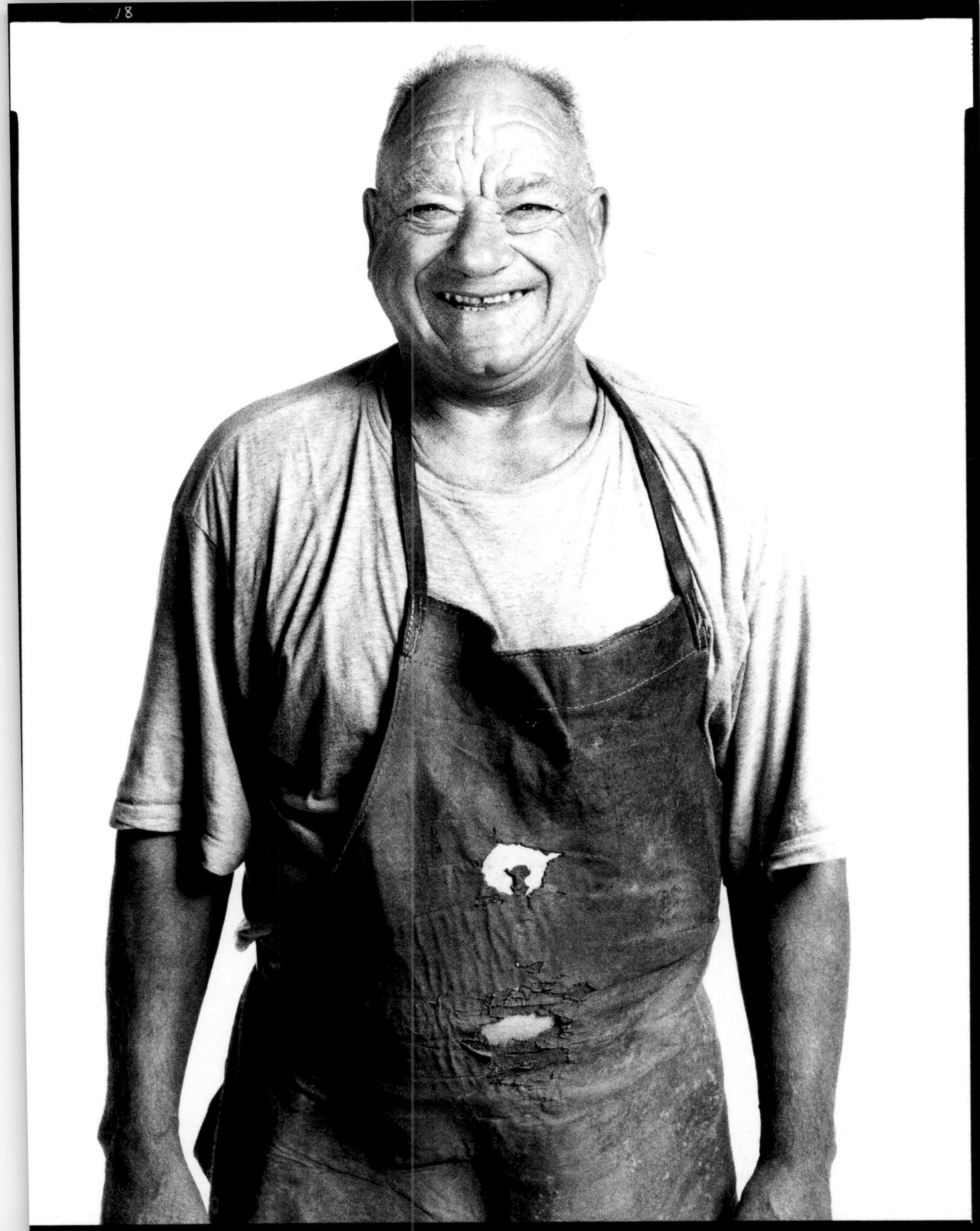

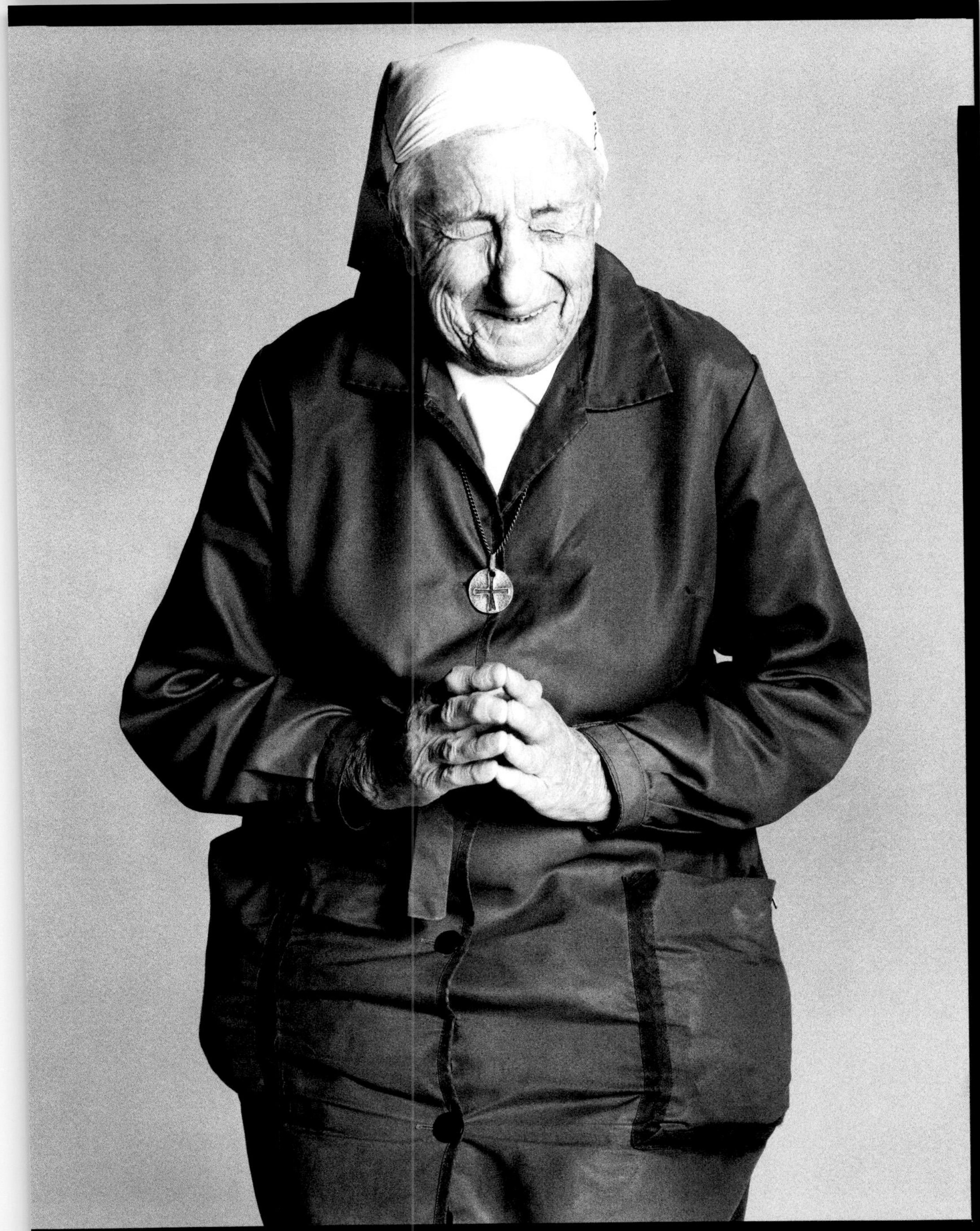

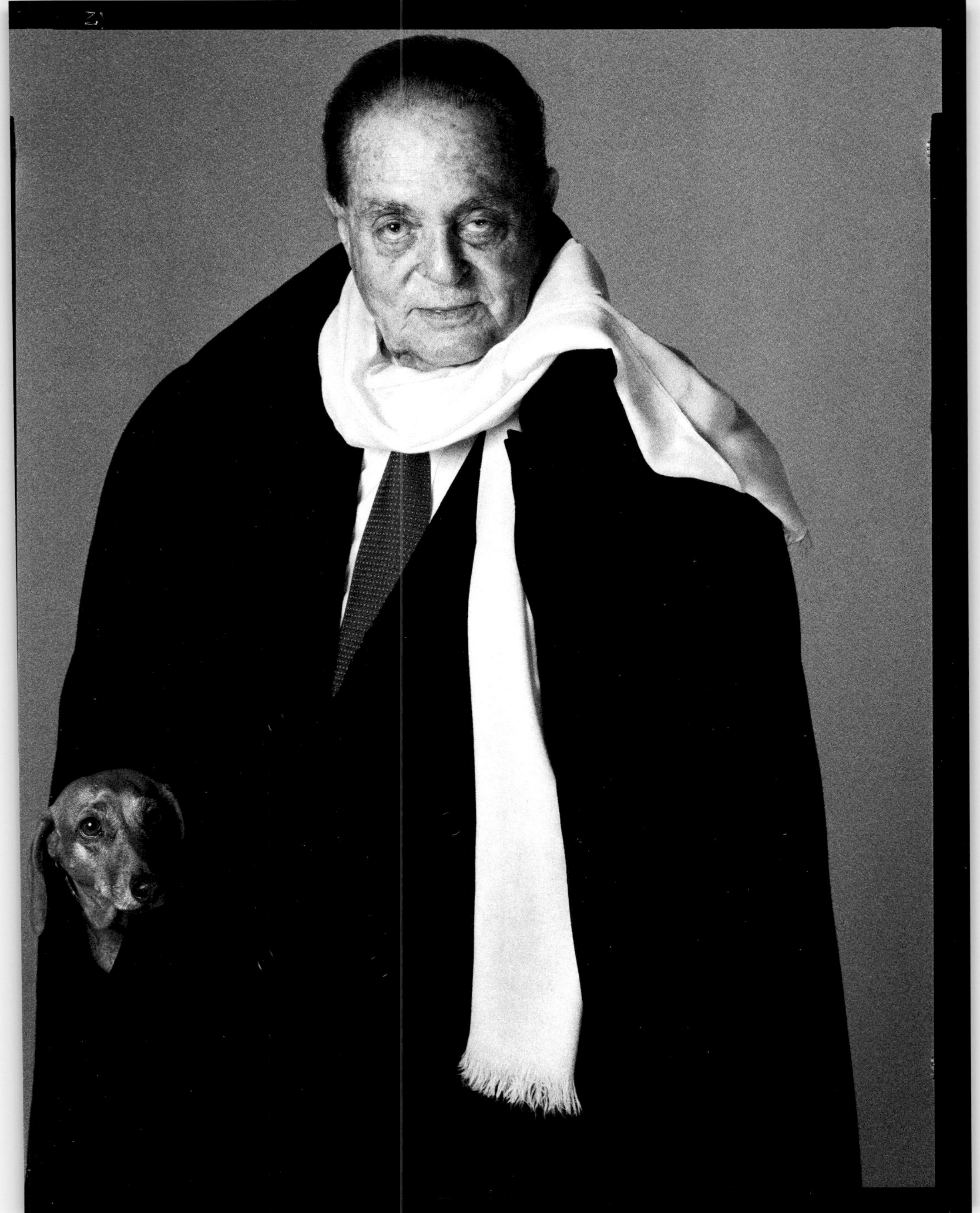

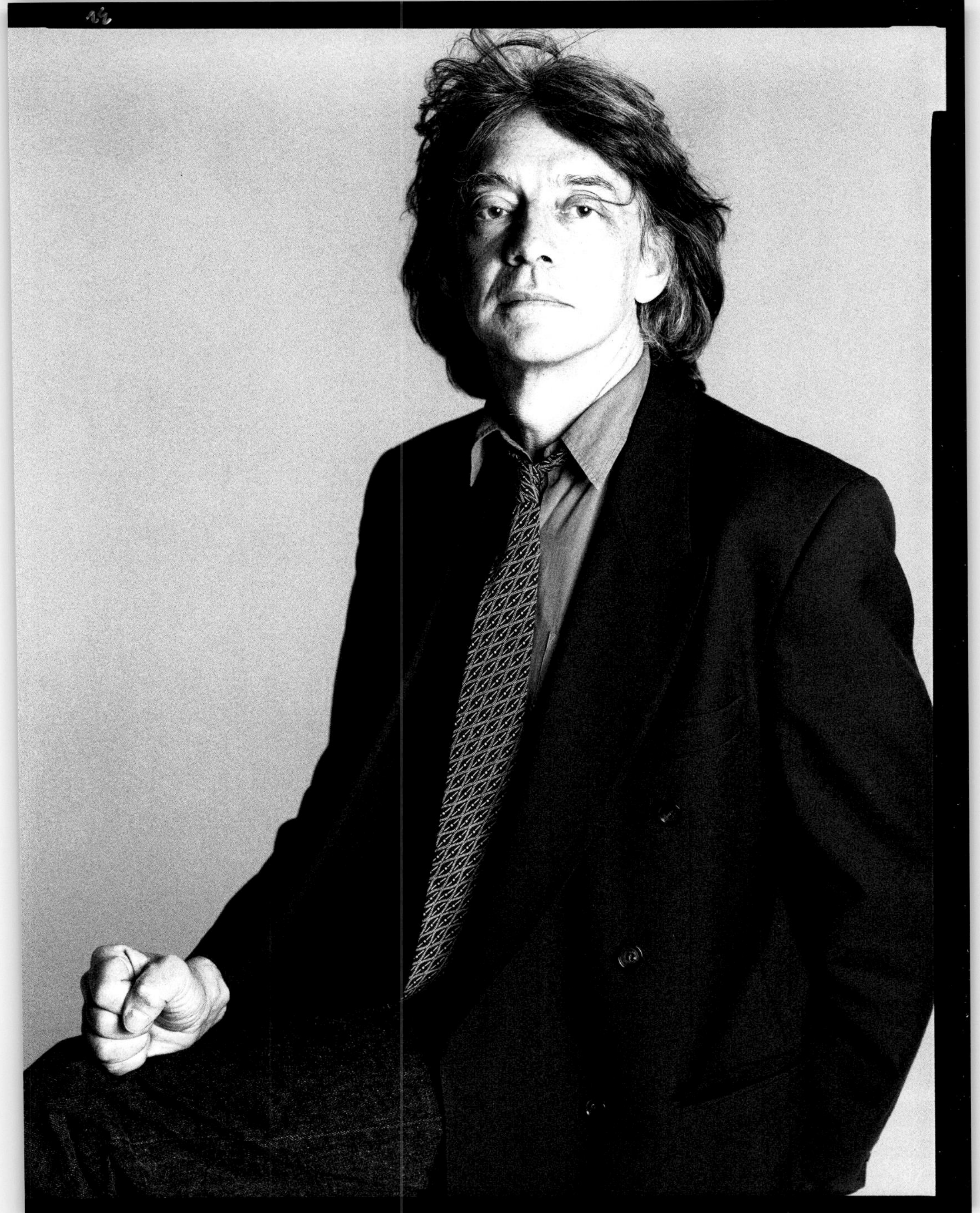

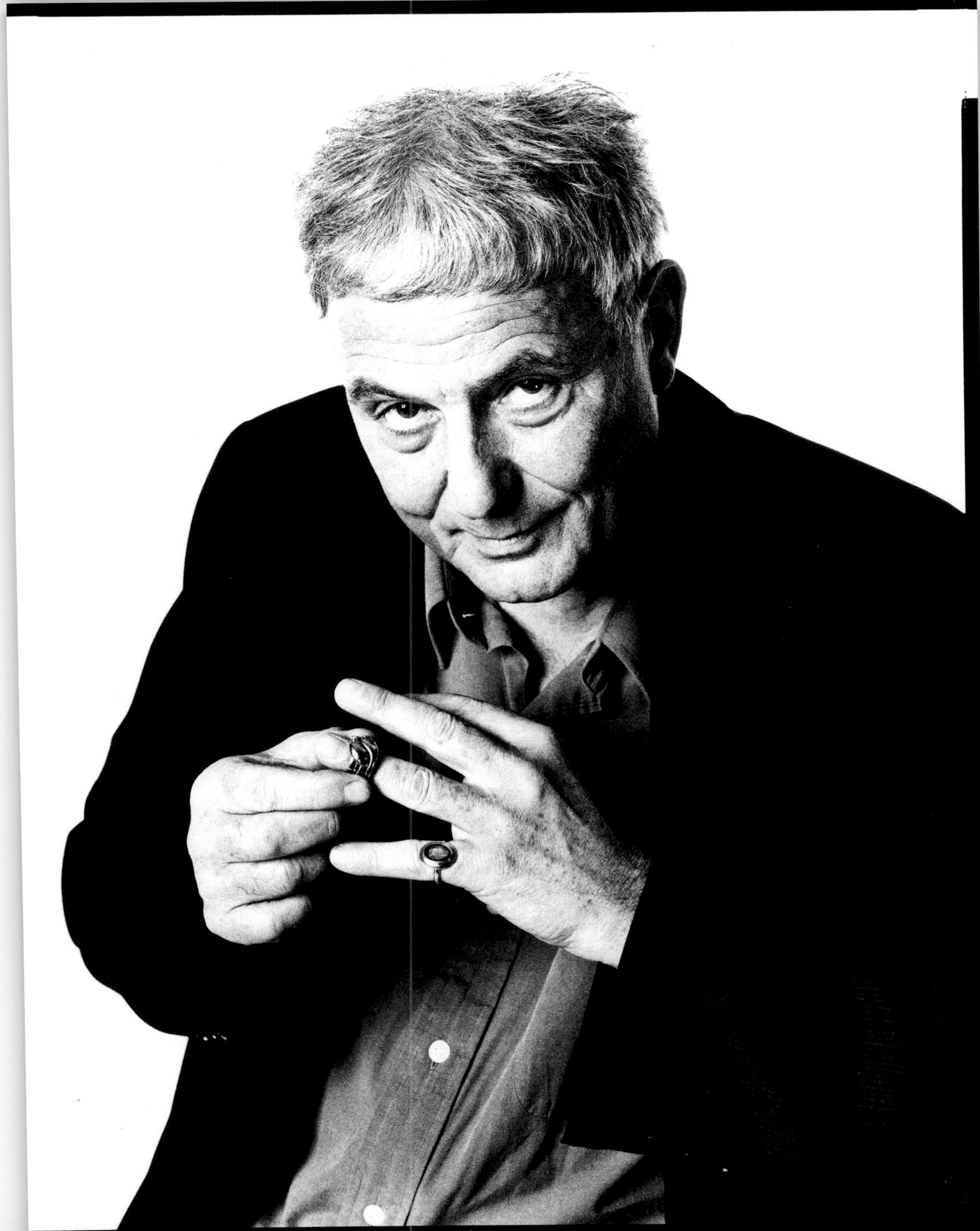

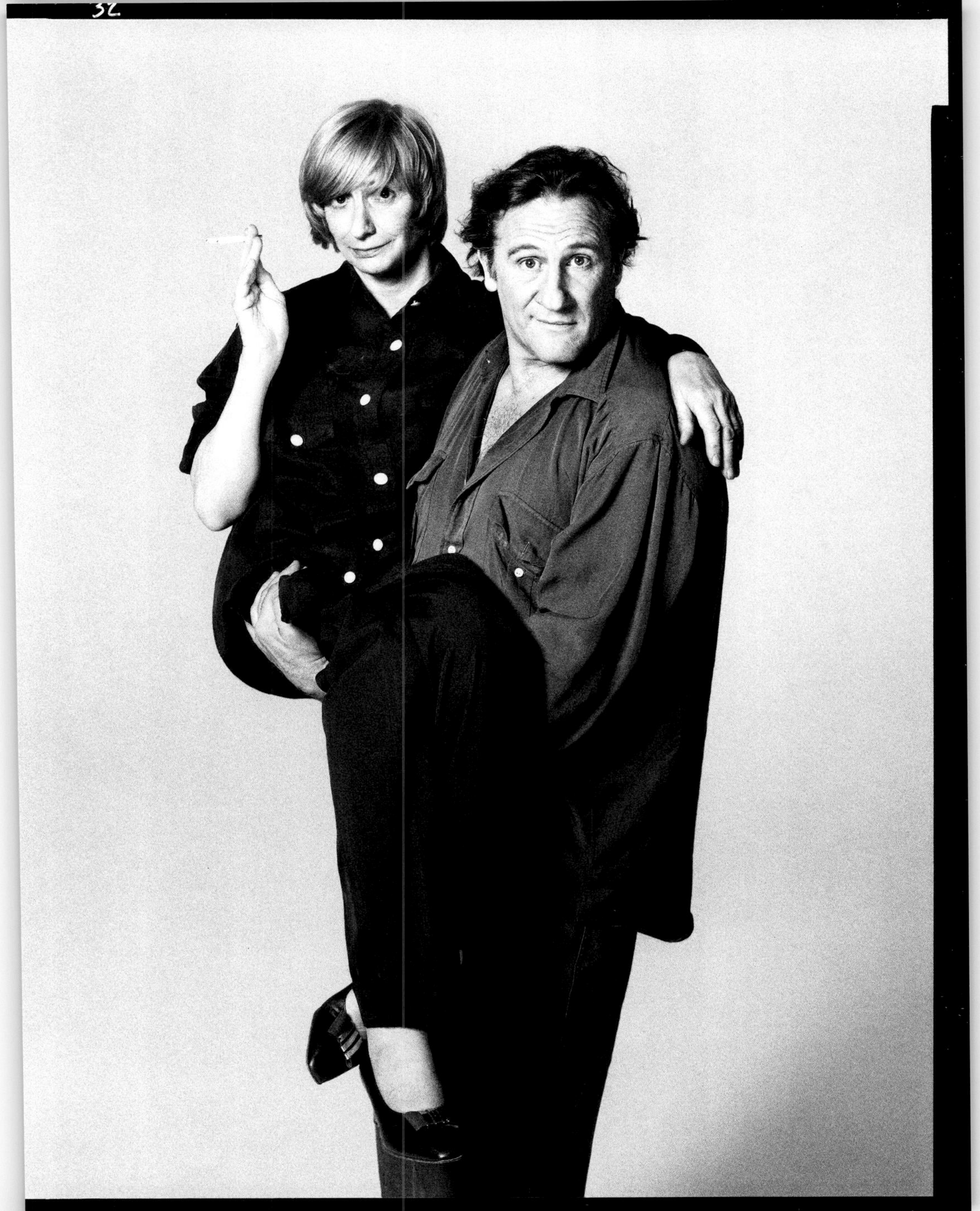

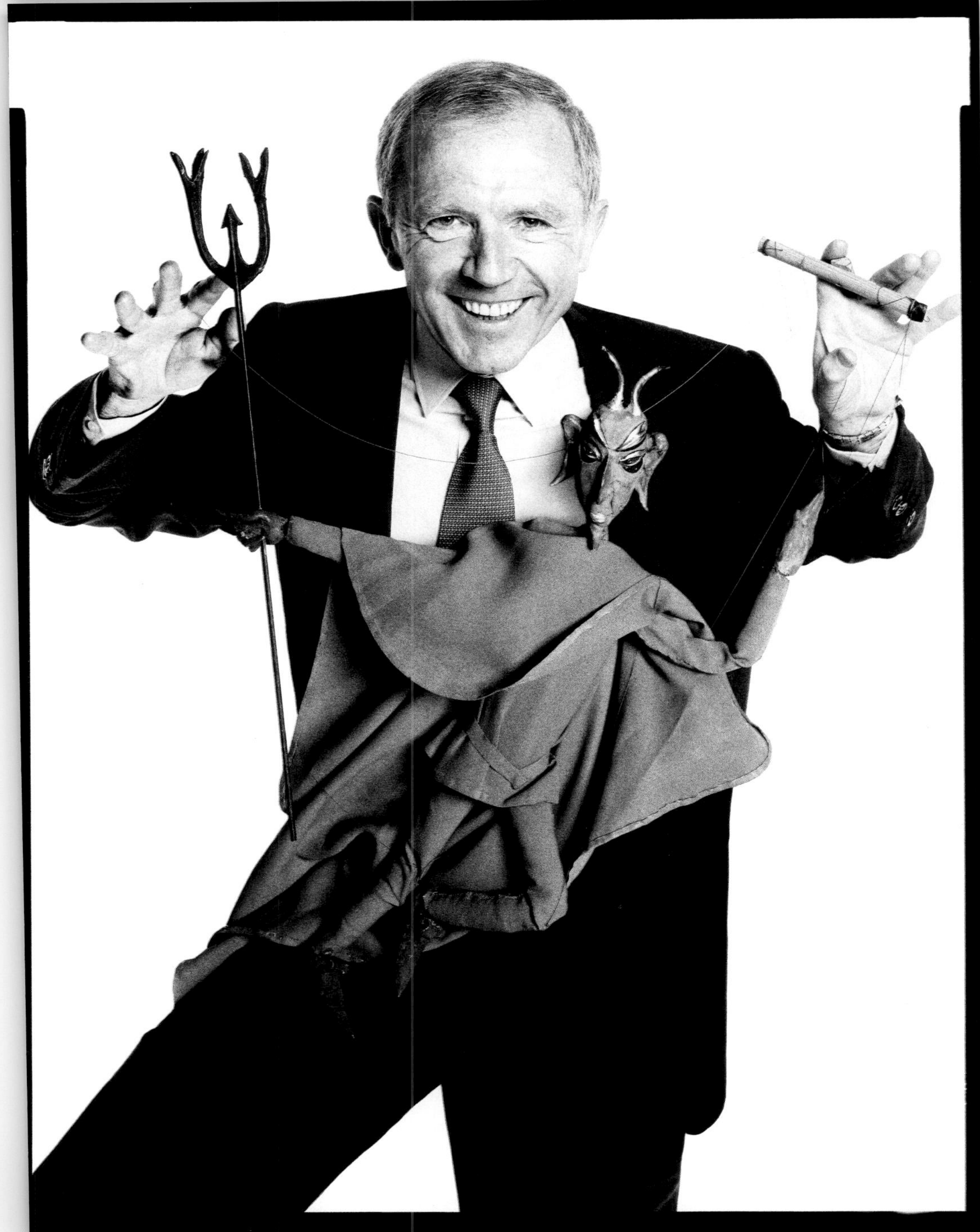

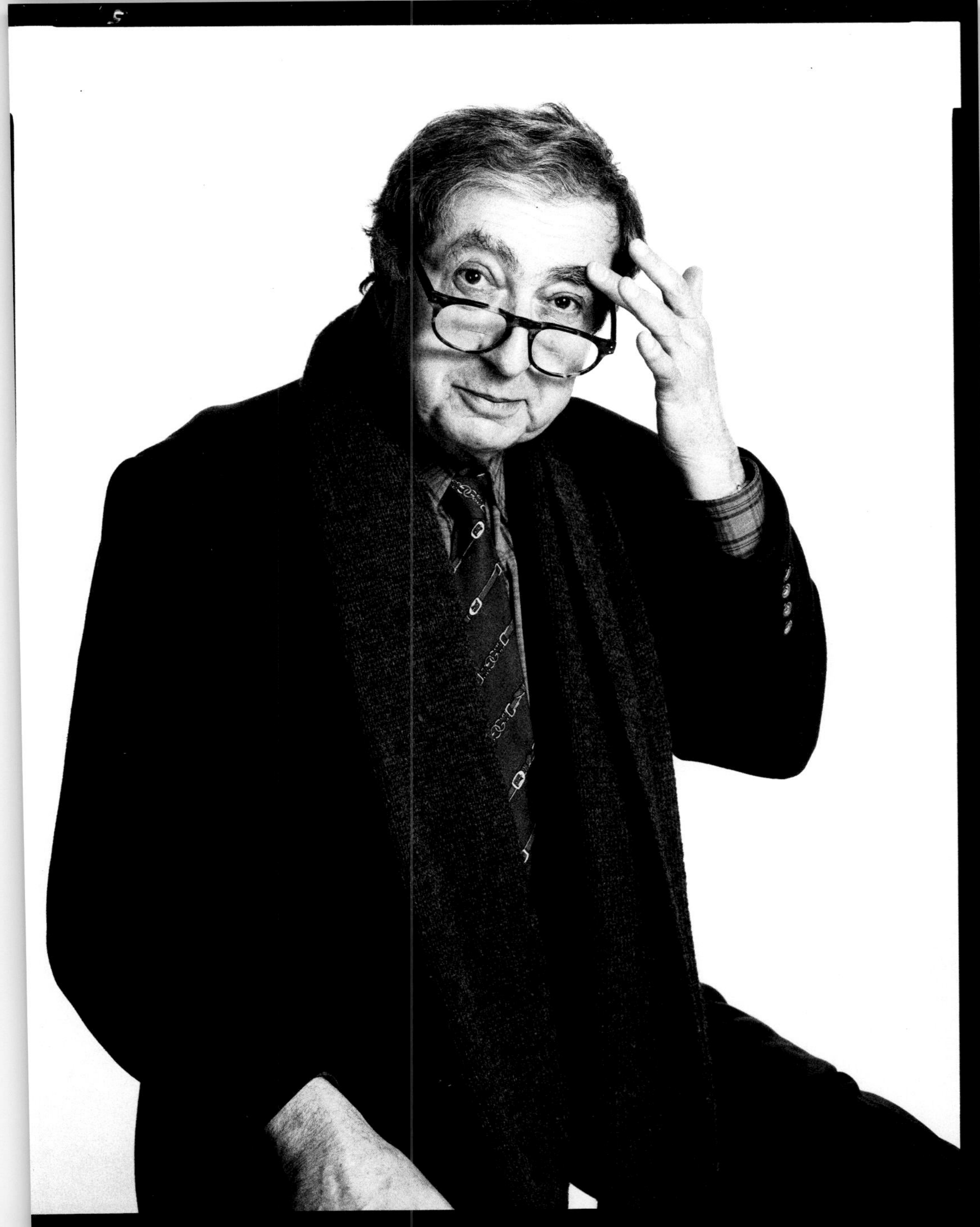

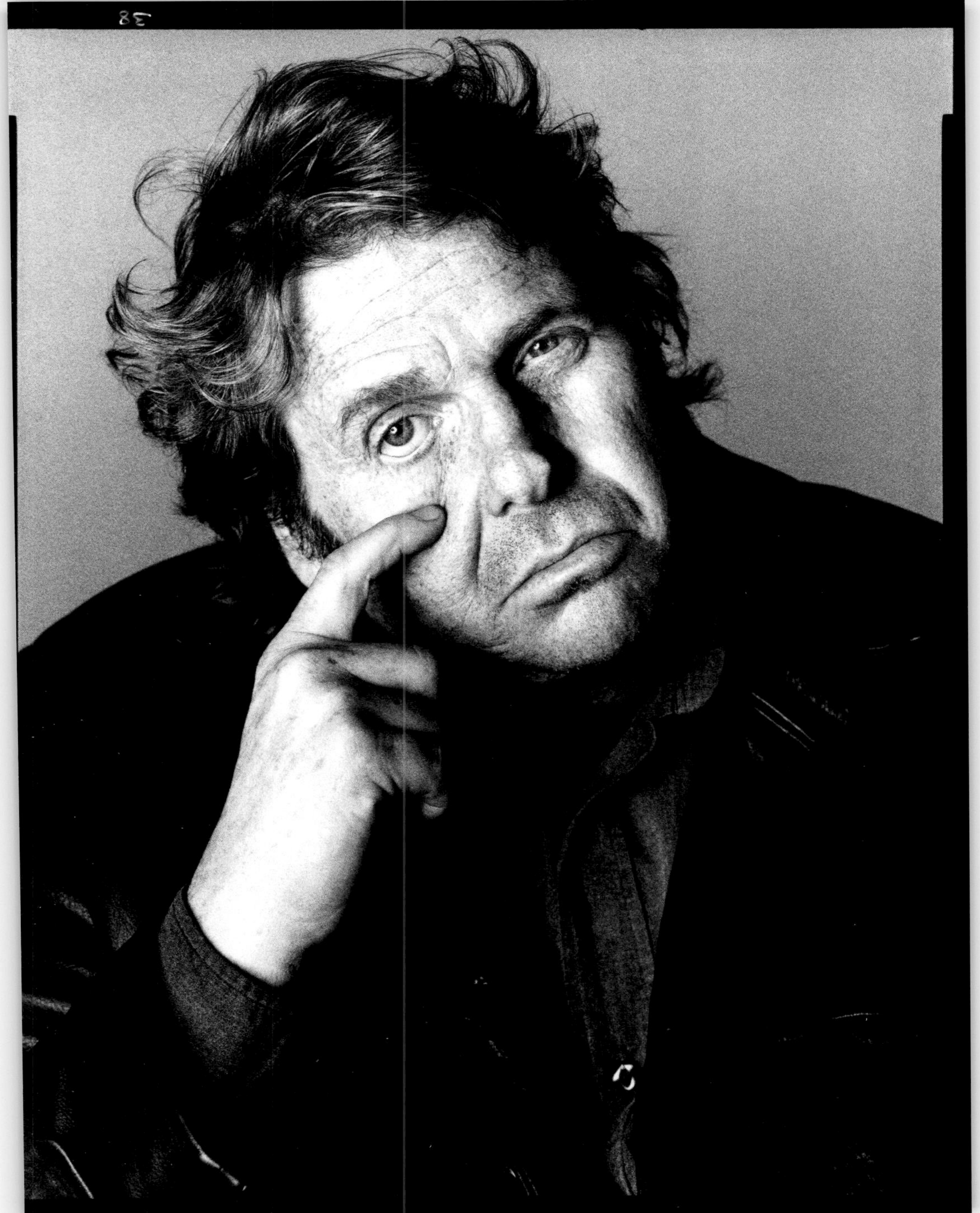

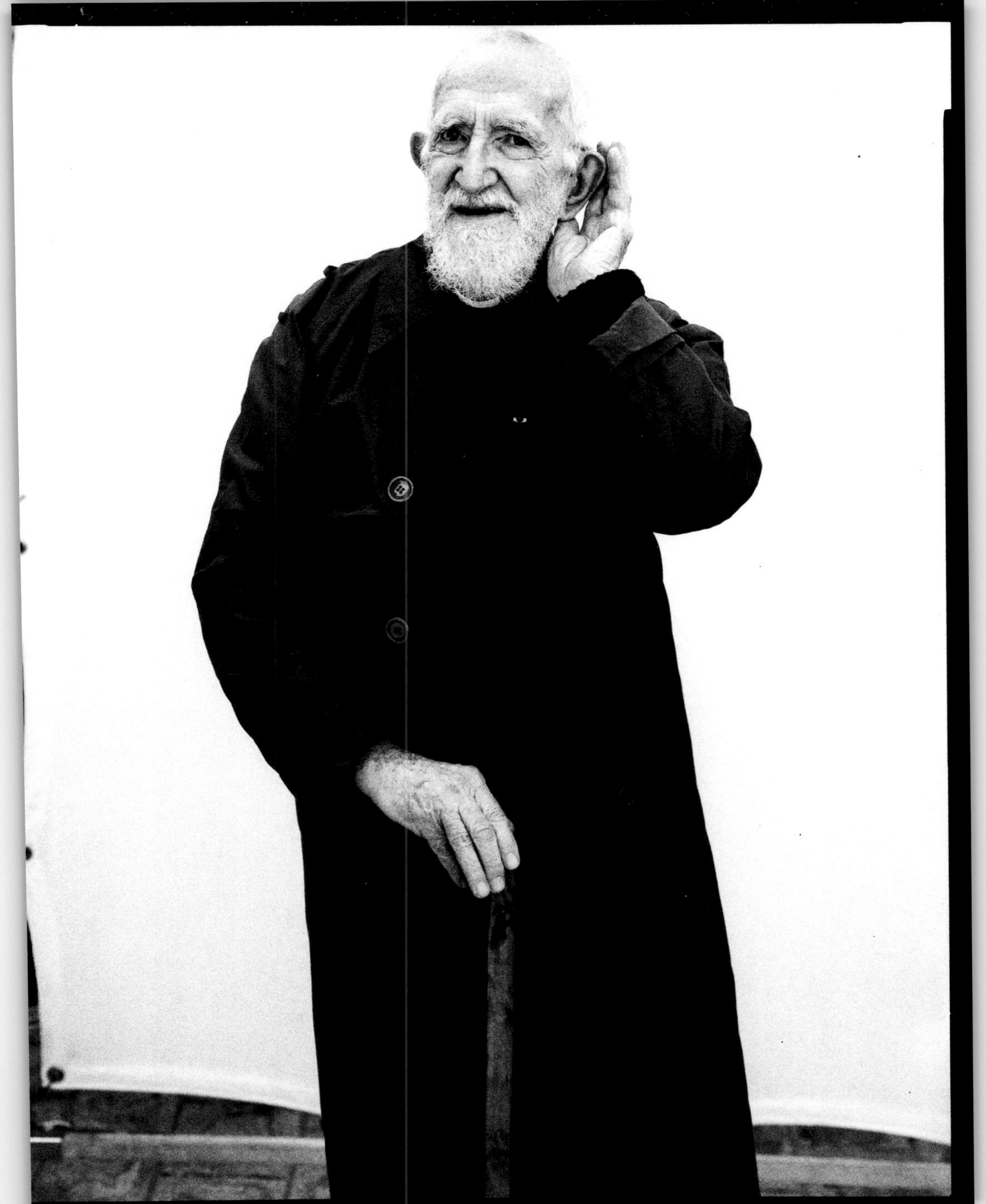

My shoot with Avedon was much more a matter of mental acrobatics. He danced, made funny faces, retreated, advanced, tried by all means to make me dizzy and to disorient me, filled with an intense vitality, in short, a master in martial art.

—

PHILIPPE SOLLERS, OCTOBER 31, 2004,
LITTÉRATURE ET POLITIQUE
(PARIS: FLAMMARION, 2014).

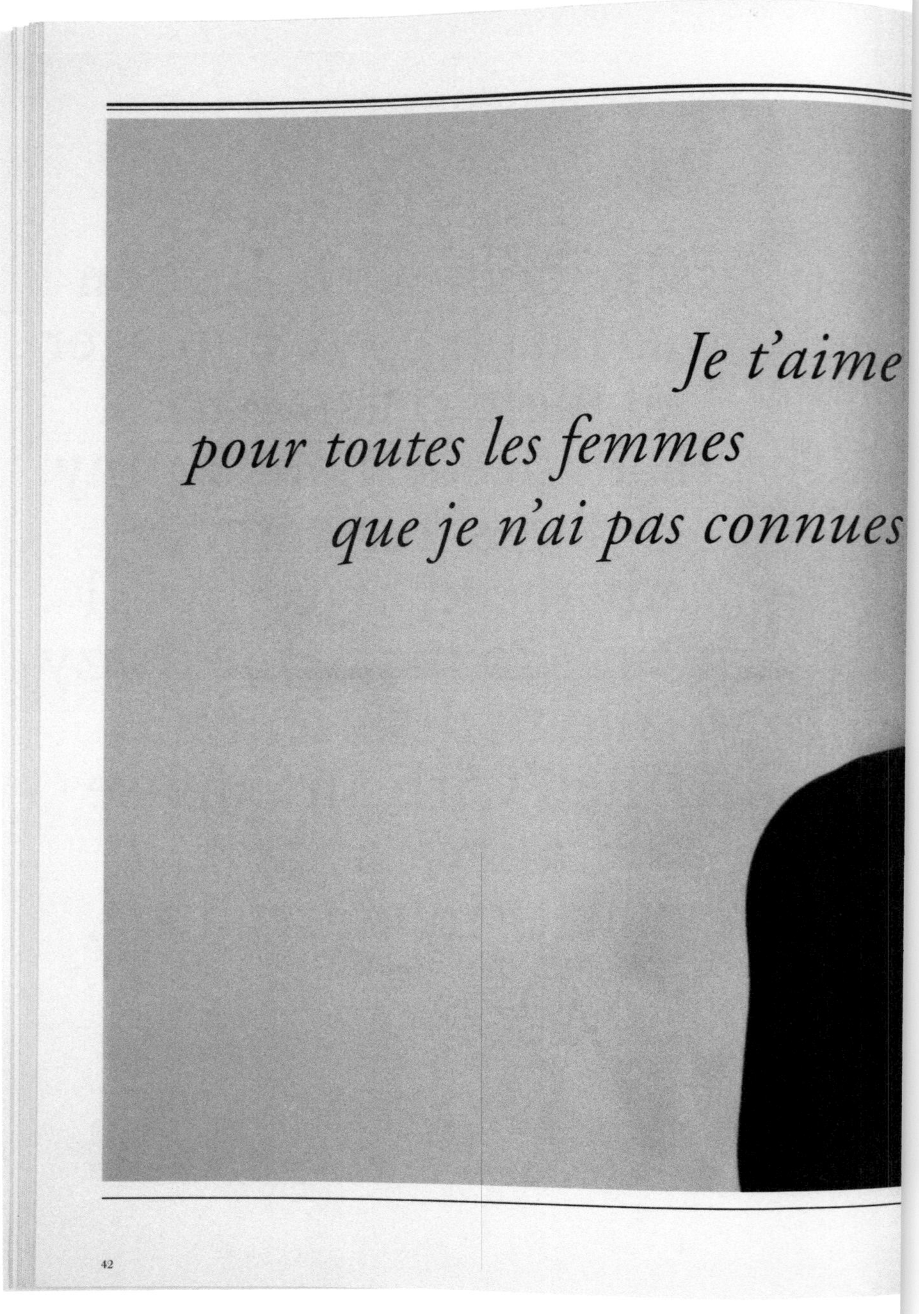

Je t'aime
pour toutes les femmes
que je n'ai pas connues

42

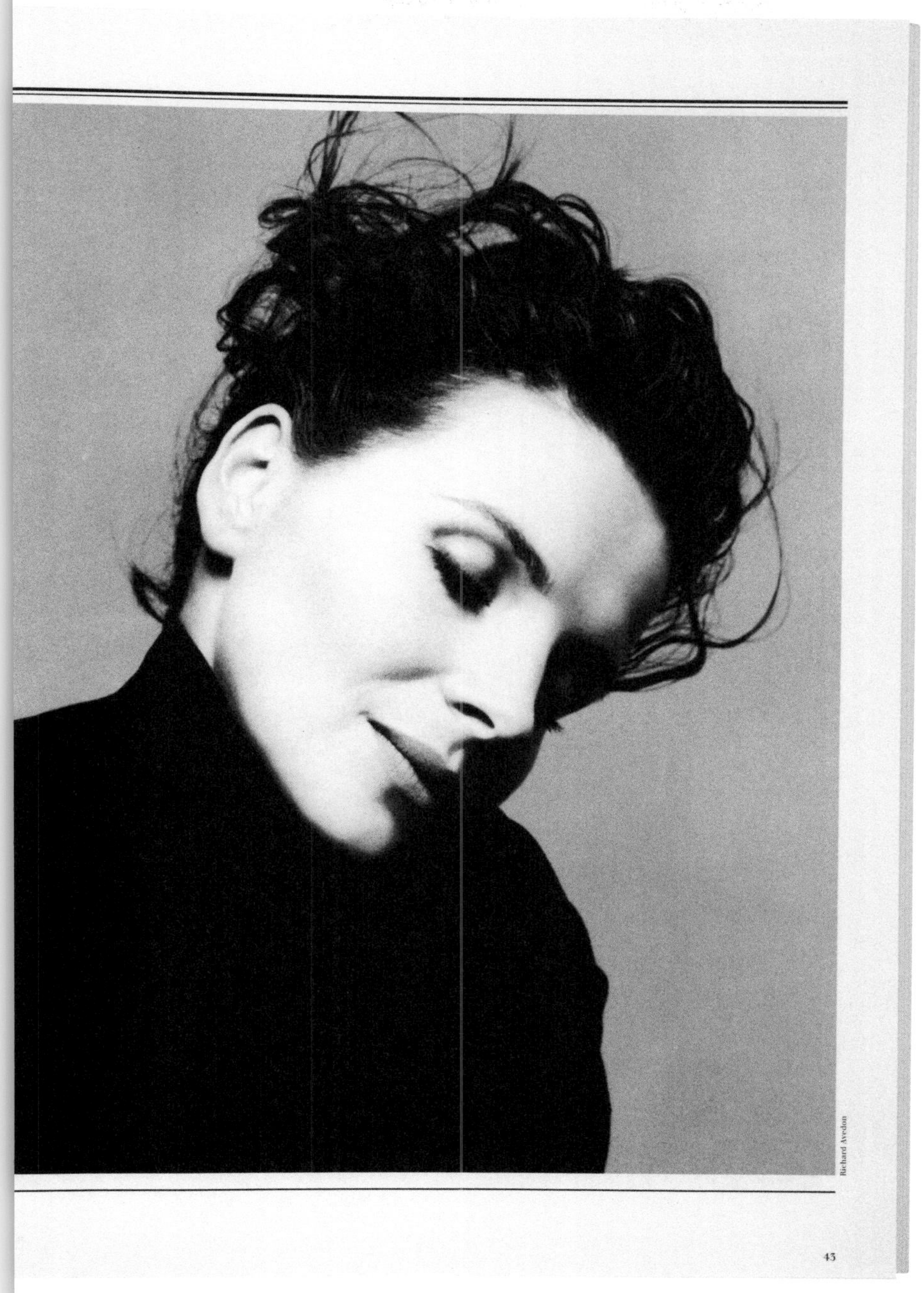

Lancôme advertisement featuring Juliette Binoche, *Egoïste*, N° 13, Tome I, 1997, pp. 42–43

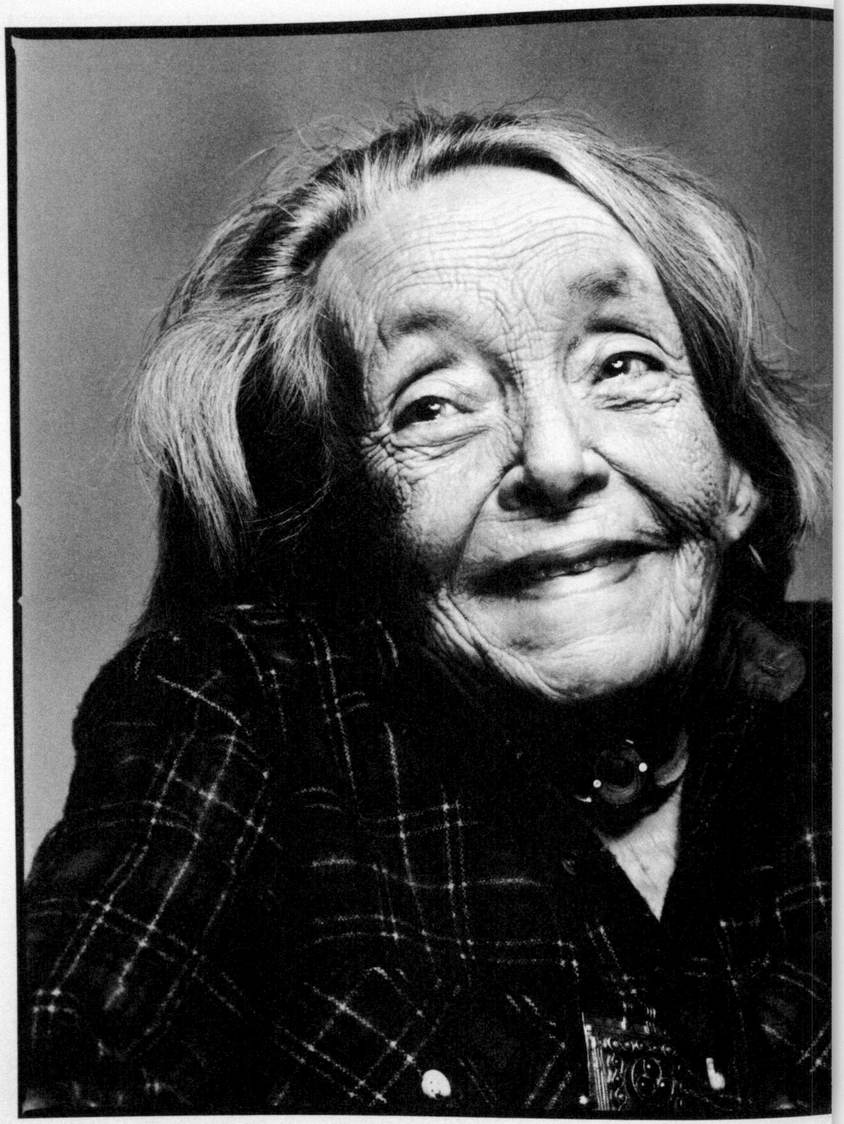

148

Richard Avedon - Paris 1993

SOUVENIR

MARGUERITE DURAS

par Marguerite Duras

Un jour, j'étais âgée déjà, dans le hall d'un lieu public,
un homme est venu vers moi.
Il s'est fait connaître et il m'a dit :
"Je vous connais depuis toujours. Tout le monde dit
que vous étiez belle lorsque vous étiez jeune,
je suis venu pour vous dire
que pour moi je vous trouve plus belle maintenant
que lorsque vous étiez jeune..."

... Au contraire d'en être effrayée j'ai vu s'opérer
ce vieillissement de mon visage avec l'intérêt que j'aurais pris
par exemple au déroulement d'une lecture...

... Ce visage-là, nouveau, je l'ai gardé. Il a été mon visage.
Il a vieilli encore bien sûr,
mais relativement moins qu'il n'aurait dû.

L'Amant

"Marguerite Duras par Marguerite Duras," *Egoïste,* N° 13, Tome II, 1997, pp. 148–49

Récit

Elle a esquissé quelques pas de Danse...

La première fois que j'ai vu M.D., c'était pour une émission du "Cinéma des cinéastes" sur *Des journées entières dans les arbres.*

Nous étions à la fin des années soixante-dix, j'étais très jeune, j'avais lu quelques-uns de ses livres. Je n'avais pas de rapports, disons, personnels avec elle.

Elle était émue par l'admiration qu'on lui témoignait, mais pas sans discernement. Lorsqu'on émettait des réserves, elle savait être cassante, vive dans la réplique, avec beaucoup d'esprit, précise avec les mots, presque dangereuse.

Beaucoup plus tard, Benoît Jacquot m'a demandé de faire l'image d'un film dont elle serait le centre. Elle lui faisait cadeau d'une histoire, l'histoire d'un jeune aviateur anglais mort à 20 ans en Normandie et enterré là.

C'était en janvier 1991. Il y eut très vite, sans doute de ma part et peut-être aussi de celle de Marguerite, un plaisir à être ensemble. Nous nous sommes beaucoup vus, Marguerite, Yann, Louido, et moi.

Elle avait une féminité intacte, sous une apparence qu'elle disait ravagée. Elle portait des jupes droites, toujours les mêmes. Souvent elle mettait une chemise à carreaux que Benoît lui avait donnée. Avec, elle ressemblait à un vieux cow-boy, elle dégainait ses doigts couverts de bagues, elle me plaisait beaucoup.

Elle téléphonait énormément, à toute heure, le matin, l'après-midi, le soir. C'était toujours urgent. Elle avait pensé à quelque chose, il fallait résoudre un problème, elle n'appelait pas pour dire : comment ça va ? cette question l'a toujours fait rigoler, elle appelait parce qu'il y avait une chose importante qu'elle devait dire ou faire, ce n'était pas pour la conversation et ça se terminait presque toujours par une proposition de dîner ici ou là : au Barone, au Munich, au Duc, ou chez nous.

Un après-midi, elle m'a appelée d'une manière plus pressante que d'habitude.

– C'est toi, j'ai un problème.

– Quoi Marguerite, c'est grave ?

– Oui, Yann n'est pas là et la télévision ne marche plus.

– C'est peut-être un branchement.

– Non, elle est foutue. Peut-être on peut la faire réparer. Je la mettrai à Neauphle ou à Trouville, mais j'en achète une autre pour ici, viens tout de suite.

Je n'avais pas envie de résister, j'y suis allée.

En fait Marguerite ne voulait pas d'une télévision, dont Yann aurait, lui, bien voulu. Il y avait, il y a peut-être encore rue du Dragon un magasin Bang & Olufsen, ce sont de très beaux écrans. La proximité de la rue Saint-Benoît rendait la chose commode pour des réparations éventuelles et en tout cas pour la livraison. Marguerite s'est habillée et nous sommes allées rue du Dragon, en voiture, puisqu'elle ne se déplaçait qu'en voiture, même de la rue Saint-Benoît à la rue du Dragon.

Nous sommes restées longtemps devant la vitrine, elle a dit que physiquement ces télés ne lui plaisaient pas et même pis que ça.

Elles étaient carrées, violentes, certaines méchantes. Nous sommes entrées, le vendeur trop courtois et presque distingué ne lui a pas plu non plus et les télécommandes que je lui ai mises dans les mains étaient trop lourdes.

– De véritables meubles, ces télécommandes !

Nous sommes ressorties et là, sur le trottoir, elle m'a dit :

– Je ne vais pas commencer maintenant à regarder des images allemandes.

C'était donc ça, l'origine présumée allemande* de ces télévisions en rendait l'achat impossible.

Dans ce quartier, la chose la plus simple était d'aller à la FNAC, y aller avec Marguerite l'était déjà beaucoup moins. Son pas de tortue, sa respiration empêchée rendaient l'expédition risquée.

Mais comme une enfant entraînée par une autre encore plus casse-cou, elle et moi nous sommes lancées à la recherche de la télé de ses rêves.

Il fallait se garer le plus près possible du sanctuaire, marcher, descendre jusqu'au rayon Hi-Fi-Télévision.

Je me sentais au début d'une longue marche à petits pas, mais tout allait bien.

Et puis là, au milieu des enceintes qui déversaient leurs décibels, Marguerite s'est arrêtée net d'avancer.

– Ça ne va plus.

– Qu'est-ce qui ne va plus, Marguerite ?

Nous distinguions au loin les écrans vibrionnants, nous touchions presque au but.

– Rien ne va plus, c'est foutu.

Le cœur m'est tombé dans les talons. Ça y est : ça devait m'arriver, elle allait avoir un malaise ici, dans le sous-sol de la FNAC, j'allais avoir tout le monde sur le dos, Yann, tout le monde.

Traîner une très vieille dame, malade, dans une grande surface, c'est criminel. J'aurais du mal à plaider quoi que ce soit d'intelligent.

Elle gémissait doucement. En fait, je devais lui serrer tellement fort le bras qu'elle aurait même dû hurler.

Je me suis approchée tout près, l'oreille contre son cou, pour percevoir ce que je pensais être son avant-dernier souffle.

Et là j'ai entendu :

– Je ne peux plus avancer, ma jupe est tombée.

J'ai baissé les yeux, sa jupe était effectivement aux chevilles.

Une bouffée de joie m'a envahie, comme si je revenais de très loin, et j'ai dû éclater de rire, elle aussi.

– C'est l'épingle double, m'a-t-elle glissé dans un fou rire.

Je l'ai entraînée entre deux baffles et à genoux j'ai raccroché l'épingle double. À partir de là nous avons beaucoup ri. Je répétais en boucle que j'avais eu peur, elle ne comprenait pas de quoi j'avais pu avoir peur, et cela nous faisait rire encore plus.

Nous sommes arrivées si joyeuses devant le rayon des télévisions que cela a contaminé le vendeur, et les télévisions qui retransmettaient un concert de valse. Marguerite commentait chaque poste, chaque image, celle-là était trop clinquante, celle-là trop vulgaire, celle-là trop rien... elle a esquissé quelques pas de danse en disant au vendeur :

– C'est tout de même agréable, les valses !

Il comprit l'invitation et fit doucement tournoyer Marguerite devant les télévisions.

Des gens ont applaudi.

Ils se sont arrêtés de danser devant l'une d'entre elles, Marguerite a dit :

– Voilà, c'est celle-là ; c'est combien ?

C'étaient les dernières mesures de la valse.

Caroline Champetier

*Bang & Olufsen est en fait une société danoise.(*N.D.L.R.*)

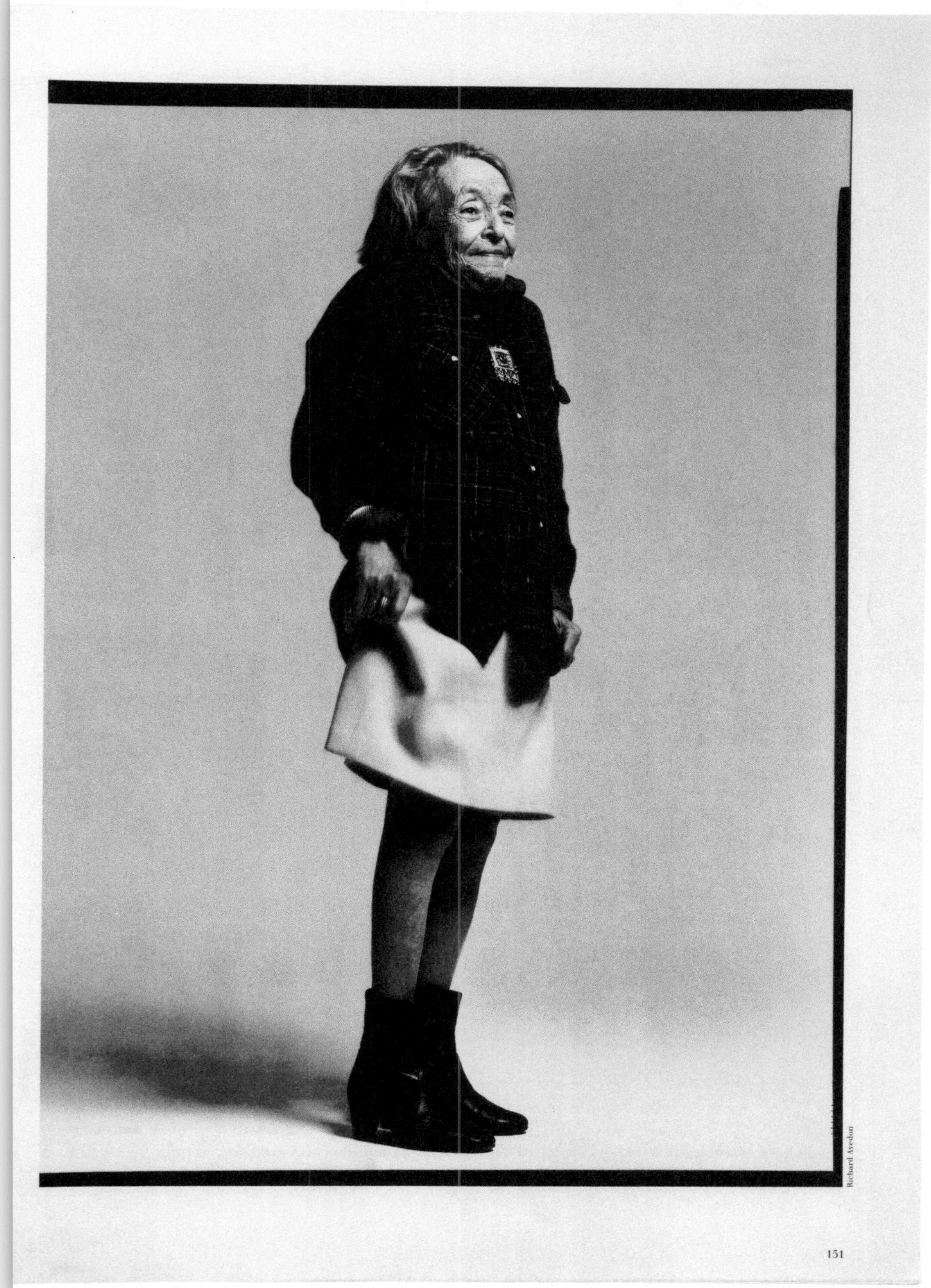

"Marguerite Duras par Marguerite Duras," *Egoïste*, N° 13, Tome II, 1997, pp. 150–51

Mise en Scène

Luc Bondy - Claude Arnaud

J'écris dans le Ciel

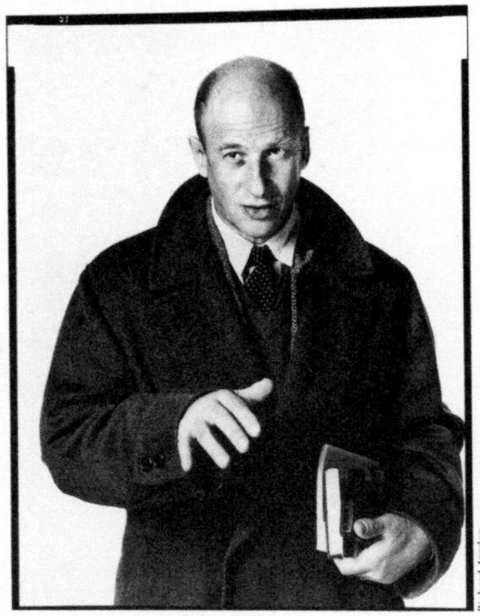

Richard Avedon

Luc Bondy ressemble à ces Luftmenschen qui planaient sur les bourgades de Galicie, et dont le corps se nourrissait seulement d'idées. On le croit en train de monter le Wozzeck *de Berg à Hambourg, il est dans le jardin de sa maison de Belleville à écrire des nouvelles. Il n'a pas fini les répétitions d'un* Don Carlos *au Châtelet qu'il est déjà à la Schaubühne pour mettre en place les décors de Gilles Aillaud. Il est de ces hommes qu'on pourrait suivre jusqu'à un aéroport, puis dans un avion en partance pour Minsk, sans même s'en apercevoir, car ils ensorcellent. Ils raisonnent à la vitesse de la terre, interprètent le mouvement des nuages, jouent avec les fuseaux horaires, spéculent sur la santé mentale du pilote, identifient un acteur que masquait la silhouette de l'hôtesse et déjà lui proposent un rôle dans une pièce d'Hofmannsthal. Personne n'est si intelligent, mais personne ne pressent aussi bien qu'en art seuls comptent le mouvement, la surprise, la ruse – et mieux encore l'innocence. Pourquoi certains hommes vivent-ils survoltés quand d'autres se contentent de sommeiller ? La flamme bleue qui court dans l'œil de Bondy éclaire tous les accidents de la réalité, des faux mouvements aux lapsus, son esprit jongle avec les références, les anecdotes, les sentences... Mais déjà je l'entends qui entre, le voilà qui parle, bouge et téléphone, le temps d'appuyer sur Play et déjà il faut le suivre dans le couloir, l'esprit souffle où il veut...*

Un jour, en Avignon, devant le Palais des papes, j'ai vu un type debout sur un tabouret qui réglait la circulation des passants : il leur donnait des indications sur la façon de faire leur promenade : à grands pas, à petits pas, titubant ou sur la pointe des pieds. Tous les festivaliers pris dans son piège s'exécutaient sagement. C'était un metteur en scène…

Je n'ai jamais compris ce qui m'a fait vouloir devenir "quelqu'un" dans le théâtre et que ce soit passé de manière aussi précoce.

C'est tout de même assez surprenant de choisir l'irréel, l'impalpable, la métamorphose, alors que l'univers nous donne tant de choses à déc vrir et à prendre comme elles so Aujourd'hui j'ai parfois même doutes sur l'acte profane de me en scène, c'est-à-dire de transfor le rythme des mouvements imposant le sien. Il n'y a que D qui en ait le droit. C'est bien la son pour laquelle les metteurs scène sont en général (et plus vieillissent) des mégalomanes.

Enfant je voulais être acteur. Je d nais des représentations dans la de notre maison de Zurich, dev un parterre d'invités. Mon souv le plus cuisant s'attache à une p que j'avais intitulée *la Clef*. Je de avoir douze-treize ans, et bran sais devant le public une des vie grosses clefs que ma mère col

200

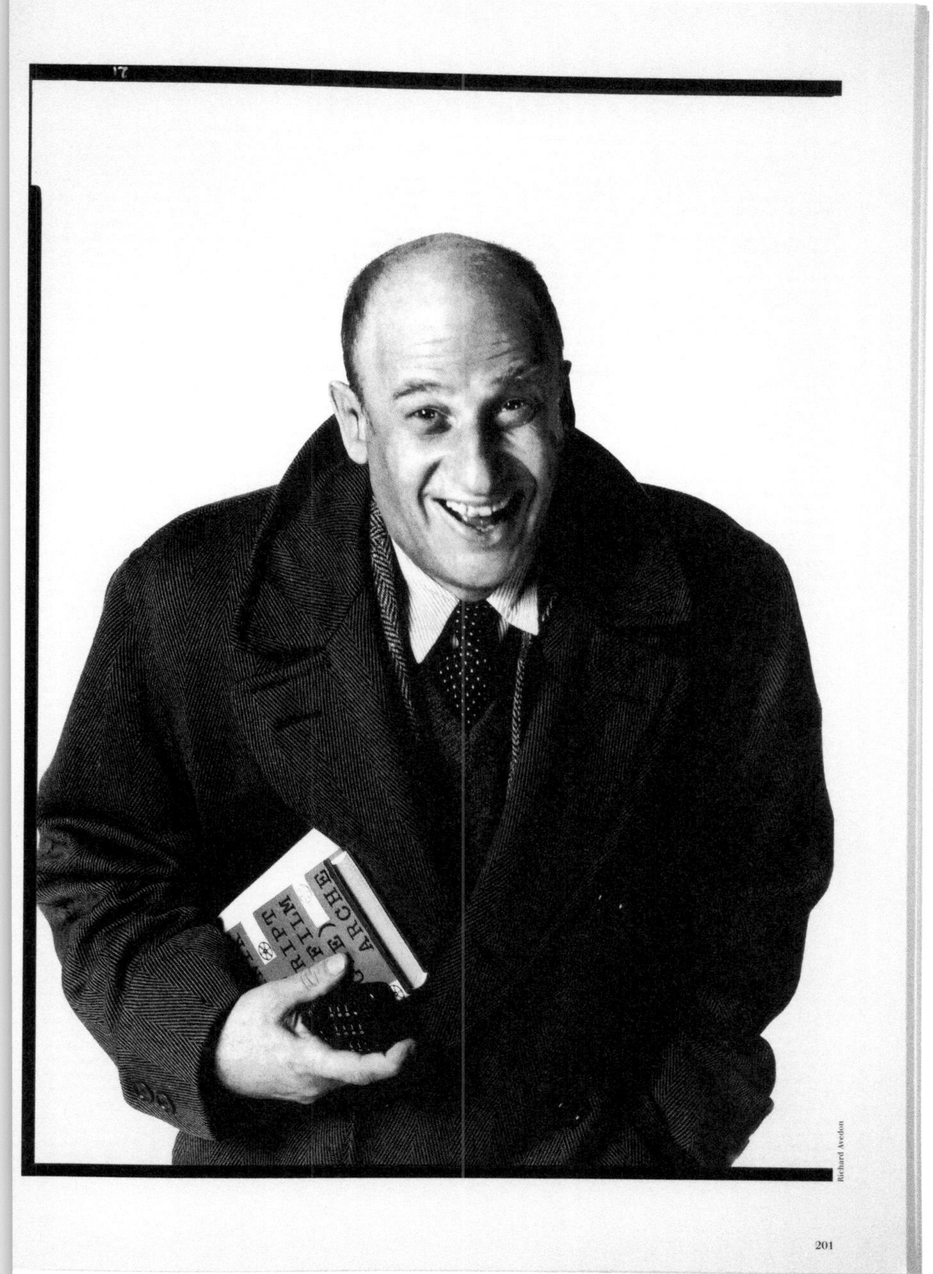

"Luc Bondy – Claude Arnaud, J'écris dans le ciel" (Luc Bondy – Claude Arnaud, I Write in the Sky), *Egoïste,* N° 13, Tome II, 1997, pp. 200–01

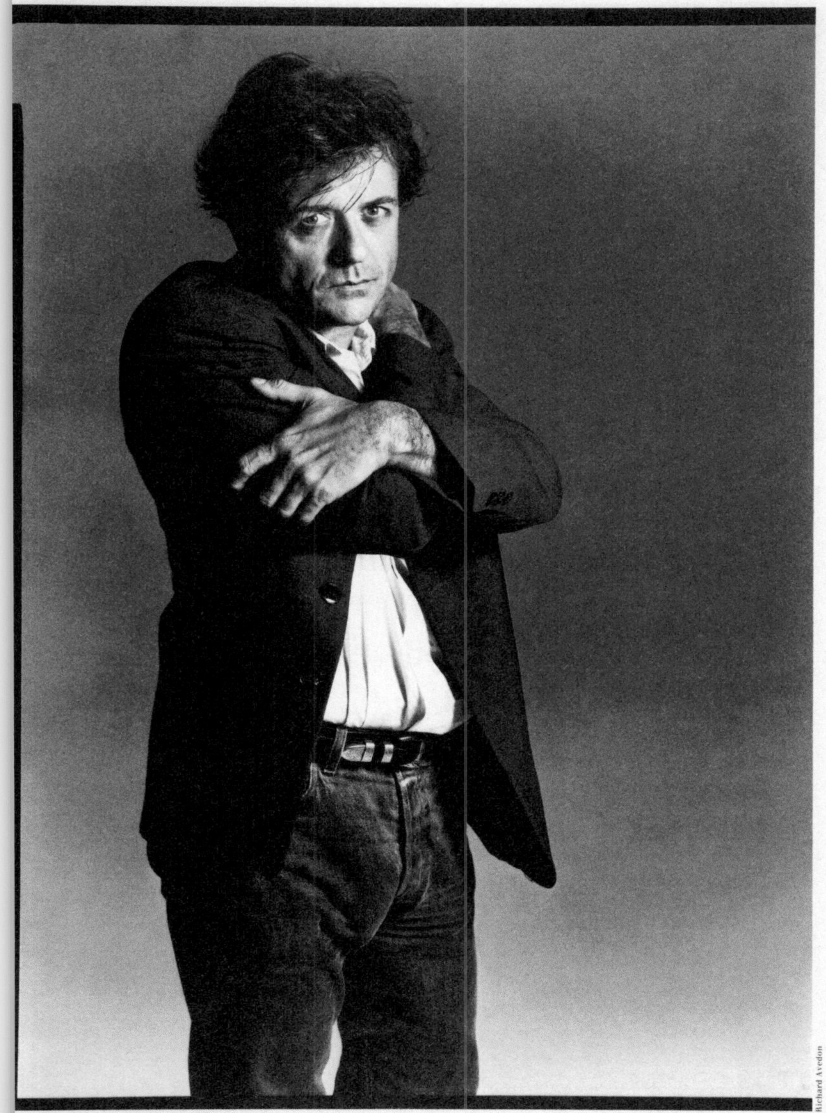

Richard Avedon

55

Patrice Chéreau, *Egoïste,* N° 12, Tome I, 1992, p. 55

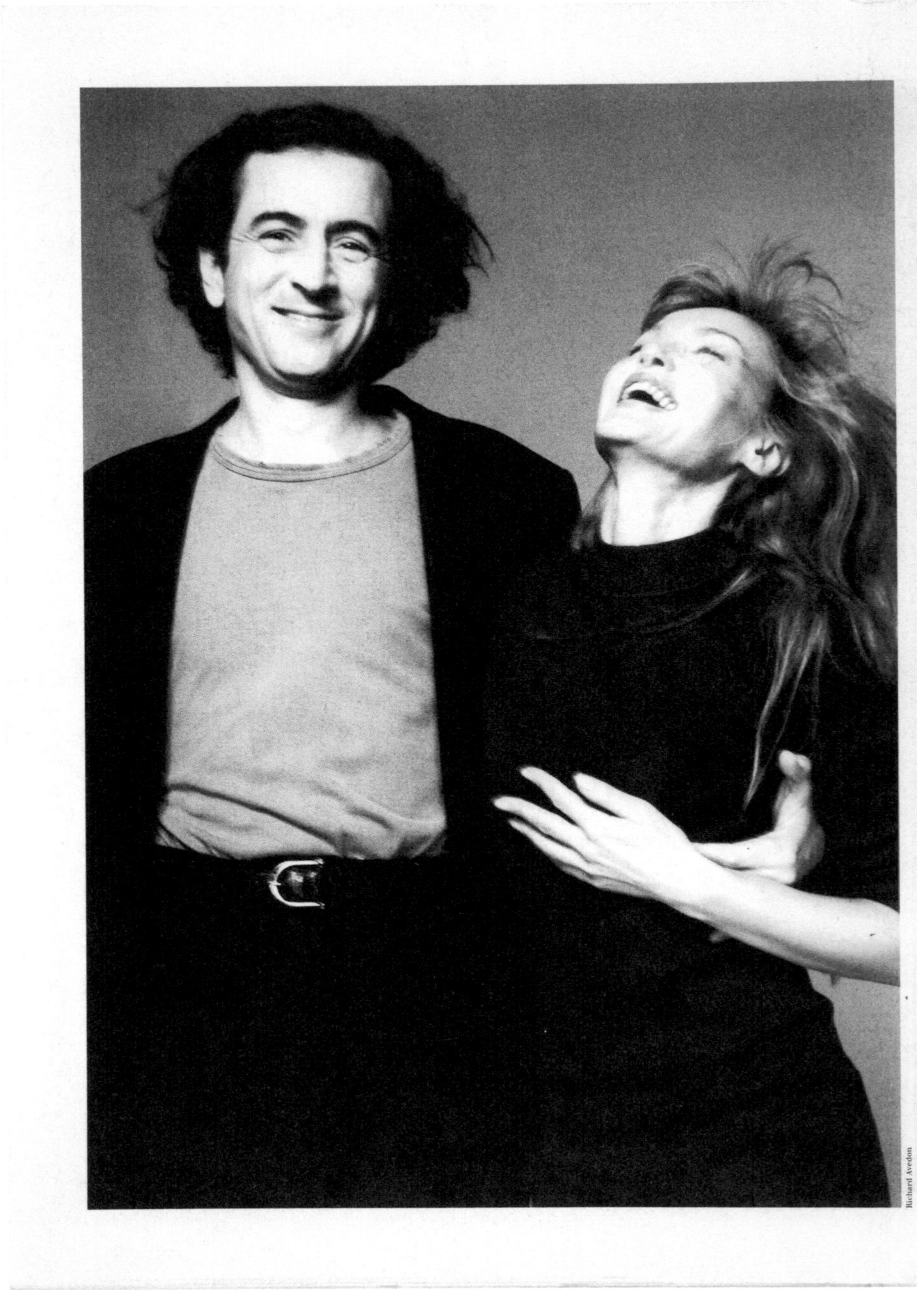

Bernard Henri Lévy and Arielle Dombasle, *Egoïste,* N° 16, Tome I, 2011, (*posthumous*), back cover

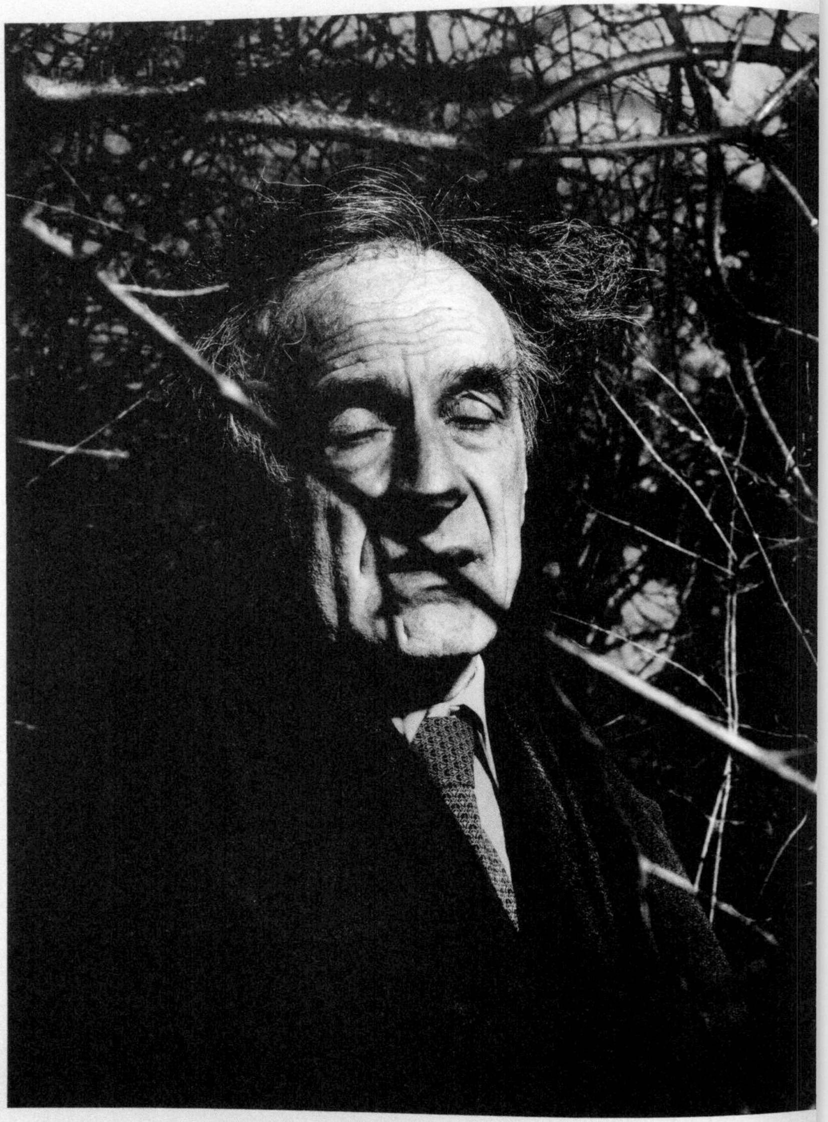

138

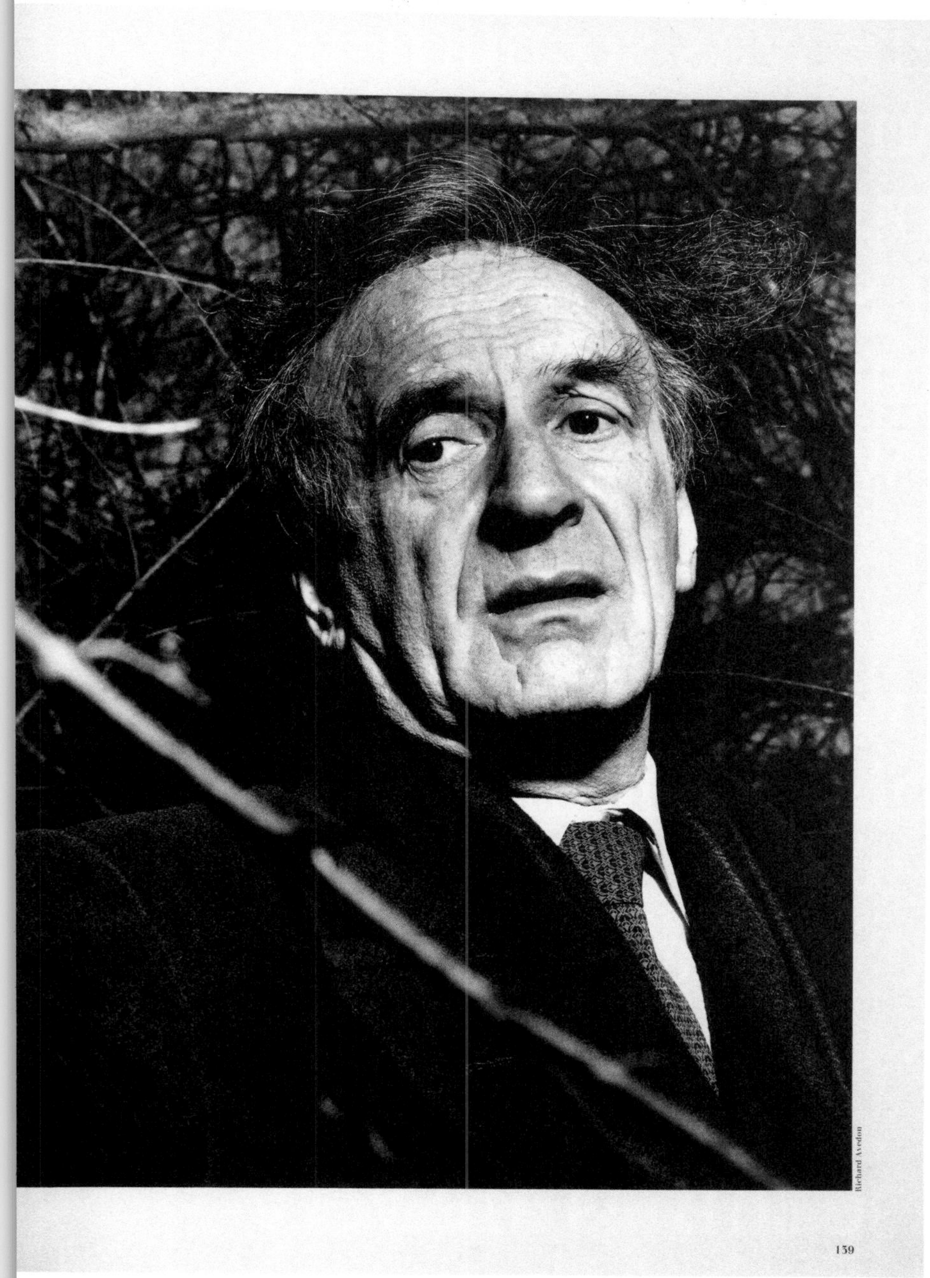

Elie Weisel, *Egoïste,* N° 12, Tome II, 1992, pp. 138–39

There was something about Adjani breaking through the branches that seemed to me a good metaphor for Wiesel. It's the way in which one part of my photography informs another. But I never realized that Isabelle Adjani breaking her way out of the forest gave me something, which was the forest that I could use with Elie Wiesel . . . These things are very instinctive, they are not intellectually formulated. I knew the branches were abrasive and hard. I had learned how they would be under the light by working with Isabelle Adjani fleeing from her demons, real or imagined. And the demons behind Elie Wiesel made it seem right for me to bring him back into those branches.

—

Richard Avedon

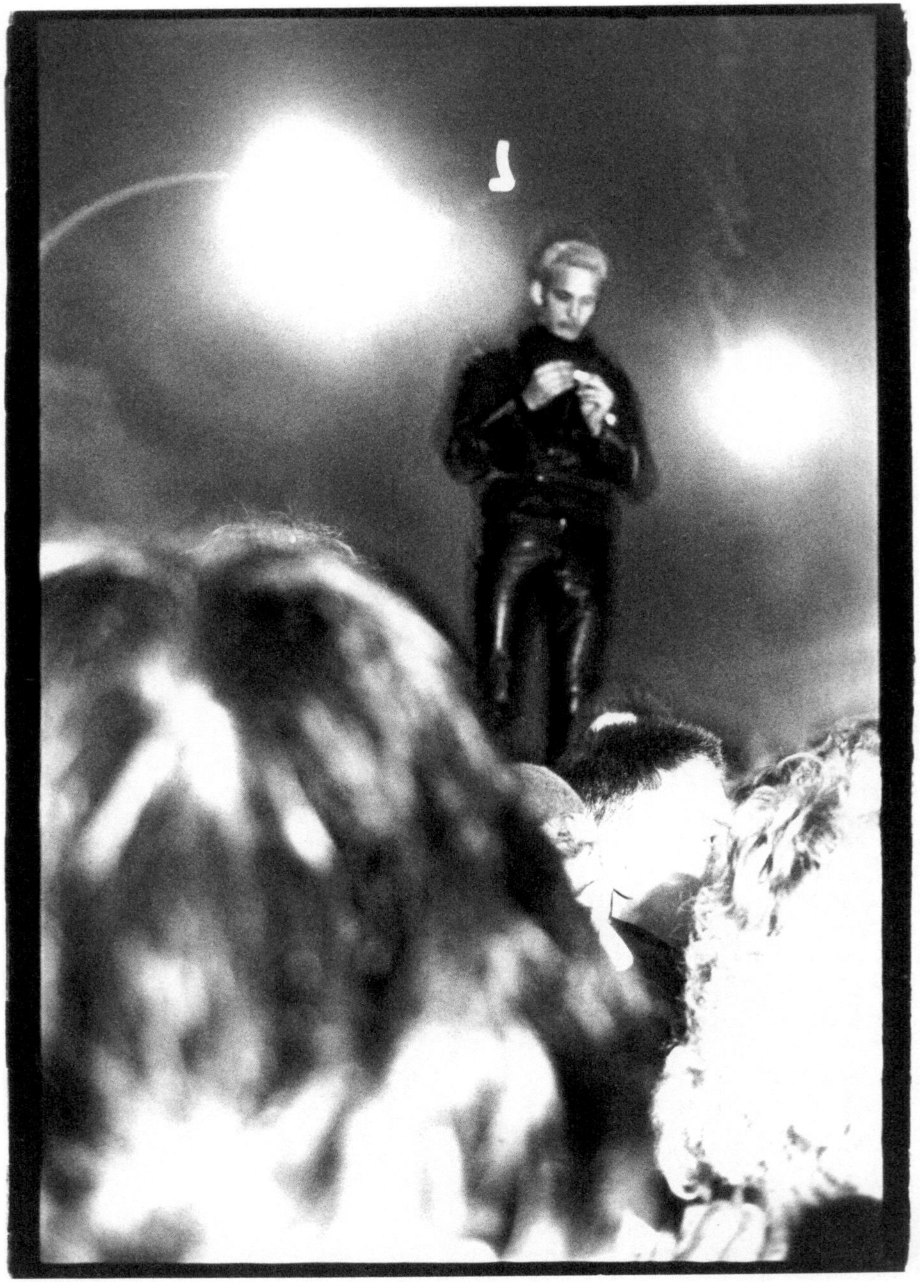

Brandenburg Gate #7, Berlin, Germany, New Year's Eve, 1989

Unter den Linden: New Year's Eve
Jean Baudrillard

There is nothing in common between a text and an image. Similarly, there is nothing in common between an event and a face. So there is the same ambiguity in putting a text opposite Richard Avedon's pictures as there is in his putting his own photographs opposite an event like the fall of the Wall. Because the specificity of photography is not to illustrate an event but to be an event itself, and the specificity of text is not to comment on an event or an image but to be, itself, a literal event, alien in its register, but which, precisely because of this, enters the same secret affinity. It is because the event, the picture and the text remain basically alien to each other, and because there is no resolution of one by the other, that they can act as strange attractors for each other and make their singular illusions converge.

Logic would have it that an event takes place, the picture illustrates it, and the text comments on it. And this is unfortunately what happens most of the time. But the poetic unfolding means that the event never exactly takes place, it remains somehow alien to itself (this is especially the case for the collapse of the Wall and of the Eastern bloc). In this sense, the event is incommensurable; it's none of our business, it comes from elsewhere and looks elsewhere. Like the faces in these photos, which are intensely watching what is happening elsewhere. Photography, when it works, of course, like Avedon's, reflects this incommensurability, this excess, this alienness of the event to itself. And to achieve this, photography must also in a way remain alien to itself. Not reflect itself, not exhaust itself in itself. Therein lies its beauty. And if the text speaks, it should also do so without saying anything — it must remain a fiction, echoing the insoluble fiction of the event, and the picture as fiction, which is its deep force.

Fiction, not testimony. Most events are only testimonies, neither "historical" nor original, but nostalgic or programmed. The photograph as testimony, the photograph as message is usually shameful, never objective, but never properly subjective either. The text/testimony only carries "information," which is the most trivial and degraded form of meaning. Nothing is more confusing than all this, which can be read indiscriminately, since everything — the act, the image, the speech — is exchanged in the same fashion, since everything "communicates" and each register loses, as a testimony, its own power of illusion and fiction.

There are no crowds in the pictures of Richard Avedon, no historical sense, no theatrical meaning. Only gestures, faces, lights. Each feature is almost isolated in its luminous space, but without any expressive desire, without any collective staging, with angles, framing, and profiles always very different. All the movements reflect a kind of intensity and excitement, as if for an unknown, unidentifiable event, which has created a scene, certainly, but which has only dispersed movements and bodies, instead of their being brought together. On the faces there is a kind of anxious expectation, reflecting the confusion of not knowing what to do with a promise that has suddenly come true, without hindrance, that happens when we no longer believe it (like Kafka's Messiah, who arrives a day late), like the unexpected Apocalypse of what we had already mourned. So, it is both the climax and the parody of History. This collision of the two Germanys is also the collision of hope and despair. This almost posthumous reunification creates a sort of no man's land, a place of collapse and disappearance, and at the same time of ghostly resurrection, visible in the faces, which are illuminated as if by the appearance of a nova, captured in their dispersion by a glow from elsewhere. Is the last photo not that of the ghost of the event, almost an atomic silhouette without shadow or depth, light and shadow completely separated here, whereas they mingle and jostle everywhere else.

To capture this historic dispersion, this paradoxical liberation experienced deep down as a catastrophe (by collapsing, the Wall reveals that it was protecting the West even more than the East; by abolishing it, History has lost its defenses, as is clear today, when it succumbs to all viruses) justifies the violent confusion of shadows and lights, but it also justifies, more deeply, the photographic acting out itself. Which for me has always remained a mystery. Just like the historic acting out is very different from the conventional event. Acting Out. All at once action, staging, "Action!" (we're filming) and out: we expel, we get rid of something. One gets the impression that in certain circumstances, like in Berlin precisely, History all of a sudden, like in the individual acting out, disposes of all its fantasies, of all its inconsistencies, by expelling them in one unpredictable, epileptic or metaleptic (whose effects submerge the causes) event, "uncanny," in which actors have the impression of being only the extras, and which makes no sense, insofar as it only a form of liquidation, of abreaction, mental or historical, to an impossible situation.

Photography, in its unrealistic instantaneity (when it accepts this unreal evidence), is totally in the transpolitical line of this event-object which is not at all the event-subject of the political sphere, with its actors and "historic" masses. Not only is photography appropriate, but it is itself in its happy moments an acting out, an acting out towards the world, a way of capturing it by expelling it, and without ever giving it a meaning. An abreaction to the world in its extreme forms, the most unusual or the most mundane, a liquidation of the world through instant exorcism, through the instantaneous fiction of its representation (not through representation itself, which only perpetuates reality, instead of forcing the illusion of it, instead of forcing it to illusion). Maybe in the act of photography it is the world itself that is acting out, which imposes its fiction on the subject. Instead of the subject remaining more or less openly the master or the conjurer of meaning, photography makes appearances meet like gazes, makes darkness and light cancel each other out — and, in doing so, it expunges the event of its meaning, it expunges the subject of its fantasies, it "acts the world out." It thus establishes a material affinity between the world and us, insofar as the former is a continual acting out.

A mere face is already an acting out: we expel our life in the features of our face, or of our body, or of our writing (some never do, and that is their misfortune). Richard Avedon has always succeeded in capturing this vital (fatal) acting out in the faces he has photographed. He always managed to find the photographic act that matches the physical or physiognomical acting out of his characters. Here, he finds this reversibility of the image and the world, in a so-called "historic" event, in the insoluble fiction of this event.

—

JEAN BAUDRILLARD, "UNTER DEN LINDEN: NEW YEAR'S EVE 1990," *EGOÏSTE* N° 9, TOME I, 1992: 106.

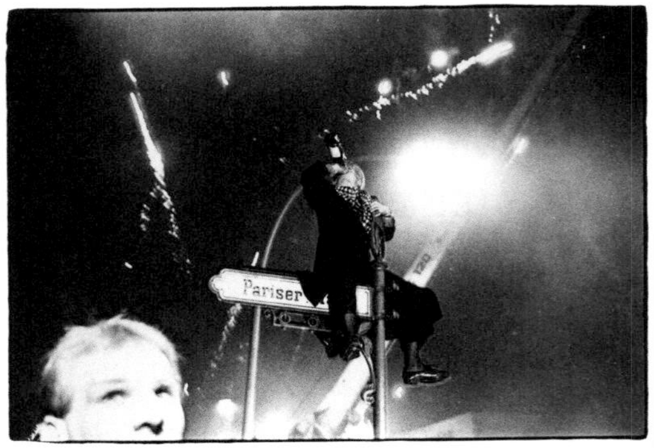
Pariser

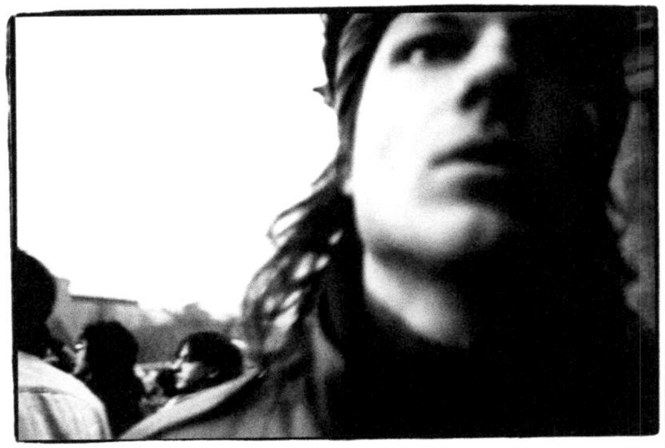

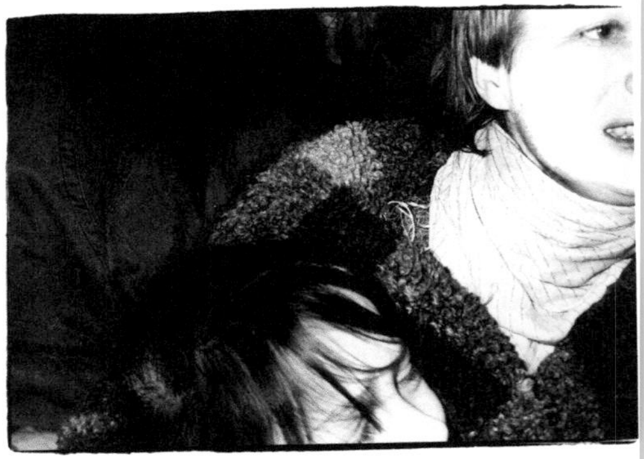

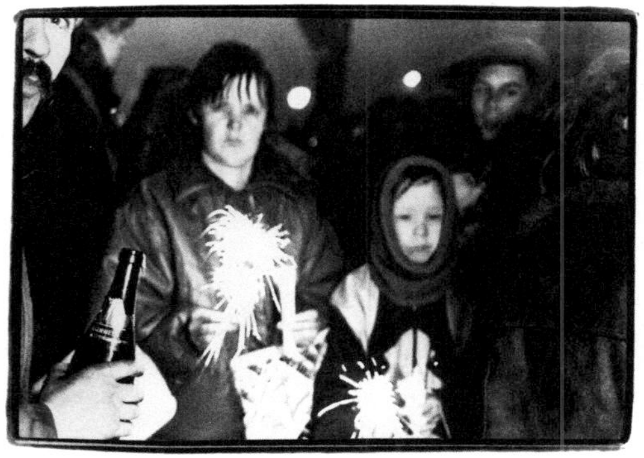
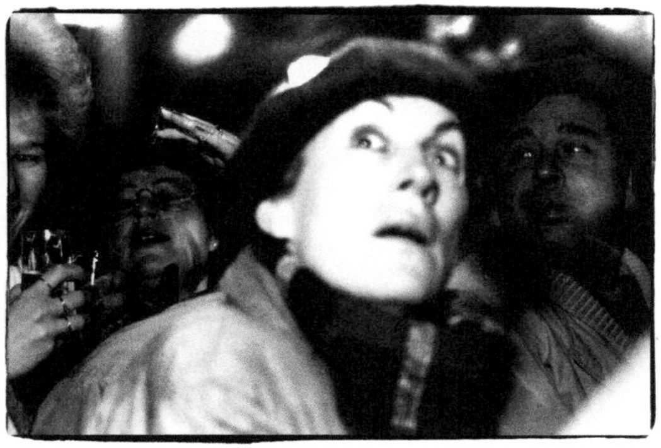
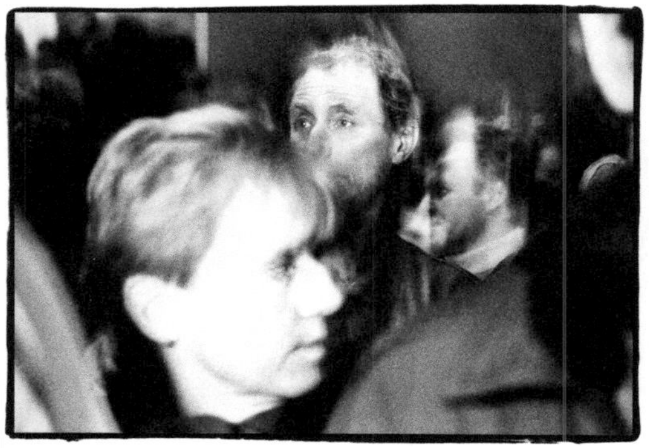
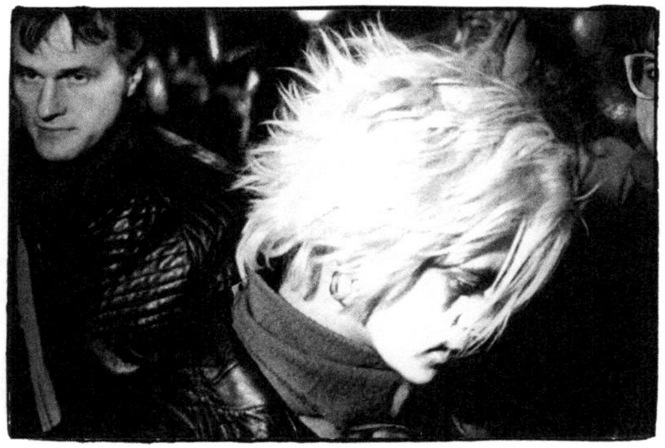
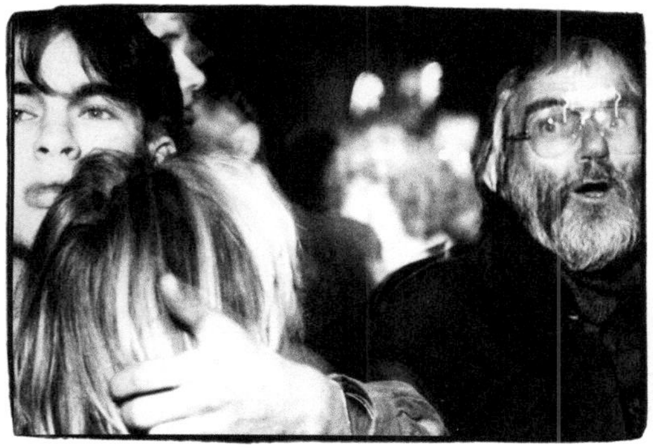
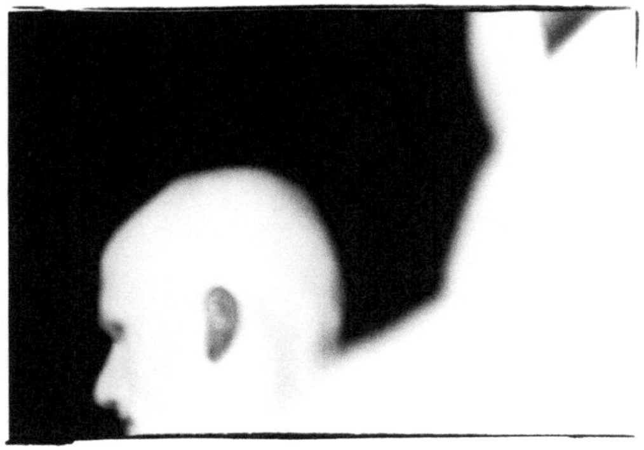

Brandenburg Gate, Berlin, Germany, New Year's Eve, 1989 (contact prints)

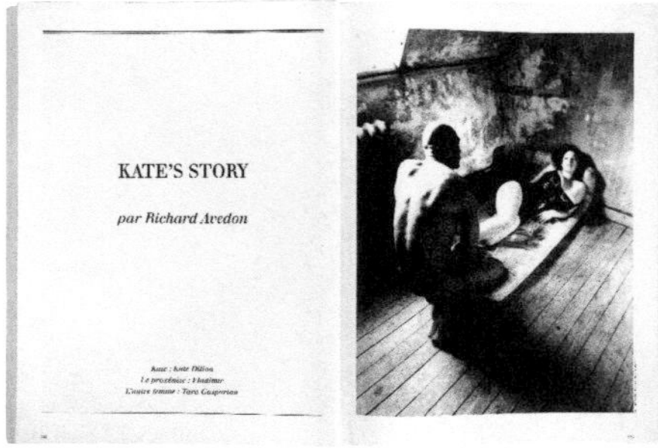

KATE'S STORY
par Richard Avedon
Kate : Kate Dillon

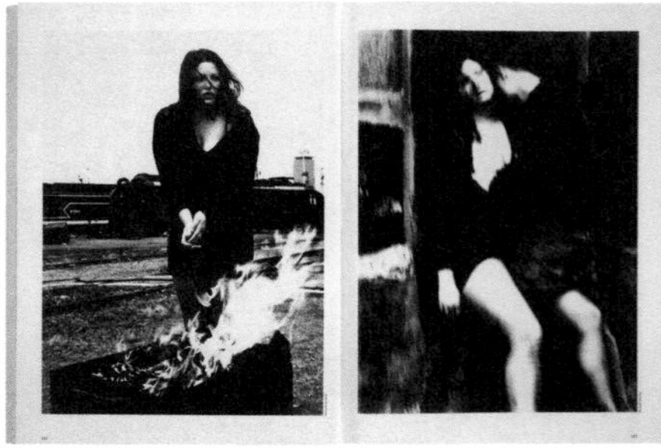

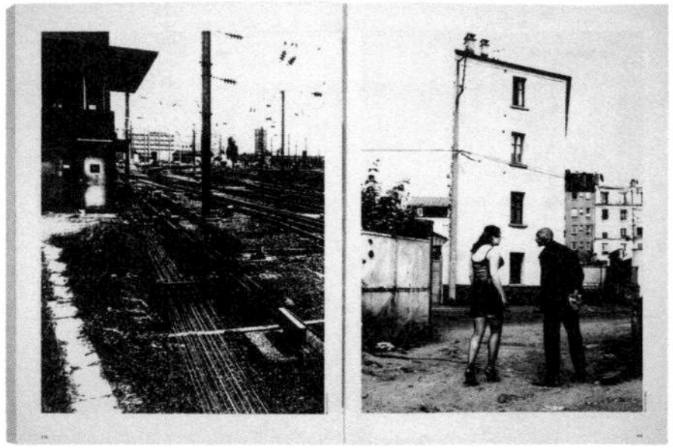

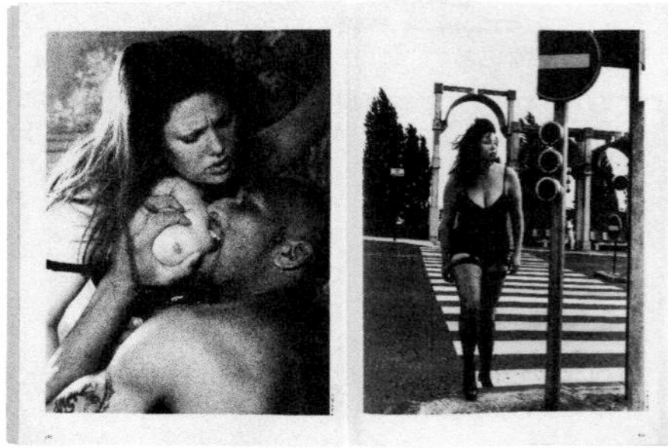

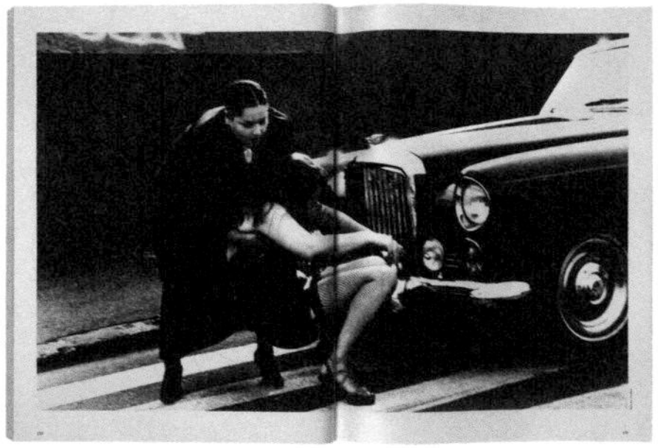

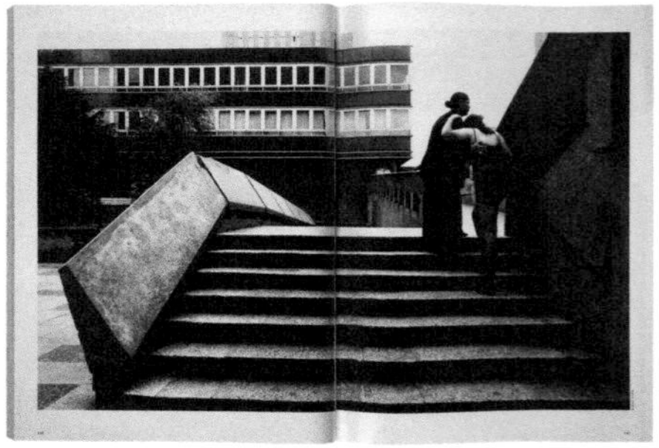

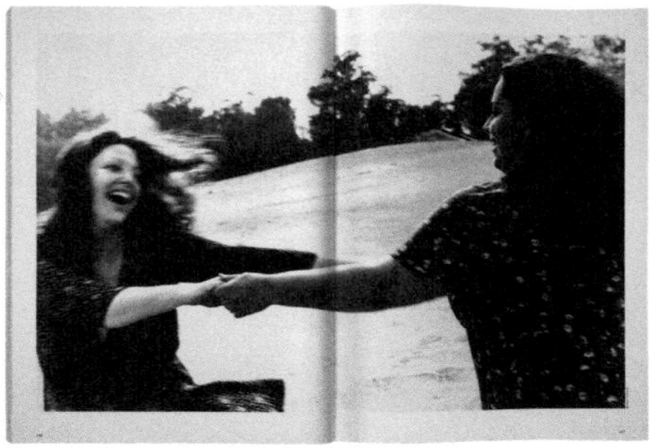

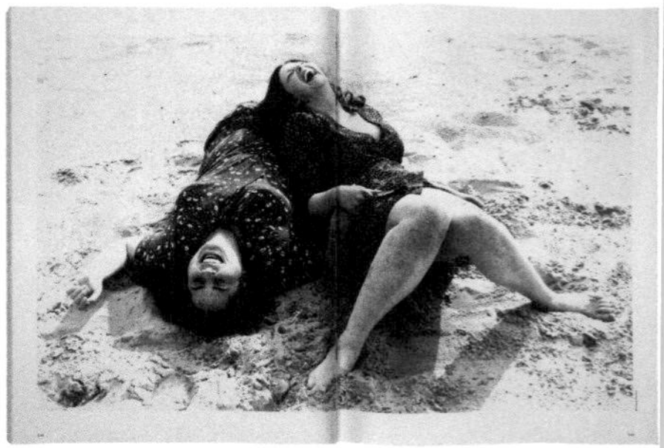

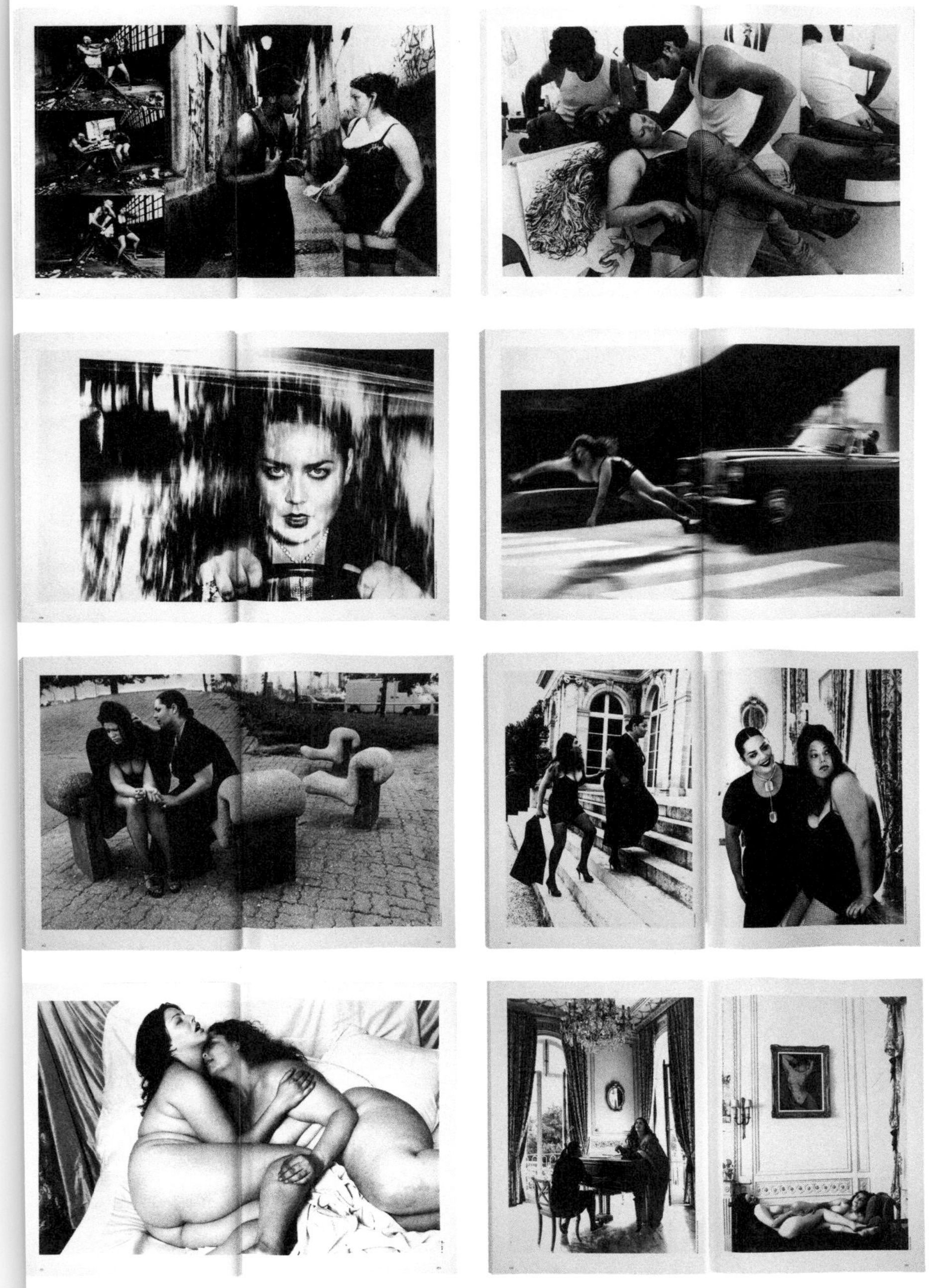

"Kate's Story par Richard Avedon," *Egoïste,* N° 14, Tome I, 2000, spreads for pp. 123–45

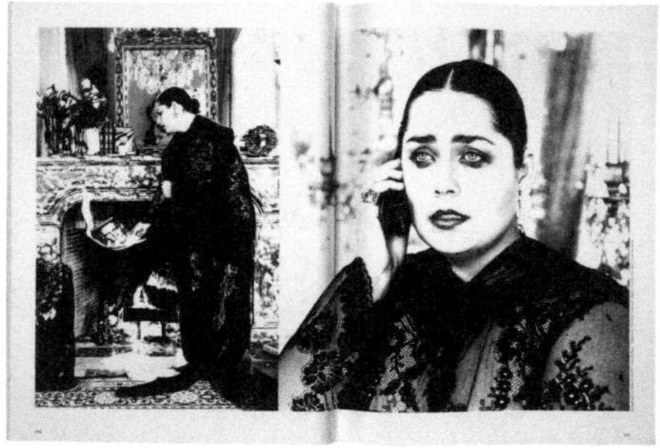

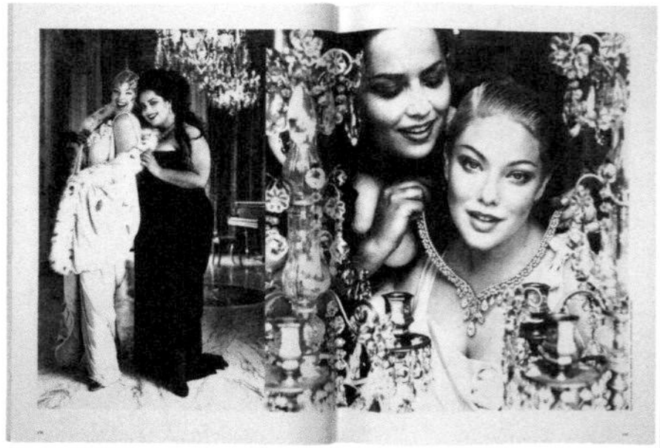

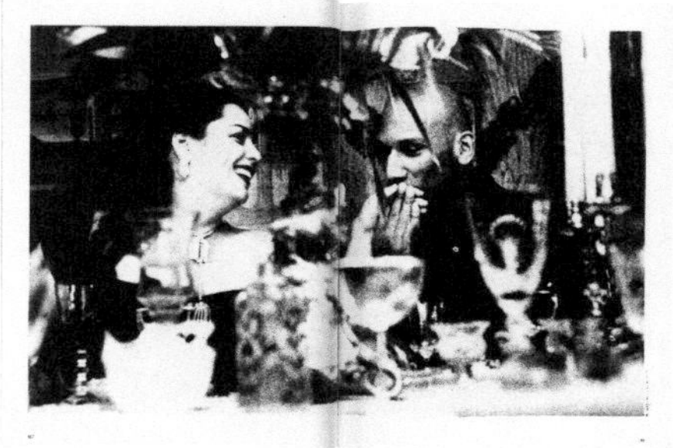

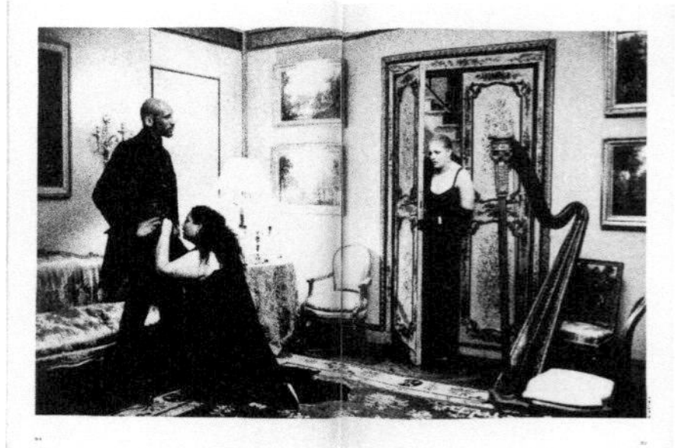

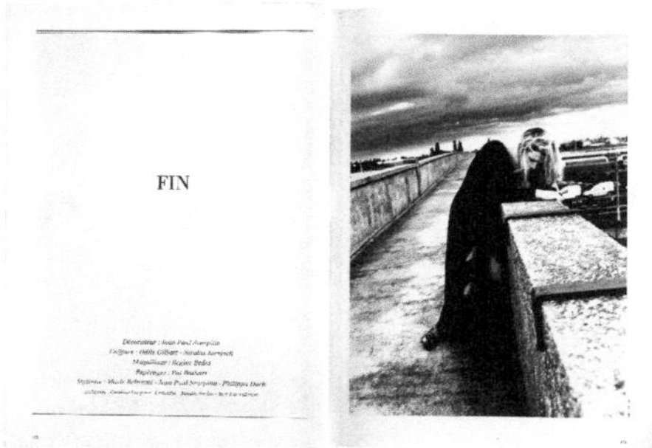

FIN

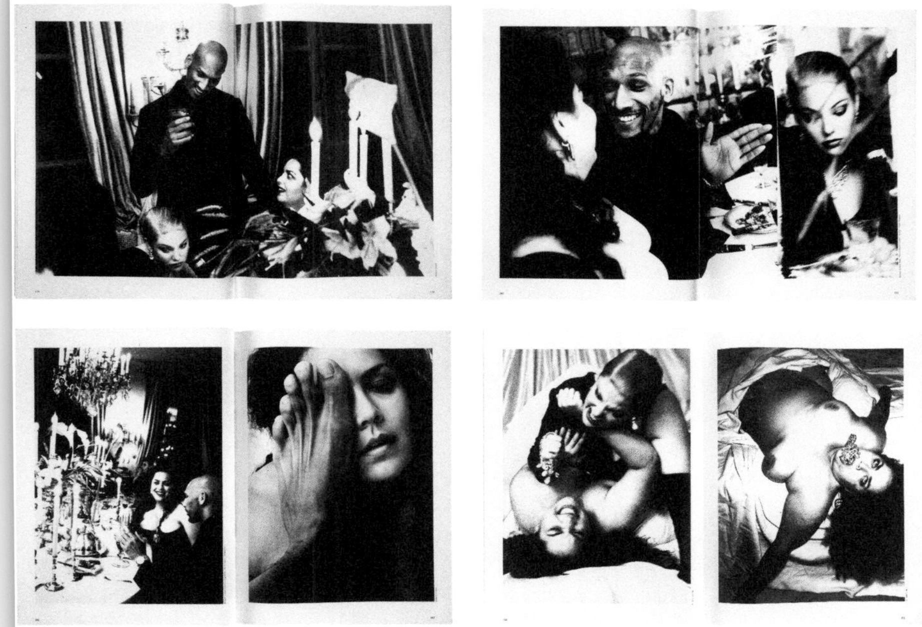

"Kate's Story par Richard Avedon," *Egoïste,* N° 14, Tome I, 2000, spreads for pp. 146–171

KATE'S STORY

par Richard Avedon

Kate : Kate Dillon
Le proxénète : Vladimir
L'autre femme : Tara Gasparian

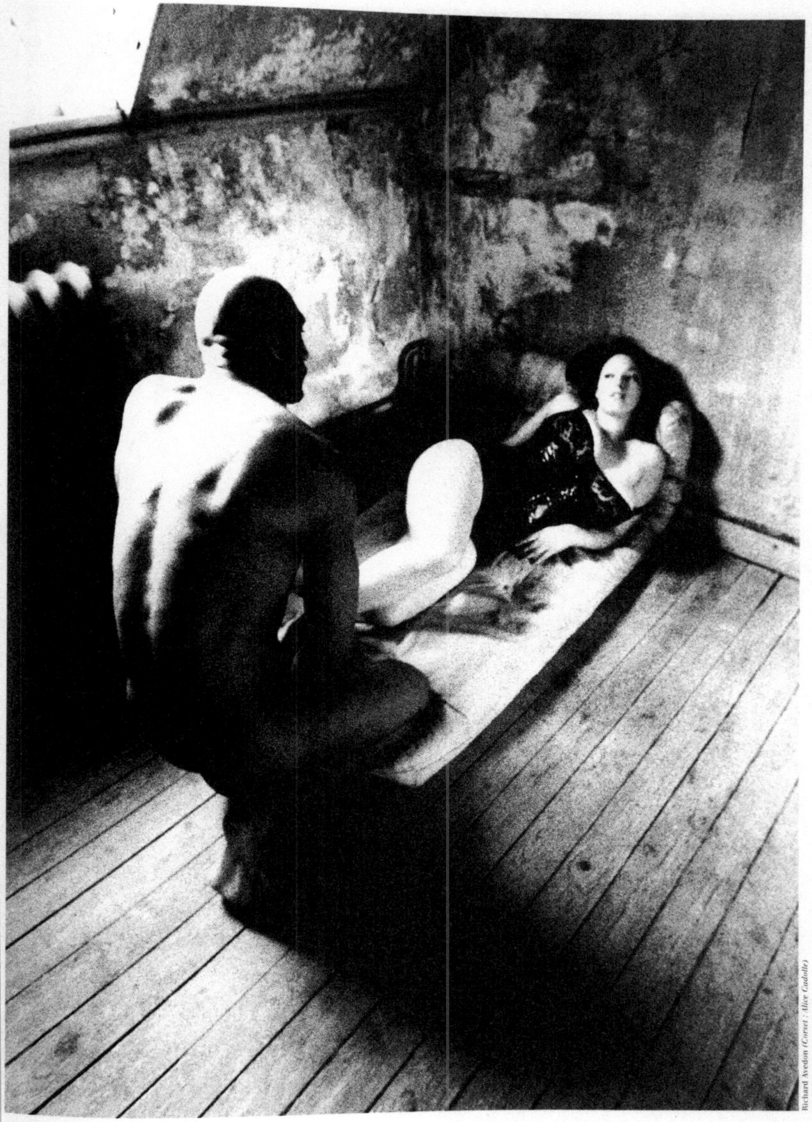

Richard Avedon (*Corset : Alice Cadolle*)

123

"Kate's Story par Richard Avedon," *Egoïste*, N° 14, Tome I, 2000, pp. 123–24

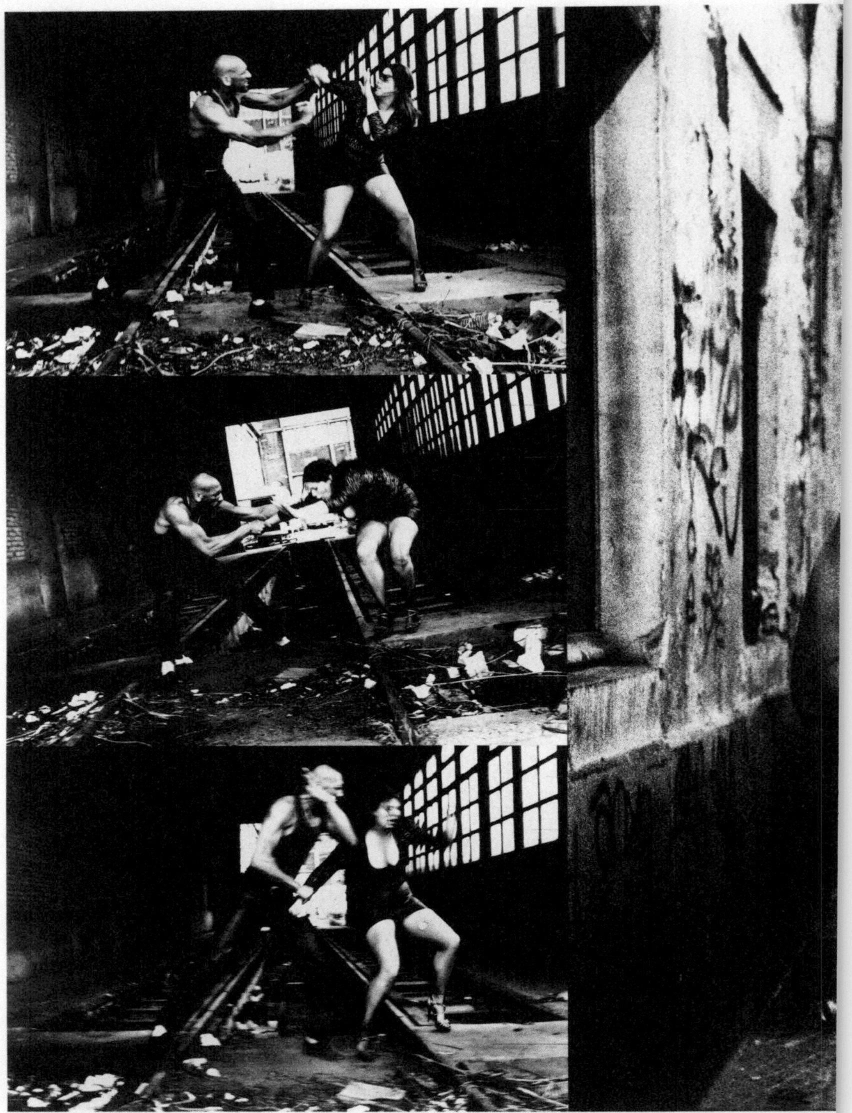

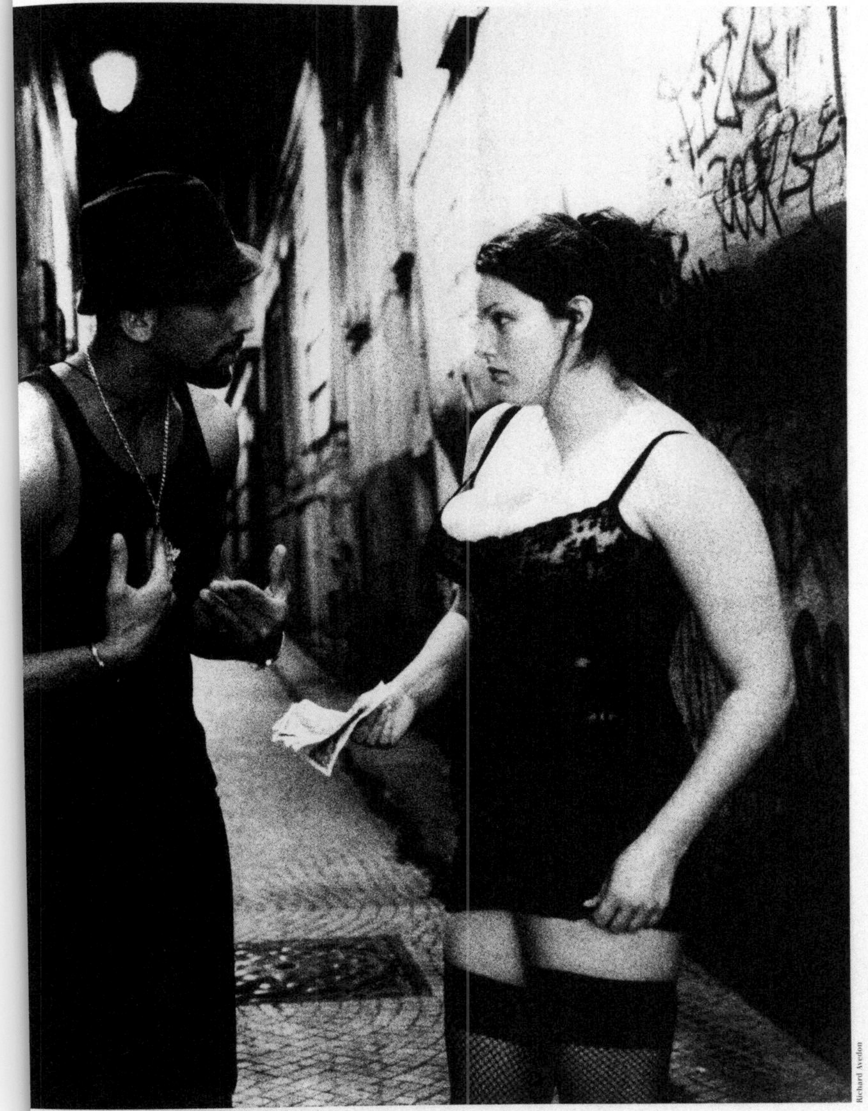

127

"Kate's Story par Richard Avedon," *Egoïste*, N° 14, Tome I, 2000, pp. 126–27

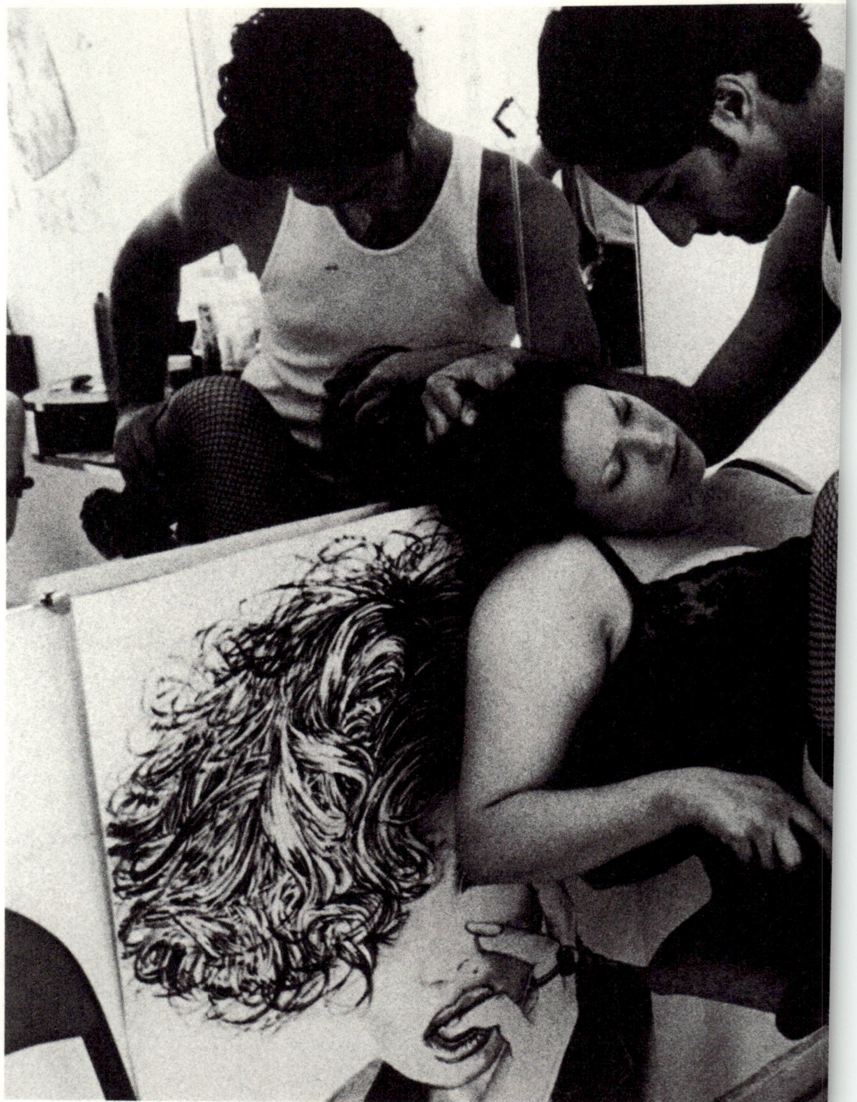

128

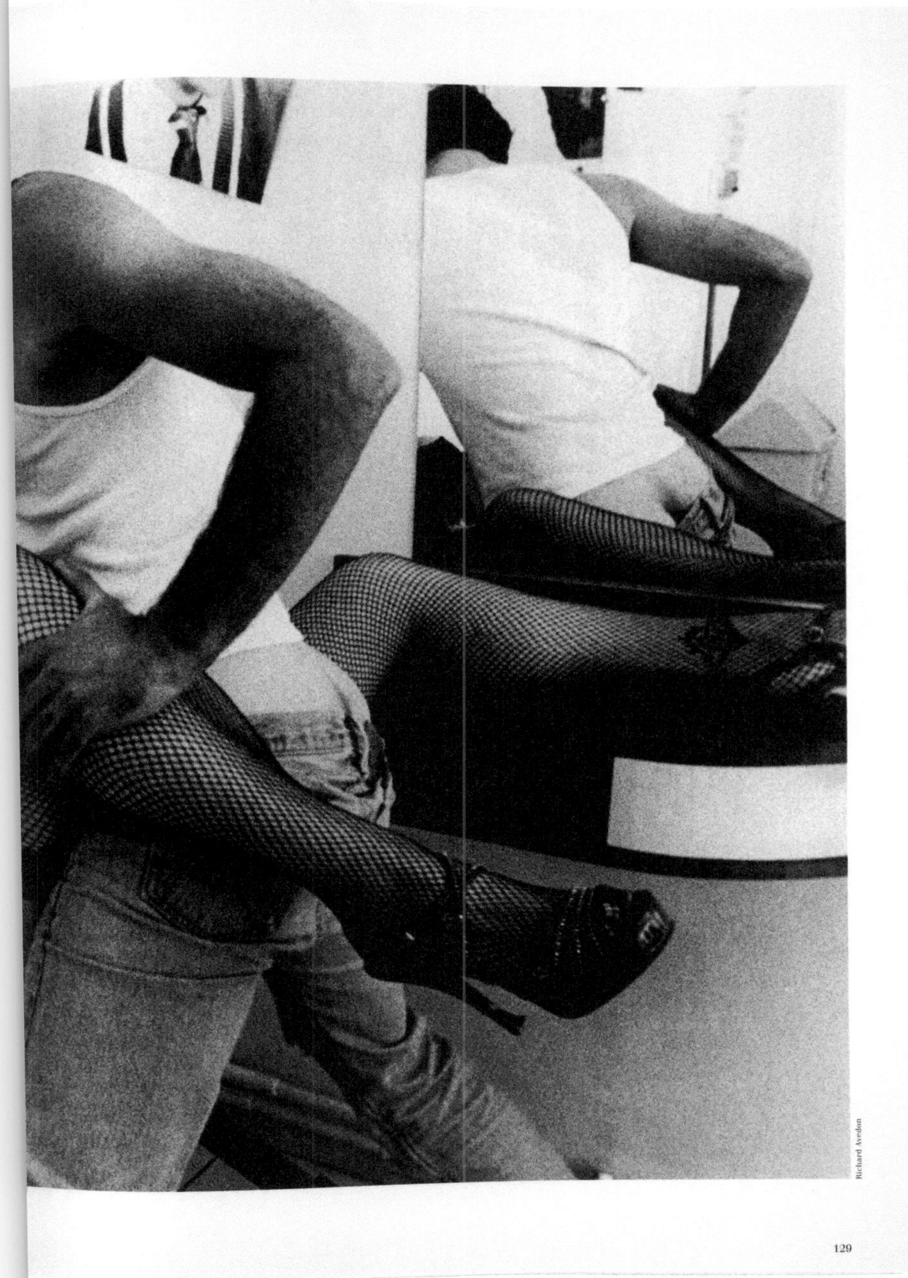

"Kate's Story par Richard Avedon," *Egoïste,* N° 14, Tome I, 2000, pp. 128–29

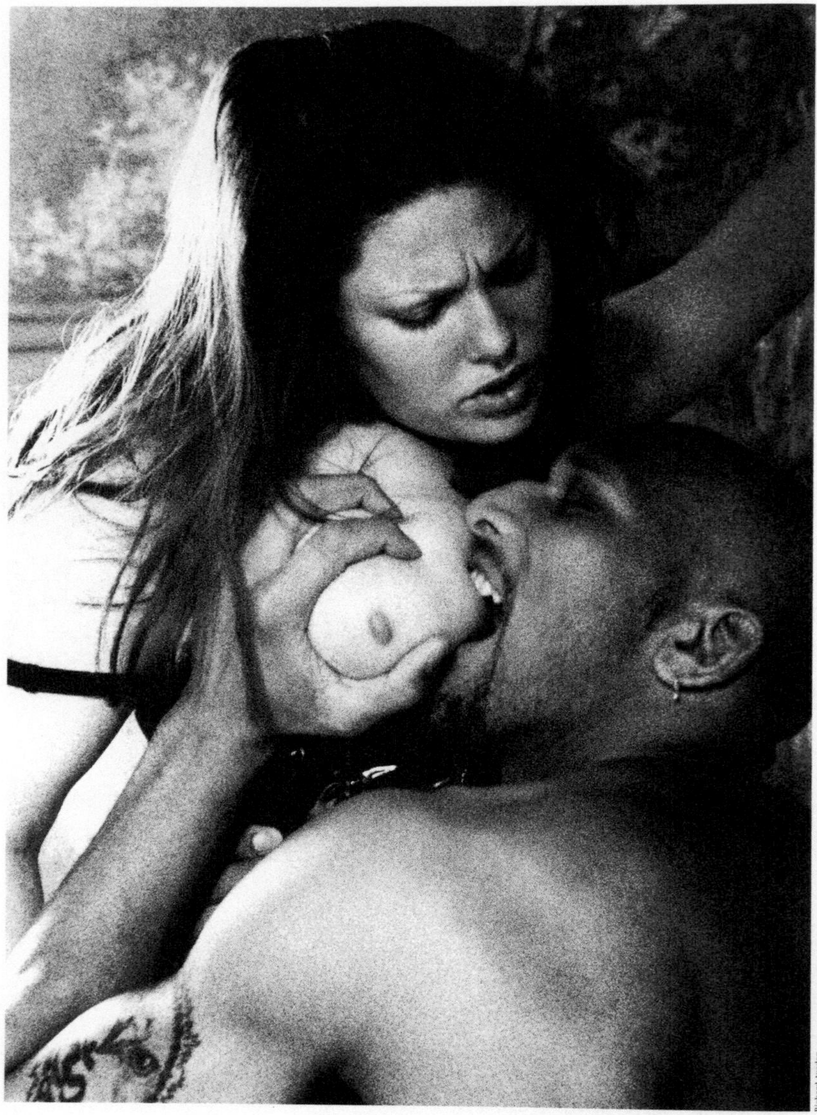

Richard Avedon

132

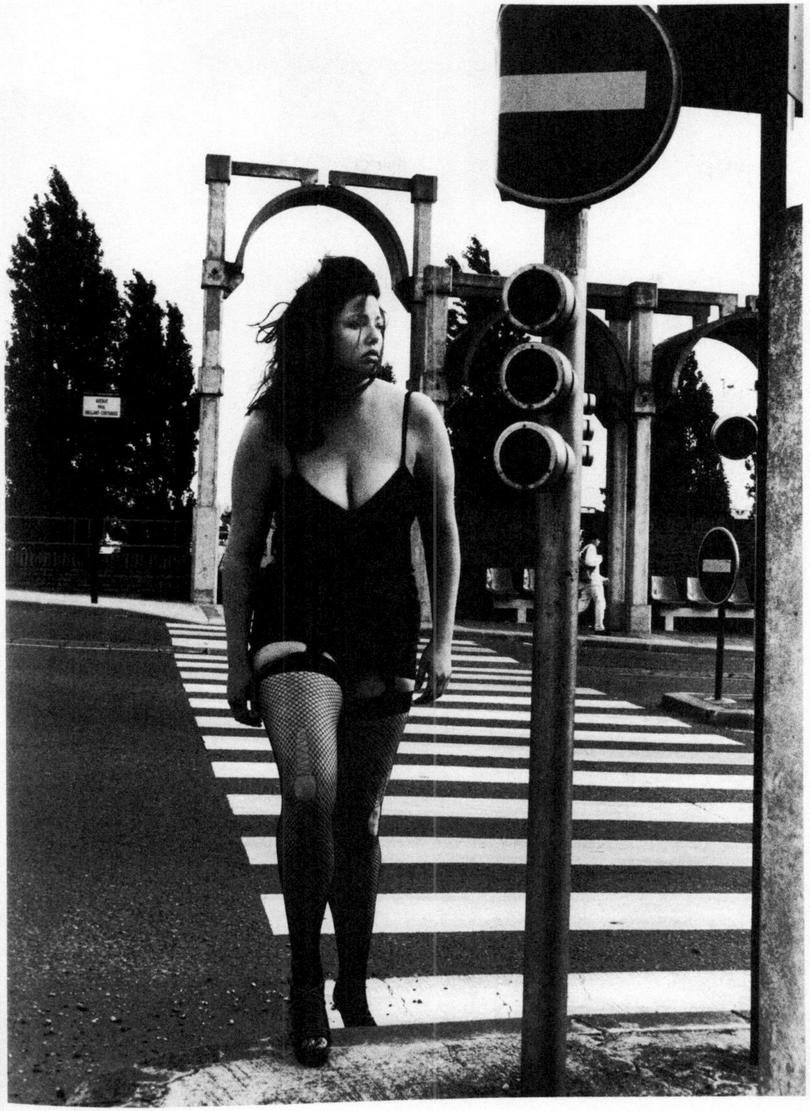

Richard Avedon

133

"Kate's Story par Richard Avedon," *Egoïste*, N° 14, Tome I, 2000, pp. 132–33

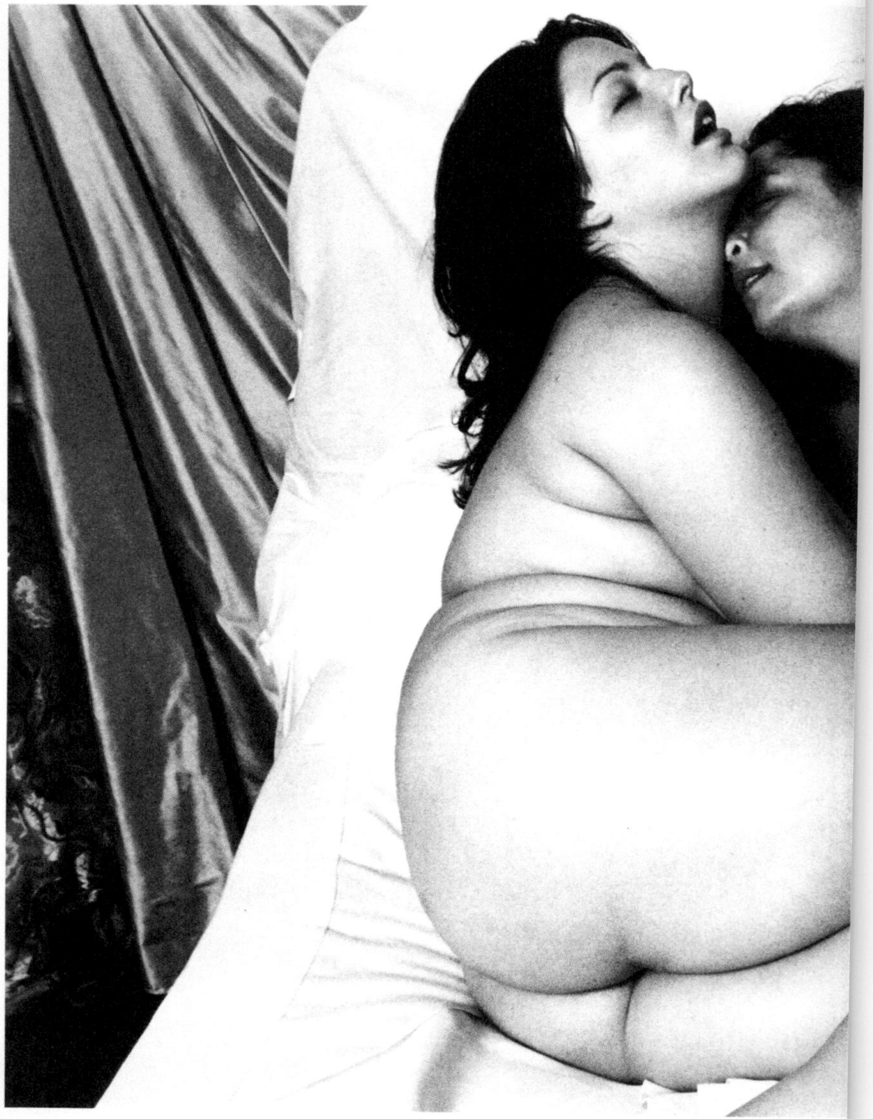

150

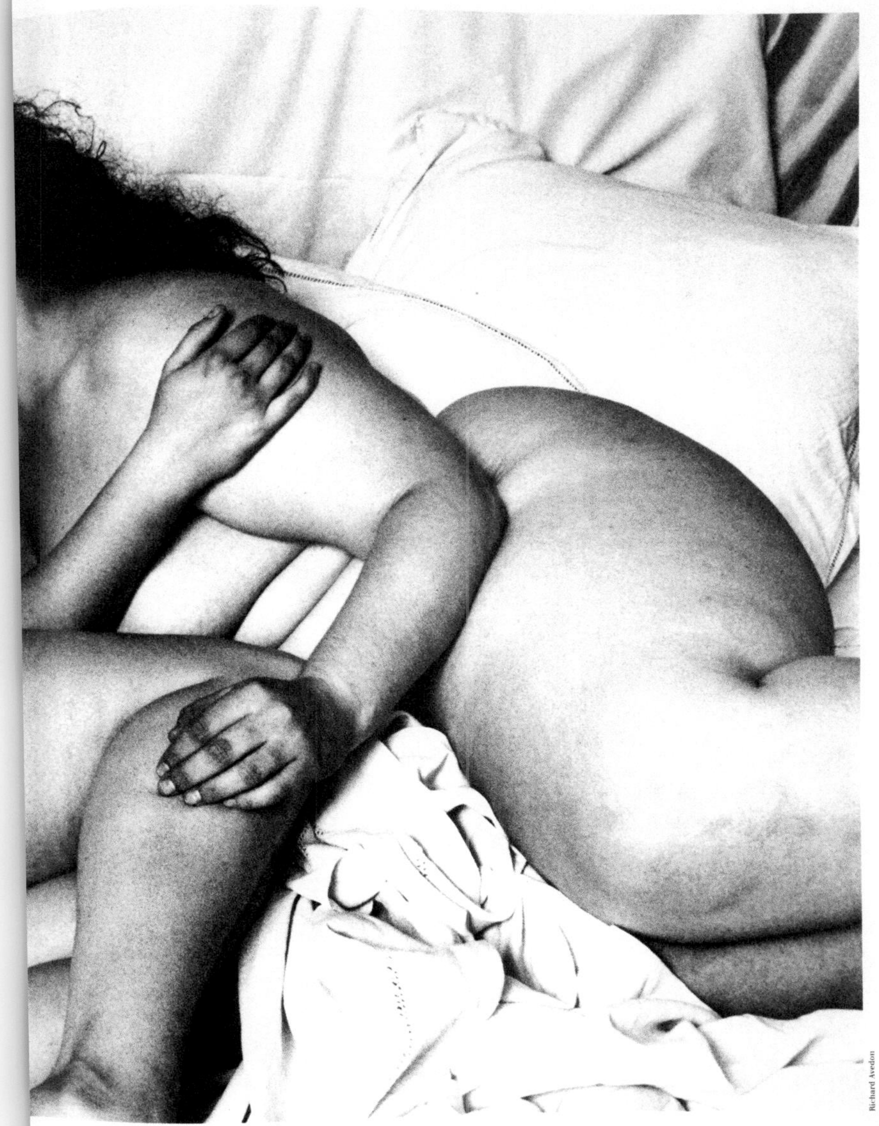

"Kate's Story par Richard Avedon," *Egoïste*, N° 14, Tome I, 2000, pp. 150–51

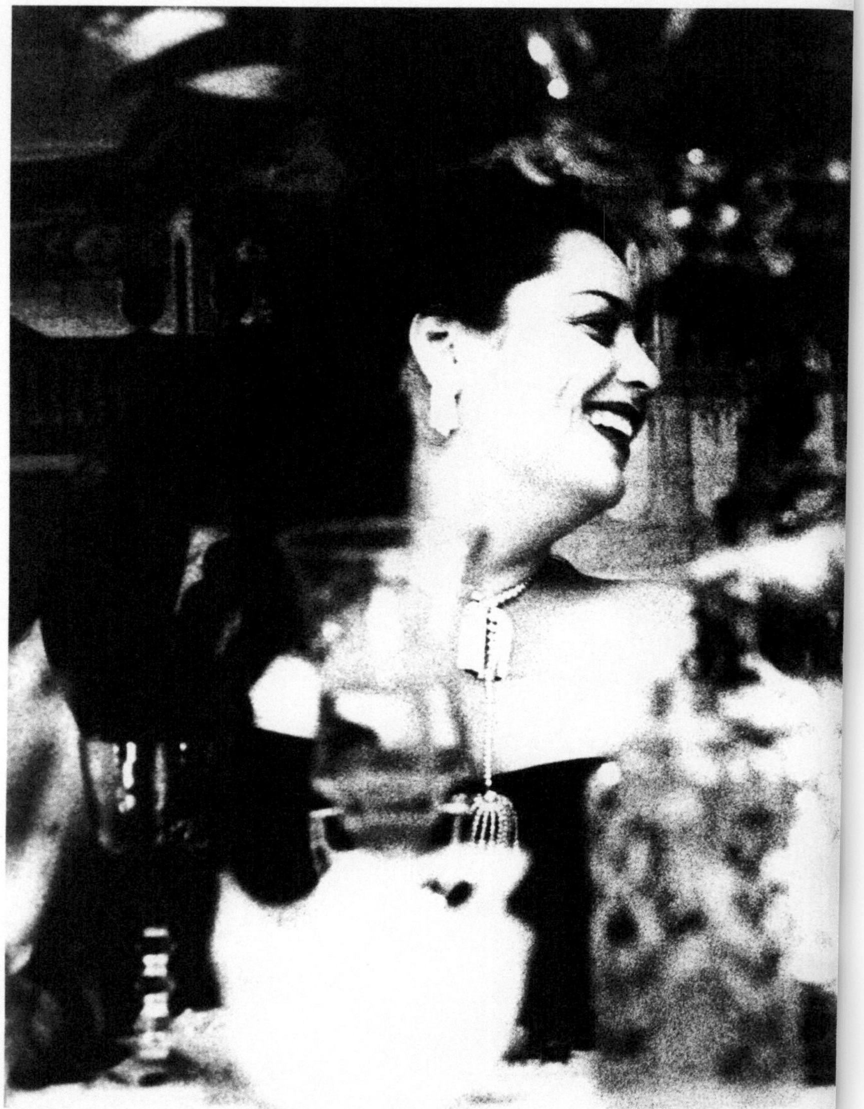

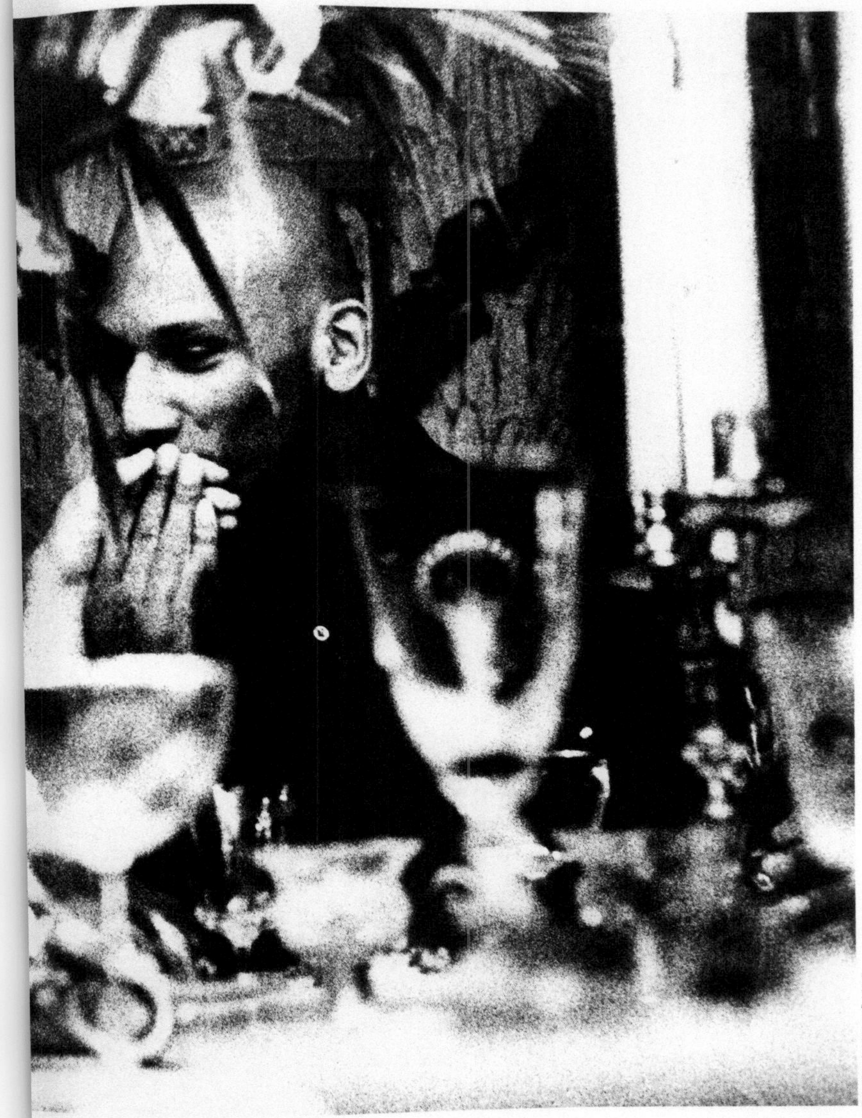

Richard Avedon (*verres : Baccarat*)

163

"Kate's Story par Richard Avedon," *Egoïste*, N° 14, Tome I, 2000, pp. 162–63

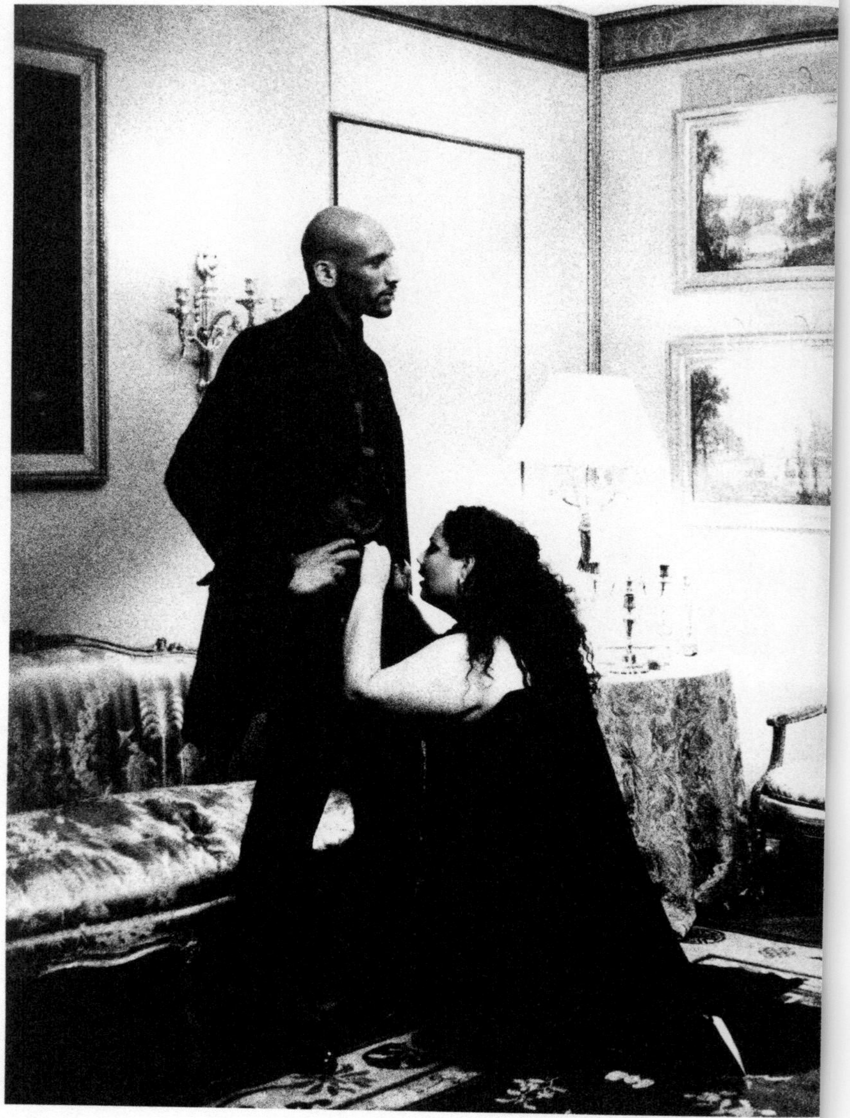

164

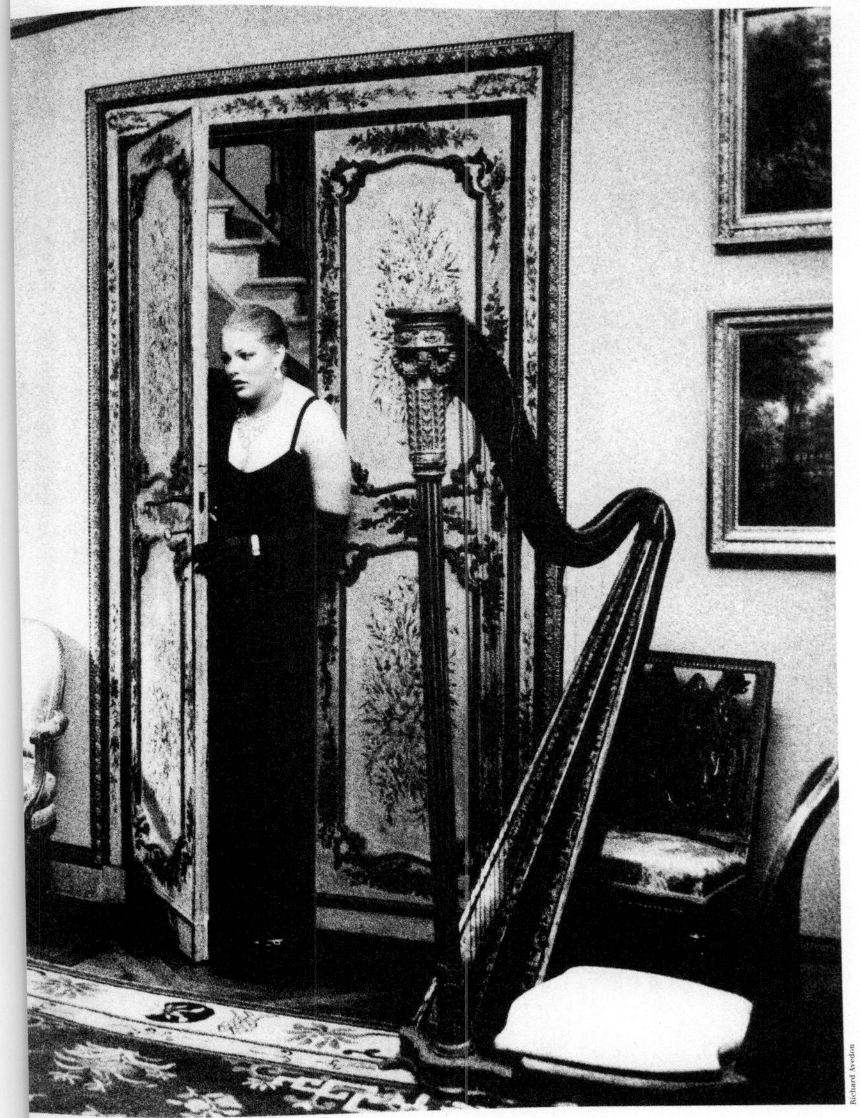

"Kate's Story par Richard Avedon," *Egoïste,* N° 14, Tome I, 2000, pp. 164–65

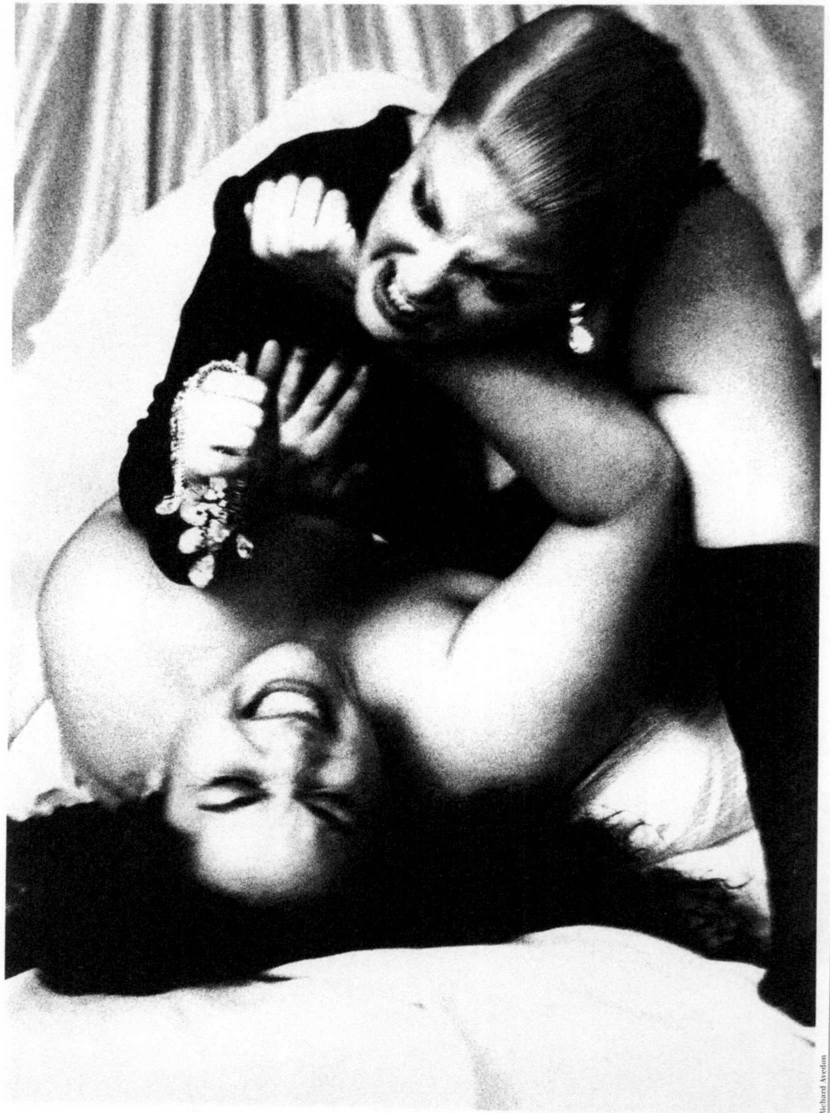

Richard Avedon

168

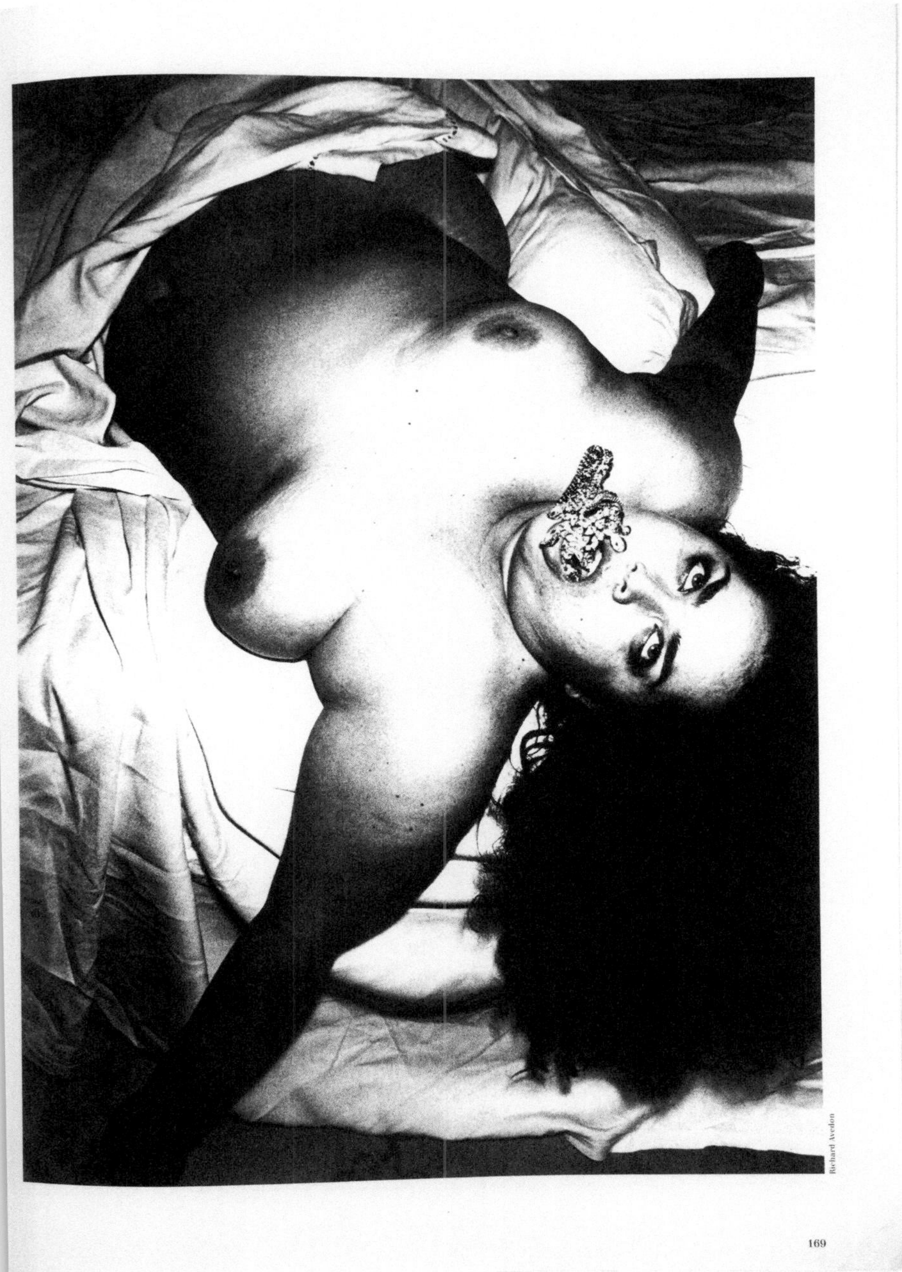

"Kate's Story par Richard Avedon," *Egoïste*, N° 14, Tome I, 2000, pp. 168–69

FIN

Décorateur : Jean-Paul Scarpitta
Coiffure : Odile Gilbert - Nicolas Jürnjack
Maquillage : Régine Bedot
Repérages : Pat Boshart
Stylisme : Marie Beltrami - Jean-Paul Scarpitta - Philippa Duck
assistants : Caroline Vacquier - Christelle - Amédée Sovissi - Jean-Luc Villemot

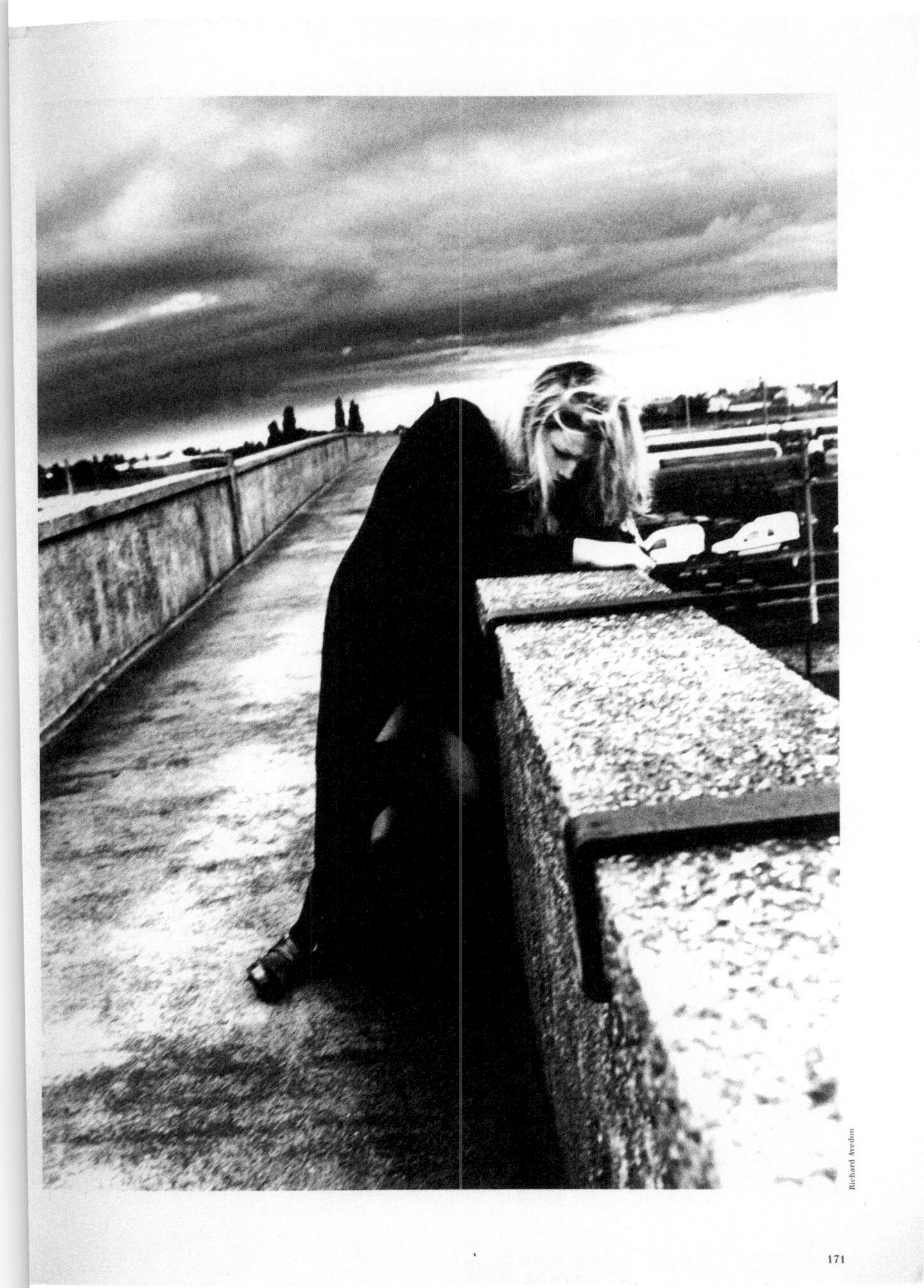

"Kate's Story par Richard Avedon," *Egoïste,* N° 14, Tome I, 2000, pp. 170–71

Dear Doe,
About Kate, the real Kate.

She was a fat girl from the midwest, whose family moved to Santa Barbara. She found herself surrounded by blonde, tanned gorgeous, beach bunnies. No one paid any attention to her, and she must have been a beautiful child, which may have something to do with her decision to become thin and beautiful. And she did. And she became anorexic and a successful model, with covers of *Glamour* and beauty contracts, and starving herself. One day, she looked in the mirror and didn't recognize the person she'd become and decided that since she was born a big woman, she was not only to give up modeling and go back to her original weight, but work for the Fat Women's Liberation movement. And that's how I found her.

The other beauty in the story, the Rich One, is her friend — a hostess in a Santa Barbara restaurant, with no experience posing.

You should have seen them in Paris. You should have seen them eat!! It would have done your heart good.

Love, Dick

—

RICHARD AVEDON, LETTER TO HIS EX-WIFE DOE SIEGEL, MARCH 16, 2001.

Taking someone's portrait can in some ways end up being like taking on a bit of his magic. The shot gives you the momentary feeling of seizing power; you feel stronger, less alone. I recently photographed André Glucksmann. I wanted his brain,

I wanted his look, I even wanted his wife. I made do with his tie. I love that tie. And I wear it every time I have to put up a fight, every time I feel I have to conjure up the "good Glucksmann."

—

Richard Avedon

Nicole Wisniak: An Interview

Robert M. Rubin

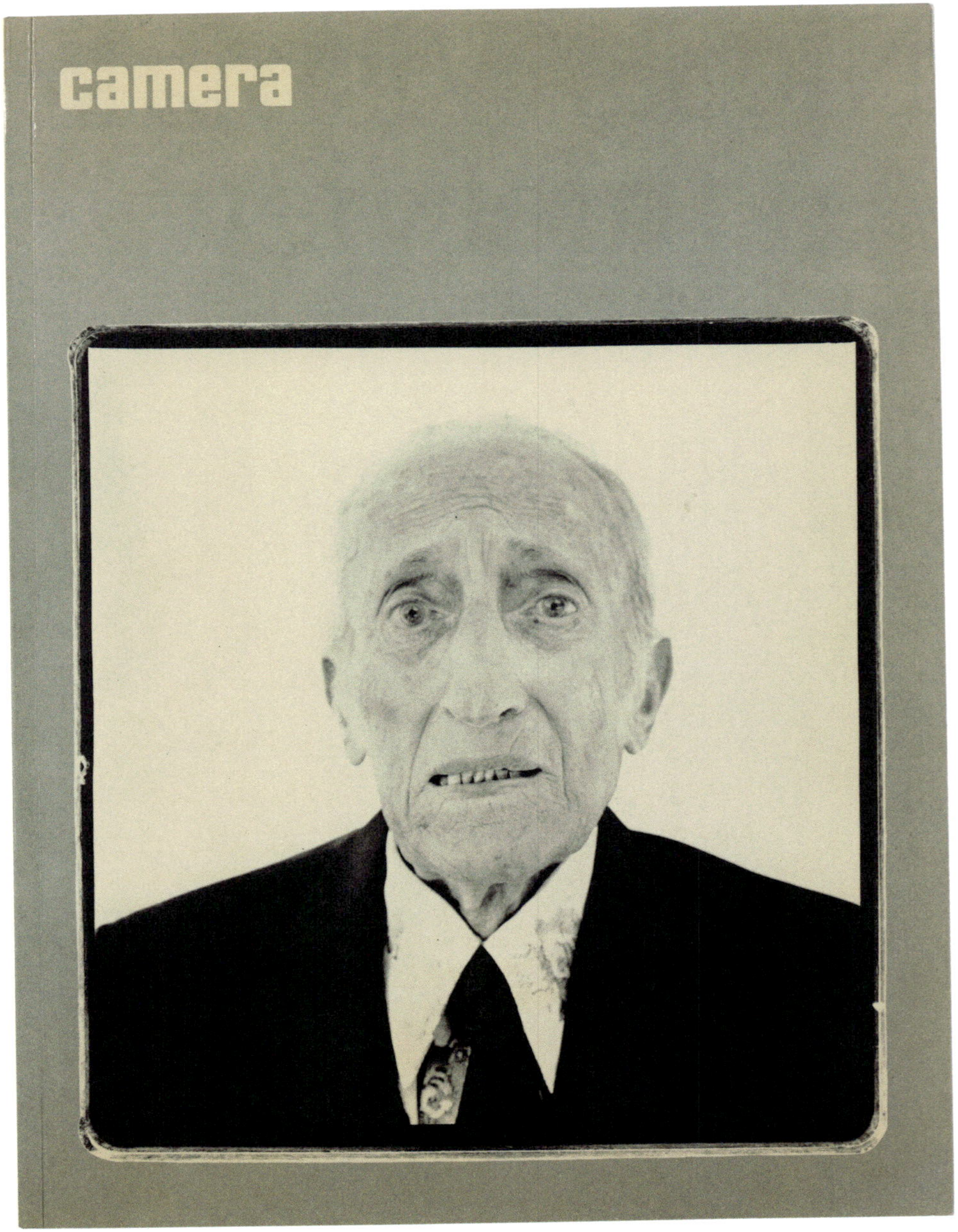

Jacob Israel Avedon, Sarasota, Florida, August 25, 1973 on the cover of *Camera*, number 11, 1974

June 22, 2016, Paris

ROBERT M. RUBIN: Tell me how you discovered Avedon.

NICOLE WISNIAK: It was in the library of a vacation home. I was overwhelmed by the photographs of his dying father. That was how death could be photographed, death colonizing a face. The fact that it was his father was even more moving. When I knew his work better, I was able to study his fashion photographs, his portraits . . . and I wondered: So who is this artist who, with such mastery, is able to show the march of death, frivolity, joie de vivre? I was struck by the breadth of his universe and the genius with which he operated in each area of photography. I was already working with photographers I admired, like Helmut Newton and also Guy Bourdin, but they expressed themselves within a defined universe. There was no limit to Avedon's virtuosity: fashion, portraiture, politics, a sharp sense for metaphor . . .

When we'd go to a shoot, he knew exactly what he was going to do before making an image. Either because he had rehearsed it with an assistant in his studio, or because he had thought about the way in which a gesture could symbolize the role or the nature of a character. The cover photograph of Depardieu naked took exactly three minutes. He came in and left. I thought he had argued with Depardieu. No. He said to me, "It's a wrap." I was amazed! In fact, he had developed the picture in his studio with an assistant, the lights, the position . . . He knew exactly what he was doing. When he photographed a politician, he knew what he wanted to show, what there was that was most cynical or opportunistic in political life: shake every hand, and sometimes any which one. When he photographed a woman who was on the verge of madness, he immediately captured her unbalanced. Of everyone I met, of every artist, he's the one who worked with the most intelligence, with incredible brio, with a kind of inspired mastery . . . That had never been seen before in other artists, at least not to that extent.

RMR: Let's talk about the photographs of the fall of the Berlin wall. How did that happen? He had never photographed history in the making before. Yes, he had gone to Vietnam, and he had photographed the depths of America, but those were portraits on the side.

NW: I wanted him to go to Berlin. I thought it would fascinate him. We talked about politics often. He always said, "It has to mean something." He always wanted there to be a certain subtext to his photographs — a jumping-off point for further reflection.

For many, the event, the fall of the wall — was a harbinger of hope. But what he photographed above all was doubt, confusion, anxiety.

RMR: There's something a bit Dionysian in those photographs. You don't know where they're heading.

NW: Yes. That's true. It's a pessimistic question mark, what's going to happen next.

RMR: It's only now that we realize he was able to see the complexity of the moment.

NW: The external aspect of things, to him, was often a trap. He always went looking beyond appearances, even though he thought appearances in themselves expressed a part of the truth.

Those photographs were taken after the wall came down, on New Year's Eve. For the first time, the passage was opened in both directions. We walked through the crowd together, from East Berlin to West Berlin, on Unter den Linden. He held my arm with one hand, and his camera with the other.

Taking Avedon to Berlin for the wall coming down was a unique editorial opportunity for *Egoïste*. I then asked Jean Baudrillard for a text, which shed new light on his pictures.

RMR: So it was you, in fact, who launched the Avedon exhibition at the Carnegie in 1991, one of the most interesting exhibitions ever on his work. He, who was so concerned with massive solo shows, found himself among photographers from one or two generations after.

NW: Dick was a genius well before meeting me. He took his first photographs before I was even born. I consider myself very lucky that he accepted my invitation to work for *Egoïste*. It so happens that — in part because of the chemistry between us, and maybe because I wasn't just interested in fashion and makeup — I was able to have a tiny bit of an influence on his work, which he would have continued in a different way without me in any case.

RMR: Certainly. But there are very specific connections between the work he did for *Egoïste* and, for example, the selection of Baudrillard's text. I was struck by Baudrillard's *America* [1989] and its correspondence with Avedon's *In the American West* series. Some of the book's propositions seem not only to define the photographic project but also to explain why there was so much Anglo-Saxon criticism of it at the time.

NW: Yes. That work went against the idea that America was the land of prosperity.

RMR: Let's talk about the Volpi Ball, which was photographed the following year, in 1991.

NW: I was invited to the Ball that year. Then I remembered that two years before, Avedon had told me about his wish to return to that Proustian world he had documented in the 1950s. So I proposed that he accompany me. He set up his studio at the Palazzo Volpi.

When we returned to Paris, we looked at the contact sheets of the photos taken that night. And he told me me: "Nicole, there's not one picture!" I had tears in my eyes. "That can't be," I said to him. And then, with nail scissors, at the bar of the Ritz Hotel, he started making new images. What had first looked like the social diary in *Vogue* began turning into iconic, unforgettable images.

RMR: And Proust?

NW: Avedon was obsessed with Proust. It's obvious that the Proustian angle was in his mind when he went to photograph the Volpi Ball, The Last Ball. The same is true with that portrait of Alexis de Redé . . . When Avedon photographed a person, he was photographing a world. And if that world was nearing extinction, his interest was even keener.

All the work for *Egoïste* was the happy chemistry between my needs and his obsessions, both propelled by mutual generosity. Two things in particular made him trust me: I had studied history and I had taken care of Picasso's estate. And I was constantly impressed.

It was a wonderful gift seeing his work, seeing the appetite he had for faces, those he came across in the street or in a café. It was fascinating watching him read life.

RMR: Can you talk about "Kate's Story"?

NW: That was at the moment when you started finding waif models. We thought we ought to present other kinds of women's bodies, and to emphasize their beauty. He chose two very buxom women, and they became the actresses in a short scene we had written together.

When we began conceiving of the project, he thought he would do a series like the one for *Vogue*, with Anjelica Huston in a wagon in Ireland [*Vogue*, October 15, 1969]. So I told him that if he wanted to photograph unusual places, there were landscapes on the outskirts of Paris that were photogenic and dramatically symbolic. One of the pictures in Kate's Story is taken on a bridge in Drancy — the site of her suicide. He liked to be able to infuse his photographs with sense of the subliminal.

He insisted we go photograph Franco's tomb in Madrid. He had friends in the past who had joined the International Brigades [during the Spanish Civil War]. It was important to him. His biography is extremely linked to his work: the asylums are connected with his sister, Franco's tomb with his friends who volunteered. He was very political.

RMR: And "Kate's Story" is a good counterpart to "Paris Pursuit," which he did almost forty years earlier. The idea of the ciné-roman —

NW: Yes, that's true.

RMR: And what do you think about his relationship with France?

NW: He adored France — he was a gourmand, an epicurean. We visited France by car, going through the villages and sleeping in people's homes.

Contrary to what you're saying [in the essay on Avedon and France], I don't think Avedon had any bitterness toward France. He couldn't care less that the Legion d'Honneur was awarded to James Baldwin. I don't agree with you about that.

RMR: Ok, let's say the overall characteristic of genius is allowing for several perspectives. Everyone has their own Avedon.

NW: Yes. But it is true that he thought French museums should have given him a major retrospective.

In any case, he knew that in the long run, he'd win every battle in posterity. He was aware of the quality of his work. Sooner or later, it would become obvious that he was unique, that his work is hugely diverse, that it is timeless and universal.

To me, Avedon is *the* photographer of the twentieth century, and of centuries to come.

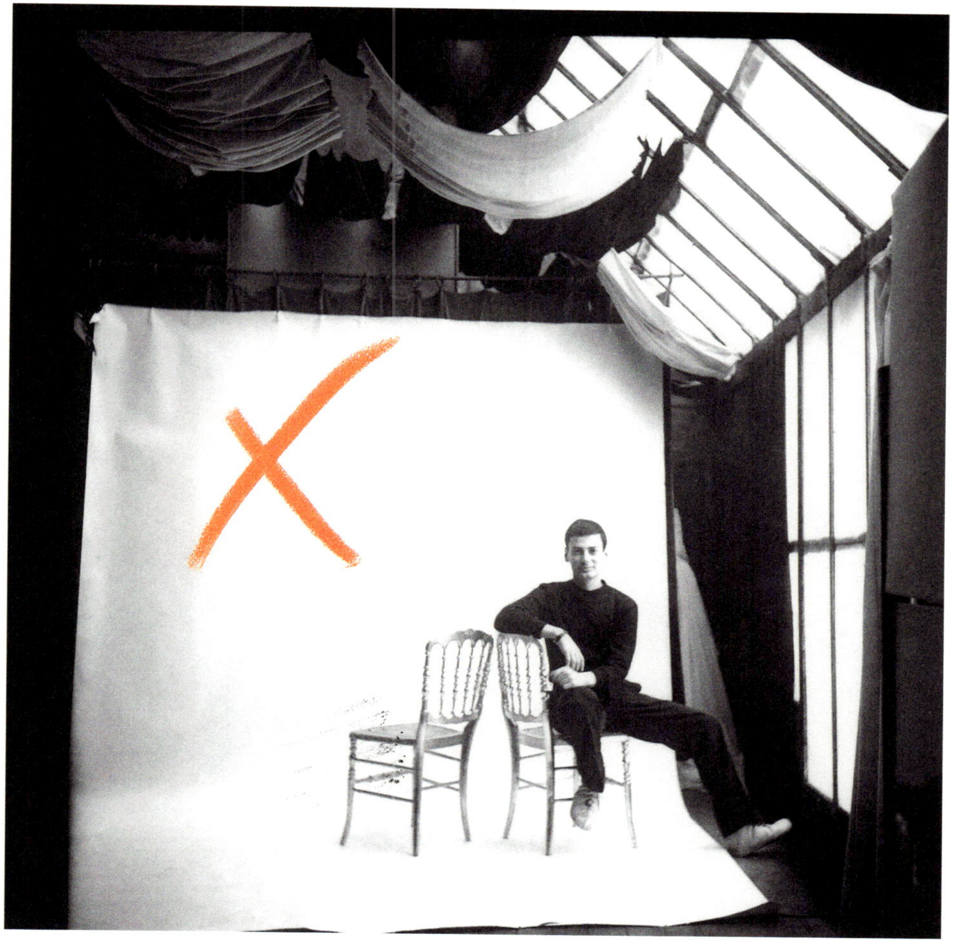

Richard Avedon in his Paris studio, c. 1948

Contemporary books do not keep. The quality in them which makes for their success is the first to go; they turn overnight. Therefore one must look for some quality which improves with time.

—

CYRIL CONNOLLY, *ENEMIES OF PROMISE* (NEW YORK: MACMILLAN, 1948): 4.

**Avedon and France:
A Selective Chronology**

1923
Richard Avedon is born in New York City on May 15.

1924
Alexey Brodovitch wins first prize in a poster competition called *Le Bal Banal*, beating Pablo Picasso. Between 1928 and 1930, Brodovitch is in charge of advertising for the Paris department store Aux Trois Quartiers.

1925
Janet Flanner is hired as Paris correspondent for *The New Yorker* and starts her "Letter from Paris" column under the pseudonym of Genêt.

1934
Brodovitch, in the U.S. since 1930, is appointed Art Director of *Harper's Bazaar* by its new Editor-in-Chief, Carmel Snow. Diana Vreeland joins them in 1936. Christian Bérard, Marcel Vertès and Colette become regular contributors. The magazine also publishes drawings by Jean Cocteau.

Henry Miller, *Tropic of Cancer*.

1937
Avedon starts at DeWitt Clinton High School in the Bronx.

Jean Anouilh, *Le Voyageur sans Bagage* (The Traveler without Luggage). Jean Giraudoux, *Électre* (Electra). Jean Renoir, *La Grande Illusion* (The Grand Illusion).

1938
Jean Anouilh, *Le Bal des Voleurs* (Thieves' Carnival). Jean Renoir, *La Bête Humaine* (The Human Beast).

1939
Coco Chanel closes her couture house.

Jean Giraudoux, *Ondine*.
Jean Renoir, *La Règle du Jeu* (The Rules of the Game).

1940
Carmel Snow travels to France for her "Paris Report" on the couture collections.

1942
Avedon serves in the U.S. Merchant Marine, where his job involves taking thousands of portraits and I.D. photographs.

1943
Colette, *Gigi*.

1944
Upon his return to civilian life in New York City, Avedon marries Dorcas Nowell (who changes her first name to Doe), and encourages her to become a model. He enrolls in the New School for Social Research, where he studies photography under Alexey Brodovitch.

Carmel Snow travels to Paris that winter for the couture collections.

Jean Anouilh, *Antigone*.
Igor Stravinsky, *Babel*.
Jean Giraudoux dies.

1945
Alexey Brodovitch hires Avedon as a photographer for *Harper's Bazaar*, publishing Avedon's first pictures in the April and June issues of *Junior Bazaar*.

Alexey Brodovitch, *Ballet*.

Day of Paris: Photographs by André Kertész, designed by Brodovitch.

Jean Giraudoux, *La Folle de Chaillot* (The Madwoman of Chaillot). Igor Stravinsky, *Symphony in Three Movements*.

1946
René Clément and Jean Cocteau, *La Belle et la Bête* (Beauty and the Beast).

1947
In August Avedon makes his first trip to Paris to photograph the haute couture collections. He photographs Christian Bérard with models wearing Christian Dior's "New Look."

In February Christian Dior and his assistant, Pierre Cardin, present Dior's spring-summer runway show, including the *Corolle* collection and the *Bar* suit. A comment by Carmel Snow leads to the term the "New Look."

René Clair, *Le Silence est d'Or* (Man About Town). Jean Genet, *Les Bonnes* (The Maids).

1948
In January, February and June Avedon returns to Paris and photographs the Comtesse Maxime de la Falaise and Coco Chanel.

Samuel Beckett, *Murphy*. Marcel Jouhandeau, *Scènes de la Vie Conjugale* (Scenes from Conjugal Life). Jean Cocteau, *Les Parents Terribles*. Igor Stravinsky, *Mass*. James Baldwin moves to Paris.

1949
While continuing to photograph for *Harper's Bazaar*, Avedon is also named Staff Editor and photographer at *Theatre Arts*. In February, he photographs *The Madwoman of Chaillot* in New York. A portrait from the series is used for its June cover.

Avedon and Doe separate.

In April Carmel Snow is named Chevalier of the Légion d'Honneur by the Consul General of France, Ludovic Chancel.

Jean Genet, *Le Journal du Voleur* (The Thief's Journal). Jacques Tati, *Jour de Fête* (The Big Day). Henry Miller, *Sexus*.

Christian Bérard dies.

1950

In March and September – November, Avedon travels to Paris.

Avedon photographs Marie-Louise Bousquet, Zizi Jeanmaire, and Marcel Jouhandeau.

Pierre Cardin starts his own couture house.

Marguerite Duras, *Un Barrage contre le Pacifique* (The Sea Wall). Eugène Ionesco, *La Cantatrice Chauve* (The Bald Soprano). René Clair, *La Beauté du Diable* (Beauty and the Devil). Jean Cocteau, *Orphée* (Orpheus). Jean-Pierre Melville, *Les Enfants Terribles*.

1951

In January Avedon marries Evelyn Franklin and the two travel to Paris.

Eugène Ionesco, *Les Chaises* (The Chairs).

Nicole Wisniak is born.

1952

In August Avedon travels to Paris and photographs Jean-Louis Barrault.

Samuel Beckett, *En Attendant Godot* (Waiting for Godot). René Clair, *Belles de Nuit* (Beauties of the Night). Henri Cartier-Bresson, Images à la sauvette (The Decisive Moment).

1953

In July and August Avedon returns to Paris and travels to Menton, a town in the South of France.

In New York Avedon makes his first portraits of Jean Renoir.

Chanel re-opens her couture house.

Roland Barthes, *Le Degré Zéro de l'Écriture* (Writing Degree Zero). Alain Robbe-Grillet, *Les Gommes* (The Erasers). Jacques Tati, *Les Vacances de M. Hulot* (Monsieur Hulot's Holiday).

1954

In March Avedon photographs Janet Flanner in New York.

Carmel Snow is now publishing her "Paris Report" regularly in *Harper's Bazaar.*

Public campaigns in the war on poverty led by Abbé Pierre and his Emmaus movement in winter.

François Sagan, Bonjour Tristesse. Cecil Beaton, *The Glass of Fashion* (translated in French by Denise Bourdet)

Colette dies.

1955

Avedon and Evelyn travel to Paris in August and see the Picasso exhibition at the Musée des Arts Décoratifs.

Alain Robbe-Grillet, *Le Voyeur* (The Voyeur). Jean Renoir, *French Cancan.*

1956

During the summer the movie *Funny Face* is filmed in Paris. The script is based on Avedon's life. Avedon serves as its visual consultant and creates the title sequence.

In August, while in Paris, Avedon photographs Suzy Parker. The series will be published in Richard Avedon: *Made in France* (2001).

In New York Avedon photographs Jacques Cousteau.

Cousteau's *World without Sun*, co-directed by Louis Malle, wins the Palme d'Or at the Cannes Film Festival, and the Oscar for Best Documentary.

Jacques Villon (Marcel Duchamp's brother) wins the grand prize for Painting at the Venice Biennale.

Alain Resnais, *Nuit et Brouillard* (Night and Fog). Roger Vadim, *And God Created Woman.*

1957

In March Avedon travels to Paris.

In its November issue *Esquire* publishes photographs made in a Mustoscope photo booth as "directed" by Avedon, including Marilyn Monroe (who appears topless), Bert Lahr, and the threesome Mel Ferrer, Audrey Hepburn and Truman Capote.

Following its premiere at Cannes in May, *Funny Face* (Drôle de Frimousse) is released in November in France.

Christian Dior dies in October. His young assistant, Yves Saint Laurent, is named head of the fashion house in November.

Carmel Snow leaves *Harper's Bazaar.*

Roland Barthes, *Mythologies* (Mythologies). Samuel Beckett *Fin de Partie* (Endgame). Marcel Pagnol, *La Gloire de mon Père* (My Father's Glory). Alain Robbe-Grillet, *La Jalousie* (Jealousy). René Clair, *Porte des Lilas* (Gates of Paris). Raymond Rouleau, *Les Sorcières de Salem* (The Crucible) with Simone Signoret and Yves Montand.

1958

In April Avedon travels to France and photographs Pablo Picasso in Beaulieu.

Avedon photographs Marcel Duchamp, René Clair and Alberto Giacometti in New York.

Robert Delpire Éditions publishes Robert Frank's *Les Américains.* The book will be published in the U.S. the following year.

Vincente Minnelli, *Gigi*, with Leslie Caron and Maurice Chevalier. Louis Malle, *Les Amants* (The Lovers) and *Ascenseur pour l'Échafaud* (Elevator to the Gallows). Jacques Tati, *Mon Oncle* (My Uncle).

1959

In January Avedon travels to Paris and photographs Bernard Buffet, Eugène Ionesco, Yves Saint Laurent, Brigitte Bardot, Zizi Jeanmaire, Marc Chagall, Georges Braque, and Jacques Tati. Several of these portraits appear in the March *Harper's Bazaar.*

In August Avedon returns to Paris for the "Paris Pursuit: A Love Farce" spread with Audrey Hepburn, Mel Ferrer and Buster Keaton, which appears in the September *Harper's Bazaar.* In October he takes Yves Montand and Simone Signoret's portraits. He publishes his first monograph, *Observations*, with an essay by Truman Capote.

François Truffaut, *Les 400 Coups* (The 400 Blows). Alain Resnais, *Hiroshima mon Amour.* Claude Chabrol *A Double Tour* (*Leda*). Jean-Pierre Mocky, *Les Drageurs*, with Anouk Aimée.

Yves Montand enjoys success on Broadway with his premiere one-man show.

1960

In July Avedon travels to Paris and photographs Jacqueline de Ribes. When he returns to New York, he photographs François Truffaut.

Zizi Jeanmaire presents her famous music hall number in Paris, "Mon Truc en Plumes," wearing costumes by Yves Saint Laurent.

Jean Cocteau, *Testament d'Orphée* (Testament of Orpheus). François Truffaut, *Tirez sur le Pianiste* (Shoot the Piano Player).

1961

Three Avedon prints are included in the *Salon International du Portrait Photographique* at the Bibliothèque Nationale de France, alongside with photographs by more than 300 other artists like Brassaï, Robert Doisneau, Guy Bourdin, William Klein, Ansel Adams and Imogen Cunningham, etc.

In May Avedon photographs Jacqueline de Ribes and Raymundo de Larrain in New York. In summer, he travels to Paris to photograph Nureyev, members of the French press and the House of Dior for the September *Harper's Bazaar*

In June Rudolf Nureyev defects to France. He is quickly hired by Raymundo de Cuevas, the new director of the Grand Ballet Marquis du Cuevas, to dance in *Sleeping Beauty.* Paris audiences hail Nureyev's "leap to freedom."

Claude Chabrol, *Les Godeluraux* (Wise Guys). Alain Resnais, *L'Année Dernière à Marienbad* (Last Year in Marienbad).

Carmel Snow dies.

1962

In July Avedon travels to Paris and photographs Jeanne Moreau.

The first Avedon exhibition, *Richard Avedon* opens in November at the Smithsonian Institution in Washington D.C.

François Truffaut, *Jules et Jim.* Jean Renoir, *Le Caporal Épinglé* (The Elusive Corporal).

1963

Jacques Henri Lartigue (69 years old) has his first exhibition at the Museum of Modern Art in New York.

Bertrand Tavernier interviews Stanley Donen about *Funny Face* in the May issue of *Cahiers du Cinéma.*

Charles Aznavour sings his first concert in the United States at Carnegie Hall in New York, launching his international career is launched.

Jean Cocteau dies.

1964
Avedon publishes his second monograph, *Nothing Personal*, with text by former DeWitt Clinton schoolmate James Baldwin. Avedon's exhibition, *Avedon: A Collage*, opens at McCann Erickson advertising agency in New York.

1965
Avedon guest-edits and photographs the April issue of *Harper's Bazaar.*

In summer, Avedon travels to Paris. Some of his prints appear in that summer's *Section d'Art Photographique* exhibition at the Musée Réattu in Arles.

1966
Avedon leaves *Harper's Bazaar* and begins working for *Vogue*. His first cover, for the March issue, is of Barbra Streisand.

In November, in New York, Avedon meets Jacques Henri Lartigue for the first time.

William Klein, *Who Are You Polly Maggoo?*

1967
In January Avedon visits Lartigue in Paris and sees the retrospective *Hommage à Pablo Picasso* at the Grand Palais.

From February to March, Avedon and Marvin Israel teach a photography master class at Avedon's New York studio.

In March issue of *Harper's Bazaar*, Lartigue publishes his first "official" fashion photograph.

Claude Picasso becomes Avedon's assistant in New York.

Roland Barthes, *Système de la Mode* (The Fashion System).

1968
In January Avedon travels to Paris and takes a portrait of Penelope Tree wearing a mask by Emanuel Ungaro. Lartigue is invited to photograph the preparations.

In March, the project of the book on Lartigue photography is decided. From May 17–30, Avedon works in Paris with Bea Feitler on *Diary of a Century.*

France is in the throes of a vast social movement that leads to the dissolution of the National Assembly on May 30.

In September Avedon photographs Catherine Deneuve in Los Angeles.

1969
Avedon photographs Andy Warhol and members of The Factory.

Michel Auder marries Viva.

1970
In Paris in February, from June-July and September-October, Avedon photographs Alexey Brodovitch, Loulou de la Falaise, Catherine Deneuve and Jeanne Moreau.

Richard Avedon, the first museum retrospective of his work, opens at the Minneapolis Institute of Art in July.

Diary of a Century is published in December.

1971
Avedon travels to Saigon, South Vietnam and photographs the U.S. Mission Council.

In July Avedon photographs Catherine Deneuve and Robert Bresson.

Henri Cartier-Bresson is awarded the Prix Nadar for the book *Vive la France.*

The Grand Palais in Paris holds a major retrospective of Francis Bacon's work.

In April Alexey Brodovitch dies in France.

1972
Avedon participates in an antiwar demonstration in Washington D.C., and is arrested and jailed for civil disobedience.

Jean Renoir sits for Avedon for a second portrait in Beverly Hills.

1973
In June Avedon travels to Paris and photographs Catherine Deneuve. Chanel uses images from the session for an ad campaign.

Alice in Wonderland: The Forming of a Company and the Making of a Play, with photographs by Avedon and text by Doon Arbus, is published.

The French edition of *Diary of a Century*, re-titled *Instants de ma Vie*, is finally published.

In April, Pablo Picasso dies.

In September, Avedon's father dies.

1974
Avedon has his first show in New York, at the Museum of Modern Art, *Jacob Israel Avedon*, consisting of 8 portraits of his father, taken during the last years of his life.

Third portrait sitting with Jean Renoir.

Avedon photographs Aurore Clément for *Vogue*.

Lartigue takes the official portrait of President Valéry Giscard d'Estaing.

1975

The Marlborough Gallery holds the first large New York exhibition of Avedon's work, *Portraits 1969–1975*. The show travels throughout the U.S., as well as to Japan and Canada.

Avedon photographs Isabelle Adjani in October.

Lartigue 8 x 80 opens is at the Musée des Arts Décoratif. It is Lartigue's first major retrospective in France.

François Truffaut, *L'Histoire d'Adèle H.* (The Story of Adele H.). Marguerite Duras, *India Song*.

Marie-Louise Bousquet dies.

1976

Portraits: Richard Avedon, with text by Harold Rosenberg, is published.

Avedon's series, "The Family," is published in *Rolling Stone*.

Diana Vreeland receives the Légion d'Honneur.

1977

French *Photo* features a port–folio of Avedon portraits with text by Roland Barthes in its January issue.

Avedon travels to Paris in December.

1978

Avedon travels to Paris in January and April and photographs Loulou de la Falaise.

In July Avedon begins his famous series, *In the American West*.

In November the Metropolitan Museum of Art holds *Avedon: Photographs 1947–1977* and the same-titled accompanying book is published. This retrospective exhibition of his fashion photography then travels throughout the United States and to Japan.

1979

In April Avedon photographs Samuel Beckett.

Avedon is awarded the Prix Nadar for his book *Photographs 1947–1977*.

1980

In July Avedon travels to Paris and photographs Paloma Picasso.

Roland Barthes, *La Chambre Claire: Note sur la Photographie* (Camera Lucida: Reflections on Photography).

1983

Yannick Noah wins Rolland-Garros (the French Open).

1984

Nicole Wisniak, the founder of the magazine Egoïste interviews Avedon.

Marguerite Duras, *L'Amant* (The Lover).

Truman Capote dies.

1985

In January Avedon begins working for *Egoïste* and will become one the magazine's principal photographers. Issue no. 9 features his self-portrait on the cover, his interview with founder Nicole Wisniak, "Un Portrait est une Opinion," and the first appearance of images from *In the American West*.

In September *In the American West* is exhibited at the Amon Carter Museum of American Art in Fort Worth, Texas. The exhibition travels throughout the US.

1986

For MoMA's exhibition *Vienna 1900*, Avedon gives a lecture on portraiture and Egon Schiele that becomes the essay, "Borrowed Dogs." *Grand Street* will publish it the following year.

On the same day, both James Baldwin and Leonard Bernstein receive the Légion d'honneur.

Jean Baudrillard, *Amérique* (America).

Jacques Henri Lartigue dies.

1987

Egoïste issue no. 10 features an Avedon portrait of Andy Warhol on the cover, and his famous mural of the Warhol Factory members inside.

James Baldwin dies.

1989

The cover of *Egoïste* issue no. 11 is Avedon's portrait of Isabelle Adjani.

Avedon travels to Berlin to photograph the first New Year's Eve there since the fall of the Berlin Wall.

Samuel Beckett dies.

1991
Avedon photographs Sylvie Guillem in New York in March.

During the summer, he travels to Venice to photograph the Volpi Ball, one of the oldest balls still held for the European aristocracy.

In October the Carnegie International in Pittsburgh exhibits photographs from Avedon's series on the fall of the Berlin Wall.

1992
Avedon is named staff photographer of The New Yorker.

Issue no. 12, vol. 1 of *Egoïste* has Avedon's portrait of Yannick Noah on the cover, and features Avedon's photographs of Sylvie Guillem, Patrice Chéreau, and Jean Genet, as well as "Unter den Linden," his series on the fall of the Berlin Wall, with text by Jean Baudrillard.

Issue no. 12, vol. 2 of *Egoïste* has Avedon's portrait of André Glucksmann on the cover.

The Fondation Abbé Pierre is created.

1993
Avedon's *An Autobiography* is published, comprising fifty years of his work.

Avedon photographs Marguerite Duras in Paris in May.

The 24th Rencontres d'Arles features a selection of Avedon's portraits of America, and for the event, Michel Guerrin and Henry Béhar interview Avedon for *Le Monde*.

The Fondation Soeur Emmanuelle is created.

1994
The retrospective *Richard Avedon Evidence: 1944–1994* opens at the Whitney Museum of American Art in New York and travels to several cities in Europe (though not Paris), including the Museum Ludwig in Cologne, the Palazzo Reale in Milan, and finally the National Portrait Gallery in London, before returning to the U.S. at the Minneapolis Institute of Art.

Avedon is awarded the Prix Nadar for *Evidence: 1944–1994*.

Patrice Chéreau, *La Reine Margot*. Philippe Sollers, *La Guerre du Goût*.

1995
Avedon takes portraits of Juliette Binoche, the new face of the Lancôme perfume Poème (and shoots the campaign that same year), and Daniel Cohn-Bendit, who had been appointed European deputy in 1994.

The documentary *Richard Avedon: Darkness and Light*, is released. It is produced by PBS and directed by Helen Whitney.

François Sagan publishes her last novel, *Le Miroir Égaré*. Jean-Paul Rappeneau, Le Hussard sur le toit (The Horseman on the Roof) avec Juliette Binoche.

1996
Marguerite Duras dies.

1997
Egoïste no. 13, vol. 1 publishes Avedon's portraits of Juliette Binoche, Daniel Cohn-Bendit and Bernard Frank. The following issue features Avedon's photographs of Cirque du Soleil, as well as his portraits of Marguerite Duras and Luc Bondy.

1998
Avedon photographs Maurice Béjart.

François Pinault becomes the owner of Christie's Auction House.

1999
Avedon: *The Sixties*, long in development, is published, with text by Doon Arbus.

John Galliano is named head designer of Dior.

2000
Issue no. 14, vol. 1 of *Egoïste* has Avedon's portrait of Gérard Depardieu on the cover, as well as more portraits of Depardieu and Françoise Sagan, Philippe Sollers, John Galliano, François Pinault, and Alexis de Rédé inside. The issue also publishes Avedon's long series, "Kate's Story," created partly in Drancy.

2001
The exhibition *Richard Avedon: Made in France* opens at the Fraenkel Gallery in San Francisco. The accompanying book is published in limited edition.

2002
In September the exhibition *Richard Avedon: Portraits* opens at the Metropolitan Museum of Art.

2003
Lartigue albums are shown in Centre Pompidou, Mnam, Paris in *Jacques Henri Lartigue, 1894-1986, L'Album d'une vie (Lartigue: Album of a Century)*.

2004
Avedon dies on October 1 at the age of 81.

Acknowledgments

Robert M. Rubin

I first met Richard Avedon fifty years ago. John, his son, and I were at boarding school together. I was a boy from a blue-collar New Jersey family trying to break my suburban chains. When John took me home to New York City for the holidays, there he was: Richard Avedon. My first thought was: Why couldn't this glamorous man be *my* father? He treated me as if I had something to say, not — as my own father did — as if I were merely a ticking adolescent time bomb.

When I graduated from college, Dick was there, but because another Avedon family friend happened to be in my class. I tagged along. I remember us riding around New Haven in a limousine. The driver wore a black suit and cap. This was 1974, well before car services: only Aristotle Onassis rode in a chauffeured limousine. Dick was wearing this fabulous sheepskin coat from the old Abercrombie & Fitch. You can see him wearing it in Robert Frank's 1973 photograph of him and John, taken in Nova Scotia.

A few years later, Avedon took my picture in the late 1970s. Again, not because I was anyone, but because he was helping John's and my friend Fred Iseman launch a magazine. Fred rounded up a bunch of young New York City professionals to pose as ourselves. I was the commodities trader at leisure (which, in real life, I was, minus the leisure). The magazine never got past the dummy stage, but I have a work print of that image somewhere.

During Avedon's lifetime, I had no real understanding of what he was trying to do. He was the guy who photographed the Beatles (John and I listened to *The White Album* incessantly back then) and made a lot of money taking cool pictures. Not trusting anyone over thirty, I was perplexed by his interest in the so-called "Movement." How can you be a rebel if your father approves?

I took his eventual museification for granted. On my fortieth birthday, I was given a copy of his book, *Autobiography*, beautifully and personally inscribed to me by Avedon himself. Fred had arranged it.

Over time, Dick looked less and less like "Avedon" and more like the other fathers of my middle-aged friends (though he dressed better). Meanwhile, I had come to love my own father, a quiet, modest man who gave me plenty of space in which to grow up. I recognize now that having a famous parent, especially one so preoccupied with his own legacy, can be a burden as well as a gift.

In 2012, John asked me to write an essay on his father and Alan Ginsberg, whose family was the subject of one of Avedon's great mural portraits. My qualification for the job rested entirely on a show I had curated at the Bibliothèque nationale de France (BnF) in 2011, *Richard Prince: American Prayer.* Prince owns a treasure trove of rare books and manuscripts by the Beats, who were the spiritual descendants of French bohemians, and the show focused on his private library. So here I am again in 2016, working the French angle of American culture at the BnF.

Like *American Prayer*, this exhibition would not have seen the light of day without the vision and encouragement of Bruno Racine, President of the BnF, who initiated the project before retiring earlier this year. Our relationship goes back even further, to his tenure as President of Centre Pompidou (2002–2007), during which time the Richard Avedon Foundation made a generous gift to France of twelve works. His successor, Laurence Engel, has been no less supportive and engaged in this ongoing Franco-American collaboration.

All those who knew Avedon better than I did have been extremely gracious and generous in sharing their recollections and materials.

John Avedon has been my friend for fifty years. I don't have many of those.

Nicole Wisniak, with whom Avedon collaborated so successfully in *Egoïste*, has been of immeasurable help to me in framing this body of work in the larger context of Avedon's career. I hope she feels the *Egoïste* section of the exhibition and catalog does her justice.

The Board of the Richard Avedon Foundation—John and Laura Avedon, Elsie Walker, Andrew Wylie, and Executive Director James

Martin have been remarkable in their enthusiasm for this project. James in particular went the extra mile for me on many occasions. Since I know how inundated the foundation is with requests (sometimes in the form of demands), his single-minded commitment to making this the best exhibition and book possible meant a great deal to me. Given his encyclopedic knowledge of Avedon's life and work, it was a challenge for me to unearth material he had not seen. I came to do so just for the pleasure of seeing his reaction. Avedon's high school yearbook didn't make the cut for the show, but it brought a smile to his face. His team, including Jennifer DiCocco, Katrina Dumas, Erin Harris, Jenica Heintzelman, Maggie Merrell, Nova Burns, Audrey Nevada Chaney, Brian De Pinto, Ann Giordano, and Kipp Wettstein were no less diligent.

Renata Adler's careful consideration of my text made it much better.

Michel Guerrin's 1993 interview with Avedon is the cornerstone of my narrative. Michel remains the preeminent French authority on Avedon.

David Adjaye and his project director, Yohannes Bereket, both of whom I had the pleasure of working with on *American Prayer*, delivered another brilliant installation. Only David could have reconciled Avedon's expressionistic and minimalist sides into a coherent visual and spatial whole. Julie Boidin executed the plan with her usual grace under enormous pressure.

Marcel Hermans and Cornelia Blatter of COMA Amsterdam/New York envisioned and designed a catalog unlike any other — one that will endure long after the show has been archived. Their counterintuitive choices have been vindicated by the end result. Nicole Jedinak took the publishing logistics in hand and, as with our two previous collaborations, produced a superb bibliographic object.

Quentin Bajac introduced me to Marianne Le Galliard, who became an essential collaborator on this project. Her narrative of Lartigue is groundbreaking, and her work on French photographers and *Harper's Bazaar* will, no doubt, be equally eye-opening. Thank you, Quentin, and thank you, Marianne.

Nakki Goranin, owner of the wonderful and authentic Mutoscope photobooth and author of *American Photobooth*, the last word on the subject, didn't flinch when I asked to borrow the beast and send it to France for the exhibition. Rick Kershner served as curatorial air traffic controller during its restoration and transport. Jennifer Baker did a sensitive job of stabilizing it for public display without robbing it of the witness marks of time. Fritz Dietl helped get it to Paris.

Larry McAllister of Paramount, Sean Ferrer and Luca Dotti of the Audrey Hepburn Children's Fund, and Jonathan Reichman helped organize the *Funny Face* component of the exhibition.

D.A. and Frazier Pennebaker generously allowed unseen Avedon footage to be shown. Kudos to Michael Chaiken for bringing it to me.

Thank you, Hiro, for the loan of your Smithsonian film.

Thank you, Michel Brodovitch, for sharing your archives.

Jeffrey Fraenkel of Fraenkel Gallery — who produced one of my favorite Avedon volumes, *Made in France* — kindly lent his treasured Avedon keepsake, and generously shared his recollections with me.

Thanks are due as well to these institutional lenders: Musée d'Orsay, Paris; Association des Amis de Jacques Henri Lartigue / Ministère de la Culture, Charenton; Centre Georges Pompidou, Paris; Museum of the Moving Image, New York; and Parsons School of Design, New York.

There will undoubtedly be Patrons too late to thank as of publication date, but the Terra Foundation for American Art's early support gave the project much-needed momentum. The Fondation Louis Roederer said yes in a heartbeat, given its longstanding loyalty not only to the BnF but also to *Egoïste*. Arnaud Brillois helped underwrite this catalog early on.

I'm sure all of the above join me in expressing our delight that Avedon and France have come together at the BnF, this essential site of cultural memory that has figured so prominently in our ever-evolving understanding of the unique role of photography in the history of the arts.

Index of Names

Credits

All photography and words by Richard Avedon © 2016 The Richard Avedon Foundation.

Photography credits

Front cover, 78–89, 96–97, 100–01, 104–15, 118–19, 122–31, 134–43, 146–57 Funny Face © Paramount Pictures. All rights reserved. Richard Avedon © 2016 The Richard Avedon Foundation; 16 Private collection. Photo by Genevieve Hanson; 18–19 © Popular Photography. Photo by Gene Pyle / All rights reserved; 20 © Paramount Pictures, collection Margaret Herrick Library, Academy of Motion Picture Arts and Sciences; 22 © Ralph Morse, LIFE Picture Collection / Getty Images; 26 (top) © Alexey Brodovitch, courtesy Michel Brodovitch. Photo courtesy William Gregory, Bookseller; 26 (bottom) © Alexey Brodovitch. Courtesy Michel Brodovitch. Courtesy Fraenkel Gallery. Photo by Genevieve Hanson; 30, 36 (top), 46 (bottom), 75, 274–75, 537 Courtesy The Richard Avedon Foundation; 32 Photography Jacques Henri Lartigue © Ministère de la Culture – France / AAJHL. Photo by Marianne le Galliard; 36 (bottom) Richard Avedon, 1993, photography by Irving Penn/ © Condé Nast Publications/ Paris-Match, courtesy Marianne Le Galliard; 46 (top and middle), 48 (bottom), 52 (top), 54 (bottom), 60 (top and middle), 62 (top and middle), 456–59, 462–79, 484–85, 518–19, 534–36 Photography Jacques Henri Lartigue © Ministère de la Culture – France / AAJHL. Photo by La Chambre Noire; 48 (top), 487, 505 © Georges Tourdjman, SAIF, 2016. Collection J. H. Lartigue. Photo by La Chambre Noire; 48 (middle) © Harper's Bazaar, 1967, previously published by Harper's Bazaar, reprinted with permission of Hearst Communications, Inc. Photo Jacques Henri Lartigue / Bibliothèque nationale de France; 50–51, 520, 522, 524, 527 Collection J. H. Lartigue © Ministère de la Culture – France / AAJHL. Photo by La Chambre Noire; 52 (bottom) Photo by Richard Avedon © Ministère de la Culture – France / AAJHL. Photo by La Chambre Noire; 54 (bottom) © Ministère de la Culture – France / AAJHL. Private collection, photo by Mark Lyon; 56 Fondation J. H. Lartigue / Fondation de France. Photo by Marianne Le Galliard; 60 (bottom), 62 (bottom) Photography Jacques Henri Lartigue © Ministère de la Culture – France / AAJHL. Photo by Marianne Le Galliard; 72, courtesy Nicole Wisniak; 76–77, 92, 211 © Paramount Pictures Productions records and Hedda Hopper papers of the Margaret Herrick Library, Academy of Motion Picture Arts and Sciences; 214 © Cahiers du Cinéma. Photo Bibliothèque nationale de France; 215 © Dance Magazine. Photo Bibliothèque nationale de France; 216 © Columbia, 1955, Private Collection. Photo by Genevieve Hanson; 217 © Helena Rubinstein/ The Advertising Archives; 239 Courtesy Fraenkel Gallery. Photo by Genevieve Hanson; 240–41 © Harper's Bazaar, 1956, previously published by Harper's Bazaar, reprinted with permission of Hearst Communications, Inc. Photo Bibliothèque nationale de France; 244–45 © Alexey Brodovitch, courtesy Michel Brodovitch. Photo courtesy Swann Auction Galleries; 248 © Harper's Bazaar, 1940, previously published by Harper's Bazaar, reprinted with permission of Hearst Communications, Inc. Photo Bibliothèque nationale de France; 249 © Ronny Jaques / Trunk Archive © Harper's Bazaar, 1949, previously published by Harper's Bazaar, reprinted with permission of Hearst Communications, Inc. Musée des Arts décoratifs. Photo Musée des Arts décoratifs / Cyrille Bernard; 252 © Hiro, The Richard Avedon Foundation; 254–55 © Walter Sanders, The LIFE Picture Collection / Getty Images; 258–59 © Henri Cartier-Bresson / Magnum Photos; 260 © Robert Doisneau / Rapho; 266 Courtesy The Richard Avedon Foundation, photo by Genevieve Hanson; 269 Christian Bérard © ADAGP, Paris 2016, Photo Bibliothèque nationale de France; 276–77, 280–81, 282–83 © Harper's Bazaar, 1948, previously published by Harper's Bazaar, reprinted with permission of Hearst Communications, Inc. Musée des Arts décoratifs. Photo Musée des Arts décoratifs / Cyrille Bernard; 278–89 © Harper's Bazaar, 1949, previously published by Harper's Bazaar, reprinted with permission of Hearst Communications, Inc. Musée des Arts décoratifs. Photo Musée des Arts décoratifs / Cyrille Bernard; 342 © Jean Cocteau, Comité Jean Cocteau, The Richard Avedon Foundation; 348–51, 356–59, 368–69, 392–99 © Harper's Bazaar, 1959, previously published by Harper's Bazaar, reprinted with permission of Hearst Communications, Inc. Photo Bibliothèque nationale de France; 352–53 © Harper's Bazaar, 1961, previously published by Harper's Bazaar, reprinted with permission of Hearst Communications, Inc. Photo Bibliothèque nationale de France; 354–55 © Harper's

Bazaar, 1955, previously published by Harper's Bazaar, reprinted with permission of Hearst Communications, Inc. Photo Bibliothèque nationale de France; 360–61 © Harper's Bazaar, 1954, previously published by Harper's Bazaar, reprinted with permission of Hearst Communications, Inc. Photo Bibliothèque nationale de France; 362–63, 364–65 © Harper's Bazaar, 1960, previously published by Harper's Bazaar, reprinted with permission of Hearst Communications, Inc. Photo Bibliothèque nationale de France; 366–67 © Harper's Bazaar, 1963, previously published by Harper's Bazaar, reprinted with permission of Hearst Communications, Inc. Photo Bibliothèque nationale de France; 373–85 © Richard Avedon. Photo by Genevieve Hanson; 408–09 Richard Avedon © Esquire, 1957, previously published by Esquire, reprinted with permission of Hearst Communications, Inc. Photo by Genevieve Hanson; 424 © Harper's Bazaar, 1965, previously published by Harper's Bazaar, reprinted with permission of Hearst Communications, Inc. Photo Bibliothèque nationale de France; 425 © Harper's Bazaar, 1965, previously published by Harper's Bazaar, reprinted with permission of Hearst Communications, Inc. Courtesy The Richard Avedon Foundation; 426–27 © Harper's Bazaar, 1965 / Stan Vanderbeek, previously published by Harper's Bazaar, reprinted with permission of Hearst Communications, Inc. Photo Bibliothèque nationale de France; 428–29 Courtesy The Richard Avedon Foundation; 431 Courtesy The Richard Avedon Foundation. Private collection. Photo by Genevieve Hanson; 450–51, Pierre-Louis Pierson / Christian Bérard © ADAGP, Paris 2016 / Photo © Musée d'Orsay, Dist. RMN – Grand Palais / Alexis Brandt; 452–53, Christian Bérard © ADAGP, Paris 2016 / Photo © Musée d'Orsay, Dist. RMN – Grand Palais / Alexis Brandt; 480–83 Courtesy The Richard Avedon Foundation, Collection J. H. Lartigue – AAJHL. Photo La Chambre Noire; 486–87 Courtesy The Richard Avedon Foundation. Photography Jacques Henri Lartigue © Ministère de la Culture - France / AAJHL. Photo by Marianne le Galliard; 494–513, 521, 523, 525 Photography Jacques Henri Lartigue © Ministère de la Culture - France / AAJHL. Photo by Genevieve Hanson; 532–33 © Jacques Henri Lartigue, Courtesy The Richard Avedon Foundation; 538 Private collection. Photo by Mark Lyon; 539 Private collection. Photo by Genevieve Hanson; 597 © Richard Avedon, Courtesy Nicole Wisniak; 598–601, 604–09, 622–27, 630–32, 676–87, 714–27, 739–59 © Egoïste, Courtesy The Richard Avedon Foundation; Photo by Genevieve Hanson; 766 © Camera, 1974.

AAJHL/ Donation Lartigue: On June 26, 1979, Jacques Henri Lartigue donated his collection of photographs, diaries and photographic equipment to the French state. The Association des Amis de Jacques Henri Lartigue, known as Donation Jacques Henri Lartigue conserves and manages the collection under the supervision of the French Ministry of Culture.

Text credits

11, 205, 267 © Janet Flanner, Paris-Journal 1944–1955, The New Yorker; 18–19 © Popular Photography, Text John Durniak. All rights reserved; 69, 233, 422–23, 460–61, 574–75, 762–63 © Michel Guerrin/ Le Monde, Michel Guerrin; 73–74 courtesy The Richard Avedon Foundation; 91 © Jean-Patrick Manchette, Journal 1966–1974, Gallimard; 158–59 © Éric Rohmer/ Arts et spectacles; 206–07 © Bertrand Tavernier and Stanley Donen, courtesy Cahiers du Cinéma and Bertrand Tavernier; 213, Richard Avedon, audio interview, Minneapolis, March 31, 1970 © The Richard Avedon Foundation; 218–19, 234–35, 236–38 Richard Avedon © The Richard Avedon Foundation and Fraenkel Gallery; 250–51 © Denise Bourdet, Plon; 253, 256–57 © Calvin Tomkins, The New Yorker; 261 Previously published by Harper's Bazaar, reprinted with permission of Hearst Communications, Inc.; 263 © Carmel Snow with Mary Louise Aswell, courtesy McGraw-Hill; 270–71 Richard Avedon, unpublished interview, February 2, 1972 © The Richard Avedon Foundation; 346–46, 603, 610–19 Richard Avedon, Un Portrait est une opinion © Egoïste and The Richard Avedon Foundation; 370–71 Avedon, unpublished interview, January 14, 1971 © The Richard Avedon Foundation; 386–87 Richard Avedon to Truman Capote, courtesy of the Truman Capote estate / The Richard Avedon Foundation; 389 Avedon, unpublished interview for PBS series, American Masters, February 1, 1995 © The Richard Avedon Foundation; 475 Jacques Henri Lartigue, Collection J. H. Lartigue © Ministère de la Culture - France/

AAJHL; 479 Jacques Henri Lartigue © Ministère de la Culture - France/ AAJHL; 489 Avedon, in Independent, February 26, 1987; 492–93 Richard Avedon © The Richard Avedon Foundation; 514–15, 674–75, 728–29 unpublished interview for PBS American Masters, February 1, 1995 © The Richard Avedon Foundation; 528–33 Collection J. H. Lartigue © Ministère de la Culture - France/ AAJHL; 541 Avedon, in San Jose Mercury News, March 25, 1986; 569–71 © Roland Barthes, Photo, January 1977; 581 Avedon, "A Conversation: The Constructed Moment," with Adam Gopnick, the Metropolitan Museum of Art, October 8, 2002; 583–92 Richard Avedon, "Borrowed Dogs," Grand Street 7, no. 1, autumn 1987 © The Richard Avedon Foundation; 621 © Jean Baudrillard, Amérique/ Éditions Grasset & Fasquelle, 1986; 629 Marcel Proust, courtesy Gallimard; 633 Richard Avedon © The Richard Avedon Foundation; 634–35 Avedon, Famous Photographers magazine, 1967; 713 © Philippe Sollers, Littérature et politique, Flammarion, 2014; 731–35 Jean Baudrillard, courtesy Egoïste; 761 Avedon letter to Doe Siegel, March 16, 2001, courtesy The Richard Avedon Foundation; 773 Cyril Connolly, Enemies of Promise, courtesy Macmillan.

Avedon's France:
Old World, New Look

Published on the occasion
of the exhibition:
La France d'Avedon:
Vieux monde, New Look

October 18, 2016–February 26, 2017

Bibliothèque nationale de France
Quai François Mauriac
75013 Paris, France
www.bnf.fr/

This exhibition was organized thanks to the support of the Terra Foundation for American Art and the Fondation Louis Roederer. This book also received the support of Mr. Arnaud Brillois, for which we are grateful.

TERRA
FOUNDATION FOR AMERICAN ART

FONDATION
LOUIS
ROEDERER
GRAND MÉCÈNE DE LA CULTURE

Liberté • Égalité • Fraternité
RÉPUBLIQUE FRANÇAISE

Ministère
Culture
Communication

Distributed by Abrams,
an imprint of ABRAMS

ABRAMS
The Art of Books

115 West 18th Street
New York, NY 10011
www.abramsbooks.com

ISBN: 978-1-4197-2600-2

Catalog

Editors: Robert M. Rubin
and Marianne Le Galliard
Managing editor:
Nicole Jedinak
Art and text coordinators:
Gwennina Lussot, Isabelle
Le Jeune, Marianne Le Galliard

Consulting editor:
Jana Martin
Consulting translator:
Molly Stevens

Concept and Design:
COMA Amsterdam/New York
Color separation:
Echelon Color
Printing:
ORO Graphic Project Management

The authors and publisher gratefully acknowledge the permissions granted to reproduce the copyright material in this book. Every effort has been made to trace copyright holders and to obtain their permission for the use of copyright material. The publisher apologizes for any errors or omissions in the above list and would be grateful if notified of any corrections that should be incorporated in future reprints or editions of this book.

Exhibition

La France d'Avedon:
Vieux monde, New Look

Curators:
Robert M. Rubin and
Marianne Le Galliard
Exhibition design:
Adjaye Associates
(David Adjaye and Yohannes
Bereket, Project Manager)
Production:
Exhibition services of
the Bibliothèque nationale
de France, under the direction
of Anne-Hélène Rigogne
General Coordination:
Anne Manouvrier
Executive Scenography:
Julie Boidin
Graphics:
Bastien Morin
Registry of Works:
Vincent Desjardins
Framing and Mounting:
Serge Derouault, assisted
by Lucie Balavoine-Coutel,
Nathalie Grassi, Damien Lebrun,
Vincent Moreau, Charly Thicot
Preparation Documents and
Framing:
Eric Vannereau assisted by Eric
Rousseau and Olivier Paitreault

Lenders to the Exhibition

United States
The Richard Avedon Foundation,
New York
Museum of the Moving Image,
New York
The New School, Archives &
Special Collections, New York
John Avedon
Jeffrey Fraenkel
Nakki Goranin
Robert M. Rubin

France
Donation Jacques Henri Lartigue
Musée d'Orsay
Centre Pompidou, Musée
national d'art moderne/Centre
de création industrielle
Nicole Wisniak
Michel Brodovitch
Marianne Le Galliard